Genealogical Guide
to the
Early Settlers of America

WITH A
BRIEF HISTORY OF THOSE OF THE
FIRST GENERATION

*And references to the various local histories and other sources
of information where additional data may be found.*

By

HENRY WHITTEMORE

Excerpted and Reprinted from
The Spirit of '76

CLEARFIELD

Excerpted and Reprinted From

The Spirit of '76

Volumes V—XII, September, 1898—May, 1906.

Reprinted
Genealogical Publishing Company, Inc.
1967

Reprinted for
Clearfield Company, Inc. by
Genealogical Publishing Co., Inc.
Baltimore, Maryland
1995, 1997, 2001

Library of Congress Catalogue Card Number 67-23072
International Standard Book Number: 0-8063-0378-6

Made in the United States of America

Reprinted from copies lent to us by the
Minnesota Historical Society and the Library of Congress

Publisher's Preface

Of the many books on genealogical research that we have published, we feel great pleasure in bringing to the attention of genealogists this work by a well known authority which has been virtually unknown to the genealogical world. THE SPIRIT OF '76, from which this work was excerpted, is in itself an extremely rare periodical and few complete sets are available in libraries in this country. We found no mention of this work in any bibliography.

We know little of the origins of this work other than from the information contained in the preface to the original work printed on the following page. It was, undoubtedly, an ambitious undertaking; and there can be little doubt that the part published is well done and should furnish the genealogist with a great deal of reference material on the names given. It is extremely unfortunate that the author did not complete this work which, as will be seen, ends with the name of "RAM." As is common with a great deal of other valuable material buried in various periodicals, this work is little known to the public.

That the work is of importance can easily be ascertained through a study of its contents. It contains all the essential features of previously published books and has a brief history of the early settlers with references to various books and other sources of information where complete data may be found. It therefore helps to locate much data on family records which could not otherwise be found except at the expenditure of a great deal of time and energy.

Genealogical Publishing Company
Baltimore, Maryland 1967

PREFACE TO THE ORIGINAL EDITION

The importance of a reliable work of reference for persons in search of genealogical information will be best appreciated when it is known that in comparing the references of a publication of this character under a single letter of the alphabet over one hundred errors and omissions were found.

In addition to the genealogical matter contained in this work one page of each number will be devoted to an explanation of heraldic terms, their origin and sentiment expressed by them.

This work will contain all the essential features (with many additions) of Savage's Genealogical Dictionary and other works long out of print; with a brief history of the early settlers and references to the various books and other sources of information where complete data may be found; thus enabling any person by following the instructions given to obtain a history of their own families at a comparatively small cost.

Sample pages are furnished with this number of THE SPIRIT OF '76, and the work will be commenced with the October number. It will be arranged alphabetically and each issue will contain the history of several families. Parties who desire information of their families in advance of publication, before the names are reached in alphabetical order, can write to the author for terms, etc., who will also, if desired, make the researches and give the line from the ancestor to the present time, together with information of Revolutionary ancestors.

Henry Whittemore
Brooklyn, N. Y. 1898

THIS work will contain all the essential features (with many additions) of Savage's Genealogical Dictionary and other works long out of print; with a brief history of the early settlers and references to the various books and other sources of information where complete data may be found; thus enabling any person by following the instructions given to obtain a history of their own families at a comparatively small cost.

It will be arranged alphabetically and will contain the history of several families. Parties who desire information of their families in advance of publication, before the names are reached in alphabetical order, can write to the author for terms, etc., who will also, if desired, make the researches and give the line from the ancestor to the present time, together with information of Revolutionary ancestors. HENRY WHITTEMORE, 487 Third street, Brooklyn, N. Y.

ABBY.

ABBE ABBY.—Richard Abbe of Windham was born February 9, 1682. He was son of John, who had land deeded to him in Windham, July 3, in 1696. In the deed he is said to be from Wendham, Mass. His parents John and Hannah Abbe were dismissed from the church in Wenham at its organization December 10, 1700. He married November 11, 1703, Mary Gunnings, now Jennings, and died childless July 10, 1737. He was a prominent citizen of the town. Ref. N. E. Gen. Reg. vol. VII, 325.

JOHN ABBY, was of Salem, Mass., 1630.

SAMUEL ABBY, of Wenham, Mass., died 1698, leaving widow Mary and children Mary, Samuel, Thomas, Eleazer, Ebenezer, Mercy, Sarah, Hepzibah, Abigail, John, Benjamin, Jonathan. He was of Salem village, now Danvers, Mass., when admitted freeman 1690

OBADIAH ABBY, of Enfield, 1682, married Sarah, widow of Joseph Warrener.

THOMAS ABBY, of Enfield, perhaps brother of Obadiah, had Sarah, Thomas, Mary, John, Tabitha. Several of this name served with the Connecticut troops in the revolution.

REFERENCES.

Savage's Gen. Dict. vol. I, 6; American Ancestry IX, 44; Stiles' History Windsor, vol. II, 9, 831; Weaver's History, Windham 9; Hinman's Puritan Settlers 13.

ABBETT.

ABBETT.—Canad. Gen. 34—6, 49—53.

CALEB ABBETT, of Dedham, Mass., may have been a son of Benjamin, removed in 1668, to Norwich, Conn., died there. He married July, 1669, Margaret, probably daughter of John Post of Saybrook. Had issue Samuel, 1672; Experience, Caleb, 1677; John, 1678; Theophilus, 1680; Joanna, Abigail, Hannah, Caleb (1st), died August 17, 1731.

JOSHUA ABBETT, of Norwich, perhaps brother of Caleb, married 1677, Experience daughter of Nehemiah Smith, of New London.

REFERENCES.

MASSACHUSETTS.—Barrus' Goshen 133.
NEW HAMPSHIRE.—Merrill's History, Acworth, 1780.
CONNECTICUT.—Caulkins' History, Norwich 209; Hines' Lebanon, Address 143; Hurd's History, New

London County, 509; Sedgwick's History. Sharon, 61; Whittemore's History, Middlesex County, 198; Hinman's Conn. Settlers, 16.
NEW YORK.—Young's Chatauqua County, 307, 478.
ILLINOIS.—Powers' History, Sangamon, 75.
OTHER WORKS.—Savage's Gen. Dic. vol I, 6; Walworth's Hyde Gen. 1044, 1065; Bliss' Gen., 664.

ABBOT—ABBOTT.

ABBOT—ABBOTT.—The name of Abbot signifies its origin, and there is no doubt that it was originally spelt with one " t." The Coat Armor of Baron Colchester, of Colchester, Essex, England, is described as Arms—Gules on a chevron between three pears or, as many crosses raguly azure, within a tressure flory, of the second. Crest—Out of a ducal coronet or, a unicorn's head ermine maned and tufted of the first, between six ostrich feathers argent quilled or, Supporters—On either side a unicorn ermine maned, hoofed and tufted or, gorged with a collar azure, within another gemel flory counter flory, gules therefrom a chain, reflexed over the back, gold, and charged on the shoulder with a cross raguly of the third. Motto—Deo patria, amicis.

The Abbot Genealogy, 1847, gives a partial line of six early settlers in America of this name; these are George, of Andover, Mass.; George, of Rowley, Mass.; Thomas, of Andover, Mass.; Arthur, of Ipswich, Mass.; Robert, of Branford, Conn., and George, of Norwalk, Conn.

Among those associated with Rev. Mr. Davenport in the management of the Massachusett's Colony, was Sir Maurice Abbot, brother of Dr. George Abbot, Archbishof of Canterbury.

GEORGE ABBOT, of Andover, Mass., born in Yorkshire, England, 1615, died at Andover, December 24, 1681. He emigrated to New England about 1640, and settled in Andover of which he was an original proprietor. He married in 1647, Hannah, daughter of William and Annie Chandler, and had issue John, George, William, Benjamin, Timothy, Thomas, Nathaniel.

GEORGE ABBOT, of Rowley, Mass., emigrated with his three sons, George, Nehemiah, and Thomas, and settled in Rowley, Mass., died 1647.

ARTHUR ABBOT, of Marblehead, removed to Ipswich, Mass., and joined Winthrop in 1634, in the settlement of that town.

DANIEL ABBOT, of Providence, R. I., came with the Winthrop fleet in 1630 to Cambridge, and removed to Providence, R. I., 1639, and died there.

ROBERT ABBOT, was of Watertown, Mass., 1634. Wethersfield, Conn., 1640, and New Haven, 1642.

GEORGE ABBOT, was of Windsor, Conn., 1640.

JAMES ABBOTT, of Long Island, born in Somersetshire, England, emigrated to America about 1690—5, and settled on Long Island, where he married and had five sons and two daughters.

JOHN ABBOTT, of Burlington County, N. J., was born in Nottingham, England, 1663, died in Burlington County, August 16, 1739. Came to America in ship " Bristol Merchant," 1684, acquired a large estate, and left to his sons nearly 1000 acres and much personal property. He married May 26, 1696, Anni Mauleverer, of Scarboro, England, daughter of Edmund and Anni (Pearson) Mauleverer, who came from France to England with William the Conqueror.

REFERENCES.

MASSACHUSETTS.—Barry's History, Framingham, Mass., 165; Bond's Watertown, Mass., vol. I, 673, 901; Brown's Bedford, Mass., Families I Hazen's History, Billerica, Mass., 2; Hodgman's History, Westford, Mass., 435; Hudson's History, Lexington, Mass., 5.
NEW HAMPSHIRE —Bouton's Sermons at Concord, 59; Bouton's History. Concord. 620: Dow's History, Hampton, 583; Hayward's History, Hancock, 297; Hill's History, Mason, 199; Livermore's History, Wilton, 526; Morrison's History, Windham, 300; Secomb's History of Amherst, 477; Smith's History of Peterborough, 4.
MAINE.—Eaton's History, Thomaston. 128: Lapham's History, Bethel, 458; Lapham's History, Rumford, 286; Lapham's History, Woodstock, 169.
CONNECTICUT.—Hinman's Conn. Settlers, 14; Stiles' History, Windsor II, 10; Weaver's History, Wendham, 26.
OTHER WORKS.—Savage's Gen. Dic. vol. I, 1; Poor's His. and Gen. Researches, 84; Chandler Gen., 4-9, 410; Dudley, Arch. Collections, plate 5.
MASSACHUSETTS.—Stearn's His., Ashburnham, 581; Abbott's His., Andover, Mass., 28; Eaton's His., Reading, Mass., 52; Hammatt Papers, Ipswich, Mass., 9; Page's His., Cambridge, Mass., 477; Page's Hardwick, Mass., 321; Wyman's Charlestown, Mass., Gens. vol. I, p. 1.
VERMONT.—Bass' History, Bramtree, 109.
MAINE.—Butler's His., Farmington, Me., 349; Lapham's History, Norway, 454; Lapham's History, Paris, 492; Ridlon's Harrison, Me., 24.
NEW HAMPSHIRE.—Hayward's History, Gesum 253; Read's History, Swanzey, 271; Runnel's History, Sanbornton, vol. II, 1; Sanderson's History, Charleston, 275; Stearn's History, Rindge, 423; Washington, N. H., History, 270, 695; Cochran's History, Antrim, 331; Coggswell's History, Henniker, 438; Coffin's History. Boscawen, 462; Bedford, Centennial, 287; Worcester's History, Hollis, 363.
RHODE ISLAND.—Austin's R. I. Gen. Dic., 234.
CONNECTICUT.—Waldo's History, Tolland, 128.
CANADA.—Hubbard's Stanstead County, 261.
OTHER PUBLICATIONS.—Savage's Gen. Dic., vol. I, p. 1.   American Ancestry I, 1; IV, 18, 93; V, 182; VI, 200; VII, 238; X, 60, 121; Whitman Gen., 457.
ABBOTT.—Canad. Gen., 34—6, 49—53.

ABDY.

MATTHEW ABDY, of Boston, came in the Abigail, 1635. He married Tabitha, daughter of Robert Reynolds of Boston. He had issue Mary, Tabitha, and Matthew.

REFERENCES.

Savage Gen. Dic. vol. I, 6.

ABEIL.

ABEIL.—See Munsell's History, Albany, vol. IX, 93; Williamson Family; Heroes of the Revolution and their Descendants.
ABEL ABELL.—Robert Abel, of Weymouth, came probably in the fleet with Winthrop, desired administration, October 19, 1630; and was made freeman May 18, following. He had Abraham and Mary. He removed to Rehoboth, and died there August, 1663, leaving widow and four children.
ROBERT ABELL, of Rehoboth, 1668, was Lieut. of the company under Samuel Gallop in the romantic exhibition of Sir William Phipps, 1690, against Quebec. He had Dorothy, born 1677, Joanna, born 1682.
BENJAMIN ABELL, of Norwich, Conn., 1670.
ABERCROMBY.—Sir Temple's Whately, 195.
ABERNETHY.—William Abernethe, a Scotchman, was an early settler at Branford, and removed to Walingford, Conn. He married 1st Sarah, Feb., 17, 1763; 2nd Elizabeth, and had issue Elizabeth, October 15, 1673, William, Jr., July 23, 1675; Sarah, 1677; Mary, 1679; Samuel, Jan. 10, 1683; Daniel, Sept. 30, 1686; Susannah, 1689.

REFERENCES.

Davis' History, Wallingford, Conn., 613; Hinman's Conn. Settlers, 17; Orcutt's History, Torrington, Conn., 637.

SAMUEL ABORN, or ABBORN, was probably at Tolland, Conn., soon after it was settled in 1713, and while it was a part of Hartford County. His estate was inventoried at £ 500. By his wife Martha he had, John, Samuel, Elizabeth and Abigail.

REFERENCES.

Hinman's Early Settlers, 18.   Waldo's Tolland, Conn., 130; Wyman's, Charlestown, Mass., Gen. vol. I, 2.
ABRAMSE.—Barton's Genealogy, 156.
ABRAMS.—Runnel's, Sanbornton, II, 7.
ABRAHAMS.—Wyman's, Charlestown, Mass., I, 3.
ABRIEL.—John ABRIEL, of Chatham, N. J., born 1772, died 1860. See American Ancestry, vol. II, 1.
ACHORN.—See Eaton's, Thomaston, Me., 128.
ACKER.—See Ruttenber's Newburgh, N. Y., 282; American Ancestry II, 1; Raymond's Tarrytown Monument, 101.
ACKERMAN, or AKERMAN.—Stephen Acreman of Newbury, Mass., married December 17, 1684, Sarah, probably widow of Amos Stickney.
ABRAHAM D. ACKERMAN, of New York, born Jan. 2, 1755. Served with Gen. Wayne at the storming of Stony Point. His father was born at Holland in 1700.

REFERENCES.

See Roe's Sketches of Rose, N. Y., 206; American Ancestry II, 1; Si vage's Gen. Dic. vol. I, 6.

ACKERLY.

ACKERLY.—Henry Ackerly, was of New Haven, Conn., 1640; Stamford, 1641; Greenwich, Conn., 1656.
ROBERT ACKERLY, or Accerly, of Brookhaven, L. I., was admitted freeman of Connecticut jurisdiction, 1664. He was an early settler of Stamford, Conn., with Capt. Underhill and Slauson as early as 1641—2. He was in the 3d company of settlers.

REFERENCES.

Savage's Gen. Dic. vol. I, 7; Hinman's Early Settlers, 18.
ACKERT.—Smith's, Rhinebeck, N. Y., 194.
ACKEY.—Egle's, Lebanon, Pa., 233.
ACKLEY.—Nicholas Ackley was in Hartford 1655, and lived for a time at 30 Mile Island—Haddam—and had a six acre lot toward Saybrook.

REFERENCES.

Savage's His., Dic. I, 7; Hinman's Conn. Settlers 19; Lapham's History, Rumford, Me., 293; Sedgwick's History, Sharon, Conn., 61; Smith Genealogy, (1890), 37, 135; Whittmore's, Middlesex County, Conn.

ACLY.

ACLY.—Abram Acly, born in England 1754, came to America on a British man-of-war, and settled at Sharon, Conn. He was a drum major, and at one time a prisoner on board the prison-ship " Jersey."
REFERENCES.—American Ancestry II, 1.

ACRES.—Henry Acres, or Ackers, of Newbury, Mass., married, March 13, 1674, Hannah, daughter of Thomas Silver. Had Catharine, Mary and John.
REFERENCES.
Savage's Gen. Dic. vol. I, 8; Shourd's, Fenwick, N. J., 18.

ACTOR.

JOHN ACTOR, was of North Yarmouth, 1685.
REFERENCES.—Savages's Gen. Dic. vol. I, 8; Shourd's, Fenwick, N. J., 18.
ACY.—See Essex, Mass., Coll. XIX, 298.

ADAM.

ADAM.—The surname of Adam is of great antiquity in Scotland, as proved by many documents in the public records. Duncan Adam, son of Alexander Adam, lived in the reign of King Robert Bruce, and had four sons, Robert, John, Reginald, and Duncan, from whom all the Adams, Adamsons, and Adies, in Scotland are descended.

For the American ancestor see Adam Genealogy, 1848, by William Adam.

ADAMS.—This family is very numerous both in England and America, and owing to the similarity and repetition of Christian names it is almost impossible to locate all the original settlers. By far the largest number are descendants of Henry Adams of Braintree. This family claims descent in a direct line from Ap. Adam who came out of the " Marches of Wales."*

The earliest record of the English branch of the Adam's family is that of John Ap Adam, of Charlton. Adam in Somersetshire, who married Elizabeth, daughter of and heiress to John Lord Gourmy, of Beviston and Tidenhaur, County of Gloucester, who was summoned to

Adams.

*Lords of the Marches were noblemen, who in the early ages inhabited and secured the Marches of Wales and Scotland, ruling as if they were petty kings, with their private laws, these were subsequently abolished.

Parliament as Baron of the Realm, 1296 to 1307. In the upper part of a Gothic window on the southeast side of Sidenham church, near Chopston, the name of JONES AB ADAM, 1310; and " Arms, argent on a cross gules five mullets or," of Lord Ap Adam, are still to be found beautifully excented in stained glass of great thickness and in perfect preservation.

This is probably one of the oldest church edifies in England. It originally stood within the boundary of Wales, but at a later period, the boundary line was changed, and it now stands on England soil.

HENRY ADAMS, of Braintree, (now Quincy), Mass., was the progenitor of the largest branch of the Adams family in this country. He is said to have emigrated to New England about 1634, and on Feb. 1641, was granted forty acres of land by the town of Boston, of which Braintree was then a part. He brought with him eight sons, and was the great-great-grandfather of John Adams, second President of the United States, who erected a granite column to his memory in the churchyard at Braintree, on which was inscribed the following:

In memory of HENRY ADAMS, who took his flight from the Dragon of persecution in Devonshire, England, and alighted with eight sons near Mount Walloston. One of the sons returned to England, and after taking some time to explore the country, four removed to Medfield and the neighboring towns; two to Chelmsford. One only, Joseph, who lies here at his left hand, remained here, who was an original proprietor in the township of Braintree, 1639.

This stone and several others have been placed in this yard by a great-grandson from a veneration of the piety, humility, sympathy, prudence, patience, temperance, frugality, industry, and perseverance of his ancestors, in hope of recommending an emulation of their virtues to their posterity.

The children of Henry Adams of Braintree. were:
HENRY (2), born 1604: settled at Medfield, Mass.
THOMAS, born in England, 1612; settled at Chelmsford, Mass.
SAMUEL, born 1617, settled at Chelmsford, died 1666.
JONATHAN, born 1619, settled at Medfield.
PETER, born 1622, settled at Medfield.
JOHN, born 1624, settled in Concord; afterward West Cambridge.
JOSEPH, of Braintree, now Quincy, Mass., who died and was buried there.
EDWARD, born 1620, settled at Medfield; died 1716.
Ursula, named in her father's will.

Among the other branches of the Adams family of which there does not appear to be any direct connection are:
JOHN, who came to Plymouth in the ship "Fortune," November 11, 1621.
WILLIAM, of Cambridge, 1635; removed to Ipswich, Mass., before 1642.
ROBERT, of Ipswich, 1635; Salem, 1638; Newbury, 1640.
RICHARD, of Weymouth, 1635.
RICHARD, of Salem, came in the ship "Abigail," 1635.
JEREMY, Braintree, 1632; Cambridge, 1635; Hartford, Conn., 1636.
RALPH, Elizabeth City, Va., 1623.
RALPH, Jones Island, Va., 1623.
ROBERT, Martin's Hundred, 1624.

RICHARD, age 22, embarked for Virginia in ship "Globe," of London, August 6, 1638.

JAMES, Londonderry, N. H., born in Argyleshire, Scotland, died at Londonderry, N. H., 1742; came to New England 1724.

FRANCIS, of Charles County, Md., born about 1690; died 1766.

DAVID, of Mass., born in Beverstone, England, June 8, 1536, died in Mass., July 27, 1611, son of Nathaniel.

REFERENCES.

MAINE.—Bradbury's, Kennebunkport, 224; Butler's History, Farmington, 360; Cushman's History, Sheepscot, 353; Eaton's History, Thomaston, 129; Farrow's History, Isleborough, 166; Lapham's History, Rumford, 294; Lapham's History, Woodstock, 170; Milliken's Naraguagus Valley, 18; Sibley's History, Union, 430.

NEW HAMPSHIRE.—Aldrich's History, Walpole; Cochran's History, Antrim, 333; Coggswell's History, Henniker, 440; Cutler's History, Jaffrey, 213; Hayward's History, Gilsum, 253; Hill's History, Mason, 199; Kidder's, New Ipswich, 289; Lancaster's History, Gilmanton, 255; Leonard's History, Dublin, 309; Livermore's History, Wilton, 297; Merill's History, Acworth, 178; Norton's History, Fitzwilliam, 453; Parker's History, Londonderry, 254; Read's History, Swanzey, 271; Runnel's History, Saubornton; Saunderson's, Charlestown, 276; Secomb's History, Amherst, 480; Stearn's History, Rindge, 523; Washington, N. H. History, 271; Wheeler's History, Newport, N. H., 285; Worcester's History of Hollis, 363.

VERMONT.—Adams' History, Fairhaven, 281; Bass' History, Braintree, Vt., 109; Caverly's History, Pittsford, 690; Heminway's, Vermont, Gazetteer, v. 396; Heminway's Gen. Record, 27; Hollister's History, Pawlet, Vt., 156; Joslin's History, Poultney, Vt., 197.

MASSACHUSETTS.—Barry's History, Framingham, 166; Ballou's History, Milford, 515; Benedict's History, Sutton, Mass., 582; Blake's History, Franklin, 228; Bond's, Watertown, Mass.; Butler's History, Groton 384; Chandler's History, Sutton, 343; Cutler's History, Arlington, 183; Davis' Landmarks of Plymouth, 3; Deane's History, Scituate, 211; Drake's History of Boston; Draper's History, Spencer, 159; Emery's Newbury Reminescence, 54; Fox's History, Dunstable, Mass., 237; Hammat Papers, Ipswich, 9; Hazen's History, Billerica, 3; Herrick's History, Gardner, 330; Hodgman's History, Westford, 436; Hudson's History, Lexington, 6; Jackson's History of Newton, 231; Jameson's History, Midway, 443; Marvin's History, Winchendon, 445; Morse's Sherborn Settlers, 1; Morse's Memorial Appendix, 32; Paige's History, Cambridge, 477; Pierce's History, Grafton, 443; Sawtelle's History, Townsend, 427; Shattuck's History, Concord, 361; Stearn's History, Ashburnham, 582; Stone's History, Hubbardston, 219; Simple's North Brookfield, 489; Ward's History, Shrewsbury, 212; Washburn's History, Leicester, 343; Wyman's, Charlestown, vol. I, 4.

CONNECTICUT.—Bronson's History, Waterbury, 458; Brown's West Simsbury, 7; Caulkin's History, New London, 486; Gold's History, Cornwall, 312; Hinman's Conn. Settlers, 20; Huntington's Stamford Families, 5; Orcutt's History, Stratford, 1115; Porter's Hartford Settlers, 1; Schenck's History, Fairfield, 349; Stile's History, Windsor, vol. II, 10; Todd's History, Riddway, 173; Weaver's History, Windham, 29.

NEW YORK.—Cleveland's History, Yates County, 610; N. Y. Gen. Biog. Record, vol. X, 9; Pearson's Schenectady Families 1.

NEW JERSEY.—Salter's History, Monmouth County, 1; Whittemore's History, Montclair, 221.

ILLINOIS.—Powers' History, Sangamon, 76.

VIRGINIA.—Richmond Standard I, 44; III, 15.

OTHER WORKS.—American Ancestry, vol. I, 1; vol. II, 1; vol. IV, 76, 124, 157, 205; vol. V, 37, 98, 175; vol. VII, 221; vol. VIII, 58; vol. IX, 152, 213; vol. X, 191; Cleveland Genealogy, 208; Driver Gen., 514; Granite Monthly, IV, 312; Gould's Stiles Gen., 341; Leland Gen., 192; Locke Gen., 48, 60, 148--50; Loomis Gen. Female Branches, 697; Muzzey's Reminescence; Paxton's Marshall Gen., 37; Savage's Gen. Dic., VI, 8; Thayer's Memorial, 1835, 37--48, 173--4; Tilley's Magazine of N. E. History; Trubee Gen., 93; Vinton Memorial, 295; Vinton's Giles Gen., 519; Vinton's Richardson Family, 884; Whitmore's Copps Hill Epitaphs; Wight Gen., 15 58, 60; N. E. History and Genealogy Reg. II, 228, 321, 351; VII, 39, 351; VIII, 41, 283; IX, 126; X, 89; XI, 53; XIV, 360; XV, 244; XXXIII, 410; XXXIV, 66; XLI, 90; XLIV, 209; XLVIII, 190.

Adams Family of Kingston, Mass., 1861; John Adams and his descendants, 1874; Thomas Adams. Amherst, 1880; William Adams, Ipswich, 1881; Whittemore's History, Adams Family, 1893; Descendants of James and William Adams of Londonderry N. H., 1894; Adams and Evarts Families, 1894; Robert Adams Family of Newbury, 1895, Adams Genealogy.

ADDINGTON.

ISAAC ADDINGTON, of Boston, 1640; freeman 1650. He married Ann, daughter of Elder Thomas Leverett, and had Isaac, Ann, Rebecca, Sarah.

ISAAC ADDINGTON, only son of Isaac and Ann Addington was born Jan. 22, 1645. He was bred for a surgeon, but was little known in that capacity. He was a member of the Council and Secretary of the Colony many years, and was appointed judge of the highest court in 1702, and its chief next year.

REFERENCES.

Savage's Gen. Dic. I, 17; Leverett Memoir, 31; Addington Gen., 1850.

ADDLEMAN.—Young's, Wayne, Ind., 217.

ADEE.—Baird's History, Rye, N. Y., 451.

ADDIS.

WILLIAM ADDIS, of Gloucester, Mass., 1642, was one of the chief inhabitants, perhaps went home for a short time, but in 1658—62, lived at New London, Conn., as a brewer. He had two daughters, Millicent, who married November 28, 1642. William Southmayd, next William Ash, and last Thomas Beebe, who were all of New London; and Ann, who married, at Boston, Ambrose Dart.

REFERENCES.

Savage's Gen. Dic. vol. I, 18.

ADEY.

WILLIAM ADEY, of Plymouth, was fined in 1636 for working on Sunday.

REFERENCES.

Savage's Gen. Dic., 18.

ADFORD.—Reference. Deane's, Scituate, Mass. 211.

ADGATE.

THOMAS ADGATE, of Saybrook, was a deacon of the church there, 1659; had Eliza, 1651; Hannah, 1653; he married 2d Mary, widow of Richard Bushnell, daughter of Matthew Marvin, and removed to Norwich where he had Abigail, Sarah, Rebecca, and Thomas Marvin.

REFERENCES.

Savage's Gen. Dic., 18; Caulkin's, Norwich, Conn., 155; Hinman's Conn. Settlers, 27.

ADGER.

THOMAS ADGER, at Pemaquid, took oath of fidelity, July 1674.

ADKINS.

JOSIAH ADKINS. of Middletown, Conn., died September 12, 1690; leaving seven children, minors, Sarah, Abigail, Solomon, Josiah, Benjamin, Ephraim. His wife was Elizabeth Wetmore or Whitmore.

THOMAS ADKINS. came first to Hartford and was located at East Hartford, 1682, died 1694. His estate was appraised at £ 182. 15s. His children were Mary, Thomas, William, Jane, Sarah, Josiah and Benoni.

REFERENCES.

Savage's Gen. Dic. vol. I, 18; Hinman's Conn. Settlers, 27; Timlow's History, Southington, Conn., I—III; Temple's History, Whately, Mass., 195. (see also Atkins.)

ADSIT.

MARTIN ADSIT, was of Chatham, N. Y., born 1761. See American Ancestry vol. II, 2.

AFRICA.

CHRISTOPHER AFRICA, born in Germany, lived at Germantown, Pa., and other places. Reference, American Ancestry, vol. VI, 54.

ADVERD or ADFORD.

HENRY ADVERD or ADFORD, of Scituate, 1640, married 1643 Thomasine Manson, and had son Experience, daughters Mary, Elizabeth and Sarah. He died at Rehoboth, 1653.

REFERENCES.

Savage's Gen. Dic. vol. I, 19.

AGARD.

AGARD.—This name was first in Connecticut, about 1700, spelled also Aguard.

REFERENCES.

Hinman's Early Settlers of Conn., 29; Orcutt's Torington, Conn., 638; Weaver's History, Windham, 30.

AGER.

WILLIAM AGER or EAGER, was admitted freeman, May 18, 1631.

REFERENCES.

Stearn's History, Rindge, N. H., 429; Stearn's Ashburnham, Mass., 594.

AGNEW.

ANDREW AGNEW, constable of Lochman, has the hereditary office of sheriff of Wigtown conferred on him 1451.

Arms—Argent a chevron between two cinquefoils in chief gules and a saltier, couped in base azure. *Crest*— An eagle issuant and regardant, ppr. *Supporters*—Two heraldic tigers proper, collared and chained or, *Motto* —Consilis, non impetu, (with counsel, not with rashness).

JOHN R. AGNEW, was the founder of the Pennsylvania and New York branch of this family. He came to this country about 1783; settling first in Philadelphia, and then in New York city. He was the progenitor of the eminent eye and ear specialist, Cornelius R. Agnew, M. D., of New York.

NINENAN AGNEW, of Kettery, 1676, was held in esteem sufficient to be made appraiser with Capt. John Wincoll's estates of Roger Plaisted, as well as of Richard Soyer, that year.

REFERENCES.

Savage's Gen. Dic., vol. I, 17.

ACKEN,

EDWARD ACKEN, of Londonderry, N. H., was born in Ireland, 1660, died at Londonderry, N. H., 1747. He was among the founders of Londonderry, N. H., to which place he emigrated in 1720. He was an elder in the church, and a prominent citizen, holding various local offices. He married Barbara Edwards, who died 1744.

REFERENCES.

Parker's History, Londonderry, N. H., 255; Runnel's Saubornton, N. H., II, 10; Secomb's History, Amherst, N. H., 481; Wheeler's History, Newport, N. H., 286; Chase's History, Chester, N. H., 462; Bedford, N. H., Centennial, 279; Cochran's History, Antrim, N. H., 336; Heminway's Vt. Gazeteer, V; Hinman's Conn. Settlers, 29; Paige's History, Hardwick, Mass., 322; American Ancestry, IV, 105; Smith's Dutchess County, N. Y., 498.

AINSWORTH.

ANCHOR AINSWORTH, was a resident of Boston, 1645. His lot was sold there in 1647.

DANIEL AINSWORTH, was of Rexbury, Mass., 1648; later of Dedham; died November 13, 1680.

REFERENCES.

Savage's Gen. Dic. vol. I, 19; Longmeadow, Mass., Centennial; Hinman's Conn. Settlers, 29; Eagle's Penn. Gen. I, 4; Cutler's History, Jaffray, N. H., 211; Ainsworth Gen. 1894.

ALBESON.—See Deane's, Scituate, Mass., 211.
AKEN.—See American Ancestry, II, 2.
AKERS.—See Lapham's, Norway, Me., 455.
AKERLY.—See American Ancestry X, 130, 132.
AKINS.—Salter's Monmouth County, N. J.

ALBEE or ALBY.

BENJAMIN ALBEE or ALBY, of Braintree, Mass., 1641, was made freeman. May 18, 1642; may have been of Mindon or Swanzey, 1669.

REFERENCES.

Sanderson's, Charlestown, N. H., 277; Read's History, Swanzey, N. H., 273; Machias, Me., Centennial 152; Eaton's History, Thomaston, Mass., 131; Ballou's Milford, 522; Savage's Gen. Dic. I, 20.
ALBERTS.—See Bergen's, Kings County, 8.

ALBESON or ALLBERSON.

NICHOLAS ALBESON or ALLBERSON, was of Scituate, Mass., he was distinguished as the Swede. He was supposed to have been the father of John of Yarmouth, Mass.

REFERENCES.

Savage's Gen. Dic. vol. I, 20; Deane's Scituate, Mass., 211.

ALBERTSON.—This was one of the Holland families, settled at Musketa Cove and Rockaway, N. J.

REFERENCES.

Clement's, Newtown, N. J., Settlers American Ancestry, IX, 72; Davis' Landmarks of Plymouth, 4.
ALBIN.—See Coggswell's Hennicker, 445.
ALBRA.—See Brooks' History, Medford, Mass, 499; American Ancestry, VII, 209; IX, 22.

ALBOROW or ALBRO.

JOHN ALBRO or ALBOROW, was of Portsmouth, R. I., in 1655, was an Assistant, 1671, and one of the council appointed by King James II.

REFERENCES.

Newport His. Magazine, IV, 238; Austin's Allied Families 1; Austin's R. I. Gen. Dic., 234; Savage's Gen. Dic. I, 20.
ALBURTIS.—See Riker's, Newtown, 395.

ALCOCK.

GEORGE ALCOCK, of Roxbury, Mass., came in the fleet with Winthrop, 1630. He was a physician and represented at the first court, May 14, 1634.
FRANCIS ALCOCK, came in the Bevis, 1638, aged 26.
SAMUEL ALCOCK, of Kittery, Me., 1652, made freeman of Mass., and was of York, 1659.
THOMAS ALCOCK, brother of George, came with Winthrop.

REFERENCES.

Hayward's History, Hancock, N. H., 298; Brownson's, Waterbury, 459; Hinman's Conn. Settlers, 30; Ellis, Roxbury, Mass., 90; N. E. His. Gen. Reg., XXXVI, 400; Prime's Sands Gen., 56; Savage's Gen. Dict, I, 21.
Arms—Gules a fesse between three cocks' heads erased argent, braked and crested or, Crest—A cock ermine braked and membered or, Motto—Vigilate.
ALCOTT.—See Tuttle Family, 673; Orcutt's Wolcott, Conn., 425.

ALDEN.

JOHN ALDEN, of Plymouth, passenger in the "Mayflower," 1620, had not been associated at Leyden with the Pilgrims, but was hired at Southampton as a cooper with the right of staying on this side or returning. Bradford refers to him as " being a hopeful young man was much desired, but left to his own liking to go or stay when he came here." He was the last male survivor of the compact. He lived most of his days at Duxbury. He was Assistant for the Colony, 1633, to Gov. Winslow, and served 42 years in that office, to every Governor after Carow. His courtship and marriage to Priscilla, daughter of William Mullins or Molines, while serving in the capacity of proxy to Capt. Miles Standish is well known. His descendants are quite numerous.

Arms—Gules a mullet argent between three crescents ermine within a bordure engrailed of the second. Crest—Out of a ducal coronet or, a demi lion gules.

REFERENCES.

MASSACHUSETTS.—Davis' Landmarks of Plymouth, 4; Freeman's Cape Cod., II, 222; Kingman's, N. Bridgewater, 443; Mitchell's, Bridgewater, 85; Paige's History, Hardwick, 324; Thatcher's History, Plymouth, 157.
MAINE.—Pierce's History, Gorham, 153; Silbey's History, Elmar, 430; Maine His. and Gen. Rec. VII, 132; Eaton's, Thomaston, 131.
VERMONT.—Heminway's Vt. Gazeteer, IV, 163.
CONNECTICUT.—Hines' Lebanon Address, 143.
OTHER PUBLICATIONS.—Alden Genealogy. Alden Chart; Alden's American Epitaphs; Ellis Gen., 364; American Ancestry, vol. I, 1; VI, 81; X, 176; Thayer'sMemorial, (1835); Walworth's Hyde Gen., 632; Whitman, Gen., 55; N. E. His. and Gen. Reg., 269.

ALDERMAN.

JOHN ALDERMAN, was of Salem, 1637, freeman in Mass., 1639; admitted to the church, February 17, 1637; died 1657.
GRACE ALDERMAN, came to New England in the "Paul of London," bound for Virginia in 1635.
WILLIAM ALDERMAN, was of Farmington and Simsbury, Conn., died about 1697, leaving Thomas, William, Sarah, Joseph.

REFERENCES.

Hinman's Conn. Settlers, 31.

ALDIS.

NATHAN ALDIS, was of Dedham, Mass., 1640, or sooner. He was made freeman May 13, 1640, and was chosen one of the first two deacons, died March 15, 1676. He had sons John, Daniel, and perhaps others.

REFERENCES.

Savage's Gen. Dic. vol. I, 24.

ALDRICH or ALDRIDGE.

GEORGE ALDRICH was of Dorchester, Mass., made freeman December 7, 1636. He resided at Braintree, Mass., and was one of the first settlers at Minden in 1663. By wife Catharine he had Meriam, Experience, Sarah, Peter, Mercy, Meriam, Jacob, Mattithiah.
GEORGE ALDRICH.—Swanzey, 1669.
HENRY ALDRICH, of Dedham, was freeman, 1645. He had Samuel, born March 10, 1645.

REFERENCES.

MASSACHUSETTS.—Pierce's History, Grafton, 448; Mitchell's History, Bridgewater, 90; Ballou's History, Milford, 537.

NEW HAMPSHIRE.—Bassett's History, Richmond, 256; Hayward's History, Gilsum, 254; Read's History, Swanzey, 273.

RHODE ISLAND.—Austin's R. I. Gen. Dict. 1; Austin's Allied Families, 3; Richardson's Woonsocket, 205.

VERMONT.—McKeen's History, Bradford, 310.

NEW YORK.—Roe's Sketches of Rose, 130.

OTHER WORKS.—Holden's Capron Family, 192; Hubbard's Stanstead, Canada, 318; Mowry Gen. 209; American Ancestry, VIII, 231; Savage's Gen. Dic. I, 25.

ALDWORTH.—See Salesbury's Mem., 1885.

ALEWORTH.

FRANCIS ALEWORTH, of Dorchester, was made freeman, May 18, 1631; went home the following year.

ALEXANDER.

The family known as Alexander of Powis, claims to be a branch of the same root as the Earls of Stirling, and inherits the lands of Powis from the heiress of Mayne, whose progenitors, descending from the Mayne of Lockwood, were settled near Stirling, and have been landed proprietors in that neighborhood since the commencement of the fifteenth century.

It was from this branch of the Alexander family, that General Alexander, Lord Stirling, of the Revolutionary Army claimed descent, a full account of which is given in the Life of Lord Stirling, published by the New Jersey Historical Society, 1847.

Arms—Per pale argent and sable a chevron, and in base a crescent, all counterchanged quartering Mac Donald. *Crest*—A bear argent erect ppr. *Motto*—Per mare per terras.

For Mac Donald, an eagle displayed with two heads gules.

GEORGE ALEXANDER, of Windsor, married March 18, 1642, Susanna Sage, and had Mary, Daniel, Jan. 12, 1651; Nathaniel, 1652, Sarah, 1654. His father was a Scotchman.

ARTHUR ALEXANDER, was of Scarborough; was constable 1658, was killed by the Indians 1675; leaving widow Ann and children.

ANDREW ALEXANDER, was of Scarborough, 1651, had by wife Agnes—John, Andrew, Matthew, Elizabeth, Joanna. He called his plantation Dunster. He was constable, 1661, and Lieutenant, was killed by the Indians with his brother Arthur, October, 1675.

THOMAS ALEXANDER, was of Taunton, 1665.

REFERENCES.

NEW HAMPSHIRE.—Hayward's History, Gilsum, 254; Merrill's History, Acworth, 179; Morrison's History, Windham, 305; Coggswell's History, Henniker, 445; Cochran's History, Antrim, 339, 46; Norton's History, Fitzwilliam, 454; Read's History, Swanzey, 272; Secomb's History, Amherst, 483; Stark's History, Dumbarton, 252.

MASSACHUSETTS.—Hyde's History, Brimfield, 469; Davis' Landmarks of Plymouth, 5; Judd's History, Hadley, 447; Temple's History, Northfield, 385; Ward's History Shrewsbury, 212; Wyman's Charlestown, I, 15.

CONNECTICUT.—Hinman's Conn. Settlers, 31; Stiles' History, Windsor, II, 12.

ILLINOIS.—Powers', Sangamon County, 76.

PENNSYLVANIA.—Plumb's History, Hanover, 387; Egle's History, Reg Int. Penn., II, 19.

NEW YORK.—Roe's Sketches of Rose, 287.

VIRGINIA.—Richmond, Va., Standard, vol. I, 39, II, 47, III, 2, 5, 7, 36, 37. Hayden's Virginia Genealogies, 180, 192. Foote's Sketches, Virginia, II, 100.

OTHER WORKS.—Wille's Washington Families, 183, 255; Slaughter's, Randolph, Fairfax, 2, 100; Paxton's Marshall Gen., 74, 248; James' Gen., 377; Green's Kentucky Families; Goodwin's Foote's Gen., 219; Good's Gen., 212, 482; De Bow's Review, XXVI, 133; American Ancestry, vol. I, 1; IV, 82; VI, 148; VIII, 142; IX, 56; N. Y. Gen. and Bio. Rec. X, 13; Savage's Gen. Dic. I, 25; Alexander Gen.

ALFORD.

WILLIAM ALFORD, was of Salem, 1635, came the year before from London, a member of the Skinner's company there, a merchant here. He brought with him a valuable letter from Francis Kisbey to his friend John Winthrop, son of the Governor. He lived for a time in New Haven but returned to Boston. By his wife Mary, he had Nathaniel, Samuel, Bithia, Elisha, Mary, Elizabeth; by another wife he had Ann and John.

REFERENCES.

Wyman's Charlestown, Mass., Gen. I, 16; Brown's Settlers, West Simsbury, Conn., 10; Eaton's Annals of Warren, Me., 498.

ALGER.

Among the early settlers on the coast of Maine were two brothers Andrew and Arthur Alger, they are believed to have come from Dunston, in Norfolk, England.

ANDREW ALGER, was living in Saes, as early as 1640, and was there styled a surveyor. In 1651 he with his brother purchased of the Indians a tract of land lying within the limits of Scarborough, containing about a thousand acres. Andrew removed from Saes to his estate in Scarborough in 1654. He was constable and selectman, and in 1668 was commissioned Lieut. He had by his wife Agnes—John, Andrew, Matthew, Elizabeth, Joanna.

ARTHUR ALGER was constable of Scarborough, 1658, grand-juryman 1661, and in 1691—2 was a representative to the General Court at Boston. Had no children.

REFERENCES.

N. E. His. and Gen. Reg., vol. XXIX, 270; XXXI, 101; Mitchell's History, Bridgewater, Mass., 91; Marvin's History, Winchendon, Mass., 445; Alger Gen., 1876; Salter's History, Monmouth County, N. J., 111; Boyd's History, Conesus, N. Y., 139; Savage's Gen. Dic. I, 27.

ALKIRE.—See Powers' History, Sangamon, Ill., 78.

ALLAIRE.—See Bolton's History, Westchester County, N. Y., I, 429. Savage's Gen. Dic., vol. I, 28.

ALLABEN.—See Bouton Gen., 342.

ALLARD.—See Adams' History, Fairhaven, Vt., 290; Savage's Gen. Dic., 1, 28; Adams' Haven Gen., 38; Barry's History, Framingham, Mass., 168; Temple's History of Brookfield, Mass., 493.

ALLDS.—See Cochran's History of Antrim, N. H., 340; Smith's History of Petersborough, N. H., 78.

ALLT.

JOHN ALLT or AULT, of Portsmouth, 1651, was sent out by John Mason, the Patentee of New Hampshire; lived at Dover most of his days after 1640. By his wife Remembrance he had issue John and Remembrance.

ALLEYNE, ALLYN, ALLAN, ALLEN, ALLIN, ALLING.

ALANUS de BUCHENHALL, who held the lordship of Buchenhall, (now Buckenhall), in Staffordshire, in the reign of King Edward I., is stated to have been the ancestor of the numerous branches of Allan, Allen, Allyn, Alleyn, and Alleyne. The original spelling of the name appears to have been Alleyne.

ALLEYNE.—This family bore *Arms*—Per chevron gules and ermine in chief, two lions' heads erased or, *Crest*—Out of a ducal coronet a horse's head argent. *Motto*—Non tua te moveant sed publica vota.

EDWARD ALLEYNE, of Dedham, 1636, was one of the founders of the church, November 8, 1638; made freeman March 13, following with prefix of respect at the same time with his pastor, Rev. John Allin spelt with an "e" in the last syllable to whom he may have had near relations. He was representative four years, 1639—42, died in the latter year.

REFERENCES.

Winslow Memorial, 286; Savage's Gen. Dic., vol. I, 43.

JOHN ALLIN, of Dedham, Mass., the first minister, came over in 1637, was freeman March 13, 1639, and advanced April 24, following. His second wife to whom he was married, November 8, 1653, was the widow of Gov. Thomas Dudley. They had Daniel, Benjamin and Eleazer.

REFERENCES.

Savage's Gen. Dic., vol. I, 40.

ALLIN.—Hon. Matthew Allin, was an early and important settler at Hartford as early as 1638. He drew 110 acres of land in the Hartford land division, 1639. He was of Cambridge, 1632, and may have been a son of Samuel of Chelmsford, Co Essex, England. Was made freeman March 4, 1635, represented at March General Court, 1636, removed probably next year to Hartford, and then to Windsor, representing that town

at the General Court, 1648 to '57; Assistant, 1658—67; chosen Commissioner for United Colonies, 1660—4; he died 1671. His children were. John, Thomas, Mary and Benjamin Newbury.

REFERENCES.

Stiles' History, Windsor, II, 27; Orcutt's History, Torrington, Conn., 639; Hurd's History, New London County, Conn., 533; Hinman's Conn. Settlers, 41; Caulkin's History, Norwich, Conn., 156; Freeman's History, Cape Cod, Mass., II, 274; Candee's Genealogy, 121; Loomis Genealogy, Female Branches, 557, 805; Swift's Barnstable Families, I, 5.

ALLINE.—See Millikin's, Naraguagus, 15.

WILLIAM ALLAN, born in Scotland, 1720; died at Halifax, N. Y., 1790. He came to America 1749, and was one of the early settlers of Halifax. He was a Major in the British army. He married Isabella, daughter of Sir Eustace Maxwell of Scotland. He left several descendants, who reside in the New England States.

REFERENCES.

Dennysville, Maine, Centennial, 101; Kidder's Mem. Col. John Allan, 25; American Ancestry, IV, 178; VI, 8; Allan Genealogy, 1867.

ALLEN.—Samuel Allen of Windsor, Conn., was the progenitor of Colonels Ethan and Ira Allen, both distinguished in the war of the Revolution, and also as the chief founders of the state of Vermont. Samuel Allen was a native of Braintree, Essex Co., England, born about 1588; came to Cambridge, Mass., 1632, was a brother of Col. Matthew Allyn, of Cambridge, Mass., afterwards of Windsor and Hartford, Conn., and of Dea Thomas Allyn of Middletown, Conn.

Ancient Windsor held the distinct families of this name and the difference in the spelling of the name by the same family has led to great confusion in tracing this line of descendants.

ALEXANDER ALLEN, a Scotchman, was of Windsor, Conn., 1689, married Mary Grant: Benjamin Allen was of Groton, Conn., 1674; Bozoan Allen was of Hingham, Mass., 1638; Daniel Allen was of Boston, Daniel Allen of Swanzey, 1673; Edward Allen of Ipswich came from Scotland, 1636; Francis Allen was of Sandwich, 1645; George Allen, of Weymouth, 1641, removed to Boston; Henry Allen, of Boston, 1642; Hope Allen, of Boston, 1641; Issac of Rehoboth, 1673; James Allen, of Dedham, Mass., 1639; James Allen, of Boston, 1652; John Allen, of Plymouth, 1633; John Allen, of Dorchester, 1632; John Allen, of Springfield, 1639; John Allen, of Northampton, 1669; Jonah Allen, of Taunton, Mass., before 1663; Joseph Allen, of Newport, R. I., 1633; Joseph Allen, of Gloucester, 1674; Matthew Allen, of Sandwich, 1643; Nathaniel Allen, of Dedham, 1646; Nehemiah Allen, of Swanzey, 1675; Nicholas Allen, of Dorchester, married July 3, 1663, Mary widow of Robert Pond; Peter Allen, of Roxbury; Ralph Allen, of Newport, R. I., 1639; Robert Allen, of Salisbury, and New Haven; Samuel Allen, of Newport; Walter Allen, of Newbury, 1640; William Allen, Salem, Mass., 1626; William Allen, of Concord, Mass., 1659.

REFERENCES.

MAINE.—Bangor, Me. His. Magazine V, 62-4, 181; Butler's History, Farmington, 363; Corliss' North Yarmouth; Eaton's History, Thomaston, 131; Eaton's Annals Warren, 2d ed., 499; Hatch's History, Industry, Me., 471; Lapham's History, Bethel, 460; Lapham's History, Paris, 497; Thurston's History, Winthrop, 172; Maine's Genealogy, I, 9, 60.

NEW HAMPSHIRE.—Bassett's History, Richmond, 267; Coggswell's History, Henniker, 446; Hayward's History, Gilsum, 254; Hill's History, Mason, 199; Leonard's History, Dublin, 311; Merrill's History, Acworth, 180; Morrison's History, Windham, 307; Norton's History, Fitzwilliam, 455; Saunderson's, Charlestown, 278; Stearn's History, Rindge, 429; Wheeler's History, Newport, 287; Aldrich's History, Walpole, 186.

VERMONT.—Bars' History, Braintree, 110; David's History, Reading, 117; Hollister's History, Pawlet, 157; Joslin's History, Poultney, 198; Williams' History, Danley, 101; Adams', Fairhaven, 284; Heminway's Gen. Record, 68.

MASSACHUSETTS.—Hammatt Papers, Ipswich 15; Morse's, Sherborn, Mass., 10; Paige's History, Hardwick, Mass., 325; Temple's History, North Brookfield, 494; Temple's History, Northfield, 393; Temple's History, Whately, 196; Temple's History, Palmer, 408; Babson's History, Gloucester, 55; Draper's History, Spencer, 160; Hudson's History, Lexington, 8; Hyde's History, Brimfield, 367; Ballou's History, Milford, 539; Barry's History, Framingham, 167; Bend's History, Watertown, 3; Mitchell's Bridgewater, 93; Pierce's History, Grafton, 449; Benedict's History, Sutton, 583; Blake's History, Franklin, 231; Cutler's History, Arlington, 189; Doggett's History, Attleborough, 87; Davis' Landmarks of Plymouth, 5; Deane's History, Scituate, 212; Freeman's Cape Cod, II, 46; Hazen's History, Bellirica, 3; Jackson's History, Newton, Mass., 233; Jameson's History, Midway, 451; Kingman's North Bridgewater, 446; Stearn's Ashburnham, 594; Stone's History, Hubbardston, 221; Wall's Reminescences, Worcester, 347; Ward's History, Shrewsbury, 214; Washburn's History, Leicester, 343; Wyman's, Charlestown, vol. I, 16.

RHODE ISLAND.—Newport, R. I. Magazine, 191; Narragansett's Hist. Magazine II, 279; Austin's Ancestries, I; Austin's R. I. Gen. Dic. 2; Austin's Allied Families, 6.

CONNECTICUT.—Cothren's Hist. Woodbury, II, 1469; Stiles' History, Windsor, II, 13; Timlow's Sketches, Southington, 13; Weaver's History, Windham, 30; Davis' History, Wallingford, 614; Middlefield Conn. History; Orcutt's, New Milford, 639; Orcutt's History, Stratford, 1115; Orcutt's History, Torrington, 639.

NEW YORK.—Young's Chautauqua County, 350; Sprague's History, Gloversville, 107; Cleveland's Yates County, 332; Boyd's History, Consensus, 140.

PENNSYLVANIA.—Clyde's Irish Settlement, 10; Davis' History, Bucks County, 144; Egle's Penn. Gen., 7; Futhey's History, Chester County, 462.

NEW JERSEY.—Littell's Passaic Valley, 3; Salter's History, Monmouth County, II; Whittemore's Founders and Builders of the Oranges, 380.

GREEN'S KENTUCKY FAMILIES.—Hayden's Virginia Genealogies; Hubbard's, Stanstead, Canada, 145; Powers' Sangamon, Ill., 79.

OTHER PUBLICATIONS.—N. E. Hist. and Gen. Reg., X, 225; XXV, 144; XXX, 444. XLVII, 86; Essex Inst. Hist. Coll. I, 187; XXIV, 223, 302; XXV, 44; XXVII, 31; Whitman Gen., 194, 208; Watkins' Gen., 19; Ward's Gen. of Rice Family, 15, 16; Vinton Memorial, 303; Thompson Gen., (1890), 236; Stray's Gen., 967; Stoddard's, J. Allen Biog., 1883; Spooner Memorial, 101; Spooner's Gen., I, 350; Putnam's Hist. Magazine, I, 286; Salem Press Hist. and Gen. Rec. II, 102; Savage's Gen. Dic. I, 28; Minor's Philps Purchase, 204; Loomis' Gen. Female Branches,

675; Hayden's Weitzell's Gen. Gould's Stiles Gen. 397; Green's Gen., (1894). Glover Gen. 401; Driver Gen. 190; Cleveland Gen., 204; Chandler Gen., 563; Bulkley's Browne's Mem., 91; Boyd Gen., 225; American Ancestry, vol. I, 1; II, 2; IV, 131, 171, 180, 208; V, 27; VI, 60, 154, 157; VII, 105, 225, 283; VIII, 102, 107, 213; IX, 89, 119. Descendants of George Allen, of Boston, 1868; Allen Family of Medfield, 1869, 1896; Allen and Witter Families. 1872 ; Samuel Allen, of Windsor, and his Descendants, 1876; George Allen of Sandwich, Mass., and his descendants; Jolley Allen, of Boston, 1883; Stephen Allen, of New Bedford, and his Descendants, 1887; Capt. Nathaniel Allen, of Boston, Mass., and his descendants; Allen Family of Dedham and Medfield, Mass., 1896; Walter Allen, of Newbury, Mass., and his descendants, 1896; John Allen and Phebe Deul of Cambridge and Peru, N. Y., 1897; Whittemore's Founders and Builders of the Oranges, 380.

ALLING.

Roger Alling at the very beginning of the settlement, 1639, signed the compact. He was sergeant, and deacon, and treasurer of the Colony, 1661; and some years after. He died September 27, 1676. He married Mary, daughter probably of Thomas Nash. Had issue Mary, Samuel, John, Sarah, Elizabeth and Susanna. Samuel, the eldest son was one of the early settlers of Newark, N. J.

REFERENCES.

Dodd's History of East Haven, Conn., 101; Davis' History, Wallingford, Conn., 614; Hamden's Conn. History, 237; Savage's Gen. Dic. I. 40; Tuttle Family, of Conn., 620; Chapman's Trowbridge, Gen. 33, 45; American Ancestry, VIII, 206, Alling Genealogy, Early Records of Newark, N. J.

ALLERTON.

ISAAC ALLERTON, born about 1583, died, New Haven, 1659, one of the pilgrims in the Mayflower, at Plymouth, 1620, at one time the richest of the Colony, was an Assistant, 1621, the sole officer for three years under the Governor. He treated with Massasoit and made several trips to England as the agent of the Colony to purchase the rights of the adventurers, to secure patents for lands, and to bring over the rest of the congregation at Leyden. In 1630 he had a dispute with the colony and was dismissed from the service. He afterwards engaged in the coast trading service.

By his wife Mary, he had Bartholomew, Remember and Mary. His first wife died in 1620, and in 1626 he married Fear, daughter of Elde William Brewster.

REFERENCES.

Davis' Landmarks of Plymouth, 6; Signers of the Mayflower Compact, 20; Mitchell's History, Bridgewater, Mass., 356; Savage's Gen. Dic. I, 40; N. E. Hist. and Gen. Reg., VII, 265; XLIV, 290; Allerton Gen.

ALLEY.

HUGH ALLEY, of Lynn, Mass., came in the Abigail, 1635, from London, aged 27. He had Mary, John, Martha, Sarah, Hugh, Solomon, Hannah, Jacob.

REFERENCES.

Wyman's, Charlestown, Mass., Gen., I, 19; Lawrence and Bartlett Mem., 158; Coggswell's Henniker, 446; Savage's Gen. Dic. I, 39.

ALLIS.

WILLIAM ALLIS or ALLLICE, of Braintree, Mass., had grant from Boston, of twelve acres for three heads. He was made freeman, May 13, 1640; selectman 1662, Lieut. of cavalry, deacon. He removed to Hadley, now Hatfield, 1661, died 1678. By his wife Mary, he had John, Samuel, Josiah, William, Hannah. His will was dated at Hartford, Conn.

REFERENCES.

Temple's History, Whately, Mass., 31, 196; Judd's History, Hadley, Mass., 447; Kellogg's Mem. Elder John White, 101; Hinman's Conn. Settlers, 48; American Ancestry, II, 2; Savage's Gen. Dic. I, 41.

ALLISON.

This family is a scion of Alison of New Hall in Anguishire, Scotland. A branch of the family settled in Ireland, the descendants of whom emigrated to this country.

JOHN ALLISON, of Hartford, purchased lands of Samuel Graham, in Hartford, in 1726.

JAMES ALLISON, was of Boston, 1644, and had a son James, born in 1650.

REFERENCES.

Smith's History, Petersborough, N. H., 8; Leonard's History, Dublin, N. H., 312; Clyde's Irish Settlement, Pa., 11; Morse's Memorial Appendix No. 11; Allison Gen. Beers' His., Rockland Co., N. Y., 335; Powers' Hist., Sangamon Co., Ill., 80; Allison Gen., 1893.

ALLMY.—See Salter's, Monmouth, N. J., 111.

ALMY.

WILLIAM ALMY, of Portsmouth, R. I., perhaps as early as 1631, went home and came again 1635, in the Abigail, aged 34, with wife Andrey, aged 32, and children Annis and Christopher; removed, 1637, probably to Sandwich, and was freeman of Portsmouth, R. I., 1655. His will names, Christopher, John, Job, Ann, and Catharine.

REFERENCES.

Austin's R. I. Gen. Dic., 236; Savage's Gen. Dic., vol. I, 45; Spooner Gen., I, 403; American Ancestry, IV, 189; Heroes of the Revolution and their descendants; Empire State Society, S. A. R., 75.

ALDRICKS.—See Egle's Penn. Gens., 13; Amer. Ancestry, VI, 93.

ALSOBROOK.—See Richmond Standard, IV, 3.

ALSOP.

One Hugh de Alsop went with King Richard I. to the Holy Land, and the king for his good service in the conquest of Acre, bestowed upon him the Order of Knighthood, and for the further argumentation of his honor, gave him an escutcheon.

JOSEPH ALSOP, of New Haven, came at the age of 14 to Boston in the Elizabeth and Ann, 1635, from London went to New Haven early, took oath of fidelity in 1644. Before 1647 he married Elizabeth, daughter of William Preston, and had Joseph, Elizabeth, Sarah, Mary, Abigail, Hannah, John, Lydia, Daniel, Joanna. He died November 8, 1638.

REFERENCES.

N. E. His. and Gen. Reg., XLVI, 366; Savage's Gen. Dic. I, 45; Whittemore's Middlesex County, Conn.,

156; Riker's, Newtown, N. Y., 334; Lamb's His., New York City, I, 740.

ALSTON.

DAVID ALSTON, was a Captain in the British army; settled on Staten Island about the beginning of the revolution.

REFERENCES.

Clute's His., Staten Island, 338.

ALVORD.

ALEXANDER ALVORD, of Windsor, married October 27, 1646, Mary, daughter of Richard Vore or Voar, and had Abigail, John, Mary, Thomas, Elizabeth, Benjamin and Sarah. He removed to Northampton and there had Jeremiah, Ebenezer, and Jonathan.

BENEDICTUS ALVORD, of Windsor, 1637, joined the Windsor church, 1641; was juror, April 1643; sergeant in the Pequot fight, 1637; constable, 1666; married, November 26, 1640, Jane Newton. Had Jonathan, Benedict, Josias, Elizabeth, Jeremy.

REFERENCES.

Hinman's Conn. Settlers, 32; Stiles' His., Windsor, vol. II, 34; Alvord's Gen. 1864; Boyd's Annals of Winchester, Conn., 62, 397; Matthew's His., Cornwall, Conn., 284; Phenix's Whitney Family, Conn., 1, 712; Judd's His., Hadley, Mass., 448; Temple's His., Northfield, 398; Eaton's Annals of Warren, Me., 375; Kellogg's White Descendants, 46, 72; Savage's Gen. Dic. I, 46; Nash Gen., 85; Whittemore's His., Middlesex County, Conn., 199.

ALWARD.—See Littell's Passaic Valley Gen., 7; Bouton's Gen., 420; Amer. Ancestry, VI, 10.

ALYSWORTH.—Alysworth Gen., (1840).

AMADON.—See Busult, Richmond, 271; Norton's His., Fitzwilliam, N. H., 457.

AMBLER.

RICHARD AMBLER, was of Watertown, Mass., and of Boston, 1643. By wife Sarah he had Sarah, Abraham. He removed to Stamford, Conn., and was made freeman 1669.

REFERENCES.

Meade's Old Families of Virginia, I, 103; Huntington's Stamford Conn. Families, 5; Hinman's Conn. Settlers, 48; N. E. His. and Gen. Reg., XXXIX, 333; Savage's Gen. Dic. I, 48; Richmond, Va. Standard, I, 39, III, 44; Paxton's Marshall Gen., 42, 251, 262; Amer. Ancestry, vol. II, 2, IV, 135.

AMBRY.

ROBERT AMBRY, was of New Haven, Conn., 1643, where the name often appears Emery or Emry. He took the oath of fidelity 1644. By wife Mary he had Joseph, Mary, and John. He removed to Stamford and there had Moses.

REFERENCES.

Savage's Gen. Dic. I, 48.

AMBROSE.

HENRY AMBROSE, was of Hampton. 1641, or earlier; was admitted freeman 1642, lived at Boston 1654, Charlestown 1656. Had considerable property. Had Samuel, Ebenezer, Henry.

REFERENCES.

Bouton's His. of Concord, N. H., 631; Chase's His. of Chester, N. H., 464; Savage's Gen. Dic., I, 48; Hatch's His. of Industry.

AMERMAN.—See Bergen's Kings County, N. Y., 10.

AMERY or EMERY.—See Emery's Reminescences of Newbury, Mass., 134.

AMES.

WILLIAM AMES, of Cambridge, came in the Mary Ann of Great Yarmouth, 1637, with his mother Joane, widow of Rev. Williams, D. D. He was born in Burton, Somersetshire, England, October 6, 1605, died at Braintree, Mass., Jan. 11, 1653. He had a son John, who lived at West Bridgewater, Mass.

REFERENCES.

MAINE.—Lapham's His. Norway, 455; Dearborn's His., Parsonfield, 365; Eaton's His., Thomaston, 132; Farrow's His. Isleborough, 166; Hatch's His. Industry, 500; Bangor His. Magazine, V, 43.

NEW HAMPSHIRE.—Coffin's His., Boscawen, 466; Hayward's His., Hancock, 300; Hill's His. of Mason, 190; Leonard's His., Dublin, 312; Smith's, Peterborough, 9; Washington, N. H. His., 275; Worcester's His. Hollis, 364.

VERMONT.—Joslyn's His., Poultney, 199.

MASSACHUSETTS.—Winsor's His., Duxbury, 220; Stearn's His., Ashburnham, 595; Paige's His., Cambridge, 479; Mitchell's, Bridgewater, 99; Kingman's North Bridgewater, 437; Davis' Landmarks of Plymouth, 6; Butler's His., Groton, 384, 468.

CONNECTICUT.—Andrews' His., New Britain, Conn., 188; Hinman's Conn. Settlers, 49; Weaver's His., Windham, 39.

INDIANA.—Ball's Lake County, 444.

OTHER PUBLICATIONS.—Ames Chart., 1851; Ames Gen., Montague Gen., 553; Poor's His. Researches, 83, 120; Savage's Gen. Dic., I, 49; N. E. His. and Gen. Reg., XVI, 255; American Ancestry, vol. I, 2; IV, 43.

AMIDON, AMIDOWN, AMADOWN.

ROGER AMADOWN, of Salem, 1637, Weymouth, 1640, where by wife Sarah he had Sarah. 1640, and at Boston, Lydia, 1643; removed 1648 to Rehoboth, where he probably had several children. He died Nov. 13, 1673.

AMIDON.—See Bass' Braintree, Vt., 110; Temple's North Brookfield, Mass., 495.

AMMIDOWN.—Paige's His., Hardwick, Mass., 328, Hayward's His., Gilsum, N. H., 256; Child's Gen., 346; Ammidown Gen.; Ammidown's Coll., II, 225.

AMORY.

SIMON AMORY, of Boston, was made freeman, 1672. Had wife Mary.

REFERENCES.

Wyman's, Charlestown, Mass., vol. I, 20; Heraldic Journal, vol. II, 101. Amory Gen.; N. E. His. and Gen. Reg., X, 59.

AMOS.

HUGH AMOS, of Boston, was made freeman 1666, was of the 2nd church. Had John baptized there; removed to Norwich, where he had Mary and Daniel, born 1673. He lived in what is now Preston.

REFERENCES.

Savage's Gen. Dic., vol. I, 50; Powers' Sangamon, Ill., 81.

AMSBURY.—See Eaton's Thomaston, Me.

AMSDEN.

ISAAC AMSDEN, of Cambridge, married June 8, 1654, Frances Perriman, and had Isaac 1656, Jacob 1657.

REFERENCES.

Temple's His., Brookfield, Mass., 495; Paige's His. Cambridge, Mass., 479; Judd's His., Hadley, Mass., 448; Hudson's His., Marlboro, Mass., 308; Heminway's Vermont Gazeteer, V, 161; Davis' Reading, Vt., 118; Huron and Erie Counties, Ohio, 391; Rice Gen., 243; Savage's Gen. Dic., vol. I, 50; N. E. His. and Gen. Reg., XV, 21.

AMY or AMEE.

JOHN AMEY, of Woburn, Mass., 1649. By wife Martha, daughter of Edward Johnson, the historian, had Mary, 1650; removed to Boston 1653, had John, 1654; Martha, 1655; William, 1657.

ANABLE.—See Anable Genealogy.

ANDERSON.

This family is supposed to be of Danish extraction, and to have settled in early times, in Northumberland and Lincolnshire, which counties were peopled by Scandinavians. They bore *Arms*—Argent a chevron, between three crosses, flory, sable. *Crest*—A spaniel dog, passant, or. *Motto*—Guaviter.

JOHN ANDERSON, a Scotch-Irish emigrant, settled in Watertown, Mass., and married, July 16, 1706, Rebecca Wright, (born 1680), and had Abraham born 1708, and two daughters. By his 2d wife, Mary Aplin, he had Richard and John.

ROBERT ANDERSON, of Goldmine, Va., son of Richard, was born in New Kent, C. H., about 1660, married Mary Overton.

JOHN ANDERSON, of Boston, 1647, was a shipwright, and was permitted in 1652 to build a wharf. He married Mary Hodges of Charlestown.

REFERENCES.

MAINE.—Wheeler's His., Brunswick, 827; Eaton's Annals of Warren, 499.

NEW HAMPSHIRE.—Chase's His., Chester, 464; Eaton's His., Candia, 51; Morrison's His., Windham, 307; Parker's, Londonderry, 259.

MASSACHUSETTS.—Hyde's His. Address at Ware, 52.

CONNECTICUT.—Stiles', Windsor, II, 37; Weaver's His., Windham, 41.

NEW YORK.—Baird's His., Rye, 452; Cleveland's His., Yates County, 512; Pomfrey, N. Y., Reunion, 251.

NEW JERSEY.—Cooley's Trenton Settlers, 5; Salter's, Monmouth County, iii.

PENNSYLVANIA.—Futher and Cope's Chester County, 463; Eagle's Penn. Gens., 24.

ILLINOIS.—Powers' Sangamon County, 83.

VIRGINIA.—Crawford Family of Virginia, 87; Richmond, Va., Standard, II, 49; III, 24, 28, 31, 33, 35, 39, 48.

OTHER PUBLICATIONS.—Anderson's Genealogy, 1880;. American Ancestry, vol. II, 3; VII, 239; VIII, 230; Champion Gen.; Cinc., Ohio, Criterion, (1888), II, 313; Gilmer's Georgians, 103; Green's Kentucky Families; Old Kent, Md., 367; Opdyck Gen., 180; Paxton's Marshall Gen., Salisbury Memorial, II, 535; Wight Gen., 129; N. E. Hist. and Gen. Reg. XLIII, 198.

ANDRUS.—See Clyde's Irish Settlers, Pa., 11.

ANDREW.

JOHN ANDREW, was of Wickford, 1674.

NICHOLAS ANDREW, of Marblehead, was made freeman there, 1683.

WILLIAM ANDREW, of Cambridge, mariner, was made freeman 1634; he died before 1655. By wife Mary he had Samuel and perhaps other children.

REFERENCES.

Paige's His., Cambridge, Mass., 480; Life of Gov., J. A. Andrew, 1868; Gold's His., Cornwall, Conn., 320; Plumb's His., Hanover, Penn., 387; Austin's R. I. Gen. Dic., 3; Burnham's Andrew Gen., 1869; N. E. His. and Gen. Reg., XXIII, 11.

ANDREWS.

One branch of the Andrews family sprang from Andrew of Charwelton, Co. Northampton, founded by Ralph Andrew, of Gray's Inn, son of Thomas Andrew of Carlisle, anno 1286, as appears from a certificate under the hand and seal of John Andrew, son of Sir John Andrew, of Charyelton, now among the archives of the College of Arms. *Arms.*—A saltire or, surmounted of another vert. *Crest*—A black moor's head in profile, couped at the shoulders, and wreathed about the temples all ppr.

EDWARD ANDREWS, of Newport, R. I., 1639, removed to Saco, Me., 1650.

EDWARD ANDREWS, of Hartford, 1655, was made freeman, 1657.

FRANCIS ANDREWS, of Hartford, Conn., 1639, had issue John, 1646; Thomas, 1648; he removed later to Fairfield.

HENRY ANDREWS, of Taunton, Mass., was an original purchaser; representative 1639, and for the four years following.

JEDEDIAH ANDREWS, was of Dover, N. H., 1657.

JOHN ANDREWS, was of Lynn, Mass., 1652.

JOHN ANDREWS, of Ipswich, Joseph of Hingham; Nicholas of Marblehead; Robert of Ipswich, 1635; Samuel of Saco, 1635; Samuel of Marlborough, and Thomas of Dorchester, Mass., 1685, all original settlers.

WILLIAM ANDREWS, of New Haven, signed the compact, 1639. He was one of the founders of the church and active in military service, and kept the ordinary.

REFERENCES.

MAINE.—Lapham's His., Woodstock, 170; Lapham's His., Rumford, 300; Lapham's His., Paris, 493; Lapham's His., Norway, 457; Lapham's His., Bethel, 461; Eaton's His., Thomaston, 135; Eaton's Annals of Warren, 501; Machias, Me., Centennial, 152; Maine His. and Gen. Rec., III, 194, 257; IV, 8, 77, 209, 236; V, 22, 162.

NEW HAMPSHIRE.—Coggswell's Henniker, 447; Coggswell's New Boston, 437.

MASSACHUSETTS.—Wyman's Charlestown, I, 21; Ward's His., Shrewsbury, 221; Pierce's His., Grafton, 450; Perley's His., Boxford, 24; Hyde's His., Brimfield, 368; Hammott Papers, Ipswich, 11; Ballou's His., Milford, 542; Babson's His., Gloucester, 57.

CONNECTICUT.—Schenck's His., Fairfield, 350; Timlow's Sketches of Southington 3; Huntington's Stanford, Conn. Settlers, 6; Hinman's Conn. Settlers, 51; Dodd's His., East Haven, 101; Davis' History, Wallingford, 437; Boyd's Annals of Winchester, 105; Andrews' New Britain, 151, 195, 233.

NEW YORK.—Roe's Sketches of Rose, 141; Cleveland's His., Yates County, 485.

OTHER PUBLICATIONS.—Walker Family, 215; Vinton's Richardson Memorial, 555; Tuttle Gen., 129; Thomas Family of Maryland; Savage's Gen. Dic. I, 51; Ransom Gen., 40; Loomis' Gen. Female Branches, 715; Hale's Lawrence Family, 10; Green's Kentucky Families; Goode's Gen., 93, 306, 475; Eagle's Penn. Gens., 4; Austin's R. I. Gen. Dic., 3; American Ancestry, vol. I, 2; II, 3; IV, 80, 82, 188; VI, 40, 45; VII, 123; VIII, 108; X, 36; N. E. His and Gen. Reg., XL,21; Genealogy of John and Mary Andrews of Farmington, 1872; Genealogy of John and Hannah Andrews of Boston; Genealogy of Robert Andrews of Ipswich, Mass., Genealogy of John Andrews of Maryland, 1893; Andrew Gen., 1867, 1872, 1887, 1890, 1893.

ANDRIES.—See Bergen's Kings County, N. Y.,

ANDROSS.—See Stiles' His., Windsor, Conn., 11, 38; McKeen's, Bradford, 172.

ANDROVETTE.—See Clute's Staten Island, 339.

ANDRUS.

REFERENCES.

Williams' His., Danby, Vt., 103; Joslin's His., Poultney, Vt., 200; Hollister's Pawlet, Vt., 159; Andrews, New Britain, Conn., 139, 160, 172; Hinman's Conn. Settlers, 54; Tunlow's His., Southington, Conn., iii, 12; Cleveland's Yates County. N. Y., 531, 685; Chandler's Gen., 310; American Ancestry, vol. II, 3; N. E. His. and Gen. Reg., XV, 242.

ANGELL.

Thomas Angell, of Providence, was one of the earliest settlers with Roger Williams, freeman, 1655, and constable. He had issue James, John, Amphyllis, Mar; Deborah, Alice, Margery.

REFERENCES.

Austin's Ancestral Dic., I, Austin's Ancestries, 101; Austin's R. I. Gen. Dic., 4; Wheeler's His., Newport, N. H., 289; Young's Chatauqua County, N. Y., 416; Savage's Gen. Dic., I, 57; Driver Gen., 346; American Ancestry, vol. II, 3; Angell Gen.

ANGEOME.—See Bolton's Westchester County, N. Y., 706; Joslin's His. Poultney, Vt., 200.

ANGER.—Dodds East Haven, Conn., 102.

ANGIER.

JOHN ANGIER, of Boston, married 1651, Hannah, daughter of William Aspinwall, and had John, born 1652.

JONATHAN ANGIER, Salem, 1668.

JOSEPH ANGIER, of Medford, Mass., 1684, removed to Dorchester. By wife Elizabeth, he had Elizabeth, Margaret, Joseph, 1702; Benjamin.

REFERENCES.

Wyman's Charlestown Gen., I, 22; Stearn's His., Ashburnham, 595; Paige's His., Cambridge; Mitchell's His., Bridgewater, Mass., 105, Hudson's His., Lexington, Mass., 8; Bond's His. Watertown, Mass., 8; Barry's Framingham, Mass., 168; Baylie's His., New Plymouth, IV, 89; Merrill's His. Acworth, N. H., 180; Norton's His., Fitzwilliam, N. H., 459.

ANGUS.—See Cleveland's His., Yates County, N. Y., 181; American Ancestry, vol. I, 2.

ANNABLE.

ANTHONY ANNABLE, came in the Ann, 1623, with wife Jane and daughters Sarah and Hannah, and was one of the first settlers at Scituate, 1630; and a founder of the church there, Jan. 8, 1635, was representative, 1639. Removed with his minister Rev. John Lathrop to Barnstable, of which he was a representative in 1646, and often afterwards. He had Susanna, Samuel, Ezekiel.

REFERENCES.

Swift's Barnstable Families, I, 13; Freeman's His., Cape Cod., Mass., II, 272; Deane's, Scituate, Mass., 213; Savage's Gen. Dic., I, 158; Ellis Gen., 92, 365.

ANNAN.

ANNAN.—See Smith's, Petersborough, 14.

ANNAS.—See Smith's, Lapham's Bethel, Me.

ANNES.—American Ancestry, VII, 193, 208.

ANNESBY.—American Ancestry, vol. I, 2.

ANNIN.—Annin Celebration, 1866.

ANNIS.

CHARLES ANNIS, of Newbury, was born 1638, at Enniskillen, Ireland. He married May 15, 1666, Sarah, daughter of Aquila Chase, and had Priscilla, Hannah, and others.

REFERENCES.

Eaton's Warren, Me., 504; Morrison's His., Windham, N. H., 314; Savage's Gen. Dic., I, 59.

ANTES.—See Dotterer's Perkomen, Pa., 51.

ANTHOINE.—See Cochran's Antrim, 341.

ANTHON.—See Anthon Gen.

ANTHONY.

JOHN ANTHONY, of Portsmouth, R. I., was freeman, 1655; was born at Hempstead near London, 1607. He had John, Joseph, Abraham and Susanna.

JOSEPH ANTHONY, brother of John, settled in Portsmouth, R. I., married April 5, 1676, Mary, daughter of Thomas Waite, and had John, 1678; Joseph, 1682; Susanna, 1684.

REFERENCES.

Hayward's His., Hancock, N. H., 310; Peck and Earll's Fall River, Mass., 223; Cooley's Settlers, Trenton, N. J., 7; Austin's R. I. Gen. Dic., 4; Austin's Ancestries, 3; Gifford's Our Patronymics, 23; Roome's Gen., 222; Life of Rev. William Smith; Savage's Gen. Dic., I, 59; N. E. His. and Gen. Reg. XXXI, 416.

ANTILL.—See N. E. His. and Gen. Reg., XIX, 165.

ANTLE.—See Powers' Sangamon Co., 84.

ANTONIDES.—See Salter's, Monmouth, N. J., IV.

ANTRAM.

THOMAS ANTRAM, of Salem, Mass., came in the James, from Southampton, 1635. He is called a weaver of Salisbury, County Wilts, in the ship's clearance. He had a grant of land 1637, made freeman, 1642; died 1663. He had Obadiah, Mary, John.

REFERENCES.

Savage's Gen. Dic., I, 60.

ANTRIM.—Salter's, Monmouth, N. J., IV.

APLEY.

EZEKIEL APLEY, born in England, came to America and settled in New London, Conn., married Judith Quincy, and had son John.

REFERENCES.

American Ancestry, vol. II, 4.

APLIN.

JOHN APLIN, was born in Taunton, England, 1710; came to America and settled in Brooklyn, Conn. He married April 2, 1760, Sarah Bowen; and had twelve children, among whom was John (2).

REFERENCES.

American Ancestry, IV, 28.

APPLE.—See Davis' Bucks County, Pa., 57.

APPLEGATE.

RICHARD APPLEGATE, born in New Jersey of English parentage, served in the New Jersey Line, Continental army in the Revolution. Moved to Albany County, N. Y. He married Miss Wiggins and had Daniel and other children.

JOHN APPLEGATE, of Gravesend, L. I., was of Oyster Bay, 1685. He bought house and land at Fairfield in 1662, and lived there in 1670.

REFERENCES.

Bergen's Kings Co., N. Y. Settlers, 13; Salter's His. Monmouth County, N. J., IV; American Ancestry, VIII, 41; Savage's Gen. Dic., I, 60.

APPLEMAN.—See Mellich Gen., 705.

APPLETON.

SAMUEL APPLETON, of Ipswich, Mass., son of Thomas, of Little Waldingfield, Co. Suffolk, Engl., was born in 1586; came to New England in 1635, made freeman 1636, chosen representative, 1637; died at Rowley, 1670. He had John, Samuel, Sarah, Judith, Martha. The Suffolk family of Appleton bore Arms—Argent a fesse sable between three apples gules stalked and leaved vert. Crest—An elephant's head couped sable eared or, in the mouth a snake vert, wreathed about the trunk.

REFERENCES.

Temple's His., North Brookfield, Mass., ? Paige's His., Cambridge, Mass., 482; Hammott Papers, Ipswich, Mass., 16; Secomb's His. of Amherst, N. H., 484; Leonard's His. of Dublin, N. H., 313; Kidder's, New Ipswich, N. H., 294; American Ancestry, VI, 103; Cults Gen. 112; Savage's Gen. Dic., I, 60; Appletons Gen., 1850, 1867, 1873, 1874; Appleton, Chart., 1864; Heraldic Journal, I, 97; N. E. His. and Gen. Reg., XXVII, 36.

APPLIN.

JOHN APPLIN, of Watertown, Mass., married November 23, 1671, Bethshua, daughter of Thomas Bartlett. He had John, Bethshua, Mary, Hannah, Thomas, Edward, Abiel, Mehitable, John. He was asked, in April, 1703, to keep a school at Groton, and was a short time at Littleton.

REFERENCES.

Temple's His., Palmer, Mass., 407; Bond's Watertown, Mass., 9; Read's His., Swanzey, N. H., 278; Savage's Gen. Dic., I, 62.

APTHORP.

CHARLES APTHORP, of Boston, Mass., was born in England, 1678; married Grizelle Eastwich, and had John.

REFERENCES.

Bridgeman's Kinks Chapel Epit., 276; Wentworth Gen., I, 519; American Ancestry, V, 4.

ARBUCKLE.—See Secomb's Amherst, 485.

ARCHER.

HENRY ARCHER, of Roxbury, Mass., married December 4, 1639, Elizabeth, daughter of John Stow, and had Rachel, John, Isaac, Theophilus.

JOHN ARCHER, of Portsmouth, R. I., was made freeman, 1655.

JOHN ARCHER, of Salem, 1668, had a grant of land, 1676. He had Benjamin and Thomas.

SAMUEL ARCHER, of Salem, Mass., 1630, was admitted as freeman, October 19, of that year. He was marshal in 1630. By his wife Susanna he had Samuel, and probably others.

REFERENCES.

Millikin's Narraguagus Valley, Me., 19; Bolton's Westchester County, N. Y., II 707; Powers' Sangamon, Ill., 85; Meade's Old Families of Va., 198; Richmond, Va., Critic, 1888; Richmond, Va., Standard, III, 89; Robertson's Pocahontas Descendants; Sullivant Gen. (1874), 81; Driver Gen., 217; Heraldic Journal, III, 71; American Ancestry, II, 4; VI, 165; Savage's Gen. Dic., I, 62.

ARCHIBALD.—See Morrison's His. of Windham, N. H., 315; Miller's Colchester County, N. S., 34-108 Hayward's, Hancock, 311.

ARENTS.—See Bergen's Kings County, N. Y., 11.

AREY.—See Freeman's His., Cape Cod, Mass., II, 163; Eaton's His., Thomaston, Me., 135; Bangor His. Magazine, IV, 211.

ARMINGTON.—American Ancestry, V, 150; N. E. His. and Gen. Reg., XXII, 354.

ARMISTEAD.—See Carter Family Tree; Richmond Standard, II, 38, 41; III, 38; Hayden's Virginia Genealogies, 530; Slaughter's St. Marks Parish, 184; Paxton's Marshall Gen., 250, 316; Keith's Harrison Ancestry.

ARMATAGE or ARMITAGE.

ELEAZER ARMITAGE, of Lynn, Mass., married 1669, Hannah Needham.

GODFREY ARMITAGE, of Lynn, 1630; Boston, 1639; married Sarah, daughter of William Webb, and had Rebecca and Samuel.

JOSEPH ARMITAGE, of Lynn, 1630, had John and Rebecca.

REFERENCES.

American Ancestry, vol. I, 2; Savage's Gen. Dic., I, 63.

ARMOUR.—See Morrison's Windham, 315.

ARMS.

WILLIAM ARMS, of Hatfield, Mass., was a soldier in King Philip's war, 1676, and served under Capt. William Turner. He married, 1677, Joanna Hawks, and had eight children there. He removed to Sunderland, thence to Deerfield, where he died 1731. Among the children mentioned are John, Daniel and William.

REFERENCES.

Hudson's His., Lexington, Mass., 9; Judd's His., Hadley, Mass., 448; Hubbard's Stanstead, Canada, 141; Kellogg's White Memorial, 100; Strong Family Gen., 1318; Nash Gen., 43; American Ancestry, III, 47; Savage's Gen. Dic., I, 63; Arms Gen. by Edward W. Arms, Troy.

ARMSBEE, ARMSBY, ARMESBEY.

THOMAS AMSBURY, or ARMSBEY, was of Taunton, Mass., 1668. His children were Thomas, born 1669; Mary, Rebecca, Judith.

REFERENCES.

Savage's Gen. Dic., vol. I, 63; Benedicts Sutton, Mass., 583.

ARMSTRONG.

Tradition states that the original surname of this family was Fairbairn, and that it was changed to Armstrong on the following occasion: An ancient King of Scotland having his horse killed under him in battle, was immediately remounted by Fairbairn (a man of powerful physique,) on his horse. For his timely assistance the king amply rewarded him with lands on the Borders, and to perpetuate the memory of so important a service, as well as the manner in which it was performed (for Fairbairn took the king by the thigh and set him on the saddle,) his royal master gave him the appellation of ARMSTRONG—strong-of-arm—and assigned him for a crest " an armed hand and arm, in the hand a leg and foot in armour, couped at the thigh—all ppr." The most complete coat armour of the family of the present time is Arms—Sable three dexter arms conjoined at the shoulders and flexed in triangle or, hands clenched (or cuffed) argent, the hands clenched ppr. Crest—A dexter arm vambraced in armour, argent the hand ppr. Motto—Vi et armis.

JONATHAN ARMSTRONG, of Westerly or Pawcatuck, R. I., settled in the debatable part of the

Narragansett territory, called in the native speech Mesquamicuck, by the English Squamicuck, claimed by Connecticut jurisdiction as belonging to their plantation of Stonington. He removed in 1670 or 1678 to Norwich, probably as land was granted to him there. He probably removed afterward to Roxbury, Mass., where his daughter Mercy died, October 2, 1694, and Martha died December, 1709.

BENJAMIN ARMSTRONG, of Norwich, Conn., by wife Rachel had issue, Benjamin, born November, 1674; John, December 5, 1678; Joseph, December 10, 1684; Stephen, March 21, 1686; Benjamin (1,) deceased, November 5, 1717; Benjamin, Jr., settled at Windham.

GREGORY ARMSTRONG, of Plymouth, Mass., died November 5, 1650.

MATTHEW ARMSTRONG, of Boston, a mariner, came there probably from Maryland, 1664, sold his estate in Somerset County, Md., in 1672.

NATHAN ARMSTRONG, the pioneer, was born in 1717, near Londonderry, in the province of Ulster, Ireland. He was a weaver by trade, a Scotch-Irishman by race, and a Protestant by religious faith. He lived several years in the central part of New Jersey, and removed about 1744 to the northwestern part of the province to a section known as the Harwick Patent. He built a long cabin and moved on his plantation May 17, 1748, and engaged in farming. He was an industrious and prudent man, managing his affairs with much economy and thrift, leaving quite an estate to his children. He died at his homestead, near Johnsonburg, Warren County, N. J., August 11, 1777. He married Uphamy Wryght, born in Ireland May 3, 1724. They had issue, Elizabeth, George, John, William, Mary, Hannah and Sarah.

MASSACHUSETTS.—Armstrongs who served in the War of the Revolution: Adam, Archibald, Ebenezer, Ebenezer, Elias, Francis, George, George, James, James, James, John (14,) Joseph, Richard, Samuel (2,) Simon, Thomas, Thomas, Timothy (5,) William (4.)

CONNECTICUT.—Armstrongs: Amos, Asa, Bela, Benjamin, Daniel, Ebenezer, Elias, James, Jeremiah, John, Jonathan, Mariam, Nabby, Palmer, Phineas, Rufus, Simeon, Stephen, William, Zacheus.

NEW JERSEY.—Armstrongs: Enoch, George, Isaac, James (2,) John (2,) Robert, Thomas, William, William.

REFERENCES.

NEW JERSEY.—Armstrong Genealogy, by William Clinton Armstrong.

CONNECTICUT.—Hinman's Connecticut Settlers, 57; Weaver's History of Windham, 41.

NEW YORK.—Cleveland's History of Yates County, 740; Eager's History of Orange County, 427; Roe's Sketches of Rose, N. Y., 12.

NEW HAMPSHIRE.—Morrison's History, Windham, 317.

VERMONT.—Joslin's History of Poultney, 201.

PENNSYLVANIA.—Clyde's Irish Settlement of Pennsylvania, 12; Davis' History of Bucks County, Pa., 564.

ILLINOIS.—Powers' History of Sangamon County, Ill., 87.

OTHER PUBLICATIONS.—Coke Family, 90-9; 101-7; Paxton's Marshall Gen.; Savage's Gen. Dic., 1-63; Slaughter's St. Mark's Parish; Walworth's Hyde Genealogy.

ARNOLD.

THOMAS ARNOLD, of Watertown, arrived from Virginia, having come first from London, May, 1635 on the Plain Joan, bringing Thomas, Nicholas, and Susanna. By his second wife, Phebe, daughter of George Parkhurst, he had Ichabod, Richard, John, Ebenezer, and perhaps others.

One branch of the Arnold family bore *Arms*—Gules a chevron ermine between three pheons or, *Crest*—A demi-leopard, reguardant ppr., bezantée holding a pheon or, *Motto*—Ult vivas vigila.

WILLIAM ARNOLD, of Hingham, Mass., 1635, and Providence, R. I., was a brother of the above named Thomas. He was born in County Nottingham, Eng., December 21, 1615. He married Damaris, daughter of Stukily Wescott, and settled in Providence 1636. He was the richest man in the Colony; and by his thorough acquaintance with the manners and languages of the aborigines, became the most effective auxiliary in all negotiations with them. In 1653 he removed to Newport, was chosen Assistant next year, and in 1663, made by the royal charter President, and elected annually for eight years. He was the ancestor of Benedict Arnold of the American and later of the British army. He had issue Godgift, Josiah, Benedict, Freelove, Oliver, Caleb, and others.

REFERENCES.

MAINE.—Eaton's His., Thomaston, 136.

NEW HAMPSHIRE.—Hayward's His., Gilsum, 256; Bassett's His., Richmond, 273; Aldrich's His., Walpole, 189.

MASSACHUSETTS.—Wyman's Charlestown Gens. I, 23; Windsor's His., Duxbury, 221; Page's His., Hardwick, 329; Hudson's His., Marlboro, 309; Freeman's His., Cape Cod, II, 187; Benedict's His., Sutton, 583; Barry's, Framingham, 170.

VERMONT.—Heminway's Vt. Gazetter, V.

CONNECTICUT.—Weaver's His., Windham, 42; Orcutt's His., Stratford, 11; Hinman's Conn. Settlers, 58; Field's His., Haddam, 43.

RHODE ISLAND.—Austin's Ancestral Dictionary, 2; Austin's R. I. Gen. Dic., 240; Austin's Allied Families, 12; Richardson's Woonsocket, 187; Rhode Island His. Society Coll., III, 294.

NEW YORK.—Boyd's His. Consensus, 141; Collins' His. Hillsdale, App., 30; Jones' His. of N. Y. in the Rev. War, 746; Munsell's His. Coll. of Albany, IV, 94.

PENNSYLVANIA.—Futhey and Cope's Chester County, 464.

NEW JERSEY.—Salter's His., Monmouth County, V.

OTHER PUBLICATIONS.—Tuttle Family, 329; Thayer Memorial (1835), 49; Savage's Gen. Dic., I, 64; Loomis Gen. Female Branches, 683; Holden's Capron Family, 251; Greene Gen., 1894; Glover Gen., 338; Bartlett's Wanton Family, 141; American Ancestry, II, 4; IV, 110; VI, 31; VIII, 160; IX, 210, 214; Arnold Chart., (1877) by G. C. Arnold; Arnold Gen., 1869, 1879.

ARNOUX.

JEAN B. ARNOUX, a native of Marseilles, France, came to this country with Count de Rochambeau, during the Revolution, and served under him as captain. After the war he settled in Vergennes, Vt.

REFERENCES.

American Ancestry, VI, 23.

ARROWSMITH.—See Salter's, Monmouth, N. J.

ARTCHER.—American Ancestry, I, 2.

ARTHUR.

JOHN ARTHUR, of Salem, Mass., married Priscilla, daughter of John Gardner. After his death the family moved to Nantucket.

REFERENCES.

Savage's Gen. Dic., vol. I; Ely Gen., 171.

ARTSELL.

JOHN ARTSELL, of Springfield, Mass., sworn fidelity, December 31, 1678.

ASBURY.—See Wyman's, Charlestown, Mass., I, 24; Willis' Washington Gen., 241; Benney Gen., 93.

ASHBRIDGE.—See Futhey's, Chester, Pa., 465.

ASHBY.

ANTHONY ASHBY, of Salem, 1665, married Abigail, daughter of Richard Hutchinson, and had issue Gershom, Abigail, and probably Benjamin.

REFERENCES.

Temple's His., North Brookfield, Mass., 496; Essex Inst. Coll., XVI, 88; Hayden's Virginia Genealogies, 449; Savage's Gen. Dic.

ASHCRAFT.

JOHN ASHCRAFT, of Stonington, 1662, married Hannah Osborne, and had issue Hannah, Ephraim, Mary

REFERENCES.

Temple's His. of Whately, Mass., 198; Savage's Gen. Dic. I, 68.

ASH or ASHE.

WILLIAM ASH, of Dover, N. H., married at Salisbury, 1667, Mary Bartlett, as supposed.

REFERENCES.

Wheeler's, North Carolina, 279; Savage's Gen. Dic., vol. I.

ASHER.—Smith's Rhinebeck, N. Y., 196.

ASHDOWN.

JOHN ASHDOWN, of Weymouth, Mass., served in King Philip's war and was at the famous Falls Fight.

REFERENCES.

Savage's Gen. Dic., vol. I, 68.

ASHFIELD.

WILLIAM ASHFIELD, of Malden, Mass.; by wife Jane, had issue, Mary and perhaps others.

REFERENCES.

Savage's Gen. Dic., vol. I, 68.

ASHLITT.—See Savage's Gen. Dic., vol. I, 69.

ASHLEY.

ROBERT ASHLEY, of Springfield, Mass., 1639, may have been of Roxbury, Mass. He had issue, David, Mary, Jonathan, Sarah, Joseph.

REFERENCES.

Hinman's Conn. Settlers, 61; Weaver's His., Windham, Conn., 44; Longmeadow, Mass., Centen., 4; West Springfield, Mass., Centen., 114; Goodwin's Olcott Family 44; Dwight Gen., 820; Champion Gen.; Amer. Ancestry, II, 4; VI, 184; Joslin's His., Poultney, Vt., 202; Savage's Gen. Dic., vol. I, 68; N. E. His. and Gen. Reg., II, 394; XXXI, 318; Whittemore's Founders and Builders of the Oranges, 456; Ashley Gen.

ASHEMEAD.—See Martin's Chester, Pa., 441; Wiswell's Ashmead Sermon (1870).

ASHTON.

HENRY ASHTON, of Boston, 1673, from County Lancaster, Eng., was of Providence, 1676.

JAMES ASHTON, of Providence, 1639, was made freeman, 1655; swore alligeance to Charles II, May 1666; and perhaps removed to New Jersey.

THOMAS ASHTON, of Providence, R. I., 1639, was a proprietor.

REFERENCES.

Salter's His., Monmouth County, N. J., VI; Hayden's Virginia Genealogies, 630; De Bow's Review, XXVI, 131; Austin's R. I., Gen. Dic., 5; Austin's Ancestries, III; American Ancestry, IV, 231; Savage's Gen. Dic., I, 69.

ASTLETT.

JOHN ASTLETT, of Newbury, Mass., married October 8, 1648, Rebecca Ayer, of Haverhill; removed to Andover, and had Hannah, Rebecca, Mary, John, Sarah, Ruth, Samuel.

REFERENCES.

ASKAM.—See Plumb's, Hanover, Pa., 388.

ASKIN.—See Hall Gen. (1892), 88.

ASPENWALL or ASPINWALL.

WILLIAM ASPINWALL, of Charlestown, 1630, probably came in the fleet with Winthrop. He removed to Boston, made freeman, 1632; went to Rhode Island and was Secretary of that Colony. He was at New Haven, 1641; returned to Boston, where he was recorder. He had Edward, 1630; Hannah, and perhaps other children.

PETER ASPINWALL, of Dorchester, Mass., came from Foxleth Park, near Liverpool, England; was an early settler of Boston; purchased with Robert Sharp, the large grant of William Colburn. He married Alice Sharp, and had issue, Samuel, Peter, Nathaniel, Thomas, Mehitable, Elizabeth, Eleazer and Joseph (twins), Mary, Timothy.

REFERENCES.

Weaver's His. Windham, Conn., 47; Hinman's Conn. Settlers, 74; Wentworth Gen. I, 464; Stow Gen. 463; Montague Gen., 445; Savage's Gen. Dic., I, 69; N. E. His. and Gen. Reg., XLVII, 342; Amer. Ancestry IX, 240.

ASPER.—See Amer. Ancestry, IX, 229.

ASTEN.—See Hill's His. Mason, N. H., 200.

ASTOR.

The founder of this family in America was John Jacob Astor, born in the village of Waldorf, Grand Duchy of Baden, Germany, July 17, 1763; came to this country in January 1783, and settled in New York city. He married in 1785, Sarah Todd, daughter of Adam Todd and Margaret Dodge, his wife. Their children were John Jacob Jr., William Backhouse, and three daughters, one of whom became the Countess of Rumpff, another was married to Rev. John Bristed, and another to Walter Langdon.

REFERENCES:—Green's Todd Gen.; N. Y. Gen. Rec. XXII, 115; XXIII, 15.

ASTWOOD.

JAMES ASTWOOD, of Roxbury, came to this country with his wife Sarah in 1638. Had issue James, John, Joseph, Sarah, Mary.

JOHN ASTWOOD, of Roxbury, came in the "Hopewell," 1635, from Stanstead Abbey, Co. Herts, made freeman 1636, removed to Milford 1639, and there married Sarah, widow of Sylvester Baldwin. He was representative 1643, afterwards Assistant of the Colony and Commissioner of the United Colonies.

REFERENCES:—Ellis' His. Roxbury, 91; Savage's Gen. Dic. I, 71.

ATCHINSON.

JOHN ATCHINSON, of Hatfield, 1672, was killed by the Indians 19th September, 1677, leaving children Elizabeth, Mary, John, Benoni.

REFERENCES:—Miner's His. of Phelps and Gorham's Purchase, 419; Savage's Gen. Dic. vol. I, 72; Long Meadow Centen. 5.

ATHEARN.

JOHN ATHEARN, of Martha's Vineyard, came there from New Hampshire; married Mary Butler; was representative 1632; first under the new charter. He had issue Solomon, Jettero, Zereah, and it may be others.

ATHERTON.

HUMPHREY ATHERTON, 1636, came perhaps from Preston, in Lancashire; was freeman 1638. Assistant 1664, Captain 1650, and 1656 he succeeded Sedgwick as Major-General. He had issue Jonathan, Catharine, Rest, Increase, Thankful, Hope, Mary, Watching, Patience, Consider.

REFERENCES:—Chandler's His. Shirley, Mass., 344; Hazen's His. of Billerica, Mass., 4; Paige's His. Cambridge, Mass., 579; Secomb's His. of Amherst, N. H., 486; Warren's His. Waterford, Me., 227; Sedgwick's His. Sharon, Conn., 61; Bassett's Richmond, 273; Pope Gen. 322; Wentworth Gen. I, 195; N. E. His. and Gen. Reg. XXXV, 67.

ATKINS.

HENRY ATKINS, of Yarmouth, 1641, removed to Plymouth, Mass.; married July 9, 1647, Elizabeth—, and had Mary, Samuel, Isaac; he married 2d, Bethia Lennell, and had Desire, John, Nathaniel, Joseph, Thomas, Mary, and Samuel again, 1679.

There was a THOMAS ATKINS, of Boston.

REFERENCES:—Freeman's Cape Cod, Mass., II, 164, 359; Emery's Newbury, Mass., Reminiscences; Atkins' His. Hawley, Mass., 65; Rich's His. Truro, Mass., 5; Whitmore's Copps Hill Epitaphs; Eaton's Annals, Warren, Me., 504; Orcutt's His. Wolcott, Conn., 439; Middle-field, Conn. His.; Timlow's Sketches Southington, Conn., 1; Vinton's Giles Mem., 135, 146; Sears' Gen. 60; Amer. Ancestry VIII, 103; Savage's Gen. Dic. I, 73; Atkins Gen.

ATKINSON.

LUKE ATKINSON, of New Haven, Conn., was one of the earliest settlers; signed the compact, 1639. He married Mary, daughter of Richard Platt, of Milford, and had Mary, Hannah, Sarah. He removed to Middletown, Conn., where his widow married Thomas Whitmore.

THEODORE ATKINSON, of Boston, 1634, was a feltmaker, who came in the employ of John Newgate from Bury, Co. Lancaster; made freeman, 1642.

REFERENCES:—Buxton, Me., Cent. 183; Hatch's His. Industry, Me., 501; Coffin's His. Boscawen, N. H., 468; Runnel's His. Sanbornton, N. H., II, 12; Hinman's Conn. Settlers, 75; Slaughter's Bristol Parish, Va., 137; Smith's Gen. of William Smith, 88; Wentworth Gen., I, 318; Savage's Gen. Dic. I, 74; Little Gen. 120, 281; Quint's Atkinson Gen.; Atkinson Gen. 1890.

ATKINSON. *Arms*—Ermine, on as a fesse sable three pheons argent. *Crest*—A pheon or, *Motto*—Nil sine labore.

ATLEE. See Holstein Gen.; Atlee Family, 1884.

ALTWATER—ATWATER.

DAVID ATWATER, of New Haven, 1638, came from London, signed the plantation covenant 4th June, 1639. His children were Mercy, Damaris, Jonathan, Abigail, Samuel, Ebenezer, Joshua.

JOSHUA ATWATER, brother of David, was a mendicant from London. Came to New Haven, 1638, signed the plantation covenant, 1639. He married, 1651, Mary, daughter of Rev. Adam Blackman, of Stratford, and had Ann, Samuel, Joshua, Mary, and others. He removed to Milford, 1655, and was Treasurer of the Colony. He removed in 1659 to Boston.

REFERENCES:—Corliss' North Yarmouth, Me.; Hinman's Conn. Settlers, 76; Orcutt's His. of Torrington, 642; Timlow's Sketches Southington, Conn., 14; Tuttle Family of Conn., 31, 621; Davis' His. Wallingford, Conn., 626; Collins' His. Hillsdale, N. Y., App. 31; Wentworth Gen. II, 712; Amer. Ancestry, III, 3; IX, 232; Dwight's Strong Gen. 83; Savage's Gen. Dic. I, 75; Atwater Gen. 1851, 1873.

ATWELL.

BENJAMIN ATWELL, of New London, by wife Mary, had Thomas, Mary, William, John, Joseph, Richard, Samuel, Benjamin.

REFERENCES:—Worcester's His. Hollis, N. H., 364; Corliss' North Yarmouth, Me.; Caulkins' His. New London, Conn., 305; Vinton Memorial Families, 204; Amer. Ancestry, V, 172; Savage's Gen. Dic. I, 76.

ATWOOD.

THOMAS ATWOOD, of Hartford, 1664, was a physician. In 1668 he settled in Wethersfield, and by his wife Abigail had Abigail, Andrew, Jonathan and Joseah.

PHILIP ATWOOD, of Malden, Mass., 1653, came from London, in the "Planter", 1635; aged 13, or in the "Planter", aged 12. He had Rachel, Mary, Philip, Abigail, Oliver.

STEPHEN ATWOOD, the founder of the Cape Cod family of this name, settled at Plymouth about 1643. He was one of the founders of Eastham, on the east side of

Cape Cod Bay, nearly opposite Plymouth. The place is now known as Wellsfleet. The Atwood homestead stood near the spot where the exploring party of the Pilgrims had their first encounter with the Indians previous to the landing at Plymouth. Stephen Atwood married Abigail Dunham, daughter of John Dunham, at Plymouth, Nov. 16, 1644.

REFERENCES.

NEW HAMPSHIRE.—Cochran's His. Antrim, 342; Bedford, N. H., Centennial, 284; Merrill's His. Acworth, 182; Washington, N. H., His., 277.

MAINE.—Bangor His. Magazine IV, 211.

MASSACHUSETTS.—Ballou's His. Milford, 544; Davis' Landmarks of Plymouth, 7; Freeman's Cape Cod, II, 373, 685; Hammatt Papers, Ipswich, 14; Rich's His. of Truro, 519; Temple's His. Brookfield, 496; Wyman's Charlestown, Mass., I, 16.

CONNECTICUT.—Cothren's Woodbury, I, 490; II, 1471; Weaver's His. Windham, 48.

OTHER PUBLICATIONS.—Whitmore's Copps Hill Epitaphs; Walker Memorials, 23; Sears Gen., 62; Savage's Gen. Dic. I, 77; N. E. His. and Gen. Reg. XV, 241; Amer. Ancestry, vol. II, 4; X, 183; Atwood Gen., 1889; Atwood Reunion, 1866. The Founders and Builders of the Oranges by H. Whittemore, 440.

AUCHMUTY.

SAMUEL AUCHMUTY, of New York, son of Robert of Boston, was born in Boston 1725, died in New York City 1777. He was rector of Trinity church and an adherent of the British Government during the Revolution. He married Mary, daughter of Robert Nichols, a descendant of Col. Nichols, to whom the island of Manhattan was surrendered by the Dutch.

REFERENCES:—Lamb's His. New York City, I, 751; Amer. Ancestry, V, 175; Updyke's Narragansett, R. I., Ch. 148.

AUDLEY.

EDMUND AUDLEY was of Lynn, 1641.

JOHN AUDLEY, of Boston, 1632.

AUGER. AUGIER. AUGUR.

WILLIAM AUGUR, was of Salem, 1636, perhaps earlier, was admitted freeman May 18, 1631, and took the name of Agar.

NICHOLAS AUGUR, of New Haven, 1643, was a physician and trader; swore allegiance Aug. 5, 1644. He had brothers or nephews, John and Robert.

REFERENCES:—Middlefield, Conn., His.; Savage's Gen. Dic. I, 57, 78.

AUGUSTINE.

JOHN AUGUSTINE, of Reading, 1677, came from the Isle of Jersey. He served in the company of Turner in the latter part of Philip's war. He married Jan. 10, 1678, Eliza, daughter of John Brown, of Watertown. He left widow, Elizabeth, and children, Samuel, John, Ebenezer, Thomas.

REFERENCES:—Savage's Gen. Dic. I, 79.

AUMACK. See Salter's Monmouth, N. J., VI.

AUNGST. See Brubacher Gen. 171.

AULT, or OLT.

JOHN AULT, of Portsmouth, R. I., 1631, was sent out by Mason, the royal proprietor, living at Dover, N. H., 1648 to 1657. By wife Remembrance he had John and Remembrance.

REFERENCES:—Savage's Gen. Dic. I, 80.

AUSTIN.

JEREMIAH AUSTIN, of Exeter, R. I., died there 1754.

ANTHONY AUSTIN, of Rowley, Mass., was made freeman 1669. He had issue, Richard, Anthony, John, Nathaniel, Elizabeth, Esther.

FRANCIS AUSTIN, of Dedham, removed to Hampton 1640, and had by his wife Isabella, Jemima and Sophia.

JOHN AUSTIN, of New London, Conn., 1647, removed in 1651 to Greenwich, and next to Stamford, died Aug. 25, 1657.

JOHN AUSTIN, of New Haven, married 1667, Mercy, daughter of first Joshua Atwater, and had John, died soon, David, Joshua, Mercy, John and Hannah, twins, Mercy, again.

REFERENCES.

MAINE.—Cushman's Sheepscott, 353; Eaton's His. of Thomaston, 137; Lapham's His. Rumford, 301.

NEW HAMPSHIRE.—Cochran's His. of Antrim, 344; Hayward's His. Gilsum, 257; Hayward's His. Hancock, 311; Secomb's His. of Amherst, 489; Worcester's His. Hollis, 364.

VERMONT.—Joslin's His. Poultney, 204.

MASSACHUSETTS.—Wyman's Charlestown, I, 28.

CONNECTICUT.—Boyd's Annals of Winchester, 42; Dodd's His. of East Haven, 103; Hinman's Conn. Settlers, 81; Orcutt's His. of Torrington, 642; Tuttle Family of Conn., 625; Weaver's His. Windham, 49.

RHODE ISLAND.—Austin's Ancestral Dictionary, 5; Austin's Allied Families, 20; Austin's R. I. Gen. Dic. 246; Austin and Whittaker Chart (1881); Newport His. Mag., IV, 227.

OTHER PUBLICATIONS.—Hubbard's Stanstead County, Canada, 268; Roe's Sketches of Rose, N. Y., 294; Whitney Gen. (1860), Appendix; Walworth Hyde Gen. 1006; Penn. Mag. IV, 484; Loomis Gen. Female Branches, 763; Ely Gen. 184; Dwight's Strong Gen.; Dwight Gen., 542; Corliss' Gen. Appendix; Amer. Ancestry vol. I, 2; VI, 71; X, 202; Savage's Gen. Dic. I, 80.

AVARY. See Amer. Ancestry, VIII, 94.

AVERY.

CHRISTOPHER AVERY, of Gloucester, a weaver, came from Salisbury in Co. Hants, Eng., to Gloucester, Mass., was selectman, 1646, and for seven years following. He removed to Boston, and in 1666 to New London, Conn.

WILLIAM AVERY, of Dedham, Mass., was a physician and apothecary; was a member of the Artillery Company, 1654, Lieutenant, 1655, of the town's company; freeman, 1677. He had issue William, 1646, Mary, Robert, Jonathan, Rachel, Hannah, Ebenezer.

Arms—Ermine, or, a pale engrailed azure three lions' heads couped or. *Crest*—A leopard couchant argent bezantée, ducally gorged or.

REFERENCES.

MASSACHUSETTS.—Freeman's His. Cape Cod, II, 558; Hammatt Papers Ipswich, 15; Rich's His. Truro, 520; Wyman's Charlestown, I, 40; Babson's His. Gloucester, Mass., 58; Allen's Worcester Assoc., 152.

CONNECTICUT.—Hurd's New London County, Conn., 474; Calkin's His. of New London, 381; Hinman's Conn. Settlers, 88; Sedgwick's His. Sharon, 62; Hines' Lebanon, Conn., Address (1880), 144.

OTHER PUBLICATIONS.—Wentworth Gen., II, 18; Walworth Hyde Gen., 256; Upham Gen., 40; Strong

Gen., 376; Smith Gen. (1889), 99; Pompey, N. Y., Reunion (1875), 253; Oxford, N. H., Centennial, 103; Morgan and Avery Gen. (1851); Machias, Me., Centen. Celebration, 153; Ellis Gen. 148; Bridgman's King's Chapel Epit., 301; Blake's Mendon Association, 124; Amer. Ancestry, II, 4; V, 9; VIII, 50; IX, 27; X, 202; The Averys of Groton, 1888; The Averys of Groton, 1894; The Groton Averys, 1893; Dedham Branch of the Avery Family, 1893; N. E. His. and Gen. Reg. XXVI, 197.

AVERED. See Boyd's His. Winchester, Conn., 47.

AVERILL.

WILLIAM AVERILL, of Ipswich, Mass., died 1653, leaving wife Abigail, and seven children.
REFERENCES:—Savage's Gen. Dic., I, 82; Bradbury's Kennebunkport, Me., 225; Cushman's Sheepscott, Me., 354; Eaton's His. Thomaston, Me., 137; Gregory's His. Northfield, Vt., 78; Heminway's Vt. Gazeteer, IV, 618; Livermore's His. Wilton, N. H., 298; Secomb's His. Amherst, N. H., 489; Cothren's His. Woodbury, Conn., 484; Hinman's Conn. Settlers, 86; Weaver's His. Windham, Conn., 50; Machias, Me., Centennial Celebration, 153; Savage's Gen. Dic., I, 82; Amer. Ancestry, VIII, 224; IX, 35, 49.

AVIS.

JOHN AVIS served on the Conn. River, in King Philip's war.
REFERENCES:—Savage's Gen. Dic., I, 83.

ARISTON.

JOHN ARISTON, of Reading, was made freeman, 1685.
REFERENCES:—Savage's Gen. Dic., I, 84.

AWARDS.

RICHARD AWARDS, of Newport and Boston.
REFERENCES:—Savage's Gen. Dic.

AWE. See Egle's Penn. Gens., 32.

AWKLEY.

MILES AWKLEY, of Boston, by wife Mary, had Elizabeth, 1635; Miles, 1638.
REFERENCES:—Savage's Gen. Dic., I, 84.

AXEY.

JAMES AXEY, of Lynn, 1630; representative 1634; died 1667.
REFERENCES:—Savage's Gen. Dic., I, 84.

AXTELL.

THOMAS AXTELL, of Sudbury, Mass., died 1646; had wife Mary and seven children.
REFERENCES:—Hudson's His. Marlborough, Mass., 310;Jamison's His. Medway, Mass., 451; Pierson's His. Grafton, Mass., 451; Savage's Gen. Dic., I, 84; Amer. Ancestry, VII, 29, 95; Appleton's Axtell Gen.; N. E. Gen. Reg., XXII, 143; XLIV, 50.

AYER.

The family of Ayer, of this country, appears to be of a different line from that of Ayres, but they, no doubt, have a common origin.
The family of Ayer settled at Haverhill, Mass. William Ayer, of Bow, Concord, and Newbury, N. H., born 1753, a revolutionary soldier, was a native of Haverhill.

REFERENCES:—Bouton's His. Concord, N. H., 630; Washington, N. H., His. 278; Lapham's His. Bethel, Me., 464; Lapham's His. Norway, Me., 458; Wyman's Charlestown, Mass., Gens., I, 40; Judd's His. Hadley, Mass., 449; Chase's Haverhill, Mass., 73, 216, 274, 615; Huntington's Stamford, Conn., Families, 7; Titcomb's Early New England People, 279; Hubbard's Stanstead County, Canada, 196; Guild's Stiles Gen., 380; Corliss' Gen. 240; Amer. Ancestry, IV, 188; VI, 10, 24; Ayer (James) Biography (1892); Savage's Gen. Dic., I, 84; N. E. His. and Gen. Reg. XVII, 307; XIX, 28.

AYRES.

JOHN AYERS or AYRES, of Salisbury, Mass., 1640; of Ipswich, 1646; Haverhill 1647, where he died 1657. In his will he names wife Hannah and children, John, Nathaniel, Hannah, Rebecca, Mary, Obadiah, Robert, Thomas, Peter.

SAMUEL AYERS, of Newbury, Mass., by wife Abigail had Stephen; by wife Sarah had Jabez.
REERENCES:—Temple's North Brookfield, Mass., 496; Hammatt Papers, Ipswich, Mass., 13; Bangor, Me., His. Mag. VI, 29; Merrill's His. Acworth, N. H., 182; Cleveland's His. Yates County, N. Y., 706; Whittemore's His. Montclair, N. J., 213; Montague Gen. 613; Egle's Penn. Gens., 40; Caldwell Gen. Record, 66; Austin's R. I. Gen. Dic., 8; Ayres Gen., 1870.

AYLESBURY. See Powers' Sangamon, 80.

AYLETT.

JOHN AYLET, of Boston, a merchant, married Nov. 21, 1654, Mary, daughter of Capt. Thomas Hawkins, and had Mary, born 1655.
REFERENCES:—Savage's Gen. Dic., I, 85; Richmond Standard II, 34, 40, 49; Slaughter's St. Marks Parish, 189.

AYLSWORTH. See Austin's R. I. Gen. Dic., 6; Bulkley's Brown Mem. 14; Aylsworth Gen.

AYRAULT.

NICHOLAS AYRAULT or AYROULD, a physician, driven by the revocation of the edict of Nantes to fly his native land, was probably at Rochelle, 1686, or earlier. He married at Providence, R. I., Marian Breton and had Peter, Nicholas, and other children.
REFERENCES:—Savage's Gen. Dic. I, 85; Austin's R. I. Gen. Dic. 7; Hinman's Conn. Settlers, 90.

AZELL.

HUMPHREY AZELL, of Kittery, Me., 1682, was one of the founders of the Baptist church there.
REFERENCES:—Savage's Gen. Dic. I, 85.

BABB.

PHILIP BABB, of Kittery, 1652, was associated the following year, under commission from Mass. with Major Bryan Pendleton, Nicholas Shapleigh, and others in the government of the Isle of Shoals, and lived there 1666.

JONATHAN BABB, of Springfield, took the oath of allegiance with Samuel, perhaps his brother, Dec. 31, 1678.
REFERENCES:—Savage's Gen. Dic. I, 85.

BABBIDGE.

CHRISTOPHER BABBIDGE or BABRIDGE, of Salem, Mass., was made freeman 1665. By his wife Agnes he had Ruth, 1664, John, 1666.

REFERENCES:—Savage's Gen. Dic. I, 85; Wheeler's His. Brunswick, Me., 828; Farrow's His. Isleborough, Me., 168; Eaton's His., Thomaston, Me., 138; Driver Gen. 229; Corliss' North Yarmouth, Me.

BABCOCK.

JAMES BABCOCK (2), of Portsmouth and Westerly, R. I., born 1610, was the son of James (1), of Essex Co., Eng., who emigrated to Dorchester, Mass., in 1623, and died 1660; James (2), the son, was of Dorchester, 1635; Portsmouth, R. I., 1640; and of Westerly, R. I., 1660, where he died June 12, 1679.

The original spelling of the name was probably Badcock, and both names appear on the Rhode Island records.

REFERENCES:—Austin's Ancestries, 7; Austin's R. I. Gen. Dic. 8; Irish's Sketch of Richmond, R. I., 88; Wyman's Charlestown, Mass., Gens., I, 43; Hudson's His. Lexington, Mass., 9; Temple's His. North Brookfield, Mass., 497; Weaver's His. Windham, Conn., 50; Sedgwick's His. Sharon, Conn., 62; Hinman's Conn. Settlers, 92; Joslyn's His. Poultney, Vt., 206; His. Greene County, N. Y., 448; Yates County, N. Y., 697; Roe's Sketches of Rose, N. Y., 95; Greene Gen. (1894); Douglass Gen. 132; Stanton Gen. 425, 561; Wight Gen. 3, 79; Amer. Ancestry, vol. I, 3; II, 5; IV, 191; V, 170; IX, 197; Savage's Gen. Dic. I. 86; N. E. His. and Gen. Reg. XIV, 23; XXIX, 114; Babcock Gen. 1844, 1861; Windham, Conn. Gens., 50.

BADCOCK.

ROBERT BADCOCK, of Dorchester, 1648, had Nathaniel, 1658, Ebenezer, 1663, Elizabeth, George. This name appears on the Portsmouth, R. I., records and is probably the same family as the Babcock.

REFERENCES:—Morse's Sherbourne, Mass., Settlers 10; Norton's His. Fitzwilliam, N. H., 462; Hinman's Conn. Settlers, 106; Savage's Gen. Dic. I, 92; N. E. His. and Gen. Reg. XIX, 215; Badcock Gen. 1881.

BABSON.

JAMES BABSON, of Gloucester, Mass., is supposed to have settled there with his mother Isabel, a widow who had lands there in 1644. He married Nov. 16, 1647, Elenor Hill, and had James, 1648, Elenor, Philip, Sarah, Thomas, John, Richard, Elizabeth, Ebenezer. His son Thomas served in Philip's war.

REFERENCES:—Babson's Gloucester, Mass., 59; Savage's Gen. Dic. I, 87.

BACHE.

RICHARD BACHE, of Penn., born Feb. 23, 1737, merchant, a man of considerable importance and standing, married Sarah, daughter of Dr. Benjamin Franklin, had eight children, among whom was Benjamin Franklin and Dr. Franklin Bache, the distinguished chemist.

REFERENCES:—Meade's Old Churches, VIII, 374; Amer. Ancestry, V, 162; Franklin Ancestry, 1889; N. E. His. and Gen. Reg. VIII, 374.

BACHELDER. BACHELLER.

HENRY BATCHELDER, of Ipswich, Mass., a brewer, from Dover, County Kent, Eng., came over in 1636, with his wife Martha and four servants, and became the founder of a large line of this name. In his will May 15, 1696, he names John, Joseph, Hannah.

WILLIAM BATCHELOR, of Charlestown, 1634, was freeman, 1644. By his wife Jane he had Seaborn and Abigail; by wife Rachel he had Joseph.

REFERENCES:—Farrow's Isleborough, 160; Washington, N. H., 281; Secomb's His. Amherst, N. H., 496; Swift's Barnstable, Mass., I, 39; Amer. Ancestry II, 5.

BACHMAN. See Davis' His. Bucks County, Pa., 389; Egle's His. Lebanon County, Pa., 235; Amer. Ancestry II, 5.

BACKUS.

WILLIAM BACKUS, of Saybrook and Norwich, Conn., was born in England, died in Norwich 1664, was in Saybrook, 1637; was one of the 35 plantation settlers who purchased land from the Indians. He married Sarah Charles, daughter of John Charles of Branford, 1673. His son, Lieut. William Backus, married Elizabeth Pratt, eldest child of Lieut. William Pratt, one of the original settlers of Saybrook. He had there William and Stephen; removed to Norwich 1660; died there 1641.

REFERENCES:—Hinman's Conn. Settlers, 93; Caulkin's Norwich, Conn., 157; Weaver's His. Windham, Conn., 58; Butler's His. Farmington, Me., 368; Munsell's Albany, IV, 99; Walworth's Hyde Gen., 419, 537, 707, 920; Huntington Gen., 74; Goodwin's Gen. Notes, 303; Savage's Gen. Dic., I, 89; Chapman's Pratt Gen., 54; Amer. Ancestry, III, 103; V, 185, 235; VII, 247; VIII, 159, 164; Backus Gen. Windham, Conn., Gens., 58.

BACON.

Of this family Burke says: " Various conjectures have been hazarded as to the origin of Bacon, but to little purpose. But it matters not, the antiquity of the family is beyond dispute; and there are few houses in the kingdom more distinguished by the production of great and eminent men. Besides Friar Bacon, the marvel of his day, Sir Nicholas Bacon, and the great Lord Bacon, there were five other extraordinary personages of the same family."

This family bore Arms—Gules on a chief argent two mullets, pierced, sable. Crest—A boar, passant, ermine. Motto—Mediocria firma.

ANDREW BACON, of Hartford, Conn., one of the original proprietors, born, probably, in Rutlandshire, Eng., had, perhaps, been of Cambridge. He was a representative 1642 to '56, and soon after removed to Hadley, Mass., and died 1669. His wife Elizabeth was widow of Timothy Standley.

NATHANIEL BACON, Middletown, Conn., 1653, is called son of William of the parish of Stretton, County Rutland, Eng. By wife Ann, daughter of Thomas Miller, he had Nathaniel, 1655, Hannah, Andrew, Nathaniel again, 1659, whose name was changed for Thomas; John, Andrew again, Abigail, Lydia. He was a nephew of Andrew and had part of his uncle's estate.

WILLIAM BACON, of Salem, Mass., 1640. He had married Rebecca, daughter of Thomas Porter, and had Isaac, 1641, and William. He died in 1653. They lived in Dublin, and on the outbreak of the Irish rebellion, she was sent over here, says tradition, and her husband followed her.

MICHAEL or MIGELL BACON, of Dedham, Mass., 1640, brought, it is said, from Ireland four children, Michael, Daniel, John and Samuel.

REFERENCES.

MAINE.—Lapham's His. Norway, 458; Pierce's His. Gorham, 154; Corliss' North Yarmouth.

NEW HAMPSHIRE.—Washington, N. H., His. 282; Hayward's His. Hancock, 312; Cutter's His. of Jaffrey, 220, Coggswell's His. Henniker, 448.

MASSACHUSETTS.—Wyman's Charlestown Gen., I, 43; Temple's Whately, 198; Temple's North Brookfield, 502; Sewall's His. Woburn, 592; Paige's His. Cambridge, 482; Jackson's His. Newton, Mass., 234; Hyde's His. Brimfield, 369; Hudson's His. Lexington, 9; Herrick's His. Gardner, 330; Hazen's His. Billerica, 4; Freeman's Cape Cod, I, 352; II, 264; Davis' Landmarks Plymouth, 9; Brown's Bedford, Mass., Families, 2; Blake's His. Franklin, 231; Barry's His. Framingham, 170; Benedict's His. Sutton, 584; Swift's Barnstable Families I, 21, 38.

CONNECTICUT.—Orcutt's His. Torrington, 643; Hinman's Conn. Settlers, 97; Cothren's Ancient Woodbury, 516; II, 1471; Brown's West Simsbury Settlers, 11; Sedgwick's Sharon, 62; Middlefield, Conn., His.

VIRGINIA.—Campbell's His. Virginia, 311, 344; Neil's Virginia Carolorum, 243; Richmond, Va., Standard, I, 44; II, 19, 20, 30, 38; III, 5, 26, 43.

OTHER PUBLICATIONS.—Leland Gen. 210; Killog Mem. of Elder J. White, 39; Keith Harrison Ancestry; Goode Gen. 472; Champion Gen.; Ammidown His. Coll., I, 455; Amer. Ancestry, I, 3; Bacon Gen. 1845; N. E. His. and Gen. Reg. II, 388; XXXVII, 189; L, 465.

BACOT. See Gregg's Old Cheraws, 105; His. of Hudson County, N. J.

BADGER.

GILES BADGER, of Newbury, 1635, married Elizabeth, daughter of Edmond Greenleaf, and had John, 1643. He had another son John, who left descendants.

REFERENCES:—Lancaster's Gilmanton, N. H., 256; Runnel's His. Sanbornton, N. H., II, 15; Wyman's Charlestown, Mass., Gens., I, 44; Chase's Haverhill, Mass., 615; Whitmore's Copps Hill Epitaphs; Maine Genealogist, 1875-6, 70; Weaver's His. Windham, Conn., 62; Wentworth Gen. II, 95; Savage's Gen. Dic. I, 93; N. H. His. Soc. Collections, VI, 124; Badger (Rev. Joseph Memoir, 1841); Amer. Ancestry, IV, 166, 208; Windham, Conn., Gens., 42.

BADGLEY. Littell's Passaic Valley, 12.

BADLAM.

WILLIAM BADLAM; by wife Joan had John. 1687. REFERENCES:—Savage's Gen. Dic. I, 92; Whitman Gen., 25.

BADMAN.

JOHN BADMAN, of Boston, by wife Sarah had Lydia, 1656.

REFERENCES:—Savage's Gen. Dic. I, 93.

BAGBY. See N. E. His. and Gen. Reg. XXXVIII, 97.

BAGG.

JOHN BAGG, of Springfield, Mass., married, 1659, Hannah, daughter of Henry Burt, and had ten children, among whom were Daniel, John, Hannah.

REFERENCES:—Loomis Gen.,.Female Branches, 641; West Springfield, Mass., Centen., 109; Amer. Ancestry, VI, 11; Savage's Gen. Dic. I, 93.

BAGLEY.

ORLANDO BAGLEY, of Salisbury, Mass., 1654, married Sarah, daughter of Anthony Colby, and had Orlando and others.

SAMUEL BAGLEY, of Weymouth, Mass., by wife Mary had Samuel, 1658, and perhaps more.

REFERENCES:—Worcester's His. Hollis, N. H., 365; Hayward's Hancock, 314; Savage's Gen. Dic. I, 93.

BAGNALL.

WALTER BAGNALL, of Scarborough, 1628, had at Richmond Isle great dealings with the Indians, who subsequently killed him.

REFERENCES:—Savage's Gen. Dic. I, 94; Davis' Plymouth, Mass., 9.

BAGWELL. See Bagwell Gen.

BAHAN. See Morrison's Windham, 327.

BAILEY.

RICHARD BAILEY, of Rowley, Mass., born in Bishopstown, Eng., died in Rowley, Mass., 1650; is supposed to have come from Yorkshire, Eng., about 1630 in the ship "Bevis." He was one of the company that set up the first cloth mill in America. He married Edna Halstead, and had Frances, Joseph and other children.

JOHN BAILEY, came from Chippenham, Eng., in the ship "Angel Gabriel" about 1639; was wrecked at Pemaquid, Me.; settled at Salisbury, Mass.; removed to Newbury about 1650. John, his son, who came with him had issue Sarah, John, James, Joseph, 1648, Joshua, 1653, and Isaac, 1654.

THOMAS BAILEY, of Weymouth, Mass., was freeman 1640. By wife Ruth, he had Christian, 1662, Samuel, Mary and Sarah.

REFERENCES.

MAINE.—Butler's His. Farmington, 371; Corliss' North Yarmouth; Cushman's His. Sheepscott, 355; Hanson's His. Gardiner, 72, 106; Hatch's His. Industry, 307; Wheeler's His. Brunswick, 828.

NEW HAMPSHIRE.—Cutter's His. Jaffray, 222; Hayward's His. Hancock, 314; Merrill's His. Acworth, 183; Morrison's His. Windham, 378; Read's His. Swanzey, 281; Washington, N. H., His. 285.

VERMONT.—Bass' His. Braintree, 111; Joslin's His. Poultney, 206.

MASSACHUSETTS.—Wyman's Charlestown Gens. I, 45; Mitchell's His. Bridgwater, 107; Hudson's His. Lexington, 10; Essex Inst. His. Coll., XIX, 299; Deane's His. Scituate, 213; Coffin's His. Newbury, 294; Barry's His. Hanover, 199; Ballou's His. Milford, 545.

CONNECTICUT.—Sedgwick's His. Sharon, 62; Middlefield His.; Hinman's Conn. Settlers, 108; Caulkin's His. New London, 220; Field, Haddam, Conn., 43; Hines' Lebanon, Conn., Address, 144.

OTHER PUBLICATIONS.—Austin's R. I. Gen. Dic. 9; Newport His. Mag. IV, 146; Bolton's Westchester County, N. Y., II, 708; Futhey's His. Chester County, Pa., 467; Slaughter's St. Marks Parish, Va., 160; Littell's Passaic Valley, N. J., 17; Whitman Gen., 181; Root Gen. 515; Poor Gen.; Poor's His. Researches, 77-161; Little Gen., 111; Kinne Gen. 91; Dunster Gen. 201; Chapman's Weeks Gen. 128; Dudley Gen.; Savage's Gen. Dic. I, 94; Amer. Ancestry, I, 3; II, 5; V, 177; VI, 73, 135; VII, 139; VIII, 228; X, 148; Descendants of Richard Bailey, 1867; Ancestry of Joseph Trowbridge Bailey, 1892; Bailey Gathering, Andover, Mass., 1894; Descendants of William Bailey of Newport, 1895; Bailey Gathering, Rowley, Mass., 1896.

BAILIC. See Bulloch Gen.

BAILY. See Amer. Ancestry V, 195; Jackson Gen. 228, 243. See also Baley, Bagley.

BAIN. See Amer. Ancestry II, 5.

BAINBRIDGE. Referring to Commodore Bainbridge, U. S. Navy; his biographer says: "The family of

Bainbridge possess one of the finest and most ancient pedegrees that can be traced among the Commoners of Great Britain.

REFERENCES:—N. E. His. and Gen. Reg., XXII, 18.

BAIRD. See Roe's Sketches of Rose, N. Y., 72; Salter's His. Monmouth County, N. J., VII; Miller's Colchester County, N. S., 167; Meginnes Biog. Annals, 64.

BAKER.

ALEXANDER BAKER, a ropemaker, came in the "Elizabeth and Ann", 1635, from London, with wife Elizabeth and children, Elizabeth, Christian; had also Alexander, Samuel, John, Joshua, Hannah, William, Benjamin, Joseph.

EDWARD BAKER, came to Lynn, Mass., with George Winthrop in 1630; had a son Timothy, who settled in Northampton, Mass.

THOMAS BAKER, came from England and settled first on Long Island and removed to Connecticut Farms, now Union, N. J.

THOMAS BAKER, of Roxbury, Mass., born in Kent, Eng., came to America 1635, settled at Roxbury. Had Thomas, Elizabeth and Sarah, and perhaps others.

Arms—Azure on a saltire engrailed sable, five escallops of the field, on a chief of the second, a lion passant of the first. *Crest*—A dexter arm embowed, vested, azure, cuffed, argent holding in the hand, ppr., an arrow of the last.

REFERENCES.

MAINE.--Warren's His. Waterford, 229; Corliss' North Yarmouth; Milliken's Narraguagus Valley, 24; Eaton's His. Thomaston, 138; Bangor His. Mag. IV, 211.

NEW HAMPSHIRE.—Smith's His. Petersborough, 15; Bouton's His. Concord, 632; Hayward's His. Gilsum, 257; Hayward's His. Hancock, 315; Cochran's His. Antrim, 346; Coggswell's His. Henniker, 450; Cutter's His. Jaffray, 226; Runnel's Sanbornton, II, 15.

VERMONT.—Hollister's His. Pawlet, 162; Williams' His. Danby, 104.

MASSACHUSETTS.—Lewis' His. Lynn, 116; Rich's His. Truro, 521; Wyman's Charlestown, Mass., Gens. 47; Ward's His. Shrewsbury, 238; Swift's Barnstable Families I, 60; Stearns' His. Ashburnham, 596; Morse's Sherborn Settlers, 11; Hyde's His. Brimfield, 370; Stone's His. Hubbardston, 224; Sewall's His. Woburn, 592; Saunderson's His. Charlestown, 281; Pierce's His. Grafton, 454; Hudson's His. Marlboro, 311; Herrick's His. of Gardner, 332; Hammatt Papers Ipswich, 22; Freeman's Cape Cod, II, 203, 707; Ellis' His. Roxbury, 91; Chandler's His. Shirley, 347; Blake's His. Franklin, 232; Atkins His. Hawley, 45; Windsor's His. Duxbury, 222.

CONNECTICUT.—Stiles His. Windsor, II, 39; Cothren's His. of Woodbury, 502; Caulkin's His. New London, 362; Hinman's Conn. Settlers, 110; Waldo's His. Tolland, 77; Weaver's His. Windham, 65; Windham, Conn., Gens., 65.

OTHER PUBLICATIONS.—Hedge's Address at East Hampton, N. Y.; Pompey, N. Y., Reunion (1875), 403; Roe's Sketches of Rose, N. Y., 147; Austin's R. I. Gen. Dic., 10; Littel's Passaic Valley; Martin's His. Chester, Pa., 408; Blackman's Susquehanna County, Pa., 54; Futhey's His. Chester County, Pa., 469; Power's Sangamon County, Ill., 87; Young's His. Chatauqua, N. Y., 352; Winslow Gen., II, App. 34; Whitmore's Copps Hill Epitaphs; Wentworth Gen. 396; Walker Memorial,

175; Pope Gen. Otis Gen. (1851); Leland Gen., 57; Dwight Gen., 606; Binney Gen., 17; Savage's Gen. Dic. I, 95; Amer. Ancestry, I, 3; II, 6; III, 111, 126; IV, 169; VI, 51, 74, 93, 133; VII, 9, 24, 269; VIII, 34, 113; X, 57; Baker Gen., 1867; 1870; 1889; 1896; V, 190; XXVIII, 205; XLIII, 279; N. E. His and Gen. Reg., XXXVII, 237.

BALCH.

JOHN BALCH, of Salem, Mass., one of the earliest settlers of Mass., from the vicinity of Bridgewater, Co. Somerset, Eng., came in 1623, with Robert Gorges to make establishment at Fort Ann, Nantucket; he removed with Roger Conant to plant at Salem on Beverly side; made freeman, 1631. By his wife Margaret he had Benjamin, 1629; John, Freeborn.

REFERENCES:—Stone's His. Beverly, Mass., 23; Deane's His. Scituate, Mass., 215; Barry's His. Framingham, Mass., 171; Essex Inst. Coll., I, 151; XVII, 3; Weaver's His. Windham, Conn., 70; Hinman's Conn. Settlers, 112; Wentworth Gen., I, 272; Poor's His. Researches, 78, 86; Morris' His. Windham, N. H., 330; Amer. Ancestry, I, 4; III, 217; Savage's Gen. Dic. I, 101; N. E. His. and Gen. Reg. IX, 233; Balch Family Chart, 1890; Balch Leaflets, 1895; Windham, Conn. Gens., 70.

BALCON.

ALEXANDER BALCON, of Providence, R. I., called "Jim," when he swore allegiance 1682; he removed to that part of Rihoboth, now Attleborough, and married Sarah, daughter of John Woodward; had William, 1692; Catharine, Alexander, John, Baruch, Sarah, Joseph.

REFERENCES:—Daggett's His. Attleborough, Mass., 88; Austin's R. I. Gen. Dic. 10; Boyd's His. Winchester, Conn., 266; Weaver's His. Windham, Conn., 68; Amer. Ancestry IX, 203; Savage's Gen. Dic. I, 101; Balcon Family of Attleborough, Mass., 1882; Windham Conn. Gens., 68.

BALCOMB. See Stone's Hubbardston, 225.
BALDEY. Hubbell Gen. 302.
BALDRIDGE. See Hollister's Pawlet, Vt., 163.

BALDWIN.

The name Baldwin is said to be derived from the words *Bald*, quick or speedy, and *win*, an old world signifying victor or conqueror—the true signification being "the speedy conqueror or victor."

The Baldwins, Earls of Flanders, were contemporary with Alfred the Great, whose son, Baldwin 2d, married the daughter of Robert of France, whose daughter Mathilda married William the Conqueror. Baldwin, Archbishop of Canterbury, with a train of 200 horses and 300 foot, his banner inscribed with the name of Thomas O'Becket, went on a crusade with Richard Coeur de Lion, in 1120.

Arms—Argent a saltier sable. *Crest*—A cockatrice ppr. wattled combed, and beaked or, ducally gorged and lined of the last. *Motto*—Je n'oublierai pas."

RICHARD BALDWIN, of Milford, Conn., 1640, came in the "Martin" to Boston, 1638. He married Eliza Alsop, sister of Joseph Alsop the first, of New Haven; and had Mary, Elizabeth, Sylvanus, 1646, Sarah, Temperance, Mary, John, Theophilus, Zachariah, Martha, Barnabus.

JOSEPH BALDWIN, of Milford, 1639, by wife Hannah had Joseph 1640, Benjamin 1642, Hannah, Mary, Elizabeth, Martha, Jonathan, David, Sarah. He removed to Hadley, Mass.

NATHANIEL BALDWIN, of Milford, 1639, had John, 1640, Daniel, 1644, Nathaniel, 1645, Abigail; by his 2d wife Joanna Westcoat, he had Sarah, Deborah, Samuel. He lived at Fairfield, 1654.

HENRY BALDWIN, of Woburn, Mass., was, it is said, from Devonshire, Eng. He married in 1649, Phebe, eldest daughter of Ezekiel Richardson, and had Susanna, Phebe, John 1656, Daniel 1659, Timothy, Mary, Henry, Abigail, Ruth, Benjamin.

JOHN BALDWIN, of Salem, Mass., married 1664, Arabella, daughter of John Norman, and had Hannah, John.

JOHN BALDWIN, of Guilford, Conn., married April 1653, Hannah Birchard, and removed to Norwich, Conn. He had John, Hannah and Thomas.

REFERENCES.

CONNECTICUT.—Weaver's His. Windham, 70; Orcutt's His. Torrington, 643; Orcutt's His. Stratford, 1116; Orcutt's New Milford, 640; Orcutt's His. Derby, 693; Caulkin's His. New London, 303; Caulkin's His. Norwich, 161; Hine's Lebanon Address, 144; Hinman's Conn. Settlers, 113; Sharpe's Seymour, 157, 223; Gold's His. Cornwall, 275.

MASSACHUSETTS.—Draper's His. Spencer, 174; Essex Inst. Coll. XVII, 7; Hazen's His. Billerica, 6; Temple's His. Palmer, 419; Bond's Watertown, 11; Hodgman's His. Westford, 437; Judd's His. Hadley, 449; Sewall's His. Woburn, 388, 593; Stearns' His. Ashburnham, 597; Temple's His. North Brookfield, 502; Temple's His. Palmer, 419; Ward's His. Shrewsbury, 246; Washburn's His. Leicester, 350; Barry's His. Hanover, 206; Wyman's Charlestown Gens., I, 49.

NEW HAMPSHIRE.—Saunderson's Charlestown, N. H., 282; Secomb's His. Amherst, 490; Wheeler's His. Newport, 292; Cochran's His. Antrim, 347; Cutter's His. Jaffray, 227; Hayward's His. Hancock, 321; Livermore's His. Wilton, 298; Morrison's His. Windham, 331.

NEW JERSEY.—N. J. His. Society, Suppt., VI, 107; His. Essex and Hudson Counties, vol. II, 717, 785; Atkinson's His. Newark; Littell's Passaic Valley, 26; Whittemore's His. Montclair, 189; The Founders and Builders of the Oranges, 42.

OTHER PUBLICATIONS.—Young's Chautauqua, N. Y., 225, 535; Hayden's Virginia Genealogies, 504; Peyton's Augusta, Va., 329; Richmond, Va., Standard, III, 51; McKeen's His. Bradford, Vt., 141; Cope Family of Penn., 40, 63, 144; Paxton's Marshall Gen.; Pickering Gen.; Powers' Sangamon, Ill., 92; His. Greene County, N. Y., 717, 785; Prentice Gen., 411; Prescott Memorial, 121; Rice Gen. 354; Rodman Gen. 79; Strong Gen. 906; Tuttle Family, 157, 629; Vinton Gen.; Vinton's Richardson Family, 38, 51; Walworth Hyde Gen., I, 338; Ward's Rice Family, 354; Hubbard's Stanstead County, Can., 297; Kitchell Gen. 33; Goodwin's Foote Gen., 240; Amer. Ancestry, I, 4; IV, 97; VII, 125, 190; VIII, 54, 69; X, 57; N. E. Gen. Reg., XXV, 153; XXVI, 294; XXVII, 148; XXXVIII, 160, 289, 372; Baldwin's Dennison Family, 127; Nathaniel Baldwin and his Descendants, 1871; Sylvester Baldwin, of Stonington, Conn., 1872; Descendants of John Baldwin, of Stonington, 1880; Baldwin Genealogy from 1500 to 1881; Baldwin Gen. Supplement, 1889; Windham Conn., Gens., 70.

BALES. See Livermore's Wilton, 302.

BALKHAM. See Bangor His. Mag. III, 203.

BALL.

ALLING BALL, of New Haven, 1643, had by his wife Dorothy, John 1656, Eliphalet, Alling, Mary or Mercy.

EDWARD BALL, of Branford, Conn., removed 1667 to Newark, N. J., and had Caleb, Abigail, Joseph, Lydia, Moses, Thomas.

FRANCIS BALL, of Dorchester, Mass., removed to Springfield, married Abigail, daughter of Henry Burt, and had Jonathan, Samuel. His widow married Benjamin Mun, and next Lieut. Thomas Stebbins.

Col. WILLIAM BALL, of Virginia, was a merchant and planter and Colonel, 1672. His sons were Richard, William and Joseph.

In Col. William L. Stone's His. of Saratoga, N. Y., p. 349, he states that the Rev. Eliphalet Ball, was a third cousin of Gen. Washington. The claim to relationship between the Virginia and New England families rests chiefly on the similarity of Arms. Those of Col. William Ball, of Virginia, were: Arms—Argent a lion passant sable, on a chief of the second three mullets of the first. Crest—Out of the clouds proper a demi lion rampant sable, powdered with estoiles argent, holding a globe, or. Motto—Coeb unique tueri.

The New England family of Balls had Arms—Argent a lion passant sable, on a chief of the second three mullets of the first. Crest—A stag trippant ppr. Motto— Semper Cavete.

REFERENCES.

NEW HAMPSHIRE.—Worcester's His. of Hollis, 365; Merrill's His. of Acworth, 184; Hill's His. of Mason, 200; Washington, N. H., His., 291; Blood's His. Temple, 203; Hayward's His. Hancock, 324; Coggswell's His. of Henniker, 452; Cochran's His. of Antrim, 351.

MASSACHUSETTS.—Temple's His. North Brookfield, 502; Ballou's His. Milford, 549; Ward's His. Shrewsbury, 234; Barry's His. Framingham, 171; Bond's His. Watertown, 11; Reed's His. Rutland, 139; Draper's His. Spencer, 177; Wyman's Charleston, I, 50.

CONNECTICUT.—Hinman's Conn. Settlers, 122; Dodd's His. of East Haven, 104; Tuttle Family of Conn., 143, 628.

NEW JERSEY.—His. Essex and Hudson Counties, vol. II, 782; N. J. His. Society Coll. vol. VI, supplement, 110; Littell's Passaic Valley, 31, 491.

VIRGINIA.—Hayden's Virginia Genealogies, 45; Meade's Old Families of Virginia, II, 126; Richmond, Va., Standard, III, 29.

OTHER PUBLICATIONS.—Ball's Maternal Ancestry of Washington; Jewitt's Ball Gen. 1867; Ball (1853), Gen., chart (1891); Edward Ball of Block Island, R. I., 1891; Austin, R. I., Gen. Dic., 11; Ball's Lake County, Ind., 438; Sylvester's His. of Ulster County, N. Y., 108; Southern Bivouac (1886), 727; Powers' His. Sangamon, Ill., 93; Green's Kentucky Families; Phoenix's Whiting Family, I, 285; Goode Gen. 176; Pompey's N. Y. Reunion, 267; Ely Gen. 243; Carter Family Tree; Savage's Gen. Dic. I, 105; Amer. Ancestry, I, 4; II, 6; V, 221; VI, 105; VIII, 72; X, 148; N. E. His. and Gen. Reg. IX, 158; His. Greene County, N. Y., 782.

BALLAUER.

CHARLES BALLAUER, of Culpepper Co., Va., a soldier of the Revolution, married Martha, daughter of Samuel, Lampton, and had issue Willis and Blanche. REFERENCES:—Amer. Ancestry, VII, 245.

BALLENTINE.

WILLIAM BALLANTINE, of Boston, 1652, called "a Scotch gentleman from Ayr," was one of the founders of the Charity Society, of that nation in 1657. He married July 23, 1652, Hannah, daughter of Angel Holland,

and had John 1653, William 1655, David, Elizabeth, Benjamin, Hannah, William, Susanna, Jonathan.
REFERENCES:—Savage's Gen. Dic. I, 107; N. E. His. and Gen. Reg. VI, 371; Hinman's Conn. Settlers, 117.

BALLARD.

WILLIAM BALLARD, of London, supposed to be son of William Ballard of Lynn, Mass., 1630, came on the "James" from London, 1635, aged 32, with wife Elizabeth, 26, and children Esther and John; settled in Andover, Mass., and had Joseph and other children; he died July 10, 1689.
REFERENCES:—Barry's His. Framingham, Mass., 172; Wyman's Charlestown, Mass., Gens., I, 52; Whitmore's Copps Hill Epitaphs; Adenus' Andover, Mass., 27; Livermore's His. Wilton, N. H., 304; Bouton's His. Concord, N. H., 633; Lapham's His. Bethel, Me., 465; Weaver's His. Windham, Conn., 73; Neil's Virginia Carolorum, 317; Locke Gen. 56, 105; Chandler Gen. 158; Savage's Gen. Dic. I, 108; Adenus' Haven Gen., 28; Amer. Ancestry, III, 186; VI, 75; Andrews Gen. (1890), 140-2; Windham, Conn. Gens., 73.

BALLATT. See Wyman's Charlestown Gen., I, 53.

BALLIET. See Balyard Gen.

BALLOCH. See Amer. Ancestry, VIII, 101.

BALLOIN. See Wyman's Charlestown Gens., I, 54.

BALLORD. Amer. Ancestry, VI, 114.

BALLOU.

MATURIN BALLOU was of Providence 1639; married Hannah, daughter of Robert and Catharine Pike, and had James 1652.
REFERENCES:—Read's His. of Swanzey, N. H., 283; Basset's His. Richmond, 277; Austin's R. I. Gen. Dic. 12; Paige's His. Hardwick, Mass., 330; Ballou's His. Milford, Mass., 556; Pickering Gen.; Faxan Gen., 101; Paxton's Marshall Gen., 303; Ballou Gen., 1888; Amer. Ancestry, IV, 222; VI, 129, 158.

BALSTONE.

WILLIAM BALSTONE, of Boston, came probably with Winthrop's fleet; took the oath of fidelity May 18, 1630. By his wife Elizabeth, he had Peleg, William, 1633, Mary Mehitable, Meribah.
REFERENCES:—See Savage's Gen. Dic., I, 109.

BALYARD. See Balyard Gen. 1873.

BAME. See Amer. Ancestry II, 153.

BAMFORD. Runnel's Sanbornton.

BANCKER. Pearson's Schenectady Settlers, 4; Munsell's Albany IV, 94; N. Y. Gen. and Bio. Rec. II, 68.

BANCKSON. Martin's Chester, Pa., 30.

BANCROFT.

THOMAS BANCROFT, born in England, 1622, died at Reading, Mass., 1691; was at Dedham, 1647; removed to Reading 1647. He married 1st 1647, Alice Bacon, of Dedham; 2d 1648, Elizabeth Metcalf, of Dedham; had Thomas and other children.

JOHN BANCROFT, of Lynn, with wife Jane, came in the "James" from London, April, 1632; died about 1637, leaving widow, and son John and Thomas.

NATHANIEL BANCROFT, of Westfield, married 1675, Hannah Gardner, probably daughter of Samuel Gardner, of Hadley, Mass., died Feb. 10, 1724. Had Nathaniel, Benjamin, Elizabeth, Edward.

REFERENCES.
MASSACHUSETTS.—Herrick's His. of Gardner, Mass., 331; Stearn's His. Ashburnham, 598; Wyman's Charlestown Gens., I, 54; Ballou's His. Milford, 560; Hill's Old Dunstable, 131; Fox's His. Dunstable, 240; Eaton's His. Reading, 43; Green's Early Groton, Mass., Settlers, 1; Green's Groton, Mass., Epitaphs, 235; Benedict's His. Sutton, 584; Butler's His. Groton, 385; Temple's His. Northfield, 399; Tyngsboro, Mass., Centen. Rec., 13; Wall's Remin. of Worcester, Mass., 141.

NEW HAMPSHIRE.—Hayward's His. Gilsum, 239; Stearn's His. Rindge, 433.

CONNECTICUT. Hinman's Conn. Settler's, 123; Orcutt's His. of Torrington, 644; Stile's His. Windsor, II, 40.

OTHER PUBLICATIONS.—Bancroft and Alling Gen., 1883; Holton's Farwell Gen. 41; Ely Gen. 33; Dwight Gen. 885; Chandler Gen. 469; Driver Gen. 885; Vinton's Upton Gen. 475; Loomis Gen., Female Branches, 707; Lapham's His. of Norway, Me., 459; Vinton's Richardson Memorial, 86; Locke Gen. 29, 51; Kellogg's Memorial of Elder J. White, 57; Savage's Gen. Dic., I, 110; Amer. Ancestry, I, 4; V, 156; VIII, 200.

BANDELL. See Brown's West Simsbury, 29.

BANE. Jordan's Leighton Gen.

BANGS.

EDWARD BANGS, of Plymouth, born perhaps 1592, at Chichester, County Sussex, Eng., came in the "Ann," 1626. He removed with Gov. Prence, 1644, to Eastham. He was a shipwright, and directed the labor, it is said, on the first vessel built in the Colony. He married, after 1627, Lydia, daughter of Robert Hicks, and had Rebecca, John, Sarah, Jonathan, 1640, Lydia, Hannah, Joshua, Bethia, Mercy, Applux.

JONATHAN BANGS, brother of Edward, married at Eastham, Mary, daughter of Samuel Mays, of Barnstable, and had Edward 1665, Rebecca 1668; Mary Jonathan, 1673; Hannah, Lamosin, Samuel, Mercy, Elizabeth, Sarah, Lydia.
REFERENCES:—Pratt's His. of Eastham, Mass., 18; Dudley's Gen. Bangs Family; Freeman's Cape Cod. Mass., I, 639; II, 512; Lincoln's His. Worcester, Mass., 198; Rich's His. Truro, Mass., 520; Paige's His., Hardwick, Mass., 330; Baylie's New Plymouth II, 220; Atkins' His. Hawley, Mass., 48; Pierce's His. Gorham, Me., 155; Lapham's His. Norway, Me., 459; Hubbard's Stanstead County, Can., 117; Bangs Autobiography, 311; Amer. Ancestry, III, 99; IV, 128; Preble Gen. 57, 245; Savage's Gen. Dic. I, 111; N. E. His. and Gen. Reg. VIII, 368; X, 157.

BANISTER.

THOMAS BANISTER, of Boston, 1685, by wife Sarah had Samuel 1686, Mary, Hannah.
REFERENCES:—Temple's His. North Brookfield, Mass., 503; Barry's His. Framingham, Mass., 175; Barry's His. Goshen, Mass., 134; Hudson's His. Marlboro, Mass., 312; Ward's His. Shrewsbury, Mass., 247; Jamison's His. Midway, Mass., 451; Campbell's Virginia, 724; Ely Gen. 137, 286; Richmond, Va., Standard, II, 15; Slaughter's Bristol Parish, 143; Amer. Ancestry, VII, 207; Bland Papers, I, 27; Savage's Gen. Dic. I, 112.

BANKHEAD. See Hayden's Virginia Genealogies, 448; Page Gen. 240.

BANKS.

JOHN BANKS, of Windsor, Conn., one of the first settlers, married a daughter of Charles Taintor, of Wethersfield; he was town clerk, 1643. He removed to Fairfield, of which town he was a representative 1651-56; removed to Rye, N. Y., and was representative from that town 1670-3. His will mentions wife Mary and children, John, Samuel, Obadiah, Benjamin, Susanna, and Mary Taylor.

REFERENCES:—Baird's Rye, N. Y., 395; Hinman's Puritan Settlers Conn., 125; Schenk's His. Fairfield, Conn., 351; Todd's His. of Reading, Conn., 174; Corliss' His. Yarmouth, Me.; Dearborn's Parsonfield, Me., 326, 365; Read's His. Swanzey, N. H., 286; Slaughter's Life of Fry, 56; Jones Gen. 92; Savage's Gen. Dic. I, 112; Banks' Gen. Family of Maine, 1890; N. E. His. and Gen. Reg., XLIV, 258.

BANNER. See Washington, N. H., His., 293.

BANTA.

GILBERT BANTA, of Boston, by wife Mercy had Mary, Gilbert, 1694; William, 1698; Elizabeth.

REFERENCES:—Savage's Gen. Dic. I, 113; Banta Gen. 1893; Pearson's Schenectady, N. Y., Settlers, 6; Amer. Ancestry, III, 65.

BAPTIST. See Goode Gen. 234; Neil's Virginia Carolorum, 377.

BARAGER. See Amer. Ancestry, II, 158.

BARBER.

GEORGE BARBER, of Dedham, 1643, freeman 1647, married 24th Nov. 1642, Elizabeth Clark, and had Mary, Samuel 1647, John, Elizabeth. He removed to Medfield and there had Hannah, Zachariah 1658, Abigail. He was a representative to the General Court and chief military officer.

THOMAS BARBER, of Windsor, came on the Elizabeth and had James 1687, Patience and Ebenezer.

THOMAS BARBER, of Windsor came on the "Christian," 1635, aged 21, and resided first at Dorchester. He was engaged in the Pequot war under Stoughton. He married 1640, Joan, and had John, Thomas 1644, Sarah, Samuel, Mary. He died 1662.

THOMAS BARBER, of Gloucester, 1662, removed in 1667 to Newbury, married in 1671, Elizabeth; he removed to Suffield, Conn., and there had Joseph and Benjamin, twins. John 1684, Moses 1687.

REFERENCES.

CONNECTICUT.—Brown's West Simsbury, 18; Orcutt's His. Torrington, 645; Stiles's His. Windsor, II, 50; Hinman's Conn. Settlers, 126.

NEW HAMPSHIRE.—Hayward's His. Hancock, 327; Smith's His. of Petersborough, 16.

MASSACHUSETTS.—Wyman's Charlestown, I, 55; Temple's His. Palmer 422; Whitemore's Copps Hill Epitaphs; Temple's His. Northfield, 400; James' His. Midway, 452; Ballou's His. Milford, 561.

OTHER PUBLICATIONS.—Irish's His. Richmond, R. I., 89; Austin's R. I. Gen. Dic. 13; Clyde's Irish Settlement, Pa., 14; Pompey, N. Y., Reunion, 283; Wight Gen. 16; Rockwood Family, 23; Loomis' Gen. Female Branches, 264; Humphrey's Gen. 332; Howe's Barber and Eno Gen. 1893; Greene Gen.; Savage's Gen. Dic. I, 113; Amer. Ancestry, I, 4; IV, 192; VII, 25; Barber's Atlas Gen. 104; Gen. Robert Barber, Pa. Barber-Eno Family, 1893; N. E. Gen. Dic. XXXVII, 28.

BARBOUR.

THOMAS BARBOUR, born about 1614, died 1662; settled in Windsor 1635; removed to Simsbury. He had Thomas, who married Mary Philps, daughter of William Philps.

REFERENCES:—Orcutt's His. Torrington, Conn. 648; Collins' His. Hillsdale, N. Y., App. 33; Moore's Sherborn, Mass., Settlers, 12; Slaughter's St. Mark's Parish, Va., 118; Kitchell Gen.-17; Smith and Dean, Jour. of Portland, 57; Green's Kentucky Families; Faxton Gen. 73; Barber's My Wife and Mother, 1885; Amer. Ancestry, VI, 88; IX, 145.

BARBERIE. See Whitehead's Perth Amboy, N. J. 124.

BARBRE. See Power's Sangamon, Ill., 95.

BARCALOW. See Honeyman's Our Home, 408.

BARCLAY. N. Y. Gen. and Biog. Rec. III, 21; Riker's Annals of Newton, N. Y., 319; Holgate's Amer. Gen. 122.

BARDELLE. See Barber's Atlee Gen. 70.

BARD.

JOHN BARD, of Lynn, Mass., had John, born 29th Jan. 1678.

BARDEN.

BARDEN. See also Borden and Burden.

WILLIAM BARDEN, of Marshfield, 1643, removed to Barnstable, Mass. Married, Feb. 1661, Deborah Barker, and had Mercy, Deborah, John, Stephan, Abraham, 1674, Joseph, 1675, Ann.

REFERENCES:—Amer. Ancestry, II, 6; Savage's Gen. Dic. I, 114; His. Richmond, N. H., 299; Cleveland's His. Yates County, N. Y., 184, Essex Inst. Coll. VII, 213.

BARDING.

NATHANIEL BARDING, was of Hartford, 1636, though not an original proprietor. He had Sarah by his first wife. His second wife was Abigail, widow of William Andrews, the schoolmaster. His daughter married, 1645, Thomas Spencer, who called a son Nathaniel Barding to perpetuate the name.

BARDWELL.

ROBERT BARDWELL, of Hartford, was a soldier in Philip's war, 1676, and was in the Falls Fight under Capt. Turner. He married, 1676, Mary, daughter of William Gull, and had Ebenezer, Samuel, John, Thomas, Mary, Sarah, Esther, Thankful, Abigail. He died, 1726.

REFERENCES:—Savage's Gen. Dic. I, 114; Amer. Ancestry, III, 198; IX, 159, 175; Barrers' His. Goshen, Mass., 134; Doolittle's Belchertown, Mass., 266; Aldrich's Walpole, Mass., 191; Judd's His. Hadley, Mass., 450; Hollister's Pawlet, Vt., 164.

BARENTS. See Bergen's Kings County, N. Y., 19.

BAREFOOT. Walter Barefoot, of Great Island, 1660, was counsel of the Colony 1682.

BARGE.

GILES BARGE, of Scarborough, married Eleanor, widow of Jonas Barclay; was selectman, 1669; representative, 1682; moved to Dorchester.

REFERENCES:—Savage's Gen. Dic. I, 114.

BARGER.

PHILIP BARGER, of Boston, a Huguenot, about 1685, came to Casco with Pierre Boudoin. He died

1703, leaving widow Margaret, and probably Philip, who died, 1720.

REFERENCES:—Savage's Gen. Dic. I, 114; Power's Sangamon, Ill., 95.

BAHRET. See Munsell's Albany IV, 95.

BARHEYT. See Amer. Ancestry, 1, 4; Pearson's Schenectady, 7.

BARINGER. See Amer. Ancestry, II, 6.

BARKALOW. Salter's Monmouth, N. J.

BARKELOO. Davis's Bucks County, Pa., 201; Bergen's Kings County, N. Y., Settlers, 20; Bergen Gen. 153.

BARKER.

EDWARD BARKER, of Boston, 1650; by wife, Jane, had Elizabeth, Mary, John, Sarah, Thomas, 1657.

JAMES BARKER, of Rowley, Mass., freeman, 1640; died, 1678, leaving wife,Mary; children, Barzillai, James, Nathaniel, Eunice, Grace.

THOMAS BARKER, of Boston, by wife Jane, had Thomas, Aug. 23, 1657.

RICHARD BARKER, of Andover, Mass., 1643, was one of the founders of the church there. By his wife Joanna, he had John, William, Richard, Ebenezer, Stephen, Benjamin, Sarah, Esther Hannah.

JOHN BARKER, of Duxbury, Mass., married, 1632, Ann, daughter of John Williams, of Scituate; removed to Marshfield, 1638. He had Deborah, John, 1650.

ROBERT BARKER, of Duxbury, 1648, brother of above, had Robert, Francis, Isaac, Rebecca.

ISAAC BARKER, of Duxbury, married, Dec. 28, 1665, Judith, daughter of Gov. Thomas Prence, and had Rebecca, Lydia, Judith, Martha, Francis, Samuel, Isaac, Jabez, Robert.

JAMES BARKER, of Newport, 1651, a friend of John Clark, named in the Royal Charter, 1663, when he was assistant and was chosen Deputy Governor, 1678. His first wife was a daughter of Hon. Jeremiah Clark. His second wife was Sarah, daughter of William Jeffrey. He had James and perhaps others.

REFERENCES.

CONNECTICUT.—Davis's His. Wallingford, 635; Windham County Gens. 77.

NEW HAMPSHIRE.—Washington, N. H., His, 691; Stearns' His. Rindge, 438; Secomb's His. Amherst, 493; Morrison's His. Windham, 381; Livermore's His. Wilton, 305; Hayward's His. Hancock, 327; Coggswell's His. Henniker, 453; Cochran's His. Antrim, 352; Blood's His. Temple, 203.

MAINE.—Warren's His. Waterford, 230; Cushman's His. Sheepscott, 355; Eaton's His. Thomaston, 139; Hanson's His. Gardener, 150; Lapham's His. Rumford, 302; Lapham's His. Bethel, 475, 652.

MASSACHUSETTS.—Temple's His. Palmer, 426; Winser's His. Duxbury, 223; Charlestown Gens. by Wyman, I, 56; Whitmore's Copp's Hill Epitaphs; Swift's Barnstable Families, I, 64; Deane's His. Scituate, 216; Barry's His. Hanover, 206; Ballou's His. Milford, 564; Abbot's Andover, 20.

NEW YORK.—Cleveland's Yates County, 398, 677; Bolton's His. Westchester County, 501; Young's Chautauqua County, 479.

RHODE ISLAND.—Newport His. Mag. I, 37; Austin's Allied Families, 26; Austin's R. I. Gen. Dic. 14; Austin's Ancestries, 9.

OTHER PUBLICATIONS.—Savage's Gen. Dic. I, 115; N. E. His. and Gen. Reg. XXIV, 297; Amer. Ancestry, I, 5; Andrews' Gen. 1890, 4, 100, 145; Buckingham Gen. 215; Essex Institute Coll. XIX, 304; Goodwin's Foote Family Gen. 189; Guild Stiles Gen. 288; Kellogg's Mem. of Elder John White, 90; Rodman Gen. 127; Memorial of Josiah Barker, of Charlestown, Mass., 1893; His. Greene County, N. Y., 205.

BARKLEY. Richmond Standard, III, 20.

BARKSDALE. Goode Gen. 78.

BARLESS. Roe's Sketches of Rose, 272.

BARLOW.

ANDREW BARLOW, of Rochester, Mass., by wife Beulah, had Elizabeth, Mary, Shubael, 1691, Nathan.

EDWARD BARLOW, of Malden, married Mary, daughter of James Pemberton, before 1660.

JAMES BARLOW, of Suffield, Conn., married, Jan. 10, 1688, Sarah, daughter of Thomas Huxley, had James, John, of Fairfield, Elizabeth, Frost, Martha, Ruth, Isabella, Chapman.

THOMAS BARLOW, of Fairfield, 1653, by wife Rose, had Phebe, Deborah, Mary.

REFERENCES:—Hurd's His. Fairfield, Conn., 577; Schenck's His. Fairfield, 352; Todd's His. Redding, 174; Hinman's Conn. Settlers, 131; Orcutt's His. Stratford, 1117; Wyman's Charlestown, Mass., Gens. I, 589; Paige's His. Harwick, 331; Freeman's His. Cape Cod, Mass., II, 78; Bolton's His. Westchester County, N. Y., II, 209; Beckwith's Creoles, 15; Hill and Barlow Gen., 1880; Amer. Ancestry, VIII, 211; IX, 88; Savage's Gen. Dic. I, 116; Barlow Gen. 1891.

BARNABY.

JAMES BARNABY, of Plymouth, married June 6, 1647, Lydia, daughter of Robert Bartlett, and had James and Stephen.

REFERENCES:—Savage's Gen. Dic. I, 117; N. E. Gen. Reg. XVIII, 361; Pierce's (E. W.) Contributions, 5; Amer. Ancestry, V, 190; Davis, Landmarks of Plymouth, Mass., 10; Barnaby Family, 1864.

BARNARD.

BARTHOLOMEW BARNARD, of Boston, had Matthew and perhaps others.

FRANCIS BARNARD, of Hartford, Conn., 1644, removed about 1659 to Hadley, Mass., made freeman, 1666. He married Hannah, sister of Matthew and Reynold Marvin, and had Thomas, Samuel, Joseph, Hannah, John, Sarah. He was ancestor of all the divines of this name from Harvard.

JOHN BARNARD, of Watertown, came in 1634, aged 30, with wife Phebe, and sons John and Samuel, in the "Elizabeth" from Ipswich. He had here Hannah, Mary, Joseph, Benjamin.

RICHARD BARNARD, of Springfield, had Joseph.

ROBERT BARNARD, of Salisbury, Mass., by wife Joanna, had John 1642. He removed to Nantucket.

ROBERT BARNARD, of Andover, Mass., one of the founders of the church there, 1645, had Stephen, John, Hannah.

THOMAS BARNARD, of Salisbury, by wife Helen, had Thomas, Nathaniel, Martha and Mary, twins, 1645; Sarah, Hannah, Ruth.

REFERENCES.

CONNECTICUT.—Stiles' His. of Windsor, II, 58, Waldo's His. Tolland, 88; Hinman's Conn. Settlers, 132.

MASSACHUSETTS.—Temple's His. North Brookfield, 504; Temple's His. Whatley, 203; Wyman's Charlestown Gen. I, 59; Whitmore's Copps Hill Epitaphs; Pierce's His. Grafton, 455; Judd's His. Hadley, 450; Hudson's His. Marlboro, 313; Bond's His. Watertown, 14; Benedict's His. Sutton, 584; Barry's His. Framingham, 175; Abbott's Andover, 20.

NEW HAMPSHIRE.—Merrill's His. of Ackworth, 184; Norton's His. Fitzwilliam, 462; Secomb's His. Amherst, 494.

OTHER PUBLICATIONS.—Futhey's His. Chester County, Pa., 473; Smith's His. Delaware County, Pa., 44; Martin's Chester, Pa., 407; Eaton's His. Thomaston, Me., 139; Caverly's His. of Pittsford, Vt., 692; Wentworth's Gen. I, 110; Maris' Gen. 62; Loomis' Gen. Female Branches, 635; Leach's Morton Ancestry; Amer. Ancestry, II, 6; IV, 83; Heraldic Journal, III, 106; Savage's Gen. Dic. I, 118; N. E. His. and Gen. Rec. XV, 269.

BARNES.

BARNES. The name of Barnes is derived from the Norse bjorne, a warrior.

THOMAS BARNES was an original settler of Hartford, Conn., 1639; served with the colonists in the Pequot fight; he was Sergeant of the train band at Farmington, Conn.; freeman 1669, and was probably the first of the family in America. He had Benjamin, Joseph and Thomas.

JOHN BARNES, of Plymouth, Mass., married Mary Plummer, had John, Jonathan, 1643; Lydia, Hannah, Mary.

WILLIAM BARNES, of Salisbury, 1640, by wife Rachel, had Mary, William, Hannah, Deborah, Jonathan, Rachel, Sarah, John, Rebecca.

REFERENCES.

CONNECTICUT.—Wood's His. East Haven, 104; Orcutt's His. New Milford, 648; Orcutt's His. Wolcott, 446; Sedgwick's His. Sharon, 62; Stiles' His. Windsor, II, 59; Timlow's Southington, 17; His. Middlefield; Hinman's Conn. Settlers, 141.

MASSACHUSETTS.—Hudson's His. Marlborough, 314; Draper's His. Spencer, 173; Davis' Landmarks of Plymouth, 10; Mitchell's His. Bridgewater, 356; Paige's His. Hardwick, 331; Stone's His. Hubbardston, 226; Temple's His. North Brookfield, 505; Ward's His. Shrewsbury, 243; Wyman's Charlestown, Mass., Gens. I, 60; Mitchell's His. Bridgewater, 356.

MAINE.—Easton's His. Thomaston, 139; Hansen's His. Gardner, 111; Bangor His. Mag.

NEW HAMPSHIRE.—Norton's His. Fitzwilliam, 462; Livermore's His. Wilton, 307; Cochran's His. Antrim, 357; Coggswell's His. Henniker, 453; Washington's N. H., His. Bedford Centen.

NEW YORK.—Howell's His. Southampton, 202; Clute's His. Staten Island, 341; Cleveland's His. Yates County, 129; Bond's His. Rye, 453; Hedge's East Hampton (1850); Roe's Sketches of Roe, 200.

VERMONT.—Williams' His. Danby, 110; Adams' His. Fairhaven; Caverley's Pittsford, 691.

OTHER PUBLICATIONS.—Austin's R. I. Gen. Dic. 15; Hayden's Virginia Gens. 719; Power's His. Sangamon, Ill., 97; Young's His. Wayne County, Ind., 337; Wentworth's Gen. I, 247; Tuttle's Gen. 632; Montague's Gen. 427; Driver Gen. 117; Hoyt's Gen. 123, 132; Dawson's Gen. 90; Douglass' Gen. 330; Savage's

Gen. Dic. I, 121; Amer. Ancestry, I, 5; II, 6; IV, 3, 172; V, 152, 162; IX, 20.

BARNETT.

ROBERT BARNETT was an early settler of Nantucket, Mass.

REFERENCES:—Aldrich's His. Walpole, N. H., 190; Hayward's His.; Hancock's N. H., 333; Stiles' His. Windsor, Conn., II, 60; Young's His. Warsaw, N. Y. 264; Egle's Penn. Gens. 49; Gilmer's Georgians, 130; Power's His. Sangamon County, Ill., 96; Walworth's Hyde Gen. 498, 505; Amer. Ancestry, I, 7.

BARNEY.

JACOB BARNEY was of Salem; freeman 1634. Was representative at the Genl. Court, 1635-8-47-53, also 1673.

REFERENCES:—Washington, N. H., His. 295; Merril's His. Acworth's, N. H., 185; Hayward's His. Hancock, N. H., 334; Bassett's His. Richmond, N. H., 306; Amer. Ancestry, VI, 17; Savage's Gen. Dic. 109, 123.

BARNHILL. See Cunnahill Gen. 109; Miller's Colchester County, N. S., 184.

BARNUM.

THOMAS BARNUM was one of the original eight settlers of Danbury, Conn., 1684, and was the ancestor of Phineas T. Barnum. He died there Dec. 26, 1695. Had issue Thomas 1663, Francis, Richard, John, Ebenezer, Hannah.

REFERENCES:—Orcutt's His. Stratford, Conn., 1117; Hinman's Conn. Settlers, 144; Emery's Taunton, Mass., Ministry, II, 8; Cleveland Gen. 235; Roe's Sketches of Rose, N. Y., 162; Savage's Gen. Dic. I, 124; Amer. Ancestry VI, 196.

BARNWELL.

JOHN BARNWELL, of South Carolina, born in Ireland, a younger son of the House of Trimleson in Ireland, who emigrated to America after the battle of Boyne, received a grant of land in South Carolina, 1705; married Miss Berners, daughter of an English merchant in Charlestown, S. C. See Amer. Ancestry V, 89.

BARR. See Bedford, N. H., Centen. 289; Driver Gen. 263; Temple's His. North Brookfield, Mass., 511; Whittemore's Founders and Builders of the Oranges, 319.

BARRADAL. See Meade's Families, I, 198.

BARRAND. See Hanson's Old Kent, 171; Richmond, Va., Standard, II, 45.

BARRE. See Van Brunt Family, 44.

BARREL.

GEORGE BARREL, of Boston, was made freeman May 10, 1643. He had a daughter Ann.

JOHN BARRELL, of Watertown, by wife Eliza, had Abigail.

REFERENCES:—Savage's Gen. Dic. I, 124; Barry's Hanover, Mass., 208; Stearn's His. Ashburnham, Mass., 599.

BARRELL. See Wyman's Charlestown, Mass., Gens. I, 60; Deane's His. Scituate, Mass., 217; French's His. Turner, Me., 58; Savage's Gen. Dic. I, 124.

BARRETT.

BENJAMIN BARRETT, of Hatfield, Mass., was a soldier under Capt. Turner, 1676. He removed to Deerfield and died in 1690, leaving children, Benjamin, John, Jonathan, Sarah, Rebecca.

HUMPHREY BARRETT, of Concord, Mass., 1640; freeman 1657, died Nov. 1662, settled in Marlborough. He had issue Thomas, Humphrey, John.

JOHN BARRETT, of Malden, Mass., 1653; removed to Wells and there made constable 1657, representative to the Genl. Court 1681. His wife was daughter of Edward Attlefield. They had John.

JOHN BARRETT, of Chelmsford, Mass., by wife Susan had Lydia 1659; Samuel, June 16, 1660.

WALTER BARETT, of Cambridge, Mass., by wife Sarah, daughter of Robert Champey, had Lydia, John 1660.

REFERENCES.

CONNECTICUT.—Stiles' His. Windsor, II, 60; Hinman's Conn. Settlers, 145.

MASSACHUSETTS.—Paige's His. Cambridge, 483; Potter's Old Families of Concord; Shattuck's His. Concord, 363; Stearn's His. Ashburnham, 600; Wyman's Charlestown, Mass., Gens.; Temple's His. Northfield, 402; Temple's His. North Brookfield, 511; Mitchell's His. Bridgewater, 108; Hudson's His. Lexington, 10; Hodgman's His. Westford, 437; Goss' Melrose, Mass., Address, 13; Barry's His. Framingham, 175; Chandlers' His. Shirley, 348.

MAINE.—Sibley's His. Union, 431; Eaton's His. Thomaston, 140.

NEW HAMPSHIRE.—Cochran's His. Antrim, 357; Hayward's His. Gilsum, 260; Hill's His. Mason, 200; Kidder's New Ipswich, 330; Livermore's His. Wilton, 308; Secomb's His. Amherst, 495; Washington, N. H., His. 301, 691.

OTHER PUBLICATIONS.—N. E. His. and Gen. Reg. XLII, 257; Williams' His. Danby, Vt. 109; Munsell's Albany Coll. IV, 94; Locke's Gen. 107; Dwight Gen. 602; Barret's Gen. (1888), 296; Savage's Gen. Dic. I, 124; Amer. Ancestry, I, 5; II, 7; III, 68, 72; VI, 167; X, 99, 233.

BARRITT. See Amer. Ancestry, IX, 25.

BARRINGER. See Wheeler's Eminent North Carolinians, 967; Wheeler's North Carolina, II, 67.

BARRON.

ELLIS BARRON, of Watertown, freeman, June 2, 1641. Brought from England, Ellis, Mary, Susanna.

ELLIS BARRON, son of Ellis, born in England, came with his father to this country and settled in Woodbridge, N. J., about 1690. He married Mary, daughter of Ephraim Andrews, one of the original freeholders to whom the patents for the town were granted, 1670. Had Samuel.

REFERENCES.

MASSACHUSETTS.—Hodgman's His. Westford, 437; Butler's His. Groton, 386; Wyman's Charlestown Gens. I, 63; Green's Groton, Mass., Epitaphs, 236; Green's Early Groton, Mass., Settlers, 2; Bond's Watertown, 17.

NEW HAMPSHIRE.—Washington, N. H., His. 302; Hayward's His. Gilsum, 260; Bedford, N. H., Centen, 290; Secomb's His. Amherst, 493; Saunderson's Charleston, N. H., 282; Worcester's His. Hollis. N. H., 365.

OTHER PUBLICATIONS.—McKeen's His. Bradford, Vt., 130; Wells' Family Antiquities; Amer. Ancestry, V, 53; VII, 111; Savage's Gen. Dic. I, 126.

BARROWS.

JOHN BARROWS was of Plymouth, Mass., moved to Salem. By wife Deborah he had Robert, Benajah, John, Ebenezer, and two daughters.

REFERENCES.

CONNECTICUT.—Weaver's His. Windham, 74, 90; Sedgwick's His. Sharon, 62; Hinman's Conn. Settlers, 146; Windham, Conn. Gens., 74.

MASSACHUSETTS.—Barrus' His. Goshen, 138; Dagget's His. Attleborough, 87; Davis's Landmarks of Plymouth, 13; Hyde's His. Brimfield, 469; Wyman's Charlestown, Mass., Gens., I, 63.

MAINE.—Eaton's Annuals of Warren, 504; Eaton's His. Thomaston, 140; Lapham's His. Norway, 459; Lapham's His. Paris, 501; Maine His. and Gen. Rec. VII, 134; Thurston's His. Winthrop, 173.

OTHER PUBLICATIONS. — Pompey, N. Y., Reunion, 258; Power's Sangamon County, Ill., 98; Amer. Ancestry, VI, 22; IX, 139; Savage's Gen. Dic. J. 125.

BARRUS. See Bassett's Richmond, 300.

BARRY. See Wyman's Charlestown Gens. I, 63; Bass' His. Braintree, Vt., 110; Barry's Hanover, Mass., 419; Temple's North Brookfield, Mass., 511; Amer. Ancestry, vol. X, 200.

BARSHAM.

WILLIAM BARSHAM, of Watertown, Mass., came, it is thought, in 1630; freeman March 9, 1637. Had children John, Hannah, William, Joshua 1641. Susanna, Nathaniel, Sarah, Mary, Rebecca, Elizabeth.

REFERENCES.—See Savage's Gen. Dic. I, 127.

BARSTOW.

GEORGE BARSTOW came from England in the "Freelove," 1635; aged 21; had a grant of land at Dedham, Mass., 1636; removed to Scituate. He married Susanna, daughter of Thomas Marritt or Maryett, of Cambridge. He had Margaret 1652.

JOHN BARSTOW or BARSTOE, of Cambridge, youngest brother of George, by . wife Hannah, had Michael 1653, John, Jeremiah.

WILLIAM BARSTOW, brother of George and John, came with them in 1635. By wife Anna he had Joseph 1639, Mary, Patience. He removed to Scituate and had Sarah, Deborah, William, Martha.

REFERENCES.—Winsor's His. Duxbury, Mass., 224; Barry's Hanover, Mass., 208; Temple's His. North Brookfield, Mass., 572; Deane's His. Scituate, Mass., 218; Corliss' North Yarmouth, Me., Cushman's Sheepscott, Me., 356; Wheeler's His. Brunswick, Me., 829; Sedgwick's His. Sharon, Conn., 63; Walworth's Hyde Gen. 44; Amer. Ancestry, II, 7; Savage's Gen. Dic. I, 128.

BARTHOLOMEW.

HENRY BARTHOLOMEW, of Salem, Mass., 1635; is said to have arrived that year, made freeman 17th May, 1637, then 36 years old. Was representative in 1645, and for 17 years more. By wife Elizabeth, he had Elizabeth 1641, Hannah, John 1644; Abraham, Eleazer, Abigail, William, Elizabeth again 1654, Henry.

WILLIAM BARTHOLOMEW, of Ipswich, came from London in 1634, on the ship with Rev. John Lathrop, Ann Hutchinson and others, and was a witness against her. He was made freeman 1635. He moved to

Boston about 1660, died in Charlestown, 1681. He had Mary.

REFERENCES.—Davis' His. Wallingford, Conn., 650; Orcutt's His. Wolcott, Conn., 449; Paige's His. Hardwick, Mass., 336; Hammatt Papers, Ipswich, Mass., 25; Collins' Hillsdale, N. Y., App. 32; Austin's Allied Families, R. I., 35; Bartholomew Gen. 1885; Bartholomew Address, 1882; Savage's Gen. Dic. I, 129; Amer. Ancestry, VI, 192; VII, 46; X, 14, 185.

BARTIN. See Winser's Duxbury, Mass.

BARTLETT.

CHRISTOPHER BARTLETT, of Newbury, Mass., 1635; married April 16, 1645, Mary, and had Mary, Ann, Martha, Christopher 1655, Jonathan 1657. He married second Dec. 19, 1663, Mary Hoyt, and had John 1665; died soon.

JOHN BARTLETT, of Newbury, Mass., 1635, came in the "Mary and John" from London; he was of County Kent; made freeman 1639. By his wife Joan, he had John.

NATHANIEL BARTLETT, of Newbury, had James, 1677.

RICHARD BARTLETT, of Newbury, 1637, brother of the first Christopher, had Richard, John, Christopher, Joanna and Samuel.

It is said that five Robert Bartletts came to this country about the same time, settling at different points.

ROBERT BARTLETT, of Plymouth. came in the "Ann," 1623; married Mary, daughter of Richard Warren, and had Benjamin, Joseph, Rebecca, Mary, Sarah, Elizabeth, Lydia, Mercy.

ROBERT BARTLETT, of Hartford, an original proprietor, had been of Cambridge, 1635, came probably on the "Lion." He had Samuel, Nathaniel, Abigail, Deborah 1640. He removed to Northampton 1665; and was killed by the Indians, March, 1676.

THOMAS BARTLETT, of Watertown 1631, freeman 1635. By wife Hannah, had Hannah 1639; Mehitabel, Hannah again 1642, Bartholomew 1647, Abigail 1651. He was often selectman, died April, 1654.

JOHN BARTLETT, of Windsor, Conn., 1640, was brother of George Bartlett, of Guilford. He had Isaiah 1641, Benjamin 1643, Hepzibah 1646, Jehoida 1649, Mehitabel.

Lieut. GEORGE BARTLETT, of Guilford, 1641. Branford 1649. He married Sep. 14, 1650, Mary, daughter of Abraham Cruttenden, and had Eizabeth 1652; Mary, John, Hannah, Daniel 1665, Abraham, Deborah. He was Lieut. representative 1665, deacon, died 3d Aug., 1669.

REFERENCES.

CONNECTICUT.—Todd's His. Redding, 177; Hinman's Conn. Settlers; Stiles' His. Windsor II, 61; Hine's Lebanon Address, 144.

MASSACHUSETTS.—Mitchell's Bridgewater, 109, 337; Judd's His. Hadley, 451; Benedict's His. Sutton, 584; Chase's His. Haverhill, 620; Coffin's His. Newbury, 295; Davis' Landmarks of Plymouth, 15; Emery's Newbury, 31; Hudson's His. Marlboro, 320; Wyman's Charlestown Gens. 64; Windsor's His. Duxbury, 225; Temple's His. Whately, 210; Temple's His. Brookfield, 512; Paige's His. Hardwick, 334; Paige's His. Cambridge, 484; Jackson's His. Newton, Mass.. 238.

MAINE.—Bangor His. Mag. IV, 214; Corliss' North Yarmouth; Eaton's His. Thomaston, 142; Lapham's

His. Bethel, 466, 651; Lapham's His. Norway, 460; Lapham's His. Rumford,303; Lapham's His.Woodstock,174.

NEW HAMPSHIRE.—Kidder's His. New Ipswich, 334; Wheeler's His. Newport, 296; Coggswell's His. Henniker, 457; Coggswell's His. Northwood, 622; Coggswell's Nottingham, 167; Wayward's His. Hancock, 336.

NEW YORK.—Collins' His. Hillsdale, App. 34; Young's His. Warsaw, 235; Cleveland's Yates County, 397.

OTHER PUBLICATIONS.—Bartlett's Gen.; Bartlett Russell Gen.; Narragansett, R. I., His. Reg. VI, 30; Norton's His. Knox County, Ohio, 320; Pierce's E. W. Contributions, 22; Strong's Gen., 582, 766, 770, 780; Titcomb's Early N. E. People, 185; Williams' His. Danby, Vt., 106; Worcester Mag. and His. Jour. II, 84; Hubbard's Stanstead County, Can., 197; Guild's Stile's Gen. 25; Ellis' Gen. 370; Cutts' Gen. 162; Chapman's Weeks Gen. 129; Neally's Chart; Savage's Gen. Dic. I, 180; Austin's Ancestral Dic. 6; Loomis' Gen. Female Branches, 689; Amer. Ancestry I, 5; II, 7; VIII, 40, 229; N. E. His. and Gen. Reg. XL, 197.

BARTLIT, Foot Gen. Supp. 1867, 21.

BARTLEY, See Morrison's Windham, 334; Bartley's Schenectady, N. Y., Settlers, 10.

BARTOL.

WILLIAM BARTOLL, of Lynn, Mass. married Susanna Waterbury; married 2d Susanna—had issue Susanna 1666, William, John, Robert, Thomas, Sarah, Mary, Alice, Andrew and others.

REFERENCES:—Savage's Gen. Dic. I, 133, Corliss' North Yarmouth, Me.

BARTON.

JAMES BARTON 1688 of Newton, a ropemaker, had a good estate, died 1729, aged 86. By wife Margaret he had Margaret, John 1686, and others.

RUFUS BARTON of Providence, R. I., had fled from persecution by the Dutch at Manhattan and settled in 1640, at Portsmouth, R. I. He had Elizabeth, Benjamin, Margaret and others.

REFERENCES:—Whittemore's Middlesex County, Conn., 200, Austin's R. I. Gen. Dic. 250; Austin's Ancestries, II; Washburn's His. Leicester, Mass., 346; Jackson's His. Newton, Mass., 236; Draper's His. Spencer, Mass., 173; Benedict's His. Sutton, Mass., 586; Barry's His. Framingham, Mass., 176; Lapham's His. Bethel, Me., 474; Lapham's His. Norway, Me., 450; Wheeler's His Croyden, N. H., Centen. 73; Wheeler's His. Newport, N. H., 294; Baird's His. Rye, N. Y., 396; N. Y. Gen. and Biog. Rec. III, 30; Baetjer's Carteret Gen. 17; Whitman Gen. 153; Amer. Ancestry II. 7; IX, 129; Paxton's Marshall Gen. 256, 353; Heraldic Journal IV (1868), 130.

BARTON. See N. Y. Gen. Biog. Rec. III, 30; V, 147; Penn. Mag. XIV, 214; Bolton's Westchester County, N. Y. II, 350; Whitehead, Perth Amboy, N. J., 138; Amer. Ancestry III, 4; Barton Gen. N. E. His. and Gen. Reg. III, 20; V, 147.

BARTRAM.

JOHN BARTRAM, of Sheffield, had Hannah, 1668, and perhaps others.

WILLAM BARTRAM, of Lynn, Mass., by wife Sarah, had Rebecca, Esther, Ellen, 1660.

REFERENCES:—Todd's His. Redding, Conn., 178; Schenck's His. Fairfield, Conn., 353; Smith's His. Del. Co., Pa., 44; Savage's Gen. Dic. I, 134; Maris Gen.

BARZIZA.   See Carter Fam. Tree.

BASCOM.

THOMAS BASCOM, of Dorchester, Mass, 1634, came perhaps in July, 1663, with the company that settled at Dorchester, and removed thence to Windsor. There had Thomas, 1642, Hepzibah, 1644. Removed to Northampton about 1661 and died there.
REFERENCES:—Temple's His. Northfield, Mass., 403; Freeman's His. Cape Cod, Mass., II, 727; Edwards' Southampton, Mass., Wheeler's His. Newport, N. H., 296; Harris Ancestry W. C. Harris; Savage's Gen. Dic. I, 134; Bascom Gen.

BASFORD.   See Chase's Chester, N. H., 405.

BASHAW.   See Powers' Sangamon, Ill., 98.

BASHFORD.   See Amer. Ancestry II, 7.

BASKERVILLE.   Goode Gen. 288; Richmond, Va., Standard, III, 44.

BASKIN.   See Goode Gen. 300.

BASS.

SAMUEL BASS, was of Braintree, 1632, representative to the General Court 1641, and often later. By wife Ann he had Samuel, Mary, Hannah, John, Thomas, Joseph, Sarah.
REFERENCES.—Bass' His. Braintree, Vermont, III; Mitchell's Bridgewater, Mass., 110; Barry's His. Hanover, Mass., 244; Washburn's His. Leicester, Mass., 344; Hayward's His. Hancock, N. H., 338; Hinman's Conn. Settlers, 159; Weaver's His. Windham, Conn., 93; Windham, Conn., Genealogies, 99; Whitmore's Copps Hill Epitaphs, Richmond, Va., Standard, II, 46; Arber's John Smith's Works; Crane's Rawson Gen. 30; Neil's Virginia Carolorum; Neil's Virginia Vetusta; Thayer's Memorial (1835), 53; Savage's Gen. Dic. I, 135.

BASSAM.

THOMAS BASSAM, of Windsor, Conn., had Abigail 1640; Thomas 1642; Hepzibah 1644.
REFERENCES:—Savage's Gen. Dic. vol. I, 136.

BASTARD.

JOSEPH BASTARD, of Fairfield, Conn., married 1685, Hannah, widow of Esbon Wakemir, died 1647. See Savage's Gen. Dic. vol. I, 136.

BASTAVO.

JOSEPH BASTAVO, of Cambridge, Mass., by wife Mary, had Mary 1640; he removed to Boston 1647, and had Joseph 1647, Benjamin 1652, Susannah 1654 and John 1657.

BASHFORD.   See N. E. Gen. Reg. vol. XIII, 190.

BASSAKER.

PETER BASSAKER, of Boston, Mass., 1633, removed before 1643 to Hartford, was afterwards at Warwich. Had Mary, Abigail and Peter.

BASSETT.

JOHN BASSETT, of New Haven, Conn., 1647, died 1653, leaving Robert and perhaps other children.

THOMAS BASSETT, of Windsor, Conn., 1641, came in the "Christian" 1635, settled in Dorchester and removed to Fairfield, Conn. Names of children not known.

WILLIAM BASSETT, of Plymouth, came in the

"Fortune" 1621 with wife Elizabeth. Had Sarah, William and Elizabeth. Sarah married 1648 Peregrene White.

WILLIAM BASSETT, of Lynn, Mass., 1640, had William, John, 1653, Miriam, Mary, Hannah, Samuel, Rachel.

REFERENCES.

CONNECTICUT.—Weaver's His. Windham, Conn., 93; Sharpe's His. Seymour, Conn., 205; Orcutt's His. Stratford, Conn., II, 21; Orcutt's His. Derby, 696; Hamden, Conn., His. 228; Andrews' His. New Britain, 380; Hinman's Conn. Settlers, 159; Windham Genealogies, 93.

MASSACHUSETTS.—Davis' Landmarks of Plymouth, 22; Freeman's Cape Cod I, 333; II, 142; Lewis' His. Lynn, Mass., 184; Mitchell's His. Bridgewater, III; Paige's His. Hardwich, 334; Wyman's Charlestown, Mass., Gens. I, 67; Swift's Barnstable Families I, 41; Wyman's Charlestown, Mass., Gens. I, 67.

NEW HAMPSHIRE.—Bassett's His. Richmond, 307; Hayward's His. Hancock, 339.

OTHER PUBLICATIONS—Baird's His. Rye,N.Y., 396; Bassett's Chart by Leeds (1886); Shourd's Fenwick Colony, N. J., 45; Wilkesbarre, Pa., His. Rec. I, 123; Walker Gen. 179; Preble Gen. 260; Munsell's Albany Coll. IV, 95; Keith's Harrison Ancestry; Ellis Gen. 407; Carter Family Tree; Amer. Ancestry II, 8.

BASTER.   See Austin's R. I. Gen. Dic. 15.

BASTON.   See Corliss' North Yarmouth, Me.

BATCHELDER.

JOSEPH BATCHELDER, of Winham, Mass., born in Canterbury, Eng., emigrated to New England in 1637 and settled at Winham, Mass. He was the first representative at the General Court from Winham, and was a leading man in town affairs. He had Ebenezer and other children.

REFERENCES:—Morse's Sherborn, Mass., Settlers 14; Eaton's His. Reading, Mass., 45; Chase's His. Chester, N. H., 467; Dow's His. Hampton, N. H., 588; Fullerton's His. Raymond, N. H., 303; Kidder's His. New Ipswich, N. H., 235; Livermore's His. Wilton, N. H., 312; Whitmore's Batchelder Gen.; Morrison's His. Windham,N.H., 226; Runnel's His. Sanbornton, N. H., II, 20; McKeene's His. Bradford, Vt., 374; Hubbard's Stanstead County, Can., 209, 285; Coggswell's Nottingham 333,626; Austin's Allied Families, R. I., 36; Fisk Gen. 135; Leland Magazine, 88, 125; Morse Gen. Appendix No. 24; Amer. Ancestry III, 139; VI, 41; VIII, 16; Whitmore's Batchelder Gen. 1864, 1873.

BATCHELLER, Temple's His. North Brookfield, Mass., 515; Pierce's His. Grafton, Mass., 455; Benedict's His. Sutton, Mass., 587; Norton's His. Fitzwilliam, N.H., 463; Leland Magazine 81; Dwight Gen. 1000; Sanborn Gen. 1894; Cushing's Dic. T. Batcheller (1864) 30; N. E. His. and Gen. Reg. XXVII, 364.

BATCHELOR.   See Freeman's Cape Cod, Mass., II, 179; Bass' Braintree, Vt., 115; Savage's Gen. Dic. vol. I.

BATE.   See Hudson's His. Lexington, Mass., 10; Barry's Hanover, Mass., 245; Chapman Gen. 254.

BATEMAN.

EDWARD BATEMAN, of Maine, was one of the purchasers from the Indian Sachem, Robin Hood, of the region about Woolwich 1654.

ELEAZER BATEMAN, of Woburn, Mass., married Nov. 1686, Elizabeth, daughter of Joseph Wright, and had Elizabeth 1686, Mary, Joseph 1699, Martha, Thomas 1704, Ruth 1707.

JOHN BATEMAN, of Boston, by wife Hannah had John 1644, Hannah, Elizabeth, Sarah, Richard, Mary, William, Joseph.

THOMAS BATEMAN, of Concord, Mass., had by wife Martha, Thomas, Peter, John, Ebenezer.

WILLIAM BATEMAN, of Concord, brother of above made freeman 1641; removed to Fairfield, Conn., 1650; names in his will "Thomas now of Concord."

REFERENCES:—Wyman's Charlestown Gens. I, 67; Hinman's Conn. Settlers 151; Amer. Ancestry II, 8; Savage's Gen. Dic. I, 137.

BATES.

CLEMENT BATES, came from Herts or Kent, Eng., in the Elizabeth 1635, aged 40, with children James, Clement, Richard, Joseph. Had here Samuel and perhaps others.

EDWARD BATES, of Boston, came in the "Griffin," 1637; had John 1642.

JOHN BATES, of Haddam and Stamford, Conn. 1669, had John 1668 and Solomon 1670.

JOHN BATES, of New London, had John 1679 Solomon 1680, Sarah 1682.

ROBERT BATES, of Wethersfield, Conn., 1640, removed to Stamford, and died there June 11, 1675; was one of the first purchasers of Stamford 1640.

ROBERT BATES, of Lynn, Mass., had John, died 1672, Rebecca born 1673, Sarah 1676.

REFERENCES.

CONNECTICUT.—Huntington's Stamford, Conn., Families. 8; Sedgwick's His. Sharon, 63; Stiles' His. Windsor II, 68; Todd's His. Redding 182; Field's His. Haddam 45; Hinman's Puritan Settlers 152.

MASSACHUSETTS.—Ballou's His. Milford 569; Barry's His. Hanover, 245; Deane's His. Scituate, 219; Hyde's His. Brimfield 387; Mitchell's His. Bridgewater 113; Stearn's His. Ashburnham, 605; Temple's His. North Brookfield 518; Swift's Barnstable Families, I, 145; Davis' Landmarks of Plymouth, 23.

NEW HAMPSHIRE.—Cutter's His. of Jaffray, 231; Hayward's His. Gilsum, 262; Norton's His. Fitzwilliam, 797.

OTHER PUBLICATIONS.—Clement's Newtown, N.J., Settlers; Richmond, Va., Standard II, 44; Whitman Gen. 159, 245; Powers' Sangamon County, Ill., 99; Missouri Biog. Dic. Loomis's Gen. Female Branches, 681; Leland Gen. 116; Hurlbut Gen. 407; Butler Gen. (1888) 76; Bates and Fletcher Gen. 1892, Amer. Ancestry vol. I, 5; II, 8; VI, 68, 195; IX, 130; N. E. His. and Gen. Reg. XXXI, 141; XXIX, 255.

BATH. See Pierson's Schenectady, N. Y., 13; N. E. His. and Gen. Reg., vol. XXXVIII, 199; XXXIX, 164.

BATHRICK. Wyman's Charlestown Gens. vol. I, 68; Page's His. Cambridge, Mass., 485; Cutter's His. Arlington, Mass., 191; Champion Gen., Amer. Ancestry vol. II, 8.

BATHURST. See Richmond, Va., Standard vol. V, 24; Jones Gen. (1891), 143.

BATSON.

STEPHEN BATSON, of Saco, 1636, removed to Kennebunk, Me., 1653; was made freeman that year.

He had son John, daughters Elizabeth, Ashley, Margery, Mary.

REFERENCES:—N.E.His. and Gen. Reg. vol. XXVIII, 159; Savage's Gen. Dic. vol. I, 139.

BATT.

CHRISTOPHER BATT, of Newbury, Mass., came from Salisbury, County Wilts, 1638, aged 37, with wife Ann and sister Dorothy. He had John 1641, Paul and Barnabas, twins, 1643; Christopher, Ann, Samuel, Jane, Sarah, Abigail, Timothy, Ebenezer, Elizabeth.

See Savage's Gen. Dic. vol.I, 140.

BATTE. See Slaughter's Bristol Parish, 206; Richmond, Va., Standard, vol. III, 33, 40; N. E. His. and Gen. Reg. vol. XXXVIII, 199; XXXIX, 164.

BATELL or BATELLE.

THOMAS BATTELLE, of Dedham, Mass., 1642, freeman, 1654; married 1648 Mary, daughter of John Fisher, and had Mary 1650, John 1653, Sarah 1654, Jonathan 1658, Martha 1660.

REFERENCES:—Leland Magazine 178; Cotthren's Woodbury, Conn., 1471; Savage's Gen. Dic. vol. I, 140; Orcutt's His. Torrington, Conn., 649; Amer. Ancestry, vol. III, 134.

BATTLE. See Wheeler's His. North Carolina, Amer. Ancestry, vol. VIII, 217.

BATTLES. Ballou's Milford, Mass., 570; Bass' His. Braintree, Vt., 115; Davis' Landmarks of Plymouth, Mass., 25; Kingman's North Bridgewater, Mass., 457; Mitchell's His. Bridgewater, Mass., 13; Norton's His. Fitzwilliam, N. H., 464; Wheeler's Eminent North Carolinians, 162; Porter Gen. (1878) 68; Pickering Gen.

BATTEN.

BENJAMIN BATTEN, of Boston, Mass., merchant married Oct. 1671. Elizabeth, daughter of John Cullick, Esq.

JOHN BATTEN, of Lynn, Mass., had John 1671.

BATTER.

EDMUND BATTER, of Salem, came from Salisbury, county Wilts, Eng., in the "James," April 1635, with wife Sarah, and was made freeman the same year; he was representative to the General Court 1637, and for 16 years more. His wife died Nov. 20, 1669. He married 2d, Jan. 8, 1670, Mary, daughter of Major-General Daniel Gookin. Had Edmond 1671. Edmond Sen. died 1685, aged 76. He had by former wife, Daniel, Mary, Elizabeth. See Savage's Gen. Dic. vol. I, 141.

BATTERSON.

GEORGE BATTERSON, together with his brother William, were sons of James Batterson, of Scotland. They settled in Fairfield, Conn. George married Mary Oysterbanks, and had George and other children.

REFERENCES.—Stiles' His. Windsor, Conn., vol. II, 68; Hinman's Conn. Settlers, 155; Amer. Ancestry, vol. III, 4; V, 181.

BATTERTON. See Powers' Sangamon Co., Ill., 100.

BATTEY. See Austin's R. I. Gen. Dic. 16.

BATTING.

WILLIAM BATTING, of Saco, 1659; Scarborough 1660.

BANDER. See Montgomery, N. Y., 152.

BAULSTONE. See Austin's R. I. Dic. 16; Savage's Gen. Dic. vol. I, 109.

BAXTER.

DANIEL BAXTER, of Salem, Mass., 1639, by wife Elizabeth, had Elizabeth 1644, Susanna 1646, Rebecca and Priscilla 1652.

GEORGE BAXTER, of Providence, R. I., 1650, was constituted umpire between the Dutch colony of New Netherlands and New Haven Colony for settlement of boundary. He carried the royal charter 1663, from Boston to New York.

GREGORY BAXTER, 1630, came probably in the fleet with Winthrop, March 6, 1632. By wife Margaret Paddy (died Feb. 1662) he had Bethulia or Bethia 1632, Abigail 1634, John 1639. He removed next year to Braintree and died Jan. 29, 1659.

JOHN BAXTER, of Salem, Mass., married Nov. 25, 1667, Abigail Whitney, and had issue John 1668, Abigail 1670, Elizabeth 1673, Mary.

NICHOLAS BAXTER, of Boston, 1639, by wife Ann, had Mary 1640, who married Thomas Buttolph. REFERENCES:—Wyman's Charlestown, Mass., Gens. vol. I, 69; Draper's His. Spencer, Mass., 181; Read's His. Swanzey, N. H., 287; Bradbury's Kennebunkport, Me., 224; Cleveland's Yates County, N. Y., 746; Hinman's Conn. Settlers, 162; Hubbard's His. Stanstead, Can. 148; Bergen's Kings County, N. Y., Settlers, 23; Childs' Gen. 460; Amer. Ancestry, vol. I, 5; VI, 53; Savage's Gen. Dic. vol. I, 141; N. E. His. and Gen. Reg. XX, 157; Memorial of the Baxter Family, 1879.

BAY.

THOMAS BAY, of Dedham, Mass., by wife Ann had Ruth 1643. Thomas 1646. He removed later to Boston.

REFERENCES:—Savage's Gen. Dic. vol. I, 142; Willard's Med. Annals, 213.

BAYARD. Lamb's His. New York City, vol. I, 343, 696; Bolton's His. Westchester County, N. Y., vol. II, 709; Cleveland's His. Yates County, N. Y., 694; Valentine's New York Common Council Manual (1853), 390; Mallory's Bohemian Manor, 46; N. Y. Gen. Rec. vol. X, 36; XVI, 49; Amer. Ancestry, vol. III, 78; Bayard Gen. 1885.

BAYLES.

JOHN BAYLES, of Setauket, N. Y., was the first of the name on Long Island. He resided at Southold, N. Y., 1656-61, was also at Huntington and Jamaica a few years; magistrate of Setauket 1673. See Amer. Ancestry VI, 10.

BAYLEY.

GUIDO BAYLEY, by his wife Elizabeth had Elizabeth 1642, Joseph 1644.

JAMES BAYLEY, of Rowley, Mass., by wife Lydia, had John 1642, James 1650, Thomas, Samuel. Damaris, Lydia, and perhaps others.

JOHN BAYLEY, of Salisbury, Mass., was a weaver from Chippenham, County Wilts; came in the "Angel Gabriel" from Bristol, April 1635, and was cast away at Pemaquid in the great storm of August 15, of that year. He removed 1650 to Newbury, where probably he had been residing before settlement of Salisbury, and died 2d Nov. next year. His wife never came over the ocean, and he was afraid to go back for her and his other children.

In his will he tried to tempt them hither by parts of his estate. His sons John and Henry came with him.

THOMAS BAYLEY, of New London 1652, married June 10, 1656, Lydia, daughter of William Redfyn or Redfield, had Mary 1657, Thomas 1653, John 1661. REFERENCES:—Gage's His. Rowley, Mass., 438; Bradbury's His. Kennebunkport, Me., 226; Bangor His. Mag. IV, 137; Wise Biog.; Porter's Hartford, Conn., Settlers 4; Redfield Gen. 7; Savage's Gen. Dic. vol. I, 142.

BAYLIES. See Amer. Ancestry V, 44.

BAYLOR. See Meade's Old Churches, Va., 464; Page Gen. 64; Richmond Va., Standard III, 2, 23.

BAYNE. See Amer. Ancestry VIII, 95.

BAYTOP. See Richmond Standard, vol. III, 9; VII, 5.

BAYSEY.

JOHN BAYSEY, of Hartford, an original proprietor, by wife Eliza, had Lydia, Mary, Elizabeth.

BEACH.

RICHARD BEACH, of New Haven, 1639, one of the signers of the original compact, married about 1640, the widow of Andrew Hull. Had Mary, Benjamin 1644, Azariah 1646, Mercy 1648. Removed to New London 1667.

THOMAS BEACH, of Milford 1648, brother of Richard, had lived at New Haven, and there had by wife Sarah, daughter of Dea. Richard Platt, had Sarah 1654, John 1655, Mary 1657, Samuel 1660, Zophar 1662.

REFERENCES.

CONNECTICUT.—Hinman's Conn. Settlers 163; Orcutt's His. Derby, 699; Orcutt's His. New Milford, 648; Orcutt's His. Stratford vol. II, 23; Orcutt's His. Torrington, 649, 663; Todd's His. Redding, 182; Boyd's Annals Winchester, 33, 186; Davis' His. Wallingford, 635; Sharpe's His. Seymour, 158.

OTHER PUBLICATIONS.—Temple's His. Northfield, Mass., 464; Littell's Passaic Valley Gens. 35; Walker Family, 163; Tanner Gen. 10; Strong Gen. 886; Loomis Gen. Female Branches, 740; Humphreys' Gen. 278; Ely Gen. 385; Hall's Genealogical Notes 156; Boltwood's Noble Gen. 319; Amer. Ancestry, vol., II, 9; VII, 5; IX, 68, 136; X. 72; Powers' Sangamon County, Ill., 202; Savage's Gen. Dic. vol. I, 144; His. Greene County, N. Y., 368.

BEACHAM. See Wyman's Charlestown Gens. 70.

BEADLE.

NATHANIEL BEADLE, of Salem, Mass., married April 20, 1671, Mary Hicks, perhaps daughter of Richard Hicks, of Boston; had Thomas 1672, Mary, Nathaniel 1675, Elizabeth, John 1683.

SAMUEL BEADLE, of Charlestown, removed to Salem. By wife Susannah he had Abigail 1661.

THOMAS BEADLE, of Salem, Mass., perhaps brother of Nathaniel, married Sept. 18, 1679, Elizabeth, daughter of Abraham Drake, of Hampton; had Elizabeth 1681, Mary, Benjamin 1687, Thomas 1690, John 1692. Thomas Beadle was Captain 1686, traded to Barbadoes, died at Gloucester 1700.

REFERENCES:—Hinman's Conn. Settlers 164; Davis' Wallingford, Conn., 651; Wyman's Charlestown, Mass., Gen. vol. I, 70; Savage's Gen. Dic. vol. I, 144.

BEAL.

ABRAHAM BEALE, of Charlestown, Mass., by wife Catharine, had Abraham 1657, Isaac 1662.

JOHN BEALE, of Hingham, Mass., came from Old Hingham, Eng., in the "Dilligent" 1638, with five sons and three daughters; was made freeman March 13, 1639. Had issue Jacob 1642, and Rebecca.

REFERENCES:—Wyman's Charlestown, Mass., Gens. vol. I, 71; Kingman's North Bridgewater, Mass., 447; Mitchell's His. Bridgewater, Mass., 113; Ballou's Milford, Mass., 573; Hobart's His. Abington, Mass., 243; Jackson's His. Newton, Mass., 447; Lapham's His. Norway, Me., 463; Read's His. Swanzey, N. H., 288; Futhrey's His. Chester County, Pa., 479; Martin's Chester, Pa., 264; Me. His. and Gen. Rec. V, 241; Paxton Marshall Gen. 311; Porter Gen. by J. W. Porter, 36; Redfield Gen. 90;Yates' Family Memor.;Beal's Gen.1865,Savage's Gen. Dic. vol. I, 145.

BEALE. See Butler's His. Farmington, Me., 376.

BEALES. See Temple's His. Whately, Mass., 205; Hudson's His. Lexington, Mass., II; Stearn's His. Ashburnham, Mass., 606; Dyer's His. Plainfield, Mass., Bassett's His. Richmond, N. H., 360; Joslin's His. of Poultney, Vt., 211; Savage's Gen. Dic. vol. I, 145; Bouton Gen. 169.

BEAM. See Powers' His. Sangamon, Ill., 104 Roome Gen. II; Amer. Ancestry vol. VIII, 135.

BEAMAN.

GAMALIEL BEAMAN, came on the "Elizabeth and Ann" 1635; the name is spelt at the London Custom House Bement. By wife Sarah he had Thomas 1649, Joseph 1651, Gamaliel, Mary, Sarah. He removed to Lancaster, Mass., and there had Noah 1661, Thankful 1663, and perhaps John.

WILLIAM BEAMAN, of Saybrook, Conn., came in the "Elizabeth" 1635, aged 27. He married Dec. 9, 1643, Lydia, daughter of Nicholas Danforth, and had Lydia 1645, Mary Elizabeth, Deborah, Abigail 1655, Samuel 1657, Rebecca. His wife was the only female named among eight grantees of Saybrook in the will of Joshua, son of Uncas the Indian Sachem.

REFERENCES:—Ward's His. Shrewsbury, Mass., 248; Hudson's His. Marlboro, Mass., 322; Temple's His. Northfield, Mass., 405; Adams' Fairhaven, Vt., 300; Joslin's His. Poultney, Vt., 212; Keyes' Gen. Reg. 10; Savage's Gen. Dic. vol. I, 147.

BEAMOND.

SIMON BEAMOND, of Springfield, Mass., married 1655, Alice Young, and had John 1657, Daniel 1659, Thomas, Joseph, Benjamin 1671, besides three daughters.

REFERENCES:—Savage's Gen. Dic. vol. I, 147; Stiles' Windsor, Conn., II, 69.

BEAMSLEY.

WILLAM BEAMSLEY, of Boston, 1632, was made freeman May 25, 1636. By his wife Ann he had Ann 1633, Grace, Mercy 1637, Samuel and Habakuk, twins, 1641.

REFERENCES:—See Savage's Gen. Dic. vol. I, 47.

BEAN.

LEWIS BEAN, came from the Isle of Jersey about

1670 to Boston, Mass., where he died leaving a widow and three sons, Lewis, Ebenezer and Joseph. Lewis settled in York, Me.

REFERENCES:—Fullerton's His. of Raymard, N. H., 187; Lancaster's His. Gilmartin, N. H., 257; Runnel's Sanbornton, N. H., vol. II, 27; Coggswell's His. Nottingham, N. H., 334; Coggswell's His. Henniker, N. H., 458; Chase's His. Chester, N. H., 467; Eaton's His. Thomaston, Me., 143; Lapham's His. Bethel, Me., 478, 652; Lapham's His. Rumford, Me., 304; Bangor, Me., His. Mag. vol. I, 159; Amer. Ancestry, vol. IV, 119; VI, 53; Guild's Stiles' Gen. 121; Otis Gen.; Poore Gen. 88; Wentworth Gen. vol. II, 15.

BEANE. See Austin's Allied Families 39.

BEARCE.

AUGUSTINE BEARCE, of Barnstable, Mass., came in the "Confidence" 1638, aged 20, from Southhamptonshire, Eng., and joined Lathrop's church April 1643; had issue Mary 1640, Martha, Priscilla, Sarah, Abigail, Hannah, Joseph 1652, Esther, Lydia, Rebecca. James.

REFERENCES:—Savage's Gen. Dic. vol. I, 147; Mitchell's His. Bridgewater, Mass., 115; Lapham's His. Woodstock, Me., 175; Lapham's Norway, Me.,

BEARD. See Hazen's His. Billerica, Mass., 9; Sedgwick's His. Sharon, Conn., 63; Orcutt's His. Stratford, Conn., 1129; Coggswell's His. New Boston, 380; Livermore's His. Wilton, N.H., 314; Norton's His. Fitzwilliam, N. H., 464; Washington, N. H., His. 302; Young's His. Wayne County, Ind., 237, 325; Savage's Gen. Dic. vol. I, 148.

BEARDSLEY.

WILLIAM BEARDSLEY, of Stratford, Conn., came in the "Planter," 1635, aged 30, and settled in Stratford, Conn. He was a representative 1645 and often after. He was made freeman 1656. His will, dated Sept. 28, 1660, named wife and sons Daniel, John, Joseph and Samuel.

REFERENCES:—Orcutt's His. Derby, Conn., 701; Orcutt's His. Stratford, Conn., 1130; Orcutt's His. New Milford, Conn., 649; Sedgwick's His. Sharon, Conn., 63; Norton's His. Knox County, Ohio, 359; Leavenworth Gen. 104; Savage's Gen. Dic. vol. I,148; Amer. Ancestry, vol. I, 5; VI, 56; VII, 40; Beardsley Gen. 1867.

BEARSE. See Swift's Barnstable Families, vol. I, 52; Freeman's Cape Cod, Mass., vol. II, 297; Boyd's Consensus, N. Y., 143; Savage's Gen. Dic. 149; Bearse Gen. 1871.

BEATON. See Morrison's Windham, 857.

BEATTY. Egle's Penn. Gens. 63; Cooley's Trenton, N. J., Gens. 8; Beatty Gen. 1873.

BEATTIE. See Eaton's Thomaston, Me., 143; Lapham's His. Bethel, Me., 487.

BEAUCHAMP.

EDWARD BEAUCHAMP, of Salem, Mass., was made a freeman 1643. By wife Mary, he had Samuel 1641, died 1662. Mary 1647, Elizabeth.

JOHN BEAUCHAMP, a Huguenot, brought most of his children with him to New England. By wife Marguerite, he had Catharine 1687, Peter 1702. He removed after 1711 to Hartford, and there died 1740, aged 88, leaving a large estate. See Hinman's Early Settlers, 168; Savage's Gen. Dic. vol. I, 149.

BEAREMONT.   See Davis' Wallingford, Conn., 635.

BEAUTIETTE.   See His. North Brookfield, Mass., 253.

BEAUVELT.   See Cole Gen. 32, 74.

BEAVAY.   N. E. His. and Gen. Reg. XXXVII, 236.

BEAVER.

JOHN BEAVER, came from Germany to America, with his two brothers, De Walt and Jacob, and settled near Harleysville, Montgomery Co., Pa., and died about 1827. See Amer. Ancestry, vol. I, 6; II, 9; III, 191.

BEBOUT.   See Littell's Passaic Valley, 37.

BECK.

ALEXANDER BECK, of Boston, Sept. 3, 1634, by wife Elizabeth Hinds, of Roxbury, had Ephraim and Deliverance, twins, bap. June 7, 1640.

HENRY BECK, of Dover, came in the "Blessing" 1635, aged 18. He married Ann Frost, and had Joshua, Thomas, Caleb, Henry, Mary.

REFERENCES:—Pearson's Schenectady, N. Y., Settlers 10; N. E. His. and Gen. Reg. XI, 256; Goode Gen. 257; Savage's Gen. Dic. vol. I, 150.

BECKER. See Pearson's Schenectady, N.Y., Settlers 11; Munsell's Albany Coll. IV, 95; Collins' His. Hillsdale, N. Y., App. 35; Brabacher Gen. 181; Bouton Gen. 246; Amer. Ancestry vol. II, 9. His. Greene County, N.Y.,449.

BECKET.

JOHN BECKET, of Salem, a shipwright, died there in 1683, aged 57, leaving widow Margaret, and children William, Mary, Sarah, John, and Harriet. Savage's Gen. Dic. vol. I, 151; Life of Rev. William Smith; Essex Inst. Coll. VIII, 139.

BECKFORD.

JOHN BECKFORD, of Dover, 1647, was in 1669, of that part called Oyster River, now Denham, Mass., was freeman 1671. He had issue John, Joseph. See Davis' Gen. 245; N. E. His. and Gen. Reg. V, 451; Savage's Gen. Dic. vol. I, 151.

BECKLEY,

RICHARD BECKLEY, of New Haven, 1639, removed to Wallingford before 1668. His second wife was a daughter of John Deming. They had issue, Sarah, 1657, John 1642, Mary, Benjamin 1650, Nathaniel, Hannah 1656. See Hinman's Conn. Settlers 175; Andrews' New Britain, Conn., 297; N. E. His. and Gen. Reg. XVI, 20; Savage's Gen. Dic. vol. I, 151.

BECKMAN. See Runnell's His. Sanbornton, N. H., vol. II, 32; His. Greene County, N. Y., 118.

BECKWITH.

MATTHEW BECKWITH, of New London, Conn., 1652, was of Hartford 1658, and was there made freeman; had lived there in 1639. He removed to Branford in 1648 and was one of the founders of the church there. He removed thence to Lynn, Mass., and died there Oct. 21, 1680, aged 70. He had issue, Matthew, John, Joseph, and two daughters.

REFERENCES:—Caulkins' His. New London, Conn., 298; Hayward's His. of Gilsum, N. H., 262. Merrill's His. of Acworth, N. H., 186; Slaughter's Bristol Parish, Va., 131; Walworth's Hyde Gen. 1003; Heminway's Vermont Gaz. vol. V, part 3, p. 39; Champion Gen. Bulkley's Brown Mem. 66, 104; Amer. Ancestry vol. II, 10; VI, 63;

VIII, 21, 67; Savage's Gen. Dic. vol. I, 151; Beckwith Gen.

BECKWORTH. See Hinman's Early Settlers, Conn.

BEDDOE. See Cleveland's Yates County, N. Y., 465.

BEDE. See Cleveland's Yates County, N. Y., 516.

BEDELL.

ROBERT BEDELL, of New London, 1648, had perhaps been at Wethersfield, where he was among the first settlers. He had Robert, born 1642. His. Greene County, N. Y., 449.

REFERENCES:—Littel's Passaic Valley, N. J., Gens. 39, Clute's His. Staten Island, N. Y., 342; Bunker's L. I., Genealogies, 172; Keith's Harrison Ancestries; Savage's Gen. Dic. vol. I, 152; Bedell Gen.

BEDFORD. See Littel's Passaic Valley, N. J., Gens. 45; Ormsby Gen. 21; Kulp's Wyoming Families.

BEDINGER. See Powers' Sangamon County, Ill., 105; Welles' Washington Gen. 243.

BEDLE. See Salter's Monmouth County, N. J.

BEDWELL. (See also Bidwell.)

SAMUEL BEDWELL of Boston, married Feb. 2, 1654, Mary Hodgkinson, and had perhaps that Samuel, of Middletown, Conn., who died about April 5, 1715.

BEEBE.

JAMES BEEBE, of Hadley, Mass., married Oct. 24, 1667, Mary, daughter of Robert Bollwood, and had Rebecca 1670, Samuel 1672, Mary 1675.

JAMES BEEBE, of Stratford, Conn., married Dec. 19, 1674, Sarah, daughter of the first Thomas Benedict, and had Sarah 1680, and James. He removed to Norwalk, and thence to Danbury, Conn.

JOHN BEEBE, of New London, Conn., 1671, married Abigail, daughter of James York, of Stonnington, and had John, Benjamin, Rebecca. He was twenty years Sergeant and Lieutenant 1690. He died 1708.

SAMUEL BEEBE, of New London, brother of above married Agnes, daughter of William Keeny, had also a second wife, Mary. Had issue Samuel, William, Nathaniel, Thomas, Jonathan, Agnes, Ann, Susanna and Hannah.

THOMAS BEEBE, another brother, 1651, married Milicent, widow first of William Southmayd and second of William Ash, daughter of William Addis. Had Thomas and Mary.

REFERENCES:—Orcutt's His. Stratford, Conn., 1142; Litchfield County, Conn., His. 166; Field's His. Haddam, Conn., 47; Caulkin's His. New London, Conn., 338; Hinman's Conn. Settlers, 172; Phenix Whitney Family, Conn., 170; Wilbraham, Mass., Centen. 292; Griffin's Journal, Southold, L. I., 200; Paul's His. Wells, Vt., 64; Amer. Ancestry, vol. II, 10, 153; VI, 196; VII, 188; VIII, 24; Savage's Gen. Dic. vol. I, 153.

BEECHER.

ISAAC BEECHER, of New Haven, had Isaac 1650, Samuel 1652, Eleazer 1655.

THOMAS BEECHER, of Charlestown, Mass., was freeman 1632. He had been engaged as captain of the "Talbot" 1629, in bringing passengers to this country and next year with Winthrop's fleet, when his wife Christian who had been a widow of Thomas Cappes, came with him and was one of the first ten members of the church. He was one of the earliest selectmen of the town, and at the first General Court, May 14, 1634, and served several sessions. He was made Captain of the Castle 1635, died 1637. It is supposed that Revs. Lyman and Henry Ward Beecher were descendants of this ancestor.

REFERENCES:—Orcutt's His. New Milford, Conn., 650; Orcutt's His. Wolcutt, Conn., 450; Sharpe's His. of Seymour, Conn., 221; Tuttle Family of Conn., 153, 634; Strong Gen. 144; Goodwin's Foote Gen. 155; Dawson Gen. 83; Ammidown Family, 26; Savage's Gen. Dic. vol. I, 153; Amer. Ancestry, vol. I, 6; V, 105; VII, 176.

BEEFORD.

RICHARD BEEFORD, of Gloucester, by wife Mary, had John, Mary, Hannah, Ruth, Nathaniel, Richard. See Babson's Gloucester 61; Savage's Gen. Dic. vol. I, 153.

BEEDE. See Livermore's His. Wilton, N. H., 315; Otis. Gen. 8, 51; Hatch's Industry, Me., 509.

BEEKMAN. See N. Y. Gen. and Biog. Rec. XVI, 133; XVII, 281; XIX, 41. Smith's His. Dutchess County, N. Y., 389; Schoonmaker's His. Kingston, N. Y., 472; Sylvester's His. of Ulster County, N. Y., 171; Talcott's N. Y. and N. E. Families, I; Lamb's His. New York, vol. I, 416; Munsell's Albany Coll. IV, 96; Bergen's Kings County Settlers, 25; Holgate's American Gen. 66; Honeyman's Our Home, 490; Amer. Ancestry, vol.III, 4; Pearson's Schenectady, N. Y., Settlers, 12; Beekman Gen.

BEERE. See Salter's His. Monmouth County, N. J., 17; Austin's R. I. Gen. Dic. 17.

BEERS.

ANTHONY BEERS, of Watertown, Mass., 1646, by wife Elizabeth, had Samuel 1647, died soon, Ephraim 1648, John 1652, Esther, Samuel.

RICHARD BEERS, of Watertown, made freeman March, 1637; served in the Pequot war; was representative 1663. He had Sarah, Mary, Eleazer, Elauthair, Jabez, Elizabeth, Richard, Abigail. He was a captain, and was killed in King Philip's war at Squakeag, now Northfield, Mass., Sept. 4, 1675.

ROBERT BEER, of Rehoboth, Mass., married Jan. 25, 1673, Elizabeth Bullock, perhaps daughter of Richard, and had Benjamin.

REFERENCES:—Schenck's His. Fairfield, Conn., 353; Orcutt's His. Stratford, Conn., 1143; Orcutt's His. New Milford, Conn.,651; Hinman's Conn. Settlers, 174; Gold's His. Cornwall, Conn., 315 Cothren's His. Woodbury, Conn., 513; Washburn's His. Leicester, Mass., 344; Bond's His. Watertown, Mass.,19; Draper's His. Spencer, Mass., 180; Powers' His. Sangamon County, Ill., 113; Trubee Gen. 97; Mansfield Gen. 49; Barton Gen. Appendix, 197; Savage's Gen. Dic. vol. I, 154.

BECHONEY.

PETER BECHONEY, of Watertown, by wife Sarah, had Sarah born 1688, Peter 1690. See Savage's Gen. Dic. vol. I, 155.

BECHUP. See Powers' Sangamon County, Ill., 118.

BECSON. See Young's Wayne, Ind., 327.

BEHEE. See Plumb's Hanover, Pa., 389.

BEIGHTON.

SAMUEL BEIGHTON, of Boston, by wife Ann, had John 1684, Samuel, Ann, James, Ebenezer. See Savage's Gen. Dic. vol. I, 156.

BELCHER.

ANDREW BELCHER, of Sudbury, Mass., 1639, married 1649 Elizabeth, daughter of Nicholas Danforth, of Cambridge, and had Ellen 1640, Jerima 1642, Martha, Mary, Andrew, Ann. He died June 26, 1780.

EDWARD BELCHER, of Boston, 1630, came, perhaps, in the fleet with Winthrop; was made freeman with prefix of respect, May 18, 1731.

JEREMY BELCHER, of Ipswich, came in the "Susan and Ellen" 1631, aged 22; was made freeman 1639. By first wife he had Samuel H. 1659, Jeremy and John, and perhaps more.

RICHARD BELCHER, youngest son of the first married March 20, 1680, Mary Simpson, probably daughter of Thomas.

REFERENCES:—Temple's His. North Brookfield, Mass., 524; Temple's His. Northfield, Mass., 405; Hammatt Papers of Ipswich, Mass., 177; Barry's His. Framingham, Mass., 177; Paige's His. Cambridge, Mass., 486; Wyman's Charlestown, Mass., Gens. vol. I, 73; Butler's Farmington, Me., 377; Bass' His. Braintree, Vt., 117; Hinman's Conn. Settlers, 177; Goode Gen. 232; Thayer's Memorial 21; Thornton's Tabular Pedigree 1850; Vinton's Giles Fam. 263; Whitmore's Belcher Gen. 1878; Amer. Ancestry, vol. II, 10; IV, 211; V, 120; N. E. His. and Gen. Reg. vol. III, 281; XI, 335; XXVII, 239; XXVIII, 204.

WILLIAM BELCHER, of Wethersfield, 1646, by wife Thomasine had Samuel 1647, Daniel 1648, John 1650, Susanna, Mary and Nathaniel 1654.

REFERENCES:—Andrews' His. New Britain, Conn., 184, 236; Hinman's Conn. Settlers, 179; Temple's His. Northfield, Mass., 405; Temple's His. Whately, Mass., 205; Sprague's His. Gloversville, N. Y., 108; Smith's His. Dutchess County, N. Y., 498; Goodwin's Foot Family, 49; Nash Gen. 67; Amer. Ancestry, vol. II, 10; VIII, 213; Savage's Gen. Dic. vol. I, 157; N. E. His. and Gen. Reg. XV, 246.

BELDEN.

RICHARD BELDEN, of Wethersfield, 1640, had Samuel and probably John, both born in England.

BELDING.

JOHN K. BELDING, of Canaan, was born in Saybrook 1762, died 1830; married Martha Dean and had Chester and others.

REFERENCES:—Temple's His. of Whately, Mass., 26; Huntington's Stamford, Conn., Families,10;Hemenway's Vermont Gaz. V, 310; Judd's His. Hadley, Mass., 452; Read's His. Swanzey, N. H., 288; Ellis Gen. 117, 170, 180, 371; Amer. Ancestry, vol. I, 6; II, 10; N. E. His. and Gen. Reg. XV, 296.

BELFIELD. See Jones' Gen. (1891) 182; Richmond, Va., Standard, IV, 19.

BELKNAP.

ABRAHAM BELKNAP, of Lynn, Mass., 1647, removed to Salem, where he died 1643. He had Abraham, Jeremy, Joseph, Samuel, and probably Hannah.

REFERENCES:—Stiles' His. Windsor, Conn., vol. II, 70; Barry's His. Framingham, Mass., 178; Winchester, Mass., Rec. vol. II, 272; Wyman's Charlestown, Mass., Gens. vol. I, 73; Cutter's His. Arlington, Mass., 192; Leonard's His. Doblin, N. H., 316; Wheeler's His. Newport, N. H., 300; Cleveland's His. Yates County, N. Y., 231; Ruttenberger's His. Newburg, N. Y., 357; Ruttenberger's Orange County, N. Y., 357; Hemenway's Vermont Gaz. vol. V, 107; Hubbard's Stanstead County, Can., 326; Vinton's Richardson Gen. 488; Wentworth Gen. vol. II, 111; Whitney Gen. 1860; Savage's Gen. Dic. vol. I, 158; N. E. His. and Gen. Reg. XIII, 17; XXVII, 351; XXVIII, 90; XLIV, 400; XLIX, 68; X, 80.

BELL.

FRANCIS BELL, of Stamford, Conn., had been early at Wallingford, Conn.; was Lieut. 1666; but not freeman of Conn. Colony before 1676; though he was admitted to that of New Haven Col. 1647. By his wife Rebecca he had Jonathan.

JAMES BELL, of New Haven, took oath of fidelity 1644. He was a brother of Abraham, and may have removed to Taunton, Mass., where there was one of this name. He had Jane 1658, John 1660, James 1663, Nathaniel, Sarah, Elizabeth, Mary, Joseph, Esther.

ROBERT BELL, of Hartford, Conn., had John, Robert and Mary.

SHADRACH BELL, of Portsmouth, N. H., had by wife Rachel, Shadrach 1685, Elizabeth, Mesheck, and Benjamin.

THOMAS BELL, of Roxbury, Mass., was freeman 1636. He had issue Sarah 1640, John 1643.

THOMAS BELL, of Boston, 1637, by wife Ann, had Thomas 1644, Hopestill, Moremercy.

REFERENCES.

CONNECTICUT.—Timlow's His. Southington, 26; Huntington's Stamford Settlers, 10; Hinman's Conn. Settlers, 186.

MASSACHUSETTS.—Ellis' His. Roxbury, 91; Temple's His. Brookfield 524; Temple's His. Palmer, 422; Wyman's Charlestown Gens. vol. I, 75.

NEW HAMPSHIRE.—Chase's His. Chester, 468; Cockran's His. Antrim, 360; Coggswell's His. Henniker, 469; Hayward's His. Hancock 340; Parker's His. Londonderry, 262; Secomb's His. Amherst, 500; Washington, N. H., His. 303.

OTHER PUBLICATIONS.—Slaughter's St. Mark's Parish, Va., 125; Richmond, Va., Standard, vol. III, 16; Peyton's His. Augusta County, Va., 311; Greene's Kentucky Families; Powers' Sangamon County, Ill., 106; Spooner Gen. vol. I, 269; Paxton's Marshall Gen. 297; Munsell's Albany Coll. IV, 96; Kilbourne Gen. 441; Dwight Gen. 237; Cunnabell Gen. 33, Amer. Ancestry, vol. I, 6; II, 11; Savage's Gen. Dic. vol. I, 159; N. E. His. and Gen. Reg. XXIII, 253; Young's His. Chautauqua, N. Y., 503.

BELLAMY.

MATTHEW BELLAMY, of New Haven, was schoolmaster at Stamford 1658. He married at New Haven, 1671, Bethia, daughter of Timothy Ford, and had Matthew, 1672, Mary. He had a grant of land at Saybrook 1675.

REFERENCES:—Cothren's His. Woodbury, Conn., 507. Davis' His. Wallingford, Conn., 652; Hinman's Conn. Settlers 182; Paul's His. of Wells, Vt., 64; Savage's Gen. Dic. vol. I, 160.

BELLAS.   Amer. Ancestry vol. X, 24.

BELLINGHAM.

RICHARD BELLINGHAM, of Boston, had been recorder at Old Boston, Eng., 1625 to 1633. He came to New England with his wife and son Samuel 1633. He was selectman 1634; was representative to the General Court, Deputy Governor 1635, and several times after, in all ten years, of which, from 1665 to 1672, besides being Ass't Major-General. He died in 1672 aged 80, the last survivor of the patentees in the charter. For second wife he married Penelope, the young sister of Herbert Pelham, Esq., who had embarked May 16, 1635, aged 16 in the "Susan and Ellen." By her he had Hannah 1642, John 1661 and Grace. His son Samuel was of the earliest class of Harvard 1642.

REFERENCES:—Essex Coll. XIX, 307; Savage's Gen. Dic. vol. I, 161; Fairfield County, Conn., 693.

BELLIS.   See Amer. Ancestry vol. IV, 134.

BELLOWS.

JOHN BELLOWS, of Concord, 1645, came in the "Hopewell," from London 1635, aged 12. He married May 9, 1665, Mary Wood, of Marlborough, and had Mary, Isaac 1663, John, Thomas, Eleazer 1671, Nathaniel.

REFERENCES:—Aldrich's Walpole, Mass., 193; Barry's His. Framingham, Mass., 180; Bond's His. Watertown, Mass., 532; Hudson's His. Marlborough, Mass., 322; Stone's His. Hubbardston, Mass., 227; Temple's His. North Brookfield, Mass., 524; Ward's His. Shrewsbury, Mass., 244; Saunders' Charlestown, N. H., 284; Hubbard's Stanstead County, Can., 327; Bellows' Gen. 1885, 1888; Dinsmore's Hartwell Gen.; Strong Gen. 1162; Amer. Ancestry vol. I, 6; II, 11; Savage's Gen. Dic. vol. I, 162.

BELSCHER.   See Goode Gen. 232.

BELSHAW.   See Ball's Lake County, Ind.

BEMAN.   See Buckingham Gen. 146.

BEMAS.   Caulkin's His. New London, Conn., 283.

BEMENT.   See Hinman's Conn. Settlers, 188.

BEMIS.

JOHN BEMIS, of Watertown, Mass., married Mary. daughter of Robert Harrington, and had Beriah 1681, Susanna, Joseph 1684, John, Mary, Samuel, Lydia, Hannah, Isaac, Abraham, 1703, Susanna and Hannah, twins, 1705. He resided in that part which became Waltham.

JOSEPH BEMIS, of Watertown, 1640, by wife Sarah, had Sarah 1643, Mary, Martha, Joseph 1651, Rebecca, Ephraim 1656, John 1659.

REFERENCES.

MASSACHUSETTS.—Wyman's Charlestown, Mass., Gens. vol. I, 76; Temple's His. North Brookfield Mass., 525; Stearn's Ashburnham, 607; Draper's His. Spencer, 161; Cutter's His. Arlington, 193; Bond's His. Watertown, 20; Barry's His. Framingham, 180; Westminster, Mass., Centen. 17.

NEW HAMPSHIRE.—Leonard's His. Dublin, 316; Norton's His. Fitzwilliam, 465; Stearn's His. Rindge, 441.

OTHER PUBLICATIONS.—Hinman's Conn., Settlers, 190; Windham Conn. Gens. 94; Heminway's Vermont Gaz. vol. V, 62; Lapham's His. Paris, Me., 504; Vinten's Richardson Memorial 97; Amer. Ancestry vol. II, 11; VI, 132; IX, 100; Dunster Gen. 146; Savage's Gen. Dic. vol. I, 163.

BEMUS.   See Young's Chautauqua County, N. Y., 320.

BENDALL.

EDWARD BENDALL, of Boston, 1630, came probably in the fleet with Winthrop; was made freeman

1634. By wife Ann, who died in 1637, he had Freegrace 1635; by wife Mary, from Roxbury, Mass., he had Reform 1639, Hopedfor 1641, Moremercy 1642, Restore 1649. He was a man of uncompromising enterprise; he projected and used a diving bell from the wreck of a ship before the dock called Bendall's, being the chief place of trade. He died in 1682. See Savage's Gen. Dict. vol. I, 164.

BENDER. See Hudson's Hist. Marlboro, Mass., 325; Roe's Sketches of Rose, N. Y., 120; Amer. Ancestry, vol. I, 6.

BENEDICT.

THOMAS BENEDICT, of Norwalk, Conn., was of Southold, L. I., before 1650. He came about 1636 to Mass., at the age of 22, and soon after married Mary Bridgham, a fellow passenger. He was the only son, it is said, of William, of Nottinghamshire. He had Thomas, John, Samuel, James, Daniel, Betty, Mary, Sarah, Rebecca, all born at Southold; and after living a short time at Huntington and Jamaica, he removed in 1665, to Norwalk, and there was deacon, selectman, town clerk, and representative at the General Court 1670.

REFERENCES.

CONNECTICUT.—Todd's*Hist. Redding, 183; Hall's Records of Norwalk, 308; Bronsen's Hist. of Waterbury, 463; Boyd's Annals of Winchester, 71; Hinman's Conn. Settlers, 196.

NEW YORK.—Young's Hist. of Chautauqua, 321; Lamb's Hist. of New York, vol. I, 102; Cleveland's Yates County, 484, 539; Bolton's Westchester County, vol. II, 501.

OTHER PUBLICATIONS.—Huron and Erie Counries, Ohio, 173; Loomis' Gen. Female Branches, 787; Morris' Bontecow Gen. 95, 180; Chapman's Trowbridge Family, 128; Savage's Gen. Dict. vol. I, 164; Amer. Ancestry, vol. I, 6; II, 11; IV, 29; VI, 110; 199, 202; VIII, 56; IX, 62, 186; X, 9; Benedict Genealogy.

BENEY. Binney Genealogy.

BENEZIT. Davis' Bucks County, Pa., 149.

BENHAM.

JOHN BENHAM, of Dorchester, probably came in the "Mary and John" 1630; made freeman 1631. By first wife he had Joseph and John. He removed in 1640 to New Haven and married at Boston, as second wife, in 1659, Margery, widow of Thomas Alcock, of Dedham.

REFERENCES.

Hinman's Conn. Settlers, 195; Hamden, Conn. Hist. 236; Davis' Hist. Wallingford, Conn., 653, 941; Power's Hist. Sangamon County, Ill., 109; Morris' Bontecow Gen. 41, 149; Tuttle Family, 641; Dimond Gen. 87; Amer. Ancestry, vol. II, 11; X, 109; Savage's Gen. Dict. vol. I, 155.

BENJAMIN.

JOHN BENJAMIN, of Watertown, Mass., came in the "Lion," Sept. 16, 1632, to Boston, and was made freeman November following. On May 20, of next year, he was appointed Constable by the General Court in Cambridge. He removed about 1637 to Watertown; died 1643. He had John 1620, Abigail, Samuel 1628, and Mary; also born here, Joseph, Joshua 1642, Caleb, Abel.

REFERENCES.

CONNECTICUT.—Stiles' Hist. Windsor, vol. II, 71;

Orcutt's Hist. Stratford, 1146; Hinman's Conn. Settlers, 196.

MASSACHUSETTS.—Stearn's Hist. Ashburnham, 610; Bond's Hist. Watertown, 26; Paige's Hist. Hardwick, 336; Swift's Barnstable Families, vol. I, 143; Wyman's Charlestown, Mass., Gens. vol. I, 77.

OTHER PUBLICATIONS.—Norton's Hist. Fitzwilliam, N. H., 466; Roe's Sketches of Rose, N. Y., 43; Washburne's Livermore, Me., 17; Burke and Alvord Gen. 187; Whitman Gen. 563; Amer. Ancestry, V, 227; VIII, 110; Savage's Gen. Dict. vol. 1, 165.

BENMORE.

CHARLES BENMORE, of Boston, by wife Elizabeth, had Lydia 1677, Stephen 1678, Martha.

BENNER. See Eaton's Annals of Warren, Me., 504; Smith's Hist. of Rhinebeck, N. Y., 172; Dennysville, Me., Centen. 102; Barry's Hanover, Mass., 258.

BENNETT.

AMBROSE BENNETT, of Boston, married, in 1653, Mary Seymour, and had John 1654, Ambrose 1656.

DAVID BENNETT, of Rowley, Mass., a physician, by first wife Mary, had David and Sarah, by second wife, Rebecca, daughter of Capt. Roger Sherman and sister of Sir William Phips, had Spencer 1685.

HENRY BENNETT, of Lyme, Conn., married, Jan. 27, 1673, Sarah Champion, eldest daughter of Henry and had Caleb 1675, Rose, John 1680, Love, Dorothy, Henry 1691.

JAMES BENNETT, of Concord, Mass., was made freeman 1639. By wife Hannah, eldest daughter of the first Thomas Wheeler, he had Hannah 1640, Thomas 1642. He removed with his father to Fairfield 1642, and there had two more children.

JOHN BENNETT, of Stonington, Conn., had William 1660, John 1666, Joseph 1681 and others.

RICHARD BENNETT, of Salem, Mass., 1636, probably removed soon to Boston. By wife Sybil he had Peter 1649, Susanna 1651, Richard 1653.

RICHARD BENNETT, of Newport, by wife Rebecca, had Robert 1650, and perhaps others.

SAMUEL BENNETT, of Lynn, came in the "James" from London 1635, aged 24; owned a large farm at Chelsea. He had Samuel, Elisha, John and perhaps Lydia.

REFERENCES.

CONNECTICUT.—Weaver's Hist. Windham, 94; Sedgwick's Hist. Sharon, 64; Orcutt's Hist. Stratford, 1148; Orcutt's Hist. New Milford, 651; Hinman's Conn. Settlers, 198; Windham Gens. 94.

MASSACHUSETTS.—Stearns' Hist. Ashburnham, 613; Stearns' Hubbardston 228; Wyman's Charlestown Gens. vol. I, 78; Ward's Hist. Shrewsbury, 229; Hudson's Hist. Lexington, Mass., 11; Hazen's Hist. Billerica, 11; Hammatt Papers Ipswich, 27; Chandler's Hist. Shirley, 351; Butler's Hist. Groton, 386; Barry's Hist. Framingham, 180; Ballou's Hist. Milford, 577; Batson's Hist. Gloucester, 62; Whitmore's Copps Hill Epitaphs, Tyngsboro Centen. Rec. 16.

NEW HAMPSHIRE.—Coggswell's Hist. Northwood, 639; Hayward's Hist. Hancock, 342; Bassett's Hist. Richmond, 311; Norton's Hist. Fitzwilliam, 466; Read's Hist. Swanzey, 290; Secomb's Hist. Amherst, 501; Washington, N. H., Hist. 304; Worcester's Hist. Hollis, 366.

NEW YORK.—Bergen's Kings County Settlers, 27; Cleveland's Hist. Yates County, 688.

OTHER PUBLICATIONS.—Eaton's Hist. Thomaston, Me., 143; Lapham's Hist. Bethel, Me., 465; Lapham's Hist. Norway, 465; Ridlon's Harrison, Me., Settlers, 25; Austin's R. I. Gen. Dict. 18; Futhey's Chester County, Pa., 480; Heminway's Vermont Gaz. V, 99, 187, 398; Hollister's Pawlet, Vt., 165; Kulp's Wyoming Valley Families; Neil's Virginia Carolorum, 304; Plumb's Hist. Hanover, Pa., 391; Power's Sangamon, Ill., 110; Salter's Hist. Monmouth County, N. J., IX; Slaughter's St. Mark's Parish, Va., 38; Smith's Hist. Delaware County, Pa., 44; Vermont Hist. Gaz. V, 99; Maris Gen. 77; Champion Gen. Caverno Gen. 26; Buckminster's Hastings Family, 101; Bolton Gen. 44; Amer. Ancestry, vol. I, 7; II, 11; VI, 176, Savage's Gen. Dict. vol. I, 166; N. E. Hist. and Gen. Reg. XXIX, 165; XXVIII, 201.

BENNEY.   See Amer. Ancestry, VIII, 92; Binney Gen.

BENNING.   See Wentworth Gen. I, 65.

BENNOCK.   Bangor Hist. Mag. vol. III, 236.

BENOIT.   Temple's Hist. North Brookfield, Mass., 526; Munsell's Albany, IV, 97.

BENSEN.   Munsell's Albany Coll. IV, 96; Amer. Ancestry, vol. I, 7; Pearson's Schenectady, N.Y., Settlers, 13.

BENSON.

JOHN BENSON. of Hingham, Mass., came from Southampton, Eng., 1638, in the "Confidence," aged 30, with wife Mary and children, John and Mary, under 4 years. Had grant of land at Hingham.

JOHN BENSON, of Rochester, by wife Elizabeth, had Mary, Sarah, Ebenezer 1693, Joseph and Benjamin, twins, 1697, Bennett 1698, Martha, Joshua, Caleb, Samuel.

REFERENCES:—Mitchell's Hist. Bridgewater, Mass., 115; Deane's Hist. Scituate, Mass., 220; Davis' Landmarks of Plymouth, 26; Barry's Hist. Framingham, 181; Bradbury's Kennebunkport, Me., 227; Dearborn's Hist. Parsonfield, Me., 453; Hatch's Hist. Industry, Me., 512; Lapham's Hist. Norway, 466; Lapham's Hist. Paris, Me., 506; Bassett's Hist. Richmond, N. H., 313; Riker's Hist. Harlem, N. Y., 480; Williams' Hist. Danby, Vt., 111; Talcott's N. Y. and N. E. Families, 8; Bergen Gen. 80; Amer. Ancestry, vol. I, 7; II, 11; Savage's Gen. Dict. I, 68; Benson Gen.

BENT.

JOHN BENT, of Sudbury, Mass., came in the "Confidence" 1638, aged 35, from Southampton, Eng., with wife Martha and children Robert, William, Peter, John and Ann, all under 12. Was made freeman 1640; had in this country, Joseph, Martha and perhaps others.

JOSEPH BENT, of Marlborough, youngest brother of John, by wife Elizabeth, had Experience 1673, Joseph 1675. He was killed that year by the accidental discharge of a gun.

REFERENCES:—Hudson's Hist. Marlborough, Mass., 324; Barry's Hist. Framingham, Mass., 181, 453; Lapham's Hist. Paris, Me., 508; Norton's Hist. Fitzwilliam, N. H., 467; Glover Gen. 340; Savage's Gen. Dict. vol. I, 169, N. E. Hist. and Gen. Reg. XLVIII, 288; XLIX, 65; Bent Gen.

BENTLEY.

WILLIAM BENTLEY, came to Boston, 1635, in the "Freelove," with John, aged 17, and Alice 15.

REFERENCES:—Wyman's Charlestown, Mass., Gens. vol. I, 79; Eaton's Hist. Thomaston, Me., 145; Young's Chautauqua, N. Y.,. 233; Thomas Gen. Maryland, 37; Robertson's Pocahontas Descendants; Austin's R. I. Gen. Dict. 19; Stanton Gen. 129; Savage's Gen. Dict. vol. I, 160.

BENTON.

ANDREW BENTON, of Milford, Conn., 1639, removed about 1660, to Hartford, and died there 1683. By first wife he had Andrew, Samuel, Joseph, Mary and Dorothy; and by second wife, Ann, had Ebenezer, Lydia, Hannah.

REFERENCES:—Waldo's Hist.Tolland, Conn., 80; Stiles' Hist. Windsor, Conn., II, 71; Hinman's Conn. Settlers, 201; Talcott's, N. Y. and N. E. Families, 485; Bass' Hist. Braintree, Vt., 117; Benton's Hist. Guildhall, Vt., 265; Matthews' Hist. Cornwell, Vt., 284; Cleveland's Yates County, N. Y., 262; Peyton's Hist. Augusta County, Va., 305; Richmond, Va., Standard II, 7; Green's Kentucky Families; Hubbard's Stanstead County, Can., 125; Paxton's Marshall Gen. 64; Missouri Biog. Dict. 5; Amer. Ancestry, vol. I, 7; IV, 236; VII, 173; Savage's Gen. Dict. vol. I, 169; N. E. Hist. and Gen. Reg. XVI, 18; Washington, N. H., Hist. 305.

BENTZEN.   See Green's Todd Gen.

BEAN.   See Ridlon's Saco Valley, Me., Settlements, 456.

BERGEN.

HANS HANSEN BERGEN, came from Holland to New Amsterdam in one of the fleet belonging to the West India Company, 1633; he married, in 1639, Sarah Rapalie. Had Michael Hansen and others.

REFERENCES:—Bergen Settlers, Kings County, N. Y., 31; Stile's Hist. Brooklyn, N. Y., Amer. Ancestry, V, 199; VI, 151; N. Y. Gen. and Biog. Rec. X, 152; Power's Sangamon County, Ill., 114; Bergen Gen.

BERGH.   See Smith's Hist. Rhinebeck, N. Y., 178; N. Y. Gen. and Biog. Rec. XIX, 122.

BERKLEY.   Richmond, Va., Standard, vol. I, 47, 49; III, 4, 48; IV, 2; Page Gen. 144, 149; Carter Family Tree.

BERNABEN.   See Barton Gen.

BERNARD.   Richmond, Va., Standard, vol. III, 26; Robertson's Pocahontas Descendants; Eaton's Thomaston, Me., 145.

BERNAN.

GABRIEL BERNAN, of Newport, R. I., son of Andre, born at New Rochelle, in France, April 6, 1644; escaped shortly before the revocation of the Edict of Nantes, though for his religion he suffered two years' imprisonment. He settled in Boston, where he resided some years. In 1718 he was one of the chief supporters of the Church of England at Kingston, R. I. He died in his 92d year at Providence, R. I. By his first wife Esther, daughter of Francois Leroy, of Rochelle, he had ten children, of which he brought eight, and by second wife Mary Harris, four more.

REFERENCES:—Austin's R. I. Gen. Dict. 19; Ammidown Coll. I, 125; Rhode Island Hist. Coll. III, 315; Savage's Gen. Dict. vol. I, 170.

BERRIAN.   See Bolton's Hist. Westchester County, N. Y., vol. II, 799.

BERRIEN.   Riker's Annals of Newtown, N. Y., 338; Bergen's Kings County, N. Y., 34.

BERRINGER.   Smith's Hist. Rhinebeck, N. Y., 190; Munsell's Albany Coll. IV, 197.

BERRY.

BDWARD BERRY, of Salem and Marblehead, had Edward, born in England, married, about 1668, Elizabeth, widow of Roger Haskell.

RICHARD BERRY, of Barnstable or Yarmouth, 1643, had John 1652, Joseph, Nathaniel and others.

SAMUEL BERRY, of Yarmouth, married Elizabeth, daughter of John Bell, and had Elizabeth, Pauline, John, Samuel, Desire.

THOMAS BERRY, of Boston, a mariner, by wife Grace, had Thomas 1663.

REFERENCES.

MASSACHUSETTS.—Swift's Barnstable Families, vol. I, 136; Paige's Hist. Hardwick, 336; Freeman's Cape Cod, II, 198, 207; Barry's Hist. Framingham, 184.

MAINE.—Eaton's Hist. Thomaston, 145; Hanson's Hist. Gardiner, 79, 81; Lapham's Hist. Bethel, 488; Lapham's Hist. Norway, 469; Lapham's Hist. Paris, 510; Lapham's Hist. Woodstock, 176; Machias, Me., Centen. Celebration, 154; Maine Genealogist, vol. II, 6; Wheeler's Hist. Brunswick, 829.

NEW HAMPSHIRE.—Morrison's Hist. Windham, 336; Dow's Hist. Hampton, 600; Chase's Hist. Chester, 471; Coggswell's Hist. Henniker, 460.

OTHER PUBLICATIONS.—Hinman's Conn. Settlers, 204; Clayton's Hist. Bergen County, N. J., 232; Guild's Stiles Gen. 37; Lawrence and Bartlett Mem. 23; Oneida Society, N. Y., vol. II, 127; Roome Gen. 7, 24; Amer. Ancestry, VI, 17; VIII, 137; Savage's Gen. Dict. vol. I, 70; N. Y. Gen. and Biog. Rec. XV, 49.

BERTHOLD. See Beckwith's Creoles, 62.

BERTINE. Bolton's Hist. Westchester County, N. Y., vol. II, 710.

BERTRAM. Hurd's Hist. Fairfield, Conn., 578.

BERTRAND. Hayden's Va. Gens. 334.

BESBEDGE.

THOMAS BESBEDGE, of Scituate, Mass., came in the "Hercules" 1635, with six children and three servants, embarked at Sandwich, county Kent. He was deacon of the first church at Scituate, which he joined in 1637. He removed to Duxbury, Mass., and was representative to the Gen. Court 1643. See Savage's Gen. Dict. vol. I, 171.

BESSAC. See Bessac Gen.

BESSE. Lapham's Bethel, Me., 489; Freeman's Cape Cod, vol. II, 74.

BESSEE. Mitchell's Hist. Bridgewater, Mass., 116.

BESSEY. Lapham's Hist. Paris, Me., 513; N. E. Hist. and Gen. Reg. XXXVII, 377.

BEST. Amer. Ancestry, vol. II, 11, 153. Savage's Gen. Dict. vol. I, 175.

BETHUNE. See Bethune Gen.; Duffield's Golden Wedding; Morrison's Hist. Windham, N. H., 337.

BETTIS. See Temple's North Brookfield, Mass., 526.

BETTS.

RICHARD BETTS, of Ipswich, 1646, is said to have come from Hemel Hempstead, county Herts. He settled in Newtown, L. I., 1656; was in high esteem there many years. By his wife Joanna, he had Richard, Thomas, Joanna.

WILLIAM BETTS, of Dorchester, was first at Scituate and removed thence to Barnstable. He married, Feb.

1639, Alice, a maiden of the Bay, and removed with his minister to Barnstable, and there had Hannah 1640, Samuel 1643, Hope 1645.

REFERENCES.

CONNECTICUT.—Todd's Hist. of Redding, Conn., 184; Sedgwick's Hist. Sharon, 64; Hall's Records of Norwalk, 274; Hinman's Conn. Settlers, 205, 440.

NEW YORK.—Bergen's Settlers of Kings County, 33; Riker's Annals of Newtown, N. Y., 373; N. Y. Gen. and Biog. Rec. XIX, 164.

OTHER PUBLICATIONS.—Swift's Barnstable, Mass., Families, vol. I, 88; Paige's Hist. Cambridge, Mass., 488; Smith's Gen. of William Smith, 57, 78; Hollister's Pawlet, Vt., 166; Amer. Ancestry, vol. II, 153; V, 43; VII, 205; Savage's Gen. Dict. vol. I, 172; Bett's Gen.

BEVANS.

BENJAMIN BEVANS, of Farmington, Conn., had Benjamin and John. Martin's Chester, Pa., 42; Savage's Gen. Dict. vol. I, 173; Orcutt's Hist. Stratford, Conn., 1149; Power's Hist. Sangamon County, Ill., 117.

BEVERIDGE. Eaton's Thomaston, Me., 146.

BEVERLY. Carter Family Tree; Meade's Old Churches, Va., II, 481; Neil's Virginia Carolorum; Va. Mag. of Hist. and Biog. vol. II (1895).

BEVERSTOCK. Hayward's Gilsum, 264.

BEVIER. Amer. Ancestry, VI, 58.

BEVIN. Whittemore's Middlesex County, Conn., 201; Hinman's Conn. Settlers, 207.

BEVOISE. Bergen's Kings County, N. Y., 85.

BIBB. Gilmer's Georgians, 108.

BIBBINS. Weaver's Hist. Windham, Conn., 96; Hinman's Conn. Settlers, 267.

BIBBETT. Temple's North Brookfield, Mass., 500.

BICE. Power's Sangamon County, Ill., 117.

BICKFORD. Eaton's Annals of Warren, Me., 505; Bradbury's Kennebunkport, Me., Herrick's Hist. Gardner, Mass., 335; Coggswell's Hist. Henniker, N. H., 462; Coggswell's Hist. Nottingham, N. H., 641; Runnel's Hist. Sanbornton, N. H., II, 33; Wentworth Gen. II, 519.

BICKNALL. Wyman's Charlestown, Mass., Gens. 81.

BICKNELL. John Bicknell, of Weymouth, by wife Mary, had Naomi 1667, Ruth, Joanna, Experience, Zachary 1668, Thomas 1670, Elizabeth, Mary.

REFERENCES:—Ballou's Hist. Milford, Mass., 578; Amer. Ancestry, V, 182; VI, 83; Bicknell Gen.

BICKWELL. Savage's Gen. Dict. vol. I, 174.

BICKNOR.

WILLIAM BICKNOR, of Charlestown, Mass., 1638, died Aug. 16, 1659, leaving widow Martha, by whom he had Benjamin 1656, Martha 1658. See Savage's Gen. Dict. vol. I, 174.

BIDDLE.

JOHN BIDDLE, of Hartford, 1639, died 1687, leaving John, Joseph, Samuel and Daniel, and daughters Sarah, Hannah, Waddam, and Mary Meekins.

REFERENCES:—Savage's Gen. Dict. vol. I, 174; Amer. Ancestry, vol. III, 212; VI, 44; Biddle Gen.

BIDDLESTONE. See Savage's Gen. Dict. vol. I, 187.

BIDLOCK.   Weaver's Hist. Windham, Conn., 99;
Ransom Gen. 34; Windham, Conn. Gens. 99.

BIDWELL.

JOHN BIDWELL, of Hartford, was an early settler
there, had his home lot of four acres in 1639,had a house
lot and tan yard then 1640 and owned land in East
Hartford.   He married Sarah, daughter of John and
Mary Wilcox, and had issue John 1641, Joseph, Samuel,
Sarah, Hannah, Mary, Daniel 1655.
REFERENCES:—Stiles' Hist. Windsor, Conn., II, 72;
Amer. Ancestry, IX, 3 to 18; Andrews' New Britain,
Conn., 384; Brown's West Simbury, Conn., Settlers, 13;
Hinman's Conn. Settlers, 209; Read's Hist. Swanzey, N.
H., 293; N. E. Hist. and Gen. Reg. XXVII, 192.

BIGELOW.

JOHN BIGELOW, of Watertown, 1636, was the son
of Randle Bigelow, in Wrentham, County Suffolk, Eng.,
and was baptized 1617.   He married, Oct. 1642, Mary,
daughter of John Warren, and had John, Jonathan 1646,
Mary, Daniel 1650, Samuel, Joshua 1655, Elizabeth,
Sarah, James, Martha, Abigail, Hannah.

JONATHAN BIGELOW, brother of the above,
married, about 1671, Rebecca, daughter of Serg't John
Shepard, and had Jonathan 1673, Rebecca, John, Mary.
For second wife he took Mary, daughter of Samuel Olcott, and had Abigail 1690, Daniel 1693, Samuel 1695.

SAMUEL BIGELOW, of Watertown, brother of the
above, married, Jan. 1674, Mary, daughter of Thomas
Flagg, and had John 1675, Mary, Samuel 1679, Sarah
Thomas, Martha, Abigail, Isaac and Deliverance.

REFERENCES.

MASSACHUSETTS.—Temple's Hist. North Brookfield, Mass., 526, Watt's Reminiscences of Worcester,
44; Westminster Centen. 22; Stearn's Hist. Ashburnham, 615; Pierce's Hist. Grafton, Mass., 458; Morse's
Sherborne Settlers, 15; Keyes' West Boylston Reg. 14;
Hudson's Hist. Marlborough,325;Draper's Hist.Spencer,
181; Bond's Hist. Watertown, 39; Barry's Hist. Framingham, 184; Allen's Worcester, Mass., Association, 95.

OTHER PUBLICATIONS.—Hurd's Hist. New
London, Conn., 399; Hinman's Conn. Settlers, 210; Hayward's Hist. Hancock, N. H., 345; Norton's Hist. Fitzwilliam, N. H., 470; Sylvester's Hist. Ulster County, N.
Y., Adams' Hist. Fairhaven, Vt., 313; Bass' Hist. Braintree, Vt., 117; Vinton's Richardson Gen. 644; Tuttle Gen.
444; Amer.Ancestry, vol. I, 7; II, 12; IV, 192, 205; V,
126; VII, 94; VIII, 76, 85; Savage's Gen. Dict. vol. I,
175; N. E. Hist. and Gen. Reg. III, 196, XLII, 79.
Bigelow Gen.

BIGG.   N. E. Hist. and Gen. Reg. XXIX, 253;
Bigg Gen.

BIGGS.

WILLIAM BIGGS, of Middletown, Conn., died 1681,
leaving children William, Mary, Thomas, Elizabeth,
Sarah and John.
REFERENCES:—Savage's Gen. Dict. vol. I, 176; Neff
Gen. 266; Hinman's Conn. Settlers, 214.

BIGNAL.   Merrill's Ackworth, N. H., 187.

BIGSBY.   Amer. Ancestry, vol. I, 8.

BILL.

JAMES BILL, of Boston, came probably with his
mother in 1638.   By wife Mehitable he had James 1651,

Jonathan, Joseph, Joshua.   He was made freeman 1638.

THOMAS BILL, of Boston, 1657, married, Jan. 14,
1653, widow Elizabeth Nichols, and had Samuel 1658.
By wife Abigail, daughter of Michael Willis, he had Sam-
uel 1659, Mary 1661, Thomas 1664, Susanna, Michael,
James 1669.   He died Oct. 29, 1696.
REFERENCES:—Whittemore's Hist. Middlesex County,
Conn., 201; Hurd's Hist. New London, Conn., 509; Hine's
Lebanon, Conn., Address (1880), 145; Caulkins' Hist.
New London, Conn., 320; Hayward's Hist. Gilsum, N.
H., 265; Bass' Hist. Braintree, Vt., 118; Vinton's Richard-
son Memorial 374; Spooner Gen. vol. I, 71; Huntington
Gen. 110; Hayes' Wells Gen. 111; Bill Gen.; Amer. Ances-
try, V, 21; VII, 138; VIII, 98; Savage's Dict. vol. I,
177; Windham, Conn., Gens. 102.

BILLINGS.

ROGER BILLINGS, of Dorchester, 1640, was made
freeman 1643.   By wife Mary he had Mary 1640.   By
second wife Hannah he had Mary again, Hannah,
Joseph, Ebenezer, Roger 1657, Elizabeth 1650, Zifforah.

WILLIAM BILLINGS, of Dorchester, or Braintree,
Mass., was a proprietor 1654 of Lancaster, Mass.   He
married at Dorchester, Feb. 12, 1658 Mary.   He removed
probably to New London and Stonington, Conn., and
had there William, Joseph, Mary and Lydia.

REFERENCES.

CONNECTICUT.—Hurd's Hist. New London,
Conn., 415; Hinman's Conn. Settlers, 216; Weaver's Hist.
Windham, Conn., 231.

MASSACHUSETTS.—Stearns' Hist. Ashburnham,
615; Barrus' Hist. Goshen, 137; Judd's Hist. Hadley, 454;
Paige's Hist. Hardwick, 337; Whitmore's Epitaphs.

MAINE.—Lapham's Hist. Bethel, 489; Lapham's
Hist. Paris, 516; Lapham's Hist.Woodstock, 49; Warren's
Hist. Waterford, 231; Bangor Hist. Mag. vol. I, 13.

OTHER PUBLICATIONS.—Hayward's Hist. Han-
cock, N. H., 348; Austin's R. I. Gen. Dict. 21; Pompey's
N. Y. Reunion, 286; Powers' Sangamon County, Ill., 118;
Thayer Memorial, 67, Loomis' Gen. Female Branches
650; Dwight's Gen. of Dwight, 763; Dunster Gen. 60;
Savage's Gen. Dict. vol. I, 177; N. E. Hist. and Gen. Reg.
VII, 272; XXXI, 319; XLV, 259; Windham, Conn.,
Gens. 102.

BILLINGTON.

JOHN BILLINGTON, of Plymouth, 1620, came in
the "Mayflower" with wife Helen and two sons.   John,
who died before his father, but after the division of property in 1627.
REFERENCES:—Hayden's Virginia Gens. 84; Davis'
Landmarks of Plymouth, 28; Bangor, Me., Hist. Mag.
IV, 216; Savage's Gen. Dict. vol. I, 169.

BILLS.

THOMAS BILLS, of Barnstable, Mass., perhaps son
of William, married Oct. 3, 1672, Anna, probably
daughter of William Twining, and had Ann 1673, Eliza-
beth 1675.   His wife died Sept. 1, 1675, and he married
May 2, 1676, Joanna Twining, daughter of another
William, and had Nathaniel 1677, Mary, Mehitable,
Thomas 1684, Gersham, Joannis.   Most of these were
born at Eastham, Mass.
REFERENCES:—Secomb's Hist. of Amherst, N. H., 501;
Savage's Gen. Dict. vol. I, 179.

BILYEU.   Powers' Hist. Sangamon County, Ill. 118.

BINGHAM.

THOMAS BINGHAM, of Norwich, Conn., married, Dec. 12, 1666, Mary Rudd, and had Thomas 1667, Abiel 1669, Mary, Jonathan 1674, Ann, Abigail, Nathaniel, Deborah, Samuel, Joseph, Stephen 1690. He removed to Windham and died there June 16, 1730, aged 88.

REFERENCES:—Caulkins' Hist. Norwich, Conn., 164; Hines' Lebanon, Conn., Address, 146; Hinman's Conn. Settlers, 218; Hayward's Hist. Gilsum, N. H., 268; Matthews' Hist. Cornwell, Vt., 286; Walworth's Hyde Gen. 57, 203, 1039; Granite Monthly, V, 353; Savage's Gen. Dict. vol. I, 180; N. E. Hist. and Gen. Reg. XLIX, 333; Amer. Ancestry, vol. I, 8; X, 155.

BINGLEY.

WILLIAM BINGLEY, of Newbury, Mass., 1659, married,Feb.27,1660,Elizabeth Preston and had William Feb. 24, 1662, and probably Elizabeth. See Savage's Gen. Dict. vol I, 180.

BINNEY.

JOHN BINNEY, of Hull, Eng., came over before 1679. By wife Mary, he had John 1680, Samuel, Mercy, Isaac 1685, Thomas and Eliza. He died Nov. 10, 1698.

SAMUEL BINNEY, brother of above, married, Nov. 11, 1701, Rebecca Vickers. He had Elizabeth 1702, Samuel 1704, Isaac, Rebecca, Caleb.

REFERENCES:—Ballou's Hist. of Milford, Mass., 579; Wyman's Charlestown, Mass., Gens. vol. I, 83; Life of Rev. William Smith; Bridgeman's Granary Burial Ground; Amer. Ancestry, VIII, 36; Savage's Gen. Dict. vol. I, 180; Binney Gen.

BIRCH.

THOMAS BIRCH, of Dorchester, Mass., who died Oct. 3, 1657, refers in his will 1654, to Joseph, Jeremiah, and Mary. See Roome Gen. 288; Savage's Gen. Dict. vol. I, 181.

BURCH. Amer. Ancestry, vol. II, 18; Orcutt's Hist. of Stratford, Conn., 1166; Powers' Hist. Sangamon County, Ill., 159.

BIRCHARD or BURCHARD.

THOMAS BIRCHARD or Burchard, of Roxbury, Mass., came in the "Freelove" from London 1635, aged 40, with wife Mary 38, and children, Elizabeth, Mary, Sarah, Susan, John, Ann. His name is given in the custom-house at London as Buchard. He wrote it Birchwood. He removed to Hartford, Conn., where he had been an original proprietor. He removed thence to Saybrook, Conn., and represented that town at the General Court 1650-1.

REFERENCES:—Caulkins' Hist. Norwich, Conn., 165; Hines' Lebanon, Conn., Hist. Address, 146; Hinman's Conn. Settlers, 221; Walworth's Hyde Gen. 41; Savage's Gen. Dict. vol. I, 181; Ely Gen. 166, 351.

BIRD.

JOHN BIRD, came from England with his brother Thomas about 1700, and bought plantations in Brandywine Hundred, also the plantation known as Vertrede Hook, Wilmington, Del. He married Margaret and had John and other children.

REFERENCES.

MAINE.—Eaton's Hist. Thomaston, 147; Eaton's Annals of Warren, 505; Lapham's Hist. Bethel, 490; Lapham's Hist. Norway, 466; Lapham's Hist. Paris, 518.

MASSACHUSETTS.—Bond's Hist. Watertown, 41; Temple's Hist. Brookfield, 529; Wyman's Charlestown Gens. vol. I, 84; Deane's Hist. Scituate, 221.

OTHER PUBLICATIONS.—Hinman's Conn.Settlers 223;New Haven Colony Collections,vol. I, 1134; Powers' Sangamon County, Ill., 119; Glover Gen. 170, 425; Blake Gen.; Pope Gen.; Underwood's Pollard Gen.; Baird's Hist. Rye, N. Y., 423; Savage's Gen. Dict. vol. I, 182; N.E. Hist. and Gen. Reg. XXV, 21, 151; Amer. Ancestry, IV, 85.

BIRDLEY.

GILES BIRDLEY, of Ipswich, Mass., 1648, had wife Elizabeth and children Andrew 1657, James, Giles, John 1668.

BIRDSALL.

NATHAN BIRDSALL or BURCHELL, was one of the seven purchasers of Matinecock, L. I., 1666. He married in New Haven, Conn., Temperance, daughter of Richard and Eliza (Alsop) Baldwin, grand-daughter of Sylvester and Sarah (Ryan) Baldwin. They had issue Benjamin, Stephen, Samuel, Nathaniel, William and Nathan.

REFERENCES:—Cleveland's Hist. Yates County, N. Y., 650; Collins' Hist. Hillsdale, N. Y., 45; Ruttenber's Hist. of Orange, N. Y., 368; Baird's Hist. of Rye, N. Y., 454; Bolton's Hist. Westchester County, N. Y., vol. II, 710; Amer. Ancestry, IX, 71; Bunker's L. I. Genealogies, 177.

BIRDSEY.

Deacon JOHN BIRDSEY, is said to have come from Reading, Berkshire, England, to America in 1636, and settled first in Wethersfield, Conn., where he married Phillipa, daughter of Rev. Henry Smith. Tradition says his brother came with him and remarried in Wethersfield, and that the brother's children were all daughters, and one of them married Joseph Hawley, the first of the name in Stratford. John Birdsey removed to Milford, Conn., and thence to Stratford in 1649. He married Alice Tomlinson, widow of Henry Tomlinson. She died Jan. 25, 1698. He died April 4, 1690, aged 74 years. They had John, born March 28, 1641; Johannah, born Nov. 18, 1642.

REFERENCES:—Orcutt's Hist. of Stratford, Conn., 1149; Hinman's Conn. Settlers, 227; Middlefield, Conn., Hist.; Pompey, N. Y., Reunion (1875) 273. Savage's Gen. Dict. vol. I, 183.

BIRGE.

RICHARD BIRGE, 1636, had probably been of Dorchester. He married Oct. 5, 1641, Elizabeth, daughter of William Gaylord, and had Daniel 1644, Elizabeth, Jeremy, John, Joseph.

REFERENCES:—Stiles' Hist. Windsor, Conn., II, 74; Orcutt's Hist. Torrington, Conn., 650; Hinman's Conn. Settlers, 228; Loomis' Gen. Female Branches, 363; Kilbourne Family, 72; Goodwin Foote Gen. 113; Amer. Ancestry, II, 12; X, 200; Savage's Gen. Dict. vol. I, 183.

BINNEY. Green's Kentucky Families;Orcutt's Hist. Torrington, Conn., 652.

BIRON. See Stearns' Hist. Ashburnham, Mass., 617.

BIRRELL. See Stearns' Hist. Ashburnham, Mass., 617.

BISBEE. Wheeler's Hist. Brunswick, Me., 829; Warren's Hist. Waterford, Me., 232; Ridlon's Settlers of Harrison, Me., 25; Lapham's Hist. of Paris, Me., 517; Lapham's Hist. Bethel, Me., 489; Eaton's Annals of

Warren, 205; Mitchell's Hist. Bridgewater, Mass., 117; Winsor's Hist. Duxbury, Mass., 227; Dyer's Hist. Plainfield, Mass.; Bassett's Hist. Richmond, N.H., 14; Vinton's Giles Memorial, 197; Lawrence & Bartlett Mem. 95, 134; Amer. Ancestry, III, 157; Bisbee Gen.

BISCO.   Lapham's Hist. Paris, Me., 519.

BISCOE.   Bond's Watertown, Mass., 42, 683; Aldrich's Walpole, N. H., 213; Draper's Hist. Spencer, Mass., 176.

BISHOP.

EDWARD BISHOP, of Salem, Mass., was one of the founders of the church at Beverly.   He had issue Hannah, Edward 1648, Mary.

JAMES BISHOP, of New Haven, 1648, was Secretary of the Colony 1651; representative at the General Court 1665, in the first session after union with Conn., was Assistant 1668, Deputy Governor 1683 until his death, June 22, 1691.   He had children born at Branford and New Haven.   Grace 1653, Sarah, Elizabeth, Abigail, John 1662, Ruth.   He married Dec. 12, 1665, Elizabeth, daughter of Micah Tompkins, of Milford, and had Samuel 1666, Mary 1669, James 1671, Rebecca 1673.

JAMES BISHOP, of Duxbury, Mass., 1679, had Ebenezer, Abigail, John, Hudson.

JOHN BISHOP, a carpenter, of Newbury, married, Oct. 1647, Rebecca, widow of Samuel Scullard, and had John 1648, Rebecca 1650, Joanna 1652, Hannah, Elizabeth, Jonathan 1657, Noah, David.   He removed first to Nantucket, and thence, with other neighbors, to found the town Woodbridge, N. J., from which he was the first representative in the Assembly 1668; a councillor under Governor Cartaret 1672.   His son John of Rahway, was of Governor Hamilton's Council 1693.

JOHN BISHOP, of Boston, was chosen minister at Stamford, Conn., whither he went on foot.   By his wife Rebecca he had Stephen, Joseph, Ebenezer, Benjamin. His second wife was Joanna, daughter of Capt. Thomas Willet, widow of Rev. Peter Prudden, of Milford, Conn. He preached at Stamford nearly fifty years.

JOHN BISHOP, of Guilford 1659, had by wife Ann, John and Stephen.   He died before 1661.

NATHANIEL BISHOP, currier, of Boston, 1634, owned a lot at Ipswich, Mass., 1638, but preferred Boston. He was made freeman 1645.   By wife Alice, daughter of James Mattocks, he had Sarah 1635, Ruth, Joseph 1642, Benjamin, John, Samuel, Hannah, Rebecca.

RICHARD BISHOP, was of Salem, Mass., 1635, freeman 1642, died 1674.   By first wife he had Thomas, John and Nathaniel.

THOMAS BISHOP, of Ipswich, 1636, was a representative to the General Court 1656.   He died in 1671, leaving widow Margaret, and children Samuel, John, Thomas, Job, Nathaniel.

THOMAS BISHOP, of Roxbury, by wife Prudence, had son Thomas.

TOWNSEND BISHOP, of Salem, Mass., was made freeman 1635.   He was a representative to the General Court 1636.   He had issue, Leah 1637, John 1642.

REFERENCES.

CONNECTICUT.—Dodd's Hist. of East Haven, 170; Huntington's Stamford Settlers, 12; Hinman's Conn. Settlers, 232.

MASSACHUSETTS.—Winsor's Hist. Duxbury, 228; Temple's Hist. Palmer, 429; Hammatt Papers Ipswich,

28; Davis' Landmarks Plymouth, 28; Daggett's Hist. Attleboro, 88; Brooks' Hist. Melford, 501.

NEW HAMPSHIRE.—Bassett's Hist. Richmond 315; Norton's Hist. Fitzwilliam, 474; Read's Hist. Swanzey, 293; Coffin's Hist. Boscowen, 476.

OTHER PUBLICATIONS.—Howell's Hist. Southampton, N. Y., 206; Pompey, N. Y., Re-union, 259; Roe's Sketches of Rose, 117; Thurston's Hist. of Winthrop, Me., 174; Whitehead's Hist. Perth Amboy, N. J., 364; Whitman Gen. 1056; Walworth's Hyde Gen. 369; Morris' Bontecou Gen. 115; Maltby Gen. (1895) 51; Cutts' Gen.; Savage's Gen. Dict. vol. I, 183.

BISPHAM.   Wyman's Charlestown, Mass., Gens. 86; Bispham Gen. (1890) 348.

BISS.

JAMES BISS, of Boston, Mass., by wife Jemima had Martha, born Febry. 23, 1668.   Savage's Gen. Dict. vol. I, 187.

BISSELL.

JOHN BISSELL, of Windsor, Conn., born in Somerset, Eng., died at Windsor, Oct. 3, 1677, aged 85.   He came to Plymouth Colony with Rev. Ephraim Hewett, 1628, moved to Windsor 1640, was deputy to General Court 1642, and later.   He was a member of Windsor troop of horse, 1657, Captain of Windsor Dragoons in King Philip's war 1675.   Quartermaster Hartford County troop of horse 1677.   He had John, Thomas, Samuel, Nathaniel 1640, Mary and Joice.   The grandfather of John Bissell went from France to England, about the time of the massacre of St. Bartholomew 1572.   His Coat Armour, as registered at the College of Heralds, was, *Arms*—Gules on a bend argent, three escallops, sable, *Crest*—A demi-eagle with wings displayed, sable, charged on the neck with an escallop or *Motto*—In recto decus.

THOMAS BISSELL, brother of above, was born in England.   Married, Oct. 11, 1655, Abigail, daughter of Deacon John Moore, and had Thomas 1656, Abigail, John 1661, Joseph, Elizabeth, Benjamin, Sarah, Ephraim 1680, Isaac.   Abigail married Nathaniel Gaylord. Savage's Gen. Dict. vol. I, 187.

REFERENCES:—Hist. Litchfield County, Conn., 1881; Hinman's Conn. Settlers 230; Hines' Lebanon, Conn. Hist. Address 146; Orcutt's Hist. Torrington, Conn., 653; Stiles' Hist. Windsor, II, 76, 406; Norton's Hist. Fitzwilliam, N. H., 475; Loomis Gen. Female Branches, 289, 609; Oxford, N. H., Centen. Cel. 103; Strong Family, 1473; Kellogg's White Descendants, 30; Goodwin Gen. of Olcott Family, 29; Dwight's Gen. Dwight, 412; Amer. Ancestry, vol. III, 125; IV, 106; V, 112; Savage's Gen. Dict. vol. I, 186.

BISSETT.   Cleveland's Yates County, N. Y., 155.

BITGOOD.   Warden Gen. 73.

BITLEY.   Cleveland's Hist. Yates County, N.Y., 531.

BITTING.   Perkiomen Region, Pa., 59.

BITTLESTONE.   Paige's Hist. Cambridge, Mass., 488.

DANIEL BIXBY, of Andover, married, Dec. 2, 1674, Hannah, probably daughter of Thomas Chandler, and had Daniel, Thomas, David and Joseph.

REFERENCES.

MASSACHUSETTS—Ward's Hist. Shrewsbury, 240; Stearn's Hist. Ashburnham, 618; Perley's Hist. Boxford, 28; Marvin's Hist. Winchendon, 447; Jackson's Hist. Newton, 242; Hodgman's Hist. Westford, 438; Bond's

Hist. Watertown, 78; Benedict's Hist. Sutton, 590; Barry's Hist. Framingham, 188.

OTHER PUBLICATIONS.—Leonard's Hist. Dublin, N. H., 318; Washington, N. H., Hist. 692; Adams' Haven Gen. 37; Dudley Gen. 115; Guild's Stiles' Gen. 385; Savage's Gen. Dict. vol. I, 188; Bixby Family.

BLACHLEY. Clayton's Hist. Bergen, N. J., 359.

BLACHLEY. Huntington's Stamford, Conn., Settlers, 12.

BLACK.

JOHN BLACK, of Charlestown, Mass., 1634, had wife Susanna. He was probably the same John who was at Salem, 1636. He had probably a son John and other children.

REFERENCES:—Bangor, Me., Hist. Mag. IV, 65; Lapham's Hist. Paris, Me., 520; Eaton's Hist. Thomaston, Me., 147; Stearn's Hist. Ashburnham, Mass., 618; Barry's Hist. Framingham, Mass., 189; Read's Hist. Swanzey, N. H., 294; Penn. Mag. vol. I, 121; Powers' Hist. Sangamon County, Ill., 122; Slaughter's Bristol Parish, Va., 170; Old Kent, Maryland, 175, 183; Amer. Ancestry, IX, 166; Savage's Gen. Dict. vol. I, 188; Saco Valley, Me., Settlements and Families, 466.

BLACKBEACH, John, of Salem, Mass., 1634, was made freeman May 6, 1635, he was an active merchant. He was a representative at the General Court 1636. By wife Elizabeth he had John, Exercise 1637, Joshua 1639, Benoni, Elizabeth and Solomon. He removed to Boston and thence to Hartford; died at Wethersfield, Conn., 1683. Savage's Gen. Dict. vol. I, 189.

BLACKBURN. See Paxton's Marshall Gen. 365; Hayden's Va. Gens. 633; Meade's Old Families, Va., II, 208.

BLACKFAN. Davis' Bucks County, Pa., 299.

BLACKFORD. Wyman's Charlestown, Mass., Gens. vol. I, 86; Swift's Barnstable, Mass., Families, vol. I, 99; Freeman's Cape Cod, Mass., 298; Paxton's Marshall Gen. 285.

BLACKINGTON. Cutter's Hist. Arlington, Mass., 193; Dagget's Hist. Attleboro, Mass., 88; Eaton's Hist. Thomaston, Me., 148.

BLACKLEACH. Orcutt's Hist. Stratford, Conn., 1155; Raymond's Burritt Sketch.

BLACKLEY or BLAKESLEY, Samuel, of New Haven, married, Dec. 3, 1650, Hannah Potter. He lived first at Guilford, and there had John 1651; at New Haven he had Mary, Samuel, Ebenezer, Hannah. Savage's Gen. Dict. vol. I, 189.

BLACKMAN, John, of Dorchester 1640, perhaps earlier by wife Mary, daughter of Robert Pond, had John 1656, Jonathan, Sarah, Joseph, Mary, Benjamin 1655. REFERENCES:—Sedgwick's Hist. Sharon, Conn., 64; Boyd's Annals Winchester, Conn., 131; Hinman's Conn. Settlers, 244; Davis' Landmarks of Plymouth, Mass., 28; Plumb's Hist. Hanover, Pa., 398; Loomis Gen. Female Branches, 533; Amer. Ancestry, IV, 238; Savage's Gen. Dict. vol. I, 190; Blackman Gen.

BLACKMAR. Austin's R. I. Gen. Dict. 21; Temple's Hist. North Brookfield, Mass., 529.

BLACKMORE, William, of Scituate 1665, came that year from England, married Elizabeth Banks and had Peter 1667, John, Phebe, William 1675. He was killed by the Indians April 21, 1676. REFERENCES:—Deane's Hist. Scituate, Mass., 221; Dawson Gen. 267; Savage's Gen. Dict. vol. I, 190.

BLACKSTONE. Austin's R. I. Dict. 21; Corliss' North Yarmouth, Me., Blackstone (Wm.) Biog. 1886; Blackstone Gen.

BLACKWELL, Michael or Myles, of Sandwich, Mass., had John, Joshua and Jane. REFERENCES:—Spooner's Mem. of W. Spooner, 60; Riker's Annals of Newtown, N. Y., 354; Freeman's Cape Cod, 164; Hayden's Virginia Gens. 265; Savage's Gen. Dict. vol. I, 190.

BLACKWOOD. Dennysville, Me., 102.

BLAGG. See Orcutt's Stratford, Conn., 1156.

BLAGUE. Joseph, of Saybrook, Conn., married, Feb. 10, 1685, Martha Kirtland, daughter probably of Nathaniel and had Elizabeth 1687, Mary 1692, Joseph 1694. Savage's Gen. Dict. I, 190.

BLAINE. Egle's Hist. Reg. Int. Penn. vol. II, 145; Robinson's Family Memorial (1867).

BLAIR.

DAVID BLAIR, of Blandford, Mass., was a native of Scotland. He had a son Robert who was of Blandford. REFERENCES:—Gibb's Blandford, Mass. Hist. 56; Smith's Hist. of Petersborough, N. H., 18; Strong Gen. 1322; Cleveland's Hist. Yates County, N. Y., 599; Clyde's Irish Settlement, Pa., 17; Greene's Kentucky Families; Miller's Colchester County, N. S., 167; Richmond, Va. Standard, II, 7; Page Gen. 72; Balling Gen. 33; Amer. Ancestry IV, 142.

BLAISDELL.

BLAISDELL, Henry of Salisbury, by wife Mary had Ebenezer 1657, Mary, Henry. He removed to Amesbury, and was made freeman there 1690.

RALPH BLAISDELL, of Salisbury, 1640, but part of that year was living at York. By wife Elizabeth he had Mary 1642, Ralph 1643, and perhaps Henry and Sarah.

REFERENCES:—Runnel's Hist. Sanbornton, N. H., vol. II, 35; Eaton's Hist. Thomaston, Me., 150; Corliss' Hist. North Yarmouth, Me., 150; Coggswell's Hist. Henniker, 462; Palmer Gen. (1886) 42; Savage's Gen. Dict. vol. I, 19.

BLAKE.

BLAKE, George, of Gloucester, 1640, was selectman 1644. By wife Dorothy, he had Rebecca 1641, Deborah, Prudence, Elizabeth, Mary, Thomas 1658, and Ruth. He removed to Andover.

JOSEPH BLAKE, of Hampton, died Feb. 11, 1673. In his will he named wife Deborah, and children Timothy, Israel, John, Joshua and Deborah.

JOHN BLAKE, of Middletown, Conn., married 1673, Sarah, daughter of Richard Hall, and had Mercy, Nov. 16, 1675, Sarah, Mary, Elizabeth, Abigail, John, Jonathan 1685, Stephen, Richard.

WILLIAM BLAKE, of Dorchester, Mass., who came in 1630, in the "Mary and John," was eldest son of Giles, of Little Baddon, county Essex, and brought with him William, born 1620, James 1623, John, Edward, and perhaps Ann. He was a very useful citizen; was freeman 1639, selectman.

REFERENCES.

CONNECTICUT.—Orcutt's Hist. Torrington, 655; Hist. Middlefield, Conn., Hist. Hamden, Conn., 237; Hinman's Conn. Settlers, 246; Boyd's Annals Winchester, 208.

MASSACHUSETTS.—Wyman's Charlestown Gens. vol. I, 87; Temple's Hist. North Brookfield, 530; Jameson's Hist. Medway, 455; Hobart's Hist. Abington, 351; Blake's Hist. Franklin, 234; Barrus' Hist. Goshen, 135; Ballou's Hist. Milford, 581; Babson's Hist. Gloucester, 62; Brown's Bedford Families, 5.

MAINE.—Sibley's Hist. Union, 432; Lapham's Hist. Norway, 467; Lapham's Hist. Paris, 521; Lapham's Hist. Bethel, 491; Eaton's Annals Warren, 506; Butler's Hist. Farmington, 387; Bangor Hist. Mag. II, 1; Maine Genealogist, II, 129.

NEW HAMPSHIRE.— Coggswell's Hist. Northwood, 645; Fullerton's Hist. Raymond, 185; Hayward's Hist. Gilsum, 268; Norton's Hist. Fitzwilliam, 476; Read's Hist. Swanzey, 294; Runnel's Hist. Sanbornton, II, 36; Stearn's Hist. Rindge, 444; Chase Hist. Cluster, 472; Dow's Hist. Hampton, 601.

OTHER PUBLICATIONS.—Heminway's Vt. Gaz., V, 29; Pierce's My Ancestors, (1864); Pope Gen. 319; Rice Gen.; Sanborn Gen. (1894); Vinton's Richardson Family, 179; Glover Gen. 427; Amer. Ancestry, vol. I, 8; II, 13; IV, 86, 115; V, 29, 200; IX, 238; Savage's Gen. Dict. vol. I, 192; N. E. Hist. and Gen. Reg. VI, 372; XI, 182; XV, 110; XXI, 292; XLV, 35; Blake Gen.

BLAKELY.   Hollister's Pawlet, Vt., 167; Cothren's Woodbury, Conn., 504.

BLAKEMAN.

ADAM BLAKEMAN, was born in Staffordshire, Eng., matriculated at Christ's College, Oxford, May 28, 1617. He began preaching in his 19th year. He was in Guilford, Conn., 1640, and was the first minister of Stratford, Conn. His children were Mary, James, Samuel, Benjamin, John and Deliverance.

REFERENCES:—Goodwin's Gen. Notes, 1; Orcutt's Hist. Stratford, 1151; Savage's Gen. Dict. vol. I, 194.

BLAKESLEE, Thomas, of Connecticut, born in England, died in Boston, Mass., came to Mass. from London 1635, resided at Hartford, Conn., 1640, moved to New Haven 1643, to Brandford in 1645. He married Susanna Hall, and had Aaron and other children.

REFERENCES:—Davis' Hist. of Wallingford, Conn., 656; Bronson's Hist. Waterbury, Conn., 469; Tuttle Family of Conn., 27, 639; White Gen. (1892) 9; Amer. Ancestry, VIII, 40; Blakeslee Gen.; Savage's Gen. Dict. vol. I, 189.

BLAKEY.   See Watkin's Gen. 37.

BLAKISTON.   See Holstein Gen.

BLANCHARD.

THOMAS BLANCHARD, came in the "Jonathan" from London in 1639, with several children, among whom was Thomas. His second wife was widow Agnes Barnes, a sister of John Bent. In his will he mentions widow Mary, and children Nathaniel, Samuel, George.

REFERENCES.

CONNECTICUT.—Huntington's Stamford Settlers, 16; Hinman's Conn. Settlers, 249.

MAINE.—Corliss' North Yarmouth; Hanson's Hist. Gardener, 128; Lapham's Hist. Rumford, 305.

MASSACHUSETTS.—Wyman's Charlestown Gens., 88; Temple's Hist. Palmer, 428; Morse's Sherborn, 16; Mitchell's Hist. Bridgewater, 118; Hudson's Hist. Lexington, 12; Hobart's Hist. of Abington, 353; Hazen's Hist. Billerica, 12; Fox's Hist. of Dunstable, 237; Brooks' Hist. Medford, 502; Abbott's Hist. Andover, 39.

NEW HAMPSHIRE.—Chase's Hist. Chester, 472; Cochran's Hist. of Antrim, 363; Coggswell's Hist. of Henniker, 462; Livermore's Hist. of Wilton, 317; Merrill's Hist. of Acworth, 187; Morrison's Hist. Windham, 345; Runnel's Sanbornton, II, 39; Secomb's Hist. of Amherst, 503; Washington, N. H. Hist. 306; Wheeler's Croydon Centen., 79; Worcester's Hist. of Hollis, 366.

OTHER PUBLICATIONS.—Bass' Hist. Braintree, Vt., 118; Miller's Colchester County, N. S., 254; Young's Hist. of Wayne Co., Ind., 442; Thayer Memorial, 14; Pierce Gen. (1894); Barbour's My Wife and Mother, App. 27; Amer. Ancestry, vol. I, 8: VIII, 95; IX, 26 27, 29; Savage's Gen. Dict. vol. I, 195; N. E. Hist. and Gen. Reg. X, 152.

BLAND.

BLAND. John, of Sudbury 1641, died in 1667, leaving widow Joanna, by whom he had Annabel and Isabel. See Savage's Gen. Dict. vol. I, 197; Amer. Ancestry, vol. I, 8.

REFERENCES:—Slaughter's Bristol Parish, Va., 147; Richmond, Va., Standard, II, 14; III, 38; Richmond. Va., Critic, (1888); Robertson's Pocahontas Descendants; Meade's Old Churches of Va., vol. I, 446; Campbell's Hist. of Virginia, 670; N. E. Hist. and Gen. Reg. XXVI, 34; Goode Gen. 54; Bland Papers, 13, 145.

BLANDEN. See Jackson's Newton, Mass., 243.

BLANDFORD, John, of Sudbury 1641, an original proprietor, came in the "Confidence" 1638, from Southampton, aged 27. He married widow Dorothy Wright, and had Sarah 1643, Hannah, John 1646, Stephen 1649, and perhaps more. Savage's Gen. Dict. vol. I, 197.

BLANDING. See Bassett's Richmond, 316; Norton's Hist. of Fitzwilliam, N. H., 477.

BLANEY.

BLANEY, John, of Lynn 1659, married. July 1660, Hannah King, perhaps daughter of Daniel the first, and had John 1661, Daniel 1664, Henry, Hannah, Joseph 1670, and Elizabeth. For second wife he married 1678, Elizabeth, widow of Thomas Purchas.

REFERENCES:—Wyman's Charlestown, Mass., Gens., 381; Johnson's Hist. Bristol, Me., 388; Essex Hist. Coll. XVI, 90.

BLANSHAU. See Schoonmaster's Kingston.

BLANTON or BLANTAINE, William, of Boston, 1640, a carpenter from Upton, in county Worcester, Eng., was made freeman 1643. By wife Phebe, he had William, Phebe and Mary. He owned land in that part of Boston, near Brookline, and was engaged in the iron works of Taunton. See Savage's Gen. Dict. vol. I, 197.

BLASDEL. Hudson's Hist. Lexington, Mass., 12; Chase's Chester, N. H.

BLASHFIELD. Corliss' North Yarmouth; Hyde's Hist. of Brimfield, Mass., 381.

BLASS. See Amer. Ancestry, II, 113.

BLATCHFORD.

BLATCHFORD, Peter, of New London, Conn., had served in 1637, before that town was settled in the Pequot war, when very young, for which he had a grant of land and was constable, and a valued citizen. He removed to Haddam, in 1669, and represented that town at the General Court 1670. He died in 1671, leaving widow Hannah, daughter of Isaac Willey and children Joanna, Peter, Mary.

REFERENCES:—Savage's Gen. Dict. vol. I, 198; Amer. Ancestry, IX, 190; Blatchford Gen.

BLATEHLEY.

BLATEHLEY, Thomas, of Hartford, Conn., 1640, removed to New Haven 1643, and took the oath of fidelity the next year, but in two years more was of Branford, encouraging the removal of others to Newark, N. J., but did not go himself. He was a representative at the General Court, 1667-89. By wife Susanna he had Aaron, Moses 1650, Meriam, Abigail. He lived for a time in Guilford and died at Boston 1674, probably on a trading visit. See Hinman's Puritan Settlers, 240; Savage's Gen. Dict. vol. I, 198.

BLAUVELT. See Cole Gen. 74.

BLAXTON.

BLAXTON, William, of Boston 1625 or 6, was bred at Emanuel, often called the Puritan College, where he had his degree 1617, and was probably ordained in England. He settled first in Boston, where he continued four or five years and was admitted freeman May 1631. He removed in 1634 to Providence, R. I., and later to Cumberland and returned to Boston. He married, July 4, 1659, Sarah widow of John Stephenson and had an only son John. William died, May 22, 1675, a few weeks before the great Indian war, in which his plantation was destroyed.

REFERENCES:—Savage's Gen. Dict. vol. I, 198; Armory's William Blaxton.

BLAY. See Old Kent, Md., 313.

BLAZO. Dearborn's Parsonfield, 366.

BLEECKER. Bolton's Hist. Westchester County. N. Y., 810; Holgate's American Gens. 87; Munsell's Coll. of Albany, vol. I, 277; IV, 98.

BLETHEN. See Whitman Gen. 197.

BLIN. Hinman's Conn. Settlers, 250; N. E. Hist. and Gen. Reg. XVI, 19.

BLINCOE. Goode Gen. 205.

BLINMAN.

BLINMAN, Richard, of Gloucester, Mass., came from Chepstow, in county Monmouth, Eng., where he had preached with much effect. He reached Plymouth, Mass., in 1640, and crossed the opposite side of the bay to Gloucester. He had a grant of land in 1641, and was made freeman Oct. 7, 1641. By wife Mary he had Jeremiah 1642, Ezekiel 1643, Azrikam 1646. He removed to New London, Conn., in 1650, and drew thither many of his Gloucester friends. He removed later to New Haven and died in Bristol, Conn., in a good old age. See Savage's Gen. Dict. vol. I, 199.

BLINN. Hudson's Lexington, Mass., 12; N. E. Hist. and Gen. Reg. XVI, 19; Amer. Ancestry, II, 13.

BLISH.

BLISH, or BLUSH, Abraham, by wife Ann, who died May 26, 1651, had Sarah 1641, Joseph 1648. By second wife Hannah, widow of John Barker, of Duxbury, he had Abraham, born 1654. His second wife died March 16, 1658, and he married, Jan. 4, 1659, Alice Derby. He died Sept. 7, 1683.

REFERENCES:—Hayward's Hist. Gilsum, N. H., 269. Savage's Gen. Dict. vol. I, 200.

BLISS.

GEORGE BLISS, of Lynn, Mass., removed in 1637 to Sandwich, was of Newport, R. I., 1649, then aged 58; he appears in the list of freemen 1655. His son John married Damaris, daughter of Benedict Arnold the first, and had Freelove, born Nov. 17, 1672.

THOMAS BLISS, of Hartford, Conn., was an early but not an original settler. He was in Braintree, now Quincy, Mass. In 1639 or 1640, he is first mentioned in Connecticut, with Thomas Jr. By his wife Margaret he had Ann, who married, April 29, 1642, Robert Chapman, of Saybrook, Conn., Mary born 1646; Thomas, Nathaniel, Lawrence, Samuel, Sarah, Elizabeth, Hannah, John.

REFERENCES.

CONNECTICUT.—Caulkins' Hist. Norwich, 167; Hinman's Conn. Settlers, 253; Stiles' Hist. of Windsor, II, 107; Hines' Lebanon, Conn., Address (1880), 147. MASSACHUSETTS.—Wilbraham Centen. 296, 304; West Springfield Centen., 124; Temple's Hist. North Brookfield, 530; Longmeadow Centen. (1883), 6; Hyde's Hist. Brimfield, 371; Freeman's Cape Cod, II, 276, 292. OTHER PUBLICATIONS.—Austin's R. I. Gen. Dict. 22; Joslin's Hist. Poultney, Vt.; McKeen's Hist. of Bradford, Vt., 223; Wetmore Gen. 257; Warren-Clarke Gen. 28; Stebbins Gen. 19; Spooner Gen. I, 391; Morris and Flynn Gen. 25; Kellogg's White Descendants, 47; Hayward's Hist. Gilsum, N. H., 270; Evans' Fox Gen. 206; Dwight Gen. 882; Barbour's My Wife and Mother, App. 62; Amer. Ancestry, IV, 119; V, 131; N. E. Hist. and Gen. Reg. XXXI, 320; 417; XXXII, 67, 175.

BLIVEN, Edward, of Westerly, R. I., married Anna Ross, and had Arnold and perhaps others. See Amer. Ancestry, V, 117.

BLODGET.

BLODGET, or BLOGGET, Thomas, of Cambridge, Mass., came in the "Increase" from London, 1635, aged 30, with wife Susanna and children, Daniel, Samuel, and was admitted freeman 1636. He had here Susanna 1637, Thomas died 1639.

REFERENCES

CONNECTICUT.—Hinman's Conn. Settlers, 258; Stiles' Hist. Windsor, II, 108. MASSACHUSETTS.—Sewall's Hist. Woburn, 593; Stearn's Hist. Ashburnham, 618; Paige's Hist. Cambridge, 489; Temple's Hist. Palmer, 425; Wyman's Charlestown Gens. I, 93; Hyde's Hist. Brimfield, 382; Hudson's Hist. Lexington, 13; Hodgman's Hist. Westford, 438. NEW HAMPSHIRE.—Norton's Hist. Fitzwilliam, 479; Hayward's Hist. Hancock, 350; Cutter's Hist. Jaffrey, 234. OTHER PUBLICATIONS.—Plumb's Hist. Hanover, Pa., 390; Penn. Mag. IV, 382; Guild's Stiles Gen. 39; Life of Rev. William Smith; Loomis Gen. and Female Branches, 672; Amer. Ancestry, IX, 69; 77, 82; Savage's Gen. Dict. vol. I, 202.

BLOEMENDAL. Munsell's Albany, IV, 98.

BLOIS, or BLOYS, Edmund, of Watertown, Mass., was made freeman 1639. By wife Mary, he had Richard, who came on the "Francis" from Ipswich, Eng., 1634. His wife died May 1675, and he married Sept. following Ruth, daughter of Hugh Parsons. He had a son

Edmund, who was of Watertown, Mass. See Savage's Gen. Dict. vol. I, 203.

BLOOD.

BLOOD, James, of Concord, Mass., made freeman June 2, 1641. He had a son James, who married 1657, Hannah, daughter of Oliver Purchis, of Lynn.

RICHARD BLOOD, a brother of James, of Concord, by wife Isabel, had Mary 1662, Nathaniel, Elizabeth and Joseph. He was the chief of the original proprietors. Died Dec. 7, 1683.

ROBERT BLOOD, brother of James, married, April 8, 1653, Elizabeth, daughter of Major Simon Willard, and had Mary, Elizabeth, Sarah, Robert 1660; Simon, Joseah or Joshua, John, Ellen, Samuel, James, Ebenezer, Jonathan, Abigail.

REFERENCES.

MASSACHUSETTS.—Stone's Hist. of Hubbardston, 229; Butler's Hist. Groton, 387, 468; Green's Early Mass. Settlers, 3; Green's Groton, Mass., Epitaphs, 237; Potter's Old Families of Concord, (1887), Shattuck's Hist. Concord, 364; Temple's Hist. North Brookfield, 530.

NEW HAMPSHIRE.—Washington, N. H., Hist. 309; Worcester's of Hollis, 366; Oxford, N. H., Centen., 104; Merrill's Hist. of Ackworth, 188; Livermore's Hist. Wilton, 323; Hill's Hist. Mason, 198; Hayward's Hist. Hancock, 352; Hayward's Hist. Gilsum, 272; Blood's Hist. Temple, 203.

OTHER PUBLICATIONS.—Eaton's Hist. Thomaston, Me., 151; Dunster Gen. 209; Shattuck Family, 368; Amer. Ancestry, III, 6; Savage's Gen. Dict. vol. I, 204.

BLOODGOOD.

BLOODGOOD, Capt. Francis Bloetgoot, the founder of the Bloodgood family of America, was born in Holland 1638, died at Flushing, N. Y., Nov. 29, 1676. He came from Amsterdam to New York in 1658, and settled at Flushing, 1659. He was Secretary to the colonies on the Delaware 1659, Schepen of Flushing 1653, chief military officer there 1674, deputy to New Orange, etc. He died of wounds received in an Indian skirmish. He married in 1657, Lysabeth Jans, of Gonda, Holland, and had Geertie 1658, Arientje, Isabella, Judith, William, Neeltie, John, Lysbeth. See Amer. Ancestry, IV, 118; V, 236.

BLOOM. See Bergen's Kings County, N. Y., 37.

BLOOMER. See Baird's Hist. Rye, N. Y., 396.

BLOMFIELD, or BLUMFIELD, Henry was of Salem, 1638. This name in the third generation is Bloomfield.

THOMAS BLOMFIELD, an early settler of Newbury, died in 1639, leaving a lame daughter and son Thomas.

WILLIAM BLOMFIELD, of Hartford, Conn., came in the "Elizabeth" 1634 from Ipswich, county Suffolk, with wife Susan and children, Sarah, John, Samuel, born 1647. He removed to New London, Conn., and thence to Newtown, L. I. See Hinman's Early Settlers of Conn. 260; Savage's Gen. Dict. vol. I, 203.

BLOOMINGDALE. See Amer. Ancestry, vol. I, 8.

BLOSS.

EDMUND BLOSS, of Watertown, Mass., 1681, is supposed to have come from Suffolk County, England, and to have arrived here prior to 1634. The earliest record of him being when he was admitted freeman at Watertown, Mass., May 22, 1639.

REFERENCES:—N. E. Hist. and Gen. Reg. XLI, 298; Wentworth Gen. vol. I, 364; Amer. Ancestry, V, 40; Bloss Gen.

BLOSSOM.

THOMAS BLOSSOM, one of the Pilgrims, who came from Leyden to Plymouth, but being on board the "Speedwell," was disappointed of passage in the "Mayflower," from England, and soon went back to encourage immigration of the residue. He came again in 1629, probably in the "Mayflower." By his wife Ann, he had Thomas, and perhaps others.

REFERENCES:—Mitchell's Hist. Bridgewater, Mass., 118; Freeman's Hist. Cape Cod, Mass., II, 260; Hollister's Hist. Powlet, Vt., 169; Paul's Hist. Wells, Vt., 65; Swift's Barnstable Families, vol. I, 75; Amer. Ancestry, VII, 183; Savage's Gen. Dict. vol. I, 205.

BLOTT, Robert, of Charlestown 1634, came in 1632, probably, to Roxbury, Mass., and was made freeman 1635. He married Susanna, who died 1660. He died 1665. He had Mary and other children. See Savage's Gen. Dict. vol. I, 205.

BLOUNT.

WALTER BLOUNT, of Norwich, Conn., son of Elijha, was born in Salem, Mass., died in Troy, Mich. He served in Capt. Canfield's Regiment during the Revolution. He married Deborah Herrick, of Salem, Mass., and had Walter and other children.

REFERENCES:—Thurston's Hist. of Winthrop, Me., 175; Hubbard's Stanstead County, Can., 175; Wheeler's North Carolinians, LVII, LXI, 130; Amer. Ancestry, VIII, 100.

BLOWERS.

BLOWERS, John, of Barnstable, Mass., 1643, was of Boston, 1654. By wife Tabitha he had Tabitha 1655, Mary, John 1659, and Thomas 1665.

PYAM BLOWERS, of Cambridge, Mass., for his services in discovering on the coast of Carolina, 1663; he had a grant of five hundred acres there, but probably never claimed them. He married, March 31, 1668, Elizabeth, daughter of Andrew Belcher, and had Thomas 1669, Samuel 1671, Jonathan 1673, Ann; Hannah and others. See Page's Hist. Cambridge, Mass., 489; Savage's Gen. Dict. vol. I, 206.

BLUE. See Powers' Hist. Sangamon Co., Ill., 124.

BLUNT, William, of Andover, Mass., 1668, by wife Elizabeth, had William, who died 1738, aged 67, Samuel and Handborough.

REFERENCES:—Butler's Hist. Farmington, Me., 392; Sibley's Hist. Union, Me., 433; Brewster's Hist. Portsmouth, N. H., II, 90; Secomb's Hist. Amherst, N. H., 508; Amer. Ancestry, II, 13; V, 134; Savage's Gen. Dict. vol. I, 206.

BLUSH. See Swift's Barnstable, Mass., 89.

BLY, John, of Salem, a brickmaker, married, perhaps as second wife 1665, Rebecca Golt or Gott, and had Benjamin 1666, Mary, Rebecca, Edmond 1672, Hannah, William. See Savage's Gen. Dict. vol. I, 206.

BLYE. See Eaton's Thomaston, Me., 151.

BLYTHE. Essex Inst. Coll. XVI, 95.

BOODEN, or BODEN, Ambrose, of Scarborough, 1658, was killed by the Indians 1675. He left a son Ambrose. See Savage's Gen. Dict. vol. I, 206.

BOARDMAN.

SAMUEL BOARDMAN, was one of the first settlers at Wethersfield, Conn., 1636.

THOMAS BOARDMAN, of Yarmouth, Mass., 1643, a carpenter, from London, was first at Plymouth, 1634, at Sandwich 1638. He had by wife Lucy a daughter, Elizabeth. He married second, Elizabeth, daughter of Lieut. John Cole. By first wife he had Thomas, Susanna and Thankful.

REFERENCES:—Timlow's Sketches of Southington, Conn., 27; Sedgwick's Hist. Sharon, Conn., 64; Hinman's Conn. Settlers, 261; Butler's Hist. Farmington, Me., 394; Farrow's Hist. Isleborough, Me., 169; Hatch's Hist. Industry, Me., 513; Paige's Hist. Cambridge, Mass., 490; Whitney's Lawrence Wills; Salisbury Gen.; Amer. Ancestry, VII, 15; Boardman Gen. 1849, 1885; N. E. Hist. and Gen. Reg. XV, 244. Savage's Gen. Dict. vol. I, 207.

BLOUNT. N. E. Gen. Reg. XII, 31.

BOAS. Egle's Penn. Gens. 82.

BOBB. Plumb's Hist. Hanover, Pa., 388.

BABBIT, Edward, of Taunton, Mass., 1643, married, 1654, Sarah, daughter of Miles Farne, of Boston, and had Edward, Sarah, Hannah, Damaris, 1663, Elkanah, Dorcas, Esther, Ruth, Deliverance. Savage's Gen. Dict. vol. I, 207.

BOCKEE. Smith's Hist. Dutchess County, N. Y., 124.

BOCKES. Munsell's Albany, VI, 99.

BODEN. See Driver Gen. 114.

BODFISH. Freeman's Hist. Cape Cod, Mass., II, 142, 300, 329, 471; Swift's Barnstable Families, vol. I, 68; Savage's Gen. Dict. vol. I, 211.

BODGE. Wyman's Charlestown, Mass., Gens. 95.

BODIE. Hubbard's Stanstead County, Can., 244.

BODINE. Salter's Hist. Monmouth County, N. J., X; Maginnis' West Branch Valley, Pa., 529; Clute's Staten Island, N. Y., 344.

BODKIN. William, of Boston, by wife Mary, had John, born March 25, 1680, and Elizabeth, born 1682. Savage's Gen. Dict. vol. I, 208.

BODLE. See Riker Gen. 12.

BODMAN, John, of Boston, by wife Sarah, had John 1645, Benjamin, Manoah 1647, Joseph 1653.

BODMAN, William, of Watertown, Mass., by wife Frances, had Rebecca 1643. Savage's Gen. Dict. vol. I, 207.

BODWELL.

BODWELL, Henry, of Newbury, Mass., was in Capt. Lathrop's company, called the flower of Essex, in the battle of Sept. 18, 1675, at Bloody Brook, and severely wounded. He married, May 4, 1681, Bethia, daughter of John Emery, and had Bethia 1682, removed to Andover, and had Henry and Joseph, who died 1685.

REFERENCES:—Hubbard's Stanstead County, Can., 220; Lapham's Hist. Norway, Me., 469; Cochran's Hist. Antrim, N. H., 365; Runnel's Hist. Sanbornton, N. H., II, 40; Humphrey Gen. 323; Bodwell C. J. R. Biog. 39.

BOEHM. See Boehm Memorial.

BOGARDUS. See Sedgwick's Hist. Sharon. Conn., 65; Schoonmaker's Hist. Kingston, N. Y., 473; Munsell's Albany, N. Y., Coll. IV, 99; Gale Gen. 182; Amer. Ancestry, II, 13.

BOGART.

TUNIS BOGART, son of Guisbert, of Heidkop, province of Utrecht, Holland, emigrated to this country 1652. He married, first Sarah, daughter of Joris Jansen Rapalie, and widow of Hans Hansen Bergen; he married, second, Nov. 11, 1687, Goertje Jans, widow of Derick Dey, and had Gysbert, and other children.

REFERENCES:—Talcott's N. Y. and N. E. Families, 22; Munsell's Albany Coll. IV, 100; Clute's Hist. Staten Island, N. Y., 346; Amer. Ancestry, III, 174; IV, 226.

BOGERT.

CORNELIUS BOGERT, came from Schoendewoert, South Holland, to Albany, N. Y., about 1641, and died there in 1665. He left a son Jacob C. and perhaps other children.

REFERENCES:—Riker's Hist. of Harlem, N. Y., 491; Roome Gen. 144; Cole Gen. 1041; Amer. Ancestry, IV, 134; N. Y. Gen. and Biog. Rec. IX, 191.

BOGERS. Lindsay Gen. 114.

BOGGS.

JAMES BOGGS, son of Ezekiel, a native of Ireland, was born in Delaware, Jan. 22, 1740, died in Halifax, N. S. He resided in Shrewsbury N. J., until the beginning of the Revolutionary War, when he entered the British army as surgeon, and served until the close of the war. He then removed to Halifax. He was highly esteemed as a physician, and was a prominent member of the N. J. Medical Society. He married Mary, daughter of Hon. Robert Hunter Morris, chief justice of New Jersey. He left a son Robert, who settled in New Brunswick, N. J.

REFERENCES:—Norton's Hist. Knox County, Ohio, 370; Eaton's Hist. of Thomaston, Me., 152; Eaton's Annals of Warren, Me., 507; Hayden's Virginia Genealogies, 362; Amer. Ancestry, VII, 22.

BOGMAN. See Bogman Gen.

BOGUE.

JOHN BOGUE, of East Haddam, Conn., born in Glasgow, Scotland, settled in East Haddam, 1680, and was a representative to the Colonial Legislature. He married Rebecca Walkley, daughter probably of Richard Walkley, of Haddam. He had a son Rev. Ebenezer, a graduate of Yale, who married Damaris, daughter of Capt. Samuel Cook, of Wallingford, Conn.

BOHONON.

BOHONON, or BOHANNON, John of Boston, by wife Mary, had Margaret, John 1661, Patrick 1665, Abigail, James 1670.

REFERENCES:—Caverly's Hist. of Pittsford, Vt., 693. Bohonon Gen.

BOICE. See Amer. Ancestry, II, 13.

BOIDEN. Temple's Hist. Palmer, Mass., 427.

BOIES. Gibbs' Blandford, Mass., Address 55; Ely Gen., 236; Strong Gen. 450; Amer. Ancestry, II, 13.

BOLAND. Sedgwick's Sharon, Conn. 65.

BOLL. Powers' Hist. Sangamon, Ill., 125.

BOLLES.

THOMAS BOLLES, of New London, Conn., 1667, his wife Zipporah, and eldest two children, Mary and Joseph, were murdered, June 6, 1678, by John Stodder, a young man, who on his confession was executed therefor. His youngest son John, who was saved was the progenitor of this family in America.

REFERENCES:—Caulkins' Hist. New London, Conn., 368; Hinman's Conn. Settlers, 285; Wyman's Charlestown, Mass., Gens. vol. I, 97; Bassett's Hist. Richmond, N. H., 348; Read's Hist. Swanzey, N. H., 295; Tuttle Gen. 707; Bolles Gen.; Amer. Ancestry, III, 6; Savage's Gen. Dict. vol. I, 208.

BOLLING.

ROBERT BOLLING, of Kippax, Prince George County, Va., born in England, Dec. 26, 1646, died at Kippix, July 17, 1709. He married first, the daughter of Thomas Rolfe, grand-daughter of Pocahontas, he married second 1681, Anne, daughter of John Slith, of Brunswick Co., Va. He had a son Robert, and this name has continued in the family for several generations.

REFERENCES:—Meade's Old Churches of Virginia, vol. I, 78; Richmond, Va., Standard, vol. II, 12, 32; III, 33, 36, 37; Hayden's Virginia Genealogies; Robertson's Pocahontas' Descendants; Slaughter's Bristol Parish, Va., 140; N. E. Hist. and Gen. Reg. XXVI, 35; Lapham's Hist. Paris, Me., 525; Goode Gen. 64; Amer. Ancestry, V, 32; Bolling Family, 1868.

BOLMER. Roome Gen. 225.

BOLSTER. Ridlon's Settlers of Harrison, Me., 26; Lapham's Hist. Rumford, Me., 307; Lapham's Hist. Norway, Me., 468.

BOLT, Francis, of Milford, Conn., came to Boston, in the "Martin," 1638, and with the Baldwins, his fellow-passengers, soon removed thither. By wife Sarah, had Philip and Susanna. Savage's Gen. Dict. vol. I, 208.

BOLTON.

BOLTON, or BOULTON, Nicholas, of Dorchester, Mass., was made freeman 1644. By wife Elizabeth, he had Thankful 1649, John, Experience, Willis.

WILLIAM BOLTON, of Newbury, married, Jan. 16, 1655, Jane Bartlett, who died 1659. He had Mary 1655, who died Sept. 6, 1659, had Mary, born 1655, married second, Nov. 1659, Mary Dennison, and had William 1665, Ruth, Elizabeth, Sarah, Hannah, Joseph.

REFERENCES:—Bolton's Hist. Westchester County, N. Y., vol. II, 711; Bolton Gen.; Mitchell's Hist. Bridgewater, Mass., 118; Wyman's Charlestown, Mass., Gens. vol. I, 98; Chandler's Hist. Shirley, Mass., 357; Bangor, Me., Mag., IV, 212; Bass' Hist. Braintree, Vt., 119; Heraldic Journal, II, 110; Martindale's Hist. Byberry, Pa., 233; Douglass Gen. 175; Amer. Ancestry, III, 63, 109; IX, 45; Savage's Gen. Dict. vol. I, 208.

BOLLING. N. E. Hist. and Gen. Reg. XXVI, 35.

BOLTWOOD. N. E. Hist. Gen. Reg. V, 101.

BOLTWOOD.

ROBERT BOLTWOOD, of Hartford, 1648, removed in 1659 to Hadley, Mass., made freeman 1661, died 1684. He was an enterprising and brave man. By wife Mary, who died in 1687, he had Samuel, Sarah, Lydia, Martha, Mary.

REFERENCES:—Temple's Hist. Northfield, Mass., 409; Judd's Hist. Amherst, Mass., 455; Boltwood's Noble Gen. 276, 342; Hinman's Conn. Settlers, 288; Amer. Ancestry, vol. 1, 8; Savage's Gen. Dict. vol. I, 208.

BOMBURGER. Harris' Hist. Lancaster, Pa., 62; Egle's Penn. Gens. 91; Brubacher Gen. 113.

BOMGARDNER. Britz Gen. 8, 45.

BOND.

GRIMESTONE, of Boston, by wife Elizabeth, had Elizabeth 1683, Joseph 1685, Mary.

JOHN BOND, of Newbury, Mass., married, Aug. 5, 1649; Esther Blakely, and had John 1650, Thomas 1652, Joseph, Esther, Mary, Abigail. He removed to Rowley and thence to Haverhill and died 1675.

WILLIAM BOND, of Watertown, Mass., 1649, third son of Thomas, of Bury St. Edwards, in County Suffolk, baptized there, Sept. 3, 1625, at St. James' Church, came probably, in 1630, in the fleet with Winthrop. He married, Feb. 7, 1650, Sarah, daughter of Nathaniel Briscoe. He was often representative in the colonial days, in the counsel of safety during the insurrection against Andros, and first speaker of the House after the new Charter. He was a man of great energy. His second wife was Elizabeth, widow of John Nevinson. His children were, William 1650, John 1652, Thomas, Elizabeth, Nathaniel, Sarah, Jonas, Mary.

REFERENCES.

MASSACHUSETTS.—Stearns' Hist. Ashburnham, 619; Temple's Hist. North Brookfield, 31; Temple's Hist. of Palmer, 427; Washburne's Hist. Leicester, 347; Paige's Hist. Hardwick, 340; Hyde's Hist. Brimfield, 384; Hudson's Hist. Lexington, 16; Bond's Hist. Watertown, 45; 686; Benedict's Hist. Sutton, 590; Harris' Watertown Epitaphs, 6.

MAINE.—Washburne's Notes on Livermore, 30; Lapham's Hist. Bethel, 493; Bradbury's Kennebunkport, 228.

NEW HAMPSHIRE.—Hayward's Hist. Hancock, 353; Hayward's Hist. Gilsum, 273; Saunderson's Charlestown, 287.

OTHER PUBLICATIONS.—Hinman's Conn. Settlers, 288; Hatfield's Elizabeth, N. J., 69; Pearson's Schenectady, N. Y., Settlers, 15; Hayden's Virginia Genealogies, 167, 184; Bond and Price Gen.; Buckminster's Hastings Family; Chase (Ira) Memorial, 97; Life of Rev. Wm. Smith; Salisbury Memorial; Segourney Gen.; Young's Hist. Wayne County, Ind., 202; Savage's Gen. Dict. vol. I, 209; Amer. Ancestry, vol. I, 8; V, 62; VI, 104; VIII, 12.

BONDURANT. Power's Hist. Sangamon, Ill., 124.

BONESTELL. Smith's Hist. Rhinebeck, 213.

BONHAM, George, of Plymouth, married, Dec. 20, 1644, as second wife Sarah, daughter of George Morton, and had Ruth, Patience, Sarah. Savage's Gen. Dict. vol. I, 211.

BONNELL. Baetjer's Cartaret Gen. 23; Littell's Passaic Valley, 46; Bradbury's Bonnell Family (1875).

BONNER.

JOHN BONNER, of Boston, by wife Mary, had Jane or John 1686, died soon, Jonah 1687, Mary 1689. He removed to Cambridge and there had Jane 1691, John 1693, Thomas 1696.

REFERENCES:—Paige's Hist. Cambridge, Mass., 489; N. E. Hist. and Gen. Reg. V, 174; Hayward's Hist. Hancock, 353.

BONNETT. Bolton's Hist. Westchester County, N. Y., 489.

BONNYCASTLE. Slaughter's St. Mark's.
BONSALL. Smith's Del. Co., Pa., 447.
BONTECON. Bontecon Gen.; Campbell Gen. 119.
BONTHYON. Bonthyon Gen.; Folsim's Hist. Saco,
Me., 113; N. E. Hist. and Gen. Reg. XXXVIII.
BOODEN. Bangor Hist. Mag. IV. 215.
BOODEY. Caverley's Boody Gen.; Hayward's Hist.
Gilsum, N. H., 273.
BOOGE, Hinman's Conn. Settlers, 291; Field's Hist.
Haddam, Conn., 47; N. Y. Gen. and Biog. Rec. III., 62;
Patterson's Booge Gen.
BOOKER. Wheeler's Hist. Brunswick, 830.
BOOM. Munsell's Albany Coll. IV., 101.
BOOMER. Austin's R. I. Gen. Dict. 23; Joslin's Hist.
Poultney, Vt., 219.
BOONE. Jenkin's Hist. Gwynedd, Pa., 325; Slaugh-
ter's St. Mark's, Va., III., 17, 21; Amer. Ancestry, V., 72.
BOOREM. Salter's Hist. Monmouth, N. J., 10.
BOORN. Bassett's Richmond, 322.
BOOSY:—JAMES BOOSY, of Wethersfield, 1635, by
wife Alice had Joseph, born, perhaps, before he settled at
Wethersfield; Mary 1635, Hannah, Sarah, James 1646.
He was a representative to the General Court from 1639
till his death 1649.
   REFERENCES:—Hinman's Conn. Settler's, 292; Sav-
age's Gen. Dict. vol. I., 211.
BOOTFISH or BODFISH:—ROBERT BOOTFISH, of
Lynn, Mas., was made freeman May 6, 1655. He removed
to Sandwich, Mass., 1637, and died about 1651. Had Jo-
seph and probably others. Savage's Gen. Dict. vol. I., 211.
BOOTH:—JOHN BOOTH, of Scituate, Mass., 1656, had
Joseph 1659, John, Benjamin, Abraham 1671, Eliza,
Mary, Grace, Judith.
   MICHAEL BOOTH, of Roxbury, Mass., had Martha
1688.
   RICHARD BOOTH, of Stratford, Conn., 1640, married
a sister of the first Joseph Hawley, and had Elizabeth
1641, Ann, Ephraim 1648, Ebenezer, John, Joseph 1656,
Bertha, Joanna. He was selectman 1669, and in freeman's
list of the same year he testified that he was 80 years old
in 1687.
   ROBERT BOOTH, of Exeter, 1645, removed to Saco,
1653, or earlier, of which town he was a representative
1659. He died 1692. aged 68. He was some years the
preacher. He married Deborah——, and had Simon,
Robert. Mary Pennewell, Elinor, Martha, Rebecca, Robert.
   SIMEON BOOTH, of Fairfield, or perhaps Hartford,
married January 5, 1664, Rebecca, daughter of Daniel
Frost, who died Dec. 25, 1688. He removed to Enfield,
of which he was an early settler. He had William 1664,
Zachariah 1666, Elizabeth and Mary.
   REFERENCES:—CONNECTICUT. Sharpe's Hist. Seymour 156; Stile's Hist. Windsor, vol. II, page 111; Or-
cutt's Hist. Stratford 1156: Orcutt's Hist New Milford
802; Hinman's Conn. Settlers. 203; Cothren's Ancient
Woodbury 508, 1474; Andrew's Hist. New Britain 126,
182.
   OTHER PUBLICATIONS:—Deane's Hist. Scituate, Mass.,
222; Long Meadow. Mass., Centen. (1883) 14; Wetmore
Gen. 112; Trubee Gen. 100: Pierce's (E. W.) Contribu-
tions 26; Goode Gen. 50 e; Dwight's Life of E. G. Booth;
Ames' Ancestry VI. 48, 150, IX. 75; N. E. Hist. and Gen.
Reg. XXXII., 176: Savage's Gen. Dict. vol. I. 212; Booth
Assoc. Report (1869): Booth Gen.
   BOOTHBY:—Lapham's Hist. Norway, Me., 469;
Dearborn's Parsonfield 366; Ridlon's Saco Valley. Me.,
Settlements and Families 469.
   BOOTMAN, Jeremiah, of Salem, Mass., married Oct.

8, 1659, Esther Lambert, and had Mary 1660, Jeremy
1662, Mather, Martha 1655. Savage's Gen. Dict. vol. I.
212.
   BORDEN:—RICHARD BORDEN (or Burden) emigrant
to Rhode Island 1638, died 1671. Settled at Portsmouth.
He was Assistant 1653-54; General Treasurer 1654; Commissioner 1654, '56, '57; Deputy to General Assembly
1667-70. Later obtained a patent of land in New Jersey,
which John Throckmorton, Richard Stout, Obadiah
Holmes, Robert Carr, James Ashton, John Tilton and
Samuel Spicer, all from Rhode Island. By his wife Joan
he had Matthew, born May 1638—"The first English child
born in Rhode Island;" John 1640, Joseph 1643, Sarah,
Samuel 1645, Benjamin 1649, Annie 1654.
   JOHN BORDEN came from Kent, Eng., in the Elizabeth and Ann in 1635, aged 28, with wife Jane and children, Matthew, 5, and Elizabeth, 3; but it is not known
where he settled. The name is found in Southampton in
1650 and in 1660 in Lynn, Conn.
   THOMAS BORDEN, of Providence, R. I., 1663,
married June 20, 1664, Mary, daughter of William Harris, of the same, and had Mary, 1664, Dinah, Wiliam,
1668, Joseph, 1669, Mercy, Experience, Meribah, 1676.
   REFERENCES:—Swift's Barnstable Families, Mass., Vol
I, 64; Peck and Earll's Fall River, Mass., 224; Fowler's
Sketch of Fall River, Mass; Salter's Hist. Monmouth
County, N. J., XI.; Austin's R. I. Gen. Dic., 23; Davis
Gen. 80; Walker Family, 150; Savage's Gen. Dict.
Vol. I, 13; Amer. Ancestry, III, 136; IX, 241.
   BORDLEY:—Thomas Family of Maryland, 38; Han-
son's Old Kent. Md., 81; Bordley Gen.
   BORDMANN:—Thomas Bordman, of Ipswich, was
made freeman in 1635; representative, 1636; removed to
Barnstable, and there married. March 3, 1645, Hannah,
daughter of Anthony Anable. Had Hannah, 1646; Thom-
as, 1648; Samuel, 1651; Desiré, Mary, Mehitable, Tristan,
1661. Savage's Gen. Dic. vol. I, 213.
   BOREEL. Green's Todd Gen.
   BOREL:—Samuel Borel, of Boston, by wife Matilda
had Deborah, bap. 1st Feb., 1691; Samuel, 1693; Catharine, Michael, 1699; John, Isabella, Samuel again, Nathaniel, 1711. Savage's Gen. Dic. vol. I, 213.
   BOREMAN or BARDMAN:—Samuel Bardman of
Ipswich, Mass., 1639, removed probably to Wethersfield,
with son Isaac, born 1642; had there Mary, 1644; Samuel,
1648; Joseph, John, Sarah, Daniel, Jonathan, 1661; Na-
thaniel, 1660; Martha, 1666. Savage's Gen. Dic. vol. I,
213; Hammett Papers, 30.
   BORIGHT. Amer. Ancestry, II, 14.
   BORLAND. Wyman's Charlestown, Mass., Gens. I,
99; Paige's Hist. Cambridge, Mass., 493; Vinton's Giles
Fam. 335; Colt's Gen. 60: Cushman's Sheepscott, 358.
   BORMAN. Hinman's Conn. Settlers, 265.
   BOROUGHS. Hubbard's Hist. Stanstead, 314.
   BOROUGH. Clement's Newtown, N. J.
   BORTHWICK:—James Borthwick of Rensselaerville
came to America in 1773. He was a farmer and took part
in the Revolution. He was the son of Richard of Mussel-
burgh, Scotland. He, James, married Margaret Byers
and had George.
   BORTLE:—Philip Bortle, of Taghkanick, born 1750,
died 1844; married Helen Van Deusen of Claverack. See
American Ancestry II, 153.
   BORTON. Cregar's Haine's Ances. 20.
   BOS. Munsell's Albany Collect. IV, 101.
   BOSS. Austin's R. I. Gen. Dic. 24; R. I. Hist. Mag.
VII, 59.
   BOSSON. Pickering Gen.
   BOSTON. Guild's Stiles Gen. 38.

BOSTWICK:—Arthur Bostwick came from County Chester, Eng., according to tradition, with son John to Stratford and settled there before 1650. By former wife he had John and other children, among them one said to be Arthur and another, Zachariah.

REFERENCES:—Orcutt's Hist. Stratford, Conn. 1161; Orcutt's Hist. New Milford, Conn., 659; Hinman's Conn. Settlers, 297; Winsor's Hist. Duxbury, Mass., 229; Bostwick Gen. (1851); Ruggles' Gen.; Amer. Ancestry II, 14; Phenix Whitney Family of Conn, vol. I, 153; Savage's Gen. vol. I, 215.

BOSWELL:—Samuel Boswell was of Bedford 1663 and of Rowley. See Hinman's Conn. Settlers, 301.

BOSWORTH:— Benjamin Bosworth of Hingham 1635, came perhaps in the Elizabeth Dorcas with Henry Sewall and sons Jonathan and Nathaniel.

JOSEPH BOSWORTH, of Hull, perhaps youngest brother of Benjamin, was at Rehoboth, Mass., and there had Joseph born, 1679, and Elizabeth, 1681. He was made freeman in 1680.

ZACHEUS or ZACHARIAH · BOSWORTH was in Boston 1630; probably came in the fleet with Winthrop; was made freeman May 25, 1636. He was important enough to be disarmed Nov. 1637; died 28 July, 1655. By his wife Ann he had daughters Restored, 1638; Elizabeth, 1640; Samuel, 1643; Sarah, who died July, 1645, having been baptized the 27th of July at three days old.

REFERENCES:—Hine's Lebanon, Conn., Hist. Address, 1880; Davis' Landmarks of Plymouth, Mass., 29; Hammatt Papers, Ipswich. Mass., 31; Mitchell's Hist. Bridgewater, Mass., 119; Eaton's Annals Warren, Me., 509; Norton's Hist. Fitzwilliam, N. H., 482; Joslin's Hist Poultney, Vt., 219; Dennysville, Me., Centen., 102; Child Gen. 125; Savage's Gen. Dic. I, 215.

BOTHWELL. Temple's Hist. North Brookfield, Mass., 534; Amer. Ancestry, vol. I, 9.

BOTOLPH. Stiles' Windsor, Conn., II, 114.

BOTSFORD:—HENRY BOTSFORD, of Milford, 1639, had by wife Elizabeth, who joined the church 1640, Elanthan, 1641; Elizabeth and Mary, probably twins, May 21, 1643; Hannah, 1645; Esther, 1647; Ruth, 1649.

REFERENCES:—Cleveland's Yates County, N. Y., 122; Sedgwick's Hist. Sharon, Conn., 65; Savage's Gen. Dic I, 217.

BOTTAM. Walworth's Hyde Gen., 368.

BOTTS. Austin's Allied Families, 39; Goode Gen. 367, 424.

BOTTUM:—DANIEL BOTTOM, of Norwich, Conn.; an early settler. He was surveyor of the town 1702, member of the First Cong. Church 1718. He married at Norwich, Feb 15, 1692, Elizabeth Lamb. See Amer. Ancestry VI, 96.

BOUCHER. Amer. Ancestry, II., 14.

BONDE. See Barber's Atlee Gen. 3.

BOUDINOL. Alden's Epitaphs. vol. I, 101.

BOUGHEY. N. E. Hist. and Gen. Reg. V., 307. See Benton.

BOUGHTON:—NICHOLAS BOUGHTON, Baron Montague de Naton of France, was born 1580, and had three sons, Herard, John and Noel.

JOHN BROUGHTON, of Norwalk, Conn., son of Nicholas, fled from France during the Huguenot persecution in England and sailed for Boston on the ship Assurance, arriving in December, 1635, and afterwards settled in Norwalk. He married first Joan Turney, 1656; second Abagail Maron; third, in 1673, Mrs. Mary Stevenson, and left among other children a son Eliazer.

REFERENCES:—Bouton and Boughton Gen. (1890), 684

pages; Leavenworth Gen. 190; Smith Gen. (1870), Amer. Ancestry IV., 221; VI., 194, 201.

JOHN BOUTON (same ancestry as above) of Norwalk, Conn., born in France, 1615, died in Danbury, 1704-5. He was an influential citizen, a representative to the General Court of Conn. He married June 1, 1656,. Abagail, daughter of Matthew Marvin of London, Eng., and had John and other children.

REFERENCES:—Bouton Gen. (1886) (1890) page 68; Hall's Records of Norwalk, Conn., 182, 306; Hinman's Conn. Settlers, 304; Huntington's Stamford, Conn,, 16; Sedgwick's Hist. Sharon, Conn., 66; Amer. Ancestry, vol. I, 9; vol VIII, 198; Savage's Gen. Dic. vol. I, 220.

BOUTON. Newport Hist. Mag. IV, 138.

BOUKER. Ward's Hist. Shrewsbury, 225.

BOULDIN. See Richmond, Va., Standard III, 14, 16, 45; Hayden's Virginia Gens, 312; Goode Gen. 121, 195.

BOULTER. Nathaniel, of Hampton, Mass., 1644, died 14 March, 1693; by wife Grace had Mary, Nathaniel, Hannah, Elizabeth, 1669, John, 1672.

THOMAS BOULTER, of Weymouth, Mass., by his wife Experience had Hannah, 1662; and by wife Hannah had Experience 1672, and Ebenezer. He was one of the first projectors of settlement of Mendon, Mass.. 1660.

REFERENCES:—Dow's Hist. Hampton, N. H., 612; Savage's Gen. Dic. vol. I, 217.

BOULTON. See BOLTON. Nicholas Boulton, of Dorchester. Mass., 1643, was made freeman 1644. By wife Elizabeth had Thankful 1649. John, Elizabeth.

REFERENCES:—Savage's Gen. Dic vol I., 218; N. E. Gen. Reg., XXXVIII, 199.

BOUND, William, of Salem, Mass., was made freeman 1637. He had by wife Ann, James 1636. Andrew 1638, Philip 1640. He married 2d 1669 Mary Haverlad. Savage's Gen. Dict. vol. I. 218.

BOURKE:—See Bullach Gen.

BOURMAN:—Swift's Barnstable, Mass., vol. I. 80.

BOURN:—Read's Hist. of Swanzy, N. H., 296. Bourne Gen.

BOULTES:—Saco Valley, Me., Settlements 516.

BOURNE, Jared or Gerald, of Boston, 1630, was made freeman 1635. He had John, born 1643. He resided in what is now Brookline, and was constable there in 1654. He had there Jarat or Jared 1651.

NEHEMIAH BOURNE, of Charleston, 1638, shipbuilder, removed to Boston 1640; made freeman 1641; went to England in 1644, and served in the army of the Parliament as Major Rainsborough's regulars. By wife Hannah he had Nehemiah 1640, Hannah 1641.

RICHARD BOURNE, of Lynn, 1637, removed to Sandwich, Mass., and was the first instructor of the Indians at Mashpee, beginning in 1658; he was ordained by Eliot and Collen. He married, July, 1677, Ruth Winslow,widow of Jonathan, daughter of William Sargent, and had Job, Elisha, 1641, and Shearjashub 1643. He died 1682.

THOMAS BOURNE, of Marshfield. Mass., came from Co. Kent, Eng.; made foreman at Plymouth 1637. He was a man of substance and repute. By wife Elizabeth who died in 1660. aged 70, he had Elizabeth, John and Martha, who married 1st John Bradford, son of the Governor, 2d Thomas Tracy, of Norwich, Conn. He had also Elizabeth, who married 9 Dec., 1638, Robert Waterman. Ann, Margaret, who married Josiah Winslow, brother of Gov. Edward; and Lydia, married Nathaniel Tilden.

REFERENCES: — Winsor's Hist. Duxbury, Mass.. 229; Swift's Barnstable, Mass., Families vol. I. 104, 140; Freeman's Hist. Cape Cod vol. I. 697, II. 128; Whitman Gen. 138; Tanner Gen. 22; Spooner's Memorial of W. Spooner 117; Amer. Ancestry V. 141; Savage's Gen.

Dict. vol. I. 218; N. E. Hist. and Gen. Reg. XIV. 82; XXVII. 26, XXVIII 1.

BOUTELL:—James Boutell emigrated to New England in 1632, and settled in Salem and Lynn, Mass., and afterwards in Reading. The name, which was originally Bontville, and so appears on the roll of Battle Abbey, and the family is of Norman descent. The termination of the name was changed at a later date and became Bontwell. James Boutell married Alice ————, and had a son John, born at Reading 1645, who served in the Narragansett war.

BOUTELL, BOUTWELL:—John Boutwell, of Cambridge, Mass., by wife Margaret had Mary, born Oct. 26, 1646, and John, died 1674.

James Boutwell of Salem and Lynn, Mass., 1635, was made freeman 14 March, 1639, died 1651. In his will of 22 Aug., 1651, he names wife Alice, son James and John and Sarah.

REFERENCES:—Benedict's His. Sutton, Mass., 591; Hayward's His. Hancock, N. H., 359; Am. Ances. V, 150; Secomb's His. Amherst, N. H., 509. For Boutwell see Runnell's His. Sanbornton, N. H., II, 44; Norton's His. Fitzwilliam, N. H., 483; Hayward's His. Hancock, N. H., 373; Cochran's His. Antrim, N. H., 366; Eaton's His. Reading, Mass., 47; Barry's His. Framingham, Mass., 188; Savage's Gen. Dic. vol. I, 219.

BOUTINNEAU, Stephen, of Boston, a Huguenot merchant came from La Rochelle in 1686, accompanied by his friend Baudoin, 1690, to Boston and married 22 Aug., 1708, Mary, and had six daughters and four sons, among whom were Anna, James 1711, John 1713, Mary 1715, Elizabeth, Mary, Stephen 1721, Peter, Thomas, Isaac. Savage's Gen. Dic. vol. I, 218; N. E. His. and Gen. Reg. VIII. 24.

BOVIE. See Munsell's Albany Coll. IV, 101; Pearson's Schenectady, N. Y., 17.

BOW. See Hinman's Conn. Settlers, 301.

BOWDEN. Howell's Southampton, 205.

BOWDITCH. William Bowditch, of Salem, 1639 probably from Devonshire, had a grant of land in 1643 By wife, Sarah, he had Nathaniel, 1643; but left only one child, Wiliam, probably older, born in England. His only surviving child, William, born Sept. 1663, was eminent at Salem for usefulness. He married 30 Aug., 1668, Mary, daughter of Thomas Gardner, and had Ebenezer 1703 His son Hobakuk was father of Nathaniel, the great American astronomer.

REFERENCES:—Mitchell's His. Bridgewater, Mass., 119; Amer. Ancestry IV, 94; Savage's Gen. Dic. vol. I 220.

BOWDOIN:—Pierre or Peter Bowdoin had been a physician at La Rochelle before the revocation of the Edict of Nantes, on which he fled forthwith to Ireland 1685. He came the next year to Casco with wife, Elizabeth, together with two sons, John, who settled in Virginia, and James, and two daughters. Two years later he, with several Huguenots, removed to Boston. He was a prosperous merchant, died 1706.

REFERENCES:—Whitmore's Temple and Bowdoin Family; Winthop's Address at Bowdoin College; Wyman's Charlestown Gens.; Gens., Hyde's Address at Ware Mass., 53; Bridgman's Granary Epitaphs I; Heraldie Journal. vol. II. 136; Me. His. Soc. Col., vol. I, 185; Mass His. Coll. 3rd series II, 49; Bowdoin Gen. (1887) (1894); Meade's Old Churches, Va., vol. I, 259; N. E His. and Gen. Reg. VIII, 247; X, 79; XI, 43; Savage's Gen. Dic. vol. I, 221.

BOWE:—Alexander Bowe, of Charlestown, removed to Middletown 1678. By wife, Sarah, he had Samuel, 1660, Sarah, Mary, Rebecca, Ann.

REFERENCES:—Stiles' His. Windsor, Conn., II, 114; Savage's Gen. Dic. vol. I, 222.

BOWEN:—Griffith Bowen, 1638, from Llangenydd, Glamorganshire, was made freeman May 22, 1639. By wife, Margaret, he had Esther 1639, Abagail 1641, Peniel 1644, Henry. He was some years at Roxbury, Mass., but went home and lived in London 1670.

OBADIAH BOWEN, of Sevanzey, representative 1681, had been of Rehoboth, Mass., 1657. He was an active member of the Baptist communion. He had Obadiah and Isaac.

THOMAS BOWEN, of Salem, 1648, was of New London, Conn., 1657. He removed to Rehoboth, Mass., where he died 1663. In his will he names son Richard and brother Obadiah.

REFERENCES.

MASSACHUSETTS.—Barry's His. Framingham, 190; Wyman's Charlestown Gens. vol. I, 101.

NEW HAMPSHIRE.—Bassett's His. of Richmond, 325; Saunderson's Charlestown, 289.

OTHER PUBLICATIONS:—Austin's Ancestral Dictionary 7; Shroud's Fenwick Colony, N. J., 517; Young's His. Wayne County, Ind., 285; Power's His. Sangamon County, Ill., 126; Hinman's Conn. Settlers, 281; Hughes and Allied Families, 185; Johnson Gen. 16; Montague Gen. 518; Davis Gen. 157; Cincinnati Ohio Criterion (1888) Ill., 750; Chandler Gen. 312; Adams' Fairhaven, Vt., 283; Amer. Ancestry VIII, 97, 114; Savage's Gen. Dic. vol. I, 222; N. E. His. and Gen. Reg. XLVII, 458; Bowen Gen. by E. C. Bowen.

BOWER. Stiles' His. Windsor II, 115; Sharpe's His. Seymour, Conn., 186; Howell's His. Southampton, 423; Kilbourne's Bower Family (1856).

BOWERS:—George Bowers, of Plymouth 1639, removed to Cambridge, where his wife, Barbara, died 25 March, 1644; he married 2nd, April 15, 1649, Eliza Worthington. He had issue Jerathmeel, born May, 1650; Benannel. 1649; Patience, Silence and, perhaps, Matthew.

REFERENCES.

MASSACHUSETTS.—Wyman's Charlestown Gens. vol. I, 102; Paige's His. Cambridge, 493; Hazen's His. Billerica, 14; Butler's His. Groton, 389, 469.

NEW HAMPSHIRE.—Hayward's His. Hancock, 373; Merrell's His. Ackworth, 189; Runnel's His. Sanbornton, II, 46; Smith's His. Petersborough, 21; Stearn's His. Rindge, 451.

OTHER PUBLICATIONS.—Bangor (Me.) His. Mag. II, 119; Eaton's His. Thomaston, Me., 152; Hinman's Conn. Settlers, 302; Watson's Johnson and other Families (1872); Amer. Ancestry IX, 190; Savage's Gen. Dic. vol. I, 223.

BOWES. Paige's His. Cambridge, Mass., 494; Heraldie Journal vol. I, 109; N. E. His. and Gen. Reg. X, 81, 129.

BOWERMAN. Freeman's His. Cape Cod, 151; Swift's Barnstable, Mass., Families, vol. I, 80; Spooner Gen. vol. I, 60, 367; N. E. His. and Gen. Reg. XXXI, 281.

BOWIE. Slaughter's St. Mark's, 149; Thomas Family of Md., 391.

BOWKER:—Benjamin Bowker, of Scituate, Mass., born there Feb. 14, 1739, married 1st, Hannah Sparrowhawk, and had Benjamin, Elisha, Hannah, Esther and Joel; he married 2nd, Mrs. Anna Sylvester, and had Polly, Joshua, Charlotte and (dau) Silvester.

REFERENCES.

MASSACHUSETTS.—Ballou's His. Milford, 588; Barry's His. Hanover, 259; Deane's His. Scituate, 223; Hudson's His. Marlboro, 330; Temple' His. North Brookfield, 534, OTHER PUBLICATIONS.—Saunder's His. Charlestown, N. H., 289; Norton's His. Fitzwilliam, N. H., Lapham's His. Paris, Me., 529, Salter's His. Monmouth Co., N. J., XI; Machias, Me., Cent., 155; Amer. Ancestry IV, 152.

BOWLES:—John Bowles, of Roxbury, Mass. was made freeman 1640. He was a ruling elder in the church in 1680. He married 1st Dorothy; married 2d, April 2, 1650, Elizabeth, daughter of Isaac Heath, and had Elizabeth 1651, Isaac 1652, John 1653, Mary 1655.

REFERENCES:—Bangor (Me.) His. Mag. V, 28; Bowles Gen. (1851); Wyman's Charlestown, Mass., Gens. vol. I, 103; Hinman's Conn. Settlers, 282; Thornton's Bowles Family (1854); Thomas Gen. 39; N. E. His. and Gen. Reg. II, 192; N. E. Gen. Rec. IV, 24; Savage's Gen. Dic. vol. I, 224.

BOWLING. Power's His. Sangamon County, Ill. 126.

BOWMAN:—Nathaniel Bowman, of Watertown. Mass., came probably in the fleet with Winthrop 1630; made freeman that year. By wife, Ann, he had Francis, Mary, Joanna, Nathaniel 1641, Benjamin.

REFERENCES.

MASSACHUSETTS.—Stearn's His. Ashburnham, 620; Wyman's Charlestown, Gens. vol. I, 103; Pierce's His. Grafton, 462; Paige's His. Cambridge, 404; Hudson's His. Lexington, 17; Hazen's His. Bellerica, 16; Cutter's His. Arlington, 195; Bond's His. of Watertown, 689.
NEW HAMPSHIRE.—Coggswell's His. of Henniker, 464; Saunderson's His. Charlestown, 290; Wheeler's His. of Newport, 306.
OTHER PUBLICATIONS.—Hinman's Conn. Settler. 303; North's His. of Augusta, Me., 807; Ruttenber's His. of Orange, N. Y., 390; Hayden's Memorial of Ann E. Sweitzer; Green's Kentucky Families; Savage's Dic vol. I, 224; Bowman Gen. (1885); Amer. Ancestry, X, 94

BOWNE:—William Bowne came from Massachusetts with Lady Deborah Moody and others, who settled in Salem, Mass. in 1637. Removed to Gravesend, L. I., in 1643, of which town he was magistrate in 1651-'55, '57. '61. He was the first patentee of Middletown, N. J., to which place he and his sons removed. He died there 1677 Issue: John, known as "Capt. Bowne," James and Andrew, Deputy Governor of East Jersey 1699; Governor, 1701.

REFERENCES:—Whitehead's His. of East Jersey; Salter's His. of Monmouth County, N. J.; Old Times in Old Monmouth; Early Settlers of Kings County, N. Y., p. 44-5; Bergen Family p. 501; Thompson's His. Long Island, 385; Bergen's His. of Kings County, N. Y., 441; Bunker's L. I. Genealogies, 184; Thomas Family of Md. 40; N. E. His. and Gen. Reg. XXV, 294; N. Y. Gen. and Biog. Rec. IV, 24.

BOWYER. Sharp's His. Seymour, Conn., 185.
BOWZER. Paige Gen., 163.
BOYES or BOYCE:—Joseph Boyce, of Salem, Mass. 1639, was made freeman 1642. He had issue Esther 1641 Elizabeth 1642, Joseph 1644. Benjamin 1647.

Samuel Boyce, of Saybrook Co., married Lydia, daughter of Willian Beamond, and had Joseph, Samuel 1673, Michael.

REFERENCES:—Norton's His. Fitzwilliam. N. H., 487; Hayward's His. of Hancock, N. H., 382; Bassett's His. of Richmond, 332; Essex, Mass., His. Coll. XIX, 308;

Hemenway's, Vt., Gaz., IV, 179; Williams' His. Danby, Vt., III, 12; Goode Gen. 301; Montague Gen. 210; Savage's Gen. Dic. vol. I, 225.

BOYD:—James Boyd, of Newburyport, Mass., born at Kilmarnock, Scotland, May 3, 1732; died at Boston, Mass., Sep. 30, 1798; came to America 1756, with a grant from King George II. of several thousand acres of land in St. Andrews, New Brunswick; this parchment with the seal of George II. is still in the family; the lands were confiscated during the Revolutionary war. He built the Kelmarnock House at St. Andrew, where he resided in the summer, and at Newburyport in the winter. He was the son of Robert, son of William, 9th Lord Boyd of Kilmarnock, Scotland, a direct descendant from the Kings of Scotland, through Lord Robert Boyd, who was the regent of Scotland during the minority of James III, his son. James Boyd, the emigrant, married Aug. 11, 1757, Susanna Coffin, and had Robert, of Portland, Me., and other children.

REFERENCES.

MASSACHUSETTS.—Temple's His. North Brookfield, 534; Jameson's His. Medway, 456.
OTHER PUBLICATIONS.—Boyd's Annals of Winchester, Conn., 312; Boyd Gen. (1884); Boyd's His. Consensus, N. Y., 144; Cleveland's His. Yates County, N. Y., 299, 505; Baird's His. of Rye, N. Y., 397; Brewster's His. of Portsmouth, N. H., II, 166; Chase's His. of Chester, N. H., 475; Cochran's His. of Antrim, N. H., 370; Clyde's Irish Settlement, Pa., 18; Egle's Penn Gens., 97; Futhey's Chester County, Pa., 485; Meginness' West Branch, Pa., 34; Bangor, (Me.) His. Mag., vol. I, 113; Power's His. Sangamon County, Ill., 127; Richmond ,Va., Standard III, 27, 43; Young's His. Wayne County, Ind., 227, 238; Smith Gen. 135;Goode Gen. 142; Amer. Ancestry III, 74; VI, 30, 174.

BOYDEN:—Thomas Boyden, of Watertown, came in the Francis from Ipswich, 1634, aged 21; made freeman 1647. By wife Frances he had Thomas 1639, Mary 1641, Rebecca, Nathaniel, 1650. He removed to Boston 1651, and had Jonathan there 1652, and Sarah 1654.

REFERENCES:—Wall's Remin. of Worcester, Mass., 353; Bond's His. of Watertown, Mass., 90; Hill's Dedham, Mass., Records; Hatch's His. of Industry, Me., 516; Hemenway's Vermont Gaz., V, 37; Amer. Ancestry, IX, 142; Savage's Gen. Dic., vol. I, 225; Boyden Gen. (1879).

BOYER. Power's His. Sangamon Co., Ill., 128.
BOYKETT:—Jarvis Boykett, of New Haven, Conn., a carpenter, came first to Charlestown, Mass., with one servant in 1635-6, from Charington in Kent. He removed in 1639 to New Haven and then had Nathaniel 1641, Bethia 1643, Sarah 1646. See Savage's Gen. Dic., vol. I, 226.

BOYKIN. Baptist Encyclopedia.
BOYLE. Littell's Passaic Valley, 53.
BOYLES. Eaton's His. Thomaston, Me., 153; Hayward's His. Hancock, N. H., 382.
BOYLSTON:—Thomas Boylston, son of Thomas, perhaps of London, who was son of Henry, of Litchfield, came in the Defense from London 1635, aged 20. By wife Sarah he had Elizabeth 1640, Sarah, Thomas 1645. He died 1653. His father was a clothworker of London, as described in the deed of house and ground to his agent. Sep. 1639, from Gregory Slone.

REFERENCES:—Bond's His. Watertown, Mass., 702; Wyman's Charlestown, Mass., Gens., vol. I, 105; Vinton Memorial 308; Savage's Gen. Dic. vol. I. 226; N. E. His. and Gen. Reg. VII, 145, 351.

BOYNTON:—William Boynton, of Rowley, was made

freeman May 13, 1640, said to have been born 1605. By wife Eliza, he had sons Caleb and Joshua. He bought in 1657, at Newbury, a farm of John Clark; his wife died at Salisbury, 1687.

REFERENCES.

MASSACHUSETTS.—Temple's His. North Brookfield 535; Marvin's His. Winchenden, 448; Hodgman's His. Westford, 439; Butler's His. Groton, 469; Ballou's His Milford, 502; Emery's His. Newbury, 321; Essex Int. His. Coll. XX, 63.
NEW HAMPSHIRE.—Blood's His. of Temple, 206; Hayward's His. Hancock, 383; Little's His. of Warren, 554; Livermore His. Wilton, 324; Morrison's His. Windham, 347; Norton's His. Fitzwilliam, 488; Runnell's His. Sanbornton II, 479; Secomb's His. Amherst, 514; Smith's His. Petersborough, 22; Worcester's His. Hollis, 367
OTHER PUBLICATIONS.—Bedford N. H. Centen. 292; Burton, Me., Centen. 175; Dwight's Strong Gen. 429; Eaton's His. Thomaston, Me., 153; Hubbard's His. Stanstead, Can., 187; Machias, Me., Centen., 155; Roe's Sketches of Rose, N. Y., 144; Amer. Ancestry, II, 15, VI, 172; Savage's Gen. Dic. vol. I, 226; Boynton Gen. (1884) Saco Valley, Me., Settlements, 518.

BRABROOK:—John Brabrook, of Watertown, by wife Elizabeth, had Elizabeth 1640, John 1642, Thomas 1643. He was first at Hampton, 1640, removed to Newbury, where lived his uncle, Henry Short, and died there June 28, 1662. Savage's Gen. Dic. vol. I, 226.

BRACE. Tuttle Family of Conn., 89; Orcutt's His. of Torrington, Conn., 656; Hinman's Conn. Settlers, 307; Loomis Gen. Female Branches, 742; Leavenworth Gen. 65; Kellogg's White Descendants, 66; Pompey, N. Y., Reunion, 263.

BRACY or BRACIE:—John Bracy, of Wethersfield, Conn., 1647, was first of New Haven, where he with the prefix of respect first settled in 1644, and had there Susanna and John baptized Sep. 1647. He removed to Wethersfield, where his mother, Phebe Martin; whose father, William Bisby, of London, had bought an estate for her, and her children by former husband. Other children of Bracy, by same Phebe, were Thomas, probably a Stephen Constant, Phebe.
STEPHEN BRACY, of Swanzey, Mass., 1669, removed to Hartford, Conn., where he died 1692, leaving Stephen, John, Henry, besides daughters Elishaba, Phebe, Elizabeth and Ann.
REFERENCES:—Milliken's Norraguagus, 15; Savage's Gen. Dic. vol. I, 227.

BRACKENBURY:—John Brackenbury, of Charlestown and Boston, married July 17, 1655, Amie or Emma, daughter of John Anderson, and had John born 1657, who lived at Charlestown, Mass., where his wife Dorcas died June 30, 1682, aged 25. He had enlisted 1676 in the company of the brave Capt. Turner, but was discharged before marching far.
RICHARD BRACKENBURY, of Salem, Mass., came in the Abigail with Gov. Endicott, arriving Sep. 5, 1628, made freeman 1634. He was one of the founders of the church at Beverly. He died in 1685, aged 83. By wife Ellen he had Hannah 1651 and Miles.
REFERENCES:—Wyman's Charlestown, Mass., Gens vol. I, 108; Malden, Mass., Centen. 239; Savage's Gen Dic. vol. I, 228; N. E. His. and Gen. Reg. XLVI, 178.

BRACKETT:—Peter Brackett, of Braintree, Mass., was made freeman May 10, 1643. He represented his town at the General Court, in 1644, and often after that and also the town of Scarborough in 1673-4. He was a

deacon of the church. By first wife Priscilla, he had Martha, Peter, John, 1641, Joseph 1642, and probably other children.
RICHARD BRACKETT, of Boston, Mass., 1652, probably brother of the first Peter, was made freeman May 25, 1636. He was dismissed, with wife Alice, to Braintree church, Dec. 5, 1641; ordained deacon of the church, July 21, 1642; was town clerk many years and third captain of the town. He died March 5, 1691, aged 80 years. By wife Alice, who died 1690, aged 76, he had Hannah 1635, Peter and John, perhaps twins, both baptized May 7, 1637; Rachel 1639, Mary 1642, James and Josiah July 8, 1662, Sarah.
THOMAS BRACKETT, of Salem, Mass., punished for attendance at Quaker worship, 1658 had Thomas baptized 7 Dec., 1645, Mary 1649, Joseph 1651, Lydia.
ANTHONY BRACKETT, son of Anthony of Portsmouth, 1640, was of Falmouth 1662. He married Ann, daughter of Michael Milton. He was lieutenant and captain in the war, and was finally killed at his house 21 Sep. 1689. His son Anthony was also lieutenant and captain in Indian hostilities.

REFERENCES.

MASSACHUSETTS.—Hazen's His. Billerica, 17; Gibb's His. Blanford, 65; Paige's His. Cambridge, 496; Hill's Dedham Records.
MAINE.—Dearborn's His. Parsonfield, 451; Eaton's Annals of Warren, 509; Johnson's His. Bristol, 384; Ridlon's Harrison, Me., Settlers, 34.
NEW HAMPSHIRE.—Cochran's His. of Antrim, 376; Dow's His. of Hampton, 614; Smith's His. of Petersborough, 23.
OTHER PUBLICATIONS.—Austin's Allied Families, R. I. 40; Bass' His. Braintree, Vt., 120; Brackett Gen. (1860); Chapman's Wells Gen. 129; Hughes and Allied Families, 235; Odiorne Gen.; Richardson Gen.; Smith and Deane's Journal, 365; Wentworth Gen. vol. I, 461; Savage's Gen. Dic. vol. I, 228; Amer. Ancestry IX, 242; Saco Valley, (Me.), Settlements and Families, 520.

BRADBROOK. Savage's Gen. Dic. vol. I, 229.

BRADBURY. Thomas Bradbury, of Salisbury, an original proprietor, probably came from Ipswich, Mass., was made freeman May 13, 1640; was a representative to the General Court 1651, and six years more; was Recorder for the county of Norfolk, when New Hampshire was a part of Massachusetts. His wife Mary, after 56 years of exemplary life, was accused of witchcraft in the dark hours of 1692, but her age was not sufficient to condemn her. She was acquitted and died 20 Dec., 1700. The children were Wymond born 1637, Judith 1638, Thomas 1640, Mary 1642, Jane 1645, Jacob 1647, William 1649, Elizabeth 1651, John 1654, Ann 1656, Jabez 1658.

REFERENCES.

MAINE.—Corliss' North Yarmouth Mag. 718; Eaton's His. of Thomaston, 154; Goodwin's His. of Baxter, 384; Hatch's His. of Industry, 520; Lapham's His. of Norway, 470; Lapham's His. of Paris, 531; North's His. of Augusta, 810; Baxter, Me., Centen. 231.
OTHER PUBLICATIONS.—Wyman's Charlestown, Mass., Gens. vol. I, 109; Worcester's His. Hollis, N. H., 368; Young's His. Wayne Co., Ind., 239; Dawson's His. Mag. (1858) 214; Cutis Gen. 193; Bradbury Gen. 1890; Amer. Ancestry, III, 132; IV, 39; VIII, 216; N. E. His. and Gen. Reg. XXIII, 262; Savage's Gen. Dic. vol. I, 229.

BRADFORD:—Governor William Bradford, of the Mayflower, was the progenitor of nearly, if not quite, all the Bradfords of New England. No connection direct has been traced between him and William Bradford, the Quaker printer of Philadelphia and New York.

The name of Bradford is derived from the Saxon Bradenford, or Broadenford, and is doubtless very ancient. Two towns of considerable size in England are known by this name—one in Wiltshire near Bath; the other in Yorkham near Leeds. The latter is supposed to have been the locality from whence originated the great founder of the name in the United States.

The family was doubtless one of considerable antiquity. With the exception of three or four generations previous to that of Gov. Bradford, little is known of the early history of the family. The fact that Burke gives twelve different coats of arms belonging to the Bradfords is an evidence that they were a family of some distinction. The Yorkshire and Wiltshire branches of the family have the arms as those described as belonging to the Governor William Bradford line, viz: *Arms*—Argent on a fesse sable three stags' heads erased. *Crest*—A stag's head erased or.

GOVERNOR WILLIAM BRADFORD, son of William and Alice (Hanson) Bradford, was born in the village of Austerfield, Yorkshire, England, March 29, 1590. His father died the following year, and he was then adopted into the family of his grandfather, William, and after the latter's death in 1596, he was placed in the family of his uncle, Robert. He early became associated with Elder William Brewster and other non-conformists, and when but eighteen years of age he suffered imprisonment in Boston, Lincolnshire, for his religious belief. He finally escaped and reached Holland, where he apprenticed himself to a Frenchman, who taught him the art of silk weaving, and soon after reaching his majority he started in business for himself. His first marriage to Dorothy May, of Witezbuts, England, took place Nov. 13, 1613. The "bans" were published in Leyden, announcing the coming marriage as follows: November 15, 1613, William Bradford fustian maker, young man from Osterfeldt in England, affianced to Dorothy May from Wetezbuts, England. There was a sad ending to this his first love, for soon after the arrival of the Mayflower, and while her husband was absent on an expedition around Cape Cod Harbor, Dorothy fell overboard and was drowned.

From this time forward William Bradford's part in the fortunes of the community were important and powerful. After the first Governor, William Carver, died, Bradford was elected to that office, which he held by annual election until his death, excepting the years 1633, '34, '36, '38 and '44. He took a prominent part in all the councils which were held at his house, and in all the affairs, civic, political and military. From his house at the foot of Burial Hill, each Sabbath morning the little company of worshipers who all assembled there, marched in procession up the steep ascent to its top, where the religious services were held.

One of Gov. Bradford's first acts on assuming the executive was to send an embassy, July, 1621, to confirm the league entered into with the Indian Sachem Massasoit, the most influential and powerful of the native chiefs. His friendly relations with the Indians, who had known the English only as kidnappers, were essential to the continued existence of the colony and its future prosperity. When a famine threatened the colonists two years later, he obtained assistance from the Indians.

In 1624 the Governor and his assistants were constituted a judicial court, and afterwards the supreme tribunal of the colony; in 1629 legislation, in which up to that date all the freemen took part, was vested in the General Court, to which all of the towns sent representatives.

In 1629 a patent was obtained from the New England Council—a band of noblemen who in 1620 received from King James absolute property in the country lying between 40 and 48 degrees of north latitude—conferring upon William Bradford, his heirs, associates and assigns the title to the land on which Plymouth plantation was situated. In 1640, at the request of the General Court, Governor Bradford conveyed to it the title of the colony, reserving to himself his proportion as a proprietor.

By his wife, Dorothy May, the Pilgrim Gov. Bradford had only one child.

John Bradford born before the inauguration. He was of Duxbury 1645, and in 1652 he was a deputy to the General Court and a Lieutenant. He removed to Marshfield and represented that town at the General Court in 1653. He married Martha, daughter of Thomas and Martha Bourne, and in 1653 removed to Norwich, Conn.

Gov. Bradford married 2d, Aug. 14, 1623, Alice, daughter of Alexander Carpenter of Wrentham, England, the widow of Edward Southworth. By this marriage he had William, Mercy and Joseph.

Major William Bradford, the oldest child of Governor William and Alice (Southworth nee Carpenter) Bradford, was born June 17, 1684. He was next to Miles Standish the chief military man in the colony, and in the Indian wars, in which he took a prominent part he held the rank of Major. He was Assistant Treasurer and Deputy Governor of Plymouth Colony from 1682 to 1686 and from 1689 to 1691, and the latter year was one of the Council of Massachusetts. He married 1st Alice, daughter of Thomas Richards; 2d, widow ―――― Wiswall. By his first wife he had:

John, born Feb. 20, 1651, married Mercy, daughter of Joseph Warren.

William, born March 11, 1654.

Thomas, died in 1708, married Anna, daughter of Rev. James Fitch.

Samuel, born 1668, died April 11, 1714; married Hannah, daughter of John and Elizabeth Rogers.

Alice was married March 29, 1680, to Rev. William Adams, of Dedham, Mass. After his death she married Major James Fitch, son of Rev. James Fitch, of Saybrook and Norwich, Conn.

Hannah, born probably about 1662, was married Nov. 28, 1682, to Joshua Ripley, of Hingham.

Mercy, born about 1663, was married to Samuel Steel of Hartford, Conn.

Melatiah, born about 1665, was married to John Steel, of Norwich, Conn.

Mary, born about 1667, was married to William Hunt.

Sarah, born about 1669, was married to Kenelm Baker, of Marshfield, Mass.

Joseph, only child of Major William by the second marriage—widow Wiswall. They resided in Norwich, Conn.

Israel, married Sarah Bartlett, of Duxbury, Conn.

Ephraim, born about 1684, married Feb. 18, 1710, Elizabeth Bartlett; resided in Kingston.

David, born probably in Kingston about 1689; married in 1714, Elizabeth Finney.

Hezekiah, born about 1691; married Mary Chandler, of Duxbury, Mass.

REFERENCES.

CONNECTICUT. Caulkins' His. of Norwich, Conn., 169; Gold's His. of Cornwall, Conn., 303; Hine's Lebanon, Conn. Address (1880) 147; Hinman's Conn. Settlers, 311.
MAINE. Butler's His. of Framington, 395; Eaton's His. of Thomaston, 154; French's His. of Turner, 57.
MASSACHUSETTS.—Winsor's His. of Duxbury, 230; Thacher's His. of Plymouth, 108; Mitchell's His. of Bridgewater, 358; Davis' Landmark of Plymouth, 30.
NEW HAMPSHIRE.—Morrison's His. of Winham, 348; Hayward's His. of Hancock, 385; Coggswell's His. of New Boston, 132; Secomb's His. of Amherst, 516; Washington, N. H., His., 310.
OTHER PUBLICATIONS.—Futhey's His. of Chester Co., Pa., 486; Moore's American Governors, vol. I, 88; Power's His. Sangamon County, Ill., 129; Slaughter's St Mark's Parish, Va., 122; Stebbins Gen. 11; Spooner Gen. 11; Rice Gen.; Morton's New England Memorial, 180; Morse's Gen. of Richards Family, 14; Dwight's Strong Gen. 294, 950; Dwight's Gen. of Dwight, 208; Dudley's Archeolog. Coll. pl. 4; Amer. Ancestry V, 34,223, 237; VI, 137; VII, 229, 241; VIII, 103; IX, 106; Savage's Gen Dic. vol. I, 230; N. Y. Gen. and Biog. Rec. IV, 133, 183; N. E. His. and Gen. Reg. IV, 39, 233; IX, 127, 218; XIV, 174; XLVIII, 196. A Gen. Memoir of the Descendants of Gov. William Bradford (1850) 27 pages. One branch of the Descendants of Gov. William Bradford. 1895; 29 pages; Genealogical Memoirs of William Bradford the Printer (1873) 8 pages.

WILLIAM BRADFORD, the printer, son of William and Annie Bradford, was born in Leicestershire, Eng., May 23, 1663; died in 1752. There is no evidence that he was immediately related to the Pilgrim, but both, no doubt, had a common origin. He served an apprenticeship with Andrew Sorole, printer and publisher of Quaker books in Grace Church street, London. It is believed that he came over with William Penn and his company in the ship "Welcome." He was recommended as "a sober young man who comes to Pennsylvania to set up the trade of printing Friends' books," etc. In 1686 he published Burnyeat's Epistle, with the imprint "Printed and sold by William Bradford, near Philadelphia." He removed to New York in 1693 and was appointed Royal Printer in Oct., 1725. He established the New York Gazette, which was the first newspaper printed in the colony. He was buried by the side of his wife in Trinity church-yard, New York city, where a simple slab marks his resting place. His son Andrew, who learned the trade of his father and became a partner, removed in 1712 to Philadelphia. On Dec. 19, 1719, he published the first number of the *American Weekly Mercury*—the first newspaper founded in the Middle States, which he continued until his death.

WILLIAM BRADFORD, JR., brother of Andrew, born 1688, was a printer and seaman. He served an apprenticeship with his father, but, owing to failing health, adopted a seafaring life. He had a son William.

WILLIAM BRADFORD (3), son of William, Jr., was born in New York City, 1719. He learned the art of printing with his uncle Andrew and became his partner in 1739. In 1742 he started the *Pennsylvania Journal* and *Weekly Advertiser*. He earnestly espoused the cause of American Independence and his paper bore as a heading from July. 1774, to Oct., 1775, a peculiar device.

He served as Major in a Philadelphia regiment of militia at the battle of Trenton, was wounded at Princeton, and returned home as colonel of his regiment. He died in Philadelphia, Sept. 25, 1791, and was buried in the Second Presbyterian churchyard on Arch street.

BRADHURST:—Ralph Bradhurst of Roxbury, Mass., married June 13, 1677. Hannah, daughter of John Gore, and had Rhoda, 1678, Dorothy 1680, Hanah, Abagail. His wife died July 10, 1686, and he married 2d Martha, who died Aug. 6, 1693. He married 3d Hannah. Savage's Gen. Dic. vol. I, 231.

BRADING:—James Brading, of Newbury, Mass., removed to Boston, 1659. He married Oct. 11 of that year Hannah, daughter of Joseph Rock, and had Elizabeth, James 1662, and Joseph.

BRADISH:—Robert Bradish, of Cambridge, 1635, by wife Mary, who died Sept., 1638, had Joseph. By wife Vashti he had Samuel, 1640, died 1642, John 1645.

REFERENCES:—Barry's His. Framingham, Mass., 190; Paige's His. of Hardwick, Mass., 341; Paige's His. of Cambridge, Mass., 496; Temple's His. of North Brookfield, Mass., 535; Wyman's His. of Charlestown, Mass., vol. I, 110.

BRADFOURTH. N. E. Gen. Reg. IV, 177.
BRADFUTE. Carter Family Tree.
BRADLEE. Bradlee Gen. (1878).
BRADLEY:—Daniel Bradley, of Haverhill, Mass., came in the Elizabeth from London, 1635, aged 20. He was killed by the Indians Aug. 13, 1689. He maried May 21, 1662, probably Mary, daughter of John Williams, and had several children.

FRANCIS BRADLEY, of Fairfield, Conn., was made freeman 1664; he was of Branford 1660, and removed thence to Fairfield. He married Ruth, daughter of John Barlow of the same. By his will Jan. 4, 1689, he names John. Frencis, Daniel, Joseph, Ruth and Abagail.

ISAAC BRADLEY, of Branford, 1667, removed to New Haven 1683, where his name was long continued by a multitude of descendants. He had Isaac, William, Samuel, Daniel 1696, Sarah, Elizabeth.

JOSEPH BRADLEY, of Haverhill, Mass., had a garrison at his house, which was surprised Feb. 8, 1704, when his wife, for the second time, was taken by the Indians and carried away; her infant child, born after her captivity, dying of want. He had Abraham, of Concord, N. H. His children, Joseph, Martha and Sarah, were killed by the Indians.

PETER BRADLEY, of New London, Conn., a mariner, by wife Eliza, who is believed to have been a daughter of Jonathan Brewster, had Elizabeth, 1655, Peter 1658 and Lucretia.

STEPHEN BRADLEY, of Guilford, Conn., and New Haven, swore fidelity 1660. He married Nov. 9, 1663, Hannah, daughter of George Smith, of New Haven, and had Hannah 1664, Sarah, Stephen 1668. Daniel 1670, Elizabeth, Abraham. He died June 20, 1702.

WILLIAM BRADLEY, of New Haven, Conn., married Feb. 18, 1645. Alice Pritchard, perhaps daughter of Roger Pritchard, of Springfield, and had Joseph, 1646, Martha, Abraham 1650, Mary, Benjamin, Esther, Nathaniel, Sarah. He died 1691.

REFERENCES.

CONNECTICUT.—Caulkin's His. New London, Conn 278; Dodd's His. of East Haven, 106; Hamden, Conn., His.,-240; Hinman's Conn. Settlers; Kilburn's His. Litchfield, 154; Orcutt's His. of Derby, 703; Orcutt's His. of Torrington, 656; Orcutt's His. of Walcott, 453; Schenck's

His. of Fairfield, 354; Timlow's His. of Southington, 28; Tuttle Family of Conn., 148, 643.

NEW HAMPSHIRE.—Bouton's His. of Concord 634, Fiske's His. of Amherst, 136.

OTHER PUBLICATIONS.—Maine His. and Gen. Rec. III, 35; Mitchell's His. of Bridgewater, Mass. 120; Titcomb's Early N. E. People, 256; Heminway's Vt. Gaz. V.; Power's Sangamon County, Ill., 16, 131; Meade's Old Families of Va.; Bass' His. of Braintree, Vt., 119; Montague Gen: 133; Redfield Gen. 19; Amer. Ancestry, vol. I, 9; II, 15; V, 13, 210, 228; VIII, 145; IX, 36.

BRADSHAW.   See Wyman's Charlestown, Mass.. Gens. vol. I, 113; Temple's His. of North Brookfield Mass., 535; Brook's His. of Medford, Mass., 504; Hudson's His. of Lexington, Mass., 21; Paige's His. of Cambridge Mass., 498; Savage's Gen. Dic. vol. I, 234.

BRADSTREET:—Humphrey Bradstreet, of Ipswich Mass., came in the Elizabeth from Ipswich, Eng., 1634 aged 40, with wife Bridget and children Hannah, John. Martha, Mary; had here Moses, Sarah, 1638, and Rebecca. He was admitted a freeman May 6, 1635; was a representative to the General Court, 1635; died 1655.

SIMON BRADSTREET, of Ipswich, Mass., and Boston was born March, 1603, at Herbling in Lincolnshire, Eng., and was the son of Simon, a minister. He was bred at Emanuel Cambridge University, graduated with the degree of A. B. in 1620; came to New England in the fleet with Winthrop, 1630; chosen an assistant March 18, and so continued by annual election 48 years; he was secretary Aug. 23, 1630, to 1636; Deputy Governor, 1673-8; Governor 1679 to 1686. and again after the rising against Sir Edmund Andros, 1689-92. He died March 27, 1697. By his first wife, Ann, daughter of Gov. Thomas Dudley (a lady of some ability for poetical talent, who died Sept. 16, 1672, at Andover), had issue Samuel 1653, Dorothy, who married June 14, 1654, Rev. Seaborn Collin; Sarah, Simon, born Sept. 28, 1640; Hannah, Dudley 1648, John July 31, 1652.

REFERENCES.

MASSACHUSETTS.—Abbott's His. of Andover, 17; Brook's His. of Medford, 505; Drake's His. of Boston (1856); Hammatt Papers, Ipswich, 32; Paige's His. of Cambridge, 498; Wyman's Charlestown, Mass., Gens., 115; Essex Inst. His. Coll. XXIV, 66.

OTHER PUBLICATIONS. Chase's His. of Chester, N. H., 475; Hinman's Conn. Settlers, 317; Hanson's His. of Gardiner, Me., 131; Moore's American Governors, vol I, 388; Dudley Gen. (1848) 116; Savage's Gen. Dic. vol. I, 235; Amer. Ancestry V, 117; VII, 187, 195; N. E. His. and Gen. Reg. vol. I, 75; VIII, 312; IX. 43, 113; XLVIII. 168; Saco Valley (Me) Settlements and Families, 523.

BRADT.   Amer. Ancestry, vol. I, 9.

BRADWAY.   Shourd's Fenwick Colony, 35.

BRADY. Coggswell's His. of Henniker, 469; Orcutt's His. of Torrington, Conn., 657; Meginnes' West Branch, Pa., 568.

BRAGAN.   Riker's His. of Newtown.

BRAGDON. Goodwin's Baxter, Maine, 378; Jordan's Leightin Gen; Saco Valley (Me.) Settlements and Families, 523.

BRAGG.   Wheeler's His. of North Carolina II. 441; Wheeler's Eminent North Carolinians. 456; Ballou's His. Milford Mass., 495; Hammatt Papers of Ipswich, Mass. 34; Temple's His. of North Brookfield, Mass., 536; Ward's His. of Shrewsbury, Mass., 227; Stiles' His. of Windsor, Conn., II, 116; Wheeler's Croyden, N. H., Centen, 78.

BRAGHAM.   Pearson's His. of Schenectady, N. Y., 19.

BRAINARD or BRAINERD:—Daniel Brainard, of Hartford, removed to Hadam, Conn., of which he was an early settler. He married in 1665, Hannah, daughter of Jared Spencer. Had issue Daniel 1665, Hannah, 1667, James 1669, Joshua, 1671, William 1673, Caleb 1675, Hezikiah 1682, Elijah 1686. He was a deacon and died April 1, 1715, aged 74.

REFERENCES:—Field's His. of Haddam, Conn., 44; Hinman's Conn. Settlers, 329; Whittemore's His. of Middlesex County, Conn., 202, 323, 406; Phenix's Whitney Family of Conn., vol. I, 147; Temple's His. of Palmer, Mass., 422; Washington N. His., 313; Thurston's His. of Winthrop, Me., 175; Butler's His. of Farmington, Me., 397; Huntington Gen., 203; Savage's Gen. Dic. 237; Brainerd Gen. (1857); Amer. Ancestry, vol. I, 95; V, 230; VI, 47; IX, 18, 165; XI, 143.

BRAISTED.   Chute's Staten Island, p. 347.

BRACKENRIDGE.   Hyde's His. of Ware, Mass., 49

BRALEY.   Braley Gen. (1878).

BRAMAN.   Clark's His. of Norton, Mass., 76.

BRAME or BREAM:—Benjamin Bream, of Boston, had wife Ann and son Benjamin, who were jointly made administrators Oct. 6, 1693. Savage's Gen. Dic. vol. I, 237.

BRAMBALL:—George Bramball of Dover, 1670, Casco 1678, was killed by the Indians 1689. He left widow Martha, and children Joseph, George, Hannah and Joshua.

REFERENCES:—Davis' Landmark of Plymouth, 39; Hurlbut Gen., 424. Savage's Gen. Dic. vol. I, 237.

BRANCH:—Peter Branch, a carpenter from Holden, near Tinterden in Kent, died on board the ship Castle very soon after arrival. He names son John.

REFERENCES:—Meade's Old Families of Va.; Robertson's Pocahontas' Descendants; Goode Gen. 468; Amer. Ancestry, VII, 162; XI, 180; Savage's Gen. Dic. vol. I, 237.

BRAMAN.   N. E. His. and Gen. Reg. II, 119.

BRAND:—Benjamin Brand, son of John Brand, Esq., of Edwardston, next parish to Groton, came with Winthrop in the Arabella in 1650; requested admission as a freeman Oct. 19, at first General Court.

THADDEUS BRAND, of Lynn, by wife Sarah had Elizabeth 1673, Mary 1675. Savage's Gen. Dic. vol. I, 238.

BRANDIGO.   Andrew's His. of New Britain, 130.

BRANDON:—William Brandon, of Weymouth, by wife Mary, had Thomas, Sarah, May, Hannah; died 1646 Savage's Gen. Dic. vol. I, 238.

BRANDOW.   His. of Green Co., N. Y., 418.

BRANDT:—Christain A. Brandt. a Hessian, born in Germany, came to America with the British Army, deserted to the Revolutionary army, and at the close of the war received a pension for military services. His son Benjamin joined the community of Shakers. He died at New Lebanon, 1851.

REFERENCES:—Amer. Ancestry, II. 15; Dotterer's Perkiomen Region, Pa., 37; Temple's His. of North Brookfield, Mass., 536.

BRANN.   Sir Eaton's Thomaston, Me., 155.

BRANNE:—Michael Branne was of Dover 1655, and had Michael 1643, and perhaps others. He was living in 1655. See Savage's Gen. Dic. vol. I, 238.

BRANSON.   See Power's His. Sangamon County, Ill. 132.

BRASHEAR.   Green's Kentucky Families.

BRASIER.   Wyman's Charlestown, Mass., Gens. 117

BRASSEY. Boddington's Brassey Gen.

BRASTOW. Bangor His. Mag. II, 135; N. E. His and Gen. Reg. XIII, 249.

BRATT. Munsell's Albany IV. 101; Pearson's Schenectady Settlers, 19, 26.

BRATTLE. Thomas Brattle of Charlestown, Mass., 1656, removed next year to Boston; married Elizabeth, daughter of Capt. William Tynig; had Thomas 1658, Elizabeth, William 1662, Catharine, Bethia, Mary, Edward 1670. He was a captain, and one of the founders of the third or Old South Church.

REFERENCES:—Wyman's Charlestown, Mass., Gens., vol. I, 119; Paige's His. of Cambridge, Mass., 499; Hinman's Conn. Settlers, 321; Bridgman's King's Chapel Epitaphs, 259; Bridgman's Granary Epitaphs, 317; Savage's Gen. Dic. vol. I, 238; Brattle Gen. 267.

BRAWNER Power's Hist. Sangamon County, Ill., 135.

BRAXTON. Campbell's Spottswood Papers, 21; Meade's Old Families of Va.; Richmond, Va., Standard III, 329; Carter Family Tree.

BRAY:—John Bray, of Kittery, a shipwright, kept an inn 1674; removed in the war to Gloucester, perhaps there married, 10 Nov. 1679, Margaret Lambert, as second wife, had Margery, who married in 1680, William, father of Sir William Pepperell.

ROBERT BRAY, of Salem, 1668, by wife Thomasin, had Daniel born 29 Nov., 1673, and perhaps others. He was lost at sea in 1692.

THOMAS BRAY, of Gloucester, shipwright, married May 3, 1646, Mary Wilson, and had Mary 1647, Thomas 1649, John 1654, Nathaniel 1656, Thomas 1659, Hannah 1662, Esther 1664. He died Nov. 30, 1691.

REFERENCES:—Ridlon's Hist. of Harrison, Me., 28; Maine Hist. and Gen. Rec. III, 248; IV, 25; Corliss' Hist. of North Yarmouth, Me.; Babson's Hist. of Gloucester, Mass., 63; Salter's Hist. of Monmouth County, N. J., XI; Essex Inst. Hist. Coll VIII, 82; Andrew's Hist. of New Britain, Conn., 303; Driver Gen. 251; Poor Gen. 65; Savage's Gen. Dic. vol. I, 289; N. E. Hist. and Gen. Reg. XII, 370.

BRAYTON:—Francis Brayton, of Portsmouth, R. I., 1643; had by wife Mary, Francis, Stephen, Elizabeth, Sarah, Mary.

REFERENCES:—Austin's Ancestral Dict. 8; Austin's R. I. Gen. Dict. 251; Mowry Richard Gen. 198; Savage's Gen. Dict. vol. I, 240.

BRAZIER:—Edward Brazier, of Charlestown, Mass., 1658, had probably Thomas 1660, Abigail 1664, Rebecca 1667. He died May3, 1689. Savage's Gen. Dict. vol. I, 240.

BRAZELTON. Iowa Hist. Atlas, 263.

BREAD. Hinman's Conn. Settlers, 321.

BREAKENRIDGE. Temple's Hist. of Palmer, Mass., 415; Breakenridge Gen. (1887). See also Breckenridge.

BREARLEY. Cooley's Gens. of Trenton, N. J., 13; Brearley Chart 1886.

BRECHIN:—James Brechin, of Halifax and Chester N. S., was born at Aberdeen, Scotland, died at Halifax or Chester, N. S. about 1796; married soon after 1788, Susanna (Tufts) Levy, widow of Nathan Levy, of Chester, N. S. Had James (21). Amer. Ancestry. IV, 218.

BRECK:—Edward Breck, of Dorchester, 1636; was admitted freeman, 1639; came probably from Ashton in County Devon. He was an officer of the town 1642, 5, 6. He died 1662, leaving Robert, whom he brought from London, John, Mary, Elizabeth and Susanna.

THOMAS BRECK, of Dorchester, Mass., married Feb. 12, 1657, Mary, daughter of John Hill, and had Mary 1657; he removed to Medfield, and there had Susanna 1667, John 1671, Bethia 1673, Nathaniel and Samuel, twins, 1782.

REFERENCES:—Allen's Hist. of Worcester, Mass., 36; Barry's Hist. of Framingham, Mass., 190; Hudson's Hist. of Marlboro, Mass., 332; Morse's Hist. Sherborn, Mass., 16; Wheeler's Croydan, N. H., Centen. 80; Wheeler's Hist. of Newport, N. N., 307; Amer. Ancestry, V, 16; IX, 178; Savage's Gen. Dict. vol. I, 240; N. E. Hist. and Gen. Reg. V, 396; Breck Gen. (1889).

BRECKENRIDGE. See also Breakenridge.

REFERENCES:—Meade's Old Families of Va., II, 474; Peyton's Hist. of Augusta County, Va., 304; Richmond Va. Standard, II, 7; Green's Kentucky Families; Collin's Kentucky, 214; Power's Hist. of Sangamon County, Ill., 136; Paxton's Marshall Gen. 71; Preston Gen. (1864).

BREDANE:—Bryan Bredane, of Malden, 1671, had Samuel, born that year. Savage's Gen. Dict. vol. I, 241.

BREED:—Allen Breed, of Lynn, 1630; born 1601; died 1691; married March 28, 1656, Elizabeth Knight, and had Allen, Timothy, Joseph, John.

REFERENCES:—Wyman's Charlestown, Mass., Gens., vol. I, 120; Washington N. H. Hist., 315; Stearn's Hist. of Rindge, N. H., 452; Coggswell's Hist. of Henniker N. H., 470; Cochran's Hist. of Antrim, N. H., 378; Dwight Gen. 1108; Amer. Ancestry, VI, 14; Savage's Gen. Dict. vol. I, 241; Breed Family Meeting (1872); Breed Family Chart (1888).

BREESE. Salter's Hist. of Monmouth County, N. J., XII; Salisbury Family Memorials, II, 475; Oneida Hist. Society Trans., II, 97; Amer. Ancestry, V, 158; IX, 178.

BREEZE. Munsell's Albany, IV, 104.

BRENNAN. Smith's Petersborough, 25.

BRENNEMAN. Brubacher Gen. 102.

BRENT. Richmond, Va., Standard, II, 49; Richmond, Va., Critic (1898); Meade's Old Families of Va.; Old Ken., Md., 17; Paxton's Marshall Gen. 377; Goode Gen. 239; De Bow's Review, May (1859); Cincinnati, O., Criterion (1888), III, 751.

BRENTON:—Governor William Brenton was of Boston, 1633; came perhaps in the Griffin, with Collin, as he joined the church a few years after the teacher. He was admitted freeman 1634; representative 1635; Selectman 1634. He went to Rhode Island and was there in high office 1638 and presided 1639. He returned to Boston 1650-8. He contributed more than any other inhabitant except Henry Webb, to subscription for the erection of town house. He was the Governor of Rhode Island 1666-7-8; he lived at Saunton 1670-2 and died at Newport 1684. On the Merrimack river is a large tract of land called Brenton's farm, now the town of Litchfield, in New Hampshire, was granted to him 1658; and the southern point of Rhode Island was named by him Hammersmith (from his birthplace near London), where great fortifications are erected for security of Newport harbor, is usually known as Brentons. He married Martha, daughter of Thomas Burton, and had Mehitable 1652, Jahleel 1655, Elizabeth, William, Ebenezer, Sarah, married Rev Joseph Eliot, of Guilford, Conn.; Abigail, John.

WILLIAM BRENTON, his son, a mariner, by wife Hannah, had Samuel and Jahleel, born Oct. 22, 1729 died Jan. 1802; was a Rear Admiral in the British Navy and father of Sir Jahleel Brenton, born at Newport; 22 Aug., 1770.

REFERENCES:—Austin's R. I. Dict. 252; R. I. Hist. Society Coll. III, 265; Heraldic Journal III, 173; Hall's Genealogical Notes 104; Dwight's Strong Gen. 359; Savage's Gen. Dict., vol. I, 242.

BRETT. WILLIAM BRETT, of Duxbury, May 1640, removed to Bridgewater, of which he was one of the first proprietors, 1645. He was a representative to the General Court, 1661. He was a Ruling Elder, and often preached when the Rev. Mr. Keith was unable. He died Dec. 17, 1681, aged 63. By wife Margaret he had William, Elihu, Nathaniel, Alice, Lydia, Hannah.
REFERENCES:—Kingman's Hist. North Bridgewater, Mass., 452; Mitchell's Hist. of Bridgewater, Mass., 120; Lapham's Hist. of Paris, Me., 532; Richmond, Va., Standard, III, 36; Savage's Gen. Dict. vol. I, 243.

BRETTON:—PHILIP LE BRETTON, a French Huguenot from Rochelle, dropped the "Le" from his name. In his will, Aug. 6, 1736, he refers to his advanced age and provides for his children, Peter, Daniel, Mary, Elizabeth, Rachael, Sarah, Jane, Ann, and for a son-in-law, Edward Dumaresque. Savage's Gen. Dict. vol. I, 243.

BRITZ. Britz, Gen. 1890.

BREVARD. Wheeler's N. Car. II, 237.

BREVOORT. Riker's Hist. Harlem, N. Y., 494; Green's Todd Gen.; Roome Gen. 227; N. Y. Gen. and Biog. Rec. VII, 58.

BREWER:—DANIEL BREWER, of Roxbury, Mass., came in the "Lion" with his wife; arrived at Boston Sept. 16, 1632; admitted freeman May 14, 1634, died early in 1646; names in his will of January 12 of that year, wife Joanna, who died Feb. 7, 1639, aged 37; son Daniel, born probably in England; Nathaniel born May 1, 1635; and daughters Ann, Joanna and Sarah.

JOHN BREWER, of Cambridge, Mass., by wife Ann had John, born 10 Oct., 1642, Hannah 1645. He removed probably to Sudbury, and married, Oct. 23, 1647, Mary, daughter of the first John Whitmore, and had Mary 1648, William Oct. 6, 1653, Sarah 1658.

THOMAS BREWER, of Ipswich, 1642, was admitted freeman 1652 when the Colonial record calls him of Roxbury. His daughter Mary married 1656 William Lane; Sarah married 1657, Thomas Webster, of Hampton.

THOMAS BREWER, of Lynn, married Dec. 4, 1682. Elizabeth Graves and had Mary, born 1684, Rebecca, Crispus, Thomas John.

REFERENCES.

MASSACHUSETTS.—Wilbraham Centen. Cel. 293; Ward's Hist. of Shrewsbury, 245; Temple's Hist. of North Brookfield, 537; Barry's Hist. of Framingham, 191; Bond's Hist. of Watertown. 92; Draper's Hist. of Spencer, 179; Ellis' Hist. of Roxbury, 92; Hammat Papers Ipswich, Me., 39.
OTHER PUBLICATIONS.—Hinman's Conn. Settlers, 32; Andrew's Hist. of New Britain, Conn., 206; Norten's Hist. of Fitzwilliam, N. H., 489; Stearn's Hist. of Rindge. N. H., 453; Ward's Rice Family, 11; Strong Gen., 1284; Bangor, Me., Hist. Mag. vol. I, 130; Bolton's Hist. of Westchester County, N. Y., II, 711; Ely Gen. 93, 215; Kellog's White Descendants, 73; Lock Gen., 35; Savage's Gen. Dict. vol. I, 243; N. E. Hist. and Gen. Reg. XXX. 422; Am. Ancestry, vol. XI, 91.

BREWSTER:—FRANCIS BREWSTER, of New Haven, 1640, came from London probably with his wife Lucy and family, including nine persons. He is supposed to have been the father of Nathaniel, who graduated in the first class at Harvard 1642, and of Joseph. His widow married Thomas Pell.

NATHANIEL BREWSTER, son of Francis, of New Haven, went to England, where he was settled as a minister at Abby, in County Norfolk. He returned and was settled at Brookhaven in 1665. He married Sarah, daughter of Roger Ludlow ,and had John, Timothy, Daniel.

ELDER WILLIAM BREWSTER, of the "Mayflower," one of the earliest of the distinguished Puritan laymen in England, was probably born in 1563, at Scrooby, in Nottinghamshire, at the manor hall of which village belonged to the archbishop of York. He afterwards long resided at the same house at which Cardinal Woolsey had made his last stop before reaching home in his final journey on compulsory retirement from court, after banishment by King Henry VIII. Elder Brewster was of good family, his coat of arms being identical with that of the ancient Suffolk branch. He entered Cambridge University and remained there for a short time,.and about 1584 entered the service of William Davison, Ambassador, and afterwards Secretary of State to Queen Elizabeth, and with him visited the Netherlands, remaining in his service two years. He then abandoned politics, devoted himself earnestly to the cause of religion and was the first prominent layman who rejected conformity to the ceremonies of the Church of England. He filled for a time the position of postmaster at Scrooby, and continued until his associate separatists had become obnoxious to the ecclesiastical authorities, and in 1607 he embarked with them and his young friend Bradford in a sloop at Boston, bound for Holland, intending to flee the country. But the captain of the vessel betrayed them and Brewster with others was arrested, imprisoned and bound over for trial. In the summer of 1608 he sailed from Hull and reached Amsterdam in safety. Having spent most of his substance in effecting his own escape and aiding his poorer associates, he was obliged to resort to teaching for a living. With the aid of friends he set up a printing press and printed a series of religious books that were contraband in England. He was ruling elder of the church at Leyden.

Through the assistance of his friend, Sir Edwin Sandys, treasurer of the Virginia company, he obtained a grant of land in North America, and in September, 1620, he set sail in the "Mayflower" with the first company of Pilgrims, landing at Plymouth Dec. 21, 1620.

Brewster was Ruling Elder of the church, and until 1629 acted as teacher and minister, enduring the hardships of the memorable first winter with wonderful courage and cheerfulness. His family which came on the "Mayflower" consisted of his wife; Lucretia, wife of Jonathan, a son who came out in the "Fortune" in 1621, and two sons, Wrestling and Love.

His daughters Patience and Fear came in the "Ann," 1623, and on Aug. 6 of the following 'year Patience married Thomas Prince, afterwards Governor. Fear married in 1626 Isaac Allerton, the first Associate of Governor William Bradford. His other children were Jonathan and Wrestling.

Love Brewster married, March 15, 1634. Sarah, daughter of William Collier. He moved to Duxbury, Mass., and had issue, three sons and one daughter.

JONATHAN BREWSTER, the eldest son of Elder William Brewster, was born at Scrooby, in County Nottingham. He went with his father to Holland, where he was left to the care of two sisters, with his own family. He came in the "Fortune" in 1621. He was Associate Judge. and established by appointment a trading post on the lands purchased of Uncas, chief of the Mohigans, and afterwards called Brewster's Neck. He gave notice to John Winthrop, governor of the fort at Saybrook, of the evil designs of the Piquots.

He settled subsequently in Duxbury, Mass., where he was was a representative of the first General Court in 1639; removing thence to New London, Conn., before 1640. By wife Lucretia he had William and Mary, born in Holland; Jonathan, Benjamin, Grace, Ruth, Hannah, Elizabeth.

REFERENCES.

CONNECTICUT.—Caulkin's Hist. of New London, 276; Caulkin's Hist. of Norwich; 115 (1867) 211; Gold' Hist. Cornwall, 272; Hine's Lebanon, Conn., Address (1880) 147; Hinman's Conn. Settlers, 327; Hurd's Hist. of New London County, 510.

MASSACHUSETTS.—Winsor's Hist. of Duxbury, 234; Davis' Landmarks of Plymouth, 40; Mitchell's Hist. of Bridgewater, 361.

OTHER PUBLICATIONS.—Frisby's Hist. of Middlebury, Vt., 24; Elderkin Gen., 90; Eaton's Hist. of Thomaston, Me., 156; Steele's Life of Brewster (1857), 350; Wetmore Gen., 552; Brewster's Golden Wedding (1860); Dudley Archa. Coll. Plate 4; Strong Gen., 131, 606, 623; Amer. Ancestry, VII, 38; Savage's Gen. Dict. vol. I, 214; N. E. Hist. and Gen. Reg. L 360.

BRIANT. Cutter's Jaffray, N. H., 236; N. E. Hist. and Gen. Reg. XLVIII, 40.

BRICK. Shourd's Fenwick, N. J., 42.

BRICKER:—NATHANIEL BRICKER, of Newberry, Mass., had Nathaniel 1673, died young; John May 3, 1676; James and Mary, twins, Dec. 11, 1679; Nathaniel again Sep. 23, 1683; drowned at 4 years old. Savage's Gen. Dict. vol. I, 247.

BRICKNALL:—EDWARD BRICKNALL, of Boston, 1681, by wife Mary had Edward, born Dec. 20, 1682; John 1684, Mary 1689. The name is often written Bicknell. See Savage's Gen. Dict. vol. I, 247.

BRICE. Old Kent, Maryland, 3.

BRICKER. Norton's Knox County, O., 348.

BRICKETT. Chase's Chester, N. H., 480.

BRIDGE:—Edward Bridge, of Roxbury, Mass., had by wife Mary, children, Mary 1637, Thomas 1639 and perhaps others. He died Dec. 20, 1683, aged 82.

REV. THOMAS BRIDGE, a merchant of Boston, was born at Hackney, near London, 1657. Came to New England and was educated at Hartford. Received his degree of A. B., 1675. After preaching in Jamaica and New Providence, Bermuda and West Jersey, he became minister of the first church at Boston and was ordained May 10, 1705; died 1715 of apoplexy.

WILLIAM BRIDGE, of Watertown, Mass., 1636, Boston 1643, had a son Peter born Jan., 1644.

REFERENCES.

MASSACHUSETTS.—Wyman's Charlestown Gen. vol. I, 425; Temple's Hist. of Northfield, 410; Stearn's Hist. of Ashburnham, 620; Paige's Hist. of Hardwick, 341; Paige's Hist. of Cambridge, 500; Hudson's Hist. of Lexington, 21; Green's Early Settlers of Groton, 3; Green's Groton, Mass., Epitaphs, 327; Bend's Hist. of Watertown, 93; Allen's Hist. of Worcester, 86.

OTHER PUBLICATIONS.—Willis' Law and Lawyers of Maine, 462; North's Hist. of Augusta, Me., 811; Haywood's Hist. of Gilsum, N. H., 275; Bridgeman's King's Chapel Epit., 260; Whitney Gen., 1860, Appendix; Amer. Ancestry, vol. I, 9; VI, 140; Bridge Gen.

BRIDGES.—EDMUND BRIDGES, of Lynn, Mass., came in the "James" from London, 1635, aged 23; admitted freeman Sept. 7, 1639. By his first wife, Alice, he had Edmund, born about 1637. and John; and perhaps by second wife, Elizabeth at Rowley, had Mehitable 1641; Bethia; Obadiah, 1646; Faith; Hackaliah ,who was lost at sea about 1671, and Josiah. His wife died Dec. 1664, at Ipswich; and by the third wife, whom he married April 6, 1665, Mary Littlehale, probably widow of Richard, may have had Mary. In his will, Jan. 13, 1685, he names John, Josiah, Faith Black, Bethia and Mary.

REFERENCES:—Temple's Hist. of North Brookfield, Mass., 537; Hammatt Papers of Ipswich, Mass., 36; Draper's Hist. of Spencer, Mass., 179; Barry's Hist. of Framingham, Mass., 193; Demingsville M. E. Centen., 103; Eaton's Hist. of Thomaston, Me., 157; Powers' Hist. of Sangamon County, Ill., 138; Rockford Gen., 129; Stickney Gen., 451; Savage's Gen. Dict. vol. I, 247; N. E. Hist. and Gen. Reg. VIII, 252; XXXVIII, 63.

BRIDGEHAM:—HENRY BRIDGEHAM, of Dorchester, Mass., was admitted freeman 1643; removed to Boston 1644; was a member of the artillery company 1644; constable 1653; Captain. He died Jan., 1671, leaving a good estate. By wife Elizabeth, who survived him, he had Jonathan, John, 1645; Joseph 1652; Benjamin 1654; Hopestill 1658; Samuel 1661; Nathaniel 1662; James 1664.

JOSEPH BRIDGEHAM, of Boston, brother of Henry, was deacon and Ruling Elder of the first church. His widow, daughter of John Wensley, married Dec. 8, 1712, Hon. Thomas Cushing. See Savage's Gen. Dict. vol. I. 249.

BRIDGER. Savage's Gen. Dict. vol. I, 250; Wyman's Charlestown Gen. vol. I, 126.

BRIDGER. Livimore's Wilton, 325; Meade's Old Families of Va., I, 305; Richmond, Va., Standard, II, 45; III, 37; N. E. Hist. and Gen. Reg. VIII, 253.

BRIDGMAN:—JAMES BRIDGMAN, of Hartford, 1641 or earlier, was of Springfield 1646. His children born at Hartford were Sarah, John, born 1645; Thomas 1647; Martha 1649; Mary 1652. He removed to Northampton, Mass., 1654, and had there James 1655; Patience 1656; Hezekiah 1658.

REFERENCES.—Doolittle's Hist. Belchertown, Mass., 255; Temple's Hist. of Northfield, Mass., 412; Hammatt Papers, Ipswich, Mass., 37; Hinman's Conn. Settlers, 336; Strong Gen., 826; Savage's Gen. Dict. vol. I, 250; N. E. Hist. Gen. Reg. vol. XVI, 135.

BRIERSLEY:—JOHN BRIERSLEY, of Gloucester, by wife Elizabeth had John 1653; Benjamin 1660; Mary 1661.

BRIGDEN:—THOMAS BRIGDEN, of Charlestown, Mass., was of Feversham, Kent, England. Came in the "Hercules" 1635, from Sandwich with wife Thomasine and two children; admitted freeman March 3, 1636, and died 20 June, 1668. He had Zachary 1639. His will May 1, 1665, names son Thomas and his children Thomas, Zachary and John, daughter Mary, wife of Henry Kimball; and her children, Zachary, Mary and Sarah; and daughter Sarah.

ZACHARIAH BRIGDEN, son of the first Thomas, was a preacher at Stonington, died 1663.

BRIES. See Munsell's Albany Coll. vol. IV, 104

BRIGGS:—CLEMENT BRIGGS, of Plymouth, came in the "Fortune," 1621; probably young; removed to Dorchester and then married, 1630 or 31, Joan Allen. Thomas Stoughton, constable, who officiated at the ceremony, was fined for the same £5 at the March term of the Court 1631. Briggs removed to Weymouth 1633, and had Thomas 1633, Jonathan 1635, John, David, 1640, Clement 1643.

JOHN BRIGGS, of Newport, R. I., 1638, or Portsmouth 1650, was admitted freeman there 1655, had Thomas and other children.

REFERENCES.

MASSACHUSETTS.—Winsor's Hist. of Duxbury, 237; Temple's Hist. of North Brookfield, 537; Freeman's Hist. Cape Cod, Mass., vol. II, 68, 608; Deane's His. of Scituate, 225; Davis' Landmarks of Plymouth, 45; Clark's Hist. of Norton, 77; Barry's Hist. of Hanover, 209; Essex Inst. Coll. VI, 171.

MAINE.—Washburn's Notes on Livermore, 41; Lapham's Hist. of Woodstock, 182; Lapham's Hist. of Paris, 535; Lapham's Hist. of Norway, 471; North's Hist. of Augusta, Me., 816.

OTHER PUBLICATIONS.—Huntington's Stamford, Conn., Settlers, 17; Hinman's Conn. Settlers, 337; Haywood's Gilsum, N. H., 276; Saunderson's Hist. of Charlestown, N. H., 291; Austin's Allied Families, 43; Austin's R. I. Gen. Dict., 25; Livermore's Hist. Block Island, R. I., 321; Adam's Hist. of Fair Haven, Vt., 310; Roe's sketches of Rose, N. Y., 125; Cleveland's Hist. of Yates County, N. Y., 655; Ely Gen., 190; Guild's Stites Gen., 313; Sear's Gen., 162; Vinton's Giles Gen., 216; Amer. Ancestry, vol. I, 10; II, 15; III, 70; V, 18; VI, 52; VII, 13; IX, 125; Savage's Gen. Dict. vol. I, 251; Brigg's Gen., 1870-1880-1887.

BRIGHAM:—THOMAS BRIGHAM, of Cambridge, Mass., came in the "Susan and Ellen," 1635, aged 32; admitted freeman April 18, 1636. By wife Mercy Hurd, he had Thomas 1642, John 1645, Mary Hannah, Samuel 1653.

REFERENCES.

MASSACHUSETTS.—Hudson's Hist. of Lexington. 26; Hudson's Hist. of Marlborough, 332; Paige's Hist. of Cambridge, 501; Pierce's Hist. of Grafton, 452; Stone's Hist. of Hubbardston, 230; Temple's Hist. of North Brookfield, 538; Ward's Hist. of Shrewsbury, 234; WorcesterMagazine, II, 151.

NEW HAMPSHIRE.—Hayward's Hist. of Gilsum, 276; Merrill's Hist. of Acworth, 191; Norton's Hist. of Fitwilliam, 491; Stearn's Hist. of Rindge, 454.

OTHER PUBLICATIONS.—Hemminway's Vermont Gaz., IV, 181; V, 715; Warren's Hist. of Waterford, Me., 232; Young's Chautauqua, N. Y., 537; Ward's Gen. of Rien Family, 11; Morse's Gen. of Grout Family, 15; Morse's Gen. of Brigham Family, 1859; Amer. Ancestry vol. I, 10; Savage's Gen. Dict. vol. I, 252.

BRIGHT:—FRANCIS BRIGHT, of Charlestown, Mass., son of Edward, of London, was bred at Oxford and matriculated at New College, Feb. 18, 1625,aged 22, and was instructed in divinity by the famous Rev. John Davenport. He came from Rayleigh, in Essex, with wife and two children to Salem, in the "Lion's Whelp," became discouraged and went home on the "Lion" 1630.

HENRY BRIGHT, of Charlestown. 1630, came probably from Ipswich, in County Suffolk, England: son of Henry, of Bury St. Edmunds. He came in the fleet with Winthrop and was very early; No. 48, enrolled in the church,

but removed not long after to Watertown and there married, in 1634, Ann, daughter of Henry Goldstone. Had issue Abigail 1637, Mary 1639, John 1641, Ann 1644, Beriah 1651. He was admitted a freeman May 6, 1635. He was a deacon of the church and was held in high esteem. He died Oct. 9, 1686, age 84.

REFERENCES:—Bond's Hist. of Watertown, Mass., 96; 706; Harris' Watertown, Mass., Epitaphs, 7; Heraldic Journal, vol. I (1865), 81; Holton's Farwell Gen., 113; Richmond, Va., Standard, III, 6; Savage's Gen. Dict. vol. I, 253; Bright's of England (1858) Bright Gen. 1848.

BRIGHTON:—SAMUEL BRIGHTON, of Boston, by wife Ann had James 1690, Ebenezer 1692. Savage's Gen. Dict. vol. I, 253.

BRIMSMEAD:—JOHN BRIMSMEAD, or Brisman, was of Charlestown, Mass., 1637; admitted freeman May 2, 1638. By wife Mary he had Mary 1640, John 1643, Daniel and Zachary. He removed to Stratford, Conn., before 1650, and was representative to the Grand Court 1669-71. and died in 1673, leaving a good estate to widow Mary and children John, Daniel, Paul, Samuel, Mary.

See Savage's Gen. Dict. vol. I, 251.

BRIGHTMAN. See Austin's R. I. Dict., 27.

BRILL. See Smith's Hist. Dutchess Co., N. Y., 499.

BRIMBLECORM. Pierce's Grafton, 468.

BRIMMER. Bangor, Me., Mag. IV, 73; Ely Gen., 193; Sigourny Gen., 22.

BRINCKERHOFF. See Buger's Hist. Kings Co. Settlers, 48; Riker's Annals of Newtown, L. I., 290; Winfield's Hist. of Hudson County, N. J., 526; Brinckerhoff Gen., 1887; Amer. Ancestry, vol. III, 72, 222, 224; IV, 16.

BRINGHURT. See Claypole Gen.

BRINK. Schoonmaker's Hist. of Kingston, N. Y., 473; Sylvester's Hist. of Ulster County, N. Y., 337; Amer. Ancestry, vol. II, 15.

BRINLEY:—FRANCIS BRINLEY, of Newport, R. I., was the son of Thomas, an auditor of the revenues of Kings Charles I. and II., as appears by the inscription on his tomb in the middle aisle of the church at Datchett, Co. Bricks, between Colnbrook and Windsor, England. Francis, above mentioned, was the eldest son and was born Nov. 5, 1632. He probably escaped from the evils brought on the family by the loyalty of his father, but went back to England, probably in 1655; came again in the "Speedwell" to Boston 27th of July next year. He married Hannah Carr, probably daughter of Caleb Carr, of Newport, and had Thomas and William. He was an Assistant of R. I. 1672. He died 1719.

THOMAS BRINLEY, his son, was of Boston, and was a member of the Artillery Company. He was one of the founders of Kings Chapel, 1686. He went to England and there married Mary Apthorp and had Elizabeth, Francis, born 1690 at London, bred at Eton. He died of smallpox 1693. The widow with her two sons came to reside with their grandfather, and after his death she lived at Roxbury with her son, who had five sons and two daughters.

REFERENCES:—Austin's Ancestral Dict., 9; Austin's R. I. Gen. Dict., 256; Bridgeman's King's Chapel, 219; Heraldic Journal, II, 31; Salter's Hist. of Monmouth County, N. J., XII; Tyngsboro, Mass., Centen. Record. 5; Wentworth Gen., vol. I. 529; Savage's Gen. Dict., vol. I, 255.

BRINSMADE. Cathern's Woodbury, Conn., 1474; Hinman's Conn. Settlers, 338; Orcutt's Hist. of Stratford. Conn., 1163; Savage's Gen. Dict., vol. I, 254; Walworth's Hyde Gen. 945.

BROCKETT:—JOHN BROCKETT, of New Haven, 1639, was a signer of the first covenant. He had issue, John 1643, Benjamin 1645, Mary 1646, Silence 1648, Abigail 1650, Samuel 1652, Jabiz 1654. He was one of the earliest settlers of Wallingford, as was his son Samuel. The father died 1690, aged 80.

BROCKETT. Davis' Hist. of Wallingford, Conn., 658; Orcutt's Hist. of Wolcott, Conn., 456; Timlow's Hist. of Southington, Conn., 31; Tuttle Family of Conn., 546, 642; Savage's Gen. Dict., vol. I, 257.

BROCKHOLST. N. Y. Biog. Rec., IX, 115.

BROCKLEBANK. Gage's Hist. of Rowley, Mass., 439; Stearn's Hist. of Ashburnham, Mass., 621; Stearn's Hist. of Rindge, N. H., 456; Savage's Gen. Dict., vol. I, 253; Essex Hist. Coll., 138.

BROCKS. Munsell's Albany, IV, 105.

BROCKWAY:—WOOLSTONE BROCKWAY, Saybrooke 1644, by wife Hannah had Hannah 1664, William 1666, Woolstone 1668, Mary 1670, Bridget 1672, Richard 1673, Elizabeth 1676, Sarah 1679, Deborah 1682.

REFERENCES:—Hinman's Conn. Settlers, 340; Sedgweck's Hist. of Sharon, Conn., 66; Andrews' Hist. of New Britain, Conn., 309; Young's Hist. Chautauqua County, N. Y., 519; Washington, N. H., Hist., 315; Amer. Ancestry, III, 222; IV, 133; V, 100; VI, 81; Brockway Gen., 1887-1888-1890; Savage's Gen. Dict., 258.

BRODHEAD:—Daniel Brodhead of Esopus, N. Y., born at Yorkshire, Eng.; died at Esopus July 14, 1667. He was captain of grenadiers in the British army 1660, officer of the expeditionary force which took New York from the Dutch 1664; commandant of the post at Esopus, N. Y., until his death, 1667. He married Ann, daughter of Francis Tye and Lettos Salmon, of England, and had Richard and other children.

REFERENCES:—Sylvester's Hist. of Ulster County, N. Y., 114; Schoonmacher's Hist. of Kingston, N. Y., 473; Heraldic Journal III (1867), Brodhead's Delaware Water Gap, 240; Amer. Ancestry I.., 165; V, 204.

BROGDEN. See Old Kent, Md., 88; Wheeler's eminent North Carolinians, 466.

BROMFIELD:—EDWARD BROMFIELD, of Boston, 1675, was third son of Henry, who was son of Arthur. Edward was born Jan. 10, 1649, at Haywood house in the New Forest, Hants. He was a merchant and a gentleman of esteem; representative to the General Court 1695, a member of the Council 1708. His second wife, to whom he was married 1683, was Mary, daughter of Rev. Samuel Danforth. Had Sarah, Edward and others.

REFERENCES:—Bridgeman's King's Chapel; Heraldic Journal III, 187; N. E. Hist and Gen. Reg., V, 100; XIII, 35; XXV, 182, 329; XXVI, 37, 141;Savage's Gen. Dict. vol I, 258; Slade's Bromfield Family, 1871.

BROMLEY:—LUKE BROMLEY, of Stonington, Conn., married Hannah, daughter of Thomas Stafford; married second, Thomasine Packer, and had Thomasine, 1692; William, 1693; Thomas, 1695.

REFERENCES:—Hollister's Hist. Pawlet, Vt.., 112; Williams' Hist. of Danby, Vt., 112.

BRONAUGH. Hayden's Virginia Genealogies, 534.

BRONCK. Hist. of Greene County, N. Y., 421; Munsell's Albany, IV, 104.

BRONK. Amer. Ancestry, I, 10.

BRONSON:—JOHN BRONSON, of Hartford, Conn., died Nov. 28. 1680; came with Hooker in 1636, and took part in the Pequot war 1637. He was deputy to the General Court in 1673, and several times afterwards. He r.-

BRINTNALL:—THOMAS BRINTNALL, of Boston, by wife Esther had Samuel 1665, Thomas 1669, Nathaniel 1671, John 1673, Joseph 1674, Mehitable 1685.

REFERENCES:—Barry's Hist of Framingham, Mass., 194; Savage's Gen. Dict., vol. I, 255; Wyman's Charlestown, Mass., Gens., vol. I, 131; Willard Gen. 280, 390.

BRINTNELL. Clark's Hist. of Norton, Mass., 78.

BRINTON. Smith's Hist. of Delaware County, Pa., 449; Futhey's Hist. of Chester County, Pa., 486; Cope's Record of Cope Family, 242; Life of Rev. William Smith; Amer. Ancestry, vol. II, 15; Brenton Gen.

BRISBIN. Lindsay Gen.; Amer. Ancestry, V, 57.

BRISCO:—BENJAMIN BRISCO, of Boston, married 1656, Sarah, daughter of Philip Long, and had Hannah 1658, Sarah 1660, William 1663, Ann 1664, Mary 1665, John 1667, Rebecca 1669, Benjamin 1671, Susanna 1674.

NATHANIEL BRISCO, of Watertown, had, by wife Eliza, Nathaniel, Mary, John, Sarah. He was a rich tanner, selectman 1643; Savage's Gen. Dict., vol. I.

BRISCO. Stone's Hist. of Beverly, Mass., 36; Harrison's Kent, Md., 121; Hayden's Virginia Genealogies, 135; Savage's Gen. Dict., vol. I, 255.

BRISE. Ruggles Gen.

BRISTED. Greene's Todd Gen.

BRISTOL. Davis' Hist. of Wallingford, Conn., 657; Hamden, Conn., Hist., 241; Wheeler's Croyden, N. H., Centen., 83; Young's Hist. of Warsaw, N. Y., 238; Adams' Hist. of Fair Haven, Vt., 303; Guild's Stiles Gen., 26; Moore's Bontecon Gen.; Redfield Gen., 36; Amer. Ancestry, II, 16.

BRISTOW:—HENRY BRISTOW was of New Haven, 1647, and had Rebecca 1650, .Samuel 1651, Mary 1653; by his second wife, Lydia Brown, whom he married 1656, he had Lydia 1658, John 1659, Mary 1661, Hannah 1663, Abigail 1666. Savage's Gen. Dict., vol. I, 256.

BRITTON. Ward's Hist. of Shrewsbury, Mass., 249; Stearn's Hist. of Ashburnham, Mass., 620; Read's Hist. of Swanzey, N. H., 299; Life of Rev. William Smith: Power's Hist. of Sangamon County, Ill., 140; Clute's Staten Island, 348.

BRITT. Power's Hist. of Sangamon County, Ill., 141.

BRITTEN. Sewell's Hist. of Woburn, Mass., 504.

BRITTEN. Littell's Passaic Valley, N. J., 55.

BROADNAX. Meade's Old Farms of Va., Slaughter's Bristol Parish, Va.

BROADUS. Slaughter's St. Mark's Va., 194.

BROADWELL. Littell's Passaic Valley, N. J., 59; Power's Hist. of Sangamon County, Ill., 142.

BROADY. Amer. Ancestry, IX, 125.

BROCK:—HENRY BROCK, of Dedham, 1644, died 1652, leaving wife Elizabeth and children John, Elizabeth, Ann.

REFERENCES:—Norton's Hist. of Fitzwilliam, N. H., 496; Wentworth Gen., vol. I, 205, 671; Williams' Hist. of Danby, Vt., 116; Amer. Ancestry, vol. VII, 153; Savage's Gen. Dict., vol. I, 257.

BROCKENBOROUGH. Mead's Old Churches of Va., II, 474; Richmond, Va., Standard, II, 34; III, 29; Hayden's Virginia Genealogies, 110; Paxton's Marshall Gen., 106; Goode Gen., 402.

BROCKLEBANK:—JOHN BROCKLEBANK, of Rowley, had Samuel, born 1655.

SAMUEL BROCKLEBANK was a deacon, a captain, and was killed in Philip's war, leaving Samuel, born 1653. Francis 1655, Hannah, Mary, Elizabeth, Sarah, Joseph 1674. Savage's Gen. Dict., vol. I, 256.

sided in Farmington, Conn., after 1641. He had a son John of Waterbury and Farmington.

REFERENCES.

CONNECTICUT.—Andrew's Hist. of New Britain, 184, 340; Boyd's Annals of Winchester, 109; Bronson . ...st. of Waterbury, Conn., 469; Brown's West Simsbury,Conn. Settlers, 469; Cothren's Hist of Woodbury, 503; Hinman's Conn. Settlers, 341; Orcutt's Hist of Stratford, 1164; Orcutt's Hist. of Wolcott, 458; Timlow's Hist. of Southington, 32.
OTHER PUBLICATIONS.—Goodwin's Olcott Family, 25; Morris and Flint Gen. 15; Young's Hist. of Warsaw, 239; Savage's Gen. Dict., vol. I, 279, 801; N. E. Hist. and Gen. Reg., XXXV, 361.

BROOKE:—JOHN BROOKE, of Limerick, Pa., born at Hugg, Yorkshire, England, died in Gloucester County, N. J. He was a Quaker who came to Pennsylvania in Sept., 1699, with wife Francis and two sons, leaving a son and two daughters in England; purchased 750 acres in Lemerick township, Pa. Both he and his wife died shortly after their arrival, leaving son Matthew, of Lemerick, Pa.

REFERENCES:—Thomas family of Maryland, 41; Paxton's Marshall Gen., 143; Page, 129; Meade's Old Families of Va.; Goode Gen. 314; Amer. Ancestry, IV, 128.

BROOKER. Orcutt's Hist of Stonington, Conn., 657; Amer. Ancestry II, 16.

BROOKING or BROOKEN:—JOHN BROOKING, of Boston, 1658, by wife Elizabeth had Elizabeth 1660, John 1662, Christian 1667, Mary 1670, Abagail 1671, Mercy 1676, Jonathan 1678, William 1681. Savage's Gen. Dict. vol. I, 279.

BROOKINS. Paul's Hist. of Wells, Vt.

BROOKS:—EBENEZER BROOKS, of Woburn, by wife Martha had Eunice 1688, John 1690, Ebenezer 1691, Eleazer 1694, Martha 1697, Eunice 1700, Priscilla 1702.

GILBERT BROOKS came in the Blessing from London, 1635. He married Elizabeth, said to have been a daughter of Gov. Edward Winslow. He had Gilbert, John Elizabeth 1645, Sarah 1646, Mary 1649, Rachel 1650, Bathsheba 1655, Rebecca, 1657, Hannah 1659.

HENRY BROOKS, of Concord, freeman 1639; had Joseph 1641.

HENRY BROOKS, of Wallingford, married Dec. 21, 1676, Hannah Blockley, and had Thomas 1679.

JOHN BROOKS, of Windsor, married May, 1652, Susanna Hanmore, and had John 1660, Samuel 1663, Elizabeth 1664, Mary 1665, Irvanna 1669, Lydia 1672, Susanna, 1675.

ROBERT BROOKS, of New London, Conn., came in 1635 with wife Ann and seven children.

ROBERT BROOKS of Plymouth, married Eliza, daughter of Gov. Edward Winslow, and had John 1657.

CAPT. ROBERT BROOKS, of Concord, was admitted freeman 1636, when he was an inhabitant of Watertown. He owned estate at Medford and Watertown as early as 1634. He was a captain and representative to the General Court 1642, and six years more. By wife Grace he had Caleb, born 1632, Gershaw, Joshua, Mary.

THOMAS BROOKS, of Haddam, Conn., was among the first settlers there and may have come in the "Susan and Ellen," 1635, aged 18. Supposed to have been a brother of Richard, of Lynn. He had a house at New London, 1659, but had gone 1661, with wife Lucy. He married Alice, daughter of Jared Spencer next year and had Sar-

ah 1662, Thomas 1664, Mary 1666, and Alice 1668. His widow married 1673, Thomas Shaler.   .

WILLIAM BROOKS, of Scituate, Mass., came in the "Blessing," 1635, aged 20; perhaps a brother of Gilbert. He was of Marshfield 1643. He married widow Susanna Dunham of Plymouth, and had Hannah 1645, Nathaniel 1646, Mary 1647, Sarah 1650, Marian 1652, Deborah 1654, Thomas 1657, Irvanna 1659.

REFERENCES.

CONNECTICUT.—Field's Hist. of Hadam, 44; Orcutt's Hist. of Stratford, 1164; Orcutt's Hist. of Torrington, 660; Orcutt's Hist. of Wolcott, 457; Hinman's Conn. Settlers, 348.
MAINE.—Bangor Hist. Mag., vol. I, 154; Lapham's Hist. of Norway, 472; Lapham's Hist. of Woodstock, 183; North's Hist. of Augusta, 817; Buxten, Me., Memorial, 156.
MASSACHUSETTS.—Wyman's Charlestown Gens. vol. I, 132; Temple's Hist. of Northfield, 413; Stearn's Hist. of Ashburnham, 621; Shattuck's Hist. of Concord, 364; Sewell's Hist. of Woburn, 594; Barry's Hist. of Hanover, 260; Bond s Hist. of Watertown, 719; Brook's Hist. of Medford, 506; Cutter's Hist. of Arlington, 197; Deane's Hist. of Scituate, 223; Essex Inst. Coll. XXI, 24; Freeman's Hist. of Cape Cod, vol. I, 666; Hazen's Hist. of Billinea, 18; Herrick s Hist. of Gardiner, 338; Pierce's Hist. of Grafton, 469; Potter's Old Families of Concord
NEW HAMPSHIRE.—Washington, N. H., Hist. 322; Stearn's Hist. of Rindge,456; Secomb's Hist. of Amherst, 510, Cochran's Hist. of Antrim, 379; Coggswell's Hist. of Henniker, 470; Hayward's Hist. of Hancock, 388; Livermore's Hist. of Wilton, 326; Merrill's Hist. of Acworth, 191; Norton's Hist. of Fitzwilliam, 496.
OTHER PUBLICATIONS.—Austin's R. I. Gen. Dict. 27; Locke Gen., 37; Porter Gen. 209; Powers' Hist of Sangamon County, Ill., 144; Prentice Gen., 404; Ransom Gen. 37; Amer. Ancestry, vol. I, 10; III, 77; V, 127; VI, 134, 260; VIII, 20, 49, 172; IX, 122; X, 167; Savage's Gen. Dict. vol. I, 259; N. E. Hist. and Gen. Reg. III, 401; V, 355; IX, 153; XXX, 466; Upham Gen., 44; Walworth's Hyde Gen., 322.

BROWN. Babson's Gloucester, Mass., 281; Martin's Chester, Pa., 281.

BROOMALL. Maris Gen. 57, 141, 220.

BROSS. Amer. Ancestry, IV, 71; VIII, 209.

BROTHWELL. Orcutt's Hist. of Stratford, Conn., 1350.

BROUGHTON:—JOHN BROUGHTON, of Northampton, was among the earliest settlers; married Hannah, eldest daughter of Thomas Bascom.

THOMAS BROUGHTON, of Watertown, 1643; came from Gravesend below London, 1635, to Virginia in the "America." By wife Mary, daughter of Nathaniel Briscoe, he had Elizabeth 1646; removed to Boston 1650. Had Mary, Thomas, 1653, Nathaniel, 1654, Thomas again 1656, Hannah 1658, Sarah 1660, Patience 1663. He was a merchant of great business; owned the mills at Salmon Falls; died 1700, aged 84.

REFERENCES:—Stearn's Hist. of Ashburnham, Mass., 627; Joshua Brown's Poultney, Vt., 221; Hinman's Conn. Settlers, 351; Paul's Hist. of Wells, Vt., 67; Savage's Gen. Dict. vol. I, 263; N. E. Hist. and Gen. Reg., XXXVIII, 298, Broughton Gen.

BROWER. Munsell's Albany IV, 105; Pearson s Schenectady, N. Y., Settlers, 26, Roome Gen., 160;

N. Y. Gen. and Biog. Rec. IX, 126.

BROWER:—WILLIAM BROWER, of Albany, born probably atEnkhuizen, died at Albany, Aug. 1, 1668; owned property in New Amsterdam in 1655; moved to Albany in 1657. It is a tradition in the family that he was the eldest son of Jacob, probably the famous Jacob Derksz, son of Dirk Jansz Brower, son of Jan Groot Albertszoon, burgomaster of Enkhuizen.

REFERENCES:—Bergen's Settlers King's County, N. Y., 51; Salter's Hist. of Monmouth County, N. J., XIII; Davis' Hist of Burk's County, Pa., 670; N. Y. Gen. Biog. Reg. VIII, 132; IX, 126; Amer. Ancestry, vol. I, 18; IV, 20.

BROWDER. Montague Gen., 660.

BROWN:—ABRAHAM BROWN, of Boston, merchant, arrived first time June 20, 1650, and married, August 19, 1653. Jane Skipper; had Mary, 1654. Went back that year and was taken by Barbary pirates, but soon was ransomed, and the following year returned to Boston, and had Jane 1657. He was admitted freeman 1654. He married May 1, 1666, Rebecca, daughter of Hezekiah Usher, and had Hezekiah 1661, Rebecca 1663, Elizabeth 1664.

ANDREW BROWN, of Scarborough, 1658, was constable 1670. and had in 1663, sons Andrew, John, Joseph, Charles and another.

CHAD BROWN came to Boston probably before 1658 and was afterwards one of the incorporators of Providence, R. I. He brought wife Elizabeth and son John, aged 8. He also had Jeremiah, Judah, alias Chad, and Daniel.

CHRISTIAN BROWN, of Salisbury, Mass. one of the first settlers, 1640, died 1641. She brought with her sons Henry, George and William.

DANIEL BROWN, of Providence, R. I., 1646, married Dec. 25. 1669, Alice Herenden, probably daughter of Benjamin, and had Judah, Sarah 1677, Jeremiah and perhaps others.

FRANCIS BROWN, of New Haven. 1639, died 1668. By wife Mary he had John 1640, Eleazer 1642, Samuel, Ebenezer, Lydia.

FRANCIS BROWN, of Stamford, Conn., 1660, constable 1663, representative to the General Court 1665-6-7-9 He married Martha, widow of John Clipman, and had Joseph.

HENRY BROWN, of Salisbury, Mass., born 1615. came with his mother and was an original proprietor of Salisbury, Mass., 1639; was a brother of George, of Haverhill. By wife Abigail he had Nathaniel 1642. Abigail 1644, Jonathan 1646, Philip 1648. Abraham 1656, Sarah 1654. Henry 1659.

HENRY BROWN, of Providence, swore allegiance in June, 1668: had Richard. Joseph, and probably Henry.

HUGH BROWN. of Boston, by wife Sarah had Job 1651. Hugh 1652. Sarah 1653.

JAMES BROWN, of Boston, 1630. number 61 in the church list, was admitted freeman 1634. By wife Grace he had James. 1645.

JAMES BROWN, of Charlestown. Mass.. 1632. admitted to the church 1634. freeman 1636: had by wife Elizabeth. John 1639. Mary 1640.

JAMES BROWN. of Charlestown. by wife Judith had John 1638. James 1647. Nathaniel 1648.

JAMES BROWN, of Hartford. May 1678. married Ian. 7. 1674. Remembrance Brook. and had Mary 1677 Abigail 1678. Thankful 1682. Sarah 1683, James 1685, Miner,-

well 1636, Hannah 1688, Mercy 1690, Elizabeth 1693, John 1695.

JAMES BROWN, of Branford, 1679, a landholder, may have removed and been of Norwalk, 1687. Had issue Isaac 1690, James.

JOHN BROWN, of Watertown, 1632, arrived Sept. 16, 1652, at Boston from London in the Leon; was admitted freeman Sept. 3, 1634. By wife Dorothy he had Hannah 1634, Mary 1637, James.

JOHN BROWN, of Salem, 1637, was admitted freeman 1638. He was a ruling elder of the church. He had John, 1638. James 1640.

JOHN BROWN, of Milford, Conn., 1648, had Mary, Esther, Joseph 1652, Mary, 1653 John 1655, Hannah, Phebe.

JOHN BROWN, of Cambridge, Mass., called a Scotchman, married April 24, 1665, Esther, daughter of Thomas Makepeace. He had Elizabeth 1657, Sarah 1661, Mary 1662, John 1664, Esther 1667, Thomas, 1669, Daniel 1671, Deborah 1673, Abigail 1675, Joseph 1677. He removed to Falmouth and later to Watertown. In his will, 1697, he mentions John, Thomas, Daniel, Joseph, Deborah.

JOHN BROWN, of Reading, married 1659 Elizabeth, the daughter of John Osgood, of Andover, and had Elizabeth, Sarah, Mary 1671. He was a captain. He was admitted freeman 1679, representative to the General Court 1679-80-82-83; died 1717, aged 81.

JOHN BROWN, of Salem, married 1669, Hannah, daughter of Francis Collins, and had Priscilla 1669, Margaret 1671, Joseph 1673, William 1677, Hannah 1678, Mary 1680. He was a representative from Marblehead under the new charter 1692 and for Salem 1707-9-13.

CAPT. JOHN BROWN, of Duxbury, Mass., by wife Ann had Ann 1673, John 1675.

CAPT. JOHN BROWN, of Swanzey, or Rehoboth, had John 1673.

JOHN BROWN, of Billeriea, Mass, married 22 April, 1682, Elizabeth, daughter of George Polley, and had John 1684, Elizabeth 1687, Hannah 1689.

JOHN BROWN, of Roxbury, Mass., by wife Elizabeth had Edmund 1687.

JOHN BROWN, of Stonington, married 1692, Elizabeth, daughter of Ephraim Miner, and had Jonathan 1695, Elizabeth 1697, Hepzebah 1699, John 1701, Ichabod 1704, Prudence 1707, Jedediah 1709, Mehitable 1716.

NATHANIEL BROWN, of Hartford, Conn., 1647, married 1647, Elinor, daughter of Richard Watts, removed to Middleton 1654, thence to Springfield, Mass., had Thomas 1655, Hannah 1657, Nathaniel 1654, John 1657, Benoni 1659.

NATHANIEL BROWN, of Ipswich, Mass., married Dec. 16, 1673, Judith Perkins, and had James 1685; was admitted freeman 1685, and perhaps was of Rowley later.

NICHOLAS BROWN, of Lynn, Mass., 1630, was admitted freeman 1638; was a representative 1641; removed to Reading 1644; died 1673. By wife Elizabeth he had John, Josiah, Edward, Elizabeth and Joseph.

PETER BROWN, of New Haven, 1639. had Mercy 1645, Elizabeth 1647; may have had Thomas and Hackaliah. His widow married Nicholas Knapp.

PETER BROWN, of Windsor, Conn., married July 15, 1658, Mary, daughter of Jonathan Gilbert, and had Peter 1667, John 1669, Jonathan 1670. Cornelius 1672. Esther 1673, Elizabeth 1676. Deborah 1679, Sarah 1681, all living at the time of his death.

RICHARD BROWN, of Watertown, Mass., came in the fleet with Winthrop; was admitted freeman 1631; was a

Ruling Elder in the church. He had Thomas and others.

SAMUEL BROWN, of Eastham, married Feb. 19, 1683, Martha Harding, and had Samuel 1690 and others.

STEPHEN BROWN, of Newbury, Mass., in his will, Aug. 3, 1656, names wife Sarah, and children, Sarah, Abigail, Ann, Mary, John, Stephen.

THOMAS BROWN, of Newbury, came from Southampton, England, 1655, in the "James"; was admitted freeman 1659. By wife Mary he had Mary 1659, Isaac, Francis.

THOMAS BROWN, of Concord, Mass., 1638, perhaps brother of Rev. Edmund Brown, was among the original proprietors of Sudbury, 1637; was admitted freeman 1639. By wife Bridget he had Boaz 1642, perhaps Jabez 1644, Mary 1646, Eleazer 1649, Thomas 1651. He removed probably to Cambridge and died there Nov. 3, 1688.

THOMAS BROWN, of Cambridge, married 1656. Martha, widow of Richard Oldham, and had Mehitable 1661, Mary 1663, Ebenezer 1665, Ischabod 1666, Martha 1668.

THOMAS BROWN, of Stonington, Conn., by wife Hannah had Samuel 1678, Hannah 1680, Mary 1683, Jerusha 1687, Sarah 1689, Thomas 1692, Elizabeth 1694. David 1696, Priscilla 1699, Humphrey 1701.

WILLIAM BROWN, of Boston, was in the employ of Gov. Winthrop. By wife Thomasine he had Sarah 1634.

WILLIAM BROWN, of Sudbury, Mass., an original proprietor, married Nov. 15, 1641. Mary, daughter of Thomas Besbeech or Bisby; had Mary, Thomas 1644, William Edmund, Hopestill, Susanna, Elizabeth, 1659. He was a deacon, Captain and representative under the new charter.

WILLIAM BROWN, of Gloucester, a selectman 1644, married July 15, 1646, Mary, widow of the first Abraham Robinson, had Mary 1649.

WILLIAM BROWN, of Plymouth, married July 16, 1649, Mary Murdock, and had Mary 1650, George 1652, William 1654, Samuel 1656, also John, James, Mercy.

WILLIAM BROWN, of Salisbury, 1641, brother of George of Haverhill, married 1645-6 Elizabeth Munford, and had Mary 1647, Ephraim 1650, Martha 1654, Elizabeth 1656, Sarah 1658.

WILLIAM BROWN, of Boston and Salem, had James. He died 1662, leaving widow Hannah and six children.

WILLIAM BROWN, of Salem, by wife Sarah had John 1669, Joseph 1672, Benjamin 1674.

WILLIAM BROWN, of Charlestown, married Feb. 29, 1672. Mary Goodwin, and had Job 1675.

REFERENCES.

CONNECTICUT.—Andrews' Hist. of New Britain, 225; Bronson's Hist. of Waterbury, 478; Brown's West Simsbury Settlers, 14; Davis' Hist. of Wallingford. 662; Dodd's Hist. of East Haven, 110; Hine's Lebanon, Conn., Address (1880), 148; Hinman's Conn. Settlers, 357; Huntington's Stamford, Conn., Families, 17; Orcutt's Stratford, II. 16; Orcutt's Hist. of Torrington, 660; Stile's Hist. of Windsor, V, 117; Tuttle Family of Conn., 637.

MAINE.—Bradbury's Kennebunkport, 229; Corliiss' North Yarmouth; Dearborn's Hist. of Parsonfield. 367; Eaton's Hist. of Thomaston, 158; Farrow's Hist. of Ilesborough. 173; Hatch's Hist. of Industry, 521; Johnston Hist of Bristol, 236; Lapham's Hist. of Bethel, 404, 652; Lapham's Hist. of Norway, 472; Lapham's Hist. of

MASSACHUSETTS. — Wyman's Charlestown, Mass., Gens., vol. I, 136; Winsor's Hist. of Duxbury, 238; Chase's Hist. of Haverhill, 248, 624; Chandler's Hist. of Shirley, 359; Babson's Hist. of Gloucester, 64; Ballou's Hist. of Milford, 602; Barry's Hist. of Framingham, 195; Brown's Medford Families, 5; Cutter's Hist of Arlington, 197; Davis' Landmarks of Plymouth, 45; Freeman's Hist. of Cape Cod, II, 371; Hammat Papers, Ipswich, 38; Hazen's Hist. of Bellerica, 18; Hobart's Hist. of Abington, 357; Hudson's Hist. of Lexington, 27; Hudson's Hist. of Marlboro', 346; Jackson's Hist. of Newton. 245; Marvin's Hist. of Winchendon, 450; Mitchell's Hist. of Bridgewater, 122; Morse's Sherbourne, 18; Paige's Hist. of Cambridge, 502; Pierce's Hist. of Grafton, 471; Potter's Old Families of Concord; Reed's Hist of Rutland. 144; Stearn's Hist. of Ashburnham, 628; Stone's Hist. of Hubbardstone, 231; Temple's Hist of North Brookfield, 539; Temple's Hist. of Palmer, 412; Temple's Hist. of Whately, 211; Washburn's Hist. of Leicester, 345; Whitmore's Copp's Hill Epitaphs; Paige's Hist. of Cambridge, 502; Essex Hist. Coll., VIII, 33.

NEW HAMPSHIRE.—Worcester's Hist. of Hollis, 368; Wheeler's Hist. of Newport, 309; Washington, N. H., Hist., 322; Bassett's Richmond; Blood's Hist. of Temple, 207; Chase's Hist. of Chester, 476; Cochran's Hist. of Antrim. 380; Coggswell's Hist. of Henniker, 471; Coggswell's Hist. of Nottingham, 335; Cushman's Hist. of Sheepscott, 359; Doro's Hist. of Hampton, 615; Eaton's Hist. of Candia, 53; Fiske's Hist. of Amherst, N. H., 138; Fullerton's Hist. of Raymond, 173; Hayward's Hist. of Gilsum, 278; Kidder's Hist. of New Ipswich, N. H., 339; Livermore's Hist. of Wilton, 327; Merrill's Hist. of Ackworth, 192; Hayward's Hist of Hancock, 403; Runnell's Hist. of Sanbornton, vol. 1, 471; Secomb's Hist. of Amherst, 520; Stark's Hist. of Dunbarton, 252; Stearn's Hist. of Ringe, 458; Read's Hist. of Swanzey, 300; Saunderson's Charlestown, 293; Norton's Hist. of Fitzwilliam, 497.

NEW YORK.—Baird's Hist. of Rye, 399; Balton's Hist. of Westchester County, vol., II, 713; Cleveland's Hist. of Yate's County, 128, 306, 462; Rutlenber's Hist. of Orange County, 389; Smith's Hist. of Rhinebeck, 203.

RHODE ISLAND.—Austin's Ancestries, 13; Austin's R. I, Gen. Dict., 27, 258.

VERMONT.—Bangor Hist. Mag., II, 43. 224; IV, 213; Bass' Hist. of Braintree, 120; Hemenway's Vt. Gazette, V, 710; Hollister's Hist. of Pawlet, 171; William's Hist. of Danby, 115; Caverley's Hist. of Pittsford, 693.

OTHER PUBLICATIONS.—Slaughter's St. Ann Parish, Virginia, 183; Richmond, Virginia, Standard, volume II. 7, 10; volume III. 6; Peyton's Hist. of Augusta County. 304; Foote's Sketches of Va., 2d series, 99; Hayden's Va. Gen., 147; Hayden's Oliver Brown Biog. (1822); Hubbard's Stanstead County, Conn., 194; Littell's Passaic Valley Gen., 61; Salter's Hist. of Monmouth County, N. J., XIII; Plumb's Hist. of Hanover, Pa., 395; Power's Hist. of Sangamon County, Ill., 151; Alexander Gen., 123; Ammedown Family, 345; Ball's Hist. of Lake County. Ind., 422; Barbour's My Wife and Mother, 68; Bouton Gen., 474; Carter Family Tree; the Clark Family of Watertown. 46, 82; Clyde's Irish Settlement of Pa., 22; Crane's Rawson Family. 58; Douglass Gen. 143, 158; Egle's Hist. Reg. Int. Pa. 11. 47; Greene's Gen.; Greene's Kentucky Families; Heraldic Journal. II, 24, 95; Holden's Capron Family, 187; Humphrey Gen., 301, 464; Kirk Gen., 56, 116; Loome's Gen., II. 166, 703; Miller's Colchester, N. S., 262; Muzzey's Reminis-

BROWN. References continued, Muzzey's Reminiscences, Nash. Gen. 81; Rockwood Gen., 104,Thomas Family of Maryland, 45; Willis' Washington Gen. 219, 237; Wentworth Gen., 134, 237; Whitman Gen., 123; Wight Gen., 114; Savage's Gen. Dict. I, 264; N; E. Hist. and Gen. Reg. VI, 232; VII, 312; IX, 219; XXIX, 184; Amer. Ancestry, vol. I, 10; II, 16; IV, 182, 215; VI, 182; VII, 71, 176; VIII, 78, 152, 242; IX, 23, 39, 190; X, 160; XI, 10, 23, 70, 169; Brown Assoc. Report, 1866, 1888; Cope's Gen. of Brown Family, 1864; Brown Gen. 1851, 1860, 1864, 1879, 1885, 1893.

BROWNE. Bond's Hist. of Watertown, Mass., 120; Eaton's Hist. of Reading, Mass., 49; Essex Inst. Coll., VIII, 225; XX, 151; Meade's Old Families of Va.; Slaughter's Bristol Parish, Va., 170; Richmond, Va., Standard, II, 17; III, 7, Morrison's Hist. of Windham, N. H., 348; Welles' Washington Gen. 219; Hughes Gen. 65; Driver Gen. 296; Amer. Ancestry, VII, 56; N. E. Hist. and Gen. Reg. XXXV, 352; XXIX, 184; XLIV, 281; Brown Gen. 1887, 1888.

BROWNBACK. Rittenhouse Gen. 237.

BROWNELL:—Thomas Brownell, of Portsmouth, R. I., was a freeman 1655. He had a son,

GEORGE BROWNELL, who married Dec. 4, 1673, Susanna, daughter of Richard Pierce, and had Susanna 1676, Sarah 1687, Mary, Martha, Thomas 1688, Joseph 1690, Wait 1693.

REFERENCES:—Austin's Ances. Dict.; Austin's R. I. Gen. Dict. 29; Pierce's Contributions, 30; Savage's Gen. Dict. vol. I, 279; Brownell Gen. 1892.

BROWNING:—Henry Browning, of New Haven, had baptized in right his wife, Hannah Jan. 5, 1640; Zephaniah 1640; Ebenezer 1646, next year he sold his estate to William Judson and probably went home.

NATHANIEL BROWNING, of Portsmouth, R. I., was admitted freeman 1655, he married Sarah, daughter of William Freeborn, and may have had Samuel.

REFERENCES:—Hyde's Hist. of Brimfield, Mass., 380; Reed's Hist. of Rutland, Mass., 152; Stone's Hist. of Hubbardston, Mass., 235; Orcutt's Hist. of New Milford, Conn., 668, 802; Austin's R. I. Gen. Dict. 262; Jones Gen. 1897, 192; Amer. Ancestry, V, 146; Savage's Gen. Dict. vol. I, 279.

BROWNSON or BRUNSON:—John Brunson, of Hartford, removed to Farmington, Conn., and was one of the founders of the church there, Oct. 15, 1652. He died 1680, having Abraham, born 1647, also Jacob, John, Isaac, and daughters Mary, Dorcas and Sarah. He settled at Waterbury.

RICHARD BRUNSON, of Farmington, brother of John, had Abigail, John, Cornelius, Hannah.

REFERENCES:—Boyd's Hist. of Winchester, 109; Joslin's Hist. of Poultney, Vt., 226.

BRUCE:—John Bruce, of Sudbury, by wife Elizabeth, had Hannah 1672, Mary 1680, Eunice 1684, Martha 1685; may have had son earlier.

ROGER BRUCE, of Marlborough, Mass., by wife Elizabeth, had Samuel 1691, Abigail 1693. He removed to Framingham, Mass., and had Elisha 1695, Rebecca 1698, Sarah 1700, Daniel 1701, Thomas 1704, Hannah 1706, Deliverance 1709, David 1711.

REFERENCES.

MASSACHUSETTS.—Washburne's Hist. of Leicester. 344; Temple's Hist. of North Brookfield, 539; Pierce's Hist. of Grafton, 472; Paige's Hist. of Hardwick, 342;

Hudson's Hist. of Marlboro, 347; Barry's Hist. of Framingham, 197.

NEW HAMPSHIRE.—Washington, N. H., Hist. 323, Smith's Hist. of Petersboro, 267; Secomb's Hist. of Amherst, 521; Runnell's Hist. of Sanbornton, vol. I, 142; Norton's Hist. of Fitzwilliam, 498; Hayward's Hist. of Gilsum, 278.

OTHER PUBLICATIONS.—Vinton's Upton Mem. 504; Richmond, Va., Standard, II, 47; Power's Hist. of Sangamon County, Ill., 153; Locke Gen. 43, 151; Green's Todd and other Gens.; Blake Gen. 47, 69; Bass'Hist. of Braintree, Vt., 121; Bangor Hist. Mag. III, 91; Amer. Ancestry, II, 17; VI, 36; Savage's Gen. Dict. vol. I, 280.

BRUEN:—Obadiah Bruen, of Gloucester, came to New England in 1640, probably with Rev. Richard Blueman; settled first at Marshfield, Mass., and asked for admission as freeman of Plymouth jurisdiction, March 1641, but speedily went to the opposite side of the Bay. He was admitted freeman May 19, 1642, selectman 1642, and for several years following. He was representative to the General Court, 1647-8-9 and 1651; the latter year with his spiritual guide. He removed to New London, and there was town-clerk fifteen years; was often represented at the General Court, and was named in the royal charter 1662; but having purchased, June 11, 1667, with an association the lands in East Jersey, now comprised in the city of Newark, he removed thence. He was the youngest son of John Bruen, Esq., of Bruen, Stapleford, Cheshire, baptized Dec. 25, 1606, at Faroe, near Chester. He became a draper at Shrewsbury, in the adjoining county of Salop. By wife Sarah, he had Mary, Rebecca, Hannah 1644, John 1646. He was living in 1680.

REFERENCES:—Hinman's Conn. Settlers, 331; Babson's Hist. Gloucester, Mass., 65; N. J. Hist. Soc. Coll. VI, 112; Davenport Gen. 251; Baldwin Gen. 841; Amer. Ancestry, V, 37; Bruen, John, Biog. 1857; Savage's Gen. Dict. vol. I, 280.

BRUBACHER. Brubacher Gen. 1884.

BRUNDAGE. Baird's Hist. of Rye, N. Y., 398.

BRUNNER. Neff Gen. 310.

BRUNK. Power's Hist. of Sangamon Co., Ill., 153.

BRUNSEN. Andrews' Hist. of New Britain, Conn., 225.

BRUSH:—George Brush, of Woburn, Mass., said to be a Scotchman, married Dec. 20, 1659, Elizabeth daughter of William Clark, and had Elizabeth 1663, Mary 1665, William 1667, John 1670, Elizabeth again 1672, Joseph 1676, Samuel 1680, Margery 1684, Lydia 1687. He was admitted freeman 1690, died Aug. 13, 1692.

REFERENCES:—Meade's Hist. of Greenwich, Conn., 315; Sewall's Hist. of Woburn, Mass., 595; Smith's Hist. of Dutchess County, N. Y., 125; Phenix's Whitney Family, Conn., vol. I, 274; Savage's Gen. Dict. vol. I, 281.

BRUSE. Amer. Ancestry, II, 17.

BRUSSY. Munsell's Albany Coll., IV, 105.

BRUYN. Sylvester's Hist. of Ulster County, N. Y., 259; Schoonmaker's Hist. of Kingston, N. Y., 473; N. Y. Gen. and Biog. Rec. XX, 26; Amer. Ancestry, IV. 213.

BRYAN:—Alexander Bryan, of Milford, 1639, was a man of influence in the New Haven Colony, and after the union of Connecticut was Assistant 1668-73. His wife Ann, died 1661, and he married the widow of Samuel Fitch, the school-master of Hartford, and died 1679, at great age. He had Richard and other children.

REFERENCES:—Slaughter's Bristol Parish, Va., 109; Hayden's Virginia Gens., 203; Power's Hist. of Sangamon County, Ill., 154; Bulloch Gen.; Baldwin Gen. Supp. 1313; Amer. Ancestry, II, 17; Savage's Gen. Dict. 281; Bryan Gen. 1889.

BRYANT:—John Bryant, of Scituate, Mass., 1639, married Nov. 14. 1643, Mary daughter of George Lewis, of Barnstable, Mass., and had John 1644, Hannah 1646, Sarah 1648, Martha 1652, Samuel 1654. He was a representative to the General Court 1677-8.

STEPHEN BRYANT, of Duxbury, 1643, removed to Plymouth 1650, married Abigail, daughter of John Shaw, and had John 1650, Mary 1654, Stephen 1658, Sarah 1659 Lydia 1662, Elizabeth 1665.

WILLIAM BRYANT, of Boston, taverner, by wife Hannah, who survived him, had Hannah 1683, Benjamin 1686, William 1687, John 1689; he died 1697.

Arms.—Azure on a cross, a cinquefoil between four lozenges, gules. *Crest.*—A flag azure charged with a saltire argent.

REFERENCES.

MASSACHUSETTS.—Davis' Landmarks of Plymouth, 46; Deane's Hist. of Scituate, 227; Eaton's Hist. of Reading, 56; Hudson's Hist. of Lexington, 30; Kingman's Hist. of North Bridgewater, 448; Mitchell's Hist. of Bridgewater, Mass., 123; Temple's Hist. of North Brookfield, 541; Swift's Barnstable Families, vol. I, 140; Winsor's Hist. of Duxbury, 238; Wyman's Charlestown, Mass., Gens., I, 146.

MAINE.—Eaton's Hist. of Thomaston, 162; Hatch's Hist. of Industry, 523; Lapham's Hist. of Bethel, 496; Lapham's Hist. of Paris, 540; Lapham's Hist. of Woodstock, 185; Cushman's Hist. of Sheepscott, 359; Machias Centen. Celebration, 156.

NEW HAMPSHIRE.—Bassett's Hist. of Richmond, 338; Cochran's Hist. of Antrim, 385; Hayward's Hist. of Gilsum, 279; Read's Hist. of Swanzey, 299.

OTHER PUBLICATIONS.—Hinman's Conn. Settlers, 360; Whitehead's Hist. of Perth Amboy, N. J., 145; Stanton Gen. 276; Savage's Gen. Dict. vol. I, 282; Amer. Ancestry, vol. I, 11; VI, 193; VII, 131; VIII, 129; IX, 226; N. E. Hist. and Gen. Reg. XXIV, 315; XXXV, 37; XLVIII, 46.

BRYER:—Elisha Bryer, of New Hampshire, 1689, probably lived at Portsmouth, when he married Oct. 4, 1689, Abigail Drew, perhaps daughter of James Drew, and had Margaret 1693, Abigail 1695, Samuel 1697, Sarah 1700, Mary 1702.

RICHARD BRYER, of Newbury, married Dec. 21, 1665, Eleanor Wright, who died Aug. 20, 1672, and had Richard 1667, Elizabeth 1669, Ruth 1670.

REFERENCES:—Austin's R. I. Gen. Dict. 30; Cutt's Gen. 28; Savage's Gen. Dict. vol. I, 283.

BUCH. Heinecke Gen. 29.

BUCHMAN. Lamb's Hist. of New York City, vol. I, 740; Roe's Sketches of Rose, N. Y., 88; Old Kent, Maryland, 49; Hist. of Clarmont, Ohio, 367; Salisbury Gen.; Amer. Ancestry, VI, 23; Buchanan Gen. 1849.

BUCHER. Egle's Hist. of Lebanon County, Pa., 236; Egle's Penn. Gens. 103; Brubacher Gen. 19.

BUCK:—Emanuel or Enoch Buck, of Wethersfield, by wife Sarah, had Ezekiel 1650, John 1652, Jonathan

1655, and by second wife Mary, daughter of John Kirby, of Middletown, had David, 1667, Sarah 1668, Hannah 1671, Elizabeth 1676, Thomas 1678, Abigail 1682.

EPHRAIM BUCK, of Woburn, Mass., married Jan. 1, 1671, Sarah Brooks, and had Sarah 1674, Ephraim 1676, John 1680, Samuel 1682, Eunice 1685, Ebenezer 1689 Mary 1691.

HENRY BUCK, of Wethersfield, married Oct. 31, 1660, Elizabeth, daughter of Josiah Churchill, and had Samuel 1664, Martha 1667, Elizabeth 1670, Mary 1673, Sarah 1678, Ruth 1681, Mehitable 1684, and Henry. He died July 7, 1712.

ISAAC BUCK, of Scituate, Mass., 1647, was town-clerk 1663-4-5. He bore arms in 1643; was Lieutenant 1676. repulsed the Indian assault on the town, died 1695, leaving widow Frances and children Thomas, Joseph, Jonathan, Benjamin, Elizabeth, Ruth and Deborah.

JOHN BUCK, of Hingham, brother of above, came probably in the same ship; he removed in 1650 to Scituate, Mass., and married Elizabeth, daughter of Samuel Holbrook, of Weymouth; had Elizabeth, born 1653, Mary 1655, Joseph 1657, John 1659, Hannah 1661, Susanna 1664, Benjamin 1665, Deborah 1670, Robert 1672, Rachel 1674. He married 1693, the widow of Edward Dalty, who was probably Sarah, sister of the famous Elder Faunce. He died 1697.

ROGER BUCK, of Cambridge, came in the Increase 1635, aged 18, perhaps son of William. He had Mary 1638, died 1669, John 1644, Ephraim 1646, Mary 1648, Ruth 1653, Elizabeth 1657, and perhaps others.

WILLIAM BUCK, of Cambridge, came in the Irene 1635, had Roger and others.

REFERENCES.

MAINE.—Lapham's Hist. of Woodstock, 185; Lapham's Hist. of Paris, 542; Lapham's Hist. of Norway 476; Bangor Hist. Mag. vol. II, 21, 142; VI, 51.

OTHER PUBLICATIONS.—Blackman's Hist. of Susquehanna County, Pa., 58; Davis' Hist. of Buck's County. Pa., 542; Sewall's Hist. of Woburn, Mass., 596; Paige's Hist. of Cambridge, Mass., 503; Mitchell's Hist. of Bridgewater, Mass., 125; Deane's Hist. of Scituate. Mass., 229; Timlow's Hist. of Southington, Conn., 34; Orcutt's Hist. of New Milford, Conn., 671; Hinman's Conn. Settlers, 364; Caverly's Hist. of Pittsford, Vt., 190; Crane's Rawsen Gen. 190; Montague Gen. 567; Penn. Mag. XII, 496; Walworth Hyde Gen. 1117; Savage's Gen. Dict. vol. I, 283; Amer. Ancestry, vol. I, 11; III, 93, 144; N. E. Hist. and Gen. Reg. XV, 297; Buck Gen. 1889, 1893.

BUCKALEW. Salter's Hist. Monmouth County, N. J., 13.

BUCKBEE. Amer. Ancestry, II, 17.

BUCKINGHAM:—Thomas Buckingham, of Milford 1639, was one of the chief men. He had Thomas 1646 He died in 1657, on a visit to Boston.

Rev. THOMAS BUCKINGHAM, of Saybrook, son of the preceding, was minister there 1669; died April 1, 1709. He was among the founders of Yale College at Saybrook. By wife Esther, daughter of Thomas Hosmer, of Hartford, whom he married Sept. 20, 1666, he had Esther 1668, Thomas 1670, David 1672, Stephen 1675, Samuel 1679, Hezekiah 1682, Temperance 1685, Ann 1687.

THOMAS BUCKINGHAM, of Hartford, married Nov. 29, 1699, Ann, daughter of Rev. Isaac Foster, died 1731, leaving only son Joseph.

Arms.—Per pale gules and sable a swan with wings

expanded argent ducally gorged and chained or.

REFERENCES:—Cothren's Woodbury, Conn., II, 1472; Hinman's Conn. Settlers, 371; Orcutt's Hist. of New Milford, Conn., 673; Bronson's Hist. of Waterbury, Conn.; Savage's Gen. Dict. vol. I, 284; Buckingham Gen.

BUCKLAND:—Benjamin Buckland, of Braintree, married Rachel, daughter of John Wheatley, had Leah and perhaps removed to Rehoboth and there had David, born 1675.

THOMAS BUCKLAND, admitted freeman 1635, was probably of Dorchester, but removed soon after to Windsor, Conn., served in the Pequot war 1637. He married Temperance, daughter of Nicholas Denslow, and had Timothy 1639, Elizabeth 1641, Temperance 1642, Mary 1644, Nicholas 1647, Sarah 1649, Hannah 1634.

WILLIAM BUCKLAND, Hartford, died 1691, leaving William and Charles.

REFERENCES:—Stiles' Hist. of Windsor, Conn., II, 122; Hinman's Conn. Settlers, 275; Eaton's Hist. of Warren, 380; Joslin's Hist. of Poultney, Vt., 227; Hubbard's Stanstead County, Can., 324; Savage's Gen. Dict vol. I, 285.

BUCKLEY:— Joseph Buckley, of Boston, merchant, married Joanna, daughter of Richard Shute, widow of Nathaniel Nichols. In his will he provided for Joseph, Richard, Thomas.

REFERENCES:—Whitmore's Copps Hill Epitaphs; Thomas Gen. of Md., 45; Roe's Sketches of Rose, N. Y., 48; Copman's Bulkley Gen.; Amer. Ancestry, III, 17; Savage's Gen. Dict. vol. I, 286.

BUCKLIN. Eaton's Hist. of Thomaston, Me., 162; Eaton's Hist. of Warren, Me., 510; Williams' Hist. of Danby, Vt., 117.

BUCKLYN. Amer. Ancestry, VII, 162.

BUCKMAN:—William Buckman, of Charlestown, had by first wife John, by second wife Sarah—had Josea 1641, Elizabeth 1644, Mercy 1648, Sarah 1650, William 1652, Mehitable 1654, Edward 1657, Samuel 1660.

REFERENCES:—Cutter's Hist. of Arlington, Mass., 198; Hudson's Hist. of Lexington, Mass., 31; Jameson's Hist. of Medway, Mass., 456; Benedict's Hist. of Salton, Mass., 591; Power's Hist. of Sangamon County, Ill., 157.

BUCKMINSTER:—Thomas Buckmenster, of Scituate, Mass., by his wife Joan, had James, Zachariah, Elizabeth, Mary.

REFERENCES:—Barry's Hist. of Framingham, Mass., 199; Allen's Worcester, Mass., Ass'n, 81; Clark Family of Watertown, Mass., 22; Cochran's Hist. of Antrim, N. H., 387; Wood Gen. 217; Alden's Epitaphs, II; Savage's Gen. Dict. vol. I, 286.

BUCKNAM. Hist. North Yarmouth, Mass., 111; Wyman's Hist. Charlestown, Mass., I, 147.

BUCKNER. Meade's Old Families of Va.; Goode Gen.

BUCKWALTER. Futhey's Chester, 484.

BUDD. Bolton's Hist. of Westchester County, N. Y., II, 715; Baird's Hist. of Rye, N. Y., 403; Neff Gen. 196; Amer. Ancestry, vol. V, 59; Savage's Gen. Dict. vol. I, 287.

BUDDINGTON. Savage's Gen. Dict. vol. I, 287.

BUDLEY:—Giles Budley, of Ipswich 1648, had wife Elizabeth, and children Andrew 1657, James 1660, John,

Giles. Savage's Gen. Dict. vol. I, 287.

BUDLONG:—Francis Budlong, of Warwick, married 1669, Rebecca, widow of Joseph Howard, and had John and other children.

JOHN BUDLONG, son of the preceding, had John, Moses and Daniel.

REFERENCES:—Austin's R. I. Gen. Dict. 264; Amer. Ancestry, II, 16; Savage's Gen. Dict. vol. I, 288.

BUEL or BUELL:—William Buell, of Windsor, Conn., was one of the first settlers of the town. By wife Mary, he had Samuel 1641, Mary 1642, Peter 1644, Hannah 1647, Hepzibah 1649, Sarah 1653, Abigail 1656.

CONNECTICUT.—Hine's Lebanon, Conn., Address 149; Hinman's Conn. Settlers, 368; Sedgwick's Hist. of Sharon, 66; Stiles' Hist. of Windsor, II, 126; Brown's West Simsbury Settlers, 30.

OTHER PUBLICATIONS.—Cleveland's Hist. of Yates County, N. Y., 207; Eager's Hist. of Orange County, N. Y., 338; Wheeler's Hist. of Newport, N. H., 312; Kilbourne Family, 113; Barbour's My Wife and Mother, App., 63; Loomis' Gen. Female Branches, 301; Walworth's Hyde Gen. 1128; Welles' Amer. Family Antiquities; Amer. Ancestry, vol. I, 2; Savage's Gen. Dict. vol. I, 288; Wells' Buell Gen. 1881.

BUFFAM. Amer. Ancestry, 229; Savage's Gen. Dict. vol. I, 288.

BUFFER. Bassett's Hist. of Richmond, N. H.

BUFFINGTON:—Thomas Buffington or Boranton, by wife Sarah Southwick, had Thomas 1672, Benjamin 1675, Abigail 1695.

REFERENCES:—Egle's Pa. Gens.; V, 233; Futhey's Chester, Pa., 480; Savage's Gen. Dict. vol. I, 289.

BUFFUM:—Caleb Buffum, son, perhaps, of the first Robert, married in 1672, Hannah, daughter of the first Joseph Pope, and Caleb, born 1672.

REFERENCES:—Aldrich's Walpole, Mass., 216; Bassett's Hist. of Richmond, N. H., 340; Richardson's Hist. of Woonsocket, R. I., 267; Williams' Hist. of Danby, Vt., 118; Austin's Allied Families R. I., 43; Amer. Ancestry, VI, 192; Savage's Gen. Dict. vol. I, 289.

BUFORD. Paxton's Marshall Gen. 179, 291; Greene's Kentucky Families, Goode Gen.

BUGBEE:—Edward Bugbee, of Roxbury, Mass., born in England, about 1594, came to Boston in ship "Francis" in 1634, with wife Rebecca, settled in Roxbury; died Jan. 26, 1669. He had Sarah and Joseph.

EDWARD BUGBY, of Roxbury, Mass., by wife Abigail, daughter of Richard Hall, had Abigail 1694, John 1696, and other children.

REFERENCES:—Austin's Allied Families R.I., 45; Hayward's Hist. of Hancock, N. H., 405; Livermore's Hist. of Wilton, N. H., 330; Amer. Ancestry, III, 75; IV, 175; Savage's Gen. Dict. vol. I, 289; Bugby Gen.; Bulger Austin's R. I. Gen. Dict. 30.

BULKLEY:—Peter Bulkley, of Concord, Mass., the first minister there, son of Edward, D. D., of Odell, of Witley, Bedfordshire, England, born June 31, 1583, was bred at St. John's College, Cambridge, Eng. He had a considerable estate from his father, a moderate non-conformist, who he succeeded in his native parish, and served at that altar twenty years, through favor of Lord Keifer William, then Bishop of London. He came in the "Susan and Ann" 1635, and gave his age as 50. He was first at Cambridge, and installed at Concord, 1637; died March 9, 1659. His widow removed to New London, Conn., and bought a house there 1663, died 1669. By first wife Jane, daughter of Thomas Allen, of Goldington, he had Edward, Thomas, Nathaniel 1618, George, Daniel, Jabez, Joseph; by wife Grace, daughter of Sir Richard Chetwood or Chetwoode, he had Gershom 1636, Eleazer 1638, Dorothy 1640, Peter 1643.

WILLIAM BULKLEY, of Ipswich, Mass., 1648, had William, who died in 1660. He removed to Salem, and died June 2, 1702, aged 80. His wife Sarah, who came in 1648, was in 1692 indicted for witchcraft but acquitted.

REFERENCES:—N. E. Hist. and Gen. Reg. XLII, 82; XVI, 135; XXIII, 299; Hinman's Conn. Settlers, 378; Champion Gen.; Hall's Gen. Notes, 82, 168; Kulp's Wyoming Valley Families; Schenck's Hist. of Fairfield, Conn., 358; Smith Gen. by Wellington Smith; Truber Gen. 110; Redfield Gen. 55; Loomis' Gen. Female Branches, 726; Printree Gen. 278; Ruggles' Gen.; Bulkley's Brown Mem. 143; Fowler's Chauncey Mem.; Heraldic Journal, 1865; Amer. Ancestry, VIII, 208, V, 134; Savage's Gen. Dict. vol. I, 296; Bulkley Gen.

BULL:—Henry Bull, of Roxbury, Mass., came in the "James" from London 1635, aged 25; admitted freeman, May 17, 1637. He was among the Boston majority of heretics disarmed; went to Rhode Island with Miss Hutchinson; was one of the purchasers 1638, his being the 18th name of the signers of the contract or covenant for civil government in that year. He was Governor of the Colony in 1685, and died Jan. 9, 1694. By wife Elizabeth, who died 1665, he had Jireh 1638, at Portsmouth, Henry, Esther, Mary.

JOHN BULL, of Boston, 1638, felt-maker, married Mary daughter of Nicholas Baxter, had James 1665, Mary 1667, Mehitable 1670, John 1672, Henry 1674, Margaret 1676, Martha 1678, Samuel 1680, Jonathan 1683.

JOSEPH BULL, of Hartford, Conn., married April 11, 1671, Sarah Manning, of Cambridge, and had Sarah 1672, Joseph 1675, Daniel 1677, Caleb 1680, and may have been at Wickford, R. I., 1674.

ROBERT BULL, of Saybrook, Conn., 1649, married in December of that year Phebe——; had Mary 1651, John 1653, Phebe 1655, Robert 1663.

THOMAS BULL, of Hartford, Conn., came in the "Hopewell," Capt. Babb; embarked at London 1635, aged 25, was of Boston or Cambridge first, but accompanied Hooker next May. He served well in the Pequot war 1637, and in 1675; was in command at Saybrook, when Andros attempted to gain the place for his master, the Duke of York, but was prevented by the determined stand taken by Bull. He died in 1684. His wife was Susanna. In his will he names children Thomas, David, of Saybrook 1651, Jonathan 1649, Joseph of Hartford, Ruth, wife of Andrew Boardman, of Cambridge, Abigail Buck, and a third daughter Bunce.

WILLIAM BULL, of Cambridge, Mass., had by wife Blyth, Rebecca 1644, John 1647, Mary 1649, William 1652, Samuel 1654, Elisha 1657. His widow died Sept. 23, 1690, aged 72.

Arms.—Azure three bulls' heads erased argent, attired or, between as many amulets in fesse of the last. *Crest.*—A bull's head, erased sable charged with six amulets or, one, two, and three.

REFERENCES:—Orcutt's Hist. of New Milford, Conn., 677; Hinman's Conn. Settlers, 386; Cothren's Hist. of Woodbury, Conn., 511; Austin's R. I. Ancestries, 15; Austin's R. I. Gen. Dict. 30, 264; Eager's Hist. of Orange

County, N. Y., 483; Futhey's Hist. of Chester County, Pa., 489; Hayden's Virginia Gens. 206; Barbour's My Wife and Mother, App. 41; Chapman Gen. 188; Green's Todd and Other Families; N. E. Hist. Reg. IV, 250; Newport Hist. Mag. IV, 134; R. I. Hist. Mag. V, 12; R. I. Hist. Society Coll. III, 307; 398; Williams' Hist. of Danby, Vt., 119; Young's Hist. of Wayne County, Ind., 338; Amer. Ancestry, vol. I, 11; II, 17; Paige's Hist. of Cambridge, Mass., 504; Savage's Gen. Dict. vol. 1, 292.

BULLA. Young's Wayne County, Ind., 338.

BULLARD:—Benjamin Bullard, of Watertown, Mass., about 1642, married a daughter of Henry Thorpe; removed to Medfield; admitted freeman 1668; perhaps had son Benjamin by former wife.

BENJAMIN BULLARD, of Dedham, son of preceding, married 1659, Martha Pidge, daughter of Thomas, and had Samuel 1667, Benjamin 1670, Hannah 1672, Eleazer 1676. He married second in 1677, Elizabeth, and had John 1678, Elizabeth 1682, Mary 1684, Malachi 1686, Isaac 1688. He lived in that part of Dedham, which was early made Medfield.

WILLIAM BULLARD, of Dedham, Mass., 1636, was admitted freeman 1640; had Isaac, Nathaniel, Elizabeth, who married Moses Collier, of Woodbridge, N. J., Mary.

REFERENCES.

MASSACHUSETTS.—Jameson's Hist. of Medway, 457; Bond's Hist. of Watertown, 147; Benedict's Hist. of Sutton, 592; Barry's Hist. of Framingham, 203; Ballou's Hist. of Milford, 606; Hill's Dedham Records; Morse's Sherbourne Settlers, 22, 57; Wyman's Charlestown Gens. vol. I, 149.

OTHER PUBLICATIONS.—Secomb's Hist. of Amherst, N. H., 522; Read's Hist. of Swanzey, N. H., 302; Hayward's Hist. of Hancock, 407; Hill's Hist. of Mason, N. H., 200; Powers' Hist. of Sangamon County, Ill., 158; Wight Gen. 23; Smith Gen. by Wellington Smith; Leland Magazine or Gen. 181; Bullard Gen. 1878; Amer. Ancestry, V, 142; Savage's Gen. Dict. vol. I, 294.

BULLEN:—Samuel Bullen, Dedham, Mass., was admitted freeman 1641; married August 10, 1641, Mary, daughter of Samuel Morse, and had Mary 1642, Samuel 1644, Elizabeth 1647, Joseph 1651, Ephraim 1653, Meletiah 1655, Elisha 1657, Eleazer 1662, Bethia 1664, and John. He died Jan. 16, 1692.

REFERENCES:—Lapham's Hist. of Norway, Me., 477; Butler's Hist. of Farmington, Me., 398; Morse's Hist. of Sherborn, Mass., 19; Barry's Hist. of Framingham, 205; Jameson's Hist. of Medway, Mass., 460; Stiles' Hist. of Windsor, Conn., vol. II, 127; Hinman's Conn. Settlers, 402; Crane's Rawson Family, 52; Savage's Gen. Dict. vol. I, 296.

BULLINGTON. Neill's Va. Carolor, 46.

BULLIS:—Philip Bullis of Boston, mariner, married Dec. 3, 1663, Judith, daughter of John Hart, widow of Robert Ratchell, and had Elizabeth 1664, John 1669, Thomas 1671, Rachel 1673. He served in Gillam's Company on the Connecticut River 1676, and the next year was at Boston.

REFERENCES:—Amer. Ancestry, II, 17; Savage's Gen. Dict. vol. I, 297.

BUTLITT. Slaughter's Fry Gen.; Richmond, Va., Standard, III, 16; Hayden's Virginia Gens., 597; Green's Kentucky Families.

BULLOCH. Amer. Ancestry, VII, 75; Bulloch Gen. 1892.

BULLOCH:—Henry Bulloch, of Charlestown, Mass., came in the "Abigail" 1635, a husbandman from Co. Essex, England, aged 40, with wife Susan 42, and children Henry who died 1657, Mary 6, Thomas 2; removed after 1638 to Salem and there had a grant of land 1643; died Dec. 27, 1663.

REFERENCES:—Bassett's Hist. of Richmond, N. H., 349; Eaton's Hist. of Thomaston, Me., 163; Baird's Hist. of Rye, N. Y., 406; Hubbard's Hist. Stanstead County, Can., 236; Adams' Hist. of Fairhaven, Vt., 295; Drivers' Gen. 294; Amer. Ancestry, vol. I, 11; 18; VI, 21; VII, 46; Savage's Gen. Dict. vol. I, 297.

BULSEN. Munsell's Albany Coll. IV, 106; Pearson's Schenectady, N. Y., Settlers, 30.

BUMP. Bassett's Richmond, N. H., 35.

BUMPASS:—Edward Bumpass, of Plymouth, came in the "Fortune" 1621, lived on Duxbury side before 1636, but most of his days at Marshfield. He had Faith 1631, Sarah, John 1636, Edward 1638, Joseph 1639, Jacob 1644, Hannah 1646, and perhaps Thomas. He was with the first purchasers of Dartmouth 1652.

REFERENCES:—Swift's Barnstable, Mass., Families, vol. I, 857; Savage's Gen. Dict. vol. I, 297.

BUMPUS. Lapham's Hist. of Paris, Me., 542; Winsor's Hist. of Duxbury, Mass., 239.

BUMSTEAD:—Edward Bumstead, of Boston, was admitted freeman 1640, had Joseph 1653.

THOMAS BUMSTEAD, of Roxbury, Mass., came to New England 1640, with two small children, Thomas and Jeremiah, and daughter Hannah. By wife Susanna he had Mary 1642, he removed to Boston and had Mercy 1650, Joseph 1653. He was a member of the Artillery Company 1647, and died 1677.

REFERENCES:—N. E. Hist. and Gen. Reg. XV, 193; Savage's Gen. Dict. vol. I, 298.

BUNBURY. Wentworth Gen. vol. I, 325.

BUNCE:—Thomas Bunce, of Hartford, 1636, served the next year in the Pequot war, and married a daughter of Captain Thomas Bull, under whom he served in that war. He had Thomas, John, Sarah, Mary 1645, Elizabeth.

REFERENCES:—Hinman's Conn. Settlers, 403; Tuttle Gen. 658; Savage's Gen. Dict. vol. I, 298.

BUNDY:—John Bundy, of Plymouth, 1643, removed to Boston. By wife Martha he had Martha 1649, Mary 1653. He removed to Taunton and had James 1664, Sarah 1669.

REFERENCES:—Aldrich's Hist. Walpole, N. H., 218; Savage's Gen. Dict. vol. I, 298.

BUNKER:—George Bunker, of Charlestown, Mass., 1634, was admitted freeman 1635. As a supporter of Wheelwright, he was disarmed Nov. 1637, yet in May following, the General Court made him constable of Charlestown, and by the end of the year he had a grant from the General Court of 50 acres. By his wife Judith (whom he probably brought from England, with his son John) he had Benjamin 1635, Jonathan 1638. His wife died 1646 and he married second, Margaret, widow of Edward Howe, of Watertown. He died 1664-5.

REFERENCES:—Wyman's Charlestown, Mass., Gens., vol. I, 150; Paige's Hist. of Cambridge, Mass., 504; Eaton's Hist. of Thomaston, Me., 163; Farrow's Hist. of Isleborough, Me., 174; Lapham's Hist. of Rumford, Me., 309; Runnel's Hist. of Sanbornton, N. H., II, 57;

Austin's Allied Families, R. I., 49; Savage's Gen. Dict. vol. I, 298.

BUNN or BUNNS:—Matthew Bunn, of Hull, by wife Esther, had Matthew 1659, Nathaniel 1664, Esther 1665. Savage's Gen. Dict. vol. I, 219.

BUNNELL. Hinman's Conn. Settlers, 405; Dwight's Strong Gen. 319; Davis' Hist. of Wallingford, Conn., 633.

BUNT. Amer. Ancestry, II, 18.

BUNTEN. Stark's Dunbarton, N. H., 219.

BURBANK:—John Burbank, of Rowley, was admitted freeman May 13, 1640. In his will he names wife Jemima, children: John, Caleb and Lydia.

REFERENCES.

MASSACHUSETTS.—Benedict's Hist. of Sutton, 611; Davis' Landmarks of Plymouth, 47; Hudson's Hist. of Lexington, 32; Temple's Hist. of North Brookfield, 541.

OTHER PUBLICATIONS.—Bradbury's Hist. of Kennebunkport, Me., 231; Dearborn's Hist. of Parsonfield, Me., 367, 451; Lapham's Hist. of Bethel, Me., 497; Coffin's Hist. of Boscawen, 476; Morrison's Hist. of Windham, N. H., 351; Norton's Hist. of Fitzwilliam, N. H., 498, 799; Washington, N. H., Hist. 323; Hinman's Conn. Settlers, 406; Clute's Hist. of Staten Island, N. Y., 349; Slaughter's St. Mark's Parish, Va., 160; Little Gen. 95; Amer. Ancestry, III, 194; Savage's Gen. Dict. vol. I, 300; Burbank Gen. 1880.

BURBECK. Amer. Ancestry, VII, 79; Glover Gen. 312; Whitmore's Copps Hill Epitaphs.

BURBEE. Norton's Hist. of Fitzwilliam, 500.

BURBEEN:—John Burbeen, of Woburn, Mass., a tailor, came from Scotland, married 1660, Sarah Gould, and had Mary, 1661, John 1663, James 1668, and perhaps others. He died Jan. 8, 1714.

REFERENCES:—Sewall's Hist. of Woburn, Mass., 595; Savage's Gen. vol. I, 301; Burbeen Gen. 1892.

BURCH:—George Burch, of Salem, by wife Elizabeth, had Elizabeth 1662, John 1664, Mary 1667, Abigail 1669, George 1671.

REFERENCES:—Amer. Ancestry, II, 18; Orcutt's Hist. of Stratford, Conn., 1166; Power's Hist. of Sangamon County, Ill., 159; Savage's Gen. Dict. vol. I, 301.

BURCHAN. N. E. Hist. and Gen. Reg. XL, 406.

BURCHARD. Ely Gen. 166, 351.

BURD. Hist. Reg. of Penn. II, 214.

BURDEN:—George Burden, of Boston, came in the "Abigail" 1635, aged 20. He was admitted to the church 1637, and made freeman May 17, following. In Nov. he was disarmed for heresy, yet not driven away. By wife Ann he had Elisha 1639, Ezekiel 1641, Joseph and Benjamin (twins) 1643, Hannah 1645.

ROBERT BURDEN, of Lynn, married about 1650, Hannah, daughter of William Witler.

REFERENCES:—Green's Kentucky Families; Savage's Gen. Dict. vol. I, 301.

BURDGE. Amer. Ancestry, III, 66; Bangor Hist. Mag. III, 88; Cope Family, 92, 192.

BURDICK:—Robert Burdick, of Newport, was admitted freeman May 22, 1655, removed to Westerly before 1661, married Ruth, daughter of Samuel Hubbard, of Newport, and had Robert, Hubbard, Thomas, Benjamin and Samuel, besides Naomi who married Jonathan Rogers.

REFERENCES:—Green Gen.; Austin's R. I. Gen. Dict. 31; Savage's Gen. Dict. vol. I, 301; Walworth Hyde Gen. 516; N. E. Hist. and Gen. Reg. XIV, 24; Amer. Ancestry, vol. I, 12; Savage's Gen. Dict. vol. I, 301.

BURDING. Eaton's Hist. of Thomaston, Me., 147.

BURDITT or BURDETT:—Robert Burdett, of Malden, married Nov. 1653, Hannah Winter, and had Thomas 1655, Hannah 1656, Joseph, Mary, Sarah, Ruth 1666. He died 16th of June next year.

REFERENCES:—Caverly's Hist. of Pittsford, 694; Wyman's Hist. Charlestown, Mass., vol. I, 156; Savage's Gen. Dict. vol. I, 302.

BURDEN. Benedict's Hist. of Sutton, Mass., 611.

BURDOO. Hudson's Hist. of Lexington, 33.

BURGARTT. Munsell's Albany Coll. IV, 106.

BURGE:—Thomas Burge, of Lynn, removed 1637, to Sandwich, with children Joseph and perhaps Jacob. He was of the chief men of the town, a representative to the General Court 1646 and died 1685, presumed to be 82 years old.

REFERENCES:—Hodgman's Hist. of Westford, 440; Savage's Gen. Dict. vol. I, 302.

BURGES or BURGISS:—Francis Burgiss, of Boston, by wife Joyce had Benjamin 1654.

JAMES BURGISS, came probably in the "Hopewell," from London 1635, aged 14. He married 1652, Lydia Mead, daughter of Gabriel Mead, and had John 1654, Benjamin 1655, John again 1657. He died Nov. 27, 1690.

REFERENCES.

MASSACHUSETTS.—Barrus' Hist. of Goshen, 136; Barry's Hist. of Hanover, 136; Davis' Landmarks of Plymouth, 48; Paige's Hist. of Hardwick, 343; Stearn's Hist. of Ashburnham, 628; Winsor's Hist. of Duxbury, 239; Freeman's Hist. of Cape Cod, II, 91, 150, 228.

OTHER PUBLICATIONS.—Farrow's Hist. of Islesborough, Me., 175; Eaton's Hist. of Warren, Me., 511; Austin's R. I. Gen. Dict. 31; Hayward's Hist. of Hancock, N. H., 410; Hinman's Conn. Settlers, 409; Cleveland Gen. 159; Amer. Ancestry, V, 213; VIII, 214; Savage's Gen. Dict. vol. I, 302; Burgess Gen. 1865.

BURGERT. Amer. Ancestry, II, 18; Munsell's Albany Coll. IV, 106.

BURGHARDT. Hist. of Great Barrington, 107.

BURGHER. Clute's Hist. of Staten Island, 351.

BURGWIN. Amer. Ancestry, VII, 223.

BURHARAS. Sylvester's Hist. of Ulster County, N. Y., 298; Schoonmaker's Hist. of Kingston, N. Y., 474; Amer Ancestry, III, 162; Burham's Gen.

BURK. Baird's Hist. of Rye, 454.

BURKE:—Richard Burke, of Concord, had grant of land in 1686, at Stow. He married at Northampton, Sept. 1687, Sarah, widow of Nehemiah Allen, daughter of Thomas Woodford, had John, born 1689, also Richard and Jonathan, born earlier.

REFERENCES:—Temple's Hist. of North Brookfield, Mass., 54; Savage's Gen. Dict. vol. I, 302; Burke Gen.

BURKETT. Eaton's Hist. of Thomaston, Me., 164.

BURKHARDT. Power's Hist. of Sangamon County, Ill., 160.

BURKHOLDER. Brubacher Gen. 53.

BURKS. Heminway's Vermont Gazeter, V.

BURLEIGH. Temple's Hist. of Palmer, Mass., 430; Runnel's Hist. of Sanbornton, N. H., II, 58; Childs' Gen. 165.

BURLESON. Hinman's Conn. Settlers, 409.

BURLEY. Hammatt Papers, Ipswich, Mass., 35; Hurd's Hist. of Rockingham County, N. H., 402; Chapman's Wicks Gen. 131; Caldwell Gen. 70; Burley Gen. 1880.

BURLING. Thomas Gen. Notes, 1878.

BURLINGHAM or BURLINGAINE:—Roger Burlingham, of Stonington 1654, Warwick 1660. By wife Mary had John 1664, Thomas 1667.

REFERENCES:—Austin's R. I. Gen. Dict. 32; Savage's Gen. Dict. vol. I, 303.

BURMAN:—Thomas Burman, of Barnstable, in his will May 9, 1663, makes wife Hannah executrix and names children: Thomas, Tristram, Samuel and daughters Hannah, Desire, Mary and Mehitable. Savage's Gen. Dict. vol. I, 303.

BURNAP:—Robert Burnap, of Reading, Mass., brought from England, Thomas 1624, Richard 1627. By wife Ann at Reading, Mass., he had Sarah 1653, Robert 1658, and Mary 1661.

REFERENCES:—Stearn's Hist. of Ashburnham, Mass., 631; Eaton's Hist. of Reading, Mass., 568; Benedict's Hist. of Sutton, Mass., 613; Heminway's Vt. Gaz. vol. V; Hinman's Conn. Settlers, 410; Savage's Gen. Dict. vol. I, 303.

BURNELL:—William Burnell, of Boston, had John, Samuel, Sarah.

Savage's Gen. Dict. vol. I, 304.

BURNET. Hinman's Conn. Settlers, 411.

BURNETT. Temple's Hist. of North Brookfield, Mass., 542; Howell's Hist. of Southampton, N. Y., 206; Egle's Penn. Gens. 607; Dod Gen. 88.

BURNHAM:—Thomas Burnham, of Ipswich 1647, married Mary, daughter of John Tuttle, and had Ruth 1658, Joseph 1660, Nathaniel 1662, Sarah 1664, Esther 1666, also Thomas, John, James, Mary, Joanna and Abigail. He died 1694. He served in the Pequot war.

THOMAS BURNHAM, of Hartford, removed to Windsor, after middle age, and died in 1688, leaving Thomas, John, Samuel, William and Richard, besides four daughters.

REFERENCES.

MASSACHUSETTS.—Hammatt Papers, Ipswich, 44; Crowell's Hist. of Essex, 313; Barry's Hist. of Framingham, 204.

MAINE.—Redlon's Hist. of Harrison, 31; Machias, Me., Centen. Cel. 156; Lapham's Hist. of Bethel, 499; Eaton's Hist. of Thomaston, 164; Dearborn's Hist. of Parsonfield, 368; Bradbury's Hist. of Kennebunkport, 231; Bangor, Me., Hist. Mag. V, 182.

NEW HAMPSHIRE.—Stearn's Hist. of Rindge, 461; Stark's Hist. of Dunbarton, 238; Morrison's Hist. of Windham, 352; Livermore's Hist. of Welton, 330; Cochran's Hist. of Antrim, 388.

OTHER PUBLICATIONS.—Andrews' Hist. of New Britain, Conn., 23; Gold's Hist. of Cornwall, Conn., 252; Hinman's Conn. Settlers, 412; Stiles' Hist. of Windsor, Conn., II, 128; Davis' Hist. of Reading, Vt., 121; Andrews' Gen. 177; Burnham Gen. 1869, 1884; Frisbie's Hist. of Middlebury, Vt., 40; Huntington Gen. 149; Kellogg's White Gen. 118; Leland Gen. 181; Loomis' Gen. Female Branches, 224; Tanner Gen. 39; Tuttle Gen. 35; Wood Gen. 62; Amer. Ancestry, vol. I, 12; III, 87; N. E. Hist. and Gen. Reg. XVI, 22; Savage's Gen. Dict. vol. I, 304.

BURNS. Wyman's Charlestown, Mass., Gens. vol. I, 156; Secomb's Hist. of Amherst, N. H., 523; Livermore's Hist. of Wilton, N. H., 331; Cochran's Hist. of Antrim, N. H., 391; Eaton's Hist. of Thomaston, Me., 164; Lancaster's Hist. of Rowley, Mass., 258.

BURPEE. Essex Inst. Coll. XX, 215; Eaton's Hist. of Thomaston, Me., 165; Eaton's Hist. of Candia, N. H., 57; Chase's Hist. of Chester, N. H., 480.

BURRAGE:—John Burrage, of Charlestown, Mass., 1637; admitted freeman 1642, by wife Mary had Mary 1641, Hannah 1643, Elizabeth and Nathaniel 1655, died next year. By second wife Joanna who died Dec. 25, 1689, aged 66, he had Mary 1657, Sarah 1659. He died January 1658.

THOMAS BURRAGE, of Lynn, by wife Elizabeth whom he married 1687, had Elizabeth, John, Thomas, Mary, Bethia and Ruth.

BURRAGE. Wyman's Charlestown, Mass., Gens. vol. I, 157; Amer. Ancestry, V, 23, 87; Savage's Gen. Dict. vol. I, 308; Burrage Gen. 1877.

BURR:—Benjamin Burr, an early settler of Hartford, had Samuel; made freeman with his father 1638, and Thomas 1646, also daughters Mary and Hannah.

JOHN BURR, of Roxbury 1650, came probably in the fleet with Winthrop; requested admission as freeman 19th of Oct. that year and was sworn May 18, following. He was a carpenter, appointed in 1633, by the Colonial government to see to the bridges between Boston and Roxbury. In 1636, he removed with Pyndian to the foundation of Springfield, and for that town not supposed to belong to Massachusetts in 1638, he was representative at Hartford, and soon after went to Fairfield, of which he was a representative 1641-5-6, and probably died soon after. Three sons: John, Daniel and Nathaniel are known, and perhaps there were other children.

JONATHAN BURR, of Dorchester, Mass., born at Redgrave in County Suffolk, it is said, bred at Corpus Christi, in Cambridge University, where he took his degree in 1623, and 1627 was rector of Rickingshall, in his native land, but was silenced by his primate Laud and came with wife Frances and three young children to New England, in 1639. In the second following winter he was called to be colleague with Mather, but died Aug. 9, 1641, aged 36, leaving Jonathan 1631, John and Simon, who were born in England, and Mary, born about 1640 at Dorchester.

SIMON BURR, of Hingham, Mass., had several children of whom Simon and John were the only survivors.

Arms.—Ermine on a chief indented sable two lions rampant. *Crest.*—A lion's head ppr. collared or. rampant. *Crest.*—A lion's head ppr. collared on.

REFERENCES.

CONNECTICUT.—Stiles' Hist. of Windsor, II, 132; Sedgwick's Hist. of Sharon, 67; Schenck's Hist. of Fairfield, 359; Orcutt's Hist. of Farrington, 66; Hurd's Hist. of Fairfield, 580; Hinman's Conn. Settler's, 427; Todd's Hist. of Redding, 184.

MASSACHUSETTS.—Wyman's Charlestown Gens., vol. I, 57; Temple's Hist. of Northfield; Paige's Hist. of Cambridge, 595; Mitchell's Hist. of Bridgewater, 125; Jameson's Hist. of Medway, 461; Freeman's Hist. of Cape Cod, vol. I, 694.

OTHER PUBLICATIONS.—Bangor Hist. Mag. III, 87; Sprague's Hist. of Gloversville, N. Y.; Goodwin Gen. of Olcutt Family, 57; Redfield Gen., 56; Tuttle Gen. 385; Loomis' Gen. Female Branches, 565; Amer. Ancestry, VII, 7, 105; Savage's Gen. Dict. vol. I, 305; N. E. Hist. and Gen. Reg. V, 472; Burr Gen. 1878, 1891.

BURRALL. Hinman's Conn. Settlers, 481. Bass' Hist. of Braintree, Vt., 122.

BURRIER. Plumb's Hist. of Hanover, Pa., 389.

BURRILL:—George Burrill, of Lynn, 1630, was one of the richest planters, brought probably from England. He and his wife Mary died in 1653, leaving sons George and Francis, born in England, and John, born in Lynn, 1631.

WILLIAM BURRILL, of New Haven, Conn., had Mary 1650, and Ebenezer 1653. The names of John and Samuel are mentioned as New Haven proprietors 1685.

REFERENCES:—Lewis' Hist. of Lynn, Mass., 116, 492; Ballou's Hist. of Milford, 608; Andrews' Hist. of New Britain, Conn., 109, 352; Savage's Gen. Dict. vol. I, 308.

BURLINGTON. Austin's Ancestral Dict.; Austin's R. I. Gen. Dict. 33.

BURRITT:—William Burritt, of Stratford, Conn., an early settler, died 1651, leaving widow Elizabeth, who survived thirty years, and in her will of Sept. 1681, names sons Stephen and John and daughter Mary Smith.

REFERENCES.

CONNECTICUT.—Tuttle Gen. of Conn. 123; Todd's Hist. of Redding, 187; Orcutt's Hist. of Stratford, 1168; Orcutt's Hist. of Derby, 705; Hinman's Conn. Settlers, 436; Fairfield Co., Hist. Society Amer. Report, 1892, p. 3; Cothren's Hist. of Woodbury, 510.

OTHER PUBLICATIONS.—Plumb's Hist. of Hanover, Pa., Morris's Bontecou Gen.; Burritt Gen.

BURROWS or BURROUGHS:—George Burrows or Burroughs, of Roxbury, Mass., bred at Harvard College, where he had his A. B. 1670, was says Savage, the most prominent victim of the diabolical fanaticism of 1692. By wife whose name is not known he had Rebecca 1674. George 1675. He preached at Falmouth 1674 or '76, where for his good services he had grant of 200 acres of land, and when the Indians destroyed that town Aug. 11. of that year, he escaped to Bang's Island in the harbor, whence he wrote the details of the disaster sent by Major Pendleton, to the Governor and Counsel at Boston. In Salisbury he had another child Hannah, by wife Hannah, and was invited Nov., 1680, to preach at Salem village, near Danvers, and there had Elizabeth. He returned to Falmouth, in 1683. On May 8, 1692, he was sent to Boston, charged with the offence of witchery, kept nine weeks in prison, tried Aug. 3, at Salem and by a court. unduly organized, was condemned in a few days and hanged on the 19th of that month.

JEREMIAH BURROUGHS, of Scituate, 1647, married May, 1651, a daughter perhaps of Thomas Huel, of Hingham, and had Jeremiah 1652, John 1653, Elizabeth 1655 and Mary 1657. He died 1660.

ROBERT BURROUGHS, of Wethersfield, Conn., married 1645, Mary, widow of Samuel Ireland. He removed to New London, 1650, and had John and perhaps others.

REFERENCES.
CONNECTICUT.—Hurd's Hist. of New London, 476; Stiles' Hist. of Windsor, II, 134; Orcutt's Hist. of Stratford, 1167; Hinman's Conn. Settlers, 424; Caulkins' Hist. of New London, 301.

OTHER PUBLICATIONS.—Hayward's Hist. of Gilsum, N. H., 279; Wyman's Charlestown, Mass., Gens., 159; Salter's Hist. of Monmouth County, N. J., XIV; Littell's Passaic Valley Gens. 64; Cooley's Trenton, N. J., 17; Maine Hist. Soc. Coll. vol. I, 175; Riker's Annals of Newtown, N. Y., 283; Davis' Hist. of Bucks County, Pa., 235; Davis' Gen. (1889) 93; Cunnabel Gen. 110; Wentworth Gen. II, 445; Savage's Gen. Dict. vol. I, 310; Amer. Ancestry, vol. I, 12; II, 18; VIII, 199; Burrow's Gen. 1872.

BURROW.   Smith Gen. 93.

BURSLEY or BURSLEM:—John Bursley or Burslem was an early settler at Weymouth, reckoned some three or four years among old planters and was soon after at Dorchester; requested admission as freeman, Oct. 19, 1630, and was sworn May 18, following. When first mentioned, he is called "Mr." and was a representative at the General Court in 1636.   He married at Sandwich, Mass., 1639, Joanna, daughter of Rev. Joseph Hull, of Barnstable. He had issue Mary 1643, Joanna 1646, Elizabeth 1649 and John April 11, 1652; he also had probably Temperance and Jemima.   He was at Exeter 1643, at Hampton of Kettery 1647, and returned to Barnstable, where he died 1650.

REFERENCES:—Swift's Barnstable Families, 127; Freeman's Hist. of Cape Cod, Mass., 290; Savage's Gen. Dict. vol. I, 312.

BURT:—George Burt, of Lynn, Mass., died Nov. 2, 1661, leaving George, who went to Sandwich; Hugh, Edward and Lewis.

HENRY BURT, of Roxbury, had his home burned, for which loss the General Court made a grant to the town of 8 pounds sterling, in Nov. 1639. He removed to Springfield, Mass., the next year and was there clerk of the writs, and died April 30, 1662.   His widow Ulalia died Aug. 29, 1690, and among his children are found the names of Jonathan, David, Nathaniel, Sarah, Abigail, Elizabeth, Patience, Mercy, Hannah, Dorcas.

RICHARD BURT, of Taunton, one of the purchasers 1639, died before 1675, had Richard and probably James.

REFERENCES:—Hyde's Hist. of Brimfield, Mass., 385; Longmeadow, Mass., Centen. 16; Temple's Hist. of Northfield, Mass., 414; Wyman's Charlestown, Mass. Gens., vol. I, 160; Chandler's Hist. of Shirley, Mass., 364; Butler's Hist. of Groton, Mass., 391; Davis' Landmarks of Plymouth, 50; Aldrich's Hist. of Walpole, N. H., 219; Hayward's Hist. of Hancock, N. H., 413; Eager's Hist. of Orange County, N. Y., 425; Power's Hist. of Sangamon County, Ill., 162; Loomis' Gen. of Female Branches, 521; Kellogg's White Descendants, 118; Holton's Winslow, Mass., 460; Ely Gen. 91; Savage's Gen. Dict. vol. I, 312; Amer. Ancestry, vol. I, 12; VI, 60; VIII, 77, 79; N. E. Hist. and Gen. Reg. XXXII, 302; Burt Gen. 1892, 1893.

BURTON:—Thomas Burton, of Hingham, Mass., married Margaret, daughter of John Otis, and had Hannah 1641, Phebe 1644, Ruth 1646.

WILLIAM BURTON, of Warwick, married Ann or Hannah, daughter of John Wicks, and had Susannah, Elder, and perhaps younger children he had, as, Elizabeth, who married 1674, Thomas Hedger, Hannah, who

married a carpenter, John, born 1697, Elkanah, Rose.

REFERENCES:—North's Hist. of Augusta, Me., 820; Eaton's Hist. of Thomaston, Me., 165; Eaton's Annals of Warren, 512; Wyman's Charlestown, Mass., Gens. vol. I, 160; Austin's Allied Families, 51; Austin's R. I. Gen. Dict. 267; Corliss' North Yarmouth, Me.; Collins' Hist. of Hillsdale, N. Y., 61; Livermore's Hist. of Wilton, N. H., 332; Sprague's Hist. of Gloversville, N. Y., 109; Hinman's Conn. Settlers, 437; Orcutt's Hist. of Stratford, Conn., 1169; Power's Hist. of Sangamon County, Ill., 163; Our Ancestors, 8; Wheeler's Hist. of North Carolina, II, 163; Savage's Gen. Dict. vol. I, 314; Amer. Ancestry, III, 158; V, 180, 237.

BURTT.   Livermore's Hist. of Wilton, N. H., 339.

BURWELL:—John Burwell, of 1639, had Samuel 1640, Ephraim 1644, Nathaniel 1646, Elizabeth 1647. Before settling in Massachusetts he had sons, John and Zacharia.

REFERENCES:—Campbell's Hist. of Va. 550; Richmond, Va., Standard, vol. I, 40; II, 38; III, 42; IV, 2; Meade's Old Families of Va. vol. I, 353; II, 290; Chase's Hist. of Chester, N. H., 480; Hinman's Conn. Settlers, 438; Carter Family Tree; Goode Gen. 65; Keith's Harrison Ancestry; Jones Gen. (1891) 45; Page Gen. 64, 144; Paxton's Marshall Gen. 102, 252; Amer. Ancestry, IV, 67; Savage's Gen. Dict. vol. I, 316; Burwell Family Tree, 1870.

BUSBY:—Nicholas Busby, of Watertown, a weaver, came from old Norwich to Boston, June 20, 1637, then aged 50, and four children, Nicholas, John, Abraham and Sarah. He was admitted a freeman, March 1638; selectman 1640-41; removed to Boston 1646, constable there 1649, and died Aug. 28, 1657.

Savage's Gen. Dict. vol. I, 316.

BUSCOTT.   Austin's Allied Families, 52; Austin's R. I. Gen. Dict. 83.

BUSH:—Edward Bush, of Salem, married Oct. 17, 1665, Mary Hyde, and had Edward 1667. He married Aug. 1, 1678, young widow Elizabeth Pittman, who long survived him, and Elizabeth 1678, Edward 1682, Ann 1683, Benjamin 1685, Edward 1687, Esewick 1693.

JOHN BUSH, of Cambridge, took oath of fidelity 1652. He had by wife Elizabeth, Joseph 1654, Elizabeth 1657, Daniel 1659, Abiah 1661, Mary 1662.

REFERENCES:—Caulkin's Hist. of Norwich, Conn., 213; Hinman's Conn. Settlers, 441; Meade's Hist. of Greenwich, Conn., 306; Ward's Hist. of Shrewsbury, Mass., 242; Temple's Hist. of North Brookfield, 543; Paige's Hist. of Cambridge, Mass., 505; Hudson's Hist. of Marlborough, Mass., 349; Draper's Hist. of Spencer, Mass., 182; Bolton's Hist. of Westchester County, N. Y., II, 509; Cleveland's Hist. of Yates County, N. Y., 314, 529; Clute's Hist. of Staten Island, N. Y., 351; Ely Gen. 120; Loomis' Gen. Female Branches, 637; Paxton's Marshall Gen. 269; Amer. Ancestry, IV, 163; V, 111; Savage's Gen. Dict. vol. I, 316.

BUSHMAN.   Corliss' Hist. of North Yarmouth, Me.

BUSHROD:—Peter Bushrod, was a soldier in Capt. William Turner's company, April, 1676, and was in the Falls Fight. After the war he married Elizabeth, daughter of William Hannum, and had Elizabeth 1681, Samuel 1684, Hannah, Abigail 1689. Both he and his wife died 1690.

REFERENCES:—Hayden's Virginia Gens., 636; Savage's Gen. Dict. vol. I, 320.

BUSHNELL:—Francis Bushnell, of Guilford, 1639, died 1646. He brought from England, son Frances and daughter Rebecca, who married John Lud, of Hartford, and died soon.

FRANCES BUSHNELL, of Saybrook, son of Mr. Burt, first Francis was born in England, and had Samuel and five daughters. He was a deacon and had favor with the Indians.

REFERENCES:—Caulkins' Hist. of Norwich, Conn., 213; Hinman's Conn. Settlers, 444; Norwich, Conn., Jubilee, 202; Hine's Lebanon, Conn., Hist. Address, 149; Collins' Hist. of Hillsdale, N. Y., App., 45; Walworth's Hyde Gen. 7, 919; Tuttle Gen. 867; N. E. Hist. and Gen. Reg. IV, 19; Amer. Ancestry, II, 18; IV, 145; IX, 207; Savage's Gen. Dict. vol. I, 307.

BUSS or BUSSEY:—William Buss or Bussey, of Concord, Mass., admitted freeman 1639, was Lieutenant and died June 30, 1638. By wife Ann he had Richard 1640, Ann 1642, Nathaniel 1647, Joseph 1649.

REFERENCES:—Livermore's Hist. of Wilton, N. H., 330; Smith's Hist. of Petersborough, N. H., 27; Savage's Gen. Dict. vol. I, 319.

BUSKIRK. Boyd's Consensus, N. Y., 145.

BUSSELL. Bangor, Me., Hist. Mag. III, 136.

BUSSING. Roome Gen. 117; Riker's Hist. of Harlem, N. Y., 497; Amer. Ancestry, VI, 6.

BUSSWELL:—Isaac Busswell or Buzzell, was admitted freeman Oct. 9, 1640; perhaps brought sons Samuel and William, from England, and here married Mary Estow, probably daughter of William. By second or third wife he had Mary 1645, Isaac 1650 and Mary.

REFERENCES:—Stearns' Hist. of Rindge, N. H., 462; Eaton's Hist. of Candia, N. H., 57; Merrill's Hist. of Acworth, N. H., 193; Runnell's Hist. of Sanbornton, N. H., II, 77; Guild's Stiles Gen. 14; Driver Gen. 151; Savage's Gen. Dict. vol. I, 319.

BUTLER. Henry Butler came to New England, about 1642, from some part of Kent, married Ann, daughter of John Holman, and had John. He taught school at Dorchester.

JOHN BUTLER, of Boston, was a member of the artillery company 1644. "Perhaps this freeman of 1649," says Savage, "said to have been a physician." He was probably of Hartford, Conn., 1666, admitted freeman there 1669; removed to Branford, there died 1680. By two wives he had four daughters and sons, John, Richard, Jonathan and Jonas.

NICHOLAS BUTLER, of Dorchester, came from Eastwell in Co. Kent; it is said, with wife Joyce, three children, of whom one was John, and five servants, 1636, admitted freeman 1639, removed 1651 to Martha's Vineyard.

PETER BUTLER, of Boston, married Mary, daughter of William Alford and had Peter, Hannah, Samuel and Mary.

RICHARD BUTLER, of Cambridge, 1632, was admitted freeman 1634, removed to Hartford, Conn., before 1643; was a representative to the General Court, 1656-60, a deacon of the church, and died Aug. 6, 1684. By first wife he had Thomas, Samuel and Nathaniel; by second wife, Elizabeth, he had Joseph, Daniel, Mary, Elizabeth, Hannah.

WILLIAM BUTLER, of Ipswich, married 1675, Sarah, and had William 1677, Thomas 1682. He was admitted freeman 1682.

Arms.—Argent three covered cups in bend between two bendlets, engrailed sable. *Crest.*—A demi-cockatrice couped, vert, comb, beak, wattles and ducally gorged or. *Motto.*—Liberté toute entière.

REFERENCES.

CONNECTICUT.—Andrews' Hist. of New Britain, 275, 280; Caulkins' Hist. of New London, 342; Cothren's Hist. of Woodbury, III, 1472; Stiles' Hist. of Windsor, II, 135; Hinman's Conn. Settlers, 454.

MAINE.—Butler's Hist. of Farmington, 399; Corliss' Hist. of North Yarmouth; Eaton's Hist. of Thomaston, 166; Hatch's Hist. of Industry, 525; Sibley's Hist. of Union, 435; Maine Hist. and Gen. Reg. III, 134; IV, 226.

MASSACHUSETTS.—Stearns' Hist. of Ashburnham, 631; Swift's Barnstable Families, vol. I, 144; Ward's Hist. of Shrewsbury, 241; Whitmore's Copps Hill Epitaphs; Hammatt Papers of Ipswich, 40; Freeman's Hist. of Cape Cod, II, 68, 485, 772; Barry's Hist. of Framingham, 205.

NEW HAMPSHIRE.—Hayward's Hist. of Gilsum, 280; Hayward's Hist. of Hancock, 423; Norton's Hist. of Fitzwilliam, 500; Coggswell's Hist. of Henniker, 475; Coggswell's Hist. of Nottingham, 236; Coffin's Hist. of Boscawen, 481; Cochrane's Hist. of Antrim, 395.

OTHER PUBLICATIONS.—Pompey's, N. Y., Reunion, 272, 405; Howell's Hist. of Southampton, N. Y., 209; Clute's Hist. of Staten Island, N. Y., 353; Egle's Hist. Reg. Interior of Penn. vol. I, 1; Futhey's Hist. of Chester County, Pa., 492; Kulp's Wyoming Valley Families, Pa., Mag. of Hist. VII, 1; Green's Kentucky Families; Heminway's Vt. Gaz. V, 89; McKeen's Hist. of Bradford, Vt., 359; Collins' Hist. of Kentucky, II, 120; Austin's Allied Families, R. I., 53; Andrews Gen. (1890) 83; Meade's Old Families of Va.; Power's Hist. of Sangamon County, Ill., 164; Bridgman's Granary Epitaphs, 260, 271; Buckingham Gen. 205; Cutt's Gen. 72, 139, 261; Paxton's Marshall Gen. 227; Poore Gen. 14; Sigourney Gen.; Walworth's Hyde Gen. vol. I, 522; Wentworth Gen. vol. I, 655; Amer. Ancestry, II, 19; III, 7; VIII, 69, 214, IX, 122, 191; X, 41, 170; XI, 24; Savage's Gen. Dict. vol. I, 320; N. E. Hist. and Gen. Reg. vol. I, 167; II, 355; III, 73, 353; XVI, 17; XXVIII, 330; Butler Gen. 1849, 1886, 1887, 1888.

BUTT:—Richard Butt, of Dorchester, Mass., by wife Deliverance, who died 1699, had Jerebiah or Sherebiah 1675, Bachariah and Hannah (twins) 1680; Mary 1682, Joseph 1684. Savage's Gen. Dict. vol. I, 321.

BUTMAN. Guild's Stiles' Gen. 384; Babson's Hist. of Gloucester, Mass., 66.

BUTRICH. Shattock's Hist. of Concord, 366.

BUTTERFIELD:—Benjamin Butterfield, of Charlestown, 1638, prospected settlement at Woburn 1640, with others; admitted freeman 1643; had Mary, Nathaniel 1643, Samuel 1647, Joseph 1649, removed in 1654 to Chelmsford, where his wife Ann died May 19, 1660. He married June 1663, Hannah, widow of Thomas Whittemore of Malden.

REFERENCES.

MASSACHUSETTS.—Brown's Bedford Families, 6; Cutler's Hist. of Arlington, 190; Hodgman's Hist. of Westford, 440; Paige's Hist. of Cambridge, 505; Sewall's Hist. of Woburn, 597; Tyngsboro, Mass., Centen. Rec. 5; Wyman's Charlestown, Mass., Gens. 161.

NEW HAMPSHIRE.—Norton's Hist. of Fitzwilliam, 500; Livermore's Hist. of Wilton, 343; Hayward's Hist. of Hancock, 427; Chase's Hist. of Chester, 480.

OTHER PUBLICATIONS.—Washington, N. H., Hist. 329; Phenix's Whitney Family of Conn., vol. I, 299; Heminway Vt. Gaz., V, 189; Butler's Hist. of Farmington, Me., 407; Butterfield Gen.; Chandler Gen., 330; Dunster Gen., 253; Locke Gen., 78; Amer. Ancestry, IX, 68; Savage's Gen. Dict. vol. I, 322; N. E. Hist. and Gen. Reg. XLIV, 33.

BUTLERS. Hudson's Hist. of Lexington, Mass., 34; Sewall's Hist. of Woburn, Mass., 596.

BUTTERWORTH:—John Butterworth, of Rehoboth, 1643, was one of the founders of the first Baptist church 1663, in Swanzey, Mass. He had a son John, who married Hannah Wheaton, and had John 1679, Elizabeth 1683, and perhaps others.

REFERENCES:—Savage's Gen. Dict. vol. I, 323; N. E. Hist. and Gen. Reg. XLI, 191.

BUTTOLPH:—Thomas Buttolph, of Boston, a leather-dresser, or glover, came in the "Abigail," from London, 1635, aged 32, with wife Ann, 24; he had Thomas 1637, John 1640, Abigail 1643, Mehitable 1651. He was admitted freeman 1641, was constable 1647 and died 1667.

REFERENCES:—Hinman's Conn. Settlers, 461; Whitney Family of Conn. vol. I, 115; Savage's Gen. Dict. vol. I, 323.

BUTTON:—Matthias Button, of Boston, by wife Lettia, had Mary 1634, Daniel 1635. He was of Ipswich 1639, and afterwards at Haverhill, where he died 1672. PETER BUTTON, of New London, Conn., had Peter 1688, Mary 1689, Matthias 1692, and daughter Eliphal 1694.

ROBERT BUTTON, of Salem, Mass., was admitted freeman 1642; married Abigail, daughter of widow Alice Vermaes, and had Samuel 1642; Abigail 1644, Hannah 1645, Sarah 1648. He was a merchant of Boston and did a large business, was constable 1650.

REFERENCES:—Williams' Hist. of Danby, Vt., 120; Paul's Hist. of Wells, Vt., 68; Savage's Gen. Dict. vol. I, 324.

BUTTRICK:—William Buttrick, of Concord, came probably in the "Susan and Ellen" 1635. He married 1646, Sarah Bateman, who died 1664. Had Mary, William, John 1653, Samuel 1655, Edward 1657, Sarah.

REFERENCES:—Stearn's Hist. of Rindge, N. H., 403; Stearns' Hist. of Ashburnham, 631; Potter's Old Families of Concord, Mass., Morrison's Hist. of Windham, 854.

BUTTS. Paul's Hist. of Wells, Vt., 70; Austin's R. I., Gen. Dict. 34; Amer. Ancestry, vol. VIII, 59; Savage's Gen. Dict. vol. I, 322.

BUTTRY:—Nicholas Buttry, of Cambridge, Mass., probably came in the "James" from London, in 1635, aged 33, with wife Martha, 28, and Grace aged 1 year. He had probably a son John, of Reading, Mass., who had issue John 1660 and Elizabeth 1662.

Savage's Gen. Dict. vol. I, 322.

BUXTON:—Anthony Buxton, of Salem, Mass., by wife Elizabeth, had several children, who died. Among those who survived were John, Lydia, Mary, Sarah.

CLEMENT BUXTON, of Stamford, Conn., 1650, died 1657. He had daughters Sarah and Vinty, besides son Clement.

REFERENCES:—Temple's Hist. of North Brookfield, Mass., 545; Benedict's Hist. of Fulton, Mass., 615; Hunt-

ington's Stamford, Conn., Families, 20; Coggswell's Hist. of Henniker, N. H., 476; Coggswell's Hist. of New Boston, N. H., 401; Hayward's Hist. of Hancock, N. H., 427; Eaton's Annals of Warren, Me., 514; Cleveland's Hist. of Yates County, N. Y., 676; Young's Hist. of Warsaw, N. Y., 242; Heminway's Vt. Gaz. V; Paul's Hist. of Wells, Vt., 70; Williams' Hist. Danby, Vt., 121; Savage's Gen. Dict. vol. I, 323.

BUZZELL. Dearborn's Hist. of Parsonfield, Me., 369, Coggswell's Hist. of Nottingham, N. H., 650; Caverne Gen. 20; Guild's Stiles' Gen. 371.

BRYAN:—George Bryan, of Salem, Mass., was admitted freeman May 18, 1642. He had Abraham 1644, and Abigail. He removed to Chelmsford.

REFERENCES:—Norton's Hist. of Fitzwilliam, 501. Savage's Gen. Dict. vol. I, 135.

BYARD. Dunster Gen. 175.

BYERS. Egle's Penn. Gens. 689; Hayden's Weitzell Gen.

BYFIELD. Savage's Gen. Dict. vol. I, 325.

BYINGTON. Orcutt's Wolcott, Conn., 465.

BYLES:—Joshua Byles, of Boston, came from Winchester, Co. Hants, with wife Sarah and had James 1699, Sarah 1701, and Samuel 1703, and others who died. For his second wife he married Elizabeth, widow of William Greenough, daughter of Rev. Increase Mather, and had a son Mather bap. March 16, 1707. He was a minister of some note and a wit of remarkable character, in Boston.

REFERENCES:—Babson's Hist. of Gloucester, Mass., 66; Savage's Gen. Dict. vol. I, 326.

BYRAM:—Nicholas Byram, of Weymouth, Mass., 1638, a physician, married a daughter of Abraham Shaw, of Dedham. He removed about 1662 to Bridgewater. He was a captain of the train band. His second wife was a sister of Rev. James Keith. He died 1687. He had Abigail, Nicholas, Ebenezer, Josiah, Joseph, Mary, besides a daughter Bass. He also had daughter Experience.

REFERENCES:—Mitchell's Hist. of Bridgewater, Mass., 127; Hanson's Hist. of Gardiner, Me., 156; Littell's Passaic Valley, N. J., Gens. 65; Amer. Ancestry, III, 8; Savage's Gen. Dict. vol. I, 326.

BYRD. Campbell's Hist. of Virginia, 420, 712; Meade's Old Families of Va., vol. I, 315; II, 290; Richmond, Va., Critic, 1888; Sketches of Lynchburg, Va., 299; Slaughter's Bristol Parish, Va., 296; Prescott's Page Gen.; Paxton's Marshall Gen.; Balch's Prov. Papers, 128; N. E. Hist. and Gen. Reg. XXXV, 162; XXXVIII, 308.

BYRNE. Drover Gen. 270.

BYRON. Corliss' North Yarmouth, Me.

BYTHEWOOD. N. E. Hist. and Gen. Reg. XL, 299.

CABANNE. See Beckworth's Creoles, 71.

CABELL:—George Cabell, of Boston, was among the taxable inhabitants 1695.

JOHN CABELL, of Springfield 1636, had come to New England, in 1631, or earlier, and had John, born 1641. He removed soon after to Fairfield, Conn., where both, father and son are in the list of freemen 1669. The son who wrote his name Cable, died 1673.

REFERENCES:—Schenck's Hist. of Fairfield, Conn., 362; Eaton's Hist. of Thomaston, Me., 170; Campbell's

Hist. of Va., 626; Meade's Old Families of Va., vol. I, 60; Sketches of Lynchburg, Va., 206; Richmond, Va., Standard, vol. I, 37, 41; II, 12, 17, 19, 40; III, 14, 34; Robertson's Pocahontas' Descendants; Slaughter's Fry Gen. 23; Amer. Ancestry, IV, 65; V, 97, 98; VIII, 204.

CABLE. Filley's Mag. of N. E. Hist. III, 135; Cable Family, 1893.

CABOT. Dwight Gen. 579; Pickerny Gen. N. E. Hist. and Gen. Reg. IX, 335.

CADMAN. Austin's R. I. Gen. Dict., 268; Amer. Ancestry, II, 19.

CADMUS. Winfield's Hist. of Hudson County, N. J., 555.

CADWALLADER. Penn. Mag. VI, 209; X, 1; Cooley's Hist. of Trenton, 23; Life of Rev. William Smith.

CADWELL:—Thomas Cadwell, of Hartford, Conn., married 1658, Elizabeth, widow of Robert Wilson, daughter of Deacon Edward Stibbing and had Mary 1659, Edward 1660, Thomas 1662, Edmond 1664, Matthew 1668, Abigail 1670, Elizabeth 1672, Samuel 1675, Hannah 1677, Mehitable 1679. He died 1694.

REFERENCES:—Stiles' Hist. of Windsor, Conn., II, 135; Hinman's Conn. Settlers, 465; Andrews' Hist. of New Britain, Conn., 252; Kellogg's Memorial of John White, 102; Savage's Gen. Dict. vol. I, 327.

CADY:—James Cady, of Hingham, 1635, came, it is said, from Wales, with three sons, removed to Boston, with wife Margaret and Mary. He soon after removed to Yarmouth, Mass.

NICHOLAS CADY, of Watertown, Mass., 1645, had by wife Judith, daughter of William Knapp, John 1651, Judith 1653, James 1655, Nicholas 1657, died soon; Daniel 1659, Ezekiel 1662, Nicholas again 1664, Joseph 1666, and probably Aaron. He sold his estate in 1668, and removed to Groton.

REFERENCES:—Stiles' Hist. of Windsor, II, 136; Butler's Hist. of Groton, Mass., 391; Hayward's Hist. of Gilsum, N. H., 280; Bass' Hist. of Braintree, Vt., 122; Adams' Hist. of Fairhaven, Vt., 322; Little Gen. 56; Savage's Gen. Dict. vol. I, 327.

CAFFINGE or CAFFINCH:—John, of Guilford, 1639, was an original proprietor. He was of New Haven, 1643, a man of some importance. He married Mary, perhaps daughter of the first William Foster and had Sarah, Mary, Elizabeth 1657.

THOMAS, of New Haven, brother of the above, had a good estate. He died in 1657, having son John.

Savage's Gen. Dict. vol. I, 327.

CAHILL. Norton's Hist. of Fitzwilliam, 503.

CAINE or CAYNE:—Christopher, of Cambridge, was admitted freeman 1639, died 1653. By wife Margery, who died 1687, aged 70, he had Jonathan 1640, Nathaniel 1642, Deborah 1647, and Esther.

REFERENCES:—Savage's Gen. Dict. vol. I, 328; Temple's Hist. of North Brookfield, Mass., 547.

CALLAWAY. Dawson Gen. 101.

CALDER. Wyman's Charlestown, Mass., Gens., 164.

CALDERWOOD. Eaton's Annals of Warren, Me., 514; Eaton's Hist. of Thomaston, Me., 170.

CALDWELL:—John Caldwell, of Ipswich, Mass., was admitted freeman 1677. He married Sarah, daughter of John Dillingham, and had Sarah 1658, John, Ann 1661, Dillingham 1667, William 1669, Mary 1672, Elizabeth 1675.

REFERENCES.

MASSACHUSETTS.—Stearns' Hist. of Ashburnham, 632; Temple's Hist. of Northfield, 416; Wyman's Charlestown, Mass., Gens., 165; Hammatt Papers of Ipswich, 44; Hudson's Hist. of Lexington, 34.

NEW HAMPSHIRE.—Stark's Hist. of Dunbarton, 240; Smith's Hist. of Petersborough, 28; Secomb's Hist. of Amherst, 525; Coggswell's Hist. of Henniker, 477; Cochrane's Hist. of Antrim, 399.

OTHER PUBLICATIONS.—Lapham's Hist. of Paris, Me., 545; North's Hist. of Augusta, Me., 822; Egle's Penn. Gens., 611; Power's Hist. of Sangamon County, Ill., 165; Richmond, Va., Standard, II, 34; Dwight Gen. 436; Savage's Gen. Dict. vol. I, 328; Hist. of Essex and Hudson Counties, N. J., vol. II, 43; Amer. Ancestry, V, 187; IX, 32; Caldwell Family, by Albert Welles 1881; Caldwell Family of Ipswich, Mass., 1873; Caldwell Family, by Albert Welles, 1881; The Early Caldwells of Nottingham, Eng., 1885.

CALIF or CALFE:—Robert, of Roxbury, Mass., had four sons, Joseph, John, Jeremiah, and Robert. The latter was the first physician of Rowley, Mass., and had by wife Mary, Robert 1693, Joseph 1695, Samuel 1697, Ebenezer, Peter, Mary.

REFERENCES:—Wyman's Charlestown's Mass., Gens., 166; Hammatt Papers of Ipswich, Mass., 46; Runnel's Hist. of Sanbornton, N. H., II, 79; Chase's Hist. of Chester, N. H., 481; Drake's Witchcraft Delusions, II, 28; Savage's Gen. Dict. vol. I, 329; Amer. Ancestry, V, 143; XI, 172; N. E. Hist. and Gen. Reg. IV, 16.

CALHOUN. Stearn's Hist. of Rindge, N. H,, 464; Gold's Hist. of Cornwall, Conn., 276; Power's Hist. of Sangamon County, Ill., 167; Marshall Gen. (1884) 64; Childs Gen. 809; Hist. of John C. Calhoun.

CALKINS:—Hugh Calkins, born in England 1600, came to America in 1640, with a Welsh colony of which the pastor was Richard Blinman, and settled at New London, Conn. He had John and other children.

REFERENCES:—Sedgwick's Hist. of Sharon, Conn., 47; Hines' Lebanon, Conn., Address (1880), 150; Temple's Hist. of Palmer, Mass., 438; Babson's Hist. of Gloucester, Mass., 67; Heminway's Vt. Gaz., IV, 850; Williams' Hist. of Danby, Vt., 121; Read's Hist. of Swanzey, N. H., 305; Wentworth Gen. vol. I, 354; Walworth's Hyde Gen. 956, 1011; Boltwood Noble Gen. 364; Amer. Ancestry, II, 20.

CALL:—Thomas Call, of Charlestown, on Mistick side, a tilemaker or husbandman, came to New England in 1636, with wife Bennet, and three children, from Taversham, in Kent, England. He was admitted freeman 1640, perhaps lived at Concord 1645, but soon went back to Charlestown to marry Joanna, widow of Daniel Shepardson, who died 1661. He died 1676, aged 79. He had a son Thomas born in England.

REFERENCES:—Wyman's Charlestown, Mass., Gens., vol. I, 166; Morrison's Hist. of Windham, N. H., 355; Runnel's Hist. of Sanbornton, N. H., II, 84; Wheeler's Hist. of Newport, N. H., 322; Malden, Mass., Bi-Centen, 240; Savage's Gen. Dict. vol. I, 329.

CALLAWAY. Meade's Old Families, Va., Richmond, Va., Standard, 17, 21.

CALLENDER:—Ellis Callender, of Boston, was one of the founders of the first Baptist Church in Boston, where some time from 1708, he served as teacher. He was admitted freeman 1690. He had John and probably other children.

REFERENCES:—Temple's Hist. of Northfield, Mass., 416; Amer. Ancestry, II, 20; Savage's Gen. Dict. vol. I, 330.

CALLER. Southwick Gen. 481.

CALLERMAN. Powers' Hist. of Sangamon County, Ill., 169.

CALLEY. Wyman's Charlestown, Mass., Gens., vol. I, 173.

CALVERLY. Runnel's Hist. of Sanbornton, N. H., 87.

CALVERT. Richmond, Va., Standard, III, 50; Neill's Terra Mariæ; Heraldic Journal, III, 18, 21.

CALVIN. N. E. Hist. and Gen. Reg. XXVII, 136.

CAMBURN. Salter's Hist. of Monmouth County, N. J., XV.

CAMERON. Amer. Ancestry, vol. I, 12.

CAMMANN. Amer. Ancestry, V, 68.

CAMMET. Swift's Hist. of Barnstable, Mass., vol. I, 249.

CAMP:—Edward Camp, of New Haven, 1643, had Edward 1650, Mary 1652, Sarah 1655, and perhaps more.

JOHN CAMP, of Hartford, was admitted freeman 1669. He married probably Mary, daughter of Robert Sanford, and had Hannah 1672, John 1675, Sarah 1677, Joseph 1679, Mary 1682, James 1686, Samuel 1691, Abigail 1699.

NICHOLAS CAMP, of Milford, Conn., 1639, married as his second wife Catharine, widow of Anthony Thompson, and had Samuel 1655, Joseph 1658, Mary 1660, John and Sarah, twins, baptized 1662, Abigail 1662.

WILLIAM CAMP, of New London, Conn., 1683, married Elizabeth, daughter of Richard Smith, and died Oct. 9, 1713, leaving sons William and James.

REFERENCES.

CONNECTICUT.—Sedgwick's Hist. of Sharon, 67; Orcutt's Hist. of New Milford, 678; Middlefield, Conn., Hist. Hinman's Conn. Settlers, 470; Andrews' Hist. of New Britain, Conn., 207, 376; Boyd's Annals of Winchester, 330.

OTHER PUBLICATIONS.—Norton's Hist. of Fitzwilliam, N. H., 503; Littell's Passaic Valley, N. J., 66; Hubbard's Hist. of Stanstead County, Conn., 169; Baldwin Gen. Supp. 1262; Savage's Gen. Dict. vol. I, 381; Amer. Ancestry, IV, 22; V, 172; IX, 48, 183; XI, 86; N. E. Hist. and Gen. Reg. XII, 27; N. J. Hist. Coll. VI, 113.

CAMPBELL:—Duncan Campbell, of Boston, 1685, a bookseller, from Scotland, arrived there 1686. Under commission from home, he was made postmaster for our side of the world. By wife Susanna, he had William 1687, Archibald 1689, Matthew 1691, Susanna 1696, Agnes 1699.

JOHN CAMPBELL, of Boston, 1695, is supposed to have been a brother of Duncan. He was postmaster, but better known as proprietor of the "Boston Newsletter," the earliest Gazette on the west side of the ocean, printed by Bartholomew Green, first issued April 17, 1704. By wife Mary, John Campbell had Elizabeth 1696 and Mary 1704.

REFERENCES.

MAINE.—Bangor Hist. Mag. vol. I, 79; III, 181; IV, 90; Cushman's Hist. of Sheepscot, 360; Eaton's Hist. of Thomaston, 170; Milliken's Narraguagus Valley, 9.

MASSACHUSETTS.—Barry's Hist. of Framingham, 205; Dyer's Hist. of Plainfield; Wyman's Charlestown, Mass., Gens. vol. I, 174; Aldrich's Hist. Walpole, 222.

NEW HAMPSHIRE.—Secomb's Hist. of Amherst, 526, Morrison's Hist. of Windham, 356; Merrill's Hist. of Acworth, 194; Cochrane's Hist. of Antrim, 400; Coggswell's Hist. of Henniker, 478; Coggswell's Hist. of New Boston, 412.

OTHER PUBLICATIONS.—Egle's Penn. Gens. 526; Heminway's Vt., Gaz., V, 344; Joslin's Hist. of Poultney, Vt., 229; Pearson's Schenectady, N. Y., Settlers, 32; Roe's Sketches of Rose, N. Y., 264; Foote's Sketches of Va., 2d series, 117; Hayden's Va. Gens. 17; Meade's Old Churches of Va., II, 160; Peyton's Hist. of Augusta County, Va., 307; Richmond, Va., Standard, vol. I, 30, 32, 35, 38; II, 39, 45, 47, 49; III, 1, 5, 7, 39, 44, IV, 3; Slaughter's St. Mark's Parish, Va., vol. I, 188; Green's Kentucky Families; Power's Hist. of Sangamon County, Ill., 16, 170; Heraldic Journal, III, 151; Munsell's Albany Coll. IV, 107; Ely Gen. 269; Ammidown Hist. Coll. vol. I, 240; Butler Gen. (1888) 52, 69; Amer. Ancestry, IV, 49; VI, 87; VIII, 156; IX, 190; Savage's Gen. Dict. vol. I, 331; N. E. Hist. and Gen. Reg. XXXII, 275; Campbell's Spottswood Papers, 25; Robert Campbell and his Descendants 1888; Campfield, N. J., Hist. Coll., VI, 141.

CAMPSEY. Jameson's Hist. of Medway, Mass., 462.

CANADA. Hinman's Conn. Settlers, 472.

CANEDY. Power's Hist. of Sangamon County, Ill., 177.

CANBY. Davis' Hist. of Bucks County, Pa., 274; Amer. Ancestry, VII, 158; Wm. Canby of Delaware and His Descendants, 1883.

CANDAGE. Eaton's Hist. of Thomaston, Me., 171; Bangor, Me., Hist. Mag., IV, 129; V, 182; Amer. Ancestry, III, 156; Candage Gen. 1889.

CANDEE. Amer. Ancestry, VIII, 115; Candee Family (1882); Descendants of Zacheus Candee of New Haven, Conn.

CANDELL. Roome Gen. 108.

CANDISH. Bangor, Me., Hist. Mag. IV, 129.

CANDLER. Amer. Ancestry, VI, 188, 197; VII, 228; Descendants of Col. William Candler of Georgia, 1890.

CANE. Page's Hist. of Cambridge, Mass., 506.

CANFIELD (Sometimes written CAMPFIELD). Matthew Canfield, of New Haven, 1644, married Sarah, daughter of Richard Treat, (father of Gov. Treat), of Wethersfield, and had Samuel 1645, Sarah, Ebenezer 1649, Matthew 1650, Hannah 1651, Rachel 1652. He removed to Norwalk and there had Jonathan and Mary. He was a representative at the General Court in 1654, until the union of the Connecticut and New Haven colonies in the Royal Charter, where this name is inserted and after that union 1665-6, he removed to Newark, N. J., and died there 1673.

THOMAS CANFIELD, of Milford, 1646, perhaps brother of Matthew, was an early but not first settler. He was a representative to the General Court 1673-4. By wife Phebe, he had Jeremiah.

REFERENCES:—Cothren's Hist. of Woodbury, Conn., II, 1490; Orcutt's Hist. of Derby, Conn., 706; Orcutt's Hist. of New Milford, Conn., 670; Sedgwick's Hist. of Sharon, Conn., 67; Sharpe's Hist. of Seymour, Conn., 193; N. J. Hist. Coll. VI, 114; Whittemore's Founders and Builders of the Oranges, N. J., 48; Power's Hist. of Sangamon County, Ill., 176; Joslin's Hist. of Poultney, Vt., 230; Smith Gen. by Wellington Smith; Humphrey Gen. 197; Buckingham Gen. 239; Amer. Ancestry, VI, 153; Savage's Gen. Dict. vol. I, 332; Canfield Gen. 1897.

CANNEY:—Thomas Canney, of Portsmouth, N. H., 1631, sent over by Mason, the patentee, was of Dover, 1644. He had Thomas 1645, Joseph and Mary.

REFERENCES:—N. E. Hist. and Gen. Reg. V, 452. Savage's Gen. Dict. vol. I, 352.

CANNON. Orcutt's Hist. of Stratford, Conn., 1172; Davis' Hist. of Wallingford, Conn., 665; Page's Hist. of Hardwick, Mass., 344; Clute's Hist. of Staten Island, N. Y., 354; Swift's Barnstable, Mass., Families, vol. I, 250; Trowbridge Gen. 102.

CANTERBURY:—William Canterbury, of Lynn, 1641, was afterwards of Salem, and died 1663, leaving widow, Beatrice, and children John, Ruth and Rebecca.

REFERENCES:—Power's Hist. Sangamon Co., Ill., 177; Savage's Gen. Dict. I, 333.

CANTINE. Schoonmaker's Hist. of Kingston; Sylvester's Hist. of Ulster County, N. Y., 252.

CANTRALL. Power's Hist. of Sangamon County, Ill., 183.

CAPHART. Wheeler's Eminent North Carolinians, 220; Goode Gen. 243.

CAPELL. Hudson's Hist. of Lexington, Mass., 35; Cleveland's Hist. of Yates County, N. Y., 707.

JAMES CAPEN, of Charlestown, Mass., by wife Hannah, had James 1683.

JOHN CAPEN, the only son of the first Bernard, came as is supposed before his father and was admitted freeman 1634. He married 1637. Redigon or Radigan Clap and had John 1639. His wife died 1645, and he married 2d, Mary, daughter of Samuel Bass, of Braintree, Sept. 20, 1647, and had Samuel 1648, Bernard 1650, Preserved 1657, Joseph 1658, Hannah 1662. He was of the artillery company 1646, deacon 1656, Captain of the train band; representative to the General Court, 1671-5-8. He died April 6, 1692.

REFERENCES:—Wyman's Charlestown, Mass., Gens., vol. I, 175; Whitmore's Copps Hill Epitaphs; Washburn's Hist. of Leicester, Mass., 350; Draper's Hist. of Spencer, Mass., 186; Clapp's Jones' Hill, Mass., 59; Adams' Hist. of Fairhaven, 346; Lapham's Hist. of Bethel, Me., 499; Clapp Gen. 15; Glover Gen. 373; Thayer's Memorial, (1835), 75; Savage's Gen. Dict. vol. I, 333; N. E. Hist. and Gen. Reg. II, 80; V, 397; XX, 246.

CAPEWELL. Cothren's Ancient Woodbury, Conn., I, 75.

CAPPS. Power's Hist. of Sangamon County, Ill., 185.

CAPRON:—Benfield Capron, of Rehoboth, Mass., that part which became Attleborough, about 1680, had by wife Elizabeth, who died 1635, Benfield, Joseph, Elizabeth, Edward, John, Jonathan and Sarah.

REFERENCES:—Daggett's Hist. of Attleboro, Mass., 89; Chapin's Uxbridge, Mass., Address, 165; Bassett's Hist. of Richmond, N. H., 383; Read's Hist. of Swanzey, N. H., 305, Richardson's Hist. of Woonsocket, R. I., 308; Oneida County Hist. Soc. Trans., II, 120; Capron Gen. 1859.

CARD. Babson's Hist. of Gloucester, Mass., 67; Austin's Allied Families, R. I., 55; Austin's R. I. Gen. Dict. 270.

CARDELL. Walworth's Hyde Gen. 529.

CARDER:—Richard Carder, of Roxbury, Mass., removed early to Boston, was admitted freeman 1636. As a supporter of the so-called heresies of Wheelwright and Hutchinson, he was disfranchised in 1637, and went to Rhode Island. He was one of the eighteen original purchasers of the Island of Aquidneck, and partner in the civil compact. In 1643 he was engaged in the purchase of Warwick, with Gorton and others, and for sustaining his and their right, was made prisoner, brought to Boston, and sentenced to be incarcerated at Roxbury, in irons, not to depart on pain of death. The government discharged him and his fellow-sufferers the next year with sentence of banishment on pain of forfeiting life on coming back. By wife Mary he had John, Sarah, James 1655, Mary, Joseph. He died at Newport 1675.

REFERENCES:—Austin's R. I. Gen. Dict. 270; Savage's Gen. Dict. vol. I, 334.

CAREW. Walworth's Hyde Gen. 1038.

CAREY. Wyman's Charlestown, Mass., Gens., vol. I, 176; Ward's Hist. of Shrewsbury, Mass., 262; Temple's Hist. of Northfield, Mass., 417; Hinman's Conn. Settlers, 485; Morrison's Hist. of Windham, N. H., 374; Washington, N. H., Hist. 329; Smith's Hist. of Petersborough, N. H., 30; Plumb's Hist. of Hanover, Pa., 403; Dudley's Archeolog. Coll. Plate, 5; Evans' Fox Gen., 142; Thomas Family of Md., 52; Alden's Epitaphs, II, 251; Poole Gen. 126.

CARY:—James Cary of Charlestown, Mass., 1639, came, as tradition says, from Bristol, England. By wife Elinor he had John 1642, Nathaniel 1645, Jonathan 1647, Elizabeth 1648, Elinor.

JOHN CARY, of Bridgewater, Mass., is said to have come from the neighborhood of Bristol, England, at the age of 25; was at Duxbury, Mass., 1637, having there a grant of land. He married 1644, Elizabeth, daughter of Francis Godfrey, and had John 1645, Francis 1647, Elizabeth 1649, James 1652, Mary 1654, Jonathan 1656, David 1658, Hannah 1657, Joseph 1663, Rebecca 1665, Sarah 1667, and Mehitable 1670. He was the first town clerk, and early his name was written Carew. He soon followed the English pronunciation and wrote his name Carey.

Arms.—Argent on a bend engrailed sable, three roses of the field, in the sinister chief an anchor of the second. Crest.—A swan ppr. wings erect, on the breast a rose sable.

REFERENCES.

MASSACHUSETTS.—Winsor's Hist. of Duxbury, Mass., 241; Ward's Hist. of Shrewsbury, 263; Temple's Hist. of North Brookfield, 550; Perley's Hist. of Roxford, 72; Mitchell's Hist. of Bridgewater, 130; Kingman's Hist. of North Bridgewater, 463; Jameson's Hist. of Medway, 462.

OTHER PUBLICATIONS.—Collins' Hillsdale, N. Y., app. 46; Lapham's Hist. of Paris, Me., 549, 559;Meade's Old Churches of Va., vol. I, 455; Richmond, Va., Critic, 1888; Richmond, Va.; Standard, II, 41; III, 31; Robertson's Pocahontas Descendants; Slaughter's Life of Fairfax, 67, 72; Southern Bivouac, May, 1886, 733; Welles' Amer. Family Antiq. vol. I, 17; Prescott's Page Gen., 93, 239; Goode Gen., 281; Green Todd Gen.; Lawrence and Bartlett Mem. 109; Keith's Harrison Ancestry, Amer. Ancestry, III, 142; IX, 49; Savage's Gen. Dict. vol. I, 344; Cary Gen. 1874; N. E. Hist. and Gen. Reg. XLV, 322; XLIX, 401.

CARGILL.   Richardson's Woonsocket, R. I., 308; Cushman's Hist. of Sheepscot, Me., 362.

CARHART.   Baird's Hist. of Rye, N. Y., 455; Amer. Ancestry, vol. I, 12; II, 20; Carhart Gen. 1880.

CARKIN.   Livermore's Hist. of Wilton, N. H., 344.

CARLE.   Little's Hist. of Warren, N. H., 67; Old Kent, Md., 232; Hull's Trenton, N. J.

CARLETON:—Edward Carleton, of Rowley, Mass., was admitted freeman 1642.   He was a representative to the General Court, 1644-7.   His son Edward was the first birth recorded in the town.

REFERENCES:—Hazen's Hist. of Billerica, Mass., 21; Wyman's Charlestown, Mass., Gens., 181; Bangor, Me., Hist. Mag. V, 183; Eaton's Hist. of Thomaston, Me., 177, 673; Essex Inst. Hist. Coll., 1883; Merrill's Hist. of Acworth, N. H., 197; Secomb's Hist. of Amherst, 528; Stearns' Hist. of Rindge, N. H., 466; Poor's Hist. Researches, 89, 134; Amer. Ancestry, VIII, 236.

CARLEY.   Smith's Hist. of Petersborough, N.H., 31; Washington, N. H., Hist. 330; Heminway's Vt. Gaz., V, 721; Hayward's Hancock, 430.

CARLIN.   Goode Gen. 267.

CARLISLE.   Aldrich's Hist. of Walpole, 224; Green's Kentucky Families.

CARLL.   Shroud's Hist. of Fenwick, N. J., 521.

CARLTON.   Hayward's Hist. of Hancock, N. H., 434; Essex Hist. Coll. XX, 249.

CARMAN:—John Carman, of Roxbury, Mass., came to New England, in 1631, probably with Eliot in the "Lion."   By wife Florence, he had John 1633, Abigail 1635, Caleb 1639.   He removed to Long Island, and was that patentee of Hempstead, whose son Caleb, born there Jan. 9, 1646, was blind from birth, the first child born there of European parents.

REFERENCES:—Bunker's L. I. Gens.. 164; N. Y. Gen. and Bio. Rec. XIII, 48.

CARNES:—Thomas Carnes, of New Haven, married Mary Brown, and had Elizabeth 1684, Alexander 1685, Joseph 1687.

REFERENCES:—Wyman's Charlestown, Mass., Gens. vol. I, 184; Coggswell's Henniker, 487.

CARNEY.   Cushman's Sheepscot, 363; Eaton's Hist. of Thomaston, Me., 172.

CARROLL.   Amer. Ancestry, II, 20.

CARPENTER:—David Carpenter, of Farmington, Conn., died Jan. 22, 1651, leaving children Elizabeth, born 1644, David 1647, Mary 1650.

WILLIAM CARPENTER, of Weymouth, Mass., came in the "Bevis" 1638, from Southampton, aged 62, from Harwell, says the clearance at the custom-house, with William 33, probably his son, Abigail his wife 32, and four children of four years old or less.   He was admitted freeman 1640, was a representative at the General Court 1641 -43; died 1659.   His will names William, John, Joseph, and others.

REFERENCES.

MASSACHUSETTS.—Ballou's Hist. of Milford, 610; Barrus' Hist. of Goshen, 143; Benedict's Hist. of Sutton, 615; Daggett's Hist. of Attleboro, 89; Paige's Hist. of Hardwick, 344; Wyman's Charlestown, Mass., Gens., vol. I, 185; Adams' Hist. of Fairhaven, 344.

NEW HAMPSHIRE.—Read's Hist. of Swanzey, 307; Hayward's Hist. of Gilsum, 281; Aldrich's Hist. of Walpole, 227.

NEW YORK.—Baird's Hist. of Rye, 455; Bolton's Hist. of Westchester County, II, 716; Ruttenber's Hist. of Newburgh, 293; Ruttenber's Hist. of Orange County, 380; Smith's Hist. of Dutchess Co., 380.

OTHER PUBLICATIONS.—Andrews' Hist. of New Britain, Conn., 334; Hinman's Conn. Settlers, 487; Austin's R. I. Gen. Dict., 35; Clement's Newtown, N. J., Settlers; Futhey's Hist. of Chester County, Pa., 494; Lapham's Hist. of Paris, Me.; Penn. Mag. VI, 453; R. I. Hist. Mag. VI, 205; Power's Hist. of Sangamon County, Ill., 187; Austin's Allied Families, R. I., 56; Caverly's Hist. of Pittsford, Vt., 694; Bliss Gen. 646; Dawson Gen. 60; Greene Gen.; Guild's Stiles Gen., 378; Hoagland Gen., 269; Hughes Gen. 88, 185; Huron and Erie Counties, Ohio, 514; Loomis' Gen. Female Branches, 618; Mott Gen.; Rodman Gen., 116; Strong Gen., 452; Vinton Gen., 480; Wentworth Gen., vol. I, 469; Savage's Gen. Dict. vol. I, 335; N. E. Hist. and Gen. Reg. IX, 52; N. Y. Bio. Rec. XIII, 48; Amer. Ancestry, II, 20; III, 214; V, 152; IX; 73; X, 102, 159, 198; Smith and Lloyd's Carpenter Gen. (1870); Carpenter Gen., 1877, 1883.

CARR:—Caleb Carr, of Newport, R. I.; may be that passenger in the "Elizabeth and Ann" (1635) from London, aged 11, among the freemen 1655, chosen Treasurer of the Colony 1661, Assistant 1678, and Governor in May, 1695, died Dec. following.   By wife Mercy, he had Nicholas, Caleb, John, Edward, Samuel, Mercy, and by wife Sarah, he had Francis, James, Elizabeth and Sarah.

GEORGE CARR, of Ipswich, 1633, removed with first settlers, to Salisbury, where he was held in high esteem. By wife Elizabeth, he had Elizabeth 1642, George 1644, Richard 1646, William 1648, James 1650, Mary 1652, Sarah 1654, John 1656, Richard again 1659, Ann 1661; he died April 4, 1682.

REFERENCES.

MAINE.—Eaton's Hist. of Thomaston, 172; Bradbury's Hist. of Kennebunkport, 233; Bangor Hist. Mag. vol. I, 9.

MASSACHUSETTS.—Kingman's Hist. of North Bridgewater. 469; Mitchell's Hist. of Bridgewater, 129.

NEW HAMPSHIRE.—Wheeler's Hist. of Newport, 324; Washington, N. H., Hist., 330; Runnel's Hist. of Sanbornton, II, 96; Hayward's Hist. of Hancock, 436; Eaton's Hist. of Candia, 58; Cochrane's Hist. of Antrim, 402; Chase's Hist. of Chester, 483; N. H. Hist. Society Coll., VII, 377.

OTHER PUBLICATIONS.—Austin's R. I. Ancestries, 75; Austin's R. I. Gen. Dict. 37; Newport, Hist. Mag., III, 243; Hinman's Conn. Settlers, 489; Clyde's Irish Settlement of Pa., 383; Davis' Hist. of Bucks County, Pa., 421;

Meade's Old Families of Va.; Richmond, Va., Standard, III, 19; Va. Mag. and Biog. II, (1895); Tilley's N. E. Notes and Queries, vol. I, 65; Wentworth Gen., vol. I, 62; Otis Gen. Amer. Ancestry, VII, 68; VIII, 215; Savage's Gen. Dict., vol. I, 338; N. E. Hist. and Gen. Reg. V, 200; XXIX, 128.

CARRIEL. Benedict's Hist. of Sutton, Mass., 616; Sibley's Hist. of Union, Me., 439; Saunderson's Hist. of Charlestown, N. H., 297; Dwight Gen. 949.

CARRIER. Hazen's Hist. of Billerica, Mass., 22; Hinman's Conn. Settlers, 490; Sedgwick's Hist. of Sharon, Conn., 69; Walworth's Hyde Gen. 554; Nash Gen. 75; Amer. Ancestry, IX, 19.

CARRINGTON:—Edward Carrington, of Charlestown, Mass., was admitted freeman 1636. By wife Elizabeth, he had Elizabeth 1639, Sarah 1643, and probably others. He was a representative to the General Court, 1651.

REFERENCES:—Andrews' Hist. of New Britain, Conn., Davis' Hist. of Wallingford, Conn.; Hinman's Conn. Settlers, 491; Orcutt's Hist. of New Milford, Conn., 686; Campbell's Hist. of Virginia, 624; Foote's Sketches of Va., 2d series, 575; Meade's Old Families of Va., II, 29; Richmond, Va., Standard, vol. I, 45; II, 7, 35, 37; III, 14, 15, 26, 27; Slaughter's St. Mark's Parish, 164; Greene's Kentucky Families; Goode Gen. 128, 249; Paxton's Marshall Gen. 104; Sullivan Gen. Memorial, 247; Tuttle Gen. 69; Watkins' Gen., 28.

CARROLL. Eaton's Hist. of Warren, Me., 515; Old Kent, Md., 137.

CARRUT. Temple's Hist. of North Brookfield, Mass., 547.

CARRUTH. Carruth Gen. (1880).

CARSLEY. Ridlon's Hist. of Harrison, Me., 43; Swift's Barnstable, Mass., Farms, vol. I, 147.

CARSON. Wheeler's Eminent North Carolinians, 88; Power's Hist. of Sangamon County, Ill., 188; Green's Kentucky Families.

CARTER:—John Carter, of Charlestown, Mass., was among the early settlers of Woburn, Mass. He was admitted freeman 1644. By wife Elizabeth, he had Mary 1647, Abigail 1648, Hannah 1651, John 1653.

JOSHUA CARTER, of Dorchester, Mass., was admitted freeman 1634, removed to Windsor, Conn., and died there July 5, 1647, leaving Joshua, Elias and Elisha.

SAMUEL CARTER, of Charlestown, Mass., was admitted freeman 1647, member of the artillery company 1648. He had issue Hannah 1640, Samuel 1642, Zachary 1644, Mary 1645, and perhaps others.

THOMAS CARTER, of Charlestown, Mass., was admitted freeman 1637. By wife Ann, who died in 1679, in her 72nd year, he had Ann 1640, Elizabeth 1642, Thomas 1644, and perhaps others. He died 1694, in his 88th year.

Rev. THOMAS CARTER, of Woburn, Mass., the first minister there, was bred at St. John's College, Cambridge, Eng. He was ordained at Watertown, Mass., 1642, and died there Sept. 5, 1684, aged 74. By wife Mary he had Samuel 1640, Judith, Mary 1648, Abigail 1649, Deborah 1651, Timothy 1653, Thomas 1655.

Arms.—Argent on a chevron between three cart-wheels vert. *Crest.*—On a mount vert, a greyhound sejant

argent sustaining a shield of the last, charged with a cart-wheel vert.

REFERENCES.

CONNECTICUT.—Timlow's Hist. of Southington, 38; Orcutt's Hist. of Wolcott, 467; Hinman's Conn. Settlers, 492; Davis' Hist. of Wallingford, 665; Andrews' Hist. of New Britain, 200.

MAINE.—Bangor, Me., Hist. Mag. V, 183; Lapham's Hist. of Bethel, 499; Lapham's Hist. of Norway, 478; Lapham's Hist. of Paris, 546.

MASSACHUSETTS.—Hyde's Hist. of Brimfield, 388; Sewall's Hist. of Woburn, 124, 599; Wyman's Charlestown Gens., vol. I, 186; Ballou's Hist. of Milford, 612; Benedict's Hist. of Sutton, 617; Bond's Hist. of Watertown, 150; Cutter's Hist. of Arlington, 201; Atkin's Hist. of Hawley, 60.

NEW HAMPSHIRE.—Stearns' Hist. of Rindge, 468; Smith's Hist. of Petersborough, 33; Secomb's Hist. of Amherst, 530; Read's Hist. of Swanzey, 310; Norton's Hist. of Fitzwilliam, 504; Coggswell's Hist. of Hinneker, 487; Coffin's Hist. of Boscawen, 4L2; Bouton's Hist. of Concord, 636.

OTHER PUBLICATIONS.—Ruttenber's Hist. of Newburgh, N. Y., 297; Ruttenber's Hist. of Orange County, N. Y., 384; Powers' Hist. of Sangamon County, Ill., 189; Campbell's Hist. of Virginia, 412; Campbell's Spottswood Papers; Carter Tree of Virginia, 1884; Hayden's Virginia Genealogies, 130, 140; Meade's Old Churches of Va., II, 110; Richmond, Va., Critic, (1888); Richmond Standard, II, 16, 42; III, 38; IV, 2; Slaughter's St. Mark's Parish, Va., 121; Futhey's Hist. of Chester County, Pa., 494; Prescott's Page Gen., 59, 74, 138; Cope Family, 30, 38, 57, 130; Cregar's Haine's Ancestry, 54; Cutter Gen., 44; Jones Gen. (1891), 159; Kellogg's White Descendants, 40; Vinton's Richardson Family, 574, 663; Welles' Washington Gen., 176; Cutt's Gen., 154; Amer. Ancestry, VI, 148; XI, 174, 163; Savage's Gen. Dict. vol. I, 340; Carter Gen. N. E. Hist. and Gen. Reg. XVII, 51.

CARTERET. Wyman's Charlestown, Mass., Gens. vol. I, 193; Hatfield's Hist. of Elizabeth, N. J., 110; N. J. Hist. Soc. Proc., 2d series I; Carteret Gen. 1887.

CARTHRAE. Green's Kentucky Families.

CARTLAND. Dearborn's Hist. Parsonfield, 369.

CARTMELL. Power's Hist. of Sangamon County, Ill., 193.

CARTWRIGHT:—Edward Cartwright, of Nantucket, had Sampson 1678, Susanna 1681, Edward 1683, Mary 1687.

NICHOLAS CARTWRIGHT, of Nantucket, Mass., died Sept. 10, 1706, leaving Sarah, born 1695, Elinor 1697, Hope 1699, Lydia 1701, Nicholas 1706.

REFERENCES:—Sedgwick's Hist. of Sharon, Conn., 70; Power's Hist. of Sangamon County, Ill., 190; Savage's Gen. Dict. vol. I, 343.

CARUTHERS. Richmond, Va., Standard, III, 2, 25; Paxton's Marshall Gen., 158; Green's Kentucky Families.

CARVER:—Robert Carver, of Marshfield, Mass., had a grant of land 1638, was admitted freeman 1644. He had issue John and William. He died 1680, aged 85.

REFERENCES:—Winsor's Hist. of Duxbury, Mass., 240; Mitchell's Hist. of Bridgewater, Mass., 129, 362; Davis' Landmarks of Plymouth, Mass., 51; Hodgman's Hist. of

Westford, Mass., 441; Washburn's Notes on Livermore, Me., 17; Davis' Hist. of Bucks County, Pa., 279; Martindale's Hist. of Byberry, Pa., 243; Power's Hist. of Sangamon County, Ill., 193; Hollister's Hist. of Pawlet, Vt., 173; Smith's Gen. of Wm. Smith, 99; Savage's Gen. Dict. vol. I, 343.

CARYL. Heminway's Vt. Gaz., V, 163; Wight Gen. 80.

CASE:—Ebenezer Case, of Roxbury, Mass., married 1690, Patience, daughter of James Draper, and had Mary 1691, Jonathan 1693, and perhaps others.

JOHN CASE, of New London, Conn., 1656, removed next year to Windsor, and married Sarah, daughter of William Spencer, he had Elizabeth, born 1658, Mary 1660, John 1662, William 1665, Samuel 1667, Richard 1669, Bartholomew 1670, Joseph 1674, Sarah 1676, Abigail 1682. The last five were born at Simsbury, whence he removed. He was constable there 1669, representative to the General Court 1670, and for several years after.

JOSEPH CASE, of Narragansett, in that part near Kingstown, had Joseph, born 1678, William 1684, Mary, Hannah, Margaret, John 1692, Emanuel 1699.

RICHARD CASE, of Hartford, perhaps brother of the first John, married Elizabeth, daughter of John Purchase. He was propounded for freeman 1671, died March 30, 1694, leaving Richard, John, Mary.

REFERENCES:—Hinman's Conn. Settlers, 497; Brown's West Simsbury, Conn., Settlers, 35; Stiles' Hist. of Windsor, II, 140; Eaton's Hist. of Thomaston, Me., 173; Lapham's Hist. of Norway, Me., 478; Cochrane's Hist. of Antrim, N. H., 407; Austin's R. I. Gen. Dict. 273; Narragansett Hist. Reg. vol. I, 208; Rhode Island Hist. Soc. Coll., III, 309; Griffin's Journal of Southold, L. I., 175; Sprague's Hist. of Gloversville, N. Y., 112; Goodwin Gen. Notes, 275; Humphrey Gen. 246; Amer. Ancestry, II, 161; V, 153, 221; VIII, 81; XI, 174; Savage's Gen. Dict. vol. I, 345.

CASEY. Tilley's Mag. of N.E. Hist., III, 83; Austin's Ancestral Dict., 13; Austin's R. I. Gen. Dict., 40; Bartlett's Wanton Family, 121; Amer. Ancestry, III, 8.

CASH:—William Cash, of Salem, a mariner, married Oct., 1667, Elizabeth, daughter perhaps of Richard, had William, born 1669, John and Elizabeth (twins) 1672, Mary and Ann (twins) 1675, Esther 1679, Elizabeth 1693.

REFERENCES:—Stickney's Hist. of Minisink, N. Y., 170; Driver Gen., 253, 265; Savage's Gen. Dict., vol. I, 347.

CASHOW. Amer. Ancestry, IX, 243.

CASKIE. Welles' Washington Gen., 230.

CASLEY. Freeman's Hist. of Cape Cod, II, 208.

CASS:—John Cass, of Hampton, 1644, married Martha, daughter of Thomas Philbrick, and had John, Samuel 1659, Joseph, Martha, Jonathan, Ebenezer, Abigail, Mercy, Mary. Of this line Hon. Lewis Cass was a descendant.

REFERENCES:—Runnell's Hist. of Sanbornton, N. H., II, 99; Dow's Hist. of Hampton, N. H., 632, 1064; Bassett's Hist. of Richmond, N. H., 356; Palmer Gen. (1886), 51; Amer. Ancestry, vol. I, 13; XI, 93; Savage's Gen. Dict., vol. I, 347.

CASSELL. Amer. Ancestry, IX, 164.

CASSON. Wheeler's Eminent North Carolinians, 88.

CAST. Eaton's Hist. of Candia, N. H., 60; Power's Hist. of Sangamon County, Ill., 195; Hubbard's Stanstead County, Quebec, 184; Savage's Gen. Dict., vol. I, 347.

CASSITY. Power's Hist. of Sangamon County, Ill., 195.

CASTLE. Temple's Hist. of Whately, Mass., 213; Cothren's Hist. of Woodbury, Conn., II, 1486; Bronson's Hist. of Waterbury, Conn., 481; Amer. Ancestry, IX, 65.

CASTNER. Jenkins' Hist. of Gwynedd, Pa., 373; Cleveland's Hist. of Yates County, N. Y., 667.

CASWELL:—Thomas Caswell, of Taunton, Mass., had Stephen 1649, Thomas 1651, Peter 1652, Mary 1654, John 1656, Sarah 1658, William 1660, Samuel 1663, Elizabeth 1665, Abigail 1666, Esther 1669.

REFERENCES:—Eaton's Annals of Warren, Me., 515; Ridlon's Harrison, Me., Settlers, 50; Clark's Hist. of Norton, Mass., 375; Wyman's Charlestown, Mass., Gens., vol. I, 194; Trisby's Hist. of Middlebury, Vt., 66; Hubbard's Hist. of Stanstead County, Canada, 172; Pierce's (E. W.) Contributions, 36; Savage's Gen. Dict., vol. I, 348; N. E. Gen. Reg., IV, 29.

CATCHPOLE. Roe's Sketches of Rose, N. Y., 139.

CATES. Runnel's Hist. of Sanbornton, N. H., II, 102. Coggswell's Hist. of Nottingham, N. H., 329; Eaton's Hist. of Thomaston, Me., 173; Caverno Gen., 334.

CATESBY. Richmond, Va., Standard, II, 51; Jones Gen. (1891), 17.

CATLAND. Eaton's Hist. of Thomaston, Me., 173.

CATLETT. Hayden's Virginia Gens., 244; Meade's Old Families Va.; Slaughter's St. Mark's Parish, Va, 156; Carter Family Tree.

CATLIN:—John Catlin, of Hartford, Conn., was constable 1662, and often selectman, had issue John and Mary.

REFERENCES:—Hinman's Conn. Settlers, 503; Tuttle Gen. 617; Baldwin's Candee Gen. 141; Amer. Ancestry, IX, 204; Savage's Gen. Dict., vol. I, 348.

CATELL. Shroud's Fenwick Colony, 61.

CAULDWELL. Littell's Passaic Valley Gens., 68.

CAUFFMAN. Rodenbough's Autumn Leaves.

CAULKINS:—Hugh Caulkins, of Gloucester, Mass., probably a Welshman, came with Rev. Richard Blinman, and settled first at Marshfield, removed next year to Lynn was admitted freeman 1642, at Gloucester. He was selectman 1643, and representative to the General Court 1650-2. He removed to New London before beginning to serve under this last election and was selectman and representative half the years of his residence there, and town clerk for all. He removed in 1662, to Norwich, and was one of the first deacons on organizing the church. He represented this town at the General Court 1663-4. He died in 1690, aged 90. He brought his wife Ann from England and children John, Sarah, Mary, and probably more. He had born at Gloucester, David, Deborah 1643.

REFERENCES:—Hinman's Conn. Settlers, 511; Caulkins' Hist. of Norwich, Conn., 171; Caulkins' Hist. of New London, Conn., 361; Smith Gen. (1889), 95; Bill Gen., 196; Savage's Gen. Dict., vol. I, 349.

CAVE. Hayden's Virginia Gens., 13; Slaughter's St. Mark's Parish, Va., 122.

CAVENDER. Hayward's Hist. of Hancock, N. H., 437.

CAVENDISH. Bangor, Me., Mag., IV, 129.

CAVERLEY. Strong Gen., 859.

CAVERLY. Runnel's Hist. of Sanbornton, N. H., II, 109; Brown's West Simsbury Settlers, 56; Amer. Ancestry, VI, 69; Caverly Gen., (1880).

CAVERNO. Caverno Gen., (1874).

CAVINS. Amer. Ancestry, IX, 40.

CAWLEY. Runnel's Hist. Sanbornton, N. H., 87.

CAZIER. Egle's Penn. Gens., 453.

CENTER:—John Center, of Boston, had by wife Mary, John 1682, Jonathan 1685, by wife Ruth, he had Elenor 1687, Ruth 1692, Sarah 1695, Jeremiah 1697.
REFERENCES:—Wyman's Charlestown, Mass., Gens., vol. I, 195; Livermore's Hist. of Wilton, N. H., 345; Hinman's Conn. Settlers, 513.

CHACE. Spooner Gen., vol. I, 46; Amer. Ancestry, II, 21.

CHADBOURNE. Eaton's Hist. of Thomaston, Me., 174; Ridlon's Settlers of Harrison, Me., 38; Pierce's Hist. of Gorman, Me., 159; Wentworth Gen. vol. I, 389; Savage's Gen. Dict., vol. I, 350; N. E. Hist. and Gen. Reg., XIII, 139, 339.

CHADDOCK. Roe's Sketches of Rose, N. Y., 67; Barry's Hist. of Hanover, 263.

CHADWELL:—Thomas Chadwell, of Lynn, Mass., 1630, had by wife Margaret, who died 1658, Moses, born 1637, Benjamin and Thomas. He removed to Boston and married Barbara, widow of John Brimblecorn, who had been the widow of George Davis, and after uniting with the church of Charlestown, was made freeman 1872.
REFERENCES:—Bond's Hist. of Watertown, Mass., 150; Savage's Gen. Dict., vol. I, 350.

CHADWICK:—Charles Chadwick, probably came in Gov. Winthrop's fleet, was sworn freeman of the Colony 1630, was selectman 1637, representative to the General Court 1657-9, died April 10, 1682, aged 85. By wife Elizabeth he had John, Thomas, and perhaps others.

JAMES CHADWICK, of Malden, Mass., a soldier of Mosley's company, was wounded in the great swamp fight Dec. 19, 1675. He married Feb. 1677, Hannah Butler and had Jemima 1687, Benjamin 1689, Abigail 1692, and perhaps others. He was admitted freeman 1690.

JOHN CHADWICK, of Watertown, Mass., probably brother of Charles, born in England, called Sergeant. By wife Joan, who died 1674, he had Elizabeth 1648, Sarah 1650, James 1653. He was admitted freeman 1656, removed early to Malden, Mass., and died 1680, aged 79.

THOMAS CHADWICK, of Newbury, Mass., brother of John, married 1674, Sarah Wolcott, and had Sarah 1675, Thomas 1677, he removed to Watertown, and there had John 1680, Elizabeth 1682, Richard 1687, Daniel 1689, Jonathan 1691.
REFERENCES:—Wyman's Charlestown, Mass., Gens., 196; Hinman's Conn. Settlers, 514; Coffin's Hist. of Boscawen, N. H., 485; Coggswell's Hist. of Nottingham, N. H., 344; Stearns' Hist. of Rindge, N. H., 470; Bass' Hist. of Braintree, Vt., 124; Salter's Hist. of Monmouth County, N. J., XVI; Champion Gen.; Cutt's Gen., 138; Thurston

Gen., (1892), 210; Wentworth Gen., II, 282, 501; Amer. Ancestry, II, 21; Savage's Gen. Dict., vol. I, 351.

CHAFFEE:—Thomas Chaffee, of Hingham, Mass., 1637, removed to Swanzey, Mass., before 1660. He had, it is supposed, sons Joseph and Nathaniel.
REFERENCES:—Stiles' Hist. of Windsor, Conn., II, 143; Sedgwick's Hist. of Sharon, Conn., 70; Hinman's Conn. Settlers, 516; Caverly's Hist. of Pittsford, Vt., 696; Davis Gen., 478; Morris and Flint Gen., 23; Walker Gen. 181; Amer. Ancestry, II, 13; VII, 93.

CHAFFIN. Aldrich's Hist. of Walpole, N. H., 228; Stearns' Hist. of Ashburnham, Mass., 634.

CHALKLEY. Sewall's Hist. of Woburn, Mass., 509.

CHALICE or CHILLIS, Philip, of Salisbury, Mass., was at Ipswich, 1637, then 20 years old. He married Mary, daughter of William Sargent, and had John 1655, Philip 1658, William 1663, Lydia 1665, Thomas.
REFERENCES:—Savage's Gen. Dict., vol. I, 353.

CHALMER. Mackin's Me. Centen., 158.

CHALKER:—Alexander Chalker, of Saybrook, Conn., married 1649, Catharine Post, probably daughter of Stephen, and had Stephen 1650, Samuel, Mary Abraham 1655, Catharine 1657, Sarah 1659, Alexander 1666.
REFERENCES:—Hinman's Conn. Settlers, 517; Savage's Gen. Dict., vol. I, 352.

CHAMBERLAIN:—Edmund, or Edward Chamberlain, of Woburn, Mass., freeman 1665, was in Mosley's company in the campaign of Dec., 1675. He married 1647, at Roxbury, Mass., Mary Turner, perhaps sister of John, and had Mary 1648, Sarah 1649, Jacob 1658. He married 2d, Hannah Burden, in 1670, at Malden, and there had Susanna, Edmund 1676.

JOHN CHAMBERLAIN, of Boston, 1651, married May, 1653, Ann, daughter of William Brown, and had Ann 1654, Elizabeth 1656; he was imprisoned as a Quaker, 1659, he may have removed to Newport, R. I., where was a John, who by wife Catharine had Susanna 1664, Peleg 1666, Jane 1667.

JOSEPH CHAMBERLAIN, of Hadley, a soldier there on service 1676, married 1688, Mercy, daughter of John Dickinson, and had Sarah, born 1693, John 1700, removed to Colchester and died 1752, aged 87.

RICHARD CHAMBERLAIN, of Braintree, Mass., had removed to Roxbury, and there had Benjamin, Joseph, Mary, Rebecca, Ann, Mehitable 1666. He removed to Sudbury, and died 1673.

THOMAS CHAMBERLAIN, of Newton, Mass., married 1682, Elizabeth, daughter of Thomas Hammond, and had Thomas 1683, Elizabeth 1686, Rebecca 1689, Mary 1693, Sarah 1695, John 1698.

Arms.—Argent an armed arm couped at the shoulders in fesse or, in the hand ppr. a rose gules leaved and stalked vert. *Crest.*—A greyhound's head erased argent, round his neck a belt azure buckled or.

REFERENCES.

CONNECTICUT.—Stiles' Hist. of Windsor, II, 143; Sedgwick's Hist. of Sharon, 70; Hinman's Conn. Settlers, 518.

MASSACHUSETTS.—Sewall's Hist. of Woburn, Mass., 599; Stearn's Hist. of Ashburnham, 634; Temple's Hist. of Northfield, 418; Barry's Hist. of Hanover, 264; Hazen's Hist. of Billerica, 23; Jackson's Hist. of Newton,

253; Morse's Sherborn, Mass., Settlers, 58; Paige's Hist. of Hardwick, 345.

OTHER PUBLICATIONS.

Austin's Allied Families, R. I., 59; Saunderson's Hist. of Charlestown, N. H., 304; Washington, N. H., Hist. 333; Wheeler's Hist. of Newport, N. H., 328; Hanson's Old Kent, Md., 288; Meade's Old Families of Va., Salter's Hist. of Monmouth County, N. J., XVII; Child Gen. 244; Cleveland Gen. 184; Shattuck Gen. 372; Whitman Gen., 429, 452; Savage's Gen. Dict., vol. I, 352.

CHAMBERLAIN:—Richard, of Braintree, 1642, afterwards of Roxbury and Sudbury, spelt his name LAINE, while his descendants have contracted the name to LIN. He had a son Joseph, who was one of the founders of Oxford, Mass.

REFERENCES:—Mitchell's Hist. of Bridgewater, Mass., 134; Hodgman's Hist. of Westford, Mass., 441; Wyman's Charlestown, Mass., Gens., vol. I, 197; Butler's Hist. of Groton, Mass., 392; Brown's Bedford, Mass., Families, 6; Austin's R. I. Gen. Dict., 40; Roe's Sketches of Rose, N. Y., 60; Futhey's Hist. of Chester County, Pa., 496; Hubbard's Hist. Stanstead County, Can., 131, 275; Dunster Gen. 197; Dwight Gen. 500; Palmer and Trimble Gen.; 101, 125; Amer. Ancestry, IX, 146.

CHAMBERS:—John Chambers, of Trenton, N. J., born in 1677, left Scotland during the latter part of the 17th century and settled in county Antrim, Ireland; from thence he emigrated to America and settled in Trenton, N. J., 1729. He had a son Alexander, a man of considerable prominence and a Commissary of State troops in the War of the Revolution.

REFERENCES:—Hall's Trenton, N. J., Pres. Church, 158; Cooley's Trenton, N. J., Gens. 29; Futhey's Hist. of Chester County, Pa., 496; Wyman's Charlestown, Mass., Gens., vol. I, 199; Barber Gen. 39; Amer. Ancestry, VII, 252; N. Y. Gen. and Bio. Rec., III, 57.

CHAMPE. Richmond, Va., Standard, III, 11.

CHAMPERNON. Essex Inst. Coll., XVI, 17.

CHAMPERNOWE. N. E. Hist. and Gen. Reg., XXVII, 322; XXIX, 45.

CHAMBLESS. Shroud's Fenwick Col., N. J., 57.

CHAMPION:—Henry Champion, of Saybrook, married 1647, and had Sarah, born 1649, Mary 1651, Henry 1654, Thomas 1656, Stephen 1658. He married 2d, in 1698, Deborah.

REFERENCES:—Hinman's Conn. Settlers, 520; West Springfield, Mass., Centen. 114; Field's Hist. of Haddam, Conn., 47; Clement's Newtown, N. J., Settlers; Ely Gen. 164, 347; Amer. Ancestry, VII, 17, 42; Savage's Gen. Dict. vol. I, 355; Campion Genealogy, 1891.

CHAMPLAIN. Amer. Ancestry, V, 90.

CHAMPLIN:—Jeffrey Champlin, of Portsmouth, and Newport, R. I., was admitted freeman Sept. 14, 1640. He was probably of Westerly, in 1668, with sons Jeffrey, William and Christopher. He died before 1695.

REFERENCES:—Austin's R. I. Dict. V, 90; Austin's Ancestral Dict., 14; Updyke's Narragansett's R. I. Ch., 111; Livermore's Block Island, R. I., 325; Sylvester's Hist. of Ulster Co., N. Y., 141; Cleveland's Hist. Yates County, N. Y., 539; N. E. Hist. and Gen. Reg. XIV, 24; Savage's Gen. Dict. vol. I, 355.

CHAMPNEY:—John Champney, of Cambridge, Mass., 1635, died early, leaving widow Joan, by whom he had Mary, Sarah, John and Joseph.

RICHARD CHAMPNEY, of Cambridge, Mass., perhaps brother of John, came in the "Defence" 1635, probably with wife Jane, and child Esther, in company with Rev. Thomas Shepard. He was admitted freeman 1636. He was a ruling elder in the church, owned estate at Billerica. He had Samuel 1635, Sarah 1638, Mary 1639, John 1641, Lydia, Daniel 1645. He died 1669.

REFERENCES:—Paige's Hist. of Cambridge, Mass., 506; Wyman's Charlestown, Mass., Gens., vol. I, 200; Kidder's New Ipswich, Mass., 343; Chapman's Trowbridge Gen., 239; Savage's Gen. Dict. vol. I, 356; Champney Family, 1867.

CHANDLER:—Edmund Chandler, of Duxbury, Mass., 1633, had Benjamin, Samuel, Joseph, Sarah, Ann, Mary, Ruth. He was at Scituate 1650, but died 1662, at Duxbury.

ROGER CHANDLER, of Concord, married 1671, Mary Simonds, and had Mary 1672, Samuel 1673, Abigail 1674. He had removed before 1679, to Billerica, and was admitted freeman 1682.

WILLIAM CHANDLER, of Roxbury, Mass., came to New England in 1637, with wife Annis or Hannah, and children Hannah, born about 1629, Thomas 1630, John, William 1636, and had here Sarah 1640. He died 1642.

WILLIAM CHANDLER, of Newbury, Mass., had three wives named Mary, and had children Esther 1652, William, Joseph, Samuel 1672, Mary 1674.

REFERENCES:

MASSACHUSETTS.—Hodgman's Hist. of Westford, 442; Mitchell's Hist. of Bridgewater, 136; Hudson's Hist. of Lexington, 35; Wall's Hist. of Worcester, Mass., 62; Winsor's Hist. of Duxbury, 241; Hazen's Hist. of Billerica, 24; Davis' Landmarks of Plymouth, 53; Chandler's Hist. of Shirley, 366; Abbot's Hist. of Andover, Mass., 32.

MAINE.—Eaton's Hist. of Thomaston, 174; Butler's Hist. of Farmington, 420; Corliss' Hist. of North Yarmouth; Lapham's Hist. of Bethel, 501; North's Hist. of Augusta, 823; Thomaston's Hist. of Winthrop, 177.

NEW HAMPSHIRE.—Secomb's Hist. of Amherst, 531; Norton's Hist. of Fitzwilliam, 507; Livermore's Hist. of Wilton, 346; Kidder's Hist. of New Ipswich, 348; Hill's Hist. of Mason, 201; Hayward's Hist. of Gilsum, 283; Coggswell's Hist. of Henniker, 491; Coffin's Hist. of Boscawen, 487; Cochran's Hist. of Antrim, 409; Bouton's Hist. of Concord, 638.

OTHER PUBLICATIONS.

Larned's Hist. of Windham, Conn.; Hinman's Conn. Settlers, 530; Redford, N. H., Centen. 294; Futhey's Hist. of Chester County, Pa., 497; Penn. Mag., IX, 234; Stiles' Hist. of Windsor, Conn., 244; Granite Monthly, IV, 129; Heraldic Journal, vol. I, 72; Dodd Gen., 113; Chapman's Trowbridge Gen. 48; Backus Gen. 141; Nash Gen. 149; Walworth Hyde Gen., 891; Winslow Gen., II, 715; Abbot's Hist. of Andover, Mass., 32; Amer. Ancestry, VII, 214; IX, 103, 179; X, 60, 173; Savage's Gen. Dict. vol. I, 356; N. E. Hist. and Gen. Reg. XV, 329; XXXIII, 68, 381; XXVII, 227; Chandler Family, 1883.

CHANNELL. Hubbard's Hist. of Stanstead County, Canada, 147.

CHANNING. Walworth's Hyde Gen., 753; Austin's R. I. Ancestries, 17; N. E. Hist. and Gen. Reg. VIII, 318.

CHAPIN:—Samuel Chapin, of Roxbury, Mass., 1638, brought from England, wife Cicily or Sisley, and children Henry, Josiah, David, Catharine, Sarah, Joseph, 1642. He removed that year to Springfield and there had Hannah 1644. He was admitted freeman 1641, was a proprietor of Westfield 1660, a deacon in the church and a man of distinction. He died 1675.

REFERENCES.

MASACHUSETTS.—Temple's Hist. of Palmer, 433; Temple's Hist. of Whitley, 213; Temple's Hist. of Northfield, 419; Wall's Hist. of Worcester, 337; Ballou's Hist. of Milford, 614; Wilbraham Centen. 297; West Springfield Centen. 115.

NEW HAMPSHIRE.—Wheeler's Hist. of Newport, 330; Cochran's Hist. of Antrim, 410; Hayward's Hist. of Gilsum, 284; Washington, N. H., Hist. 334.

OTHER PUBLICATIONS.—Roe's Sketches of Rose, N. Y., 36; Young's Hist. of Warsaw, N. Y., 246; Boyd's Hist. of Consensus, N. Y., 146; Barbour's My Wife and Mother, 52, 64; Dwight Gen. 334, 341; Ellis Gen. 374; Morris and Flint Gen., 87; Nash Gen., 87; Stiles' Hist. of Windsor, II, 145; Thurston Gen. (1892), 364; Savage's Gen. Dict. vol. I, 359; Amer. Ancestry, II, 21; VII, 27, 110; VIII, 67; XI, 181; Ely Gen. 50, 54, 94, 105, 116, 238; N. E. Hist. and Gen. Reg. XV, 356; Chapin Gen. 1862,`1895.

CHAPLIN:—Hugh Chaplin, of Rowley, Mass., came probably with Rev. Ezekiel Rogers, in 1638, was admitted freeman 1642. By wife Elizabeth, he had John 1643, Joseph 1646, Thomas 1648, and Jonathan 1651. He died before March 31, 1657, when his will made two years before was probated.

REFERENCS:—N. E. Hist. and Gen. Reg. vol. IV, 175; Gage's Hist. of Rowley, Mass., 430; Essex, Mass., Hist. Coll. XX, 219; Paige's Hist. of Cambridge, Mass., 508; Paige's Hist. of Hardwick, Mass.. 347; Waterford, Me., Centen. 240; Ridlon's Harrison, Me., Settlers, 37; Poor's Merrimac Valley, 97; Stearn's Hist. of Rindge, N. H., 472; Norton's Hist. of Fitzwilliam, N. H., 507; Davis' Hist. of Reading, Vt., 126; Chandler's Hist. of Shirley, 365; Savage's Gen. Dict. vol. I, 360.

CHAPLER. Eaton's Hist. of Thomaston, Me., 174.

CHAPMAN:—Edward Chapman, of Windsor, Conn., 1662, married in England, it is said, Elizabeth Fox, and had Henry 1663, Mary 1665, Elizabeth January 1668, Simon 1669, Hannah 1671, Margaret 1673, Sarah 1675. He was admitted freeman 1667, and killed in the great Narragansett fight, December 19, of that year.

EDWARD CHAPMAN, of Ipswich, 1642, married Mary, daughter of Mark Symonds, and had Symonds, Nathaniel, Mary, Samuel and John.

RALPH CHAPMAN, of Marshfield, Mass., came in the "Elizabeth" 1635, from London, aged 20, of Southwark, in Surry, close to London, and settled first at Duxbury, Mass., married there November 23, 1642, the earliest marriage in that place, Lydia Wills or Willis, and had Mary 1643, Sarah 1645, Isaac 1647, Lydia 1649, Ralph 1654.

RICHARD CHAPMAN, of Braintree, Mass., by wife Mary, had Susan 1640, Hope 1655, Richard, killed by the Indians. His will (1669), mentions wife Joan and son Richard.

ROBERT CHAPMAN, of Saybrook, Conn., married 29th April, 1642, Anne, daughter of Thomas Bliss, of Hartford, and had John, born 1644, Robert 1646, Ann 1648, Hannah 1650, Nathaniel 1653, Mary 1655, Sarah 1657. He was a Captain of the train band, a representative to the General Court, 1652, and most of the years to 1673, Assistant, 1681-5. He died Oct. 13, 1687, aged 70.

THOMAS CHAPMAN, of Charlestown, Mass., seived a short time in Turner's company as a soldier, 1676. By wife Sarah, he had Sarah, Elizabeth 1680, Mercy 1681, Thomas 1683, and posthumous daughter Abiel 1687.

WILLIAM CHAPMAN, of New London, Conn., 1656, was annmong the freemen of 1669. He died December 18, 1699. He had issue John, William, Samuel, Jeremiah, Joseph, Sarah, Rebecca.

JOHN CHAPMAN was impressed on board of a British man-of-war, while on a visit to London, and brought to America. While the ship was lying in the harbor of Boston, he made his escape by jumping overboard and traveled on foot to Wakefield, R. I., where he was sheltered and kindly treated by Samuel Alden. He subsequently removed to North Stonington, Conn., where he died in 1760, leaving a son Thomas, born about 1721, who settled in Bolton, Tolland County, Conn.

REFERENCES.

CONNECTICUT.—Sedgwick's Hist. of Sharon, 71; Caulkin's Hist. of New London, 340; Field's Hist. of Haddam, 47; Orcutt's Hist. of Stratford, 1172; Stiles' Hist. of Windsor, II, 147; Timlow's Hist. of Southington, 43; Waldo's Hist. of Tolland, 62; Whittemore's Hist. of Middlesex County, Conn., 573.

MASSACHUSETTS.—Temple's Hist. of Whately, 213; Winsor's Hist. of Duxbury, 244; Wyman's Charlestown Gens., vol. I, 201; Rich's Hist. of Truro, 521; Lyman's Hist. of Easthampton, 187; Hammatt Papers, Ipswich, 48; Freeman's Hist. of Cape Cod, II, 220, 711; Essex Inst. Hist. Coll. XVI, 95; Barry's Hist. of Hanover, 266; Ballou's Hist. of Milford, 632; Swift's Barnstable Families, vol. I, 151.

MAINE.—Lapham's Hist. of Bethel, 503; Maine Genealogist, III, 129; Eaton's Hist. of Thomaston, 175; Cushman's Hist. of Sheepscot, 364.

NEW HAMPSHIRE.—Washington, N. H., Hist. 334; Dow's Hist. of Hampton, 633; Fiske Gen. of Amherst, 138; Hayward's Hist. of Gilsum, 286; Runnel's Hist. of Sanborton, II, 111; Smith's Hist. of Petersboro, 34.

OTHER PUBLICATIONS.—Austins R. I. Gen. Dict. 41; Davis' Hist. of Bucks County, Pa., 252, 701; Richmond, Va., Standard, II, 47; III, 35; Hubbard's Hist. of Stanstead County, Canada, 327; Wentworth Gen., vol. I, 245; Thurston Gen. (1892), 180, 294; Strong Gen., 1084; Kellog's White Gen. 62; Goode Gen. 346; Cutt's Gen., 149; Buckingham Gen., 167; Chapman Weeks Gen. 132; Amer. Ancestry, vol. I, 13; III, 9; IV, 201; IX, 65; Savage's Gen. Dict. vol. I, 361; N. E. Hist. and Gen. Reg., IV, 21; Chapman Gen. 1854, 1876, 1878, 1893.

CHAPPELL:—George Chappell, of Wethersfield, came in the "Christian" 1635, from London, aged 20, and two years later is found apprenticed to learn the trade of carpenter, with Francis Stiles, of Windsor, who had come in the same ship, and perhaps, paid for his transportation. Fifteen years later he removed to New London, Conn., with wife Margery and children, Mary, Rachel, John and George, born 1654, and there had

Elizabeth 1656, Esther 1662, Sarah 1666, Nathaniel 1668, and Caleb 1671. He died 1709.

WILLIAM CHAPPELL, of New London, 1659, perhaps brother of George, had by wife Christian, Mary 1669, John 1672, Christian 1681, and perhaps more.

REFERENCES:—Hinman's Conn. Settlers, 546; Sedgwick's Hist. of Sharon, Conn., 72; Hine's Lebanon, Conn., Address, 150; Caulkins' Hist. of New London, Conn., 325, 352; Loomis Gen. Female Branches, 816, 919; Savage's Gen. Dict. vol. I, 363.

CHARD:—William Chard, of Weymouth, Mass., was admitted freeman 1654, had first wife Grace, died Jan. 1656, he married Nov., 1656, Elizabeth, daughter of Matthew Pratt, and had Thomas 1657, Caleb 1660, Mary 1663, Samuel 1666, Joanna 1667, Patience 1671, Hugh 1675. See Savage's Gen. Dict. vol. I, 364.

CHARDAVOYNE.   Roome Gen., 109.

CHARLES.   Hyde's Hist. of Brimfield, Mass., 389.

CHARLOT.   Amer. Ancestry, II, 21.

CHARLTON.   Stiles' Journal of Windsor, II, 149.

CHARLTON.   Stiles' Hist. of Windsor, II, 149.

CHARRUAND.   Cartaret Gen., 28.

CHASE:—Aquila Chase, Hampton, a mariner from Cornwall, England, married Ann, daughter of John Wheeler, had Sarah, removed in 1646 to Newbury, Mass., and there had Ann, 1647, Priscilla, Mary, Aquila 1652, Thomas 1654, John 1655, Elizabeth 1657, Ruth 1660, Daniel 1661, Moses 1663. He died August 29, 1670, aged 52.

THOMAS CHASE, supposed to be the elder brother of the first Aquila, married Elizabeth, daughter of Thomas Philbrick, and had Thomas 1643, Joseph 1645, Isaac 1647, James 1649, Abraham 1651. He died 1652.

CHATFIELD:—George Chatfield, of Guilford, Conn., 1640, married Sarah, daughter of John Bishop, who died 1657, without issue; he married 2d, 1659, Isabel, daughter of Samuel Nettleton, and had John 1661, George 1668, and Mercy 1671. He died June 1671, at Killingworth, to which place he removed in 1663.

WILLIAM CHASE, of Roxbury, Mass., came in the fleet with Winthrop, and was made freeman 1634. He brought wife Mary and son William. He removed to Scituate, thence to Yarmouth, Mass., where he was appointed Constable 1639. He had a son Benjamin, born about 1640. He died 1659.

REFERENCES.

MASSACHUSETTS.—Hammatt Papers, Ipswich, 49; Peck and Earl's Fall River, Mass., 244; Poor's Hist. of Merrimac Valley, 138; Temple's Hist. of North Brookfield, 552; Wyman's Charlestown Gens., vol. I, 209; Freeman's Hist. of Cape Cod, II, 188; Davis' Landmarks of Plymouth, 53; Coffin's Hist. of Newbury, 297; Chase's Hist. of Haverhill, 624; Chandler's Hist. of Shirley, 369; Benedict's Hist. of Sutton, 620; Ballou's Hist. of Milford, 634.

MAINE.—Washburn's Hist. of Livermore, 25; Pierce's Hist. of Gorham, 158; Lapham's Hist. of Woodstock, 190; Lapham's Hist. of Paris, 562; Lapham's Hist. of Norway, 478; Lapham's Hist. of Bethel, 502; Cushman's Hist. of Sheepscot, 365; Corliss' Hist. of North Yarmouth.

NEW HAMPSHIRE.—Wheeler's Hist. of Newport, 329; Runnel's Hist. of Sanbornton, II, 114; Stark's Hist. of Dunbarton, 228; Norton's Hist. of Fitzwilliam, 510; Hayward's Hist. of Gilsum, 286; Dow's Hist. of Hampton, 684; Coggswell's Hist. of Nottingham, 347; Coggswell's Hist. of Henniker, 492; Chase's Hist. of Chester, 483; Alrich's Hist. of Walpole, 229; Washington, N. H., Hist. 335; Machias, Me., Centen. 157.

OTHER PUBLICATIONS.—Stiles' Hist. of Windsor, Conn., II, 149; Updyke's Narragansett Church, R. I., 109; Bass' Hist. of Braintree, Vt., 123; Heminway's Vt. Gaz., V, 716; Williams' Hist. of Danby, Vt., 123; Cleveland's Hist. of Yates County, N. Y., 560; Wood Gen., 43; Usher's Lawrence Estate, App.; Titcomb's Early New England People, 286; Spaulding Memorial, 522; Prescott Memorial of Dr. Prescott, 553; Norway Gen., 217; In Mem. Prof. Ira Chase, App.; Hill's Lawrence-Townley Estate; Heraldic Journal, IV, 153; Ely Gen. 191; Driver Gen., 263; Amer. Ancestry, vol. I, 13; III, 9; V, 92, 184; VII, 217; VIII, 126; Savage's Gen. Dict., vol. I, 364; N. E. Hist. and Gen. Reg., vol. I, 68; Chase Gen., 1867, 1869, 1874, 1878, 1886, 1894.

CHASTAIN.   Virg. Hist. Coll., V, 193.

CHATFIELD.

REFERENCES:—Hinman's Conn. Settlers, 560; Orcutt's Hist. of Derby, Conn., 709; Hedges' Hist. of Easthampton, L. I.; Howell's Hist. of Southampton, N. Y., 210; Dwight Gen., 678; Savage's Gen. Dict. vol. I, 366.

CHATTERTON.   Roe's Sketches of Rose, N. Y., 17.

CHATTERTON.   Hamden, Conn., Hist., 242; Merrill's Hist. Acworth, N. H., 198.

CHAULER.   Green's Todd Gen.

CHAUNCEY:—Charles Chauncey, of Scituate, Mass., son of George and Agnes Welch Chauncey, was born at Yardly, in County Herts, November 5, 1592, was bred at Westminster school and saved on November 5, 1605, by the discovery of the Gunpowder plot; he took his degree of A. B. at Trinity College, Cambridge, 1613; A. M., 1617; B. D., 1624. He was early at Marston, St. Lawrence, and had the vicarage of Ware in his native shire 1627, and from that valuable living, for non-conformity in non-essentials he was forced by Archbishop Laud. He came to New England in 1637, and preached for a time at Plymouth, but in 1641, was called to Scituate, Mass., and remained there for twelve years and in 1654, became the first President of Harvard College, at Cambridge. It is said that he was descended from a family that came in with the conquest, and was the great uncle of Sir Henry Chauncey, author of the history of Hertfordshire, in two volumes. His wife was Catharine, (married 1630), daughter of Robert Eyre, Esq., of Wilts, barrister at law, by his wife Ann, daughter of John Still, Bishop of Bath and Wills. The Chauncey family bore: Arms.—Gules a cross bottonée or, on a chief, azure a lion passant of the second. Crest.—Out of a ducal coronet or, a griffin, head and wings endorsed bendy gules and azure beaked of the first.

The children of President Charles Chauncey were Sarah, born 1631, Isaac August 23, 1632, Ichabod 1651, Barnabas 1637, Nathaniel and Elanthan (twins), 1639, Israel, Hannah.

REFERENCES.

CONNECTICUT.—Fowler's Hist. of Durham, 110; Hinman's Conn. Settlers, 524; Orcutt's Hist. of Stratford,

1173; Stiles' Hist. of Windsor, II, 150; Tuttle Family of Conn., 109.

OTHER PUBLICATIONS.—Paige's Hist. of Cambridge, Mass., I, 508; Judge's Hist. of Hadley, Mass., 459; Strong Gen., 1279; Heraldic Journal, vol. I, 187; Hill's Gen. Notes, 87; Goodwin's Olcott Gen., 52; Darling Memorial; Cutt's Gen., 101; Brewster Rambles, 280; Savage's Gen. Dict. vol. I, 336; N. E. Hist. and Gen. Reg. X, 105, 257, 251, 323; XI, 148; Chauncey Gen.

CHECKLEY:—John Checkley, of Boston, 1645, married March 5, 1652, Ann, daughter of Simon Eyre, and had John 1653, Samuel 1661, Ann 1669. He died January 1, 1685, aged 75.

ANTHONY CHECKLEY, a merchant of Boston, son of William, of a small parish, called Preston Capes, in the west of Northamptonshire, England, was born 1636, and came to New England, with his uncle John, and settled in Boston, where he was Captain of the Artillery company. He married Hannah, daughter of Rev. John Wheelwright, and had John 1664, Sarah 1668, Elizabeth 1672, Mary 1673, Hannah 1674; he married 2d in 1678, Lydia, widow of Benjamin Gibbs, daughter of Joshua Scottow. He was chosen in 1689, Attorney General.

REFERENCES:—Drake's Hist. of Boston, Mass., 459; N. E. Hist. and Gen. Reg. II, 349; XV, 13; Savage's Gen. Dict. vol. I, 370; Checkley Gen. 1848.

CHIDSEY:—John Chidsey, of New Haven, 1644, had by wife Elizabeth, Joseph born 1655, Mary 1659, Caleb 1661, Hannah 1664, Ebenezer 1666, and Sarah, who was married in 1683, to Samuel Alling, being his second wife.

REFERENCES:—Dodd's Hist. of East Haven, Conn., 111; Hinman's Conn. Settlers, 551; Savage's Gen. Dict.

CHENEY:—John Cheney, of Watertown, Mass., died 1675, had issue John and Ebenezer.

THOMAS CHENEY, of Roxbury, married January 11, 1656, Jane Atkinson. He was of Cambridge, where he had Margaret 1656, perhaps Thomas and William, Jane 1669, Joseph 1671, Hannah 1673, Benjamin 1676, Ebenezer 1678.

WILLIAM CHENEY, of Roxbury, had John 1640, Mehitable 1643, Joseph 1647, and probably more. He was admitted freeman 1666, and died next year, aged 63. See Hinman's Conn. Settlers, 562.

CHEESBOROUGH:—William Cheesborough, of Boston, came from Boston, County Lincoln, England, with wife Ann, and arrived in the fleet with Winthrop. He had married 1620, Ann Stevenson, and they had in England, Mary born 1622, Martha 1623, David and Jonathan (twins) 1624, Samuel 1627, Nathaniel 1630. He was admitted freeman 1631, and the same day his house was burned. His children born in Boston were John 1632, Elisha 1637, at Braintree, he had Joseph 1640. He removed to Rehoboth in 1643, in 1650 to Pawcatuck, where he was the earliest settler in that part of New London, called Stonington. He died 1667.

REFERENCES:—Wetmore Gen., 113; Savage's Gen. Dict. vol. I, 373.

CHEEVER:—Daniel Cheever, came to New England in 1637, with his brother Bartholomew. By wife Esther, he had Mary 1646, Lydia 1647, James, Mary 1656, John 1659, Israel 1662, Elizabeth, Sarah.

REFERENCES:—Freeman's Hist. of Cape Cod, Mass., II, 403; Page's Hist. of Cambridge, Mass., 509; Temple's

Hist. of North Brookfield, Mass., 552; Hammatt Papers of Ipswich, Mass., 54; Cutts' Gen.; Driver Gen., 435; Essex Inst. Hist. Coll., V, 236; Bill Gen., 68; Savage's Gen. Dict. vol. I, 370; N. E. Hist. and Gen. Reg., XXXII, 90; XXXIII, 164; XXXVI, 305; XXXVIII, 170; XLI, 65; Chever Pedegree, 1878; Ezekiel Cheever and some of his Descendants, 1896; Bartholomew and Richard Cheever and Descendants, 1882.

CHECKLEY. N. E. Hist. and Gen. Reg., II, 349.

CHENERY:—Lambert Chenery, born 1593, of Dedham, Mass., came from England, in 1630, and settled first in Watertown, Mass., and was one of the original proprietors of Dedham, Mass., to which place he removed in 1635, and died there, January 30, 1673. He had a son John, who was killed in King Philip's war. John married Sarah, the widow of Thomas Boylston.

REFERENCES:—Montague Gen., 512; Damon Gen., 124; Amer. Ancestry, VIII, 68, 70.

CHENNEVARD. Hinman's Conn. Settlers, 555.

CHENEY:—William Cheney, of Milford, Mass., was born in Medfield, Mass., July 27, 1670, moved to Mendon, about 1695, and returned to Milford, when he died, about 1756. By his wife Margaret, he had William and other children.

REFERENCES.

MASSACHUSETTS.—Stearn's Hist. of Ashburnham, 635; Coffin's Hist. of Newbury, 298; Ballou's Hist. of Milford, 634; Ellis's Hist. of Roxbury, 93; Harris's Watertown Epitaphs, 11; Jackson's Hist. of Newton, 255; Paige's Hist. of Cambridge, 509; N. E. Hist. and Gen. Reg., XXII, 139.

NEW HAMPSHIRE.—Wheeler's Hist. of Newport, 335; Washington, N. H., Hist. 337; Runnel's Hist. of Sanbornton, II, 122; Norton's Hist. of Fitzwilliam, 511; Cochrane's Hist. of Antrim, 411; Coggswell's Hist. of Henniker, 496; Hayward's Hist. of Hancock, 438; Smith's Hist. of Petersborough, 36.

OTHER PUBLICATIONS.—Young's Hist. of Chautauqua, 438; Goodwin's Olcott.Gen., 20: Amer. Ancestry, II, 21; VIII, 36; IX, 221; N. E. Hist. and Gen. Reg., XXII, 139; Pope Gen.

CHEESBROUGH. Hinman's Conn. Settlers, 566; Stonington, Conn., Centen. 289; Baldwin's Denison Gen. 10; Stanton Gen., 483, 562; Wetmore Gen., 113; Amer. Ancestry, VII, 133, 247; VIII, 205; IX, 195, 198; X, 178.

CHESHOLME. Paige's Hist. of Cambridge, Mass., 509.

CHESLEY:—Philip Chesley, of Dover, 1642, had by wife Elizabeth, Thomas 1644, Philip 1646, Esther, Mary and Elizabeth. After 1661, he had second wife Sarah, and probably third wife Joanna, in 1673.

REFERENCES:—Temple's Hist. of North Brookfield, Mass., 553; Lapham's Hist. of Paris, Me., 556; Hatch's Hist. of Industry, Me., 539; Paxton's Marshall Gen., 310; Wentworth Gen., vol. I, 221; II, 90; Chapman's Weeks Gen., 133; Otis Gen.; Savage's Gen. Dict. vol. I, 375; N. E. Hist. and Gen. Reg., V, 205, 453.

CHESMAN. Chesman Gen., 1893.

CHESTER:—Leonard Chester, of Watertown, Mass., son of John, of Blaby, County Leicester, and his wife Dorothy, sister of Thomas Hooker, came to New England before 1635. He had John 1635, Dorcas 1637,

Prudence 1643, Eunice 1645. He died 1648, aged 38.

SAMUEL CHESTER, of New London, Conn., 1663, mariner, was also a competent surveyor. He had by first wife Mary, John, Susanna, Samuel, Mercy 1673. By wife Hannah, who survived him, he had Hannah 1695, Jonathan 1697. In his will the first son named is Abraham.

REFERENCES:—Paige's Hist. of Cambridge, Mass., 510; Bond's Hist. of Watertown, Mass., 735; Caulkins' Hist. of New London, Conn., 353; Hinman's Conn. Settlers, 567; Talcott's Gen. Notes, 492; Walworth Hyde Gen., 442; Huntington Gen., 167; Goodwin's Gen. Notes, 8; Aiden's Epitaphs, IV, 145; Savage's Gen. Dict., vol. I, 375; Amer. Ancestry, vol. I, 13; IV, 157; VIII, 5; N. E. Hist. and Gen. Reg., XXII, 338; Chester Gen., 1886; Chester Chart.

CHESTNEY. See Amer. Ancestry, vol. I, 13.

CHESTON. Thomas Family of Md., 53.

CHETWOOD. Witmore Gen., 421.

CHEVALIER. Penn. Mag., VII, 483.

CHEW. Richmond, Va., Critic (1888); Thomas Gen., 55, 170.

CHEWTE. N. E. Hist. and Gen. Reg., XIII, 103, 123.

CHENNEY. Futhey's Hist. of Chester, Pa., 497.

CHICHESTER:—James Chichester, was of Taunton, Mass., 1643, Salem, 1650, when Mary, probably his wife, united with the church and on April 21 his children John, James, Mary and Martha were baptized, as also Sarah, in May, 1651, James 1652, William 1653, Elizabeth 1654, Susanna 1657; but perhaps one, two or more of them were children of William.

REFERENCES:—Hayden's Vir. Gens., 92; Huntington's Hist. of Stamford, Conn., 21; Savage's Gen. Dict., vol. I, 376.

CHICK:—Richard Chick, of Roxbury, Mass., was born 1638, died 1686, aged 48. He had a son Richard.

REFERENCES:—Savage's Gen. Dict. vol. I, 376.

CHICKLEY. Southern Bivouac (1886), 649.

CHICKERING:—Francis Chickering, of Dedham, was admitted freeman 1640, member of Artillery company, 1643, representative to General Court, 1644-53. He came probably in 1637, from County Suffolk, bringing wife Ann, daughter of John Fisk, of England, and sister John, the first minister of Wenham, Mass., with her children Ann and Mary. Here they had Elizabeth 1638, Bethia 1640, Esther 1643, Mercy 1648.

HENRY CHICKERING, of Dedham, Mass., perhaps brother of Francis, had a grant of land at Salem, 1640, admitted freeman 1641. He was one of the first deacons at Dedham, was representative to the General Court, 1642-4 and '51. By wife Ann, he had son John.

NATHANIEL CHICKERING, of Dedham, married 1666, Mary, daughter of Samuel Judson. In December, 1674, he married Lydia, daughter of Daniel Fisher, and had Prudence 1675, Nathaniel 1677, Lydia 1678, Mary 1680, John 1682, Abigail 1685, Daniel 1687, Samuel 1689. He was admitted freeman 1681; died 1699.

REFERENCES:—Sewall's Hist. of Woburn, Mass., 461; Wyman's Charlestown, Mass., Gens., vol. I, 212; Kidder's

Hist. of New Ipswich, N. H., 532; Secomb's Hist. of Amherst, N. H., 532; Dedham Hist. Mag., III, 117; Wight Gen., 25; Savage's Gen. Dict. vol. I, 376; Amer. Ancestry, VI, 194.

CHIDELL. Leland Gen., 162.

CHIDSEY. Cleveland's Hist. of Yates Sounty, N. Y., 699; Rodenburgh's Autumn Leaves.

CHILD or CHILDS:—Benjamin Childs, of Roxbury, Mass., son of Benjamin, of England, lived at Muddy River plantation, now Brookline, Mass. By wife Mary, he had Ephraim, who was killed by the Indians at Northfield, September 4, 1675, with Captain Burr. Children: Benjamin, Joshua 1659, Mary 1660, Elizabeth 1664, Margaret 1666, Mehitable 1669, John 1671.

JOHN CHILDS, of Swanzey, Mass., 1669, had by wife Martha, Jeremiah, born September 2, 1683.

JOHN CHILDS, of Watertown, Mass., by first wife Mary, had Mary 1664, and by second wife, married 1668, Mary Warren, eldest daughter of Daniel Warren, he had John 1669, Elizabeth 1670, Daniel 1687. He died Oct. 15, 1676, aged 40.

JOSEPH CHILDS, of Watertown, Mass., married 1654, Sarah Platts, and had Joseph, born January 7, 1659. He was admitted freeman 1654, and died 1698.

REFERENCES.

MASSACHUSETTS.—Pierce's Hist. of Grafton, 473; Wyman's Charlestown, Mass., Gens., vol. I, 213; Swift's Barnstable Families, vol. I, 183; Paige's Hist. of Hardwick, 347; Keyes' West Boylston Reg., 15; Jackson's Hist. of Newton, 361; Hudson's Hist. of Lexington, 41; Herrick's Hist. of Gardner, 339; Freeman's Hist. of Cape Cod, vol. II, 303; Cutter's Hist. of Arlington, 203; Barry's Hist. of Framingham, 206; Bond's Hist. of Watertown, 87, 152.

OTHER PUBLICATIONS.—Coggswell's Hist. of Henniker, N. H., 497; Blood's Hist. of Temple, 211; Butler's Hist. of Farmington, Me., 422; French's Hist. of Turner, Me., 52; North's Hist of Augusta, Me., 826; Orcutt's Hist. of Torrington, Conn., 666; Hinman's Conn. Settlers, 571; Powers' Hist. of Sangamon County, Ill., 198; Bridgman's Granary Burial Ground, 200; Hubbard's Hist. of Stanstead County, Canada, 144, 308; Spooner Gen. vol. I, 198; Morris Gen.; Guild's Stiles Gen., 291; Dwight Gen., 515; Amer. Ancestry, vol. III, 200; V, 106; VII, 144; XI, 92; Savage's Gen. Dict. vol. I, 377; Child Gen., 1881.

CHILER. Stearn's Hist. of Ashburnham, Mass., 636.

CHILSON or CHILSTONE:—John Chilstone, of Lynn, Mass., married July 28, 1667, Sarah, daughter of the first Joseph Jenks, and had Joseph 1670, Sarah 1673.

REFERENCES:—Middlefield, Conn., Hist.; Southwick Gen., 191, 307; Savage's Gen. Dict. vol. I, 377.

CHILTON:—James Chilton, a passenger in the "Mayflower," after signing the immortal compact died at Cape Cod, December 8, 1620, and his wife died soon after landing. His daughter Mary married John Winslow, and in 1650, Bradford says, she had nine children.

REFERENCES:—Pilgrim Rec. Soc. Bulletin; Savage's Gen. Dict., vol. I, 377.

CHINNERY. Bond's Hist. of Watertown Mass., 157.

CHINN. Hayden's Virginia Gens., 75.

CHIPMAN:—John Chipman, of Barnstable, had been at Plymouth or Yarmouth, a few years before 1630, and may have resided at other towns, since he stated Feb. 8, 1652, that it was 21 years ago that he came from England, and was now about 37 years old. He probably came with Allerton, in the "White Angel" or in the "Friendship," that had sailed at the same time from Barnstable, in Devon, but had put back and so reached here a few days later. He married Hope, second daughter of John Howland, of the "Mayflower" and had Elizabeth, born June 24, 1647, besides one or two more, for he speaks of more than one before Hope, baptized 1652, Lydia 1654, John 1657, Hannah 1659, Samuel 1662, Ruth 1663, Bethia 1666, Mercy 1668, John again March 3, 1670, Desire 1673. His father Thomas had a good estate near Dorchester, in County Dorset. He was long a Ruling Elder and a Representative to the General Court, 1663 to 1669, every year except 1667. He died January 8, 1684.

REFERENCES:—Stone's Hist. of Beverly, Mass., 271; Freeman's Hist. of Cape Cod, Mass., II, 164, 289; Essex Inst. Coll., XI, 263; Heminway Gen. Record, 68; Lapham's Hist. Paris, Me., 557; Hinman's Conn. Settlers, 514; Kilbourn's Hist. of Litchfield, Conn., 70; Pierce Gen., 1894; Savage's Gen. Dict., vol. I, 380; N. E. Hist. and Gen. Reg., IV, 23; VI, 272; XV, 79; XVII, 90.

CHIPP. Amer. Ancestry, II, 21.

CHISOLM:—Alexander, with other Scotchmen, emigrated to America after the battle of Culloden, where the chief of the clan was killed. He had a son Alexander Robert, of Chisolm Island, S. C., who owned a large estate in South Carolina and Georgia, and is buried in Sheldon Church, which was burned during the Revolutionary war by the British.

REFERENCES:—Amer. Ancestry, V, 69; Cleveland's Hist. of Yates County, N. Y., 215.

CHITTENDEN:—Thomas Chittenden, a linenweaver, from some part of County Kent, England, came it is said, from London, in the "Increase" 1635, aged 51, with wife Rebecca 40, and children Isaac, age 14, and Henry 6.

WILLIAM CHITTENDEN, of Guilford, Conn., came from East Guilford, in County Sussex, adjourning Rye, on the British Channel, near the border of Kent, with wife Joan, daughter of Dr. Jacob Sheaffe, of Cranbrook in Kent, and sister of Jacob Sheaffe, and of the wife of Rev. Henry Whitfield, with whom they came to Boston, 1638. He soon went to New Haven, was the founder of the church at Guilford, Conn., June 1, 1639, and trustee of the land purchased from the Indians for the settlement. He had been a soldier in the Netherlands and reached the rank of Major. Here he was made Lieutenant of the force of New Haven Colony, and a Magistrate for the rest of his days. He was a representative to the General Court for 27 sessions, between 1643 and 1661, and died in February of that year. His children were Thomas, Nathaniel, John, Joanna, Elizabeth, Mary, Joseph and Hannah (twins), April 12, 1652, Deborah 1653.

REFERENCES:—Hinman's Conn. Settlers, 578; Deane's Hist. of Scituate, Mass., 232; Kellogg's White Memorial, 38; Warden Gen., 62; Baldwin Gen., 530; Amer. Ancestry, II, 22; V, 16; VIII, 47; Chittenden Gen.

CHOATE:—John, of Ipswich, 1648, was then 24 years old, and is first mentioned as contributing to instruction

in the military art. He came probably from Sudbury, County Suffolk, on the border of Essex, not far from the former home of Governor Winthrop. He was Sergeant of the train band. By wife Ann, he had John 1661, Samuel, Mary, Thomas, Sarah, Margaret, Joseph and probably Benjamin.

REFERENCES:—Stearns' Hist. of Ashburnham, Mass., 636; Wyman's Charlestown, Mass., Gens., vol. I, 214; Washburn's Hist. of Leicester, Mass., 351; Hammatt Papers of Ipswich, Mass., 50; Coffin's Hist. of Boscawen, N. H., 489; N. E. Hist. and Gen. Reg., XV, 293; Savage's Gen. Dict., vol. 1, 383; Amer. Ancestry, V, 122; 211; VI, 146, 185.

CHOUTEAU. Beckwith's Creoles, 7.

CHRISLER. Amer. Ancestry, vol. I, 14.

CHRISMAN. Green's Kentucky Families; Plumb's Hist. of Hanover, Pa., 402.

CHRISMAN. Slaughter's St. Mark's Parish, Va., 188; Meade's Old Families of Va.'; Richmond, Va., Standard, II, 43; Peyton's Hist. of Augusta County, Va., 313; Green's Kentucky Families; Pearson's Schenectady, N. Y., Settlers, 35.

CHRISTIE. Cochran's Hist. of Antrim, 413; Hubbard's Hist. of Stanstead County, Canada, 241; Miller's Colchester, N. S., 243; Morrison Gen., 252.

CHRISTOPHER. Clute's Staten Island, 354.

CHRISTOPHERS:—Christopher, of New London. 1667, a mariner from Devonshire, England, brought from Barbadoes, wife Mary, and children Richard, John and Mary. His wife died July 13, 1676, aged 54, and he married 2d, Elizabeth, widow of Peter Bradley, daughter of Jonathan Brewster. He died July 23, 1687, aged 55.

JEFFREY CHRISTOPHERS, brother of the above Christopher, came at the same time with him and had daughters Margaret, Joanna and another, beside only son, Jeffrey, who married and died 1690, of small pox, with his wife within three weeks, leaving no children. He was 55 years old in 1676, and removed in old age with two daughters living in 1700, at Southold, L. I.

RICHARD CHRISTOPHER, of Boston, by wife Ann, had Deborah 1685, Lydia 1687, and Henry 1688. He was a householder in 1695.

REFERENCES:—Hinman's Conn. Settlers, 582; Caulkins Hist. of New London, 316; Savage's Gen. Dict. vol. I, 383.

CHRYSTIE. Freeman's Hist. of Cape Cod, Mass., II, 144; Morrison's Hist. of Windham, N. H., 409; Amer. Ancestry, V, 152.

CHUBBUCK:—Thomas, of Charlestown, 1634, by wife Alice, had Nathaniel 1635; he removed next year to Hingham, and there was made freeman 1672, and died 1676, leaving sons Nathaniel and John, besides daughters Sarah, who married October 6, 1657, Jeremiah, Fitch, Rebecca, wife of William Husey, and Mary, who married Thomas Lincoln.

REFERENCES:—Stiles' Hist. of Windsor, II, 151; Savage's Gen. Dict. vol. I, 384.

CHURCH:—Richard, of Plymouth, 1633, had probably come to Massachusetts in the fleet with Winthrop, for he requested admission as freeman Oct. 19, 1630, but did not take the oath at that time. He removed from Weymouth to Plymouth, and was received as free-man of that Colony Oct. 4, 1632. He was engaged as a carpenter in building the earliest church edifice at Plymouth. He served in the Pequot war, sold his estate at Plymouth, in 1649, and was at Charlestown, 1653, and for final residence settled at Hingham. He married Elizabeth, daughter of Richard Warren, who probably came in the "Ann" 1623. Besides Joseph, he had Benjamin, the great soldier, born 1639, Caleb, Nathaniel, Hannah 1647, Abigail, Charles 1659, Deborah 1657.

RICHARD CHURCH, of Hartford, Conn., an original proprietor, removed, about 1660, to Hadley, Mass., and died there Dec. 1667. His widow Ann, died March 10, 1684, aged 83, and in his will four children only are mentioned, viz: Edward, John, Mary and Samuel, all probably born in England.

GARRETT or JARED CHURCH, of Watertown, 1637, was born 1611; admitted freeman 1649. By wife Sarah he had John 1638, Samuel 1640, Sarah 1643, Mary 1644, Jonathan 1646, David 1657.

JOHN CHURCH, of Dover, 1662, at Salisbury, married November 29, 1664, Abigail, daughter of John Severance, and had Jonathan 1666, John 1668, Ebenezer 1670, Abigail 1672. He was taken by the Indians in the war of 1689 and escaped, but was killed May 7, 1696, by the Indians near his own home.

REFERENCES.

CONNECTICUT.—Sedgwick's Hist. of Sharon, 72; Porter's Hartford Settlers, 2; Orcutt's Hist. of Torrington, 677; Hinman's Conn. Settlers, 583; Field's Hist. of Haddam, 46; Cothren's Hist. of Woodbury, 526.

MASSACHUSETTS.—Davis' Landmarks of Plymouth, 54; Bond's Hist. of Watertown, 158; Winsor's Hist. of Duxbury, 245; Stone's Hist. of Hubbardston, 237; Reed's Hist. of Rutland, 135; Paige's Hist. of Hardwick, 348; Mitchell's Hist. of Bridgewater, 363; Judd's Hist. of Hadley, 460; Hudson's Hist. of Marlborough, 350; Freeman's Hist. of Cape Cod, II, 357; Deane's Hist. of Scituate, 233; Baylie's New Plymouth, IV, 123, 129, 230; Barry's Hist. of Hanover, 267.

OTHER PUBLICATIONS.—Butler's Hist. of Farmington, Me., 424; North's Hist. of Augusta, Me., 828; Wheeler's Hist. of Newport, N. H., 342; Austin's R. I. Gen. Dict. 44; Adam's Hist. of Fairhaven, Vt., 326; Collins' Hist. of Hillsdale, N. Y., app. 51; Winslow Gen., II, 975; Montague Gen., 64; Mack Gen., 53; Little Gen., 154; Goodwin's Olcott Gen., 56; Barnard's My Wife and I, 42; Savage's Gen. Dict. vol. I, 384; N. E. Hist. and Gen. Reg., vol. XI, 152; Amer. Ancestry, III, 203; VI, 12, 46; XI, 183; Church's King Philip's War, XLV—VII; Church Family, 1878; Church Family of Tiverton, R. I., 1887; Church Gen. Preliminary.

CHURCHILL or CHURCHALL, Josiah, of Wethersfield, Conn., married 1638, Elizabeth, daughter of Nathaniel Foote, and had Mary 1639, Elizabeth 1642, Hannah 1644, Ann 1647, Joseph 1649, Benjamin 1652, Sarah 1657. He died January 1, 1686.

REFERENCES.

MAINE.—Dearborn's Hist. of Parsonfield, 369; Lapham's Hist. of Norway, 479; Lapham's Hist. of Paris, 557; Lapham's Hist. of Woodstock, 103.

OTHER PUBLICATIONS.—Hinman's Conn. Settlers, 590; Orcutt's Hist. of Wolcott, Conn., 471; Andrews' Hist. of New Britain, Conn., 164, 215; Mitchell's Hist. of Bridgewater, Mass., 136; Davis' Landmarks of Ply-

mouth, Mass., 54; Coggswell's Hist. of Nottingham, N. H., 353; Powers' Hist. of Sangamon County, Ill., 198; Sprague's Hist. of Gloversville, N. Y., 113; Hayden's Virginia Genealogies, 253; Hurlbut Gen., 405; Kilbourn Gen., 254; Savage's Gen. Dict., vol. I, 386; N. E. Hist. and Gen. Reg., XXXV, 301; Amer. Ancestry, vol. I, 14; VII, 44; XI, 109; Churchill Gen., 1887.

CHURCHMAN. Futhey's Chester, Pa., 497; Johnston's Cecil County, Md., 525; Rodenbough's Autumn Leaves.

CHUTE:—Lionel, of Ipswich, 1639, the earliest school-master there, made his will September 4, 1644, having by his wife Rose, daughter of Robert Baker, son James. A genealogy of this name traces it back to 1268, before the first King Edward.

REFERENCES:—Hammatt Papers of Ipswich, Mass., 53; Gage's Hist. of Rowley, Mass., 440; Heraldic Journal, vol. I, 142; Maine Hist. and Gen. Rec., III, 290; VII, 54; Thurston Gen., (1892) 17, 40; Amer. Ancestry, III, 62; Savage's Gen. Dict. vol. I, 387; N. E. Hist. and Gen. Reg., XIII, 123.

CILLEY or SEELEY:—John, of Isle of Shoals, 1647, born in England, died in England or at sea, 1670; commander of ship "Dolphin"; attorney 1659; owned property on Starr Island, which was sold May 3, and June 19, 1651; bought land on the Great Island, near Portsmouth, N. H., 1660. He had a son, Thomas Seally of Hampton and Andover, N. H., died at Nottingham; married July 2, 1697, Ann, daughter of John and Mary (Bradbury) Stanyon, and had Joseph and other children.

REFERENCES:—Dow's Hist. of Hampton, N. H., 637; Coggswell's Hist. of Nottingham, N. H., 175, 354; Coggswell's Hist. of Henniker, N. H., 502; Eaton's Hist. of Thomaston, Me., 176; Maine Genealogist, II, 121; III, 85; Neally Chart; Amer. Ancestry, V, 138; VI, 194; IX, 168; Cilley Gen.

CIST:—Charles, of Philadelphia, Pa., born at St. Petersburg, Russia, August 15, 1758; died at Fort Allen, Pa., December 2, 1805; graduate of University of Halle; came to America 1773. He was a publisher. Among his works were "Paine's American Crisis;" "The American Herald," 1784, one of the first magazines in America; "The Columbian Magazine," 1786. It is said that he discovered and introduced anthracite coal. He was public printer for the United States, during the administration of John Adams. He was commissioned under Congress to sign Continental currency. He married June 7, 1781, Mary Weiss, daughter of John Jacob and Mary Elizabeth Weiss, and sister of John Jacob Weiss, the first deputy quartermaster general of the United States under Greene, in his southern campaign. He left a son Charles.

REFERENCES:—Amer. Ancestry, VII, 48.

CLAAS. Bergen's Hist. of Kings County, N. Y., 61.

CLAFLIN. Hudson's Hist. of Lexington, Mass., 42; Morse's Sherborn, Mass., Settlers, 59; Barry's Hist. of Framingham, Mass., 207; Ballou's Hist. of Milford, 646; Hayden's Virginia Gens., 169.

CLOGGETT. Wheeler's Hist. of Newport, N. H., 343; Secomb's Hist. of Amherst, N. H., 588.

CLAGHORN:—James, of Barnstable, Mass., an early settler, married January 6, 1654, Abigail Lombard, probably daughter of Thomas, and had James, Mary 1655, Elizabeth 1658, Sarah 1660, Robert 1661 and Shubael.

REFERENCES:—Swift's Barnstable Families, 180; Savage's Gen. Dict., vol. I, 388.

CLAIBORNE: Meade's Old Families, Va.; Neill's Virginia Carolorum, 49; Richmond, Va., Standard, vol. II, 4, 52; III, 38; IV, 3; Slaughter's Bristol Parish, Va., 164; Virg. Mag. of Hist. vol. I, 1894; Campbell's Virginia, 324; Carter Family Tree, Goode Gen.

CLAP:—Roger, of Dorchester, Mass., 1630, came in the "Mary and John," from Plymouth, England, March 20, 1630, was born at Salcomb Regis, England, on the coast of Devonshire, April 6, 1609, the youngest of five sons. He arrived at Nantucket, Mass., May 30, with his Reverend friends Maverick and Warham. He married November 6, 1633, Joanna, daughter of Thomas Ford, a fellow-passenger, and had issue Samuel 1634, William 1636, Elizabeth 1638, Experience 1640, Waitstill 1641, Preserved 1643, Experience again 1645, Hopestill 1647, Wait 1649, Thanks 1651, Desire 1652, Thomas 1655, Unite 1656, Supply 1661. He was a member of the artillery company 1646, its Lieutenant 1658, Captain of the Castle 1665, on demand of Davenport, in whose post he continued until the usurpation of Andros, when he relinquished it. He was a representative many years between 1652 and 1673, and died February 2, 1692.

EDWARD CLAP, of Dorchester, brother of Capt. Roger, came in 1633, and was made freeman December 7, 1636, selectman 1637. He was deacon of the church for some twenty-five years. By first wife Prudence, he had issue John, Nicholas, Richard, Thomas, Elizabeth, born 1634, Prudence 1637, Ezra 1640, Nehemiah 1646, Susanna 1648; by second wife Susan, he had Esther 1656, Abigail 1659, Joshua 1661, Jonathan 1664, the last three died young. He died January 8, 1665, and his widow died June 16, 1688.

INCREASE CLAP, of Barnstable, Mass., married Oct. 1675, Elizabeth, widow of Nathaniel Goodspeed, and had John 1676, Charity 1678, Benjamin, Thomas Jan., 1684.

THOMAS CLAP, of Weymouth, Mass., brother of Ambrose, John, Nicholas and Richard, was born at Dorchester, in Dorsetshire, was admitted freeman at Weymouth, March 13, 1639, he had Thomas 1639. He removed to Scituate, and was deacon there 1647, representative to the General Court 1649. His children were Samuel, Elizabeth, Prudence, Eleazer (killed in the Rehoboth fight, March 26, 1676) John 1658, Abigail 1660. He died 1684, aged 87.

RICHARD CLAP, of Dorchester, 1636, brother of Nicholas, had Richard, Elizabeth and Deborah.

REFERENCES:—Deane's Hist. of Scituate, Mass., 234; Judd's Hist. of Dudley, Mass., 402; Swift's Barnstable Families, vol. I, 249; Lyman's Hist. of Easthampton, Mass., 141; Emery's Taunton Ministry, vol. I, 292; Bridgman's King's Chapel Epitaphs, 239; Hinman's Conn. Settlers, 598; Bolton's Hist. of Westchester County, N. Y., II, 509; Blake Gen., 58; Pope Gen., 323; Trumbell Gen., 15; Savage's Gen. Dict., vol. I, 388; N. E. Hist. and Gen. Reg., XIV, 275; XV, 225.

CLAPP:—Gilbert, of Stuyvesant, born about 1740, came from Rhode Island to New York, about 1765; had son Eddy.

REFERENCES.

MASSACHUSETTS.—Lyman's Easthampton, Mass., 141; Hill's Dedham, Mass., Records; Wright's Hist. of Easthampton, Mass., 28; Wyman's Charlestown, Mass., Gens., vol. I, 216,

OTHER PUBLICATIONS.—Stiles' Hist. of Windsor, Conn., II, 151; Baird's Hist. of Rye, N. Y., 457; Strong Gen., 339, 389, 574, 1239; Ransom Gen.; Pope Gen.; Pompey, N. Y., Reunion, 295; Loomis' Gen. Female Branches, 753; Leach's Morton Ancestry; Hayes' Wells Gen., 192; N. E. Hist. and Gen. Reg., XLIII, 429; Amer. Ancestry, vol. I, 14; II, 22; III, 375; Clapp Gen. 1876.

CLAPPER. Roe's Sketches of Rose, N. Y., 190; Amer. Ancestry, vol. I, 14; II, 22.

CLARK:—Arthur, admitted freeman May 13, 1640. Had been at Hampton, removed 1643, to Boston. He died 1655. By wife Sarah, he had Sarah 1644 and Samuel 1646.

CHRISTOPHER CLARK, of Boston, mariner, by wife Rebecca, had Dorothy 1650, John 1652, Peter 1654, Rebecca 1657, Christopher 1660, Daniel 1662, Elizabeth 1663, Mary or Mercy 1657. He was admitted freeman 1673, a merchant often voyaging between England and our country. On one of his passages was in the "Speedwell," embarked at London, May 30, and landed at Boston, July 27, 1656.

DANIEL CLARK, of Windsor, Conn., came in 1639, in company with Rev. Ephraim Hunt. He married that year Mary, daughter of Thomas Newbury, and had Josiah 1649, Elizabeth 1651, Daniel 1654, John 1656; Mary 1658, Samuel 1661, Sarah 1663, Nathaniel 1666; killed by the Indians 1691. He was representative 1657-61, Secretary of the Colony 1658-63, Assistant 1662-4, Capt. of the Cavalry troop 1664. He died Aug. 12, 1710, aged 87.

EDMUND CLARK, of Gloucester, 1650, was town-clerk 1656. By wife Agnes, he had Abigail and Joseph, born 1650. He died 1667.

GEORGE CLARK, of Milford, 1639, husbandman, had George and six daughters; died August 1690, leaving a good estate.

GEORGE CLARK, of Roxbury, Mass., was a fellmonger, was an inhabitant of Boston, before 1695, died 1696. By wife Ann, he had George, Elizabeth, Mary, Richard.

HUGH CLARK, of Watertown, Mass., 1640, by wife Elizabeth, had John 1641, Uriah 1644, Elizabeth 1648. He owned estate in Cambridge, but removed to Roxbury, 1657; was admitted freeman 1660, member of artillery company, 1666.

JAMES CLARK, of New Haven, formed with Gov. Eaton and company, the civil compact June 4, but removed before 1669, to Stratford. May have had children in both places.

JAMES CLARK, of Boston, by wife Elinor, had Martha 1648, Hannah 1649, James 1652, Samuel 1654, John 1656, Abigail 1658, ? ? ? ? 1660, Aaron 1663. He died December 18, 1674.

JEREMIAH CLARK, of Newport, R. I., 1640, had been at Portsmouth, 1638, before Newport was settled. He was first constable of the town, treasurer of the colony, 1647, and Assistant 1648, when he was chief officer. He died January 1652, having Walter, born 1639, Jeremiah, Latham, Weston 1648, James 1649, and daughters Francis, Mary, Sarah 1651.

JOHN CLARK, of Cambridge, was admitted freeman, Nov. 6, 1632, removed in 1636, to Hartford, with Hooker, thence, perhaps, to Milford, where his daughter Elizabeth married William Pratt.

JOHN CLARK, of New Haven, 1639, may have come in the "Elizabeth," to Boston, from Ipswich, in Co. Suffolk, 1634, aged 22, and was made clerk of the military company, February 1648. He had John 1637, Samuel 1639, and Esther 1646.

JOHN CLARK, of Newbury, 1638, who came before this from England, married Martha, sister of Sir Richard Saltonstall. He was admitted freeman 1639, and perhaps was representative the same year. He removed ten years after to Boston, and was noted for keeping fine horses. He died November, 1664. By wife Martha, he had John and Jemima.

JOHN CLARK, of Hartford, an original proprietor, removed to Farmington, and died there Nov. 22, 1712, at a great age. He had John, Matthew and nine daughters.

JOHN CLARK, of Saybrook, 1640, may have before been at Wethersfield, and later at Milford. He was representative from Saybrook to the General Court, 1651 to 1664. He is named in the royal charter of 1662, removed to Milford, which town he also represented at the General Court. He had John, Joseph, and Rebecca.

JOHN CLARK, of Springfield, Mass., married 1647, Elizabeth, daughter of Rowland Stebbins, and died 1684, leaving John, Sarah (born 1649) and Mary.

JOHN CLARK, of New Haven, Conn., married 1661, Sarah, daughter of George Smith, had son John, born 1686.

JOHN CLARK, of Roxbury, Mass., married Nov. 18, 1680, Lydia Buckminster, and had Elizabeth 1681, John 1683, Samuel 1686.

JONATHAN CLARK, of Newbury, Mass., married 1683, Lydia Titcomb, and had Oliver 1684, Samuel 1688, Jonathan 1689, Lydia 1691, Elizabeth 1694.

JOSEPH CLARK, of Dedham, Mass., may first have been at Dorchester. By wife Alice, he had Joseph 1642, Benjamin 1644, Ephraim 1646, Daniel 1647, Mary 1649, Sarah 1651. He removed to Medfield, Mass., and there had John 1652, Nathaniel 1658, Rebecca 1660. He was admitted freeman 1653. He married 2nd, in 1663, Mary Allen, and had Joseph 1664, John again 1666, Jonathan 1669. By third wife, Mary, he had Esther 1671, Thomas 1672.

NATHANIEL CLARK, of Newbury, Mass., was admitted freeman 1668. He married 1663, Elizabeth, daughter of Henry Somerby, and had Nathaniel 1666, Thomas 1668, John 1670, Henry 1673, Daniel 1675, Sarah 1678, Josiah 1682, Elizabeth 1684, Judith 1687, Mary 1689. He died on board the ship "Six Friends," soon after sailing in the expedition against Quebec, August 25, 1690, from an injury. He was aged 46.

NICHOLAS CLARK, of Cambridge, arrived at Boston, September 16, in the "Lion," removed to Hartford, where tradition says, he built 1635, the first frame house for Captain Talcott. He died July 2, 1680, having son Thomas and one or two daughters.

PIERCY or PERCIVAL CLARK, of Boston, was admitted freeman 1675. By wife Elizabeth, he had John 1665, Mary 1667, Robert 1673, Ruhama 1678, Gamaliel, Sarah, Mercy. His will was dated November 17, 1700.

RICHARD CLARK, of Rowley, by wife Alice, had Judah 1644, and John 1650, besides three daughters.

ROBERT CLARK, of Stratford, admitted freeman 1669. He married 1st, Sarah, widow of Francis Stiles. By second wife, he had John 1684, Hannah 1687. He died 1694.

THADDEUS CLARK, of Falmouth, Mass., married 1663, Elizabeth, daughter of Michael Milton. He was Lieutenant in the Indian war, 1689, and was killed by them at Falmouth, in 1690. He had son Isaac.

THOMAS CLARK, of Plymouth, came in the "Ann" 1623, married Susanna, daughter of widow Mary Ring, and had Andrew, James, Susanna, William, John and Nathaniel. He was a representative 1651-5. He married second wife 1664, widow Alice Nichols, daughter of Richard Hallett, lived in 1670, at Harwich, where he had a third wife, Elizabeth Crow, and died March 24, 1697, aged 92.

THOMAS CLARK, of Boston, merchant, had first lived at Dorchester, 1636, selectman about 1641 and '2, member of the Artillery company 1638, admitted freeman March 14, 1639, was a captain in 1653, and afterward head of the Boston regiment. He was representative to the General Court 1651, and, many years more; speaker in 1662, and several years later; chosen Assistant 1673, and died July 28, 1678. His first wife was Mary, by whom he had Mehitable 1640, Elizabeth May 22, 1642, Deborah 1644, Thomas, Leah and others.

THOMAS CLARK, of Boston, a blacksmith, lived at Winisemet, near Chelsea. By wife Elizabeth, he had Cornelius 1639, Jacob 1642, Rachel 1646, and perhaps Benjamin.

THOMAS CLARK, of Boston, called "Jr.," but though born in England, may not be the son of Hon. Thomas, yet he lived some time earlier or later, at Dorchester. He was of the artillery company 1644; more than once its captain; representative to the General Court 1673-6, and died March 13, 1683. He was one of the wealthiest merchants of Boston, and by his will of Aug. 15, 1679, it is judged that only two children were then living, Mehitable Warren and Elizabeth, who had married Mr. John Freak.

THOMAS CLARK, of Reading, Mass., by wife Elizabeth, had Thomas.

THOMAS CLARK, of Scituate, 1674, supposed to be a son or grandson of the mate of the Mayflower, married Martha, daughter of Richard Curtis, and had Thomas, Joseph, Daniel, Samuel, Nathaniel, Mercy, Deborah, Rachel, Ann, Charity, Mary. He served in King Philip's war.

WILLIAM CLARK, of Dorchester, was selectman 1646-7, removed in 1659, to Northampton, represented that town at the General Court, 1663, and for thirteen years more, but not consecutively. He was Lieut. in King Philip's war. By wife Sarah, he had Jonathan 1639, Nathaniel 1642, Experience 1643, Increase 1646, Rebecca 1648, John 1651, Samuel 1653, William 1656, Sarah 1659. His wife died Sept. 6, 1675, and he married Nov. 15, 1676, Sarah, widow of Thomas Cooper, of Springfield. He died July 18, 1690, aged 81.

WILLIAM CLARK, of Lynn, 1640, had Hannah, Sarah, Mary, William, Elizabeth, Martha, John.

WILLIAM CLARK, of Hartford, 1639, removed to Haddam, died 1681, leaving William, John, Joseph, Thomas and several daughters.

WILLIAM CLARK, of Boston, married 1661, Martha, daughter of George Farr, of Lynn, and had Samuel 1663, Mary 1668.

WILLIAM CLARK, of Saybrook, married March 7, 1678, Hannah, daughter of the Secretary Francis Griswold.

REFERENCES.

CONNECTICUT.—Orcutt's Hist. of Derby, 710; Orcutt's Hist. of New Milford, 794; Stiles' Hist. of Windsor, II, 153; Timlow's Hist. of Southington, 49; Whittemore's Hist. of Middlesex County, 204; Andrews' Hist. of New Britain, 193, 253; Bronson's Hist. of Waterbury, 483; Brown's West Simsbury Settlers, 55; Field's Hist. of Haddam, 44; Gold's Hist. of Cornwall, 273; Hinman's Conn. Settlers, 600; Middlefield Hist.

MAINE.—Hatch's Hist. of Industry, 540; Lapham's Hist. of Bethel, 512; Lapham's Hist. of Paris, 550; Lapham's Hist. of Woodstock, 193; North's Hist. of Augusta, 829; Pierce's Hist. of Gorham, 191; Wheeler's Hist. of Brunswick, 830; Eaton's Annals of Warren, 517; Eaton's Hist. of Thomaston, 176; Farrow's Hist. of Isleborough, 188; Hanson's Hist. of Gardiner, 137.

MASSACHUSETTS.—Paige's Hist. of Cambridge, 510; Paige's Hist. of Hardwick, 348; Gage's Hist. of Rowley, 440; Babson's Hist. of Gloucester, 68; Draper's Hist. of Spencer, 183; Freeman's Hist. of Cape Cod; II, 524, 756; Essex Inst. Coll., XXVI, 59; Dyer's Hist. of Plainfield; Deane's Hist. of Scituate, 237; Davis' Landmarks of Plymouth, 59; Chase's Hist. of Haverhill, 275; Ballou's Hist. of Milford, 653; Barry's Hist. of Framingham, 206; Barry's Hist. of Hanover, 268; Wyman's Charlestown Gens., I, 217; Lyman's Hist. of Easthampton, 152; Mitchell Hist. of Bridgewater, 365; Wright's Hist. of Easthampton, 29; Sewall's Hist. of Woburn, 509; Whitmore's Copps Hill Epitaphs; Stearn's Hist. of Ashburnham, 636; Winsor's Hist. of Duxbury, 246; Harris' Watertown Epitaphs, 12; Herrick's Hist. of Gardner, 340; Hudson's Hist. of Lexington, 42; Jackson's Hist. of Newton, 257; Jameson's Hist. of Medway, 462; Temple's Hist. of Palmer, 434; Stone's Hist. of Hubbardston, 238; Judd's Hist. of Hadley, 462; Morse's Sherborn Settlers, 59; Blake's Hist. of Franklin, 236; Bond's Hist. of Watertown, 159; Brown's Medford, Mass., Families, 7; Temple's Hist. of North Brookfield, 554; Pierce's Hist. of Grafton, 473.

NEW HAMPSHIRE.—Parker's Hist. of Londonderry, 264; Stearn's Hist. of Rindge, 416; Washington, N. H., Hist., 341; Cochrane's Hist. of Antrim, 417; Eaton's Hist. of Candia, 61; Coggswell Hist. of Nottingham, 651; Coggswell's New Boston, 369; Aldrich's Hist. of Walpole, 230; Hayward's Hist. of Gilsum, 287; Hayward's Hist. of Hancock, 439; Kidder's Hist. of New Ipswich, 353; Lancaster's Hist. of Gilmartin, 260; Leonard's Hist. of Dublin, 322; Livermore's Hist. of Wilton, 349; Merrill's Hist. of Ackworth, N. H., 499; Morrison's Hist. of Windham, 377; Runnell's Sanbornton, N. H., 129; Saunder's Hist. of Charlestown, 309; Secomb's Hist. of Amherst, 544; Read's Hist. of Swanzey, 311; Norton's Hist. of Fitzwilliam, 512; Leonard's Hist. of Dublin, 322.

NEW YORK.—Stickney's Minisinck Region, N. Y., 121; Howell's Hist. of Southampton, 211; Collins' Hist. of Hillsdale, App., 48; Bolton's Hist. Westchester County, N. Y., II, 717; Baird's Hist. of Rye, 499; Avon, N. Y., Record, 30; Boyd's Hist. of Consensus, 147; Cleveland's Hist. of Yates County, 481; N. Y. Gen. and Biog. Rec., XIX, 170.

NEW JERSEY.—Shroud's Fenwick Colony, 525; Littel's Passaic Valley, 75; Cooley's Trenton, N. J., Gens., 39.

VERMONT.—Williams' Hist. of Danby, 125; Vt. Hist. Gaz., V, 95; McKeens' Hist. of Bradford, 162, 391, 382; Hollister's Hist. of Pawlet, 175; Heminway's Vermont Gaz., V, 95; Frisbie's Hist. of Middletown, 74; Paul's Hist. of Wells, 71; Jennings' Vt. Memorial; Joslin's Hist. of Poultney, 281.

OTHER PUBLICATIONS.—Slaughter's St. Mark's Parish, Va., 190; Richmond, Va., Standard, III, 39; R. I. Hist. Soc. Coll., III, 313; R. I. Hist. Mag., VII, 125; Hubbard's Hist. of Stanstead County, Canada, 198; Wight Gen., 13; Wheeler's Eminent North Carolinians, XII; Wentworth Gen., vol. I, 222; Tuttle Family, 2; Strong Family, 1439; Stoddard Gen. (1865), 13, 26; Stephen's Gen., 45; Stanton Gen., 206; Smith Gen. by Wellington Smith; Sim's Gen. Notes on Clark, 1870; Sears' Gen., 86; Robinson Gen., (1837); Rice Gen.; Palmer and Tremble Gen., 130; Morse Mem., Appendix No. 15½ Mag. of Am. Hist., XXII, 246; Mack Gen., 48; Locke Gen., 58, 141, 300; Leland Mag., 164; Kellog's White Memorial, 27, 51, 70, 111; Huntington Gen., 86; Guild's Stiles Gen., 209, 241; Greene Gen.; Goodwin's Gen. Notes, 23; Gifford's Our Patronymics, 19; Elderkin Gen.; Dwight Gen., 274; Cutts' Gen., 177; Chapin Gen.; Champion Gen.; Bridgman's Granary epitaphs, 307; Barbour's My Wife and Mother, App., 35; Ball's Lake County, Ind., (1884), 404; Alexander Gen., 78; Amer. Ancestry, vol. I, 14, 11, 22; III, 94; V, 212, 236; VI, 95; VIII, 24, 63, 153, 203; IX, 137, 159, 185; X, 121, 139, 196, 198; XI, 185, 222; N. E. Hist. and Gen. Reg., XIV, 25; XVI, 140; XXXIII, 226; Gen. David Clark of Northampton; Hugh Clark of Watertown, 1866; Thomas Clark of Milford, 1870; George Clark and Daniel Kellogg, 1877; William Clark of Haddam, 1880; John Clark of Farmington, 1882; Simon Clark of Amherst, 1883; Gen. Emmons Clark of New York City, 1891; Samuel Clark, Sen. of Hempstead, L. I., 1891, 1892.

REFERENCES.

CONNECTICUT.—Orcutt's Hist. of Stratford, 1174; Stiles' Hist. of Windsor, II, 834.

MASSACHUSETTS.—Atkins' Hist. of Hawley, 52; Hammatt Papers, Ipswich, 62; Cutter's Hist. of Arlington, 204; Essex Inst. Coll., XVI, 270; XX, 222.

RHODE ISLAND.—Newport Hist. Mag., vol. I, 75, 129; Irish's Hist. of Richmond, 129; Austin's Allied Families, 61; Austin's R. I. Gen., Dict., 43; Austin's Ancestries, 126.

OTHER PUBLICATIONS.—Richmond, Va., Standard, II, 39; Meade's Old Families of Va.; Cushman's Hist. of Sheepscott, Me., 366; Heraldic Journal, II, 75; Green Gen.; Goode Gen., 239, 375; Chapman's Weeks Gen., 134; Pompey's N. Y. Re-union, 291; Pope Gen.; Preble Gen. 253; Salisbury Gen.; Tuttle Gen., 350; Amer. Ancestry, vol. I, 14; III, 122, 133; IV, 143; V, 155; VII, 51, 73; IX, 32; X, 159; XI, 185, 222; Warren Clark Gen., 42; Voyage of Geo. Clarke to America, preface, 71; Turner's Clarke Gen., (1881); Huntington's Warren Clarke Gen., 1894; Greenwood's Clarke Gen.; Thomas Clarke; Rev. Dorcas Clarke; Stephen Clarke, 1878; Clarke Family, 1879, 1884; Nathaniel Clarke of Newbury, 1883; Jeremy Clarke's Family of R. I., 1881.

CLARKSON. N. Y. Gen. and Biog. Rec., X, 156; Lamb's Hist. of N. Y. City, 385; Coggswell's Hist. of Henniker, N. H., 502; Paxton's Marshall Gen., 99; Clarkson Biog., 1890.

CLARY.—John, of Watertown, Mass., married Feb. 5, 1644, Sarah Cady or as Cora Bond says Mary Cassell, and had Sarah, 1647, John and Gershom. He removed to Hadley, and died 1690.

REFERENCES.—Temple's Hist. of Northfield, Mass., 464; Judd's Hist. of Hadley, Mass., 434; Kidder's Hist.

of New Ipswich, N. H., 351, 385; Wentworth Gen., II, 104; Savage's Gen. Dict., vol. I, 405.

CLASON. Amer. Ancestry, VIII, 81; Clason Gen., 1892.

CLAUSON. Stickney's Hist. of Minisink, 139.

CLAWSON. Huntington, Stamford, Conn. Settlers, 22; Amer. Ancestry, IX, 88.

CLAUW. Munsell's Albany Coll., IV, 107.

CLAY:—Joseph, of Guilford, married April 18, 1670, Mary Law, and had Mary 1671, Sarah 1674. He died April 30, 1695. His wife died 1692.

REFERENCES:—Stearn's Hist. of Rindge, N. H., 477; Runnel's Hist. of Sanbornton, N. H., II, 152; Chase's Hist. of Chester, N. H., 492; Bangor, Me., Hist. Mag. V, 184; Hanson's Hist. of Gardiner, Me., 170; Colton's Life of Henry Clay, vol. I, 17; Green's Kentucky Families; Holstein Gen.; Walker Gen., 131.

CLAYES. Cunnabell Gen., 13; Norton's Hist. of Fitzwilliam, N. H., 514.

CLAYPOOLE. Claypoole Gen., 1893.

CLAYTON. Slaughter's Hist. of St. Mark's Parish, Va., 125; Futhey's Hist. of Chester County, Pa., 498; Butler's Hist. of Farmington, Mass., 428; Powers' Hist. of Sangamon County, Ill., 16, 205.

CLEARWATER. Amer. Ancestry, III, 95.

CLEARY. Roe's Sketches of Rose, N. Y., 41.

CLEAVER. Futhey's Sketches of Chester, Pa., 498; Jenkins' Hist. of Gwynedd, Pa., 365.

CLEAVES. Secomb's Hist. of Amherst, N. H., 539; Lapham's Hist. of Norway, Me., 480; Corliss' Hist. of North Yarmouth, Me.; Chandler Gen., 23.

CLEEMAN. Richmond Standard, II, 32.

CLEEVES. Austin's Allied Families, 65.

CLEMANS. Paul's Hist. of Wells, Vt., 75.

CLEMENCE. Austin's R. I. Gen. Dict., 48.

CLEMENT. Chase's Hist. of Haverhill, Mass., 275; Ballou's Hist. of Milford, Mass., 661; Stark's Hist. of Dunbarton, N. H., 241; Runnel's Hist. of Sanbornton, N. H., 156; Hayward's Hist. of Hancock, N. H., 449; Clement's Newtown, N. J., Settlers; 'Pompey's N. Y. Reunion, 289; Pearson's Schenectady, N. Y., Settlers, 37; Hubbard's Hist. of Stanstead County, Canada, 313; Poor's Merrimac Valley, 142; Savage's Gen. Dict., vol. I, 407.

CLEMENTS CLEMENS:—Abraham, of Newbury, married March 10, 1683, Hannah Gove, daughter, probably, of Edward, of Hampton, and had Edmund 1684; removed to Hampton, and there had seven more.

AUSTIN or AUGUSTINE CLEMENT, of Dorchester, came from Southampton, England, in the "James" of London, April, 1635. By wife Elizabeth, he had Elizabeth, Samuel, born 1635, John. He was admitted freeman 1636.

REFERENCES:—Powers' Hist. of Sangamon County, Ill., 206; Dow's Hist. of Hampton, N. H., 638; Eaton's Warren, Me., 517; Wentworth Gen., I, 125; Ely Gen., 323.

CLEMONS. Hinman's Conn. Settlers, 617.

CLENDENNEN. Clyde's Irish Settlement, Pa.; Hist. Reg. of Penn., vol. I, 36; Morrison Gen., 254.

CLEVES or CLEAVES:—William, of Beverly, married Martha, daughter of 'Giles Corcy, and had John 1676, Elinor 1678, Martha 1681. He married second, Margaret, sister of the first wife, and had William 1686, Hannah 1688, Robert 1689, Ebenezer 1691, Benjamin 1693.

REFERENCES:—Savage's Gen. Dict. vol. I, 408.

CLEAVELAND:—Moses, of Woburn, came, says family tradition, from Ipswich, County Suffolk, Eng. He married Sept. 26, 1648, Ann, daughter of Edward Winn, and had Moses 1651, Hannah 1653, Aaron 1655, Samuel 1657, Mirriam 1659, Joanna 1661, Edward 1663, Josiah 1667, Isaac 1669, Joanna again 1670, Enoch 1671. He died January 9, 1702.

REFERENCES:—Wyman's Charlestown, Mass., Gens., vol. I, 219; Paige's Hist. of Hardwick, Mass., 350; Ballou's Hist. of Milford, Mass., 662; Hinman's Conn. Settlers, 618; Cleveland's Hist. of Yates County, N. Y., 206; Young's Hist. of Chautauqua, N. Y., 300; Adams' Hist. of Fairhaven, Vt., 316; Bass' Hist. of Braintree, 125; Hollister's Hist. of Pawlet, Vt., 177; Joslin's Hist. of Poultney, Vt., 241; Gifford's Our Patronymics, 10; Champion Gen.; Child Gen., 807; Ely Gen., 323; Hubbard's Hist. of Stanstead County, Canada, 303; Kelly Gen., 1892; Lindsay Gen.; Putnam's Hist. Mag., vol. I, 158; Walworth Hyde Gen., 399; Vinton's Richardson Gen., 192; Amer. Ancestry, vol. I, 15; III, 10, 186; V, 41; Cleveland Gen.; Benjamin Cleveland, 1879; Moses Cleveland of Woburn, 1881; Lineage of Hon. Grover Cleveland, 1884; Gen. Moses Cleveland of Canterbury, 1885.

CLEVER. Cochrane's Hist. of Antrim, 419.

CLEVERLY. Bass' Hist. of Braintree, Vt., 125; Binney Gen., 59; Amer. Ancestry, V, 95.

CLIFFORD:—George, of Boston, was a member of the artillery company, 1644. He had son John, born 1646.

REFERENCES:—Stark's Hist. of Dunbarton, N. H., 249; Lancaster's Hist. of Gilmartin, N. H., 259; Dow's Hist. of Hampton, N. H., 638; Chase's Hist. of Chester, N. H., 493; Caverly's Hist. of Pittsford, Vt., 696; Lapham's Hist. of Paris, Me., 558; Hubbard's Hist. of Stanstead County, Canada, 319; Stone's Hist. of Hubbardston, Mass., 252.

CLIFT. Mitchell's Hist. of Bridgewater, Mass., 137; Amer. Ancestry, III, 10; XI, 25.

CLIFTON. Austin's R. I. Gen. Dict., 48.

CLINCH. Pearson's Schenectady, 28.

CLINE. Powers' Hist. of Sangamon, Ill., 206.

CLINTON. Eager's Hist. of Orange County, N. Y., 628; Campbell's Life of Gov. Clinton, 19; Valentine's N. Y. City Manual (1853), 415; Alden's Am. Epitaphs, V, 276; Amer. Ancestry, VI, 52; XI, 182; N. Y. Gen. Reg. XII, 95; XIII, 5, 173, 80; Whittemore's Heroes of the Revolution and their Descendants.

CLESBY or CLEESBY:—Ezekiel, of Boston, was brought by his uncle John in 1670, aged 7. By wife Sarah, he had Ezekiel 1689. He was admitted freeman 1690.

REFERENCES:—Savage's Gen. Dict. vol. I, 410.

CLOCK. Huntington's Hist. of Stamford, Conn., 23; Whittemore's Heroes of the Revolution and their Descendants; Amer. Ancestry, XI, 9.

CLOGSTON. Hist. of Washington, N. H., 342.

CLOPTON. N. E. Hist. and Gen. Reg., XVIII, 184.

CLOSE. Mead's Hist. of Greenwich, Conn., 307; Bolton's Hist. of Westchester County, N. Y., vol. II, 717.

CLOSS. Roe's Sketches of Rose, N. Y., 314.

CLOUGH:—Ebenezer, of Boston, by wife Martha, had John 1694, Martha 1695, Mary 1697, Ebenezer 1699, John 1704, William 1707, Susannah 1709, Mary 1711, Elizabeth 1714, Ebenezer again 1716, John 1720.

JOHN CLOUGH, of Watertown, came in the "Elizabeth" 1635, aged 22; admitted freeman 1642. By wife Jane he had Elizabeth 1642, Mary 1644, Sarah 1646, John 1648, Thomas, Martha, Samuel. He died 1691.

WILLIAM CLOUGH, of Charlestown, Mass., by wife Mary, had Mary 1657, Joseph 1659, Benjamin 1662, Samuel 1665, Nathaniel 1668.

REFERENCES:—Wyman's Charlestown, Mass., Gens., 222; Whitmore's Copps Hill Epitaphs; Runnel's Hist. of Sanbornton, N. H., II, 159; Coggswell's Hist. of Henniker, N. H., 506; Bangor, Me., Hist. Mag. V, 185; Eaton's Hist. of Thomaston, Me., 177; Eaton's Hist. of Warren, Me., 517; Niven's Little Britain, N. Y. Church (1859); Champion Gen.; N. E. Hist. and Gen. Reg., VIII, 79; Savage's Gen. Dict. vol. I, 410.

CLOUD. Futhey's Hist. of Chester County, Pa., 500.

CLOUTMAN:—Thomas, of Salem, by wife Eliza, had Thomas 1683, John 1685, Mary 1691, Joseph 1693.
REFERENCES:—Pierce's Hist. of Gorham, Me., 161; Savage's Gen. Dict. vol. I, 410.

CLOW. Amer. Ancestry, vol. II, 24.

CLOWES. Bunker's L. I. Gens., 186-8.

CLOYES or CLOYCE:—John, of Watertown, mariner, was of Charlestown, 1658, Falmouth, 1660. By wife Abigail, had John 1638, Peter 1640, Nathaniel 1640, Abigail, Sarah. By second wife Jane, said to be widow Spurwell, had Thomas, Mary, Martha. He was probably killed by the Indians 1676.

REFERENCES:—Barry's Hist. of Framingham, Mass., 210.

CLUM. Hall's Trenton, N. J., Presbyterian Church, 249; Amer. Ancestry, vol. I, 15.

CLUTE. Pearson's Schenectady, N. Y., Settlers, 38, 45; Munsell's Albany, N. Y., Coll. IX, 108.

CLUXTON. Sedgwick's Hist. of Sharon, Conn., 72.

CLYDE. Washington, N. H. History, 343; Hayward's Hist. of Gilsum, N. H., 288; Hayward's Hist. of Hancock, N. H., 449; Morrison's Hist. of Windham, N. H., 380; Martin's Hist. of Chester, Pa., 267; Clyde's Irish Settlement of Pa., 29; Clyde Family of Pa. (1880).

CLEYMER. Amer. Ancestry, V, 45; Penn. Mag., IX, 358.

COALL. Thomas Gen., 65.

COALTER. Slaughter's Hist. of Bristol, 160.

COAN. Amer. Ancestry, V, 116, 128; IX, 189.

COATE. Thomas Family of Md., 65.

COATES:—Thomas, of Philadelphia, son of Henry, of England, baptized in Sproxton, Eng., Sept. 26, 1659, died in Philadelphia, July 22, 1719; came from England, 1682, settled in Philadelphia, where he purchased several pieces of real estate. He was a Quaker; married Oct. 1, 1694, Beulah, daughter of Thomas and Elizabeth Jacques, and had Samuel.

THOMAS COATES, of Lynn, Mass., had sons John, James and Thomas.

REFERENCES:—Futhey's Hist. of Chester County, Pa., 501; Pierce's Hist. of Gorham, Me., 157; Cleveland's Hist. of Yates County, N. Y., 495; Powers' Hist. of Sangamon County, Ill., 209; Crane's Rawson Gen., 201; Cunnabell Gen., 83; Holstein Gen.; Plumstead Gen., 61; Amer. Ancestry, VIII, 111; Savage's Gen. Dict. vol. I, 412.

COBB:—Augustine, of Taunton, Mass., 1670, had Elizabeth 1671, Morgan 1673, Samuel 1675, Bethia 1678, Mercy 1680, Abigail 1684.

HENRY COBB, of Barnstable, one of the first settlers, was of Plymouth, 1629, of Scituate, in 1633, and one of the founders of the church there 1635; was chosen deacon. By wife Patience, probably daughter of James Hurst, he had John 1632, James 1635, Mary 1637, Hannah 1639, Patience 1642, Gershom 1645, Eleazer 1648. He married 2d, Sarah, daughter of Samuel Hinckley, and had Mehitable, Samuel 1654, Jonathan 1660, Sarah 1663, Henry 1665, Mehitable again 1667, Experience 1671. He was a representative to the General Court, 1664, and six years more.

JOHN COBB, of Plymouth, married Aug. 28, 1658, Martha Nelson, and had John 1662, Samuel, Israel, Elizabeth, Elisha, James.

REFERENCES.

MAINE.—Lapham's Hist. of Norway, 481; Pierce's Hist. of Gorham, 158; Bangor Hist. Mag., IV, 1; Eaton's Hist. of Thomaston, II, 178; Eaton's Hist. of Warren, 518.

MASSACHUSETTS.—Swift's Barnstable Families, vol. I, 166; Freeman's Hist. of Cape Cod, II, 274, 340, 763; Hobert's Hist. of Abington, 360; Kingman's Hist. of North Bridgewater, 475; Morse's Hist. of Sherborn, 62; Ballou's Hist. of Milford, 664; Clark's Hist. of Norton, 79; Davis' Landmarks of Plymouth, 63; Deane's Hist. of Scituate, 238; Paige's Hist. of Hardwick, 351; Pratt's Hist. of Easthampton, 27; Rich's Hist. of Truro, 523.

OTHER PUBLICATIONS.—Waldo's Hist. of Tolland, Conn., 97; Adams' Hist. of Fairhaven, Vt., 341; Hollister's Hist. Pawlet, 178; Bass' Hist. of Braintree, Vt., 125; Hayward's Hist. of Hancock, N. H., 450; Runnel's Hist. of Sanbornton, N. H., vol. I, 473; Richmond, Va., Standard, II, 23; Amer. Ancestry, IV, 179; V, 91; VI, 64; VII, 251; X, 182; XI, 64; Savage's Gen. Dict. vol. I, 412; N. E. Hist. and Gen. Reg. II, 389.

COBBETT:—Thomas, of Lynn, Mass., a man of high esteem, was born at Newbury, in County Bucks, Eng., and was bred at Oxford. He married Elizabeth, and had Samuel, Thomas, Elizabeth, John and Eleazer. After a long service at Lynn, he removed to Ipswich, to fill the place of Nathaniel Rogers in 1656, and was there minister until his death, Nov. 5, 1685.

REFERENCES:—Hammatt Papers, 54; Hinman's Conn. Settlers, 626; Savage's Gen. Dict. vol. I, 414.

COBBLE:—Edward, of Salisbury, by wife Judith, had Edward 1652, Benjamin 1655, Sarah 1657, Judith 1659, Elizabeth 1663, Edward again 1666.

REFERENCES:—Savage's Gen. Dict. vol. I, 415.

COBHAM:—Josiah, of Salisbury, by wife Mary, had Mary 1640, Joseph 1642, Martha 1643, Moses 1645, Sarah 1646, Joshua 1648, Mary 1652.

REFERENCES:—Savage's Gen. Dict. vol. I, 415.

COBBS. Slaughter's Hist. of Bristol, 45.

COBLA. Pierce Gen., 1894.

COBLEIGH. Stearn's Hist. of Ashburnham, Mass., 639; Norton's Hist. of Fitzwilliam, 514.

COBOURNE. Smith Hist. of Delaware, Pa., 454.

COBURN:—Edward, of Darcut, Mass., born 1618, died February 17, 1700; came to America 1635, and settled at Ipswich, Mass., 1638, and moved thence to Dracut. Had son John.

REFERENCES:—Livermore's Hist. of Wilton, N. H., 357; Eaton's Hist. of Thomaston, Me., II, 179; Farrow's Hist. of Islesborough, Me., 189; Eaton's Hist. of Warren, Me., 520; Lapham's Hist. of Norway, Me., 482; Hinman's Conn. Settlers, 627; Bass' Hist. of Braintree, Vt., 126; Amer. Ancestry, II, 24, V, 228.

COCHRAN:—Thomas, born at Coleraine, Ireland, came with his brother John to America,a from Ireland, whence they had removed from Scotland, in the time of King James. They were lineal descendants of Earl Dundonald. He had Samuel.

REFERENCES:—Secomb's Hist. of Amherst, N. H., 539; Morrison's Hist. of Windham, N. H., 390; Hayward's Hist. of Hancock, N. H., 451; Coggswell's Hist. of New Boston, N. H., 356; Cochrane's Hist. of Antrim, N. H., 421; Aldrich's Hist. of Walpole, Mass., 231; Cothren's Hist. of Woodbury, Conn., 519; Eaton's Hist. of Thomaston, Me., II, 179; Futhey's Hist. of Chester, Pa., 500; Martin's Hist. of Chester, Pa., 319; Peyton's Hist. of Augusta County, Va., 312; Aldrich's Rev. William Smith's Biography; Marshall Gen., 1884, 62; Amer. Ancestry, II, 24; IV, 194; VI, 80.

COCK:—James Cock, of Killingworth, N. Y., died about 1698, was at Setauket, 1659, at Oyster Bay, 1662, purchased land at Killingworth, near Matinecock 1669. He married Sarah, and had Mary (married John Bowne), Thomas, John, James, Henry.

REFERENCES:—Bunker's L. I. Gens., 188; Bolton's Hist. of Westchester County, N. Y., II, 718; Miller's Colchester County, N. S., 150; Amer. Ancestry, IX, 75; X, 75, 81; N. Y. Gen. and Biog. Rec. IV, 18, 189; VIII, 9.

COCKE. Slaughter's Bristol Parish, Va., 173, 184; Virginia Hist. Coll., V, 194; Richmond, Va., Standard, II, 31, 35, 37, 40, 44, 52; III, 8, 20, 40; Old Kent, Md., 172; Watkins' Gen., 21; Jones Gen. (1891) 121.

COCKS. Amer. Ancestry, IX, 73.

COCKRELL. Richmond Standard, IV, 3.

COCKERUM:—William, of Hingham, 1635, went home, and came again in the "Mary Ann," of Yarmouth, when he calls himself of Southold. He was made freeman March 13, 1639, sailed for home again Oct., 1642. In 1657, he conveyed his estate to his son William.

REFERENCES:—Savage's Gen. Dict., vol. I, 416.

CODDINGTON:—William, of Boston, an Assistant, of the company chosen in England 1630, and came with Winthrop. His first wife and two children died. In 1633, he married Mary and had Benjah 1636. Children by his third wife were Nathaniel 1653, Mary 1654, Thomas 1655, John 1656, Noah 1658, Ann 1663. He was treasurer of the Colony 1634-6, represented Boston at the General Court and early the following year went to Rhode Island, where he was made Governor. In 1649, he went to England and some years after his return he was elected Governor. He died in office, Nov., 1678, aged 77.

REFERENCES:—Updyke's Narragansett Church, R. I., 164; Austin's R. I. Gen. Dict., 276; Mott Gen.; Amer. Ancestry, VII, 103; IX, 131; Savage's Gen. Dict., vol. I, 415; Turner's William Coddington, 9; N. E. Hist. and Gen. Reg., XXVIII, 18.

CODMAN:—Robert, of Salem, Mass., had grant of land, and in 1641, he removed to Salisbury, and in 1650, to Hartford, Conn., in 1654-6, to Saybrook, and afterward to Edgartown, where he died in 1678. He had Benjamin 1641, James 1644, Joseph, Stephen.

REFERENCES:—Wyman's Charlestown, Mass., Gens., 224; Washington, N. H. Hist., 349; Pierce's Hist. of Gorham, Me., 161; Joslin's Hist. of Poultney, Vt., 242; Amer. Ancestry, III, 133; VI, 91; Savage's Gen. Dict., vol. I, 416.

CODMER. Savage's Gen. Dict., vol. I, 417.

CODNER:—Edward, of New London, 1651, removed in 1659, to Saybrook. By wife Priscilla, he had son Lawrence.

RICHARD CODNER, of Swanzey, married May 23, 1671, Phebe, daughter of Rufus Barton, of Warwick, and had Richard 1676, Elizabeth 1678, Savoy 1679.

REFERENCES:—Savage's Gen. Dict., vol. I, 417.

CODRINGTON. Richmond, Va., Standard, II, 35, 37.

CODY. Hughes Gen., 183.

COE:—Matthew, of Portsmouth, 1645, removed to Gloucester, and married June 15, 1647, Elizabeth, daughter of Thomas Wakeley, and had John 1649, Sarah 1651, Abigail 1658, Matthew 1661.

ROBERT COE, of Watertown, 1634, came that year in the "Frances" from Ipswich, aged 38, with wife Ann, 43, and children John aged 8, Robert 7, and Benjamin. He removed to Wethersfield, Conn., in 1635-6, and after some years to Stamford or Stratford, and later to Jamaica. He was Sheriff 1669-72.

REFERENCES.

CONNECTICUT.—Hist. ,of Litchfield County, (1881) 724; Hinman's Conn. Settlers, 627; Middlefield, Conn. Hist.; Orcutt's Hist. of Stratford, 1176; Orcutt's Hist. of Torrington, 668; Boyd's Annals of Winchester, 51.

OTHER PUBLICATIONS.—Boyd's Hist. of Consensus, N. Y., 148; Baird's Hist. of Rye, N. Y., 407; Babson's Hist. of Gloucester, Mass., 69; Bent's Hist. of Whiteside County, Ill., 261; Bolton's Hist. Westchester County, N. Y., II; 717; Coggswell's Hist. of Nottingham, N. H., 656; Amer. Ancestry, VII, 100; Savage's Gen. Dict. vol. I, 417; Coe Gen., 1856, 1859.

COELY. N. Y. Gen. and Biog. Rec., IX, 153.

COERTE. Bergen Gen., 61.

COEYMAN. Messler's Hist. Somerset, N. J., 19.

COEYMANS. Munsell's Albany, IV, 109.

COFFIN:—Tristram, of Nantucket, born, it is said, at Brudon, near Plymouth, County Devon, about 1605 or 1609; he was son of Peter and Joanna. He married Dionis Stevens, and had Peter 1631, Tristram 1632, Elizabeth, James 1640, and John. He was first at Salisbury, removing thence to Haverhill, where he had Mary, born 1645, John again 1647. He removed in 1648, to Newbury, where Stephen was born 1652, again removed to Salisbury, there was county magistrate, and finally removed 1660, to Nantucket with his aged mother and four children, and died there Oct., 1681.

REFERENCES.

MASSACHUSETTS.—Coffin's Hist. of Newbury, 298; Wyman's Charlestown Gens., 226; Babson's Hist. of Gloucester, 69.

NEW HAMPSHIRE.—Wheeler's Hist. of Newport, 346; Stearn's Hist. of Rindge, 478; Dow's Hist. of Hampton, 640; Coffin's Hist. of Boscawen, 491.

OTHER PUBLICATIONS.—Heraldic Journal, III, 49; Lapham's Hist. of Bethel, Me., 513; Maine Hist. Soc. Coll., IV, 240; Austin's Allied Families, R. I., 67; Crane's Rawson Gen., 39; Morse Mem., Appendix 89; Buxton Centen., 211; Champion Gen.; Amer. Ancestry, vol. I, 15; II, 15; VII, 125; XI, 194, Savage's Gen. Dict., vol. I, 418; N. E. Hist. and Gen. Reg., II, 336; XXIV, 149, 305; XXV, 90; Woodman's Coffin Memorial, 1855; Armory's Life of Sir Isaac Coffin; Coffin Wills, by Appleton, 1893; Coffin Family, 1881.

COFFMAN. Palmer Gen. (1875), 169.

COGAN. N. E. Gen. Reg., XLIII, 310.

COGGAN or COGAN:—Henry, of Barnstable, Mass., 1639, by wife Abigail, had Abigail, John 1643, Henry 1646. He went home for a visit and died there 1649.

JOHN COGGAN, of Boston, had first been of Dorchester 1632, was admitted freeman Nov. 5, 1633. By his wife Ann, he had Ann and Lydia. He married March 10, 1652, Martha, widow of Gov. Winthrop, who before had been the widow of Thomas Coztemere, and by her had Caleb 1652. He died 1658.

JOHN COGGAN, of Charlestown, married Dec. 22, 1664, Mary Long, perhaps daughter of the second Robert. He was a householder 1678. His children Henry and John, lived at Woburn.

REFERENCES:—Savage's Gen. Dict. vol. I, 420.

COGGIN. Swift's Barnstable Families, vol. I, 189; Freeman's Hist. of Cape Cod, Mass., II, 260; Bangor, Me., Hist. Mag., V, 186; Secomb's Hist. of Amherst, N. H., 541; Amer. Ancestry, VI, 34.

COGGESHALL:—John, of Roxbury, a mercer, from County Essex, England, came in the "Lion," Sept. 16, 1632, and was admitted freeman Nov. 6, following. He removed with his wife Mary to Boston, and had Hananiel 1635, Wait 1636, Bedaiah 1637. He was a representative in the first General Court 1634, and several sessions after; but in 1637, sympathizing with Wheelwright, he was expelled from his seat; disarmed and next year banished, then went to Rhode Island, was chosen Assistant 1641, and in 1647, President of the Colony, and was one of the chief men at Newport, treasurer of the Colony. He died, after filling other honorable places, in Nov., 1689.

REFERENCES:—Tilley's Mag. of N. E. Hist., II, 99;

R. I. Hist. Mag. V, 173; Newport, R I. Hist. Mag., (1889), 195; Austin's R. I. Dict., 49; Savage's Gen. Dict. vol. I, 421.

COGGSHALL. Coggshall Chart.

COGSHAL. Stamford, Conn., Families, 24.

COGHILL. Coghhill Gen.

COGGSWELL:—John, of Ipswich, came from Bristol 1635, in the "Angel Gabriel," was wrecked Aug. 15, at Pemaquid. He was admitted freeman March 3, 1636, and died Nov. 29, 1669. His widow died June 2, 1676. He brought William, born 1619, John 1623, Edward 1629, Mary, Hannah, Abigail, Sarah.

SAMUEL COGGSWELL, of Saybrook, married Oct. 27, 1668, Susanna Hearn, and had Hannah 1670, Susanna 1672, Wastall 1674, Samuel 1677, Robert 1679, Joseph 1682, Nathaniel 1684, John 1688.

REFERENCES.

NEW HAMPSHIRE.—Runnel's Hist. of Sanbornton, II, 161; Morrison's Hist. of Windham, 403; Lancaster's Hist. of Gilmantown, 258; Coffin's Hist. of Boscawen, 495; Coggswell's Hist. of Henniker, 509; Coggswell's of Nottingham, 659.

OTHER PUBLICATIONS.—Andrews' Hist. of New Britain, Conn., 342; Hinman's Conn. Settlers, 635; Granite Monthly, IX, 185; Chase's Hist. of Haverhill, Mass., 226; Hammatt Papers of Ipswich, Mass., 59; Timlow's Hist. of Southington, Conn., 61; Orcutt's Hist. of New Milford, Conn., 687; Kellogg's White Mem., 108; Kellogg's W. Coggswell Sermon, 10; Knight's Memorial of Frederick Knight; Montague Gen., 462; Otis Gen., (1851); Wentworth Gen., II, 92; Savage's Gen. Dict., vol. I, 422; Coggswell Gen.; Amer. Ancestry, vol. I, 15; IV, 108; VIII, 200; N. E. Hist. and Gen. Reg., IV, 291; V, 207; VI, 101.

COHOON. Hayward's Hist. of Hancock, 452; Stiles' Hist. of Windsor, II, 157.

COIT:—John, of Salem, Mass., was a shipwright. In 1644, he removed to Gloucester, and was selectman there 1648; he removed to New London, Conn., 1651, and died there 1659, leaving John, Joseph, Mary.

REFERENCES:—Caulkins' Hist. of New London, Conn., 275; Hinman's Conn. Settlers, 630; Babson's Hist. of Gloucester, Mass., 71; Bartlett's Wanton Family, 151; Prentice Gen., 280; Chandler Gen., 53; Bill Gen., 180; Walworth Hyde Gen., 1112; Amer. Ancestry, V, 10; Savage's Gen. Dict., vol. I, 422; Coit Gen. (1874) 1895.

COKER:—Robert, of Newbury, came in the "Mary and John," in 1634, died May 16, 1680, aged 74. By wife Catharine, who died May 2, 1678, he had Joseph 1640, Sarah 1643, Hannah 1645, Benjamin 1650.

REFERENCES:—Little Gen., 196; Savage's Gen. Dict., vol. I, 423.

CALBRON or COLBURN:—John, of Dedham, Mass., married 1672, Experience, only daughter of Henry Leland, of Sherborn, and had John 1675, Ebenezer 1677, Deborah 1680, Hannah 1683, Bethia 1686, Daniel 1689, Experience 1692.

WILLIAM COLBURN, of Boston, came in the fleet 1630, with Winthrop, having been active in the engagement to embark 1629. He was chosen deacon and ruling elder of the church; admitted freeman 1630. He died 1662. His surviving children were Sarah Pierce, wife of William, Mary, Turin or Turell, who had been the wife of John Barrell, and Elizabeth Paine.

REFERENCES.

NEW HAMPSHIRE.—Worcester's Hist. of Hollis, 369; Stearn's Hist. of Rindge, 480; Norton's Hist. of Fitzwilliam, 516; Basset's Hist. of Richmond, 369.

OTHER PUBLICATIONS.—Ballou's Hist. of Milford, Mass., 665; Fox's Hist. of Dunstable, Mass., 240; Adams' Fairhaven, 330; Hill's Dedham, Mass., Records, I; Hanson's Hist. of Gardiner, Me., 71; Bangor, Me., Hist. Mag., V, 186; Powers' Hist. of Sangamon County, Ill., 211; Amer. Ancestry, IV, 136, 187; XI, 7; Roe's Sketches of Rose, N. Y., 200; Savage's Gen. Dict., vol. I, 423.

COLBY:—Anthony, of Boston, 1630, probably came with the Winthrop fleet. He was admitted freeman at Cambridge, 1634, removed to Salisbury, and there by wife Susanna, had Isaac 1640, Rebecca 1643, Mary 1647, Thomas 1651, Sarah 1654. He previously had John, bap. 1633. He died February 1, 1661.

REFERENCES.

NEW HAMPSHIRE.—Runnell's Hist. of Sanbornton, II, 161; Hayward's Hist. of Hancock, 452; Eaton's Hist. of Candia, 63; Coggswell's Hist. of Henniker, 516; Chase's Hist. of Chester, 493; Lapham's Hist. of Rumford, Me., 312; Eaton's Hist. of Thomaston, Me., 180; McKeen's Hist. of Bradford, Vt., 282; Hubbard's Hist. of Stanstead County, Canada, 151; Child Gen., 151; Child Gen., 586; Savage's Gen. Dict., vol. I, 444.

COLCORD:—Edward, of Exeter, 1638, removed in 1640 to Dover, 1644 to Hampton, to Saco 1668, and back to Hampton in 1673. He was born about 1617, and died 1682. He had Hannah 1665, Sarah 1668, Mary 1670, Mehitable 1677, Shuah 1660, Deborah 1664, Abigail 1677, Jonathan, Samuel.

REFERENCES:—Hayward's Hist. of Hancock, N. H., 459; Dow's Hist. of Hampton, N. H., 643; Coggswell's Hist. of Nottingham, 198; Dearborn's Hist. of Parsonfield, Me., 370; Savage's Gen. Dict., vol. I, 424.

COLDAM or COLDHAM, was of Lynn, Mass., 1630; a miller, member of artillery company 1645. He had a son Clement, who settled in Gloucester.

REFERENCES:—Ruttenber's Hist. of Orange County, N. Y., 355; Lamb's Hist. of New York City, vol. 1, 521; Alden's Epitaphs, V, 268; Ruggle's Gen.; N. Y. Gen. and Biog. Rec., IV, 161; Colden Gen.

COLDWELL. Amer. Ancestry, VII, 148.

COLE:—Alexander, of Salem, Mass., 1685, a Scot, from Dunbarton, married Bethia, widow if Henry Silsbee, and had Alexander. The father died 1687.

ARTHUR COLE, of Cambridge, Mass., by wife Lydia, had Arthur 1674, Daniel 1676.

DANIEL COLE, of Yarmouth, Mass., removed to Eastham, 1643, was brother of Job; he was the first town clerk, representative to the General Court, 1652, and six years more. By wife Ruth, he had John 1644, Timothy 1646, Hepzibah 1649, Ruth 1651, Israel 1653, James 1655, Mary 1659, William 1663. He died 1694, aged 80.

HENRY COLE, of Sandwich, perhaps went to Middletown, Conn., and there married 1646, Sarah Rusco, probably daughter of William Rusco, and had Henry 1647, James 1650, John 1652, William 1653, Sarah 1654, Samuel 1656, Mary 1658, Joanna 1661, Abigail 1664, Rebecca 1667. He removed to Wallingford, and died there 1676.

HENRY COLE, of Boston, by wife Mary, had Ann

1687, Henry 1689, Mary 1690, and perhaps more.

ISAAC COLE, of Charlestown, Mass., came from Sandwich, County Kent, in 1635, in the "Hercules" with wife Joanna and two children. He had here Abraham 1636, Isaac 1637, Mary 1639, Jacob 1641, Elizabeth 1643. He was admitted freeman 1659, and died 1674.

JACOB COLE, of Charlestown, Mass., by wife Sarah, daughter of John Train, of Watertown, had Sarah, Abigail, Hannah, Jacob 1677. He had been a soldier in Mosley's camp, in the great Narragansett fight, Dec. 19, 1675.

JOHN COLE, of Boston, by wife Joan, had Sarah, born 1642, John 1643, may have removed soon or died.

JOHN COLE, of Hartford, had Sarah, bap. 1647, Mary 1654. He was constable 1657, and admitted freeman the same year; died 1685. In his will he names children: John, of Farmington; Samuel and Nathaniel, of Hartford; Job, in England; Ann and Lydia.

JOHN COLE, of Boston, married 1659, Susanna, daughter of Nicholas Upshur; had John, born 1661.

JOHN COLE, of Hadley, 1666, admitted freeman that year. He is also called Cowles. He was called a farmer, to distinguish him from the other John, the carpenter, who both lived in Hartford, and the object of change in the surname was to prevent confusion, but it increased the trouble. He had John, Samuel and perhaps others.

JOHN COLE, of Boston, married Mary, daughter of the brave John Gallop, killed in the decisive battle of Philip's war; had Samuel 1684, Thomas 1686, Mary 1688.

JOHN COLE, of Gloucester, by wife Mehitable, had Daniel 1669.

RICE or RISE COLE, of Charlestown, 1630, member of the church at Boston, dismissed in 1632 to form the new church at Charlestown, was admitted freeman 1633, and died 1646. His widow is called Harold Colles. In his will he names son John and grandchildren.

ROBERT COLE, of Roxbury, Mass., came in the fleet with Winthrop, and was admitted freeman 1630. He went to Providence, R. I., and became one of the founders of the Baptist Church there. By wife Mary, he had John, Daniel, Nathaniel, Robert, Sarah, Ann, Elizabeth. He died 1654.

ROBERT COLE, of Boston, by wife Ann, had daughter Staines 1681, son Staines 1682, Richard 1685.

SAMPSON COLE, of Boston, 1673, married Elizabeth, daughter of Edward Weeden, and had Elizabeth 1679, David 1683, Jonathan 1686.

SAMUEL COLE, of Boston, came inthe fleet with Winthrop, and with his wife Ann, formed the church as Nos. 40 and 41 of the members; admitted freeman 1630. The first house of entertainment in Boston was opened by him 1633. His will, 1666, mentions John, Elizabeth and Elisha.

WILLIAM COLE, of Boston, by wife Martha, had William 1687, and others.

REFERENCES.

MASSACHUSETTS.—Sewall's Hist. of Woburn, 605; Winsor's Hist. of Duxbury, 247; Wyman's Charlestown, Mass., Gens. vol. I, 228; Deane's Hist. of Scituate, 238; Freeman's Hist. of Cape Cod, II, 373; Kingman's Hist. of North Bridgewater, 477; Mitchell's Hist. of Bridgewater, 137; Rich's Hist. of Truro, 523; Davis' Landmarks of Plymouth, 66; Brown's Bedford, Mass., Families, 7; Barry's Hist. of Framingham, 213; Benedict's Hist. of Sutton, 627.

MAINE.—Thurston's Hist. of Winthrop, 178; Lapham's Hist. of Woodstock, 195; Lapham's Hist. of Paris; Lapham's Hist. of Norway, 483; Corliss' Hist. of North Yarmouth, 965; Bangor Hist. Mag., IV, 216.

NEW HAMPSHIRE.—Dow's Hist. of Hampton, 644; Cochrane's Hist. of Antrim, 431; Bassett's Hist. of Richmond, 370.

NEW YORK.—Boyd's Hist. of Consensus, 149; Cleveland's Hist. of Yates County, 203, 496; Clute's Hist. of Staten Island, 356; Gummer's Hist. of Deerport, 78; Schoonmaker's Hist. of Kingston, 475; Smith's Hist. of Dutchess County, 497.

RHODE ISLAND.—Austin's R. I. Gen. Dict., 50; Austin's Ancestral Dict., 15; Narragansett Hist. Reg., II, 179; Updyke's Narragansett Church, R. I., 105.

OTHER PUBLICATIONS.—Timlow's Hist. of Southington, Conn., 64; Hinman's Conn. Settlers, 658; Richmond, Va., Standard, II, 4, 31, 32; Littell's Passaic Valley Gens., 80; Clement's Newtown, N. J., Settlers; Heminway's Vt. Gaz., V; Hubbard's Hist. of Stanstead County, Can., 197; Leland Gen., 253; Pope Gen.; Ressaguin Gen. 55; Salisbury Gen.; Guild's Stile's Gen., 325; Barton Gen., part II, 143; Amer. Ancestry, vol. I, 15; II, 25; III, 11; VII, 274; VIII, 58, 144; IX, 74; X, 46, 68, 196; Cole Gen., 1876.

COLES:—Robert, of Warwick, R. I., came with Winthrop's fleet to Ipswich, Mass., was admitted freeman 1631. He was at Providence Plantations, R. I., with Roger Williams; was one of the received purchasers of Warwick, R. I. He died in 1654. He married Mary, supposed to have been the sister of Christopher Hawxhurst, and after the death of Robert, to have married Matthias Harvey and removed to Long Island. By his wife Mary, Robert Coles had Daniel, John, Deliverance, Ann, Robert and Sarah.

REFERENCES:—Thompson's Hist. of Long Island, vol. I, 510; Davis' Hist. of Wallingford, Conn., 719; Middlefield, Conn., Hist.; Shourd's Fenwick Colony, N. J., 64; Slaughter's St. Mark's Parish, Va., 186; Richmond, Va., Standard, III, 26; Meade's Old Families of Va., II, 15; Amer. Ancestry, IX, 77, 80; X, 82; Cole Gen.

COLESWORTHY. N. E. Hist. and Gen. Reg., XV, 330.

COLEMAN:—Thomas, of Newbury, from Marlborough, in Wiltshire, arrived at Boston, June 3, 1635, in the "James," from Southampton, came out under contract with Sir Richard Saltonstall and others, to keep their cattle, in which he was negligent and unfaithful as the Court ruled, yet was admitted freeman May 17, 1637, by wife Susanna, who died Nov. 17, 1650, had Tobias, born 1638; Benjamin, May 1, 1640; Joseph, Dec. 2, 1642; John, 1644; Isaac, Feb. 20, 1647, before mentioned; and Joanna; removed to Hampton, married July 11, 1651, Mary, widow of Edmund Johnson, who died Jan. 30, 1663; and he took for third wife Margery, daughter of Philip Fowler (widow of Thomas Rowell, of Andover, who had been widow of first Christopher Osgood, of Andover). He removed to Nantucket before 1663, there died 1682, aged 83. Perhaps Susanna, who died Jan. 2, 1643, was his daughter. Coffin says he spelled his name "Coultman," but was probably Coaleman, or Coulman.

THOMAS COLEMAN, of Wethersfield 1639, representative 1652 and '6, removed to Hadley, freeman 1661, there died 1674, leaving good estates to two sons before mentioned and three daughters of whom Sarah married the second Richard Treat, one married Philip Davis, of Hartford; and Deborah married Daniel Gunn, of Milford. Part of the property was at Evesham, Worcestershire, England. His second wife was widow Frances Welles, by whom he had only Deborah. Mrs. Welles had Thomas, John, Mary, who married Jonathan Gilbert, before her marriage with Coleman.

REFERENCES.

MASSACHUSETTS.—Stone's Hist. of Hubbardston, 204; Temple's Hist. of Whately, 27; Swift's Barnstable Families, vol. I, 195; Stearn's Hist. of Ashburnham, 639; Freeman's Hist. of Cape Cod, II, 286; Judd's Hist. of Hadley, 464.

OTHER PUBLICATIONS.—Boyd's Hist. of Consensus, N. Y., 149; Cleveland's Hist. of Yates County, N. Y., 246; Egle's Hist. of Lebanon County, Pa., 237; Slaughter's St. Mark's Parish, Va., 128; Slaughter's Bristol Parish, Va., 202; Meade's Old Families of Va.; Sedgwick's Hist. of Sharon, Conn., 72; Paxton's Marshall Gen., 130, 236; Robertson's Pocahontas' Descendants; Cooley's Trenton, N. J., Gens., 41; Power's Hist. of Sangamon Co., Ill., 209; Round's Hist. of Sanbornton, N. H., II, 176; Ely Gen., 23, 47; Savage's Gen. Dict., vol. I, 430; N. E. Hist. and Gen. Reg., XII, 129; XVI, 141; Coleman Gen. (1867).

COLEY:—Samuel, of Milford, 1639, one of the first settlers, joined the church 1640, married Ann, daughter of James Prudden, had Peter, baptized 1641; Abilene 1643, Samuel 1646, Sarah 1648, Mary 1651, Hannah 1654, and Thomas 1657; and died in 1684. In his will of 1678, and in the will of his widow 1689, the same seven children are named. Abilene married Japhet Chapin, Sarah married a Baldwin; Mary married first Peter Simpson and second John Stream, and Hannah married Joseph Garnsey.

REFERENCES:—Schenk's Hist. of Fairfield, Conn., 362; Power's Hist. of Sangamon County, Ill., 210; Amer. Ancestry, VIII, 131.

COLIE. Amer. Ancestry, VI, 30.

COLFAX:—William, of Wethersfield, Conn., 1645. had several children born there and died before 1661.

COLGATE. Norwich, Conn., Jubilee, 200; Whittemore's Founders and Builders of the Oranges.

COLGRAVE. Amer. Ancestry, II, 25.

COLLAMORE, COLLEMORE or CULLIMORE.

COLLAMORE:—Anthony, of Scituate, nephew of Peter, born in England, married 1666, Sarah daughter of Isaac Chittenden, had Mary, born 1667, Peter 1671, Sarah 1673, Martha 1677 and Elizabeth 1679; was captain of militia, master of a vessel, and perished by wreck Dec. 16, 1693, on a ledge, still called Collamer's, near his home. Mary married Robert Stetson.

ISAAC COLLAMORE, Boston, 1636, shipwright, written Cullimer, in our old book of possessions, and Colimer, in Colonial Records, in 1638, had grant of lot at Braintree for four heads: freeman 1643; had wife Margaret, who died Dec. 13, 1651; and he married Jan. 22, 1652, Margery Page.

JAMES COLLAMORE, of Salem 1668.

PETER COLLAMORE, of Scituate, married 1695, Abigail, daughter of Tobias Davis, of Roxbury.

REFERENCES:—Eaton's Hist. of Thomaston, Me., 181;

Deane's Hist. of Scituate, Mass., 239; Savage's Gen. Dict., vol. I, 432.

COLLANE:—Matthew, of Isle of Shoals, died about Dec. 25, 1650; and the Court at Kittery, appointed March 11, following Teague Mohonas admor.

REFERENCES:—Savage's Gen. Dict., vol. I, 432.

COLLAR:—John, of Cambridge, by wife Hannah, probably daughter of James Cutler, had John, born Mar. 6, 1661, and Thomas Dec. 14, 1663; perhaps others; as probably in Boston, Jane July 20, 1681. Hannah, probably his daughter, married June 16, 1679, James Cutting.

REFERENCES:—Savage's Gen. Dict., vol. I, 433; Barry's Hist. of Framingham, Mass., 214; Boyd's Hist. of Consensus, N. Y., 150.

COLLIER:—Ambrose, embarked at Barbados, for Boston, March 11, 1679, in the society.

JOSEPH COLLIER, of Salisbury, had Mary, born April 9, 1662, who probably died young, and he removed to Hartford, about 1666, died Nov. 16, 1691, leaving Joseph aged 23; Mary (Phelps), 22, Sarah 18, Elizabeth 16, Abel 14, John 12, Abigail 9, Susanna 7, and Ann 4½. His wife was, I presume, Elizabeth, daughter of Robert Sanford, of Hartford.

THOMAS COLLIER, of Hingham, 1635, freeman 1646, died April 6, 1647, the date of his will as in Genealogical Register, VII, 173-4, appears (tho. IX, 172, the abstract of record of death is one year earlier), aged 71, leaves wife and daughter Susanna, son Moses and Thomas.

WILLIAM COLLIER, of Duxbury, a merchant of London, came 1633, having for several years acted as one of the adventurers, and had so generous a spirit, as not to be content with making profit by the enterprise of pilgrims, unless he shared their hardships. Whether he brought wife from home, or had any here, is doubtful; but four daughters came, of excellent character, Sarah, who married March 15, or May, 1634, Love Brewster; Rebecca, married March 15, or May, 1634, Job Cole; Mary, married April 1, 1635, Thomas Prence, afterwards the governor and surveyor to 1676, being his second wife, but tradition makes her widow of Samuel Freeman; and Elizabeth, married Nov. 2, 1637, Constant Southworth. He was assistant 28 years, between 1634 and 1665, and one of the two plenipotentiaries at the first meeting of the Cong. of Unit. Col., 1643, among the first purchasers of Dartmouth, 1652, and died 1670.

REFERENCES:—Savage's Gen. Dict., vol. I, 432; Winsor's Hist. Duxbury, Mass., 248; Rose's Sketches of Rose, N. Y., 291; Munsell's Albany, N. Y., Coll., IV, 109; Hinman's Conn. Settlers, 661; Dudley's Arch. and Gen. Coll. plate, 4; Amer. Ancestry, vol. I, 16; II, 25.

COLLEY. Eaton's Thomaston, Me., 181.

COLLICOTT or COLLACOT:—Edward Collicott, Hampton 1642; Historical Collections, N. H., II, 214.

RICHARD COLLICOTT, of Dorchester, freeman Mar. 4, 1633, was sergeant in the Pequot war artillery company 1637,selectman 1636,representative 1637,removed before 1656 to Boston, was representative for Falmouth 1669, and Saco 1672, died July 7,1686,aged 83,as his gravestone on Copp's Hill reports. His will of April 23, preceding, is good for names of grandchildren who might be lost for want of it. His first wife Joanna, died Aug. 5, 1640, and by another wife Thomasin, who survived him, he had daughter Experience, born Sept. 29, 1641, son

Dependence July 5, 1643, who died before his father; and Preserved, baptized Jan. 28, 1649; Elizabeth and Bethia. Experience married Richard Miles; Elizabeth married Richard Hall; and Bethia married July 21, 1692, Rev. Daniel Gookin, as his second wife. Winthrop II, 336; Hutchinson, II, 515. The record gives the name Colcott sometimes.

REFERENCES:—Savage's Gen. Dict., vol. I, 432.

COLLINS:—Anthony, of New Hampshire, of the Grand Jury, 1684. The death, March 22, 1700, of aged widow Collins is mentioned in Pike's Ms. Journal.

BENJAMIN COLLINS, of Salisbury, married Nov. 5, 1668, Martha, daughter of John Eaton, had Mary, born Jan. 8, 1670, John 1673, Samuel Jan., 1676, Ann April 1, 1679, Benjamin May 29, 1681, and Ephraim Sept. 30, 1683, and the father died Dec. 10, following.

BENJAMIN COLLINS, of Lynn, freeman 1691, married Sept. 25, 1673, Priscilla Kirtland, had Susanna, born July 9, 1674, William Oct. 14, 1676, died at 12 days; the mother died soon after, and he married Sept. 5, 1677, widow Elizabeth Putnam, had Priscilla, May 2, 1679, Elizabeth Jan. 3, 1682, and Benjamin Dec. 5, 1684.

BERNARD COLLINS, of New London, drowned 1660.

CHRISTOPHER COLLINS, of Boston, had in 1640, grant of lot for two heads at Braintree; Saco 1660, was constable of Scarborough 1664, there died 1666, aged 58, under some suspicion of murder by a neighbor, who on trial was acquitted and the jury say, "the said Collins was slain by misadventure and culpable of his own death." He left good estates and son Christopher and Moses. See the valua. History of Scarborough, by Wm. S. Southgate, in Maine Historical Collections, III. His widow Jane returned good inventory of 422 pounds sterling, 14 shillings, including 23 cows.

DANIEL COLLINS, of Enfield, 1683, died May 3, 1690, aged about 42, leaving widow Sarah, daughter of Thomas Tibbals, who next year married Joseph Warriner, and children Daniel, Patience, Nathan born 1683, and Sarah 1686.

EBENEZER COLLINS, of New Haven, married about 1683, Ann, widow of John Trowbridge, daughter of Gov. Leete, had Mehitable, and a posthumous child.

EDWARD COLLINS, of Cambridge, 1638, freeman May 18, 1640, was deacon representative 1654-70; except '61, lived many years on plantation of Gov. Cradock, at Medford, and at last purchased it, sold to Richard Russell 1600 acres, and other parts to others. Mather, Magn., IV, 8; in his whole chapter on the twin sons John and Nathaniel, does not equal in value the few lines of 'Mitchell, from whom we learn, his wife was Martha, and child Daniel, about 9 years old when his parents united in his church possibly father of Phebe, who died at Cambridge, Jan. 5, 1654; lived at Koenigsberg, in Prussia; John, Harvard College 1649; Samuel, lived in Scotland for some years; and Sibyl, wife of Rev. John Whiting, all born in England; beside these, Martha born Sept. 1639; Nathaniel, March 7, 1643, Harvard College 1660; Abigail, Sept. 1644; and Edward 1646, all baptized here. Abigail married probably in 1663, John Willet, son of Capt. Thomas, who died Feb. 2, 1664; and Martha, it is thought, married Rev. Joshua Moody. The patriarch died at Charlestown, April 9, 1689, aged about eighty-six.

ELIZUR COLLINS, of Warwick, 1644, son of that widow Ann Collins, who married John Smyth, President of the College of R. I., 1649. On the death of his mother's husband she and her son had the estate of Smyth. Of him I learn, that, in 1667, his age was 45; had married Sarah Wright, who brought him Thomas, born Oct. 26, 1664; Elizur June 11, 1666; William March 8, 1668; Ann, March 4, 1670, who married Jan. 7, 1686, the second John Potter, and Elizabeth Nov. 1, 1672.

FRANCIS COLLINS, of Salem, 1637, had Hannah, who married June 30, though another account says Jan. 27, 1669, John Brown of Salem; asked permission in 1687, on the strength of his half century's residence to keep a house of entertainment and ten years later a widow Collins, probably his, of thte same town, had the same leave.

HENRY COLLINS, of Lynn, came in the Abigail, 1635, aged 29, with wife Ann, 30; and children Henry 5, John 3, Margery 2, and four servants, says the London custom house record; freeman March 9, 1637, died Feb. 1687, leaving Henry, John and Joseph.

HUGH COLLINS, of Norwich, or perhaps Lyme, a devisee in the will of young Joshua Uncas, the Mohegan sachem, for which see Geneal. Reg., XIII, 236; but I find nothing more.

JAMES COLLINS, Salem, a shipmaster, lost at sea, 1685.

JOHN COLLINS, of Gloucester, may have had grant of land at Salem, 1643, had wife Joan, son John, born perhaps in England; James, born Sept. 16, 1643, Mary March 8, 1646. Selectman 1646 and '70, beside often intermediate years freeman 1646. Died March 25, 1675, and his widow died May 25, 1695. Joan, probably his daughter married Dec. 25, 1661, Robert Scamp, and died Nov. 9, 1663, Mary, probably another daughter, married June 15, 1665, Josiah Elwell.

JOHN COLLINS, of Boston, brother of Edward, artillery company 1644, had besides eldest son John, by wife Susanna, Thomas, baptized April 5, 1646, 7 months old, and at same time, Susanna, about 3 years and 12 days old; and Elizabeth April 16, 1648, about 8 days old, was a shoemaker, and died March 29, 1670. In 1640, he had grant of lot at Braintree, for three heads. His daughter Susanna, married March 25, 1662, Thomas Walker.

JOHN COLLINS, of New London, 1680-3.

JOSEPH COLLINS, of Eastham, married March 20, 1672, Duty Knowles, had Sarah, born Jan. 2, 1673; John Dec. 18, 1674, Lydia, July, 1676, Joseph, June, 1678, Hannah, Feb., 1680, Jonathan, Aug. 20, 1682, Jane, March 3, 1684, Benjamin, Feb. 6, 1687, and James, March 10, 1689, died at three weeks.

PETER COLLINS, of New London, 1650, is not thought to be son of any in our country, nor to have had wife or children at his death, May or June, 1655, dividing his property among John Gager and other neighbor.

PETER COLLINS, of Pemaquid, in 1674, swore fidelity to Massachusetts.

SAMUEL COLLINS, of New London, 1680-3; perhaps removed to Lyme, married Aug. 6, 1695, Rebecca, widow of Joseph Hunt, of Duxbury, who died June 15, preceding.

THOMAS COLLINS, of Boston, 1677, merchant.

REFERENCES.

MAINE.—Hatch's Hist. of Industry, 542; Farrow's Hist. of Isleborough, 189; Eaton's Hist. of Thomaston, 182.

MASSACHUSETTS.—Page's Hist. of Hardwick, 353; Paige's Hist. of Cambridge, 511; Rich's Hist. of Truro, 522; Wyman's Charlestown, Mass., Gens., vol. I, 231; Davis' Landmarks of Plymouth, 68; Babson's Hist. of Gloucester, 72; Freeman's Hist. of Cape Cod, II, 373, 598.

NEW HAMPSHIRE.—Norton's Hist. of Fitzwilliam, 518; Hayward's Hist. of Hancock, 460; Coggswell's Hist. of Nottingham, 355; Washington, N. H., Hist., 344.

CONNECTICUT.—Dodd's Hist. of East Haven, 114; Orcutt's Hist. of New Milford, 688; Stiles' Hist. of Windsor, II, 158; Hinman's Conn. Settlers, 664.

OTHER PUBLICATIONS.—Hough's Hist. of Lewis County, N. Y., 230; Cleveland's Hist. of Yates County, N. Y., 317; Roe's Hist. of Rose, N. Y., 269; Irish Hist. of Richmond, R. I., 91; Austin's R. I. Gen. Dict., 51; Clement's Newtown, N. J., Settlers; Putnam's Hist. Mag. V, 30; Hubbard's Hist. of Stanstead County, Can., 200; Huntington Gen., 129; Hall's Genealogical Notes, 76; Goodwin's Foote Gen., 240; Walworth's Hyde Gen., vol. I, 297; Amer. Ancestry, vol. I, 16; II, 26; IV, 189; VII, 172; IX, 184, 196, 199; X, 146; XI, 161; N. E. Hist. and Gen. Reg., V, 95; XI, 335; XVI, 141; Collins' Gen.

COLLIN. Amer. Ancestry, II, 26; Collins' Hist. of Hillsdale, N. Y., 16; App. I.

COLLINGSWOOD. Davis' Landmarks of Plymouth, 68.

COLLIS. Hyde's Brimfield, Mass., 391; Temple's Hist. of Palmer, Mass., 433.

COLLYER. Baird's Hist. of Rye, N. Y., 407.

COLLISHAW:—William, of Boston, 1633, came, possibly at the same time as Cotton, with wife Ann, and Sarah Morrice, her daughter, for the three were received into our church the month following the admission of our teacher; freeman March 4, 1634. No more is known.

REFERENCES:—Savage's Gen. Dict., vol. I.

COLMAN:—Edward, of Boston, married Oct. 27, 1648, Margaret, daughter of Thomas Lumbard of Barnstable, had Elizabeth Jan. 28, 1652; Mary, Sept. 12, 1653, died under four years; Martha, Aug. 8, 1655; James, Jan. 31, 1657; and other children, certainly Abigail, named in will of grandfather Lumbard.

JOSEPH COLMAN, of Scituate, shoemaker, came in 1635 or '36, from Sandwich, in Kent, with wife Sarah, and four children, was first at Charlestown, but went, 1638 to Scituate, thence removed, perhaps, to Norwich, before 1690; had at Sandwich, Joseph, Zechariah, Thomas and several daughters.

WILLIAM COLMAN, of Boston, came with wife Elizabeth, in the "Arabella," 1671, from London, had Mary, born Dec. 3, 1671, and Benjamin, Oct. 19, 1673, Harvard College, 1692. They were from Satterly, in Norfolk, and perhaps brought John. Five of this name, in 1834, had been graduates at Harvard and nine at other N. E. Colleges.

REFERENCES:—Emery's Penn. Newbury, Mass., 151; Deane's Hist. of Scituate, Mass., 241; Essex Inst. Hist. Coll., XX, 226; Hinman's Conn. Settlers, 658; Dawson Gen., 155; Thurston Gen., (1892) 80; Savage's Gen. Dict., vol. 1, 437; N. E. Hist. and Gen. Reg., XII, 129; XVI, 141.

COLESWORTHY. N. E. Hist. and Gen. Reg., XV, 330.

COLQUHOUN. Richmond Standard, II, 32.

COLQUITT. Goode Gen., 98.

COLSON:—Adam, of Reading, an early settler, married Sept. 7, 1668, Mary, had Josiah, born March 6, 1673, died in few months; Elizabeth, Oct. 9, 1676; Lydia, March 31, 1680; and David, April 26, 1682; and died March 1, 1687.

NATHANIEL COLSON, of Newport, by wife Susanna, had Ann, born June 8, 1678.

REFERENCES:—Eaton's Thomaston, Me., 182; Millikin's Narraguages Valley, Me., 2.

COLT or COULT.

COLT:—John, of Windsor, 1668, lived to old age, had Sarah, baptized at Hartford, says Hinman, Feb. 7, 1647, and several sons of whom one or more settled at Lyme. In his second edition 672-8, Hinman gives many names of descendants yet with no precision of line. But the original is quite mythical. The settler was born in Colchester, Co. Essex, about 50 minutes from London, came to Dorchester, when about 11 years old, removed to Hartford about 1638, as says the book, with no inherent probability, but it is sure to encourage distrust of such tale, that he is made great-great-great-grandson of a peer of England, who was dispossessed of his estate, etc. Such examples may, I hope, be shunned and not imitated. Mr. Hinman had too respectable a name to encourage the relations of such old wives' inventions.

REFERENCES:—Wadsworth Hyde Gen., 101; Loomis' Gen. Female Branches, 149; Orcutt's Hist. of Torrington, Conn., 657; Tuttle Gen., 182; Hinman's Conn. Settlers, 672; Savage's Gen. Dict., vol. I, 437.

COLTMAN:—John, of Wethersfield, 1645, a schoolmaster, who had been a servant with Leonard Chester, or his widow Mary, who in her will of Nov. 20, 1688, then widow of Hon. Richard Russell, remembered his servant near fifty years before. His daughter Mary married May 1, 1684, John Nash of Norwalk, and died about 1688, or '9, leaving widow and three daughters.

REFERENCES:—Savage's Gen. Dict., 438.

COLTON:—George, of Springfield, 1644, came from Sutton Coldfield, as is said, Co. Warwick, about 8 minutes from Birmingham, married Deborah Gardner, had Isaac, born 1646; Ephraim, 1648; Mary, or Mercy, Sept. 22, 1649; Thomas, 1651; Sarah, 1653; Deborah, 1655; Hepzibah, 1657; John, 1659; and Benjamin, 1661; died young; was freeman 1665, a grantee of Suffield, 1670, called "quartermaster" in the record report 1669-71, and '7. His wife died Sept. 5, 1689, and he married 1692, Lydia, daughter of deacon Samuel Wright, widow of John Lamb, who had been widow of John Norton, and before him of Lawrence Bliss; died Dec. 17, 1699.

REFERENCES:—Cothren's Hist. of Woodbury, Conn., II, 1478, 1605; Adams' Hist. of Fairhaven, Vt., 327; Hinman's Conn. Settlers, 678; Stiles' Hist. of Windsor, Conn., II, 159; Long Meadow, Mass., Centen. 27; Chandler Gen., 83; Ely Gen., 46, 101; Wentworth Gen., II, 55; Morris and Flint Gen., 39; Amer. Ancestry, II, 26; Savage's Gen. Dict., vol. I, 438; N. E. Hist. and Gen. Reg., XXXIII, 202, 319, 416; XXXIV, 31, 187.

COLVILLE. Amer. Ancestry, II, 26.

COLVIN. Williams' Hist. of Danby, Vt., 125; Rose's Sketches of Rose, N. Y., 30; Austin's R. I. Gen Dict., 52; Wight Gen., 175; Amer. Ancestry, vol. I, 16.

COLWELL:—Robert of Providence, R. I., admitted freeman 1658.

SAMUEL COLWELL, embarked at Barbadoes, March 21, 1678.

REFERENCES:—Mitchell's Hist. of Bridgewater, Mass., 138; Austin's R. I. Gen. Dict. 58; Amer. Ancestry, IV, 104.

COMBERBACH.

THOMAS COMBERBACH, came from Norwich, 1637, aged 16, in the employment of Michael Metcalf. Savage's Gen. Dict. vol. I.

COMBS, COMBE, COOMES, or COOMBS.

COMBS:—George, of Charlestown, died July 27, 1659, was perhaps only a transient man.

JOHN COMBS, Plymouth, freeman 1633, is called gentleman, next year had wife Sarah, and son Francis, seems to have died before 1645, when William Spooner, who was his servant in 1642, was by the Court ordered to have charge of the children of Combs, and in 1666, the son Francis got grant of land in his father's right.

JOHN COMBS, Boston, cooper, married Feb. 24, 1662, Elizabeth, widow of Thomas Barlow, had Elizabeth, born Nov. 30, 1662; John, July 20, 1664, probably the freeman 1690; and Mary, Nov. 28, 1666; and he died May, 16, 1668. He spent much of Barlow's estate and the Court ordered provision for Barlow's only child and his widow who married John Warren as his second wife and died early in 1672.

JOHN COMBS, Northampton, had there twelve children, removed to Springfield, and had one more, born 1714. Sometimes this name has "e" final, instead of "s"; and other variations.

REFERENCES:—Temple's Hist. of North Brookfield, Mass., 556; Cochrane's Hist. of Antrim, N. H., 431.

COMEE or COMY.

COMEE:—David, of Woburn, had Mary, born Jan. 30, 1663; removed to Concord, 1664, died 1690. His daughter Mary, married May 24, 1688, Joshua Kibby. This may be the same name as the next.

REFERENCES:—Herrick's Hist. of Gardiner, Mass., 340; Hudson's Hist. of Lexington, Mass., 340.

JOHN COMER, Weymouth, perhaps the same as the preceding, by wife Sarah, had Sarah, born July 10, 1662.

JOHN COMER, Newport, a Baptist preacher 1656.

JOHN COMER, Boston, by wife Elinor, had John, born Aug. 12, 1674; William, Nov. 28, 1678; Thomas Sept. 6, 1680, and Mary Dec. 15, 1685.

RICHARD COMER, perhaps of Ipswich 1651, married a daughter of Humphrey Gilbert.

REFERENCES:—Cleveland's Hist. of Yates County, N. Y., 720; Savage's Gen. Dict. vol. I, 437.

COMEGGS. Old Kent, Md., 224.

COMERFORD. Hist. Sanbornton, N. H., 177.

COMERY. Eaton's Hist. of Warren, Me., 520.

COMINGS. Hodgman's Westford, 443.

COMMONS. Young's Wayne, Ind.

COMLY. Martindale's Byberry, 250.

COMPTON.

COMPTON:—John, of Roxbury, freeman Sept. 3,

1634, had wife Susanna, in Roxbury church record, spelled Cumpton, as also in list of freeman; removed to Boston, was disarmed with the majority in 1637. Winth. I, 248. Snow's Hist. 108. His daughter Abigail, married Jan. 30, 1652, Joseph Brisco, but the father was probably dead though his widow lived to Nov. 1664.

WILLIAM COMPTON, Ipswich, bought land in 1662, of Daniel Ladd.

REFERENCES:—Savage's Gen. Dict., vol. I, 439.

COMSTOCK.

COMSTOCK:—Christopher, of Fairfield, 1661, married Oct. 6, 1663, Hannah, daughter of Richard Platt, of Milford, had Daniel, born July 21, 1664; Hannah. July 15, 1666; Abigail, January 27, 1669, died at 20 years; Mary, Feb. 19, 1671; Elizabeth Oct. 7, 1674; Mercy, Nov. 12, 1676; and Samuel, Feb. 6, 1680; had good estate, kept a tavern, and died Dec. 28, 1702.

JOHN COMSTOCK, Weymouth, 1639, indenture served of Henry Russell, sat down at Saybrook, E. part, now Lyme, had Abigail, born Apr. 12, 1662; Elizabeth June 9, 1665; William, Jan. 9, 1669; Christian, Dec. 11, 1671; Hannah, Feb. 22, 1673; John, Sept. 30, 1676; and Samuel July 6, 1678. Abigail married June 24, 1679, William Peake.

SAMUEL COMSTOCK, of Wethersfield, 1648.

WILLIAM COMSTOCK, of Wethersfield, came from England, and there lived several years with wife Elizabeth, and probably son William and Daniel, removed 1649, to New London. His son William, had William, left widow Abigail, who married a Huntley of Lyme.

REFERENCES.

CONNECTICUT.—Sedgwick's Hist. of Sharon, 273; Orcutt's Hist. of New Milford,689; Hinman's Conn. Settlers, 682; Hall's Hist. of Norwalk, 185; Caulkins' Hist. of New London, 205.

MASSACHUSETTS.—Ballou's Hist. of Milford, 667.

NEW HAMPSHIRE.—Hayward's Hist. of Gilsum, 289; Hayward's Hist. of Hancock, 461; Wheeler's Hist. of Newport, 348. Bassett's Hist. of Richmond, 378.

OTHER PUBLICATIONS.—Turner's Philip Purchase, N. Y., 223; Cleveland's Hist. Yates County, N. Y., 460; Richardson's Hist. of Woonsocket, R. I., 242; Austin's R. I. Gen. Dict., 280; Austin's Ancestral Dict., 16; Bulkley's Brown Mem., 19; Bangor Hist. Mag., IV, 125; Champion Gen.; Morris Gen.; Amer. Ancestry, vol. I, 16; V, 88; VII, 155; XI, 202; Savage's Gen. Dict., vol. I, 439.

CONNABLE. Connable Gen.

CONARD. Conard Gen.

CONARY. Eaton's Hist. of Thomaston, Me., 184.

CONDE. Amer. Ancestry, vol. I, 16.

CONDIT. Dodd Gen., 91, 182; Condit Gen., 1885; Whittemore's Founders and Builders of the Oranges, N. J.

CONANT.

CONANT:—Christopher, of Plymouth, 1623, came in the Ann, had share in division of land next year but was gone in 1627, perhaps to Cape Ann, for he had not shared in the division of cattle that year. But if he had gone home, he must have come back to our country, for he was on the first jury for criminal trial here, impanneled for the case of Walter Palmer, for manslaughter, Nov. 1630, having been in 1623, at Plymouth, next at Nantasket, thence removed to Cape Ann, there resided between one and two years and removed to Naumkeag, about 1627. He was son of Richard and Agnes, brother it is said of Dr. John of the great Assembly of Divines at Westminster, born in the hundred of E. Budleigh, baptized at the parish church of the same, in Devonshire, April 9, 1593; appointed 1625, governor, agent, or superintendent for the Dorchester projector of the plantation as Endicott, who superseded him, was, 1629, for the Governor and Comptroller of Mass. before the coming of Winthrop, the first Charter Governor in the country. (Felt. I, 106; Hubbard, 109, 10.) Gibbs says his grandfather John, was of French, i. e. Norman, extraction, his ancestors for many generations having been at Gittisham, between Honiton and Ottery St. Mary's. He requested to be freeman Oct. 19,1630, was admitted May 18 following, was representative at the first general Court of Mass., 1634, died Nov. 19, 1679, in 87th year at Beverly (which he earnestly desired to be named Budleigh). Young, Chronicle 24, gives him four sons, I think, he had five; but even the assiduous fondness of Felt, in a Memorandum of great diligence filling fourteen pages of Geneal. Reg., II, has not furnished complete family account. His abstract of the will, made March 1, 1678, refers to son Exercise and children; son Lot's ten children;grandchildren John,son of Roger;grandchild Joshua Conant, whose father may have been John, or Roger; daughters Elizabeth Conant, probably never married; Mary, widow of the second William Dodge, and her five children; Sarah, and her children John and four daughters; a grandchild Rebecca Conant, whose father may have been either of the sons, John or Roger, beside cousin Mary, wife of Hilliard Verin, but whose daughter is unknown; Adoniram Veren, and his sister Hannah, with her two children and three daughters of his cousin James Mason, deceased and it is equally unknown who she was. Of Exercise, perhaps the third son, born at Cape Ann, about 1636, baptized Dec. 24, 1637; Joshua; and Lot, above, is all that is known to me; John was of Beverly church, 1671, probably died before his father; Roger, the first born child at Salem, is spoken next. His wife Sarah, but neither he nor wife united early with the church.

REFERENCES.

MASSACHUSETTS.—Wyman's Charlestown Gens., vol. I, 232; Stone's Hist. of Beverly, Mass., 18; Stearn's Hist. Ashburnham, 641; Mitchell's Hist. of Bridgewater, 138; Herrick's Hist. of Gardner, 342; Paige's Hist. of Hardwick, 354.

OTHER PUBLICATIONS:—Cochrane's Hist. of Antrim, 434; Worcester's Hist. of Hollis, N. H., 370; Eaton's Hist. of Thomaston, Me., 182; Hollister's Hist. of Pawlet, Vt., 180; Powers' Hist. of Sangamon County, Ill., 210; Whitman Gen., 101; Hinman's Conn. Settlers, 691; Amer. Ancestry, IV, 101, 111, 167; VII, 106; Savage's Gen. Dict., vol. I, 440; Conant Chart, 1884; Conant Gen. 1887.

CONDY.

CONDY:—Samuel, of Marblehead, 1668-74.

THOMAS CONDY, a soldier in Turner's company, Feb. 1676, probably of Boston.

WILLIAM CONDY, of New London, had a lot granted 1664, was master of a vessel in the West Indies trade, married Mary, daughter of Ralph Parker, had Richard, William, Ebenezer and Ralph, all baptized March 23,

1673; removed to Boston, was master of a vessel going to London, in 1679, taken by the Algerines; died Aug. 26, 1685.

REFERENCES:—Caulkin's Hist. of New London, Conn. 353; Pearson's Schenectady, N. Y., Families, 47.

CONDON. Eaton's Hist. of Thomaston, Me., 183.

CONCKLIN.

CONCKLIN:—Ananias, of Salem, 1638, freeman May 18, 1642, had Lewis, baptized April 30, 1643; Jacob and Elizabeth, March 18, 1649; removed to Long Island.

JEREMIAH CONCKLIN, of Long Island, married Mary, daughter of Lyon Gardiner, died 1712, in 78th year.

JOHN CONKLIN, of Salem, perhaps, at least he is in Felt's list, as having grant of land 1640, and he and Ananias, probably his sons were there in 1645; was of Southold, L. I., admitted freeman of Conn. 1662, as was John Jr., perhaps his son.

REFERENCES:—Savage's Gen. Dict., vol. I, 440; Amer. Ancestry, X, 63.

CONKLIN. Cleveland's Yates County, N. Y., 491; Hedge's Hist. of East Hampton, N. Y., Address; Littell's Passaic Valley, N. J., 83, 499; Pompey, N. Y., Reunion, 288; Powers' Hist. of Sangamon County, Ill., 215; Frey Gen., 34; Amer. Ancestry, vol. I, 16; II, 26; X, 63; Savage's Gen. Dict., vol. I, 441.

CONKLING. Essex Inst. Coll., XXXI, 43; Sedgwick's Hist. of Sharon, Conn., 73; Hays' Wells Gen., 89.

CONN. Cochrane's Hist. Antrim, N. H., 435; Stearns' Hist. of Ashburnham, Mass., 643.

CONNABLE. Cunnabell Gen.

CONE:—Daniel, Haddam, by wife Mehitable, daughter of Jared Spencer, had Ruth, born Jan. 7, 1663; Hannah, Apr. 6 or 8 1664; Daniel, Jan. 21, 1666; Jared, Jan. 7, 1668; Rebecca, Feb. 6, 1670; Ebenezer; Jared, again, 1674; Nathaniel; Stephen; Caleb about 1680; and died Oct. 24, 1706, aged 80.

REFERENCES.

CONNECTICUT.—Field's Hist. of Haddam, Conn., 44; Hinman's Conn. Settlers, 693; Andrews' Hist. of New Britain, 249; Whittemore's Hist. of Middlesex County, 321.

OTHER PUBLICATIONS.—Paul's Hist. of Wells, Vt., 78; Loomis Gen. Female Branches, 523; Walworth Hyde Gen., 783; Smith Gen. (1890) 19; Hurlbut Gen., 413; Humphrey Gen., 344; Heminway's Vt. Gaz., V; Savage's Gen. Dict., vol. I, 441; Amer. Ancestry, IV, 25; IX, 134.

CONELLY. Powers' Hist. Sangamon County, Ill., 217.

CONEY. Breckinridge Gen., 63.

CONGDON. Austin's R. I.Gen. Dict., 53; Austin's Allied Families, R. I., 53; Newport Hist. Mag., 236.

CONGER. Williams' Danby, Vt., 129.

CONEY.

CONEY:—James, of Braintree, had Joshua, born April, 1640, died Dec. 1642; Patience and Experience, twin daughters, Aug. 1642, and James, died Dec. 1642.

JEREMY CONEY, Exeter, took oath of allegiance Nov. 30, 1677.

JOHN CONEY, of Boston, cooper, married June 20, 1654, Elizabeth, daughter of Robert Nash, had John, born Jan. 5, 1656; Sarah, May 22, 1660; Joseph, April 27, 1662; Elizabeth, April 2, 1664; William, July 5, 1665; Thomas, Sept. 26, 1667; Mary, March 10, 1669; Rebecca, June 18, 1670; Elizabeth again, Feb. 24, 1672 and Benjamin, Oct., 1673.

REFERENCES:—Savage's Gen. Dict. vol. I, 442.

CONIGRAVE.

CONIGRAVE:—Walter, of Warwick, was on the freeman's list 1655, and soon after at Newport; but no more can be heard of him, e xcept that he was Captain 1661;and so strange a name would be observed if perpetuated in any record as it is when made worse in Col. Rec. R. I., 1,455, where it is distorted to Cemigrave.

REFERENCES:—Savage's Gen. Dict. vol. I, 442.

CONLEY or CONNELLY.

CONLEY:—Abraham, of Kittery, 1640, took oath of fidelity 1652, constable 1647-59; by Sullivan, 343, written Cunley.

REFERENCES:—Savage's Gen. Dict. vol. I, 442.

CONNEBALL.

CONNEBALL:—John, of Boston, a soldier of Turner's company in the Falls fight, March 1676, was of Old South church and freeman 1690, died April 10, 1724, aged 75. His son Samuel, had his share of land in Bernardston, granted 1736, for those in that bloody field. The name now is Cunnable.

REFERENCES:—Savage's Gen. Dict. vol. I, 443.

CONNELL:—Thomas. See Cornhill.

CONNER.

CONNER:—Cornelius, of Exeter, quite early removed to Salisbury, there, by wife Sarah, had Sarah, born Aug. 23, 1659; John, Dec. 8, 1660; Samuel, Feb. 12, 1662; Mary Dec. 27, 1663; Elizabeth Feb. 26, 1665; Rebecca, April 10, 1668; Ruth, May 16, 1670; Jeremiah, Nov. 6, 1672; a daughter probably Ursula, in record Husly, Aug. 10, 1673; Cornelius, Aug. 12, 1675 and Dorothy, Nov. 1, 1676. Ruth married 1687, Thomas Clough, of Salisbury, as his second wife.

WILLIAM CONNER, of Plymouth, came in the Fortune 1621, but died or more probably removed before 1627, as he has no part of division of cattle.

REFERENCES:—Dearborn's Hist. of Parsonfield, Me., 372; Runnel's Hist. of Sanbornton, N. H., II, 178; Clute's Hist. of Staten Island, 357; Old Kent, Md., 79; Wheeler's Hist. of North Carolina, II, 82; Savage's Gen. Dict., vol. I, 443.

CONNOR. Willis' Amer. Family Antiquities; Bell's Hist. of Exeter, N. H., 7; Coggswell's Hist. of Henniker, N. H., 525; Amer. Ancestry, IV, 14.

CONNET. Littell's Passaic Valley Gens., 89; Amer. Ancestry, VI, 144; Conant Gen., 563.

CONOVER. Willis' Amer. Family Antiquities; Heroes of the Revolution and their Descendants; Salter's Hist. of Monmouth County, N. J., XX; Roome Gen., 140; Bergen Gen., 140.

CONRAD. Amer. Ancestry, VII, 197; VIII, 78; Conrad Gen.

CONROY. Worcester's Hist. of Hollis, N. H., 370; Temple's Hist. of North Brookfield, Mass., 556.

CONNOWAY.

CONNOWAY:—Jeremiah, of Charlestown, 1678. Ann, perhaps his widow, died July 21, 1692, aged 58.

REFERENCES:—Savage's Gen. Dict. vol. I, 443.

CONSTABLE.

CONSTABLE:—Thomas, of Boston, died about 1650 and his widow Ann, married Philip Long, who came from Ipswich. At New Haven, 1643, was a Mrs. Constable.

REFERENCES:—Hugh's Hist. of Lewis County, N. Y., 238; Old Kent, Md., 85; Bartow Gen., 197.

CONSAULUS. Pearson's Schenectady, N. Y., Fam., 48; Munsell's Albany, IV, 127.

CONSTANT. Powers' Hist. of Sangamon County, Ill., 218.

CONTESSE. Richmond Standard, vol. I, 49.

CONSTANTINE. History of Ashburnham, Mass., 645.

CONVERS or CONVERSE.

CONVERS:—Allen, of Woburn, freeman 1644, who, Felt says, had grant of land at Salem, 1639, had Zechary, born Oct. 11, 1642; Elizabeth March 7, 1645, died young; Sarah, July 11, 1647; Joseph, May 31, 1649; Mary, Sept. 26, 1651, died soon; Theophilus, Sept. 21, 1652, died soon; Samuel, Sept. 20, 1653; Mary, again, Nov. 26, 1655; Hannah, March 13, 1660. He died April 19, 1679, and his wife died three days after, probably of small-pox.

EDWARD CONVERS, of Charlestown, came in the fleet with Winthrop, 1630, with wife Sarah, and children; requested Oct. 19, to be, and, May 18, following was admitted freeman. They were dismissed from our church to be among the first of that in Charlestown, where he was selectman 1634-40, had grant of first ferry to Boston in 1631, removed 1643 to Woburn, was representative 1660, and deacon. His wife Sarah, died Jan. 14, 1662. He may have been father of all in this region, except Allen, and perhaps, was his brother; died Aug. 10, 1663. His daughter Mary, married Dec. 19, 1643, Simon Thompson, who died 1658; she married a Sheldon next year. His will, of Aug. 1659, names wife Sarah, sons Josiah, James and Samuel, Edward, son of James. as well as alludes to others, children of daughter Mary Thompson, who was then wife of Sheldon, kinsmen Allen Convers and John Parker, kinswoman Sarah Smith.

ZECHARIAH CONVERS, of Woburn, married June 12, 1667, Hannah Bateman, daughter of John, of Boston, who died Jan. 1, 1679, had Zechariah, born Nov. 4, 1670; Elizabeth, Oct. 29, 1672; Ruth. Oct. 3, 1674, died at 3 months; and he died Jan. 22, 1679. Of this name, spelled sometimes with "i" for "e" and often with final "e," though the soldier wrote it, as I have; two had. in 1834, been graduates at Harvard and eight at other New England colleges.

REFERENCES.

MASSACHUSETTS.—Sewall's Hist. of Woburn. 72, 176; Drapers Hist. of Spencer. 188; Hyde's Hist. of Brimfield, 391; Temple's Hist. of North Brookfield, 557; Washburn's Hist. of Leicester, 353; Winchester Record, vol. I. 233; Wyman's Charlestown Gens., vol. I, 234; Temple's Hist. of North Brookfield, 557.

NEW HAMPSHIRE.—Stearn's Hist. of Rindge, 482; Hayward's Hist. of Gilsum, 280; Sanderson's Hist. of Charlestown, 311; Secomb's Hist. of Amherst, 543.

OTHER PUBLICATIONS.—Roe's Sketches of Rose, N. Y., 195; Hubbard's Hist. of Stanstead County, N. Y., 302; Heminway Gen., 55; Vinton's Richardson Gen., 248; Walworth's Hyde Gen., 633; Amer. Ancestry, vol. I, 16; X, 67; Converse Gen.

CONWAY.

CONWAY:—Edwin, of Worcestershire, Eng., married Martha, daughter of William Eltonhead, of Eltonhead, Eng., had son Edwin of Virginia, born 1694, died 1698, married Sarah, daughter of Capt. Henry Fleete. His son Edwin married Annie Ball, half sister of Mary Ball, mother of Washington.

REFERENCES:—Slaughter's St. Mark's Parish, Va., 129; 158; Meade's Old Families of Va.; Hayden's Virginia Genealogies, 222; Norton's Hist. of Knox County, Ohio, 297; Bassett's Hist. of Richmond, N. H., 370; Carter Family Tree; Amer. Ancestry, IV, 204.

CONY. North's Hist. of Augusta, Me., 836; Maine Hist. Rec., vol. I, 207; Butler's Hist. of Farmington, 430; Guild Gen., 29; Cony Gen.

CONYN. Munsell's Albany, IV, 109.

CONYNGHAM. Penn. Mag., VII, 204; Kulp's Wyoming Valley.

COOK or COOKE.

COOK:—Aaron, of Dorchester, freeman May 6, 1635, removed 1636, with the great.body of others, to Windsor, married there a daughter of Thomas Ford, had Joanna, baptized Aug. 5, 1638; Aaron, Feb. 21, 1641; Miriam, March 12, 1643; Moses. Nov. 16, 1645; Samuel Nov. 21, 1650; Elizabeth, Aug. 7. 1653; and Noah, June 14, 1657; the last three by second wife Joan, daughter of Nicholas Denslow, who died April 1676. He had graduated at Mussaco, now Simsbury, but was discouraged probably by a controversy and removed to Northampton 1661, was a proprietor 1667, at Westfield. representative 1668; by a third wife Elizabeth, married Dec. 2, 1679, daughter of John Nash, of New Haven, had no children; married fourth wife 1688, Rebecca, widow of Philip Smith, daughter of Nathaniel Foote; was captain and Mayor; and died Sept. 5, 1690, aged 80. Miriam married Nov. 8, 1661, Joseph Leeds and Elizabeth married probably Samuel Parsons.

CALEB COOK, of Watertown, married July 31, 1685. Mary Parmenter, had Caleb, born April 1, 1686.

ELKANAH COOK, of Boston, 1658.

FRANCIS COOK, of Plymouth, came in the Mayflower, 1620. with one child, John: his wife Esther, and other children Jacob, Jane, and Esther, coming in the Ann, 1623, so that he counted six shares in division of lands 1624: and in 1626, was born Mary, and he had seven shares at division of cattle. He was called by Bradford, "a very old man," in 1650, who saw his "children's children having children." and had married in Holland, a native of the Netherlands, of the Walloon Church, was one of the first purchasers of Dartmouth, 1652, and of Middleborough, 1662: died April 7, 1663. His will, of Dec. 7, 1659, made wife Esther and son John executors. Jane married about 1628, Experience Mitchell; Esther married Nov., 1644, Richard Wright; and Mary married Dec. 26, 1645, John Thomson, who died June 16, 1696, aged 80, and she died March 21, 1715.

GEORGE COOK, of Cambridge, came in the "Defence," 1635, aged 25, with elder brother Joseph, in Harlakenden's company, in the ship's clearance at the London custom house called with others, servants of Harlakenden for description of the government, no doubt, for in the year following our record gives both the prefix of respectable; freeman March 3, 1636; representative 1636-42-5, and speaker 1645, artillery company 1643, captain, by wife Alice, had Elizabeth, born March 27, 1640, who died August following; Thomas, born June 19, 1642, died at 2 months; Joseph Dec. 27, 1643; Elizabeth again, August 21, 1644; and Mary August 15, 1646. He went home, and was a colonel on service in Ireland, there died or was killed 1652. His daughter Mary, married, it is said, Samuel Annesley, Esq., of Westminster, called "her mother's younger brother," with whom she was living 1691; and Elizabeth married Rev. John Quick of St. Giles, Cripplegate, London. Administration on his estate here was granted 1653, to President Dunster and Joseph Cooke.

GREGORY COOK, of Cambridge, shoemaker, by wife Mary, who died August 17, 1681, had Stephen, born about 1647; and Susanna, who died Nov. 13, 1674; lived in that part now Newton, in 1672; next year was of Watertown, yet had some years been at Mendon, was there selectman 1669; of Watertown again, 1684, and at Cambridge was selectman 1678, and after; married Nov. 1, 1681, widow Susanna Goodwin, and died Jan. 1, 1691, and his widow married Sept. 15, following Henry Spring.

HENRY COOK, of Salem, 1638, married June, 1639, Judith Burdsall, died Dec. 25, 1661, when his inventory is produced and his children named with their ages, Isaac, 22; Samuel 20; John, 14; Judith, 18; Rachel, 16; Mary and Martha, 12; Henry 8; and Hannah 4.

ISAAC COOK, of Salem, married May 3, 1664, Elizabeth, daughter of Anthony Buxton, had Elizabeth, born Sept. 23, 1665; Isaac, Jan. 9, 1667, and Mary Nov. 12, 1668.

JAMES COOK, of Boston, died Dec. 15, 1690.

JOHN COOK, of Plymouth, 1633, called senior, probably removed 1643, to Rehoboth, is not known to have been relative of the succeeding. Perhaps he removed to Warwick, was town-sergeant 1651, freeman there 1655, and probably died that year, for his widow Mary married 1656, Thomas Relph. He left son John, and daughter Elizabeth, who married Dec. 24, 1666, John Harrod.

JOHN COOK, of Salem, 1637, came, perhaps, in thte Abigail, 1635, aged 27, freeman May 18, 1642, had Sarah, baptized Sept. 19, 1640; Elizabeth May 16, 1641; and Mary, Oct. 22, 1643. He died, I suppose, in 1650, when his inventory was brought in.

. JOHN COOK, of Ipswich, 1664.

JOHN COOK, of Portsmouth, R. I., 1655, of whom I learn no more, unless that he has wife Ruth in 1682, then was 51 years old, and John Jr., probably his son, was 26, and other sons Joseph and Thomas, beside several daughters, and his will was recorded 1691. As early as 1647, he was made one of two "water bailies" of the Colony, if there be no mistake. One John, a young man, Winth. II, 97, says, was killed by accident at Boston, June 23, 1643; and a John was at Windsor, 1644.

JOHN COOK, of Boston, was of the vestry of King's Chapel, 1689; and a John, a soldier in the company of Moseley, Dec., 1675, and again in Philip's war, 1676, at Hadley; may have been of Gloucester, married Feb. 2,

1680, and Mary Elwell, had John, born Nov. 20, 1680.

JOHN COOK, of Middletown, at his death Jan. 16, 1705, left children John and Mary, of full age; Daniel 14 years; Sarah, 12; Ebenezer, 7. His wife Hannah, daughter of Capt. Daniel Harris, could not have been the first. His will was made Aug. 15, 1698.

JOHN COOK, of Hampton, married Nov. 26, 1686, Mary Downs.

JOSEPH COOK, of Cambridge, elder brother of George, came in the Defence, 1635, of George. They were of Earl's Colne in Essex, and there had enjoyed the spiritual guidance of Shepard, who came in the same ship "Freeman," March 3, 1636; representative 1636-40, artillery company 1640; had wife Elizabeth and children Elizabeth, March 16, or August, 1645; Mary Jan. 30, 1647; Grace Dec. 9, 1648, died soon; Grace, again May 1, 1650; and Ruth; all baptized at Cambridge. I think it not unlikely, that after administration on his brother's estate he went home.

JOSEPH COOK, of Wells, swore allegiance, 1680.

JOSIAH COOK, of Plymouth, married Sept. 16, 1635, Elizabeth, widow of Stephen Deane, daughter of widow Mary King, freeman 1637, removed with Gov. Prence to Eastham, had Josiah and Ann, who married Jan. 18, 1655, Mark Snow, and died July 7, 1656; Bethia, who married April 4, 1660, Joseph Harding; and died Oct. 17, 1673; and his widow died about 1687.

NATHANIEL COOK, of Windsor, married June 29, 1649, Lydia, daughter of Richard Vore, had Sarah, born June 28, 1650; Lydia, Jan. 9, 1653; Hannah, Sept. 21, 1655; Nathaniel, May 13, 1658; Abigail, March 1, 1680; John, August 3, 1662; and Josiah, Dec. 22, 1664. He was admitted freeman of Conn., 1650, and died May 19, 1688. The widow died June 14, 1698. Sarah married June 30, 1670, Samuel Baker; Lydia died unmarried before 24 years; Hannah married Thomas Buckland the younger, who died May 28, 1676; and she next married Joseph Baker, who died Dec. 11, 1691; and she married third husband John Loomis; and Abigail married Joshua Pomeroy, and next, David Hoyt, and next, Nathaniel Royce.

PEYTON COOK, of Saco, 1635, called gentleman, was clerk of the assembly of Lygonia 1648. Folsom, 32.

PHILIP COOK, of Cambridge, freeman 1647, died Feb. 10, 1667, by wife Mary, daughter of Barnabas Lamson, had Mary, born July 26, 1652; Philip, Aug. 19, 1654; Samuel; Hannah, July 4, 1657; and Sarah; all except Philip, who probably died young, baptized at Cambridge: also Philip again, baptized May 5, 1661; John, Aug. 30, 1663; and Barnabas, June 4, 1665; as in matchless Mitchell's register appears, but it must be, that he had two daughters named Hannah, for town record shows daughter of Hannah, July 13, 1654, and brother of Samuel, 1655. Sarah died May 12, 1661. His will of July 18, before his death disposes of children John, 3 years old; Philip, 5; and Hannah, 9; leaving widow Mary, to bring up others to trades. A discrepance between Mitchell and the inscription on gravestone of second Philip may be observed if Harris, 57, has correctly given it, that he died March 25, 1718, aged 55 years, 10 months, 25 days, so that by such computation he was born April 30, 1662. Probably the gravestone is false, Mitchell may be following and we may suppose he was baptized at 5 days old.

RALPH COOK, of Charlestown, 1640, may have had wife Sarah, admission of the church Nov. 30, 1643.

RICHARD COOK, of Charlestown, came in the Jonathan, 1639, aged 31, joined with the children May 30, 1641, lived on Malden side, had wife Frances, and daughter Mary, born May, 1649; was of friends of Marmaduke Matthew's preaching, and died Oct. 14, 1658. His will names children of his wife by former husband Isaac, Thomas, Elizabeth and Sarah, Wheeler; but, I think, the sons were born in England. Elizabeth married Sept. 12, 1659, William Greene; and Sarah married Dec. 18, 1660, John Greene. His widow married Sept. 5, 1659, Thomas Green; and his only daughter Mary, married 1666, Samuel Green.

RICHARD COOK, of Boston, tailor, came, it is said, from Gloucestershire, freeman March 4, 1635, artillery company 1643, lieutenant, 1656, representative for Dover, 1670; by wife Elizabeth, had Elhanan, born June 30, baptized July 17, 1636, died Nov. following; Elisha, before mentioned Sept. 16, baptized Nov. 5, 1637, Harvard College 1657; Elkanah, baptized Sept. 12, 1640, but the town record gives a false date of birth; Joseph, born 2d, baptized May 8, 1642, who may have been Harvard College 1660, or 61; and Benjamin, baptized August 4, 1644, about 5 days old, died May following. His will, made Dec. 18, 1671, probate Dec. 25, 1673, names wife Elizabeth and only child Elisha, beside brothers William and Walter, in England. His widow died Oct. 7, 1690, in 75th year.

RICHARD COOK, of Norwich, had grant of lot 1680, in the part now Preston, and son Obed, born Feb. 1, 1681.

ROBERT COOK, of Charlestown, freeman June 2, 1641, by wife Sarah, had Samuel, born Aug. 10, 1644. I feel some hesitation in this case, whether he and Richard were not one, for Richard is not in the Colonial record as freeman, which would not, however, be very surprising though rather observing; but how Robert, whose name is not found in the church, was admitted freeman is strange.

ROBERT COOK, of Portsmouth, R. I., married Dec. 5, 1678, Tamar, daughter of John Tyler of Bristol, had Mary, born June 27, 1682; Miriam, Dec. 9, 1689; and Samuel, Dec. 19, 1695.

ROGER COOK, of Marshfield, 1643.

SAMSON COOK, of Gloucester, died Jan. 26, 1674.

SAMUEL COOK, of Dedham, 1640, called gentleman late of Dublin, in Ireland, when his executors conveyed his estate, 1652.

SAMUEL COOK, of New Haven, m. Hope, May 2, 1667, daughter of Edward Parker, had Samuel, born March 3, 1668; John, Dec. 3, 1669; and a daughter without name; removed to Wallingford, 1673, where the residue of his children named in his will, twelve in all, were born: Mary Ives, Judith, Isaac, Joseph, Hope, Israel, Mabel, Benjamin, Ephraim and Elizabeth. A second wife Mary, he had, but we know not, which of these children, if any, were hers. He made his will March, 1703, and soon died.

STEPHEN COOK, of Mendon, freeman 1673, perhaps brother of Gregory, removed to Watertown, was one of founders of the second church, a deacon, and died April 24, 1714.

THOMAS COOK, of Salem, was dead Sept. 1650, when inventory of 40 pound sterling was returned. Perhaps he was unmarried.

THOMAS COOK, of Taunton 1639, proprietor with Thomas jr. in 1643, probably both removed to Portsmouth, R. I., early, was called captain and in 1659 honored with commission to run the West line of the Colony.

THOMAS COOK, of Watertown, had daughter before 1647, and may be that mariner who died at Boston, Feb. 1646.

THOMAS COOK, of Guilford, of whose early years I know not the residence, brought two children Thomas jr. and Sarah, who married Thomas Hall. There he married Mar. 30, 1668, second wife Hannah Lindon, who died July 7, 1676, and he died Dec. 1, 1692.

THOMAS COOK, of Windsor, of whom no connection with any other of the name is known, had wife and daughter Martha, who died Nov. 8, 1683; and Mary, another daughter died Mar. 10, 1689; and he died Nov. 18, 1697. He had good estate and probably left children to enjoy it.

THOMAS COOK, of Braintree, one of a military watch 1689.

WALTER COOK, Weymouth 1643, freeman 1653, had Ebenezer, born May 30, 1656; Walter, Sept. 10, 1657; and Nicholas, the last born Feb. 9, 1660.

WILLIAM COOK, of Maine 1665. Eleven of this name

WILLIAM COOK, of Maine 1665. Eleven of this name, a few included without final "e", had been graduates at Harvard, nineteen at Yale, and twenty-two at other New England colleges among whom were twelve clergymen.

REFERENCES.

CONNECTICUT.—Orcutt's Hist. of Torrington, 677; Stiles' Hist. of Windsor, II, 161; Timlow's Southington, 63; Boyd's Annals of Winchester, 302; Bronson's Hist. of Waterbury, 485; Hinman's Conn. Settlers, 698; Davis'Hist. of Wallingford, 671; Andrews' Hist. of New Britain, 207.

MASSACHUSETTS.—Stearn's Hist. of Ashburnham, 648; Temple's Hist. of Northfield, 424; Wyman's Charlestown Gens. 235; Babson's Hist. of Gloucester, 74; Ballou's Hist. of Milford, 668; Davis' Landmarks of Plymouth, 69; Dyer's Hist. of Plainfield; Fox's Hist. of Dunstable, 242; Freeman's Hist. of Cape Cod, II, 366, 389, 642; Hazen's Hist. of Billerica, 25; Hobart's Hist. of Abington, 363; Judd's Hist. of Hadley, 465; Mitchell's Hist. of Bridgewater, 141; Paige's. Hist. of Cambridge, 513; Rich's Hist. of Truro, 424.

NEW HAMPSHIRE.—Read's Hist. of Swanzey, 313; Kidder's Hist. of New Ipswich, 352; Bassett's Hist. of Richmond, 371.

VERMONT.—Williams' Hist. of Danby, 130; Hollister's Hist. of Pawlet, 179; Heminway's Vt. Gazeteer, V. 36.

OTHER PUBLICATIONS.—Pearson's Schenectady, N. Y., Settlers, 49; Howell's Hist. of Southampton, N. Y., 212; Richardson's Hist. of Woonsocket, R. I., 224; Austin's R. I., Gen. Dict. 54, 282; Hubbard's Hist. of Stanstead County, Can., 288; Cope Gen. of Pa., 44, 78, 157, 175; Chapman's Trowbridge Gen., 39, Cooley's Trenton, N. J., Gens., 42; Humphrey Gen., 281; Kellog's White Gen., 77; Nash Gen., 33; Strong Gen., 389, 1380; Poole Gen., 92; Tuttle Gen., 645; Amer. Ancestry, vol. I, 16; II, 27; VI, 21; IX, 106, 214; X, 91; XI, 186; Savage's Gen. Dict., vol. I, 455; Cook Gen.

COOKE:—Nicholas of Providence, R. I., born there Feb. 5, 1717; died there Sept. 14, 1782; Governor of Rhode Island 1775; a descendant of Daniel Cooke, of Saybrook, Conn., supposed to be son of John Cooke, of England.

REFERENCES.

MASSACHUSETTS.—Temple's Hist. of North Brookfield, 558; Cutter's Hist. of Arlington, 205; Jackson's Hist. of Newton, 247; Bond's Hist. of Watertown, 163.

OTHER PUBLICATIONS.—Slaughter's St. Mark's Parish, Va., 155; Welles' Amer. Antiq.; Old Kent, Md., 244; Kellogg White Gen., 148; Driver Gen., 508; Cutter Gen., 290; Bartlett and Russell Families; Baldwin Candee Gen., 149; Amer. Ancestry, IV, 92; Cooke Gen.

COCKERY.

COCKERY:—Henry, (an odd name), married at Charlestown, Oct. 22, 1657; Hannah Long, daughter of the first Robert.

REFERENCES:—Wyman's Charlestown Gens., 237; Savage's Gen. Dict., vol. 1, 450.

COOKS. Paul's Hist. of Wells, Vt., 75.

COCKSON. Farrow's Hist. of Isleborough, 189.

COOLEDGE or COOLIDGE.

COOLEDGE:—John, of Watertown, may be youngest son of William, gentleman of Cottenham, County Cambridge, baptized Sept. 16, 1604, son of good lineage; freeman May 25, 1636, selectman 1639, and often after, representative 1658, died May 7, 1691, left widow Mary, by her had John; Nathaniel; Simon; all, perhaps, born in England; Mary, born Oct. 14, 1637; Stephen, Oct. 28, 1639; Obadiah, April 15, 1642; and Jonathan, March 10, 1647. In this will, made Nov. 19, 1681, probated June 16, 1691, he names all the children but Obadiah, who died 1663, unmarried; and Mary, who married Sept. 19, 1655, Isaac Mixer, and died Nov. 2, 1660, but her children Sarah and Mary are mentioned.

REFERENCES:—Hudson's Hist. of Lexington, Mass., 47; Morse's Mem. Appendix; Cochrane's Hist. of Antrim, 436; Savage's Gen. Dict., vol. I, 451.

COOLIDGE. Stearn's Hist. of Ashburnham, 210; Morse's Sherborn, Mass., Settlers, 62; Paige's Hist. of Cambridge, Mass., 516; Jackson's Hist. of Newton, Mass., 251; Bond's Hist. of Watertown, Mass., 165, 743; Barry's Hist. of Framingham, Mass., 251; Washburne's Notes of Livermore, Me., 31; Waterford, Me., Centen. 56; Harris' Watertown, Mass., Epitaphs, 14; Heyward's Hist. of Hancock, N. H., 462; Norton's Hist. of Fitzwilliam, N. H., 521; Leland Gen., 270; Greene's Todd Gen.; Converse Gen.; Clarke's Watertown Gen., 73, 124.

REFERENCES:—Amer. Ancestry, X, 92.

COOLEY.

COOLEY:—Benjamin, of Springfield, 1646, died Aug. 17, 1684; by wife Sarah, who died 6 days after, had Bethia, born Jan. 16, 1644; Obadiah, Jan. 27, 1647; Eliakim, Jan. 8, 1649; Daniel, May 2, 1651; Sarah, Feb. 27, 1654; Benjamin, Sept. 1, 1656; Mary, June 22, 1659; and Joseph, March 6, 1662; all living at his death. Bethia married Dec. 15, 1664, Henry Chapin.

DENNIS COOLEY, of Stonington, written Coolie, died 1683.

HENRY COOLEY, of Boston, 1670, cooper, had wife Rebecca, who survived. He died before Nov., 1677.

JOHN COOLEY, of Ipswich, 1638, removed to Salem, died March, 1654.

PETER COOLEY, of Fairfield, freeman of Conn., 1664.

WILLIAM COOLEY, of Mass., 1634. Felt. He was a mariner, of New London, 1652, and called himself in 1664, about 60. Eight of this name had been graduates at some of the New England Colleges.

RFERENCES:—Stiles' Hist. of Windsor, Conn., II, 166; Hinman's Conn. Settlers, 704; Temple's Hist. of Palmer, Mass., 435; West Springfield, Mass., Centen, 115; Atkin's Hist. of Hawley, Mass., 56; Longmeadow, Mass., Centen. 47; Sanderson's Hist. of Charlestown, N. H., 312; Caverly's Hist. of Pittsford, Vt., 697; Cooley's Trenton, N. J., Gen., 44; Buckingham Gen., 260; Chapman Gen., 53; Ely Gen., 150, 321; Goodwin's Olcott Gen., 26; Guild's Stiles' Gen., 193 Warren-Clarke Gen., 49; Strong Gen., 1325; Amer. Ancestry, vol. I, 15; N. E. Hist. and Gen. Reg., XXV, 25; XXXIV, 386; Savage's GeGn. Dict., vol. I, 453.

COOMBS.

COOMBS:—Alister, of Maine, 1665.

HENRY COOMBS, of Marblehead, 1647.

HUMPHREY COOMBS, of Salem, 1668, married July 29, 1695, Bathshua, daughter of Richard Raymond; had Hannah, born May 26, 1660.

JOHN COOMBS, of Plymouth, 1630, married that year Sarah, daughter of Cuthbert Cuthbertson, was taxed 1633 and '4.

JOHN COOMBS, of Boston, married Feb. 24, 1662, Elizabeth, widow of Thomas Barlow, diminished her property, but lived not long.

JOHN COOMBS, of Sherborn, 1676. Bigelow, 38.

THOMAS COOMBS, of Maine, 1665. Often this name appears Combs.

REFERENCES:—Farrow's Hist. of Isleborough, Me., 175; Eaton's Hist. of Thomaston, Me., 184; Derby's White Haskell and Coomb's Families; Longmeadow, Mass., Centen. 56; N. E. Hist. and Gen. Reg., XXXV, 161; L, 210.

COON. Munsell's Albany Coll., IV, 138; Marshall Gen., 142; Greene Gen.; Amer. Ancestry, II, 127.

COONS. Amer. Ancestry, II, 27.

COOPER.

COOPER:—Anthony, of Hingham, 1635, came with wife, four sons, four daughters and four servants (any one of whose names I would gladly learn) from old Hingham, died very early, for his inventory was taken February 26, 1636.

BENJAMIN COOPER, of Salem, was of Brampton, in the east part of Suffolk, came from Yarmouth, in the "Mary Ann," 1637, aged 50, with wife Elizabeth 48, and five children, Lawrence, Mercy, Rebecca, Benjamin and Francis Fillingham, his son-in-law, aged 32, his sister aged 48, and two servants, John Filin and Philemon Dickerson. Of the father or children we know no more, but the son-in-law, and Dickerson are mentioned shortly after at Salem; he died soon, and his inventory taken Sept. 27, of that year shows good estate.

JOHN COOPER, of Watertown, died 1637, in his 80th year it is said, but this may be traditional error for Thomas.

JOHN COOPER, of Lynn, came, 1635, in the "Hopewell," captain Bundock, aged 41, with wife and children Mary, 13; John, 10; Thomas, 7; and Martha, 5. He was from Olney, Co. Buckshire; freeman Dec. 8, 1636; was one of the purchasers from the Indians for the projectors of the Colony at Southampton, L. I., and there was living 1664.

JOHN COOPER, of Cambridge, came with sister Lydia, after their father's death in company of Gregory Stone, who married their mother Lydia. His sister married David Fiske. He was freeman May 18, 1642, constable, selectman, very many years deacon, town clerk from 1669 to his death Aug. 22, 1691; by wife Ann, daughter of Nathaniel Sparhawk, had Ann, born Nov. 16, 1643, who married Edward Pinson; Mary, Sept. 11, 1645; Samuel, Jan. 3, 1654; John, 1656; Nathaniel, baptized May 8, 1659, died Dec. 19, 1661; Lydia, April 13, 1663; and Hannah Dec. 29, 1667.

JOHN COOPER, of Scituate, married 1634, Priscilla, widow of William Wright, who was a sister of Gov. Bradford's wife Alice; removed 1639 to Barnstable, there died without children. His will was made 1676.

JOHN COOPER, of New Haven, 1639, was agent for iron works, representative 1664-7, had Mary, born 1631, probably in England, baptized Aug. 15, 1641; Hannah, 1638, who was baptized at same time with Mary, and married 1661, John Potter; and Sarah, baptized Sept. 21, 1645, who married 1662, Samuel Hemenway, and he died Nov. 23, 1689.

JOHN COOPER, of Weymouth, whose will in Genealogical Register, V, 303, seems to show that he was only transient visitor in autumn of 1653.

JOHN COOPER, of Duxbury, 1666.

NATHANIEL COOPER, of Rehoboth, had Thomas, born July 12, 1676; Abijah, May 1, 1677, died soon.

PETER COOPER, of Rowley, 1643, came 1635 in the "Susan and Ellen," aged 28, may have removed to Rehoboth, there buried Feb. 28, 1678.

SIMON COOPER, of Newport, 1663, a physician, married Jan. 20, 1664, Mary Tucker, called in the Friend's record of Shelter Island, who may have been daughter of that John of Watertown and Hingham, had Robert, born Oct. 10, 1664; Joseph Feb. 4, 1667; Mary, July 20, 1669; and Simon, April 1, 1672.

THOMAS COOPER, of Watertown, buried June 20, 1637, aged 80, as the record says.

THOMAS COOPER, of Hingham, came in the "Diligent," 1638, with wife, two children and two servants from Old Hingham, removed perhaps 1643, to Rehoboth, was representative 1652 and '53; married Oct. 17, 1656, for second wife Ann, widow of Zaccheus Bosworth. He was deacon and buried third wife Elizabeth, Feb. 1, 1681. Davis, in Morton's Memorial, 442; Baylies, II, 198.

THOMAS COOPER, of Boston, came, perhaps, in the "Christian," 1635, aged 18, was probably early at Windsor, removed 1641, to Springfield, freeman 1649, a lieutenant killed by the Indians, Oct. 5, 1675. His daughter Rebecca, married July 12, 1677, John Clark of Northampton.

Another THOMAS COOPER, of Boston, had probably married a widow Smith of Watertown, for Matthew Smith is called on the record of his death son-in-law of Thomas Cooper, in May, 1658.

TIMOTHY COOPER, of Lynn, 1637, died March, 1659, had John, born 1647; Timothy, 1651; and four daughters.

TIMOTHY COOPER, of Springfield, 1668.

TIMOTHY COOPER, of Groton, married June 2, 1669, Sarah Morse, daughter of Joseph of Watertown, had Timothy, born March 24, 1670; John, March 5, 1672, died next month; Sarah, March 20, 1673; and John, May 5, 1675.

WILLIAM COOPER, of Piscataqua, one of the men sent over 1631, or earlier, by Mason for settler of his plantation. Belknap I, 425; and probably Winthrop, I, 120, mentioned the loss of same man in a storm. Six of this name had been graduates at Harvard and two at other New England colleges.

REFERENCES.

MASSACHUSETTS.—Paige's Hist. of Cambridge, 510; Davis' Landmarks of Plymouth, 70; Essex Inst. Coll., XX, 226; Freeman's Hist. of Cape Cod, II, 276; Wyman's Charlestown Gens., vol. I, 238; Hudson's Hist. of Lexington, 47.

MAINE.—Machias Centen. 158; Maine Hist. and Gen. Rec., II, 85; Bangor Hist. Mag., II, 40; V, 45; Cushman's Hist. of Sheepscott, 369; Eaton's Annals of Warren, 521; Eaton's Hist. of Thomaston, 1868; Hanson's Hist. of Gardner, 137.

OTHER PUBLICATIONS.—Wheeler's Croyden, N. H., Centen. 84; Washington, N. H., Hist., 347; Bolton's Hist. of Westchester County, N. Y., II, 718; Howell's Hist. of Southampton, N. Y., 217; Munsell's N. Y. Coll., IV, 110; Austin's R. I. Gen. Dict., 54; Clement's Newton, N. J., Settlers; Futhey's Hist. of Chester County, Pa., 502; Hinman's Conn. Settlers, 705; Goode Gen., 156; Hist. of Preble County, Ohio, 192; Leland Gen., 117; Littell's Passaic Valley, 90; Powers' Hist. of Sangamon County, Ill., 248; Morrison Gen., 248; Roome Gen., 135; Amer. Ancestry, vol. I, 17; II, 27; IV, 80; V, 212; VII, 231; VIII, 56; IX, 149; Savage's Gen. Dict., vol. I, 543; Cooper Chart, 1879; Cooper Gen.; N. E. Gen. Reg., XLIV, 53.

COOTE. Heraldic Journal, I, 166; III, 24.

COPE.

COPE:—Edward, of Providence, 1640, or probably earlier, by 2 or 3 years. Sometimes this spelling is used for the family name of Copp, which see.

REFERENCES:—Savage's Gen. Dict., vol. I, 543; Futhey's Hist. of Chester, Pa., 502; Amer. Ancestry, IV, 137; V, 24; IX, 183; Cope Chart, 1879; Cope Gen.

COPELAND.

COPELAND:—John, of Boston, came in July, 1656, in the "Speedwell," aged 28, from London, a Quaker. He was next year banished from Plymouth Colony and whipped in Massachusetts.

LAWRENCE COPELAND, of Braintree, married Dec. 12, 1651, Lydia Townsend, sadly perverted so Feb. 16, 1654, in Genealogical Register, XII, 110, had Thomas, born May 10, 1652, (Genealogical Register, XI, 334,) died next month; Thomas again, Aug. 12, 1654, or Feb. 6 or 8, 1655; Richard, July 11, 1672; and Abigail, 1674. This last married Nov. 23, 1715, says Thayer, but the name of her husband is, I think, an impossible one. Ephraim, his son died unmarried of small-pox, on board a ship of his fleet, before the sailing of the disastrous expedition of Sir William Phips, 1690; he died Dec. 30, 1699, born, says the record, "in the reign of our gracious sovereign

Queen Elizabeth of blessed memory." Farmer, who was much indebted to Chief Justice Sewall's fondness for instances of unusual longevity, refers to his diary, as saying he was 110. Perhaps this is mistaken. In the diary of Marshall, called Fairfield's, by Dr. Harris, when he presented it to the Historical Society, I read, under date Jan. 1, 1700, (so that it seems he was wise enough to be half a century ahead of the law in reckoning the beginning of a year), "old Lawrence Copeland buried aged 100 years, who died last Saturday." Marshall was a townsman, and his authority may be sufficient; but the grave-stone also says Dec. 30, 1699, 100 years old. His wife Lydia, died Jan. 8, 1688.

REFERENCES:—Merrill's Hist. of Ackworth, N. H., 202; Hayward's Hist. of Hancock, 463; Eaton's Annals of Warren, Me., 521; French's Hist. of Turner, Me., 52; Washington, N. H., Hist. 347; Deane's Hist. of Scituate, Mass., 242; Kingman's Hist. of North Bridgewater, 470; Mitchell's Hist. of Bridgewater, Mass., 141; Bangor Hist. Mag., vol. I, 137; Bass' Hist. of Braintree, Vt., 126; Binney Gen.; Thayer's Memorial, 1835; Savage's Gen. Dict., vol. I, 465.

COPIE.

COPIE:—James, probably of Braintree, freeman, May 13, 1640.

REFERENCES:—Savage's Gen. Dict., vol. I, 546.

COPLEY.

COPLEY:—Thomas, of Springfield, son of a widow Elizabeth, who married 1650, Nathaniel Phelps of Windsor, and with her husband removed to Northampton, where her daughter Elizabeth married 1665, Praisever Turner, and second Samuel Langton in 1676, and for third husband had David Alexander. But the son was of Springfield, 1672, married at Westfield, Nov. 13, 1672, and had Thomas, born July 28, 1678; removed to Suffield 1679, there died Nov. 29, 1712, leaving Thomas, Matthew and Samuel.

REFERENCES:—Hinman's Conn. Settlers, 709; Savage's Gen. Dict., vol. I, 456.

COPERTHWAITE. Cregar's Haines Gen.

COPP.

COPP:—Richard, perhaps brother of William, came in the "Blessing," 1635, aged 24, but no more is known of him.

WILLIAM COPP, of Boston, came, probably, in the "Blessing," 1635, a shoemaker, from London, aged 26, freeman June 2, 1641; by wife Judith, had Joanna, probably Ann and David, perhaps born in England; Naomi, baptized July 5, 1640 (the day after his joining with the church) who died Oct. 8, 1653; Jonathan, Aug. 23, 1640; Rebecca, born May 6, 1641; Ruth, 24, baptized Nov. 26, 1643; and Lydia, July, 1646; Ann married Aug. 11, 1646, Herman Atwood. His estate was in part of that beautiful hill which bore his name; and he died March, 1670. On the 27th of the month following, his will was probated, which had been made Oct. 31, 1662, and David was executor.

REFERENCES:—Runnel's Hist. of Sanbornton, N. H., II, 182; Morrison's Hist. of Windham, N. H., 304; Whitmore's Copp's Hill Epitaphs; Hubbard's Hist. of Stanstead County, Canada, 233; Amer. Ancestry, VII, 152; N. E. Hist. and Gen. Reg., X, 369; Savage's Gen. Dict., vol. I, 456.

COPPOCK. Pott's Carter Gen., 169.

CORBEE, or CORBY.

CORBEE:—William, of Haddam, an early settler in 1640, was indentured servant of James Olmstead, at Hartford; died 1674, leaving William, 18 years old; John, 16; Mary, 12; Samuel, 9; and Hannah, 6. Hinman, 20. The name has been written Corbey, and Corbe.

REFERENCES:—Savage's Gen. Dict., vol. I, 457.

CORBESSON.

CORBESSON:—Samuel, of Maine, 1665.

REFERENCES:—Savage's Gen. Dict., vol. I, 457.

CORBETT.

CORBETT:—Abraham, of Portsmouth, disaffected to Massachusetts in 1665, when the royal commissioners came to New England, occasioned much trouble.

CLEMENT CORBETT, of Boston, married March 7, 1655, Dorcas, daughter of Thomas Buckmaster. See Corbin.

ROBERT CORBETT, of Weymouth, a soldier in Philip's war, 1675 and '76, in service on Connecticut River.

REFERENCES:—Sedgwick's Hist. of Sharon, Conn., 73; Collin's Hist. of Hillsdale, N. Y., App., 50; Ballou's Hist. of Milford, Mass., 628; Butler's Hist. of Farmington, Me., 434; Miller's Hist. of Colchester County, N. S., 211.

CORBIN or CORBYN.

CORBIN:—Clement, of Boston, in Muddy river grants, worshipped at Roxbury, where he had baptized Jabez, Feb. 23, 1668; Dorcas, Nov. 13, 1670; Joanna, Feb. 9, 1672; and Margaret, Mar. 21, 1673. Probably he had others earlier, as John, a soldier in Johnson's company, Dec. 1675.

ROBERT CORBIN, of Casco 1663, a man of consequence there many years married Lydia, daughter of Richard Martin, had no issue, was killed by the Indians Aug. 1676, and his wife taken prisoner. Hubbard, Wars, 33; Willis, I, 129, 143. Perhaps he was at Boston, Aug. 1637, master of the "Speedwell". Winthrop II, 348.

REFERENCES:—Sanderson's Hist. of Charlestown, N. H., 313; Wheeler's Hist. of Newport, N. H., 351; Boyd's Annals of Winchester, Conn., 113; Mead's Old Families of Va., II, 145; Wight Gen. 69; Richmond, Va., Standard, III, 20, 38; Dwight Gen. 592; Davis Gen. 16, 60, 70; Carter Family Tree; Amer. Ancestry, I, 17.

CORDELL:—Hayden's Virginia Gens. 638; Richmond, Va., Standard, III, 6.

CORDES:—Wyman's Charlestown, Mass., Gens. 240; Pierce Gen. 1894.

COREY:—Washington, N. H., History, 448; Norton's Hist. of Fitzwilliam, N. H., 523; Leonard's Hist. of Dublin, N. H., 325; Hayward's Hist. of Gilsum, N. H., 290; Bassett's Hist. of Richmond, N. H., 376; Stearn's Hist. of Ashburnham, Mass., 650; Hodgman's Hist. of Westford, Mass., 443; Bond's Hist. of Watertown, Mass., 187, 749; Brown's Bedford Mass., Families, 7; Hist. of Somerset County, N. J., 853; Walker Gen. 52; Ammidown Mem. 53; Savage's Gen. Dict. vol. I, 459.

CORIEL:—Littell's Passaic Valley, 92.

CORLESS, or CORLISS.

GEORGE CORLESS, of Haverhill 1645, had wife Joane. His daughter Mary married Jan. 23, 1665; William Neff, who died 1689; and eight years after she was taken prisoner by the Indians and partook in the heroic act of Mrs. Duston, and died Oct. 22, 1722. Another daughter married Thomas Eastman; and another married Samuel Ladd; and Huldah Corless probably another daughter married Nov. 5, 1679, Samuel Kingsbury. Descendants of sixth generation still living on his farm.

REFERENCES:—Poor's Hist. of Merrimac Valley, 104; Oxford, N. H., Centen. 105; Morrison's Hist. of Windham, N. H., 405; Corliss' North Yarmouth, Me., 285; McKeen's Hist. of Bradford, Vt., 287; Amer. Ancestry, VI, 101; VII, 84, 210, 226; XI, 74; Corliss Gen.

ELIJAH CORLET, son of Henry of London, bred at Lincoln College Oxford, where he was matriculated Mar. 16, 1627; was schoolmaster from 1641, when New England First Fruits, written 1642, takes notice of his merit in that service until he died Feb. 24, 1687, aged 76, as one account tells, or by another in 78th year. He was freeman 1645; by wife Barbara, daughter probably of Wiliam Cutter, had Rebecca, born Aug. 14, 1644; Hepzibah; and Ammi Ruhamah, Harvard Colege 1670. This son taught the grammar school at Plymouth, 1672, and died at Cambridge in office of tutor, Feb. 1, 1679. Hepzibah married May 21, 1673, James Minot, and June 4, 1684; Daniel Champney.

REFERENCES:—Savage's Gen. Dict., vol. I, 459; Paige's Hist. of Cambridge, Mass., 517.

CORLEW:—Deane's Hist. of Scituate, Mass., 243.

CORLEY:—Hudson's Hist. of Lexington, Mass., 35.

COUNTER:—Edward, of Salem, 1668. Savage's Gen. Dict., vol. I, 463.

COUNTS:—Edward, of Charlestown, mar. Feb. 25, 1663, Sarah, daughter of Richard Adams of Malden, had Samuel, born July, 1671; Sarah and Elizabeth, all baptized June 10, 1677. He lived some time at Malden. Savage's Gen. Dict., vol. I, 463.

COURSER:—Archelaus, of Lancaster, had estate in Boston, and, I think, was of Charlestown, 1658, where the record has the name Hercules; removed to Lancaster 1664, or earlier.

WILLIAM COURSER, of Boston, shoemaker, came in the Elizabeth and Ann, 1635, aged 26, joined with the church a week after Vane, but was not of his side two years later; freeman May 25, 1636, was allowed to be innholder; had Deliverance, born March 4, 1638; Joanna, Feb. 9, 1640; and John, baptized May 8, 1642, about four days old, but the dates of birth suspiciously concur with the church record of baptism and the originality of one or the other may well be doubted.

REFERENCES:—Savage's Gen. Dict., vol. I, 463.

COURTEOUS:—Thomas, of York, freeman of Massachusetts, 1652; and in 1680, swore allegiance to the king.

WILLIAM COURTEOUS, of Newbury, died Dec. 31, 1654.

REFERENCES:—Savage's Gen. Dict., vol. I, 464.

COURTER. Amer. Ancestry, VIII, 138.

COUSINS. Morse's Sherborn, Mass., Settlers, 65; Corliss' Hist. of North Yarmouth, Me.

COUTANT. Sylvester's Hist. of Ulster County, N. Y., 250.

COWENHOVEN. Willes' American Family Antiquity; Hist. of Monmouth County, N. J.; Roome Gen., 139.

COVENHOVEN. Hist. of Monmouth County, N. J.; Meginnes' Hist. of West Branch Valley, Pa., 618.

COVE:—Francis, of Salisbury, 1650. Savage's Gen. Dict., vol. I, 464.

COVELL:—John, of Marblehead, 1668.

COVELL:—Philip, of Malden, married Nov. 26, 1688, Elizabeth, daughter of Philip Atwood of the same, had Sarah, born April 13, 1689; but in Geneal. Reg., VI, 338, his name is printed Fowle, as it had been, p. 336.

REFERENCES:—Freeman's Hist. of Cape Cod, II, 297; Rose's Sketches of Rose, N. Y., 157.

COVIL. N. E. Hist. and Gen. Reg., XXXI, 280.

COVERT. Amer. Ancestry, vol. I, 17.

COVENTRY:—Jonathan, of Marshfield, 1651. Thacher's Hist. of Plymouth, 106. Savage's Gen. Dict., vol. I, 465.

COVEY:—James, of Boston, had grant of lot at Braintree, for four heads, in 1640. Savage's Gen. Dict., vol. I, 465; Austin's R. I. Gen. Dict., 58.

COVINGTON:—John, of Ipswich, 1635. Felt, II.

REFERENCES:—Davis' Landmarks of Plymou.h, Mass., 73; Baldwin Gen., 1056; Savage's Gen. Dict., vol. I, 465.

COWARD. Salter's Hist. of Monmouth County, N. J.

COWDALL:—John, of Boston, 1644, married 1655, Mary, widow of William Davis, was that year freeman of Newport, and at New London, 1659 and '60, but removed.

COWDEN. Egle's Penn. Gens., 121.

COWDRY:—William, of Lynn, 1630, was born about 1602, perhaps was of Weymouth, 1640, removed to Reading, 1642; there was selectman, town-clerk and representative, 1651, yet I find no admission as freeman; died 1687; had Nathaniel, Mathias and Bethia, perhaps others.

COWDREY. Hodgman's Hist. of Westford, Mass., 443; Eaton's Hist. of Reading, Mass., 58; Amer. Ancestry, III, 121.

COWDRY. Wyman's Charlestown, Mass., Gens., vol. I, 245; Hazen's Hist. of Billerica, Mass., 26; Coggswell's Hist. of Henniker, 533; Paul's Hist. of Wells, Vt., 79.

COWDRICK. Amer. Ancestry, VI, 14.

COWELL:—Edward, of Boston, 1645, cord-wainer, by wife Margaret, had John. Joseph, Elizabeth, born Aug. 17, 1653, died next year, and Wil'iam, perhaps the youngest, born June 28, 1655; was captain some time in Philip's War; died Sept. 12, 1691. Perhaps he took second wife Sarah Hobart, married at Hingham, June, 1668.

EZRA COWELL, of Plymouth, 1643, able to bear arms.

JOSEPH COWELL, of Woburn, married Feb. 27, 1685, Alice Palmer, had Elizabeth, born Nov. 25, 1686; Alice, April 6, 1689; Philip, Feb. 12, 1692, died very soon; Joseph, Dec. 9, 1694; Sarah, August, 1698; and perhaps removed.

REFERENCES:—Herrick's Hist. of Gardner, Me., 344; Hall's Trenton, N. J., Presb. Church, 233; Amer. Ancestry, vol. I, 18; Savage's Gen. Dict., vol. I, 466.

COWEN:—John, of Scituate, a Scotchman, purchased estate there, and married 1656, Rebecca, widow of Richard Man, had Joseph, born 1657; Mary, 1659; John, 1662; Israel, 1664 and Rebecca, 1666. Joseph was killed in

Philip's War, at Rehoboth fight, 1676. Rebecca married Dec. 19, 1693, Obediah Hawes, of Dorchester.

REFERENCES:—Deane's Hist. of Scituate, Mass., 243.

COWENHOVEN. See Cowenhoven, Covenhoven, Conover, Riker's Annals of Newtown, N. Y., 362; Bergen's Kings County, N. Y., Settlers, 76; Bergen Gen., 133; Welles' American Family Antiquities.

COWING. Eaton's Hist. of Thomaston, Me., 188; Mitchell's Hist. of Bridgewater, Mass., 143; Cleveland's Hist. of Yates County, N. Y., 549.

COWLAND:—Ralph, of Portsmouth, R. I., in Dr. Stiles's list of freemen, 1655, had married Alice, widow of Sampson Shotten, and by second wife, Sarah, had Mary, who became wife of John Greene of Newport, and Sarah, daughter by the former husband of his second wife, married Henry Greene.

REFERENCES:—Austin's R. I. Gen. Dict., 58; Savage's Gen. Dict., vol. I, 466.

COWLES:—John, of Farmington, 1652, removed about 1664, to Hadfield, died September, 1677, leaving widow Hannah, who died at Hatfield, 1684; John, of Hatfield, freeman 1690, who married Deborah, daughter of Robert Bartlett, of Hartford; Samuel of Farmington; besides four daughters. One had married Nathaniel Goodwin, of Hartford; Esther, another daughter, married Thomas Bull. This person was thought to be the brother of James Cole, and so was his own name; but the records vary to Coale, Cowle, Coales, Colles, Cowles, Coule, or Coules, the descendants have generally adopted the "w," sometimes without the "e."

JOHN, senior, and JOHN, junior, were at Hadley, 1668.

ROBERT COWLES, of Plymouth, 1633.

REFERENCES:—Orcutt's Hist. of Torrington, Conn., 680; Andrews' Hist. of New Britain, Conn., 230; Davis' Hist. of Wallingford, Conn., 719; Judd's Hist. of Hadley, Mass., 471; Doolittle's Hist. of Belchertown, Mass., 270; Hubbard's Hist. of Stanstead County, Canada, 138; Morse Mem., 166; Amer. Ancestry, vol. I, 18; VII, 218; VIII, 225; IX, 28; Cole Gen. by F. T. Cole; Cowles Chart, 1893.

COWLEY:—Abraham, of Maine, 1656. Maine Historical Collections, I, 292.

AMBROSE COWLEY, of Boston, 1660.

HENRY COWLEY, of Marblehead, 1660, brother of the preceding.

REFERENCES:—Savage's Gen. Dict., vol. I, 466; Cowley Gen., 1881.

COWMAN. Thomas Family of Md., 67.

COWPLAND. Martin's Hist. of Chester, 271.

COX:—Edward, of Boston, 1672, mariner, had wife Margaret, and died June, 1675.

FRANCIS COX, embarked at Barbados, August 25, 1679, for New England, but he may only have been a transient visitor.

GEORGE COX, of Salem, married Sept. 10, 1671, Mary, eldest child of John Ingersoll.

JOHN COX, of Boston, by wife Mary, had Philip, born February 9, 1674, died 1690.

JOHN COX, of Pemaquid, took the oath of fidelity to Massachusetts, 1674.

JOSEPH COX, of Boston, freeman 1673, married Nov. 10, 1659, Susannah, daughter of Nicholas Upshall, had Nicholas, Susannah, Elizabeth, Ann, born June 10, 1676; Joseph, Sept. 15, 1670, posthumous, and Mary, and died January 15, 1679.

MOSES COX, of Hampden, 1639, then a young man unmarried. In 1657, his wife Alice, son John, and six other persons, going in a boat from Hampton, Oct. 20, were all drowned. He died May 28, 1687, "aged about 93 years," is the addendum in the report, Genealogical Register, VII, 117, the latitude of which phrase may justify a subtraction, if not of twenty, certainly of ten years. Alice, perhaps his daughter, married May 24, 1662, Matthew Abady; another daughter, married Francis Jenness; and his daughter Leah, married Dec. 13, 1681, James Perkins of the same, and died Feb. 19, 1749, aged 88.

RICHARD COX, of Salem, 1645, Felt.

ROBERT COX, of Boston, mariner, freeman 1666, by wife Martha, had Elizabeth, born April 13, 1677.

THOMAS COX, of Pemaquid, with two others, named Thomas, took oath of fidelity 1674. Perhaps he had been driven by the Indian hostilities to Boston, there, by wife Martha, had Jacob, born January 4, 1678.

MATTHEW COX, of Boston, 1653, came, it is said, in 1638, aged 15, married August 29, 1654, Elizabeth Roberts, had Matthew, born Sept. 5, 1656; Richard, Sept. 6, 1658; John, Sept. 2, 1666; and Samuel, February 19, 1668.

RICHARD COX, of Salisbury, brother of Matthew, came with him, it is said, in 1638, aged 13, lived some years at Boston, before and after 1650; when he was at Salisbury; there, by wife Martha, had Caleb, born August 13, 1666; was of Brookfield, 1673, there killed by the Indians, Aug. 2, 1675. Perhaps he and his brother were brought by sister Mary, who married John Lake of Boston.

WILLIAM COX was one of the first settlers, 1637 at Taunton.

REFERENCES.

MASSACHUSETTS.—Page's Hist. of Hardwick, 355; Paige's Hist. of Cambridge, 518; Wyman's Charlestown, Gens., vol. I, 245; Bond's Hist. of Watertown; Davis' Landmarks of Plymouth, 73; Malden, Mass., Bi-Centen 243.

OTHER PUBLICATIONS.—Lapham's Hist. of Norway, Me., 484; Eaton's Annals of Warren, Me., 525; North's Hist. of Augusta, Me., 840; Joslin's Hist. of Poultney, Vt., 241; Futhey's Hist. of Chester County, Pa., 505; Young's Hist. of Wayne County, Ind., 340; Miller's Hist. of Colchester County, N. S., 299; Preble's Life of John Cox (1871:) Preble Gen., 240; Maris Gen., 110; Amer. Ancestry, vol. I, 18; II, 28; VI, 113; IX, 81; XI, 26.

COXE. Hall's Trenton, N. J., Pres. Church, 236; Penn. Mag., V, 457; Amer. Ancestry, II, 28.

COY. Barry's Hist. of Framingham, Mass., 215.

COYE. Hyde's Hist. of Brimfield, Mass., 391.

COYTEMORE:—Thomas, of Charlestown, 1636, son of widow Catharine Coytemore, whose family name was Myles, and her second husband Rowland Coytemore, but by former husband, A. Gray, she had Parnell, wife of Increase Nowell and Catharine, wife of Thos. Graves; and by Coytemore: Elizabeth, who was first wife of William

married a Williams.' She made her will April 28, 1658, and died Nov. 28, 1659. He was of artillery company 1639, freeman May 13, 1640, selectman and representative that year and once or twice afterwards, was master of good estate, an enterprising merchant, went on several voyages to distant lands, and was lost on a voyage to Malaga, by shipwreck, December 27, 1645, on the coast of Spain; by wife Martha, daughter of Captain Rainsborough, married doubtless in England, had Thomas, born February 25, 1642, baptized next day; and William, February 6, 1643, died in six days. His inventory shows Feb. 6, 1643, died in six days. His inventory shows 1266 pounds sterling, 9 sh., 7 p. His widow married Dec., 1647, Governor Winthrop, brought him son Joshua, who died within two years, and married next, March 10, 1651, John Coggan, bore him Joshua, Caleb, and Sarah; and after his death in 1658, wished to be married again, as related by Rev. John Davenport; and, it is said, poisoned herself for ill-success. The will of his mother aids our research for genealogy. Its date is April 30, 1658, and names the four children of William Tyng, who had married her eldest daughter Elizabeth; five of Increase Nowell; five of Thomas Graves, who were all the living grandchildren; besides the daughters, Sarah Williams, to whom she gave land at Woburn; Parnell Nowell; and Catharine Graves, as also Martha, the widow of Coggan, who had before been widow of her son Thomas, and of Governor Winthrop.

REFERENCES:—Savage's Gen. Dict., vol. I, 467.

COZENS. Morse Mem. Appendix, 49; Savage's Gen. Dict.. vol. I, 468.

COZZINS. Hinman's Conn. Settlers, 739; Barry's Hist. of Framingham, Mass., 216; Spooner Gen., vol. I, 405.

CRABB:—Henry, of Boston, married January 1, 1658, Hannah, the daughter of Thomas Emmons, had Samuel, named in the will of his grandfather Emmons, January 20, 1661.

JOHN CRABB, of Dorchester, 1630, came, I presume, in the "Mary and John," requested October 19th to be made freeman, but probably went home soon, at least never took the oath; though Dr. Harris, who finds him in town records, 1632, says he removed to Connecticut. As this could not be before 1635, it is liable to doubt.

RICHARD CRABB, of Wethersfield, was representative 1639, '40 and '41; sold estate 1643, and removed probably to Stamford, and in 1655, was of Greenwich. See Hinman, 127; Savage's Gen. Dict., vol. I, 468.

CRABTREE:—John, of Boston 1639, a joiner, by wife Alice, had John, born October 23, 1639; and Deliverance, September 3, 1641, died within two years. He died late in 1656, and his widow married February 11, 1657, Joshua Hewes. Savage's Gen. Dict., vol. I, 468.

CRACKBONE:—Gilbert, of Dorchester, freeman, December, 1636, removed soon to Cambridge, had, perhaps, the four, whose death is on record. Mary, May 30, Judith, July 7, both of 1653; Hannah September 24, 1658; and Benjamin, April 27, 1661; yet we know not who was mother of either. But as he married June 17, 1656, Elizabeth Cooledge, it is clear the first two were by former wife; and of the last named we may doubt for two reasons, that in his register, Matchless says: "his son Benjamin was about five or six years old, when his father joined here," though he leaves it uncertain how old he was when that was written, still we might infer,

that he was continued in life. Next, we know that one Benjamin Crackbone was killed by the Indians, Sept. 4, 1675, at Northfield, under Captain Beers, and probably was that man's son. He died January 9, 1672. His will, of December 20, with codicil of January 2, preceding, names son Benjamin and his children Joseph and Sarah. His widow was Elizabeth. Savage's Gen. Dict., vol. I, 468.

CRACKSTONE or CRAXTON.

CRACKSTONE:—John, of Plymouth, came in the "Mayflower," 1620, with son of same name, died before end of March following. Savage's Gen. Dict., vol. I, 469.

CRAFORD or CRAFFORD.

CRAFORD:—John, of Dover, 1671.

MORDECAI CRAFORD, of Salem, in 1663, had wife Judith.

MUNGO CRAFORD, of Boston, 1686, a Scotchman, had been some years here apprentice, or a servant of John Smith, the mason, and this year was allowed to be an inhabitant. By wife Mary, he had Elizabeth, born May 19, 1681, who died young; was, I believe, among the adherents of Andros, imprisoned April, 1689, but did not go home, and is among the taxed 1695; by second wife Susannah, had only child Mary, who married Stephen Paine, and died 1712. The inventory of 109 pounds sterl. 9 sh. 10 p. had drugs and medicines for two-fifths. His widow Susannah made her will August 27, 1713, probated September 15, afterwards making daughter Mary and her husband Stephen executor, giving all to Mary, except 20 pound sterl. to each of the grandchildren. An early settler, Mr. Craford, probably of Watertown, had been drowned. See Winthrop I, 138, and Lieutenant Feake, and three other gentlemen of that town, by order of October 6, 1684, were to be taken inventory of his estate for the Court.

STEPHEN CRAFORD, of Kittery, 1640, died at Isle of Shoals. 1647, leaving widow and one child. Savage's Gen. Dict., vol. I, 469.

CRADOCK. N. E. Hist. and Gen. Reg., VIII, 25; IX, 122; X, 231; Heraldic Journal, vol. I, 1865; Robert Cradock Biog. (1856.)

CRAFT. Jackson's Hist. of Newton, Mass., 263; Hodgson's Hist. of Westford, Mass., 443; Judd's Hist. of Hadley, Mass., 473; Roe's Sketches of Rose, N. Y., 214; Hinman's Conn. Settlers, 741.

CRAFTS:—Griffin, of Roxbury, 1630, came probably with wife Alice and daughter Hannah, in the fleet with Winthrop, freeman, May 18, 1631; had John, born July 10, 1630, the earliest birth in town record; Mary, Oct. 10, 1632; Abigail, March 28, 1634; Samuel, December 12, 1637; and Moses, April 28, 1641; was lieutenant, selectman, representative 1663-7, artillery company, 1668, and died 1690, leaving widow Dorcus, his third or fourth wife, who died December 30, 1697; but he had former wife, for he married July 15, 1673, Ursula, widow of William Robinson of Dorchester, being her fourth husband; and in the record is Alice Crafts, died March 26, 1673, aged 73. In his will, made May 18, 1689, probated November 9, 1690, of which Samuel was executor, he names Abigail, who had first married January 24, 1651, John Ruggles, as wife of Edward Adams; Hannah, as wife of Nathaniel Wilson; and grandchild Ephraim, son of John. Apostle Eliot, spells his name "Crofts;" in some other records "e" is used for "s" final; and often the first five letters made the name.

THOMAS CRAFTS, of Hadley, 1678, died 1692, leaving six children, of whom only John was of Hatfield, had issue. Five of this name had, in 1833, been graduates at Harvard and four at the other New England Colleges.

REFERENCES:—Mitchell's Hist. of Bridgewater, Mass., 143; Kingman's Hist. of North Bridgewater, Mass., 473; Ellis' Hist. of Roxbury, Mass., 94; Temple's Hist. of Whately, Mass., vol. I, 469; Cothren's Ancient Woodbury, Conn., vol. I, 525; II, 1476; Chandler Gen., 275; Ruggle's Gen., Driver Gen., 305; Dows' Gen., 185; Savage's Gen. Dict., vol. I, 469; Craft's Gen., 1893.

CRAGG:—John, embarked at Barbados for New England, January 31, 1679, perhaps only transient visitor. Savage's Gen. Dict., vol. I, 469.

CRAGGAN:—John, of Woburn, married November 4, 1661, Sarah Dawes, had Abigail, born August 4, 1662; Sarah, August 10, 1664; Elizabeth, August 3, 1666; Mercy, March 25, 1669; Ann, August 6, 1673; John, Sept. 19, 1677; and Rachel and Leah, twins, March 14, 1680, both died in four days. Savage's Gen. Dict., vol. I, 470.

CRAGEN. Kidder's Hist. of New Ipswich, Mass., 353.

CRAGIN. Sewall's Hist. of Woburn, Mass., 607; Stearn's Hist. of Rindge, N. H., 192; Smith's Hist. of Peterborough, N. H., 42; Livermore's Hist. of Wilton, N. H., 353; Hayward's Hist. of Hancock, N. H., 465; Blood's Hist. of Temple, N. H., 213; Amer. Ancestry, vol. I, 18; VIII, 87; Cragin Gen., 1860.

CRAIG:—James and his brother Thomas Craig, were early settlers in Pennsylvania; the former in Allen township, Burk County, Pa., and the latter in 1728, went to the Forks of the Delaware and settled what was afterwards known as the Irish and later as Craig's Settlement.

REFERENCES:—Clyde's Irish Settlement, Pa., 35; Littell's Passaic Valley, 98; Butler's Hist. of Farmington Me., 440; Hayward's Hist. of Hancock, N. H., 468; Ooggswell's Hist. of Henniker, N. H., 534; Chase's Hist. of Chester, N. H., 496; Egle's Penn. Gens., 484; Draper's Hist. of Spencer, Mass., 189; Washburn's Hist. of Leicester, Mass., 352; Washington, N. H., Hist., 350; North's Hist. of Augusta, Me., 842; Bass' Hist. of Braintree, Vt., 128; Prentice Gen., Amer. Ancestry, vol. XI, 136.

CRAGBORE. Paige's Hist. of Cambridge, Mass., 518.

CRAIGUE. Hayward's Hist. of Hancock, N. H., 469.

CRAIK. Hayden's Virginia Gens., 341; Slaughter's Fry Memoir., 76.

CRAIN. Egle's Penn. Gens., 117; Washington, N H., Hist., 352.

CRADLE. Hayden's Virginia Gen., 117.

CRAM—John, of Boston, 1637, executor 1639, Hampton, 1658, died March 5, 1682. In 1665 he had wife Esther, children Benjamin, Thomas, Lydia and Mary

REFERENCES.

NEW HAMPSHIRE.—Washington, N. H., Hist., 350; Dow's Hist. of Hampton, 649; Coggswell's Hist. of Nottingham, 338; Cochrane's Hist. of Antrim, 439; Runnel's Hist. of Sanbornton, II, 187; Morrill's Hist. of Ackworth, 203; Livermore's Hist. of Wilton, 353; Hurd's Hist. of Rockingham County, 446; Hayward's Hist. of Hancock 470; Fullerton's Hist. of Raymond, 193.

OTHER PUBLICATIONS.—Bass' Hist. of Braintree, Vt. 128; Poor's Hist. of Merrimac Valley, 104; Savage's Gen. Dict., 570.

CRAMER. Smith's Hist. of Rhinebeck, N. Y., 198.

CRAMPTON:—Dennis, of Guilford, 1656, married September 16, 1660, Mary, daughter of John Parmelee, had Hannah, Elizabeth and Nathaniel, this last born March, 1667, and she died on the 16th of the same month. By second wife Sarah, widow of Nicholas Munger, had Sarah, born December 17, 1669; Thomas, November 25, 1672; and John, June 16, 1675; lived some years at Killingworth, but went back to Guilford before marriage of third wife Frances, was living there 1685; and died Jan. 31, 1690, leaving good estate. He is the man called by Kellond and Kirk (to whom Governor Endicott had issued warrant for arrest of Whalley and Goffe, the regicides,) Dennis Scranton, when they made report of their unsuccessful errand. Of this document not exceeded in curious detail by any in New England history, see Hutchinson Collection, 334. Elizabeth married 1686, John Lee, of Westfield, as his second wife, and Sarah married John Evarts, as his second wife.

JOHN CRAMPTON, of Norwalk, 1672, was a soldier in Philip's War, had lived 1661, at Fairfield, there married Hannah, daughter of Francis Andrews, and by her had Hannah, born 1662, who married March 5, 1680, Benjamin Scribner, or Scrivener; and for second wife married October 8, 1676, Sarah, daughter of John Rockwell, of Stamford, had Sarah, born September 10, 1679; Abigail, August 9, 1681; and John, January 7, 1683.

SAMUEL CRAMPTON, a soldier of Lothrop's company, killed at Bloody Brook, September 18, 1675.

REFERENCES:—Amer. Ancestry, IX, 220; Stone Gen., 16; Savage's Gen. Dict., vol. I, 471.

CRAMER. Smith's Hist. of Rhinebeck, N. Y., 198.

CRAMWELL:—John, of Boston, died 1639. Another John Cramwell, of Boston, by wife Rebecca, had Rebecca, born July 20, 1654. But this is more probable Cromwell.

REFERENCES:—Savage's Gen. Dict., vol. I, 471.

CRANBERRY.

CRANBERRY:—Nathaniel, killed by the Indians at Deerfield, September, 1675, was probably a soldier.

REFERENCES:—Savage's Gen. Dict., vol. I, 471.

CRANCH.

CRANCH:—Andrew, of New Hampshire, born about 1646, was of grand jury 1684 and '85.

REFERENCES:—Alden's Am. Epitaphs, III, 13; Savage's Gen. Dict., vol. I, 471.

CRANCE. Am. Ancestry, II, 28.

CRANDALL.

CRANDALL:—James, of Westerly, 1675, or before. John Crandall, of Providence, 1637, married Elizabeth, daughter of Samuel Gorton, and adopted his opinion, I suppose, for in August, 1651, he is imprisoned at Boston for a Baptist, freeman at Newport, 1655, removed to Westerly, preached as 7th day Baptist and died 1676. He had two daughters, of whom one married Job Babcock; and other, Josiah Witter. Other children were John, Jeremiah, Peter, Joseph and Eber.

REFERENCES:—Hayward's Hist. of Gilsum, N. H., 293; Austin's Allied Families, R. I., 74; Austin's R. I. Gen. Dict., 58; Long Meadow, Mass., Centen., 57; Waldo's Hist. of Tolland, Conn., 86; Williams' Hist. of Danby, Vt., 132; Roe's Sketches of Rose, N. Y., 203; Greene Gen.; Stanton Gen., 490; Amer. Ancestry, II, 28, IV, 95.

CRANDON. Davis' Landmarks of Plymouth, 74.

COP.NEILISEN. Bergen's Hist. of Kings County, N. Y., 69.

CORNELIUS. Bunker's L. I. Genealogies, 192; Amer. Ancestry, II, 27.

CORNELL.

CORNELL:—Samuel, of Dartmouth, took oath of fidelity 1684.

THOMAS CORNELL, of Boston, 1639, removed to Portsmouth, R. I., 1654, or earlier; was freeman there 1655, perhaps had Thomas Jr., of whom, perhaps, that he was hanged for murder of his mother is all that is now wished to be known.

REFERENCES:—Baird's Hist. of Rye, N. Y., 454; Bolton's Hist. of Westchester County, N. Y., II, 719; Bergen's Kings County, N. Y., Settlers, 71; Hazen's Hist. of Billerica, Mass., 26; Austin's R. I. Gen. Dict., 54; Prime's Sands Gen., 69; Amer. Ancestry, vol. I, 17; III, 123, 139; IV, 33, 145; Savage's Gen. Dict., vol. I, 457.

CORNELLY.

CORNELLY:—William, of Duxbury, 1637. Winsor, 248, 306, with strange spelling at the first.

REFERENCES:—Savage's Gen. Dict., vol. I, 458.

COURNEY or CURNEY.

CORNEY:—John, of Falmouth, had Elisha, born 1668; removed to Salem or Gloucester. Willis. I, 209. At Gloucester he married Nov. 18, 1670, Abigail Skilling; had Elisha, born Sept. 25, 1672; Abigail, February 8, 1676, and John, Sept. 27, 1678, died at 2 weeks.

REFERENCES:—Savage's Gen. Dict., vol. I, 458.

CORNHILL.

CORNHILL:—Richard, of Newtown, L. I., 1666.

SAMUEL CORNHILL, of Salem, 1638, born about 1616, freeman June 2, 1641, was one of the founders of the church in Beverly. 1667. had Samuel, which was of Beverly, 1657; and Sarah, baptized June 4, 1643.

THOMAS CORNHILL, of Boston, 1638, then allowed to keep an ordinary; had land at Mt. Woliaston, now Braintree, probably accompanied Mrs. Hutchinson to Rhode Island, then to Long Island, and there, in 1643, was cut off by the Indians. Perhaps the spelling is sometimes Connell.

REFERENCES:—Savage's Gen. Dict., vol. I, 458.

CORNFORTH. Hatch's Hist. of Industry, Me., 562.

CORNING. Hinman's Conn. Settlers, 713; Bliss Gen., 691; Amer.Ancestry, vol. I, 17; IX, 210.

CORNISH.

CORNISH:—Edward, servant of John Harris, embarked at Barbados, May 28, 1679, for Boston, in the "William and John."

JAMES CORNISH, of Saybrook, 1662, school-master, at Northampton, 1664, where his wife died Dec. 28, of that year, removed to Westfield, freeman 1669; in 1678 was desired at Norwalk, for some service and in Andros's time was clerk of the County Court, had Gabriel, who was under age in 1667; James, born 1663, who went to Simsbury; and perhaps other children.

REFERENCES:—Gen. Register of the first settlers of New England, page 69; Stiles' Hist. of Ancient Windsor, Conn., pages 228, 398, 399, 400.

In an account of town debts Stiles' Ancient Windsor, February, 1660-'61, occurs an item of 4 pounds sterling, 10 shillings, to Mr. Cornish, for schooling. This was probably James Cornish, whom we find mentioned at different times and places along the river as a schoolmaster. He was for some time a resident of Windsor.

RICHARD CORNISH, of Mass., 1634, surety for his wife's behavior (Hutch. I, 436,) may be the same which Winthrop II, 210, tells of, as removed from Weymouth, to York, there murdered, 1644.

SAMUEL CORNISH, of Salem, 1637, had daughter Remember, baptized May 3, 1640; and Samuel, March 14, 1641. Possibly in Felt, I, 174, or Colonial Records or Church Records of baptism, Corning and Cornish may be confused.

THOMAS CORNISH, of Gloucester, married Sept. 4, 1641, Mary, daughter of John Stone, had John, born Sept. 1, 1642; was of Exeter, 1652.

REFERENCES:—Hinman's Conn. Settlers, 722; Davis' Landmarks of Plymouth, 70; Savage's Gen. Dict., vol. I, 458.

CORNU. Stearn's Hist. of Ashburnham, Mass., 655.

CORNWALL. Goodwin's Foote Gen., 245; Hinman's Conn. Settlers, 724; Hall's Genealogical Notes, 152; N. E. Hist. and Gen. Reg., XLIX, 39; Andrews' Hist. of New Britain, Conn., 229.

CORNWALLES. Neil's Carolorum, a, 99.

CORNWELL.

CORNWELL:—Thomas, of Portsmouth, R. I., died before 1873.

WILLIAM CORNWELL, of Roxbury, 1634, when his wife was Joan, removed to Hartford, 1639, thence to Middletown, was representative 1654, '64 and '65, died February 21, 1678, leaving widow Mary, son John, born April, 1640; William, June 24, 1678, Samuel, Sept., 1642; Jacob, Sept., 1646; Thomas, Sept., 1648; beside Sarah, Oct., 1647, who married Oct. 16, 1675, Daniel Hubbard; Esther married 1671, John Wilcox of the same, and next, 1678, John Stow of the same; and Elizabeth, who married John Hall.

REFERENCES:—Middlefield, Conn. Hist.; Kellogg's White Gen., 27; Amer. Ancestry, II, 28; Savage's Gen. Dict., vol. I, 459.

CORP. Austin's R. I. Gen. Dict., 56.

CORRELL. Power's Hist. of Sangamon County, Ill., 228.

CORRINGTON.

CORRINGTON:—John, came in the "Susan and Ellen," 1635, aged 33, with wife Mary, 33.

REFERENCES:—Savage's Gen. Dict., vol. I, 459.

CORSE.

CORSE:—James, of Deerfield, before 1690, married Elizabeth, daughter of John Catlin of the same, died May 15, 1696, leaving Ebenezer, James and Elizabeth.

REFERENCES:—Temple's Hist. of Northfield, Mass., 425; Savage's Gen. Dict., vol. I, 459.

CORSEN. Clute's Hist. of Staten Island, 358.

CORSER. Coffin's Hist. of Boscawen, 497; Amer. Ancestry, X, 43.

CORSON. Davis' Hist. of Bucks County, Pa., 357; Neff Gen., 316; Amer. Ancestry, IX, 163.

CORSS. Amer. Ancestry, IX, 54.

CORTEIS. Barry's Hist. of Hanover, Mass., 272.

CORTELYOU. Clute's Hist. of Staten Island, N. Y., 363; Bergen's Kings County, N. Y., Settlers, 74; Hist. of Somerset County, N. J., 806; Bergen Gen., 90, 128, 150; Honeyman's Our Home, 242; Van Brunt Gen., 18.

CORTHELL. Barry's Hist. of Hanover, 271; Whitman Gen., 141; Hobart's Hist. of Abington, Mass., 365.

CORTLANDT. Heraldic Jour., III, 70, 150.

CORTWRIGHT. Gumaer's Deer Park, 69.

CORWIN. Hinman's Conn. Settlers, 788; Essex Inst. Hist. Coll., XVII, 331; Cleveland's Hist. of Yates County, N. Y., 556; Corwin Gen.

CURWIN. Savage's Gen. Dict., vol. I, 488; N. E. Hist. and Gen. Reg., X, 304.

CURWEN. Heraldic Journal, vol. I, 1865, 144; Drake's Hist. of Boston, Mass.; Essex Inst. Coll., II, 228; Vinton's Giles Mem., 339.

CORWITH. Howell's Hist. of Southampton, 226.

CORY, COREE, COUREE or COREY.

CORY:—Abraham, of Southold, L. I., 1662, was made freeman of Connecticut that year, married Margaret, daughter of Jeffry Christophers, and Margaret, who married Willoughby Lynde of Saybrook.

GILES CORY, of Salem, 1649, had daughter Deliverance, born August 5, 1658, by wife Margaret; and married second wife April 11, 1664, Mary Britz, who died August 27, 1684, aged 63. He had third wife Martha, who was admitted to the church at the village now Danvers, April 27, 1690, imprisoned in March, 1692, convicted and hanged for witchcraft on the Thursday following the suffering of her husband. At the age of almost 77, he was the victim of that execrable fanaticism of 1692. When the preposterous indictment was read, he stood mute, though he had before said he was not guilty; and was, by force of sentence, under the cruel old common law, pressed to death, Felt says, "On Sept. 19, (other accounts 16th, which must be wrong,) being the only person who ever endured that barbarous process in Massachusetts. On July 25th, he confirmed the will made in prison April 24th, preceding, giving estate to his son-in-law William Cleves, of Beverly, and John Moulton, of Salem. He was a member of the first church by which of course he was excommunicated, Sept. 18, the day before his dreadful fate; and so long did the infernal delusion last, that this sentence was erased by vote only at the end of 20 years though in case of his wife's membership of another church the malignity lasted but eleven years." Felt II, 475-85. Hutch. II, 59. Calef, More Wonders of Invisible World, 217, 18. The late Hon. Daniel P. King, of Danvers, occupied the homestead of poor Cory. In Essex Hist. Coll., I, 56, is petition of his daughter Elizabeth for self and other children. His daughter Martha married Cleves.

JOHN and THOMAS CORY, were of Chelmsford, 1691; but I know no more of either.

WILLIAM CORY, of Portsmouth, R. I., had Michael, born April 21, 1688; and no more is heard of him.

REFERENCES:—Stearn's Hist. of Rindge, N. H., 469; Littell's Passaic Valley, 94; Austin's R. I. Gen. Dict., 56.

COSIN, COZENS or COUSINS.

COSIN:—Abraham, of Sherborn, married at Woburn, November 19, 1684, Mary Eames, had Abraham, born August 22, 1685; Isaac, June 2, 1688; Jacob and Joseph, twins, August 13, 1692, and Mary, May 10, 1695. Morse thinks him son of Isaac, of Rowley, and that he had served in the war against Philip. Though the two points are not utterly inconsistent I look on their concurrence as improbable.

EDMUND COSIN, of Boston, lived at Pulling Point, married 1656 or '57, Margaret Bird, servant to John Grover, of Rumney Marsh.

FRANCIS COSIN, was of artillery company 1640.

GEORGE COSIN, whose name is Coussens in the custom house records, came in the "James," from Southampton to Boston, arrived June 3, 1635.

ISAAC COSIN, of Rowley, about 1650, was from Marlborough, in Wiltshire, went to New London, where he had a grant of lot, 1651, but did not take it, and went back to Rowley; had wife Ann, in 1658, on the Boston records of marriage (when the date is omitted though we may be sure it was 1657,) called Hunt, formerly wife of John Edwards; but on the same record appears, that by former wife Elizabeth, who died Dec. 14, 1656, he had Sarah, born August 31, preceding.

JOHN COSIN, of Casco, in that part now North Yarmouth, 1645, born about 1596, died at York, 1689.

REFERENCES:—Wills, I, 44, 55, 65, 231.

MATTHEW COSIN, of Boston, 1656.

RICHARD COSIN, of Saybrook, married March 7, 1678, Mary, daughter of Alexander Chalker, had Hannah, born March 17, 1679; Sarah, May 10, 1683, and Bethia, Nov. 4, 1685. Sarah was born at Block Island.

WILLIAM COSIN, of Boston, 1649.

REFERENCES:—Savage's Gen. Dict., vol. I, 460.

COSGROVE. Barlow Gen.

COSMORE.

COSMORE:—John, of Southampton, L. I., an Assistant of Connecticut, 1647-58, except 51, 2, 3 and 4, when perhaps, he was gone from this country. Strange is it, that we know no more.

REFERENCES:—Hinman's Conn. Settlers, 727; Savage's Gen. Dict., vol. I, 460.

COSSER.

COSSER:—Hercules, of Boston, 1659.

WILLIAM COSSER, of Boston, 1657. Two Scots, of whose names I see not any other mention except that they were early members of the Charity Society, preserved in Drake's History of Boston, 455. Yet the name may be Courser, to whom one of the references in the Index points.

REFERENCES:—Savage's Gen. Dict., vol. I, 461.

COSSETT. Cossett Gen.

COSTER. Amer. Ancestry, VIII, 240; Munsell's Albany Coll., IV, 110.

COST. Turner's Phelps Purchase, 228.

COSTIN or COSTING.

COSTIN:—William, of Concord, had Sarah, and Phebe, about 1642, perhaps was of Boston, in 1654, called Castine, and at Wickford, 1674.

REFERENCES:—Savage's Gen. Dict., vol. I, 462.

COTELLE. Swift's Barnstable, Mass., vol. I, 250.

COTHEAL. Amer. Ancestry, IX, 141.

COTHILL.

COTHILL:—John, a person named in Hutch. I, 354, as one of Sir E. Andros's Council, but as no such name is heard of, we may fear this a typographical error, for Hutch. could not be wrong on such a point.

REFERENCES:—Savage's Gen. Dict., vol. I, 462.

COTHREN. Hinman's Conn. Settlers, 730; Butler's Hist. of Farmington, Me., 437; Amer. Ancestry, V, 215; Cothren's Hist. of Ancient Woodbury, Conn., II, 1482.

COTTA, COTTY or COTTEY.

COTTA:—John, of Boston, freeman 1671, married 1668, Mary, daughter of Jeremiah Moore, artillery company 1679, died Nov. 20, 1723, aged 77.

ROBERT COTTA, of Salem, freeman May 6, 1635, probably had wife Joan and a son whose name is not given, baptized January 28, 1638; Bathshua, March 24, 1639; Mary, September 20, 1640; Peter, May 1, 1642: Obadiah, September 10, 1643; and John, May 11, 1645.

REFERENCES:—Savage's Gen. Dict., vol. I, 462.

COTTER.

COTTER:—William, of New London, 1660-8, had wife Elinor.

REFERENCES:—Gold's Hist. of Cornwall, Conn., 275; Savage's Gen. Dict., vol. I, 462.

COTTERILL, COTTEREL or COTTRELL.

COTTERILL:—Francis, of Wells, 1668.

NICHOLAS COTTERILL, of Newport, 1639, freeman 1655, removed to Westerly, 1669, and died 1715. His children were Nicholas, Gershom; Mary, who married Edward Larkin, of Newport; Elizabeth, John, Samuel, Nathaniel and Dorothy.

ROBERT COTTERILL, of Providence, 1645. Savage's Gen. Dict., vol. I, 462.

COTTRELL. Farrow's Hist. of Isleborough, Me., 190; Austin's R. I. Gen. Dict., 57; Amer. Anestry, vol. I, 17.

COTTRILL. Heminway's Vt. Gaz., IV, 520.

COTTING. Hudson's Hist. of Marlborough, Mass., 351; Cutter's Arlington, 208.

COTTLE.

COTTLE:—Edward, of Nantucket, had Judith, born April 13, 1670; Lydia, May 17, 1672; Ann, March 3, 1674; and John, Sept. 7, 1675. Dorothy, perhaps his wife, died October 1, 1681. But he had first lived at Salisbury, there by wife Judith, had Edward, born January 17, 1652, died in a few months; Mary, Nov. 1, 1653; Benjamin, March 2, 1655; Sarah, March, 1657; Judith, March 5, 1659, probably died young; Elizabeth April 19, 1663; and Edward, again, Sept. 28, 1666.

WILLIAM COTTLE, of Newbury, came in the "Con-

fidence," 1638, from Southampton, aged 12, as servant of John Saunders. He was son of Edward, of the city of Salisbury, Wiltshire, who died June 15, 1653; had Ezra, born May 5, 1662; Ann, July 12, 1663; and Susanna, Aug. 1665, and died April 30, 1668.

REFERENCES:—Poor's Hist. of Merrimac Valley, 169; Morrison's Hist. of Windham, N. H., 408; Hatch's Hist. of Industry, Me., 565; Amer. Ancestry, VIII, 206.

COTTON.

COTTON:—John, of Boston, the most distinguished divine that came from England in the first age, born at Derby, December 4, 1585, son of Rowland Cotton, Esq., was entered at the University of Cambridge, when 14 years old, bred at Trinity College, where he took his A. M., 1606, became fellow of Emanuel, after spending, as he says, fourteen years at Cambridge, preached at Boston, Lincolnshire, twenty-one years, from 1612, being by the choice of the corporation made vicar; came with several of his parish in the "Griffin," arrived Sept. 4, 1633, with wife Sarah and their first child named at baptism Seaborn, (from the circumstance of his birth,) received at the church on Sunday following, Sept. 8; on October 10, was ordained teacher of that church, freeman May 4, 1634, died Dec. 23, 1652, yet the old copy of town records of which, I presume, no original has been known for 150 years, has it 15. His daughter ensuing on taking cold in crossing the ferry as he went to preach a few days before at Cambridge. His will of Nov. 30, of that year with codicil of Dec. 12, mentioned the four children, Seaborn, John, Elizabeth and Mary, with wife Sarah, and "house and garden in the market-place of Boston, in Lincolnshire," as well as the "small part of my house, which Sir Henry Vane built, whilst he sojourned with me," and at his departure gave by deed, to son Seaborn; and also mentioned cousin Henry Smith, and cousin John Angier, with his wife and children all living at his house and kinswoman Martha Mellowes, who I judge to be widow of Abraham. But the name of grandchild Betty Day, in the codicil can only be explained by supposing that his wife had by former husband a daughter who had married a Day and had this child. We know she was not grandchild in natural descent. He lived 18 years with wife Elizabeth Horrocks, and had no children; by second wife, widow Sarah Story, who outlived him, and married August 26, 1656, Richard Mather, outlived him, and died May 27, 1676, had the son before mentioned born on the ocean, August 12, 1633, baptized 4 days after he reached port: Sarah, born Sept. 12, baptized Sept. 20, 1635, betrothed to Jonathan Mitchell, but died of small-pox, Jan. 20, 1650; Elizabeth 9, baptized Dec. 10, 1637; John, March 15, baptized March 22, 1640, Harvard College, 1657; Mary or Maria, February 16, baptized February 20, 1642; and Rowland, about 6 days old, baptized Dec. 24, 1643, died of small-pox, Jan. 29, 1650. Elizabeth married Oct. 12, 165, Jeremiah Eggington, died Aug. 31, following, having Elizabeth born Aug. 15, who died soon; Maria married March 6 1663, Rev. Increase Mather, and died April 4, 1714. Twenty-one of his descendants in the male line (beside the many thro male or female of the Mather blood, and many grand-daughters and other females,) had been in 1818, graduates at Harvard, of whom two thirds were clergymen.

THOMAS COTTON, of Roxbury, had Thomas, born April 21, 1664, may be he who died at Chelmsford, Sept. 30, 1687.

WILLIAM COTTON, of Boston, a butcher, may have been before joining our church in May, 1647, first at Gloucester, for one William, either this or the next, owned land in 1642, at that place, where no more is told of him; born about 1610, freeman 1647, artillery company 1650, by wife Ann, had Mary, born Dec., 1641; John, Dec. 1643; William, May 31, 1646, died young; the three baptized May 16, 1647; Sarah, March 19, 1649; William, again, February 23, 1651, who died at 6 months; Rebecca, January 2, 1653; William, again, February 4, 1655; Thomas, Jan. 18, 1657; Hannah, 1660; and Benjamin, baptized March 25, 1666. John, his son may have been of Concord, 1665, and 1679, perhaps the freeman of 1680, belonged to second church of Boston. Mary, his daughter, married March 7, 1660, John Matson.

WILLIAM COTTON, a witness, Dec. 12, 1653, at Weymouth, to will of Joseph Shaw, is not known for anything else.

WILLIAM COTTON, of Portsmouth, 1640, of the Grand Jury, 1669, died about 1677.

WILLIAM COTTON, of Boston, possibly the same as first, by wife Mary, had John, born 1666; and Jeremiah, 1670.

REFERENCES.

MASSACHUSETTS.—Jackson's Hist. of Newton, 251; Freeman's Hist. of Cape Cod, vol. I, 361; II, 276; Davis' Landmarks of Plymouth, 72; Allen's Worcester Asso., 154; Sewell's Hist. of Woburn, 337; Heraldic Journal, IV, 49.

OTHER PUBLICATIONS.—Hinman's Conn. Settlers, 734; Pierce's Hist. of Gorham, Me., 158; Lapham's Hist. of Woodstock, Me., 196; Dow's Hist. of Hampton, N. H., 646; Durant's Hist. of Lawrence County, Pa., 180; Norton's Hist. of Knox County, Ohio, 297; Vinton's Giles Mem., 77; Wetmore Gen., 327; Dudley Gen., 121; Kellogg's White Gen., 52; Drake's Cotton Pedigree, 1856; Savage's Gen. Dict., vol. I, 462; N. E. Hist. and Gen. Reg., vol. I, 164; IV, 92; XLIX, 180; Amer. Ancestry, VIII, 128; IX, 124, 170; Cotton Gen.

COTYMORE.   Dunstable Bi-Centen., 171.

COUCH.

COUCH:—John, of York, freeman 1652.

ROBERT COUCH, of New Hampshire, 1656-69.

SIMON COUCH, of Fairfield, freeman 1664. In the Colonial Record his name has an "r."

THOMAS COUCH, of Wethersfield, 1666, and died there 1687; had Susanna, then 20 years old; Simon, 18; Rebecca, 15; Hannah, 13; Thomas, 12; Mary, 11; Sarah, 8; Abigail, 6; and Martha, 3. Hinman, I, 27.

REFERENCES: — Hinman's Conn. Settlers, 787; Schenck's Hist. of Fairfield, Conn., 363; Todd's Hist. of Redding, Conn., 187; Richmond, Va., Standard, vol. I, 46; Nash Gen., 117; Coffin's Hist. of Boscawen, N. H., 510; Jessup Gen., 97.

COUES.   Brewster's Hist. of Portsmouth, 245.

COUGHLIN.   Stearn's Hist. of Ashburnham, Mass., 655.

COUGHTREY.   Amer. Ancestry, vol. I, 17.

COUNCE.   Wyman's Charlestown, Mass., Gens., vol. I, 244; Eaton's Hist. of Thomaston, Me., 188; Eaton's Annals of Warren, Me., 524.

COUNCIL.   Powers' Hist. of Sangamon County, Ill., 230.

COURTENAY.   Richmond, Va., Standard, III, 6; Amer. Ancestry, VI, 171.

CRANE.

CRANE:—Benjamin, of Medfield, 1649, married Sept. 12, 1656, Elinor Breck, probably daughter of Edward, of Dorchester, removed to Wethersfield, freeman of Connecticut, 1658, died May 31, 1691, leaving Benjamin, Jonathan, Joseph, John, Abraham, Jacob, Israel, Elizabeth and Mary. Perhaps he lived some years late in life at Taunton, for his son John there took his wife, and (which is better ground for the inference), there Samuel Hackett married, March 28, 1690, his daughter Mary.

CHRISTIAN CRANE, of Cambridge, 1647. But I doubt, that Farmer was deluded into deriving this name from Christopher Cane, which see.

HENRY CRANE, of Dorchester, 1658, in Milton, 1667-77, married a daughter of Stephen Kingsley.

HENRY CRANE, of Guilford, 1664, was, perhaps father of that Mercy, who married October 30, 1701, John Hoadley, the second.

JASPER CRANE, of New Haven, 1639, had beside Hannah, who married Thomas Huntington, Deliverance, baptized June 14, 1642; Mercy, March 1, 1645; Micah, November 3, 1647; and Jasper, born 1651; removed to Branford, in 1668, had been representative of New Hampshire 1650, an assistant of New Haven Colony ten years before, and of the United Colony of Connecticut, three years.

JOHN CRANE, a youth, came to Boston in the Speedwell, 1656, aged 11, from London, of whom I hear no more.

JOHN CRANE, of Braintree or Dorchester, married Dec. 13, 1686, Hannah, daughter of the second James Leonard, and no more is known.

JONATHAN CRANE, of Norwich, 1680, married Dec. 19, 1678, Deborah, eldest daughter of Francis Griswold, had Sarah, Jonathan, John and Mary. Perhaps he had been first of Killingworth.

NATHANIEL CRANE, of Newton, by wife Mary, had Thomas, born February 27, 1687.

WILLIAM CRANE, a soldier in Philip's War, from some eastern part of the colony, was at Northampton, April, 1676.

REFERENCES.

CONNECTICUT.—Stile's Hist. of Windsor, II, 167; Orcutt's Hist. of Stratford, 1177; Orcutt's Hist. of New Milford, 689; Cothren's Hist. of Woodbury, II, 1483; Hinman's Conn. Settlers, 742.

NEW HAMPSHIRE.—Washington, N. H., Hist., 52, 362; Bassett's Hist. of Richmond, 377; Norton's Hist. of Fitzwilliam, 624; Smith's Hist. of Petersborough, 445.

OTHER PUBLICATIONS.—Mitchell's Hist. of Bridgewater, Mass., 143; Jameson's Hist. of Medway, Mass., 468; Longmeadow, Mass., Centen. 57; Eaton's Annals of Warren, Me., 526; Littell's Passaic Valley, N. J., Gens., 100, 498; Whittemore's Hist. of Montclair, N. J., 179; Coll. N. J. Hist. Society, VI; Supplement, 115; Thayer Memorial, 36; Trubee Gen., 113; Goode Gen., 152, 291; Smith's Life of Zena Crane, 55; Amer. Ancestry, vol. I, 18; III, 11, 119; IV, 20; V, 157; VI, 68; VIII, 33; IX, 129; Savage's Gen. Dict., vol. I, 471; N. E. Hist. and Gen.

Reg., XXVII, 76; XLI, 176; XLVI, 216; XLVII, 78, 325; Crane Gen.

CRANMER. Cregar's White Gen.

CRANNELL. Munsell's Albany Coll., IV, 110; Am. Ancestry, vol. I, 18.

CRANFIELD.

CRANFIELD:—Edward, of New Hampshire, came in October, 1682, as lieutenant-governor, swayed tyrannically till he went home 1685, died before 1704. Belknap I, 91-115; Chalmers, 493-7. Savage's Gen. Dict., vol. I, 471.

CRANIVER.

CRANIVER:—Richard, of Salem, married April 7, 1665, Elizabeth Woolland, as given for the name of w. had William, born December 27 following; Elizabeth, September 13, 1668; Richard, July 12, 1671; and Edward, March 28, 1674.

REFERENCES:—Savage's Gen. Dict., vol. I, 471.

CRANSTON.

CRANSTON:—John, of Newport, 1651, among freemen 1655, married Mary, daughter of Jeremiah Clark, was a physician, chosen Governor 1679; by fond tradition called descendant through his grandfather, John of Poole, from Lord William Cranston; died March 12, 1680, aged 54. His widow married John Stanton, died April 7, 1711.

WALTER CRANSTON, of Woburn, married June 4, 1683, Mary, daughter of George Brush of the same.

REFERENCES:—Hudson's Hist. of Marlborough, Mass., 352; Narr. Hist. Reg., VII, 342; Heraldic Journal, III, 59; Draper's Hist. of Spencer, Mass., 187; Martin's Hist. of Chester, Pa., 108; Austin's R. I. Gen. Dict., 60; Austin's Ancestries, 87; Montague Gen., 432; Amer. Ancestry, V, 83; Savage's Gen. Dict., vol. I, 472.

CRANWELL.

CRANWELL:—John, of Boston, 1630, probably came in the fleet with Winthrop, requested admission as freeman October 19, 1630; took the oath March 4, 1634, had lot at Muddy River, 1638; and as he is no more mentioned I suppose him the same person above, called Cramwell, in the town record of his death.

REFERENCES:—Savage's Gen. Dict., vol. I, 472.

CRAPO. Spooner Gen., vol. I, 176.

CRAPSER. Amer. Ancestry, II, 29.

CRARY.

CRARY:—Peter, of New London, 1676, married Dec. 1677. Christobel, daughter of John Gallup, the second, had Peter, John, William, Robert, Christobel, Margaret, and Ann, all living at his death, 1708.

REFERENCES:—Hinman's Conn. Settlers, 752; Savage's Gen. Dict., vol. I, 472.

CRATER. Crater Gen., 1894.

CRATHORNE. Penn. Mag., IV, 491.

CRAVER. Amer. Ancestry, vol. I, 119; II, 29.

CRAW.

CRAW:—Robert, of Newport, 1651. Savage's Gen. Dict., vol. I, 472.

CRAWLEY.

CRAWLEY:—Thomas, of Exeter, 1639, had several children, of whom the name of Phebe only is known. He probably went to Maine, where, in 1677, the Indian tenderness to one of the name is related. Belknap I, 20. 147.

REFERENCES:—Savage's Gen. Dict., vol. I, 473.

CRAWFORD:—Aaron, of Rutland, Mass., born at Tyrone, Ireland, about 1680, came to America in the spring of 1713, with sons Samuel, John and Alexander. He was of 3d generation of Alexander Crawford, second son of Malcom Crawford of Kilberny, Scotland, who was the fifteenth generation from Johannes de Crawford, who lived about 1140, younger brother of Domenic Galfridus, Feudal Lord of Crawfurd or Crawford.

REFERENCES.

NEW YORK.—Ruttenber's Hist. of Newburgh, 311, Pearson's Schenectady, N. Y., Settlers, 51; N. Y. Gen. and Biog. Rec., XVI, 110.

OTHER PUBLICATIONS.—Eaton's Annals of Warren, Me., 527; Lapham's Hist. of Paris, Me., 353; Bangor Hist. Mag., vol. I, 144; Ward's Hist. of Shrewsbury, Mass., 262; Reed's Hist. of Rutland, Mass., 155; Austin's R. I. Gen. Dict., 61; Chase's Hist. of Chester, N. H., 498; Heminway's Vt. Gaz., V, 245; Richmond, Va., Standard, II, 6; III, 28; Peyton's Hist. of Augusta County, Va., 314; Meade's Old Families of Va.; Crawford Gen. of Virginia Branch (1883;) Hayden's Weitzel Gen.; Gilmore's Georgians, 123; Amer. Ancestry, V, 71; X, 184.

CRAYFOOT.

Mr. CRAYFOOT, perhaps CRAWFORD, with whose prefix of respectability we would gladly purchase a Christian name, came in 1634, by the same ship with Simon Willard. Possibly the name was at Springfield Crowfoot. See that.

REFERENCES:—Savage's Gen. Dict., vol. I, 473.

CREAMER. Driver Gen., 276.

CREETMAN. Miller's Hist. of Colchester, 365.

CREGIER. Munsell's Albany, IV, 111.

CREGO. Amer. Ancestry, II, 29; Moore's Bontecou Gen., 164.

CREHORE.

CREHORE:—Teague, of Milton, 1670, had wife Mary, daughter of Robert Spurr, perhaps had Timothy.

REFERENCES:—Stearn's Hist. of Ashburnham, Mass., 655; Aldrich's Hist. of Walpole, 232; Amer. Ancestry, VI, 106; Crehore Gen.

CREIGH. Egle's Penn. Gens., 528, 536; Amer. Ancestry, VI, 202.

CREIGHTON. Eaton's Hist. of Thomaston, Me., 190; Eaton's Hist. of Warren, Me., 529; Odiorne Gen.

CRENSHAW. Richmond, Va., Standard, II, 30; III. 29; Goode Gen., 78.

CRESAP. Amer. Ancestry, V, 27.

CRESSON. Read's Hist. of Swanzey, N. H., 316; Cresson Gen.

CRESEY or CRESSEY.

CRESEY:—Michael, of Ipswich, died 1670, as Coffin says. Perhaps he had Michael and William, who were taxed at Rowley, 1691.

REFERENCES:— Huntington's Conn., Settlers, 26; Pierce's Hist. of Gorham, Me., 159; Coggswell's Hist. of Henniker, 534; Guild's Stiles' Gen., 87; N. E. Hist. and Gen. Reg., XXXI, 197; Cressy Gen.; Savage's Gen. Dict., vol. I, 473.

CRISSEY. Timlow's Hist. of Southington, Conn., 72; Young's Hist. of Chautauqua, N. Y., 563; Boyd's Hist. of Winchester, Conn., 270; Amer. Ancestry, IX, 72.

CRIBB:—John, came in the "Christian," 1635, aged 30. Savage's Gen. Dict., vol. I, 473.

CRIE. Eaton's Hist. of Thomaston, Me., 190.

CRICK:—Andrew Crick, of Topsfield, died 1658.

CRICK:—Edward, of Boston, artillery company, 1674, ensign in Philip's War, of Turner's company on Connecticut River, lieutenant with a command of 34 men at Wells, September 7, 1676, and a captain afterwards, died May 6, 1702.

REFERENCES:—Savage's Gen. Dict., vol. I, 474.

CRIPPIN.

CRIPPIN:—Thomas, of Haddam, had been there many years prior to April, 1689, when he gives deed of land to Shubael Rowley, who had married his eldest daughter Catharine. He had also, Mary, who married Jan. 28, 1690, Samuel Corbee, beside Mercy, Experience, Thomas and Jabez; but no dates can be heard of except as to the baptisms, when the subjects were adults.

CRIPPIN. Hinman's Conn. Settlers, 754; Sedgwick's Hist. of Sharon, Conn., 73; Loomis Gen. Female Branches, 693; Caverly's Hist. of Pittsford, Vt., 698; Amer. Ancestry, vol. I, 19.

CRIPS:—George, of Plymouth, 1643, was able to bear arms. Savage says: "Perhaps this should be Crisp or Crispe."

REFERENCES:—Savage's Gen. Dict., vol. I, 474; Clute's Hist. of Staten Island, N. Y., 44.

CRISP or CRISPE.

CRISP:—Benjamin, of Watertown, 1630, freeman 1646, had by wife Bridget, Elizabeth, born January 8, 1637; Mary, May 20, 1638; Jonathan, January 29, 1640; Eleazer, January 14, 1642; Mehitable, January 21, 1646; and Zechariah. From Bond we learn, that in 1630, he was servant of Major Gibbons, and perhaps, came as early as 1629; late in life removed to Groton, but was returned before 1682 to Watertown, and had married Joanna, widow of William Longley. Elizabeth married Sept. 27 or 29, 1657, George Lawrence.

RICHARD CRISP, of Boston, merchant, came from Jamaica, married 1666, Hannah, widow of Benjamin Richards, daughter of William Hudson, Jr., and in 1671, married Sarah, youngest daughter of Rev. John Wheelwright, and lived not long afterwards, I presume; had Sarah, born September 15, 1672, who married April 11, 1695; William Harris, and next, April 5, 1722, President Leverett; and next, July 15, 1725, Hon. John Clark; and for fourth husband, May 6, 1731, Rev. Benjamin Colman, and she died April 24, 1744.

RICHARD CRISP, of Boston, permitted to teach fencing, 1686. 3 Mass. Hist. Coll., VIII, 157. A Joanna Crisp died at Charlestown, April 8, 1698, aged 78. Perhaps she was widow of Benjamin, driven from Groton by the Indians.

CRISLER. Roe's Sketches of Rose, N. Y., 276.

CRISPEL. Schoonmaker's Hist. of Kingston, N. Y., 476; N. Y. Gen. and Biog. Rec., XXI, 83.

CRISPIN. Davis' Hist. of Bucks County, Pa., 300.

CRITCHELT:—Henry, of Boston, 1678, was of second church.

REFERENCES:—Chase's Hist. of Chester, N. H., 499.

CRITCHFIELD. Norton's Hist. of Knox County, Ohio, 322.

CRITTENDIN:—Abraham, (2) son of Abraham, (1,) was born in England, 1635, came to New England 1639, and settled in Guilford, Conn. He married May 16, 1661, Susannah, daughter of Thomas Grayson, of New Haven, who came to America, July 26, 1637, in company with John Davenport, Theophilus Eaton and others.

REFERENCES:—Hinman's Conn. Settlers, 755; Atkins' Hist. of Hawley, Mass., 67; Joslin's Hist. of Poultney, Vt., 243; Green's Kentucky Families; Richmond, Va., Standard, II, 7; Amer. Ancestry, VI, 206.

CROAKHAM, CROWKHAM or CROCUM.

CROAKHAM:—Frances, of Boston, 1665, married widow Joan Waller, to whose son Thomas he gave his estate, died about 1669. By Joan he had Hannah, born February 15, 1657, probably died young.

JOHN CROAKHAM, of Boston, married Rebecca, daughter of Abraham Josselyn, died December, 1678, without issue. His widow married Thomas Harris next year.

REFERENCES:—Savage's Gen. Dict., vol. I, 474.

CROADE.

JOHN CROADE, of Salem, married March 17, 1659, Elizabeth, daughter of Walter Price, had Elizabeth, born October 21, 1661, baptized April 27, 1662; John, June 14, baptized June 21, 1663; Hannah, July 14, baptized July 23, 1665; and Jonathan, born January 14, 1668; was freeman 1663, and died 1670. His widow married John Ruck.

RICHARD CROADE, of Boston, 1644, merchant, son of Richard, of Frampton, County Dorset, England, came from Bristol, had lived first at Hingham, there married Frances, daughter of William Hersey, May 29, 1656, and had John, born November 26, 1657, and others; but removed to Salem, there had Sarah, February 3, baptized February 18, 1666; William, born February 9, 1668, Hannah, November 14, 1671; and John again, February 25, 1673. He was licensed, 1678, to keep an inn, died 1689, aged 61, leaving widow Frances, and children, Hannah, Richard, William, John, Judith and Sarah. His daughter Judith, married Joseph Neal, and died before her father.

REFERENCES:—Savage's Gen. Dict., vol. I, 474.

CHRITCHLEY, CRUTCHLEY or CROYCHLEY.

CRITCHLEY:—Richard, of Boston, blacksmith, freeman May 19, 1642, married August, 1639, Alice, widow of William Dinely, had Samuel, born December 25, 1640; Joseph, May 3, baptized May 7, 1643, and died August 1645. But by another wife, for Alice died March 26,

1645, and his wife Jane, was admitted member of our church, November 27, 1647, had Jane, 1647; Elizabeth, November 28, baptized December 11, 1653; Mary, Jan. 18, baptized March 2, 1656, and John, 1657. He lived at Rumney Marsh, now Chelsea.

REFERENCES:—Savage's Gen. Dict., vol. I, 474.

CROCKER.

CROCKER:—Daniel, of Boston, married November 30, 1660, Sarah Baldwin, died at Marshfield, February 5, 1692. Another Daniel Crocker, of Salem, died probably November, 1681.

EDWARD CROCKER, of Boston, was the public executioner, 1684. In July, 1690, Edward of Salem, perhaps his son, was killed by the Indians at Casco or Falmouth.

FRANCIS CROCKER, of Barnstable, 1643, of age to bear arms. His wife died March, 1693, at Marshfield.

JOHN CROCKER, of Scituate, 1636, had William, born 1637; Elizabeth, 1639; Samuel, 1642; Job, 1644; Josiah, 1647; Eleazer, 1650, and Joseph, 1654; removed probably to Barnstable. (Deane.) But one of necessity distrusts the names and dates of all the children except the first, because they so wonderfully concur with those of his brother William's children, and in his will of Feb. 10, 1669, I find good reason, for he gives to his wife Joan, and to six children of his brother William, viz: John, Job, Samuel, Josiah, Elisha and Joseph; made Job executor, and names no children of his own.

RICHARD CROCKER, of Marblehead, 1674.

THOMAS CROCKER, of New London, 1660, by wife Rachel, had Mary, born March 4, 1669; Thomas, Sept. 1, 1670; John, 1672; William, 1675, died young; Samuel, July 27, 1676; William again, 1680, and Andrew, baptized April 1, 1683; was constable 1684, called in 1693, about 60 years old, died January 18, 1716.

WILLIAM CROCKER, ofBarnstable, brother of first John and tradition makes their arrival 1634, was first at Scituate, united with the church, December 25, 1636, by wife Alice, had John, born May 3, baptized June 11, 1637; and at Barnstable, Elizabeth, September 22, baptized Dec. 22, 1639, died at 18 years; Samuel, born July 3, 1642; Job March 9, 1645; Josiah, September 19, 1647; Eleazer, July 21, 1650, and Joseph, 1654; was representative 1670, '71 and 74. Twelve of this name had, in 1834, been graduated at Harvard, and five at Yale.

REFERENCES.

MASSACHUSETTS.—Kingman's Hist. of North Bridgewater, 480; Barry's Hist. of Hanover, 271; Swift's Barnstable Families, vol. I, 200; Freeman's Hist. of Cape Cod II, 281.

OTHER PUBLICATIONS.—Lapham's Hist. of Paris, Me., 563; Machias, Me., Centen., 159; Bangor Hist. Mag. V, 27; Eaton's Annals of Warren, Me., 531; Eaton's Hist. of Thomaston, Me., 195; Caulkins' Hist. of New London, Conn., 361; Sedgwick's Hist. of Sharon, Conn., 74; Hinman's Conn. Settlers, 755; Hollister's Hist. of Pawlet, Vt., 181; Holton's Winslow Mem., vol. I, 264; Emery's Hist. of Taunton Ministry, vol. I, 330; Amer. Ancestry, II, 29; XI, 135; Young's Hist. of Warsaw, N. Y., 251; Savage's Gen. Dict., vol. I, 474; N. E. Hist. and Gen. Reg., II, 389.

CROCKETT.

CROCKETT:—Thomas, of Kittery, 1648, York, 1652.

Hazard's Historical Collections, vol. I, 575; Belknap's N. H., I, 425, shows him here in 1633.

REFERENCES:—Pierce's Hist. of Gorham, Me., 160; Eaton's Hist. of Thomastown, Me., 191; Lapham's Hist. of Woodstock, Me., 197; Lapham's Hist. of Norway, Me., 484; Runnel's Hist. of Sanbornton, N. H., II, 189; Hayward's Hist. of Hancock, N. H., 471; Coggswell's Hist. of Nottingham; Peyton's Hist. of Augusta County, Va., 288; Wentworth Gen., II, 5, 91.

CROFOOT. Hough's Hist. of Lewis County, N. Y., 231; Hinman's Conn. Settlers, 767.

CROFF. Williams' Hist. of Danby, Vt., 133.

CROFT.

CROFT:—George, of Wickford, 1674.

THOMAS CROFT, of Hadley, married December 6, 1683, Abigail, daughter of John Dickinson, first of the same, had John, born November 8, 1684; Mary, February 2, 1686; Abigail September 29, 1688; Thomas February 27, 1690, died at 24 years; Elizabeth, April 17, 1691; and Benoin, Oct. 22, 1692. He died February 27, 1693, and his widow married November 30, 1704, Samuel Crofoot.

WILLIAM CROFT, of Lynn, 1650 to '75, had married Ann, widow of Thomas Ivory the first,who made her will June 25,1675, in which she names her son Thomas Ivory, daughter Sarah Chadwell, son Theophilus Bailey, and son John Burrill. Yet that will was not probated before November 26, 1689, the same time with his will of March 5, preceding, in which also are named the Ivory, Chadwell, Bailey and Burrell connections with additional gift to "cousins, the eldest childen each of Peter, Nathaniel, Samuel and William Frothingham;" but the relation is less easily discovered.

REFERENCES:—Orcutt's Hist. of Derby, Conn., 713; Savage's Gen. Dict., vol. I, 475.

CROMBIE. Coggswell's Hist. of New Boston, N. H., 374; Blood's Hist. of Temple, N. H., 215; Chase's Hist. of Chester, N. H., 500.

CROMPTON. Dawson Gen.

CROMWELL.

CROMWELL:—Giles, of Newbury, an early settler, whose wife died June 14, 1648. She was probably mother of all his children, but he married September 10, 1648, Alice Wiseman, who died June 6, 1669. He had Argentine, who married November 25, 1662, Benjamin Cram; Dorothy and Philip, probably older, as well as Thomas; and, perhaps, John; and died February 25, 1673. Dorothy died at Salem, September 27, 1673, aged 67, as the gravestone has it.

JOHN CROMWELL, of Boston, by wife Rebecca, had Rebecca, born July 20, 1654.

PHILIP CROMWELL, of Dover, 1657-74, married Elizabeth, daughter of Thomas Laighton, had Ann, born Aug. 19, 1674; and was probably, too old to have more, called 74 in 1686. By former wife or wives, he, perhaps, had enough children, of which Sarah, that married Timothy Wentworth, may have been one.

SAMUEL CROMWELL, of Massachusetts, freeman Sept. 3, 1634.

THOMAS CROMWELL, of Boston, mariner, styled himself of London, made a large fortune by privateering, came hither to enjoy it, 1646, had wife Ann, daughter

Elizabeth, and died before October 10, 1649. His will of August 29, was probated October 26, of that year. Winthrop, II, 264, says that he was brought into the world by the Caesarian operation, and never saw father or mother. His widow soon married Robert Knight, of Boston, and shortly after his death 1655, married John Joyliffe. His daughter Elizabeth married August 18, 1659, Richard Price, sometimes the name in our records appears, as it sounded, Crumwell.

REFERENCES:—Bolton's Hist. of Westchester County, N. Y., II, 724; Baird's Hist. of Rye, N. Y., 458; Dwight's Strong Gen., 160; Wentworth Gen., vol. I, 157; Savage's Gen. Dict., vol. I, 476; American Ancestry, vol. XI, 192.

CRONSIE. Amer. Ancestry, vol. IV, 241.

CROODE. Walker Mem., 144; Savage's Gen. Dict., vol. I, 476.

CROOK. Evans' Fox Gen., 108.

CROOKER.

CROOKER:—Francis, of Scituate, married 1647, Mary Gaunt, of Barnstable, perhaps daughter of Peter, removed soon after 1648, it is thought, to Marshfield. See Deane for curious note about his health.

WILLIAM CROOKER, of Stratford, an original proprietor, of which no more is known, but that he lived at New Haven, in 1647, sold to Henry Wakelyn his land.

REFERENCES:—Lapham's Hist. of Norway, Me., 487; Lapham's Hist. of Bethel, Me., 514; Barry's Hist. of Hanover, Mass., 271; Bassett's Hist. of Richmond, N. H., 378; Secomb's Hist. of Amherst, N. H., 545; Hinman's Conn. Settlers, 758; Amer. Ancestry, XI, 186; N. E. Hist. and Gen. Reg., XII, 68.

CROPPER. Hamilton's Biog. of H. A. Wise.

CROSBY.

CROSBY:—Anthony, of Rowley, 1643, surgeon, had Anthony, who was 23 years old in 1659; Joseph, 25 in 1665; and probably Hannah, who married December 1, 1655, John Johnson. Perhaps his widow Prudence was second wife of Edward Carlton.

HENRY CROSBY, of Salem, married June 5, 1683, Deliverance, probably daughter of Giles Cory, had Henry, born May 14, 1684.

SIMON CROSBY, of Cambridge, came in the "Susan and Ellen," 1635, aged 26; with wife Ann, 25; and son Thomas, 8 weeks; freeman March 3, 1636; had Simon, born August, 1637; and Joseph, February, 1639; selectman 1636 and '38, died September, 1639. His young widow married Rev. William Tompson, of Braintree. His estate by several mesne conveyances passed 1707, to Rev. William Brattle, being that partly occupied now by the Brattle house.

THOMAS CROSBY, of Cambridge, 1640, perhaps removed to Rowley. Twelve of this name had been graduated in 1834, at Harvard, and twelve at the other New England Colleges.

REFERENCES.

MASSACHUSETTS.—Paige's Hist. of Cambridge, 519; Stearns' Hist. of Ashburnham, 656; Atkins' Hist. of Hawley, 62; Freeman's Hist. of Cape Cod, II, 213, 365; Ballou's Hist. of Milford, 690; Essex Inst. Coll., XX, 230; Gibbs' Hist. of Blandford, 61; Hazen's Hist. of Billerica, 27; Hudson's Hist. of Lexington, 47; Ward's Hist. of Shrewsbury, 255; Saunderson's Hist. Charlestown, 245, 315.

NEW HAMPSHIRE.—Secomb's Hist. of Amherst, 547; Norton's Hist. of Fitzwilliam, 525; Dow's Hist. of Hampton, 651; Cutter's Hist. of Jaffray, 257.

OTHER PUBLICATIONS.—Bangor, Me., Hist. Mag., vol. I, 81; II, 105; Heminway's Vermont Gaz., V, 86; Maine Hist. and Gen. Rec., IV, 160; Hinman's Conn. Settlers, 759; Martin's Hist. of Chester, Pa., 208; Dudley's Arch. Gen. Coll., Plate I; Locke Gen., 112; Warren, Clarke Gen., 51; Adams' Haven Gen., 23; Amer. Ancestry, vol. I, 19; III, 11; IV, 236; VI, 67; XI, 187; N. Y. Gen. and Biog. Rec., XVIII, 87; Savage's Gen. Dict., vol. I, 476.

CROSSCUM:—George, of Marblehead, 1653, a fisherman. Savage's Gen. Dict., vol. I, 476.

CROSSMAN. Amer. Ancestry, VI, 197.

CROSS.

CROSS:—Henry, came in the "Increase," 1635, carpenter, aged 20.

JOHN CROSS, of Watertown, came in the "Elizabeth," from Ipswich, 1634, aged 50, with wife Ann, 38; but second wife Mary had Mary, born May 10, 1641; he died September 15, 1640. His widow married 1642, Robert Saunderson, the silversmith, died November 13, 1669.

JOHN CROSS, of Ipswich, 1635, by wife Ann, had Ann, baptized October 9, 1638; removed to Hampton, freeman September 6, 1639, representative 1640, perhaps in 1642 at Dover and back again to Ipswich, died 1652. His inventory of September, was of 382 pound sterling, 5 sh. 2 p.; and the only child Susannah, married Thomas Hammond.

JOHN CROSS, of Windsor, 1645, had, perhaps, been at Stamford.

JOHN CROSS, of Wells, was constable there 1647, died about 1676, leaving widow Frances, and sons John and Joseph, of which John died soon after his father.

JOHN CROSS, of Boston, 1663, a brewer.

JOHN CROSS, a soldier of Moseley's company, Dec., 1675.

JOSEPH CROSS, of Plymouth, 1638, removed, perhaps, to Maine, was constable at Wells, 1670.

NATHANIEL CROSS, brother of John, of Windsor.

PETER CROSS, of Ipswich, 1673.

PETER CROSS, of Norwich, had grant of lot, 1680.

RICHARD CROSS, of Salem, married November 24, 1670, Jane Pudeater, had Elizabeth, born August 17 following; and John, April 12, 1673.

ROBERT CROSS, of Ipswich, 1639, had served in the Pequot War; by wife who died October 29, 1677, had several children, but names of only Robert, perhaps eldest, Martha, who married William Durgin Durkee, Stephen and Ralph, born February, 1659, probably youngest, have reached me.

SAMUEL CROSS, was, perhaps, first at Stamford, went to Windsor, married July 12, 1677, Elizabeth, widow of Edward Chapman, had Hannah, born June 11, 1678, died at 2 years; and Samuel, born and died December 10, 1679; died 1707, without children.

STEPHEN CROSS, of Boston, married 1690, Mary, widow of Robert Lawrence, daughter of John Phillips, of Dorchester, who had been widow of George Munjoy, of Falmouth.

WILLIAM CROSS, of Hartford, 1645, says Hinman, 19, was of Fairfield, 1649, there he died about 1655, leaving widow and perhaps children.

REFERENCES:—Mitchell's Hist. of Bridgewater, Mass., 144; Hammatt Papers Ipswich, Mass., 66; Lapham's Hist. of Bethel, Me., 515; Pierce's Hist. of Gorham, Me., 160; Read's Hist. of Swanzey, N. H., 316; Hayward's Hist. of Hancock, N. H., 471; Runnel's Hist. of Sanbornton, N. H., II, 196; Oxford, N. H., Centen., 108; Hinman's Conn. Settlers, 761; Paul's Hist. of Wells, Vt., 82; Power's Hist. of Sangamon County, Ill., 236; Stiles' Hist. of Windsor, Conn., II, 168; Preble Gen., 242; Savage's Gen. Dict., vol. I. 477.

CROSSETT. Read's Hist. of Swanzey, N. H., 319; Chase's Hist. of Chester, N. H., 500.

CROSSING.

CROSSING:—William, embarked at Barbados, for Boston, April 1, 1679, in the ship "Blessing," but was not probably an inhabitant. Savage's Gen. Dict. vol. I, 477.

CROSSMAN.

CROSSMAN:—John, of Taunton, one of the first purchasers about 1639, had Robert.

REFERENCES:—N. Y. Gen. and Biog. Rec., XXII, 77; Benedict's Hist. of Sutton, 628; Savage's Gen. Dict., vol. I, 478.

CROSSTHWAYTE or CROSWAIT.

CROSSTHWAYTE:—Charles, of Boston, by wife Judith, had George, born June 16, 1671; George, again, March 3, 1676; Charles, February 3, 1678; and John, May 7, 1680, but of him I see no more. Savage's Gen. Dict., vol. I, 478.

CROSWELL.

CROSWELL:—Thomas, of Charlestown, had wife Priscilla, daughter of Deacon John Upham, who died December 8, 1717, aged 75.

REFERENCES:—Davis' Landmarks of Plymouth, Mass., 75; Butler's Hist. of Farmington. 444; Wyman's Charlestown, Mass., Gens., 249; Hinman's Conn. Settlers, 760.

CROTCHERON Clute's Hist. of Staten Island, 364.

CROUTCH. CROWCH, or CROUCH, (See Couch.)

CROUTCH:—William. of Charlestown, 1654, by wife Sarah, married February 21, 1657, had David, January 16, 1659; Mary, baptized December 22, 1661; Elizabeth, September 4, 1664; Richard and Hannah, twins, March 17, 1667; Joseph, August 22, 1669; and William, born November 16, 1678. A widow Croutch was living there in 1678, and in a different house. a William, perhaps her son. The name was continued in Charlestown, for I find the grave-stone of Jonathan there, who died Nov. 25, 1714, aged 58.

REFERENCES:—Wyman's Charlestown, Mass., Gens., vol. I, 250; Hyde's Hist. of Brimfield, Mass., 393; Eaton's Hist. of Thomaston. Me., 195; Hayward's Hist. of Gilsum, N. H., 204; Read's Hist. of Swanzey, N. H., 319; Cleveland's Hist. of Yates County, N. Y., 388; Richmond, Va., Standard, IV, 2.

CROUSE. Hist. of Ross and Highland County, O.

CROW:—Christopher Crow, of Windsor, freeman of Connecticut, 1658, married January 15, 1657, Mary, daughter of Benjamin Burr; died 1680, leaving Samuel, Benoni, Thomas ,and four daughters. Hinman, 127 says he died 1681, and gives the ages of the children Samuel, 21 years; Mary, 18; Hannah, 15; Martha, 14; Benoni, 12; Margaret, 11; and Thomas, 5. His widow married Josiah Clark, of Windsor, and Mary, married John Clark, brother of Josiah.

ELI CROW, a soldier from some Eastern part of the Colony, was at Northampton, April, 1676.

JOHN CROW, of Charlestown, 1635, whose wife Elishua, came, says Frothingham, 84, in the preceding year, and we see in Budington, she was received in the church, January 4, of this year; had Moses, baptized June 24, 1637, who probably died young; John, perhaps 1638, in which year he removed to the new plantation of Yarmouth, in Plymouth Colony, became freeman 1640, representative 1641-3, and died January, 1673; had, I presume, born at Yarmouth, Samuel and Thomas, perhaps more children.

JOHN CROW, of Hartford, an original proprietor, was, perhaps, there in 1637 or '38, married Elizabeth, only child of William Goodwin, the famous ruling Elder, had sons John, Samuel, Daniel and Nathaniel, daughters Esther, who married Giles Hamlin, of Middletown; Sarah, born Mar. 1, 1647; Ann or Hannah, July 13, 1649, who married Thomas Dickinson of Hadley; Mehitable, married Samuel Partridge, of Hadley; Elizabeth, 1650, married William Warren, and not, next, Phineas Wilson, as sometimes said; Mary, married Noah Coleman, of Hadley, and, next, September 16, 1680, Peter Montague; Sarah, married Daniel White, of Hatfield; and Ruth, married William Gaylord, and next, John Hadlhey, both of Hadley. Here are one son and one daughter more than Porter mentioned, beside that the intermarriages in several cases the daughters are different from his. He tells us, that Warren, the husband of Elizabeth, died 1689, and she married Phineas Wilson, who died in 1691, and she died 1727. He sided with his father-in-law in the religious controversy, and with him went to plant Hadley, became freeman of Massachusetts, 1666, but many years afterwards removed back to Hartford, there died January 16, 1686. His son Daniel, died 1693, leaving widow but no children.

THOMAS CROW, of Yarmouth. His estate is still enjoyed by descendants. See Crowell.

WILLIAM CROW, of Plymouth, 1643, able to bear arms, married April 1, 1664, Hannah, daughter of first Josiah Winslow, had no children, died January, 1684, aged about 55. says Savage his grave-stone, in his will mentioned brothers Samuel, Robert and Thomas, all of Coventry, England.

YELVERTON or ELVERTON CROW, of Plymouth, had, in 1643, been of Yarmouth, there had Thomas and Elizabeth, twins, born May 9, 1649; representative 1663. Baylies, II, 55.

REFERENCES:—Hinman's Conn. Settlers, 763; Porter's Hartford Conn. Settlers, 3; Stile's Hist. of Windsor, Conn., 576; Talcott's N. Y. and N. E. Families, 495; Judd's Hist. of Dudley, Mass., 474; Powers' Hist. of Sangamon County, Ill., 234; Miller's Hist. of Colchester County, N. S., 199; Barlow's My Wife and Mother, 32; Dwight Gen., 112; Savage's Gen. Dict., vol. I, 479.

CROWDER. Powers' Hist. of Sangamon County, Ill., 237.

CROWELL:—John Crowell, of Yarmouth. See Crow.

THOMAS CROWELL, of Yarmouth, perhaps brother of John, by wife Agnes, had (beside, perhaps, others), John, Thomas and Lydia; died March 9, 1690, leaving widow and those children. Lydia married February, 1677, Ebenezer, Goodspeed.

CROWFOOT:—Joseph Crowfoot, of Springfield, 1658, freeman 1672, died April 8, 1678, leaving Joseph, Mary, John, Samuel, James, Daniel, Matthew and David. He married April 14, 1658, Mary Hillier.

REFERENCES:—Wheeler's Hist. of Newport, N. H., 354; Morrison's Hist. of Windham, N. H., 414; Atkins' Hist. of Hawley, Mass., 61; Freeman's Hist. of Cape Cod, II, 192, 708; Paige's Hist. of Hardwick, Mass., 355; Hinman's Conn. Settlers, 768; Middlefield, Conn., Hist.; Bangor, Me., Hist. Mag., IV, 216; Austin's Allied Families of R. I., 78; Wheeler's Eminent North Carolinians, 203; Wheeler's Hist. of North Carolina, II, 199; Sear's Gen., 41, 143; Amer. Ancestry, IV, 210; Savage's Gen. Dict., vol. I, 480.

CROWFOOT. Savage's Gen. Dict., vol. I, 480.

CROWL. Powers' Hist. of Sangamon County, Ill., 235.

CROWLEY. Williams' Hist. of Danby, Vt., 133.

CROWNE:—William Crowne, of Boston, 1657, came with a patent of September 8, 1656, from his Highness, Oliver, Lord Protector, etc., in conjunction with the Sieur de La Tour, and Col. Thomas Temple. He was to have, in division of this grand province of Acadia, all West of Machias for 30 leagues, including Penobscot, and up Machias river 180 leagues on its West bank; was freeman 1660, and had more productive, though narrower, estate by grant of the Colony 500 acres near Sudbury, in 1662, and by purchase of 1674, at Mendham, See valuable paper in Genealogical Register, VI, 46, about his serving as friend of New England. But I do not concur with the writer in claiming his son John, the poet, "as an American by birth," who in my opinion, preceded the first coming of his father hither.

REFERENCES:—Savage's Gen. Dict., vol. I, 480

CROWNINSHIELD. Hudson's Hist. of Lexington, Mass., 48; Driver Gen., 268, 327; Amer. Ancestry, IV, 126.

CROZER. Crozer Gen. (1886), 29.

CROZIER. Martin's Hist. of Chester, Pa., 454; Davis' Hist. of Bucks County, Pa., 109; Cleveland's Hist. of Yates Co., N. Y., 339.

CROWTHER:—John Crowther, of Portsmouth, 1631, sent by Mason, the patentee, was there 1640.

REFERENCES:—Savage's Gen. Dict., vol. I, 480.

CRUFTS:—William Crufts, Kittery, 1687.

REFERENCES:—Savage's Gen. Dict., vol. I, 481.

CRUGER . N. Y. Gen. and Biog. Rec., VI, 74, 180; XXIII, 147; Lamb's Hist. of New York City, vol. I, 517; Cruger Chart, 1892.

CRUMB or CROMB:—Daniel Crumb, of Westerly, 1669, married Alice, widow of Richard Haughton; but

by a former wife, I suppose, had William, and a daughter who married Edward Austin. He died 1713, and his widow died January 29, 1716.

REFERENCES:—Savage's Gen. Dict., vol. I, 480; Hist. Rockland County, N. Y.

CRUMBIE. Stearn's Hist. of Rindge, N. H., 493.

CRUMP. Temple's Hist. of Whately, Mass., 223.

CRUMRINE. Amer. Ancestry, VI, 153.

CRUSER. Clute's Hist. of Staten Island, N. Y., 366.

CRUTCHER. Amer. Ancestry, IX, 20.

CRUTTENDEN:—Abraham Cruttenden, of Guilford, 1639, brought wife Mary, and one or more children from England, died January, 1683; had, probably Abraham, Isaac, Mary, Elizabeth, Hannah, Deborah and Thomas, who died unmarried February 8, 1698. Mary married George Bartlett, and died September 11, 1689; Elizabeth married John Graves; Hannah married George Highland; and Deborah, died April 24, 1658, probably unmarried. His second wife, married May 31, 1665, was Joanna, widow of William Chittenden, who died August 16, 1668.

REFERENCES:—Savage's Gen. Dict., vol. I, 481.

CUBBERLY. Clute's Hist. of Staten Island, 368.

CUDDEBACK. Amer. Ancestry, VII, 31, 171, 213; Gumaer's Hist .of Deerpark, N. Y., 41; Stickney's Hist. of Menesink, N. Y., 133.

CUDWORTH:—James Cudworth, of Scituate, 1634, by Deane, is supposed to have come in the Charles, with Hatherly, 1632, a very valuable man, joined the church January 18, 1635, with his wife who bore him James, baptized May 3, 1635, under his own roof, probably the place where the congregation then worshiped; Mary, July 23, 1637; Jonathan, September 16, 1638, died in a few days; Israel, April 18, 1641; Joanna, March 26, 1643; beside a son buried very young, June 24, 1644; and others, certainly Hannah, and another Jonathan, of whom we find not the baptism; representative 1649-56, and again in 1659, when for his tenderness to the Quakers, he was rejected; an Assistant 1656-8, captain of the militia and in the early part of Philip's war commander of the whole force of Plymouth Colony, in 1681 deputy-governor, died 1682. He was in London, as Colonial agent, where he died of small-pox soon after his arrival, and he had served as Commissioner of the United Colonies, in 1657. Baylies I, 280; IV, 13-15. Mary married 1660, Robert Whitcomb, of Scituate. He had taken wife in England, a daughter of Rev. Dr. Stoughton, as is inferred from a letter in Genealogical Register, XIV, 101, and removed with Lothrop to Barnstable, but after few years went back to Scituate. In his will, early in 1682, he gives to James, Israel, Jonathan and daughters Hannah, Jones and four children of daughter Mary Whitcomb.

REFERENCES:—Swift's Barnstable Families, vol. I, 232; Deane's Hist. of Scituate, Mass., 245, 251; Stearn's Hist. of Rindge, N. H., 494; Guild's Stile's Gen., 474; Amer. Ancestry, III, 170; Savage's Gen. Dict., vol I, 481.

CULBERTSON. Amer. Ancestry, V, 39; VII, 124; Culbertson Gen., 1893.

CULLEN. James, was a soldier in Turner's company 1676, King Philip's war.

REFERENCES:—Savage's Gen. Dict., vol. 1, 482; Richmond, Va., Standard, IV, 3.

CULLICK:—John Cullick, of Hartford, 1639, a captain, representative, 1644, '46 and '47, Assistant and Secretary 1648, and several years afterwards, married May 20, 1648, Elizabeth, sister not daughter (as I had said in note upon Winthrop's History, I, 228, of Edition 1853, having been misled by some Connecticut author,) of George Fenwick, Esq., of Saybrook, probably as 2d wife, had John, born May 4, 1649, Harvard College, 1668; and Elizabeth, July 15, 1652; removed to Boston, where he was received into the church November 27, 1659, with his wife and two elder children John and Mary. I suppose it was an elder daughter Hannah, who married May 20, 1660, Pelitiah Glover. He was from Felstead, Essex, served as Commissioner of the United Colonies for Connecticut, and died at Boston, January 23, 1663. His widow married Richard Ely, and much contention followed about the estate. His daughter Elizabeth married October, 1671, Benjamin Batten, of Boston.

REFERENCES:—Porter's Hartford, Conn., Settlers, 4; Hinman's Conn. Settlers, 769; Savage's Gen. Dict., vol. I, 482.

CULLIVER:—John, of Boston, 1658. mariner.

REFERENCES:—Savage's Gen. Dict., vol. I, 481.

CULVER:—Edward Culver, of Dedham, wheelwright, had John, born April 15, 1640; Joshua, January 12, 1643; Samuel, January 9, 1645; Gershom, baptized December 3, 1648; and Hannah, April 11, 1652, both at Roxbury, whither he had removed, but next year went to New London, where he had Joseph and perhaps, Edward. His wife was Ann: and he died 1685, near the head of Mistick, on Groton side of the town.

REFERENCES:—Hinman's Conn. Settlers, 762; Hurd's Hist. of New London County, Conn., 511; Hine's Lebanon, Conn., Address, 131; Davis' Hist. of Wallingford, Conn., 720; Caulkin's Hist. of New London, Conn., 309; Howell's Hist. of Southampton, N. Y., 228; Smith's Hist. of Dutchess County, N. Y., 247; Joslin's Hist. of Poultney Vt., 244; Paul's Hist. of Wells, Vt., 83; Strong Gen., 915; Amer. Ancestry, vol. I, 20, X, 204.

CUMBY or CUMBEE:—Humphrey Cumby, of Boston, mariner, by wife Sarah, had John, born January 23, 1651; Robert, February 14, 1655; and Esther, March 1, 1657; was living 1673.

REFERENCES:—Savage's Gen. Dict., vol. I, 482.

CUMINS. Hall's Trenton, N. J., Pres. Church, 194.

CUMING. Goode Gen., 192; Amer. Ancestry, IV, 242.

CUMMINGS, CUMINGS, CUMMENS, or with single "m," with or without "s," and

COMYNS:—David Cummings, of Dorchester, 1664, died September 12, 1690. Elizabeth, probably his wife, died November 13, 1689.

ISAAC CUMMINGS, of Ipswich, freeman May 18, 1642, may have been at Watertown, before and after, at Topsfield, for in 1661. Isaac senior, a deacon and Isaac junior, (who by wife Mary had a son, born November 3, in that year, and was living in 1686,) were there. In his will of 1676, he names son Isaac, son-in-law John Jewett, husband of Elizabeth, and John Pease, husband of Ann.

RICHARD CUMMINGS, of Isle of Shoals, joined with Thomas Turpin in purchase of all estate of Francis Williams, of Portsmouth, in December, 1645, and in short time removed to Massachusetts, freeman 1669, but went back, I presume, to Maine, and died at Scarborough, 1676, where his property was not small.

WILLIAM CUMMINGS, of Salem, 1637, probably the supporter of Wheelwright, disarmed that year. Ann, possibly his daughter, married October 8, 1669, at Salem, John Pease. Seven of this name, with its various spelling, had been graduated at Harvard, in 1820, and eleven at other New England colleges.

REFERENCES.

MAINE.—Corliss' Hist. of North Yarmouth; Lapham's Hist. of Bethel, 516; Lapham's Hist. of Norway, 488; Lapham's Hist. of Paris, 564; Lapham's Hist. of Woodstock, 198; Sibley's Hist. of Union, 441; Ridlon's Hist. of Harrison, Me., Settlers, 54.

MASSACHUSETTS.—Temple's Hist. of Palmer, 432; Paige's Hist. of Hardwick, 356; Temple's Hist. of North Brookfield, 560; Stearn's Hist. of Ashburnham, 660; Perley's Hist. of Boxford, 29; Butler's Hist. of Groton, 393; Hudson's Hist. of Lexington, 278; Hyde's Hist. Address, Ware, Mass., 48; Draper's Hist. of Spencer, 186; Fox's Hist. of Dunstable, 240; Hazen's Hist. of Billerica, 32; Benedict's Hist. of Sutton, 629; Tyngsbow, Mass., Centen., 18.

NEW HAMPSHIRE.—Kidder's Hist. of New Ipswich, 355; Hayward's Hist. of Hancock, 473; Cochrane's Hist. of Antrim, 441; Worcester's Hist. of Hollis, 371; Merrill's Hist. of Acworth, 204; Read's Hist. of Swanzey, 320; Norton's Hist. of Fitzwilliam, 520.

OTHER PUBLICATIONS.—McKeen's Hist. of Bradford, Vt., 390; Powers' Hist. of Sangamon County, Ill., 241; Richmond, Va., Standard, III, 2; Alden's Epitaphs, V, 215; Dinsmore's Hartwell Gen.; Green's Kentucky Families; Morrison's Gen., 231; Spooner Gen., vol. I, 356; Amer. Ancestry, VI, 55, 178; N. E. Hist. and Gen. Reg., XXXIX, 334; Savage's Gen. Dict., vol. I, 483; Cummings Gen.

CUMMINS. Cleveland's Hist. of Topsfield, 27.

CUNDY:—Samuel Cundy, of Marblehead, 1674.

REFERENCES:—Savage's Gen. Dict., vol. I, 483.

CUNLIFF, CUNLITH or CUNDLIEF:—Henry Cunliff, of Dorchester, freeman 1644, when the record has Cunlithe or Cunlithe, as Mr. Paige reads it; by wife Susanna, had Susannah, born March 15, 1645; removed with early settlers 1659, to Northampton, was one of the founders of the church June 18, 1661, there died September 14, 1673. His widow died November 19, 1675. His only child Susanna, had been bethrothed to Eldad Pomeroy, who died 1662, and she married 1663. Matthew Cole; and December 12, 1665, John Webb, Jr.

REFERENCES:—Savage's Gen. Dict., vol. I, 483.

CUNNABEL. Savage's Gen. Dict., vol. I, 484; Cunnabel Gen.

CUNNINGHAM:—Andrew Cunningham, of Boston, 1684.

PATRICK CUNNINGHAM, of Springfield, died September 12, 1685. Sprague. Four of this name had been graduated at Harvard, and one at Yale, in 1834.

REFERENCES:—Temple's Hist. of North Brookfield, Mass., 561; Draper's Hist. of Spencer, Mass., 183; Davis' Landmarks of Plymouth, Mass., 77; Cushman's Hist. of Sheepscott, Me., 370; Hinman's Conn. Settlers, 775; Stark's Hist. of Dunbarton, N. H., 243; Smith's Hist. of Petersborough, N. H., 45; Futhey's Hist. of Chester County, Pa., 508; Wyman's Charlestown, Mass., Gens., vol. I, 252; Amer. Ancestry, V, 65; Savage's Gen. Dict., vol. I, 484.

CUNNYNGHAM. Roberdeau Gen.

CUNRED. Canad Gen.

CURNEY or CORNEY:—John Curney, of Gloucester, married November 18, 1670, Abigail Skilling, perhaps daughter of Thomas, had Elisha, born September 12, 1672; Abigail, February 8, 1676; John, September 27, 1678, died in a few days; Mary, 1682; and Babson thinks, another son John married 1713, Mary Cook, perhaps daughter of John; and he died 1722.

REFERENCES:—Savage's Gen. Dict., vol. I, 484.

CURRIE. Richmond, Va., Standard, V, 20; Hayden's Virginia Gens., 239; Paxton's Marshall Gen.

CURRIER:—Richard Currier, of Salisbury, 1640, by wife Ann, had Hannah, born July 8, 1643; Thomas, March 8, 1646, and earlier, probably Sarah, who married June 23, 1659, Samuel Fogg, of Hampton; and he died May 17, 1689. Hannah, married June 23, 1659, Samuel Foote.

SAMUEL CURRIER, of Haverhill, married 1670, Mary, daughter of Thomas Hardy. Martha, of Andover, was one of the victims of the baneful superstition about witchcraft, executed August 19, 1692, at the same time with Rev. George Burrows, suffering by the same horrid delusion. Yet her punishment was, to some extent, less than his, as the greater culprit met the malediction of Cotton Mather, the church inquisitor.

REFERENCES.

NEW HAMPSHIRE:—Runnel's Hist. of Sanbornton, 201; Merrill's Hist. of Acworth, 205; Lancaster's Hist. of Gilmanton, 260; Fullerton's Hist. of Raymond, 192; Coggswell's Hist. of Nottingham, 369; Coggswell's Hist. of Henniker, 535; Chase's Hist. of Chester, 501.

OTHER PUBLICATIONS.—Thurston's Hist. of Winthrop, Me., 179; Hazen's Hist. of Billerica, Mass., 33; Poor's Hist. of Merrimac Valley, 115; Butler's Hist. of Farmington, Me., 446; Hubbard's Hist. of Stanstead County, Can., 277; Wentworth Gen., II, 99; Amer. Ancestry, III, 12; Savage's Gen. Dict., vol. I, 484.

CURRY. Runnel's Hist. of Sanbornton, N.H., II, 202.

CURTENIUS. Oneida Hist. Society, Col., II, 132.

CURTIN. Egle's Penn. Gens., 251; Amer. Ancestry, VII, 81.

CURTIS, CURTICE, CURTISE or CURTIZE:—Deodate Curtis, of Braintree, about 1643, had Solomon; and by wife Rebecca, had Ruth, born January 8, 1648.

FRANCIS CURTIS, of Plymouth, married December 28. 1671, Hannah Smith, had John, born July 26, 1673; Benjamin, August 11, 1675; Francis, middle April, 1679; Elizabeth, June 15, 1681; and Elisha, March, 1683.

GEORGE CURTIS, of Boston, freeman, May 13, 1640, joined our church August 4 preceding, called "servant to our teacher Mr. John Cotton." He had grant of lot for two heads, December 30, 1640, when, probably, he was recently married at Muddy river.

HENRY CURTIS, of Watertown, 1636, an original proprietor of Sudbury, married Mary, daughter of Nicholas Guy, had Ephraim, born March 31, 1642; John, 1644; and Joseph, 1647; named in their grand-mother's will, 1666; and died May 8, 1678.

HENRY CURTIS, of Windsor, married May 13, 1645, Elizabeth Abell; had Samuel, born April 26, 1649; Nathaniel, July 15, 1651; removed to Northampton, and died November 30, 1661, leaving widow Elizabeth, (who married June 22, 1662, Richard Weller, from Windsor,) and these sons, of which Samuel died September 11, 1680.

HENRY CURTIS, of Boston, by wife Jane, had John, born July 2, 1657.

HENRY CURTIS, of Marblehead, perhaps went to Pemaquid, before 1674, where he and Henry Jr., in that year took the oath of fidelity.

JOHN CURTIS, of Dover, admitted an inhabitant April 24, 1656, but, perhaps, as no more is heard of him there, he removed to Roxbury.

JOHN CURTIS, of Stratford, 1650-85. Trumbull, I, 105, says he came from Roxbury, and had John, born October, 1642. But all of it seems erroneous. He was really son of widow Curtis; had, says the preposterous tradition, daughter Elizabeth, old enough to marry John, the eldest son of Governor Thomas Welles, bearing to him several children, and, next, married March 19, 1663, John Wilcoxson. Almost every word of Trumbull, and of Cothren, borrowed from Trumbull, in relation to the Roxbury derivation of John,and William, is wrong; and must have been a tradition of the middle of the eighteenth century. Yet a true John of Stratford, by wife Elizabeth, who died as Cothren, tells, 1682, beside that John, of 1642, had Israel, April, 1644; Elizabeth, May, 1647, (who by tradition became wife of John Welles, eldest son of the Governor, bore him one son in 1648, the year after her own birth, and twins 1651); Thomas, January, 1649; Joseph, November, 1650; Benjamin, September, 1652; and Hannah, February, 1654 or 5. None of this must be rejected but perhaps when Cothren adds, that he died December 6, 1707, aged 96 years, and that his widow Margaret, died 1714, acquiescence of our judgment may not be so easy.

JOHN CURTIS, of Topsfield, married December 4, 1672, Sarah Locke, freeman 1690.

NATHANIEL CURTIS, of Northampton, 1668, was a soldier, killed September 2, 1675, at Northfield, by the Indians, but who was his father is not known.

RICHARD CURTIS, of Dorchester, 1642, freeman 1647, by wife Elizabeth, had Elizabeth, born July 17, 1643. His wife died May 28, 1657; and he married September 25 following, Sarah had Isaac, June 17, 1658; and Joseph, September 4, 1661.

RICHARD CURTIS, of Salem, there had, by wife Sarah, Caleb, born September 24. 1646; and Sarah, March 19, 1650; both baptized April 21, 1650; Samuel, April 1. baptized May 18, 1651; Richard, February 14, baptized 20, February 1653; Sarah, again, baptized April 15, 1655; Hannah, born September 16, 1656, baptized Jan. 25 following; John, born February 2, 1659, died soon; John again, born June 4, 1660, died soon; and Mary, born February 11, 1663.

RICHARD CURTIS, of Boston, 1657, had wife Sarah, probably widow of John Strange.

RICHARD CURTIS, Marblehead, 1648, removed to Scituate, married 1649,Ann, daughter of John Hallet, had Ann, born 1649; Elizabeth, 1651; John, December 1, 1653; Mary, 1655; Martha, 1657; Thomas, March 18, 1659; Deborah, 1661; and Sarah, 1663; and he died 1693. His will of 1692 provides for second wife Lydia, the two sons, and daughters Ann, Elizabeth Brooks, wife of Nathaniel; Mary Badcocke; and Martha Clark, wife of Thomas. So it is inferred that the youngest two daughters died before their father.

RICHARD CURTIS, of Wallingford, had three sons and a daughter who married Nathaniel Howe, but of the four, only Isaac is named. The father died September 17, 1681.

SAMUEL CURTIS, of Northampton, 1668.

THEOPHILUS CURTIS, of Woburn, freeman 1684.

THOMAS CURTIS, of Wethersfield, an early settler, had John, born 1639; James, 1641; Joseph, 1644; Samuel, 1646; Isaac, 1647; Elizabeth and Ruth, all living November 13, 1681, at his daughters in Wallingford, whither he removed 1670. Elizabeth married May 26, 1674, John Stoddard; Ruth, married Eleazur Kimberly, the Secretary of the Colony.

THOMAS CURTIS, of York, removed to Scituate, there had Elizabeth, baptized 1649; and Samuel, 1659, went back to York, 1663; had Benjamin, 1684. With some of Courteous, he is seen swearing allegiance to Massachusetts, 1652, in Colonial Records, IV, pt. I, 129.

WILLIAM CURTIS, of Roxbury, 1632, came in "Lion," arrived at Boston, September 16, with wife Sarah. and children Thomas, Mary, John and Philip, freeman March 4, 1633, first named in the list of that day; had here, says Ellis, Hannah, Elizabeth and Isaac, born July 22, 1641. His eldest son William, who came in 1631, perhaps with Eliot in the "Lion," was a hopeful scholar, but God took him in 1634," says the church record. Thomas, died June 26, 1650, of "long and tedious consumption," says the church record, unmarried, it is presumed. His daughter Hannah married Aug. 25, 1651, William Geary, and Elizabeth married, December 14, 1659, John Newell. He died December 8, 1672, aged 80; and his widow died March 20 or 26 following, aged 73.

WILLIAM CURTIS, of Stratford, 1642-1702, son of a widow Curtis, that came, so I presume, from England, with John and this son, by Trumbull. I. 105 said to have come from Roxbury, erroneous. as must be thought for his observance on John. But Cothren shows that he, of Stratford (who may never have seen Roxbury), was one of the grantees of Woodbury, in 1672, though he removed not from Stratford, but died there December 21, 1702, in his will of six days preceding named his children Sarah, who was born October, 1642; Jonathan, February, 1644; Joshua, October, 1646; Abigail, April, 1650; Daniel, November, 1652; Elizabeth, February, 1654; Ebenezer, July, 1657; Zechariah, November, 1659; and Josiah, August, 1662. Who was his father is uncertain. His second wife was Sarah, widow of William Goodrich, but all the children were by first wife, whose name is not seen. Both husband and wife died 1702, as is said.

WILLIAM CURTIS, of Scituate, 1643, brother of Richard, had Joseph, born 1664; Benjamin, 1666; William, 1668; John, 1670; Miriam, 1673; Mehitabe, 1675; Stephen. 1677; Sarah, 1679; and Samuel, 1681.

WILLIAM CURTIS, of Salem, by wife Alice, had Ann,

born August 30, 1658; Sarah, October 13, 1660, died soon; William, December 26, 1662; Abigail, about Aug. 15, 1664; John, May 14, 1666; Elizabeth, January, 1668; and Hannah, August, 1670; was one of the troop in 1678.

ZACHEUS CURTIS, of Salem, came in the "James" from Southampton, 1635, was from Downton, in Wiltshire, had grant of land 1646, but probably removed to Gloucester, there by wife Joan had Mary, born May 12, 1659, who married April 19, 1677, at Salem, Richard Friend. Of this name, ten had been graduated at Harvard, in 1834, and 19 in other New England colleges.

REFERENCES.

MASSACHUSETTS.—Draper's Hist. of Spencer, 183; Deane's Hist. of Scituate, 251; Kingman's Hist. of North Bridgewater, 476; Mitchell's Hist. of Bridgewater, 144; Perley's Hist. of Boxford, 35; Winsor's Hist. of Duxbury, 249; Wyman's Charlestown Gens., vol. I, 253; Davis' Landmarks of Plymouth, 75; Ellis' Hist. of Roxbury, 183; Barry's Hist. of Hanover, 272.

MAINE.—Lapham's Hist. of Paris, 569; Lapham's Hist. of Woodstock, 200; Eaton's Hist. of Thomaston, 197; Bradbury's Hist. of Kennebunkport, 235; Corliss' Hist. of North Yarmouth; Cushman's Hist. of Sheepscott, 371.

NEW HAMPSHIRE.—Washington, N. H., Hist., 362; Secomb's Hist. of Amherst, 622; Runnel's Hist. of Sanbornton, II, 205; Read's Hist. of Swanzey, 322; Livermore's Hist. of Wilton, 356; Cochrane's Hist. of Antrim, 442.

CONNECTICUT.—Davis' Hist. of Wallingford, 722; Hinman's Conn. Settlers, 776; Mead's Hist. of Greenwich, 309; Dodd's Hist. of East Haven, 115; Huntington's Stamford Settlers, 27; Orcutt's Hist. of Derby, 715; Orcutt's Hist. of Wolcott, 472; Sedgwick's Hist. of Sharon, 74; Brown's West Simsbury Settlers, 31; Cothren's Hist. of Woodbury, 531.

OTHER PUBLICATIONS.—Bass' Hist. of Braintree, Vt., 128; Deacon's Stoddard Gen.: Guild's Calvin Ancestry, 8; Hall's Gen. Notes, 168; Meade's Old Churches of Va., vol. I, 262; Ransom Gen., 46; Rodman Gen., 112; Upham Gen., 52; Wadsworth Hyde Gen., 599; Amer. Ancestry, vol. I, 20; II, 29; III, 69; IX, 240; XI, 213; N. E. Hist. and Gen. Reg., XII, 283; XVI, 137; Savage's Gen. Dict., vol. I, 484; Curtis Gen.

CURTISS. Orcutt's Hist. of Torrington, Conn., 681; Orcutt's Hist. of Stratford, Conn., 1178, 1351; Cothren's Hist. of Woodbury, Conn., 1486; Andrews' cester, Mass., 32; Wheeler's Hist. of Brunswick, Me., 831; Hubbard's Hist. of Stanstead County, Canada, 168; Trubee Gen., 115; Montague Gen., 539; Amer. Ancestry, IX, 195; N. E. Hist. and Gen. Reg., XLIII, 321.

CURWIN or CORWIN:—George Curwin, of Salem, 1638, came with wife Elizabeth. who had been widow of John White, and daughter Abigail from Workington, in Cumberland, where he was born December 10, 1610, had John, born July 25 or 28, 1638; Jonathan, November 14, 1640, baptized January 17 following; Abigail, Nov. 30, 1643; Hannah, born January 1, baptized January 4, 1646; and Elizabeth, July 2, 1648. His wife whose family name was Herbert, it is said of Nort'rampton, died Sept. 15, 1668; and by second wife Elizabeth Brooks, widow of Robert, daughter of Governor Edward Winslow, married September 22, 1669, he had Penelope, born August 7, baptized October 2, 1670; Susanna, December 10, 1672, baptized January, 1673; and George, born 1674, died soon; was freeman 1665, representative 1666, 7, 9, 70, 2, 4 and 6; a selectman; captain in Philip's war, and died January 3 or 6, 1685, leaving large estate. Abigail married August 28, 1663, Eleazur Hacho.ne, and, next, Hon. James Russell; Hannah married, December 29, 1664, William Browne, and died November 21, 1692; Penelope married Josiah Wolcott; and Susanna married Edward Lyde, of Boston, and died early. More light is wanted as to Abigail's second husband than the Genealogical Register affords, as also for the marriage of Samuel Andrews to another child of Curwin's wife.

MATTHIAS CURWIN, of Southold, Long Island, had been early at Ipswich, it is said.

SAMUEL CURWIN, of Boston, died November 16, 1698. Often this name is written Corwin, sometimes Currin, to conform to sound. The Curwens were a very ancient family in Cumberland, and the name being nearly. or quite, extinct, it was assumed two or three generations since by Mr. Christian of the Isle of Man, who was a member of Parliament of some distinction, 60 years ago.

REFERENCES:—Savage's Gen. Dict., vol. I, 488.

CUSHING:—David Cushing, of Exeter, 1655.

MATTHEW CUSHING, of Hingham, 1638, from Hingham, in County Norfolk, son of Peter, born in 1588, the year of the Spanish Armada, married, August 5, 1613, Nazareth Pitcher, had, as by register of old Hingham appears, Daniel, baptized April 20, 1619; Jeremiah, Jan. 1, 1621; Matthew, April 5, 1623; Deborah, February 17, 1625; and John, whose baptism is. I believe. omitted, and I have heard that it was in a neighboring parish; came in the "Diligent," embarked at Gravesend, April 26, and landed at Boston, August 10, 1638, with that wife and those children. He is the ancestor of all the myriads of this name in New England, and thence indefinitely spread; and died December 30, 1660. His widow died 1681, aged 95, as is said. Her sister, widow Frances Ricroft, came in the same voyage, but died in a few weeks after arrival. In his will all the children, except Deborah, who married, May, 1648, Matthew Briggs, are named as living; and the share to this son-in-law was large.

THEOPHILUS CUSHING, of Hingham, came in the "Griffin," 1633, with Gov. Haynes, at whose farm he lived some years. He was from old Hingham, and died March, 1679, aged about 100 years, of which he was blind for 25, had, it is thought, no children.

REFERENCES.

MASSACHUSETTS.—Temple's Hist. of North Brookfield, 561; Stearn's of Ashburnham, 661; Barry's Hist. of Hanover, 288; Davis' Landmarks of Plymouth. 76; Ward's Hist. of Shrewsbury, 259; Winsor's Hist. of Duxbury, 249; Mitchell's Hist. of Bridgewater, 366; Bond's Hist. of Watertown, 189; Freeman's Hist. of Cape Cod, II, 128; Dean's Hist. of Scituate, 25.

MAINE.—Wheeler's Hist .of Brunswick, 831; Bangor Hist. Mag., V, 185; Eaton's Annals of Warren. 531.

OTHER PUBLICATIONS.—Benney Gen.; Bridgman's Copps Hill Epitaphs, 223; Bridgman's Granary Epitaphs, 13; Buckingham Gen.. 242; Heraldic Journal. II, 123; IV, 55; Saunderson's Hist. of Charlestown. N. H.: 318; Page Gen., 197; Whitmore's Copps Hill Epitaphs; Sumner Gen..·57; Turner Gen., 1852; Amer. Ancestry,, VII, 70; X, 6, 202; XI, 26; N. E. Hist. and Gen. Reg., VIII, 41; XIX, 39; XV, 25; Savage's Gen. Dict., vol. I, 489.

CUSHMAN:—James Cushman, of Scituate, from 1639 to '48, says Deane. His will, April 25, 1648, probated May 24 following, names only cousins. It is not easy to offer a reasonable conjecture what he was.

ROBERT CUSHMAN, of Plymouth, one of the most active promoters of the migration from Holland in 1620 of the pilgrims in the "Mayflower," of which he was one, but when adverse circumstances compelled that ship to put back, he gave up his place for the good of other companions in the "Speedwell," which was abandoned; came next year in the "Fortune," arrived November 10, the first ship after the "Mayflower," with son Thomas, yet stayed only one month, went home in the same little bark, and came again no more. He had married at Leyden, June 3, 1617, Mary Singleton (on the Dutch records spelled Chingelton), of Sandwich, he being designated a woolcarder at Canterbury, both in County Kent. The first sermon preached in New England, was by him, on the highly appropriate subject of self-denial. He was constant in serving at London for the emigrants and in December 1624 spoke of his hope of coming in the next season; but Governor Bradford notes, that he was dead before receipt of his answer from Plymouth of June 1625; and his family came soon after to partake in the fortunes of the plantation. By general consent, he was assigned a share in the division of land with the comers of the "Mayflower." Davis, in Morton's Memorial, 128; Young's Chronicles of the Pilgrims, 99, 249. Twelve of this name had been graduatetd at the New England colleges in 1834.

REFERENCES.

MAINE:—Lapham's Hist. of Woodstock, 202; Lapham's Hist. of Paris, 570; Lapham's Hist. of Norway, 490; Lapham's Hist. of Bethel, 517; Eaton's Annals of Warren. 531; Butler's Hist. of Farmington, 448; Corliss' Hist. of North Yarmouth; Thurston's Hist. of Winthrop.

OTHER PUBLICATIONS.

Winsor's Hist. of Duxbury, Mass., 249; Stearns' Hist. of Ashburnham, Mass., 633; Mitchell's Hist. of Bridgewater, Mass., 372; Adams' Hist. of Fairhaven, Vt., 334; Bass Hist. of Braintree, Vt., 129; Barrus' Hist. of Goshen, Mass., 142; Cushman Gen. 1855; Adams' Gen. (1861) 23; Cushman Monument Proc. (1859); Davis' Landmarks of Plymouth, Mass., 77; Amer. Ancestry, vol. I, 20; III, 12; V, 39; IX, 99; XI, 75; Savage's Gen. Dict. vol. I, 491; Cushman Gen.

CUSTIS.—Meade's Old Churches of Va., vol. I, 262; Richmond, Va., Standard. III, 150; Neil's Virginia Carolorum, 208; Paxten's Marshall Gen. 264; Potter's Amer. Monthly, VI, 85; Custis' G. W. P. Reminiscences, 113.

CUTHBERT:—Hayward's Hist. of Gilsum, N. H., 294.

CUTHBERTSON:—Cuthbert Cuthbertson, of Plymouth, came in the "Ann," 1623, and in the division of lands, next season, was counted for six heads, if the records be right, yet at division of cattle, 1627, he. and wife Sarah, who. I presume, had been widow of Digory Priest (that died at Plymouth January 1, 1621), and married November 21 following, at Leyden; and son Samuel are all; but we may suppose, that some daughters had been married in the interval, and at this division are counted by other names. Sarah, his daughter, married 1630, John Coombs, it is said, and another married Phineas Pratt. He was a Dutchman, united with the fathers at Leyden, and Winslow and gives his name, as, perhaps, in earlier life, the man wrote it, Godbert Godbertson. He died before October 23, 1633, the date of inventory of both himself and wife, so that she was probably dead a short time before. By descendants the last syllable of the surname is now rejected. Davis, in Morton, 379. Savage's Gen. Dict. vol. I, 491.

CUTLER:—James Cutler, of Watertown, by wife Ann, had James, born November 6, 1635; Hannah, July 26, 1638; Elizabeth, January 28, 1640, died soon; and Mary, March 29, 1643. His wife died September in the following year, and he married March 9, 1645, Mary, widow about 1648; Sarah, Joanna, Jemima, John, March 19, and perhaps one or more of the latest were by third wife Phebe, 1663; Samuel, November 18, 1664; Phebe, daughter of John Page. He had removed 1648, to an outlying plantation, called Cambridge Farms, now Lexington, and there his will of November 24, 1684, calling himself 78 years old, was made, and yet not probated before August 20, 1694. Ann married, probably, John Coller; Elizabeth married John Parmenter, of Sudbury; Sarah married Thomas White; and Joanna, married Philip Russell.

JOHN CUTLER, of Hingham, came in 1637, with wife, seven children and one servant, from some part of Norfolk, Eng., and died, I suppose, about 1671, for next year his widow Mary, then became Hewet, joined with son Nathaniel, of Reading, Samuel, of Topsfield and Thomas, of Charlestown, in sale of the estate at Hingham.

JOHN CUTLER, of Woburn, married September 3, 1650, Olive Thompson, had Mary, born August 7, 1651, died young; Susanna, March 22, 1653; and Mary, again, May 5, 1663. He died of small-pox, 1678 or 9. Mary married June 20, 1684, another record says March 2, 1684, Matthew Smith.

JOHN CUTLER, of Woburn, perhaps, married May 12, 1682, Susanna Baker, probably daughter of John, but may have removed after having John, born December 7, 1684, died soon.

JOHN CUTLER, of Hingham, a surgeon, who changed his name from John Demesmaker, married January 4, 1675, Mary, daughter of Edward Cowell, had John, born August 6, 1676; Peter, July 7, 1679; Mary, July 24, 1682; Hannah, June, 1685; Abigail, November 1, 1687, died in few months: David, November 1, 1689; Ruth, February 22, 1692; Elizabeth, September 7, 1695; and Abigail, again, May 30, 1699, the last two at Boston, to which he removed for permanent residence, and here died 1717. His widow had administration of his good estate November 30, of that year. His elder son John, followed the father's profession. married August 21, 1716, Joanna, widow of Thomas Richards, whose maiden name was Dodd, but had no issue.

ROBERT CUTLER, of Charlestown. 1637, freeman May 2, 1638. deacon 1659, died March 7, 1665, leaving widow Rebecca and children John, Rebecca, married 1649, Abraham Errington: Hannah. married August 29, 1654, Matthew Griffin; and Nathaniel, baptized November 8, 1640, Harvard Coll. gr. 1663. He had good estate, by his will, made May 1, preceding his death, distributing to wife. four children and to grand-children, beside bequeathing to officers of the church.

SAMUEL CUTLER, of Marblehead, 1654, was 71 years old in 1700.

SAMUEL CUTLER, of Charlestown, by wife Dorothy,

had Samuel, baptized December 9, 1683, born May 4, same year; Abraham, born July 6, 1685, baptized in Boston, at Old South Church, January 3 following. His wife was daughter of Abraham Bell, and they were married June 30, 1681. After his death she married Dec. 3, 1698, Josiah Treadway.

REFERENCES.

MAINE.—Eaton's Hist. of Thomaston, 197; Hatch's Hist. of Industry, 567; Butler's Hist. of Farmington, 451.

MASSACHUSETTS.—Paige's Hist. of Cambridge, 521; Ward's Hist. of Shrewsbury, 260; Paige's Hist. of Hardwick, 357; Wyman's Charlestown, Mass., Gens., vol. I, 254; Stearns' Hist. of Ashburnham, 669; Sewall's Hist. of Woburn, 607; Temple's Hist. of North Brookfield, 562; Pierce's Hist. of Grafton, 474; Barry's Hist. of Hanover, 291; Judd's Hist. of Hadley, 474; Eaton's Hist. of Reading, 60; Dunstable Bi-Centen. 160; Cutter's Hist. of Arlington, 211; Brown's Bedford, Mass., Families, 7; Bond's Hist. of Watertown, 189; Hudson's Hist. of Lexington, 48; Morse's Sherborn, Mass., Settlers, 67.

NEW HAMPSHIRE.—Stearn's Hist. of Rindge, 498; Kidder's Hist. of New Ipswich, 356; Norton's Hist. of FitzWilliam, 527; Morrison's Hist. of Windham, 417; Smith's Hist. of Petersborough, 48.

OTHER PUBLICATIONS.—Hinman's Conn. Settlers, 790; Morse's Mass. Appendix, 64; Benton's Hist. of Guildhall, Vt., 217; Heminway's Vt. Gaz., V, 393; Avon, N. Y., Gen. Rec., (1871); Upham Gen., 38; Rockwood Gen., 62, 102; Whitney Gen., (1860); Driver Gen., 421; Amer. Ancestry, vol. I. IV. 19; IV, 87; Savage's Gen. Dict., vol. I, 493; N. E. Hist. and Gen. Reg., IV, 175; VII, 297; VIII, 259.

CUTTER:—Richard Cutter. of Cambridge, freeman June 2, 1641, artillery company 1643; by his first wife Elizabeth, had Elizabeth, born July 15, 1645, died at 18 years; Samuel, January 3, 1647; Thomas, July 19, 1648, died soon; William, February 22, 1650; Ephraim, Gershom and Mary; all, says Mitchell, born and baptized in this church, except Thomas. His wife died March 5, 1662, not 1663, as Harris Epitaphs, I., has it, aged about 42, and he married February 14, 1663, Harris, 23 (which was before the death of Elizabeth, as by him given), Frances, widow of Isaac Amsden, had Nathaniel, December 11, 1663, baptized January 24, 1664; Rebecca, September 5, baptized October 8, 1665; Hepzibah, November 11, baptized December 1, 1667, died at 3 months; Elizabeth. born March 1, 1669; Hepzibah, again, August 15, 1671; Sarah, August 31, 1673; and Ruhamah; and he died June 16, 1693, aged about 72. Frances, his widow, outlived him; and his daughter Mary married Nathaniel Sanger; Rebecca married December 19, 1688, Thomas Fillebrown; Elizabeth married a Hall; and Sarah married December 5, 1700, James Locke, of Woburn.

WILLIAM CUTTER, of Cambridge, 1636, freeman April 18, 1634, artillery company 1638, brother of the preceding, was living some years later; had grant 1648, of land in Cambridge, and in short time afterward went home, and sent power of attorney in 1653, to his brother Corlet, from Newycastle on Tyne. Elizabeth, I think, his mother, who died January 10, 1664, in her will of February 16 preceding, called herself about 87 years. says she has lived now about 20 years with Mr. Elijah Corlet, who married her daughter Barbara, and gives them all her little property. making the daughter executrix.

REFERENCES:—Paige's Hist. of Cambridge, Mass., 519; Draper's Hist. of Spencer, 188; Cutter's Hist. of Arlington, Mass., 211; Wyman's Hist. of Charlestown, Mass., vol. I, 260; Cutter's Hist. of Jaffrey, N. H., 261; Eaton's Annals of Warren, Me., 532; Corliss' Hist. of North Yarmouth, Me., 764; Powers' Hist. of Sangamon County, Ill., 240; Amer. Ancestry, IV, 112; VII, 54; Savage's Gen. Dict., vol. I, 496; N. E. Hist. and Gen. Reg., XXVIII, 259.

CUTTING:—John Cutting, of Watertown, 1636, afterward at Charlestown, thence removed, was about 1642, at Newbury, had Sarah, married James Brown, and Mary, married November 9, 1657, Samuel Moody. He made many voyages, and brought very many passengers from England, and died November 20, 1659. His widow, Mary, married John Miller, and died March 6, 1664.

JOHN CUTTING, of Boston, 1655.

RICHARD CUTTING, of Watertown, came in the "Elizabeth," from Ipswich, 1634, a youth of 11 years, under the care of Henry Kimball; by wife Sarah, who died November 4, 1685, aged 60, had James, born January 26, 1648; John, Susanna; Sarah, September 2, 1661; and Lydia, September 1, 1666, beside Zechariah, who may have been the eldest. He made his will June 24, 1694, in which he mentioned the four children alive, and child of John, named John, and child of Sarah, named Elizabeth. Susanna married June 2, 1672, Peter Newcombe, of Braintree; Sarah married March 5, 1683, John Barnard, Jr., and died May 6, 1694; and Lydia married Henry Spring.

WILLIAM CUTTING, a passenger in the "Elizabeth," from Ipswich, 1634, aged 26. It may be asked if he were related to Richard Young, who came in the same ship with him, or of John, who was master of the Francis, which sailed on the same day from the same port, and both reached Boston the same day, without loss of any passengers. Yet where the answer will come from, or what it will be, is beyond conjecture.

REFERENCES.

MASSACHUSETTS.—Ward's Hist. of Shrewsbury, 259; Bond's Hist. of Watertown, 193; Barry's Hist. of Framingham, 216; Stearns' Hist. of Ashburnham, 672; Washburn's Hist. of Leicester, 351; Westminster, Mass., Centen. 29.

OTHER PUBLICATIONS.—Washington, N. H., Hist., 363; Wheeler's Croyden, N. H., Centen. 70; Wheeler's Hist. of Newport, N. H., 358; Norton's Hist. of Fitzwilliam, N. H., 528; Eaton's Annals of Warren, Me., 532; Hubbard's Hist. of Stanstead County, Can., 330; Amer. Ancestry, IV, 142; V, 110; VIII, 46; IX, 169.

CUTT:—(or Cutts in modern days) John Cutt, of Portsmouth, son of that Richard, a member of Oliver's Parliament, 1654, in which year he died, was a merchant from Wales, married July 30, 1662, Hannah Star, had John, born June 30, 1663; Elizabeth, November 30, 1664, died next year; Hannah, July 29, 1666; Mary, November 17, 1669, and Samuel; was appointed by the crown, 1679, president of the province, undertook the office next year and died March 27, 1681, leaving large estate. A second wife Ursula survived, but was killed by the Indians, 1694, on a Saturday, as Mather tells, VII, 86; and from Belknap we may guess it was on July 21. Hannah married February 16, 1681, Richard Waldron, died February 14, 1683, and Mary married July 1, 1687. Samuel Penhallow. Belknap I, 90, 91, 141; Chalmers, 490

ROBERT CUTT, of Portsmouth, brother of John, went to Barbados, from New England, came back, lived at Kittery, about 1663, built many vessels; by second wife Mary, had Richard. Elizabeth, who married Humphrey Eliot. Robert: Bridget, who married Rev. William Scriven: Mary and Sarah. His will, of June 18, 1674, probated July 6 following, names son Richard, also, so that we may assume he was born by former wife. In the inventory of 890 pounds sterling, large for that neighborhood, are included eight negro slaves, but their aggregate value is only 111 pounds sterl. His widow married Francis Champernoon.

REFERENCES:—Savage's Gen. Dict., vol. I, 494.

CUTTS. Hatch's Hist. of Industry, Me., 569; Maine Hist. and Gen. Rec., IV, 294; Brewster's Hist. of Portsmouth, N. H., II, 142; Wheeler's Hist. of Newport, N. H., 357; Richmond, Va., Standard, III, 6; Slaughter's Hist. of St. Mark's Parish, Va., 186; Wentworth Gen., vol. I, 312; Amer. Ancestry, IV, 138; N. E. Hist. and Gen. Reg., II, 276; Savage's Gen. Dict., vol. I, 294; Cutts Gen., (1892.)

CUYLER. John, the ancestor, settled in Albany, and had a son John.

REFERENCES:—Pearson's Schenectady, N. Y., Settlers, 52; Munsell's Albany, N. Y., Coll., IV, 111; N. Y. Gen. and Biog. Rec., IV, 179; Amer. Ancestry, V, 133.

—————:o:—————

DABNEY, Cornelius (spelled d'Aubigne) of Wales, born in France, a descendant of Theodore Agrippa d'Aubigne, came to Virginia from Wales, heaving fled from France after the Revocation of the Edict of Nantes. He had a son, George D.

REFERENCES:—Richmond, Va., Standard, II, 34; III, 24; Meade's Old Families of Va.; Sketches of Lynchburg, Va., 245; Slaughter's St. Mark's Parish, Va., 186; Paige Gen., 163; Gilsum's Georgians, 166; Amer. Ancestry, VI, 91, 166; Dabney Gen., 1888.

DADE, DAVY, DADY, or DAWDY, and even DANDY:—William Dade, of Charlestown, 1630, a butcher, came in the fleet with Winthrop, probably, for his name stands on the list of the Boston church next after John Winthrop, Jr., who came, however, in 1631; and he was of the 35 earliest members of the church of Charlestown, freeman April 1, 1633; by wife Dorothy, had Benjamin, baptized March 24, 1635; Nathaniel, January 22, 1637; and Zechary, born May 16, 1644; died April, 1682, aged 77, leaving estate to wife Dorothy, son William and daughter Abigail. Frothingham, 79.

REFERENCES:—Hayden's Virginia Gens., 731; Slaughter's St. Mark's Parish, Va., 158; Savage's Gen. Dict., vol. II, 1.

DADEY. Wyman's Charlestown, Mass., Gens., 271.

DADNUM. Barry's Hist. of Framingham, Mass., 217.

DAFFORNE or DAFFERN:—John Dafforne, of Boston, by wife Mary, had Mary, born 15, baptized April 22, 1677; John, 3, baptized August 5, 1678; Isaac, November 20, baptized December 5, 1680; and Richard, whose birth is not known, but baptized June 10, 1683. Perhaps he had been driven away from some frontier settlement in the Indian War and went back. Yet in the great fire of March, 1760, one of the sufferers, as we see in Drake's valuable History of Boston, page 652, was Isaac Dafforne, perhaps grand-son of John.

REFERENCES:—Savage's Gen. Dict., II, 2.

DAGAN:—Richard Dagan, of Scituate, 1690, had Elizabeth, born 1693; and Thomas, 1694. Deane tells little more.

REFERENCES:—Savage's Gen. Dict., II, 2.

DAGGGETT or DOGGETT:—As on record at Watertown, but Doghead or Doged, at Plymouth; John Daggett, of Watertown, 1630, probably came in the fleet with Winthrop, for October 19, he desired admission, and May 18, 1631, was made freeman; removed perhaps with Mayhew to the Vineyard, and 1645, to Rehoboth, was representative 1648. He married at Plymouth, August 29, 1667, probably was second wife, widow of Bathsheba Pratt, then called himself of Martha's Vineyard.

THOMAS DAGGETT, of Concord, came as servant of Thomas Oliver, 1637, aged 30, from Norwich, England. His wife died August 23, 1642. Thirteen of this name had been graduated at Yale, 1828; of which Rev. Naphtali, who died November 25, 1780, was President from 1766 to 1777.

REFERENCES:—Hinman's Conn. Settlers, 793; Sebley's Hist. of Union, Me., 443; Hatch's Hist. of Industry, Me., 570; Eaton's Hist. of Thomaston, Me., II, 197; Benedict's Hist. of Sutton, Mass., 630; Daggett's Hist. of Attleboro, Mass., 89; Tuttle Family of Conn., 648; Savage's Gen. Dict., II, 2.

DAILLE:—Peter Daille, of Boston, first minister of the Huguenot or French Protestant church, came about 1686, died May 20, 1715, in his 66th year, says the Newsletter of May 23, but in the contemporary note of Rev. William Cooper, aged about 70; had three wives, Esther Latonice, married probably in France, who died December 14, 1896; Psyche, died August 31, 1713; and Martha, who survived. James Bowdoin was executor of his will made April 20, preceding, in which is named his brother Paul Daille Vaugelade, of Amsfort, in Holland. Neal History of Puritans, IV, 250, mentioned a Daille of Paris. Snow History of Boston, 201; Three Massachusetts Historical Collections, II, 52; Worcester Magazine, II, 349.

REFERENCES:—Savage's Gen. Dict., II. 2.

DAILEY. Austin's R. I., Gen. Dict., 62; Whitman's Gen., 22.

DAIN. Jameson's Hist. of Midway, Mass., 468.

DAINS. Cleveland's Hist. of Yates County, N. Y., 132.

DAKIN, DAKYNGS or DAKING:—Thomas Dakin, of Concord, had Joseph, John, Samuel and Sarah, this last born October 8, 1659; perhaps all were by wife Sarah, who died ten days after last birth. He married June 11, 1660, widow Susan Stratten, and may have had one of the children by last named wife.

REFERENCES:—Hill's Hist. of Mason, N. H., 201; Trowbridge Gen., 189.

DALAND. Driver Gen., 273.

DALE:—John Dale, of Salem, 1682, Felt.

ROBERT DALE, of Woburn, married November 30, 1680, Joanna, daughter of John Farrar, had Martha, born February 9, 1684; Abigail, July 29, 1687; Joanna, July 26, 1690; and Rebecca, January 24, 1698, and he died February 9, 1700.

REFERENCES:—Ballou's Hist. of Milford, Mass., 693;

Collins' Hist. of Newbury, Mass., 300; Livermore's Hist. of Welton, N. H., 356; Penn. Mag., IV, 494; Meade's Old Families of Va., vol. I, 278; N. E. Hist. and Gen. Reg., XXVII, 427; Savage's Gen. Dict., vol II, 3.

DALEY. Norton's Hist. of Fitzwilliam, N. H., 529; Amer. Ancestry, II, 29.

DALLAS. Dallas Gen.

DALISSON or DALISON:—Gilbert Dalisson, of Milford, about 1647, as Lambert presumes, but at Boston, we learn by record, married widow Margaret Story, Oct. 24, 1661; perhaps later in life he had wife Mary, and good estate, but no children, died 1689, gave his property, after decease of wife, to John Barton, of Salem; and he to pay 10 pounds sterling, to Thomas Marshall, yet no relationship is known with either of them.

DALKIN:—......Dalkin, of Medford, the escape of whose life from drowning is told by Winthrop, II, 162.

REFERENCES:—Savage's Gen. Dict., II, 3.

DALTON or DOLTON:—Philemon Dalton, of Watertown, linen-weaver, came in the "Increase," 1635, aged 45; with wife Hannah, 35, and Samuel, 5½; removed to Dedham, probably in 1637, thence to Hampton, 1640, and perhaps to Ipswich, at least there he died June 4, 1662, by injury from a fall of a tree shortly before. He was freeman March 3, 1636, had second wife Dorothy, left only three children, of which probably one was Philemon, of Hampton, 1685. His widow married November 25, 1662, Godfrey Dearborn.

WILLIAM DALTON, an Irish youth, brought in the "Goodfellow," sold by the shipmaster, George Bell, to Samuel Symonds, May 10, 1654, having been sent by command of the English Government, after the triumphs of Cromwell, in Ireland.

REFERENCES:—Timlow's Hist. of Southington, Conn., 87; Runnel's Hist. of Sanbornton, N. H., II, 207; Dow's Hist. of Hampton, N. H., 653; Dearborn's Hist. of Parsonfield, Me., 379; Driver Gen., 135, 437; Amer. Ancestry, IV, 216; V, 79; IX, 37; N. E. Hist. and Gen. Reg., XXVII, 364; Savage's Gen. Dict., II, 3; Whitmore's Dalton Gen., 1873.

DAME, DAMME or DAM:—John Dame, of Dover, 1640, or earlier, by wife Elizabeth, had John, Elizabeth, born May 1, 1649; Mary, Sept. 4, 1651; William, Oct. 4, 1653; Susanna, December 14, 1661; and Judith, November 15, 1666; was freeman 1672; deacon, died January 27, 1690, in advanced age. Judith married July 6, 1684, Thomas Tibbets, and died before middle age. Formerly the name was written as sometimes it is now, Dam.

REFERENCES:—Wheeler's Hist. of Newport, N. H., 362; Wentworth Gen., vol. I, 450; Page Gen., 198; Amer. Ancestry, VII, 189; N. E. Hist. and Gen. Reg., V, 456; Savage's Gen. Dict., II, 3; Dame Gen.

DAMAN. Hill's Dedham, Mass., Records; Deane's Hist. of Scituate, Mass., 260.

DAMEN. Bergen's Hist. of Kings County, N. Y., 83.

DAMERON. Amer. Ancestry, IV, 58.

DAMERILL:—Humphrey Damerill, of Boston, a master mariner, appraiser of whose estate, to be divided between wife and children, was had April 27, 1654. His widow Sarah married Sept. 15, 1654, John Hawkins.

REFERENCES:—Savage's Gen. Dict., II, 3.

DAMON, DAMMAN, DAMAN or DAMING:— Edward Damon, of Marblehead, 1674. Dana, 8.

JOHN DAMON, of Scituate, 1643, came with sister Hannah, minors, under care of William Gilson, their uncle, one of the chief men of the town, as early as 1633, and had his estate. He married June, 1644, Catharine, daughter of Henry Merritt, had Deborah, born April 25, 1645; John, November 3, 1647; Zechary, 1649, died soon; Mary, July, 1651; Daniel, February, 1653; Zechary again, 1654; and his wife died. He married 1659, Martha Howland, had son Experience, born 1662; Silence, 1663; Ebenezer, 1665; Ichabod, 1668; Margaret, 1670; and Hannah, 1672. He was representative 1675-6, and died 1677, and his widow married Peter Bacon, of Taunton. John was on service in Philip's war. Ebenezer married a daughter of Bacon, but was weak, and his estate was in his mother's hands, not managed by him, as Deane tells. Deborah married 1666, Thomas Woodworth; Experience and Ichabod, also, had sons of same names.

JOHN DAMON, of Reading, freeman 1645, had John, who died January 14, 1652; and John, again, born March 18, 1652; daughter Abiah, August 26, 1654; Samuel, June 23, 1656; Joseph, August 18, 1661; probably also others; was a deacon, and died 1708. In the Reading family the "m" is doubled.

DANA:—Richard Dana, of Cambridge, married Anna Bullard, had John, born April 15, 1649, died in six months; Hannah, July 8, 1651; Samuel, October 13, 1653, died next month; Jacob, February 2, 1655; Joseph, May 21, 1656; Benjamin, February 20, baptized April 8, 1660; Elizabeth, April 27, 1662; Daniel, March 20, baptized April 3, 1663; daughter Abiah, died young; Deliverance, March 5, 1667; Sarah, who died January 11, 1670; and Sarah again, January 1, 1671; twelve in all, of which one daughter, probably Hannah, married Samuel Oldham; one, perhaps Elizabeth, perhaps Deliverance, married Daniel Woodward; and Sarah, married Samuel Hyde. The time of his death, by a fall in his barn, is given April 2, 1690, but the partition of the estate was not before April 15, 1695, when division to widow and four sons, beside Oldham, Woodward and Hyde is found. Thirteen of this family had been graduated in 1839, at Harvard, and thirteen at other New England Colleges.

REFERENCES.

MASSACHUSETTS.—Temple's Hist. of North Brookfield, 562; Wyman's Charlestown Gens., vol. I, 273; Cutter's Hist. of Arlington, 226; Barry's Hist. of Hanover, 291; Davis' Landmarks of Plymouth, 79; Eaton's Hist. of Reading, 60; Hudson's Hist. of Lexington, 55.

OTHER PUBLICATIONS.—Secomb's Hist. of Amherst, N. H., 553; Norton's Hist. of Fitzwilliam, N. H., 529, 801; Fiske's Hist. of Amherst, N. H., Gen., 141; Bolton Gen., 26; Savage's Gen. Dict., II, 4; Damon Gen.

DANA:—Richard, came to America, about 1640, and was the progenitor of this family in America. He had a son Benjamin, who married Mary Buckminster.

REFERENCES.

MASSACHUSETTS.—Stearn's Hist. of Ashburnham, 673; Wyman's Charlestown, Mass., Gens., vol. I, 274; Paige's Hist. of Cambridge, 526; Hill's Dedham, Mass., Record; Jackson's Hist. of Newtown, 264.

OTHER PUBLICATIONS.—Larned's Hist. of Windham County, Conn.; Secomb's Hist. of Amherst, N. H., 554; Oxford, N. H., Centen. 110; Joslin's Hist. of Poultney,

Vt., 244; Hinman's Conn. Settlers, 795; Strong Gen., 400; Leland Gen., 21; Dwight Gen., 665, 796, 800; Darling Memorial, 101; Chapman's Trowbridge Gen., 262; Chandler Gen., 104, 293; Amer. Ancestry, IX, 169; Savage's Gen. Dict., II, 4; Darling's Dana Gen., (1888); Dana Gen.

DAND:—John Dand, of Boston, 1641, clerk in the prothonotary's office (but I hear not where), gave much trouble by joining others in petition for enlargement of privilege 1645. Winslow describes him as living in another man's house at board hire. He was not a freeholder. See our General Court's Declaration in Hutchinson's Collections, 211, one of the most curious papers in that invaluable collection. We might presume, on his ill-success in Massachusetts, that he went home, but Farmer says he was of Dover, 1654. Winthrop, II, 262, 92-5. The learned author of "Gens Sylvestrina," one of the most agreeable books of genealogy ever printed, says, the Dands were "the most considerable family in the sixteenth century at Mansfield in Nottinghamshire." Yet there were mersers, as he tells.

REFERENCES:—Savage's Gen. Dict., II, 4.

DANDRIDGE. Richmond, Va., Standard, II, 10, 12, 21; Robertson's Pocahontas Descendants; Meade's Old Families of Va.; Spootswood Gen., 23; Willis' Washington Gen., 259.

DANDY:—William Dandy, of Charlestown, probably called Davy in Frothingham, 181, was in 1680 one of the tything men of the town. See Dady.

REFERENCES:—Savage's Gen. Dict., II, 5.

DANE:—John Dane, of Roxbury, from County Essex, England, came 1636, bringing children of a deceased wife, Francis, Elizabeth, and John; was perhaps the freeman of June 2, 1641, married July 2, 1643, Ann, or Hannah, or Annis, widow of William Chandler, and died, says the town record; buried, says the church record, September 14, 1658. His will, of a week preceding, probated October 16, names only those children, of which he calls Elizabeth, Howe, perhaps wife of the second Abraham, of Roxbury. Perhaps he had removed a short time to Ipswich, and came back to Roxbury. His widow had third husband John Parmenter, of Sudbury, and died March 15, 1683.

THOMAS DANE, of Concord, had, I suppose, by wife Elizabeth, a daughter born February 24, 1643, and certainly by her had Hannah, March 18, 1645, if this be the real name of him, printed Dann in the Genealogical Register, VIII, 347, with which confer Genealogical Register, IV, 271.

WILLIAM DANE, of Woburn, had Martha, born August 17, 1671; William, July 5, 1673; Samuel, July 26, 1675; John, June 25, 1677; Sarah in 1687, by wife Martha. Great difficulty occurs in turning over the records, by frequent substitution of Dean, or Deane, or Daine, for Dane and the reverse.

REFERENCES.

MASSACHUSETTS.—Hammatt Papers of Ipswich, 67; Temple's Hist. of North Brookfield, 563; Babson's Hist. of Gloucester, 324; Abbott's Hist. of Andover, 324.

OTHER PUBLICATIONS.—Hayward's Hist. of Hancock, N. H., 482; Coggswell's Hist. of New Boston, 421; Poor's Hist. Researches, 81; Chandler Gen., 108; N. E. Hist. and Gen. Reg., VIII, 148; XVIII, 263; Savage's Gen. Dict., II, 5; Spalding's F. Dane Sermon, 1875; Dane Memorial.

DANFORTH:—Nicholas Danforth, of Cambridge, from Framlingham, County Suffolk, came 1634, freeman March 3, 1636, representative 1636 and 7, died April, 1638, leaving Thomas, who was born 1622; Samuel, September, 1626, Harvard College, 1643; Jonathan, February 29, 1628; Ann, probably 1620, wife of Matthew Bridge; Lydia, wife of William Beaman; and the eldest, Elizabeth, 1618, wife of Andrew Belcher, grand-mother of Gov. Jonathan. His wife Elizabeth had died 1629, in England.

WILLIAM DANFORTH, of Newbury, 1667, born only 14 years before at London, perhaps was soldier in December 1675, of Johnson's company; by first wife who died Oct. 18, 1678, had no children; by second wife Sarah Thurlo, had William, Mary, Richard, born January 31, 1680; John, December 8, 1681, died October 1, 1772; Jonathan, May 18, 1685; Thomas, September 11, 1688; Francis, March, 15 1691; and Joseph, May 12, 1694. Descendants, says Farmer, are in New Hampshire, and some of them spell their name Danford. Eleven of this name graduated at Harvard, all are male line descendants of Nicholas.

REFERENCES.

MASSACHUSETTS.—Paige's Hist. of Hardwick, 358; Paige's Hist. of Cambridge, 529; Wyman's Charlestown, Mass., Gens., vol. I, 275; Hudson's Hist. of Lexington, 55; Hazen's Hist. of Billerica, 34; Davis' Landmarks of Plymouth, 79; Balie's Hist. of North Plymouth, 79; Bond's Hist. of Watertown, 196; Emerson's Taunton, Mass., Ministry, vol. I, 177; Tyngboro, Mass. Centen., 19.

NEW HAMPSHIRE.—Worcester's Hist. of Hollis, 372; Coffin's Hist. of Boscawen, 516; Hayward's Hist. of Hancock, 483; Runnell's Hist. of Sanbornton, II, 209; Secomb's Hist. of Amherst, 556; Stearns' Hist. of Rindge, 500; Washington, N. H., Hist., 364.

OTHER PUBLICATIONS.—Lapham's Hist. of Norway, Me., 491; Bradbury's Hist. of Kennebunkport, Me., 236; Farmer's Hist. Coll., II, 269; N. E. Hist. and Gen. Reg., VII, 315; Savage's Gen. Dict., II, 7; Danforth Family Meeting, (1886); Harris' Danforth Gen., 1853; Amer. Ancestry, XI, 189.

DANGERFIELD. Meade's Old Families of Virginia, vol. I, 405; Richmond, Va., Standard, III, 6.

DANIEL or DANIELS:—David Daniel, of Dover, 1661-72.

JAMES DANIEL, of Exeter, took oath of allegiance, November 30, 1677.

JOSEPH DANIEL, of Falmouth, 1680. Willis, I, 217. Perhaps he had been of Medfield, 1649-78.

JOHN DANIEL, of New London, 1663, married January 19, 1665, Mary, daughter of George Chappel, had John, born January 19, 1666; Mary, October 12, 1667; Thomas, December 30, 1669; Christian, March 3, 1671; Hannah, April 20, 1674; Rachel, February 27, 1676; Sarah, February 10, 1679; Jonathan, October 15, 1682; and Clement, whose date is not given; and died 1709 or 10.

RICHARD DANIEL, of Billerica, 1675, lived also at Andover, and is spoken of by Gookin, in his account of the Indians.

ROBERT DANIEL, of Watertown, removed 1651, to Cambridge, freeman March 14, 1639; his wife Elizabeth, died October 2, 1643, and he died at Cambridge, July 6, 1655. His will of three days before names widow of uncertain letters, like Reana Andrews, whom he had mar-

ried only May 2, of the year 1654, and five children, Elizabeth, wife of Thomas Fanning; Samuel, and minors Joseph, Sarah and Mary, the last of which was born September 2, 1642. His widow married Edmund Frost, as his third wife.

STEPHEN DANIEL, of Saybrook, perhaps, 1650; removed to New Haven, married Anna or Hannah, daughter of Thomas Gregson, had Joanna, born September 1, 1652; Elizabeth, October 1, 1655; Rebecca, January 30, baptized February 28, 1658; and perhaps removed, but the family did not, for Joanna, married there December 7, 1671, John Glover; Elizabeth, married May 9, 1682, John Winston; and Rebecca, married the same day, John Thompson; and Grigson's widow gave, 1692, some property to her daughter Anna Daniel.

STEPHEN DANIEL, at Salem, 1668, to a petition against imposts signed his name, and no more is known of him.

THOMAS DANIEL, of Kittery, 1652, removed to Portsmouth, married Bridget, daughter of Richard Cutt; was a captain, and of the first council, 1680, under President John Cutt. His widow married December 11, 1684, Thomas Graffort.

WENTWORTH DANIEL, of Lynn, 1640. Lewis.

WILLIAM DANIEL, of Dorchester, freeman 1648, married Catharine, daughter of John Grinoway. A daughter married John Kingsley, and died 1671. Alice Daniels, had, say Felt, grant of land, 1637, at Salem. Distinction of family with, or without final "s" is probably not universally observed.

REFERENCES.

MASSACHUSETTS.—Paige's Hist. of Cambridge, 532; Jameson's Hist. of Medway, 468; Ballou's Hist. of Milford, 694; Morse's Sherborn, Mass., Settlers, 71.

OTHER PUBLICATIONS.—Hayden's Virginia Gens., 292; Richmond, Va., Standard, vol. I, 32; III, 51; Hinman's Conn. Settlers, 796; Runnel's Hist. Sanbornton, N. H., II, 211; Goode Gen., 49, 104; Baldwin Gen., 362; N. E. Hist. and Gen. Reg., XXVIII, 185; Amer. Ancestry, V, 149; Daniell Gen., 1874.

DANIELS:—Robert, of Watertown, Mass., married Rachel Partridge, and had Joseph, of Medfield, Mass.

REFERENCES:—Jameson's Hist. of Medway, Mass., 471; Temple's Hist. of North Brookfield, Mass., 565; Lapham's Hist. of Paris, Me., 573; Sibley's Hist. of Union, Me., 446; Blake's Hist. of Franklin, N. H., 238; Livermore's Hist. of Wilton, N. H., 358; Boyd's Hist. of Consensus, N. Y., 151; Caulkin's Hist. of New London, Conn., 351; Norton's Hist. of Knox County, Ohio, 326; Munsell's Albany, N. Y., Coll., IV, 112; Austin's Allied Families, R. I., 79; Leland Gen., 215, 271; Montague Gen., 379; Amer. Ancestry, V, 31; XV, 5; Savage's Gen. Dict., II, 9.

DANIELSON. Hyde's Hist. of Brimfield, 303; Whitman Gen., 633.

DANN. Bouton Gen., 442; Huntington's Stamford, Conn., Settlers, 27.

DANTS or DANKS:—Robert Dants, of Northampton, 1671, married Elizabeth, widow of John Webb, had Mehitable; Robert, who died 1675; Elizabeth, born 1677; Robert, 1680; and Mercy, 1682. Elizabeth, mother or daughter, died December, 1691; and he died February 24, 1692. The name was long kept up, but is now extinct at Northampton, yet whence he came is unknown. A Robert Dants, perhaps his father, was freeman May 10,

1643, of course belonging to some Eastern town of the Colony. Savage's Gen. Dict., II, 9.

DARKE:—Thomas Darke, of Weymouth, of early, but not known date. Savage's Gen. Dict., II, 9.

DARLEY:—Dennis Darley, of Braintree, an early settler, says Farmer.

EDWARD DARLEY, of Boston, married January 25, 1660, Susanna Hooke.

REFERENCES:—Kingman's Hist. of North Bridgewater, Mass.,; Washman's Notes on Livermore, 221.

DARKIN. Shourd's Fenwick Colony, N. J., 224.

DARBY. Westminster, Mass., Centen. 29.

DARLING:—George Darling, of Lynn, 1650-70, had Joseph, born March, 1667; was of Marblehead, 1674. Lewis and Dana, 8.

JOHN DARLING, of Braintree, 1660-90, may have been brother of George, and had wife Catharine.

JOHN DARLING, of Fairfield, married Elizabeth, daughter of James Beers, the first. Thirteen of this name had been graduated at the New England Colleges in 1828.

REFERENCES.

MASSACHUSETTS.—Temple's Hist. of Palmer, 444; Marwin's Hist. of Winchenden, 452; Hudson's Hist. of Marlborough, 352; Wyman's Charlestown Gens., vol. I, 276; Jameson's Hist. of Medway, 480; Blake's Hist. of Franklin, 240; Benedict's Hist. of Sutten, 631; Barry's Hist. of Framingham, 219; Ballou's Hist. of Milford, 703.

OTHER PUBLICATIONS.—Bradbury's Kennebunkport, Me., 237; Bangor, Me., Hist. Magazine, V, 187; Runnel's Hist. of Sanbornton, N. H., vol. I, 215; Stearn's Hist. of Rindge, N. H., 501; Coggswell's Hist. of Henniker, N. H., 535; Darling Gen., 1888; Young's Hist. of Warsaw, N. Y., 258; Leland Gen., 89; Kulp's Wyoming Valley Families; Amer. Ancestry, III, 18; IV, 42.

DARLINGTON. Futhey's Hist. of Chester County, Pa., 509; Smith's Hist. of Delaware County, Pa., 455; Cope Gen. of Pa., 68, 148, 208; Amer. Ancestry, IX, 242; Maris Gen., 153; Darlington Gen., 1853.

DARMAN:—John Darman, of Braintree, had John, born 1664, died young; Joseph, 1645; and John, again, 1653. Savage's Gen. Dict., II, 10.

DARNALL.—Powers' Hist. of Sangamon County, Ill., 242.

DARREL:—John Darrel, came in the "Mary Ann" from Great Yarmouth, 1637, desiring to go to Salem; but no more is known.

DARRAH. Hayward's Hist. of Hancock, N. H., 484; Bedford, N. H., Centen. 297; Saunderson's Charlestown, N. H., 320; Davis' Hist. of Bucks County, Pa., 553; Amer. Ancestry, VII, 214.

DARRIN. Champion Gen.; Amer. Ancestry, VII, 49.

DARROW or DARRAH:—George Darrow, of New London, 1676, by wife Mary, had Mary, baptized Dec., 1678; George, October, 1680; Nicholas, May, 1683; Jane, April, 1692; beside Richard; was a serj.   , died about 1704.

REFERENCES:—Walworth's Hyde Gen., 762; Dodd's

Hist. of East Haven, Conn., 116; Caulkin's Hist. of New London, Conn., 347; Amer. Ancestry, II, 29.

DART:—Ambrose Dart, of Boston, married June 24, 1653, Ann, daughter of William Addis, of Gloucester, had William, born January 1, 1655.

RICHARD DART, of New London, 1664, by wife Bethia, had Dinah, born January 13, 1663; Daniel, May 3, 1666; Richard, May 7, 1667; Roger, November 22, 1670; Ebenezer, February 18, 1673; Ann, February 14, 1675; Bethia, July 30, 1677; Elizabeth, December 15, 1679; Sarah, June 10, 1681; and Mary, 1685.

REFERENCES:—Hayward's Hist. of Gilsum, N. H., 295; Amer. Ancestry, VII, 248; Savage's Gen. Dict., II, 10; Dart Gen.

DARVALL, DARVILL or DARVELL:—Robert Darvall, of Sudbury, an original proprietor, died February 26, 1662; had Elizabeth, and by wife Esther, had Mary, born May 10, 1642; and Dorothy, named in the will of their grand-father of January 16, 1662, in which he gave the mother 5 and a one-half acres of land at Norchurch, in County Herts, "commonly called "Herrot's End." Elizabeth, his daughter, perhaps by former wife, married at Sudbury, November 30, 1654, the second Peter Noyes. He also names daughter Mary Darvall, who married that year Joseph Noyes, nephew of Peter.

WILLIAM DARVALL, of Boston, 1674, merchant.

REFERENCES:—Savage's Gen. Dict., II, 10.

DARWIN. Champion Gen.

DASCOMB. Livermore's Hist. of Willis, 359.

DASKOM. Orcutt's Hist. of Stratford, Conn., 1189.

DASSETT:—John Dassett, of Braintree, one of the founders of the church September 17, 1639, freeman May 13, 1640, had Joseph, born and died December, 1642, who may have been his youngest child, for his division of lands February 24, 1640, was for seven heads. His name in Genealogical Register, IX, 142, is distorted to Deffet. He died 1677, his will of March, in that year, was probated April 27, following. It gave all to his son John. Mary, his daughter, perhaps, born in England, married John Briggs, and second Captain John Minot.

REFERENCES:—Savage's Gen. Dict., II, 11.

DAVENPORT:—Francis Davenport, of Boston, 1675, mariner, married Ann, daughter of Dr. William Snelling.

HUMPHREY DAVENPORT, of Dorchester, came from Barbados, married Rachel, daughter of Thomas Holmes, had Richard, removed to Hartford, there had Willam, and in 1667, his wife was convicted of playing cards. They removed to New York, where greater laxity might be indulged in.

JOHN DAVENPORT, of New Haven, first minister there, son of John, says Wood's Athenae Oxonienses, not, as the fondness of Mather states, mayor of Coventry, in idle attempt to magnify a great man, was born 1597. bred at Oxford, not admitted, as Mather has it, of Brazen Nose, 1611, entered 1613, at Merton College, thence after two years removed to Magdalen Hall, where he proceeded B. D. 1625, was preaching at St. Stephen's, Coleman street, London, perhaps not quite so early as the Magnalia imports; but being in 1633 complained of for nonconforming, went to Amsterdam, thence came to New England 1637, with Gov. Eaton, arrived at Boston, June 26, and next year with him settled New Haven.

Mr. Haven, the accomplished editor of Archaeologic Americana, vol. III, in preliminary remark cxxxvi, corrects that looselessness of the Magnalia as to the mayor of Coventry; yet falls into slight error as to the coming of this famous divine. On page 85, he says: "When the times grew favorable for the Puritans, he returned to England, from his refuge in Holland;" but more exact expression should be, in my judgment thus: "As the times grew not favorable for the Puritans, he returned no more to England," except to embark privily, perhaps without landing, for he dared not appear in London. After nearly 30 years of great influence in the Colony of his own planting, removed to Boston, freeman 1669, having with very injurious controversy been installed as successor of Wilson, December 9, 1668, at the first church, causing foundation of third church in Boston, gathered May 12, 1669, at Charlestown, and violent heats in the commonwealth for many years. The great body of the clergy favored the new church, as did a major part of the assistants, of six opponents, three, including Gov. Bellingham, being of the old church. He was at New Haven eager in defence of Goffe and Whalley, the regicides in 1661, and perhaps much aided in their escape. Yet a most curious, if not characteristic, letter from him furnishes no small light to the history of his acting given by Dr. Stiles, as it tends to exculpate or inculpate him according to the eyes with which it is read, in the 3 Mass. Hist. Coll. VIII, 327. With his name is frequently associated that of a cousin, possibly a brother Christopher, born 1598, a Catholic priest of great learning, not a Jesuit, under the name of Santa Clara, who died May 31, 1680. Mather, III, 52, denies that he was a brother, "as a certain Wooden Historian, in his Athenae Oxonienses has report." By this merciless punishment of honest Anthony, the immortal author of the Magnalia fully proves how much better qualified he was for executioner than judge. We know no child but John, called only son, though he certainly had youngest son Joseph, who died probably before his father, and perhaps had daughters before or after coming to New England, and he died March 15, 1670. Elizabeth, perhaps his widow, died at Boston, September 15, 1676, aged 73, if the grave-stone be correct. In the present age a descendant of the venerable father of New Haven, A. Benedict Davenport, Esq., calls himself of the 24th generation, has confidently carried the line of his family back to Orme de Davenport, 1086, or the 20th of the Conqueror. Such labors are seldom reverenced in this country.

RICHARD DAVENPORT, of Salem, came with Capt. Endicot, in the "Abigail," September, 1682, from Weymouth, in the County Dorset, a few miles from Dorchester, near where probably he was born about 1606. He was freeman September 3, 1634, ensign next month, when his friend Endicot cut out the Red Cross in the National banner, in admiration of which rashness he gave a daughter born that year, her name Truecross; lieutenant, with a happier spirit when he was wounded 1636, in the Pequot expedition, representative 1637, and that year directed to receive the arms from Wheelwright's friends; artillery company 1639; removed to Boston, 1642, and was appointed captain of the castle, where he was killed by lightning, July 15, 1665. His wife was Elizabeth, and children Nathaniel, Truecross, born 1634 or more probably '35; Experience, baptized August 27, 1637; and John, September 19, 1641, all at Salem, but the record of the church being for the earliest years lost, the baptism of the oldest child is not known; and at Boston, he had Samuel, baptized June 28, 1646;

Sarah, September 30, 1649; Elizabeth, September 13, 1652; and William, born May 11, 1656, baptized 7 days old. His widow died June 24, 1678. Truecross married November 10, 1654, Stephen Minot; and Elizabeth, married Asaph Eliot. William was a sergeant in Phips's Quebec expedition, but whether he was married is unknown and he died soon after reaching home. Prince Annals, I, 174. Johnson, W. W. P.

THOMAS DAVENPORT, of Dorchester, 1640, freeman May 18, 1642, perhaps living 1660, at Cambridge, died November 9, 1685, leaving wife Mary, who died October 4, 1691; had Sarah, born December 28, 1643; Thomas, who was killed in Philip's war December 19, 1675, in Johnson's company; Mary, baptized January 21, 1649; Charles; Mehitable, born February 14, 1657; Jonathan, March 6, 1659; Ebenezer, April 26, 1661; and John, baptized November 20, 1654. Mary married Samuel Maxfield. Often in early records, inexperienced readers will be misled by finding this name as Danfort or Damport. Five of this name had been graduated in 1834 at Harvard, and eight at the other New England Colleges.

REFERENCES.

MASSACHUSETTS.—Jackson's Hist. of Newton, 265; Ward's Hist. of Shrewsbury, 265; Benedict's Hist. of Sutton, 631; Ballou's Hist. of Milford, 705.

OTHER PUBLICATIONS. — Huntington's Stamford, Conn., Settlers, 28; Tuttle Gen. of Conn., 354; Dodd's Hist. of East Haven, Conn., 116; Hinman's Conn. Settlers, 205; Waterford, Me., Centen. 262; Thurston's Hist. of Winthrop, Me., 179; Heminway's Vt. Gaz., V, 34; Heraldic Journal, vol. I, 36; Bouton's Hist. of Westchester County, N. Y., II, 513; Hough's Hist. of Lewis County, N. Y., 148; Cutt's Gen., 232; Goodwin's Gen. Notes, 306; Huntington Gen., 96; Maltby Gen. (1895), 58; Meade's Old Families of Va., 36; Richmond, Va., Standard, II, 26; Powers' Hist. of Sangamon County, Ill., 244; Preble Gen., 235; Ransom Gen., 49; Walworth's Hyde Gen., 1060; Amer. Ancestry, II, 30; III, 102; VI, 41; VIII, 99; X, 192; XI, 190; Savage's Gen. Dict., II, 11; N. E. Hist. and Gen. Reg., III, 351; IV, 111; IX, 146; XXXIII, 25; Davenport Gen.

DAVES. Daves Biog., 1892.

DAVEY. Adams' Hist. of Fair Haven, Vt., 335.

DAVID:—John David, of Boston, known to me only as witness to the will of Major Holmes, November, 1649.

REFERENCES:—Secomb's Hist. of Amherst, N. H., 559; Savage's Gen. Dict., II, 13.

DAVIDS:—Samuel Davids, of Boston, heard of only in May, 1663; as appraiser on estate of Robert Lincoln.

REFERENCES:—Raymond's Tarrytown, N. Y., Mem., 172; Savage's Gen. Dict., II, 14.

DAVIDSON:—Nicholas, born in Dingwall Castle, Scotland, 1580; removed to Lynn, Eng., about 1605; had Nicholas, (2).

NICHOLAS DAVIDSON, (2), son of Nicholas, born in Lynn, England, 1611, settled near Charlestown, Mass., married Joan Hodges.

REFERENCES.

NEW HAMPSHIRE.—Morrison's Hist. of Windham, 425; Cutter's Hist. of Jaffrey, 298; Hayward's Hist. of Hancock, 485; Merrill's Hist. of Ackworth, 206.

OTHER PUBLICATIONS.—Young's Hist. of Warsaw, N. Y., 254; Collins' Hist. of Hillsdale, N. Y., App., 51; Wyman's Charlestown, Mass., Gens., vol. I, 277; Iowa Hist. Atlas, 264; Amer. Ancestry, VIII, 61, 129; IX, 121; Davidson Chart, 1887.

DAVIE:—Edmund Davie, of Harvard College, 1674, of whom we know nothing, but what the college catalogue of 1698 tells, that he had taken his M. D. at Padua, and was then dead. Unsatisfactory conjecture may suppose that he was younger brother of Humphrey.

GEORGE DAVIE, of Sheepscot, near Wiscasset, as early as 1653, wounded by Indians, 1676. Sullivan, 148, 298.

HUMPHREY DAVIE, of Boston, merchant, son of Sir John, who had been created a baronet, September 9, 1641, came from London 1662, possibly to encourage Rev. James Allen, freeman 1665, artillery company 1665, representative for Billerica, because he had estate there 1665-9, for Woburn 1678, probably on equal reason, an assistant 1679-86; married as second or third wife, Sarah, widow of James Richards, of Hartford, who had left large estate that caused his removal thither; had by her Humphrey and William, and died February 18, 1689. By former wife he had John, Harvard College, 1681, but whether she came with him from London, I cannot find. His widow married Hon. Jonathan Tyng.

JOHN DAVIE, of Boston, freeman May 25, 1636, a surporter of Wheelwright and Mrs. Hutchinson, punished therefor. Winthrop, I, 248. I presume he is the man admitted of the church in January before, but the Elder wrote the name Davisse, and called him joiner. Most of the names Davie or Davy, Davies or Davis, are convertable. He may have gone to Duxbury, where one of his name sold estate 1650.

SAMUEL DAVIE, of Boston, 1668.

A widow Mary, of Charlestown, had there baptized William, aged 13, on August 11, 1689.

REFERENCES:—Davis' Landmarks of Plymouth, Mass., 80; Caulkins' Hist. of New London, Conn., 415; Slaughter's Bristol Parish, 203; Wheeler's Hist. of North Carolina, 188, 198; Butler Gen., 34; Savage's Gen. Dict., II, 14.

DAVIES. Powers' Hist. of Sangamon County, Ill., 245; Amer. Ancetry, III, 14; IX, 161; Anderson, Davies and Wersler Gen.

DAVIS or DAVIES:—Anthony Davis, of Boston, died June, 1674, leaving widow Elizabeth.

BARNABY DAVIS, of Charlestown, 1636, or after, came in the Blessing, 1635, aged 36, died November 27, 1685, aged about 86. Frothingham, 152, has his name 1658, at division of wood and commons on Mistick side; and page 183, has Barnaby, Jr., probably his son, in the list of householders, 1678.

DANIEL DAVIS, of Kittery, 1649, freeman 1652.

DOLOR, DOLLARD or DOLLAR DAVIS, of Cambridge, 1634, is said to have married perhaps in England, Margery, sister of Simon Willard, if so, he was probably from Kent, and this conjecture is confirmed to me by collateral evidence. Yet the grave-yard at Benefield, in County Northampton, as Dr. Palfrey assures me, contains the names of his ancestors. He removed about 1640. and had land that year in Duxbury, and was of that church when he removed to Barnstable, and joined that August 27, 1648, with his wife, but had his daughter Ruth, baptized at Barnstable, March 24, 1645; was freeman of that Colony, 1646; and in the list of those able to bear arms 1643, is this man's name "and his sons." Who may be

intended by the last word, is not precisely understood, but probably John alone. Yet at the end of that list stand John and Nicholas, who might well, therefor, be thought brothers, certainly not sons. But two sons he did have, Simon and Samuel, both younger by much than John, who was executor of his will. Before removed to Duxbury, he lived some years at Concord, and was one of the proprietors of Groton, 1655, engaged in its first settlement, and made one of its selectmen by the General Court of the Colony. Still it is not likely, that he ever inhabited in the new plantation, but leaving his youngest son to reside at Concord, went back to Barnstable, and died there 1673. His daughter Ruth, married 1663, it is said, Stephen Hall; and Mary, who married June 15, 1653, Thomas Lewis, of Barnstable, was probably another.

EDWARD DAVIS, of Boston, married September 16, 1657, Hannah, daughter of Richard Gridley.

EPHRAIM DAVIS, of Haverhill, married December 29, 1660, Mary Johnson, of Andover, took oath of allegiance November 28, 1677, died 1681, leaving children Stephen, Ephraim, Thomas, Jonathan, Mary, Susanna and Hannah.

FRANCIS DAVIS, of Amesbury, swore allegiance Dec. 20, 1677.

GEORGE DAVIS, of Boston, 1644, blacksmith, perhaps the freeman of 1645, one of the founders of the second church, by wife Barbara, who had joined first church Aug., 1647, had Samuel, born October 17, 1651; and, if the records be not false, John, June 3, 1652; was a sergeant, died early in 1655. He throve by his trade, for the inventory valued one fourth of George Munjoy's ship "Swan," and five sixteenths of Benjamin Munjoy's ship "Delight"; and his widow married January 14, 1656, John Brimblecome, first, who was one of the witnesses to his will, and for third husband Thomas Chadwell. His will made September 23, 1654, was probated April 25 following, and anticipating the marriage of his widow again, he made various provisions for the two sons. See Genealogical Register, V, 306, and IX, 35.

GEORGE DAVIS, of Lynn, freeman 1647, had Hannah, born May 31, 1650; Sarah, September 1, 1651; removed to Reading, there had Elizabeth, January 16, 1655; Mary, January 16, 1658; John, July 20, 1660; and Susanna, May 11, 1662.

GEORGE DAVIS, of Weymouth, 1654, blacksmith.

GEORGE DAVIS, of Boston, 1650, went 1654 to North Carolina, in his will before departing, provides for wife, sons Benjamin, Joseph and five daughters.

GERSHOM DAVIS, of Cambridge, had wife Sarah, who died November 20, 1713, aged 55; son Gershom, and died February 6, 1718, aged 75.

HOPEWELL DAVIS, of Charlestown, by wife Sarah, had Joseph, baptized February, 1686; Ebenezer, May 6, 1688; Sarah, November 2, 1690; Ellen, January 14, 1694; and John, November 6, 1698.

ISAAC DAVIS, of Salem, 1637, of Beverly, 1650, perhaps was after at Carso; unless this were another whose eldest son John, born 1660, was living at Gloucester, 1733, with other sons Samuel and James, beside children of a daughter who married a Fitz, and was of Ipswich, and another daughter who married Smith. He had after first destruction of Falmouth, estate set out 1680, but on second destruction probably moved to safer quarters. Willis, I, 160, 209.

JACOB DAVIS, of Gloucester, married Jan. 20, 1662;

Elizabeth Bennet, had Jacob, born January 26, 1663; John, November 25, 1665, died soon; Elizabeth, June 27, 1667; Susanna, June 27, 1670; Moses, July 6. 1673; Mary, June 3, 1676; Aaron, January, 1679; and John, again, July 1, 1681.

JAMES DAVIS, of Newbury, freeman, March 4, 1635, removed to Haverhill, 1640, had wife Cicely, representative 1660, died January 19 or 29, 1679, aged 90. In his will of March 17, 1676, names as his children John, Ephraim, Samuel and Sarah, wife of John Page, Jr. His wife had died May 28, 1673.

JAMES DAVIS, of Hampton, 1638, freeman May 13, 1640. Belknap, I, 21. James, Jr., perhaps son of preceding, was of Hampton, 1643, may have lived at Haverhill, there took oath of allegiance, November 28, 1677.

JAMES DAVIS, of Boston, 1634, mariner, by wife Joanna, had Jacob, born July 11, 1639; and daughter Josebeth, Aug. 20, baptized Aug. 28, 1642, who married John Wing, of Boston; beside John, who died November 13, 1653.

JAMES DAVIS, of Plymouth, 1639, a tailor, may have been of Newport, the year before, had grant of land for serving in the Pequot War, but was gone in 1643.

JAMES DAVIS, of Boston, by wife Mary, had Mary, born May 7, 1647.

JAMES DAVIS, of Charlestown, 1658, had Elizabeth, baptized at 21 years, on May 6, 1694; and Patience, aged 18, on April 21, 1695.

JAMES DAVIS, of Haverhill, freeman 1666, was, perhaps son of James, the aged, of that town, may have married a daughter of John Eaton, of Haverhill, had son John, and died July 18, 1694.

JAMES DAVIS, of Gloucester, by wife Mehitable, who died June 9, 1666, had John, born March 10, 1660; James, March 16, 1662, died soon; James again, January 22, 1663, died soon; and Joseph, 1665, died soon. He married December 6, 1666, Elizabeth Bachelor, had Elizabeth born September 11, 1669; Abigail, April 13, 1672; Joseph again, January 25, 1674; Susanna, November 20, 1676; and Ebenezer, January 26, 1682; died 1717.

JAMES DAVIS, of Scituate, 1673, there married Elizabeth, daughter of William Randall, and removed to Boston.

JENKYN DAVIS, of Lynn, freeman March 9, 1637, a joiner, who had been in the employ of Mr. Humphrey, who unhappily, put his daughters to board with Davis, when he went to the West Indies; by Sarah, had John, and a daughter, and died 1662. Winthrop, II, 45. Lewis.

JOHN DAVIS, of Boston, 1635, a joiner, artillery company, 1643. I presume this to be the same man who came in the "Increase," 1635, aged 29; and perhaps was the John Davie, friend of Wheelwright, in the former article.

JOHN DAVIS, of Newbury, 1641, by wife Mary, had Mary, born October 6, 1642, died young; John, January 15, 1645; Zechary, February 22, 1646; Jeremy, June 21, 1648; Mary again, August 12, 1650; Cornelius, April 15, 1653; and Ephraim, September 29, 1655; and died November 12, 1675.

JOHN DAVIS, of Watertown, married Mary, daughter of John Spring, had Mary, born March 20, 1642, and probably John and Bnjamin, died early, as did his widow, administration being given June 19, 1656.

JOHN DAVIS, of Reading, had John, who died November 4, 1660.

JOHN DAVIS, of York, 1650, an important person, kept an inn, freeman, probably of Massachusetts, 1652. There was also another John, perhaps his son, was lieutenant-captain, and at last sergeant-major for the Province, and deputy-president 1680-85.

JOHN DAVIS, of Boston, brother, perhaps, of Edward, a joiner, by wife Return, (daughter of Richard Gridley, married April 9, 1656), had Grace, born March 4, 1657.

JOHN DAVIS, of Roxbury, 1653, a tailor.

JOHN DAVIS, of New London, 1651-64.

JOHN DAVIS, of Charlestown, 1668, fined for hospitality to a Quaker. Frothingham, 158. He may have removed soon to Westerly, where was one John, 1669.

JOHN DAVIS, of Lynn, married October 5, 1664, Sarah, daughter of Philip Kirkland, had Sarah, born November 10, 1665, died at two months; Sarah again, February 5, 1667, died at   months; Mary, July 25, 1668; Joseph, June 10, 1672, died in July of next year; John, June 16, 1674; Sarah again, February 1, 1676; Ebenezer, October 2, 1678, and Benjamin, September 27, 1681.

JOHN DAVIS, of Saco, representative 1682, "disaccepted as a scandalous person," says the record.

JOSEPH DAVIS, of Kittery, 1660, constable that year, may have been son of Nicholas.

JOSEPH DAVIS, of Boston, married May 7, 1662, Elizabeth, daughter of David Saywell, freeman 1666, artillery company 1675.

JOSEPH DAVIS, perhaps of Roxbury, there married October 28, 1670, Sarah Chamberlain, but I know not, that either belong to that place. In the neighboring Joseph, of Muddy River, had Mehitable, born February 3, 1685. Possibly he may be the man named in the letter of Rev. Edmund Browne to Gov. Leverett, printed in Genealogical Register, VII, 268, as Daby.

LAWRENCE DAVIS, of Falmouth, 1662, had Rachel, born 1663; Jacob, and perhaps others; removed to Ipswich, during the first Indian war, but came back 1681, but no more is told, only that Rachel married first Robert Haynes; and second a Wedgewood, of Hampton.

NATHANIEL DAVIS, of Mass., came in the "Mary and John," or perhaps the "Hercules," having qualified himself by taking oath of allegiance and supremacy, April 16, 1634, but where he sat down I find not. See Genealogical Register, IX, 268.

NATHANIEL DAVIS, of Charlestown, 1677, had married March 31, 1675, Mary Convers, who died November 6, 1690, aged 36; and wife Mary again who died April 18, 1721, aged 65. Nathaniel, his eldest child, baptized April 19, 1677, died at Charlestown, the same year. He had also Mary, baptized May 9, 1680; Barnabus, Dec. 1681; Sarah, July 22, 1683; Zachary, August 5, 1688; and Mary, July 16, 1695; and was one of the constables 1690.

NICHOLAS DAVIS, of Charlestown, came in the "Planter," early in 1635, aged 40, with Sarah, 48, probably his wife, and Joseph, 13, perhaps his son, with four servants, whose names are then given, was in 1640 one of the promotors of the settlement of Woburn, where his wife Sarah, died May 24, 1643, and he married July 12 following, Elizabeth, widow of Joseph Isaacs; probably he removed to York, and was there in 1652. His will, of April 27, 1667, probated March 12, 1670, refers not to any son, yet opens many remote relations, or perhaps those of his wife, as cousin Barnard, the wife of Matthew, of Boston; cousin William Locke, of Woburn, (spelled Owburne); daughter Astine's (or Austin's) children, Mary and Sarah, beside Mary, Elizabeth and Mehitable, Dodd.

NICHOLAS DAVIS, of Barnstable, able to bear arms 1643, when he is last on the list, so that possibly it may be an error, as Hamblen put him into a list of inhabitants admitted after 1660. He may have been of Newport, 1638, and there learned the strange policy of toleration in religion. In Sewel, I, 388, it is said he favored the Quakers at their first meeting. He had wife Mary, and was banished from Mass. for his peaceful pravity. At Newport he was drowned before August 9, 1672, as Roger Williams in his big book against the Quakers, page 26, tells that in his public conference, there, with the friends of George Fox, he made good use of the event.

PHILIP DAVIS, of Plymouth, 1638, removed to Duxbury after. Farmer, M. S.

PHILIP DAVIS, of Hartford, came, perhaps, in the "Confidence," from Southampton 1638, aged 12; but if so, he probably was first at Newbury, where William Isley, with whom he came, pitched his tent. He married a daughter of Thomas Coleman, of Hadley, was freeman of Connecticut, 1656, and died 1689, had two daughters but no sons.

RICHARD DAVIS, of Ipswich, 1642.

RICHARD DAVIS, of Roxbury, married about 1654, Sarah, daughter of John Burrill, had Richard, born Jan. 5, 1658, who died next year; Richard, again, May 26, 1661; and Sarah, and he died March 6, 1663, his will of February 20, being probated March 19, of that year. But there is a posthumous child and the widow married Samuel Chandler, in 1664, and he died August, 1665.

ROBERT DAVIS, of Sudbury, came in 1638, aged 30, with Margaret, perhaps his sister 26, (who married a Burnett), in the Confidence of Southampton, as servant of Peter Noyes, had wife Bridget, who survived, daughters Sarah, born April 10, 1646; and Rebecca, and died July 19, 1655. His will is of July 17, and probated October 2 of that year.

ROBERT DAVIS, of Yarmouth, 1643, or earlier, had Deborah, born January, 1646; Mary, May 28, 1648; Andrew, May, 1650; John, March 1, 1652; Robert, August, 1654; Josiah, September, 1656; Hannah, September, 1658; Sarah, October, 1660; and Tristram. Perhaps Sarah married October 23, 1679, Joseph Young.

SAMUEL DAVIS, of Watertown, removed early in 1646, to Boston, had wife Ann, who died soon; and married July 20, 1651, Sarah, daughter of Richard Thayer, of Boston, had Samuel, born March 22, 1654; William, September 4, 1656, died next year; and Sarah, December 19, 1657. Probably he was the freeman of 1645, and perhaps brother of George. It may be, that his widow married May 6, 1663, Jonathan Hayward.

SAMUEL DAVIS, of Groton, by wife Mary, had a daughter born January 31, 1662; John, March 10, 1664; Sarah, August 12, 1667; Samuel, January 10, 1669; Barnabus, April 17, 1672; and a daughter April 10, 1674; and died December 28, 1699.

SAMUEL DAVIS, of Salisbury, married December 19, 1663, Deborah, daughter of William Barnes, had Samuel,

born January 26, 1667. Perhaps he was of Amesbury, there took oath of allegiance, December 20, 1677.

SAMUEL DAVIS, of Charlestown, had served under Captain Turner, 1676, in Philip's war, but as early as November, 22, 1658, by wife Mary, had Elizabeth.

STEPHEN DAVIS, of Hartford, 1646, freeman of Connecticut, 1658.

SYLVANUS DAVIS, of Sheepscott, 1659, swore allegiance to the king 1665, wounded by the Indians 1676, at Arowsick, when Capt. Lake was killed, removed to Falmouth, 1680, there had command of the fort in the next Indian war, taken by the French and Indian combined force, May 20, 1690, carried to Canada; after his return was put into the Council by the Charter of William and Mary 1691; wrote an account of the conduct of the war, which is in the three Mass. Hist. Collections, I, 101. He lived at Hull in latter days, died 1704, leaving wife but no children. His will, April 8, 1703, probated May 6, 1704, gives all his quarter of Casco lands to three daughters of James English, each of them paying three pounds to his widow, and all his other estate to John Nelson, he "promising justice and kindness" to Davis's widow. Willis, I, 161, 209.

THEOPHILUS DAVIS, of Saco, constable in 1636. Folsom, 33, 131. It is almost certain that he soon removed.

THOMAS DAVIS, of Newbury, a sawyer, from Marlborough, in County Wiltshire, came in the "James," 1635, embarked at Southampton, in April, arrived at Boston, June 3, freeman June 2, 1641, removed next year to Haverhill, where he had son Joseph, and died 1683, aged 80. He brought, says Coffin, wife Christian from England, and his posterity is numerous. This name among the passengers from Southampton in the James, by record in State Paper Office, Somerby, read Thomas James. It seems a wild error of his or mine; but if my reading be correct, his surname may be that of the ship.

THOMAS DAVIS, of Saco, an early settler, assessed toward public worship 1636.

TOBIAS DAVIS, of Roxbury, brother of Richard, of the same, married Sarah, daughter of Isaac Morrill, had Sarah, born February 10, 1647, and his wife died January 23, by church record, but February 15, says the town, 1649. He married next, December 13, 1650, Bridget Kinsman, had John, born April 17, 1651; Tobias, June 10, 1653; Isaac, December 7, 1655; Samuel, baptized with the three preceding, June 12, 1659, who died young; Samuel again, March 24, 1661, died at 18; and Abigail, in town records said to be born September 5, 1671; was of artillery company 1666, and died April 25, 1690.

TOBIAS DAVIS, of Dover, freeman 1666.

WILLIAM DAVIS, of Boston, by wife Mary, had Abigail, born October 31, 1635, died at four years; Thomas, March 15, 1637, died young; Aaron, July 20, 1638, died next year; John, who died young, in 1641; Trine, August 10, 1642; Mary, October 3, 1644, perhaps died soon; and Thomas, again, 3, baptized September 7, 1645.

The Book of Possessions in early days shows William Sen., and William Jr., in Boston, but who was father of these children is to be determined, I fear, only by conjecture. There was a gunsmith, and one was dead November 10, 1655, when Isaac Collamore gave in the inventory of his estate only seven pounds. His widow Mary, soon married John Cowdall.

1656, in the "Speedwell," then 45 years old, and died 1664, leaving good estate. His will of March 26, 1655, made in view of a voyage to Barbadoes, thence to England, probated July 11, 1664, names wife Joan, children Daniel and Sarah, brother John, of which we know not where he was, sister-in-law Mary Hodges, wife of brother-in-law John Anderson, two nephews or nieces, perhaps not in this country, and children of brother Jeremy Davison, deceased, who was married and lived at Lynn, England, as late as 1652. An Indian sagamore gave him mortge. of Nahant. His inventory included land in Boston, Charlestown, Pemaquid and about 2100 acres near Windsor, on both sides of the Connecticut, was 1869 pounds sterling, 11 shillings, 11 pence.

PETER DAVIS, of Stonington, about 1680 or '90, was perhaps brother of Daniel, or of Thomas, who was in the same quarter at that time.

WILLIAM DAVIS, of New Haven, 1639, had John, Harvard College, 1651, the scholar, lost on his voyage to England. He died 1659, leaving widow Martha, who was sister of John Wakeman, and died 1663. His only surviving child Sarah, married William Russell, and to educate his son Noadiah, the grandmother left sixty pounds.

WILLIAM DAVIS, of Salem, 1639, had that year grant of land, probably removed to Boston or elsewhere, may be the mariner, who at Boston made his will September 14, 1655, as in Genealogical Register, V, 298, and Ib, IX, 141.

WILLIAM DAVIS, of Boston, apothecary, admitted of the church July 28, 1644, in which year he married Margaret, daughter of William Pynchon of Springfield, perhaps a second wife. By her he had seven children, of which Thomas, born September 3, 1645, may have been one; also, Benjamin, Elizabeth, Ephraim, who died Aug. 2, 1652; and William, the last, born June 25, 1653; and his wife died July 3 after. He married next, Huldah, daughter of Rev. Zechariah Symmes, had Mary, born December 3. 1656; Rebecca, August 3, 1658; Huldah, December 21, 1659; Ruth, February 12, 1662; John, June 10, 1663; and Deborah, April 13, 1665, died young; by another wife Judith, had Margaret, November 13, 1667; and perhaps Hannah. He had still another wife Sarah, and hope of progeny by her when he made his will, in which all of these children except Deborah, are mentioned. He was a man of wealth, enterprise and descretion, artillery company 1643, freeman 1645, a captain, representative for Springfield, 1652, where probably he lived some few years, also for Haverhill, 1668, was employed as commander of a troop in Ninigret's troubles, joint commissioner in 1653, with Leverett to the Dutch Government at New York, and one of the founders of the third church. His will, made May 17, 1676, probated nine days after, being only two days after his death, gave four hundred pounds to his wife Sarah, and contains many particulars. His widow married Captain Edward Palmes, of New London.

WILLIAM DAVIS, of Roxbury, probably brother of Tobias, freeman 1673, had John, born October 1, 1643; Samuel, February 21, 1645; Joseph, whose date, presumed, is October 12, 1649. His wife Elizabeth died or was buried May 4, 1658; and he married October 21, next Alice Thorp. who had William and Elizabeth, baptized June 14. 1663: but perhaps they were not living when this second wife died 1678. probably soon after birth of Jonathan, February 28, of that year. He had also, Matthew, but I know not the day of his birth, or whether

he was not by a third wife made executrix, but not named in the will of December 6, 1683, in which he mentioned all these children and that Matthew and Jonathan are under age. He died December 9, 1683, aged 66.

WILLIAM DAVIS, of Boston, by wife Mary, daughter of Nicholas Parker, had Joanna, born August 16, 1655; and I presume, that the same man by wife Susanna, had Joanna, born July 26, 1657, sold his estate in 1658, and went to Barbados.

WILLIAM DAVIS, of Marblehead, a petitioner 1668, against imposts.

WILLIAM DAVIS, of Boston, mariner, in his will Oct. 31, 1690, not probated before August 5, 1701, gives estate to wife Mary and children, not named.

WILLIAM DAVIS, of Haverhill, married December 31, 1700, Mary, daughter of John Kelly, Jr., of Newbury. In many instances, some of the above named are spelled Davies as well as Davis; and the utmost care in arranging relationship between parties with a name so widely diffused will sometimes be at fault. "A courageous soldier," is the designation of a Sergeant Davis in the Pequot war, 1637; but who can individualize him? There came in the "Elizabeth," 1635, from London to Boston, Margaret Davis, aged 32, with her son John, 9; Mary, 4; and Elizabeth, 1; the wife and family of some person who had come a year or two before, and to find the husband and father, may be the happiness of some more skillful enquirer. Twenty of this name had in 1834, been graduated at Harvard, and as many more at the other New England colleges.

REFERENCES:

MASSACHUSETTS.—Davis' Landmarks of Plymouth,81; Chandler's Hist. of Shirley, 375; Butler's Hist. of Groton, 394; Wyman's Charlestown Gens., vol. I, 278; Potter's Old Families of Concord, (1887); Reed's Hist. of Rutland 109; Rich's Hist. of Truro, 524; Temple's Hist. of Palmer,440;Temple's Hist. of North Brookfield, 565; Swift's Barnstable Families, vol.I, 276;Sewall's Hist. of Woburn, 608; Babson's Hist. of Gloucester, 75, 253; Ballou's Hist. of Milford, 709; Brown's Bedford Families. 8; Chase's Hist. of Haverhill, 276; Hammatt Papers of Ipswich, 70; Hazen's Hist. of Billerica, 39; Hudson's Hist. of Lexington, 55; Hyde's Address at Ware, 48; Hyde's Hist. of Brimfield, 470; Keyes' Hist. of West Boylston, Reg.. 16; Worcester Mag., II, 182; Whitmore's Copps Hill Epitaphs; Stone's Hist. of Hubbardstown, 259; Stearn's Hist. of Ashburnham, 674; Shattuck's Hist. of Concord, 368; Freeman's Hist. of Cape Cod, vol. I, 578; II, 321.

MAINE.—Lapham's Hist. of Woodstock, 203; Lapham's Hist. of Paris, 576; Hanson's Hist. of Gardiner. 87; Eaton's Hist. of Thomaston, II, 198; Eaton's Annals of Warren, 533; Dearborn's Hist. of Parsonfield, 373: Corliss' Hist. of North Yarmouth; Butler's Hist. of Farmington, 454; Bradbury's Hist. of Kennebunkport. 237; Hatch's Hist. of Industry, 589; North's Hist. of Augusta, 845.

NEW HAMPSHIRE.—Washington, N. H., Hist., 366; Stearn's Hist. of Rindge, 502; Secomb's Hist. of Amherst, 561; Runnell's Hist. of Sanbornton, 217; Bouton's Hist. of Concord, 641; Chase's Hist. of Chester, 503: Cochrane's Hist. of Antrim, 446; Coggswell's Hist. of Henniker. 542; Dow's Hist. of Hampton, 656; Hayward's Hist.of Gilsum,297; Hayward's Hist. of Hancock, 486; Hill's Hist. of Mason, 201; Kidder's Hist. of New Ipswich, 356; Merrill's Hist. of Acworth, 207; Morrison's

Hist. of Windham, 435; Norton's Hist. of Fitzwilliam, 533; Wheeler's Hist. of Newport, 363.

NEW YORK.—Cleveland's Hist. of Yates County, 322, 467, 718; Howell's Hist. of Southampton, 2d edition, 424; Pearson's Schenectady Settlers, 53; Stickney's Hist. of Minisinck, 167.

OTHER PUBLICATIONS.—Sedgwick's Hist. of Sharon, Conn., 75; Sharp's Hist. of Seymour, 170; Pennypacker's Hist. of Phoenixville, Pa.; Futhey's Hist. of Chester County, Pa., 515; Martin's Hist. of Chester, 146; Shroud's Fenwick Colony, N. J., 528; Littell's Passaic Valley Gens., 110; Powers' Hist. of Sangamon County, Ill., 246; Austin's R. I. Gen. Dict., 62; Hubbard's Hist. of Stanstead County, Can., 202; McKeen's Hist. of Bradford, Vt., 387; Ammidown Gen., 19; Bullock Gen.; Cope Gen., 192, 200; Cunnabel Gen., 100; Darling Memorial; Hayden's Weitzel Gen., 1883; Driver Gen., 407, 416; Greene Gen.; Jones' Gen., (1891), 60; Montague Gen., 522; Morse's Richards Gen., 121, 131; Stickney Gen., 504; Strong Gen.; Warren-Clark Gen., 55; Wood Gen., 45, 147; Wyman's Hunt Gen., 103; Amer. Ancestry, vol. I, 20; II, 30; III, 14, 206; IV, 46, 90, 206, 215; VI, 13, 33, 191; VII, 156; IX, 114, 123; X, 105, 153; XI, 27, 187, 188; Savage's Gen. Dict., II, 15; N. E. Hist. and Gen. Reg., III, 84; IX, 195; XX, 212, 219; XXI, 65; Thompson (Ebenezer) Memoirs; Eager and Davis Chart, (1859); Davis Gen.

DAVIDSON:—Nicholas Davidson, of Charlestown, 1639, one of the chief men, agent of Gov. Cradock, by wife Joanna Hodges, had Daniel and Sarah, who married March 24, 1665, Joseph Lynde, artillery company 1648, went home 1655, probably on business and came back

DAWSON:—Daniel Dawson, of Ipswich, may easily be misprinted for Davison. But Coffin, in Genealogical Register, VI, 250, calls widow, 1693, Margaret. Yet she may have been second wife of Davison.

GEORGE DAWSON, of Boston, 1679, a Quaker, who had been whipped for attending the meeting 1677.

HENRY DAWSON, of Boston, admitted of the church May 16, 1641, freeman June 2 after, a laborer, whose wife was in England. He was in the employment of William Hudson, Jr., who, when he went to serve in the Parliament's cause against the king, left the care of his family two years to this young man in consequence of which he was brought into great peril of his life, as set forth in Winthrop II, 249. Probably he repented soon, for he was in October, 1646, restored to his rank.

HENRY DAWSON, of Boston, a soldier in the company of Capt. William Turner in February, at Medfield, and on Connecticut river, April, 1676, under Capt. Pierce, freeman 1678.

ROBERT DAWSON, of New Haven, had John, born 1677, by first wife Sarah, daughter of William Tuttle, as erroneously has been said, and married next Hannah, widow of John Russell, had Thomas, born 1693.

REFERENCES:—Dodd's Hist. of East Haven, Conn., 115; Goode Gen., 85; Power's Hist. of Sangamon County, Ill., 244; Savage's Gen. Dict., II, 25; Tuttle Family, 47; Amer. Ancestry, III, 87, 102; X, 112. Dawson Gen.

DAWSTIN:—Josias Dawstin, of Medford or Reading, 1640, by the first deed in Suffolk register took grant of his message from Matthew Cradock, Esq., of London, skinner, former Gov. of Mass. Bay Colony, April 26, 1641. In Reading record of birth of his children Hannah, February 20, 1649, who died November following, and Sarah, September 25, 1653, the name is given without "w."

REFERENCES:—Savage's Gen. Dict., II, 25.

DAY:—Anthony Day, of Gloucester, 1645, had wife Susanna, and seven children, John, born April 28, 1657; Ezekiel, March 12, 1660, died soon; Ezekiel, again, May 19, 1662; Nathaniel, September 9, 1665; Elizabeth, April 2, 1667; Samuel, February 25, 1670; and Joseph, April 4, 1672; and died April 23, 1707, aged 90. His widow died December 10, 1717, aged 93.

ISAAC DAY, of Cambridge, by wife Susanna, had Robert, born October 24, 1686; and Susanna, November 28, 1688. Robert died February 4, 1688. He was a London citizen, embroiderer, but when he came, who was his wife when he removed are matters unknown. Probably he left in the summer of 1692.

Some two or three Johns can find no proper habitation, yet one is seen subscribing to memorial, 1668, at Salem, against imposts.

JOHN DAY, of Boston, 1677, a merchant, died that year, in his will of September 4, calls himself of Frome Woodlands, near Warminster, in Wiltshire, on the border of Somersetshire, and gives all his property to his brother Robert of that place; and probably had no wife or children.

NATHANIEL DAY, of Ipswich, 1637. Kimball.

RALPH DAY, of Dedham, freeman 1645, died October 28, 1677, in his will of September 12 preceding, wife Abigail, who was daughter of Daniel Pond, and children John, Ralph, Mary, who was wife of John Paine, Abigail, and son-in-law John Ruggles, are named. But his first wife was Susan, daughter of Jonathan Fairbanks, who in 1668 mentioned her four children in his will, and they are found in Dedham church records, to be Elizabeth, baptized July 3, 1648, taken with the town records that shows Mary, born November 9, 1649; Susan, 1652; and John, April 15, 1654; while the next is found Abigail, daughter of Ralph and Abigail, April, 1661.

ROBERT DAY, of Cambridge, came in the "Elizabeth," 1634, from Ipswich, aged 30, with wife Mary, 26, freeman May 6, 1635, went to Hartford, perhaps with Hooker, in 1636, or very soon after, had several lots among first proprietors. His first wife died probably before removal, and the mother of his children was Edatha, sister of Deacon Edward Stebbins. She is named in his will, May 20, 1648, which is printed in Trumbull's Colonial Records of Connecticut, I, 487; but though children are provided for, we find not names nor number. They were Thomas, Sarah, who married September, 1658, Nathaniel Gunn, of Hartford, and next November 24. 1664, Samuel Kellogg, of Hatfield, and was killed with her son Joseph, September 19, 1677. by the Indians; Mary, who married October 28. 1659, Samuel Ely, of Springfield, and next, April 12. 1694, Thomas Stebbins, and next, December 11, 1696. deacon John Coleman, of Hatfield, where she died 1725; and John. His widow married John Maynard, of Hartford, who died without children, leaving to the children of Day, "provided they carry themselves well towards" their mother, some decent estate, and next married in 1657 or 8, Elizur Holyoke, of Springfield, who she survived by twelve years, and died October 24. 1688. Of descendants of this Robert in the male line, full account is printed by Rev. George E. Day, of Northampton.

ROBERT DAY, of Ipswich, came in the "Hopewell," Capt. Bundocke, 1635, from London, aged 30, freeman June 2, 1641, was living in 1681. Perhaps Sarah, who married at Ipswich, June 17, 1674, David Fiske was his daughter Hannah, who came in the "Elizabeth and Ann," 1635, aged 20, may not have been a relative.

STEPHEN DAY, of Cambridge, the earliest printer on our side of the ocean, was a locksmith of Cambridge, England, brought over, in the "John," 1638, by Rev. Josse Glover, who died on the voyage. He began business in March, 1639, but was, I fear, unthrifty, for in 1647, the Almanac of his press purports to come from Greene became ruler in the office. Yet he was enter-his son who was very young, and the year following prising, having for his service, unluckily, been rewarded by grant of 300 acres in 1641, he was 2 years after engaged in settlement of Lancaster, and reduced to work as journeyman of Greene all his latter days .He brought from England, wife Rebecca, who had been widow of William Boardman, had Matthew, and probably after coming hither Stephen, who died December 1, 1639, and Moses. His wife died October 27, 1659, he was admitted of the church February 28, 1661, but was never freeman, and died December 22, 1668, aged 58. A catalogue of books of his printing is given by Thomas, in his History, I, 227-34.

THOMAS DAY, of Gloucester, married December 30, 1673, Mary Laughton, had Thomas, born May 27, 1675; Mary, December, 1677; and Joseph, January 24, 1680. An earlier Thomas, whose inventory was found by Coffin 1670, was perhaps father of the preceding, born about 1651, and of Sarah, about 1652, may have been of Salem, a signer of the memorial 1668, against imposts, and perhaps father of John, another signer.

TIMOTHY DAY, of Gloucester, freeman 1690, married July 24, 1679, wife Phebe had son born February 20, 1682.

WENTWORTH DAY, of Boston, 1640, has prefix of respectability on admission to the church September 22, but called a single man; soon after married, had Elizabeth, baptized September 26, 1641, at 8 days old; and Wentworth, August 13, 1643, at 6 days. He was a surgeon at Cambridge, and is honored by Rev. Mr. Hale, in his tract on Witchcraft, as saving in 1652, a woman charged with the horrid offence. Perhaps he went home, for one of this unusual name was in 1658, fined and imprisoned as one of the fifth monarchy men, setting up the imaginary reign of King Jesus to disturb the absolute throne of Oliver Cromwell, in his last years. In September, 1661, living in London, he had a legacy in the will of Edward Shrimpton.

WILLIAM DAY, of Boston, 1669, a mariner.

Of descendants of first Robert a Register was published some years since by Rev. George E. Day, who shows that nineteen had been graduated at Yale, and one at each of the colleges following. Dartmouth, Williams, Amherst and Brown, and that ten of the eleven min. (ministers?) were living at his date of publication. One at Harvard College, 1806, was the earliest of the name in that catalogue.

REFERENCES.

MASSACHUSETTS.—Dodd's Hist. of East Haven, 115; Hammatt Papers of Ipswich, 70; Hodgman's Hist. of Westford, 445; West Springfield Centen. 116; Temple's Hist. of Northfield, 428; Paige's Hist. of Cambridge, 522; Marvin's Hist. of Winchenden, 453; Babson's Hist. of Gloucester, 79; Ballou's Hist. of Milford, 711; Benedict's Hist. of Sutten, 632; Chandler's Hist. of Shirley, 384; Hill's Dedham Records.

OTHER PUBLICATIONS:—Eaton's Hist. of Thomaston, Me., II, 198; Bangor, Me., Hist. Mag., V, 186; Lapham's Hist. of Woodstock, Me., 205; Read's Hist. of Swanzey, N. H., 324; Hayward's Hist. of Gilsum, N. H., 299; Cochrane's Hist. of Antrim, N. H., 446; Stiles' Hist. of Windsor, Conn., II, 170; Sedgwick's Hist. of Sharon, Conn., 74; Timlow's Hist. of Southingham, Conn., 78; Young's Hist. of Warsaw, N. Y., 255; Powers' Hist. of Sangamon County, Ill., 247; Poor's Hist. Researches, 85, 144; Oten's Olin Gen., 161; Loomis' Gen. Female Branches, 383, 607; Littell's Passaic Valley Gens., 113; Leland Gen., 178; Ely Gen., 113, 155, 168, 205, 246, 273; Dwight Gen., 908; Dolbeare Gen., 23; Boltwood's Noble Gen., 102; Davis' Gen., 57; Amer. Ancestry, V, 84; IX, 52; XI, 37, 135, 212; Savage's Gen. Dict., II, 25; Day Gen.

DAYNES, DEANS, or DAINES:— Abraham Daynes, of New London, 1664, supposed to have come from Casco, married December 27, 1671, Sarah, daughter of William Peake, had Joanna, born February, 1672; John, baptized February, 1674; Thomas, July, 1677; removed to Norwich, there had Ebenezer, born October 27, 1680; Sarah, January 19, 1683; and Ephraim, January 15, 1686.

REFERENCES:—Savage's Gen. Dict., vol. II, 26.

DAYTON:—Ralph Dayton, of New Haven, about 1639, signed the covenant of habitancy, but not at its formation, yet lived there 10 years; was of Easthampton, L. I., 1650, and later. Sometimes the name is Daighton.

SAMUEL DAYTON, of Southampton, L. I., 1641, probably at New Haven, 1646, and Brookhaven, about 1655. Perhaps the distinguished family of New Jersey is of this stock.

REFERENCES:—Orcutt's Hist. of Stratford, Conn., 1189; Orcutt's Hist. of New Milford, Conn., 691; Meade's Hist. of Greenwich, Conn., 311; Howell's Hist. of Southampton, N. Y., 229; Hedge's Anniversary at Easthampton, N. Y.; Oxford, N. H., Centen., 109; Tuttle Family, 193; Amer. Ancestry, vol. I, 21; Savage's Gen. Dict., II, 26.

DEACON:—John Deacon, of Plymouth, of whom no more is known, but that he died 1636.

JOHN DEACON, of Lynn, came in the "Abigail," 1635, aged 25, with wife Alice, 30, who died July 27, 1657, was a blacksmith, married December 25, 1657, Elizabeth, widow of John Pickering, removed to Boston, was of Mather's Church, 1669.

REFERENCES:—Savage's Gen. Dict., vol. II, 26.

DEADY. Roe's Sketches of Rose, N. Y.

DEAKE. Amer. Ancestry, III, 76.

DEALAND. Driver Gen., 273; Felton Gen., 249.

DEALE:—Charles Deale, of Milford, 1658, was encouraged to raise tobacco by grant of land that year, perhaps had been there a year or more, had wife Pity, in 1672, but no children, and died about 1686.

WILLIAM DEALE, of Haverhill, 1662.

REFERENCES:—Savage's Gen. Dict., vol. II, 26.

DEAN, often spelled with the final "e," Daniel Dean,

of Concord, perhaps at Sudbury, 1663, a lieutenant, died November 29, 1725, aged 97. Shattuck.

GEORGE DEAN, of Salem, 1660-1686, was a cordwainer, by wife Elizabeth, had Elizabeth, born January 2, 1661, died soon; John; Thomas; George; Joseph, about 1671; Benjamin; Elizabeth and Hannah; of not one can the date of birth or death be ascertained, and gladly can we read in family records that Elizabeth married Jonathan Lambert; and that Hannah married June 11, 1701, John Cook; that John, Thomas and Joseph, had families, and of George and Benjamin only that they died before 1706.

JAMES DEAN, of Stonington, blacksmith, had John, born May 15, 1672; James, October 31, 1674; Sarah, September 4, 1676; a son whose name is not legible, November 28, 1678; Mary, 1680; Francis, 1682; William, born and died 1684; William, again, September 12, 1689, One son was inhabitant of Plainfield; another lived at North Groton, now Ledyard, who was progenitor of Hon. Silas Dean, 1758, the ambassador with Franklin in France, and of late Prof. James Dean.

JOHN DEAN, of Dorchester, 1636, came from Chard, Somersetshire, removed to Taunton, of which he was one of the first purchasers 1639, having been made freeman of the Colony, December 4, 1638; by wife Alice, who survived, had John, Thomas, Israel, Isaac, Nathaniel and Elizabeth, who married Josiah Edson, Esq., of Bridgewater, and at her death in 1734, was called about 84; and died 1660, between April 25, date of his will, and June 7, of the inventory, aged about 60.

JOHN DEAN, of Dedham, by wife Sarah, had John, born April 25, 1677; Sarah, December 13, 1678; Ebenezer, May 17, 1681; Joseph, March 14, 1683; Jeremiah, March 24, 1685; Elizabeth, October 13, 1689; and Abigail, June 12, 1694.

JOHN DEAN, of Dover, killed by the Indians, 1694, when his wife and daughter were taken, but soon escaped. Betlknap, I, 138.

JONAS DEAN, of Scituate, 1690, by Deane, in his history of Scituate, presumed to have come from Taunton, England, had Thomas, born 1691; and Ephraim, 1694; died 1697, and his widow Eunice, married 1701, deacon James Torrey.

SAMUEL DEAN, of Stamford, 1650, had John, born 1659; Joseph, 1661, and others.

SAMUEL DEAN, of Lancaster, 1653.

STEPHEN DEAN, of Plymouth, one of the first comers in the "Fortune," 1621, built the first corn mill in New England, 1632; married about 1627, Elizabeth, daughter of widow Ring, had Elizabeth, Miriam, and Susanna, and died September, 1634. His widow married Sept. 16, 1635, Josiah Cook, and died about 1687; the daughter Elizabeth married William Twining; Miriam was not married as late as 1669; Susanna married April 4, 1660; Joseph Rogers, Jr.; and next, October 23, 1663, Stephen Snow.

THOMAS DEAN, of Concord, came in the "Elizabeth and Ann," 1635, aged 32, a carpenter, by wife Elizabeth, had Sarah, a daughter perhaps Mary, born February 24, 1643; Hannah, March 18, 1646; Elizabeth, December 25, 1648; died at six months; and first born Joseph, about 1638; and had second wife Mildred, who died September 15, 1673; was freeman 1672, and died February 5, 1676. In some records the name is given Dane.

THOMAS DEAN, of Boston, a merchant of exetnsive

business, came from Hampshire, was born about 1640, married 1665, Sarah, daughter of William Brown, of Salem, had Sarah, born 1666, who went with her father to England, and there married Robert Woodward, Dean of Sarum; and Elizabeth, 1667, who probably died young; and his wife soon after, or perhaps before. He was freeman 1669, and married second wife Ann, daughter of William Farr, of London, had Thomas, born 1673; Rebecca, 1677; went home about 1678, and had James and Samuel, was some time in London, but went down to Hampshire, and died April 27, 1686. A mural monument to his memory in Frefolk church. His youngest son conveyed part of his estate here by deed from London, 1730.

THOMAS DEAN, of Charlestown, mariner, married September 15, 1668, Elizabeth, daughter of John Burrage, the first of the same, and had children John and Catharine, as by a will imperfectly appears. His inventory was of May 25, 1674. The children were brought to baptism September 9, 1677; and his widow married August 12, 1680, John Poor.

THOMAS DEAN, of Boston, married Jane, daughter of Richard Scammon of Exeter, who died October 9, 1726, had Mary, born August 20, 1692; Thomas, November 28, 1694; Jane, June 17, 1696; Elizabeth, September 20, 1697; and Jane, again, September 2, 1698; removed to Hampton Falls and Salisbury, and died about 1737. Where he was born, who was his father or grand-father is beyond my knowledge.

WALTER DEAN, of Taunton, younger brother of first John, who was from Chard, in County Somerset, 12 or 14 miles from Taunton, freeman of that Colony Dec. 4, 1638, had been with his brother first at Dorchester, married, it is said, Eleanor, daughter of Richard Strong, of Taunton, England, who had come with her brother John, had six children, of which only Benjamin, Ezra and Joseph are known, was representative 1640, perhaps, and selectman many years after; and was with his wife living so late as 1693.

WILLIAM DEAN, of Woburn, married September 1, 1670, Martha, daughter, I presume, of Thomas Bateman, of Concord, had Martha, born August 17, 1671; William, July 5, 1673; Samuel, July 26, 1675; John, June 25, 1677; and Sarah, who died young.

WILLIAM DEAN, of Boston, 1668, may have been, a few years later, of Dedham, and there married Dec. 13, 1677, Mehitable Wood, had Hannah, born December 5, 1678; Alice, October 18, 1680; Judith, November 3, 1682; Josiah, March 7, 1685; and Abigail, January 23, 1687. Rachel, a widow, came from London, 1685, in the "Planter," married October 28, 1636, Joseph Beedle, or Biddle, who, in his will provides for her daughter Martha Dean, who probably came with her mother.

REFERENCES.

MASSACHUSETTS.—Hammatt Papers of Ipswich, 67; Ballou's Hist. of Milford, 712; Essex Inst. Coll., XIII, 268; Hill's Dedham Records; Paige's Hist. of Hardwick, 360; Sewall's Hist. of Woburn, 609; Temple's Hist. of North Brookfield, 566; Freeman's Hist. of Cape Cod, II, 629; Emery's Taunton, Mass., Ministry, vol. I, 49; Ward's Hist. of Shrewsbury, 269; Wyman's Charlestown Gens., vol. I, 285; Swift's Barnstable Families, vol. I, 327.

MAINE.—Bangor Hist. Mag., IV, 248; Lapham's Hist. of Paris, 576.

NEW HAMPSHIRE.—Stearns' Hist. of Rindge, 505;

Saunderson's Hist. of Charlestown, N. H.; Hayward's Hist. of Gilsum, 300.

OTHER PUBLICATIONS.—Cleveland's Hist. of Yates County, N. Y., 302, 409; Raymond's Tarrytown, N. Y., Monument, 60; Hinman's Conn. Settlers, 206; Huntington's Stamford, Conn., Settlers, 30; Cooley's Trenton N. J., Gens., 54; Titcomb's New England People, 129; Richmond, Va., Standard, III, 17; Bunker's L. I. Genealogies, 195; Spooner Gen., vol. I, 266; Green's Todd Gen.; Driver Gen., 266; Dwight Gen., 1007; Faxan Gen., 57; Hallon's Winslow Mem., vol. I, 435; Morse Mem., Appendix, 60½; Whitman Gen., 127; Amer. Ancestry, vol. I, 21; II, 30; VI, 88; IX, 186; Savage's Gen. Dict., II, 28; N. E. Hist. and Gen. Reg., III, 375; IX, 93; XVIII, 263; XXV, 358; XXXVII, 228; XLI, 261; Pierce's Life of Gardner Dean, 1883; Dean Gen., (1887); Dean Gen., 1889.

DEAR or DEARE:—Edward Dear, Ipswich, 1683, had, before 1665, married Elizabeth, daughter of Humphrey Griffin.

PHILIP DEAR, of Salem, 1638.

REFERENCES:—Hammatt Papers, Ipswich, Mass., 76; Savage's Gen. Dict., II, 28.

DEARBORN:—Godfrey Dearborn, of Exeter, 1639, was from some part of Devon, perhaps Exeter, with wife who died 1651 or 2, and son Henry, born about 1632; and Thomas, about 1634; and perhaps, also, a daughter brought from England, had here John, born about 1642, and probably two more daughters, of which one was Sarah; was selectman in 1648, but early in 1651 was settled in Hampton, there married November 25, 1662, Dorothy, widow of Philemon Dalton, and lived in a house of which his descendants are still occupying, was a selectman and town-clerk and died February 4, 1686. His will was of December 14, 1680, and his widow died before 1696. Of his three daughters, not named in the will, but earlier provided for, one was, perhaps, Esther, wife of Richard Shortridge, of Portsmouth, (for in his will is bequest to grand-child Ann Shortridge); and Sarah, married December 9, 1659, Thomas Nudd.

REFERENCES.

NEW HAMPSHIRE.—Eaton's Hist. of Candia, 64; Dow's Hist. of Hampton, 659; Coggswell's Hist. of Nottingham, 199, 372; Chase's Hist. of Chester, 503; Fullonton's Hist. of Raymond, 197; Runnel's Hist. of Sanbornton, II, 219; New Hampshire Hist. Soc. Coll., VII, 382.

OTHER PUBLICATIONS.—Dearborn's Hist. of Parsonfield, Me., 374; Granite Monthly, VII, 124; Hanson's Hist. of Gardiner, Me., 340; Maine Hist. and Gen. Rec., III, 1, 69; Lawrence and Bartlett Mem., 176; Richardson's Vinton Gen., 396; Adams' Haven Gen., 14; Amer. Ancestry, V, 82; VI, 90; XI, 76; N. E. Hist. and Gen. Reg., II, 81, 297, 305; Savage's Gen. Dict., II, 31; Dearborn Gen.

DEARDORFF. Power's Hist. of Sangamon, Ill., 248.

DEARING or DEERING:—George Dearing, of Scarborough, 1639, had probably son Roger; and his widow Elizabeth married Jonas Bayley.

SAMUEL DEARING, of Braintree, married Bethia, daughter of Gregory Baxter, had Bethia, born April 6, 1649, and his wife died May 11, 1651. He married November 15 following, Mary Ray, and had Mary, Jan.

16, 1653; Hannah, February 14, 1655; and Sarah, June 30, 1657, who died in a few weeks. This wife died July 1, 1657, and he married November 10 next, Mary, daughter of Francis Newcomb, and had Rachel, and perhaps other children.

REFERENCES:—Bradbury's Hist. of Kennebunkport, Me. Savage's Gen. Dict., II, 31.

DEARTH. Hyde's Hist. of Brimfield, Mass., 306.

DEATH:—John Death, of Sudbury, 1672, by wife Mary, daughter of Francis Peabody, of Topsfield, had John, born January 2, 1677; Hepzibah, June 5, 1680; Lydia, March 26, 1682; Samuel, September 12, 1684; and Ruth, July 20, 1688. He removed 1678 to Sherborn; perhaps died early, and his widow married 1690, Samuel Eames. See Barry. This name was common in this part of the country, some few years since, but within a few years, by the legislature, it has been changed to How.

REFERENCES:—Barry's Hist. of Framingham, Mass., 220; Morse's Sherborn, Mass., Settlers, 74; Savage's Gen. Dict., II, 33.

DECKANE:—Nicholas Deckane, of Beverly, 1668.

REFERENCES:—Savage's Gen. Dict., II, 33.

DECKER:—John Decker, of Exeter, 1672.

REFERENCES:—Savage's Gen. Dict., II, 33.

DECROW:—Valentine Decrow, of Marshfield, married February 26, 1678 or 9, Martha Bourne, and she died March 25, 1724.

REFERENCES:—Savage's Gen. Dict., II, 30.

DEBVOISE. Hist. of Queens County, N. Y., 317; Riker's Annals of Newtown, 406; Temple's Hist. of North Brookfield, Mass., 506.

DE BLOIS. Amer. Ancestry, VII, 209.

DE BOUCHELLE. Mallery's Bohemia Manor.

DE BOW. Amer. Ancestry, VIII, 138.

DE BRUYN. Mrs. Lamb's Hist. of New York City, vol. I, 350; N. Y. Gen. and Biog. Rec., X, 856.

DE CARTARET. Corliss' Hist. of North Yarmouth, Mass.

DECKER. Whittemore's Founders and Builders of the Oranges, 289; Clute's Hist. of Staten Island, N. Y., 369; Stickney's Hist. of Minisink, N. Y., 136; Gumaer's Hist. of Deerpark, N. Y., 61; Farrow's Hist. of Isleborough, Me., 190; Amer. Ancestry, II, 30.

DEDERER. Roome Gen., 244.

DEDERICK. Hist. of Greene County, N. Y., 423; Amer. Ancestry, vol. I, 21; II, 31.

DEERING. Lapham's Hist. of Paris, Me., 579; Lapham's Hist. of Norway, Me., 492; Preble Gen., 162; Wentworth Gen., vol. I, 316; Amer. Ancestry, VI, 23; Savage's Gen. Dict., II. 33.

DEETH. Norton's Hist. of Fitzwilliam, 537.

DE FOE. Johnston's Hist. of Cecil County, 526.

DEFOREST. This family appears first in Avesnes, France where from 1559 for many years a Spanish Garrison was maintained, so that any tendency to the

Protestant faith was specially subject to cruel repression. Here, however, the De Forests and several other families embraced the Reformed doctrines.

JESSE DE FOREST, the American ancestor, married probably at Leyden, Marie du Cloux. His son Isaac, sailed for New Amsterdam, October 1, 1636, in the yacht "Rensselaerwyck," in the employ of Killian Van Rensselaër, of Amsterdam. He married in New Amsterdam June 9, 1641, Sarah du Trieux, daughter of Philip and Susannah de Cluney Trieux, and had fourteen children.

REFERENCES:—Orcutt's Hist. of Stratford, Conn., 1190; Orcutt's Hist. of New Milford, Conn., 691; Cothren's Hist. of Woodbury, Conn., II, 1491; Bronson's Hist. of Waterbury, Conn., 487; Munsell's Albany, N. Y., Coll., IV, 113; Riker's Hist. of Harlem, N. Y., 571; Talcott's N. Y. and N. E. Families, 429; Dwight Gen., 1112; Amer. Ancestry, vol. I, 24; III, 184.

DE GARMO. Munsell's Albany, IV, 114.

DE GRAAF. Pearson's Schenectady, N. Y., Settlers, 54; Munsell's Albany, N. Y., Coll., IV, 114; Hist. of Montgomery and Fulton County, N. Y., 150; Holgate's Amer. Gens., 99.

DEGROVE. Ruttenber's Hist. of Orange County, N. Y., 382; Ruttenber's Hist. of Newburgh, N. Y., 294.

DE HART. Clute's Hist. of Staten Island, N. Y., 373; Bergen's Kings County, N. Y., Settlers, 89; Bergen Gen., 108.

DE HAVEN. Atlee.Gen., 108; Holstein Gen.

DE KRAFT. Richmond, Va., Standard, III, 6, 8.

DE LA GRANGE. Munsell's Albany, N. Y., Coll., IV, 115; Amer. Ancestry, vol. I, 21.

DE GROOT. Clute's Hist. of Staten Island, 371.

DELAFIELD. N. Y. Gen. and Biog. Rec., VII, 91, 118.

DELAMATER:—Claude, of New Amsterdam, born in Richebourg, France, died in Harlem, N. Y., 1683; settled in New Amsterdam, 1652; married Hester, daughter of Peter Du Bois. Had Jacobus, who settled at Kingston, N. Y.

REFERENCES:—Riker's Hist. of Harlem, N. Y., 500; Willard's Albany Medical Annals, 272; Walworth Hyde Gen., 988; N. Y. Gen. and Biog. Rec., XX, 131; Amer. Ancestry, vol. I, 21; II, 31, 153; VIII, 22; N. E. Hist. and Gen. Reg., XIV, 41; Delamater Gen.

DELAMONT. Pearson's Hist. of Schenectady, 59.

DE LANEY. Bolton's Hist. of Westchester County, N. Y., 297; Jones' Hist. of New York City in the Rev. War, vol. I, 649; Lamb's Hist. of New York City, vol. I, 444, 532, 536, 626; Holgate's Amer. Gen., 114; N. Y. Gen. and Biog. Rec., IV, 181.

DELAND. Wyman's Charlestown, Mass., Gens., vol. I, 287; Winsor's Hist. of Duxbury, Mass., 251; Temple's Hist. of North Brookfield, Mass., 566; Driver Gen.

DE LANE. Temple's Hist. of North Brookfield, Mass., 570.

DEINS:—William Deins, named in a valuable paper on the Sturbridge black lead mine in Genealogical Reg., X, 160, as an overseer of said works, about 1657-9.

Gladly should we learn more, but it may well be despaired of; and probably the residence of this skilful man was transferred as the prosperity of the undertaking.

REFERENCES:—Savage's Gen. Dict., vol. II, 35.

DELANO, early DELANOYE, DELAUNY, or DELANOY:—Michael Delano, of New Haven, died 1667.

PHILIP DELANO, of Plymouth, came in the "Fortune," 1621, born of French or Flemish Protestant parents, but of the English church at Leyden, Winslow says, and 19 years old at his coming; was probably son of Jean and Marie de Launey, baptized December 7, 1603, in the Walloon church of Leyden; was freeman of that Colony 1632, removed soon after to Duxbury, married December 19, 1634, Esther Dewsbury, and next, 1657, Mary, widow of James Glass, daughter of William Pontus, (though Ricketson makes her daughter of James Churchill, who is wholly unknown to me); and had children (of which we are uncertain who may be elder or younger, whether all, or part, by first wife) Thomas, Mary, Philip, John, Jane, Rebecca, Jonathan, Esther, and Samuel. But as a family genealogy in MS. has been given to me, though it is confined to the descendants of Jonathan, yet as it purports to give the offspring of the Dewsbury marriage, three sons Samuel, Thomas and Jonathan, beside one daughter who died soon, it might be probable that three daughters and one son came of the second marriage. He removed to Bridgewater. was one of the purchasers of Dartmouth, 1652, and in 1662, of Middleborough, and died about 1681, aged 79 years old. Mary married November 29, 1655, Jonathan Durham. De La Noye was the name at first.

REFERENCES:—Mitchell's Hist. of Bridgewater, Mass. 373; Davis' Landmarks of Plymouth, 83; Washburne's Notes on Livermore, Me., 22; Thurston's Hist. of Winthrop, Me., 180; Waldo's Hist. of Tolland, Conn., 114; Sedgwick's Hist. of Sharon, Conn., 76; Saunderson's Hist. of Charlestown, N. H., 324; Marshall's Grant Ancestry, 161; Spooner Mem., 71; Swift Gen., 24; Amer. Ancestry, V, 11; Savage's Gen. Dict., II, 33, 45.

DELAP. Swift's Barnstable Families, vol. I, 304.

DELAPLAINE. Alden's Epitaphs, V, 173.

DELAVAN. Bolton's Hist. of Westchester County, 514; Huntington's Stamford. Conn., Settlers, 30.

DELHARDE. Essex Inst. Coll., VII, 205.

DE LONG. Lindsay Gen.

DELEVEY. Temple's Hist. of North Brookfield, Mass., 570.

DEMOREST. Cole Gen., 49, 230; Roome Gen., 15; Demorest Gen.

DEMARY. Stearn's Hist. of Rindge, N. H.

DEMERITH. Coggswell's Hist. of Nottingham, 678; Thompson's Ebenezer Memoir.

DE MILLE. Amer. Ancestry, III, 138.

DELL or DILL:—George Dell, of Salem, 1639, removed to Boston, freeman 1651, by wife Abigail, had John, born October, 1645; Samuel, August 31, 1647; Joseph, February, 1650; and Benjamin, April 27, 1652. He was an active merchant, died abroad, probably in 1654, for an imperfect will of November 3, 1653, recites that he was bound from England to Ireland, thence to Virginia, etc. He had good amount of property. Winthrop, II, 312. His widow married November 8, 1655, John Hanniford.

PETER DELL, of Chelmsford, 1691. Savage's Gen. Dict., vol. II, 35.

DEMING, DEMON or DEMENT:—John Deming, of Wethersfield, 1635, one of the chief settlers, representative very often from 1649 to 61, named in the charter of 1662, married Honour, daughter of Richard Treat, had John, born September 9, 1638; and others. His will of June 26, 1690, with probate 1705, names sons John, Jonathan, 1639; Samuel, 1646; David, Ebenezer; and five daughters, wives of John Morgan (whose name was probably Rachel); of Richard Beckley; of Thomas Hurlbut (whose name was Mary); of Thomas Wright, and probably Sarah, wife of Samuel Moody, beside some grand-children.

NICHOLAS DEMING, of Pemaquid, swore fidelity to Massachusetts, 1674.

THOMAS DEMING, of Wethersfield, perhaps brother of first John, married July 24, 1645, Mary Sheaffe, was of Farmington, and removed to Southampton, L. I., thence to Easthampton, where posterity is still living. Sometimes in the records the name is Demon or Dement, and the affinity is exceedingly difficult to be traced with exactness. Eight of this name had, in 1828, been graduated at New England colleges.

REFERENCES:—Timlow's Sketches of Southington, Conn., 80; Sedgwick's Hist. of Sharon, Conn., 76; Andrews' Hist. of New Britain, Conn., 308; Glastenbury, Conn., Centen., 162; Talcott's N. Y. and N. E. Families 499; Howell's Hist. of Southampton, L. I., 2d Ed., 411; Goodwin's Gen. Notes, 233; Champion Gen.; Elv Gen.; Amer. Ancestry, vol. I, 21; IX, 187; N. E. Hist. and Gen. Reg., XVI, 264; Savage's Gen. Dict., II, 35.

DEMITT. Lamb's Hist. of N. Y. City, vol. I, 343.

DEMOND. Hyde's Address at Ware, 52.

DEMOREST. Amer. Ancestry, II, 32.

DE MOTT. Amer. Ancestry, VIII, 140.

DEMPSEY. Stearns' Hist. of Ashburnham, Mass., 679.

DE MUNN. Beckwith's Creoles, 92.

DEMUTH. Eaton's Hist. of Thomaston, Me., 201.

DE MYER. Schoonmaker's Hist. of Kingston.

DENEGAR. Amer. Ancestry, II, 32.

DENBOW:—Salathiel Denbow, of Dover, 1665.
REFERENCES:—Savage's Gen. Dict., vol. II, 35.

DENGAYNE or DINGHAM:—Henry Dengayne, of Watertown, a physician, had grants of land in February and June, 1637, as Francis, in his Historical Sketch, 132, tells. He married April, 1641, Elizabeth widow of deacon George Alcock, and died of apoplexy, December 8, 1645, as Roxbury church record tells.

REFERENCES:—Savage's Gen. Dict., II, 35.

DENHAM:—Thomas Denham, of Rye, in Connecticut jurisdiction, in 1681 was 60 years old.

REFERENCES:—Amer. Ancestry, III, 127.

DENIO. Amer. Ancestry, VII, 185.

DENISON:—James Denison, of New Haven, married November 25, 1662, Bethia, daughter of Jarvis Boykem, had James, born August, 1664, died soon; John, November, 1665, died at 3 years; Mary, or Mercy, July 26, 1668; Sarah, April 12, 1671; Hannah, 1673; probably died young; John and James, again twins, February 6, 1677, of which James died soon; Elizabeth, November 24, 1681; and James, again, January 5, 1683, died May 8, 1719; aged 78. Sarah married 1710, Joseph Sackett; and Elizabeth married 1707, Samuel Harrison.

JOHN DENISON, of Ipswich, 1648, by Farmer, was thought to be a brother of the major-general, but I can hardly think so, unless he went home, as we know no more of him.

ROBERT DENISON, of Milford, about 1645, had Samuel born 1656; Esther, 1658; and Hannah, 1662; removed 1667 with Branford people to Newark, N. J.

THOMAS DENISON, of Kittery, 1652.

WILLIAM DENISON, of Rokbury, came with wife Margaret, and sons Daniel, Edward and. George, in 1631, and was, perhaps, in the Lion, with Winthrop's wife and eldest son, beside apostle Eliot, in the record of whose church he stands third in the list: freeman July 3, 1632, representative 1635, but in 1637 taking sides with Wheelwright, was disarmed. His wife died February 2, 1646 in the church records of Eliot's affection, called "old mother Denison"; and he died January 25, 1654.

WILLIAM DENISON, of Boston, living at Pulling Point, married October 27, 1659, Mary Parker. Of this name six had been graduated in 1834, at Harvard, but not one within 90 years, and of them I am uncertain about the parentage of Daniel, in 1690, and George, in 1693, but for the earlier has the star marq in the catalogue of 1698, at other New England colleges seven had been graduated, beside two with double "n."

REFERENCES:—Lapham's Hist. of Norway, Me., 496; Norton's Hist. of Fitzwilliam, N. H.,539; Aldrich's Hist of Walpole, N. H., 223; Stonington, Conn., Bi-Centen., 296; Whittemore's Hist. of Middlesex County, Conn., 487; Paige's Hist. of Cambridge, Mass., 534; Benton's Hist. of Guildhall, Vt., 255; Austin's R. I. Gen. Dict. 64; Prentice Gen., 404: Stanton Gen., 75, 483; Amer Ancestry, vol. I, 21: VII, 277; N. E. Hist. and Gen. Reg. XLVI, 352; Savage's Gen. Dict., II, 36; Denison Gen.

REFERENCES:—Hammatt Papers of Ipswich, Mass. 72; Ellis' Hist. of Roxbury, Mass., 95; Dodd's Hist. of East Haven, Conn., 117; Caulkin's Hist. of New London, Conn., 332; Corliss' Hist. of North Yarmouth, Me., Hughes Gen., 8; Hvde Gen., vol. I, 196; vol. II, 1015; Amer. Ancestry, IX, 153.

DENLO:—William Denlo, of Pemaquid, took oath of fidelity to Massachusetts, 1674.

REFERENCES:—Savage's Gen. Dict., II, 36.

DENMAN:—Alexander Denman, perhaps of Hampton, married about 1678, the widow of Abraham Perkins, Jr., probably daughter of Thomas Sleeper.

JOHN DENMAN, of Dorchester, had Mary, who married Clement Maxfield. But great uncertainty prevails with reference to his residence, as no success followed the search for the line in Dorchester. In the administration on estate of widow Smead by her brother Israel Stoughton, 1639, of Dorchester, this man is entitled to a share of her property, as well as his daughter Maxfield.

PHILIP DENMAN, of Derby, had born there, Mary, in 1678; Elizabeth, 1680; Sarah, 1682; Micah, 1684; and Hannah; and died 1698; in his will mentioned wife and the five children.

REFERENCES:—Savage's Gen. Dict., vol. II, 36.

DENMARK:—Patrick Denmark, of Dover, 1663. was after at Saco, had Patrick, born April 8, 1664; and James, March 13, 1666.

REFERENCES:—Savage's Gen. Dict., vol. II, 36.

DENNETT:—John Dennett, of Portsmouth, freeman 1672, had Ephraim, born August 2, 1683, who was a counsel, app. by mandamus, 1732, for New Hampshire, where the name continues.

REFERENCES:—Bangor Hist. Mag., V, 64; Lapham's Hist. of Paris, Me., 579; Savage's Gen. Dict., vol. 11, 36; Buxten's Me. Gen., 227.

DENNING:—Francis Denning, of Massachusetts, 1664. Felt.

JOHN DENNING, of Massachusetts, 1664. Felt.

WILLIAM DENNING, of Boston, 1634, was in the employment of William Brenton, and perhaps came with him the year preceding, died January 20, 1654. By his will made two days before, probated 31 of the same month, his wife Ann and son Obidiah, are mentioned. but the later absent, and the father gives him, "in case he doth not come personally into the country," for half the testator's estate, "twenty shillings and no more."

REFERENCES:—Babson's Hist. of Gloucester, Mass. 80; Savage's Gen. Dict., II, 36.

DENNIS:—Edward Dennis, of Boston, 1636, by wife Sarah, had Sarah, baptized August 9, 1640, and Mary, at six days old, July 3, 1642; Martha, born 1, baptized May 5, 1644; John, 18, baptized February 22, 1646; and Joseph, June 13, 1648. He came in the employment of William Hutchinson. His widow married August 15, 1656, Abner Ordway, of Watertown.

GEORGE DENNIS, of New London, 1680, came thither from Long Island, married January 26, 1681, Elizabeth, widow of Joshua Raymond, had Ebenezer, born Oct. 23, 1682.

JAMES DENNIS, of Boston, by wife Mary, had John, born December 6, 1653; and John, again, August 4, 1655, both died soon; may have lived at Marblehead, 1674.

LAWRENCE DENNIS, of Maine, 1665.

ROBERT DENNIS, of Yarmouth, 1643-69; had there Mary, born September 19, 1649.

THOMAS DENNIS, of Boston, 1630, came in the fleet with Winthrop, had Thomas, born on the voyage probably, therefor on the "Jewell," May 29, as related by Winthrop, I, 21; removed to New Jersey, and was a proprietor of Woodbridge, and its representative 1668. Samuel, possible his son, was of the council of that province, 1684-92.

THOMAS DENNIS, of Rowley, 1691.

WILLIAM DENNIS, of Scituate, made his will February 16, 1650, as by the abstract in Genealogical Reg., V, 335, is shown, but though his wife Judith is made Executrix, and he gives only to son-in-law William Parker and Remember, Dependence and Experience Litchfield, children of Lawrence, who married Judith, daughter of his wife no doubt, yet there may be doubt

whether any children of his married Parker or Litchfield.

REFERENCES:—Freeman's Hist. of Cape Cod, Mass., II, 700; Hammatt Papers, Ipswich, Mass., 75; Paige's Hist. of Hardwick, Mass., 361; Hayward's Hist. of Hancock, N. H., 510; Whitehead's Hist. of Perth Amboy, N. J., 364; Eaton's Hist. of Thomaston, Me., II, 201; Caulkin's Hist. of New London, Conn.. 351; Austin's R. I. Gen. Dict., 65; Savage's Gen. Dict., II, 36; Amer. Ancestry, XI, 130.

DENN. Shourd's Fenwick Colony, 142.

DENNIE. Pearson's Hist. of Schenectady, 60.

DENSLOW:—Henry Denslow, of Windsor, 1644, probably was from Dorchester, had Susanna, born Sept. 3, 1646; Mary, April 10, 1651; Ruth, Sept. 19, 1653; Abigail, February 5, 1656; Deborah, December 21, 1657; Samuel, December 19, 1659; Hannah, March 1, 1662; and Elizabeth, February 11, 1666; he was killed by the Indians, 1676. Mary married April 5, 1669, Thomas Rowley; Deborah married 1677, John Hoskins; Elizabeth married 1686, William King, of Northampton; and Hannah married 1687, Henry Burt.

JOHN DENSLOW, of Windsor, perhaps brother of the preceding, or of Nicholas, or of both, freeman of Connecticut, 1657, married June 7, 1655, Mary Eggleston, had John, born August 13, 1656; Mary, March 10, 1658; Thomas. April 22, 1661; Deborah, May 29, 1663; Joseph, April 12, 1665; Benjamin, March 30, 1668; Abraham, March 8, 1670; George, April 8, 1672; Isaac, April 12, 1674; and Abigail, November 7, 1677; and he died September 10, 1689.

NICHOLAS DENSLOW of Dorchester, 1630, perhaps came in the "Mary and John," or in the fleet with Winthrop, freeman March 4. 1633, removed about 1640. to Windsor. died March, 1677; by wife Elizabeth, who died August 13, 1669, had no sons. but two daughters. Joan, who married Aaron Cook, as his second wife, and Temperance, who married Thomas Buckland.

REFERENCES:—Stiles' Hist. of Windsor, Conn., II. 71; Austin's Allied Families, R. I., 84; Savage's Gen. Dict., II, 39.

DENNESTER. Eager's Hist. of Orange County, N. Y., 617.

DENNY. Robert, of Frederick County, Va.. born in Bucks County. Pa., 1753; died in Washington County, Ind., April 17, 1826, moved to Mercer County. Ky., 1789. married May, 1778, Rachel Thomas, and had John and others.

THOMAS DENNY, of Combs, Eng.. son of Edmund, born about 1646, married Grace Cook, and had Daniel of Leicester, Mass.

REFERENCES:—Washburne's Hist. of Leicester. Mass., II. 100; Worcester Mag. Hist. Journal. 354; Futhey's Hist. of Chester County, Pa., 518: Egle's Penn. Gens., 521; Richmond. Va., Standard. III, 7; Schenck's Hist. of Fairfield, Conn., 366; Spooner Gen., vol. I, 350; Amer. Ancestry. IV. 216; VIII, 172; Denny Gen.

DE NORMANDIE. Amer. Ancestry, VII, 98.

DANSMORE:—Thomas. of Bedford. Mass., born in the north of Ireland. died December 10. 1748, married Hannah, ———and had Abraham and other children.

REFERENCES:—Milliken's Narraguagas Valley, Me., 3; Amer. Ancestry, III, 116; VII, 82.

DENT:—Francis Dent, of Lynn, freeman May 14, 1634, died 1638, or early in 1639.

REFERENCES:—Savage's Gen. Dict., II, 39.

DENTON:—Richard Denton, of Wethersfield, about 1640, bred at the University of Cambridge, where he had his A. B. 1623, being of Catherine Hall, perhaps came over in 1638 or 9; and we fear, that the long dissension at Wethersfield about Rev. Henry Smith made it desirable for him to move about 1644, and he went to Stamford, and after a few months or years, to Hempstead, Long Island, where he died 1663. Probably he had family, perhaps son Daniel. We learn from Mather, that he had been a minister at Halifax, in Yorkshire, and most of his chapter 9, in Book III, 95 is taken up with telling that he was a little man, blind of one eye, and wrote a system of divinity. Better authority tells that he was of good family, and had, in 1631, curacy of Coley Chapel in that large parish.

RICHARD DENTON, of Dorchester, married December 11, 1657, Ruth, daughter of Thomas Tileston, died Dec. 28, 1658. His widow married October 13, 1663, Timothy Foster.

REFERENCES:—Stickney's Hist. of Menesinck, N. Y., 168; Eager's Hist. of Orange County, N. Y., 411; Savage's Gen. Dict., II, 39; Amer. Ancestry, X, 187.

DE PEYSTER. Lamb's Hist. of New York City, vol. I, 420, 517; Valentine's N. Y. Com. Council Manual, 1853, 392; 1861, 556; Amer. Ancestry, III, 83; N. Y. Gen. and Biog. Rec., IX, 124.

DE PUY. Sylvester's Hist. of Ulster County, N. Y., 228; Clute's Hist. of Staten Island, N. Y., 373; Schoonmaker's Hist. of Kingston, N. Y., 476; Broadhead's Delaware Water Gap, 235; Amer. Ancestry, X, 129; Whittemore's Heroes of the Revolution and their Descendants.

DEQUINDRE. Hall Gen.

DERBY:—Edward Derby, of Braintree, 1660, married January 25 of that year, Susanna Hooke, had Mary, Eleazer and others. This Eleazer had Eleazer, and was grand-father of Rev. Jonathan in Harvard College Catalogue, 1747, given Dorby.

FRANCIS DERBY, of Warwick, died 1663. His will of October of that year mentioned wife Ann, eldest son Francis, and other child without naming him. The widow married John Read. Her son Francis was born January 20, 1660; and Eleazer, March 21, 1662.

ROGER DERBY, of Ipswich, 1671, came from Topsham, in Devonshire, removed 1681 to Salem, there died 1698. In England he had married August 23, 1668, Lucretia Kilham or Hilman, who died May 25, 1689, and had Charles, born in England, July 27, 1669; Experience, December 18, 1671; Samuel, November 24, 1673; Roger, January 1, 1675; John, February 15, 1677; Richard, October 8, 1679; Lucretia, August 17, 1681; and Ebenezer, July 9, 1683, died at 5 years; a second wife Elizabeth, by which he had Elizabeth, March 14, 1692; Margaret, December 10, 1695; and Martha, September 11, 1697. Martha married 1719, Joshua Hicks. He was a shopkeeper, assisted by his wife in that way, and founder of the distinguished family of this name. great grand-father of Elias Hasket Derby, who died 1799, at Salem. Variation of this patronymic to Dorby and Darby, may be presumed. Nine of this name, including Rev. Jonathan Dorby, 1747, minister of Scituate, a man of great promise. great grandson of Edward, had been graduated in 1828, at Harvard and one at Bowdoin.

REFERENCES:—Stearns' Hist. of Rindge, N. H., 509; Stearns' Hist. of Ashburnham, Mass., 680; Essex Inst. Hist. Coll., III, 154, 201, 283, 289; Paul's Hist. of Wells, Vt., 85; Joslin's Hist. of Poultney, Vt., 245; Locke Gen., 66, 122; Driver Gen., 279; Amer. Ancestry, vol. I, 23, V, 109; VI, 31, 105; Austin's Allied Families, R. I., 84; Austin's R. I. Gen. Dict., 65; Savage's Gen. Dict., II, 40.

DE RIDDER.   Munsell's Albany Coll., IV, 116.

DE RIEMER.   Roome Gen., 235; N. Y. Gen. and Biog. Rec., VII, 61.

DERING or DEERING:—George Dering, of Scarborough, 1645, Maine Historical Coll., 1, 228. See Dearing.

HENRY DERING, of Boston, 1663, born, as the family genealogy has it, August 16, 1639, married June 8, 1664, Ann, widow of Ralph Benning, had Ann, born May 31, 1667; he married next, November 15, 1676, Elizabeth, widow of Theodore Atkinson, daughter of Edward Mitchelson, had Elizabeth, born January 4, 1679; Mary and Martha, twins, 1682, both died young; and Henry, October 6, 1684. He was ensign in one of the Boston Militia Companies, and he and his wife were buried 1717, in one grave; as in another were Robert Winsor and wife the same evening. Hutchinson, II, 223. Elizabeth married William Welsteed. Another Deering family, which I am unable to get an account of, was of Braintree, and spread to Wrentham.

REFERENCES:—Wood's Hist. of Long Island, 194; Amer. Ancestry, IV,, 51; Savage's Gen. Dict., II, 41.

DERMIT:—William Dermit, of Piscataqua, 1633 under Wannerton. Belknap, I, 425.

REFERENCES:—Savage's Gen. Dict., II, 40.

DERR.   Amer. Ancestry, VII, 204.

DERRICK.   Amer. Ancestry, II, 32.

DESBOROUGH:—Isaac Desborough, of Lynn, came in the Hopewell, Captain Bundock, from London, 1635, aged 18. He was of Elltisley, about 12 miles from Cambridge, England, was, no doubt, related to Major-General John, who married a sister of Oliver Cromwell, and so by the usurper, entrusted to be of his upper house; and so we may be sure went home in a few years, after 1638, when Lewis gives him residence here.

SAMUEL DESBOROUGH, of New Haven, 1639, probably from London, son of James of Elltisley in County Cambridge, England, lord of that manor, probably brother of Isaac, born November 13 or 30, 1619, was one of the early settlers of Guilford, 1641, and at the gathering of the church, June 19, 1643, though so young, he was one of the seven pillars. The name of his wife is not found, probably he had more than one; and daughter Sarah, born March, 1649; is the only record of his family. In Mather, II, cap. 12, he is called John in the list of Assistants of the Colony, but that error is less gross than that of the date 1637, which was before any part of the colony was occupied by Christians. He went home in the Autumn of 1650, with his minister Whitfield. His wife died of small-pox, late in 1654; and he married Rose, widow of Samuel Penoyer, whose brother William, a merchant of London, benefactor of Harvard College, was trustee in the marriage settlement. Being brother of John, the Major-General, who had married a sister of Cromwell, and one of the lords, he got rapid preferment, was a general officer, commissioner of revenues, and was soon chosen to parliament, in 1651, for Edinburgh, and in 1656, by Oliver's favor was returned to another of his assemblies, nicknamed Parliaments for Mid-Lothian, and rose to be Chancellor for the ancient kingdom, with 2000 lbs. sterl. annual allowance, in which station he continued some time under Richard. That successor in the royal protectorship, his brother, was one of the principal instruments of overthrow; as he had, indeed, successfully counteracted the desperate ambition of the great captain for the title of king, though he was elevated by his brother-in-law to a seat in the "other house," with the empty name of Lord. See the very copious and curious letter of Maidstone to Gov. Winthrop of Conn., 3; Mass. Hist. Coll., I, 185. How long he preserved this dignity in the conquered kingdom is not told. He died December 10, 1690, at family estate of Elsworth, Cambridgeshire. See Styles' History of the Judges, 35; Noble Memorial of the Cromwell Family, II, 254; Savage's Gen. Dict., II, 41.

DESBROSSES. Lamb's Hist. N.Y.City,vol. I, 760.

DE SHONG. Martin's Hist. of Chester, Pa., 246.

DE SILLE. Lamb's Hist. of New York City, vol. I, 167; N. Y. Gen. and Biog. Rec., VIII, 128.

DESPÉAUX. Ballou's Hist. of Milford, 715.

DETERICK. Plumb's Hist. of Hanover, Pa., 407.

DETURK. Egle's Hist. Reg. Pa., II, 92.

DE VEAUX. Bullock Gen.; De Veaux Gen., 1883.

DEVELL, DEVEL, DAVOLL or DEVILL:— William Devell, of Braintree, had John, born June 24, 1643, died at 3 weeks; probably removed to Newport, there was in list of freeman 1655.

REFERENCES:—Savage's Gen. Dict., II, 41.

DEVENS. Wyman's Charlestown, Mass. Gens., vol. I, 280; Bridge Gen., 82; Amer. Ancestry, III, 194.

DEVENISH or DAVENISH:—Thomas Devenish, of Salem, 1639, admitted with wife Mary of the church, 1641, freeman June 2 of that year, had Mary, baptized July 18, 1641; and Bethia, November 30, 1643; probably other children.

REFERENCES:—Savage's Gen. Dict., II, 41.

DEVEREUX, DEVORIX or DEVEROE:—John Devereux, of Salem, came perhaps in the fleet with Winthrop, 1630, a youth of 16, was on Marblehead side 1648, freeman 1683, and living in 1694. Probably by wife Ann, he had John, and Susanna, who married June 10, 1695, Stephen Parker, of Andover. Four of this name had been graduated in 1884, at Harvard and two at Yale. A large family of divines of this name was in Suffolk, England. 3 Mass. Hist. Coll., X, 148.

REFERENCES:—Walworth's Hyde Gen., 523; Tuttle Gen., 725; Pickering Gen.; Driver Gen., 329; Dearborn's Hist. of Parsonfield, Me., 376.

DEVOE. Munsell's Albany, N. Y. Coll., IV, 116; Richmond, Va., Standard, III, 47; Amer. Ancestry, vol. I, 22; II, 32; VI, 159; Devoe Gen.

DEVOTION:—Edward Devotion, of Roxbury, lived at that part of Boston called Muddy River, now Brookline, when he joined the church at Boston, March, 1645, then single, freeman 1645, had baptized at Boston, Edward, February 25, 1649, four days old; his wife Mary was baptized the same day at Roxbury; Elizabeth, at Boston, April 20, 1651; and at Roxbury, Martha,

March 13, 1653; Hannah, December 3, 1654; at Boston, again, Deborah, May 17, 1657, died unmarried at 25 years; John, June 26, 1659; and at Roxbury, again, Sarah, January 19, 1662; Edward, July 12, 1663; and Thomas, May 1, 1670; died September 28, 1685, aged 64. In his will made three days before, of which wife Mary and son John were executors, he mentioned also son Edward and son Thomas, daughter Sarah Griffin, but not other daughter. Of the daughters, Elizabeth married September 2 ,1674, Joseph Weld, died February 15, 1679; Martha married September 2, 1674, John Rogers, Jr., grandson of Thomas; and Hannah, married May 1, 1679, John Ruggles who had married her sister, and died December 17, 1700; but she married a Paine, after death of Ruggles, December 16, 1694.

REFERENCES:—Savage's Gen. Dict., II, 43.

DEW or DUE:—Ambrose Dew, of Boston, cordwainer, married February 10, 1652, Esther, daughter of Nicholas Barker, had Patience, born December 1, 1654.

THOMAS DEW, of Marblehead, 1668.

REFERENCES:—Savage's Gen. Dict., II, 43.

DEWER:—Thomas Dewer, of oBston, 1648, a tailor, by wife Ann. had Thomas, who died December 3, 1652; David, John, Sampson, Joseph, June 24, 1652; and Thomas, again, the last born, August 26, 1653.

REFERENCES:—Savage's Gen. Dict., II, 44.

DEWERSON:—John Dewerson, of Salisbury, 1666.

REFERENCES:—Savage's Gen. Dict., II, 44.

DE WANDALAER. Munsell's Albany Coll., IV.

DE WELL. Humphrey's Gen., 194.

DEWEES. Maris Gen., 158.

DE WEVER. Munsell's Albany Coll., IV, 117.

DEWEY:—Thomas Dewey, of Dorchester, 1633, whose name Dr. Harris read Duce, freeman May 14, 1634, removed early, perhaps with Warham to Windsor, there married March 22, 1639, widow Frances Clark, (who had only child Mary), by her had Thomas, baptized February 16, 1640; Josiah, October 10, 1641; Ann, Oct. 15, 1643; Israel, born September 25, 1645; and Jedediah, December 15, 1647; was cornet of the troop, and died or was buried April 27, 1648. His widow married November 2 or 30, 1648, George Phelps, who removed to Westfield, about 1668, and with him went all the Dewey's except the one Israel.

REFERENCES:—Heminway's Vt. Gaz., IV, 61; Binnington, Vt., Centen. (1689); Joslin's Hist. of Poultney, Vt., 246; Taylor's Hist. of Great Barrington, Mass., III, 160; Temple's Hist. of Palmer, Mass., 441; Andrews' Hist. of New Britain, Conn.; Hine's Lebanon, Conn., Address, 152; Stiles' Hist. of Windsor, Conn., II, 172; Young's Hist. of Chautauqua, N. Y., 549; Wright's Williams Gen., 32; Walworth's Hyde Gen., 720; Turner's Gen., 20; Strong Gen., 370; Loomis' Gen. Female Branches, 655, 695; Dwight Gen., 692; N. Y. Gen. and Biog. Rec., VI, 63, 129, 166; VIII, 153; Savage's Gen. Dict., II, 44.

DEWHURST:—Henry Dewhurst came in the "Defence" 1635, aged 35.

REFERENCES:—Savage's Gen. Dict., II, 44.

DEWING, sometimes DEWEN:—Andrew Dewing. of Dedham, artillery company, 1644, freeman 1646, had there baptized John, March 17, 1650, died soon; John, again, June 29, 1651; Rachel, June 27, 1658; perhaps Jonathan and others, beside one April 19, 1663, whose name (perhaps Lydia, who married December 15, 1683, John Bacon), is not given in the records, and Ann, May 6, 1666, who married February 17, 1686, Daniel Wright of the same.

REFERENCES:—Temple's Hist. of North Brookfield, Mass., 571; Hill's Dedham, Mass., Rec.; Savage's Gen. Dict., II, 44.

DE WITT. John, grand pensionary of Holland, settled in New York, 1662.

REFERENCES:—Schoonmaker's Hist. of Kingston, N. Y., 477; Bergen's Kings County, N. Y., Settlers, 97; Stickney's Hist. of Minisick, N. Y., 137; Sylvester's Hist. of Ulster County, N. Y., 396; Eager's Hist. of Orange County, N. Y., 396; Gumaer's Hist. of Deerpark, N. Y., 65; Gregg's Hist. of Old Cheraws, S. C., 97; Amer. Ancestry, vol. I, 22; II, 32; III, 160; XI, 196; N. Y. Gen. and Biog. Rec., V, 165; XVII, 251; XVIII, 13; XXI, 185; XXII, 3. De Witt Gen., 1886.

DEWOLF:—Balthazer Dewolf, of Wethersfield, 1664, removed to Lyme, 1668, then had a daughter of age to live in a neighbor's family; Edward, Simon and Stephen, which may have all, as was Simon, his son (or not), joined with him in 1678, as member of the town train band, in a petition.

EDWARD DEWOLF, of Lyme, had Simon, born Nov. 28, 1671; Charles, September 18, 1673; Benjamin, December 3, 1675; beside Edward, whose date is not on the records.

STEPHEN DEWOLF, of Lyme, 1676, had Edward, born about 1686, and by a second wife Hannah, who survived, had others, and died October 17, 1702.

REFERENCES:—Champion Gen.; Amer. Ancestry, IV, 48; Salisbury Memorials, (1888); Savage's Gen. Dict., II, 44.

DEXTER:—Francis Dexter, a youth of 13, came in the "Planter," 1635, but where he lived is unknown.

GREGORY DEXTER, of Providence, preached in the baptist church, 1643, had been a printer and stationer in London, there brought out that curious book, Roger William's Key into the language of America, and his admiration of that author induced him to accompany or follow him; was town clerk, 1654; and President the year before, died at 90 years, it is said, in 1700. His children by wife Abigail, were Stephen, born November 1, 1647; James, May 6, 1650, perhaps, but the year is not plain; John, November 6, 1652; and Abigail, September 24, 1655, who married James Angel.* But in the latter days, a descendant of the sixth generation from Gregory has enlarged the family with Pelig, 1658.

REFERENCES:—Thomas, I, 418; Knowles, 253, 270.

RICHARD DEXTER, of Boston, admitted a townsman February 28, 1642, was of Charlestown, 1644, on Mystic side, where his estate descended through five generations. By wife Bridget, one of the friends of the meek preacher Marmaduke Matthews, of Malden, he had Sarah, born November 1, 1644, and other children of whose names I know only Elizabeth, who married about 1658, James Mellen; and Alice, wife of Benjamin Mussey, both born perhaps in England, and two other children, it is said, of which one was John, born about 1640. He was, I think, grandfather of John, and father of Rev. Samuel, born at Malden, October 23, 1700, Harvard College, 1720, minister of Dedham, ordained May

6, 1724, father of Hon. Samuel, born March 16, 1726, who was distinguished as patriot before the Revolution, and died at Malden, June 10, 1810, leaving bequest to promote the study of sacred literature at Harvard College.

THOMAS DEXTER, of Lynn, 1630, came probably in the fleet with Winthrop, freeman May 18, 1631, whose name has been omitted in printed volume, because he was defranchised March 4, 1633; was one of the purchasers to promote settlement of Sandwich, 1637, but did not remove for several years, was admitted freeman of Plymouth Colony, June 1, 1658, lived at Barnstable, there had Mary, born Aug. 11, 1649, had probably other children beside Thomas and William, perhaps born in England, certainly the former; and the kindness of tradition gives doubtful grandson Richard, and great-grandson William; and died in Boston, early in 1677. Lewis, 159. Six of this name had been graduated at Harvard, and six at Yale and Brown.

REFERENCES.

MASSACHUSETTS.—Freeman's Hist. of Cape Cod, II, 78, 446; Brooks' Hist. of Medford, 510; Hudson's Hist. 78, 446; Brooks' Hist. of Milford, 510; Hudson's Hist. of Marlborough, 354; Wyman's Charlestown, Mass., Gens., vol. I, 292; Swift's Barnstable Families, vol. I, 315; Malden Bi-Centen., 246; Paige's Hist. of Hardwick, 362.

OTHER PUBLICATIONS.—Austin's Ancestral Dict., 18; Austin's R. I. Gen. Dict., 288; Heminway's Vermont Gaz., V, 356; Stiles' Hist. of Windsor, Conn., II, 172; Oneida Hist. Society Trans., II, 124; Whitman Gen., 444; N. Y. Gen. and Biog. Rec., XXII, 6; Amer. Ancestry, vol. I, 23; III, 180; VI, 121; Savage's Gen. Dict., II, 44; N. E. Hist. and Gen. Reg., VIII, 248; Dexter Gen.; Dexter Chart.

DEY. N. Y. Gen. and Biog. Record, VII, 578.

DEYARMOND. Miller's Hist. of Colchester, 187.

DEYS. Hist. of Greene County, N. Y., 451.

DE ZING. N. Y. Gen. and Biog. Rec., II, 49, 53; V, 8; Thomas Family of Maryland.

DIAMOND. Hammatt Papers of Ipswich, Mass., 77; Husdon's Hist. of Lexington, Mass., 56; Smith's Hist. of Petersborough, N. H., 53; Howell's Hist. of Southampton, L. I., second edition., 236; Amer. Ancestry, vol. I, 23.

DIBBLE, DEEBLE or DEBLE:—John Dibble, of Springfield, 1641, had (perhaps before going thither), Abraham and Samuel; and after, Zechary, born April 4, 1644; Elizabeth, 17, baptized January 18, 1646; and Sarah, (posthumous), March 21, 1647. He died Sept. 1646, and his widow married November, 1647, William Graves, of Stamford.

ROBERT DIBBLE, of Dorchester, 1634, wrote his name Deeble, freeman, May 6, 1635, was living there 1652.

REFERENCES:—Huntington's Conn. Settlers, 31; Gold's Hist. of Cornwall, Conn., 258; Orcutt's Hist. of Torrington, Conn., 682; Sedgwick's Hist. of Sharon, Conn., 76; Stiles' Hist. of Windsor, Conn., II, 174; Jessup Gen., 85, 277; Chapman's Trowbridge Gen.

DIBBLEE. Amer. Ancestry, II, 153.

DIBBS:—John Dibbs, of Salisbury, married about 1689, Hepzibah Merrill, had Michael, born May 6, 1690.

REFERENCES:—Savage's Gen. Dict., II, 46.

DICK:—William Dick, of Salem, 1668. Perhaps it is the same as Dixey.

REFERENCES:—Martin's Hist. of Chester, Pa., 394; Amer. Ancestry, II, 32; Savage's Gen. Dict., II, 46.

DIEKE. Eaton's Hist. of Warren, Me., 391.

DICKARDSON:—John Dickardson, of Plymouth, married July 10, 1651, Elizabeth, the young widow of Ephraim Hicks, daughter of John Howland.

REFERENCES:—Savage's Gen. Dict., II, 47.

DICKENS:—Jeremiah Dickens, of Windsor, often spelled Diggins, and Hinman, 21, gives date of 1648. He had a family before 1690.

NATHANIEL DICKENS, of Providence, among freemen 1655, married widow Joan Tyler, but no more is told of him.

REFERENCES:—Livermore's Hist. of Block Island, R. I., 326; Austin's R. I. Gen. Dict., 66.

DICKERMAN:—John Dickerman, of Reading, of whom Eaton tells only that he was an early settler.

THOS. S DICKERMAN, of Dorchester, 1636, a tailor, freeman March 14, 1639, had Isaac, born November, 1637, died soon; and the father died January 3, 1658. His widow Ellen, acted as administrator, and married John Bullard, of Medfield.

REFERENCES:—Mitchell's Hist. of Bridgewater, Mass., 146; Kingman's Hist. of North Bridgewater, Mass., 487; Hist. of Hamden, Conn., 242; Tuttle Family of Conn., 166, 649; Amer. Ancestry, V, 145; Savage's Gen. Dict., II, 47.

DICKERSON. Powers' Hist. of Sangamon County, Ill., 249; Chandler's Sherley Gen., 386.

DECKEY. Secomb's Hist. of Amherst, N. H., 562; Merrill's Hist. of Ackworth, N. H., 209; Morrison's Hist. of Windham, N. H., 436; Parker's Hist. of Londonderry, N. H., 267; Cochrane's Hist. of Antrim, N. H., 449; Aldrich's Hist. of Walpole, N. H., 235; Eaton's Annals of Warren, Me., 535; Futhey's Hist. of Chester County, Pa., 520; Miller's Hist. of Colchester, N. S., 309.

DICKINSON:—John Dickinson, of Salisbury, 1640, had wife Mary, who died April 16, 1647; and by her had Mary, born March 12, 1640; and John. October 20, 1642; had, perhaps, Ann, a second wife, died 1679; and he married April 14, 1681, Alice Roper, who may have been the widow of John, of Dedham; and he died December 30, 1683.

NATHANIEL DICKINSON, of Wethersfield, 1637, town-clerk, 1645, representative 1646-56, removed 1659, to Hadley, was deacon in both places, freeman 1661, lived a few years at Hatfield, but went back to Hadley, died June 16, 1676. Four children, John, Joseph, Thomas and Hannah or Ann, he took with him on first going to Wethersfield, there had other six, Samuel, born 1638; Obidiah, April 15, 1641; Nathaniel, August, 1643, or perhaps four years earlier; Nehemiah, about 1644; Hezekiah, February, 1646; and Azariah, October 4, 1648. Hannah, who in her days is called Ann, married 1) John Clary, Jr., 1670, who died at Northfield; and 2) Enos Kingsley, of Northampton.

PHILEMON DICKINSON, of Salem, tanner, came with Benjamin Cooper, of Brampton, County Suffolk, as one of his servants, (but this might be to deceive an arbitrary government), embarked May 10, 1637, in the "Mary Ann," from Yarmouth, had grant of land 1639, admitted of the church 1641, freeman June 2, 1641, married Mary daughter of Thomas Payne, of Salem, had baptized there Mary, March 20, 1642; Thomas, March 10, 1644; Elizabeth, 1646; and Peter, July, 1648; removed to Southold, L. I., and was in 1662 received as freeman of Connecticut, but his will was presented in New York, where his widow was made administrator, October 28, 1672. Uniformly this name is Dickerson in New York records, as it is found in the Augmentation Office, Westminster Hall, on the return from the custom house at Yarmouth, but the name of baptism is spelt Feleman, that seems much unlike that of the friend of St. Paul. Hon. Mahlon Dickinson, late a Senator of U. S. from New Jersey, is a descendant.

THOMAS DICKINSON, of Fairfield, had been at New Haven, 1642, and it is unknown when he removed to Fairfield, but there he died about 1658, his inventory being of September 11, leaving Thomas, three daughters, and widow Mary.

THOMAS DICKINSON, of Rowley, 1643, died 1662, leaving James and four daughters. Of thirty-one graduates of New England colleges, only three (1834) had been of Harvard.

REFERENCES.

MASSACHUSETTS.—Morse's Sherborn Settlers, 75; Judd's Hist. of Hadley, Mass., 472; Stearn's Hist. of Ashburnham, 681; Swift's Barnstable Families, vol. I, 347; Temple's Hist. of Northfield, 429; Temple's Hist. of Palmer, 442; Temple's Hist. of Whately. 223; Essex Inst. Hist. Coll., XXI, 69; Gage's Hist. of Rowley, 441.

CONNECTICUT.—Whittemore's Gen. of Middlesex County, Conn., 487; Orcutt's Hist. of Stratford, Conn., 1194; Middlefield, Conn., Hist.; Timlow's Sketches of Southington, Conn., 82; Goodwin's Gen. Notes of Connecticut, 6.

OTHER PUBLICATIONS.—Read's Hist. of Swanzey, N. H., 325; Cooley's Trenton, N. J., Gens., 55; Heminway's Vermont Gaz., V; Blake's Minden Association, 130; Goodwin's Foote Gen., 270; Humphrey's Gen., 285; Redfield Gen., 45; Penn. Mag., V, 480; Montague Gen., 504; Kellogg's White Gen., 32, 103; Leach's Morton Ancestry; Amer. Ancestry, VII, 220; IX, 50; XI, 188, 191; Savage's Gen. Dict., II, 47; N. E. Hist. and Gen. Reg., XVI, 263; Dickinson Re-union, (1883); Dickinson Gen., 1865.

DICKSON:—William Dickson, of Cambridge, freeman May 18, 1642, by wife Jane, who died December 4, 1689, aged about 73, had Lydia, Mary, born August 10, 1644, who died or was buried July 21, 1648; Abigail. March 10, 1648; Mary again. January 17, 1650; Hannah and John. March 21, 1656; all baptized, says Mitchell, in his church; and he died August 5, 1692, aged 78. Often it is Dixon.

REFERENCES:—Paige's Hist. of Cambridge, Mass., 534; Cutter's Hist. of Arlington, 231; Wyman's Charlestown, Mass., Gens., vol. I, 295; Green's Kentucky Families; Miller's Hist. of Colchester County, N. S., 248, 384; Dunster Gen., 54; Savage's Gen. Dict., II, 49; Dickson Gen.

DIDIES. Amer. Ancestry, IX, 159.

DIDLAKE. Richmond Standard, II, 46.

DIES. Hist. of Greene County, N. Y., 430.

DIFFENDERFER. Wolf Family, 101.

DIGBY. Salisbury Gen.; Heraldic Journal, II, 92.

DIGGENS. Stiles' Hist. of Windsor, Conn., II, 175.

DIGGES. Richmond, Va., Standard, II, 24; Southern Bivouac, (1886), 732; Meade's Old Churches, Va., vol. I, 238.

DIGHTON. Me. Hist. Rec., VI, 362.

DIKE, DYKE or DIKES:—Abraham Dike, of Dorchester, before 1656, when he sold part of his lot to Thomas Wiswall.

RICHARD DIKES, of Gloucester, married August 7, 1667, Rebecca Doliver, had Samuel, born November 8, 1670; Sarah, May 28, 1673; Mary, November 7, 1675; Joseph, January 29, 1678; and Job, July 3, 1680; died 1729.

REFERENCES:—Kingman's Hist. of North Bridgewater, Mass., 488; Benedict's Hist. of Sutton, Mass., 633; Babson's Hist. of Gloucester, Mass., 81; Caverly's Hist. of Pittsford, Vt., 698; Noyes Gen., (1861), 9; Amer. Ancestry, III, 173.

DILL:—George Dill, of Watertown, 1671, says Bond, died there 1716, a pauper. Perhaps it was the same as Dell.

REFERENCES:—Barry's Hist. of Hanover, Mass., 294; Brown's West Simsbury, Conn., Settlers, 59; Savage's Gen. Dict., vol. II, 49.

DILLARD. Powers' Hist. of Sangamon County, Ill., 250.

DILLAWAY. Eaton's Hist. of Thomaston, Me.

DILLEY. Plumb's Hist. of Hanover, Pa., 408.

DILLINGHAM:—Edward Dillingham, of Lynn, 1636, from Bitteswell County, Leicester, where he had estate, removed next year to Sandwich; was representative 1642, and had Henry, and John; the younger born in England, about 1630. His will of May 1, 1666, probated June 1, 1667, is abstracted in Genealogical Register, VII, 225.

JOHN DILLINGHAM, of Ipswich, who came in the fleet with Winthrop was perhaps, brother to Edward, a man of respectable condition, as is proved by the prefix, at his request, October 19, 1630, and also at admission as freeman May 18 following, came from Leicestershire, was first at Boston, being No. 71 of the list of members, and dead is written against it, so that he died soon, leaving wife Sarah, and children Edward and Sarah; but Sarah alone was living when her mother made her will at Ipswich, July 10, 1636. She married John Caldwell, and was probably a relative to Richard Saltonstall and Samuel Appleton, as may be judged from that instrument. See the Appleton family memorial.

JOHN DILLINGHAM, of New Haven, 1644.

REFERENCES:—North's Hist. of Augusta, Me., 847; Eaton's Hist. of Warren, Me.; Hammatt Papers, Ipswich, Mass., 77; Hollister's Hist. of Pawlet, Vt., 183; Savage's Gen. Dict., II, 50.

DILLON. Power's Hist. of Sangamon County, Ill., 251.

DILWORTH. Futhey's Hist. of Chester County, Pa., 251.

DIMAN, DYMOND, DIAMOND, DYAMONT or DIMOND:—John Diman, of Lynn, 1647, perhaps removed to Kittery before 1652, there called ropemaker.

JOHN DIMAN, of New London, married June 17, 1674, Rebecca, widow of Tobias Minter, daughter of James Bemis.

ROBERT DIMAN, of Roxbury. His wife Mary, died 1643.

THOMAS DIMAN, of Fairfield, lost a vessel and cargo by fire in 1656, and died 1658, had Thomas, Moses and John. It may be that he is the same person under Deming, but it is not likely.

REFERENCES:—Davis' Landmarks of Plymouth, 86; Pickering Gen.; Wight Gen.; Savage's Gen. Dict., II, 50.

DIMICK. Turner Gen. of H. Turner, 375; Ellis Gen., 375.

DIMMICK. Hyde's Hist. of Brimfield, Mass., 470; Freeman's Hist. of Cape Cod, Mass., vol. I, 618, 647; Amer. Ancestry, vol. I, 23; II, 32.

DIMMOCK, DAMUCK or DIMICK:—Thomas Dimmock, of Dorchester, 1635, selectman that year, freeman May 25, 1636; removed to Hingham 1638, next year to Scituate, and in 1640 to Barnstable, of which he was August 7, 1650, ordained ruling Elder, and representative five years, being the first from the town in December, 1640. He had Thomas, perhaps John, and certainly Timothy, baptized January, 1640, died in a few months; Mehitable, April 17, 1642; Shubael, September 15, 1644; besides a son and daughter, twins, buried without names, March 18, 1641. His noncup. (?) will give all to his wife for the reason "that the children were hers as well as his." Various spelling has this name appeared in; and it may, originally, be the same as that of Dymocke, the hereditary champion of England. who at coronations, owes the service of challenge to all competitors for the crown.

REFERENCES:—Swift's Barnstable, Mass., Families, vol. I, 328; Morrison's Hist. of Windham, N. H., 437; Amer. Ancestry, IV, 189; Savage's Gen. Dict., II, 51.

DIMOCK. Walworth's Hyde Gen., 987.

DIMON. Howell's Hist. of Southampton, L. I., 236.

DIMOND:—Thomas, the ancestor, settled at Pequonnock, near Fairfield, Conn., and bought the Bennet homestead. He was a sea-faring man; died at Fairfield, 1658, leaving son Moses, who married Abigail, daughter of Governor Andrew Ward.

REFERENCES:—Schenck's Hist. of Fairfield, Conn., 367; Cochrane's Hist. of Antrim, N. H., 453; Bouton's Hist. of Concord, N. H., 641; Amer. Ancestry, VI, 15; Dinard Gen.

DINEHART. Amer. Ancestry, II, 32.

DINLEY, DYNELEY:—William Dinely, of Boston, 1635, barber surgeon, No. 340 in the list of church members, freeman April 17, 1637, by wife Alice, had Thomas, born January 9, baptized January 17, 1636; Abigail, baptized October 8, 1637, though the town record has it born in December; and Fathergone, born December 25, 1638, in the church records of his baptism on January 6, 1639, is marked "son of our gone brother"; was one of the favorers of his fellow christian, Mrs. Hutchinson, and therefore disarmed November, 1637, died in a storm December 15 next, on Boston neck. Winthrop, I, 248, 286. Johnson's observations in his Wonder-working Providence are more ludicrous than philosophical. In August following, his widow married Richard Crichley.

REFERENCES:—Savage's Gen. Dict., II, 51.

DINGLEY:—John Dingley, of Lynn, removed to Sandwich, 1637, thence to Marshfield, about 1644, and died 1658; by wife Sarah had Jacob, Mary, who married December 19, 1654, Capt. Josiah Standish, and died the next year; Sarah, probably who married 1658, William Ford, Jr., and Hanna, who married Josiah Kean; beside probably that John, who was buried July 9, 1665. The family spread into Duxbury, and descendants remain in that neighborhood.

RICHARD DINGLEY, a Baptist minister of Newport, 1685, had come to Boston from England, removed 1694, to South Carolina. Benedict. Backus, II, 109.

REFERENCES:—Winsor's Hist. of Duxbury, Mass., 255; Me. Hist. and Gen. Rec., 120; Savage's Gen. Dict., II, 52.

DINGHAM. Pearson's Schenectady, N. Y., Settlers, 62; Munsell's Albany, N. Y., Coll., IV, 117; Amer. Ancestry, II, 33.

DINNY:—Edward Dinny, of Boston, freeman April 17, 1637.

WILLIAM DINNY, freeman March 9, 1637, brother it may seem, of the proceeding. But I have some reason for thinking this name Dennis. Savage's Gen. Dict., II, 52.

DINSDALE:—William Dinsdale, an early proprietor of Boston, whose house and garden are set out in the book of possessions; by wife Martha had John, born May, 1644; Martha, January 10, 1649; Mary, September 24, 1651; and Sarah, January 7, or June 2, 1657: freeman 1657, artillery company 1658; in 1663. was aged 47, and died at Barbadoes. Savage's Gen. Dict., II, 52.

DINSMORE. Hayward's Hist. of Hancock, N. H., 518; Morrison's Hist. of Windham, N. H., 437; Coggswell's Hist. of Henniker, N. H., 544; Cochrane's Hist. of Antrim, N. H., 453; Chase's Hist. of Chester, N. H., 509; Washington, N. H., Hist., 384; Paige's Hist. of Cambridge, Mass., 364; Eaton's Hist. of Thomaston, Me., II, 202; Keye's West Boylston, Mass., Gen. Reg., 17; Morrison's Among the Scotch-Irish; Little Gen., 159; Dinsmore Gen.

DINWIDDIE. Ball's Lake County, Ind., 425; Amer. Ancestry, VI, 15, 89; Dinwiddie Papers, III, 21.

DIODATE. N. E. Hist. and Gen. Reg., XXXV, 167; Diodate Gen.

DIODATE. Salisbury Memorials.

DISBROW, DISBORW or DESBROUGH:—Nicholas Disbrow, of Hartford, 1639, an early settler, not an original proprietor, married 1640, Mary Brunson, had Phebe, baptized December 20, 1646; Abigail, born February 1, 1649; and probably more; and, after 1669, says Porter, he married Elizabeth, widow of Thwaite Strickland; died in 1683, aged 71, and left four daughters. Mary, married Obidiah Spencer; one married Samuel Eggleston; Phebe married John Kelsey; and Abigail married Robert Flood. In the year of his death, some ridiculous mischief is, by the Magnalia, VI, 69, honored as a tragedy of witchcraft; but Cotton borrowed the nonsense from his father's Remarkable Providense, page 113. By Colonial Records of Connecticut, I, 45, he seems to have been unfortunate in his early relations.

PETER DISBROW, of Rye, in New Haven jurisdiction, 1660, of which he was one of the purchasers from the Indians, representative 1665, perhaps also for Greenwich, in 1681 was called 50 years old. He married Sarah daughter of Nicholas Knapp, of Stamford. A John Disbrow, of Rye, 1683, may have been his son; also Thomas, Fairfield, 1685, or earlier, who had wife Mercy, and son Thomas, who seems to be of age at death of his father early in 1707.

DISBROW. Porter's Hartford, Conn., Settlers, 5; Clevland's Hist. of Yates County, N. Y., 153; Bolton's Hist. of Westchester County, N. Y., vol. I, 499; Baird's Hist. of Rye, N. Y., 408; Savage's Gen. Dict., II, 53.

DISCO:—Teague Disco, of Exeter, took oath of allegiance November 30, 1677.

REFERENCES:—Savage's Gen. Dict., II, 53.

DISER:—William Diser, of Salem, 1668, perhaps ill spelled, or very rare name, signed to petition against imposts.

REFERENCES:—Savage's Gen., II, 53; Wyman's Charlestown, Mass., Gens., vol. I, 29.

DISPAW:—Henry Dispaw, of Lynn, died October 4, 1676. May have had son Henry. This seems a very strange name, found by Mr. Felt, perhaps once spelled wrong.

REFERENCES:—Savage's Gen. Dict., vol. II, 53.

DISOWAY. Clute's Hist. of Staten Island, 375.

DETMARS. Hist. Queens County, N. Y., 230; Bergen's Kings County, N. Y., Settlers.

DITSON. Hazen's Hist. of Billerica, Mass., 40.

DIVELBLISS. Powers' Hist. of Sangamon County, Ill., 253.

DIVEN:—John Diven, of Lynn, 1643, perhaps had John, died October 4, 1684. Lewis.

REFERENCES:—Savage's Gen. Dict., II, 53.

DIX:—Anthony Dix, of Plymouth, one of the first comers, 1623, in the "Ann," took a share in the division of lands next year, but not in the division of cattle, 1627, because he left the Colony and joined with Conant and other Massachusetts people, freeman May 18, 1631, was taken by the pirate Bull in 1632, but allowed easily to escape, and in 1637, was of Charlestown or Salem, had wife Tabitha, who after his death married Nathaniel Pitman; and was lost by shipwreck of his thirty ton boat on Cape Cod, December 15, 1638, the same storm in which Dinely perished at Boston. This we learn from Danforth's Almanac. See Winthrop, I. 287; who spells the name Dick which Felt prefers to give as Dike, and both Dikes and Deekes are found in some records.

EDWARD DIX, of Watertown, came probably, in the fleet with Winthrop, and was first at Boston, No. 49, among members of the church, freeman March 4, 1635, by wife Jane, whose family name was Wilkinson, had Abigail, born May 2, 1637; Mary, May 2, 1639; John, September 4, 1640; and Rebecca, February 18, 1642, had second wife Susanna, who survived him; was a selectman and died July 9, 1660. The daughters were all married, viz., Abigail, December 1, 1653, to Thomas Parks, of Cambridge; Mary, February 5, 1663; Abraham Brown, Jr.; and Rebecca, February 18, 1668, Thomas Flagg, Jr. His will of June 25, 1660, makes son John executor, but the inventory was sworn to December following, by John Wincoll, his guardian. Bond gives him another daughter Deborah, without date of birth, who married Richard Barnes of Marlborough, he says, and distinguishes him from the Boston church member by remarking that he embarked at the age of 19, on January 16, 1635, and that Jane Wilkinson, aged 20, embarked at the same time. So that there must have been two of the same name. But the member of the Boston church, and not the youth of 19, must have been that freeman, and this Deborah must have been a widow, for she was mother of Leonard, of Wethersfield.

JOHN DIX, of Taunton, 1669. Baylies, II, 241.

JOHN DIX, of Hartford, perhaps brother of Leonard, was required by court to marry Mary Birdwell, but was complained of for beating her, 1676, was still there taxed 1683; sold his house and land 1686, and one of his children, John, died 1692.

LEONARD DIX, of Wethersfield, 1645, had wife Sarah, and died December 7, 1697, leaving John, Samuel and three daughters. He had been of Branford, and had grant of land there 1648; was born probably 1624, and the will which names the daughters Mercy, Hannah, and Elizabeth, provided for the widow who died 1709.

RALPH DIX, of Ipswich, 1647, fisherman, had wife Esther and children John, born March 12, 1659; Samuel, August 28, 1661; removed next year to Reading, there had Stephen, June 18, 1664; and Stephen again, December 14, 1672; freeman 1684, and died 1688. Of his descendants are Rev. Samuel, Harvard College, 1758, and J. A. Dix, late U. S. Senator from New York.

RALPH DIX, of Malden, freeman 1685, had lived at Reading years before.

SAMUEL DIX, from Norwich, England, had leave to embark at Great Yarmouth, April 8, 1637, being aged 43 years, with wife Joane, 38; two children, Priscilla and Abigail, and two servants William Storey and Daniel Linsey, to come to Boston to inhabit, but I have not yet learned where he sat down.

WILLIAM DIX, of Hartford, perhaps brother of Leonard, a single man, died March, 1676 or 7. Six of this name had been graduated at Harvard in 1834.

REFERENCES:—Hammatt Papers of Ipswich, Mass., 76; Eaton's Hist. of Reading, Mass., 62; Bond's Hist. of Watertown, 198, 753; Coffin's Hist. of Boscawen, N. H., 518; Farrow's Hist. of Isleborough, Me., 191; Richmond, Va., Standard, II, 47; Dwight's Strong Gen., 362; Amer. Ancestry, III, 135; Savage's Gen. Dict., II, 53; Dix Chart.

DIXEY:—John Dixey, of Salem, 1639. Felt.

THOMAS DIXEY, of Salem, 1637, had there baptized, Mary, January 12, 1645; Abigail, October 1, 1648; Thomas, January 29, 1654; Margaret, March 16, 1656; and John, April 26, 1657; was of Marblehead, 1674, died 1691.

Another THOMAS, at Marblehead, signed the petition against imposts 1688, as did the Salem man. Yet perhaps it was the same man, for in such cases it is sometimes thought that more value attaches to the number than to the argument, and undue artifice is employed to swell the list. Margaret, aged 18, was one of the servants of Percival Greene, embarked at London, 1635, in the "Susan and Ellen."

WILLIAM DIXEY, of Salem, had come to Cape Ann, 1629, was next at Lynn, had baptized at Salem, Abigail, December 25, 1636; Ann, May 17, 1638; John, 1639; Elizabeth, 1641; and others; freeman May 14, 1634; was captain of Beverly, about 1677, and died 1690, aged 82.

REFERENCES:—Savage's Gen. Dict., vol. II, 54.

DIXON:—Jeremiah Dixon, of New Haven, 1639, one of the seven for founding of the church June 4, removed before 1644.

WILLIAM DIXON, probably was of Charlestown, 1633-8, Kittery, 1649, freeman 1652, died March, 1666, perhaps then of York. In his will of February 13 of that year, gave to wife Joan, son James, daughter Susanna Frost, perhaps wife of Charles, to John Brown, and to children of Henry Milbury. Seven of this name, besides four called Dickson, had, in 1834, been graduated at the New England colleges, though none of either at Harvard. See Dickson.

REFERENCES:—Power's Hist. of Sangamon County, Ill., 252; Richmond, Va., Standard, III, 16; Hubbard's Hist. of Stanstead Co., Canada; Egle's Penn. Gens., 126; Marshall Gen., 28; Goode Gen., 417; Amer. Ancestry, V, 83; Savage's Gen. Dict., II, 54; Dickson Gen.

DIXWELL:—James Dixwell, of New Haven, a proprietor 1685, unless the record be wrong, as by confusion with the assumed surname I suspect.

JOHN DIXWELL, of Dorchester, 1640, gave his share, with others, in Thompson's Island, February 7, 1642, for support of a free school.

JOHN DIXWELL, of New Haven, came in 1664, it is said, after long concealment in Europe or elsewhere, flying from prosecution as one of the regicides, but it is supposed that his first quiet residence was at Hadley, with Goffe & Whalley, under shelter of Rev. John Russell, though the length of time is unknown. At New Haven he was called by himself and others, James Davids, married November 3, 1673, I think for second wife, Joanna, widow of Benjamin Ling, with whom who died in few weeks) he obtained comfortable property, and he married again October 23, 1677, Bathsheba How, had Mary, born June 9, 1679; John, March 6, 1681; and Elizabeth, July 14, 1682, who died young. His widow died at Middletown, December 27, 1729, aged 83, so that she was 39 years younger than her husband. His concealment was perfect, but his real name was known to one or more of the chief people and confessed by himself shortly before his death March 18, 1689, in his 82d year. His only daughter Mary, married December 23, 1707, John Collins, of Middletown. The family was and is still highly respected in Kent; and in the great civil war, the head of it Sir Basil stood and suffered for the royal cause.

REFERENCES:—Hinman's Conn. Settlers; Savage's Gen. Dict., II, 54.

DI ZEREGA. Amer. Ancestry, VI, 83, 97.

DOAN. Morris Gen., 189; Penn. Mag., IX, 236.

DOANE:—Henry Doane, of Watertown, 1643.

JOHN DOANE, of Plymouth, 1630, an assistant 1633, but not after, as he declined the civil office on being chosen deacon; removed 1644 to Eastham, there was deacon and died February 21, 1686. His age was great, perhaps 95. His wife Abigail had Daniel, John, Ephraim, Lydia, who married 1645, Samuel Hicks; Abigail, born January 13, 1632, at the age of 60, became the second wife of Samuel Lothrop, outlived him many years and died January 23, 1735.

Another JOHN came in the Truelove from London, 1635, aged 16.

RICHARD DOANE, of Rhode Island, 1672.

REFERENCES:—Temple's Hist. of North Brookfield, Mass., 572; Atkin's Hist. of Hawley, Mass.; Pratt's Hist. of Eastham, Mass., 17; Maine Hist. and Gen. Rec., IV, 119, 286; Walworth Hyde Gen., 470; Chapman Gen., 52; Amer. Ancestry, vol. I, 23; III, 14; Savage's Gen. Dict., II, 55.

DOBER:—John Dober, of Springfield, had grant of land, 1643, but removed.

REFERENCES:—Savage's Gen. Dict., vol. II, 55.

DOBSON:—George Dobson, of Boston, married November 24, 1653, Mary Bostwick.
REFERENCES:—Savage's Gen. Dict., II, 55; Futhey's Hist. Chester County, Pa., 524.

DOCKHAM. Eaton's Hist. of Warren, Me., 533.

DODD, sometimes DOD:—Daniel Dodd, of Branford, 1644, by wife Mary, married about 1646, had Mary, Hannah, Daniel, all baptized at New Haven, June 1, 1651; Ebenezer, born December 11, 1651; a daughter March 29, 1653, died soon; Stephen, February 16, 1656; and Samuel, May 2, 1657. His wife died May 26, 1657, and he died January, 1666. Mary married about 1665, Aaron Blatchley. All the sons but Stephen, removed to Newark, N. J.

GEORGE DODD, of Boston, 1645, a mariner, by wife Mary, had Patience, born April 11, 1646, baptized May 16, 1647, (as the wife joined the church the day preceding) died at three months; Isaac, September 3, 1651; Mary, July 5, 1653; and Elizabeth, April 5, 1657. He died in London.

THOMAS DODD, of Marblehead, 1674.

WILLIAM DODD, of Salem, 1644.

REFERENCES:—Littell's Passaic Valley Gens., 125; Hinman's Conn. Settlers, 1st ed., 209; Baldwin Gen. Supp., 1118, 1156; Savage's Gen. Dict., II, 56; Dodd Gen.

DODDREDGE. Hayden's Va. Gens., 662.

DODDS. Powers' Hist. of Sangamon County, Ill., 253.

DODGE:—Israel Dodge, of New London, 1690.

JOHN DODGE, of Wenham, freeman 1690.

JOSIAH DODGE, a soldier of Lothrop's company, killed at Bloody Brook, September 18, 1675.

RICHARD DODGE, of Salem, 1638, perhaps brother of William, admitted of the church May, 1644, had by wife Edith probably several children earlier, and certainly John and Mary, both born perhaps in England of unknown date, but baptized July 3 of that year; Richard, born 1643; and Sarah, 1644; yet not found in freeman's list, was in 1667, one of the founders of the Beverly church; made his will in 1670, in which he names wife Edith, children Richard, Samuel, Edward, Joseph, the last three of uncertain dates, daughter Mary, wife of Zechary Herrick, beside brothers William and Michael in England. He died June 15, 1672; and his widow died June 27, 1678. Sarah married Peter Woodbury, July, 1667.

WILLIAM DODGE, of Salem, 1629, came in the Lion's Whelp, called a skillful husbandman, from Dorsetshire, when Gov. Cradock commends him to Capt. Endicott, had John, baptized December 25, 1636; William, born September 19, 1640; and Hannah, baptized July 24, 1642; was freeman April 17, 1637, lived on Beverly side, was a founder of the church there 1667. Hannah married Samuel Porter, and next, Thomas Woodbury.

REFERENCES.

MASSACHUSETTS.—Wyman's Charlestown Gens., vol. I, 298; Stearn's Hist. of Ashburnham, 682; Hammatt Papers of Ipswich, Mass., 78; Temple's Hist. of North Brookfield, 574; Atkin's Hist. of Hawley, 62; Benedict's Hist. of Sutton, 634; Chandler's Hist. of Shirley, 389.

MAINE.—Farrow's Hist. of Islesborough. 192; Eaton's Hist. of Thomaston, 202; Cushman's Hist. of Sheepscot, 373; Bangor Hist. Mag., V, 189.

NEW HAMPSHIRE.—Secomb's Hist. of Amherst, 564; Hayward's Hist. of Hancock, 521; Fiske Family of Amherst, 145; Dow's Hist. of Hampton, 674; Coggswell's Hist. of New Boston, 379; Coggswell's Hist. of Henniker, 545; Cochrane's Hist. of Antrim, 457; Washington, N. H., History, 385.

OTHER PUBLICATIONS.—Walworth's Hyde Gen., 404; Prime's Sands Gen., 73; Pompey, N. Y., Re-union, 296; Pickering Gen.; Herrick Gen.; Heminway's Vt. Gaz., V, 136; Greene's Todd Gen., 100; Driver Gen., 271; Dodge Re-union (1879); Austin's R. I. Gen. Dict., 66; Livermore's Hist. of Block Island, R. I., 327; Amer. Ancestry, III, 76, 136; VI, 144, 185, 192; VII, 242, 247; IX, 91, 138; XI, 76; N. E. Hist. and Gen. Reg., XV, 254; XLVI, 383; Savage's Gen. Dict., II, 56; Dodge Gen.

DODSON:—Anthony Dodson, of Scituate, 1650, married November 12, 1651, Mary, daughter of John Williams, Sr., had Sarah, born August 26, 1652; Gershom, February 14, 1654; Mary, 1656; Jonathan, 1659; Patience, Bethia and Eunice.

DOE:—Nicholas Doe, of Dover, 1667, at Oyster River, now Durham, by wife Martha had John, born August 25, 1669; Sampson, April 1, 1670; and Elizabeth, February 7, 1679; and he died 1691. Descendants are in the same region and some of them spell the name Dow.

REFERENCES:—Deane's Hist. of Scituate, Mass., 263; Savage's Gen. Dict., II, 57.

DOE. Lapham's Hist. of Paris, Me., 581; Lapham's Hist. of Norway, Me., 493; Dearborn's Hist. of Parsonfield, Me., 376; Runnel's Hist. of Sanbornton, N. H., II, 226.

DOGGETT. Davis' Landmarks of Plymouth, 87; Doggett Gen.

DOLACK:—Christian Dolack, Dover, 1663 and 4, was there taxed. Savage's Gen. Dict., vol. II, 57.

DOLBERY:—Andrew Dolbery, of Boston, 1677, a mariner, had wife Elizabeth, and daughter Elizabeth, baptized July 12, 1691. Savage's Gen. Dict., II, 58.

DOLBEARE. N. E. Hist. and Gen. Reg., XLVII, 24; Dolbeare Gen.

DOLBY. Chase's Hist. of Chester, N. H., 511; Coggswell's Hist. of Henniker, N. H., 551.

DOLE:—George Dole, of Lynn, removed 1637, to Sandwich.

RICHARD DOLE, of Newbury, 1639, from Thornbury, Co. Gloucester, whose father bound him apprentice for seven years to John Lowell and Mary his wife; came with Lowell, a youth, born at Bristol, 1624, a merchant, married May 3, 1647, Hannah, probably daughter of Henry Rolfe, mother of all his children (who died November, 1678), had John, born August 10, 1648; Richard, September 6, 1650; Ann, March 26, 1653; Benjamin, June 14, 1654; Joseph, August 5, 1657; William, April 10, 1660; Henry, March 9, 1663; Hannah, October 23, 1665; Apphia, December 7, 1668; and Abner, March 8. 1672. He married March 4, 1679, Hannah, widow of Capt. Samuel Brocklebank, who perhaps made him remove to Rowley; and had third wife Patience, widow of Shubael Walker.

REFERENCES:—Washington, N. H., Hist., 386; Dow's Hist. of Hampton, N. H., 675; Woodford's Hist. of Bedford, N. H., 298; Bangor, Me., Hist. Mag., IV, 217; Chandler's Hist. of Shirley, Mass., 390; Guild's Stiles' Gen., 339; Poore Gen., 16, 118; Wilder Gen., 291; Savage's Gen. Dict., II, 258.

DOLLEY. Lapham's Hist. of Rumford, Me., 316.

DOLHAFF or DOLHERT:—Christian Dolhaff, of Exeter, 1684, died August, 1708, leaving Samuel, Richard, Thomas, Mary, Prudence and Catharine.

REFERENCES:—Savage's Gen. Dict., II, 59.

DOLIBER, DELLABER or DALLIBER, now DOLIVER:—Joseph Doliber, of Salem, 1640, Marblehead, 1644, was constable 1660.

SAMUEL DOLIBER, of Marblehead, 1648, of Gloucester, 1654, there by wife Mary had Samuel, born July 9, 1658; Mary, March 26, 1662; Richard, April 18, 1665; Sarah, December 24, 1667; and John, September 2, 1671; died 1683.

WILLIAM DOLIBER, of Gloucester, married October 4, 1682, Ann, daughter of Rev. John Higginson, who was apprehended in 1692 for witchcraft, but either good sense or favor of her father saved her life.

REFERENCES:—Savage's Gen. Dict., II, 59.

DOLLEY. Lapham's Hist. of Rumford, Me., 316.

DOLLIVER. Babson's Hist. of Gloucester, 81.

DALLOPE. Runnel's Hist. of Sanbornton, N. H., II, 227; Lapham's Hist. of Rumford, Me., 315; Guild's Stiles' Gen., 329; Bell's Hist. of Exeter, N. H., 10.

DOLOFF. Hubbard's Hist. of Stanstead, 191.

DOLOVAN. Austin's R. I. Gen. Dict., 67.

DOLPH. Amer. Ancestry, VII, 118.

DOLSEN. Stickney's Hist. of Minisink.

DOMMETT:—Alexander Dommett, of Boston a mariner, was taken by the Turks, 1681, at the same time. I suppose as John Greene. Savage's Gen. Dict., II, 59.

DOMINICK. Amer. Ancestry, IV, 181; Whittemore's Heroes of the Revolution and their Descendants.

DOMING. Hedge's Hist. of Easthampton, N. Y.

DONAHUE. Eaton's Hist. of Thomaston, Me.

DONALDSON. Freeman's Hist. of Cape Cod, 467.

DONGAN. Lamb's Hist. of New York City, vol. I, 299.

DONERLY. Amer. Ancestry, II, 33.

DONN:—Hugh Donn, of Dover, 1664. Savage's Gen. Dict., II, 59.

DONNELL, DENNELL or DUNNELL:—Henry Donnell, of Kittery, 1650, freeman 1652, removed to Falmouth, married a daughter of Thomas Reading, of Saco, had Henry and Samuel.

THOMAS DONNELL, of York, 1660, took oath of fidelity to Massachusetts, 1652.

REFERENCES:—Barry's Hist. of Hanover, Mass., 294; Savage's Gen. Dict., II, 59.

DONNER. Powers' Hist. of Sangamon County, Ill., 258.

DONNOVAN. Eaton's Hist. of Thomaston, Me., Runnel's Hist. of Sanbornton, N. H., II, 229.

DOOLAN. Stearn's Hist. of Ashburnham, 682.

DOOLITTLE:—Abraham Doolittle, of Boston, went to New Haven, 1644, had Sarah, Abraham, born February 12, 1650; Elizabeth, 1652; Mary, 1654; John, June 14, 1655; Abigail, baptized May 22, 1659; these by first wife, and the following by Elizabeth Moss, his second wife, Samuel, born July 7, 1665; Joseph, 1667; Abigail again, 1669. He was representative 1668 and 72, but removed to Wallingford, 1670, there had Ebenezer, about 1672; Daniel, 1675; besides two daughters perhaps, and certainly Theophilus; and died August 11, 1690. In his will he names wife Abigail, the seven sons and three daughters, Sarah, Ebenatha, Elizabeth Brockett, and Abigail, unmarried.

JOHN DOOLITTLE, of Lynn, 1643. He removed to Boston, and in that part named Rumney marsh, now Chelsea, was constable 1653. His will of September 22, 1681, names wife Sybel, married October 30, 1674, who had been widow of Miles Nutt, of Malden, and first of John Bibble; but no children; having by contract of marriage with said Sybel bound himself that he would give house and lands at Malden, he gives that and other estate to her, beside providing for her children and grand-children. The widow died September 23, 1690. He was brother of Abraham mentioned above.

REFERENCES:—Temple's Hist. of Northfield, Mass., 433; Doolittle's Hist. of Belchertown, Mass., 273; Andrews' Hist. of New Britain, Conn.; Tuttle Family of Conn., 317, 651; Davis' Hist. of Wallingford, Conn., 726; Boyd's Annals of Winchester, Conn., 272; Orcutt's Hist. of Torrington, Conn., 682; Tilley's Mag. of New Eng. Hist., III, 151; Oneida Hist. Soc. Trans., II, 76; Doolittle Gen.; Dawson Gen., 93; N. E. Hist. and Gen. Reg., V, 293; Savge's Gen. Dict., II, 59.

DOOR. Hanson's Hist. of Gardener, Me., 75.

DORCHESTER:—Anthony Dorchester, of Springfield, came from Windsor, about 1649, where he had been some years, but had been first at Hingham perhaps, by first wife Sarah, who died November 9, 1649, had three children, and by second wife Martha, widow of Samuel Kitcherell, of Hartford, married January 2, 1651, had three more; had third wife, the widow of John Harmon. He took oath of allegiance December 31, 1678, and died August 28, 1682. The children were John, James, Mary, Benjamin, Sarah and Esther.

REFERENCES:—Temple's Hist. of Palmer, Mass., 443; Warren-Clarke Gen., 58; Savage's Gen. Dict., II, 60.

DORE. Wentworth Gen., vol. I, 278.

DOREMUS. Clayton's Hist. Bergen County, N. J., 201; Amer. Ancestry, VIII, 141, 183.

DORLAND:—John Dorland, of Salem, 1674, permitted an inn-holder that year, had early been a fisherman, married a daughter of Richard Bishop of the same, had daughter Mary, remembered in the division of the estate of the grandfather.

REFERENCES:—Bergen's Kings County, N. Y., Settlers, 101; Amer. Ancestry, II, 38.

DORMAN:—Edmund Dorman, of New Haven, 1657, married 1661, Hannah, daughter of Richard Hull, had Samuel, born 1666; John, 1667, Joseph, 1669; Benjamin, 1673; Hannah, 1677; and Mary, 1680; was a proprietor 1685. His wife and last five children were living when he died 1711.

JOHN DORMAN, of Ipswich, died probably 1652 or 3.

THOMAS DORMAN, of Ipswich, one of the earliest set-tiers, freeman March 4, 1635, removed, perhaps, to Rowley, died at Topsfield, April 25, 1670, aged 70. Daniel Bradley was his son-in-law; and Ephraim and Thomas, his two sons, were of Topsfield, 1684.

REFERENCES:—Hamatt Papers of Ipswich, Mass., 79; Perley's Hist. of Roxford, Mass., 96; Thayer's Memorial, 5; Milliken's Narraguagus Valley, Me., 2; Bradbury's Hist. Kennebunkport, Me., 239; Savage's Gen. Dict., II, 61.

DORR:—Edward Dorr, of Roxbury, perhaps came from Pemaquid, had there sworn fidelity to Mass., 1674, by wife Elizabeth, daughter of Thomas Hawley, had Edward, baptized July 4, 1680; Ann, died 1683. He lived a year or two about 1680, at Boston, but had at Roxbury, Edward again, born November 15, 1683; Ebenezer, January 25, 1688; Edmund, October 19, 1692; Harbottle, May 11, 1696; and a daughter of Clemence, July 17, 1700. He had second wife, it is said, the widow of Ebenezer Clap.

REFERENCES:—Hudson's Hist. of Lexington, Mass., 56; North's Hist. of Augusta, Me., 847; Blake's Minden Association, 84; Walworth's Hyde Gen., vol. I, 194; II, 960; Crane's Rawson Gen., 28, 82; Amer. Ancestry, vol. I, 24; II, 33; IV, 15; Savage's Gen. Dict., II, 61.

DORSET:—John Dorset, of Boston, 1676, in which year his wife died, had son John, and daughter Comfort.

REFERENCES:—Savage's Gen. Dict., II, 60.

DORYFALL or DORIFIELD:—Barnaby Doryfall, of Boston, came in the "Mary and Jane," 1633, I presume, with Coddington. There came in 1634, by the "Elizabeth," from Ipswich, Ann Doryfall, aged 24, perhaps sister of Barnaby. He lived at Braintree, then part of Boston; freeman May 25, 1636.

REFERENCES:—Savage's Gen. Dict., II, 60.

DORRANCE. Powers' Hist. of Sangamon County, Ill., 260; Kulp's Wyoming Valley, Pa., Families; Buckingham Gen., 224.

DORRINGTON. Seagrave Gen. App., 9.

DORSEY. Turner's Phelp Purchase, 392.

DOTEN. Barry's Hist. of Hanover, Mass., 294; Spooner Gen., vol. I, 441.

DOTEY, DOTY, DOTE or DOTEN:—Edward Dotey, of Plymouth, came in the "Mayflower" 1620, a London youth in the employ of Stephen Hopkins, was one of the signers of the solemn compact in Cape Cod Harbor, November 11, and was with his master in the shallop that in December following, discovered Plymouth Harbor; yet June 18 following, was party in the first duel fought in New England. He retrieved his sharacter by change from his youthful folly, married probably as second wife January 6, 1635, Faith, daughter of Tristram Clark, had William, Faith, Edward, John, Isaac, born February 8, 1648; Desire, Thomas and Joseph, April 30, 1651. Bradford says he had by second wife seven children living in 1650. He was in 1652, one of the purchasers of Dartmouth, but removed to Yarmouth, died August 23, 1655. His will of March preceeding, names only wife and Edward. His widow married March 14, 1667, John Phillips of Duxbury and outlived him.

REFERENCES:—Sedgwick's Hist. of Sharon, Conn., 76; Page's Hist. of Hardwick, Mass., 365; Davis' Landmarks of Plymouth, 87; Eaton's Annals of Warren, Me.,

2d ed., 536; Baird's Hist. of Rye, N. Y., 462; Littell's Passaic Valley Gens., 139; Amer. Ancestry, II, 33; IX, 22; X, 33; Savage's Gen. Dict., II, 61.

DONBLEDAY:—Roger Donbleday, of Boston, 1674, a currier, died November 22, 1690.

REFERENCES:—Hine's Hist. of Lebanon, Conn., 153; Wyman's Charlestown, Mass., Gens., vol. I, 300.

DOTTERER. Perkiomen Region, Pa., 57.

DOUGHERTY. Barry's Hist. of Framingham, Mass., 221.

DOUGHTY:—Francis Doughty, of Taunton, 1639, removed to Long Island, 1641, where he was hardly so well treated as the minister of the gospel should have been. Adrian Van der Donck, an official under Van Rensselaer, a patentee, who married his daughter, printed a statement of the case.

JAMES DOUGHTY, of Scituate, married August 15, 1649, Lydia, daughter of Humphrey Turner, had, between 1650 and 1670, Mary, James, Elizabeth, Martha, Lydia, Sarah, Samuel, Robert and Susanna, was a soldier in Phillip's war.

THOMAS DOUGHTY, of Dover, 1657-67. Perhaps he removed to Berwick, and Doughty's Falls may have been named for him.

REFERENCES:—Bunker's L. I. Gen., 198; Amer. Ancestry, IX, 63; X, 118.

DOUGLASS:—Henry Douglass, of Boston, freeman 1657. His daughter Ann, married September 1, 1660, Eliphalet Het.

JOHN DOUGLASS, of Dover, married September 16, 1687, a widow Nason whose husband is not of my acquaintance, nor her baptismal name as printed in the New England Register, VII, 119.

WILLIAM DOUGLASS, perhaps of Gloucester first, but of Boston 1640, cooper, freeman 1646, by wife Ann, had Ann, Robert, born 1639; Elizabeth, August 26, 1641; Sarah, April 8, 1643; and William, April 1, 1645; removed to New London, was deacon and representative 1672, and perhaps later, died July 26, 1682, aged 71. Ann, his wife, was daughter of Thomas Mable, of Ringstead, Northamtonshire.

REFERENCES:—Hinman's Conn. Settlers, 1st ed., 209; Caulkin's Hist. New London, Conn., 300; Gold's Hist. of Conwell, Conn., 241; Powers' Hist. of Sangamon County, Ill., 261; Wheeler's Hist. of Brunswick, Me., 831; Amer. Ancestry, III, 194; IV, 67; IX, 198; N. E. Hist. and Gen. Reg., XXVIII, 69, 75; Goode Gen., 354; Richmond, Va., Standard, III, 6; Meade's Old Families of Va., vol. I, 458; Hamilton's Biog. of Wise; Robertson's Pocahontas' Descendants; Ransom Gen.; Bullock Gen.; Savage's Gen. Dict., II, 63; Douglass Gen.

DOUGHREY. Morris Bontecou Gen.

DOUTHAT. Paxton's Marshall Gen.; Richmond, Va., Standard, III, 23.

DOUTHETT. Amer. Ancestry, IV, 102; IX, 96; Douthett and Ward Gen.

DOUTY. Amer. Ancestry, VIII, 45.

DOVE:—Matthew Dove, of Salem, had children baptized there, Hannah and Elizabeth, September 10, 1654; Dorcas, October 5, 1656; Bethia, May 30, 1658; Daniel, November 3, 1661; Deborah, May 20, 1666; and a daughter whose name is not known, July 1 following.

REFERENCES:—Savage Gen. Dict., vol. II, 63.

DOW:—Francis Dow, of Salisbury, in the record of proprietors, has the prefix of respectability, and is third on the list, came from the city of Salisbury Co., Wiltshire, before 1650.

HENRY Dow, of Watertown, 1637, a husbandman, aged 29, came from Ormsby in Norfolk, that year with wife Joan, who was buried June 10, 1640; four children and a servant Ann Manning, 17; freeman May 2, 1638; had Joseph, born March 20, 1639; and Thomas, and by second wife Margaret Cole, of Dedham, had Daniel, September 22, 1641; and Mary, September 14, 1643; married before 1645, another wife, widow Nudd, removed to Hampton, was representative 1655 and 6, died April 21, 1659. In his will he mentioned wife Margaret, perhaps the widow Nudd, and children Henry, born in England, 1634; Mary, at Watertown, Sept. 14, 1643; Hannah, Thomas and Jeremiah, besides Joseph, March 20, 1639; and Daniel, September 2, 1641.

HENRY Dow, of Salisbury, married December 7, 1694, Mary Mussey.

JOHN Dow, of Haverhill, married May 23, 1696, Sarah, daughter of Abraham Brown, of Salisbury.

JOHN Dow, freeman, 1666, of Haverhill, 1690.

STEPHEN Dow, freeman 1668, of Haverhill, 1690.

MATTHEW Dow, of Salem.

ROBERT Dow, of Salisbury, by wife Sarah, had Robert, born July 23, 1676; and Martha, October 1, 1678.

SAMUEL Dow, perhaps of Dover, certainly of some part of New Hampshire, by wife Abigail, had Joseph, born September 13, 1686.

SAMUEL Dow, of Hartford, married December 12, 1665, Mary, daughter of the first George Graves of the same.

SIMON Dow, of New Hampshire, by wife Sarah, had Mary, born November 19, 1686.

THOMAS Dow, of Newbury, an early settler, freeman June 22, 1642, by wife Phebe, had Stephen, born March 29, 1642; Mary, April 26, 1644; Martha, June 1, 1648; John and Thomas; removed to Haverhill, and died May 31, 1654. In his will made only two days before his death the widow Phebe and the five children (but John and James first), are mentioned, so that possibly they were older than the others.

REFERENCES.

NEW HAMPSHIRE.—Worcester's Hist. of Hollis, 372; Washington, N. H., Hist., 389; Morrison's Hist. of Windham, N. H., 510; Wheeler's Hist. of Newport, N. H., 366; Hayward's Hist. of Hancock, 531; Dow's Hist. of Hampton, 676; Coggswell's Hist. of Nottingham, 679; Bouton's Hist. of Concord; Cochrane's Hist. of Antrim, 492; Coggswell's Hist. of Henniker, 550.

OTHER PUBLICATIONS.—Talcott's Gen. Notes, 64; Munsell's Albany, N. Y., Coll., IV, 117; N. Y. Gen. and Biog. Rec., III, 82; Eaton's Hist. of Thomaston, Me., II, 204; Hudson's Hist. of Lexington, Mass., 278; Stiles' Stranahan Gen.; Titcomb's Early New England People, 238; Amer. Ancestry, vol. I, 24; III, 155; IV, 102; IX, 96; XI, 193; Savage's Gen. Dict., II, 63.

DOWD, DOUDE, DOWDE or DOWDY:—George Dowd of Concord, freeman 1645.

HENRY DOWD, of Guilford, 1639, died or was buried

August 31, 1668. By wife Elizabeth, who died 1683, had Rebecca, Mary, Sarah, John, born May 24, 1650; Thomas and Jacob, February 16, 1653; all living in 1680, beside Jeremiah, who died 1668; and Elizabeth, who died 1669.

REFERENCES:—Amer. Ancestry, V, 96; VI, 35; VII, 144; Savage's Gen. Dict., II, 64; Dowd Gen.

DOWDEN:—Leonard Dowden, of Boston, 1679, married Mercy, daughter of William Paddy, died 1682, and his widow died March 11, 1694.

REFERENCES:—Savage's Gen. Dict., II, 63.

DOWELL:—James Dowell, of Boston, 1669, mariner.

REFERENCES:—Savage's Gen. Dict., II, 64.

DOWHAM:—Deerman Dowham, of Braintree, by wife Elizabeth, had Elizabeth, born January 15, 1646; and John, 1648.

JOHN Dowham, of Braintree, perhaps brother of the preceding, by wife Dorothy, had John, or, I think, Thomas, 1644; Joseph, 1645; John, again, 1653; Mercy, 1655; Dorothy, 1659; and again Dorothy.

REFERENCES:—Savage's Gen. Dict., II, 64.

DOWNE, DOWNS or DOWNES:—Edmund Downe, of Boston, 1667, merchant.

JOHN Downe, of Boston by wife Dorothy, had Mary, 1667.

JOHN Downe, of New Haven, 1654, had John, born 1659; Samuel, 1662; Mary, 1665; Ebenezer, 1667; Deliverance and Elizabeth, twins, 1669; Hannah, 1671; John again, 1672; Daniel, 1674; Nathaniel, 1676, and Ruth, 1679.

ROBERT Downe, of Milford, 1660.

THOMAS Downe, of Boston, came in the "Defence," 1635, perhaps aged 25, by wife Catharine had Rebecca, 1652; and Thomas, 1654; was at Dover, 1657, and there had Elizabeth, 1663; and died 1697. Mary, killed by the Indians, was perhaps his daughter.

THOMAS Downe, of Dover, by wife Martha, had Gershom, 1680; he afterwards married Abigail, widow of John Hall, was killed by the Indians 1711.

WILLIAM Downe, of Massachusetts, 1635.

WILLIAM Downe, of Boston, 1676, married Hannah, eldest child of Samuel Appleton, of Ipswich.

REFERENCES:—Savage's Gen. Dict., 264; Amer. Ancestry, IX, 203.

DOWNER:—Joseph Downer, of Newbury, married 1660, Mary, daughter of John Knight, had Mary, 1662; Joseph, 1666; and Andrew, 1672.

ROBERT Downer, of Salisbury, 1665, had some years earlier been of Newbury, married 1675, Sarah, daughter of John Eaton, had John, 1681; Andrew, 1683; Samuel, 1686; Joseph, 1688; Sarah, 1690; Mary, 1696; and Joseph, 1699.

REFERENCES:—Amer. Ancestry, III, 149; Savage's Gen. Dict., II, 64.

DOWNES. Sedgwick's Hist. of Sharon, Conn., 77.

DOWNIE. Carey's Hist. of Bridgwater, Mass.

DOWNEY. Temple's Hist. of North Brookfield, Mass., 577.

DOWNING:—Benjamin Downing, of Hatfield, 1679, took the oath of allegiance and married the same year, Sarah, daughter of William Hunter.

DENNIS DOWNING, of Kittery, 1650, in 1652, swore allegiance to Massachusetts, and was killed by the Indians 1697, unless it was a son of the same name.

EMANUEL DOWNING, of Salem, from London, where he was a lawyer of the Inner Temple, inhabitant of the parish of St. Michael, Cornhill Ward, was probably son of Emanuel, a clergyman in Ireland, came in 1638, with his wife Lucy, daughter of Adam Winthrop, Esq., of Groton, in County Suffolk, where she was baptized 1601, sister of our first Governor of Massachusetts, married 1622. They were admitted of the church 1638, and he was sworn a freeman 1639, representative the same year 1640, 1641, 1644 and 1648, was proposed for an Assistant in 1641, but not chosen. His children were George, 1623 or 4; Mary, who came over in 1633; James, who came over with his uncle, the Governor, 1630; Susan, who came with Mary, Ann, Lucy, and these following born on this side of the ocean, John, 1640; and Dorcas, 1641. He went home in 1642, back next year, and went again 1644, but came back next year. The date of his death is not found, nor that of his wife, though we see proof of his request to the General Court, September 1653, for his 600 acres to be laid out, and of her living 1656, when she gave to Capt. Joseph Gardner dowry on his marriage with her daughter, and the same shows that her husband Emanuel was dead.

JOHN DOWNING, died at Boston, 1694, was a merchant from Nevis.

JOHN DOWNING, of Charlestown, to his wife Joanna, who bore him Mary, 1659, was given administration of his estate, 1663.

JOHN DOWNING, of Ipswich, married 1669, Mehitable, daughter of Richard Brabrook, had John, 1675; Margaret, 1679; and Richard.

JOHN DOWNING, of Braintree, 1673, was a soldier in Philip's war with Capt. Turner, 1676, on Connecticut River settlement at Hatfield, married soon after Mary, widow of Thomas Meakins, Jr., had Jonathan, 1677; and John, 1678.

MALCOLM DOWNING, of Lynn, a Scotchman, married 1653, Margaret Sullivan, had Mary, 1655; Hannah, 1657; Sarah, 1659; Margaret, 1661; Priscilla, 1662; Catharine, 1665; John, 1667; and Joanna, 1671.

RICHARD DOWNING, of Ipswich, died 1702, but I know nothing more of him, except that in 1664 (three years before he married) was 27 years old.

THEOPHILUS DOWNING, of Salem, 1642, had grant of land that year, and son Theophilus, 1642; Ann or Hannah, 1644; and Benjamin, 1647; in the last instance the child is noted as of Ellen Downing. He was a fisherman, and was of Marblehead part of the time.

WILLIAM DOWNING, of Boston, 1690, freeman that year.

REFERENCES.

NEW HAMPSHIRE.—Read's Hist. of Swanzey, 328; Cochrane's Hist. of Antrim, 468; Hayward's Hist. of Gilsum, 302.

OTHER PUBLICATIONS.—Bradbury's Hist. of Kennebunkport, Me., 240; Ruttenber's Hist. of Orange County, N. Y., 398; Plumb's Hist. of Hanover, Pa., 406; Poor's Hist. of Merrimac Valley, 82; Futhey's Hist. of Chester County, Pa., 525; Palmer and Trimble Gen., 345, 406; Miller's Hist. of Colchester, N. S., 338; Duren's Stoddard Gen.; Montague Gen., 34; Amer. Ancestry, II, 34; Savage's Gen. Dict., II, 65.

DOWMAN. Hayden's Virginia Gens., 72.

DOWNS. Swift's Barnstable Families, I, 24; Orcutt's Hist. of Stratford, Conn., 1195; Orcutt's Hist. of New Milford, Conn., 692; Ransom Gen.; Savage's Gen. Dict., II, 65; Wentworth Gen., vol. I, 254.

DOWNTON:—William Downton, of Salem, freeman 1668, had John, born two or three years after, was goalkeeper 1686.

REFERENCES:—Savage's Gen. Dict., II, 67.

DOWS. Amer. Ancestry, IV, 139.

DOWSE:—Francis Dowse, of Boston, in the employment of George Burden, 1640, freeman 1641, by wife Catharine, had Elizabeth, 1642; Mary, 1644; Hannah, 1646; Deborah, 1652; Naomi, 1653; Lydia, 1655; and Sarah, 1657. He removed to Charlestown, and his wife died 1698, outliving him.

LAWRENCE DOWSE, of Boston, carpenter, by wife Martha, who died at Charlestown, 1644, had Samuel, 1642; and John, 1644; married at Charlestown, Margery, daughter of Robert Rand, had Elizabeth, 1647; John, 1650; Mary, Joseph, 1654; Benjamin, 1656; Benjamin again, 1658; Nathaniel, 1658; Nathaniel, again; Jonathan, Sarah, 1663; Eleazer, 1669. He died 1692, aged 78 years, and his widow died 1714, in her 90th year.

LODOWICK DOWSE, of Sherborn, had Mary, 1683; Stephen, 1686; Martha, 1688; and Samuel, 1693.

SAMUEL DOWSE, of Portsmouth, N. H., married 1689, Sarah Berry, of Newcastle, had Joanna, 1689; Samuel, 1690; John, 1693; Ann, 1695; Solomon, 1697; Susannah, 1699, and another.

REFERENCES:—Wyman's Charlestown, Mass., Gens., vol. I, 301; Morse's Hist. of Sherburne, Mass., 78; Hazen's Hist. of Billerica, Mass., 41; Cregar's Winte Gen.; Amer. Ancestry, IV, 139; Savage's Gen. Dict., II, 68; Dowse Gen.

DOWST. Pickering Gen.

DOX. Talcott's N. Y. and N. E. Families, 166; Munsell's Albany Coll., IV, 118.

DOXY:—Thomas Doxy, of New London, 1650, by wife Catharine, had Thomas and perhaps other children, but died 1652. His widow married Daniel Lane, and the family moved to Long Island.

REFERENCES:—Savage's Gen. Dict., II, 68.

DOYLE:—Robert Doyle, perhaps of Lancaster, married 1680, Joanna, daughter of John Farrar of the same.

REFERENCES:—Temple's Hist. of North Brookfield, Mass., 597; Davis' Hist. of Buck's County, Pa., 668; Savage's Gen. Dict., II, 69.

D'OGLEY. Amer. Ancestry, VII, 232.

DOZIER. Powers' Hist. of Sangamon County, Ill., 262.

DRAKE:—Francis Drake, of Portsmouth, 1661, was of grand jury 1663, a surveyor, perhaps removed to New Jersey soon after.

JOHN DRAKE, of Dorchester or Boston, came in the fleet with Winthrop, probably, as we find his request 1630, to be made freeman, and he removed perhaps as a purchaser of Taunton, 1639, and not long after to Windsor, and there was killed 1659, leaving sons Jacob and Job and John. His widow died 1681.

ROBERT DRAKE, of Exeter, came from Devonshire, where he was born 1630, removed to Hampton, in 1654, was selectman, died 1668. His will names sons Nathaniel and Abraham, and daughters Susanna.

SAMUEL DRAKE, of Fairfield, 1650, representative 1662, removed to East Chester, 1665, had John, Samuel, and Joseph, and four daughters, of which one was Mary; wife's name was Ann.

THOMAS DRAKE, of Weymouth, by wife Jane had John, 1659; William, 1661; Joseph, 1663; Amy, 1666; and Benjamin, 1677. I think he married 1681, Millicent, widow of John Carver, daugher of William Ford. Perhaps he was of Dorchester, 1640.

A widow Joan Drake, was admitted of the church in Boston, 1634, but I know no more of her.

DRAKELEY:—Thomas Drakeley, of Woodbury, 1682, had come from Stratford, married Lydia Brooks, of New Haven, had Ann, 1697; Thomas, 1704; Robert, 1709; Mary, 1709; and William, 1714; and died 1734, aged 77. He was perhaps born in England, and his widow died 1762.

REFERENCES.

CONNECTICUT.—Whitney Family of Conn., vol. I, 100; Orcutt's Hist. of Torrington, Conn., 682; Stiles' Hist. of Windsor, Conn., II, 177.

OTHER PUBLICATIONS.—Dow's Hist. of Hampton, N. H., 688; Hurd's Hist. of Rockingham, N. H., 425; Temple's Hist. of North Brookfield, Mass., 578; Kingman's Hist. of North Bridgwater, Mass., 490; Eaton's Hist. of Thomaston, Me., II, 204; Dolton's Hist. of Westchester County, N. Y., II, 726; Bass' Hist. of Braintree, Vt., 129; Salisbury's Memorials; Littell's Passaic Valley Gens., 145; Green's Kentucky Families; Loomis' Gen. Female Branches, 309, 865; Prible Gen., 263; Barbour's My Wife and Mother, 64; Amer. Ancestry, IV., 204; Savage's Gen. Dict., II, 69; Drake Gen.; Drake Chart.

DRAKELY. Cothren's Ancient Woodbury, 539; Tuttle Gen., 574; Savage's Gen. Dict., II, 71.

DRAPER:—James Draper, of Dedham, 1683, may be the same who was a proprietor of Lancaster, 1654, and who was of Roxbury, freeman 1690, and died 1697, aged 73, says the inscription on the gravestone.

JAMES DRAPER, of Roxbury, by wife Elizabeth, had William, 1686.

MOSES DRAPER, of Roxbury, married 1685, Hannah, daughter of John Chandler, who died 1692, had Hannh, 1686; Elizabeth, 1687; and Elizabeth, again, 1688. He soon had second wife Mary, and removed to Boston, had Moses, 1693.

NATHANIEL DRAPER, of Damariscove, 1631.

NICHOLAS DRAPER, of Salem, 1637.

RICHARD DRAPER, of Boston, freeman 1690.

ROGER DRAPER, of Concord, freeman 1639, had Adam and Lydia, 1641.

CLEAR DRAPER, of Boston, 1634, aged 30.

REFERENCES.

MASSACHUSETTS.—Hill's Dedham Records; Hudson's Hist. of Lexington, 57; Temple's Hist. of North Brook-

field, 578; Wyman's Charlestown Gens., II, 308; Draper's Hist. of Spencer, 190; Ballou's Hist. of Milford, 719.

OTHER PUBLICATIONS.—Cochrane's Hist. of Antrim, N. H., 467; Washington, N. H., Hist., 389; Guild's Calvin Ancestry, 3; Chandler Gen., 51; Amer. Ancestry, vol. I, 24; VIII, 96, 158; Savage's Gen. Dict., II, 71; Draper and Preston Families, 1871; Draper Gen., 1892.

DRAWWATER:—Thomas Drawwater, of New Haven, 1668, fined for drinking unduly.

REFERENCES:—Savage's Gen. Dict., II, 71.

DRAYTON:—Henry Drayton, of Marshfield, able to bear arms, 1643.

JOHN DRAYTON, of Maine, 1642.

REFERENCES:—Savage's Gen. Dict., II, 71.

DRECKAN:—Nicholas Dreckan, came to Salem, 1660.

REFERENCES:—Savage's Gen. Dict., II, 72.

DRENNAN. Powers' Hist. of Sangamon County, Ill., 262.

DRESSER:—John Dresser, of Rowley, 1643, by wife Mary, had Mary, 1643; Samuel, 1644; Jonathan, 1647; Elizabeth, 1656; and Mary again, 1667; was a lieutenant, and died 1672.

SAMUEL DRESSER, of Salem, 1638.

REFERENCES:—Barrus' Hist. of Goshen, Mass., 144; Gage's Hist. of Rowley, Mass., 441; Essex Inst. Coll., XXI,73; Washington,N. H.,Hist., 391; Hubbard's Hist. of Stanstead County; Canada, 317; Powers' Hist. of Sangamon County, Ill., 268; Ammidown Hist. Coll., II, 220; Ammidown Gen., 29; Amer. Ancestry, V, 79.

DRET. Munsell's Albany Coll., IV, 119.

DREW:—James Drew, of Portsmouth, 1667.

JOHN DREW, of Plymouth, by wife Hannah, had Elizabeth, 1674; John, 1676; Samuel, 1678; Thomas, 1681; Nicholas, 1684; and Lemuel, 1687.

ROBERT DREW, of Boston, married 1656, by Gov. Endicott, to Jemima, daughter of John Clark.

ROSEMUND DREW, of Roxbury, married 1678, Mary Druce, daughter of Vincent, had Rosemund, a son, 1679; Jonathan, Ebenezer, Abigail; the mother died 1719, in her 70th year.

WILLIAM DREW, of Dover, 1648, died about 1669, leaving wife Elizabeth, who married 1671, William. Follet. He had Francis, 1648; John, 1651; perhaps James and William.

REFERENCES:—Winsor's Hist. of Duxbury, Mass. 256; Davis' Landmarks of Plymouth, 91; Eaton's Hist. of Thomaston, Me., 205; Dow's Hist. of Hampton, N. H., 694; Hubbard's Hist. of Stanstead County, Canada, 230, 309; Wentworth Gen., II, 292; Savage's Gen. Dict., II, 72; Amer. Ancestry, II, 34, 154; IV, 144; IX, 129.

DRINKER:—Philip Drinker, of Charlestown, 1635, came in the "Abigail," that year, aged 39, with wife Elizabeth, 32; Edward, 13; and John, 8; freeman 1637, kept the first ferry over the Mistick 1640, died 1647.

REFERENCES:—Wyman's Charlestown, Mass., Gens., vol. I, 309; Bartow Gen., Part I, 135; Savage's Gen. Dict., II, 72.

DRINKWATER. Orcutt's Hist. of New Milford, Conn., 692; Eaton's Hist. of Thomaston, Me., II, 205; Maine Hist. and Gen. Rec., III, 205; Corliss' Hist. of North Yarmouth.

DRISCOLL:—Florence Driscoll, of Windsor, or Wethersfield, died 1678, probably unmarried.

REFERENCES:—Temple's Hist. of North Brookfield, Mass., 580; Savage's Gen. Dict., II, 72.

DRIVER:—Robert Driver, of Lynn, 1630, freeman 1635, died 1680, aged 87. His wife died 1683. He had son Robert, born 1627, and perhaps John and Richard.

WILLIAM DRIVER, of Salem, 1687, died 1691, leaving wife Mary.

REFERENCES:—Driver's Gen.; Savage's Gen. Dict., II, 72.

DRODY. Freeman's Hist. of Cape Cod, Mass., 145.

DROWN. Rose's Sketches of Rose, N. Y., 212.

DROWNE:—Leonard Drowne, of Kittery, shipwright, married Elizabeth Abbott, perhaps daughter of Richard, of Portsmouth, had Solomon, 1682; Samuel, Simeon, Shem, Susanna and Mary. He was one of the founders of the first Baptist church in Maine, 1682. He had practised his trade in Boston for a dozen years when his wife died 1704; and by second wife had no children. He died 1729, aged 83.

REFERENCES:—N. Y. Gen. and Biog. Rec., XVII, 215; Whitmore's Copps Hill Epitaphs; Brewster's Hist. of Portsmouth, N. H., 139; Bartlett's Russell Gen., 119; Amer. Ancestry, II, 34; Savage's Gen. Dict., II, 74; Drowne Gen.

DRUCE:—Vincent Druce, of Hingham, 1637, freeman 1645, removed before 1652 to Cambridge, lived on South side of the river, now Newton, had share in the division of the Shawsheen lands. His children were Vincent, John, Mary.

REFERENCES:—Paige's Hist. of Cambridge, Mass., 536; Jackson's Hist. of Newton, Mass., 271; Savage's Gen. Dict., II, 74.

DRUMM. Amer. Ancestry, II, 34; III, 193.

DRUMER:—Samuel Drumer, of Lynn, died 1676.

REFERENCES:—Savage's Gen. Dict., II, 72.

DRUMMOND:—John Drummond, Boston, married 1661, widow Lydia Hallet.

REFERENCES:—N. Y. Gen. and Biog. Rec., XVI, 35; Amer. Ancestry, VI, 161; Savage's Gen. Dict., II, 73.

DRURY:—George Drury, came in the "Abigail," 1635, aged 19.

HUGH DRURY, of Boston, 1640, carpenter, freeman 1654, constable 1655 and 6, artillery company 1659, lived some years at Sudbury, there by wife Lydia, who died 1675, had John, 1646; and Thomas, married 1676, for second wife, Mary, widow of Edward Fletcher, and died 1689.

REFERENCES.

MASSACHUSETTS.—Ward's Hist. of Shrewsbury, 266; Temple's Hist. of North Brookfield, 580; Pierce's Hist. of-Grafton, 475; Draper's Hist. of Spencer, 194; Barry's Hist. of Framingham, 222.

OTHER PUBLICATIONS.—Worcester's Hist. of Hollis,

N. H., 372; Aldrich's Hist. of Walpole, N. H., 241; Norton's Hist. of Fitzwilliam, N. H., 539; Caverly's Hist. of Pittsford, Vt., 699; Turner Gen.; Ward's Rice Gen., 13; Amer. Ancestry, II, 34; III, 179; Savage's Gen. Dict., II, 73; Drury Chart; Drury Gen.

DUANE. Valentine's New York Common Council Memorial, (1853), 410; (1861), 547; Lamb's Hist. New York City.

DUBBS. Butz Gen., 83.

DU BOIS:—Louis Du Bois, born in Wicres, near Lisle, now in the province of Artois, France, October 27, 1626; died in Kingston, N. Y., 1695. He and his wife fled to Mannheim, in the Palatinate to escape persecution, and came thence to Hurley, N. Y., about 1660; in 1670, he led a colony for the settlement of New Paltz, moving thence to Kingston, N. Y., 1687. He married October 16, 1655, Catharine Blancon; died 1706. They had Abraham, Isaac, Jacob, Sarah, 1664; David, 1667; Solomon, Louis, Matthew, Rebecca, Rachel.

REFERENCES:—Hist. of Greene County, N. Y., 109; Schoonmaker's Hist. of Kingston, N. Y., 477; Shourd's Fenwick Colony, N. J., 75; Sylvester's Hist. of Ulster County, N. Y., 180; Blackman's Hist. of Susquehanna County, Pa., 66; Bass' Hist. of Braintree, Vt., 130; Amer. Ancestry, vol. I, 24; II, 34; II, 211; VI, 25; VII, 192; Du Bois Chart, 1876; Du Bois, 1860; Du Bois Reunion, 1876.

DU BOSE. Gregg's Old Cheraws, 91.

DUBOYS. Clute's Hist. of Staten Island, 376.

DUBS. Perkiomer Region, Pa., by Datterer, 21; Penn. Mag. of Hist., XVIII, 371.

DUCHE. Penn. Mag. of Hist., XII, 486.

DUCKWORTH:—Charles Duckworth, a soldier in Philip's war, of Turner's company, left at Quaboag, 1676.

REFERENCES:—Savage's Gen. Dict., II, 75.

DUDBRIDGE:—William Dudbridge, of Gloucester, had grants of land 1645 and 9.

REFERENCES:—Savage's Gen. Dict., II, 75.

DUDLEY:—Francis Dudley, of Concord, married 1655, Sarah Wheeler, had Mary, Joseph, Samuel, Sarah, John and Francis.

HUGH DUDLEY, of Springfield, in the employment of William Pynchon, married 1656, Mary, daughter perhaps of widow Elizabeth Copley, sold out his property and removed.

JOHN DUDLEY, of Charlestown, 1658, was a witness 1671, then called 55 years old. He may have married Hannah, daughter of John Poulter, and lived at Concord, yet the age would be discord with such supposition, but cannot be the man who was at Guilford, 1673, married that year Martha French, had John, 1675; Mary, 1678; Nathaniel, 1680; Ebenezer, 1682; Mercy, 1684; Jonathan, 1686; Elizabeth, 1688; and Naomi, 1690, in which year he died, all the children then living. His name was early written Deadly; and he seems not connected with other Dudelys at Guilford.

THOMAS DUDLEY, of Roxbury, third Governor of Massachusetts Bay, and second in it, according to the Royal Charter, was son of Capt. Roger, it is said, born at Northampton, England, 1576, having leave from Queen Elizabeth to volunteer, he served under Henry

IV of France, says a reputable tradition at the siege of Amiens, lived after at Northampton, but by Isaac Johnson, who names him one of the Executors of his will, is called of Chipsham Co., Rutland. He came over 1630, probably in the "Arabella," as deputy governor, was early at Newtown, or Cambridge, and a short time at Ipswich, had a mill at Watertown, at last fixed at Roxbury, was an Assistant 1635, and some years later, but deputy-governor 13 years, Governor 1634, 40, 5, and 50, and died 1653, aged 76. His wife Dorothy died 1643, aged 61, and he married April following, Catharine, widow of Samuel Hackburne, whose maiden name was Dighton, and who married 1653, Rev. John Allin, of Dedham. The children of both wives were, perhaps, Thomas, Samuel, Ann, 1612; Patience, Sarah, baptized 1620; Mercy, 1621; these all born in England by first wife, and Deborah, baptized 1645; Joseph, baptized 1647; and Paul, baptized 1650, both by 2d wife.

WILLIAM DUDLEY, of Guilford, 1639, married 1636, at Oakley in Surrey, England. Jane Lutman who came with him probably as friends of Rev. Henry Whitfield, and died 1674; had William, 1639; Joseph, 1643; Ruth, 1645; Deborah, 1647; and another child.

REFERENCES.

MASSACHUSETTS.—Shattuck's Hist. of Concord, 369; Paige's Hist. of Cambridge, 536; Barry's Hist. of Framingham, 225; Emerson's Hist. of Douglass, 212; Drake's Hist. of Boston, Benedict's Hist. of Sutton, 635; Dunstable Bi-Centen., 177; Hammatt Papers of Ipswich, 80; Hudson's Hist. of Lexington, 58.

NEW HAMPSHIRE.—Wheeler's Hist. of Newport, 367; Runnel's Hist. of Sanbornton, II, 230; Lancaster's Hist. of Gilmanton, 260; Fullerton's Hist. of Raymond, 202; Chase's Hist. of Chester, 511.

OTHER PUBLICATIONS.—Lapham's Hist. of Paris, Me., 584; Lapham's Hist. of Woodstock, Me., 707; Waterford, Me., Centen., 244; Barbour's My Wife and Mother, App., 56; Moore's Amer. Governors, vol. I, 273, 294, 402; Heraldic Journal, vol. I, 185; Davis' Hist. of Wallingford, Conn., 741; Neally Chart; Strong Gen., 756; Smith Gen., (1890), 189; Ruggle's Gen.; N. E. Hist. and Gen. Reg., vol. I, 71; X, 130; Amer. Ancestry, IV, 146; VII, 166; VIII, 11, 26; Savage's Gen. Dict., II, 75; Dudley Gen.

DUDSON:—Francis Dudson, of Boston, by wife Martha, had Samuel, 1675; and Martha, 1679.

JOSEPH DUDSON, of Boston, married Abigail, daughter of Robert Button, had Joseph, 1669; Robert, 1672; and Abigail, 1676. His widow married 1698, Barnabas Lothrop.

REFERENCES:—Savage's Gen. Dict., II, 78.

DUE. Hayward's Hancock, N. H., 532.

DUEL. Ely Gen., 188.

DUEY. Butz Gen., 4, 16.

DUFF. Powers' Hist. of Sangamon County, Ill., 269.

DUFFIE. Green's Todd Gen.

DUFFIELD. Martindale's Hist. of Byberry, Pa., 284; Duffield's Golden Wedding; Green's Todd Gen.; 122; Davis' Hist. of Bucks County, Pa.; 203; Neill's Ancestry of Henry Neill.

DUGALL or DOUGALL:—Alister Dugall, of Lynn,

perhaps a Scotch prisoner from the field of Dunbar, 1650, or of Worcester, the year following, sent over and sold here; and one of the very few who lived to bring up a family; by wife Hannah, had James, 1660; John, 1663; Joseph, 1668; Mary, 1671; Elizabeth, 1676; Allen, 1679; and Samuel, 1682.

REFERENCES.—Savage's Gen. Dict., II, 78.

DUGGAN. Temple's Hist. of North Brookfield, Mass., 580.

DUHAMEL. Amer. Ancestry, IX, 66.

DUGE. Richmond, Va., Standard, III, 20; Paxton's Marshall Gen., 178, 282; Prescott's Page Gen., 209; Green's Kentucky Families.

DULANY. Meade's Old Families of Va.

DUMBLETON:—John Dumbleton, of Springfield, 1649, came in the service of William Whiting, of Hartford, had John, 1658; and Nathaniel, 1664; besides six daughters who all married.

REFERENCES:—Savage's Gen. Dict., II, 79.

DUMARESQ. Heraldic Journal, III, 97; Amer. Ancestry, VI, 170; N. E. Hist. and Gen. Reg., XVII, 316; Dumaresq Gen.

DUMAS. Temple's Hist. of North Brookfield, Mass., 580.

DUMMER:—Richard Dummer, of Newbury, born about 1599, at Bishopstoke, Hantshire, second son of John, came in the "Whale," from Southampton, arrived 1632, and he first sat down at Roxbury, built a mill there 1633, freeman 1632, removed a short while to Boston, at the desire of his wife Mary, who died in a few years, and he then removed to Newbury with early settlers, was Assistant 1635 and 6, favored Wheelwright, and was turned out and disarmed 1637, and soon went home, came again 1638, in the "Bevis," from Southampton, then called 40 years old, with brothers and other relatives; was representative 1640, 5 and 7; married for second wife 1644, Frances, widow of Rev. Jonathan Burr of Dorchester, who died 1682, aged 70, had Jeremiah, 1645; Hannah, 1647; Richard, 1650; and William, 1639; died 1678. By former wife had Shubael, 1636.

STEPHEN DUMMER, of Newbury, brother of Richard, came in the "Bevis," from Southampton, 1638, by wife whose name was also Alice Archer, aged 35; and children Jane, 10; Dorothy, 6; Richard, 4; and Thomas, 2; freeman 1639; had Mehitable, 1640. He went home 1647.

THOMAS DUMMER, of Salisbury, brother of the preceding. came with him in the "Bevis," with Joan Dummer, who may have been his wife, age 19; had Joanna; freeman 1640.

REFERENCES:—Hammatt Papers of Ipswich, Mass., 83; Coffin's Hist. of Newbury, Mass., 301; Essex Inst. Hist. Coll., XXI, 77; Heraldic Journal, II, 34; Salisbury Family Memorial, vol. I, 215; North's Hist. of Augusta, Me., 849; N. E. Hist. and Gen. Reg., XXXV, 254, 321; Savage's Gen. Dict., II, 79; Cleveland's Dummer Academy; Dummer Academy Anniv.; Chester's Dummer Gen.

DUMOND. Schoonmaker's Hist. of Kingston, N. Y., 479; Sylvester's Hist. of Ulster County, N. Y., 102; Amer. Ancestry, VI, 12.

DU MONT. Sylvester's Hist. of Ulster County, N.

Y., 102; Life of Rachel Du Mont, 93.

DUNBAR:—Peter Dunbar, of Hingham, married 1691, daughter of John Cushing, had Elisha and others. ROBERT DUNBAR, of Hingham. had John, born 1657; and perhaps others.

REFERENCES.

MASSACHUSETTS.—Mitchell's Hist. of Bridgewater, 147; Temple's Hist. of Palmer, 144; Washburn's Hist. of Leicester, 358; Davis' Landmarks of Plymouth, 95; Hobart's Hist. of Abington, 366; Deane's Hist. of Scituate, 264; Kingman's Hist. of North Bridgewater, 181; Barry's Hist. of Hanover, 295.

NEW HAMPSHIRE.—Livermore's Hist. of Wilton, 362; Hayward's Hist. of Hancock, 533; Dow's Hist. of Hampton, 695.

OTHER PUBLICATIONS.—Miliken's Naraguagus Valley, Me., 17; Eaton's Annals of Warren, Me., 537; Eaton's Hist. of Thomaston, Me., II, 205; Munsell's Albany Coll., IV, 119; Salisbury's Memorials; Pearson's Schenectady, N. Y., Settlers, 63; Orcutt's Hist. of Torrington, Conn., 685; Slaughter's St. Mark's Parish, Va., 175; Welles' American Family Antiquities, Whitman Gen.; Winslow Gen.

DUNCAN:—Jabez Duncan, a soldier of Philip's war, of Capt. Turner's company, 1676.

JOSEPH DUNCAN, killed by the Indians, 1689.

NATHANIEL DUNCAN, of Dorchester, 1630, came, doubtless, in the "Mary and John," with the other first settlers of that town, freeman 1635, artillery company 1638, a captain, auditor general and representative, skilled in Latin and French, brought, perhaps, wife Elizabeth, son Nathaniel, also had Peter, removed to Boston about 1646, and died about 1668.

REFERENCES.

MASSACHUSETTS.—Chase's Hist. of Haverhill, 628; Barry's Hist. of Hanover, 295; Temple's Hist. of North Brookfield, 580; Babson's Hist. of Gloucester, 82.

NEW HAMPSHIRE.—Smith's Hist. of Petersborough, 60; Cochrane's Hist. of Antrim, 468; Hayward's Hist. of Hancock, 534; Merrill's Hist. of Acworth, 212; Parker's Hist. of Londonderry, 269; Eaton's Hist. of Candia, 65.

OTHER PUBLICATIONS.—Eaton's Hist. of Thomaston, Me., II, 206; Heminway's Vermont Gazeteer, V, 92; Powers' Hist. of Sangamon County, Ill., 270; Bartow Gen., 140; Amer. Ancestry, IX, 144; Savage's Gen. Dict., I, 80.

DUNKLE. Hazen's Hist. of Billerica, 42.

DUNCKLEE. Wyman's Charlestown, Mass., Gens., 570; Secomb's Hist. of Amherst, 570.

DUNDORE. Dundore Gen.

DUNEN or DUNNIN:—Jonathan Dunen, alias Singletary, Killingworth 1665, had Ruth, 1666; Eunice, 1668; and probably removed.

REFERENCES:—Savage's Gen. Dict., II, 81.

DUNGAN. Austin's Allied Families, 86; Austin's R. I. Dict., 67; Davis' Hist. of Buck's County, Pa., 359.

DUNFORD:—John Dunford, of Plymouth, 1639.

REFERENCES:—Savage's Gen. Dict., II, 81.

DUNGIN:—Thomas Dungin, of Newport, 1651, in Dr. Stiles's list of freemen there 1656.

REFERENCES:—Savage's Gen. Dict., II, 81.

DUNHAM:—Beniah Dunham, of Eastham, married 1660, Elizabeth Tilson, had Edmund, 1661; John, 1663; Elizabeth, 1664; Hannah, 1666; and Benjamin, 1667.

BENJAMIN DUNHAM, of Eastham, probably brother of Beniah, married 1660, Mary Tilson.

JOHN DUNHAM, of Plymouth, 1633, representative 1639, and often after, was deacon, among the first purchasers of Dartmouth; had wife Abigail, sons John, Beniah and Daniel, perhaps born in England; and died 1669, aged 80. He may have had a daughter Persis. His will mentions also son-in-law Stephen Wood. Persis married Benjah Pratt, 1655.

JOHN DUNHAM, of Woburn, had Patience, 1645.

JONATHAN DUNHAM, of Barnstable, married 1655, Mary, daughter of Philip Delano, who died early, and he married 1657, Mary, daughter of Henry Cobb, was representative 1689, for Middleborough, and served among the islands as minister to the Indians, but was 1694 at Edgartown.

JOSEPH DUNHAM, of Plymouth, married 1657, Mercy, daughter of Secretary Morton, who died 1667; and he married 1669, Esther Wormall.

THOMAS DUNHAM, of Plymouth, fit to bear arms 1643, married Martha, daughter of George Knott, I think.

REFERENCES.

MAINE.—Lapham's Hist. of Woodstock, 210; Hanson's Hist. of Gardiner, 158; Lapham's Hist. of Norway, 495; Lapham's Hist. of Paris, 585.

OTHER PUBLICATIONS.—Davis' Landmarks of Plymouth. Mass., 96; Hobart's Hist. of Abington. Mass., 367; Hyde's Hist. of Brimfield, Mass., 326; Bass' Hist. of Braintree, Vt., 130; Andrews' Hist. of New Britain, Conn., 157, 282; Timlow's Sketches of Southington, Conn., 84; Sedgwick's Hist. of Sharon, Conn., 77; Littell's Passaic Valley Gens., 146; Pompey, N. Y., Reunion, 301; Loomis' Gen. Female Branches, 515; Spooner Gen., vol. I, 392; Amer. Ancestry, vol. I, 23; II, 35; Savage's Gen. Dict., II, 80.

DUNK or DUNCK:—Thomas Dunk, of Guilford, 1645, Saybrook 1662, was from Kent, England, had brother John there, married Mary, widow of Thomas North, of New Haven, who had been widow of Philip Petersfield, and was a daughter of Walter Price, County Surrey, and had come to New Haven about 1644. She went to England and probably died there. He married 1677, Elizabeth Stedman, had Thomas, 1678; and his wife died same year; he died 1683.

REFERENCES:—Savage's Gen. Dict., II, 80.

DUNKIN:—John Dunkin, of Billerica, 1675, had two sons killed by the Indians, 1692.

SAMUEL DUNKIN, of Newbury, 1638, perhaps removed to Boston, had there besides other children, Thomas, 1656; and in 1672 had land in Muddy River, now Brookline. Samuel of Roxbury, probably his son.

REFERENCES:—Savage's Gen. Dict., II, 81.

DUNKELEE. Hudson's Hist. of Lexington. Mass., 59; Hayward's Hist. of Hancock. N. H., 543; Dunney Gen.; Caverly's Hist. of Pittsford, 700.

DUNLAP. Wheeler's Hist. of Brunswick, Me., 832; Chase's Hist. of Chester, N. H., 513; Cochrane's Hist. of Antrim, N. H., 476; Caverley's Hist. of Pittsford, Vt., 700; Orcutt's Hist. of Stratford, Conn., 1195; Powers' Hist. of Sangamon County, Ill., 272; Miller's Hist. of Colchester, N. S., 111.

DUNN:—Richard Dunn, of Newport, freeman 1655, Westerly, 1661.

THOMAS DUNN, of Weymouth, freeman of Mass. 1647, removed to Rehoboth, and soon to New Haven, there swore fidelity in March, 1648, next year bought estate at Fairfield, there died 1660, without wife or child and gave his property to Rev. John Jones.

REFERENCES:—Swift's Barnstable Families, vol. I, 348; Temple's Hist. of North Brookfield, Mass., 581; Eaton's Hist. of Thomaston, Me., II, 206; Temple's Hist. of North Brookfield, Mass., 581; Norton's Hist. of Fitzwilliam, N. H., 543; Austin's R. I. Gen. Dict., 68; Buxton, Me., Centen., 173; Powers' Hist. of Sangamon County, Ill., 272; Meginnes Hist., II, 24, 175; Amer. Ancestry, IX, 173; Savage's Gen. Dict., vol. II, 80.

DUNNELL. Buxton, Me., Centen., 168; Bartlett's Wanton Family, 137; Dunnel Gen.

DUNNING:—George Dunning, of New Haven, 1644, removed soon.

HICKS DUNNING, of Hingham, married 1669, Sarah, daughter of Thomas Joy, had Edmund, 1672; but in the will of Joy is called Dunham or Denham.

JONATHAN DUNNING, a soldier in Turner's company 1676.

REFERENCES:—Wheeler's Hist. of Brunswick, Me., 832; Eaton's Hist. of Thomaston, Me., II, 207; Bangor Hist. Mag., VI, 35; Stickney's Hist. of Minisinck, N. Y., 120; Sprague's Hist. of Gloversville, N. Y., 115; Amer. Ancestry, VI, 171; Savage's Gen. Dict., vol. II, 81.

DUNNY:—James Dunny, of Boston, was admitted freeman 1690.

DUNSHEE. Aldrich's Hist. of Walpole, Mass., 244.

DUNSMORE. Saunderson's Hist. of Charlestown.

DUNSPAUGH. Amer. Ancestry, II, 154.

DUNSTER:—Henry Dunster, of Cambridge, first President of Harvard College, a Lancashire man, son of Henry Balehoult, came in 1640, and resided a short time in Boston, was of Artillery company 1640, was of Cambridge before admission as freeman 1641; was bred at Magdalen College, in the University of Cambridge, had his degrees 1630 and 1634. Soon after coming he was made president 1640, compelled to resign 1654, on account of his opinions on infant baptism. He was desired to come to Ireland by the deputy Henry Cromwell and his council, and 50 pounds sterling advanced for his passage, but he was wise enough to avoid this evil, and died at Scituate, 1659, where he preached all his latter days; but his heart's desire was to be buried at Cambridge, where, in his will, he says lay the remains of some of his babes. He names as living, two sons David and Jonathan, daughter Elizabeth, sister Hills, wife of Joseph of Malden, sister Willard of Concord, and cousin Faith Dunster. His first wife Elizabeth married 1641, died 1643; and next he married 1644, Elizabeth, widow of Rev. Josse Glover, had David, 1645; Dorothy, 1648; Henry, 1650; Jonathan, 1653; and Elizabeth, 1656. Elizabeth, his widow died 1690.

RICHARD DUNSTER, of Cambridge, 1642, brother of Henry. His sisters were Elizabeth and Mary, and a third perhaps, Rose.

REFERENCES.

MASSACHUSETTS.—Page's Hist. of Cambridge, 537; Stearn's Hist. of Ashburnham, 688; Wyman's Charlestown Gens., vol. I, 312; Freeman's Hist. of Cape Cod, II, 523; Cutter's Hist. of Arlington.

OTHER PUBLICATIONS.—Titcomb's New England People, 82; N. E. Hist. and Gen. Reg., XXVII, 307; Life of Henry Dunster; Dunster Genealogy; Savage's Gen. Dict., vol. II, 81.

DUNTON:—John Dunton, of Reading, freeman 1691.

NATHANIEL DUNTON, of Reading.

ROBERT DUNTON, of Reading, 1647, perhaps father of two preceding.

SAMUEL DUNTON, of Reading, perhaps son or brother of the preceding, died 1683, had Samuel, 1647; Hannah, 1650; Nathaniel, 1656; Elizabeth, 1658; Sarah, 1660: and Mary, 1662.

REFERENCES:—Norton's Hist. of Fitzwilliam, N. H., 543; Barry's Hist. of Framingham, Mass., 226; Eaton's Hist. of Reading, Mass., 63; Cleveland's Hist. of Yates County, N. Y., 378; Savage's Gen. Dict., vol. II, 81.

DUNTZ. Amer. Ancestry, II, 35.

DUNWOODIE. Bullock Gen.; Amer. Ancestry, VI, 62, 115.

DU PONT. Biography of Rev. William Smith; Amer. Ancestry, III, 180.

DUPUY. Whittemore's Heroes of the Revolution and their Descendants; History of Dutchess County; Watkins' Gen., 25; Meade's Old Churches of Virginia. vol. I, 467; Virginia Hist. Coll., V, 151; Goode Gen., 173; Amer. Ancestry, VII, 263; VIII, 197; X, 29.

DURAND:—John Durand, of Scituate, 1547. A John Duren, who may be the same, was of New Hampshire, 1689.

WILLIAM DURAND, of Boston, 1644, is the member of our church who went to Virginia, perhaps was ruling Elder of a Congregational church there, disturbed and banished by Sir William Berkeley, the Governor, came to Boston again, 1648.

REFERENCES:—Sharpe's Hist. of Seymour, Conn., 159; Orcutt's Hist. of Derby, Conn., 718; Adams' Hist. of Fairhaven, Vt., 348; Amer. Ancestry, VII, 227; IX, 109; Savage's Gen. Dict., II, 81.

DURANT:—George Durant, of Malden, removed about 1666, to Middletown, died about 1690, had Edward.

JOHN DURANT, of Billerica, 1675, died in prison at Cambridge, 1692, during the witchcraft delusion, of which he was probably a victim.

MOSES DURANT, of Falmouth, 1690.

REFERENCES:—Temple's Hist. of Palmer, Mass., 443; Jackson's Hist. of Newton, Mass., 268; Hazen's Hist. of Billerica, Mass., 43; Secomb's Hist. of Amherst, N. H., 573; Amer. Ancestry, vol. I, 25; Savage's Gen. Dict., II, 81.

DURDALL:—Hugh Durdall, was of Newport, 1639; Savage's Gen. Dict., II, 82.

DURELL:—Nicholas Durrell was a soldier in Turner's company, 1676.

REFERENCES:—Lapham's Hist. of Paris, Me., 590; Jackson's Hist. of Newton, Mass., 270; Wentworth Gen., II, 101.

DUREN:—Andrew Duren, of Dedham, had Henry and five other children, perhaps by a daughter of John Hayward, who gives in his will to each of them, but most to Henry.

GEORGE DUREN, of Lyme, 1685, but in 1687 his widow is called Mary Durine, probably the same name, perhaps as second or third wife, was married 1678, perhaps had Edward.

REFERENCES:—Hudson's Hist. of Lexington, Mass., 60; Locke Gen., 96; Amer. Ancestry, VII, 5; Savage's Gen. Dict., II, 83.

DURFEE:—Thomas Durfee, of whom I see only the name before 1692, but know not residence, perhaps only transient, in 1679 was 36 years old.

REFERENCES:—Fowler's Hist. of Fall River, Mass., 67; Davis' Landmarks of Plymouth, Mass., 98; Peek's Fall River, Mass., Industries, 261; Turner's Philps Purchase, 382; Austin's R. I. Gen. Dict., 68; Austin's Ancestries, 19; Walker Gen., 155; Amer. Ancestry, IX, 121; Savage's Gen. Dict., II, 84.

DURGEE. Babson's Hist. of Gloucester, Mass., 82.

DURGIN, DURGY or DIRGEY:—Of Portsmouth, 1684.

JOHN DURGIN, of Ipswich, had John, 1689; and Andrew, 1692.

WILLIAM DURGIN, of Dover, 1664, was with a wife Martha, daughter of Robert Cross, at Ipswich, had Martha, 1668, probably went back to New Hampshire, there lived 1684.

REFERENCES:—Lancaster's Hist. of Gilmartin, N. H., 261; Runnel's Hist. of Sanbornton, N. H., 281; Coggswell's Hist. of Nottingham, N. H., 681; Coffin's Hist. of Boscawen, N. H., 520; Dearborn's Hist. of Parsonfield, Me., 378; Farrow's Hist. of Isleborough, Me., 200; Savage's Gen. Dict., II, 83.

DURHAM:—Humphrey Durham, of Casco, 1658, was killed by the Indians, 1676.

JOHN DURHAM, of Falmouth, about 1690, was, perhaps, son of the preceding.

THOMAS DURHAM, of Marshfield, married 1659, Sarah, daughter of Edward Bumpas.

REFERENCES:—Williamson's Hist. of Belfast, Me., 93; Cleveland's Hist. of Yates County, N. Y., 472; Champion Gen.; Savage's Gen. Dict., II, 88.

DURKEE. Wheeler's Hist. of Newport, N. H., 371; Hammatt Papers, Ipswich, Mass., 84; Walworth Hyde Gen., 92; Amer. Ancestry, III, 15; Savage's Gen. Dict., II, 83.

DURLAND. Stickney's Hist. of Minisink, N. Y., 172.

DURPEE. Wheeler's Hist. of Newport, N. H.

DURRANT. Brown's Bedford, Mass., Families.

DURREL. Bradbury's Hist. of Kennebunkport.

DURRIE. Durrie's Steel Gen., 41.

DURREN, DURRIN or DURRUM:—Ephraim Durren, of Guilford, 1672, married 1678, Elizabeth, daughter of Richard Guttridge, had Daniel, 1680; and probably others. Sometimes the name is Darwin. He was a proprietor 1685. Possibly the name is the same as Duren.

REFERENCES:—Savage's Gen. Dict., II, 84.

DURYEA. Bunker's L. I. Genealogies, 200; Bergen's Kings County, N. Y., Settlers, 103; Amer. Ancestry, IX, 77; X, 187; N. Y.Hist. and Biog. Rec., X, 62.

DUSINBURY. Baird's Hist. of Rye, N. Y., 461; Amer. Ancestry, II, 35.

DUSTAN. Clute's Hist. of Staten Island, 377.

DUSTIN or DUSTON:—Josiah Dustin, of Reading, 1647, had Josiah, 1656; perhaps others, died 1672.

THOMAS DUSTIN, of Dover, 1640, perhaps removed to Kittery, before 1652.

THOMAS DUSTIN, of Haverhill, perhaps son of the preceding, married 1677, Hannah Emerson, had thirteen children before 1699, the youngest, Martha, was killed by the Indians, who carried away the mother and nurse, and the mother killed ten of the Indian family who had charge of these prisoners, with an English youth, Samuel Leonardson.

REFERENCES:—Runnel's Hist. of Sanbornton, N. H., 243; Eaton's Hist. of Candia, N. H., 66; Cochrane's Hist. of Antrim, N. H., 481; Chase's Hist. of Chester, N. H., 513; Hayward's Hist. of Hancock, N. H., 544; Corliss' Gen.

DUSTON. Morrison's Hist. of Windham, N. H., 520; Lapham's Hist. of Bethel, Me., 520; Coggswell's Hist. of Henniker, 552.

DUTCH:—Osman Dutch, of Gloucester, 1646, by ably daughter of Walter Roper, had John, 1646; Robert, and perhaps other children; and died 1684, aged 100 or more. He had been admitted inhabitant of Newport, 1638, and there probably Esther was born, and perhaps other children.

ROBERT DUTCH, of Gloucester, by wife Mary, probably daughter of Walter Ruper, had John, 1646; Robert, 1647; Samuel, 1650; and others it is believed: removed to Ipswich, where he had Caleb, 1659; and Benjamin, 1665. He died 1686.

THOMAS DUTCH, of Edgartown, 1654.

REFERENCES:—Hammatt Papers, Ipswich, Mass., 81; Babson's Hist. of Gloucester, Mass., 83; Dearborn's Hist. of Parsonfield, Me., 378; Savage's Gen. Dict., II, 84.

DUTCHER. Ballou's Hist. of Milford, Mass., 723; Raymond's Tarrytown Monument, 89.

DUTCHFIELD or DITCHFIELD: — Thomas Dutchfield, Boston, 1644, by wife Ann, had Joan, 1644. He died, or was buried 1645, and his son was born 1645, named Posthumus.

REFERENCES:—Savage's Gen. Dict., II, 84.

DUTTON:—John Dutton, came in 1630, but I know not where he sat down.

THOMAS DUTTON, perhaps son of John, born about 1621, had first lived at Reading, there had by wife Susan, it is thought, Thomas, 1648; Mary, 1651; Susanna, 1654; John, 1656; but the following probably at Woburn, Elizabeth, 1659; Joseph, 1661; Sarah, 1662;

James, 1665; Benjamin, 1669; removed to Billerica, and his wife died 1684, aged 58; he married same year Ruth Hooper.

REFERENCES.

MASSACHUSETTS.—Temple's Hist. of Palmer, 445; Temple's Hist. of Northfield, 435; Stearn's Hist. of Ashburnham, 683; Hodgman's Hist. of Westford, 445; Hazen's Hist. of Billerica, 45; Brown's Bedford, Mass., Families, 9.

OTHER PUBLICATIONS.—Timlow's Hist. of Southington, Conn.; Davis' Hist. of Wallingford, Conn., 741; Stearns' Hist. of Rindge, N. H., 510; Hill's Hist. of Mason, N. H., 201; Hayward's Hist. of Hancock, N. H., 545; Heminway's Vermont Gazeteer, V, 41, 213; Martin's Hist. of Chester, Pa., 247, 251; Bass' Hist. of Braintree, Vt., 131; Powers' Hist. of Sangamon County, Ill., 273; Douglass Gen., 209; Dutton Gen., (1871); Maris Gen., 60, 130; Savage's Gen. Dict., II, 84.

DUTY:—William Duty, of Rowley, 1691; Savage's Gen. Dict., II, 84.

DU VAIL. N. Y. Gen. and Biog. Rec, XXII, 105.

DUYCKINCK. N. Y. Gen. and Biog. Rec., XXIII, 33; Bergen's Kings County Gens., N. Y., 105.

DWELLEY:—Richard Dwelley, of Lancaster, 1654, but perhaps he had been at Watertown, lived some years at Hingham, in 1663, removed to Scituate, served with credit in Philip's war, and died 1692. Beside Mary, baptized 1664, he had Richard, Samuel and John.

REFERENCES:—Winsor's Hist. of Duxbury, Mass., 287; Barry's Hist. of Hanover, Mass., 296; Deane's Hist. of Scituate, Mass., 265; Savage's Gen. Dict., vol. II, 85.

DWIGHT:—John Dwight, of Watertown, removed to Dedham, 1635, freeman 1639, had brought wife Hannah, who died 1656, and some children from England, John, Hannah and Timothy. He had Mary, 1635; and Sarah, 1638. In his will he names wife Elizabeth, (married 1658, widow of William Ripley, and had been widow of Thomas Thaxter, and died 1680), and only son Timothy and the three daughters.

TIMOTHY DWIGHT, perhaps brother of John, of Dedham, at Hampton, 1640, freeman 1641, representative 1652 for Medfield, where he resided many years, died 1677. In his will he names wife Dorcas, daughter of John Watson, of Roxbury, and children Timothy and John.

WILLIAM DWIGHT, of Ipswich, 1668.

REFERENCES.

MASSACHUSETTS.—Temple's Hist. of North Brookfield, 582; Stearns' Hist. of Ashburnham, 684; Long Meadow, Mass., Centen., 58; Benedict's Hist. of Sutton, 638; Chandler's Hist. of Shirley, 391; Doolittle's Hist. of Belchertown, 260.

OTHER PUBLICATIONS.—Larned's Hist. of Windham County, Conn.; Eaton's Hist. of Thomaston, Me., II, 207; Tuttle Family of Conn., 409; Strong Gen., 365, 402; Goodwin's Gen. Notes, 40; Amer. Ancestry, vol. I, 26; IV, 232, 244; IX, 57; N. Y. Gen. and Biog. Rec., XVII, 23; Savage's Gen. Dict., II, 85; Dwight Gen.

DWINNELL, DUENNELL or DUNNELL:—Michael Dwinnell, of Topsfield, 1668, by wife Mary, had Mary, 1669; Michael, 1670; Thomas, 1672; John, 1674;

Elizabeth, 1677; Magdalen, 1679; Joseph, 1681; Joanna, 1685; and Susanna, 1690.

REFERENCES:—Lapham's Hist. of Rumford, Me., 316; Savage's Gen. Dict., vol. II, 87.

DWINNEL. Poor's Hist. of Merrimac Valley, 117; Benedict's Hist. of Sutton, Mass., 638; Dunnel and Durnnel Gen., (1862); Savage's Gen. Dict., vol. II, 87.

DYAMONT:—Andrew Dyamont, of Maine, perhaps Kittery, authorized in 1680, to hold courts at Isle of Shoals, where he lived in 1671.

JOHN DYAMONT, of Kittery, 1658. The name may be same as Dimon.

REFERENCES:—Savage's Gen. Dict., II, 87.

DYCKMAN. Riker's Hist. of Harlem, N. Y., 505; Bolton's Hist. of Westchester County, N. Y., 727; Munsell's Albany Coll., IV, 119; N. Y. Gen. and Biog. Rec., XXIV, 81.

DYE. Young's Hist. of Chautauqua, N. Y., 581; Joslin's Hist. of Poultney, Vt., 254; Green Gen.

DYER:—Benjamin Dyer, of Boston, freeman 1675, his wife died 1690, her name was Mary, and he may have been son of Thomas.

GEORGE DYER, of Dorchester, sat on the jury at Court of Assistants, September, 1630, and may well be presumed to have come on the "Mary and John," requested admission as freeman and sworn October and May following. Constable 1632, had wife Elizabeth, daughters Elizabeth and Mary.

GILES DYER, of Boston, artillery company 1660, by wife Hannah, had Giles, 1674; Mary, 1677; Elizabeth, Hannah, 1683; and Giles, 1685. He was a Colonel and Sheriff of the Company, died 1713.

JOHN DYER, came in the "Christian," at the age of 28, 1635, and two years after served in the Pequot war. He probably settled at New London, before 1650, and soon after went to Long Island, where he was in 1659.

THOMAS DYER, of Weymouth, cloth-worker, said to have come as early as 1632, married Agnes Reed, who died 1667, had Mary, 1641; John, 1643; Thomas, 1645; Abigail, 1647; Sarah, 1649; Thomas, 1651; and Joseph and Benjamin, twins, 1653; was freeman 1644, representative 1646 and four years more, was deacon, and died 1676, aged 63. His widow was named Elizabeth in her will.

WILLIAM DYER, of Boston, 1635, who wrote the name Dyre, was a milliner, from London, by wife Mary, had Samuel, 1635, husband and wife united with the church 1636, next year was disarmed as a supporter of Wheelwright, defranchised, and 1638, driven to Rhode Island. Other children were William, Henry, Mahershallalhasbaz, and Charles. At Newport, he was in good esteem, Secretary of that colony, and prevailed with the government of ours in 1659, when his wife had come to Boston to preach Quakerism, and was condemned to die therefor to spare her life; but the insane desire of martyrdom led the poor woman back here in 1660 to the scaffold; serving to show how useless was the unnatural lenity of Endicott, who knew well what the honor of God demanded.

WILLIAM DYER, of Dorchester, died 1672, aged 93.

WILLIAM DYER, of Lynn, had Mary, 1673; and James, 1681.

WILLIAM DYER, of Boston, surveyor of the customs and searcher of the port 1680.

WILLIAM DYER, of Barnstable, married 1686, Mary Taylor, had Lydia, 1688; William, 1690; Jonathan, 1692; Henry, 1693; Isabel. 1695; Ebenezer, 1697; Samuel, 1698; and Judah, 1701.

REFERENCES.

MASSACHUSETTS.—Mitchell's Hist. of Bridgewater, 150; Rich's Hist. of Truro, 525; Swift's Barnstable Families, vol. I, 346; Wyman's Charlestown, Mass., Gen., vol. I, 315; Hobart's Hist. of Abbington, Mass., 372; Freeman's Hist. of Cape Cod, II, 551; Dyer's Hist. of Plainfield; Barry's Hist. of Hanover, 300; Davis Landmarks of Plymouth, 99.

OTHER PUBLICATIONS.—Runnell's Hist. of Sanbornton, N. H., II, 248; Eaton's Hist. of Thomaston, Me., II, 268; Bass' Hist. of Braintree, Vt., 131; Milliken's Narraguagus Valley, Me., 8; Brown's West Simsbury, Conn., Settlers, 57; Austin's R. I. Gen. Dict., 290; Austin's Ancestries, 21; Olin's Oliver Gen., 71; Poole Gen., 89; Amer. Ancestry, vol. I, 26; IV, 20, 52; Savage's Gen. Dict., II, 88; Dyer Gen.

DYKE. Davis' Landmarks of Plymouth, 85; Jackson's Hist. of Newton, Mass., 271; Mitchell's Hist. of Bridgewater, Mass., 146.

DYMOND. Savage's Gen. Dict., II, 88.

DYNN. Driver Gen., 281.

DYSON. Slaughter's Bristol Parish, 7.

— H —

EADER. Richmond Standard, III, 31.

EAGER. Worcester Mag. and Hist. Journal, vol. II, 152; Ward's Hist. of Shrewsbury, Mass., 272; Paige's Hist. of Cambridge, Mass., 539; Hudson's Hist. of Marlborough, Mass., 355; Pierce's Hist. of Gosham, Me., 163; Caulkin's Hist. of Norwich, Conn., 174; Coggswell's Hist. of Henniker, N. H., 555; Hayward's Hist. of Gilsum, N. H., 303; Eager's Hist. of Orange County, N. Y., 302; Eager and Davis' Charts, 1859.

EAGLE. Egle's Penn. Gens., 129.

EAGLEY. Egle's Penn. Gens., 691.

EAMES or EMMES:—Anthony Eames, of Charlestown, 1634, Hingham, 1636, freeman 1637, representative that year and the following, and 1643; was lieutenant, and about his choice as captain grew the fierce controversy that long convulsed the colony, removed to Marshfield and was representative in Plymouth Colony most of the time between 1653-61 inclusive, perhaps was father of John and of Mark. He had daughter Margery, and probably Justus, another son.

GERSHOM EAMES, of Marlborough, by wife Hannah, had Hannah, 1671; and Mary posthumous, 1677. He died 1676. His widow was daughter of Solomon Johnson and married, 1679, William Ward. He died 1676.

HENRY EAMES, of Boston, messenger of the General Court, freeman 1684, by wife Elizabeth, had William, 1674; John, Mary, Benjamin, Henry, Samuel, Nathaniel, baptized 1690; and Elizabeth, 1695.

JOHN EAMES, of Woburn, married 1650, Martha, perhaps daughter of Captain Edward Johnson, had Mary, 1650; and probably removed.

RICHARD EAMES, of Rowley, 1680.

ROBERT EAMES, of Woburn, had been of Charlestown,

1651, had wife Elizabeth, and children Samuel, 1653; John, 1654; Elizabeth, 1659; Mary, 1661; Priscilla, 1663; Samuel, 1664; Abigail, 1666; and John, 1668; removed to Chelmsford and died 1671.

ROBERT EAMES, of Andover, by wife Rebecca, had Hannah, 1661; Daniel, 1663; Robert, 1667; John, 1670; Dorothy, 1674; Jacob, 1677; Joseph, 1681; and Nathan, 1685. Commonly this family has spelt the names Ames.

THOMAS EAMES, of Dedham, by wife Margaret, had John, 1642; Mary, 1645; John, 1640; and probably other children. His wife died and he removed to Cambridge, married about 1662, Mary, widow of Jonathan Paddleford, had Thomas, 1663, removed to Sudbury, freeman 1665, there had Samuel, 1665; Margaret, 1666; Nathaniel, 1668; removed to Sherborn, had Sarah, 1670; and Lydia, 1672; he died 1680; his wife was killed by the Indians, 1676, and some children carried away captive. Sometimes name is spelled Emes.

REFERENCES.

MASSACHUSETTS.—Sewall's Hist. of Woburn, 609; Hudson's Hist. of Marlborough, 357; Ballou's Hist. of Milford, 726; Perley's Hist. of Boxford, 80; Paige's Hist. of Cambridge, 539; Barry's Hist. of Framingham, 227; Keyes' West Boylston Reg., 17; Kingman's Hist. of North Bridgewater, 496; Morse's Gen. of Sherborn, 79; Mitchell's Hist. of Bridgewater, 105.

MAINE.—Farrow's Hist. of Isleborough, 201; Butler's Hist. of Farmington, 461; Lapham's Hist. of Bethel, 521; Bangor Hist. Mag., V, 47.

OTHER PUBLICATIONS.—Reade's Hist. of Swanzey, N. H., 330; Brown's West Simsbury, Conn., Settlers, 69; Adams' Haven Gen., vol. I, 38; II, 24; Leland Gen., 27; Amer. Ancestry, vol. I, 26; Savage's Gen. Dict., II, 89; Morse Mem. Appendix, 50; Wight Gen., 104.

EARL. Stearns' Hist. of Rindge, N. H., 511; Cleveland's Hist. of Yates County, N. Y., 179.

EARLE:—Francis Earle, a soldier, 1675, in Moseley's company at the great Narragansett swamp fight.

JOHN EARLE, of Northampton, 1662, had come to Boston, 1656, aged 17, in the "Speedwell," from London, at Northampton, about 15 years, removed to unknown place, after having there married 1663, Mary, daughter of first John Webb, and had Noah, John and three daughters, of whom Mary was, perhaps, one. He may have been one of the Townsmen of Dartmouth, in 1686, or it may have been son of same name.

RALPH EARLE, of Rhode Island, 1638, among freeman 1655, had been admitted an inhabitant 1639, perhaps had sons Ralph, Thomas and William; and it is mentioned in Church's Indian wars. But in 1686, there were both Ralph, sen. and jr., among townsmen at Dartmouth, it may be doubted which of the two he meant. One, not the jr., is called the son of William. I think Ralph. of Portsmouth. R. I. 1638. that purchased 1653, of Underhill his conquest at Hartford, (from the Dutch suspicions soon after the exploit), was he who made his will 1673, naming wife Joan executrix.

ROBERT EARLE, of Boston, 1679. kept the prison 1681, and several years after; died 1698.

ROBERT EARLE, of Newport, had come in the "Hercules," I suppose, 1643, to some part of Mass., was born 1606, it is said, yet had wife in 1699, living at age of 105, however unlikely that she was so many years older. There were Roger and Samuel at Boston, 1695, of which the latter died 1706, aged 34.

WILLIAM EARLE, of Dartmouth, 1673, had Ralph, and was, perhaps, brother of Ralph the first, or he may have been his son.

REFERENCES:—Washburn's Hist. of Leicester, Mass., 359; Temple's Hist. of North Brookfield, Mass., 582; Stone's Hist. of Hubbardston, Mass., 262; Clayton's Hist. of Bergen County, N. J., 247; Amer. Ancestry, III, 168; VII, 65; XI, 100; Austin's R. I. Gen. Dict., 69; Savage's Gen. Dict., II, 91; Earle Gen.; Earl Chart. EARLL. Hughes' Gen., 201.

EARLY:—George Early, of Salem, married 1670, Abigail, daughter of Pasco Foote, had Abigail, 1671; and he died 1672.

ROBERT EARLY, who came in the "Hercules," 1634, may have reached our shore, but where he lived is not known.

REFERENCES:—Morrison's Hist. of Windham, N. H., 523; Egle's Hist. of Lebanon County, Pa.; Page Gen., 162; Savage's Gen. Dict., II, 90.

EARNEST. Power's Hist. of Sangamon County, Ill., 274.

EARTHEY. John Earthey, of Boston, was a witness to the treaty with the Indians, 1676; Savage's Gen. Dict., II, 90.

EASLEY. Power's Hist. of Sangamon County, Ill., 276.

EAST:—David East, of Boston, mariner, married Abigail, widow of Jonathan Woodbury, daughter of Henry Phillips, and administration of his estate was given her 1685. She not long after married Thomas Walter.

FRANCIS EAST, of Boston, 1636, a carpenter, freeman 1637, by wife Mary, had Samuel, 1640; Mary, 1642; Elizabeth, 1644; David, 1647; Sarah, 1649; and Daniel, 1652; he may be the man who died in 94th year; Sewall, who calls him father, puts it 1687. His last child was Rebecca, 1656.

WILLIAM EAST, of Milford, 1639, had Solomon, baptized 1648. In 1676, he had 2nd wife Mary, widow of Robert Plum, and died 1681, without children. His widow died 1708.

REFERENCES:—Savage's Gen. Dict., II, 92.

EASTEROOK. Wyman's Charlestown, Mass., Gens., vol. I, 316; Swift's Barnstable Families, vol. I, 358; Amer. Ancestry, VII, 53.

EASTLOCK. Clement's Hist. of Newtown, N. J.

EASTMAN:—Roger Eastman, an original proprietor, ancestor of all, it is believed, of the name in the land, died 1694, aged 83, and his widow Sarah, died 1698. They had John, 1640; Nathaniel, 1643; Philip, 1644; Thomas, 1646; Timothy, 1648; Joseph, 1651; Benjamin, 1653; Sarah, 1655; Samuel, 1657; and Ruth, 1662. He probably came from Southampton, 1638, on board the "Confidence," with many who sat down at Salisbury.

EASTON:—John Easton, of Hartford, had Sarah. 1670; Mary, 1672; Sarah. 1675; John, 1679; Mary, 1681; Mehitable, 1683; Abigail. 1687; and John, 1689.

JOSEPH EASTON, of Cambridge, freeman 1635, removed early to Hartford, where he had Joseph, John and perhaps other children, and was living 1685.

NICHOLAS EASTON, of Ipswich, one of the earliest settlers, a tanner, from Wales, came in the "Mary and John," 1634, freeman 1634, was representative 1635, and that year removed to Newbury, but, being a favorer of Wheelwright, was disarmed 1637, and went to Rhode Island, there in 1638, was chosen Assistant. A second wife Christian, widow of Thomas Beecher, who had been widow of Thomas Cooper of London, he married 1638, and she probably was mother of several of his children, but as she lived to 1665, we may presume that by third wife, Ann Clayton, married 1671, he had no issue. His children were John, 1621, and perhaps Daniel, Peter, Joshua, Nicholas, Mary, Patience, Elizabeth and Waite. He was President in 1672 and 3, was Governor, died 1675, aged 82. His widow Ann married Gov. Henry Bull and died 1708.

REFERENCES.

MASSACHUSETTS.—Page's Hist. of Hardwich, 308; Chase's Hist. of Haverhill, 276; Judd's Hist. of Hadley, 489.

MAINE.—Thurston's Hist. of Winthrop, 181; Lapham's Hist. of Rumford, 317; Eaton's Hist. of Thomaston, II, 208; Eaton's Annals of Warren, 538; Dennysville Centen., 103; Corliss' North Yarmouth.

NEW HAMPSHIRE.—Worcester's Hist. of Hollis, 372; Wheeler's Hist. of Newport, 373; Coffin's Hist. of Boscawen, 521; Coggswell's Hist. of Henniker, 556; Lancaster's Hist. of Gilmanton, 262; Runnel's Hist. of Sanbornton, N. H., II, 249; Secomb's Hist. of Amherst, 574; Bouton's Hist. of Concord, 645; Coggswell's Hist. of Henniker, 556.

OTHER PUBLICATIONS.—Cleveland's Hist. of Yates County, N. Y., 741; Cothren's Hist. of Woodbury, Conn., 541; Granite Monthly, V, 387; Kellog's White Gen., 47; Corliss Gen., 239; Chapman's Weeks Gen., 135; Powers' Hist. of Sangamon County, Ill., 276; Amer. Ancestry, IV, 244; VII, 187; VIII, 3; IX, 189; N. E. Hist. and Gen. Reg., XXI, 229; Savage's Gen. Dict., II, 92; Eastman Chart; Eastman Gen.

EASTOW:—William Eastow, of Newbury, freeman 1639, removed that year to Hampton, where he had representative 1644, 8 and 9, and died 1655; had Sarah, and Mary.

REFERENCES:—Austin's Ancestral Dict., 19; Austin's R. I. Gen. Dict., 292; Hammatt Papers, Ipswich, Mass., 91; Guild's (Calvin) Ancestry, 19; Locke Gen., 102; Amer. Ancestry, VIII, 167; IX, 215; Savage's Gen. Dict., II, 93.

EASTY or ESTY:—Isaac Easty, of Topsfield, 1661, perhaps son of Jeffry, freeman 1673. The name of Mary Easty, probably his wife, daughter of William Towne, tried and executed as a witch 1692, must be held in honor forever, for in her petition to Sir William Phips, the Governor, she begged not for her own life, which she knew must be vain. but only "that no more innocent blood may be shed."

JEFFRY EASTY, of Salem, 1637, had then a grant of land.

REFERENCES:—Savage's Gen. Dict., II, 93.

EASTWICK, ESTICK or ESTWICK:—Edward Eastwick, of Salem, 1640, mariner, died 1666, leaving Elizabeth, Sarah, Hannah, Esther and Edward, perhaps all by wife Elizabeth.

PHESANT EASTWICK, of Boston, 1670, of Portsmouth, 1680, was born about 1630, and wife Sarah about 15 years later. They had Nathaniel, 1682.

REFERENCES:—Savage's Gen. Dict., II, 93.

EATON:—Francis Eaton, of Plymouth, came in the "Mayflower," 1620, with wife Sarah and son Samuel, and in 1624, had Rachel. It is thought that his wife of the "Mayflower," died soon after landing, and a second wife died soon, but Bradford says that he took third wife, and had three children by her. In the division of lands 1627, this wife is called Christian, supposed to be Christian Penn, who came in the "Ann," 1623, no other in the Colony having such a name. By her he had Benjamin, 1627; and he died probably 1633, for his widow married 1634, Francis Billington.

JABEZ EATON, perhaps of Dorchester. See Heaton.

JOHN EATON, of Watertown, freeman 1636, removed to Dedham, had by wife Abigail, born there, John, 1640; and Jacob, 1642; besides other children, and died 1658, leaving John, Mary and Abigail, mentioned with their mother in his will.

JOHN EATON, of Salisbury, 1646, by wife Martha, had Esther; Thomas, 1647; Martha, 1648; Elizabeth, 1650; Ann, 1652; Sarah, 1654; Mary, 1656; Samuel, 1659; Joseph, 1661; and Ephraim, 1663; and died 1668, perhaps at Haverhill, leaving a daughter, wife of George Brown, and perhaps Ruth.

JOHN EATON, of Salisbury, by wife Mary, had Mary, 1685; James, 1691; Samuel, 1692; perhaps Martha, 1695; and Jonathan, 1698.

JOHN EATON, of Reading, by wife Elizabeth, married 1669, had Thomas, 1661; and Elizabeth, 1662; perhaps other children, freeman 1677.

JOHN EATON, of Haverhill, had a daughter who married 1660 or 70, James Davis, of the same.

JONAS EATON, of Watertown, removed to Reading, by wife Grace had Mary, 1644; John, 1645; Jonas, 1647; Jonas again, 1648; Joseph, 1651; Joshua, 1653; Jonathan, 1655; and David, 1657, was freeman 1653, and died 1674. Two Johns, at Reading, one died 1691, and the other died 1695, and we infer that one, but which is doubtful, was his son.

NATHANIEL EATON, of Cambridge, brother of Gov. Theophilus, was born about 1609, freeman 1638, the first head of Harvard College, but not dignified with title of President; on censure by the government fled to Virginia, and family went home, and died there. His wife with her children, except Benoni, followed him to Virginia, in a ship never heard of after.

SAMUEL EATON, of New Haven, brother of the preceding, son of Richard, bred at Magdalen College, Cambridge, where he had his degree 1624 and 28, came to New England, 1637, probably had wife and no children, went home after three years, had a living at Duckenfield, Co. Chester, near Manchester, until the great ejection, and died at Denton, 1665 or 6. aged 68.

THEOPHILUS EATON, of New Haven, brother of the two preceding, was born at Stony Stratford, in Co. Bucks. His father was minister there, and after at Coventry. He was deputy-governor of the East land or Baltic company in London, and by King James employed as his agent at the Court of Denmark. He had wife and child at London, and he married for second wife, Ann, widow of David Yale, daughter of Thomas Morton, Bishop of Chester, who had kindness for the Puritans. The family seat was in that shire, and the Governor in his will devises the estate at Great Budworth, in the same County. He came in 1637 to Boston,

and after went with his fellow passenger Davenport to found the settlement of New Haven, in 1639 was made Governor, and so, by annual choice was continued until his death 1658, aged 67. His will names three children only, Theophilus, Mary and Hannah, but mentions his wife, her son Thomas Yale, and son-in-law Edward Hopkins, late Governor of Connecticut, then in London. Samuel, born in London 1630, probably came with his father 1637, was the son of Theophilus also. The widow went home and died 1659. The son Theophilus, and unmarried daughter Hannah went with the mother. Theophilus, jr., lived at Dublin; but Hannah married 1659, at London, William Jones, who next year came to New Haven.

THOMAS EATON, of Reading, had Joseph, 1652.

THOMAS EATON, of Haverhill, married at Andover, 1659, Unice Singletary of Salisbury; freeman 1666; was killed by the Indians, 1698.

THOMAS EATON, of Dedham, freeman 1681.

WILLIAM EATON, of Watertown, came in 1635 or 6, from Staple in Kent, embarked at Sandwich, with wife Martha, three children, and one servant, had Daniel, 1639; and Mary, 1643; removed to Reading; was freeman 1653, had John; died 1673. He had daughter Martha, and his will mentions wife Martha, eldest son John, Daniel, daughter Mary, and two son-in-laws. The widow died 1681. William, freeman 1691, probably his son also.

An ABIGAIL EATON, aged 35, with Mary and Thomas, children, came 1635, in the "Elizabeth and Ann," following the husband and father, to us unknown.

REFERENCES.

MASSACHUSETTS.—Stearns' Hist. of Ashburnham, 694; Temple's Hist. of North Brookfield, 583; Mitchell's Hist. of Bridgewater, 373; Paige's Hist. of Cambridge, 539; Barry's Hist. of Framingham, 233; Davis' Landmarks of Plymouth, 99; Draper's Hist. of Spencer, 196; Benedict's Hist. of Sutton, 639; Bond's Hist. of Watertown, 202, 755; Eaton's Hist. of Reading, 63; Herrick's Hist. of Gardiner, 345; Hill's Dedham, Mass., Records; Wall's Reminiscences of Worcester, 360; Winsor's Hist of Duxbury, 257; Wyman's Charlestown Gens., 317.

MAINE.—Butler's Hist. of Farmington, 461; Corliss' Hist. of North Yarmouth; Lapham's Hist. of Rumford, 318; Eaton's Hist. of Thomaston, 209; Eaton's Annals of Warren, 538; Wheeler's Hist. of Brunswick, 833.

NEW HAMPSHIRE.—Washington, N. H., Hist., 392; Chase's Hist. of Chester, N. H., 514; Secomb's Hist. of Amherst, 575; Cochran's Hist. of Antrim, 482; Coggswell's Hist. of Henniker, 559; Eaton's Hist. of Candia, 67; Hayward's Hist. of Hancock, 546, 1051; Livermore's Hist. of Wilton, 363; Norton's Hist. of Fitzwilliam, 545; Read's Hist. of Swanzey, 332; Runnel's Hist. of Sanbornton, II, 256.

CONNECTICUT.—Waldo's Hist. of Tolland, 84; Brown's West Simsbury Settlers, 62; Davis' Hist. of Wallingford, 940; Hist. of Hamdon, 256; New Haven Hist. Society Papers, IV, 185; Stiles' Hist. of Windsor, II, 191.

OTHER PUBLICATIONS.—Young's Hist. of Chautauqua, N. Y., 506; N. Y. Hist. Society Coll., New Series, II, 499; Currier's Castleton, Vt., Epitaphs, 11; Davis' Gen., 52; Cleveland's Gen. of B. Cleveland, 221; Heminway's Vermont Gaz., IV, 160; Poore Gen., 84; Powers' Hist. of Sangamon County, Ill., 280; Vinton Gen., 64; Ammidown Gen., 54; Wyman's Hunt Gen,, 105; Amer.

Ancestry, III, 151, 191; IV, 144, 215; V, 82; VI, 11, 101; VIII, 130; IX, 176; N. E. Hist. and Gen. Reg., XXVII, 195; Savage's Gen. Dict., II, 95.

EAVENSON. Palmer and Trimble Gen., 49, 67, 188.

EBBING. Secomb's Hist. of New York City, vol. I, 260.

EBERHARDT. Amer. Ancestry, VII, 18; Eberhardt Gen.

EBERSOLE. Butz Gen., 121.

EBEY. Ruttenber's Hist. of Orange County, N. Y., 373; Powers' Hist. of Sangamon County, Ill., 277.

EBENATHA:—William Ebenatha. See Abernethy. Perhaps he had more children than these who took admission. Now the name is Abernethy, may have been so before 1673.

REFERENCES:—Savage's Gen. Dict., II, 98.

EBORNE or EBURNE:—George Eborne, of Hampton, 1644, died before 1647.

SAMUEL EDORNE, of Salem, born about 1614, may have resided some time about 1640 at Lynn, but had grant of land the year preceding at Salem, and there had baptized Samuel, Moses and Mary, 1648; Rebecca, 1651; and Sarah, 1656; was freeman 1665, and living 1697.

THOMAS EBORNE, of Salem, a tanner, freeman 1634, was living, but aged 1642, may have been father of Samuel preceding. See Aborne.

REFERENCES:—Savage's Gen. Dict., II, 98.

EBY. Brubacker Gen., 18.

ECCLES, ECLES, ECKLES or ECKELS:—Richard Eccles, of Cambridge, freeman 1642, by wife Mary, who died 1675, had Mary, Hannah and Martha. Timothy, perhaps only son, born 1645, died 1656.

REFERENCES:—Savage's Gen. Dict., II, 98.

ECKERSON. N. Y. Gen. and Biog. Rec., VII, 119.

EDDY:—John Eddy, of Watertown, 1633, was of Boxted, in Co. Suffield, and came in the "Handmaid," 1630, from London, arrived at Plymouth, where he continued over one year; freeman 1634, by wife Amie, had Pilgrim, 1634; Pilgrim, again; John, 1637; Benjamin, 1639; Samuel, 1640; Abigail, 1643; Sarah, Mary and Ruth. He had second wife Joanna, who died 1683, aged 80; and he died at the age of 90, 1684.

SAMUEL EDDY, of Plymouth, son of Rev. William, it is said, of Cranbrook in Kent, but lived at Boxted, Co. Suffield, came in the "Handmaid" to Plymouth, 1630, is called brother of first John, by wife Elizabeth, who died 1682, aged 81, had John, 1637; Zechariah, 1639; Caleb, 1643; Obidiah, 1645; and Hannah, 1647. He died 1688 at Swanzey, aged about 87.

REFERENCES:—Bond's Hist. of Watertown, Mass., 203, 754; Clark's Hist. of Norton, 80; Cutter's Hist. of Arlington, 235; Davis' Landmarks of Plymouth, 100; Ward's Hist. of Shrewsbury, 274; Stearn's Hist. of Ashburnham, 687; Jackson's Hist. of Newton, 273.

OTHER PUBLICATIONS.—Williams' Hist. of Danby, Vt., 141; Joslin's Hist. of Poultney, 225; Norton's Hist. of Fitzwilliam, N. H., 545; Stearns' Hist. of Rindge, N. H., 513; Maine Gen., II, 113; Clute's Hist. of Staten Island, N. Y., 378; Andrews' Hist. of New Britain, Conn., 221, 264, 275; Austin's Allied Families R. I., 87; Bangor, Me., Hist. Mag., IV, 53; Adams' Hist. of Fairhaven, Vt., 571; Walworth's Hyde Gen., 436; Cunnabel Gen., 76; Greene's Todd Gen., 129; Amer. Ancestry, VIII, 112; N. E. Hist. and Gen. Reg., VIII, 201; Savage's Gen. Dict., II, 98; Eddy Family Tree, (1880); Eddy Gen.

EDENDEN, EDDINGTON:—Edmund Edenden, of Scituate, 1641, representative 1642; removed to Boston, where his daugher Mehitable was baptized 1654; but the list of freemen 1665 calls him Roxbury. Next year among freemen from Boston, is Edm. Eddington, which I judge to be the same. He had daughters Mary, Sarah, Mehitable and Rebecca.

REFERENCES:—Savage's Gen. Dict., II, 99.

EDES:—John Edes, of Boston, by wife Catharine, had John, 1680; John, 1686; and Elizabeth, 1689.

JOHN EDES, of Charlestown, married 1647, Mary Tufts, daughter of Peter, had John, 1680; Edward, 1681; Mary, 1684; Peter, 1686; Jonathan, 1688; and Sarah, 1691; and died next year.

NICHOLAS EDES, of Southold, Long Island, 1678.

PHILIP EDES, of Newport, 1678, had been an officer in Cromwell's family, in good reputation, died 1662.

PHILIP EDES, of Casco, 1689.

WILLIAM EDES, of Salem, 1629, came in the fleet with Higginson.

WILLIAM EDES, of Boston, by wife Elizabeth, had Nicholas, 1687; and Elizabeth, 1689.

REFERENCES:—Wyman's Charlestown, Mass., Gens., vol. I, 319; Whitmore's Copps Hill Epitaphs; Cochrane's Hist. of Antrim, N. H., 484; Smith's Hist. of Petersborough, N. Y., 62; Wheeler's Hist. of Newport, N. H., 374; Bangor Hist., IV, 235; Savage's Gen. Dict., II, 100.

EDGARTON:—Richard Edgarton, of Saybrook, married 1653, Mary Sylvester, had Mary, 1656; Elizabeth, 1657; Ann or Hannah, 1659; removed next year to Norwich, there had John, 1662; Richard, 1665; Sarah, 1667; Samuel, 1670; Lydia, 1675; and Joseph, 1677.

REFERENCES:—Chandler's Hist. of Shirley, 394; Savage's Gen. Dict., II, 100.

EDGE:—Robert Edge embarked at London, 1635, aged 25, in the "Hopewell," Captain Babb. Possibly the name may be the same as Hedge; or it may be that the custom house record meant a "y" what I read "g."

REFERENCES:—Savage's Gen. Dict., II, 100; Futhey's Hist. Chester, Pa., 527.

EDGECOMB:—John Edgecomb, of New London, 1670, married 1673, Sarah, daughter of Edward Stallion, the record calls him "son of Nicholas Edgecomb, of Plymouth, Old England"; had Margaret, 1674; John, 1675; Sarah, 1678; Joanna, 1680; Nicholas; Samuel, 1690; and Thomas, died 1721.

NICHOLAS EDGECOMB, of Scarborough, 1640, took oath of submission to Massachusetts, 1658; but as I find his subscription by a mark, he was not, probably, as Farmer though. of the family of Sir Richard Edgecomb, of Mount Edgecomb, in Devonshire. Yet he may have been a dependent of that house. He removed to Saco, about 1660. In Southgate, page 25, we learn that his daughter Mary, married George Page, of Saco, and next John Ashton, of Scarborough, and that his other daughter Joanna married a Pynchon of Boston; Christopher, John, Michael and Robert, soldiers at Blackpoint, Scarborough, 1676, were, we may well imagine, his sons.

REFERENCES:—Smith Gen., 83; Eaton's Hist. of Thomaston, Me., 209; Hatch's Hist. of Industry, Me., 601; Brown's Simsbury, Conn., Settlers, 62; Caulkin's Hist. of New London, Conn., 366; Caulkin's Norwich, Conn., 227; Savage's Gen. Dict., II, 100.

EDGERLY:—Philip Edgerly, of New Hampshire, 1654.

THOMAS EDGERLY, of Dover, 1665, married that year Rebecca Holloway, or Hallowell, freeman 1672; was a magistrate. Perhaps he married 1691, after, as second wife Jane Wheedon, a daughter of John Ault, but whose widow she was, I know not.

REFERENCES:—Runnel's Hist. of Sanbornton, N. H., II, 261, Kellog Gen.; Amer. Ancestry, IV, 107; N. E. Hist. and Gen. Reg., XV, 337; XXXIV, 282; Edgerly Gen.

EDGERTON. Mitchell's Hist. of Bridgewater, Mass., 157; Atkins' Hist. of Hawley, Mass., 101; Eaton's Hist. of Thomaston, Me., II, 209; Hollister's of Pawlet, Vt., 184; Joslin's Hist. of Poultney, Vt., 256; Caulkin's Hist. of Norwich, Conn., 173; Waldo's Hist. of Tolland, Conn., 99; Plumb's Hist. of Hanover, Pa., 411; Ball's Hist. of Lake County, Ind., 385; Amer. Ancestry, III, 113.

EDGETT. Stanton Gen., 326.

EDISON. N. E. Hist. and Gen. Reg., XLVIII, 199.

EDLIN or EDLING:—David, of Leudicoes, or Ludecus Edlin, of Dover, 1659, admitted that year in spite of his outlandish name, had grant of land same year, which was in 1662 or 3, perhaps after his death, laid out to his widow Elizabeth. I suppose he was a German doctor, and that Ludecus, which remained for a family name, after rejection of Edlin, was in reality abbreviated for Ludovicus, for the abomination of a double one could not be endured even in the mist skillful deciple of Hippocrates.

REFERENCES:—Savage's Gen. Dict., II, 101.

EDMANDS. Amer. Ancestry, VII, 46; Temple's Hist. of North Brookfield, Mass., 583; Denny Gen.; Converse Gen.

EDMASTER:—John Edmaster, of Charlestown, 1678, had daughter Prudence, baptized 1687.

REFERENCES:—Savage's Gen. Dict., II, 101.

EDMISTON.   Alexander Gen., 18.

EDMONSON:—William Edmonson, of Rhode Island, 1672.

EDMOND.   Chandler Gen., 512.

EDMONDS. Wyman's Charlestown, Mass., Gens., vol. I, 324; Austin's R. I. Gen. Dict., 70; Cothren's Hist. of Woodbury, Conn., 542; Savage's Gen. Dict., II, 101.

EDMONSTON. Eager's Hist. of Orange County, N. Y., 620.

EDMUNDS, EDMONDS or EDMANDS:—Andrew Edmunds, of Providence, married 1675, Mary, daugh-

ter of Benjamin Harendean, had Mary, 1676; Sarah, 1678; William, 1681; Andrew, 1683; and Joseph, 1687; and in 1696, his widow Mary, was allowed to keep the ferry over Seekonk river.

JAMES EDMUNDS, of Boston, 1673, merchant, had been, perhaps, of Salem, 1668, but was, probably, not the man who desired employment of our governor and council 1629, who came 1629 in the fleet with Higginson, a cooper.

JAMES EDMUNDS, of Charlestown, Mass., freeman 1631, died 1677.

JOHN EDMUNDS, of Hartford, 1639.

RICHARD EDMUNDS, of Woburn, died 1689.

ROBERT EDMUNDS, of Maine, 1665, swore fidelity to Massachusetts, 1674.

SAMUEL EDMUNDS, of Concord, 1645.

WALTER EDMUNDS, of Concord, freeman 1639, had John, 1640; removed, and with wife Dorothy, was of Charlestown church, 1652; died 1667; and his widow died 1671. Most of his children were, no doubt, born in England. His daughter Mary, married 1644, Luke Potter. In his will wife and son John are made executors, but Joshua, Daniel and a daughter Potter are named.

WILLIAM EDMUNDS, of Lynn, a tailor, freeman 1635, had wife Mary, who died 1657; and he married same year at Boston, widow Ann Martin; testified in 1678, that he was in 68th year; had John, Mary, Joseph and Samuel; died 1693. Lewis marks his arrival 1630.

REFERENCES:—Williams' Hist. of Danby, Vt., 186; Barry's Hist. of Framingham. Mass., 237; Meade's Old Families of Va.: Slaughter's St. Marks Parish, Va., 140; Olin's Ohio Gen., 38; Watkins' Gen., 32.

EDRINGTON. Amer. Ancestry, VII, 238.

EDSALL or EDSELL:—Thomas Edsall, of Boston. turner, artillery company, 1652, married Elizabeth Farman, probably 1652, had Henry, 1655.

REFERENCES:—Amer. Ancestry, III, 15; Savage's Gen. Dict., II, 102.

EDSON:—Samuel Edson, of Salem, 1639, removed to Bridgewater, there was deacon, representative 1676. died 1692, aged 80; and his widow Susanna, died 1699, aged 81. He had Samuel, Joseph, Josiah, Susanna, Elizabeth, Mary, Sarah and Bethia.

REFERENCES:—Temple's Hist. of North Brookfield, Mass., 585; Temple's Hist. of Whately, Mass., 221; Mitchell's Hist. of Bridgewater, Mass., 151; Kingman's Hist. of North Bridgewater, Mass., 492; Stearns' Hist. of Ashburnham, Mass., 688; Young's Hist. of Chautauqua Co., N. Y., Nozes' Gen., 11; Savage's Gen. Dict., II, 102; Edson Gen.

EDWARDS:—Alexander Edwards, of Springfield, came from Wales, about 1640, embarked at Bristol, married 1642, Sarah, widow of John Searl, had Samuel, 1643; Hannah, 1645; Joseph, 1647; Mary, 1650; Benjamin, 1652; and Sarah, 1654; next year removed to Northampton, there had Nathaniel, 1657; and Elizabeth, 1660; and died 1690. Samuel, Joseph, Nathaniel, and the father were made freemen 1690.

EDWARD EDWARDS, of Plymouth, 1643, perhaps removed or died same year.

GRIFFIN EDWARDS, of Boston, calls, in a deed, Ann, wife of Rev. John Myles, who was sole heir of John Humphrey, his mother-in-law.

JOHN EDWARDS, of Wethersfield, 1640, had probably lived at Watertown, and by first wife, before settling at Wethersfield, had Thomas; and Abraham, 1637; and married Dorothy widow of Abraham Finch, had John, 1638; Esther, 1641; Ruth, 1643; Hannah, 1645; Joseph, 1648; and Lydia. He died 1664, and his widow married 1667 Richard Tousley, of Saybrook, and in 1676, was widow for third time.

JOHN EDWARDS, of Ipswich, married 1658, Mary Sams, had John, 1660; Mary, 1661; Elizabeth and Lucy, twins, 1667; William, 1669; Samuel, 1671; Francis, 1678; Hannah, 1681; and Frances, 1682; was freeman 1690.

JOHN EDWARDS, of Ipswich, by wife Margaret, had Thomas, 1694; and Margaret, 1695; perhaps he was of Cape Elizabeth, 1690.

JOHN EDWARDS, of Charlestown, by wife Elizabeth, had John, 1687.

MATTHEW EDWARDS, of Reading, came in the "Speed-well," 1656, from London, married 1657, Mary, daughter of John Poole, had Mary, 1659; Sarah, 1661; Matthew, 1662; and Elizabeth. He was freeman 1669, and died 1683, aged 52.

NATHANIEL EDWARDS, of Boston, merchant, a citizen of London, died 1654.

NICHOLAS EDWARDS, from Boston, died at Barbados, 1661.

RICE EDWARDS, of Salem, 1643, Boston, 1646, a joiner. His wife Joan was admitted of our church, 1647.

ROBERT EDWARDS, of Concord, came from London, in the "Hopewell," Captain Babb, in 1635, aged 22, or he may be the same who seven days earlier than his entry for Babb's ship, is, at the London custom house, certified to have taken the oath of allegiance, being aged 27, and to pass to Virginia. Possibly only one man so named was in London. He had wife Christian at Concord, Sarah, 1640; Christian, 1646; and several others, probably before as well as after. He was freeman 1642, died early, for his inventory was taken 1646.

THOMAS EDWARDS, of Salem, 1637, shoe-maker, freeman 1648, there had baptized John, 1639; Joseph, 1642; and Joshua, 1643; and probably removed to Lynn or Watertown, where he may have been before settling at Salem.

THOMAS EDWARDS, of Wethersfield, brought Elizabeth, who married 1645, John Goodrich; was of Hartford, 1648, engaged to remove 1659, with other friends of Goodwin, but went not, and in 1663 was by the Court ordered to oversee the work on bridges. His daughter Ruth married 1670, Samuel Hale.

THOMAS EDWARDS, of Boston, 1665, and several years after a master mariner, perhaps the same maltreated by the French at Tortugas, 1674, mentioned by Gov. Leverett.

THOMAS EDWARDS, of Stonington, 1667, married Mary, perhaps daughter of Henry Bridgham, of Dorchester, died 1693.

WILLIAM EDWARDS,, of Hartford, 1639, but not freeman before 1658; he was brought in childhood, says the family tradition, by his mother Ann, wife of James Cole; married Agnes, widow of William Spencer, had only child Richard, born 1647.

WILLIAM EDWARDS, of Taunton, 1643, perhaps was at Lynn five years later, but removed to Long Island, probably at Easthampton, 1650.

WILLIAM EDWARDS, of Marblehead, 1668.

REFERENCES.

MASSACHUSETTS.—Hammatt Papers Ipswich, 95; Wyman's Charlestown Gens., 330.

MAINE.—Hatch's Hist. of Industry, 602; Lapham's Hist. of Bethel, 523; Corliss' Hist. of North Yarmouth.

OTHER PUBLICATIONS.—Orcutt's Hist. of Stratford, Conn., 1195; Hinman's Conn. Settlers, 219; Stoughton's Windsor, Conn., Families, 146; Stiles' Hist. of Windsor, Conn., II, 194; Blood's Hist. of Temple, N. H., 217; Coggswell's Hist. of Henniker, N. H., 192; Howell's Hist. of Southampton, N. Y., 238; Meade's Old Families of Va.; Hayden's Virginia Gens., 98; Gregg's Hist. of Old Cheraws, S. C., 82; Futhey's Hist. of Chester County, Pa., 527; Powers' Hist. of Sangamon County, Ill., 278; Wright Gen., 174; Wetmore Gen., 516; Tuttle Gen., 374; Stoddard Gen., 4; Smith Gen. by Wellington Smith; Paxton's Marshall Gen., 122; Goode Gen., 205; Goodwin's Gen. Notes, 48; Gifford's Our Patronymies, 3; Powers' Hist. of Sangamon County, Ill., 278; Dwight Gen., 1035; Dwight Strong Gen., 1419; Chapman's Trowbridge Gen., 192; Savage's Gen. Dict., II, 102; Edward's Hist. Sketches (1894); Edward's Family Meeting; Amer. Ancestry, II, 35; VI, 54, 135; VII, 163, 164; VIII, 13; IX, 216.

EELLS, ELLS, EELS or EALES:—John Eells, of Dorchester, freeman 1634, had Samuel, 1640; removed perhaps to Hingham first, but in 1645, to Newbury, there called "beehive maker," died 1653, aged 78.

RICHARD EELLS, of Boston, died 1639, probably without wife or child. His will, the first in first volume of records, names brother John in England, and refers to three brothers and a sister as residuary legatees. But it has been argued with much plausibility, that the testators name was Hills.

REFERENCES:—Phoenix's Whitney Family of Conn., vol. I, 403; Hinman's Conn. Settlers (1846); Andrews' Hist. of New Britain, Conn., 258; Barry's Hist. of Hanover, Mass., 301; Kellogg's White Gen., 49; Savage's Gen. Dict., II, 104.

EGBERT. Clute's Hist. of Staten Island, 379.

EGBERTS. Talcott's N. Y. and N. E. Families, 182; Munsell's Albany, N. Y., Coll., IV, 119; Amer. Ancestry, V, 37.

EGERLY. Egerly Gen.

EGER:—William Eger, of Cambridge, by wife Ruth, who died 1680, aged 39, had Zerubabel, 1672; Martha, 1674; Ruth, 1677; and Sarah, 1679. He married 1680, Lydia, widow of Arthur Cole, removed to Marlborough, after having Margaret, 1681; there had several more; but as William; Zechary; Abraham; James, 1685; Jacob, Mercy, Lydia, and Esther, named in the will, as well as Zerubabel, Ruth, Sarah and Margaret, seem too many for the second wife, for whose promise of another also provision is made, one must suppose, that two or three beside those recorded at Cambridge were born of first wife at some other town. Probably this name is now Eager.

REFERENCES:—Savage's Gen. Dict., II, 100.

EGERTON. Vinton's Giles Gen., 223; Vermont Gaz., IV, 623.

EGERY. Paige's Hist. of Hardwich, Mass., 367.

EGGINGTON:—Jeremiah Eggington, of Boston, married 1655, Elizabeth, daughter of Rev. John Cotton, who died 1656, had Elizabeth, 1656. He, I suppose, removed.

REFERENCES:—Savage's Gen. Dict., II(105.

EGGLESTON:—Bagot, Bigot, Bigod or Begat Eggleston, of Dorchester, came, probably, in the "Mary and John," freeman 1631; removed with first settlers to Windsor, died 1674, near 100 years old, leaving Samuel and James, both born before he removed, and Thomas, 1638; Mary, 1641; Sarah, 1643; Rebecca, 1644; Abigail, 1648; Joseph, 1651; and Benjamin, 1653. The name of his wife is not known.

REFERENCES:—Orcutt's Hist. of Torrington, Conn., 686; Talcott's N. Y. and N. E. Families, 510; Stiles' Hist. of Windsor, Conn., II, 198, 836; Barbour's My Wife and Mother, App., 72; Williams' Hist. of Danby, Vt., 141; Meade's Old Churches of Va., II, 20; Loomis' Gen. Female Branches, 547, 679; Goodwin's Orcutt Gen., 51; Goode Gen., 279; Amer. Ancestry, V, 3; Savage's Gen. Dict., II, 105.

EGLESTON. N. Y. Gen. and Biog. Rec., XXIII, 122.

EGLE. Egle's Penn. Gens., 129.

EGLETON:—John Egleton, of Fairfield, by wife Peaceable, had John, 1657; died 1659. His widow married 1660, Daniel Silliman, and died next year. The son died unmarried.

REFERENCES:—Savage's Gen. Dict., II, 105.

EGLIN:—William Eglin, of Boston, married Phebe, daughter of Robert Williams, of the same, had Mary, 1667; Samuel, 1669, Phebe, 1673; and John, 1677.

REFERENCES:—Savage's Gen. Dict., II, 106.

EGLINTON:—Edward Eglinton, of Boston, died 1696.

REFERENCES:—Savage's Gen. Dict., II, 106.

EGELEY. Egle's Penn. Gens., 129.

EGMONT. Munsell's Albany Coll., IV, 120.

EGRON:—John Egron, of Malden, had Elizabeth, 1673.

EHLE. Whitmore Gen., 75.

EIGENBRODT. N. Y. Gen. and Biog. Rec., XVIII, 122.

EIGHMY. Amer. Ancestry, II, 35.

EKEL. Egle's Penn. Gens., 129.

ELA:—Daniel Ela, of Haverhill, 1675, perhaps several years earlier, a tanner, but in 1677, had leave to keep an ordinary. He took oath of allegiance 1677. Perhaps he had son Israel, who took oath 1677.

REFERENCES:—Parker's Hist. of Londonderry, N. H., 272; Amer. Ancestry, V, 213.

ELBRIDGE:—Thomas Elbridge, of Boston, son of Giles, merchant and joint grantee of the patent, 1632,

to Aldsworth, an Alderman of Bristol, by the President and Council of New England for Pemaquid, came, perhaps, 1650, to dispose of that in lots, of which one moiety was in 1652 to Captain Paul White, for 200 pounds sterling, and the last was in 1657. He also sold for the company, Monhigon. He was associated with the first who owned a fire engine in the metropolis 1680.

REFERENCES:—Salisbury's Memorials; Savage's Gen. Dict., vol. II, 107.

ELCOCK:—Anthony Elcock, of New Haven, 1657, had Mary, 1661; John, 1663; Thomas, 1666; and Sarah, 1669. He died not long after, for his will in mentioned 1672.

REFERENCES:—Savage's Gen. Dict., vol. II, 107.

ELDEN:—Goodwin's Hist. of Buxton, Me., 359; Buxton, Me., Centen., 149.

ELDER:—Daniel Elder, of Dorchester, married 1667, Lydia Holmes, who died 1689, had Lydia, 1668; Remember, 1669; Andrew, 1671; Lydia, 1673; Daniel, 1675; and died 1692.

REFERENCES:—Temple's Hist. of Whately, Mass., 228; Pierce's Hist. of Gorham, Me., 64; Hatch's Hist. of Industry, Me., 603; Maine Hist. and Gen. Rec., IV, 161; Egle's Penn. Gens., 151; Powers' Hist. of Sangamon County, Ill., 282; Marshall Gen., 13; Mack Gen., 66.

ELDERKIN:—John Elderkin, of Lynn, 1637, Dedham, 1641, Reading 1646, and two years later at Providence, and of New London, 1651, where he built both the first church and the first mill, finally in 1664, settled at Norwich, there also built the first church and mill, died 1687, aged 71. He had Abigail, 1641; but what his wife's name, or whether she had more children, or when she died is unknown. Yet a daughter of this wife married Daniel Comstock. He married for second wife Elizabeth, daughter of John Drake, widow of William Gaylord, and had Ann, 1661; John, 1664; Bathshua, 1665; James, 1671; and Joseph, 1672. His widow long survived him, and died 1716, aged 95.

REFERENCES:—Caulkin's Hist. of Norwich, Conn., 215; Caulkin's Hist. of New London, Conn., 117; Kellogg's White Gen., 88; Amer. Ancestry, IX, 62; Savage's Gen. Dict., II, 108; Elderkin Gen.

ELDERTON:—John Elderton, of Providence, 1645.

ELDRED:—John Eldred, of Hampton, 1640.

JOHN ELDRED, of Warwick, married Margaret, fifth daughter of Randall Houlden the first.

SAMUEL ELDRED, of Cambridge, 1646, by wife Elizabeth, had Elizabeth, 1642; Samuel, 1644; Mary, 1646; and Thomas, 1648. Taken prisoner by Connecticut, when Rhode Island was too weak to vindicate her right, he, perhaps, to serve his relatives and neighbors consented to be made a constable, until the royal justice might settle the disputed boundary.

A Mrs. Eldred is mentioned 1643, at New Haven, with family of five, and estate of 1000 pounds sterling, but not there in 1647, probably had gone home to London.

WILLIAM ELDRED, of Yarmouth, married a daughter of William Lumpkin, had Ann, about 1648; and Sarah, 1650; beside Elisha and Bethia. Very often the name is Eldridge.

REFERENCES:—Newport Hist. Mag., IV, 242; Austin's R. I. Gen. Dict., 71; Austin's Allied Families, 90; Cleveland's Hist. of Yates County, N. Y., 735; Savage's Gen. Dict., II, 107.

ELDRIDGE:—James Eldridge, of Stonington, 1670.

NATHANIEL ELDRIDGE, of Windsor, 1642, probably removed.

ROBERT ELDRIDGE, of Yarmouth, married 1649, Elizabeth, daughter of William Nickerson, had Nicholas, 1650; Mary, was, perhaps, his daughter.

SAMUEL ELDRIDGE, of Stonington, was constable, 1670

THOMAS ELDRIDGE, of Boston, 1674, ship carpenter.

REFERENCES:—Freeman's Hist. of Cape Cod, Mass., II, 598, 601, 710; Aldrich's Hist. of Walpole, 245; Bangor, Me., Hist. Mag., IV, 219, 236; Futhey's Hist. of Chester County, Pa., 530; Meade's Old Families of Va.; Richmond, Va., Standard, II, 10, 36; Robertson's Pocahontas' Descendants; Savage's Gen. Dict., II, 107.

ELERBY. Gregg's Old Cheraws, 64.

ELFORD:—John Elford, of Salem, 1636, excommunicated 1639, and probably removed with Roger Williams and other outcasts.

TRISTRAM ELFORD, of Gloucester, 1664, then aged 40 years.

REFERENCES:—Savage's Gen. Dict., II, 108.

ELGARR:—Thomas Elgarr, of Hadley, 1678, a young man, chargeable to the town, perhaps an invalid soldier of Philip's war, removed to Suffield, married about 1691, Abigail Filley, had Thomas, 1692, and perhaps others.

THOMAS ELGARR, of Windsor, 1729, probably the son of the preceding, but possibly the same.

REFERENCES:—Savage's Gen. Dict., II, 109.

ELIOT, or ELLIOT and ELLIOTT:—Andrew Eliot, of Beverly, came from Somersetshire, it is said, but no date is known, had only son Andrew, born 1651 in England; was representative 1690-2. He was of the juries, says tradition, which tried the witches, and had great mental affliction on that account the residue of his life.

DANIEL ELIOT, of Sudbury or Marlborough, married Hannah, daughter of Peter Cloyes, had Daniel, 1687; Ebenezer, 1693; John, 1695; James, 1697; Nathaniel, 1699; Jonathan, 1701; and Peter, 1704; removed to Oxford.

EDMUND ELIOT, of Salisbury, 1652, by wife Sarah, had John, 1660. He had perhaps two wives, one daughter of Jared Hadden, of Ralph Blaisdell.

FRANCIS ELIOT, of Braintree, youngest brother of the apostle John, born in England, freeman 1641, married Mary, daughter of Martin Saunders, had Mary, 1641; Rachel, 1643; John, 1650; Hannah, 1651; Mary, again, 1653; and Abigail, 1659. He was made deacon 1653, and died 1677.

JACOB ELIOT, of Boston, elder brother of Rev. John, came probably with him in the "Lion," 1631, freeman 1632, deacon 1640, which is quite observable, as he was disarmed two and a half years before, as one of the pestilent heretics that supported Wheelwright and Mrs. Hutchinson in their "opinions and revelations"; and died 1651, leaving widow Margery, who died 1661. His children were Jacob, baptized 1632, John, 1634; Hannah, 1637; Abigail, 1639; Susanna, 1641; Mehitable, 1645; Sarah, Asaph, 1651.

JOHN ELIOT, of Roxbury, the celebrated apostle of the Indians, born at Nazing, County Essex, 1603, was bred at Cambridge, pensioner at Jesus College, 1619,

where he took his A. B. 1623, came to Boston, 1631, in the Lion, freeman 1632, in November following was settled in his office of teacher, with Thomas Welde, who was made pastor July preceding. He married Ann Mumford or Mountfort, who was bethrothed to him in England, and followed him the next year. She died 1687, had Hannah, 1633; John, 1636; Joseph, 1638; Samuel 1641; Aaron, 1644; and Benjamin, 1647. Ever honorable will be the name of Eliot for the philanthropic labor of forty years in spreading among our aborigines the sentiments and in some degree the doctrines of his religion. He died 1690.

JOHN ELIOT, of Watertown, 1633, by wife Margaret, had Elizabeth, 1634; John, 1636; Ann, 1638; Samuel, 1640; Martha, 1641; and Sarah, 1643; sold his estate in 1646, and removed probably to Stamford, 1650, where wife Margaret died 1658.

JOHN ELIOT, of Amesbury, took oath of a legiance, 1677.

JOSEPH ELIOT, of New London, 1667, removed to Stonington, had, perhaps, Henry.

PHILIP ELIOT, of Roxbury, brother of the apostle, came probably early in 1635, in the "Hopewell," with his wife Elizabeth, aged 30, children Mary, 13; Elizabeth, 8; Sarah, 6; and Philip, 2. All were from Nazing, the seat of the family. He was freeman 1636; deacon; representative 1654-7, and died 1657. We may conjecture that another daughter was born on this side of the ocean.

RICHARD ELIOT, of Beverly, died 1664.

RICHARD ELIOT, of New London, 1662, transient.

ROBERT ELIOT, of Casco, 1670, of Scarborough, 1685, representative, lived at Portsmouth, and was in 1716, eldest of the council of New Hampshire. He was father of Humphrey, I think, of Jane; probably of Elizabeth.

THOMAS ELIOT, of Boston, a carpenter, by wife Hannah, had Mary, 1686.

WILLIAM ELIOT, of Ipswich, 1634, came in the "Mary and John," that year, having taken the oaths of allegiance and supremacy; was from Salisbury, in Wiltshire, was drowned next year at Cape Ann, in the wreck of the vessel with Rev. Mr. Avery.

REFERENCES.

MASSACHUSETTS.—Paige's Hist. of Cambridge, 540; Drake's Hist. of Boston, 1876; Mass. Hist. Society Coll., 2d Series II, 228; Whitmore's Copps Hill Epitaphs; Ellis' Hist. of Roxbury, 117; Jones' Hist. of Stockbridge, 131.

OTHER PUBLICATIONS.—Stiles' Hist. of Windsor, Conn., II, 207; Hall's Hist. of Mason, N. H., 201; Hall's Gen. Notes, 104, 107; Dwight Gen., 179; Dwight's Strong Gen., 359, 502; Maltby Gen., 70; Walker Gen., 26; Amer. Ancestry, III, 16; IV, 26, 111; N. E. Hist. and Gen. Reg., VIII, 45, 259; X, 355; XXVII, 124; XXVIII, 144; XXXIII, 144; XXXIX, 365; Whitmore's Tabular Eliot Family, 1857; Eliot Family, 1854; Caverley's Eliot Mem., 1881.

ELISTONE or ELLISON:—George Elistone, of Boston, freeman, 1690.

REFERENCES:—Savage's Gen. Dict., II, 110.

ELITHROP or ELITHORP:—Henry Elithorp, of Dedham, a soldier in Moseley's company, 1675. A widow Elithorp, probably his mother, married 1657, Thomas Jones of Hull.

JOHN ELITHORP, of Manchester, 1686.

NATHANIEL ELITHORP, of Ipswich, had Thomas, 1663; Abigail, 1665; Mary, 1672; and Nathaniel, 1675; aged 54, in 1686. He was of Rowley, 1691.

THOMAS ELITHORP, of Rowley, 1643, died 1668; or another Thomas, there, died 1689, and a third, quite aged, there died 1709.

REFERENCES:—Essex Inst. Coll., XXI, 78; Savage's Gen. Dict., II, 111.

ELKENBURG. Amer. Ancestry, II, 35.

ELKIN. Powers' Hist. Sangamon County, Ill., 281.

ELKINS or ELKING:—Christopher Elkins, of Scarborough, 1663.

ELEAZER ELKINS, of Exeter, 1677.

GERSHOM ELKINS, of Hampton, 1677, then took oath of allegiance.

HENRY ELKINS, of Boston, 1634, a tailor, freeman 1635, had Mary, baptized 1638, had been 1637 disarmed for supporting Wheelwright; removed to Hampton, died 1668. His will mentions sons Gershom and Eliezer. Henry was probably his son, also.

THOMAS ELKINS, of Saco, 1640, was deputy of Robert Sankey, the marshal of Gorges' Province, and in 1663, of Scarborough.

REFERENCES:—Runnel's Hist. of Sanbornton, N. H., 263; Dow's Hist. of Hampton, N. H., 697; Essex Inst. Hist. Coll., 197; Leavenworth Gen., 141; Amer. Ancestry, VII, 9; Savage's Gen. Dict., II, 112.

ELLEN:—Nicholas Ellen, of Dorchester, had Ann, 1658, wife died early and he had second wife.

REFERENCES:—Savage's Gen. Dict., II, 112.

ELLENSWOOD. Secomb's Hist. of Amherst, 577.

ELLERY:—Isaac Ellery, of Gloucester, a soldier in Appleton's company, killed at the great Narragansett fight 1675.

WILLIAM ELLERY, of Gloucester, married that year Hannah, daughter, I suppose, of William Vincent, may have had William, 1665; William, again, 1667, Benjamin, 1669; Susanna, 1673. His wife died 1675, and he married 1676, Mary, probably widow of John Coit, had Mary, 1677; and Abigail, 1679; perhaps he lived 1668, at Salem; was freeman 1672; representative 1689, and died 1696.

REFERENCES:—Wyman's Charlestown, Mass., Gens., vol. I, 331; Babson's Hist. of Gloucester, 84; Newport Hist. Mag., IV, 183; Muzzey's Reminiscences; Heraldic Journal, vol. I, 177; Bartlett's Wanton Family, 125; N. E. Hist. and Gen. Reg., XLIII, 313; Savage's Gen. Dict., II, 112; Ellery Chart.

ELLET or ELLIT:—John Ellet, of Watertown, by wife Margaret, had John, 1636; Ann, 1638; Samuel and Martha; and Sarah, 1643.

WILLIAM ELLET, by wife Sarah, had Sarah, and died 1670.

REFERENCES:—Lloyd and Carpenter Gen., 66; Savage's Gen. Dict., II, 112.

ELLICE. Jameson's Hist. of Medway, Mass., 480.

ELLICOT:—Vines Ellicot, of Boston, came in the "Supply," from London, 1679, but perhaps, only transient.

REFERENCES:—Ellicot and Thomas Gen., 69, 177; Evans' Fox Ellicot and Evans' Gen., 1882; Savage's Gen. Dict., II, 112.

ELLINGHAM:—William Ellingham, of Kittery, perhaps, of York certainly, when he submitted to Massachusetts, 1652, constable 1655.

REFERENCES:—Savage's Gen. Dict., II, 112.

ELLINGWOOD:—Ralph Ellingwood, of Salem, 1637, had Joseph, baptized 1644; Stephen, 1656; Ralph, 1657; Joseph, 1662; Mary, 1664; and Sarah, 1666; and he had other children. Probably he was the man who came over under the name of Ralph Ellwood, in the "Truelove," 1635, aged 28. He was one of the founders of Beverly church 1667, he left property by his will to widow, and children John, Benjamin, David and Elizabeth, beside some of these mentioned above.

REFERENCES:—Rose's Sketches of Rose, N. Y., 247; Lapham's Hist. of Bethel, Me., 523; Savage's Gen. Dict., II, 113.

ELLINGS or ELLINS:—Anthony Ellins, of Portsmouth, 1631, sent over by Mason, the patentee; admitted freeman of Mass., 1674.

REFERENCES:—Savage's Gen. Dict., II, 113.

ELLIOT:—Pierce's Hist. of Grafton, Mass., 477; Benedict's Hist. of Sutton, Mass., 639; Bouton's Hist. of Concord, N. H., 650; Chase's Hist. of Chester, N. H., 515; Secomb's Hist. of Amherst, N. H., 579; Lapham's Hist. of Rumford, Me., 319; Cushman's Hist. of Sheepscott, Me., 377; Babson's Hist. of Gloucester, 299; Penn. Mag., VI, 333; Sedgwick's Hist. of Sharon, Conn., 78; Walworth's Hyde Gen., 754, 937; Cope Family of Pa., 86, 190; N. E. Hist. and Gen. Reg., XLIV, 112; Savage's Gen. Dict., II, 113.

ELLIOTT:—John Elliott, the apostle to the Indians, born in England, 1604; married 1632, Ann Mountfort, came to Boston in the ship "Lion," 1631. Had Joseph and other children.

WILLIAM ELLIOT, came from Cornwall, England, to America, 1690, and was the first of this family to settle in South Carolina. He had son Thomas, who married Mary Gibbes, daughter of Chief Justice Robert Gibbes.

REFERENCES:—Wyman's Charlestown, Mass., Gens., vol. I, 322; Hazen's Hist. of Billerica, Mass., 46; Leonard's Hist. of Dublin, N. H., 328; Collins' Hist. of Boscawen, N. H., 523; Eaton's Hist. of Thomaston, Me., II, 210; Hines' Lebanon, Conn., Address, 153; Powers' Hist. of Sangamon Co., Ill., 284; Miller's Hist. of Colchester, N. S., 9, 11; Heraldic Journal, IV, 183; Dwight Gen., 987; Cutts Gen., 26, 50; Bullock Gen.; Amer. Ancestry, V, 130, 205.

ELLIS:—Arthur Ellis, came to New England, 1630.

CHRISTOPHER ELLIS, of New London, 1682.

CONSTANT ELLIS, of Ipswich, died 1686.

EDWARD ELLIS, of Boston, married 1652, Sarah, daughter of Robert Blott, had Sarah, 1654; perhaps others, certainly Edward, 1656; and Ann; he died 1695, aged 74.

FRANCIS ELLIS, of Salem, perhaps as early as 1691.

FREDERICK ELLIS, of Norwich, had grant of land, 1678

HENRY ELLIS, of Boston, mariner, 1666.

JAMES ELLIS, of Stonington, 1653, died 1694.

JOHN ELLIS, of Dedham, freeman 1641, married 1641, Susan Lumber, had John, 1646; and Hannah, 1651; was of Medfield, 1653, where his wife died 1654. He married next, 1655, Joan, widow of John Clapp, of Dorchester, had Samuel, 1660; and Joseph, 1662. He died 1697, and his widow 1704.

JOHN ELLIS, of Sandwich, married about 1645, Elizabeth, daughter of first Edmund Freeman, had, perhaps, Bennet, 1649; certainly Mordecai, 1651; Joel, 1655; and Matthias, 1657; died 1677, then called jr., yet who was the senior is unknown. His wife survived him.

JOHN ELLIS, of New London, 1664, probably removed.

JOSEPH ELLIS, of Mass., freeman 1663, may have been son of preceding.

RICHARD ELLIS, of Dedham, by wife E izabeth, married 1650, who may seem to be daughter of Lambert Genery, calls Ellis, son-in-law, had, perhaps, several children, but certainly a daughter, 1651; and Mary, 16.5.

ROGER ELLIS, of Yarmouth, had John, 1648.

THOMAS ELLIS, of Medfield, 1649, may be the same who was baptized at Wrentham, England, 1629, and married 1659, Mary, daughter of Thomas Wight, of Dedham, had Mary, 1660; Abiel, 1662; Samuel, 1664; Thomas, 1666; Patience, 1668; Ruth, 1670; Thomas, again ,1674; Joanna, 1677; and Juda. He died 1690. His widow died 1693.

THOMAS ELLIS, perhaps lived at Marblehead, 1668-74.

WILLIAM ELLIS, of Braintree.

REFERENCES.

MASSACHUSETTS.—Paige's Hist. of Hardwick. 367; Stearn's Hist. of Ashburnham, 689; Barry's Hist. of Hanover, 305; Ballou's Hist. of Milford, 726; Davis' Landmarks of Plymouth, 102; Freeman's Hist. of Cape Cod, II, 72, 132; Hull's Dedham Records; Jameson's Hist. of Medway, 489; Whitmore's Copp's Hill Epitaphs.

NEW HAMPSHIRE.—Read's Hist. of Swanzey, 333; Norton's Hist. of Fitzwilliam, 546; Hayward's Hist. of Gilsum, 304; Bassett's Hist. of Richmond, 384.

MAINE.—Bangor Hist. Mag., V, 190; Hatch's Hist. of Industry, 603; Wheeler's Hist. of Brunswick, 833; Machias Centen., 159.

VERMONT.—Heminway's Gen. Rec., 35; Heminway's Vermont Gaz., V; Adams' Fairhaven, 368.

OTHER PUBLICATIONS.—Meade's Old Churches of Va., II, 460; Titcomb's New England People, 5; Sharp's Hist. of Seymour, Conn., 164; Clement's Newtown, N. J., Settlers; Penn. Mag. of Hist. and Biog., XIV, 199; Powers' Hist. of Sangamon County, Ill., 285; Smith's Hist. of Delaware County, Pa., 458; Wight Gen., 18; Spooner Gens., vol. I, 483; Loomis' Gen. Female Branches, 779; Lawrence and Bartlett Gen., 108; Humphrey's Gen., 433; Amer. Ancestry, vol. I, 26; III, 151; V, 130; VI, 8, 193; VII, 23, 73; VIII, 219; IX, 109; X, 179; XI, 188; Savage's Gen. Dict., II, 113; Ellis Gen., 1849, 1888, 1893.

ELLISON or ELISSON:—George Ellison, of Plymouth, married Lydia, daughter of Secretary Morton.

LAWRENCE ELLISON, of Windsor, 1643, removed to Hempstead, L. I., perhaps, there died 1665. Had sons Richard, Thomas and John.

RICHARD ELLISON, of Braintree, 1646, by wife Thomasine, had Mary, 1646; Hannah, 1648; John, 1650; Sarah, 1652; Temperance, or in another record Thomasine, 1655; and Experience, 1657.

REFERENCES:—Rodman Gen., 149; Savage's Gen. Dict., II, 113.

ELLMER. Savage's Gen. Dict., II, 113.

CORRECTIONS RECEIVED
FOR GENEALOGICAL GUIDE TO DATE.

ARNOLD:—Thomas, born 1599, in Cheselbourne, Dorset Co., England. Married 1st———, married 2d Phebe Parkhurst, daughter of George and Susanna Parkhurst, died 1688. He came to America in May, 1635, in ship "Plain Joan," and settled at Watertown, Mass. In 1666-67-70-71-72 he was deputy. In 1672, a member of town council. Died in September, 1674. ELEAZER, born June 17, 1651, died August 29, 1722. Married Eleanor Smith, died 1722. Lived at Providence, R. I.

———

I wish to make a correction as a descendant of Rev. CHACE BROWN, of Rhode Island. In your issue of May, 1899, you give Chace Brown as having four sons. He also had a daughter Phoebe, who was my ancestress.

M. K. BARNEY, Arden, North Carolina.

———

I saw in your Notes on Early Settlers:—

BIXBY:—Daniel, settled in Andover, Mass., married Hannah Chandler, daughter of Thomas Chandler, etc. etc. This is all true, but he was not the original Bixby of America. Joseph Bixby, born in Bexford, England, about 1620, come from there to Ipswich, Mass., in 1637, with his father and mother Nathaniel and Mary. He married 1647, widow Sarah Wyatt Hewed, who came from Arlington, Suffolk Co., England. He settled in Rowley, (now Bexford, Mass.,) was one of the incorporators of the town of Bexford Selectman, and held other important offices. He died in Bexford, 1700.

He had the following children: Joseph W., Sarah, Nathaniel, Mary, George, Jonathan, Daniel, Benjamin and Abigail. This son Daniel married Hannah Chandler, and settled in Andover, as you stated.

A. B. BIXBY.

———

The name BOWKER, page 51. My husband's family are from people of that name, but they have little data. The grave-stone of his great grandfather, reads: "Mr. Joseph Bowker, born at Scituate, Mass., March 16, 1739; died at Georgetown, (now Phipsburg, Me.,) March 4, 1802, aged 62 years. Elizabeth Conrus Bowker, born 1739, died at Meadowbrook, November, 1831, aged 93."

It is supposed in the family she also was from Scituate. You see these dates all tally, but do not agree with yours, as you have Benjamin, born February 14, 1739, unless they were cousins. Now can you tell me anything more of the Bowker preceding? Any information would be gratefully accepted.

The Bowker arms are: "Hebrareth argent, a chevron vert, between three round buckles. Azure, by the name of Bowker, of Scotland, and descends to the name and family." This description is dated Boston, August 8th, 1728." The general surroundings and embellishment suggest to me a Boston dealer's make, but it is certainly old, as that date and treasured by them. They think their father's ancestor was Lazarus Bowker.

Mrs. G. W. PERCY, Oakland, Cal.

In your Genealogical Guide, etc., you give: "JOHN BISSEL, of Windsor, Conn., born in Somerset, England, died at Windsor, October 3, 1677 * * * * * * He had John, Thomas, Samuel, Nathaniel, 1640; Mary and Joice * * * etc.," and *Thomas Bissel*, brother of above, was born in England, married October 11, 1655, Abigail, daughter of Duncan John Moore * * * etc."

Are you not in error in stating that Thomas, who married Abigail Moore, was the brother of John. Savage gives this Thomas as the son of John, and his marriage in 1655 would indicate that he was a young man; while John at that date, was 63 years of age. I have always understood that this Thomas was the son of John the immigrant, and should not want to accept your "brother" theory without justly strong evidence. What is your authentic for the statement?

C. S. GLEASON, Seattle, Wash.

On page 64, of Genealogical Guide, next to last line, last column, "Loome's Gen." doubtless means "Loomis Gen. Female Lines."

Among the Browns in the Genealogical Guide, I fail to identify JOHN BROWN, (brother of Peter, of the Mayflower). He joined the church in Leyden, came to Plymouth, Mass., and later to Rehoboth, where he died 1662. By wife Dorothy, had James, married Lydia Howland; Mary, married Thomas Willett, 1636, and John—John was the oldest son and died before his father. John Brown received into his family the orphaned children, Mary and Priscilla, daughters of his brother Peter Brown, of the Mayflower. The second John, on page 63, seems to be the one, but does not agree with my information. Possibly, I am wrong, but if so, shall be glad to be corrected.

On page 61, of Genealogical Guide, some text under Brownson is well, the columns on that page, I see are reversed.

T. H. LOOMIS.

BOWEN:—Griffith Bowen, wife Margaret Fleming, Chas., Margaret, Francis, William, Henry, Mary, Esther, Abigail, Penuel, (not "Peniel"), Elizabeth, Deviah. He left America about 1655. He was living in London as late as 1670. Obediah Bowen was of Swanzea, not "Swanzey."

A. S. W. BRICKARD.

You mention "Nathaniel Bowman," who arrived at Watertown, with Winthrop, 1630. In the list of References following, you give "Bowman Gen." published 1885. Allow me please to correct this mistake—the "Bowman Genealogy" was published by Dr. Jesse Bowman Young, in Harrisburg, Pa., 1885.

Mr. Young descends from Christopher Bauman, who came to America from Ems, Germany, about 1754, and located in Pennsylvania. About this time, this family of "Bauman's," (meaning Builder or Architect), appropriated our name of Bowman, which was given to our family in the earliest ages of England, for the expert use of the bow, the two families being entirely different and Nathaniel and his descendants are not the family of whom the "Bowman Genealogy" was written.

For information regarding the history of the Bauman family, please refer to the Memoir of Rev. Geo. Bryant Bowman, Boston Pub. Library, 2343 11th St., page 13.

At the close of the Revolutionary War, Captain Sam. Bowman, Ebenezer and Joshua, his brohters and a nephew, Isaac Bowman, located in Wilkesbarre, Pa., and they and their descendants have filled many places

---

of responsibility in the State and Church. These men were born in Lexington and are direct descendants of Nathaniel of 1630. This is probably how much of the confusion of families came about after the Germans took the name in the same state. Knowing that you wish your references correct, I send you this statement.

SARAH BOWMAN VAN NESS.

I have been looking over your BROOKS data and notice that you have omitted the earliest Brooks that settled in this country. He was Captain Thomas Brooks of Concord, Mass. In his place I see you have a "Capt. Robert Brooks," but this is erroneous, as there never was a Captain Robert Brooks of Concord. Capt. Thos. Brooks was of Watertown, Mass., where he had a lot assigned him on the main road in 1631, but removed to Concord, before 1636. He did not buy his property at Medford, however, until 1660. He was representative to the General Court in 1642, 1643, 1644, 1654, 1659, 1660, 1661 and 1662—eight years. He also had besides the children you name a daughter Hannah, who married Thomas Fox of Watertown. Captain Thomas Brooks' fifth child was Gershom, not Gershaw, as you have it. All of these facts differ from your statements, but I have ample proof of the accuracy of my data.

I spent many ears in hunting up the Brooks family, and the result in manuscript form is before me as I write.

Now, about the other Brooks that you mention. First, Ebenezer Brooks, of Woburn, was not a first settler there, but was a grandson of Henry Brooks, who was of that town in 1649, but of Concord in 1639.

You say Henry Brooks of Concord, freeman 1639, had Joseph, 1641. There was no Joseph Brooks, son of this Henry Brooks that I have ever been able to learn of. I do not know whether you publish any corrections or not in your Genealogical Guide, but as the value of an article depends upon its accuracy, I feel justified in sending you the above corrections.

WALTER F. BROOKS, Worcester, Mass.

On page 63, I learn some startling facts about my family. The fact that John BROWN, of Watertown, arrived September 16, 1652, in the ship "Lion," is probably a misprint for 1632, and the ship "Lion," but I fail to see where you found the son James. Their oldest child was John born at Hawkedon, County Suffolk, in England, in 1631, the next Mary, born September 8, 1634, the next Mary, born March 24, 1636, the two latter at Watertown, as the records which I have seen state. John, the father "was buried ye 20th day of ye 4th month 1636," so you see there could be no James.

John Brown, of Cambridge, called a Scotchman, who married Esther Makepeace, who was the John born in England, in 1631. He lived in Cambridge, Marlboro, Falmouth and Watertown. He lived in a part of Watertown, later Lexington, which was called Scotland, hence, the name.

His son Joseph, the youngest child, was great grandfather of my great-grandfather, Joseph who was born in Lexington in 1773, and lived till 1850. The latter Joseph has many times told the family history from the emigrant down to my grandmother, who is living at the age of 93, and my father who is also alive, so I feel confident of its truth. Had you been familiar with the family you could easily have gotten this solution from either Hudson's Lexington, or Brown's History of Bedford.

MAUD L. BROWN, Chelsea, Mass.

With reference to the BOWEN family, those in this country and principally traced from Richard Bowen, of Rehoboth, Mass., (c 1640), Griffith Bowen, of Boston, (Map 1638), See:—

(1) "Memorial of the Bowen Family," by E. C. Bowen, M. D., part I. Rand, Avery & Co., Boston, 1884.

(2) "The Family of Griffith Bowen," (especially the branch of Silas Bowen, born Woodstock, Conn., 1722), by Daniel Bowen. Da Costa Printing Co., Jacksonville, Fla., 1893.

(3) "Lineage of Bowens of Woodstock; Conn.," by Edward Augustus Bowen. Riverside Press, Cambridge, Mass., 1897.

The Rev. J. E. Bowen, of West Point, New York, is and long has been engaged in the collection of Bowen data, and has a large mass of it already.

Arnold's Vital Record of Rehoboth, Mass., gives many datas, about the Richard Bowen branch.

WM. M. P. BOWEN, Providence, R. I.

I am a direct descendant according to my records taken from Todd's Burr Genealogy and various other sources it should be JEHU BURR, instead of John—(who was son of Jehu and probably came to America with his father)—otherwise the account corresponds with mine, which states that Jehu Burr came in Winthrop's fleet in 1630, was in Roxbury, 1635, where he and his wife's—Stedman's names appear as church members 1635, he was appointed overseer of arches and bridges.

In 1636, he joined the Wm. Pyncheon Colony, which planted Springfield where the records show he was a very prominent man. In 1645, he removed to Fairfield, Conn., where he also held many prominent and responsible positions at Commissioner, Representative, etc. He died about 1672, left four sons Jehu, John, Daniel and Nathaniel, and possibly daughters.

I have every reason to believe my record is right, but if it is not, I shall be glad to correct it.

Mrs. A. C. OLMSTED, Batavia, N. Y.

The statement on page 58, that Lucretia, (wife of Jonathan Brewster), came in the "Mayflower," is a mistake which should be corrected when your Genealogical Guide is published in book form. Shurtleff, Savage and Baylies, who wrote before the discovery of Gov. Bradford's manuscript history, all have the same error. The discovery in 1855, of the Bradford history, (sometimes called the "Mayflower Log,") with its carefully compiled list of the passengers of the "Mayflower," makes it certain that Lucretia and her son William, (grandson of Elder William Brewster), did not come on that vessel. Bradford's list is the supreme authority.

By an oversight, as he himself says, Mr. Davis in his "Ancient Landmarks of Plymouth," part II, page 44, repeats the same error, but on page 24, of part I, he states the facts correctly. Goodwin's "Pilgrim Republic," to which I recently called your attention, is right in this, as in most of its statements.

The above and other errors have unfortunately crept into the list given in the handsome "First Book" of the Society of Mayflower Descendants, issued 1896.

It is to be hoped that the Society will hasten to publish a new list in which these mis-statements do not occur.

G. HUNTER BARTLETT, Buffalo, N. Y.

I recently saw in the "Genealogical Guide to Early Settlers," as published in your journal for October, (vol. VI, No. 2.), page 100, the following line:

COMEGGS. Old Kent, Md., 224.

The name, as printed in your journal, is mis-spelled and should be COMEGYS—as it appears in "Old Kent of Maryland," by Hanson.

CORNELIUS COMEGYS, (referred to) was born in Lexmont, Holland, and went to Kent County, Md., about 1661, where he had a large plantation. He was naturalized, with his entire family, in 1671. (Chap. XXIX, Act of Assembly.) References:—Bacon's Laws of Maryland; Archives of Maryland, p. 241, (1689); Old Kent of (Maryland, by Hanson, p. 224; Memoirs of Long Island Historical Society, vol. 1, pp. 198-202. (Dankers & Sluyter's Journal.)

I send the corrected spelling of the name, and have mentioned the other details merely for your information as in corroboration of the true spelling of the name. Charles G. Comegys.

CHARLES G. COMEGYS, Cincinnati, Ohio.

If you will kindly compare the following dates, etc., you will see that Savage is undoubtedly mistaken in saying that MARY COULTMAN, (John 1,) married John 2, Nash (Edward 1,) in fact in the Notes under Nash, Savage himself credits John Nash with a different wife.

From Gen. Guide E. Set. of America.

John Coultman, of Wethersfield, 1645, a schoolmaster, who had been a servant with Leonard Chester . . . His daughter Mary, married May 1, 1684, John Nash, of Norwalk . . . .

From Wethersfield Records, New Eng. H. & G. Reg., vol. 1862, page 140.

John Coultman and Mary, his wife, were married September 2, 1667. Issue Mary, born November 29, 1672; Elizabeth, born January 14, 1677; Anna, born March 11, 1681.

From this you see that Mary Coultman was eleven and a half years old when John (2) Nash was married.

Hist. of Norwalk, by Sellick, page 105.

Edward 1, Nash of Norwalk, married the widow Barton, whose daughter Mary Barton married John 2, Nash, (Edward 1,) i. e. John 2, Nash of Norwalk married his step-sister Mary 1, Barton (Thomas 1).

Some of this confusion may have arisen from confusing the widow of Thomas Barton, of Fairfield, (who married Edward Nash), with the widow of another Thomas Barton, who married John Combs. Each of these widows seems to have had a daughter Mary, and both Maries appear to have been of suitable age to marry John 2, Nash.

Mary 2, Coultman, again:—

From Wethersfield Records, New Eng., H. & G. Reg., vol. 1886, page 126.

"David Sage and Mary, daughter of Jno. Coultman, was married May 3, 1693."

Hall Ancestry, p. 216, says that the David Sage who married Mary 2, Coultman (John 1), was born February 1, 1665, and was eldest son of David and Elizabeth (Kirby) Sage, of Middletown, Conn. I do not consider Hall Ancestry good authority, but this may be so.

L. BETHUNE, Buffalo, N. Y.

BYRAM:—Nicholas Byram, according to family tradition was son of an English gentleman of the County of Kent, who removed to Ireland about the time this son was born. His father sent him at the age of sixteen to visit his friends in England in charge of a man, who betrayed his trust, robbed him of his money, and sent him to the West Indies, whence he was sold to service to pay his passage, and after his term expired he made his way to New England and settled at Weymouth. He married Susanna, daughter of * Abraham Shaw of Dedham, and had Nicholas, Abigail, who married Thomas, Whitman, 1656; Deliverance, who married John Porter, 1660, Experience, who married John Willias, Susanna, who married Samuel Edson, and Mary, who married Samuel Leach,. These were all born at Weymouth. In 1660, he bought three proprietary or original purchase rights in Bridgewater . . . . . and settled there soon after. He died 1688; she died about 1698." (Hist. of Bridgewater, by Nahum Mitchell, 1840.)

* Abraham Shaw, of Dedham, made free 1637—his will on Boston Records without date, but inventory was taken in 1638, no wife named in will. (Mitchell's History.)

In your pages of the "Genealogical Guide," I notice that you have the names of HUGH CALKINS, and also Hugh Caulkins, as if they were two separate individua's. They are identically the same person. You have been misled by the fact that the name is sometimes spel'ed in both ways.　　　O. P. DICKINSON, Chicago, Ill.

On page 83, under the name CHAPIN, you give as the name of a son of Deacon Samuel Chapin, the name Joseph, 1642, it should be "Japhat, 1642," as per Chapin Genealogy and also Chapin, page 26, 27. Japhat or Japhet is quite a common name in the Chapin family.
　　　Mrs. EVA CHAPIN MAPLE, Maquon, Ill.

Under CHURCH, in the "Genealogical Guide to the Early Settlers of America," I note a most unpardonable error.
"Richard Warren, probably came in the Lion, 1623."
"Mr. Richard Warren," as he is generally sty'ed, was one of the Historical Founders of Plymouth Planta1ion, and signed the Mayflower Compact in 1620.
Let us hope the value of the Notes is not to be judged by the above statement!
　　　Mrs MORRIS P. FERRIS, Dobbs Ferry, N. Y.

RICHARD WARREN, fourth son of Christopher Warren of Greenwich, Kent, married Elizabeth Juatt, or Jewett, and came in the "Mayflower," December 22, 1620.
"1628. This year, this Mr. Richard Warren, a useful instrument in the difficulties attending the settlement of Plymouth."
"Mistress Elizabeth Warren, an aged widow, aged 90 years deceased on the 2nd of October, 1673, who having lived a Godly life, came to her grave as a shoke of corn fully ripe. She was honorably buried on the 4th of October aforesaid."

CHEEVER:—Ezekiel Cheever was born in London, Jan. 25, 1614; came to Boston in June, 1637, and to New Haven probably the next Spring and taught school there. —In list of planters he stands sixth. He removed in 1649, to Ipswich, Mass., and taught school; and to Charlestown in 1661, teaching the school there. In 1670, on invitation of the Selectmen he took charge of the school in Boston, at 60 pounds Sterling, per annum, and remained in this capacity until within a couple of years of his death, at the age of 94, August 21, 1708, having taught school for seventy-two years. His first wife Mary————, died in New Haven, January 20, 1649, and he married second November 18, 1652, Ellen Lathrop, sister of Captain Thomas Lathrop, of Bever!y; she died in Boston, September 10, 1706.
　　　T. H. LOOMIS, Brooklyn, N. Y.

I do not think you gave JOHN CLARK, a nice notice at all. He took the freeman's oath at General Court, held November 6, 1632, one of the forty-two original proprietors of Newtown, now Cambridge, March 29, 1632, see Savage's Winthrop I, 104, and d30. In Paige's Hist. of Cambridge, p. 510, John Clark owned land on corner Brattle and Mason Sts., which he sold to Edward Mason, and removed to Hartford, 1635, with the Rev. Mr. Hooker's Co., and his name is on the monument in the First Church. There is not much doubt that his second wife was Rebecca Marvin, daughter of Matthew Marvin, and his wife Alice, of Hartford, who died before him.
　　　Mrs. G. W. PERCY, Oakland; Cal.

Refering to NATHANIEL CLARK, p. 90, "Spirit of '76," for September. I find a disagreement with Clark Genealogy, G. K. Clark, Boston, T. R. Merriam & Son, which says:—
"Nathaniel Clark, who married Elizabeth Somerby, died August 25, 1690. His son Nathaniel, also married Jane Toppan, died on board of the ship "Six Friends," in October of the same year, aged 24.
　　　RUFUS W. CLARK, Detroit, Mich.

Refering to your October Number, page 103, FRANCIS COOK, of Plymouth, Mass. Please allow me to note the following for your notice.
Rev. JOHN COOKE, of Dartmouth, Mass., and son of Francis Cooke, came with his father in the "Mayflower," 1620. His mother Esther, came in the "Ann," 1623, with children Jacob, Jane and Esther. He married March 28, 1634, Sarah Warren, daughter of Richard and Elizabeth Warren, of London, Eng. Richard came in the "Mayflower," 1620, and Elizabeth and the five children came in the "Ann," 1623.
Rev. John Cooke was one of the first purchasers of Dartmouth land at "Cooksett," 1652, (now Westport), July 1, 1672, he settled an account with the town with a committee. of Lieut. John Smith, (of "Smith's Neck.") Samuel Hicks and Pelig Nipp—they "find that John Cooke shall have and forever enjoy a little is!and ca!led Ram Island in the Coaksett River, and 14 p3unds Sterling." Their children were:—
Elizabeth, born————married November 21, 1661, Daniel, the son of Edward Willcox.
Esther, born August 16, 1650.
Mercy, born July 25, 1654.
Marv, born————1657.
Sarah, born———— married Nov. 20, 1652, Arthur Hathaway.
I find your notice of Francis Cooke correct of record. I have much data and news of Dartmouth, Mass., my town of birth, and have been a student of genealogy for over 50 years—and would at anv or all times favor you with memorandum of old historic Dartmouth.
　　　H. H. H. CRAPO SMITH.

ELLMES:—Rhodolphus Ellmes, of Scituate, came in the "Planter," 1635, aged 15, married 1644, Catharine, daughter of John Whitcomb, had Sarah, 1645; Mary, 1648; Joanna, 1651; Hannah, 1653, John, 1655; Joseph, 1658; Waitstill, 1661; Jonathan, 1663; and Rhodolphus, 1668.

REFERENCES:—Deane's Hist. of Scituate, Mass., 266.

ELLMS. Eaton's Hist. of Thomaston, Me., 209.

ELLSWORTH:—Jeremiah Ellsworth, of Rowey, 1650, married 1657, Mary, widow of Hugh Smith, died 1704.

JOSIAH ELLSWORTH, of Windsor, married 1654, Elizabeth, daughter of Thomas Holcomb, had Josiah, 1655; Elizabeth, 1657; Mary, 1660; Martha, 1662; Thomas, 1665; Jonathan, 1669; John, 1671; Job, 1674; and Benjamin, 1677; died 1689, aged 60, when wife and all children were living.

REFERENCES:—Secomb's Hist. of Amherst, N. H., 580; Runnel's Hist. of Sanbornton, N. H., II, 265; Essex Inst. Col., XXI, 79, 97; Paige's Hist. of Hardwick, Mass., 368; Stiles' Hist. of Windsor, Conn., II, 208; Young's Hist. of Chautauqua County, N. Y., 419, 643; Howel's Hist. of Southampton, L. I., 2d ed., 241; Goodwin's Gen. Notes, 302; Kellogg's White Gen., 31; Loomis Gen. Female Branches, 300; Marshall's Grant Ancestry, 107; Strong Gen., 299; N. E. Hist. and Gen. Reg., V, 458; Savage's Gen. Dict., II, 114.

ELMENDORF: Sylvester's Hist. of Ulster County, N. Y., 102; Schoonmaker's Hist. of Kingston, N. Y., 479; Munsell's N. Y. Coll., IV, 120; N. Y. Gen. and Biog. Rec., XX, 101; Amer. Ancestry, vol. I, 26. Whittemore's Heroes of the Revolution and their Descendants, 136.

ELMER or ELLMER:—Edward Elmer, of Cambridge, came in the "Lion," 1632, went early to Hartford, of which he was one of the original proprietors, there had John, about 1645; Samuel, baptized 1647; Elizabeth, 1649; and Edward, 1654; removed to Northampton, there had Joseph, 1656; Mary, 1658; and he removed to Windsor, there had Sarah, about 1664. He was killed by the Indians in Philip's war, 1676. Of the wife we know not the name nor the mother.

REFERENCES:—Temple's Hist. of Northfield, Mass., 437; Hyde's Hist. of Brimfield, Mass., 397; Stiles' Hist. of Wndsor, Conn., II, 234; Orcutt's Hist. of Torrington, Conn., 687; Orcutt's Hist. of Stratford, Conn., 1197; Sedgwick's Hist. of Sharon, Conn., 78; Littell's Passaic Valley, N. J, 148; Ellis Gen., 373; Elmer Gen., 1840; Amer Ancestry, IX, 173, 223; Savage's Gen. Dict., II, 114.

ELMORE. Powers' Hist. of Sangamon County, Ill., 287; Amer. Ancestry, vol. I, 26; V, 28.

ELRICKS. Marshall Gen., 48.

ELSE or ELSIE:—Elisha Else, of Newbury, freeman, 1673.

NICHOLAS ELSE, New Haven, 1639, married as second wife, Hannah, widow of Robert Coe, of Stratford, had Samuel, 1666; died 1691. His widow died 1702.

ROGER ELSE, Yarmouth, 1643, had John, baptized 1649; admitted an inhabitant of Boston, 1654, removed to Charlestown, 1658, and died 1668.

ELSON. ELSEN or ELSING:—Abraham Elson, Wethersfield, may have been there 10 years, but died 1648, leaving two daughters His widow married 1649, Jarvis Mudge.

JAMES ELSON, of Charlestown, by wife Sarah, who died 1680, aged 38, had James, baptized 1672; and Abigail, 1674. He was, tradition says, master of a ship taken by the pirates of Algiers, 1678 or 9, and perhaps died in slavery.

JOHN ELSON, of Wethersfield, perhaps brother of Abraham, married a widow who had sons Benjamin and Job and John; had no children of his own, and died probably same time as Abraham. His widow married Thomas Wright.

JOHN ELSON, of Wells, freeman 1653, may have been the man at Cradock's plantation, 1631, called Elston; forced by the Indian hostility, 1675, to Salem, where he died 1685, leaving wdow and six children.

REFERENCES:—Savage's Gen. Dict., II, 115.

ELTHAM:—William Eltham, of Woburn, had Hannah, 1690.

REFERENCES:—Savage's Gen. Dict., II, 115.

ELSTER. Buckingham Gen., 112.

ELSWORTH. Roome Cen., 104; Amer. Ancestry, V, 154.

ELTING. Sylvester's Hist. of Ulster County, N. Y., 54; Schoonmaker's Hist. of Kingston, N. Y., 479; N. Y Gen. and Biog. Rec., XVI, 25; Amer. Ancestry, IV, 151.

ELTON:—John Elton, of Middletown, by wife Jane, had Mary, 1672; Richard, 1674; John, 1676; Richard, again, 1679; Ann, 1681; and Ebenezer, 1686.

A Mr. Elton, of Southold, L. I., 1662, was admitted freeman of Conn. that year, and may have been father of the preceding.

REFERENCES:—Cregar's White Gen.; Savage's Gen. Dict., I, 116.

ELTONHEAD. Neil's Virginia Carolorum, 251.

ELWELL:—Robert Elwell, of Dorchester, 1635, removed 1638, to Salem, there had baptized, beside two others not named, John, 1640; and Isaac, 1642; freeman 1640; removed to Gloucester, was a selectman 1648, and often after; had wife Jane, who died 1675, and he died 1683, but may have married 1676, Alice Leach. He had Samuel; Josiah; Joseph; Sarah, 1451; Thomas, baptized 1655; Jacob, born 1657; Richard, baptized 1658; and perhaps others.

REFERENCES:—Farrow's Hist. of Islesborough, Me., 203; Eaton's Hist. of Thomaston, Me., II, 211; Corliss' Hist. of North Yarmouth, Me.; Babson's Hist. of Gloucester, 87; Shaud's Hist. of Fenwick Colony, N. J., 78; Savage's Gen. Dict., II, 116.

ELWYN. Wentworth Gen., vol. I, 337.

ELY:—Nathaniel Ely, of Cambridge, 1632, freeman 1635, removed, probably, next year to Hartford, was an original proprietor, constable 1639, one of the first settlers at Norwalk, 1651, and representative 1657, but removed to Springfield three years later, and died there 1675. His widow Martha, died 1688. The only children we hear of are Samuel and Ruth; yet there may have been other daughters.

RICHARD ELY, of Saybrook, had been a merchant of Boston, 1664, and there married that year Elizabeth, widow of John Cullick, and sister of Col. Fenwick. But by a former wife, he had, perhaps, not born on our side of the water, William and Richard; he died 1684; his wife died 1683.

A Mr. ELY, a mariner, came in the "Mayflower." 1620, but not as a passenger, to abide in the land. He was hired by the Pilgrims for a year, and had no farther relation to New England. Yet, as he was not one of the crew of the vessel, but continued here till his time was out, the number is 102 besides the ship's company in that famous voyage.

REFERENCES:—Long Meadow, Mass., Centen., 58; West Springfield, Mass., Centen., 117; Orcutt's Hist. of Stratford, Conn., 1197; Saunderson's Hist. of Charlestown, N. H., 333; Darling Memorial; Goodrich's Recollections of a Lifetime, vol. I, 533; Goodwin's Olcott Gen., 16; Hall's Genealogical Notes, 106; Hill's Gen. Table of Lee Family, App. C.; Kellogg's White Gen., 65; Kitchell Gen., 52; Montague Gen., 83; Walworth's Hyde Gen., II, 838; Amer. Ancestry, III, 78; VII, 137; N. E. Hist. and Gen. Reg., XXXV, 236; Savage's Gen. Dict., II, 116; Ely Reunion; Ely Gen.

EMBLIN:—John Emblin, of Boston, minister of the first Baptist Church from 1684, to his death, 1702.

REFERENCES:—Savage's Gen. Dict., II, 116.

EMBREE. Futhey's Hist. of Chester County, Pa., 53.

EMBRY. Meade's Old Farms of Va.

EMERICK. Amer. Ancestry, II, 36.

EMERSON:—John Emerson, of Ipswich, came in the "Abigail," 1635, a baker, aged 20. It may be that he removed to Scituate, and married at Duxbury, 1638, Barbara, daughter of Rev. John Lothrop.

JOHN EMERSON, of Newbury, a lieutenant, by wife Judith, had John, 1690; Daniel, 1693; Joseph, 1696; Samuel, 1699; and Jonathan, 1702.

MICHAEL EMERSON, of Haverhill, 1656.

ROBERT EMERSON, of Haverhill, freeman 1668, who had removed from Rowley, where he was as early as 1655; was killed by the Indians, with his wife and children, Sarah and Timothy, 1697.

THOMAS EMERSON, of Ipswich, 1639, a baker, died 1666; by wife Elizabeth, had Joseph, Nathaniel and James, Thomas and John.

REFERENCES.

MASSACHUSETTS.—Hammatt Papers Ipswich, 85; Wyman's Charlestown Gens., vol. I, 334; Eaton's Hist. of Reading, 68; Babson's Hist. of Gloucester, 197; Malden Bi-Centen., 244.

MAINE.—Dearborn's Hist. of Parsonfield, 378; Poor's Hist. of Merrimac Valley, 100, 171; Redlon's Harrison Settlers, 57; Eaton's Hist. of Thomaston, II, 213.

NEW HAMPSHIRE.—Worcester's Hist. of Hollis, 373; Runnel's Hist. of Sanbornton, II, 268; Secomb's Hist. of Amherst, 581; Chase's Hist. of Chester, 516; Eaton's Hist. of Candia, 69; Fullerton's Hist. of Raymond, 215; Coggswell's Hist. of Henniker, 562; Hayward's Hist. of Hancock, 553; Kidder's Hist. of New Ipswich, 445; Morrison's Hist. of Windham, 524; Livermore's Hist. of Wilton, 363; New Hampshire Hist. Soc. Coll., VII, 378; Washington, N. H., 394; Wheeler's Hist. of Newport, 376; Aldrich's Hist. of Walpole, 245.

OTHER PUBLICATIONS.—Williams' Hist. of Danby, Vt., 142; Walker Family, 24; Turner Gen.; Thompson's Memoirs of Ebner Thompson; Poore Gen., 75; Emerson Gen.; Crane's Rawson Gen., 87; Chapin Gen., 309; Chapman's Trowbridge Gen., 309; Blake's Hist. of Mindon Assn., 271; Amer. Ancestry, V, 87; VI, 185; XI, 29; Savage's Gen. Dict., II, 117.

EMERY or EMORY:—Anthony Emery, a carpenter, of Romsey, in Hants, came in the "James," 1635,

to Boston, perhaps with wife and children, removed about 1644, to Dover, thence after 1648, to Kittery; was ferryman, kept an inn 1650, freeman 1652, constable 1658, representative 1680.

ROBERT EMERY, of New Haven. See Ambry.

GEORGE EMERY, of Salem, a physician, had, says Felt, grant of land 1637, was born 1609, and died 1687, his wife died 1673.

JAMES EMERY, of Kittery, perhaps brother of Anthony, freeman 1652, constable 1670, and representative 1676, 7, 84, 5, and 92.

JOHN EMERY, of Newbury, 1635, brother of Anthony, came in the James, 1635, freeman 1641; brought son John, had here a daughter Ebenezer, 1648; and Jonathan, 1652.

NOAH EMERY, of Kittery, perhaps son of Anthony or John, escaped from the Indians 1693.

REFERENCES.

NEW HAMPSHIRE.—Dow's Hist. of Hampton, 702; Cochrane's of Antrim, 485; Coggswell's Hist of Henniker, 564; Cutter's Hist. of Jaffray, 309; Chase's Hist. of Chester, 518; Runnell's Hist. of Sanbornton, II, 269.

MAINE.—Hatch's Hist. of Industry, 604; Eaton's Hist. of Thomaston, II, 211; Maine Hist. Soc. Coll., IV, 289; Poor's Hist. of Merrimac Valley, 119; Buxton Centen., 220; Farrow's Hist. of Islesborough, 203.

OTHER PUBLICATIONS.—Coffin's Hist. of Newbury, Mass., 301; Freeman's Hist. of Cape Cod, II, 615; Austin's R. I. Gen. Dict., 72; Benton's Hist. of Guildhall, Vt., 219; Palmer Gen., 56; Guild's Stiles Gen., 32; Dudley Gen., 122; Amer. Ancestry, 14, 37; VII, 121; IX, 212; N. E. Hist. and Gen. Reg. XXIII, 414; XXVII, 423; Savage's Gen. Dict., II, 118; Emery Gen.

EMES. Leonard's Hist. of Dublin, N. H., 330.

EMLEN. Futhey's Hist. of Chester County, Pa., 536.

EMMERSON. Williams' Hist. of Danby, 142.

EMMERTON. Drover Gen., 343; Emmerton Gen.

EMMES. Whitmore's Copp's Hill Epitaphs.

EMMET. Heraldic Journal, vol. 1, 95.

EMMETT. Whitmore's Temple Gen.

EMMONS. Bergen's Hist. Kings County, N. Y., 108.

EMMONS:—Henry Emmons, of Boston, by wife Mary, had Samuel, 1690.

THOMAS EMMONS, of Newport, 1638, probably removed to Boston, freeman 1652, died 1664, had daughter Hannah, also Elizabeth, wife Martha, sons Ben a-min, Obidiah and Samuel.

REFERENCES:—Whittemore's Hist. of Middlesex County, Conn., 321; Bradbury's Hist. of Kennebunkport, Me., 242; North's Hist. of Augusta, Me., 850; Temple's Hist. of North Brookfield, Mass., 587; Babson's Hist. of Gloucester, Mass., 90; Blake's Hist. of Mindon Association, 109; Spooner Gen., 210; Mack Gen., 16, 35; Blake Gen., 48; Savage's Gen. Dict., II, 119.

EMORY. Stearns' Hist. of Ashburnham, Mass., 692; Stearns' Hist. of Rindge, N. H., 514.

EMPIE. Willis' Washington Gen., 281; Amer. Ancestry, II, 36.

EMPY. Pearson's Hist. of Schenectady, N. Y., 65.

ENDICOTT:—Gilbert Endicott, of Reading, said to have been born 1658, at Dorchester, but we know nothing more.

JOHN ENDICOTT, perhaps from Dorchester, England, by some thought his place of birth; born about 1589; came in the "Abigail," from Weymouth, a small port in the channel, with wife and a small company of about 20 or 30 others, including women and children, to Salem, 1628. He was one of the six original purchasers of Massachusetts Bay from the Plymouth Council, March preceding, and the only one who came over for more than two years. In the Royal Charter of March following, he is named as an Assistant, one of 18, and by his associates at London in General Court, after his coming, made the head superintendent, or governor, of the first settlement at Salem, called London's plantation. He was the seventh Charter Governor of Massachusetts, 1644. Honor enough there is for Endicott, the earliest patentee who came over under the indenture from the Plymouth Company, without calling him "first Governor of Massachusetts." He was the first and only Governor of the London's Plantation, and if he ever was qualified by taking the oaths under that delegation from the Governor and Company of Massachusetts, which is unlikely and cannot be proven, he never had a successor in that office, which was merged in the superior title on arrival of Winthrop. As Assistant, he continued for 9 years, from 1630, by successive elections; except in 1635, when for his indiscreet zeal against the cross in the ensign, he was left out; but in 1636, he was made head of the first expedition against the Pequots; for the first time, in 1641, deputy-governor according to the Charter, and seven times after, and in 1644, governor for the first time, with full power according to the Charter, and again after the death of Winthrop, 1649, 51, 2, 3, and from 1655, to his death at Boston, (where he had resided for about twenty years), 1665, serving a longer period than any other of the Governors under the old Charter, and by Shirley alone exceeded, since, Endicott was of stern energy, but great prudence in secular affairs, disapproving the conduct of his friends in England, for putting to death their King, and issued warrants for the apprehension of Whalley and Goffe, the regicides, here. Much of the sad occurences of cruel scourging of the Baptists 1651, and hanging of the Quakers 1659, that fell within his administration, must be charged to Wilson and Norton, the spiritual advisers of the day. His first wife was Ann Gower, who was a cousin or niece of Matthew Cradock., first Charter Governor, died soon after coming, and she had, it is believed, no children; and he married 1630, Elizabeth Gibson, from Cambridge, England, had John, 1632; and Zerubbabel, about 1635.

WILLIAM ENDICOTT, of Boston, a mariner, in his will 1690, he mentions son-in-law John Bell, and wife Joanna.

WILLIAM ENDICOTT, of Boston, by wife Elizabeth, had William, 1686; Elizabeth, 1690; John, 1693; Elizabeth, 1699; Benjamin, 1702; Lydia, 1703; Lydia, again, 1704; Sarah, 1705; Sarah, again, 1706; and Benjamin, again, 1709.

REFERENCES:—Perley's Hist. of Boxford, Mass., 98; Moore's Mem. Am. Governors, vol. I, 363; Dunstable Bi-Centennial, 176; Felton Gen., 20; N. E. Hist. and Gen. Reg., vol. I, 263, 335; Savage's Gen. Dict., II, 120.

ENDILL:—Michael Endill, Isle of Shoals, was grand juror at Court in York, 1659.

REFERENCES:—Savage's Gen. Dict., II, 120.

ENGLAND:—John England, of New Haven, 1647, removed to Branford, died 1655, left widow, but no children. Probably another of this name in one of the Providence Plantations, had daughter Ellen, who married 1665, Jeremiah Westcott.

REFERENCES:—Powers' Hist. of Sangamon County, Ill., 289; Futhey's Hist. of Chester County, Pa., 538; Cregar's Haines Ancestry, 60; Austin's R. I. Gen. Dict., 72.

ENGLE:—Bernard Engle, of Boston, 1664, husbandman.

JAMES ENGLE, of Boston, 1662, mariner.

REFERENCES:—Cregar's Haines Gen., 18; Penn. Mag., IV, 353; Savage's Gen. Dict., II, 120.

ENGLISH or ENGLES:—Clement English, of Salem, married 1667, Mary, daughter of Richard Waters, had Mary, 1669; Elizabeth, 1671; Joseph, 1673; Benjamin, 1676; Abigail, 1680; and Clement, 1683. The father died December before, 1682.

JAMES ENGLISH, of Boston, married 1658, perhaps as second wife, Joanna, daughter of John Farnum, who was not 14 years old. We know too little of him to affirm or deny that he was dead 1698, freeman 1691.

MAUDETT ENGLISH, of Boston, by wife Jane had Hannah, 1639; Mary, 1644; his will names son Samuel, and daughter-in-law Mary; perhaps this daughter-in-law was the widow English, who married 1688, Joshua Lee.

PHILIP ENGLISH, of Salem, son of John, or Isle of Jersey, there baptized 1651, a merchant, married 1675, Mary, daughter of Richard Hollingworth, suffered very much in the blind ferocity against witchcraft. His wife was the greater sufferer, and lived very few years after escape. This was managed with skill and firmness by Rev. Joshua Moodey, then minister with Willard in the Old South Ch rch in Boston. He had second wife Sarah Ingersoll, was representative 1700, one of the contributors to the first Episcopal Church, 1734, and died 1740. He reckoned his damage by the persecution at 1500 pounds sterling, and was allowed about 20 years later 300 pounds sterling.

THOMAS ENGLISH, of Plymouth, one of the passengers of the "Mayflower," 1620, died next spring, leaving no wife nor children. He was a sailor hired by the Pilgrims.

WILLIAM ENGLISH, of Ipswich, 1638, shoemaker, freeman 1642, representative 1646 and 7, removed to Hampton, 1639, for short time, but went back to Ipswich. He may be the same who was admitted at Boston, 1652, constable 1656, with wife Sarah, joined our church 1663.

REFERENCES:—Tuttle Family of Conn., 105; Cunabell Gen., 36; Amer. Ancestry, V, 81; VI, 28; VIII, 89.

ENO, EANNO, ENNO or ENNOE:—James Eno, of Windsor, 1646, married 1648, Ann Bedwell, had Sarah, 1649; James, 1651; and John, 1654. His wife died 1657, and he had second wife 1658, widow of Thomas Holcomb, who died 1679, and he married 1680, Esther, widow of James Eggleston. He died 1682.

ENOW:—Thomas Enow, Falmouth, 1689.

REFERENCES:—Stiles' Hist. of Windsor, Conn., II, 239; Orcutt's Hist. of Torrington, 687; Andrews' Hist. of New Britain, Conn., 127; Barbor's My Wife and Mother, App., 76; Bidwell Gen., Hayden's Virginia Gens., 24; Marshall's Grant Ancestry, 109; Savage's Gen. Dict., II, 124; Howe's Barber and Eno Gen.

ENOS. Power's Hist. of Sangamon County, Ill., 288.

ENSIGN:—James Ensign, of Cambridge, 1634, freeman 1635, removed about 1639 to Hartford, had only son David, and three daughters, Sarah, Lydia, baptized 1649, and Mary; his will was probated 1671.

THOMAS ENSIGN, of Scituate, married 1639, Elizabeth Wilder, of Hingham, had Hannah, baptized 1640; Elizabeth and John. He was of Duxbury, 1656, and died 1663.

REFERENCES:—Winsor's Hist. of Duxbury, Mass., 257; Stiles' Hist. of Windsor, Conn., II, 248; Deane's Hist. of Scituate, Mass., 266; Amer. Ancestry, VII, 119; VIII, 214; Savage's Gen. Dict., II, 124.

EDSOME:—Robert Edsome, of Boston, 1646, merchant.

REFERENCES:—Savage's Gen. Dict., II, 124.

ENSOR. Mallory's Bohemia Manor.

ENSWORTH, ENDSWORTH or ENISWORTH:—Tixall, Tixoll, Texhall or Tyxhall Ensworth, so variously written in records, was of Hartford, 1681, removed 1700, to Canterbury, had baptized at Hartford, five children, and left Nathaniel, Nehemiah, Ezra and Joseph.

ENYARD. Clute's Hist. of Staten Island, 380.

ENYART. Powers' Hist. of Sangamon County, Ill., 380.

EPES or EPPES:—Daniel Epes, of Ipswich, son of Daniel, from Kent, England, came 1637 with his mother Martha, who is said to have married Samuel Symonds. He married 1644 Elizabeth, eldest daughter of Samuel Symonds, who died 1685, aged 60, by whom he had Samuel, 1647; Daniel, 1649; Nathaniel, 1650; John, 1651; Joseph, 1653; Martha, 1654; Mary, 1656; Lionel, 1657; another son, 1658; and Richard, 1659. He had second wife Lucy, daughter of Rev. John Woodbridge, widow of Rev. Simon Bradstreet, of New London; was freeman 1674, a captain, representative 1684, and died 1693, aged about 70 years.

REFERENCES:—Hammatt Papers of Ipswich, 93; Slaughter's Bristol Parish, Va., 172; Richmond, Va., Standard, II, 32; III, 16, 40; Meade's Old Families of Va.; Page Gen., 105; N. E. Hist. and Gen. Reg., XIII, 115; Savage's Gen. Dict., II, 125.

ERB. Harris' Hist. Lancaster County, Pa., 194.

ERICHZON. Pearson's Hist. of Schenectady, 63.

ERRINGTON. Paige's Hist. of Cambridge, Mass., 540.

ERSKINE. Life of Rev. William Smith.

ERVING. Prime's Bowdoin Gen.

ERTING. Cath. Hist. Coll., II, 333; Amer. Ancestry, III, 16; VI, 30.

ERRINGTON:—Abraham Errington, of Cambridge, 1649, married Rebecca, daughter of Robert Cutler, of Charlestown, had Abraham, 1652; perhaps had a second Abraham, 1654; Rebecca, Hannah, Sarah, Mary, baptized 1661; Abraham, 1663; and Jacob. He died 1677, aged 55. Ann, probably his mother, died 1653, aged 76; but his father was, perhaps, dead before she came over.

THOMAS ERRINGTON, of Lynn, 1642, was of Charlestown, 1647, but soon back to Lynn, and probably removed to Warwick, there freeman 1655.

REFERENCES:—Savage's Gen. Dict., II, 125.

ERWIN:—Edward Erwin, of Dover, 1658.

REFERENCES:—Savage's Gen. Dict., II, 125.

ESMOND. Collins' Hist. of Hillsdale, N. Y., 53.

ESSET:—William Esset, of Boston, married Ann Sheffield, died 1697.

REFERENCES:—Savage's Gen. Dict., II, 125.

ESPY. Plumb's Hist. of Hanover, Pa., 440; Kulp's Wyoming Valley Farms. Egle's Penn. Gens., 177.

ESSELSTYN. Munsell's Albany, N. Y., Coll., IV, 120; Amer. Ancestry, II, 36.

ESTABROOK or EASTERBROOK:—Joseph Estabrook, of Concord, came about 1660, from Enfield, Middlesex, England, it is said, with two brothers, graduated Harvard College, 1664, ordained about 1667, freeman 1665, married 1668, Mary, daughter of Hugh Mason, had Joseph, 1669; Benjamin, 1671; Mary, 1673; Samuel, 1675; Daniel, 1677; and Ann, 1678. He died 1711.

THOMAS ESTABROOK, of Swanzey, by wife Sarah, had Elizabeth, 1673.

REFERENCES.

MASSACHUSETTS.—Hudson's Hist. of Lexington, 61; Paige's Hist. of Cambridge, 541; Reed's Hist. of Rutland, 159; Bond's Hist. of Watertown, 204; Cutter's Hist. of Arlington, 236; Westminster, Mass., Centen., 32.

OTHER PUBLICATIONS.—Washington, N. H., Hist., 794; Norton's Hist. of Fitzwilliam, N. H., 547; Hayward's Hist. of Hancock, N. H., 563; Fowler's Chauncey Mem., 299; Heminway's Vt. Gaz., V, 146; Amer. Ancestry, VI, 62; Savage's Gen. Dict., II, 126; Estabrook Gen.

ESTERBROOK. Amer. Ancestry, VII, 56.

ESTAUGH. Clement's Hist. of Newtown, N. J.

ESTEN:—Thomas Esten, of Providence, swore allegiance 1682.

REFERENCES:—Austin's R. I. Gen. Dict., 294; Savage's Gen. Dict., II, 126.

ESTES:—Matthew Estes, of Dover, son of Robert, of Dover, England, where he was born 1645, married 1676. Philadelphia, daughter of Reginald Jenkins, had Joseph. John, 1684; Richard, 1686; and Matthew, 1689; possibly more. He probably removed to Scituate, and his wife died 1721; and he died 1723.

REFERENCES:—Lapham's Hist. of Woodstock, Me., 213; Lapham's Hist. of Bethel, Me., 525; Bassett's Hist. of Richmond, N. H., 386; Barry's Hist. of Hanover, Mass., 397; Spooner Gen., vol. I, 484; Savage's Gen. Dict., II, 126; Amer. Ancestry, III, 153, 205; IV, 42; Estes Gen.

ESTEY. Heminway's Vt. Gaz., V, 144; Amer. Ancestry, VIII, 100.

ESTY. Thurston's Hist. of Winthrop, Me., 181; Morrison's Hist. of Windham, N. H., 527; Morse Mem. Appendix X, 20; Essex Inst. Coll., XVI, 104.

ESTHERBROOKS. Hodgman's Hist. of Westford, 445.

ESTOW:—William Estow, of Hampton, 1639, died 1655; in his will names only daughters Sarah and Mary.

REFERENCES:—Savage's Gen. Dict., II, 126.

ETHEREDGE:—Edward Etheredge, of Massachusetts, 1646.

REFERENCES:—Savage's Gen. Dict., II, 126.

ETHERINGTON:—Thomas Etherington, of Kittery, was lost, with his wife in the wreck of a small vessel, 1664.

REFERENCES:—Savage's Gen. Dict., II, 127.

EUSTACE. Hayden's Virginia Genealogies, 216.

EUSTIS:—William Eustis, of Charlestown, lived at Malden, perhaps Winisemet, or Boston, 1695, had, I suppose, son William, perhaps other children, and w.fe Sarah ,who died 1713, aged 74.

REFERENCES:—Wyman's Charlestown, Mass., Gens., vol. I, 336; Reed's Hist. of Rutland, Mass., 127; N. E. Hist. and Gen. Reg., XXXII, 204; Savage's Gen. Dict., II, 127.

EVANCE:—John Evance, of New Haven, 1639, came probably, from London, signed the original compact, was one of the most wealthy inhabitants, had Daniel, baptized 1646; Mary and Stephen, 1652. He probably went home, certainly was at London, 1656, and his widow Susanna, married at London, Henry Hatsell.

REFERENCES:—Savage's Gen. Dict., II, 127.

EVAN. Smith's Delaware County, 459.

EVANS:—David Evans, of Boston, 1654, merchant, died 1663, leaving widow Mary, by whom he had David and Elizabeth, 1655; and Martha, 1657.

HENRY EVANS, of Boston, 1643, husbandman, freeman 1645; and his wife Amy, came in the year preceding, from the church of Roxbury. Administration on one Henry Evans, who was drowned 1667, was granted in Middlesex, to his widow Esther.

JOHN EVANS, of Wethersfield, 1640, may have been at Hatfield, 1678.

JOHN EVANS, of Roxbury, by wife Mary, had John, baptized 1671; Peter, 1673; Peter, again, 1674; it is thought he served in Philip's war. Perhaps he lost his wife before or after he removed to Hatfield, there married 1677, Mary, widow of Experience Hinsdale, daughter of John Hawke, had Elinor, 1678; Jonathan, 1680; and Randall, 1682; removed about 1685 to Deerfield.

JOHN EVANS, of Dover, there acted as a commissioner with others to settle York, Dover and Kittery boundary.

PHILIP EVANS, of Newbury, by wife Deborah, had William, 1687; Elizabeth, 1689; and John, 1692; the last at Ipswich.

RICHARD EVANS, of Dorchester, freeman 1643, by wife Mary, had Richard, Mary, 1641; Matthias, 1644; besides probably Hannah and Joanna.

RICHARD EVANS, of Rehoboth, had Richard, 1681.

ROBERT EVANS, of Dover, 1665, had Robert, 1665; Edward, 1667; Jonathan, 1669; and Elizabeth, 1672; all by wife Elizabeth; was killed 1689, or as another account gives it, died of cancer, 1697.

THOMAS EVANS, of Plymouth, died 1635.

THOMAS EVANS, of Dorchester, 1640, perhaps was there 1689.

THOMAS EVANS, of Salisbury, married 1686, Hannah Brown, had Ann, 1687; John, 1689; Abigail, 1692; Thomas, in 1696; and Hannah, 1698.

WILLIAM EVANS, of Taunton, 1643, probably died before 1676, or he may have been the same as William, of Gloucester, one of the selectmen, 1647-8, was of Ipswich, 1656.

REFERENCES.

MASSACHUSETTS.—Temple's Hist. of Northfield, 438; Eaton's Hist. of Reading, 69; Wyman's Charlestown

Gens., vol. I, 336; Saunderson's Hist. of Charlestown, 334.

NEW HAMPSHIRE.—Smith's Hist. of Petersborough, 66; Morrison's Hist. of Windham, 528; Runnel's Hist. of Sanbornton, II, 273.

OTHER PUBLICATIONS.—Timlow's Hist. of Southington, Conn., 90; Austin's R. I. Gen. Dict., 73; Futhey's Hist. of Chester County, Pa., 538; Jenkins' Hist. of Gwynedd, Pa., 146, 380; Lapham's Hist. of Norway, Me., 499; Rhoad's Chronicles of Phila.; Gregg's Hist. of Old Cheraws, S. C., 75; Potts' Carter Gen., 177; Maris Gen., 224; Johnston's Hist. of Cecil County, Md., 485; Jackson Gen., 188, 193; Holton's Winslow Mem., 475; Alexander Gen., 111; Amer. Ancestry, III, 65; VII, 285; IX, 201; Savage's Gen. Dict., II, 127; Fox, Ellicott an l Evans Gens.

EVARTS:—John Evarts, of Concord, freeman 1638, had John, 1640; and Judah, 1642; but other children must have been older, certainly James, and probably one or more brought from England; removed to Guilford, 1650, and died 1669. We know not the mother of his children, but at Guilford, he married Elizabeth, widow of John Parmelee, the elder. John, Judah, Daniel and heirs of James were proprietors. His daughter Elizabeth, married Peter Abbott.

REFERENCES:—Hist. of Litchfield County, Conn., 557; Whitemore's Heroes of the Revolution and their Descendants, 101; Savage's Gen. Dict., II, 128.

EVERTS. Joslin's Hist. of Poultney, Vt., 250; Goode Gen., 171; Amer. Ancestry, vol. I, 26.

EVE:—Adam Eve, of Boston, is the strange name of one who married 1694, Elizabeth, youngest daughter of William Barsham, of Watertown, had daughter Annabel, who married Jonathan Benjamin.

REFERENCES:—Savage's Gen. Dict., II, 127.

EVELETH:—John Eveleth, of Ipswich, by wife Mary, had Mary, 1683; but may have had others several years before or after; died 1745, in his 107th year. John of Ipswich, possibly, was his son.

SYLVESTER EVELETH, of Gloucester, had been a baker at Boston, 1642, at Gloucester was selectman 1647, 9 and 51; had wife Susanna, who died 1659, or 1669; by her had Isaac, Joseph, baptized 1643; and Hannah, 1644, both at Boston. He married 1672, B ridget, probably widow of first Elias Parkman.

REFERENCES:—Leonard's Hist. of Dublin, N. H., 331; Hayward's Hist. of Hancock, N. H., 565; North's Hist. of Augusta, Me., 851; Hatch's Hist. of Industry, Me., 614; Hammatt Papers, Ipswich, Mass., 94; Babson's Hist. of Gloucester, Mass., 91; Savage's Gen. Dict., II, 129.

EVELYN. Evelyn Gen.

EVERARD. Meade's Old Families Va.; N. E. Hist. and Gen. Reg., XXXVIII, 66.

EVERDEN:—Anthony Everden, of Providence, took the oath of allegiance, 1666.

RICHARD EVERDEN, of Providence, swore allegiance 1668.

THOMAS EVERDEN, of Salem, 1682, a Quaker preacher.

WALTER EVERDEN, from Kent, an aged man, employed in the manufacture of gunpowder, was of Massachusetts, 1674.

REFERENCES:—Austin's R. I. Gen. Dict., 73; Savage's Gen. Dict., II, 129.

JOHN EVERED, with a perpetual alias Webb, for surname, of Boston, from Marlborough, in Wilts, came in the "James," 1635, had large estate from 1656, as also at Chelmsford, where he was Captain, and Representative, 1663, 4 and 5, spent the last 5 or 6 years of his life in that part and died 1668. His will names wife Mary, and it may be presumed that he left no descendants.

STEPHEN EVERED, perhaps brother of the preceding, having the same alias, and coming in the same ship with him.

WILLIAM EVERED, of Charlestown, without the alias, married 1659, Sarah Fillebrown.

REFERENCES:—Savage's Gen. Dict., II, 130.

EVEREST:—Isaac Everest, of Guilford, by wife Joanna, had John, Isaac, 1667; Benjamin and Lydia, died 1697, probably.

JOB EVEREST, brother of the preceding, died 1684, unmarried.

REFERENCES:—Brown's West Simsbury, Conn., Settlers, 59; Amer. Ancestry, II, 37; Savage's Gen. Dict., II, 130.

EVERETT:—Francis Everett, of Reading, 1675, married at Cambridge, Mary Edwards.

RICHARD EVERETT, of Dedham, had, I presume, lived at Watertown, there probably, by wife Mary, had John, removed about 1636 or 7, had Mary, 1638; Samuel, 1639; Sarah, 1641; and James, 1643; the mother died soon. He married 1643, at Springfield, Mary Winch, had Sarah, again, 1644; Abigail, 1647; Israel, 1651; Ruth, 1654; and Jedediah, 1656. He died 1682.

RICHARD EVERETT, of Jamaica, L. I., had died in 1666, or earlier, for in that year Abraham Smith was appointed administrator of his estate in trust for his children. These children are not named.

WILLIAM EVERETT, whose name might be Averitt, of Kittery, 1640, was admitted a freeman of Massachusetts, 1652, when, perhaps, he was of Dover, died at sea 1674.

REFERENCES.

MASSACHUSETTS.—Hill's Dedham Records; Temple's Hist. of Northfield, 439; Morse's Gen. of Sherborn, Mass., 81; Jameson's Hist. of Medway, 482.

OTHER PUBLICATIONS.—Sedgwick's Hist. of Sharon, Conn., 79; Boyd's Annals of Winchester, Conn., 47; Eaton's Hist. of Thomaston, Me., II, 213; Lapham's Hist. of Norway, Me., 498; Norton's Hist. of Fitzwilliam, N. H., 548; Richmond, Va., Standard, IV, 5; Everett Gen.; Crawford Family of Va., 79; Amer. Ancestry, IV, 185, 217; N. E. Hist. and Gen. Reg., XIV, 215; Savage's Gen. Dict., II, 130.

EVERHART. Everhart Gen.

EVERINGHAM. Humphrey's Gen., 587.

EVERILL:—Abiel Everill, of Boston, married 1655, Elizabeth, daughter of Lieut. William Phillips, had James, 1656; and died early, for his widow married 1660, John Alden, Jr.

JAMES EVERILL, of Boston, was admitted with wife Elizabeth, of the church 1634, freeman 1635, had Ezekiel, baptized 1636; Coneniah, 1638; and Elizabeth, 1641; beside Ann or Hannah, older than either, who was born, probably, in England; was in good esteem, often one of the selectmen, died 1682 or 3.

REFERENCES:—Savage's Gen. Dict., II, 131.

EVERETT. Orcutt's Hist. of Torrington, Conn., 688; Orcutt's Hist. of New Milford, 693.

EVERTON:—William Everton, of Manchester, 1658, Charlestown, 1674, by wife Sarah, had John, Fownell, Joseph and Sarah, all baptized 1677; William, 1677; Benjamin, 1680; and by second wife Ruth Walley, married 1684, had Elizabeth, baptized 1688; and Ruth, 1691; wife died next year, and he died 1688.

REFERENCES:—Wyman's Charlestown, Mass., Gens.; Savage's Gen. Dict., II, 132.

EVERTSEN. Munsell's Albany, N. Y., Coll., IV, 120; Bergen's Kings County, N. Y., 111.

EWE:—John Ewe, of Hartford, by misadventure killed Thomas Scott, 1643, and was fined ten pounds for the widow and five for the colony.

REFERENCES:—Savage's Gen. Dict., 130.

EWELL:—Henry Ewell, of Scituate, came from Sandwich, Kent, 1635, in the "Hercules," shoemaker, united with the church 1636, was a soldier in the Pequot war 1637, married 1638, Sarah, daughter of Anthony Annable, removed to Barnstable, where his eldest son was baptized 1640; Ebenezer, 1643; Sarah, 1645; and came back 1647, had at Scituate, Hannah, 1649; Gershom, 1650; Abia, 1653; Ichabod, 1659; and Deborah, 1663. His house was burned 1676, by the Indians. His will of 1681, names the before mentioned, except John and Abia, and adds other child Eunice, and mentions wife Sarah.

JOSEPH EWELL, of Ipswich, freeman 1683.

RICHARD EWELL, of Springfield, 1668.

REFERENCES:—Freeman's Hist. of Cape Cod, Mass., II, 257; Swift's Barnstable Families, vol. I, 359; Deane's Hist. of Scituate, Mass., 267; Hayden's Virginia Gens., 333; Savage's Gen. Dict., II, 132; Ewell Gen.

EWER:—Henry Ewer, of Sandwich, 1637.

JOHN EWER, of Barnstable, died 1652.

THOMAS EWER, of Charlestown, came in the "James," from London, 1635, aged 40; with wife Sarah, daughter of William Larned, 28; and children Elizabeth, 4; and Thomas, 1½; had elder children, perhaps John, certainly Sarah; united with the church 1636, as had his wife the month before; freeman 1636; died 1638; and his widow married 1639, Thomas Lothrop, of Barnstable, where his daughter Elizabeth was buried 1641.

THOMAS EWER, of Sandwich, of whom I learn nothing but that his widow Hannah, probated his inventory 1667.

THOMAS EWER, of Barnstable, perhaps son of first Thomas, had by first wife, Thomas, 1673, and probably mother and child died soon. He married second wife Elizabeth Lovell, 1684, who died 1712, had Thomas, 1686; Shubael, 1690; John 1692; Mehitable, 1694; Nathaniel, 1695; Jonathan, 1696; Hezekiah, 1697; and Hannah, 1701; besides Sarah and Elizabeth.

REFERENCES:—Swift's Barnstable, Mass., Families, vol. I, 360; Freeman's Hist. of Cape Cod, Mass., II, 151; Austin's Allied Families of R. I., 92; Savage's Gen. Dict., II, 132.

EWILL:—John Ewill, of Newbury, 1669, died 1686. Perhaps was sometimes Ewins, and he may have been son of that William, who in 1666, was aged 46.

REFERENCES:—Savage's Gen. Dict., II, 132.

EWING. Egle's Hist. Reg. Interior of Penn., II, 206; Penn. Mag., VII, 94; Cooley's Trenton, N. J., 64; Ewing Gen.

EWINGS. Covert Hist. of Pittsford, Vt., 701.

EWINGTON:—Thomas Ewington, of Lynn, 1642, is, I think, Thomas Euington, freeman Rhode Island, 1655. REFERENCES:—Savage's Gen. Dict., II, 132.

EWSTEAD:—Richard Ewstead, of Salem, 1629, came in the fleet with Higginson.

EXELL or EXILE:—Richard Exell, of Springfield, 1646, married 1651, Hannah, widow of Thomas Reeves, had Mary, 1653; John, 1657; and Abigail, 1660; suffered in Philip's war, and removed 1676, but where is unknown, yet in 1681 he sent whale cil to Boston, perhaps from Long Island or Rhode Island.

EYER:—John, Nathaniel, Samuel Eyer, of Haverhill or Salisbury. See Ayer.

EYMANS:—Edward Eymans, of Haverhill, in 1663, was 40 years old.

EYRE, EIRE or EYERS:—Simon Eyre, of Watertown, a surgeon, came in the "Increase," 1635, from London, aged 48, with wife Dorothy, 38; and children Mary, 15; Thomas, 13; Simon, 11; Rebecca, 9; Christian, 7; Ann, 5; Benjamin, 3; and Sarah, 3 mon.hs; freeman 1637; representative 1641; selectman 1636-43; and clerk of the town 1641-5, when he soon removed to Boston, where his wife died 1650; but he had before removing Jonathan, 1638; and Dorothy, 1640. He married about 1651, Martha, daughter of William Hubbard, sister of the historian and widow of John Whittingham, of Ipswich, had Maria, 1652; and John, 1654; and died 1658. His widow died 1687.

John, Sen., and John Jr., Joseph, Nathaniel, Samuel and Timothy, who were all of Haverhill, and there took the military oath of allegiance, 1677, no doubt belong to Ayre family.

REFERENCES:—Smith's Hist. of Delaware County, Pa., 462; Meade's Old Churches of Va., vol. I, 259; Martin's Hist. of Chester County, Pa., 49; Harris' Bascom Gen., 25, 69; N. E. Hist. and Gen. Reg., XV, 13, 58; XXXVIII, 67; Savage's Gen. Dict., II, 133.

EYTON:—Samson Eyton, of Cambridge, 1650, then a student at College, who left before graduating to go to England. There he was made a fellow, but we do not know the name of the college, nor at what University.

REFERENCES:—Savage's Gen. Dict., vol. II, 133.

FABENS, FABIN or FABINS:—John Fabens, on a jury in New Hampshire, 1656, married, perhaps, one of the daughters of Edward Gilman.

ELIZABETH FABENS, came in the "Elizabeth and Ann," 1635, aged 16, but we know not the name of her father.

FABYAN is a name in New Hampshire, and John Fabyan, Esq., of the province died 1757.

REFERENCES:—Essex Inst. Coll., XVIII, 40; Savage's Gen. Dict., II, 133; Fabens' Gen.

FABER or FEBAR:—Joseph Faber, of Boston, 1637, a cooper, came in the "Elizabeth and Ann," 1635, aged 26; was fined 1638, for selling wine without a license. His wife was a principal cause of the excommunication of Capt. John Underhill.

REFERENCES:—Savage's Gen. Dict., II, 134.

FACE:—Robert Face, of Charlestown, a carpenter, died 1657, in his will gave all his property to John Fownell, the miller, with whom he lived.

REFERENCES:—Savage's Gen. Dict., II, 134.

FADDIS. Palmer and Trimble Gen., 359.

FAGAN. Powers' Hist. Sangamon County, Ill., 293.

FAHNESTOCK. Harris Hist. of Lancaster County, Pa., 202; Amer. Ancestry, VI, 18; Fahnestock Gen.

FAIRBANKS:—John Fairbanks, of Dedham, perhaps brother of Jonathan, brought from England, it is said, only daughter Mary; no more is heard of him.

JONATHAN FAIRBANKS, of Dedham, the progenitor, I presume, of all this family in New England, came with wife Grace, and probably all his six children before 1641, died 1668. His will provides for, or mentions wife Grace, eldest son John, George, Mary, Jonas and Jonathan. He was probably from West Riding of Yorkshire, as the will of his uncle George calls him of Sowerby in that part of England.

RICHARD FAIRBANKS, of Boston, 1633, probably with Elizabeth, his wife, came in the "Griffin" with Cotton; freeman 1634; artillery company 1654; had Constan:e. baptized 1636; and Zaccheus, 1639. He was a man of some distinction, disarmed 1637 for perversity in the cause of Wheelwright, but within two years made the first receiver of all letters from abroad for the whole Colony.

REFERENCES.

MASSACHUSETTS.—Stearns' Hist. of Ashburnham, 692; Hill's Dedham, Mass., Records; Barry's Hist. of Framingham, 239; Morse Gen. of Sherborn, 82; Hyde's Hist. of Brimfield, 398; Herrick's Hist. of Gardner, 347; Jameson's Hist. of Medway, 483; Keyes' W. Boylston, Mass., Reg., 18; Blake's Hist. of Franklin, 240.

NEW HAMPSHIRE.—Cochrane's Hist. of Antrim, 487; Hayward's Hist. of Gilsum, 305; Washington, N. H., Hist., 395; Smith's Hist. of Petersborough, 67; Norton's Hist. of Fitzwilliam, 549; Leonard's Hist. of Dublin, 331.

OTHER PUBLICATIONS.—Thurston's Hist. of Winthrop, Me., 181; Butler's Hist. of Farmington, 467; Austin's Allied Families R. I., 93; Leland Gen., 239; Rockwood Gen., 109; Wood Gen., 116; Amer. Ancestry, V, 122; VIII, 152; Savage's Gen. Dict., II, 135.

FAIRCHILD:—Thomas Fairchild, of Stratford, one of the first settlers, 1646, representative 1659, 60 an l often afterwards; by wife, daughter of Robert Seabrook, had Samuel, 1640; Faith, 1642; John, 1644; Thomas, 1646; Dinah, 1648; Zechariah, 1651; and Emma, 1653. He had gone home, got second wif: Catharine Cragg, a widow of London, married 1662, had by her three children.

REFERENCES:—Orcutt's Hist. of Derby, Conn., 719; Orcutt's Hist. of Stratford, Conn., 1197; Todd's Hist. of Redding, Conn., 190; Hall's Rec. of Norwalk, Conn., 222, 290; Hurd's Hist. of Fairfield County, Conn., 581, 795; Powers' Hist. of Sangamon County, Ill., 294; Dwight's Strong Gen., 105; Amer. Ancestry, vol. I, 27; III, 121; VII, 25, 47; X, 158; Savage's Gen. Dict., II, 137.

FAIRCLOUGH. Orcutt's Hist. of Wolcutt, Conn., 473.

FAIRFAX:—Thomas Fairfax, the ancestor, immigrated to Maryland, about December, 1667. He had John, of Calvert and Charles County, Md., living 1701, married Catharine Philpott, of Maryland.

REFERENCES:—Meade's Old Churches of Va., II, 106; Richmond, Va., Standard, IV. 20; Slaughter's Life of R. Fairfax, 62; Fairfax Gen.; Driver Gen., 350; Goode

Gen., 114, 378, 456; Thomas Gen., 74, 178; Lindsay Gen., 112; Amer. Ancestry, V, 114.

FAIRFIELD:—Daniel Fairfield, of Boston, by wife Elizabeth, had Mary, buried 1639; Elizabeth, born 1640; and Mary, again, 1643; was freeman 1683, unless another were the man.

DANIEL FAIRFIELD, of Salem, 1639, called a half Dutchman, the unhappy subject of severe punishment. He had liberty in 1656, to go with wife and children to England, and probably wished not to return.

DANIEL FAIRFIELD, of Weymouth, by wife Sarah, had James, 1666; a child, 1667; and Sarah, 1670. He was, probably, father of Daniel, of Braintree, born there 1662.

JOHN FAIRFIELD, of Charlestown, 1638, of Salem, 1639, freeman 1640, had John, baptized 1641; and a daughter, 1647; leaving widow Elizabeth, who married Peter Palfrey, and children Benjamin, John and Walter, both the former and latter, perhaps, born in England.

JOHN FAIRFIELD, of Newport, freeman there 1655, was of Westerly, 1669, and probably had no children, as in 1689, he gave all his property to Mary Babcock, widow of John, to obtain maintenance of himself and wife for life.

REFERENCES:—Eaton's Hist. of Reading, Mass., 70; Hudson's Hist. of Lexington, Mass., 64; Hammatt Papers of Ipswich, Mass., 105; Bradbury's Hist. of Kennebunkport, Me., 243; Maine Hist. and Gen. Rec., III, 118; IV, 1; Hayward's Hist. of Hancock, N. H., 565; Austin's R. I. Gen. Dict., 73; Savage's Gen. Dict., II, 137.

FAIRLAMB. Buckingham Gen., 253.

FAIRLY. Pearson's Hist. of Schenectady, 66.

FAIRMAN:—John Fairman, of Enfield, one of the first settlers, had James, 1683; perhaps others before, and died 1684. He wrote his name Ferman, and may have been son or grandson of John Firmin, of Watertown.

REFERENCES:—Savage's Gen. Dict., II, 137.

FAIRWEATHER or FAYERWEATHER:—Thos. Fairweather, of Boston, came early, probably in the fleet with Winthrop, freeman 1634, by wife Mary, had John, baptized 1634; and Mary, born 1636. His son Thomas, died 1638, and he died same year.

REFERENCES:—Savage's Gen. Dict., II, 138.

FALCONER:—David Falconer, of Boston, had Thomas, 1656.

REFERENCES:—Bolton's Hist. of Westchester County, N. Y., 731.

FALDOE:—Bartholomew Faldoe, a youth of 16, embarked in the "Planter," 1635, to come from London, but no more is seen of him.

REFERENCES:—Savage's Gen. Dict., II, 137.

FALES:—Spelled Vales, sometimes, James Fales, of Medfield, was freeman 1673. He may have had son James, of Dedham, who was freeman 1684.

JOHN FALES, of Wrentham, married 1684. Abigail Hawes, had John, 1685; John, again, 1689; and Joseph, 1691.

REFERENCES:—Temple's Hist. of North Brookfield, Mass., 587; Ward's Hist. of Shrewsbury, Mass., 281; Hill's Dedham, Mass., Records; Ballou's Hist. of Milford, Mass., 737; Eaton's Hist. of Thomaston, Me., II. 214.

FALIS. Stone's Hist. of Hubbardston, 265.

FALKINGBURG. Salter's Hist. of Monmouth, N.J.

FALL:—John Fall, of Swanzey, killed by the Indians, was buried 1675.

REFERENCES:—Savage's Gen. Dict., II, 138.

FALLAND:—Thomas Falland, of Yarmouth, freeman 1641, representative 1644 and 57.

REFERENCES:—Savage's Gen. Dict., II, 139.

FALLOWAY or FALLOWELL:—Gabriel Falloway, of Plymouth, came early, was freeman 1640, died 1667, aged 83. His will names wife Catharine, and grandson John. William, of Plymouth, may have been son of Gabriel, and possibly father of John, mentioned above.

REFERENCES:—Savage's Gen. Dict., II, 139.

FALLS. Durant's Hist. of Lawrence, Pa., 183.

FANCHER. Huntington's Stamford, Conn., Families, 33; Ball's Hist. of Lake County, Pa., 403; Boutcn Gen., 35.

FANE:—Henry Fane, of Boston, 1648, turner, had wife Elizabeth.

REFERENCES:—Savage's Gen. Dict., II, 140.

FANEUIL:—Andrew Faneuil, of Boston, a Huguenot merchant from Amsterdam, to which city he fled from his native Rochelle, received as inhabitant of the Colony, 1692, in company with his brothers Benjamin and John. But some uncertainty exists, whether either of his brothers ever resided in New England. He brought wife from Holland, but no issue is mentioned and his wife died 1724. He died 1739.

BENJAMIN FANEUIL, brother of Andrew, married at Kingston, 1699, Ann Bureau, and he may have been of Gabriel Bernon's French settlement at Oxford, in County Worcester, yet with many other of his countrymen he had made New Rochelle, N. Y., only 20 miles from the city, his proper home, and there were born all his eleven children. There, too, he died 1718. But his eldest son Peter, born 1700, and Benjamin, 1701, became merchants of distinction of Boston. Peter was the richest man in the Province, and gave to the town the market house known by his name.

REFERENCES:—Heraldic Journal, II, 121; Weesse's Bethune and Faneuil Gen.

FANNING:—Andrew Fanning, of Stonington, perhaps, but known only to us as embarking 1679, in the "Diligence," to come to New England.

EDMUND FANNING, of New London, 1652, is by tradition, said to have escaped from the Irish massacre, 1641, removed to Stonington before 1670, and some time after came back to New London, died 1683, leaving sons Edmund, John, Thomas and William, besides daughter Mary.

THOMAS FANNING, of Watertown, married 1655, Elizabeth, daughter of Robert Daniel, had Elizabeth, 1656; Mary, 1657; Mary, again, 1662; and Sarah, 1665. He died 1685, and his widow lived to 1722, aged 92. She was born in England.

WILLIAM FANNING, of Newbury, married 1668, Elizabeth Allen, had Joseph, 1669; Benjamin, 1671; William, 1673; James, 1676; and Elizabeth, 1681.

REFERENCES:—Caulkin's Hist. of New London, Conn., 306; Howell's Hist. of Southampton, N. Y., 2d edition, 241; Cleveland's Southold Rec., 103; Wheeler's Hist. of North Carolina, II, 332; Dorr's Life of J. F. Watson, 60; Savage's Gen. Dict., II, 140.

FANTON. Schenck's Hist. of Fairfield, Conn., 367; Bergen's Hist. of Kings County, N. Y., 112.

FAREWELL:—George Farewell, of Salem, had practised law several years, was made Clerk of the Court 1687, at Ipswich. He was imprisoned at the Revolution of 1689.
REFERENCES:—Lapham's Hist. of Bethel, Me., 529; Savage's Gen. Dict., II, 140.

FARGO:—Moses Fargo, of New London, 1690, a smith, by wife Sarah, had Moses, 1691, and eight others, whose names are not known.
REFERENCES:—Young's Hist. of Warsaw, N. Y., 257; Pompey, N. Y., Reunion, 373; Caulkin's Hist. of New London, Conn., 373; Savage's Gen. Dict., II, 140.

FARLEY:—George Farley, of Woburn, married 1641, Christian Births; who probably died soon; petitioned with many others for religious liberty 1655, removed to Billerica, before 1655, had married 1643, and by wife Beatrice, had James, 1643; Caleb, 1645; Mary, 1647; Timothy, and perhaps more children at Woburn; at Billerica, by wife Christian, had Samuel, 1655; and Mehitable, 1656; member of the Baptist church at Boston, where the spelling is Farlow. He died 1693.

MICHAEL FARLEY, of Ipswich, sent over, 1675, from England, by Richard Saltonstall, to have care of his fulling mill; had sons Meshack and Michael..
REFERENCES.
MASSACHUSETTS.—Sewall's Hist. of Woburn, 611; Hammatt Papers of Ipswich, 96; Hazen's Hist. of Billerica, 47; Hudson's Hist. of Lexington, 65.
OTHER PUBLICATIONS.—Cushman's Hist. of Sheepscott, Me., 378; Worcester's Hist. of Hollis, N. H., 373; Mellick's Story of an Old Farm, 683; Richmond, Va., Standard, II, 14; Hubbard's Hist. of Stanstead County, Canada, 173; Meade's Old Families of Va., Carter Family Tree; Tuttle Gen., XXXV; Amer. Ancestry, IV, 223; V, 112.

FARMAN:—Ralph Farman, came from London, a barber-surgeon 1635 aged 32, in the "James," with wife Alice, 28; children, Mary, 7; Thomas, 4; and Ralph, 2; but I find nothing of his residence or death, and think it not improbable that he was one of the first settlers of Andover, and his name was Farnum or Farnham.

THOMAS FARMAN, was of Milford, 1658, and may not have been son of the preceding.
REFERENCES:—Savage's Gen. Dict., II, 140.

FARMER:—Edward Farmer, of Billerica, son of John, of Ansley, or Anceley, near Atherstone, in Warwickshire, came in 1671 or 2, with his mother Isabella, a widow who married Elder Thomas Wiswall, of Newton, outlived him and died 1686, at the house of her son. He brought, perhaps, sister Isabella, and brother Thomas, certainly wife Mary, daughter Sarah, born about 1669; and probably John, 1671; had here Edward, 1674; Mary, 1675; Barbara, at Woburn, 1678; Elizabeth, 1680; Thomas, 1683; and Oliver, 1686; was a useful townsman. His wife died 1719, aged about 76, and he died 1727, aged 87.

JOHN FARMER, of Boston, a soldier, killed in the great fight of Philip's war 1675.

JOHN FARMER, of Concord, had daughter Isabel, was of Charlestown, 1677.

THOMAS FARMER, of Billerica, 1675, probably brother

of Edward, perhaps came with him, is not heard of after 1684, may have gone home.
In the Royal Charter for Virginia, 1609, are found John and George Farmer, gentlemen.
REFERENCES.
NEW HAMPSHIRE—Secomb's Hist. of Amherst, 582; Coffin's Hist. of Boscawen, 524; Hayward's Hist. of Hancock, 566; Morrison's Hist. of Windham, 529.
OTHER PUBLICATIONS.—Whitehead's Hist. of Perth Amboy, N. J., 92; Hazen's Hist. of Billerica, Mass., 49; Hudson's Hist. of Lexington, Mass., 65; Ball's Hist. of Lake County, Ind., 292; Amer. Ancestry, VII, 221; N. E. Hist. and Gen. Reg., vol. I, 22, 360; Savage's Gen. Dict., II, 141; Farmer Family.

FARNAM. Whitemore Gen., 545; Amer. Ancestry, VII, 227.

FARDEN:—Berger's Kings Co., N. Y., 112.

FARNHAM:—Ralph Farnham (Farnam or Farnum), Andover, married 1658, Elizabeth, daughter of Nicholas Holt, had Sarah, born 1661; Ralph, 1662; John, 1664; Henry, 1666, who died 1683; Hannah, 1668; besides Thomas, Ephraim, and perhaps others; and died 1692.

HENRY FARNHAM, Roxbury, artillery company 1644, freeman 1645; perhaps went to Long Island, thence to Conn.; certainly was at Killingworth 1666, and died there 1700, leaving only son, Peter.

JOHN FARNHAM, Dorchester, freeman 1640; perhaps brother of the preceding; probably one of the founders of the Second Church at Boston, 1650; by wife Elizabeth, had Elizabeth; who married 1657, Joshua Carwithee; Jonathan, born 1639; Hannah, 1642; Joanna, 1645; and Rachel, who married Thomas Martyn.

JOHN FARNHAM, Andover, married 1667.

REBECCA KENT, daughter of Stephen Kent, of Newbury, had John, born 1670, died next year; and David, died 1687. Perhaps he had second wife, Mary Tyler, and by her, Ann, who died 1696.

JOHN FARNHAM, Boston, married 1654, probably as second wife, Susanna, daughter of Thomas Arnold, of Watertown, had John, born 1655; freeman 1671; a daughter Joanna, married James English, 165-8.

JOSEPH FARNHAM, Boston, freeman 1674.

SAMUEL FARNHAM, Andover, perhaps brother of Ephraim, and son of Thomas, the first, married Hannah Holt, 1698.

THOMAS FARNHAM, Andover, probably brother of Ralph, married 1660, Elizabeth Sibborus, who died 1683; freeman 1669; and died 1686, aged about 53.

REFERENCES:—Aldrich's Hist. of Walpole, N. H., 246-8; Whitman Gen., 545; Barry's Hist. of Hanover, Mass., 310; Eaton's Hist. of Thomaston, Me., II, 221; American Ancestry, II, 37; IV, 177, 221; VI, 133; VII, 53, 227; Farnham Gen. (1886), 91 p., (1889) 141 p.; Redfield Gen., 64-7; McKeen's Hist. of Bradford, Vt., 377-80; Runnel's Hist. of Sanbornton, N. H., 274-6; Stiles' Hist. of Windsor, Conn., II, 249; Wentworth Gen. I, 443-5; Savage's Gen. Dict., II, 142.

FARNSWORTH:—Joseph Farnsworth, Dorchester, freeman 1639, by wife Elizabeth had Mary born 1637; Hannah, 1638; Rebecca, 1640; and Ruth, 1642; besides Joseph, Samuel, and perhaps others by second wife, Mary Long; was selectman 1647, and died 1660.

MATTHIAS FARNSWORTH, of Lynn and Groton, an early proprietary freeman 1670, and selectman, by wife Mary had Joseph, born 1657, died at 17 years; Mary, 1660, at Lynn; and at Groton had Samuel, 1669, and probably others. He died 1689, aged 77.

REFERENCES:—Bass' Hist. of Braintree, Vt., 132; Butler's Hist. of Groton, Mass., 395-9; Chandler's Hist. of Stanley, Mass., 409-12; American Ancestry, VI, 44; Farnsworth Gen. (1891), 122 pages; Savage's Gen. Dict., II, 143; Farrow's Hist. of Islesborough, Me., 204; Green's Groton, Mass., Epitaphs, 239-41; Norton's Hist. of Fitzwilliam, N. H., 550; Saunderson's Charlestown, N. H., 333-45; Green's Groton, Mass., Settlers, 4-7; Washington, N. H., Hist., 396-406; Wyman's Charlestown, Mass., Gen., I, 340.

REFERENCES.

MASSACHUSETTS.—Abbot's Andover, 34; Pierce's Hist. of Grafton, 477-9; Barry's Hist. of Hanover, 310.

NEW HAMPSHIRE.—Bouton's Hist. of Concord, 655-61; Hayward's Hist. of Gilsuni, 306; Leonard's Hist. of Dublin, 333; Secomb's Hist. of Amherst, 582; Smith's Hist. of Peterborough, 68.

MAINE.—Lapham's Hist. of Rumford, 324-9; Lapham's Hist. of Woodstock, 215; Joslin's Hist. of Poultney, Vt., 257-9; Whitmore's Copps Hill Epitaphs; Savage's Gen. Dict., II, 142.

FARQUHAR:—Thomas Family, of Maryland, 78.

FARR:—Benjamin Farr, Lynn, son of George, freeman 1691, married, 1680, Elizabeth, daughter of Francis Burrill, had Elizabeth, born 1682; Mary, 1684; and perhaps others.

GEORGE FARR, Salem, came in the fleet with Higginson, 1629, became farmer at Lynn, freeman 1635, died 1662, leaving wife Elizabeth, who died, 1687, and children, John, who died 1672; Lazarus, who died 1669; Benjamin; Joseph; Mary; Martha; Elizabeth; and Sarah.

JAMES FARR, Newport, 1638.

REFERENCES:—Eaton's Hist. of Thomaston, Me., II, 222; Paige's Hist. of Hardwick, Mass., 369; Read's Hist. of Swanzey, N. H., 336; Dunster Gen., 195; American Ancestry, IV, 218; Savage's Gen. Dict., II, 144.

FARRABAS:—Daniel Farrabas, Cambridge, Concord, and Marlborough, married 1660, Rebecca Perriman, who died 1677; and he married, 1679, Dorothy Rediat. By first wife he had Daniel, born 1664; Thomas, 1667; Elizabeth, 1669; Rebecca, at Concord, 1672; by the second wife, had John, born at Marlborough, 1681; Isaac, 1682; and Jonathan, 1684; he died 1687. His widow married Alexander Stewart, 1688.

REFERENCES:—Page's Cambridge, 541; Savage's Gen. Dict., II, 144.

FARRAH. Clargy's Farrah Disc. (1847).

FARRAN. Temple's Palmer, Mass., 445.

FARRAND. Cothven's Woodbury, 544; Kitchell Gen., 35-42; Savage's Gen. Dict., II, 144.

FARRAR:—George Farrar, Lancaster, son of Jacob, married, 1692, Mary Holt, of Concord; had Joseph; Daniel; George, born 1705; and Samuel, 1708.

JACOB FARRAR, Lancaster, son of the Jacob who was killed by the Indians, 1675, born in England about

1643, by wife Hannah had Jacob, born 1669; George, 1670; Joseph, 1672; and John.

JOHN FARRAR, Lancaster, 1653, brother of the preceding, perhaps was also of Woburn, had there Mary, born 1656; Jacob, 1657; died 1679; Isaac, 1659, died in a few days; Joanna, 1661; Mercy, 1663; Hannah, 1668; and Isaac, 1671. He died 1690.

THOMAS FARRAR, Lynn, 1639, whose wife Elizabeth died 1681, had Thomas; Sarah; Hannah; Susanna, born 1659; Peleg and Mehitable, twins, 1660, died soon; and Elizabeth, who died young; was freeman 1690, and died 1694.

REFERENCES.

MASSACHUSETTS.—Barry's Hist. of Framingham, 2461; Bond's Hist. of Watertown, 728; Sewall's Hist. of Woburn, 611; Ward's Hist. of Shrewsbury, 279; Stearn's Hist. of Ashburnham, 698.

NEW HAMPSHIRE.—Blood's Hist. of Temple, 218; Hayward's Hist. of Gilsum, 306; Hayward's Hist. of Hancock, 567; Kidder's Hist. of New Ipswich, 358-73; Lancaster's Hist. of Gilmanton, 264; Norton's Hist. of Fitzwilliam, 551-5; Stearn's Hist. of Rindge, 519.

MAINE.—Lapham's Hist. of Paris, 596; Lapham's Hist. of Woodstock, 216.

OTHER PUBLICATIONS:—American Ancestry, II, 154; Farrar Family (1853) 45 pages; Hemenway's Vermont Gaz., V, 85; Humphrey's Gen., 448; Neill's Virginia Carolorum, 182; N. E. Hist. and Gen. Reg., III, 212; VI, 313-28; Potter's Old Families of Concord, Mass., Richmond, Va., Standard; Southern Bivouac (1886), 646; Washington, N. H., History, 407; Savage's Gen. Dict., II, 144.

FARRELL. Pearson's Schenectady, 67; Temple's Hist. of Palmer, Mass., 458.

FARREN. Dodd's E. Haven, Conn., 118.

FARRINGTON:—Edmund Farrington, Lynn, from Olney, in Bucks, England, came in the Hopewell, 1635, aged 47, with wife Elizabeth, and children, Sarah, 14; Matthew, 12; John, 11; and Elizabeth, 8; was one of the first projectors of settlement on Long Island, 1640, perhaps went thither, but returned to Lynn, and died there 1671.

JOHN FARRINGTON, Dedham, married, 1650, Mary, daughter of William Bullard, the first, had Mary, born 1651; Sarah, 1652; John, 1654; Nathaniel, 1656; Elizabeth, 1600; Hannah, 1662; Daniel, 1664; Judith, 1666; Abigail, 1668; Benjamin, 1672; and Joseph, 1681; was freeman 1668, and died before 1686, leaving widow.

REFERENCES.

MAINE.—Eaton's Annals of Warren, 540; Eaton's Hist. of Thomaston, II, 222.

NEW HAMPSHIRE.—Cochrane's Hist. of Antrim, 489; Hist. of Washington, 406; Livermore's Hist. of Wilton, 365.

OTHER PUBLICATIONS:—Abbott's Andover, 29; Farrington Gen. (1880) 24 p.; Bolton's Westchester Co., N. Y., 732; Groton's Histor. Series, XIX, 22; Hill's Dedham, Mass., Records; Ruttenber's Hist. of Orange Co., N. Y., 405; Savage's Gen. Dict., II, 145.

FARRER. Davis's Plymouth, Mass., 105.

FARROW:—George Farrow. Ipswich, 1637, married, February 16, 1644, Ann Whitmore, perhaps daughter of the first John, had Mary, born 1645;

Martha, 1647; and George, 1650. He was, perhaps, the man killed by the Indians at Wells, 1676.

JOHN FARROW, Hingham, came from Hingham, England, 1635, with wife Frances, and one child, Mary; had here John, born 1639; Remember, baptized 1642; Hannah, 1648; and Nathan, born 1654; he died 1687. His widow died the next year.

REFERENCES:—Bangor Histor. Mag., V, 173-7, 236; Farrow's Hist. of Islesborough, Me., 205-8; Deane's Scituate, Mass., 268.

FARWELL:—Henry Farwell, Concord, freeman 1639, had wife Olive, son Joseph, born 1641; James, perhaps Henry; John; Mary; Olive; and Elizabeth; removed to Chelmsford, and died there 1670.

REFERENCES.

MASSACHUSETTS.—Butler's Hist. of Groton, 399; Chandler's Hist. of Shirley, 413-5; Stearns' Hist. of Ashburnham, 698; Fox's Hist. of Dunstable, 242.

NEW HAMPSHIRE.—Hayward's Hist. of Hancock, 568; Norton's Hist. of Fitzwilliam, 555; Saunderson's Charlestown, 345-52; Washington Hist., 408-11.

OTHER PUBLICATIONS:—American Ancestry, III, 109; IV, 188; VII, 222; Bangor Hist. Mag., V, 36; Dunstable, Mass., Bi-Centen., 95-118, 122-30; Eaton's Hist. of Thomaston, Me., II., 222; Farwell Gen. (1879) 254 p.; Hammatt Papers, Ipswich, Mass., 101; Joslin's Hist. of Poultney, Vt., 259; N. E. Hist. and Gen. Reg., XXXV, 275; Savage's Gen. Dict., II, 147.

FASSETT, JOHN, Dedham, freeman, 1654.

NATHANIEL FASSETT, Concord, N. H., 1666.

PATRICK FASSETT, Malden, had Joseph, born 1672; removed to Billerica.

REFERENCES.

MASSACHUSETTS.—Hazen's Hist. of Billerica, 51; Brown's Bedford, 9; Hodgman's Hist. of Westford, 446; Hudson's Hist. of Lexington, 66; Paige's Hist. of Hardwick, 370.

OTHER PUBLICATIONS:—Coverly's Pittsford, Vt., No. 70; Jennings' Bennington, Vt., Mem. (1869); Montague Gen., 350-3, 454; Norton's Hist. of Fitzwilliam, N. H., 556-60.

FAULKNER:—David Faulkner, Boston, perhaps son or brother of Thomas, of the same, by wife Mary, had Martha, born 1653; Mary, 1654; Thomas, 1656.

EDMUND FAULKNER, Andover, married 1648, as the record shows, but Farmer says in year previous, Dorothy Robinson, who died 1668; had Francis, born 1651; and John, 1654; probably several others, and died 1687. Mary, who married Joseph Marble, 1671; and Hannah, who married, 1689, Pasco Chubb, were perhaps his daughters.

REFERENCES:—Bangor Hist. Mag., V, 191; Hazen's Hist. of Billerica, Mass., 52; Morrison Gen., 175; Savage's Gen. Dict., II, 147.

FAUNCE:—John Faunce, Plymouth, came in the "Ann," 1623; married, 1633, Patience, daughter of George Merton, had Priscilla, who married Joseph Warren; Mary, who married, 1658, William Harlow; Patience, who married, 1661, John Holmes; Sarah, who married, 1663, Edward Dotey; Thomas, born about 1647; Elizabeth, 1648, died next year; Mercy, 1651, who married, 1667, Nathaniel Holmes; John,who died, 1654; and Joseph, 1653. He died January 18, 1687.

REFERENCES:—Freeman's Hist. of Cape Cod, Mass., II, 153; Lapham's Hist. of Norway, Me., 500; Lapham's Hist. of Paris, Me., 597; Davis' Landmarks, 106; Mitchell's Hist. of Bridgewater, Mass., 373; Savage's Gen. Dict., II, 148; Spooner Gen., I, 442, 456-8.

FAUNTLEROY. DeBow's Review, XXXVI, 130; Jones' Gen. (1891), 167-81; Meade's Old Churches of Va., II, 478-81.

FAVOR:—Philip Favor, Salisbury, married, 1689, Mary, daughter of John Osgood; had Richard, born 1690; John, 1692; and Ann, 1696.

REFERENCES:—Hayward's Hist. of Hancock, 569; Lapham's Hist. of Norway, Me., 500.

FAWCETT. Norton's Knox Co., Ohio.

FAWNE:—John Fawne, Ipswich, freeman 1635, had wife Elizabeth, and one of his daughters married Robert Clement. Savage's Gen. Dict., II, 149.

FAWER:—Barnabas Fawer (or Fower), Dorchester, came 1635, in the "James," from Bristol, with Rev. Richard Mather; was an assessor in 1638; by wife Dinah, who perhaps came with him from England, had, besides other children, Eleazer, born 1642. His wife died 9 days after; and for second wife he took, 1643, Grace, sister of Jonathan Negose; removed to Boston, and died 1654. His widow married John Johnson, of Roxbury.

REFERENCES:—Young's Chronicle of Mass., 450; Savage's Gen. Dict., II, 148.

FAXON:—Thomas Faxon (or Faxson), Braintree, freeman 1657, representative 1669; had Thomas and Richard, both perhaps brought from England, and died 1680. He had married, 1670, Sarah, widow of William Savil, who died 1697.

REFERENCES:—Faxon Gen. (1843), 24 p. (1860), 2d edit. (1880), 377 p.; Durries' Steel Gen., 66; Tuttle Family of Conn., 92-4; Kingman's N. Bridgewater, Mass., 509; Vinton Gen., 311-7; Vinton's Richardson Gen., 426; Washington, N. H., History, 411-3; Savage's Gen. Dict., II, 149.

FAY:—John Fay, Marlborough, came in the "Speedwell," 1656, from London, a youth of 8 years, living at Watertown; by wife Mary had David, who died 1676; and the mother died not long after. He married, 1678, Susanna, widow of Joseph Morse, eldest daughter of William Shattuck, had David, again, 1679, Gershom, 1681; Ruth, 1684; and Deliverance, 1686.

RICHARD FAY, Dorchester, 1634.

WILLIAM FAY, Boston, 1643.

REFERENCES.

MASSACHUSETTS.—Ballou's Hist. of Milford, 741; Hudson's Marlborough, 359-61; Hyde's Hist. of Brimfield, 399; Hazen's Hist. of Billerica, 148; Paige's Hist. of Hardwick, 370-5; Pierce's Hist. of Grafton, 479; Ward's Hist. of Shrewsbury, 281.

NEW HAMPSHIRE.—Aldrich's Walpole, 248-50; Hill's Hist. of Mason, 202; Norton's Hist. of Fitzwilliam, 560-2.

OTHER PUBLICATIONS:—Buckminster's Hasting Gen., 116-8; Jennings' Hist. of Bennington, Vt., 255-63; Rice Gen.; Young's Hist. of Chautauqua Co., N. Y., 507; Spooner Gen., I, 94, 299-322; Walworth's Hyde Gen., 479; Savage's Gen. Dict., II, 149.

FAYREWEATHER. Orcutt's Hist. of Bridgeport; Orcutt's Hist. of Stratford, Conn., 1202.

FEAKE:—Henry Feake, Lynn, 1630, freeman 1634, removed about 1637 to Sandwich, was representative 1643-4; had daughter Elizabeth, who married, 1654, John Dillingham; removed to Newtown, L. I., about 1656.

ROBERT FEAKE, Watertown, 1630; came probably in the fleet with Winthrop, made freeman in that year: married, 1632, Elizabeth, widow of Henry Winthrop, daughter of Thomas Fones, of London; was representative 1635-6, and died 1663.

REFERENCES:—Savage's Gen. Dict., II, 150.

FEARING:—John Fearing, Hingham, from Cambridge, England, it is said, came 1638, in the "Diligent," was selectman 1648, constable 1650, freeman 1652; and died 1665. He had, by wife Margaret, John, Israel, baptized 1644; Mary, baptized 1647; and Sarah, 1649.

REFERENCES:—Amer. Ancestry, VIII, 143; Davis' Landmarks of Plymouth, Mass., 106-8; Savage's Gen. Dict., II, 150.

FEARNE. Smith's Hist. of Delaware Co., 462.

FEARS. Babson's Hist. of Gloucester, 281.

FEATHERLY. Amer. Ancestry, I, 27.

FEENEY. Temple's Palmer, Mass., 459.

FEERO. Munsell's Hist. of Albany, N. Y., IV, 121.

FEILD. Goode Gen., 244; Slaughter's Bristol Parish, Va., 173-7.

FEKE. Bunker's L. I. Gens., 202.

FELCH:—Henry Felch, Watertown, 1642, Reading, 1647, may have been at Gloucester earlier, had Hannah, born 1650; Mary, 1653; Elizabeth, 1655, died at 2 yrs.; John, 1660. He removed to Boston; by wife Elizabeth had Henry, and died 1670, leaving widow.

REFERENCES:—Babson's Hist. of Gloucester, Mass., 93; Eaton's Hist. of Reading, Mass., 71; Paige's Hist. of Cambridge, Mass., 542; Felch Gen. (1881), 98 pp.; Cogswell's Hist. of Hemicker, N. H., 506; Hayward's Hist. of Hancock, N. H., 570; Amer. Ancestry, IX, 140; Savage's Gen. Dict., II, 150.

FELL REFERENCES:—Babson's Gloucester, Mass., 323; Orcutt's Hist. of Torrington, Conn., 689; Waldo's Hist. of Lollard, Conn., 75; Davis' Hist. of Bucks Co., Pa., 278; Fell Gen. (1891), 555 pp., Kulp's Wyoming Valley Families.

FELLOWS:—Richard Fellows, Hartford, 1643; removed 1659 to Springfield, soon to Northampton, and to Hatfield in 1661; died, 1663, leaving widow Ursula, and children, Richard, killed by the Indians 1675; Samuel, died unmarried; Sarah; and Mary.

SAMUEL FELLOWS, Salisbury, freeman 1645; by wife Ann had Samuel, born 1647; and he died, 1698.

WILLIAM FELLOWS, Ipswich, 1642, came in the "Planter," 1635, aged 24, had Ephraim, Samuel, Joseph, Isaac, Mary, Elizabeth, Abigail and Sarah, the last born 1657. From his will, probated 1677, it seems he left widow, but her name is not given, nor is it said whether she was mother of all the children.

REFERENCES:—Coffin's Hist. of Boscoven, N. H., 526; Dow's History of Hampton, N. H., 706; Corliss' Hist. of No. Yarmouth, Me.; Amer. Ancestry, I, 27; II, 37; IV, 188; Stearns' Hist. of Ashburnham, Mass., 699; Hammatt Papers, Ipswich, Mass., 100; Savage's Hist. of Hampton, N. H., 706; Corliss' Hist. of No. Gen. Dict., II, 151.

FELSHAW. Davis' Gen., 48.

FELMINGHAM:—Francis Felmingham (or Fellingham), Salem, 1637, came from Brampton, England, aged 32 in that year, by the "Mary Ann," from Yarmouth. Felt says that next year he had a grant of 200 acres at what is now Wenham; Savage's Gen. Dict., II, 151.

FELT:—George Felt, Charlestown, 1633, lived on the Malden side; married Elizabeth, daughter of widow Prudence Wilkinson; before 1663 had removed to Casco, Me., but soon after 1689, if not earlier, went back to Malden, and died there 1693, aged 92. By wife Elizabeth, had Elizabeth, George and Mary, all baptized 1640, and Moses, 1641. Rev. Joseph B. Felt, the historian of Salem, is supposed to be of this family, but he thinks the line cannot be traced.

REFERENCES:—Blood's Hist. of Temple, N. H., 219; Smith's Hist. of Peterborough, N. H., 70-2; Corliss' North Yarmouth, Me.; Lapham's Hist. of Woodstock, Me., 217; Amer. Ancestry, III, 127; Driver Gen., 471; Felt Gen (1893), 568 pp.; Hammatt Papers, Ipswich, Mass., 103; Savage's Gen. Dict., II, 151.

FELTHOUSEN. Pearson's Hist. of Schenectady.

FELTON:—Benjamin Felton, Salem, 1635, freeman 1639; by wife Mary had John, baptized 1640; Remember, 1643; and Benjamin, 1641.

NATHANIEL FELTON, Salem, 1633, a youth of 17 years, a brother of Benjamin, went back to England 1634, came over again next year, and died 1705, in his 90th year, leaving John, Nathaniel, Elizabeth, Ruth and Hannah. He had also, at Salem, baptized Mary, 1651, died young; Mary, again, 1658; and Susanna, 1665.

REFERENCES:—Ballou's Hist. of Milford, Mass., 742; Hudson's Hist. of Marlborough, Mass., 361-6; Norton's Hist. of Fitzwilliam, N. H.; Secomb's Hist. of Amherst, N. H., 583; Felton Gen. (1868), (1877), 19 p.; (1886), 260 p.; Amer. Ancestry, V, 74; Cunnabel Gen., 75; Savage's Gen. Dict., II. 151.

FELTZ. Amer. Ancestry, II, 38.

FENDERSON. Dearborn's Parsonsfield.

FENIMORE. Amer. Ancestry, I, 27; Penn Magazine, XVI, 377.

FENN:—Benjamin Fenn, of Dorchester, came, perhaps, 1630, in the "Mary and John," although his name is not mentioned before 1638. soon after which he removed to New Haven, and to Milford; had two wives, of whom first was Sarah, daughter of Sylvester Baldwin, who died 1663. and in 1664 he married Susanna Ward. Of the children, Benjamin, baptized 1640; Joseph, 1642; Sarah, 1645; Mary, 1647; and Martha, 1650; were of the first wife; Samuel, 1666, died soon; Samuel, again, 1667, died young; Susanna, 1669; Samuel, again, baptized 1671; and James, born 1672, were of the second wife. He was representative

1653, and died 1672. His estate was large in this country and in Bucks Co., England.

REFERENCES:—Baldwin Gen., 50, 510; Greggs Fenn Gen. (1884); Amer. Ancestry, II, 38; III, 210; Davis' Hist. of Wallingford, Conn., 743; Jessup Gen., 315-8; Tuttle Gen., 516; Savage's Gen. Dict., II, 152; 3 Mass. Hist. Collection, X, 13.

FENNER:—Arthur Fenner, of Providence, born in England, 1622, as is said, freeman 1655, swore allegiance 1667, was captured in Philip's War 1676. He had for second or third wife, Howlong, daughter of William Harris, married 1684.

JOHN FENNER, of Saybrook, had Phœbe, born 1673, certainly another daughter, and perhaps more children; died 1709, leaving wife Sarah, and one daughter, married to Gershom Palmer, and another to David Buell.

ROBERT FENNER, of Stamford, 1641.

THOMAS FENNER, of Bramford, or Wethersfield, died 1647.

WILLIAM FENNER, of Providence, brother of Arthur, was there in 1645. From one of these brothers descends Gov. Fenner.

REFERENCES:—Fenner Gen. (1886-7), 43 p.; R. I. Hist. Mag., VII, 161-83; VIII; R. I. Col. Records, Vol. I; Austin's Ancestries, 23; Austin's R. I. Gen. Dict., 74; Pompey, N. Y., Reunion, 302-4; Savage's Gen. Dict., II, 153.

FENNO. Guild's Stiles' Gen., 89; Stearns' Hist. of Rindge, N. H., 520; Lapham's Hist. of Bethel, Me., 531; Jackson's Hist. of Newton, Mass.

FENTON:—Robert Fenton, of Woburn, by wife Dorothy, had Robert, born 1688, and Frances, 1690; and probably removed.

REFERENCES:—Fenton Gen. (1867), 34 pp.; Paul's Hist. of Wells, Vt., 86; Hyde's Hist. of Briarfield, Mass., 400; Temple's Hist. of Palmer, Mass., 446; Wales, Mass., Centennial, 20; Cleveland's Yates Co., 145; Young's Chautauqua Co., N. Y., 248, 358.

FENWICK:—George Fenwick, of Saybrook, came in 1636 to Boston, from England; not, as often said, in 1635; went home the same year or the following, but came back with his wife and children, 1639, arriving at New Haven in two ships, the first and perhaps the last that ever came direct to that port from England. He had been a lawyer in England, and in high esteem for capacity and honor. He was of the ancient house of Fenwick, and enjoyed much influence in Parliament. His wife Alice died here; of the family we know only his sister Elizabeth, who married Capt. John Cuttick, 1648, and daughters Elizabeth; Dorothy; and Mary. His first wife was the Lady Alice, widow of Sir John Boteler, and daughter of Sir Edward Apsley. He died at Berwick, about 1657. Savage's Gen. Dict., II, 153; 3 Mass., Hist. Collec., I, 184.

FERGUSON:—Archibald Ferguson (or Ferginson), of Marblehead, married Mary, daughter of Moses Maverick, baptized 1640-1, died 1655-6; he died about 1698.

DANIEL FERGUSON, of Kittery, died 1676, leaving widow Mary.

HERBERT FERGUSON, of Springfield, took oath of allegiance, 1678.

REFERENCES:—N. E. Gen. Register, VIII, 270; Bedford, N. H., Centenn., 299; Egle's Penn. Gen., 189-

93; Gibb's Hist. of Blandford, Mass., 62; Smith's Hist. of Peterborough, N. H., 73-8; Temple's Hist. of Whately, Mass., 228; Amer. Ancestry, II., 38; Cleveland's Hist. of Yates Co., N. Y., 334; Marshall Gen. (1884), 44-7; Powers' Hist. of Sangamon Co., Ill., 295; Savage's Gen. Dict., II, 154; Robertson's Pocahontas Descendants.

FERNALD:—Reginald Fernald, of Portsmouth, 1631, sent over by Capt. Mason, the patentee, is the first surgeon among New Hampshire settlers, was of the grand jury, 1643, recorder 1654; died 1656, leaving wife Joanna, and sons, John, Samuel, William and Thomas.

THOMAS FERNALD, of Portsmouth, 1631, perhaps brother of the preceding.

REFERENCES:—Dearborn's Hist. of Parsonsfield, Me.; Adams' Annals of Portsmouth, 19; Amer. Ancestry, III, 193; VI, 157, 180; Jordan's Leighton Gen.; Savage's Gen. Dict., II, 154.

FERNESIDE:—John Ferneside (or Ferniside), of Duxbury, 1643, married Elizabeth, daughter of Comfort Starr, but had his first child Jacob, 1642, record at Boston, perhaps after removal thither; also Mary, 1646; Hannah, 1650; Lydia, 1653; Elizabeth, 1658, and Ruth, 1661. Of these children only three were alive 1659, when Grandfather Starr made his will. His widow died 1704, aged 83. Hannah married, 1673, Reuben Hull, of Portsmouth.

REFERENCE:—Winsor's Hist. of Duxbury, Mass., 93, 258; Savage's Gen. Dict., II, 154.

FERNAM:—Robert Fernam, of Oyster Bay, L. I., 1664, a commissioner for Connecticut.

FERNIS:—Benjamin Fernis, of Salem, 1640; possibly the name may be Ferris. Felt; Savage's Gen. Dict., II, 154.

FEROE. Amer. Ancestry, II, 38.

FERRAND. Eaton's Hist. of Thomaston, Me., 224.

FERRAR. Neill's Virginia Caralorum, 42.

FERRELL. Temple's Hist. of Palmer, Mass., 458.

FERRIS:—Jeffry Ferris, of Watertown, probably freeman 1635, was one of the first settlers at Wethersfield, removed thence to Greenwich, where his wife Susanna died 1660, and he removed to Stamford, and there died 1666, leaving children, as mentioned in his will: James, Peter, Joseph, and daughter, Mary, wife of Jonathan Lockwood.

JAMES FERRIS, of Greenwich, son of Jeffry, had estate there 1672.

ZECHARIAH FERRIS, of Charlestown, 1675; freeman 1676. married 1673, Sarah Blood, possibly daughter of Richard Blood, of Lynn; had Zechariah, baptized 1676: Sarah, 1678; and Hannah, 1680; and in deed of 1719, names sons, James, Nathaniel, and Samuel.

REFERENCES:—Meade's Hist. of Greenwich, Conn., 312; Huntington's Stamford, Conn., Settlers, 33; Ransom Gen.; Orcutt's Hist. of New Milford, Conn., 694-9; Bolton, Westchester Co., N. Y., II, 422; Smith's Hist. of Dutchess Co., N. Y., 500; Amer. Ancestry, III, 155; VII, 270; IX, 208; Savage's Gen. Dict., II, 155.

FERRY:—Charles Ferry, of Springfield, swore allegiance 1678; married, 1661, Sarah Harmon; had John, 1662; Charles, 1665; Samuel, 1667, died soon; Sarah, 1668; Mary, 1671; Gershom, 1674; Solomon, 1677, died young; Mary, again, 1680; Elizabeth, 1683; and Solomon, again, 1686; was freeman 1671, and died 1699, leaving seven children, of whom there are many descendants.

REFERENCES:—Cochrane's Hist. of Antrim, N. H., 489; Bass' Braintree, Vt., 132; Hyde's Hist. of Brimfield, Mass., 402; Lyman's Hist. of Easthampton, Mass., 185; Montague Gen., 276-81; 290-8; Temple's Hist. of Palmer, Mass., 457; Savage's Gen. Dict., II, 155.

FERSON:—Thomas Ferson (or Furson), Dover, 1644-8.

FESSENDEN:—John Fessenden, of Cambridge, from Kent, England, freeman 1641, selectman after, died 1666, without children. His widow, Jane, died 1683, aged 80.

NICHOLAS FESSENDEN, of Cambridge, born in England, probably at Canterbury, about 1650, came about 1674, perhaps with wife Margaret, to inherit estate of preceding, who was probably his uncle; had Jane, who died 1676; Hannah, died same year; Hannah again, 1677; Thomas, died 1683; Nicholas, born about 1682; Thomas, again, 1684; Margaret, 1686; Jane, 1688; Mary, 1689; William, about 1693; and Benjamin, 1701. His wife died 1717, aged 61; and he died 1719, aged 68. The name has been well perpetuated in descendants, but it has been strangely written; Hazard making it Phisenden, and the town record, Fishenden.

REFERENCES:—Eaton's Hist. of Thomaston, Me., 224; Morrison's Hist. of Windham, N. H., 530; Aldrich's Hist. of Walpole, N. H., 250-2; Freeman's Cape Cod, I, 461; 618; II, 154; Paige's Hist. of Cambridge, Mass., 542-4; Ward's Hist. of Shrewsbury, Mass., 281; Cutter's Hist. of Arlington, Mass., 237; Hudson's Hist. of Lexington, Mass., 66-9.

OTHER PUBLICATIONS:—Hemenway's Vermont Gazette, V, 110; Locke Gen., 27, 43-6, 89-91, 146, 313-6; Morse Mem., 166; Maine Hist. Soc. Coll., IV, 289; Pope Gen.; Spooner's Mem., W. Spooner, 113; Savage's Gen. Dict., II, 155.

FETTER. Amer. Ancestry, II, 155.

FEVERYEAR:—Edward Feveryear, of Salem, married, 1664. Tabitha, daughter of Nathaniel Pickman; had Priscilla, born 1665, died in two months; Elizabeth, 1666; Edmund, 1668, died 1670; John, 1670; Mary, 1673; and Edmund, again, 1676; married, 1688, second wife, Mary, widow of Joseph Hardy, daughter of John Grafton; had Grafton, born 1689; and Benjamin, 1693; and she died 1705.

REFERENCE:—Savage's Gen. Dict., II, 155.

FEYLER. Eaton's Hist. of Thomaston, Me., 225.

FICKLIN. Slaughter's St. Mark's, 164.

FIDLER. Amer. Ancestry, II, 38.

FIELD:—Alexander Field, of Charlestown, 1640, shoemaker; removed to Salem, 1642, with a wife, was freeman 1649. may have removed to New Haven; there married Gillian, widow of Richard Mansfield, and died 1666. His widow died 1670.

DARBY FIELD, of Exeter, 1638, an Irishman, the first European, probably, who went up to the summit of the White Mountains; removed about 1645 to Dover, probably, and died 1649, leaving a widow, and, tradition says, children; perhaps that Elizabeth who married, 1664, Stephen Jones: Joseph; and Zachary, born 1645.

GEORGE FIELD, Boston, probably before 1655, removed to Sudbury.

JAMES FIELD, Dedham, freeman 1683.

JOHN FIELD, Providence, 1637, probably was of Bridgewater after 1655.

JOHN FIELD, of Providence, swore allegiance 1668, and was then called junior, so that he may have been son of the preceding; and perhaps Ruth, who married John Angel, 1669, was his sister.

ZECHARIAH FIELD, of Hartford, 1639, had wife Mary; removed about 1659 to Northampton; thence 1663, to Hatfield; died 1666; had Mary, born about 1643, who married, 1663, Joshua Carter; Zechariah; John; Samuel; and Joseph.

ROBERT FIELD, of Boston, tailor, came in the "James," from Southampton, 1635; was probably at Providence, 1638, but soon after came to Boston; by wife Mary, probably daughter of Christopher Stanley, had John, baptized 1644; Robert, born 1647, died young; Thomas, died young; William, baptized 1650; Thomas, again, baptized 1651; Thomas, again, born 1652; Robert, again, 1653; John, again, baptized 1656; Elizabeth, baptized 1658; Sarah, born 1660, died young; Daniel, baptized 1662; and Sarah, again, baptized 1665.

ROBERT FIELD, of Newtown, L. I., took, with others, in 1645 a patent from the Dutch Governor, Kieft, for Flushing; had Robert; John, who removed to Bound Brook, N. J.; Hannah, who married, 1656, John Brown; Elizabeth; and Benjamin.

THOMAS FIELD, of Providence, who swore allegiance 1667, was probably nephew, certainly successor to William, at Field's Point; had one daughter and twelve sons, of whom were: Thomas, Jeremiah, William, Anthony, Charles, John, Jonathan, Joseph, and Nathaniel, all at or near Providence; did not remove in 1676, and died 1717.

ZECHARIAH FIELD, of Providence, swore allegiance 1671, and, in 1676, stayed through Philip's War; may have been of Dover, 1664; by wife Sarah had Zechariah, born 1686, and Daniel, 1690; and was living 1708.

REFERENCES.

MASSACHUSETTS.—Ballou's Hist. of Milford, 744; Bond's Hist. of Watertown, 207; Hyde's Hist. of Briarfield, 403; Judd's Hist. of Hadley, 492-4; Kingman's N. Bridgewater, 409-505; Mitchell's Hist. of Bridgewater, 158; Paige's Hist. of Hardwick, 375; Temple's Hist. of Northfield, 441-50; Temple's Hist. of Whately, 228.

MAINE.—Corliss' Hist. of No. Yarmouth; Lapham's Hist. of Paris, 599.

NEW HAMPSHIRE.—Read's Hist. of Swanzey, 337; Smith's Hist. of Peterborough, 79-83.

OTHER PUBLICATIONS:—Baird's Hist. of Rye, N. Y., 463-5; Bolton. Westchester Co., N. Y., II, 728-31; Martin's Hist. of Chester. Pa., 296; Meade's Hist. of Greenwich, Conn., 312; Slaughter's St. Mark's Parish Va., 130-2; Whittemore's Hist. of Middlesex Co.,Conn.. 408: Amer. Ancestry, II, 38; III, 97; V, 93; VI, 96; VII, 279; VIII, 157; IX, 181; Cooley's Trenton, N.

J., Gens., 66-71; Austin's R. I., Gen. Dict., 75-7; Field Gen. (1860), 105 p.; (1863), 9 p.; (1864), 15 p.; (1876), (1878), 65 p.; (1880), 147 p.; Field Chart (1882); Hemenway's Vermont Gaz., V.; Longmeadow, Mass., Centenn., 61-3; Meade's Old Families of Va.; Mellick's Story of an Old Town, 650; Morris and Flynt Gen., 33; New Eng. Hist. and Gen. Reg., XVII, 106-12; XVIII, 260; XXII, 166-73; XXXV, 239, 356-8; XLVIII, 331-6; Newfane, Vt., Centenn., 155-7; N. Yarmouth, Me., Mag., 448; Talcott's, N. Y. and N. E. Families, 561-6; Thayer's Memorial, 46; Savage's Gen. Dict., II, 155-7.

FIELDER:—Stephen Fielder, of Boston, married Mary, daughter of John Griggs, of Roxbury; had Sarah, born 1685. He lived, perhaps but a short time, and probably at Roxbury, where Sarah married John Ruggles, 1704.

REFERENCE:—Savage's Gen. Dict., II, 157.

FIFE:—REFERENCES:—Cutter's Hist. of Jaffrey, N. H., 276-8; Norton's Hist. of Fitzwilliam, N. H., 566.

FIFIELD:—Giles Fifield, of Charlestown, married, 1652, Mary, daughter of Abraham Perkins, of Hampton; had two or more children, and removed to Hampton; there had Mary, 1659, died soon; perhaps went back in a few years to Charlestown, and had there baptized, Abraham; Giles; Richard, born 1663, died soon; Richard, again, 1665; John; and Mary, again, 1667; Deborah, 1673; and Thomas, 1676; but the last two, whose mother died 1676, were by second wife, married 1672, Judith, widow of Samuel Convers, and eldest daughter of Rev. Thomas Carter; was freeman 1671, and died 1716.

WILLIAM FIFIELD, came in the "Hercules," 1634; was probably at Ipswich first, next year at Newbury, removed 1639 to Hampton; there married second wife, 1693, Hannah Cram, unless she was wife of the second William, of Hampton, who died 1715, aged 66; and died 1700, aged 85.

REFERENCES:—Lapham's Hist. of Bethel, Me., 531; Dow's Hist. of Hampton, N. H., 707-9; Bouton's Hist. of Concord, N. H., 705; Runnel's Sanbornton, N. H., II, 276-8; Washington, N. H., History, 413; Joslin's Hist. of Poultney, Vt., 261; Wyman's Charlestown, Mass., Gen., 245; Savage's Gen. Dict., II, 158.

FILBRICK. Hammatt Papers, 109.

FILER:—George Filer (or Fyler), of Northampton, a surgeon, nephew of Walter; had Judith, born 1664; and Samuel, 1666; removed to Westfield, became a Quaker, and removed probably to Shelter Island, L. I., 1674.

WALTER FILER, of Worcester, 1630, came probably in the "Mary and John," freeman 1634, removed to Windsor, 1636; had John, born 1642; and Zerubbabel, 3, baptized 1644; was representative 1661-3, and died 1683. His widow, Jane, died 1690.

REFERENCES:—Doolittle's Hist. of Belchertown, Mass., 137; Strong Gen., 1305-11; Hedge's Anniversary, Easthampton, N. Y.; Talcott's N. Y. and N. E. Families, 511; Savage's Gen. Dict., II, 158.

FILES. Eaton's Hist. of Thomaston, Me., 225; Pierce's Hist. of Gorham, Me., 165.

FILLEBROWN:—Thomas Fillebrown, of Charlestown, 1658, Cambridge, 1665, or earlier; by wife Anna had Thomas; and Mary, both born before 1666; Anna, baptized 1666, died 1685. He was freeman 1666 or '68, the name being entered at each year, and died 1713; and his widow died early in the following year; both aged 82.

REFERENCES:—Paige's Hist. of Cambridge, Mass., 544; Cutter's Hist. of Arlington, Mass., 238; Wyman's Charlestown, Mass., Gens., I, 346; Savage's Gen. Dict., II, 159.

FILLEY:—William Filley, of Windsor, 1640, or earlier, married, 1642, Margaret had Samuel, born 1643; John, 1645; Mary; Elizabeth, 1650; Abigail, 1658; Deborah, 1661; and William, 1665. Mary married, 1666, Joseph Skinner; Elizabeth, 1669, David Winchell; and Abigail, 1680, John Bissell.

REFERENCES:—Stiles' Hist. of Windsor, Conn., 250-8; Lovun's Gen. (Females), 318-26; Savage's Gen. Dict., II, 159.

FILLMORE. Caulkins' Hist. of Norwich, Conn., 229; Walworth's Hyde Gen., 398, 654, 727-9; N. E. Hist. and Gen. Reg., XI, 141-7.

FILLOW. Fillow Gen. (1888), 274 p.

FINCH:—Abraham Finch, of Wethersfield, was first, probably, at Watertown, and freeman 1634, but removed soon; was, it is said, constable 1636, in Connecticut, and fell in the Pequot War, 1637. He left only son, Abraham. His widow, Dorothy, married, 1637 or '38, John Edwards.

DANIEL FINCH, of Watertown, probably, and brother, perhaps, of first Abraham, came, it is thought, in the fleet with Winthrop; freeman 1631, removed to Wethersfield with first settlers there; was, perhaps, constable 1636; thence to Stamford, of which he was one of the original proprietors, and in 1653 to Fairfield; there married, 1657, Elizabeth, widow of John Thompson, of the same, and died 1667; in his will names son Nathaniel.

SAMUEL FINCH, of Roxbury, freeman 1634, was for some time at Wethersfield, but returned to Roxbury, and married, 1654, Judith, widow, perhaps, of William Potter, as second wife; in 1638 he had wife Martha, and six in family; died 1674.

REFERENCES:—Cleveland's Hist. of Yates Co., N. Y., 731-3; Eager's Hist. of Orange Co., N. Y., 401-3; Greene Co., N. Y., History, 309; Dodd's Hist. of E. Haven, Conn., 118; Orcutt's Hist. of Walcott, Conn., 475; Huntington's Stamford, Conn., Settlers, 34; Smith's Hist. of Peterborough, N. H., 83; Stickney's Hist. of Minesink, N. Y., 154-7; Timlow's Sketches of Southington, Conn., 91-3; Amer. Ancestry, II, 38; Savage's Gen. Dict., II, 159.

FINDLEY. Marshall Gen. (1884), 158-60.

FINEL. Joslin's Hist. of Poultney, Vt., 261.

FINGAR. Amer. Ancestry, II, 39.

FINLAY. Egle's Penn. Gens., 72; Merrill's Hist. of Acworth, N. H., 214-9.

FINLAY. Littell's Passaic Valley, 151.

FINNEY:—John Finney, an early settler in Plymouth, had, by wife Christian, who died 1649, John, born 1638. He married, 1650, for second wife, Abigail, widow of Henry Coggin; and for third, Elizabeth

Bagley, 1654, and had Jonathan, 1655; Robert, 1656; Hannah, 1657; Elizabeth, 1659; Josiah, 1661; Jeremiah, 1662; Joshua, 1665.

ROBERT FINNEY, of Plymouth, probably brother of first John, came with his mother from England, married Phebe Ripley, 1641, and had Josiah. He was representative 1657 and eight years more, deacon 1667, and died, 1688, aged 88; his widow died 1710, aged 91. The more common spelling of this name is Phinney.

REFERENCES:—Davis' Landmarks of Plymouth, 109-11; Timlow's Hist. of Southington, Conn., XCI; Futhey's Hist. of Chester, Pa., 547; Watkins Gen. 39; Amer. Ancestry, II, 40; Hines' Lebanon, Conn., Address, 153; Penn. Mag., IV, 234-40; VII, 466-71; Savage's Gen. Dict., II, 160.

FIRLY. Powers' Hist. of Sangamon, Ill., 296.

FIRMAN. Norton's Hist. of Fitzwilliam, N. H., 566.

FIRMIN:—Giles Firmin (or Firman), of Boston, came from Sudbury, England, in the fleet with Winthrop, 1630; first settled at Watertown, but removed in two years to Boston; was chosen deacon 1633, a selectman, and freeman 1634, and died same year.

JOHN FIRMIN, of Watertown, 1630, came probably in the fleet with Winthrop; was freeman 1631.

ROBERT FIRMIN, Newtown, L. I., one of the first settlers, 1645.

REFERENCES:—Hammatt Papers, Ipswich, Mass., 102; Essex Ind. Coll., XVII, 34-9; N. E. Hist. and Gen. Reg., XXV, 51-5; Savage's Gen. Dict., II, 160.

THOMAS FIRMIN, of Ipswich, freeman 1639; had wife Sarah; was a merchant of good estate; removed to Salisbury 1652.

FISH:—Thomas Fish, of Portsmouth, R. I., 1655, may be of Boston, 1656; married 1668, Grizzel, daughter of John Strange, and had Alice, born 1671; Grizzel, 1673; Hope, 1676; Preserved, 1679; and Mehitable, 1684. He died 1687.

GABRIEL FISH, of Boston, an early inhabitant, removed 1638 to Exeter, but in a short time returned to Boston; by wife Elizabeth, had Deborah, born 1642; Abel, baptized 1644.

JOHN FISH, of Lynn, removed 1637, to Sandwich, with sons Jonathan and Samuel, perhaps others, went to New London 1655, but back soon to Sandwich, and died 1663.

JONATHAN FISH, of Sandwich, brother of first John, had lived at Lynn, but at Sandwich had Nathaniel, born 1650; John; and Samuel; removed to Newtown, L. I., 1659, died about 1663. He was progenitor of Hamilton Fish, late Governor of New York.

NATHANIEL FISH, Sandwich, perhaps brother of John, had Nathaniel, born 1648; and John, 1651.

ROBERT FISH, of Portsmouth, R. I., married 1686, Mary, daughter of Zuriel Hall; had Robert, born 1690; Mary, 1693; William, 1695; Zuriel, 1697; Isaac, 1699; Alice, 1702; Jonathan, 1704; Daniel, 1707; and David, 1710.

REFERENCES.

MASSACHUSETTS.—Ballou's Hist. of Milford, 746; Freeman's Hist. of Cape Cod, II, 51, 161, 337, 478; Winsor's Hist. of Duxbury, 258.

NEW HAMPSHIRE.—Heywood's Hist. of Gilsum, 306; Morrison's Hist. of Windham, 531; Read's Hist. of Swanzey, 338.

MAINE.—Eaton's Hist. of Thomaston, II, 226; Hatch's Hist. of Industry, 617-21.

VERMONT.—Bass' Hist. of Braintree, 133; Williams' Hist. of Danby, 144-7.

OTHER PUBLICATIONS.

Austin's R. I. Gen. Dict., 78; Davis' Landmarks of Plymouth, 111; Amer. Ancestry, II, 40; V, 201; Austin's Allied Families, 95-7; Cooley's Trenton, N. J., Gens., 71-4; Hubbard's.Stanstead Co., Canada, 256; Riker's Annals of Newtown, L. I., 365-70; Walworth's Hyde Gen., 803-6; Welles' Amer. Family Antiquities; Wentworth Gen., I, 232; Savage's Gen. Dict., II, 161.

FISHER:—Anthony Fisher, of Dedham, 1637, born at Syleham Co., Suffolk, Eng.; freeman, perhaps, 1646, died 1670. In his inventory, taken same year, he was called late of Dorchester. He married, 1647, Joanna Faxon, had Mehitable, born 1648; Josiah, 1654; Sarah, 1658; and Elizabeth, 1669. The widow died 1694.

ANTHONY FISHER, of Dorchester, freeman 1645, selectman, 1664-6; died 1671, in his 80th year.

JOSHUA FISHER, of Dedham, 1639, brother of the second Anthony, born in England, freeman 1640, died 1646.

JOSHUA FISHER, born in England, of unknown family, married, 1643, perhaps, as second wife, Mary, daughter of deacon Nathan Aldis; had Mary, born 1644; Joshua, 1645; Hannah, 1647, died soon; Abigail, 1649; Joshua, again, 1651; John, 1652; and Hannah, again, 1653. He lived in the part of Dedham which became Midfield; freeman 1649, representative 1653, and for six years more; died 1674.

CORNELIUS FISHER, born in England, son of the first Anthony; freeman 1649, married 1653, Leah, perhaps, daughter of Nathaniel Heaton; had Leah, born 1656; Experience, 1658; Cornelius, 1660; Ann, 1661; Eleazer, 1663; his wife died same year. He married, 1665, Sarah, daughter of Richard Everett, who died 1676; had Dorothy, 1667; Sarah, 1668; and Jonathan, 1671, died young; was representative under the new charter, 1692, died 1699, it is said, "the first head of a family who died in the town in a natural way for 30 years."

EDWARD FISHER, of Portsmouth, R. I., freeman 1655. His daughter Ruth married, 1664, John Potter, of Warwick, and Frances, another daughter, married John Briggs, of the same.

SAMUEL FISHER, of Wrentham, by wife Meletiah, had Ebenezer, born 1670; Hannah, 1672; and Abigail, 1674; was deacon, representative 1689, and died 1703.

THOMAS FISHER, of Cambridge, 1634, came, perhaps, from Winton in England, freeman 1635, removed to Dedham, 1637.

REFERENCES.

MASSACHUSETTS.—Blake's Hist. of Franklin, 241-9; Clark's Hist. of Norton, 81; Jameson's Hist. of Medway, 484-6; Stearn's Hist. of Ashburnham, 700; Temple's Hist. of Northfield, 450.

NEW HAMPSHIRE.—Aldrich's Hist. of Walpole, 255; Bassett's Hist. of Richmond, 387; Cochrane's Hist. of Antrim, 491; Cogswell's Hist. of Henniker, 567-9; Heywood's Hist. of Hancock, 571-3; Norton's Hist. of Fitzwilliam, 566-8.

MAINE.—Corliss' Hist. of No. Yarmouth; Eaton's Annals of Warren, 541.

OTHER PUBLICATIONS.

FISHER.

Austin's R. I. Gen. Dict., 79; Bangor Hist. Magazine, V, 65-7; Cleveland's Hist. of Yates Co., N. Y., 419; Cregar's White Gen.; Amer. Ancestry, II, 40; IV, 195; VII, 237; Dedham Hist. Reg., I, 24-6; III, 187-92; IV, 17-21; 61-5; 103-7, Fisher Gen. (1890), 243 p.; Dotterer's Perkiomen Region, Pa., 26; Hill's Dedham, Mass. Records; Miller's Colchester Co., N. S., 323-7; Page Gen., 104; Plumb's Hist. of Hanover, Pa., 415; Richmond, Va., Standard, II, 2; Power's Sangamon Co., Ills., 144, 297-9; Rodman Gen., 94-6; Washington, N. H., History, 414-20; Wentworth Gen., I, 555-8; Wheeler's Hist. of No. Carolina, II, 392; Young's Hist. of Warsaw, N. Y., 261-4; Savage's Gen. Dict., II, 161-4.

FISKE:—Benjamin Fiske, of Medfield, married, 1674, Bathshun Morse; two Benjamins, and other children; possibly was son of William.

DAVID FISKE, of Watertown, 1637 or earlier, had wife Sarah, daughter of Edmund Smith, of Wrentham, County Suffolk, England; was freeman 1628; died probably 1661, leaving a son David, and a daughter who married a Fitch.

WILLIAM FISKE, of Salem, 1637, brother of Rev. John Fiske; freeman 1642; removed to Wenham, and was town clerk there; had by wife Bridget Musket, of Pelham, married in England, William, Samuel, Joseph, Benjamin, and Martha, perhaps most of them born in England; was representative 1647-50; died 1654.

JOHN FISKE, of Wenham, born about 1601, in Wangford, County Suffolk, England, married, about 1629, Ann Gipps, of Frinshell, County Norfolk, England; brought his wife and two children to Boston, 1637; resided first at Cambridge, but removed the same year to Salem; freeman 1637, and taught the grammar-school there. He had John, born 1638, died under nine years; Sarah, baptized 1640; Moses, born at Wenham, baptized at Salem, 1642; Ann, baptized 1646; Eliezur, 1647, died young; removed 1655 to Chelmsford, where his wife Ann died 1672. He died 1677.

JAMES FISKE, of Salem, 1641 or earlier, freeman 1642, removed to Haverhill; had there by wife Ann, James, born 1649; John, 1651; Ann, 1654, died soon; Ann, again, 1656; and Samuel, 1658.

PHINEAS FISKE, of Salem, 1641, or earlier, perhaps father, but frequently called brother of James; freeman 1642; removed to Wenham, 1644; was captain, representative 1653; had James, John, and Thomas, all born in England.

NATHAN FISKE, of Watertown probably brother of the first David, of an honorable family in County Suffolk, England; freeman 1643; by wife Susanna, had Nathan, born 1642; John, 1647; David, 1650; Nathaniel, 1663; and Sarah, who married Abraham Gale. He died 1676.

JOHN FISKE, of Watertown, 1648, married, 1651, Sarah, daughter of Nicholas Wyeth, of Cambridge; had Sarah, born 1653; John, 1654, died in 3 months; John again, 1655; Margaret, 1657; David, 1658; Mary, 1661; William, 1664; Martha, 1666; Elizabeth, 1669; Nathaniel, 1672; and Abigail, 1675; took the oath of fidelity, 1652, and died 1684, aged 65.

REFERENCES.

MASSACHUSETTS.—Ballou's Hist. of Milford, 748; Paige's Hist. of Hardwick, 376; Barry's Hist. of Framingham, 242-4; Cutter's Hist. of Arlington, 240-2; Hudson's Hist. of Lexington, 69-75; Butler's Hist. of Groton, 401-471; Bond's Hist. of Watertown, 208-19, 759-62; Jackson's Hist. of Newton, 277; Paige's Hist. of Cambridge, 545; Temple's Hist. of Palmer, 447-9; Pierce's Hist. of Grafton, 480.

NEW HAMPSHIRE.—Secomb's Hist. of Amherst, 584-7; Leonard's Hist. of Dublin, 335-7; Blood's Hist. of Temple, 220; Bouton's Hist. of Concord, 661; Norton's Hist. of Fitzwilliam, 658; Livermore's Hist. of Walton, 365-7; Saunderson's Charlestown, 333; Washington Hist., 203.

OTHER PUBLICATIONS.—Adam's Haven Gen., 53-5; Eaton's Hist. of Thomaston, Me., II, 225; Blake's Mendon Association, 151-3; Dunster Gen., 62-4; Hemenway's Vermont Gaz., IV, 789; Hammatt Papers, Ipswich, Mass., 104; Haven Gen., 43-5; Morse's Sherborne, Mass. Settlers, 85-7; Montague Gen., 437; Quincy, Mass., Church Anniv., 104-6; Ruttenber's Hist. of Newburgh, N. Y., 306; Tinlow's Sketches of Southington, Ct., 93; Williams' Hist. of Danby, Vt., 145-7; Amer. Ancestry, III, 219; IV, 21; V, 175; Essex Inst. Hist. Coll., VIII, 175-89; Fiske Gen. (1843) 40 pages; (1865) 151 pages; (1867) 209 pages; Leland Gen., 29-31; Heraldic Journal, III, 120-5; N. E. Hist. and Gen. Reg., IV, 180; XI, 221; Spooner's Mem. of W. Spooner, 2,025; Stiles' Hist. of Windsor, Ct., II, 259; Vinton's Giles Gen., 242; Wymmis' Charlestown, Mass., Gen., I, 348; Savage's Gen. Dict., II, 164-8.

FITCH:—James Fitch, of Saybrook, born, 1622, at Bocking, County Essex, England, was brought to New England about 1638; studied for the ministry; by wife Abigail, daughter of Rev. Henry Whitfield, had James, born 1649; Abigail, 1650; Samuel, 1655; and Dorothy, 1658. His wife died 1659, and next year he removed to Norwich, and married, 1660, Priscilla, daughter of Major John Mason; had Daniel, born 1665; John, 1667; Jeremiah, 1670; Jabez, 1672; Ann, 1675; Nathaniel, 1679; Joseph, 1681; and Eleazur, 1683. He removed to Lebanon, 1696, and died, 1702.

JAMES FITCH, of Boston, a tailor; came in the "Defence," 1635, aged 30; by wife Abigail, had Elizabeth, baptized 1636.

JOHN FITCH, of Gloucester, married widow, Mary Coit 1667, and died 1715.

JOHN FITCH, of Norwalk, 1652, perhps brother of Thomas, removed 1665, to Northampton; thence in 1660 to Hartford; married Mary, daughter of Rev. Samuel Stone; had Joseph, Nathaniel, and perhaps another son and several daughters; was representative 1662-8; then removed to Windsor, and had there a large farm, enjoyed by several generations of his descendants, and was living in 1713.

ZECHARY FITCH, of Reading, freeman 1638, had Samuel, born 1645; and Zechary, 1647; Joseph, Benjamin, John, Jeremiah, Thomas and Sarah, who married John Wessen or Weston, of Salem.

SAMUEL FITCH. Perhaps at Milford, 1644; certainly of Hartford, 1650; schoolmaster; married that year, or early in the next, Mary, widow of William Whiting; freeman 1651; representative 1654-5; died 1659. He had Samuel, who went to Milford, and Thomas, born 1652, who lived at Wethersfield. His widow married Alexander Bryan, of Milford.

THOMAS FITCH, of Norwalk, 1652, brother of Rev. James; probably came with him in 1637; freeman 1657; had Thomas, and John, and was living with them in 1688.

THOMAS FITCH, of Boston, cordwainer; by wife Martha, daughter of David Fiske, of Watertown, had Martha 1664; and Thomas, 1669. The church record calls him of Watertown; freeman 1666, and died, 1678.

REFERENCES.

MASSACHUSETTS.—Babson's Hist. of Gloucester, 93; Eaton's Hist. of Reading, 72; Hazen's Hist. of Billerican, 53; Hudson's Hist. of Lexington, 75.

NEW HAMPSHIRE.—Hayward's Hist. of Hancock, 573; Stearn's Hist. of Rindge, 521-3.

CONNECTICUT.—Caulkin's Hist. of Norwich, 148, 153; Hall's Hist. of Norwalk, 189, 191, 213; Stiles' Hist. of Windsor, II, 261-70.

OTHER PUBLICATIONS.—Amer. Ancestry, I, 27; IV. 28; Alden's Amer. Epitaphs, IV, 139; Brown's Bedford, Mass., Families, 10-12; Hine's Lebanon, Ct., Address, 154; Hollister's Hist. of Pawlet, Vt., 188-90; Huntington Gen., 107; Morse's Sherborne, Mass., Settlers, 87-9; Loomis Gen. Female Branches, 540-6; Stranahan and Fitch Gen. (1868) 49-91; Strong Gen., 311, 320-30; Thayer Memorial, 41-3, 90-102; Walworth's Hyde Gen., 262; Westcott's Life of John Fitch, 27-9, 413; Savage's Gen. Dict., II, 168-70.

FITHIAN. Howell's Hist. of Southampton, 242-5.

FITTS:—Richard Fitts, of Ipswich, removed to Newbury; married, 1654, Sarah Ordway, who died 1667; he died 1672. He had perhaps son Richard, of Salisbury.

ROBERT FITTS, of Salisbury, 1640, removed to Ipswich, and died about 1665, leaving wife Grace and a son, Abraham.

REFERENCES:—Benedict's Hist. of Sutton, Mass., 641; Paige's Hist. of Cambridge, Mass., 546; Chase's Hist. of Chester, N. H., 619-21; Fitts Gen. (1869) 91 pages; Eaton's Hist. of Candia, N. H., 77; Bass' Hist. of Braintree, Vt., 133-5; N. E. Hist. and Gen. Reg., XXII, 70-2, 161-5.

FITZGERALD. Eaton's Hist. of Thomaston, Me., II, 226; Eaton's Annals of Warren, Me., 541; Meade's Old Families of Va.

FITZHUGH. Carter Family Tree; De Bow's Review, XXVI, 133; Turner's Phelps Purchase, 365, 396; Meade's Old Churches of Va., II, 192; Richmond, Va., Standard, II, 3, 24, 35, 51; III, 2; Virginia Mag. of History (1894) I; Welle's Washington Gen., 252.
FITZPATRICK. Blake's Franklin, 249-91.

FITZ-RANDOLPH:—Edward Fitz-Randolph, of Scituate, 1637, born in Nottinghamshire, Eng., about 1614, came to New England, 1630, married 1637, Elizabeth, daughter of Elder Thomas Blossoin of Plymouth, and joined the church same year; went to Barnstable 1639, there had Nathaniel, born 1642; Mary, 1644, died young; Hannah, 1648; Mary again, 1651; John, 1653; Joseph, 1656, Thomas, 1659; and Hope, 1661. Hannah married, 1668, Jasper Taylor; and Mary married 1669, Samuel Hinckley, a second wife.

REFERENCES:—Amer. Ancestry, VI, 22; Swift's Barnstable Families, 368-70; Paxton's Marshall Gen., 235; Savage's Gen. Dict., II, 170.

FLACK:—Cotton Flack, of Boston, 1634; freeman 1640, by wife Ann, had Deborah, buried 1642; Deborah, again, born 1644, died young, and son Samuel, to whom he gave in his will, 1654, his estate in that part of the town now Brookline.

REFERENCES:—Amer. Ancestry II, 40, Savage's Gen. Dict. II, 170.

FLAGG:—Thomas Flagg, of Watertown, came 1637, with Richard Carver, from Scrotby, County Norfolk, England; by wife Mary, had John, born 1643; Bartholomew, 1645; Thomas, 1646; Michael, 1651; Eliezur, 1653; Elizabeth, 1655; Mary 1657; Rebecca, 1660; Benjamin, 1662; and Allen, 1665. Elizabeth and Mary married Joshua and Samuel, sons of John Bigelow.

REFERENCES.

MASSACHUSETTS.—Ballou's Hist. of Milford, 749; Barry's Hist. of Framingham, 244; Bond's Hist. of Watertown, 219-25, 762-4; Draper's Hist. of Spencer, 197; Pierce's Hist. of Grafton, 480-3; Sewall's Hist. of Wohnon, 611; Ward's Hist. of Shrewsbury, 278; Stone's Hist. of Hubbardston, 266.

NEW HAMPSHIRE.—Chase's Hist. of Chester, 521; Hayward's Hist. of Hancock, 574; Norton's Hist. of Fitzwilliam, 569; Worcester's Hist. of Hollis, 375.

OTHER PUBLICATIONS.—Andrews' Hist. of New Britain, Ct., 218; Bass' Hist. of Braintree, Vt., 143; Flagg Gen. (1877) 7 pages; Maine Genealogist, II, 80-7; Saunders' Gen.; N. E. Hist. and Gen. Reg., XXVII, 246; XXX, 112; North's Hist. of Augusta, Me., 852-69; Wall's Reminiscences of Worcester, Mass., 106; Savage's Gen. Dict. II, 171.

FLANDERS:—Stephen Flanders, of Salisbury, 1646, had two wives. By wife Jane, had Stephen, born, 1647; Mary, 1650; Philip, 1652; Sarah, 1654; Naomi, 1656; and John, 1659. He died, 1684.

REFERENCES:—Coffin's Hist. of Boscawen, N. H., 527-30; Bouton's Concord, N. H., 705; Cogswell's Hist. of Henniker, N. H., 569; Futhey's Hist. of Chester Co., Pa., 549; McKeen's Hist. of Bradford, Vt., 367-70; N. E. Hist. and Gen. Reg., XXVII, 170-6; Poor's Hist. of Merrimac Valley, 122; Prescott's Flanders Gen. (1873) 8 pages; Runnel's Hist. of Sanbornton, N. H., II, 278; Savage's Gen. Dict., II, 172.

FLANSBURGH. Amer. Ancestry, II, 40; Pearson's Schenectady, N. Y., Settlers, 69.

FLATMAN:—Thomas Flatman, of Salem, perhaps, 1637; removed to Braintree, where he had Elizabeth, born 1640; and Thomas, 1643; was freeman 1640.

REFERENCE:—Savage's Gen. Dict., II, 172.

FLEMING:—John Fleming, of Watertown, by wife Ann, had Sarah, born 1639; and John, 1642; was deacon, 1657; his wife died same year. Sarah married, 1654, John Barnard. He had elder children, Thomas, Mary, and Elizabeth, all living in England.

REFERENCES:—Amer. Ancestry, II, 40; Goode Gen., 211; Bolling Gen., 25; Meade's Old Families of Va.; Egle's Penn. Gens., 194-208; Temple's Hist. of Palmer, Mass., 449; Paxton's Marshall Gen., 337; Richmond,

Va., Standard, II, 20, 23; IV, 1; Robertson's Pocohontas' Descendants, Savage's Gen. Dict., II, 172.

FLETCHER:—Robert Fletcher, of Concord, 1635; constable, 1637; died, 1677, aged 84; had Luke, Francis, Samuel, and William; one, or more, no doubt, were born in England.

JOHN FLETCHER, of Wethersfield, married before 1641, Mary, daughter of Widow Joyce Ward; the old lady's will, 1640, naming sons, Edward, born in England, and Anthony, William, Robert, and John here. He removed to Milford, and joined the church there, 1641, in which year his daughter Sarah was baptized; Hannah, 1643; Elizabeth, 1645; Samuel, 1649, died young; and Abigail, 1652. He died, 1662.

JOHN FLETCHER, of Portsmouth, freeman 1669, one of the founders of the first congregational church, 1671, and deacon; was a physician, and died, 1695.

HENRY FLETCHER, of Reading, had Samuel, born 1662.

REFERENCES.

MASSACHUSETTS:—Ballou's Hist. of Milford, 750; Butler's Hist. of Groton, 401; Chandler's Hist. of Shirley, 416; Fox's Hist. of Dunstable, 243; Hazen's Hist. of Billerica, 53; Mill's Old Dunstable, 147-62; Hodgman's Hist. of Westford, 446-50; Pierce's Hist. of Grafton, 483; Reed's Hist. of Rutland, 115; Stearn's Hist. of Ashburnham, 700-2.

NEW HAMPSHIRE:—Aldrich's Hist. of Walpole, 253-5; Cochrane's Hist. of Antrim, 492-5; Hayward's Hist. of Hancock, 575; Saunderson's Hist. of Charlestown, 354; Stearn's Hist. of Rindge, 523-5; Secomb's Hist of Amherst, 587-91; Washington History, 423-8; Wheeler's Hist. of Newport, 386-8; Kidder's Hist. of New Ipswich, 374-6; Livermore's Hist. of Wilton.

MAINE:—Bradbury's Hist. of Kennebunkport, 244; Eaton's Hist. of Thomaston, II, 227; Farrow's Hist. of Islesborough, 209.

OTHER PUBLICATIONS:—Amer. Ancestry, VI, 140; 203; VII, 385; IX, 138; Bates and Fletcher Gen. (1892) 58 pages; Dunstable, Mass., Bicentenn, 157; Fletcher Gen. (1848) 24 pages; (1871) 279 pages; (1870) 12 pages; (1878) 10 pages; (1881) 600 pages; Fletcher's Hatch Gen., 22-4 Leland Gen., 61-3; Morse's Mem. Appendix, 51½; N. E. Hist. and Gen. Reg., XXII, 389; Power's Hist. of Sangamon Co., Ill, 299-303; Vinton's Richardson Gen., 111; Wood Gen., 70-7; Wyman's Charlestown, Mass., Hist. Gens., I, 348; Savage's Gen. Dict., II, 172-4.

FLAVELLING:—Ruttenber's Hist. of Orange Co., N. Y., 365.

FLINDERS:—Richard Flinders, of Salem, born about 1637, had John and Richard, who died in England.

REFERENCE:—Savage's Gen. Dict., II, 174.

FLINN. Littell's Passaic Valley, 153.

FLINT:—Henry Flint, of Braintree, came in 1635 to Boston; born at Mattock, in Derbyshire, England; freeman 1636; married Margery, eldest daughter of Joanna Hoar; had Dorothy, born 1642; Ann, 1644; Josiah, 1645; Margaret, 1647, died soon; Joanna, 1649; David, 1652, died soon; Seth, 1653; Ruth, 1655; John, and Cotton, twins, both died soon; he died 1668, and his widow, 1687.

THOMAS FLINT, of Concord, came to New England, 1636; freeman 1638; representative, 1637-40. He had perhaps one or more children born in England, besides Ephraim, born here, 1642; and John.

THOMAS FLINT, of Salem, died 1663, leaving widow and children: Thomas, Elizabeth, George, John and Joseph.

WILLIAM FLINT, of Salem, 1645; died 1673, leaving a good estate to widow and sons: Edward, born 1638; and Thomas. His daughter Alice, married, 1657, John Pickering.

REFERENCES.

MASSACHUSETTS:—Eaton's Hist. of Reading, 72-9; Marvin's Hist. of Wichendon, 454; Shattuck's Hist. of Concord, 371; Stearn's Hist. of Ashburnham, 703; Ward's Hist. of Shrewsbury, 275; Washburn's Hist. of Leicester, 365.

NEW HAMPSHIRE:—Basset's Hist. of Richmond, 388; Cochran's Hist. of Antrim, 495-9; Cogswell's Hist. of Henniker, 570; Hayward's Hist. of Hancock, 575-8; Livermore's Hist. of Wilton, 368-71; Reade's Hist. of Swanzey, 339; Secomb's Hist. of Amherst, 591-3.

MAINE:—Butler's Hist. of Farmington, 470; Eaton's Hist. of Thomeston, II, 227; Lapham's Hist. of Norway, 501.

OTHER PUBLICATIONS:—Amer. Ancestry, VI, 84; VIII, 54; Bass' Hist. of Braintree, Vt., 135-41; Driver Gen., 291-307; Brown's Bedford, Mass., Families, 12; Essex, Mass., Inst. Coll., XVI, 106-9; Flint Gen (1860) 150 pages; N. E. Hist. and Gen. Reg., XIV, 58-60; Pompey, N. Y., Reunion, 304; Potter's Old Families of Concord, Mass. (1887); Vinton's Richardson Gen., 553; Wyman's Charlestown, Mass., Gens., 349; Savage's Gen. Dict., II, 174.

FLINTNER. Hanson's List of Gardiner, Me., 82.

FLINTNER. Cutts' Gen., 202; Maine Hist. of Gen. Rec., VI, 285-92; 341-8, 417, 21.

FLOOD:—Henry Flood, of Boston, by wife Mary, had Henry, born 1666; Mary, 1668; Henry again, 1671; and Jonathan, 1673.

JOHN FLOOD, of Boston, by wife Hannah had James, born 1668; Richard, 1670; Lydia, 1672; Joseph, 1675; Benjamin, 1677; Abigail, 1679; and John, 1681.

JOHN FLOOD, of Lynn, may have removed to Salisbury, where was one of this name, aged 27, in 1679, or to Malden, where was John, freeman 1690; died 1702. By wife Sarah, he had Hugh; John, born 1665; Joseph; Daniel, born 1675; Sarah; and Abigail.

JOSEPH FLOOD, of Dorchester, perhaps brother of the preceding, had Eleazor, baptized 1638; was bailiff 1636; and removed to Lynn.

PHILIP FLOOD, of Newbury, came about 1680 from New Jersey; by wife Mary had Joseph, born 1684; Esther, 1686; Mary, 1688; Henry, 1689; John, 1693; Richard, 1696; Rachel, 1698; Philip, 1700; and Benjamin, 1705.

ROBERT FLOOD, of Wethersfield; married, 1646, Abigail, daughter of Nicholas Disbrough, of Hartford; died, 1689, leaving Robert, Abigail, John, Thomas, Mary and George. The name Flood and Floyd are used indiscriminately in record of this family.

REFERENCES:—Chandler's Hist. of Shirley, Mass., 417; Savage's Gen. Dict., II, 175.

FLORIDA. Hemenway's Vermont Gaz., V, 162.

FLORVILLE. Power's Hist. of Sangamon Co., Ill., 303.

FLOUNDERS. Austin's R. I. Gen. Dict., 79.

FLOURWAY. Richmond, Va., Standard, I, 37, III, 14; Va. Mag. of Hist. and Biog., II, 1895.

FLOWER:—Lamrock Flower (or Flowers), Hartford, 1686, had Lydia, born 1687; Lamrock, 1689; Elizabeth, 1693; John, 1695; Mary, 1697; Francis, 1700; Ann, 1703, and Joseph, 1706; and died 1716.

REFERENCES:—Smith's Hist. of Delaware Co., Pa., 436; Potts' Carter, Gen., 158; Welles' Amer. Family Autig., N. E. Hist. and Gen. Reg., XLIV, 399; Ellis Gen., 112, 152-4, LX, 373; Martin's Hist. of Chester Co., Pa., 436-44.

FLOYD:—John Floyd, of Scituate, 1640, merchant, was at Boston, 1653.

JOSEPH FLOYD, of Lyon, 1635, removed to Boston, 1666.

JOHN FLOYD, of Lynn, or Romney Marsh, now Chelsea, served as captain against the Indians, 1690, and died 1701; by wife Sarah, had Sarah, born 1662; Hugh, 1663; John, 1665; Joseph, 1667; and Joanna, 1669; perhaps, removed to Malden, and had Noah, born 1670; and Daniel, 1675; and in Boston had Mary, 1679.

RICHARD FLOYD, of Boston, 1642, by wife Lydia, had Lydia, born 1643; and three other children, dead before 1654. His inventory was taken 1662.

REFERENCES:—Aldrich's Hist. of Walpole, N. H., 252; Thompson's Hist. of Long Island, N. Y., II, 431-7; Bangor, Me., Hist. Mag., V, 191; Strong Gen., 604-6; Carter Family Tree; N. E. Hist. and Gen. Reg., XXXVIII, 74; Richmond, Va., Standard, II, 7; Wyman's Charlestown, Mass., Gens., I, 350; Savage's Gen. Dict., II, 176.

FLUCKER. Wyman's Charlestown, Mass., Gens., I, 350.

FLYNT. Amer. Ancestry, IV, 176; Morris and Flynt Gen. (1882).

FOBES:—John Fobes, of Duxbury, 1636, was early at Bridgewater; married probably before their removal, Constant, sister of Experience Mitchell; had John Edward, Mary, Caleb, William, Joshua, and Elizabeth, and died 1661 or 1662. His widow married, 1662, John Briggs.

REFERENCES:—Lapham's Hist. of Paris, Me., 601-4; Winsor's Hist. of Duxbury, Mass., 258; Mitchell's Hist. of Bridgewater, Mass., 159-63; Savage's Gen. Dict., II, 176.

FOGERTY. Eaton's Hist. of Thomaston, Me., II, 228.

FOGG:—Ralph Fogg, of Plymouth, 1633, removed to Salem, freeman 1634; by wife Susanna, had Ezekiel, baptized 1638; and David, 1640; was town treasurer 1637, and for some years engaged in municipal affairs, but about 1652 he returned to England, and died in London 1674.

SAMUEL FOGG, of Hampton, married 1659, Sarah, daughter of Richard Carrier, had Daniel, born 1660; and Seth; and died 1672.

REFERENCES.

MAINE.—Corliss' Hist. of No. Yarmouth; Dearborn's Hist. of Parsonfield, 380; Eaton's Hist. of Thomaston, II, 228.

NEW HAMPSHIRE.—Dow's Hist. of Hampton, 709-16; Fullerton's Hist. of Raymond, 223-6; Hayward's Hist. of Hancock, 579-81; Runnels' Hist. of Sanbornton, II, 279; Wheeler's Hist. of Newport, 388.

OTHER PUBLICATIONS.—Fogg's Eliot, Me., Settlers, 1-9; Maine Hist. Rec., I, 70-80; Savage's Gen. Dict., II, 177.

FOKAR:—John Fokar, a husbandman, came in the "Increase," 1635.

FOLAND. Amer. Ancestry, I, 27; II, 41.

FOBY. Temple's Hist. of Palmer, Mass., 462.

FOLGER:—John Folger, of Watertown, came from Norwich, Eng., 1635, with son Peter and wife, who was Miribah Gibbs.

PETER FOLGER, of Nantucket, son of the first John, went early from Watertown to the Vineyard, married Mary Morrill, and removed about 1663 to Nantucket, where his name has been ever since in high regard; had Eleazur, about 1646; and John 1659; and seven daughters, Joanna, Bethia, Dorcas, Bathsua, Patience, Experience and Abiah, born 1667, who married Josiah Franklin as his second wife, and was mother of the famous Benjamin Franklin.

REFERENCES:—Amer. Ancestry, I, 28; II, 41; VI, 17; N. E. Hist. and Gen. Reg., XVI, 269-78; Savage's Gen. Dict., II, 177.

FOLLANSBEE:—Thomas Follansbee, of Portsmouth, removed about 1667 to Newbury, probably bringing wife Sarah, and perhaps children, Rebecca and Thomas; had Francis, born 1677, and Hannah, 1680. Sarah, his wife, died 1683.

REFERENCES:—Follansbee Assoc. Reports (1815), 28 p.; (1869), 8 p.; Smith's Hist. of Peterborough, N. H., 84; Savage's Gen. Dict., II, 178.

FOLLANSBY. Benton's Hist. of Guildhall, Vt., 270.

FOLLEN:—Abraham Follen, Casco, 1658.

FOLLET:—William Follett, of Dover, 1651, married 1672, Elizabeth, widow of William Drew, and had son Nicholas.

PHILIP FOLLET, of Dover, 1671-5.

ROBERT FOLLET, of Salem, had Abraham, born 1671. Hatch's Hist. of Industry, Me., 621; Morse Mem. Ap-

REFERENCES:—Amer. Ancestry, IV, 127; Stone's Hist. of Hubbardston, Mass., 268; Austin's Allied Families, 99; pennix, 60; Huron and Erie Counties, Ohio, 406; Savage's Gen. Dict., II, 178.

FOLLMER. Meginners' Hist. Jour., II, 383.

FOLSOM:—John Folsom, of Hingham, born 1617, came from Old Hingham, Co. Norfolk, Eng., in the "Diligent," of Ipswich, 1638, with wife and two servants. He had married, 1636, Mary, daughter of Edward Gilman, of Old Hingham, and had here baptized, Samuel, 1641; John, Nathaniel, 1644; Israel, 1646; Peter, 1649; Mary, 1651, and Ephraim, 1654; was representative, 1654, and removed, 1659, to Exeter, where he died 1681.

REFERENCES.

NEW HAMPSHIRE.—Bell's Hist. of Exeter, 12-14; Chase's Hist. of Chester, 522-4; Cogswell's Hist. of Henniker, 571; Lancaster's Hist. of Gilmanton, 262; Fulledton's Hist. of Raymond, 226-8; Runnel's Hist. of Sanbornton, II, 280-3.

OTHER PUBLICATIONS.—Amer. Ancestry, III, 193; Chapman's Weeks Gen., 51, 136-8; Folsom Gen. (1876) (1879) (1882), 297 pages; Montague Gen., 348; Palmer Gen. (1886), 48-51; N. E. Hist. and Gen. Reg., XXX, 207-31; New Hampshire Hist. Soc. Coll., VI., 191; Savage's Gen. Dict., II, 178.

FONDA. Amer. Ancestry, I, 28; VII, 29; Munsell's Albany, N. Y., Coll., VI, 122; Pearson's Schenectady, N. Y. Settlers, 70-2.

FONDEY. Amer. Ancestry, I, 28.

FONES:—John Fones, of Kingston, 1679, one of His Maj. Justices, had wife, Margaret, sons, John, Jeremiah, Samuel, James and Daniel, and daughter, Mary, who married James Greene, of Warwick. He was, perhaps, the first comer of this name, and probably from London. He died 1703.

REFERENCES.—Austin's R. I. Gen. Dict., 79; Savage's Gen. Dict., II, 179.

FONTAINE. Bergen's Kings Co. Settlers, 115; Meade's Old Churches of Va., I, 465; Greene's Kentucky Families; Slaughter's Fry Memoirs, 48; Maury's Huguenot Memoirs (1863); Slaughter's St. Mark's Parish, 184, 189; Virginia Hist. Coll., V, 119-50; Welles' Washington Gen., 251.

FONTLEROY:—James Fontleroy, of Boston, came in the "Prudence and May," from London, 1679.

FOOTE:—Pasco Foote, of Salem, 1637, joined the Church 1653, and in the same year had his children, John, Malachi, Samuel, Elizabeth, Mary, Isaac, Pasco and Abigail, all baptized together. He died 1670.

NATHANIEL FOOTE, of Watertown, brought from England his wife Elizabeth, and children, Nathaniel, Elizabeth, Mary, Robert, Frances and Sarah; had Rebecca, born probably at Watertown; freeman 1634; removed to Wethersfield, 1636, of which he was representative 1641-4, dying in this last year. He left a good estate to his children and widow, who was the sister of John Deming, and married Thomas Welles, afterwards Governor of the Colony; she died 1683.

JOSHUA FOOTE, of Roxbury, citizen and ironmonger of London, came in 1653, removed over to Providence, and died there about 1655. He had a son Samuel, and about 1650, his daughter Elizabeth married William Sheldon, of London.

REFERENCES.

CONNECTICUT.—Caulkin's Hist. of New London, 308; Davis' Hist. of Wallingford, 745; Orcutt's Hist. of Stratford, 1202-4.

OTHER PUBLICATIONS.—Amer. Ancestry, IV, 88, 191; V, 231; Brown's W. Simsbury, Ct., Settlers, 53-6; Barbour's N. Y., Wife and Mother App., 624; Felton Gen. (1886), 247; Foote Gen. (1849) 360 p.; (1867) 32 p.;

(1886) 26 p.; Judd's Hist. of Hadley, Mass., 494; Matthew's Hist. of Cornwall, Vt., 285; Nash Gen., 42; Loomis Gen., Female Branches, 573-8; Humphrey Gen., 201-5, 346-9; Walworth's Hyde Gen., 276; N. E. Hist. and Gen. Reg., IX., 272; XXVII, 448; Young's Chautauqua Co., N. Y., 359-61; Savage's Gen. Dict., II, 179-82.

FOOTMAN:—Thomas Footman, of Dover, 1648, had wife, Catharine, and seven children, dead as early as 1668. His will was of date 1667.

REFERENCES.—Bulloch Gen.; Savage's Gen. Dict., II, 182.

FOP:—Daniel Fop, of Hingham, 1635.

REFERENCES.—Lincoln's Hist. of Hingham, Mass., 42.

FORBAS:—Alexander Forbas, of Charlestown, married 1674, Kate Robinson.

FORBES:—James Forbes, of Hartford, died 1692, leaving John, David, James, Dorothy, Mary and Sarah.

WILLIAM FORBES, of New London, 1648, removed soon.

REFERENCES.—Amer. Ancestry, III, 147; Forbes Gen. (1892) 190 p.; Bangor Hist. Mag., IV, 20; Dodd's Hist. of East Haven, Ct., 119; Dudley's Archael. Gen. Coll., plate 5; N. Y. Gen. and Biog. Rec., XXI, 159-62.

FORBUSH or FURBUSH:—Jonathan Forbush, of Marlborough, by wife Hannah, had eight children; removed to Westborough, and was deacon there, called Forbes; but the name of his father seems to have been commonly written Farrabas.

REFERENCES.—Forbes Gen.; Paige's Hist. of Hardwick, Mass., 377; Pierce's Hist. of Grafton, Mass., 484-8; Smith's Hist. of Peterborough, N. H., 858; Ward's Rice Gen., 21; Hudson's Hist. of Marlborough, Mass., 364; Temple's Hist. of N. Brookfield, Mass., 588-91.

FORCE:—Benjamin Force, of Wrentham, with wife, Eliza, came from Newport, R. I., 1690. Amer. Ancestry, VI, 80.

FORD or FORRDE:—Andrew Ford, of Weymouth, freeman 1654; by wife, Elinor, had Samuel, born 1656; Nathaniel, 1658; Ebenezer, 1660; Silence, 1661; Prudence, 1663; Jacob, 1666; Elizabeth, 1667; Israel, 1670, and Sarah, 1672; besides, probably, the eldest, Andrew, who was a proprietor 1673.

JOHN FORD, of Plymouth, one of the "first comers," with, perhaps, his widowed mother, elder brother William, and sister Martha, in the "Fortune," 1621; had wife Hannah, and died at Marshfield, 1693.

JOHN FORD, of Haverhill, 1670, was a son-in-law of Stephen Kent.

ROGER FORD, of Cambridge, died 1644.

ROBERT FORD, of Haverhill, 1677.

THOMAS FORD, of Dorchester, came in the "Mary and John," 1630. Made freeman 1631; brought children, Abigail, Joanna and Hepzibah; removed 1636 to Windsor, where he was representative, 1638-41, '44 and '54. His wife died 1643, and he married for second wife, 1644, Ann, widow of Thomas Scott, of Hartford; had, perhaps, Ann, who married, 1677, Thomas Newbury, of

Windsor; removed in old age to Northampton, and died 1776.

THOMAS FORD, of Milford, 1646, married Elizabeth, daughter of Alexander Knowles, of Fairfield; had Elizabeth, born about 1652; John, 1664; Thomas, 1656; Mary, 1658; Lydia, baptized 1660; and died 1662. His widow married 1663, Eliezer Rogers.

TIMOTHY FORD, of Charleston, 1637; removed to New Haven, 1639, and died there 1684. He had children, Matthew, Samuel, Mary, Bethia, and Elizabeth.

WILLIAM FORD, of Marshfield, 1639, son, perhaps, of the widow who came in the "Fortune," 1621; was at Duxbury, 1643; had by wife Ann, William, born about 1634; Michael, Millicent and Margaret. He was a miller at Duxbury, and an original proprietor of Bridgewater; died 1676, aged 72. His widow died 1684.

REFERENCES.

MASSACHUSETTS.—Deane's Hist. of Scituate, 269; Hobart's Hist. of Abington, 378-83; Kingman's Hist. of N. Bridgewater, 503; Mitchell's Hist. of Bridgewater, 163, 373; Temple's Hist. of Whately, 229; Winsor's Hist. of Duxbury, 259.

CONNECTICUT.—Blake's Hist. of Hamden, 245; Stiles' Hist. of Windsor, II, 270.

NEW HAMPSHIRE.—Runnell's Hist. of Sanbornton, II, 283-5.

OTHER PUBLICATIONS.—Amer. Ancestry, II, 41; V, 115; Bass' Hist. of Braintree, II, 141-3; Baldwin Gen. 1108, 1113; Goode Gen., 291; Barbour's N. Y., Wife and Mother App., 25; Collins' Hist. of Hillsdale, N. Y. App., 54-6; Davis' Landmarks of Plymouth, Mass., 111; Historical Mag. (1871), 91; Kitchell Gen., 50; Maine Hist. and Gen. Reg., III, 229; Poole Gen., 78-80; Pope Gen.; Power's Hist. of Sangamon Co., Ill., 304; Strong Gen. 17; Whitman Gen., 370; Wyman's Charleston, Mass., Gens., I, 252; Savage's Gen. Dict., II, 182-4.

FORDHAM:—Robert Fordham, of Southampton, L. I., came, perhaps, in 1640, possibly earlier; was a short time at Cambridge; was in temporary office at Sudbury, 1641; had by wife Elizabeth, Hannah, John, Jonah, Robert and Joseph. He preached at Hempstead, and may have been more there than at Southampton; his name being first in the Dutch Government patent for the town of Hempstead; and died 1674.

REFERENCES.—Howell's Hist. of Southampton, L. I., 245-7; Savage's Gen. Dict., II, 184.

FORCHAND. Amer. Ancestry, IV, 220.

FORMAN or FURMAN:—John and Josiah Forman. of Newtown, L. I., 1655.

JOHN FORMAN, of Newbury, had, as Coffin says, Abigail, born 1676, and John, 1678.

REFERENCES.—Leavenworth Gen., 338-43; Paxton's

FORREST:—Archibald Forrest, at Hatfield, perhaps Marshall Gen., 229-33; Sutter's Hist. of Monmouth Co., N. J., XXVII.

FORNEY. Wheeler's Hist. of N. Carolina, 241. transiently a soldier in King Philip's War, 1676.

REFERENCES.—Amer. Ancestry, IV, 146; Cinc., Ohio, Criterion (1888), II, 474; Powers' Hist. of Sangamon Co., Ill., 305; Runnel's Hist. of Sanbornton, N. H., I,

474; Clyde's Irish Settlers, Pa., 45; Richmond, Va., Standard. Ill., 37.

FORRISTALL. Norton's Hist. of Fitzwilliam, 570-4.

FORSAITH. Chase's Hist. of Chester, N. H., 524; Wheeler's Hist. of Newport, N. H., 389.

FORSBEE. Cole Gen., 86-90, 171-203.

FORSTER. Amer. Ancestry, VI, 204; Caulkin's Hist. of New London, Ct., 312; Egle's Penn. Gens., 209-20; Forster Gen. (1870), 25 pages; Forster's Descendants, Jacob Forster, of Charlestown, Mass.; New Eng. Gen. and Hist. Reg., XXX, 83-102; Forster's Descendants, Reginald Forster, of Ipswich, Mass.; Wyman's Charlestown. Mass., Gens.. I, 353.

FORSYTH. Forsyth Gen. (1888), 29 pages; Amer. Ancestry, III, 150; VII, 87; Cope Gen. Pa., 39, 61, 141; Granite Monthly, VIII, 251; Richmond, Va., Standard III, 23; Ruttenber's Hist. of Orange Co., N. Y., 394; Sylvester's Hist. of Ulster Co., N. Y., 106.

FORT:—Abraham Fort, of Boston, married 1656, widow Hannah Hutchinson.

REFERENCES:—Munsell's Hist. of Albany, IV, 123; Schuyler's Colonial New York, II, 367-75.

FORTH. N. E. Gen. and Hist. Reg., XXIII, 184.

FORTUNE. Powers' Hist. of Sangamon Co., Ill., 306.

FORTUNE:—Samuel Forward, of Windsor, 1670, by wife Ann, had Samuel, born 1671; and Joseph, 1674; he died 1684, and his widow, Ann, died the following year.

REFERENCES:—Holton's Wnislow Gen., 341; Stiles' Hist. of Windsor, Ct., II., 271.

FOSDICK:—Stephen Fosdick, of Charlestown, 1635; brought wife and perhaps his children; freeman 1638; had wife Sarah; sons, Thomas. John, and Samuel, and daughters, Hannah, Martha and Mary. He died 1664.

REFERENCES:—Caulkin's New London, Ct., 343; Wyman's Hist. of Charlestown, Mass., I, 354-60; Savage's Gen. Dict., II, 185.

FOSKETT:—John Foskett, of Charlestown, 1658, was a householder, 1678. Elizabeth, his wife, was admitted of the church, 1673, and their children, John, Thomas, Joshua, Robert, Elizabeth and Mary, were baptized the same year; Jonathan, 1674, and Abigail, 1680.

REFERENCES:—Hyde's Hist. of Brimfield, Mass., 403; Temple's Hist. of Palmer, Mass., 453; Wyman's Charlestown, Mass., Gen., I, 360.

FOSS:—John Foss, of Dover, 1665, had son, John, was of the grand jury 1688, and died 1699.

REFERENCES:—Chase's Hist. of Chester, N. H., 525; Little Gen., 290; Machias, Me., Centenn., 161.

FOSSETT. Johnston's Hist. of Bristol, Me., 442.

FOSSEY. Hammatt Papers, 108.

FOSTER:—Reginald, or Renold Foster. of Ipswich, came, it is said, 1638, had grant of land 1641. and brought Abraham, Reginald, William, Isaac and Jacob, besides two daughters. It appears, also, that he had a second wife, Judith, who died 1664, and who brought him, Judith, born 1660; Mary, 1662, and John, 1664. It is also stated that he married next, 1665, Sarah Martin, and had Ruth, born 1671, died in one month; Ellen, 1673; Hannah, 1675, and Nathaniel, 1678. He died 1681.

WILLIAM FOSTER, of Boston, 1644, had wife, Susanna; removed, perhaps, in a short time to Charlestown, where he was admitted of the church, 1652; married for second wife, Ann, daughter of William Brackenbury; had John, born 1656, who died 1659; Ann, 1658; Mary, 1660; Elizabeth, 1665; Deborah, baptized 1668, died soon, and John again, 1668. He died 1698, aged 80, and his widow died 1714, in her 86th year.

HOPESTILL FOSTER, of Dorchester, 1634, or earlier, had wife, Patience, who came in the "Elizabeth," 1635, aged 40, with her son, Hopestill, aged 14. He was freeman 1639, of the artillery company 1642, selectman, 1645.

CHRISTOPHER FOSTER, of Lynn, came in the "Abigail," 1635, aged 32, with wife, Frances, 25, and children, Rebecca, Nathaniel and John; was freeman 1637; removed to Long Island, N. Y., and was probably living there 1670.

BARTHOLOMEW FOSTER, of Gloucester, married 1669, Hannah, daughter of Thomas Very; had Bartholomew, born 1670; John, 1673; Thomas, 1676; Samuel, 1678; Edward, 1681, and died 1682.

EDWARD FOSTER, of Scituate, about 1633, married 1635, Lettice Hanford; had Timothy, 1636, who died next year; Timothy again 1638, died soon; Timothy again, and Elizabeth, posthumous, 1644.

EDWARD FOSTER, of Springfield, married 1661, Esther Bliss, who lived in the family of John Pynchon; was freeman 1690,. and died 1720.

SAMUEL FOSTER, of Wenham, freeman 1650, removed to Chelmsford, 1655; by wife, Esther, had there, Edward, born 1657, and Esther, 1659; had before removal, Hannah, about 1649; Samuel, about 1650, and Eli, about 1653; was representative 1679, and died 1702, aged 82.

THOMAS FOSTER, of Weymouth, freeman 1647, had Thomas, born 1640; John, 1642, and Increase.

THOMAS FOSTER, of Roxbury, married 1662, Sarah, daughter of Robert Parker; had Thomas, born 1663, died shortly; Thomas, again; Sarah, 1667; Hannah, 1669, and Jonathan, 1671; was freeman 1666.

THOMAS FOSTER, of New London, called in the record son of John Forster, of Kingsware, married 1666, Susanna, daughter of Ralph Parker; had Susanna, born 1667; Thomas, 1669; Jonathan, 1673; Mary, 1675; Edward, 1677, died soon; Samuel, 1678; Rebecca, 1681, and Ebenezer, 1683; he died 1685.

REFERENCES.

MASSACHUSETTS.—Abbott's Hist. of Andover, 38; Babson's Hist. of Gloucester, 94; Barry's Hist. of Framingham, 245; Daggett's Hist. of Attleborough, 90; Deane's Hist. of Scituate, 270; Eaton's Hist. of Reading, 79; Freeman's Hist. of Cape Cod, II, 111, 765; Hazen's Hist. of Billerica, 54; Herrick's Hist. of Gardner, 348; Hyde's Hist. of Brimfield, 404; Paige's Hist. of Cambridge, 547; Perby's Hist. of Boxford, 31; Paige's Hist. of Hardwick, 377-9; Sewall's Hist. of Woburn, 612; Stearns' Hist. of Ashburnham, 705-10; Temple's Hist. of No. Brookfield, 491-3; Temple's Hist. of Northfield, 451; Temple's Hist. of Palmer, 450-3.

NEW HAMPSHIRE.—Aldrich's Hist. of Walpole, 256-9; Blood's Hist. of Temple, 221; Cochrane's Hist. of Antrim, 499; Cogswell's Hist. of Henniker, 572-5; Eaton's Hist. of Candia, 80; Hayward's Hist. of Gilsum, 308-10; Hayward's Hist. of Hancock, 581-5; Hill's List of Mason, 202; Kidder's Hist. of New Ipswich, 376; Livermore's Hist. of Wilton, 371; Merrill's Hist. of Acworth, 216; Norton's Hist. of Fitzwilliam, 574-6; Read's Hist. of Swanzey, 340; Stearn's Hist. of Rindge, 525; Worcester's Hist. of Hollis, 375.

MAINE.—Corliss' Hist. ofNo. Yarmouth; Eaton's Hist. of Thomaston, I, 229; Lapham's Hist. of Bethel, 532-4; Lapham's Hist. of Norway, 502; Ridlon's Hist. of Harrison, 59-63; Thurston's Hist. of Winthorp, 1835.

OTHER PUBLICATIONS.—Amer. Ancestry, I, 28; II, 42; 5Carei-;,RM86tagJsmiE*D shr shr shrd hrdl rdlulushr IV, 140, 230; V, 186; VI, 40; Austin's R. I. Gen. Dict., 80; Ammidown Family, 33; Caldwell Gen. Rec., 64; Collin's Hist. of Hillsdale, N. Y., App., 56; Davis Gen., 95-8; Davis' Landmarks of Plymouth, Mass., 112; Dennysville, Me., Centenn., 103; Derby's Foster Gen. (1872), 35 pages; Driver Gen., 275; Dwight Gen., 634-60, 671-4; Foster Gen. (1871), 6 p.; (1872) 35 p.; (1876) 25 p.; (1885) 32 p.; Goodwin's Olcott Gen.; Greene's Tod Gen., Guild's Stiles Gen., 286-8, 353-7; Hammatt Papers, Ipswich, Mass., 1058; Hist. of Clermont Co., Ohio, 435; Holton's Winslow Mem., I, 148-62; Howell's Hist. of Southampton, N. Y., 247-56; Hubbard's Hist. of Stanstead Co., Canada, 137; Kilbourne Fam., 126; Leach's Morton Ancestry; Locke Gen., 64, 145, 300; Machias, Me., Centenn., 160; Milliken's Narraguagus Valley, Me., 3; Morse's Gen. Sherborn, Mass., 89; N. E. Hist. and Gen. Reg., I, 352-4; XX, 227, 308; XXV, 67-71, 394-9; XXX, 83-102; Poore Gen., 177-82; Powers' Hist. of Sangamon Co., Ill., 307-10; Rodenburgh's Autumn Leaves; Sedgwick's Hist. of Sharon, Ct., 79; Spooner's Mem. of W. Spooner, 215; Stiles' Hist. of Windsor, Ct., II, 272; Stoddard Gen. (1865), 48, 73; Swift's Barnstable Families, I, 388-90; Washington, N. H., History, 428; Whitman Gen., 432-7; Wood Gen., 47-57; Wyman's Charlestown, Mass., Gens., I, 362-6; Young's Hist. of Warsaw, N. Y., 264; Savage's Gen. Dict., II, 185-91.

FOULKE.—Hayden's Virginia Gens., 658; Jenkins' Hist. of Gwyuedd, Pa., 328, 210-47; Penn. Mag., XII, 369.

FOUNTAIN:—Aaron Fountain, of New London, 1680, married Susanna, daughter of Samuel Beebee, but after 1683 is not known.

REFERENCES:—Bolton's Hist. of Westchester, 518; Chite's Hist. of Staten Island, N. Y., 381.

FOWLE:—George Fowle, of Concord, freeman 1639; brought, probably, wife from England, and certainly a son, John; by wife, Mary, had Mary, born 1640, died. probably, young; Peter, 1641; James, 1643; Mary, again, 1646; removed to Charlestown, there probably had Abraham, Isaac, Jacob, and Elizabeth, born 1656, died soon. His wife Mary died 1677, and he died 1608, aged 72.

THOMAS FOWLE, of Boston, probably before 1635, merchant, had wife, Margaret, who was admitted of the church, 1641, and their daughter Elizabeth, and son John, were baptized same year; Mary, born 1643, and James, 1644. In 1646, in Boston, he was earnest for extension of liberties, fined heavily and went back to England in disgust.

REFERENCES:—Bond's Hist. of Watertown, Mass., 225; Fowle Mamily Reun. (1891); Hudson's Hist. of Lexington, Mass., 279; Secomb's Hist. of Amherst, N. H., 594; Sewall's Hist. of Woburn, Mass., 612-14; Savage's Gen. Dict., II, 192; Wyman's Charleston, Mass., Mass., Gens. I, 367-72.

FOWLER:—William Fowler, of Milford, 1639, one of the seven pillars at the foundation of the church in that year, after 1647, was frequently representative, lieu-tenant and at last an assistant of the colony; died 1661, leaving only William and John.

PHILIP FOWLER, of Ipswich, a clothworker, came in the ship "Mary and John," 1634, bringing, accordingt o family tradition, Benjamin, Joseph and Margaret; was freeman 1634, and died 1678; aged 80, by one report, more probably, 80. He had besides by wife, Martha, Thomas, born 1636, and Philip, about 1646; and married 1660, Mary, widow, perhaps, of George Norton.

AMBROSE FOWLER, of Windsor, married 1646, Joan Alvord; had Abigail, born 1642; John, 1648; Ma 1650; Samuel, 1652; Hannah, 1654; Elizabeth, 1656, and Ambrose, 1658, all living in 1692; was freeman of Conn., 1657, and had removed, about 1668, to Westfield, and died there 1704. His wife, Joan, died 1684.

HENRY FOWLER, of Providence. 1655, swore allegiance 1666.

FOWLER:—John Fowler, of Milford, 1639, born in England, married 1647, Mary, daughter of George Hubbard; had Abigail, born 1648, died 1651; removed to Guilford about 1649; there had Mary, born 165u Abraham, 1652; John, 1654; Mehitable, 1656, and Eliza-beth, 1658, who died at 18 years; was deacon, representa-tive 1665-73, and after; died 1677. His widow died 1713.

REFERENCES.

NEW HAMPSHIRE.—Chase's Hist. of Chester, 525; Coffin's Hist. of Boscaven, 531; Dow's Hist. of Hamp-ton, 716; History of Washington, 429-31.

CONNECTICUT.—Hurd's Hist. of New London, 511; Orcutt's Hist. of Torrington, 690-3; Stiles' Hist. of Windsor, II, 274.

NEW YORK.—Baird's Hist. of Rye, 465; Bolton's Westchester Co., II, 519; Ruttenber's Hist. of Newburgh, 274-7; Ruttenber's Hist. of Orange Co., 365-7; Howell's Southampton, 257.

OTHER PUBLICATIONS.—Amer. Ancestry, II, 43, 154; II, 17; V, 91; VI, 96; VII, 280; IX, 140; Ball's Hist. of Lake Co., II, 375; Bangor Hist. Mag., IV, 237; Bartow Gen., Part 2; Champion Gen.; Chapman's Weeks Gen. 137; Douglas Gen., 206-8; Driver Gen., 316, 370; (1889), 78 p.; Granite Mnothly, IV, 1-5; Guild's Stiles 27 p.; (1867), 12p.; (1870), 42 p.; (1883), 247 p.; Gen., 324-7, 651-3; Hammatt Papers, Ipswich, Mass., 108; Herrick Gen.; Loomis Gen., Female Branches, 688; Hine's Lebanon, Ct., Address, 154; Maltby Gen., 203; Powers' Hist. of Sangamon Co., Ill., 312; N. E. Hist. and Gen. Reg., VII, 131; XI, 247-54; Stickney's Gen. Appendix, 505; Savage's Gen. Dict., II, 193-5; Wal-worth's Hyde Gen., 709-11; Warren-Clarke Gen., 65.

FOWKE. Hayden's Virginia Gens., 155-61; Meade's Old Churches of Va., II, 482; N. E. Hist. and Gen. Reg., XXXVIII, 320; Southern Biouvac (1886), 727.

FOWLES. Eaton's Hist. of Warren, Me., 542.

FOWNES. N. E. Hist. and Gen. Reg., XVIII, 185.

FOX:—Thomas Fox, of Concord, Mass., freeman, probably, 1638; by wife, Rebecca, who died 1647, had Mary, born 1642; Elizabeth and Eliphalet; and he married in 1647, Hannah Brooks; had Hannah, born 1648; Thomas, 1650; Samuel, Mary, John, Isaac, born 1657; and died 1658.

THOMAS Fox, of Cambridge, freeman, perhaps, of 1644, selectman 1658, and often after; for second wife, married Ellen, widow of Percival Green, who died 1682, when he took another wife, Elizabeth, widow of Charles Chadwick, who died 1685, leaving him again a widower; and he died 1693, aged 85. He probably had but one child, Jabez, born 1647.

RICHARD Fox, of Wethersfield, married Beriah, daugh-ter of first Richard Smith, of the same.

REFERENCES.

MASSACHUSETTS.—Bond's Hist. of Watertown, 765; Paige's Hist. of Cambridge, 547; Sewall's Hist. of Wo-burn, 139-43, 331; Temple's Hist. of Whately, 230.

NEW HAMPSHIRE.—Cochrane's Hist. of Antrim, 500-3; Cutter's Hist. of Jaffrey, 326-8; Haywood's Hist. of Hancock, 585-91.

CONNECTICUT.—Caulkin's Hist. of New London, 370; Stiles' Hist. of Windsor, II, 274.

OTHER PUBLICATIONS.—Alden's Amer. Epitaphs, I, 229-31; Amer. Ancestry, V, 66; Brown's W. Simsbury Settlers, 62; Cleveland's Hist. of Yates Co., N. Y., 339-401; Crosby's Obituary Notices (1858), 403; Dwight's Strong Gen., 1199; Fox, Ellicott and Evans Gen. (1882), 281 pp.; Fox Gen. (1890), 31 pp.; Hayden's Virginia Genealogies, 60; Hubbard's Stanstead Co., Canada, 175; Montgomery and Fulton Cos., N. Y., 157; Palmer and Trimble Gen., 190, 261-3; Richmond, Va., Standard, III, 23; Rodman Gen., 159; Washington, N. H., History, 431; Wentworth Gen., II, 857; Savage's Gen. Dict., II, 195-7.

FOXCRAFT or FOXCROFT, of Boston, 1665, mem-ber of the Artillery Co.; married 1682, Elizabeth, daugh-ter of Gov. Danforth, who died 1721; had Francis, born 1695, and Thomas, 1697; died at Cambridge, 1727.

REFERENCES.—N. E. Hist. and Gen. Reg., VIII, 171. Paige's Hist. of Cambridge, 548-50; Vinton Gen., 124; Savage's Gen. Dict., II, 197.

FOXWELL:—Richard Foxwell, of Salem or Boston, came in the fleet with Winthrop, was made freeman 1631, perhaps went home or removed soon to Scituate, was there in 1634, having married Ann Shelley, a serv-ant, who came over that year, and had Mary, born 1635; Martha, 1638, and Ruth, 1641. He removed to Barn-stable before the birth of last; there his son John was buried 1646; and he died 1668.

RICHARD FOXWELL, probably at Piscataqua 1631, or earlier; settled at Scarborough, 1636; there married Sarah daughter of Richard Bonython; had Richard, John, Philip and five daughters, and died 1677, aged 73.

JOHN FOXWELL, of Barnstable, 1643.

REFERENCES:—Folsom's Hist. of Saco, Me., 116; N. E. Hist. and Gen. Reg., VIII, 171; Savage's Gen. Dict., II, 198; Deane's Hist. of Scituate, Mass., 272; Swift's Barnstable Families, I, 365-7.

FOY:—John Foy, of Boston, 1671, mariner, by wife Dorothy, had Elizabeth, born 1672; John, 1674; Joseph and Benjamin, twins, 1678; William, 1681; Hannah, 1683; Joseph, again, 1685; Samuel, 1688; and Samuel again, 1689. .

JEFFERY FOY, of Boston, 1676, mariner.

REFERENCES:—Savage's Gen. Dict., II, 198.

FOYE:—Wyman's Foye, Charlestown, Mass., Gen., 372.

FRAILE:—George Fraile, of Lynn, 1637, may first have been at Charlestown, by wife, Elizabeth, had Elizabeth, born 1641; Hannah, 1642, died at 19 years; Eunice, 1644; Samuel, 1646; Deborah, 1648; and Ruth, 1653. He died 1663, leaving a son George, who was killed by an accident 1669. His widow died at Salem, 1669.

REFERENCES:—Savage's Gen. Dict., II, 199.

FRAIRY. Leach's Morton Ancestry.

FRALEIGH. Amer. Ancestry, I, 29; II, 43; Smith's Hist. of Rhinebeck, N. Y., 216-18.

FRAME. Guild's Stiles Gen., 22.

FRANCE. Amer. Ancestry, I, 29.

FRANCIS:—Richard Francis, of Cambridge, was first at Dorchester; by wife Alice, had Stephen, born 1645; Sarah, 1646; John, 1650; Rebecca, and Ann; all at Cambridge; was freeman 1640, and died 1687, aged about 81.

ROBERT FRANCIS, of Wethersfield, by wife Joan, had Susanna, born 1651; Robert, 1653; and Mary, 1656; besides John, and perhaps others. His wife died 1705, and he died 1712.

FRANCIS FRANCIS, of Reading, had John, born 1657.

JOHN FRANCIS, of Braintree, about 1650; by wife, Rose, had Elizabeth, born 1657; and Susanna, 1659. His wife died same year.

REFERENCES.

MASSACHUSETTS.—Brooks' Hist. of Medford, 512-14; Cutter's Hist. of Arlington, 244; Paige's Hist. of Cambridge, 550.

CONNECTICUT.—Andrew's Hist. of New Britain, 162; Stiles' Hist. of Windsor, II, 274.

OTHER PUBLICATIONS.—Amer. Ancestry, III, 18; IV, 59; V, 16; Butch's Prov. Hist. of Pa., 41-50; Bergen's Kings Co., N. Y., Settlers, 116; Essex Inst. Hist. Coll., XXV, 123, 288-90; Old Kent, Md., 296; N. E. Hist. and Gen. Reg., XVII, 262; XXVII, 136; XLVIII, 345; Paull's Hist. of Wells, Vt., 86-9; Powers' Hist. of Sangamon Co., Ills., 313-17; Savage's Gen. Dict., II, 199; Wyman's Charlestown, Mass., Gen., I, 374.

FRANCISCO. Amer. Ancestry, II, 43.

FRANK. Corliss' Hist. of No. Yarmouth, Me.; Lapham's Hist. of Norway, Me., 503; Pearson's Schenectady, N. Y., Settlers, 73; Young's Hist. of Chautauqua Co., N. Y., 235-38.

FRANKLIN:—Josiah Franklin, of Boston, born in Eaton, Northamptonshire, Eng., 1657, came about 1683, with wife Ann and three children; Elizabeth, born 1678; Samuel, 1681; and Hannah, 1683. Followed in Boston his trade of soapboiler and maker of candles; had here Josiah, born 1685; Ann, 1687; Joseph, 1688, died soon; had John, born 1690; Peter, 1692; Mary, 1694; James, married not long after, Abiah, daughter of Peter Folger; had John, born 1690; Peter, 1692; aMry, 1694; James, 1697; Sarah, 1699; Ebenezer, 1701, died at 2 years; Thomas, 1703; Benjamin, the celebrated philosopher and statesman, 1706; Lydia, 1708; and Jane, 1712. He died 1745 and his wife Abiah died 1752 in her 85th year.

WILLIAM FRANKLIN, of Ipswich, 1634, came in the Mary and John, that year, removed to Newbury 1635, married Alice, daughter of Zobert Andrews; was a blacksmith, removed to Boston, and had Elizabeth, born 1638; was admitted to the church 1641. Perhaps his wife died before that, and by second wife, Joanna, he had John, born 1642; and Benjamin, 1643.

REFERENCES.

Bridgman's Granary Burial Ground, 323-32; Franklin Gen. (1857) 4 p.; (1889) 8 p.; Hayden's Virginia Gen., 658; Hammatt Papers, Ipswich, Mass., 110; Heraldric Journal, II, 97-9; Hubbard's Roswell Franklin (1839), 103 p.; Phoenix's Whitney Gen., I, 723; Plumb's Hist. of Hanover, Pa., 412; N. E. Gen. and Hist. Reg., VIII, 374; XI, 17-20; XVI, 273; XXVII, 246; N. Y. Gen. and Biog. Rec., XXIII, 127-30; Ransom Gen., 33, 68, 71-3; Sparks' Life of Benjamin Franklin, 546; Savage's Gen. Dict., II, 199.

FRANKS:—John Franks, married 1663, Sarah, daughter of Joseph Weld, of Roxbury; had John, born 1664; Joseph, 1666; and Sarah 1669.

JOHN FRANKS, of Boston, by wife Grace, had Deborah, born 1666.

FRARY:—John Frary, of Dedham, by wife Prudence, had Isaac, born 1638; Eleazar, 1640; Samuel, 1641; Theophilus; and probably others before these, some born in England; freeman, 1639; lived in that part of the town which became Medford, and there died at a great age.

REFERENCES:—Judd's Hist. of Hadley, Mass., 496; Morse's Frary Gen. (1850); Kellogg's White Gen., 39; Savage's Gen. Dict., II, 201; Temple's Hist. of Whateley, Mass., 230-32.

FRASER. Hubbard's Hist. of Standstead Co., Conn., 242.

FRAVOR. Amer. Ancestry, I, 29.

FRAZEE. Littell's Passaic Valley, 154-57; Powers' Hist. of Sangamon Co., Ills., 317.

FRAZER:—John Frazer, of Newbury, but removed to Rowley; after some years, married, 1685, Martha, daughter of Duncan Stuart, had Simon, born 1686; John, 1688, died young; Hannah, 1692; John again, 1694, who died at 19 years; Ebenezer, 1696; Gershom, 1697; Nathan, 1700; Abigail, 1701; and Lawson, 1704.

REFERENCES:—Amer. Ancestry, IV, 235; V, 18; Cothren's Hist. of Woodbury, Ct., 1494-97; Fathey's Hist. of Chester Co., Pa., 552; Martin's Hist. of Chester, Pa., 275; Washington, N. H., Hist., 433; Winsor's Hist. of Duxbury, Mass., 259; Savage's Gen. Dict., II, 202.

FRAZIER. Richmond, Va., Standard, IV, 2.

FREDENBURGH. Amer. Ancestry, II, 43; Cleveland's Hist. of Yates Co., N. Y., 712-14; N. Y. Gen. and Biog. Reg., XIX, 178.

FREDENRICH. Amer. Ancestry, I, 29.

FREDERICK. Plumb's Hist. of Hanover, Pa., 413.

FREAKE:—John Freake, of Boston, 1660, merchant; married 1661, Elizabeth, daughter of Capt. Thomas Clark; had Mary, born, 1662; Elizabeth, 1663; Clark, 1666; John, 1668; Jane, 1669; Mehitable, 1670; Thomas, 1672; and Mary, 1674. He died by explosion of ship from Virginia, in Boston Harbor, 1675.

REFERENCES:—Savage's Gen. Dict., II, 202.

FREEBORNE or FREEBOURNE:—William Freeborne, of Boston, came in the Frances from Ipswich, 1634, aged 40, with wife Mary, 33, and children Mary and Sarah. He first settled in Massachusetts, and was sworn freeman, 1634, when his son Gideon was probably born; was living in Boston in 1637; was in Portsmouth, R. I., in 1655, and died there 1670, aged about 80.

REFERENCES:—Savage's Gen. Dict., II, 202.

GAAS. Young's Hist. of Wayne Co., Ind., 418.

GAASBECK. Sylvester's Ulster Co., 106.

GACHET. N. E. Hist. and Gen. Reg., I, 344.

GAGE:—John Gage, of Boston, came probably in the fleet with Winthrop, removed to Ipswich, 1633, among the first settlers; was freeman 1634; had Benjamin, Daniel, Jonathan, Samuel, and probably Thomas. His wife Ann died 1658; and he married, 1658, Sarah, widow of Robert Keyes, perhaps; removed 1664 to Rowley, but his widow, Sarah, died at Newbury, 1680.

JOSIAH GAGE, at Haverhill, freeman, 1682, had son Samuel who marrried, 1674, Faith, daughter of William Stickney.

THOMAS GAGE, of Beverley, by wife Sarah, had Thomas, born 1678; Willliam, 1680; and four daughters, all at Beverley; but after his wife died he removed to Rowley, and married for second wife, Elizabeth, widow of Humphrey Hobson, had Elizabeth, born 1698.

REFERENCES.

MAINE.—Corliss' Hist. of No. Yarmouth; Lapham's Hist. of Bethel, 538.

NEW HAMPSHIRE.—Aldrich's Hist. of Walpole, 259; Livermore's Hist. of Wilton, 378-81; Norton's Hist. of Fitzwilliam, 579; Sanbornton, II, 288-92; Secomb's Hist. of Amherst, 597; History of Washington, 440-45; Coffin's Hist. of Boscowen, 534-36.

MASSACHUSETTS.—Ballou's Hist. of Milford, 769-71; Gage's Hist. of Rowley, 442.

OTHER PUBLICATIONS.—Amer. Ancestry, III, 18, 155; IV, 212, 220; V, 67; VI, 69; Cleveland's Hist. of Yates Co., N. Y., 230-37; Gage Gen. (1889), 16 p.; (1894), pamphlet; Granite Monthly, VI, 62-4; Heraldic Journal, III, 148-51; Loomis' Gen. Female Branch, 848; Wyman's Charlestown, Mass., Gen., I, 397.

GAGER:—William Gager, of Charlestown, a surgeon, came in the fleet with Winthrop, was deacon of the first church, now of Boston, and died 1630.

JOHN GAGER, of New London, son of the preceding, came probably with his father to Boston, 1630, and may

have been at Hampton. His wife, Elizabeth, is named in his will, yet she may. not have been mother of the children, six of them born before removing, 1660, to Norwich, and those, after he went, as follows: John, born 1647; Elizabeth, 1649; Sarah, 1651; Hannah, 1653, died young; Samuel, 1654; ,1657; William, 1662; Lydia, 1663; Hannah, again, 1666; and Mary, 1671. He was freeman, 1675, constable of Norwich, 1681, and died, 1703.

REFERENCES:—Walworth's Hyde Gen., 675-77, 732; Caulkin's Hist. of Norwich, Ct., 103; Sedgwick's Hist. of Sharon, Ct., 81; Hine's Lebanon, Ct., 155; Savage's Gen. Dict., II, 221.

GAGNON. Temple's Hist. of No. Brookfield, Mass., 574.

GAIGE. Amer. Ancestry, I, 30.

GAINES:—Henry Gaines, of Lynn, freeman, 1639.

SAMUEL GAINES, of Lynn, married 1665, Ann Wright; was of Hartford, 1667; removed to Haddam, had a family and there the name is still found.

REFERENCES:—Cunnabell Gen., 85; Goode Gen., 124, 290, 470; Amer. Ancestry, VII, 191; Hammatt Papers, Ipswich, Mass., 117; Richmond, Va., Standard, III, 14; Meade's Old Families of Virginia; Powers' Hist. of Sangamon Co., Ills.; Slaughter's St. Mark's Parish, 149, 164; Savage's Gen. Dict., II, 221.

GALBRAITH. Eagle's Penn. Gen., 226-40.

GALE:—Richard Gale, of Watertown, 1640, had Sarah, born 1641; Abraham; Mary; John; perhaps Abigail and Ephraim. Sarah married, 1663, Joseph Garfield; and Mary married, 1670, John Flagg.

AMBROSE GALE, of Salem, had there baptized, Benjamin and Elizabeth, 1663; Charity, 1664; and Ambrose, 1665; was one of the founders of the church at Marblehead, and lived there, 1674.

BARTHOLOMEW GALE, of Salem, married 1662, Martha, daughter of Robert Lemon, who died the same year; and he married Mary Bacon; had Abraham, born 1666; Isaac; Jacob; Bartholomew; Daniel; perhaps others.

EDMUND GALE, of Salisbury, freeman, 1666, removed perhaps to Marblehead, and went to Falmouth before 1689.

REFERENCES.

MASSACHUSETTS.—Barry's Hist. of Framingham, 249; Benedict's Hist. of Sutton, 647-49; Bond's Hist. of Watertown, 229-31; Jameson's Hist. of Medway, 487; Stearn's Hist. of Ashburnham, 711.

NEW HAMPSHIRE.—Bouton's Hist. of Concord, 662-64; Lancaster's Hist. of Gilmanton, 265; Hist. of Sanbornton, II, 292-96.

OTHER PUBLICATIONS.—Amer. Ancestry, I, 30; VI, 9; Denny Gen.; Huntington's Stamford, Ct., Settlers, 36; Gale Gen. (1866), 254 pp.; Morse's Grout Gen., 24-34; N. E. Hist. and Gen. Reg., XVIII, 189-97; Pickering Gen.; Whittemore's Hist. of Middlesex Co., Ct., 241; Savage's Gen. Dict., II, 221.

GALES. Wheeler's Hist. of No. Carolina, II, 416.

GALESPY. Gregg's Old Cheraws, S. C., 62.

GALLAUDET. N. Y. Gen. Reg., XIX, 118-21.

GALLATIN. Gallatin's Works, III (1879).

CREST: A French count's coronet.
MOTTO: Persevere.

GALLAUDET.   Bolton's Hist. of Westchester, 734.

GALL:—Ambrose Gall, perhaps of Charlestown, married, it is said, Mary, daughter of Samuel Ward, in early days, but probably the name is Gale.

GALLAWAY.   Balch's Prov. Pa., 75.

GALLIGHER.   Temple's Hist. of Palmer, Mass., 473.

GALLISON:—Elisha Gallison (or Gullison), of Falmouth, 1689, had a garrison house.

REFERENCES:—Willis' Hist. of Portland, I, 200; N. E. Gen. Reg., III, 25; Savage's Gen. Dict., II, 222; Lapham's Hist. of Norway, Me., 510; Winslow's Gen., II, 745-48.

GALLOP:—Humphrey Galllop (or Gallup), of Dorchester, 1630; came probably in the Mary and John; by wife Ann had Joseph, born, 1633.

JOHN GALLOP, of Dorchester, 1630, perhaps brother of the preceding, removed to Long Island, or part of Boston, 1632; was a fisherman and pilot. He was freeman, 1634; brought wife Christobel, who died 1655; and children, John, Samuel, Nathaniel, and Joan, who married Thomas Joy; and died 1650.

JOHN GALLOP, of Boston, 1637, served in the Pequot War, for which Connecticut made him a grant of 100 acres; married Hannah, a widow, daughter of Margaret Lake; had Hannah, born 1644; removed to New London, 1651; was of Taunton, 1643, but in a short time removed to Stonington, of which he was representative 1665 and 1667; had John, who became freeman, 1673; Benadam, born about 1656; William, 1658; Christobel; Elizabeth; Mary; and Margaret; besides Esther, born 1653, who married, 1674, Henry Hodge, of Taunton. He was killed in the Narragansett swamp fight, 1675, the hardest battle of Philip's War.

REFERENCES:—Babson's Hist. of Gloucester, Mass., 94; Temple's Hist. of Palmer, Mass., 468; Eaton's Hist. of Thomaston, Me., II, 233; Caulkin's Hist. of New London, Ct., 291; Savage's Gen. Dict., II, 222-23.

CAPTAIN JOHN GALLUP (GALLOP) THE FIRST. Born in 1590 of an ancient family, Armingers, of Dorset, Eng. Had his military education in Holland, where he served under Fairfax in war with Spain. Came to New England with Winthrop in the Dorchester Colony in 1630. He was owner and commander of the first vessel built in American waters. Like all knights and gentlemen of the West Coast he was a thorough seaman, and as such rendered great service to the infant colony, whose fishing fleets were chief sources of income and needed protection, and where Indians ravaged the coast. He received grants of land for his services, and was one of the founders of Boston. Died, Boston, January 14, 1650. His will one of the first recorded in Boston.

REFERENCES:—Hutchins' Dorset, Astor Library; Hubbard's Indian Wars; Winthrop's Journal; Palfrey's New England, etc., etc.

CAPT. JOHN GALLUP, SECOND. Born in Dorchester, Eng., in 1615; son of the preceding. Came to Boston with his mother, two brothers and sisters, 1633. Served with Mason and Stoughton in Pequot War, 1636-37. Called to become first Sheriff of Plymouth Colony in 1640. Married at Ipswich, Hannah Lake, niece of Mrs.

Winthrop and daughter of Mme. Margaret Lake, in 1643. With Winthrop, Mme. Lake, Cary Latham and others, John Gallup was a founder of New London. He moved to a grant from the General Court upon the Mystic River, where he built and planted the Whitehall estate. He led 300 Mohigans into the Narragansett's Fort fight, Dec. 19, 1675, and fell at the head of his faithful followers.

REFERENCES:—Miss Caulkin's Hist. of New London, Conn.; R. A. Wheeler's Hist. Stonington; Palfrey's Hist. New England.

GALLOW.   Sedgwick's Hist. of Stamford, Ct., 81.

GALLOWAY.   Thomas' Families of Md., 78.

GALLUP.   Amer. Ancestry, I, 30; IX, III, 113; Barry's Hist. of Framingham, Mass., 249; Gallup Gen. (1893), 329; Gregory's Hist. of Northfield, Vt., 220; Hurd's New London Co., Ct., 478; Huron and Erie Counties, Ohio, 179; Smith Gen. (1889), 123 pp.; Savage's Gen. Dict., II, 222.

GALLY:—John Gally, of Salem, 1637, had there grant of land, perhaps living on Beverly side, where John, probably his son, was freeman, 1670. His widow, Florence, died 1686, in her 80th year. His daughter Elizabeth, married Osmund Trask.

REFERENCES:—Savage's Gen. Dict., II, 223.

GALPIN:—Philip Galpin, of New Haven, married Elizabeth Smith; had Samual, born 1650; and Joseph, 1652; removed to Fairfield, 1657, then to Rye, N. Y.

REFERENCES:—Cothren's Hist. of Woodbury, Ct., 544; Orcutt's Hist. of Stratford, Ct., 1206; Baldwin Gen. Supp., 1047; Amer. Ancestry, IX, 189; Baird's Hist. of Rye, N. Y., 410; Savage's Gen. Dict., II, 223.

GALT.   Powers' Hist. of Sangamon Co., Ills., 19; Richmond, Va., Standard, III, 32.

GALUSHA:—Daniel Galusha, of Chelmsford, 1691, or earlier, removed to Dunstable; had Rachel and Daniel; said to be of Dutch origin. His house was a garrison, burned by the Indians, 1706, when Rachael was killed.

REFERENCES:—Huntington Gen., 99; Savage's Gen. Dict., II, 224; Belknap, I, 173.

GAMAGE.   Amer. Ancestry, IX, 71.

GAMBEL.   Eaton's Hist. of Thomaston, Me., 234; Eaton's Annals of Warren, Me., 545; Goode Gen., 402; Gilmer's Georgians, 34; Richmond, Va., Standard, II, 2, 51.

GAMLYN:—Robert Gamlyn (or Gamblin), of Concord, was made freeman 1634, probably then living at Roxbury. He died and was buried at Concord, 1642, but little is known of his history.

ROBERT GAMLYN, probably son of the preceding, came in the William and Francis, early in 1632, bringing his wife Elizabeth, widow of John Mayo; had Elizabeth 1634; Joseph, 1636, who died 1653; Benjamin, 1639; and Mary, 1641, who married, 1663, Thomas Baker.

REFERENCES:—Ellis's Hist. of Roxbury, Mass., 118; Savage's Gen. Dict., II, 224.

GAMBY.   Cleveland's Hist. of Yates Co., N. Y., 528

GAMMELL.   Hudson's Hist. of Lexington, 75.

GAMMETT. Miller's Colchester Co., U. S. married before 1690, Mary, daughter of John Parrott; in 1734 was of Portsmouth.

GAMMON:—Philip Gammon, of Casco, fisherman; in 1734 was of Portsmouth.

REFERENCES:—Lapham's Hist. of Norway, Me.; Ridlon's Hist. of Harrison, Me., 64; Savage's Gen. Dict., II, 224; Willis' Hist. of Portland, 294.

GAMWELL. Temple's Hist. of Palmer, Mass., 469

GANNETT:—Matthew Gannett, of Scituate, 1651, but had probably been first at Hingham; had sons, Matthew, Joseph and Rehoboth, and daughter named in his will of 1694, Hannah Adams; Abigail, wife of Jonathan Dodson; and Elizabeth Leavitt.

THOMAS GANNETT, of Duxbury, 1642, brother of the preceding, removed to Bridgewater, and died 1655, leaving widow, Sarah.

REFERENCES:—Mitchell's Hist. of Bridgewater, Mass., 166; Deane's Hist. of Scituate, Mass., 273; Harn's Bascom Gen., 45-50; Savage's Gen. Dict., II, 224.

GANO. Amer. Ancestry, VII, 229.

GANONG. Amer. Ancestry, VIII, 144; Ganong Gen. (1893), 27 pp.

GANSEVOORT. Munsell's Hist. of Albany, 124; N. Y. Gen. and Biog. Record, III, 84.

GANUNG. Cleveland's Hist. of Yates Co., N. Y., 299.

GARBER. Goode Gen., 407.

GARDENER. Pierce Gen. (1894).

GARDENIER. Amer. Ancestry, II, 44; Munsell's Albany, N. Y., Coll., IV, 125.

GARDEN:—Miles Garden, a soldier in Gallop's company, in the abortive expedition of Sir William Phips, 1690, against Quebec.

GARDINER:—Lyon (or Lion) Gardiner, of Saybrook, 1635, came in the Bachelor, of 25 tons, aged 36, with wife Mary, 34, who was daughter of Dericke Williamson, of Worden, in Holland; had David, born 1636; Mary, 1638, both at Saybrook fort; and Elizabeth, born on the island purchased from the Indians, 1639, at the east end of Long Island, since known as Gardiner's Island; the first English child born there. He lived at Easthampton longer than at Saybrook, probably living after 1642 on Long Island, and died 1663. His estate of Gardiner's Island is still enjoyed by his descendants of the ninth generation.

REFERENCES.

MASSACHUSETTS.—Babson's Hist. of Gloucester, 95; Judd's Hist. of Hadley, 497.

NEW YORK.—Hedge's Easthampton (1850); Rudenber's Hist. of Newburgh, 301-03; Rudenber's Hist. of Orange Co., 387-89; Thompson's Long Island, II, 378-81.

OTHER PUBLICATIONS.—Austin's R. I. Gen. Dict., 81; Bunker's Long Island Genealogies, 336; Gardiner Gen. (1890), 210 pp.; Chandler Gen., 57; Clement's Newtown, N. J., Settlers; Cregar's White Gen.; Gardiner Papers and Gen. (1883); Hanson's Hist. of Gardiner, Me., 83,

105; Holgate's Amer. Gen., 58; Lamb's Hist. of New York City, 570; Heraldic Journal, III, 81; IV, 97-102; Hinman's Conn. Settlers, 212; Narragansett Reg., I, 211-13; II, 306-09; E. W. Pierce's Contributions, 43-51; N. Y. Gen. and Biog. Rec., XXIII, 159-90; Preble Gen., 259; Updyke's Narragansett Churches, 125-30; 330; Savage's Gen. Dict., II, 225.

GARDNER:—Thomas Gardner, of Salem, sailed from Weymouth, Dorset Co., England, in 1623, with fourteen others, in a small vessel fitted out by "The Western Adventurers," and landed at Cape Ann. He was to "oversee the planting" in the colony, and for this reason has sometimes been called the first governor of Mass. In 1626, those who remained of the colony, removed to Nathum Keike, afterwards called Salem. He was prominent in town affairs and had extensive grants of land in Salem and Danvers. He married Margaret Frier in England, and for second wife the widow Damaris Shattuck, who died 1674. He died a month later, same year, leaving 9 children: Thomas, George, Samuel, Joseph, John, Sarah, who married Benjamin , who married Jos. Grafton, and Miriam, who married John Hill.

JOHN GARDNER, of Hingham, by wife Mary had John, baptized, 1652; Francis, 1653; Mary, 1654; Samuel, 1656; Deborah, 1657; James, perhaps, 1660; Stephen, 1662; Thomas, 1664; Benjamin, perhaps, 1666; and Christian, born, 1668. He died in same year.

RICHARD GARDNER, of Woburn, married, 1651, Ann or Hannah Blanchard, widow of Thomas, of Charlestown; had John, born 1652; Ann, 1655; Benjamin, 1656; Henry, 1658; Esther, 1659; Ruth, 1661; Hannah; Abigail; Rebecca; and Mehitable; these four probably at Charlestown; was freeman 1652; died, 1698.

RICHARD GARDNER, of Salem, perhaps son of the first Thomas, was living there, 1666, and went to Nantucket next year. Before removing he had by wife Sarah, probably daughter of Samuel Shattuck, Joseph; Sarah; Richard, born 1653; Deborah, 1658; Damaris, 1662; and James, 1664; besides Miriam; Nathaniel, 1669; Hope; and Love, 1672; he died, 1689. Sarah married Eleazer Folger; Deborah married John , and Miriam married John Worth.

SAMUEL GARDNER, of Hartford or Wethersfield, 1641, removed to Hadley, 1663, was living there, 1678; had Samuel, who died, 1676, unmarried; and Joseph, who died, 1684, leaving widow, but no children; and five daughters.

ARMS:—Sable, a chevron, ermine, between two griffins' heads, in chief, and a cross, pattée, silver, in base.

CRESTS:—A saraceu's head, cauped at the shoulders: proper. On the head a cap, turned up, red and blue, crined and bearded, sable.

MOTTO: *Præsto pro patria.*

Also: a pelican, sable, vulning itself, red.

MOTTO: *Deo non fortuna.*

REFERENCES.

MASSACHUSETTS.—Barry's Hist. of Hanover, 311; Cutter's Hist. of Arlington, 251; Hyde's Hist. of Brimfield, 404; Morse's Hist. of Sherborn, 90; Paige's Hist. of Cambridge, 557; Sewall's Hist. of Woburn, 614; Temple's Hist. of Palmer, 469-71; Wyman's Hist. of Charlestown, I, 398, 402.

NEW HAMPSHIRE.—Blood Hist. of Temple, 222; Secomb's Hist. of Amherst, 589; Stearn's Hist. of Rindge, 527.

OTHER PUBLICATIONS.—Cleveland's Hist. of Yates

Co., N. Y., 659; Collin's Hist. of Hillsdale, N. Y., 57 pp; Allen's Worcester Ass'n., 52; Austin's Allied Families, 100-2; Amer. Ancestry, I, 31; II, 44. 154; IX, 126; Dennysville, Me., C   , 104; Essex Inst. Hist. Coll., I, 190; VI, 161-3; Gardner Gen., (1858) 14 pp; Greene Gen.; Machias, Me., C   162; Kitchell Gen., 412-4; New England Hist., and Gen. Reg., XXV, 48-51; Pierce's Life of Gardner Dean (1883), 307 pp; Powers' Hist. of Sangamon Co., Ills., 321; Pickering Gen., Pode Gen., 144-6; R. I. Hist. Soc. Coll., III, 308; R. I. Hist. Mag., 217-20; Walworth's Hyde Gen., 253-5, 520-2; Whitman's Gen., 90-2; Savage's Gen. Dict., 226-31; Whitmore's Copp's Hill Epitaphs; Winchester, Mass. Record, I, 244-6; Worden Gen., 59-62.

GARFIELD:—Edward Garfield, of Watertown, died 1672, aged 97.

EDWARD GARFIELD, of Watertown, son of the preceding, born in England, freeman 1635, by wife Rebecca had Samuel; Joseph, born 1637; Rebecca 1641; Benjamin 1643; and Abigail 1646, who married John Parkhurst. His wife Rebecca died 1661, aged 55, and he married 1661, Joan, widow of Thomas Buckminster of Muddy River, now Brookline.

ARMS: Red, two bars, gold, each charged with three mascles, azure, on a canton, of the second, a leopard's face, of the third.

REFERENCES:—Bond's Hist. of Watertown, Mass., 231; Draper's Hist. of Spencer, Mass., 198-200; Ward's Hist. of Shrewsbury, Mass., 290-2; Amer. Ancestry, I, 31; III, 163, 181; IX, 190; Bridge Gen., 77; Garfield Gen. (1876) 15 pp.; (1892) 16 pp.; N. E. Hist. and Gen. Reg., XLIX, 190-204; Norton's Hist. of Fitzwilliam, N. H., 580; Thurston Gen., (1892), 32; Montague Gen., 123; Young's Hist. of Chautauqua Co., N. Y., 238; Savage's Gen. Dict. II, 231.

GARFORD:—Jarvis Garford, of Salem before 1635, had wife Ann; was freeman 1639.

REFERENCES:—Felt's Annals of Salem.

GARIT:—Power's Hist. of Sangamon Co., Ills., 322.

GARLAND:—John Garland of Hampton, married 1654, Elizabeth, widow of Thomas Chase, daughter of Thomas Philbrick; had John, born 1655; Jacob, 1656; Peter, 1659. He died 1672.

REFERENCES:—Dow's Hist. of Hampton, N. H., 720-6; Cogswell's Hist. of Henniker, N. H., 577; Caverno Gen., 12; Goode Gen., 240; Dearborn's Hist. of Parsonfield, Me., 380; Amer. Ancestry, V, 195; Meade's Old Families of Va.; Powers' Hist of Sangamon Co., Ills., 324; Savage's Gen. Dict., II, 232.

GARLICK:—Joseph Garlick, of New London, 1651, but in a few years removed to Brookhaven or Easthampton, where his wife was charged with witchcraft, 1657; but the case was referred and she sent to Hartford, and thus her life was saved.

REFERENCES:—Fruber Gen., 118-20; Orcutt's Hist. of New Milford, 795; Roc's Sketches of Rose. N. Y., 127; Savage's Gen. Dict., II, 232.

GARNER:—Edmund Garner, of Cambridge, 1635, removed before 1638.

THOMAS GARNER, merchant, of Boston, 1648.

REFERENCE:—Amer. Ancestry, II, 44, 154.

GARNETT:—John Garnett, of Hingham, 1656, had

perhaps, a daughter Mary, born 1654, who married 1683, Nathan Farrow; had probably, also, John; Samuel, born 1656; Joanna, who married 1690, Thomas Whiton; Deborah, born 1657; and Stephen, who married, 1683, Sarah Warren.

REFERENCES:—Richmond, Va., Standard, III, 11, 14, 23, 26, 93; Meade's Old Families of Va.; Slaughter's St. Mark's Parish, 134-6; Savage's Gen. Dict., II, 233.

GARNSEY:—Joseph Garner, of New Haven, 1647, removed probably to Stamford, and married 1659, Rose, widow of John Waterbury; had Joseph and perhaps other children; and died 1688.

HENRY GARNSEY, of Dorcheser, 1655, freeman 1690.

JOSEPH GARNSEY, of Milford, married, 1673, Hannah, daughter of Samuel Coby, of the same; had Joseph, born 1675; and Sarah 1678; perhaps others. He was living at Milford 1713.

WILLIAM GARNSEY, of York, freeman 1652.

REFERENCES:—Baird's Hist. of Rye, N. Y., 411; Andrews' Hist. of New Britain, Conn., Settlers, 36; Bassett's Hist. of Richmond, N. H., 391-5.

GARRABRANT:—Winfield's Hist. of Hudson Co., N. J., 520-4.

GARRATT:—Barry's Hist. of Hanover, Mass., 312.

GARRETT:—Richard Garrett (or Garrard), of Scituate, first town clerk 1636; married Lydia, daughter of Nathaniel Tilden; had Joseph, born 1648; John, 1651; Mary 1655; and Richard, 1659. He died probably at Boston 1662.

JAMES GARRETT, of Charlestown, 1637, freeman 1639; by wife Deborah had Mary, born 1638; Priscilla, 1640; James 1643. He was probably master of the ship in whose unhappy voyage to London, 1657, he perished with many others.

ROBERT GARRETT, of Boston, by wife Mary, had John, born 1643; Robert, Mary and Sarah; all mentioned in his will 1660, in which he says, "being bound on a voyage to Barbados;" yet he probably lived some years after that.

REFERENCES:—Deane's Hist. of Scituate, Mass., 274; Brown's W. Simsbury Settlers, 66-8; Futhey's Chester Co., Pa., 560; Smith's Hist. of Delaware Co., Pa., 464; M   Gen., 160; Swift's Barnstable Families, I, 449; Savage's Gen. Dict., II, 233.

GARRETSON:—John Garretson, of Boston, married 1659, Alice Willey, perhaps daughter of Isabel.

REFERENCES:—Powers' Hist. of Sangamon Co., Ills., 323; Savage's Gen. Dict., II, 234.

GARRIGUES:—Thomas' Families of Maryland, 80.

GARRINGER:—Plumb's Hist. of Hanover, Pa., 420-2.

GARRISON:—Edward Garrison, of Boston, married 1660, Joan Pullen.

REFERENCES:—Amer. Ancestry, I, 31; III, 19, 83; IV, 161; Garrison Gen., (1877) 4 pp; Clute's Hist. of Staten Island, N. Y., 384; Plumb's Hist. of Hanover, Pa., 419; N. E. Hist. and Gen. Reg., XXX, 418-21.

GARVEY:—Powers' Hist. of Sangamon Co., Ills., 325

GARVIN:—Wentworth Gen., II, 88-90.

GARY:—Andrews' Gen., (1890) 130; Wyman's Charlestown, Mass., Gens., I, 402; Norton's Hist. of Fitz william, N. H., 580; Lapham's Hist. of Norway, Me. 512.

GASCOYNE:—Edward Gascoyne, of Salem, shipwright, had grant of land 1637; by wife, Sarah, had Samuel, baptized 1639; Daniel 1640; Sarah 1643; Hannah 1646; and Edward 1648.

GASKERIE:—Schoonmaker's Hist. of Kingston, 480.

GASKILL:—Bassett's Hist. of Richmond, N. H., 395; Richard Mowry Gen., 219, 222; Southwick's Gen., 586 90; Ballou's Hist, of Milford, Mass., 162-4.

GASKINS:—Hayden's Virginia Gens., 440.

GASLEY:—Amer. Ancestry, VII, 27.

GASSETT:—N. E. Hist. and Gen. Reg., I, 344; Hayward's Hist. of Gilsum, N. H., 310; Hayward's Hist. of Hancock, N. H., 592; Morse's Mems., Appendix, 53.

GASTON:—Bay State Monthly, II, 246; Mellick's Story of an Old Farm, 635; Amer. Ancestry, V, 86, 103; Wheeler's Eminent No. Carolinians, 137-9; Wheeler's Hist. of No. Carolina, II, 114.

GATCHELL:—John Gatchell (or Getchell), of Salem, 1637, aged about 26, was of Marblehead 1648.

JONATHAN GATCHELL, of Marblehead, 1647, removed to Portsmouth, R. I., and there married 1683, Mary, widow of Gershom Wodell; had Priscilla, born in same year, and Isbell, 1685.

SAMUEL GATCHELL, of Salem, 1638, removed to Hampton, 1644, thence to Salisbury, 1648; by wife Dorcas, who died 1685, had Priscilla, born 1649; and Samuel 1657. A daughter Susanna married, 1662, Joseph Norton.

REFERENCES:—Futhey's Hist. of Chester, Pa., 561; Savage's Gen. Dict., II, 234.

GATES:—George Gates, of Haddam, an original proprietor 1662, was of Hartford 1661; by wife Sarah, daughter of Nicholas Olmstead, who died 1709, had Joseph, born 1662; Thomas 1665; John 1668; Sarah 1670; Mary 1674; George 1677; Daniel 1680; and Samuel 1683; was one of the first settler representatives 1668-73; and died 1724, in his 90th year.

STEPHEN GATES, of Hingham, 1638, came in the Diligent, with wife and two children that year; was from Old Hingham, removed to Cambridge, thence, 1654, to Lancaster, where he was constable 1657, freeman 1656. Went back to Cambridge and died there 1662. By wife Ann had Stephen, Simon, Thomas, Elizabeth, who married John Lasell; and Mary, who married John Maynard, of Sudbury.

REFERENCES.

MASSACHUSETTS:—Barry's Hist. of Framingham, 250-2; Draper's Hist. of Spencer, 198; Stearn's Hist. of Ashburnham, 711-14; Herrick's Hist. of Gardner, 349; Hudson's Hist. of Marlborough, 366; Paige's Hist. of Cambridge, 557; Stone's Hist. of Hubbardston, 270-2; Temple's Hist. of Palmer, 463-6.

NEW HAMPSHIRE:—Cochrane's Hist. of Antrim, 503; Merrill's Hist. of Acworth, 217; Hayward's Hist. of Gilsum, 311; Hayward's Hist, of Hancock, 594.

MAINE:—Eaton's Hist. of Thomaston, II, 234; Eaton's Annals of Warren, 545.

OTHER PUBLICATIONS:—Amer. Ancestry, I, 31; II, 45; V, 15; VIII, 10, 212; Chapman's Trowbridge Gen., 258; Dwight Gen., 449; Field's Hist. of Haddam, Conn., 45; Goodwin's Foote Gen., 78; Gates' Gen., (1887) 4 pp; Hemenway's Vt. Gazette, V, 55; N. E. Hist. and Gen. Reg., XXXI, 401; Phœnix's Whitney Family, I, 603; Powers' Hist. of Sangamon Co., Ills., 326; Smith's Gen., (1890) 155-9; Turner's Phelps and Gorham Purchase, 206; Whittemore's Hist. of Middlesex Co., Conn., 207; Walworth's Hyde Gen., 756; Young's Hist. of Warsaw, N. Y., 271-3; Savage's Gen. Dict., II, 235.

GATLINE:—Thomas Gatline (or Gatliffe), of Dorchester, a miller, was of Braintree 1650, died 1663. He had Jonathan; Prudent; and Mary, born 1656.

GATEWOOD:—Richmond, Va., Standard, III, 31.

GATTON:—Powers' Hist. of Sangamon Co., Ills., 326.

GAUL:—Amer. Ancestry, II, 45; Temple's Hist. of N. Brookfield, Mass., 595.

GAULT:—Temple's Hist. of N. Brookfield, Mass., 595; Granite Monthly, IX, 71; Chase's Hist. of Chester, N. H., 530.

GAUNT:—Peter Gaunt, of Lynn, removed to Sandwich, 1637, was living there 1643; had perhaps son Thomas.

REFERENCES:—American Ancestry, V, 59.

GAUTIER:—N. Y. Gen. Rec., III, 1, 10.

GAVIT:—Collin's Hist. of Hillsdale, N. Y., Appendix, 58.

GAY:—John Gay, of Watertown, freeman 1635; removed to Dedham, by wife Joanna had Samuel, born 1639; Hezekiah, 1640; perhaps Elizabeth, who married Richard Martin, 1660; Nathaniel 1642; Joanna 1645; Ebenezer 1647; Abiel and Judith, twins, 1649; John 1651; Jonathan, 1653; and Hannah, 1656. He died 1688.

SAMUEL GAY, of Roxbury, by wife Abigail, had Samuel, born 1688; and Abigail, 1689.

REFERENCES.

MASSACHUSETTS:—Blake's Hist. of Franklin, 249-51; Jameson's Hist. of Medway, 487; Paige's Hist. of Cambridge, 558; Stone's Hist. of Hubbardston, 273.

MAINE:—Butler's Hist. of Farmington, 471-6; Eaton's Hist. of Thomaston, II, 235; Hanson's Hist. of Gardiner, 156; Sibley's Hist. of Union, 451.

OTHER PUBLICATIONS:—Amer. Ancestry, I, 31; II, 154; Gay Gen., (1897) 15 pp.; Hill's Dedham, Mass., Records; Hine's Lebanon, Conn., 156; Meade's Old Families of Va.; Loomis' Gen., Female Branches, 794; N. E. Hist. and Gen. Reg., VI, 373; XXXIII, 45-47; Phœnix's Whitney Gen., I, 147; Reade's Hist. of Swanzey, N. H., 344; Sedgwick's Hist. of Sharon, Conn., 81; Washington, N. H., History, 445; Robertson's Pocahontas Descendants; Savage's Gen. Dict., II, 236.

GAYER:—William Gayer, of Nantucket, married Dorcas, daughter of Nathaniel Starbuck; had Damaris, born 1673; Dorcas 1675; and William 1677. His wife died about 1696; and he died 1710, having had a second wife, but no children by her. Damaris married 1692, Nathaniel Coffin, the progenitor of Admiral Sir Isaac Coffin; and Dorcas married, 1694, her cousin Jethro Starbuck.

REFERENCES:—Amory's Life of I. Coffin, 83-5; N. E. Hist. and Gen. Reg., XXXI, 297-302.

GAYLORD:—William Gaylord, of Dorchester, perhaps brother of John of the same, a deacon chosen at the gathering of the church 1630, in Plymouth, Eng.; came in the Mary and John; made freeman 1631, representative 1635, 6 and 8; removed to Windsor and was representative for nearly 40 sessions up to 1664; died 1673 in his 88th year. His sons, William, Samuel, Walter, and perhaps John, a daughter Elizabeth, were all born in England. The name occurs in various forms, Gaylor, Gayler, Gallard or Gallerd.

REFERENCES:—Amer. Ancestry, V, 127; VI, 48; Davis' Hist. of Wallingford, Conn., 747-50; Litchfield Co., Conn., History, 354; Gaylord and Gaillord Gen., (1872) 64 pp.; Judd's Hist. of Hadley, Mass., 497; Loomis' Gen. Female Branches, 579-84; Orcutt's Hist. of New Milford, Conn., 699-702; Orcutt's Hist. of Farrington, Conn., 699; Savage's Gen. Dict., II, 238; Stiles' Hist. of Windsro, Conn., II, 277-84, 837.

GAZZAM:—Amer. Ancestry, V, 69.

GEARS, GEER or GEERS:—George, of New London, married 1659, Sarah, daughter of Robert Allyer or Allen, of Norwich; had Sarah, born 1660; Jonathan, 1662; Joseph 1664; Hannah, 1666; Margaret 1669; Mary, 1671; Robert, 1676; Daniel; Ann, 1679; Isaac, 1681; and Jeremiah. He died 1726, having made his will 1723, in which he names as living his wife Sarah, and all his sons and daughters except Mary.

THOMAS GEARS, of Enfield, brother of George; by wife Deborah had Elizabeth, born 1685, died under 3 years, and, earlier, Shubael, who perpetuated the name; and the father died 1722, aged about 99.

GEER:—Amer. Ancestry, I, 32; Eaton's Hist. of Thomaston, Me., II, 235; Saunderson's Hist. of Charlestown, N. H., 358-60; Geer Gen., (1856) 84 pp.; Hinman's Conn. Settlers, 1st edit., 178; P Hist. of Wells, Vt., 91; Hurd's Hist. of New London, Conn., 525; Stiles' Hist. of Windsor, Conn., II, 285-7; Savage's Gen. Dict., II, 239; Wight Gen., 47.

ARMS: Red, two bars, gold, each charged with three mascles, azure, on a canton, of the second, a leopard's face, of the third.

GEARY:—Arthur, of Roxbury, had Samuel 1638, but other children, William and Nathaniel, before he came from England; was freeman 1639, died 1666, aged 67. In his will, 1664, he provides for his wife, Frances, and these three sons.

DENIS GEARY, of Lynn, came in the Abigail, 1635, aged 30, with wife Elizabeth, 22, son William, and daughters Elizabeth and Sarah. A son, Samuel, was probably born in this country. He died early and left by his will £300, to the Colony of Massachusetts.

WILLIAM GEARY, of Salam, 1639, was freeman 1641; had Samuel, born that year; Mary, 1643; and John, 1644. The name is sometimes written Gery, Gerry, and Gary.

REFERENCES:—Amer. Ancestry, II, 45.

GEDNEY:—John, of Salem, came in the Mary Ann from Yarmouth, Eng., 1637, with wife Mary, aged 25, and children Lydia, Hannah, and John; freeman 1638; had here Bartholomew 1640; Eleazar, 1642; Sarah 1644; and Eli 1648. He had a second wife, Catherine, and died 1688.

REFERENCES:—Baird's Hist. of Rye, N. Y., 468-70; Essex Inst. Hist. Coll., XVI. 241-70; Gedney and Clarke Gen., (1880) 52 pp., (reprint); Hammatt Papers, Ipswich, Mass., 118; Sylvester's Hist. of Ulster Co., N. Y., 134; Savage's Gen. Dict., 240.

GEE:—Peter Gee, of Boston, 1667, fisherman; by wife Grace, had Thomas, John and Joshua.

REFERENCES:—Norton's Hist. of Fitzwilliam, N. H., 581; Whitmore's Copp's Hill Epitaphs.

GELLING:—Power's Hist. of Sangamon Co., Ills., 328.

GELSTON:—New York Gen. and Biog. Reg., II, 131-8; Dwight Gen. 1065-76; Howell's Hist. of Southhampton, N. Y., 258-60; Strong Gen., 354.

REFERENCES:—Amer. Ancestry, II, 45; Hayward's Hist. of Hancock, N. H., 599; Austin's R. I. Gen. Dict., 83; Bangor Hist. Magazine, IV, 237; R Hist. of Sanbornton, N. H., II, 296-8; Corliss' Gen. Appendix; Paul's Hist. of Wells, Vt., 91; Plumb's Hist. of Hanover, Pa., 418; Thomas Family, Md., 81; Wheeler's Hist. of Newport, N. H., 392-4; Wyman's Charlestown, Mass., Gen., I, 404; Savage's Gen. Dict., II, 242.

GERALD:—Spare Gen., 35-9; Temple's Hist. of Palmer, Mass., 461.

GERAERD:—John, of Warwick, was a Dutchman of New Amsterdam, who about 1651 settled at Narragansett and married Maribab, daughter of Isaac Sweet, whose widow had married Ezekiel Hollman. He was freeman 1655, and left children Mary and John. There are variations of the name, Gerriard, Geriard, Geraerdi, and others.

REFERENCES:—Savage's Gen. Dict., II, 243.

GERARD:—N. Y. Gen. and Biog. Reg., V, 137; Talcott's N. Y. and N. E. Families, 80-5.

GERE:—Stanton Gen., 248.

GERMAIN:—Amer. Ancestry, I, 32; Eaton's Hist. of Thomaston, Me., II, 236.

GEROULD:—Amer. Ancestry, III, 152; VI, 8; Gerouid Gen. (1885) 85 pp.; (1890) 15 pp.; (1895) 17 pp.; Hayward's Hist. of Gilsum, N. H., 312.

GERRETSON:—Bergen's Hist of Kings Co., N. Y., 119.

GERRITSEN:—Munsell's Albany, IV, 126.

GERRISH:—William, of Newbury, from Bristol, Eng., where he was born 1617, as is said, but more probably 1620, came about 1640, was representative 1650-3, and also for Hampton, 1663 and 4. He married 1645, Joanna, widow of John Oliver; had John, born 1646; Abigail 1647; William 1648; Joseph 1650; Benjamin 1652; Elizabeth 1654; Moses 1656; Mary 1658; Ann 1660; and Judith 1662. His wife died 1677, and he removed next year to Boston, and there married Ann, widow, perhaps, of John Manning; had Henry, and died, 1687, while on a visit to Salem.

GENDALL:—Walter, of Falmouth, 1669, an enterprising trader among the Indians, was also of Scarborough, and N. Yarmouth last; representative 1683-4. and was killed by the Indians in the war of 1688.

REFERENCE:—Corliss' Hist. of No. Yarmouth, Me.

GENERY, or Chenerie:—Isaac, of Dedham, 1636, may have been first of Watertown; freeman 1645; had Isaac and John; and by second wife, Thomasin Heines, whom he married 1656, and who died 1760, had Mary, born 1659; and another daughter perhaps, who married Richard Ellis; and he died 1674.

REFERENCE:—Savage's Gen. Dict., II, 241.

GENIN:—Griffin's Journal, L. I., 183.

GENTLE:—Stearn's Hist. of Ashburnham, Mass. 714.

GEORGE:—James, of Haverhill, 1653, Salisbury 1662, was of Amesbury 1667, when he took the oath of fidelity; by wife Sarah, had Samuel, born 1666.

JOHN GEORGE, of Watertown, had Robert and Susanna who were probably born in England, where his wife may have died. He married at Watertown, Ann, widow of Henry Goldstone, and died 1647. His widow died 1670 aged 79.

JOHN GEORGE, of Charlestown 1657, was one of the founders of the first Baptist Church in Boston, 1665, died 1666. He had by wife Elizabeth, Elizabeth, Martha, John, Ruth, Hannah and Mary.

NICHOLAS GEORGE, of Dorchester, innholder, freeman 1666; had by wife Elizabeth, Nicholas and probably other children, and died perhaps 1675. His widow died 1699, in her 98th year.

PETER GEORGE, of Braintree, had Susan, born 1643; Mary 1645; Hannah 1648; John 1850, died soon; Samuel 1651; he sold his estate at Braintree and removed to Block Island.

RICHARD GEORGE, of Boston, married 1655, Mary, daughter of William Pell; had Mary, born 1656; Hannah 1661; Thomas 1663; Mary, again, 1666; and Elizabeth, 1670.

REFERENCES:—Amer. Ancestry, IV, 103, 124, 223; Coffin's Hist. of Boscowen, N. H.; Cogswell's Hist. of Nottingham, N. H., 202-380; Ball's Lake Co., Ind., 445-8; Coffin's Hist. of Newbury, Mass., 302; Cutt's Gen., 38-40, 48-50, 70-2; Eaton's Annals of Warren, Me., 545; Essex Inst. Hist. Coll., V, 27-30; Gerrish Gen., (1880 13 pp.; N. E. Hist. and Gen. Reg., VI, 258; Little Gen., 18, 100; Savage's Gen. Dict., II, 243.

GERRY:—Henry, of Salem, 1648.

REFERENCES:—Amer. Ancestry, IV, 223; Alden's Epitaphs, V, 25, 45; Vinton's Richardson Gen., 432.

GEST:—Amer. Ancestry, V, 48.

GETCHELL:—Eaton's Hist. of Thomaston, Me., II. 236; Wheeler's Hist. of Brunswick, Me., 835.

GETTY:—Marshall Gen., (1884) 219-21.

GHEEN:—Cope Family of Pa., 66, 146; Palmer and Trimble Gen., 210, 213, 402.

GHEER:—Egle's Penn. Gens., 617-20.

GHILSON:—Meade's Old Families of Richmond, Va., Standard, II, 29.

GIBB:—Andrew, of Bookhaven, L. I., 1655.

REFERENCES:—Hubbard's Hist. of Stanstead Co., Conn., 149; Thompson's Hist. of L. I., I, 415.

GIBBARD:—William, of New Haven, 1647, came

from Warwickshire, Eng.; by wife Ann, daughter of Edmund Tapp, Hannah, born 1641; Esther 1643; Mary 1645; Phebe, 1647; Sarah 1648; Rebecca 1651; Samuel 1653; Timothy 1655; John 1658; and Abigail 1660. He was representative 1652, Secretary of the Colony 1657, and Assistant, 1661, and died 1663.

REFERENCE:—Savage's Gen. Dict., II, 244.

GIBBONS:—Folsom's Hist. of Saco, Me., 112.

GIBBON:—Meade's Old Fams. of Va.

GIBBONS:—Ambrose, of Portsmouth, Eng., 1630, factor of the Company of Laconia, came that year, and his wife the following; of Dover 1648, a selectman, died 1656. His daughter, Rebecca, married Henry Sherburne.

EDWARD GIBBONS, of Charlestown, 1630, freeman 1631, removed soon to Boston, was representative 1635, of the Artillery Co., 1637, its Captain 1641, 46 and 54, Major Gen. 1649; Assistant 1650, died 1654. By wife Margaret he had Jerusha, born 1631; Jotham 1633; Edward 1636, died soon; Edward, again, 1637; and John 1641.

JAMES GIBBONS, of Saco, came in the Inverse 1635, aged 21; freeman 1653; by wife Judith, daughter of Thomas Lewis, had James, Elizabeth, Thomas, Charity, Rebecca, Rachel, Esther and Anthony.

WILLIAM GIBBONS, of Hartford, 1639, was in good esteem, and was living 1647; had wife Ursula, and daughter Sarah, born 1645, who married James Richards.

WILLIAM GIBBONS, of New Haven, signer to compact of 1639, proprietor 1685. Had Ann, who married Ellis Mew; died 1704.

REFERENCES:—Cope Gen., 55, 126; Futhey's Hist. of Chester Co., Pa., 564-9; Gibbon's Gen., (1881) 27 pp.; Savage's Gen. Dict., II, 245; Sharpless Gen., 406; Wyman's Charlestown, Mass., Gens., I, 406.

GIBBS:—Francis Gibbs, of Windsor, 1640.

GILES GIBBS, of Dorchester, 1630, came probably in the Mary and John; freeman 1634; selectman 1634; removed to Windsor, there died 1641. His will names wife Catharine, and children Gregory, Samuel, Benjamin, Sarah and Jacob, all minors; perhaps all born on our side of the ocean.

HENRY GIBBS came from old Hingham to Charlestown, 1633, servant to Edmund Hobart, died 1676.

JOHN GIBBS, of Wethersfield, a republican at the Gen. Ct., 1638.

JOHN GIBBS, of Cambridge, came in 1637, perhaps in company of Gen. Eaton, from London; had share in division of lands at Cambridge, 1638, and in short time removed to New Haven, was freeman early. First wife died 1668; no children. He married 1670, Hannah, daughter of John Punderson, and died 1690. Had Margaret, born 1684.

MATTHEW GIBBS, of Sudbury, was of Charlestown before 1654; had, by wife Mary, supposed to be daughter of Robert Bradish of Cambridge, Matthew and Thomas, twins, born 1656; Thomas died soon; Thomas again, 1660; John, Elizabeth, Hannah and Mary; and died before 1697.

ROBERT GIBBS, of Boston, merchant, born 1636 or 1639, of an ancient family in Warwickshire, said to be son of Sir Henry, came before 1660; married, 1660, Elizabeth, daughter of Jacob Sheaffe; had Margaret, born 1663; Robert, 1665; Henry, 1668; Jacob, 1672; died, 1673, aged 37. His widow married Jonathan Curwin of Salem.

SAMUEL GIBBS, of Sandwich, had Samuel, born 1649; and Sarah, 1652.

WILLIAM GIBBS, of New Haven, a hatter, swore fidel., 1654, and no more is known.

CREST: Three broken tilting spears, gold,—two in saltire, and one in pale,—ensigned with a wreath, silver and sable.

ARMS: Three battle axes, in pale silver.

REFERENCES:—Amer. Ancestry, IX, 192; Ballou's Hist. of Milford, Mass., 765-7; Barry's Hist. of Framingham, Mass., 252-6; Bemis' Hist. of Marlboro, N. H., 506; Benedict's Hist. of Sutton, Mass., 649; Bond's Watertown, Mass., Gens., 236; Daniel's Hist. of Oxford, Mass., 116; Freeman's Hist. Cape Cod, II, 147, 156, 164; Gibbs Family of Boston, (1845), 8 pp.; Gibbs Assoc. Repart (1848), 28 pp.; Gibbs Family of Boston (1879), 52 pp.; Gibbs Family Legacy (1893), 77 pp.; Gibbs Family of Bristol, Mass., (1894), 23 pp; Gibbs. Family of South Carolina, (1899) chart; Gibbs' Hist. of Blanford, Mass., 67-71; Heywood's Hist. of Westminster, Mass., 664-7; Hinman's Conn. Settlers, 1st edit., 213; Jackson's Hist. of Newton, Mass., 292; Richmond, Va., Stand., III, 28; Savage's Gen. Dict., II, 245-8; Sedgwick's Hist. of Sharon, Conn., 88; Smith's Hist. of Peterborough, N. H., 91-3; Stearn's Hist. of Ashburnham, Mass., 714; Stiles' Hist. of Windsor, Conn., II, 287; Temple's Hist. of North Brookfield, Mass., 595; Whitman's Heraldic Journal, III, 12-14, 166; Wyman's Charlestown, Mass., Gens., I, 406. See also Gibbes.

GIBSON:—Christopher Gibson, a soap boiler, of Dorchester, 1630, came probably in the Mary and John; married Margaret, daughter of James Bates; removed to Boston, 1646, and was one of the founders of the 2nd charter; died 1674.

JOHN GIBSON, of Cambridge, 1634, freeman 1637, died, 1694.

JOHN GIBSON, of Watertown, married, 1680, Hannah, daughter of Joseph Underwood; had Silence, born 1680; and Mary, 1682.

ROGER GIBSON, of New London, 1675, said to be from R. I., had William, and only daughter Thankful, who married Geo. Smith, 1682.

WILLIAM GIBSON, of Boston, 1665, or Lynn, where his son Purchas died 1665; and Aquila died, 1671; a cordwainer; was freeman 1677; probably the gifted preacher mentioned by Backus. I, 435.

REFERENCES.

NEW HAMPSHIRE.—Cochrane's Hist. of Antrim, N. H., 505; Cochrane's Hist. of Francestown, N. H., 729; Cogswell's Hist. of Henniker, N. H., 578-86; Granite Monthly of Concord, N. H., V. 329; Norton's Hist. of Fitzwilliam, N. H., 581; Runnel's Sanbornton, N. H., II, 298-301; Secomb's Hist. of Amherst, N. H., 600; Stearn's Hist. of Rindge, N. H., 529-32.

MAINE.—Lapham's Hist. of Norway, Me., 512; Ridlon's Saco Valley, Me., Families, 694.

MASSACHUSETTS.—Paige's Hist. of Cambridge, Mass., 558; Stearn's Hist. of Ashburnham, Mass., 718-20; Temple's Hist. of Palmer, Mass., 466; Wyman's Charlestown, Mass., Gens., I, 407.

OTHER PUBLICATIONS.—Amer. Ancestry, II, 45; IX, 183; Austin's R. I. Gen. Dict., I, 83; Avon, N. Y., Gen. Rec., 29; Denmore's Hartwell Gen.; Egle's Notes and Queries (1898), 205; Gibson Assoc. (1867), 20 pp.;

(1869), 4 pp.; Jackson Gen., 108-16; Joslin's Hist. of Poultney, Vt., 265; New Eng. Hist. Gen. Reg., 388-92; Peyton's Hist. of Augusta Co., Va., 306; Powers' Sangamon Co., Ills., Settlers, 328-30; Richmond, Va., Standard, II, 7; Salem, N. Y. Book of Hist., 33-5; Savage's Gen. Dict., II, 248.

GIDDINGS:—George Giddings, of Ipswich, came in the Planter, 1635, aged 25, with wife Jane; freeman 1638; representative, 1641, and 8 years more; had Thomas, John, James, Samuel, Joseph, and Mary, who married Samuel Pearce, or Pierce; he died 1676. (Name often spelled Gittings.)

JOHN GIDDINGS, of Ipswich, perhaps brother of the preceding, representative, 1653-5, died 1680, leaving 3 daughters, besides Thomas and William.

REFERENCES:—Andrew's New Britain, Conn.; Babson's Gloucester, Mass., 95; Baldwin's Gen., 1134-6; Gidding's Gen. (1882) 227 pp.; Hammatt Papers of Ipswich, Mass., 116; Joslin's Hist. of Poultney, Vt., 266-Orcutt's Hist. of New Milford, Conn., 702-7; Savage's Gen. Dict., II, 249; Wight Gen., 77.

GILBERT:—Humphrey Gilbert, of Ipswich, 1648, died 1658, leaving widow Elizabeth, who married William Raynor; and children John; Abigail; Esther and two other daughters. (Gen. Reg., XII, 370.)

JOHN GILBERT, of Dorchester, may have come in the "Mary and John," 1630; was here early with sons, Thomas and John, perhaps had Giles or Joseph born there, removed 1637 to Taunton; representative 1639; died after 1654, leaving wife Winifred. His will mentions daughter, Mary Norcross.

JOHN GILBERT, of Hartford, born in England, married 1647; Amy, daughter of Thomas Lord, died 1690, naming in will Thomas, born 1658; Joseph, 1666; James and Dorothy; records also show John, born 1648; died soon; John again, 1653; Elizabeth, 1656; Amy, 1663, probably died young.

JONATHAN GILBERT, of Hartford, brother of John of the same; born in England, married, 1646, Mary, daughter of John White, or Whight; had Jonathan, born 1648; and Mary, 1649, died young. His wife died same time, and he married, 1650, Mary Welles, of Hadley, had Sarah, born 1651; Mary; Lydia, 1654; Thomas, 1655; Nathaniel; Samuel; Ebenezer; Esther; and Rachel; was man of distinction, kept an inn, and for many years was marshal of the Colony; died 1682, aged 64.

MATTHEW GILBERT, of New Haven, 1638; one of the seven pillars for founding church; assistant of the colony, 1658; dep. gov., 1661; and died probably, 1680; had John, baptized 1644; Sarah, 1645; Rebecca, 1649; in his will he names Matthew; Samuel; Mary and Hannah. He was the only assistant who had not the distinction of being an assistant of the United Colony of Connecticut, though nominated; having failed of election after the charter of Charles II.

WILLIAM GILBERT, of Windsor, 1640, made freeman that year.

WILLIAM GILBERT, of Boston, cordwainer and merchant, 1675; had wife Rebecca, three sons, of whom William was one, died soon after his father, 1693; and Mary.

REFERENCES.

MASSACHUSETTS.—Babson's Hist. of Gloucester, Mass., 246; Davis' Landmarks of Plymouth, Mass., 116; Essex, Mass. Inst. Hist. Colls., 40-50; Hammatt's Papers of Ipswich, Mass., 113-15; Lincoln's Hist. of Hingham, Mass., II, 267; Paige's Hist. of Hardwick, Mass., 383.

NEW HAMPSHIRE.—Aldrich's Hist. of Walpole, N. H., 260-62; Cochrane's Hist. of Francestown, N. H., 730-32.

CONNECTICUT.—Andrew's Hist. of New Britain, Ct., 181, 350; Blake's Hist. of Hamden, Ct., 246-49; Middleford, Ct., Hist.; Orcutt's Hist. of Stratford, Ct., 1206.

OTHER PUBLICATION.—Adam's Fairhaven, Vt., 378-80; Am. Ancestry, VI, 158; VII, 32; VII, 130; Boyd's Hist. of Conesus, N. Y., 155; Caverly's Hist. of Pittsford, Vt., 702; Champion Gen., 295-300, 316-39; Cope Gen., 90, 192; Cutt's Gen., 214; Dickerman Gen., 173; French's Hist. of Turner, Me., 62; Gilbert Narrative (Phila. 1848), 240 pp.; Gilbert Gen., (1850) chart; Gilbert Families of New England, (1850) 23 pp.; Gilbert Families of Penn. (1864), 2 pp.; Gilmer's Georgians, 216; Kellog's White Gen., 24; Martindale's Hist. of Byberry, Pa., 289-99; New England Hist. and Gen. Reg., IV, 223-32, 339-49; XIII, 280-82; Pompey, N. Y., Reunion, 311; Savage's Gen. Dict., II, 249-52; Schenck's Hist. of Fairfield, Ct., 368; Sharpe's S. Britain, Ct., Sketches, 99; Swain Gen., 72-4; Swift's Barnstable, Mass., Families, I, 406; Talcott's N. Y. and N. E. Families, 513; Temple's Hist. of N. Brookfield, Mass., 596-602; Turner Gen., 57; Wyman's Charlestown, Mass., Gen., I, 407.

GILDERSLEEVE:—Richard Gildersleeve, of Stamford, one of the first settlers in 1641; representative 1643; had been 5 years before at Wethersfield, removed about 1646 to Hempstead, L. I., where he was 1663; had commission for administering justice.

REFERENCE.—Champion Gen., 62.

GILE, GUILE, GYLES, or GILES:—Daniel Gile, of Salem, 1689, fisherman.

EDWARD GILE, of Salem, freeman 1634, married widow Bridget Very, had baptized Mehitable, 1637; Remember, 1639; Eleazur, 1640; John, 1645; died probably 1650.

JOHN GILE, probably of Dedham, freeman 1643; was perhaps of Boston, 1654.

MATTHEW GILE, of Dover, 1643, had Mark; and died about 1667.

SAMUEL GILE, of Newbury, an early settler, removed 1640 to Haverhill, freeman 1642; married 1647; perhaps second wife, Judith Davis, had John; Samuel; Ephraim; and Sarah; died 1684.

CREST:—A lion's gamb, erased and erect; proper—charged with a baton, gold, holding an apple branch, vert, fructed. MOTTO: Libertas et patria.

REFERENCES.—Am. Ancestry, II, 46; IV, 224; Cogswell's Hist. of Nottingham, N. H., 204; Fullonton's Hist. of Raymond, N. H., 228; Guild Gen. (1887), 221-318; Walker Gen. (1895), 52-63; Warthen's Hist. of Sutton, N. H., 725.

GILFORD:—John Gilford, of Hingham, died 1660; may have been father of Susanna, baptized 1651; Paul 1653; Priscilla, 1660, died soon; Susanna married Thomas Jewett.

WILLIAM GILFORD, of Boston, by wife Mary had John, born 1653.

Also GUILFORD.

REFERENCES:—Lincoln's Hingham, II, 268; Adam's Fairhaven, 381-84; Anderson's Waterbury, 58; Draper's Hist. of Spencer, Mass., 203; Hayward's Hist. of Hancock, N. H., 624.

GILL:—Arthur Gill, of Dorchester, shipwright, removed to Boston, freeman 1641; by wife Agnes had John, born 1639; Thomas, 1644; Frances; and Nathaniel, died young. He went home about 1654, and died 1655. Frances married Henry Boyen, of Boston.

JOHN GILL, of Dorchester, 1640, freeman 1666; removed to Boston and died there 1678. By wife Ann, had Rebecca, who married Joseph Belcher.

JOHN GILL, of Salisbury, married Phebe, daughter of Isaac Buswell; had Elizabeth, 1646; John, 1647; Phebe, 1650; Samuel, 1662; Sarah, 1654; Moses, 1656; Benjamin; and Isaac, 1665.

JOHN GILL, of Boston, mariner, and merchant, 1649-77. His wife was Elizabeth Weare, or Ware, and children, Obadiah; Elizabeth; John, born 1657; William, and Thomas; unless another John had this wife and children.

THOMAS GILL, of Hingham, 1635, married Hannah, daughter of first John Otis; had Mary, baptized 1644; Sarah, same day; Hannah, 1645; Elizabeth, 1647; Thomas, born 1649; John, 1651, died young; Deborah, 1653; Samuel, 1655; Nathaniel, 1658, died soon; John, 1660; and Rachel, 1661. His wife died 1676; he, 1678.

REFERENCES.

MASSACHUSETTS.—Heywood's Hist. of Westminster, Mass., 667-69; Hoyt's Salisbury, Mass., Fams., 174-76; Lincoln's Hingham, Mass., II, 268-74; Smith's Founders of Mass. Bay, 347-49; Wyman's Charlestown, Mass., I, 408-10.

OTHER PUBLICATIONS.—Am. Ancestry, VII, 74; XI, 84; Coffin's Hist. of Boscowen, N. H., 551-53; Clement's Newtown, N. J., Settlers; Ely Gen., I, 125-27, 255-57; Gill Gen. (of Canada) (1887-89), 126 pp.; Hubbard's Hist. of Springfield, Vt., 306-11; N. E. Hist. and Gen. Reg., XXXIII, 339-41; XLVI, 212, 5; Ripley's Ingersoll Gen., 85-7; Roome Gen., 222; Savage's Gen. Dict., II, 254; Wentworth's Gen., I, 345-47; Whitmore's Copps Hill Epitaphs.

GILLAM:—Benjamin Gillam, of Boston, ship carpenter, freeman 1635, came 1634, followed by his wife Ann, and son Benjamin the next year; had Zachary here, born 1636; Ann, 1638, died soon; Ann, again, 1640; Elizabeth, 1642; and Joseph, 1644. Benjamin, second, had command of company in Philip's War.

REFERENCES:—N. E. Hist. Reg., XIX, 344; Savage's Gen. Dict., II, 255.

GILLETT or JELLETT:—Jonathan Gillett, of Dorchester, freeman 1635, removed next year to Windsor with children, Cornelius, Jonathan and Mary; there he had, Ann, baptized 1639; Joseph, 1641; Samuel, 1643; John, 1644; Abigail, 1646, died at 2 years; Jeremiah, 1648; and Josiah, 1650; was a constable 1656; died 1677.

MATTHEW GILLETT, of Dorchester, 1634, came that year in the "Mary and John," removed to Windsor 1636.

NATHAN GILLETT, of Dorchester, 1630, brother of Jonathan, came, it is said, with the Minister Maverick, and Warham, by the "Mary and John," was freeman 1634; removed to Windsor 1636; had Elizabeth, 1639; Abia, 1641; Rebecca, 1646, died young; Elias, 1649;

Sarah, 1651; Benjamin, 1653; Nathan, 1655; Rebecca, again, 1657; his wife died 1671, and he removed to Simsbury.

REFERENCES.

CONNECTICUT.—Hines' Lebanon, Ct., Hist. Address, 156; Orcutt's Hist. of Torrington, Ct., 701-4; Orcutt's Hist. of Wolcott, Ct., 482-84; Sedgwick's Hist. of Sharon, Ct., 82; Sharp's Hist. of Seymour, Ct., 199; Stiles' Hist. of Windsor, Ct., II, 289-300.

OTHER PUBLICATIONS.—Am. Ancestry, II, 154; III, 19; IX, 117; XII, 50; Barbour's My Wife and Mother, 35, 70; Dickinson Gen. (1896), 54-60; Douglas Gen., 127-29; Goode Gen., 259, 291, 4; Judd's Hist. of Hadley, Mass., 498; Loomis Gen. (1880), 420, 584, 633; Roe's Sketches of Rose, N. Y., 129; Savage's Gen. Dict., II, 255; Sheldon's Hist. of Deerfield, Mass., 172; Sprague's Hist. of Gloversville, N. Y., 117; Tucker's Hist. of Hartford, Vt., 421-25.

GILLIGAN:—Alexander Gilligan, of Marblehead, 1674.

GILLINGHAM:—James Gillingham, of Salem, probably before 1692, married that year, Rebecca, daughter of John Bly; had Rebecca, 1693; Hannah, 1694; James, 1696; Benjamin, 1697; Martha, 1699; Deborah, 1700; John, 1704; Mary, 1705; William, 1706; Jonathan, 1709; and David, 1711.

REFERENCES:—Am. Ancestry, V, 167; Penn. Magazine of History, XXIV, 224-29.

GILLAW:—John Gillaw, of Lynn, 1637, had Benjamin; John; and perhaps more children. He is, perhaps, the cowkeeper of whom good story is told in Winthrop, I, 274.

GILLOWAY:—John Gilloway, of Lynn, 1637; probably same as preceding.

GILMAN:—Edward Gilman, from Hingham, Eng., came to Boston 1638, in the "Diligent" with wife Mary, 3 sons and 2 daughters. Records show, Mary, baptized 1615; Edward, 1617; Sarah, 1622; John, 1626; Moses, 1630; and Lydia; one of these probably died in England. He was freeman 1639, removed to Rehoboth 1643, and to Ipswich soon after, where he was 1647; and after that to Exeter, there died.

ARMS:—Sable, a man's leg, in pale, crouped at the thigh.

REFERENCES.

NEW HAMPSHIRE.—Bell's Hist. of Exeter, N. H., 16-21; Cochrane's Hist. of Francestown, N. H., 733; Cogswell's Hist. of Nottingham, N. H., 283-89; Fullonton's Hist. Reymond, N. H., 229-32; Lancaster's Hist. Gilmanton, N. H., 267-72; N. H. Hist. Soc. Colls., VI, 189; Norton's Hist. of Fitzwilliam, N. H., 581; Runnel's Sanbornton, N. H., II, 304-14; Saunderson's Charlestown, N. H., 372.

MAINE.—Bangor, Me., Hist. Mag., III, 128; Corliss' N. Yarmouth, Me., Mag.; North's Hist. of Augusta, Me., 874.

OTHER PUBLICATIONS.—Am. Ancestry, III, 20; Coit Gen., 175-81; Dickerman Gen., 519-28; Driver Gen., 336; Gilman Gen. (1863), 51 pp.; do. (1864), 24 pp.; do. (1869), 324 pp.; Gilman's of England, etc. (1895), 231 pp.; Hammatt Papers of Ipswich, Mass., 115; Hemenway's Vermont Gaz., IV, 154-58; Hubbard's Hist. of Stanstead Co., Canada, 219; Little Gen., 81; N. E. Hist.

and Gen. Reg., XVIII, 258; Prescott's Paige Gen., Wentworth's Gen., I, 380-84; Whitmore's Heraldic Journal, I, 150.

GILPIN:—Anthony Gilpin, of Barnstable, had probably no wife or children, and may have been only short time in the land; died 1655.

REFERENCES:—Am. Ancestry, IV, 60; IX, 134; Fisher Gen. (1896), 41-3; Futhey's Hist. of Chester, Pa., 570; Gilpin Mems. (1853), 86 pp.; Gilpin (Henry D.) Biog. (1860), 211 pp.; Gilpin Ancestry (1870), 12 pp.; Johnson's Hist. of Cecil Co., Md., 511-13; Sharpless Gen., 232-35, 363-65; Swift's Barnstable, Mass., Families, I, 406; Thomas Gen. (1877), 83; Thomas Gen. (1896), 327.

GILSON:—Jameson, of Rehoboth, 1668, had Nathaniel, 1675.

JOSEPH GILSON, of Chelmsford, married 1660, Mary Caper; removed to Groton; had Joseph, born 1667; Sarah, 1669; John; and perhaps some earlier.

WILLIAM GILSON, of Scituate, 1631, one of the founders of the church 1635, a man of property, assistant, built the first mill in the colony for grinding corn; had wife Frances; no children; died 1640.

REFERENCES:—Butler's Groton, Mass., 402, 471; Green's Groton, Mass., Settlers, 7; Green's, Groton, Mass., Epitaphs, 241; Gilson Gen., see Jillson; Hayward's Hist. of Hancock, N. H., 601-4; Hemenway's Vt. Gazette, V; Heyward's Hist. of Westminster, Mass., 669; Norton's Hist. of Fitzwilliam, N. H., 581; Randall's Hist. of Chesterfield, N. H., 319; Ridlow's Harrison, Me., Settlers, 64-7; Savage's Gen. Dict., II, 258.

GILVIN, of Ipswich, 1639. Felt, II.

GINGELL, GINGLE, GENGILL or GINGEN:—John Gingell, of Taunton, 1639-43; removed to Dorchester, thence, perhaps, after many years, to Salem, freeman 1646; his will seems to notice no family connections. One John Gingden took the oath of fidelity 1674, at Pemaquid.

WILLIAM GINGELL, of Westerly, 1661; no more is said.

GIRDLER:—Francis Girdler, of Salem, freeman 1678, had baptized there, though he lived at Marblehead Side, George; Francis; Hannah; Benjamin; and Mary; all in 1678; Ann, 1680; John, 1684. (Name also made Grodler.)

GIRLING:—Richard Girling, of Cambridge, 1635, of whom no more is told.

GISBORNE:—Francis Gisborne, of Warwick, married 1671, Mary, daughter of John Wicks; was given 100 acres on R. I., by will of Capt. Samuel Wilbor.

GISHAP:—Edward Gishap, of West Chester, if such a name be possible, appointed commissioner 1663, by colony of Conn.

GIVAN:—John Givan, of Boston, 1684, member of the Scots Charit. Soc.

GLADING:—John Glading, of Newbury, married 1666, Elizabeth Rogers, had Susanna, born 1668; John, 1670; William, 1673; Elizabeth, 1676; Mary, 1679; Hannah, 1681.

REFERENCES:—Am. Ancestry, I, 32; Hayes' Wells Gen., 164.

GLANFIELD:—Robert Glanfield, of Salem, mariner, married 1665, Lydia Ward, had Lydia, born 1666; Abigail, 1668; Peter, 1670; Robert, 1672; and Sarah, 1675.

GLASS:—James Glass, of Plymouth, 1638, married Mary, daughter of William Pontus, had Hannah, 1647, died next year; Wybra, 1649; Hannah, again, 1651; and Mary, posthumous, 1652. He was a freeman 1648; and 1652, near the harbor, was lost in a storm. His widow married Philip Delano.

JAMES GLASS, of Boston, by wife Elizabeth, had William, 1688; Robert, 1692; Elizabeth, 1695.

RICHARD GLASS, of Pemaquid, took the oath of fidelity 1674; was of Manchester, 1686.

ROGER GLASS, of Duxbury, then of Scituate; by wife Mary, had Elizabeth; James; Emma; Mary; and John; freeman 1657; perhaps brother of first James, and died 1690.

REFERENCES:—Paul's Hist. of Welles, Vt., 92; Savage's Gen. Dict., II, 259; Temple's Hist. of N. Brookfield, Mass., 602; Windsor's Hist. of Duxbury, Mass., 262.

GLAZIER:—John Glazier, of Woburn, by wife Elizabeth, had John, 1663; Zechariah, 1666; Elizabeth, 1668; John, 1669; Ruth, 1671; Samuel, 1671; and George, 1676.

REFERENCES:—Am. Ancestry, XII; Hastings' Gen., 95-101, 164; Hemenway's Vt. Hist. Gaz., V, 525; Herrick's Hist. of Gardner, Mass., 351; Keyes' W. Boylston, Mass., Reg., 20; Sewall's Hist. of Woburn, Mass., 615; Temple's Hist. of N. Brookfield, Mass., 603; Ward's Hist. of Shrewsbury, Mass., 296.

GLEASON:—Thomas Gleanson, of Watertown, Cambridge, and Charlestown; wife Susanna; had Thomas; Joseph; John; Mary; Isaac; and William; places of birth not certain; is believed to have sworn fidelity in 1653.

REFERENCES.

MASSACHUSETTS.—Barry's Hist. of Framington, Mass., 256-60; Bond's Watertown, Mass., Gens., 236; Brown's Bedford, Mass., Fams., 13; Clarke Fam. of Watertown, 44, 79, 81; Daniel's Hist. of Oxford, Mass., 518-22; Davis' Landmarks of Plymouth, Mass., 117; Draper's Hist. of Spencer, Mass., 205; Hazen's Hist. of Billerica, Mass., 63; Hudson's Hist. of Lexington, Mass., 76; Hudson's Hist. of Marlborough, Mass., 367-69; Hyde's Hist. of Brimfield, Mass., 405; Morse's Sherborn, Mass., Settlers, 90; Paige's Hist. of Cambridge, Mass., 559; Paige's Hist. of Hardwick, Mass., 384.

OTHER PUBLICATIONS.—Am. Ancestry, VII, 173; Eaton's Hist. of Thomaston, Me., II, 237; Hayward's Hist. of Gilsum, N. H., 314; Leonard's Hist. of Dublin, N. H., 341; Norton's Hist. of Fitzwilliam, N. H., 583; Old Northwest Gen. Quarterly, III, 23-8, 68-71, 109-17; Savage's Gen. Dict., II, 260; Sibley's Hist. of Union, Me., 455-57; Walworth's Hyde Gen., 445; Washington, N. H., Hist., 446; Wight Gen., 68.

GLEN:—James Glen, of Boston, a printer, 1682. Thoms' Hist., I, 280.

GLIDDEN:—Charles Glidden; of Portsmouth, 1665,

of Exeter, 1677, when he took oath of fidelity.

REFERENCES:—Am. Ancestry, IX, 231; X, 15; Cushman's Hist. of Sheepscott, Me., 382-87; Saunderson's Charlestown, N. H., 373; Whitmore's Copps Hill Epitaphs.

GLIDE:—John Glide, a soldier, perhaps from Marlborough, under Capt. William Turner, 1676.

GLOVER:—Charles Glover, of Salem, 1632, a shipwright, arrived at Boston in the "Lion," freeman 1641; had wife, Elizabeth, removed to Gloucester, was selectman 1644 and 1645; had Samuel, born 1644. His wife died 1648, and he married, 1650, widow, Esther Saunders.

HABAKKUK GLOVER, of Boston, son of John of Dorchester, born in England, a tanner, with good estate, freeman 1650; married 1653, Hannah Eliot, had Hannah, 1654, died soon; and Rebecca, 1655.

HENRY GLOVER, of New Haven, 1647, or earlier, came, probably in the "Elizabeth," from Ipswich, 1634, aged 24; had Mary, baptized 1641; Mercy, 1643; Hannah, 1646; John, 1648; Abigail, 1651; and Sarah, 1655; was proprietor in 1685; died 1689; perhaps he was the lieutenant of Southold 1662, that year admitted as freeman of Connecticut.

JOHN GLOVER, of Dorchester, 1630, came, perhaps, in the "Mary and John;" but was a Lancashire man, and engaged in the favor of the Plant.; before embark in 1629, was a captain; representative, 1637-50, was near all same years selectman; removed to Boston; was assistant 1652-53; died next year. Had wife Ann; sons, Thomas; Nathaniel; Habakkuk, before mentioned; John; and Pelatiah; no daughters.

RALPH GLOVER, supposed to have come in the fleet with Winthrop, and to have lived at Watertown; he died before 1633.

STEPHEN GLOVER, of Gloucester, 1658, married 1663, Ruth, daughter of William Stephens, perhaps as second wife; selectman 1659, 1661, 1669, 1686; died 1686; his wife had died previously and he left no children.

REFERENCES:—Am. Ancestry, II, 46; Babson's Hist. of Gloucester, Mass., 96; Barry's Hist. of Framington, Mass., 260; Cochrane's Hist. of Francestown, N. H., 733; Davis' Gen. (1888), 158-75; Eaton's Hist. of Thomaston, Me., 238; Essex Inst. Hist. Colls., V, 130-32; Glover Gen. (1867), 602 pp.; Lapham's Hist. of Rumford, Me., 332; N. E. Hist. and Gen. Reg., XIX, 213; Orcutt's Hist. of Stratford, Ct., 1207; Paige's Hist. of Cambridge, Mass., 559; Savage's Gen. Dict., II, 261-63; Van Rensselaer's New Yorkers; Warren and Clarke Gen., 71-4.

GOAD or GOARD:—Richard Goad, of Roxbury, came in the "Elizabeth and Ann," perhaps, 1635, aged 17; married 1639, Phebe Hawes, had Hannah, born 1641; John, baptized 1643; Mary, 1644; Phebe, 1646; Joseph, 1647, died soon; Sarah, 1649; Joseph, again, 1651; Lydia, 1653; Benjamin, 1654, died soon; Benjamin, again, 1656; he died 1683.

GOBAN:—Daniel Goban, of Boston, 1684, member of the Scots' Charit. Soc.

GOBLE:—John Goble, of Concord, with son John followed their minister, Rev. John Jones, in 1644, to Fairfield.

THOMAS GOBLE, of Charlestown, after few years was of Concord, freeman 1634; by wife Alice, had 3 sons and 3 daughters, of whom Mary is known to have been baptized 1636; Sarah, 1638; Daniel, 1641; he died 1657.

GODDARD:—John Goddard, of Dover, 1631, sent by mason for his plant.; had John; Benjamin; and 3 daughters; married to John Gilman, Arthur Bennett, and James Thomas, respectively; he died 1660, leaving widow Welthea, who married   Simmons.

THOMAS GODDARD, came, in 1635, from Marlborough, in Wilts, arrived at Boston in the "James," from Southhampton, but nothing more is known.

WILLIAM GODDARD, of Watertown, came from London, 1665; he had by wife Elizabeth, who came next year, 6 children, of whom she lost 3; brought from England, William, born about 1653; Joseph, 1655; and Robert; here had Thomas, 1667; died soon; Benjamin, 1668; Elizabeth, 1671, died young; Josiah; and Edward, 1675; was a school master; died 1691; and his widow 1698.

REFERENCES.

MASSACHUSETTS.—Barry's Hist. of Framington, Mass., 261-63; Bassett's Hist. of Sutton, Mass., 649; Bond's Watertown, Mass., 237-56, 772; Davis' Landmarks of Plymouth, 119-21; Hudson's Hist. of Lex., Mass., 76; Hudson's Marlborough, Mass., 397-401; Jackson's Hist. of Newton, Mass., 299; Paige's Hist. of Cambridge, Mass., 560; Pierce's Hist. of Grafton, Mass., 488-90; Temple's Hist. of N. Brookfield, Mass., 603; Wall's Reunion of Worcester, Mass., 356-59; Ward's Hist. of Shrewsbury, Mass., 283-90; Wood's Brookline, Mass., Sketches, 363-72; Wyman's Charlestown, Mass., Gens., I, 412.

NEW HAMPSHIRE.—Hayward's Hist. of Gilsum, N. H., 314; Norton's Hist. of Fitzwilliam, N. H., 583; Read's Hist. of Swanzey, N. H., 345; Stearn's Hist. of Rindge, N. H., 533.

MAINE.—Lapham's Hist. of Bethel, Me., 540; Lapham's Hist. of Rumford, Me., 333.

OTHER PUBLICATIONS.—Am. Ancestry, V, 167; VII, 115; Austin's Ancestral Dict., 20; Barlow Gen., 229; Bulkley's Browne Mem., 104; Driver Gen., 347-52, 513; Goddard Gen. (1833), 99 pp.; Goddard and Frost Fams. (1899), 5 pp.; Kellog's White Gen., 112; N. E. Hist. and Gen. Reg., LIII, 242-45; Savage's Gen. Dict., II, 264; Updyke's Narragansett Ch., 153-57.

GODFREY:—Edward Godfrey, of Kittery and York, 1630, alderman of the city of Acomenticus; governor, 1649, of the Prov. of Maine, under George's patent, but in 1654 became freeman of Mass., voluntarily.

FRANCIS GODFREY, of Duxbury, 1638, carpenter, removed early to Bridgewater, died 1669. His will names wife, Elizabeth, and daughter of John Cary.

GEORGE GODFREY, of Eastham, had George, born 1663; Samuel, 1665; Moses, 1667; Hannah, 1669; Mary, 1672; Ruth, 1675; Richard, 1677; Jonathan, 1682; and Elizabeth, 1688.

JOHN GODFREY, at New London, in 1667, may have been an inhabitant of Andover, and born 1622; but probably was first at Ipswich and Newbury, as he came 1634, in the "Mary and John."

PETER GODFREY, of Newbury, married 1656, Mary, daughter of Thomas Brown, first white born in the town, had Andrew, born 1657; Mary, 1659, died soon; Mary, again, 1661; Margaret, 1663; Elizabeth, 1667; Peter,

1669; Joanna, 1672; James, 1677; Sarah, 1680; he died 1697, aged 66.

RICHARD GODFREY, of Taunton, 1652, married a daughter of John Turner, had Richard; John; and Robert.

WILLIAM GODFREY, of Watertown, freeman 1640; by wife Margaret had Isaac, born 1639; Sarah, 1642; removed to Hampton, was deacon, and died 1671. His will also names son John, and daughter Deborah.

REFERENCES:—Am. Ancestry, IV, 194; VII, 69; Austin's R. I. Gen. Dict., 84; Ballou's Hist. of Milford, Mass., 768-72; Bangor, Me., Hist. Mag., II, 133; Bond's Watertown, Mass., Gens., 811; Davis' Hist. of Hampton, N. H., 727-35; Freeman's Cape Cod, Mass., II, 375, 609; Gregg's Hist. of Old Cheraws, S. C., 103; Pa. Mag of Hist., IV, 211; XVIII, 24; Pierce's Biog. Contrib. 52-98; Savage's Gen. Dict., II, 265; Schenck's Hist. of Fairfield, Ct., 372-74; Walker Gen., 25.

GODING or GODDING:—George Goding, of Fairfield, 1651, may be the same as Godwin.

HENRY GODING, of Watertown, married 1663, Elizabeth Beers, perhaps daughter of Anthony; had Timothy, born 1664; and Elizabeth, 1667; who married John Morse, 1690.

RICHARD GODING, of Gloucester, 1666, who died 1709. This name may be the same as Goodwin or Godwin.

REFERENCES:—Bond's Watertown, 256; Eaton's Thomaston, Me., 239; Hudson's Hist. of Lexington, Mass., 78; Savage's Gen. Dict., II, 266; Stearn's Hist of Rindge, N. H., 534.

GODMAN:——, of New Haven. His wife, Elizabeth, was, in 1653, suspected for a witch.

GODSOE:—William Godsoe, of Salem, 1684, had wife, Elizabeth.

GODSON:—Francis Godson, of Lynn, 1634. Perhaps the family name may be the same as the preceding.

GODWIN:—Samuel Godwin, of Fairfield, 1670. REFERENCES:—Lapham's Rumford, Me., 334-36; Va. Mag. of Hist., V, 198; VI, 85.

GOE:—George Goe, of Dover, found to have been taxed there 7 or 8 years, freeman 1669.

HENRY, PETER and RALPH GOE, fishermen, of whom the first and last are said to have been sent to Piscataqua by Mason in 1631; name may be GEE. Peter may be grandfather of famous minister of Boston.

GOFFE:—Edmund Goffe, of Cambridge, came from Ipswich, in Co. Suffolk, by the "Great Hope;" embarked late, 1634, or early, 1635; was first at Watertown, had land there 1637; brought wife, Joyce, and children, Samuel and Lydia; here had Nathaniel, born 1638; probably died young. His wife died 1638, and he married Margaret, daughter of widow Isabel Wilkinson; by her had Deborah, 1639; Mary, died 1646; Hannah, 1644; and Abiah; was freeman 1636, representative 1646 and 1650; died 1658, aged 64.

JACOB GOFFE, of Wethersfield, married Margery, daughter of John Ingersoll, of Westfield, 1679; had Jacob, born 1680, died soon; Moses, 1682, died young; Mabel, 1690; Mary, 1693; and Eunice, 1696; and he died 1697. His widow married Jonathan Buck.

JOHN GOFFE, of Newbury, freeman 1639, died 1641.

His will names wife Amy and children Susan and Hannah. How he came to these shores is not known.

PHILIP GOFFE, of Wethersfield, had Jacob, born 1649; Rebecca, 1651; Philip, 1653; Moses, 1656; and Aaron, 1658; died 1674.

REFERENCES:—Bedford, N. H. Cent., 306-8; Dwight's Strong Gen., 178; Paige's Hist. of Cambridge, Mass., 56:; Savage's Gen. Dict., II, 267; Whitmore's Copps Hill Epitaphs.

GOLD:—See Gould. ARMS: On a chevron, between three roses, azure, three pineapples [sometimes thistles] slipped of the first. CREST: An eagle's head, erased azure. In the beak a pineapple.

GOLDER:—See Goulder.

GOLDHAM:—Henry Goldham, of New Haven, 1645 was soon after at Guilford; had only Susanna, who married second John Bishop.

GOLDING:—Peter Golding, of Boston, by wife, Jane, had Mary, born 1666; and Frances, 1668; and by wife, Sarah, had Elizabeth, born 1673; Windsor, 1675; Thomas, 1678; Sarah, 1679; Jane, 1684; and Mercy, in 1686; about 1690 removed to Hadley, there lived three or four years, had Abigail, born 1691; removed to Sudbury, and died 1703.

REFERENCES:—Am. Ancestry, VII, 6; Savage's Gen. Dict., II, 269.

GOLDSMITH:—John Goldsmith, of Charlestown, 1647, servant to Philip Drinker.

JOSHUA GOLDSMITH, of Salisbury, married 1667, Mary, daughter of William Huntington; at Amesbury swore alleg. 1677.

RALPH GOLDSMITH, of Mass., 1661, named in George Fox's Journal, 325.

RICHARD, of Wenham, removed 1655 to Chelmsford; killed by lightning 1673.

THOMAS GOLDSMITH, of Southampton, L. I., 1641; Salem, 1643; in 1673 was, and had long been, inhabitant of Southampton. He married, perhaps, as second wife, Susanna, widow of John Sheather, of Guilford.

ZACCHEUS GOLDSMITH, of Wenham, perhaps brother of Richard, freeman 1685, and after recov. from the usurp. of Andros, sworn again 1690.

REFERENCES:—Ballou's Milford, 772; Clement's Newtown, N. J., Settlers; Converse Gen. (1897), 43-52; Livermore's Hist. of Wilton, N. H., 381-83; Norton's Hist. of Fitzwilliam, N. H., 584; Savage's Gen. Dict., II, 269.

GOLDSTONE:—Henry Goldstone, of Watertown, came in the "Elizabeth" from Ipswich, 1634, aged 43, with wife, Ann, 45; and children, Ann, 18; and Mary, 15. He was of infirm health and died 1638, and his widow married John George, of Watertown.

REFERENCE.—Bond's Watertown, 774.

GOLDTHWAIT:—Thomas Goldthwaith, of Roxbury, 1631, probably came in the fleet the year before, was freeman 1634, removed, probably, 1637, to Salem, had there baptized Samuel, 1637; Mehitable, 1640, who died 1668, unmarried; and Elizabeth, 1642. Name has been greatly perverted in spelling.

REFERENCES:—Am. Ancestry, IV, 7; Benedict's Hist. of Sutton, Mass., 651; Goldthwaite Gen. (1899), 411 pp.; Longmeadow, Mass., Cent., 315; Wheeler's Hist. of Newport, N. H., 397.

GOLDWYER:—George Goldwyer, of Salisbury, 1650, Dover, 1658, and died 1684, probably at S. His daughter Martha probably married, 1684, second Robert Pike.

GOLIKO:—Hugh Goliko, a soldier in Turner's company, in Philip's war.

GOLT or GAULT:—William Golt, of Salem, came in the "Mary Ann," of Yarmouth, 1637, aged 29, a cordwainer of Yarmouth, Co. of Norfolk, a single man; had there baptized Deborah, and Sarah, in 1648.

GOOCH:—Edward Gooch, of Boston, 1685, well spoken of by John Dunton; called him Gouge; warden of King's Chap., 1692.

JOHN GOOCH, of York, freeman 1652, had, probably, second wife Ruth; in his will mentions sons John and James.

REFERENCES:—Bass' Hist. of Braintree, Vt., 145; Machias Me. Cent., 163; Savage's Gen. Dict., II, 270. ARMS:—Poly of eight, silver and sable, a chevron, of the first, between three greyhounds, of the second, spotted, of the field.

CREST:—A greyhound, passant, silver, spotted and colored, sable.

MOTTO:—*Virtute et fide.*

GOOD:—William Good, a soldier in Moseley's company, 1675.

ROBERT GOODE, of Massachusetts, 1646; no more said.

REFERENCES:—Am. Ancestry, III, 21; IV, 101; Goode Gen. (1887), 526 pp.; Savage's Gen. Dict., Vol. II, 270.

THOMAS GOODE, came in "Bevis" from Southampton, 1638, aged 24; may have set down at Salem, may have had wife, Abigail.

GOODALE:—Joseph Goodale, of Boston, married before 1681, Sarah, widow of Thomas Rix.

NEHEMIAH GOODALE, of Lynn, married 1673, Hannah, daughter of Richard Haven; had Martha, born 1675; Joseph, 1677; Mary, 1686; and perhaps others.

RICHARD GOODALE, of Newbury, 1638, was from Yarmouth Co., Norfolk; removed to Salisbury, among first settlers, 1639 or 1640; had wife Dorothy, who died 1655; children, Ann, who married William Allen; and Richard, of Boston; he died 1666.

RICHARD GOODALE, of Boston, mariner, one of the founders of the first Bapt. Ch., perhaps with wife Mary, in Boston, 1665; had Richard, born 1665; and Mary, who married John Ewell; may have died at Middletown, 1676.

ROBERT GOODALE, of Salem, 1637, came in the "Elizabeth" from Ipswich, 1634, aged 30, with wife, Catharine, 28; and children, Mary; Abraham; and Isaac; had one child, name unknown, baptized 1640; Jacob, 1642; and Hannah, 1648. Sometimes name is Goodall, or Goodell.

REFERENCES.

MASSACHUSETTS.—Barry's Hist. of Framingham, 263; Herrick's Hist. of Gardner, 352; Keyes' West Boylston

Reg., 21-3; Benedict's Hist. of Sutton, 651; Heyward's Hist. Westminster, 670; Hoyt's Salisbury Fams., 176; Pierce's Hist. of Grafton, 490.

OTHER PUBLICATIONS.—Am. Ancestry, VI, 176; IX, 158; Savage's Gen. Dict., II, 270; Pickering Gen.

GOODENHOUSE:—Samuel Goodenhouse, of New Haven, had probably son Samuel, who, perhaps, removed to New York before 1695. See Vangoodenhausen.

GOODENOW, GOODNOW or GOODENOUGH:—Edmund Goodenow, of Sudbury, came in the "Confidence," from Southampton, 1638, a husbandman of Dunhead, in Wilts, aged 27, with wife Ann, and sons John and Thomas; had here, born 1639, Hannah; Mary, 1640; Sarah, 1643; Joseph, 1645; and Edmund; was freeman 1640, representative 1649 and 1650; honored as a leader of the militia, died 1679.

JOHN GOODNOW, of Sudbury, brother of Edmund, came in same ship, from Semley, in Wilts, husbandman, aged 42, with wife Jane, and Lydia, and Jane, daughters, was freemän 1641, selectman 1644, died 1654. His will mentions other children, John, Joseph, David, and Benjamin.

NATHANIEL GOODENOW, perhaps son of Thomas, came in the "Speedwell" from London in 1656, aged 16.

THOMAS GOODENOW, of Sudbury, brother of second John, came in same ship with them, 1638, aged 30; brought wife Jane, son Thomas and sister Ursula, who died 1653; he was freeman 1643; by wife Jane had here Mary, born 1640; Abigail, 1642; Susanna, 1643, died soon; Sarah, 1644, died at 10 years; Samuel, 1646; Susanna, again, 1647; Elizabeth, who died 1653; and Jane; had second wife, Joanna in 1662, and he died 1663.

REFERENCES:—Am. Ancestry, VI, 39; Savage's Gen. Dict., II, 271; Ward's Hist. of Shrewsbury, 293; Draper's Hist. of Spencer, Mass., 203; Butler's Framingham, Me., 476.

GOODFELLOW:—Thomas Goodfellow, of Hartford, was there before 1639, had grant, but did not settle; died at Wethersfield 1685, leaving widow Mary, who married again.

GOODHEART:—Isbrand Goodheart, of Hartford, servant of Casper Varlett in 1658.

GOODHUE:—Nicholas Goodhue, came from London in the "James," 1635, aged 60, with Jane, probably his wife, 58, a clothworker, of whom no more is ever heard; perhaps he was father of William.

WILLIAM GOODHUE, of Ipswich, freeman 1636, had wife Margery Watson; had Joseph, born 1639; William; and Mary; had second wife, widow Mary Webb; had third wife 1683, Bethia, widow of Joseph Grafton; in 1689 he married fourth wife, Remember, widow of John Fiske, of Wenham, who died 1701. He was selectman, deacon, 1658; representative, 1666, and often after; died 1699, aged 86.

REFERENCES:—Savage's Gen. Dict., II, 272; Pickering Gen.; Goodhue Gen. (1834), 16 pp.; Goodhue Gen. (1891), 394 pp.; Am. Ancestry, XII, 16; Cogswell's Gen., 168; Chase's Chester, N. H., 533; Driver Gen., 249; Mammatt Papers of Ipswich, Mass., 119-21; Henenway's Vt. Hist. Gaz., V, 239; Perkins' Old Houses of Norwich, Ct., 463.

GOODING:—Daniel Gooding, of Kittery, 1659; may be same as Goodwin.

REFERENCES:—Corliss' No. Yarmouth, Me., Walker Gen., 39.

GOODMAN:—John Goodman, of Plymouth, 1620, passenger on "Mayflower," single man, who had division in lands; probably died before 1621.

JOHN GOODMAN, of Sudbury, married 1656, Mary, perhaps daughter of Thomas Axtell, had Hannah, born 1657.

RICHARD GOODMAN, of Cambridge, 1632, perhaps freeman 1634, removed to Hartford early, before 1640, was constable 1656, married Mary, daughter of Stephen Terry, had John, born 1661; Richard, 1662; Stephen, 1664, died soon; Mary, 1665; Thomas, 1668, died soon; removed to Hadley, it is supposed, before most of children were born; was killed by Indians 1676.

REFERENCES:—Savage's Gen. Dict., II, 274; Tuttle Gen., 95-100; Am. Ancestry, VI, 6; Whitman Gen., 600-4.

GOODRICH:—John Goodrich, of Wethersfield, 1643, married about 1645, Elizabeth, daughter of Thomas Edwards, had Elizabeth, born 1645; John, 1647; Mary, 1650; Joseph, 1653; Jonathan, and Hannah. His wife died 1670, and he married 1674, Mary, widow of John Stoddard; died 1680, and his widow married Thomas Tracy, of Norwich.

WILLIAM GOODRICH, of Wethersfield, brother of John, married 1648, Sarah, daughter of Matthew Marvin, who outlived him; had William, born 1649; other children, Elizabeth; Abigail; Mary; Sarah; John; William, again, 1661; Ephraim, 1663; and David. He was representative, 1660, 1662, 1665, and 1666. His widow became second wife of Captain William Curtis, of Stratford.

REFERENCES:—Savage's Gen. Dict., II, 274; Stiles' Hist. of Windsor, Ct., II, 300; Talcott Gen., 233-35; Adams' Fairhaven, Vt., 37; Amer. Ancestry, II, 46; IV, 239; X, 144; Boardman Gen. (1895), 693-95; Guild's Stiles Gen., 497-99; Leland Gen., 143-45; Paul's Hist. of Wells, Vt., 945; Kellog's White Gen., 78; Goodrich's Recollections, I, 523-33; Goodrich Gen. (1883), 109 pp.; Goodrich Gen. (1889), 417 pp.

GOODRIDGE:—John Goodridge, of Watertown, 1637, perhaps brother of William, had grant of land that year.

JOHN GOODRIDGE, of Boston, 1640, tailor, freeman 1642, when record had name Guttering; by wife Prudence had Joseph, 1642.

RICHARD GOODRIDGE, of Guilford, 1639; nothing else known.

ROBERT GOODRIDGE, of Boston, kept a coffee house in the main, now Washington street, where the name was always called Gutteridge; by wife Mary had Robert; Mary, 1677; Elizabeth, 1682, died soon; Elizabeth, again, 1684; and Susanna, 1686. His wife died 1701; and he married 1703, widow, Mary Thaxter, had John, born 1706; Buttolph, 1707; and Mary Ann, 1711. He died 1717, aged 72.

WILLIAM GOODRIDGE, of Watertown, 1636, by wife Margaret had Mary, perhaps born in England; Jeremy, born 1638; Joseph, 1639; and Benjamin, 1642; died probably at Newbury, before 1647; his widow married John Hull of same place.

GOODRICH (GOODRIDGE).

ARMS:—Silver, a fess, sable. In chief, three cross crosslets, fitchel, of the last.

CREST:—A blackbird: proper.

REFERENCES:—Hatch's Hist. of Industry, Me., 624-26; Heyward's Hist. of Westminster, Mass., 671; Stearn's Hist. of Rindge, N. H., 535; Savage's Gen. Dict., II, 275; Goodridge Gen. (1884), 78 pp.

GOODSELL:—Thomas Goodsell, of Branford, 1667, a youth then, married 1684, Sarah, daughter of Samuel Hemmingway, of New Haven, had Samuel, born 1685; Mary, 1686; Sarah, 1689; Lydia, 1692; Deborah, 1694; Abigail, 1697, died soon; Abigail, again, 1699; Thomas, 1702; and John 1705.

REFERENCES:—Dodd's Hist. of East Haven, Ct., 120; Savage's Gen. Dict., II, 276; Am. Ancestry, X, 50, 156.

ARMS:—Per pale, red and blue; and a fess, wavy, silver, between three crosses, formée, gold, three crescents, sable.

GOODSPEED:—Roger Goodspeed, of Barnstable, married 1641, Alice Layton, had Nathaniel, born 1642; John, 1645; Mary, 1647; Benjamin, 1649; Ruth, 1652; Ebenezer, 1655; and Elizabeth, 1658.

REFERENCES:—Freeman's Cape Cod, 479; Swift's Barnstable Fams., I, 391-405; Am. Ancestry, XI, 214; XII; Hadley Gen., 61-6; Howland Gen., 304; New Eng. Hist. and Gen. Reg., III, 86; Ransom Gen., 36; Savage's Gen. Dict., II, 276; Ruggles Gen.

GOODWIN or GOODWYN:—Adam Goodwin, of Providence, 1641, had come home with John Moulton, of Ormsby, in Co. Norfolk, as his servant, aged 20, 1637, embarked at Yarmouth.

CHRISTOPHER GOODWIN, of Charlestown, 1676, freeman 1677, married Mary or Mercy, daughter of William Crouch, had Elizabeth, born 1659; and probably Timothy, baptized 1662; Mary and Hannah, 1676; and Mercy, 1680; died 1683, aged 65.

DANIEL GOODWIN, of Berwick, kept an inn there in 1662.

EDWARD GOODWIN, of Boston, 1641, freeman 1642, was a boatman; had wife Elizabeth, and daughter Elizabeth; he died 1694.

EDWARD GOODWIN, of Salisbury, 1667, shipwright, married 1668, Susanna Wheeler, of Newburg, widow, it is supposed, of George, and probably left descendants.

JOHN GOODWIN, of Charlestown, married 1669, Martha, daughter of Benjamin Lathrop, had Nathaniel, born 1672; and Martha, 1674; John, 1677; Mercy, 1681; removed to Boston, "where four of his children, in 1688, being possessed with a spirit of childish mischief, sadly perplexed and befooled Cotton Mother, so as to cause Mrs. Glover, the washerwoman, to be convicted of dealing with the devil, and hanged. By these infant instructors the learned author was adequately prepared for the honors he gained in the doleful tragedies of 1692, enacted at Salem."—(Savage's Gen. Dict., II, 277.) Several other children he had, as perhaps a second John; Benjamin, born 1683; Hannah, 1687; and Elizabeth, 1694; he died 1712. His widow married 1714, John Pearson, and died 1728.

JOHN GOODWIN, of Reading, an early settler.

OZIAS GOODWIN, of Hartford, one of the first settlers, was born about 1596, brother of William, died about 1683, leaving son William, born in England, 1629; and Nathaniel, 1637; besides daughter Hannah.

RICHARD GOODWIN, of Gloucester, married 1666, Hannah Jones, had Hannah, born 1667; Richard, 1669; Thomas, 1672; Mary, 1675; and Eleanor, 1680.

RICHARD GOODWIN, of Amesbury, married 1667, Mary Fowler, of Salisbury.

WILLIAM GOODWIN, of Cambridge, came to Boston, in the "Lion," 1632; freeman, representative 1634, removed 1635 or 1636 to Hartford, there was in highest esteem, ardent friend of famous Hooker, removed to Hadley, 1659, thence, 1670, to Farmington. He died 1673, leaving widow Susanna, who died 1676. His only child, Elizabeth, married John Crow.

REFERENCES.

MASSACHUSETTS.—Davis' Landmarks of Plymouth, 119-21; Brown's Bedford Fams., 13; Eaton's Hist. of Reading, 80; Freeman's Hist. of Cape Cod, I, 634; Hazen's Hist. of Billerica, 64; Hudson's Hist. of Lexington, 78; Stearn's Hist. of Ashburnham, 721.

CONNECTICUT.—Stiles' Hist. of Windsor, II, 301; Sedgwick's Hist. of Sharon, 84; Orcutt's Hist. of Torrington, 704; Goodwin Fam. of Conn. (1891), 798 pp.

OTHER PUBLICATIONS.—Am. Ancestry, I, 32; III, 216; IV, 98; IX, 132, 177; XII, 18, 36; Craft's Gen., 205-7; Walker Gen., 23; Savage's Gen. Dict., II, 277; Meade's Churches of Va.

GOODWRIGHT:—Isaac Goodwright, of Kittery, 1686, mentioned as relative in will of Christopher Adams, in which he gives him two cows.

GOODYEAR:—Stephen Goodyear, of New Haven, 1638, was probably a London merchant; here chosen assistant, and, in 1641, dep. gov., in which office he served until he went home; his wife embarked 1645 in Lamberton's ship for London, was lost with all of many passengers. He married Lamberton's widow, went home 1656 or 1657, and died soon in London, leaving here Mary, born of first wife before coming to our country, who married Thomas Lake, of Boston; Elizabeth, widow of Daniel Silevant; perhaps, however, this was only daughter of Lamberton; Hannah; Stephen; Lydia; Andrew; John; and Esther.

JOHN GOODYEAR, of New Haven, probably brother, not son of the preceding, had Stephen, born 1654; besides which nothing more can be learned.

REFERENCES:—Fiske Gen., 145-47; Goodyear Gen. (1899), 250 pp.; Savage's Gen. Dict., II, 278.

GOOKIN:—Daniel Gookin, of Cambridge, born in Kent, Eng., passed probably fourteen years in Virginia from 1630, whither he went with his father, perhaps of the same name, who had grant in that colony in 1620, came to Boston in a ship 1644, with other passengers, flying from Indian massacre; freeman, called captain in records, also lived at Roxbury, where, by his wife Mary, had Elizabeth, 1645; and Hannah, 1646, died in a few weeks; he had removed to Cambridge, of which he was representative 1649, and speaker 1651, mag. gen., 1681, died 1687, aged 75. Had also children, Daniel, died 1649, few months old; Daniel, again, 1650, Harvard College, 1669; Samuel, 1652; Solomon, died 1654; Nathaniel, 1656; H. C. 1675; and Mary, older than any, who may have come from Va.

ARMS:—Red, a chevron, ermine, between three crosses, gold.

REFERENCES:—Atkins' Gen. (1891), 146-51; N. E. Hist. Reg., I, 345-52; II, 167-74; IV, 185-88; Morse's Sherborn, Mass., Settlers, 92; Richmond, Va., Standard, IV, 4; Savage's Gen. Dict., II, 278-80; Virginia Mag. of Hist., V (1898), 435; Am. Ancestry, VIII, 206.

GOOLE:—Francis Goole, of Duxbury, 1643; at Braintree, by wife Rose, had Samuel, born 1659.

GOOSE:—Isaac Goose, of Boston, freeman 1690, in which year his wife Mary, died, aged 42. He was constable 1673; fuller account may be read under Vergoose.

WILLIAM GOOSE, of Salem, 1637, was of Charlestown, 1658, had John, baptized 1659; may have had other children.

GORDON:—Alexander Gordon, of Exeter, 1677-89.

EDMUND GORDON, a passenger in the "Susan and Ellen," 1635, aged 18, of whom no more is heard.

JOHN GORDON, of Bridgewater, 1682.

NICHOLAS GORDON, of N. Hamp., 1689.

ARMS:—Quarterly—First, azure, on a fess, silver, between 3 boar's heads, couped, gold, a wolf's head, couped, sable. Second, gold, three lion's heads, erased, red. Third, gold, three crescents, within a double tressure, flory, counterflory, red. Fouth, azure, three frases, silver.

CREST:—A hart's head, affrontée: proper.

MOTTO:—Animo.

REFERENCES:—Bell's Hist. of Exeter, N. H., 21-4; Smith's Hist. of Petersborough, N. H., 93-5; Slaughter's Bristol Paris, Va., 203; Whitehead's Perth Amboy, N. J., 60-8; Am. Ancestry, III, 23, 195; IV, 155; VII, 50; VIII, 53; X, 56; Goode Gen., 122; Green's Kentucky Fams., Hall Gen. (1892), 66-72; Savage's Gen. Dict., II, 280.

GORE:—John Gore, of Roxbury, 1635, brought wife Rhoda, perhaps daughter Mary, and son John, born 1634, in England, had Obadiah, 1636, died at 10 years; Abigail, 1641, died soon; Abigail, again, 1643; Hannah, 1645; Obadiah, again, 1649, died 1653; two children unbaptized, died 1651; besides Samuel, of whom no record of birth is found. He was freeman 1637, died 1657.

REFERENCES:—Payne and Gore Gen. (1875), 423-25; Gore Gen. (1875), 8 pp., reprint; Preble Gen., 243-45; Savage's Gen. Dict., II, 280; Ellis' Hist. of Roxbury, Mass, 119.

GOREN or GORING:—Henry Goren, of Windsor, had William, born 1679; next year abandoned his family; the son went, 1710, to England in vain pursuit of estate.

GORGES:—Robert Gorges, son of Sir Ferdinando, came over in 1623, and set down with several families at Weymouth; but they were soon willing to return home, and perhaps very few, if any, continued for a second year.

THOMAS GORGES, of York, cousin of the preceding, came 1640, was first mayor of the corpo., but went home after three years. Winthrop, II, 9. In Hutch., I, 176, is a strange tradition that he came back and died here.

WILLIAM GORGES, of Saco, another nephew of Sir F., deput. with full authority for his government of Somersetshire, i.e., all the coast between the Kennebeck and Piscataqua rivers, came over in 1635. It is presumed that he soon tired of his office, and went home. See Chalmers' Polit. Ann., 472-4.

REFERENCES:—N. E. Hist. Gen. Reg., XV, 18-20; XXIX, 42-7; Savage's Gen. Dict., II, 281; Gorges Gen. (1875), 11 pp.

GORHAM, Gorum, or Goram:—Ralph Gorham, of Duxbury, 1637, probably came with son John, and Ralph, from Benefield, dist. Northamptonsh. But no more is heard of him, so that we may suppose he went home. John, it is known, settled here and had descendants.

REFERENCES:—Goodwin's Olcott Gen., 25; Gorham Fam. of Barnstable (1896), 7 pp.; Gorham Fam. of R. I. (1900), 11 pp.; Savage's Gen. Dict., II, 281; Wyman's Charlestown, Mass., I, 423-5; Austin's Allied Fams., 106-8; Am. Ancestry, X, 145; Huntington's Stamford, Ct., Settlers, 38.

GORNELL:—John Gornell, of Dorchester, lawyer, may have come 1630 in the "Mary and John," from Devonshire, or from Suffolk, with Winthrop; freeman 1643, died 1675, aged 64. His widow Jane married, 1676, Giles Burge, outlived him and died 1678. She is called on gravestone, widow of John Gornell, without reference to Burge. He had large estate.

GORNOCK:—Duncan Gornock, of New Haven, 1688, had wife Margaret, but, it is thought, no children there.

GORTON:—John Gorton, of Roxbury, had wife Mary, who died 1636; Mary, again, 1641; died young; Sarah 1644; Hannah 1646, died 1669, unmarried; Mary again 1648; Alice 1652; Elizabeth, 1654, died soon; John 1656, died before his father; and Abraham 1659. He was freeman 1669, and died 1676.

SAMUEL GORTON, an active relig. disturber of several places, born at Groton about 1600, came to Boston 1636, soon to Plymouth, thence, 1638, to Rhode Island; in 1641 was disquieting Roger Williams at Providence; in 1643, with Holden Greene, and others, made the great movement to purchase of Warwick from the Indians, which led to hostile aggress. by the governor of Mass., who took all his settlers prisoners and punished them cruel. not without some hesit. even sparing their lives. Next year he went to England with other suffer. and obtain. just assertion of his right, and had peace near 30 years for his adherents in the cloudy doctrines. (Savage's Gen. Dict., II, 283.) He had children Samuel, John, and Benjamin, besides daughters Maher, Mary, Sarah, Ann, Elizabeth, and Susanna; he died 1724, aged, as report is, 94 years.

REFERENCES:—Ely Gen., 183; Savage's Gen. Dict., II, 282; N. E. Hist. and Gen. Reg., II, 199-201; Austin's Allied Fams., 111.

GOSIER:—Bastion Gosier, earliest mention in town records is under spelling of Gazeau, as having, by wife Elizabeth, son Bartholomew, born 1686; William, 1687; John, 1689; and Elizabeth, 1690.

GOSMER:—John Gosmer, of Southampton, Long Island, 1641, took estate 1655 in Boston, which in 1658, he made over to his kinswoman Ann, widow of Richard Carter.

GOSNALL:—Henry Gosnall, of Boston, 1634, had wife Mary.

GOSNOLD:—Bartholomew Gosnold, the distinguished navigator, son and heir, as he styles himself, of Anthony G., of Grundisburg, first named in honor of his Sovereign, if he did not discover the Elizabeth Islands, S. W. of Cape Cod, and plant. a small colony on Cuttyhunk, 1602, soon given up; removed in 1606, the plantation of Virginia, and died there 1607, probably leaving *no issue*.

GOSS:—Edward Goss, of Marblehead, 1668.

JOHN Goss, of Watertown, freeman 1631, came with Winthrop, probably in 1630, and wife Sarah, and several children, of whom Joseph, and Elizabeth died; was freeman, and died 1644. His widow married Robert Nichols.

PHILIP Goss, of Roxbury, or, as may seem not unlikely, Muddy River, as the town record does not show his name. The children by his wife, Hannah Hopkins, baptized at Roxbury, were Philip, 1679; Hannah, same year; and Mary, 1680.

RICHARD Goss, of New Hampshire, 1689.

REFERENCES:—Davis' Hist. of Hampton, N. H., 736; Goss Family Romance (1886), 24 pp.; Amer. Ancestry, V, 121; Savage's Gen. Dict., II, 284; Temple's Hist. of N. Brookfield, Mass., 604; Essex Co., Mass., Register, I, (1894), 128 pp.; Lapham's Hist. of Paris, Me., 610; Lapham's Hist. of Bethel, Me., 541.

GOTOBED:—Robert Gotobed, of Concord. The origin of this rather remarkable name is not found. Nothing much is known of him; in fact, he died, 1667, without, it seems, having taken any active part in any military or civic event.

GOTT:—Charles Gott, of Salem, came in the "Abigail" with Endicott, 1628; freeman 1631, first deacon of church, representative 1635; had Deborah, baptized 1637; Charles, 1639; and Daniel, 1646; removed to Wenham, was representative for this town 1654, and died 1657 or 8.

REFERENCES:—Savage's Gen. Dict., II, 284; Amer. Ancestry, II, 44; Temple's Hist. of N. Brookfield, Mass., 605; Davis' Ancestry (1897), 37-40.

GOUGE, or GOUCH:—See Gooch, and Gutch.

GOULD, or GOLD:—Adam Gould, of Groton, by wife Rebecca, had Dorcas, born 1683, removed to Woburn, there by wife Hannah, had Thomas, born 1689; and his wife died soon.

CHRISTOPHER GOULD, of Hampton, 1660.

DANIEL GOULD, of Newport, a freeman there 1655, represent. 1672, married, 1651, Wait Coggeshall, probably daughter of the first John, had Mary, born 1653; Thomas,

1655; Daniel, 1656; John, 1659; Priscilla, 1661; Jeremy, 1664; James, 1666; Jeremy, again, 1669; Content, 1671; and Wait, 1676. The date of his death is not found.

EDWARD GOULD, of Hingham, a pailmaker, came in the "Elizabeth" from London, 1635, aged 28, was of Hawkhurst Co., Kent; living in Boston, in 1657.

FRANCIS GOULD, of Chelmsford, had been of Braintree, by wife Rose had there Hannah, born 1655; and John, 1657, who probably died young; and at C. had John, again, 1660.

HENRY GOULD, of Ipswich, by wife Sarah, married 1675, had Sarah; Elizabeth, 1677; Jane, 1679; and Joanna, 1681.

JAMES GOULD, of Haverhill, took oath of fidelity, 1677.

JARVIS GOULD, of Hingham, cardwainer, came in the "Elizabeth," 1635, aged 30, servant to Clement Bates, removed to Boston, 1656, leaving John.

JEREMIAH GOULD, of R. I., 1638, is in list of Newport freeman, 1655.

JEREMY GOULD, of Weymouth, 1639.

JOHN GOULD, a husbandman from Towcester, Northamptonsh., came in the "Defence," 1635, with wife Grace, 25; but nothing is found of his settlement.

JOHN GOULD, of Charlestown, had wife Mary in 1636, who died 1642; daughter Mary baptized 1637; Sarah, 1637; Elizabeth, 1640; Abigail, 1642; by another wife, Hannah, who died 1647, had Hannah, 1644; and John, 1647, died soon. By the same records he is favored with another John, 1648, probably by another wife, Joanna; both father and son living 1678. He may have been one of the early settlers at Reading.

JOHN GOULD, of Newport, 1655, represent. 1672, but no more can be learned of him.

JOHN GOULD, of Topsfield, only son of Zaccheus, born about 1637, in England, freeman, 1665, the greatest landholder in the neighborhood, married 1660, Sarah, perhaps daughter of John Baker, who died 1709, had John, born 1662; Sarah, 1664; Thomas, 1667; Samuel, 1670; Zaccheus, 1672; Priscilla, 1674; Joseph, 1677; Mary, 1681, and he died perhaps 1710.

JOHN GOULD, of Taunton, married Mary, daughter of Robert Crossman, 1673, had Mary, born 1674; Hannah, 1677.

JOHN GOULD, of Stamford, married a daughter of George Slawson.

NATHAN GOULD, of Fairfield, 1652, married Martha, widow of Edmund Harvey, an assistant, 1657, and every year but one following; was named for some rank in the Royal Charter of 1662; in 1670 was the richest inhabitant. He wrote his surname without the u, but perhaps the universal pronunciation caused the change. He died 1694, in his will names only son Nathan, and daughters Sarah, Deborah, Abigail and Martha.

NATHAN GOULD, of Salisbury, 1660, by wife Elizabeth, had Mary, born 1661; Elizabeth, 1664; and Samuel, 1668; was of Amesbury, 1690, freeman that year. In his will names wife Elizabeth, and children Joseph, Elizabeth, Hannah, and Samuel.

ROBERT GOULD, of Hull, married, 1666, Judith, and had second wife Jane Smith, a widow, daughter of Thomas Harris, of Boston; was freeman 1680.

THOMAS GOULD, of Boston, came in the "Jonathan," 1639, aged 32, may have been the freeman of 1641, but that is doubtful; was perhaps first of Cambridge, by wife Mary had Jacob, born 1643, died 1662.

THOMAS GOULD, of Newport, 1655, married Elizabeth, daughter of William Balstone, may have been many years of Wickford, 1674.

THOMAS GOULD, of Charlestown, with wife Hannah, joined to the church, 1640; had Hannah, baptized 1641; became a Bapt., was long imprisoned for his falling off, but ultimately discharg. with reput. He had second wife, Mary, before all his troubles were over. He died perhaps 1674, at Boston, and in his will names wife Mary, son Samuel, daughters Mary Skinner, Mehitiable Goodwin, Mary Bunker, and her two children, Abigail Shapely, son, Nathaniel Haywood, and daughter Hannah Gold.

THOMAS GOULD, of Boston, married, 1656, Frances Robinson, had probably other children, besides Ann, born about 1685, who married Nathaniel Green.

ZACCHEUS GOULD, of Lynn, 1640, had son Daniel, it is said, born about 1650, who went, probably, with other of his neighbors to Reading.

ZACCHEUS GOULD, of Weymouth, 1639.

ZACCHEUS GOULD, of Ipswich, 1644 (in that part which was soon incorp. as Topsfield), came from Hants Green, near Potter's Row, in Co. Bucks; left good estate to only son, John, and four daughters, perhaps both at Rawley and Topsfield. His daughters were Phebe, Martha, Mary, and Priscilla.

Arms: Or, on a chevron, between three roses, azure, three pineapples, [sometimes thistles], slipped of the first.
Crest: An eagle's head, erased, azure. In the beak a pineapple, or.

REFERENCES.

MASSACHUSETTS.—Chandler's Hist. of Shirley, 428; Daniel's Hist. of Oxford, 523; Temple's Hist. of N. Brookfield, 605; Marse's Sherborn, 93; Ballou's Hist. of Milford, 773-5; Cleveland's Topfield Anniv., 52.

NEW HAMPSHIRE.—Kidder's New Ipswich, 379-83; Norton's Hist. of Fitzwilliam, 585; Cochrane's Hist. of Antrim, 512; Haywood's Hist. of Hancock, 613; Stearn's Hist. of Rindge, 536-8

OTHER PUBLICATIONS:—Gould Gen., (1841), 2 pp.; (1872), 109 pp.; (1895), 353 pp.; Savage's Gen. Dict., II, 284-7; Am. Ancestry, I, 32; III, 197; IV, 178; VI, 158; Binney Gen., 24, 88-93; Dwight Gen., 976-80; Walworth's Hyde Gen., 813-6.

GOULDEN, or GOLDEN:—Roger Goulden, of R. I., captain of a vessel, did service in Philip's War, especially on August 12, 1676, when the great adversary was killed; married Penelope, daughter probably of the first Benedict Arnold.

GOULDER:—Francis Goulder, of Plymouth, 1643, died 1664. Catharine, probably his widow or daughter, died there 1651.

GOURDING:—Abraham Gourding, of Boston, 1672, mariner.

GOVE. or GOAVE:—Edward Gove, of Hampton, rep. in assembly of N. H., 1680. (See accounts of Insurrection against Royal Governor Cranfield, in Belkn., I, 98-100, and in Chalmers Polit. Ann., 495-6.) He was first of Salisbury, there had John,, born 1661; William, 1662; died next year; Hannah, 1664; and at H. had Mary, 1666; Abigail; Peniel; both died soon; Jeremiah, 1674;

died at 18 years; Ann, 1677; and Sarah, 1678. He died 1691.

JOHN GOVE, of Charlestown, probably a merchant; in his will of 1648 made shortly before his death, he names children, John, Edward, and Mary.

JOHN GOVE, of Cambridge, probably brother of Edward, married, 1658, Mary, perhaps daughter of William Aspinwall, who died 1676; had Mary, born 1659; John, 1660; Aspinwall, 1661, died soon; Nathaniel, 1662; James, 1663, died young; Nathaniel, again, 1667; he married second wife, 1677, Mary Woodhead, had Jonathan, born, 1678, who died 1681; Jonathan, again, 1682; and Sarah, 1686; his son John died 1679; his wife, 1700; he married third wife 1700, widow Elizabeth Walden, and died 1704, aged about 77.

REFERENCES:—Savage's Gen. Dict., II, 287-9; Am. Ancestry, IV, 122; Potts' Gen. (1895), 277-9; Washington, N. H., Hist., 450; Wyman's Charlestown, Mass., Gens., I, 429; Little's Hist. of Weare, N. H., 865-84; Cogswell's Hist. of Henniker, N. H., 603-5; Cogwell's Hist. of Nottingham, N. H., 206-9.

GOWING, or GOWEN:—John Gowing, of Lynn, by wife Joanna, married, 1682, had, it is said, John, Thomas, Elizabeth, Samuel, Joanna, Lois, and Timothy, but he gives no dates for them.

NATHANIEL GOWING, of Reading, freeman, 1691.

ROBERT GOWING, of Dedham, freeman 1644, by wife Elizabeth had John, baptized, 1645.

SIMON GOWING, a soldier of Appleton's company, wounded in Philip's War.

REFERENCES:—Am. Ancestry, IX, 137; XII, 16; Secomb's Hist. of Amherst, N. H., 605; Benedict's Sutton, Mass., 652; Norton's Hist. of Fitzwilliam, N. H., 585.

GOYT:—John Goyt, of Dorchester, 1635, removed perhaps 1642, or before, to Salem, where Mary, probably his wife, had Joseph and Mary; Mary, again; was of Marblehead, 1648.

GOZZARD:—Nicholas Gozzard, of Windsor, died 1693, leaving widow Elizabeth and children Elizabeth, Nathaniel, and John.

GRAFFORT:—Thomas Graffort, of Portsmouth, married, 1684, Bridget, widow of Thomas Daniel, a daughter of Richard Cutts, was a counsellor of the Prov., 1692, removed to Boston before 1695, and died 1697. His wife died 1701.

GRAFTON:—Joseph Grafton, of Salem, 1636, freeman 1637; had wife Mary, who died 1674, and child Priscilla; Joseph, baptized, 1637; John, 1639; and Nathaniel, 1642. He was an active mariner and merchant. His second wife was Bethia, widow of Captain Thomas Lathrop, daughter of Samuel Rea, or Ray.

JOSHUA GRAFTON, of Salem, 1649, perhaps brother of first Joseph.

REFERENCES:—Savage's Gen. Dict., II, 289; Pierce Gen., by West (1894); Eaton's Warren, Me., 546.

GRAHAM:—Benjamin Graham, of Hartford, married Abigail Humphrey, probably daughter of John of Simsbury, and she died, 1697.

JAMES GRAHAM, of Boston, came probably as a friend of Andro's, and was his attorney-general, but on the overthrow of that admin. was imprison. without bail.

REFERENCES:—Am. Ancestry, I, 33; VIII, 91; IX, 23; X, 101; Cleveland's Hist. of Yates Co., N. Y., 291-7; Powers' Sangamon Co., Ills. Settlers, 334; Richmond, Va., Standard, III, 5; Fowler's Chauncey Gen., 229; Lapham's Hist. of Rumford, Me., 338, 40; New Eng. Hist. and Gen. Reg., XXI, 189-91; Chase's Hist. of Chester, N. H., 534; Egle's Penn. Gens., 625; Baird's Hist. of Rye, N. Y., 466.

GRAME:—Samuel Grame, of Boston, 1641, a pewterer, joined the church, 1642, had baptized same year, daughter Mary, aged 3.

GRANGER:—Bryan Granger, of Salem, 1637.

JOHN GRANGER, of Scituate, 1640, left widow Grace, son John, and daughter Elizabeth; the son died at Marshfield, probably, in 1655.

LANCELOT GRANGER, of Ipswich, 1648, removed to Newbury, married Joanna, daughter of Robert Adams; had John, 1655; George, 1658; Elizabeth, 1662; Dorothy, 1665; Samuel, 1668; and Abraham, 1673; but he had others at Ipswich, as Thomas; Rebecca; Robert, killed at Brookfield, 1709; besides Hannah, and Mary; 11 children in all. In 1679 he removed to what is now Suffield, and died 1689.

REFERENCES:—Savage's Gen. Dict., II, 1290; Deane's Hist. of Scituate, Mass., 275; Granger Gen. (1893), 587 pp.; Amer. Ancestry, IV, 165; VIII, 86; IX, 119; X, 197.

GRANNIS:—Edward Grannis, of Hartford, married 1655, Elizabeth Andrews, had Joseph, born 1656; died young; and perhaps more; but he married, 1662, second wife, Hannah Wakefield; had Hannah; Mabel; Abigail; removed to Hadley; there had Sarah; John; removed again to Conn.; at New Haven, where the name is still to be heard, had Joseph; and Ann.

JOHN GRANNIS, of New Haven, 1670, may have been brother of the preceding.

REFERENCES:—Hughes' Gen., 161-4; Savage's Gen. Dict., II, 290; Grannis' Pedigree (1889), 15x25 inches; (1891), 17x18 inches; Dodd's East Haven, Conn., 122.

GRANT:—Christopher Grant, of Watertown, 1634, by wife Mary had Abigail, born 1635; Joshua, 1637; Caleb, 1640; and Benjamin, 1641; and by wife Sarah, had Sarah, 1643; Joseph, 1646; Mary, or Mercy, or both; and Christopher, 1649; died 1685.

EDWARD GRANT, of Boston, 1658, shipwright, married Sarah Ward, or Weare, had Experience, born 1658; and Joseph, 1661; freeman, 1672; died 1682; leaving widow and son Joseph only.

JAMES GRANT, of Boston, 1657, one of the founders of the Scot's Charit. Soc. that year.

JAMES GRANT, of Charlestown, 1658, may have been of Dover, 1657, of York, 1674, and of other town later, nothing being known at either place about him, except that at York one of that name took the oath of allegiance, 1681.

JAMES GRANT, of Dedham, 1664, died 1698, leaving widow Margaret.

MATTHEW GRANT, of Dorchester, came in the "Mary and John," 1630, with Maverick and Warham, was, we may suppose, therefore of Co. Devon; freeman, 1631, had wife and daughter Priscilla, born in England, and here had Samuel, born 1631; Tahan, 1634, removed, 1635, to Windsor, for the first plant. there; was for many years

its faithful town clerk; had John, born 1642, but records no other children; died 1681. For second wife he had Susanna, widow of William Rockwell.

PETER GRANT, of Boston, 1657; may have removed to Hartford, died 1681, leaving 6 children.

ROBERT GRANT, of Ipswich, 1685.

SAMUEL GRANT, of Boston, 1640.

SETH GRANT, of Cambridge, 1632, came with Wadsworth, Talcott, Goodwin, Olmstead, and others in the "Lion," arriving with them at Boston; removed to Hartford, an original proprietor.

REFERENCES.

MASSACHUSETTS.—Pierce's Hist. of Grafton, 495; Jameson's Hist. of Medway, 487; Barrus' Hist. of Goshen, 145; Bond's Hist. of Watertown, 260, 775; Wyman's Charestown Gens., I, 431.

NEW HAMPSHIRE.—Aldrich's Walpole, 262; Haywood's Hist. of Hancock, 613; Little's Hist. of Weare.

OTHER PUBLICATIONS.—Am. Ancestry, II, 47; VII, 72, 113; VIII, 9; VII, 30; Savage's Gen. Dict., 290-4; Grant Ancestry, (1869), 186 pp.; (1885); 17 pp.; (1893), 142 pp.; (1898), 578 pp.; Missouri Pioneer Fams., 333; Driver Gen., 85; Whitemore's Copp's Hill Epitaphs; Barbour's My Wife and Mother, app., 51; Hanson's Hist. of Gardiner, Me., 134.

GRANTHAM:—Andrew Grantham, of Newbury, died, 1668.

GRATH. See Groth.

GRAVES:—George Graves, of Hartford, an original proprietor, representative 1657 and after; had George, John, and one or two daughters; died 1673.

JOHN GRAVES, of Roxbury; came in 1633, with wife, who died soon after, and 5 children, John, Samuel, Jonathan, Sarah, and Mary, according to church records. In 1635 he married Judith Alward, or Allard, had Hannah, born 1636; was freeman 1637, and died 1644. (See Savage's Gen. Dict., II, 294-5.)

RICHARD GRAVES, of Boston, had Ruth, who married, 1656, Henry Keskeys.

ROBERT GRAVES, of Ipswich, 1638.

SAMUEL GRAVES, of Lynn, 1630, had Samuel, and probably 7 other children, of whom we have no report.

SAMUEL GRAVES, of Ipswich, 1658, feltmaker, married Grace, daughter of William Beamsley, of Boston, where he may have lived at first; had Samuel, born 1658; John, 1660; Elizabeth Hannah, 1668; and Jonathan, who died young.

THOMAS GRAVES, of Charlestown, the engineer, who laid out the place in 1629, came in the fleet with Higginson, with possibly, but not probably, wife and 5 children from Gravesend Co., Kent, arriving at Salem in June. In 1630 was made freeman; probably went home in 1632, as no more is heard of him.

THOMAS GRAVES, of Hartford, not an original proprietor; an old man, excused from train.; 1645, removed to Hadley, perhaps had not any children born here, yet had brought from England, Isaac, John, and perhaps Samuel, and a daughter, whose name is unknown, and possibly Nathaniel; he died 1662.

THOMAS GRAVES, of Charlestown, 1638, probably was 9 years before mate of the "Talbot," in which came Higginson to Salem, was, it is said, son of John, born at Ratcliffe, near London, 1605; was several years master of a ship almost constantly employed between London and Boston; was freeman 1640, married in England before 1635, Catherine Gray. He was a very active and brave man; for good service in the Eng. chan. was rewarded by Parliament with title of Rear Admiral; died at C. 1653. Had children John, Nathaniel, Thomas, Susanna, and Joseph; two others, Rebecca, and Elizabeth, are mentioned in his will.

WILLIAM GRAVES, of Dover, 1659.

Graves or Greaves. *Arms:* Gu., an eagle displayed, or [sometimes crowned, arg.]; a martlet, of the Second, for difference.

The exact meaning of the motto is: *An eagle does not catch flies.*

REFERENCES.

MASSACHUSETTS.—Wyman's Charlestown Gens., I, 332; Sewall's History of Woburn, 68-70; Heywood's Hist. of Westminster, 672-4; Craft's Hist. of Whately, 473-97; Craft's Gen., 185-7; Barry's Hist. of Framingham, 265; Ellis' Hist. of Roxbury, 129; Judd's Hist. of Hadley, 501-4.

NEW HAMPSHIRE.—Aldrich's Hist. of Walpole, 263-7; Dam's Hist. of Hampton, 739; Merrill's Hist. of Acworth, 221; Read's Hist. of Swanzey, 346-8.

OTHER PUBLICATIONS.—Am. Ancestry, I, 33; V, 49; VII, 17, 136; X, 197; XII, 19; Graves' Gen. (1896), 546 pp.; Hayden's Va. Gens.; Montague Gen., 517; Savage's Gen. Dict., II, 294-8; Graves' Family of Lynn, (1898), 3 pp.; Wentworth Gen., II, 202.

GRAY:—Edward Gray, of Plymouth, 1643, a youth, married 1651, Mary, daughter of John Winslow, who died 1663, and he married, 1665, Dorothy, daughter of Thomas Lettice, had Desire, born 1651; Mary, 1653; Elizabeth, 1658; Sarah, 1659; John, 1661; by the first wife, and Edward, 1667; Susanna, 1668, by the second, and perhaps others. He was a merchant, representative 1676-8, died 1681, and his grave stone is called the oldest now standing in the town.

HENRY GRAY, of Boston, 1638, a tailor.

HENRY GRAY, of Fairfield, 1643, married Lydia, daughter of William Frost, was representative 1656 and 7, died 1658, leaving Jacob, Henry, Levi, William and Sarah; had also Mary, who died.

JAMES GREY, of Providence, swore alleg., 1671.

JOHN GREY, of Yarmouth, 1643, married Hannah, perhaps daughter of William Lumpkin; had Benjamin, born 1648; William, 1650; and prob. Mary; Edward, John and Gideon; and died about 1674.

NICHOLAS GRAY, a soldier, probably from the E. on Conn. River, 1676.

ROBERT GRAY, of Salem, by wife Elizabeth had there baptized, Elizabeth, 1651; Joseph, 1652; Bertha, 1654; Robert, 1658; Hannah, 1659; removed to Andover; died 1718, aged 84. Another Robert Gray was fined as a Quaker, at Salem, 1669. Perhaps the same married, 1669, Hannah Holt, and had Catharine, born 1670; Henry, 1672; Jemima, 1672, died soon; and Hannah, 1675.

REFERENCES.

MASSACHUSETTS.—Abbott's Andover, 36; Barry's Hist. of Hanover, 314; Wyman's Charlestown Gens., I, 434; Temple's Hist. of Whately, 240; Gray Family of Beverly (1887), 316 pp.; Freeman's Cape Cod, II, 227, 525, 758; Davis' Landmarks of Plymouth, 121.

NEW HAMPSHIRE.—Hayward's Hist. of Hancock, 614-30; Livermore's Hist. of Wilton, 383-8; Smith's Hist. of Peterborough, 96-8.

OTHER PUBLICATIONS.—Savage's Gen. Dict., II, 298; Am. Ancestry, I, 34; II, 47; IV, 217;.VI, 17; XII; Am. Gen. Record (1897), II, 190-2; Gray Family of Sauquoit, N. Y. (1882), 13 p.; Walworth's Hyde Gen., 21; Schenck's Hist. of Fairfield, Conn., 374; Huntington's Stamford, Conn., Settlers, 38.

GRAYGOOSE.—Nathaniel Graygoose, of Boston, 1640, a single man, when admitted in August of that year into the church.

GRAZILLIER:—Ezekiel Grazillier, of Boston, probably a Huguenot, who by wife Mary had Ezekiel, born 1688. He had removed perhaps to Salem, during or before 1695.

GRELE, or GREELEY:—Andrew, of Salisbury, an original proprietor, by wife Mary had Philip, born 1644; Andrew, 1646; Mary, 1649; Joseph, 1652; Benjamin, 1654; was of Haverhill, 1669; and died 1697.

NATHANIEL GRELE, of Salisbury, 1649, perhaps brother of Andrew.

REFERENCES:—Savage's Gen. Dict., II, 299; Corliss' North Yarmouth, Me., Mag., 42-5; Livermore's Hist. of Wilton, N. H., 388; Hoyt's Salisbury, Mass., Families, 180-2; Poor's Merrimack Valley Researches, 89; Am. Ancestry, VII, 90.

GREEN:—Abraham Green, of Hampton, 1678.

BARTHOLOMEW GREEN, of Cambridge, freeman 1634; came the year before and died the year following; by wife Elizabeth had Samuel, Nathaniel, Sarah and Phœbe.

CHARLES GREEN, of Marblehead, 1668.

DANIEL GREEN, of Wickford, 1671, owned jurisdict. of R. I. in that year, probably the same, who, by wife Rebecca had Peleg, born 1690; Daniel, 1692; Jonathan, 1694; Rebecca, 1696; Rachel, 1698; Sarah, 1700; and Jonathan, again, 1705.

HENRY GREEN, of Reading, called by Winthrop "a scholar," had been in 1643, invited to go to Martha's Vineyard by its first settlement, but went not; married Frances, eldest daughter of Deacon Simon Stone; had Joanna, and Nathaniel; was the earliest minister of R.; ordained 1645, died 1648.

JAMES GREEN, of Charlestown 1646, freeman, 1647; had wife Elizabeth, sons John and James; died 1687, aged 77.

JAMES GREEN, of Boston, lived at Romney Marsh, now Chelsea, but at Dorchester married, 1661, Rebecca, daughter of Thomas Jones; had Elizabeth, born 1662; James, 1664; Rebecca, 1665; Richard, 1669; John, 1672; Esther, 1674; and Samuel, 1680; was freeman 1683, and by wife Ann had Rebecca, born 1688.

JAMES GREEN, of Portsmouth, R. I., mariner, sold land there, 1669.

JOHN GREEN, of Charlestown, came in the "James" from London, 1632, with wife Perseverance and 3 children, John, Jacob, Abigail. His wife, it is said, was daughter of Rev. Francis Johnson, a Puritan of eminence, who had fled to Amsterdam; was distinguished as town clerk, and as selectman 12 years; died 1658, aged 65.

JOHN GREEN, of Roxbury, lived with Daniel Brewer, died before 1639.

JOHN GREEN, of Providence, 1636, may be that surgeon who came from Southampton in the "James," 1635, from Salisbury, in Wilts; brought wife and 5 children, John, born 1620; Peter; James, 1629; Thomas, 1631; and Mary, probably older than the last two. He partook largely in the exertions of Gartan and his friends to obtain security for their worldly as well as spiritual rights, and went to negotiate in London in 1644 for Narragansett; died about 1658.

JOHN GREEN, of Sandwich, 1643, made his will 1660, died soon after.

JOHN GREEN, of New Haven, had John, 1651.

JOHN GREEN, of Kittery, 1652, Subm. to jurisdict. of Mass. that year.

JOHN GREEN, of Fairfield, 1648, made freeman 1662, had good estate.

JOHN GREEN, of Stamford, was representative 1668-71, and perhaps later.

JOHN GREEN, a freeman of Mass., 1654, may have been of Malden or Cambridge.

JOHN GREEN, of Sudbury, a captain in 1674.

JOHN GREEN, of Woburn, married, 1671, Sarah, daughter of John Bateman, of Boston, had Sarah, born 1672; Samuel, 1674; John, 1677; Hannah, 1679; and perhaps he removed.

JONAS GREEN, of New London, 1694, a shipmaster, married Jane, daughter of Alexander Lygan; had Samuel, and perhaps others.

JOSEPH GREEN, of Weymouth, may be he who came 1632, in the "James," with first John, of Charlestown; by wife Elizabeth, daughter of John Whitman, of the same; married 1657, had Joseph, born 1658; John, 1661; Elizabeth, 1664; Mary, 1667; and Zechary, 1671.

NICHOLAS GREEN, of York, died 1663, leaving widow Susanna, who married Jeremiah Shears, and children, whose names are not seen.

PERCIVAL GREEN, of Cambridge, brother, it is supposed, of Bartholomew the first, came in the "Susan and Ellen," 1635, aged 32, with wife Ellen, 32, and 2 servants; freeman 1636. Had John, born 1636; and Elizabeth, 1639; died 1639, when the town records make the name Perceiveall.

RALPH GREEN, of Boston, had John, born 1642; perhaps removed to Malden and there had a child baptized, 1654.

RICHARD GREEN, of Plymouth, came in the "Charity," 1622, for Weston's planta. at Weymouth, being bro.-in-l. of W.; died soon after landing.

RICHARD GREEN, of Boston, mariner, may possibly have arrived 1638, though was not admitted before 1654; by wife Rebecca had Rebecca, born 1665; and he died early in 1672.

THOMAS GREEN, of Malden, had wife Elizabeth, who died 1658, and he married 1659, Frances, widow of Richard Cook, who had been widow of Isaac Wheeler, but probably by former wife only had children. Thomas, the eldest; John, 1632; William, 1635; Henry, 1638; all probably born in Eng. Samuel, 1645; besides Elizabeth, Mary, perhaps both brought from England; Hannah; Martha; and Dorcas, 1653; and he died 1667.

THOMAS GREEN, of Malden, not son of the preceding, by wife Margaret, perhaps daughter of first Thomas Call, who died 1667; had Thomas, born 1653; John, 1659; Ephram; Mary; and Elizabeth, all minors, named in his will, 1674; he died same year; had married 1667. Elizabeth Webb for second wife, and may have been the freeman of 1670.

TOBIAS GREEN, of Hull, 1675.

WILLIAM GREEN, of Charlestown, 1640, freeman 1644, was of the part which became Woburn, by wife Hannah had Mary, born 1644; Hannah, 1647; John, 1649; William, 1651; and the father, died 1654.

WILLIAM GREEN, of Boston, mariner, had house and land there, 1659-77.

WILLIAM GREEN, of Providence, swore alleg., 1671.

WILLIAM GREEN, of Grotan, by wife Mary had William, born 1665; Ann, 1667; John, 1669; Eleazer, 1672; Elizabeth, 1680; and Hannah, 1683.

Note.—The stocks of Greens are very numerous. For further information see Savage's Gen. Dict., II, 299-307.

Arms: Argent, on a fess, azure, between three pellets, each charged with a lion's head, erased, of the first, a griffin, a passant, between two escalops, or.

Crest: A woodpecker, picking a shaft, couped, raguly and erect: all proper.

REFERENCES.

CONNECTICUT.—Caulkins' Hist. of New London, 471; Baker's Hist. of Montville, 234-9; Stiles' Hist. of Windsor, II, 345; Orcutt's Hist. of New Milford, 795; Schenck's Hist. of Fairfield, 375; Green Fam. of Bethlehem (1893), 100 pp.; Huntington's Stamford Settlers, 39.

MASSACHUSETTS.—Wyman's Charlestown, I, 435-43; Wall's Remin. of Worcester, 341-4; Stearn's Hist. of Ashburnham, 721-3; Malden Bi-Centennial, 234-7; Paige's Hist. of Cambridge, 567-9; Hudson's Hist. of Lexington, 79; Green Fam. of Malden, (1858), 80 pp.; Green Fam. of Cambridge, (1861), 5 pp.; (1876), 67 pp.; Draper's Hist. of Spencer, 200-2; Bond's Hist. of Watertown, 261; Hoyt's Salisbury Fams, 180-2.

NEW HAMPSHIRE.—Dearborn's Hist. of Salisbury, 601-5; Hill's Hist. of Mason, 202; Little's Hist. of Weare, 885-8; Runnel's Hist. of Sanbornton, H, 318; Secomb's Hist. of Amherst, 608-10; Bouton's Hist. of Concord, 664; Cogswell's Hist. of Henniker, 606.

OTHER PUBLICATIONS.—American Ancestry, II, 47; IV, 16, 43, 214; V, 132; VI, 109; VII, 55; X, 39; XI, 218; XII, 49; Cogswell's Gen., 221; Barlow Gen., 247-9; Vinton Mem., 15, 394-456; Whitmore's Copp's Hill Epitaphs; Green Fam. of Warwick, R. I., (1887), 71 pp.; Green's Todd and other Fams.; Hartwell Gen., (1887), 27 pp.; Meade's Old Churches of Va.; New Eng. Hist. and Gen. Reg., IV, 75; XV, 105-9; XVI, 12; Opdyke Gen., 214-7; Slaughter's Fry Gen.; Slaughter's Life of William Green; Spooner's Gen., I, 147-9.

GREENFIELD:—Samuel Greenfield, of Salem, a weaver, of Norwich, C. Norf'k, came in the "Mary Ann" from Yarmouth, 1637, aged 27, with wife Barbara, 35, two children, Mary, and Barbara, beside John Teed, a servant, 19; was a short time at Ipswich, but of Hampton, 1639, and of Exeter, 1645. He married second wife, Susan, widow of Humphrey Wise; had grant of land at Salem, but perhaps did not take it.

THOMAS GREENFIELD, of Sandwich, 1643.

REFERENCES:—Champion Gen., 48; Savage's Gen. Dict., II, 310.

GREENHILL:—Samuel Greenhill, came in 1634, with

wife and son Thomas, a baby; freeman 1635, went to Hartford next year, there died soon, leaving widow Rebecca and 2 children, Rebecca and Thomas.

GREENLAND:—Henry Greenland, of Newbury, born about 1628, a physician, there from 1662-75.

JOHN GREENLAND, of Charlestown, 1644, by wife Lydia, had John, born that year, who, or his father, was of Malden, freeman 1678.

GREENLEAF:—Edmund Greenleaf, of Newbury, a dyer, brought, 1635, wife Sarah, who was, it is said, named Dole, perhaps sister of Richard the first, and children Elizabeth; Judith, born 1628; Stephen, 1630; and Enoch; perhaps also Daniel; all born in England; was freeman, 1639; head of the militia under Gerrish, 1644; removed about 1650 to Boston, was admitted 1654, and died 1671.

JOHN GREENLEAF, of Boston, 1662, shipwright, married, 1666, Hannah, daughter of William Veazle, of Braintree; no mention of children.

REFERENCES.

MASSACHUSETTS.—Hudson's Hist. of Lexington, 79; Freeman's Hist. of Cape Cod, II, 214; Brook's Hist. of Medford, 515; Wyman's Charlestown Gens., I, 444.

NEW HAMPSHIRE.—Dearborn's Hist. of Salisbury, 620-2; Washington, N. H. Hist., 457-60; Little's Hist. of Weare, 88.

OTHER PUBLICATIONS.—Savage's Gen. Dict., II, 308; Amer. Ancestry, XI, 183; Greenleaf Fam. Chart, (1853); Greenleaf Gen. (1854), 116 pp.; (1896), 553 pp.; Preble Gen., 246-8.

GREENMAN, or GRINMAN:—David Greenman, early a proprietor of Taunton. Perhaps he was of Newport, freeman 1655.

EDWARD, or EDMUND GREENMAN, freeman, of Newport, 1655, Westerly, 1661, perhaps son of John, who was in R. I., 1638.

GREENOUGH:—William Greenough, of Boston, a sea captain, freeman 1669, married 1652, Elizabeth, daughter of Nicholas Upshall, had 11 children, yet no descendants of male line remain. His children were William, born 1656; William, again, 1658; Israel, 1660; Samuel, 1662, died soon; Dorothy, 1663; Elizabeth, 1664; Ann, 1669; Joseph, 1672; Mercy, 1673; Sarah, 1675; Sarah, again, 1676; all died young except Elizabeth and Mercy, who both married.

WILLIAM GREENOUGH, cousin of preceding, born in England, freeman 1673, married, 1660, Ruth, daughter of Thomas Swift, of Dorchester; had four sons and three daughters, Mary, born 1662; Ann, 1665; Luke, 1668; William, 1671; John, 1673; Samuel, 1676; and Consider, 1678. He married second wife, Elizabeth Rainsford, had Newman, 1681; Edward, called William on town records, 1684; Elizabeth, 1686; and Ann, 1688. This wife died 1688; and he married same year, Sarah Shove, of Chelmsford, and died 1693, aged 52.

REFERENCES:—Am. Ancestry, III, 23; V, 157; VI, 128; Sumner Gen. (1854), 63 pp.; N. E. Hist. and Gen. Reg., XVII, 167-9; Coffin's Hist. of Boscamen, N. H., 553; Whitman's Copp's Hill Epitaphs; Jackson's Hist. of Newton, Mass., 295.

GREENSLAD, Greenly, Greenslate, or Greensledge:—Thomas, of Scarborough, 1658, Salem, 1668.

REFERENCE:—Powers' Sangamon, 340.

GREENSMITH:—Nathaniel Greensmith, of Hartford, was probably husband then of the woman executed for a witch, 1662, "Supplying the first example of the dire delusion," in c. vii of Mather's Magn. VI, 67.

STEPHEN GREENSMITH, of Boston, 1636, arrived in colony, 1638, was more than once prosecuted for freedom of speech. [Winthrop, I, 314.]

THOMAS GREENSMITH, of Hartford, 1660.

GREENWAY, Grinaway, Grinoway, or Grinnoway:—Clement Greenway, of Saco, 1636.

JOHN GREENWAY, came probably in the "Mary and John," 1630, freeman next year; a millwright of much esteem, brought children, perhaps one or more, already married in England.

OLIVER GREENWAY, of Saco, 1636.

RICHARD GREENWAY, of Salem, 1637.

REFERENCE:—Meade's Old Fams. of Va.

GREENWOOD:—Samuel Greenwood, of Boston, 1670, who by wife Mary had Mary, born 1673, who died at 45 years unmarried; Samuel, 1677; Priscilla, 1680; Miles, 1682; Peter, 1685, died at 21 years, and Martha, 1688; probably died 1711, aged 65.

THOMAS GREENWOOD, of Cambridge, married, 1670, Hannah Ward, of Newton, had John; Thomas, born 1673. Harv. Col., 1690, min. of Rehoboth; and by second wife, Abigail, had James, born 1687; and William, 1689; was freeman 1690; and died 1693, aged 50.

Arms: Arg., a fess., between three mullets, pierced, of the field, in chief, and three ducks, passant, in base: all sa.

REFERENCES:—Am. Ancestry, III, 80; V, 121; VII, 86; VIII, 8; Savage's Gen. Dict., II, 311; Greenwood in Colonial service (1899), 11 pp.; Paige's Hist. of Cambridge, Mass., 590; Dunster Gen., 251; Butler's Hist. of Farmington, Me., 488-91.; New Eng. Hist. and Gen. Reg., XIV, 171; XV., 239; XXII, 303; Stearns' Hist. of Ashburnham, Mass., 723.

GREET:—John Greet, of Westfield; married daughter of Edmund Hart, had John, born 1671. Perhaps he came from Weymouth with Hart, but he removed soon.

GREGORY:—Elizaphal, of Windsor, 1641.

HENRY GREGORY, of Springfield, 1639, removed in few years to Stratford, and perhaps after 1650 removed again.

JOHN GREGORY, of New Haven, had Joseph, baptized 1646; and Thomas, 1648; removed 1653 to Norwalk, with all his children, probably John, Jachin, Thomas, Joseph and Sarah was representative several years after 1662, and living in 1688.

JOHN GREGORY, of Weymouth, by wife Hannah, had Hannah, born 1669.

JONAS GREGORY, of Ipswich, married 1653, Hannah Dow, and she died, 1672.

JUDAH GREGORY, of Springfield, married, 1643, Sarah Burt, and no more is known of him, but that his widow married Henry Wakeley.

Arms: A fir tree, growing out of a mount in base, vert, surmounted by a sword, in bend, ensigned by a royal crown, in the dexter chief paint: all proper. In the Sinister chief and dexter base, a lion's head, erased, az., langued, gu. Quartering Forbes: Az., three bears' heads, couped, arg., muzzled, gu.

REFERENCES:—Am. Ancestry, I, 33; Doyle's Gen., 237; Ransom Gen.; Slaughter's Fry Gen., 73; Fillow Gen., 79-83; Orcutt's Hist. of Stratford, Conn., 1208; New Eng. Hist. Gen. Reg., XXIII, 304-7; Savage's Gen. Dict., II, 312; Powers' Sangamon Co., Ills. Settlers, 342.

GRENNELL:—Matthew Grennell, of Portsmouth, R. I., among freeman of 1655. See GRINNELL.

GRICE, or GRISE:—Charles, of Braintree, freeman 1651, had wife Margery provided for in his will of 1661. A son in England is mentioned in this will.

JOSIAH GRICE, of Boston, brother of preceding, freeman, 1690, died next year.

SAMUEL GRICE, of Boston, freeman 1690.

GRIDLEY:—John Gridley, of Boston, 1681-3, was public executioner, and had a salary.

RICHARD GRIDLEY, of Boston, as early as 1631, by wife Grace had Mary, baptized 1632; Sarah, 1634; Hannah, 1636; Return, 1638; Believe, 1640; and Tremble, 1642; he was freeman 1634, and a captain.

THOMAS GRIDLEY, of Hartford, married, 1644; Mary Seymour, had Samuel, born 1647; and Thomas, 1650; removed to Farmington, thence, perhaps, to Northampton, then died.

REFERENCES:—Andrew's New Britain, 257-6; Kellog's White Gen., 84; Am. Ancestry, X, III; XII; Putnam's Hist. Mag., VI, 46-50.

GRIFFIN, or GRIFFING:—Hugh, of Sudbury, one of the first settlers, had wife Elizabeth, freeman 1645, died, 1690; names in his will children, Jonathan; Abigail, born 1640; Sarah, 1642; and Shemuel, 1645, perhaps the youngest; besides Hannah Upson, daughter of his wife Elizabeth, by former husband.

HUGH GRIFFIN, of Stratford, 1654, had John, born that year, and perhaps Thomas; a proprietor; with him, in 1685, may have been his sister.

HUMPHREY GRIFFIN, of Ipswich, 1641, who died 1665, had wife Elizabeth and children, John, Nathaniel, Samuel, Lydia, and Elizabeth.

JASPAR GRIFFIN, of Marblehead, 1674.

JOHN GRIFFIN, of Windsor, 1646, married, 1647, Ann Bancroft, had Hannah, born 1649; Mary, 1652; Sarah, 1654; John, 1656; Thomas, 1658; Abigail, 1660; Mindwell, 1663; Ruth, 1666; Ephraim, 1669, and Nathaniel, 1673; was one of the first settlers at Simsbury, where he

had grant of land as reward for his introduction of manufacture of pitch and tar; representative several years, died, 1681.

JOHN GRIFFIN, of Boston, a caulker, married, 1655, Susanna Price, had Elizabeth, born 1656; Sarah, 1659; Mary, 1662; Susanna, 1664; and Remember, 1667; he was living 1677.

MATTHEW GRIFFIN, of Saybrook, 1645, may have removed to Charlestown, there married, 1654, Hannah Cutter; had Matthew, born 1656, who died 1691; Hannah, 1657; Samuel, 1659; Elizabeth, baptized 1662; Rebecca, 1664; Richard, 1666; John, 1668; Jonathan, 1670; and Sarah, 1672.

NATHANIEL GRIFFIN, of Salisbury, married, 1671, Elizabeth Ring, of Andover, had Hannah, born 1676; Elizabeth, 1682; Maria, 1686; and Judith, 1689.

PHILIP GRIFFIN, of Salisbury, by wife Ann had Hannah, born 1653; Mary, 1655; and John, 1656; and was killed by lightning.

RICHARD GRIFFIN, of Concord, 1635, freeman 1638, representative 1639 and 40, married probably as second or third wife, 1660, widow Mary Harrod, and died the following year, aged 70 years.

RICHARD GRIFFIN, of Roxbury, had wife Mary, and children, then baptized Mary, Elizabeth and Joseph, all in 1657; Abigail, 1659; Esther, 1661; Samuel, 1663; and Hannah, 1666; was freeman, 1657; died about 1667.

SAMUEL GRIFFIN, of Charlestown, by wife Priscilla had Samuel, baptized 1687, the same day with his mother; John, 1689; Caleb, 1692; Hannah, 1693; Priscilla, 1696; and Sarah, 1699.

THOMAS GRIFFIN, of New London, 1651, removed 1654 to Stonington, died 1661, leaving Thomas and perhaps other children.

REFERENCES.

MASSACHUSETTS.—Babson's Hist. of Gloucester, 239; Hodgman's Hist. of Westfield, 450; Draper's Hist. of Spencer, 204; Wyman's Charlestown, I, 445-7.

NEW HAMPSHIRE.—Norton's Hist. of Fitzwilliam, 589; Chase's Hist. of Chester, 536; Morrison's Hist. of Windham, 554; Cogswell's Nottingham, 389.

OTHER PUBLICATIONS.—Am. Anecstry, I, 34; II, 47; IV, 165; V, 153; VI, 112; VIII, 165, 171; Chandler Gen., 95-8; Huntington Gen. (1885), 337; Nash Gen., 65. (Griffing) Am. Ancestry, VIII, 200; X, 33; Griffing Gen., (1881), 194 pp.

GRIFFITH:—Henry Griffith, of Cambridge, died, 1639.

JOSHUA GRIFFITH, of Boston, came here in the Hopewell, Captain Bundocke, from London, 1635, aged 42, with wife Alice, 42; and children Thomas, 15; William, 14; Elizabeth, 10; Mary, 6; and James, 2. Had here Elizabeth again, born 1636; Sarah 1637, and William also, who died 1638; second Elizabeth died 1640. He died 1660.

HUMPHREY GRIFFITH, of Braintree, died 1657, leaving widow Grizzell, who had been widow of Thomas Jewell.

STEPHEN GRIFFITH, of Marblehead 1674.

THOMAS GRIFFITH, of Rosbury 1639, brought wife Mary who died that year, and sons Joseph and John; married, 1640, Mary Green, and he died 1646, after long illness.

WILLIAM GRIFFITH, of Boston, cooper, freeman 1672; married daughter of John Hannaford.

WILLIAM GRIFFITH, married Thankwell, daughter of Richard Baker, of Dorchester.

REFERENCES:—Savage's Gen. Dict., II, 314; Amer. Ancestry, VI, 120; VIII, 121; Freeman's Hist. of Cape Cod, Mass., II, 524; Thomas Gen. (1884), 67; Williams' Hist. of Danbury, Vt., 150-2; Dow's Hist. of Hampton, N. H., 742; Futhey's Hist of Chester Co., Pa., 573; Waldo's Hist. of Tolland, Ct., 75-7; Daniel's Hist. of Oxford, Mass., 525.

GRIGSON, or GREGSON:—Thomas Grigson, of New Haven, came from London to Boston 1637, in company with Gov. Eaton and John Davenport, was one of the chief men, an active merchant, and an assistant of the colony, first treasurer, and first Commissioner for the Union with other N. E. colony; lived on East Side of Harbor; sailed for London 1646, with Lamberton and "divers other godly persons," of whom nothing was ever heard, the vessel having no doubt foundered. He left widow Jane, who lived to 1702, one son, Richard, and 8 daughters; Mary, baptized 1640; Phebe, 1643; Abigail, 1645; Ann, who married Stephen Daniels; Susanna, who married 1661, Abraham Cruttenden; Sarah, who married 1667, John Gilbert, but Dodd calls her wife of Whitehead; Phebe was second wife, 1673, of Rev. John Whiting, of Hartford; and next, of Rev. John Russell, of Hadley.

GRIHME, or GRIHMES:—Henry Grihme, of Hartford, 1661, had good estate, died 1684, leaving Benjamin, then aged 22; John, died about 1720; Joseph, 17; Mary, 16; Sarah, 13; Elizabeth, 10; Susanna, 7; and Rebecca, 4. This name, in the second generation, perhaps from no desire of concealment, became Graham. Yet Benjamin, who married 1684, Abigail Humphrey, is called where her interment is recorded, 1097, Grimes.

GRIMES:—Samuel Grimes, of Boston, a pewterer, by widow Francis, had Mary, born 1639; freeman 1642; spelled in church records Graine, and in town records of Boston Greames. He removed to Plymouth; there, by wife Ann, had Susanne, born 1657.

WILLIAM GRIMES, of Greenwich, died 1671, without family; gave his property to the town.

REFERENCES:—Amer. Ancestry, X. 9; Hudson's Hist. of Lexington, Mass., 80; Malley Chart, Montgomery Gen. (1897), 35-48; Read's Hist. of Swanzey, N. H.,

350; Hayward's Hist. of Gilsum, 316; Meade's Old Churches of Va., II, 370; Bemis' Hist. of Marlboro, N. H., 515.

GRIMSTONE, or GRIMSTED:—Margaret Grimstone, a widow, died at Boston, 1650.

GRINNELL:—Daniel Grinnell, of Portsmouth, R. I.

MATTHEW GRINNELL, of R. I., 1638, received as a freeman and lived at Portsmouth 1655.

GRISWOLD:—Edward Griswold, of Windsor, born at Kenilworth, in Warwickshire, 1607, as tradition says, came, it is always said, with Rev. Ephraim Huit, though it is certainly wrong, for his son George testified that he was born 1638, and "lived in his youthful years" with his father and uncle at Kenilworth, Eng. Before coming to Windsor he had Francis, George, John and Sarah, probably all born in England, and he had, at Windsor, Ann, born 1642, in which year John died there; Mary, 1644; Deborah, 1646; Joseph, 1648; Samuel, 1649; John, again, 1652; removed about 1664 to Killingworth. He was representative 1658-61 for W. and after for K. His son Francis and brother Matthew, as well as himself, were representatives in one court.

FRANCIS GRISWOLD, of Cambridge, 1639, perhaps brother of the preceding, perhaps cousin by wife Mary, had Mary, born 1639; Hannah, 1643, died at 2 mos., and Hannah, again, 1645; was freeman 1645, lived at Charlestown 1649, and died soon.

MATTHEW GRISWOLD, of Saybrook, younger brother of Edward, and perhaps of first Francis, came from Warwickshire, Kenilworth being his native place, and possibly with Rev. Ephraim Huit, married Ann, daughter of first Henry Wolcott, had two sons and three daughters, but dates of birth are unknown, except that Matthew, perhaps not the eldest, was born 1653; was representative of S. often, and of Lyme after the division of the old town; calls himself 66 years old in 1684, and died 1699; his widow then 79.

MICHAEL GRISWOLD, of Wethersfield, had Thomas, born 1646; Esther, 1648; Mary, 1650; Michael, 1652, probably died young; Abigail, 1655; Isaac, 1658; Jacob, 1660; Sarah, 1662, and Michael, again, 1667.

REFERENCES.

CONNECTICUT:—Hibbard's Hist. of Goshen, Ct., 455-9; Cathren's Hist. of Woodbury, Ct., II, 1497-9; Griswold Family of Conn. (1884), 85 pages; Caulkin's Hist. of Norwich, Ct., 176; Andrew's Hist. of New Britain, Ct., 142.

OTHER PUBLICATIONS:—Strong Gen., 1371-4; Savage's Gen. Dict., II, 316-8; Griswold Ancestry (1872), 1 sheet; Griswold Fam. of Vt. (1880), 23 pp.; Gregar's White Gen.; Amer. Ancestry, I, 34; II, 47; IV, 213; V. 63; VII, 14, 38; VIII, 75; Boyd's Hist. of Conesus, N. Y., 156; Clarke's Old King Wm. Co., Va., Families; Lane Gen. (1899), 17; Perkins' Old Houses of Norwich, Ct., 468.

ARMS:—Arg., a fess, gu., between two greyhounds, courant, sa., within a bourdure, or, as a difference.

MOTTO:—Fortiter et celeriter.

GROOM:—Nicholas Groom, of Massachusetts, died 1651, and Henry G. (it is not known whether latter was father, son or brother), had admin. of his estate in Middlesex Co.

SAMUEL GROOM, of Salisbury, 1650, a mariner, in the list of inhabs. dignified with prefix of Mr., went home to London before 1658. He may seem to be that Quaker who published in 1676, "A Glass for the People of N. E.," which in a note to his history, I, 72, Hutchinson ascribed to Gorton.

REFERENCES:—Savage's Gen. Dict., 2, 318; Hanson's Old Kent, Md., 180-3.

GROSSE:—Clement Grosse, of Boston, son of Isaac, born in England, married before 1649; had Isaac, who was a cordwainer; by wife Mary had Edmund, born 1656, and Elizabeth, 1658; William, 1665; Edmund, again, 1669, and Ann, 1671.

EDMUND GROSSE, of Boston, elder brother of preceding mariner, by wife Catharine, had Isaac, born 1642; Susanna, 1644; perhaps Thomas; Hannah; Lydia, baptized 1650; by wife Ann had Mary, born 1652; Elizabeth, 1654; John, 1655. He died same year.

SIMON GROSSE, of Hingham, married, 1675, Mary Bond, had Simon, born 1676; Thomas, 1678; John, 1681; Josiah, 1683; Micah, 1686; Alice, 1689, and Abigail, 1692. Descendants are known at Scituate.

REFERENCES:—Savage's Gen. Dict., II, 318; Wismer Gen., 9; Amer. Ancestry, X, 67; Barry's Hist. of Hanover, Mass., 314; Sahler and Gross Gen. (1895), 38 pp.

GROSVENQR:—John Grosvenor, of Roxbury, came as family tradition tells from County Chester; by wife Esther had William, born 1673, Harvard College, 1693; Susanna, 1681; a child, 1683, died soon; Ebenezer, 1684; Thomas, 1687, died soon; and Joseph, 1689, and he died 1691. The name is Norman, meaning great hunter, and the English peerage is rich with it.

REFERENCES:—Davis Gen., 147; Clarke Family (1866), 39; Whitman Gen., 105-7; Thurston Gen. (1892), 458-60; Savage's Gen. Dict., II, 319.

GROTH (if such a name be possible, or misprinted, for Growth or Grath).

JOHN GROTH, of Salisbury, married, 1674, Elizabeth, daughter probably of John Eaton; had Elizabeth, born 1674; was adm. to practice medicine, 1679, at Hampton. Perhaps he was a German and called doctor; may have died early, and William Hutchins perhaps married his widow, 1685.

GROUT:—John Grout, of Watertown; by wife Mary had John, born 1641, and Mary, 1643; was at Sudbury, 1643, freeman 1665, selectman, several years town clerk and a captain; was 70 years old in 1689; died 1697.

WILLIAM GROUT, of Charlestown, 1664; had wife Sarah.

REFERENCES:—Amer. Ancestry, II, 48; Savage's Gen. Dict., II, 319; Grout Gen. (1858), 86 pp.; Morse's, Sherborn, Mass., Settlers, 95; Wall's Reminis. of Worcester, Mass., 108; Pierce's Hist. of Grafton, Mass., 495; Saunderson's Charlestown, N. H., 375-81; Warren and Clarke Gen., 77-84; Barry's Hist. of Framingham, Mass., 267.

GROVE:—Edward Grove, of Salem, was of Boston, a soldier in Col. Service at the fort, 1636, died 1686; in his will names wife Elizabeth and only child, Mary, wife of William Hirst, of Salem, and her son Grove.

GROVER:—Andrew Grover, of Malden, married, 1674, Hannah Hills.

EDMUND GROVER, of Salem, 1633; had Naomi, Mary and Lydia, all baptized 1646, and Deborah, 1648; lived on Beverly Side; perhaps his wife was Margaret, and he may have had other children; was freeman 1678, and died 1683, aged 82.

JOHN GROVER, of Boston, 1640; by wife Elizabeth, had John, born 1641; Elizabeth, and Lydia, 1644; removed to Boston, the part called Rumney Marsh; died 1686, aged 80.

SAMUEL GROVER, of whom it is only known that he came from London, aged 16, in 1635, by the Truelove.

SIMON GROVER, of Malden; freeman 1690; had been a soldier in Philip's War, and was in the famous Falls fight; by wife Sarah, had Mary, born 1687, and Simon, 1691; he died 1717, aged about 63 years.

STEPHEN GROVER, of Charlestown, or Malden, 1658; was a soldier at Hadley in 1676; by wife Sarah, had Hannah, born 1686, and John, 1689.

THOMAS GROVER, of Charlestown, Malden Side; by wife Elizabeth, had Lazarus, born 1642; Elizabeth, 1652; Thomas, 1653; John, 1656, died young; Grace, 1658; and he died 1661.

REFERENCES:—Savage's Gen. Dict., II, 320; Wakefield Gen., 191; Norton's Hist. of Fitzwilliam, N. H., 589-91; Ely Gen., 319; Babson's Gen., 273; Daniel's Hist. of Oxford, Mass., 526.

GROVES:—John Groves, of Kittery; married Martha, daughter of Michael Mitton; removed to Little Compton.

MATTHEW GROVES, a soldier in Philip's War on Connecticut River.

PHILIP GROVES, of Hartford, early settler; was representative 1642 and often after, but for Stratford, whither he removed before 1650, was rul. elder; died 1676; provides in will for wife Ann and grandchildren, Nathaniel, Hannah, Sarah and Ruth. In codicil gives to his daughter Elizabeth Porter, mother of above children, and to her son John.

REFERENCES:—Hyde's Brimfield, Mass., 407; Savage's Gen. Dict., II, 321.

GRAW:—John Graw, of Ipswich; married, 1669, Hannah, daughter of Robert Lord, of the same; had John, born next year, died soon; Samuel, 1671; John, again, 1673; Joseph, 1677; Hannah, 1680; Nathaniel, 1683; Thomas, 1685, and William, 1690; and died 1727.

REFERENCES:—Norton's Hist. of Fitzwilliam, N. H., 590; Savage's Gen. Dict., II, 321; Daniel's Oxford, Mass., 526.

GRUBB:—Gabriel Grubb, Isle of Shoals, 1677, or earlier, we may suppose, for he died about that year.

THOMAS GRUBB, of Boston, 1633, leather dresser, numbered 160, when he and wife Ann united with the ch., freeman 1634; had daughter Abiah, baptized 1637, and died that night; John, born 1638; Samuel, 1641; John, again, died 1644; Elizabeth, baptized 1644, died soon; Heman, baptized 1646, died soon. He was of some consequence, constable in 1646. Probably outlived all of his children.

REFERENCES:—Amer. Ancestry, IV, 125; IX, 46; Power's Sangamon Co., Ill., Settlers, 345; Wyman's Charlestown, Mass., Gens. I, 449; Grubb Gen. (1893), 12 pp.

GRUMAN, GRUMMAN, or GROWMAN:—John Gruman, of Fairfield; freeman 1664; had good estate; married Sarah, daughter of Michael Try, with whom he had gained it. Lived long after 1670, and died without children, although he had had some.

REFERENCES:—Schenck's Fairfield, Ct., 375; Savage's Gen. Dict., II, 321.

GRUMWELL:—John Grumwell, a freeman of Conn., 1658, of whom more is unknown.

GRUNDY:—Robert Grundy, of Roxbury; had there baptized Elizabeth, 1679; John, 1681; Robert, 1683; Edmund, 1685, and Rebecca, 1687.

GUERNSEY:—James Guernsey, of Suffield; married, 1693, Mary, widow of Joseph Eastman, daughter of Hon. Peter Tilton; had many quarrels with his wife, but probably no children by her.

JOSEPH GUERNSEY, of Milford, 1640, or by Lambert, 1673.

REFERENCES:—Kasson Gen., 29-31; Anderson's Waterbury, 58; Bronson's Hist. of Waterbury, Ct., 491.

GUILD:—John Guild, of Dedham, weaver; perhaps freeman 1643; spelt Guile. Died 1682; had also estate in Wrentham and Medfield; left children, Samuel, John and Elizabeth.

REFERENCES:—Daniel's Hist. of Oxford, Mass., 526; Aldrich's Walpole, N. H., 269; Amer. Ancestry, VI, 39, 56, 152, 155, 187; Guild Fam. of Dedham (1867), 132 pp; Guild Fam. of W. Dedham (1873), 21 pp.; Guild Gen. (1887), 381 pp.; Guild ancestry (1891), 42 pp; Washington, N. H., Hist., 461.

GUILE:—Abraham Guile, of Watertown; freeman 1682. See Gile.

REFERENCE:—Guild Gen., 221-318.

GULL:—William Gull, of Wethersfield, 1649; married, after 1654, Elizabeth, widow of Nathaniel Foote, daughter of Lieut. Samuel Smith; had no sons but several daughters, certainly Mary and Ann, before removing to Hadley in 1663; there had Esther, born 1665, and Mercy, 1668; was freeman 1673.

GULLIFORD, GULLIFER or GULLIVER:—Anthony Gulliford, of Dorchester, 1656; lived in that part which is now Milton; freeman 1666; had wife Elinor, daughter of Stephen Kingsley, and many children, of whom we know the dates of but few. Stephen; Samuel, who died, 1676, and Stephen admin. his estate; Lydia; Jonathan, born 1659; a man of some distinction and representative for Milton; Nathaniel; Hannah; Mary, and Elizabeth. He died 1706, aged 87.

REFERENCES:—Hayward's Hist. of Hancock, N. H., 624; Draper's Hist. of Spencer, Mass., 203; Adams' Fairhaven, 381-4; Temple's N. Brookfield; Walker Gen., 77; Winsor's Hist. of Duxbury, Mass., 249.

GULLY:—Jacob Gully, of Boston; by wife Mercy had Jacob, born 1677, and Mary, 1680; and no more is known.

GULTHORP:—Ralph Gulthorp, of Boston; adm. inhab., 1643.

GUNLITHE:—Henry Gunlithe, of Dorchester. (See Cunliffe.)

GUNN:—Jasper Gunn, of Roxbury, came in the Defence, 1635, aged 29, with Ann, 25, perhaps his wife, though the church record does not mention her; perhaps his sister; was freeman 1636. At London Custom House name was written Goun. Perhaps he visited Milford, 1639; after ten years he removed to Hartford; there was physician some time, and after 1659 removed to Milford; died 1670, leaving one daughter, Mehitable Fenn; four sons, Jobanna, Abel, Daniel and Samuel.

THOMAS GUNN, of Dorchester; freeman 1635; removed to Windsor; had Elizabeth, who died 1640; Elizabeth, again, 1640, died young; Deborah, 1642; Mehitable, 1644, and John, 1647; removed to Westfield; there his wife died, 1678, and he died 1681.

REFERENCES:—Savage's Gen. Dict., II, 323; Stiles' Hist. of Windsor, Ct., II, 362; Baker Gen. (1867), 52-4; Orcutt's Hist. of Derby, Ct., 723; Montague Gen., 380-7, 513-7; Hayward's Hist. of Gilsum, N. H., 319; Anderson's Waterbury, Ct., I, 59; Read's Hist. of Swanzey, N. H., 352.

GUNNISON, or GULLISON:—Hugh Gunnison, of Boston, 1634; on adm. to ch. next year is titled "Serv. to our br. Richard Bellingham;" freeman 1636; by wife Elizabeth, who died 1646, had Sarah, born 1638; Elizabeth, 1640, and Deborah, 1642; besides two sons, Joseph and Elihu. In 1646 he was of artillery comp.; in 1651, removed to Kittery; was representative for Wells in 1654. It is presumed his son Elihu was a proprietor of Falmouth in 1689, when name appears Gullison; also, elsewhere, Gallison.

REFERENCES:—Amer. Ancestry, VI, 67; Savage's Gen. Dict., II, 324; Cutt's Gen., 182-4; Gunnison Gen. (1880), 222 pp.

GUNTER:—Lester Gunter, a youth of 13; emb. at London, 1635, for N. E. in the Truelove.

GUPPIE, GUPPY, or GUPPEY:—John, of Weymouth; freeman 1653; removed to Charlestown, where, in 1678, was "goodman Guppy," who had wife Elizabeth. He had been of Salem, there had wife Abigail, and by her had Abigail, born 1672, and Elizabeth, 1675; but perhaps this John was son of Reuben, and not the Weymouth man.

REUBEN GUPPY, of Salem, 1648; by wife Ellen, had John, born that year, and Reuben, 1651; was living in 1684, in 85th year.

ROBERT GUPPY, of Salem, 1647. The name is said to be found also at Dover.

GURLEY:—William Gurley, of Boston, 1653; but no record of birth, death, marriage or property.

WILLIAM GURLEY, of Northampton, 1679; brought up in family of Rev. Solomon Stoddard, but most indistinct is the tradition that he was born about 1665, though neither parent nor other relat. is known, and was brought from Scotland; married, 1684, Esther Ingersoll; had Samuel, born 1686; and was drowned next year. His widow married Benoni Jones, who, with two of her children, were killed in the assault on Northampton, 1704, when she was taken, carried to Canada by the Indians; there died.

REFERENCES:—Savage's Gen. Dict., II, 324; Walworth's Hyde Gen., 886; Amer. Ancestry, III, 24; Gurley Gen. (1897), 285 pp.

GURNALL:—John Gurnall, of Dorchester. See *Garnell*.

GURNEY:—Edward Gurney, of Cambridge, 1636.

JOHN GURNEY, of Braintree, an early inhab.; may be that apprent. of John Newgate; born 1615; mentioned by Winthrop, II, 345. He died 1663. His wife, 1664.

JOHN GURNEY, of Welmouth; by wife Elizabeth had Elizabeth, born 1689.

RICHARD GURNEY, of Weymouth; by wife Rebecca, daughter probably of John Taylor, first of same, had Joseph, born 1665, and Mary, 1667; freeman 1681.

REFERENCES:—Poole Gen., 83; Barry's Hanover, Mass., 315; Hobart's Hist. of Abington, Mass., 383-6; Lapham's Hist of Norway, Me., 515.

GUSTIN:—John Gustin, of Falmouth. See Augustine.

REFERENCES:—Maine Hist. and Gen. Recorder, VI, 353-5; Hubbard's Stanstead, Canada, 225.

GUTCH:—Robert Gutch, of Salem, 1638, had bapt. these: John, 1641; Patience, 1643; Lydia, 1645; Magdalen, 1647; Elizabeth, 1648; Deborah, 1652; and Sarah, 1654; was freeman 1642; removed to the E. beyond Casco, bt. from Indians land near mouth of Kennebec River. This may be the same name as Gouch, Gooch or Gouge, in sound nearly alike.

GUTTERIDGE:—See Goodridge.

GUTTERSON:—John Gutterson, of Andover, married, 1689, Abigail Buckmaster, had Abigail, who died 1694; and Samuel, died 1700.

WILLIAM GUTTERSON, of Ipswich, 1648, died 1666; had William, born 1658, died young; Mary 1660; John 1662; and Sarah 1665.

REFERENCES:—Cogswell's Henniker, 607; Little's Hist. of Weare, N. H., 889.

GUY:—Henry Guy, of Charlestown, 1652, merchant.

JOHN GUY, of Casco, 1663-75; a tenant of Robert Jordan. See Willis, I, 94, 141; and Gen. Reg., V, 264.

NICHOLAS GUY, of Watertown, came in the Confidence of London, 1638, aged 50, with wife, Jane, 30; daughter Mary, and two servants, from Upton, in Hants; emb. at Southampton, was deacon, freeman 1639; died 1659; his widow lived to 1669.

REFERENCES:—Savage's Gen. Dict., II, 325; Shourd's Fenwick's Colony, N. J., 80; Goodwin's Foote Gen., 185; Temple's Hist. of N. Crookfield, Mass., 609.

GWIN:—John Gwin, of Charlestown, 1646.

THOMAS GWIN, of Boston, 1660, married Elizabeth, daughter of Benjamin Gillam, who died 1669, leaving two children.

REFERENCE:—Hayden's Va. Gens., 469.

GYLES:—Edward and Matthew, assigned to Giles.

THOMAS GYLES, of Salem, had daughter Hannah, married 1650, Thomas Very of Gloucester.

THOMAS GYLES, an active promoter of settlement at Kennebec, called Pejepscat, now Brunswick, 1666, may have been son of the preceding, was killed at Pemaquid by the Indians, 1689; had besides Samuel, his youngest,

then absent, three sons. James, the third, then 14, was taken at the same time, and escaped three years after; was retaken, and tortured to death. Thomas, the eldest, escaped, and John escaped with life, but with ten years' captivity; and many years later this last printed a memoir of his father in 1736. Thomas' widow was taken captive and never heard of again. The two daughters, Mary and Margaret, were taken captive; but were redeemed and afterward in Boston.

REFERENCES:—Savage's Gen. Dict., II, 325-6; Whitmore's Copps Hill Epitaphs; Giles Memorial, 101-51.

HABBERFIELD:—William Habberfield, of Boston, 1683, clothier, had wife Mary, and we suppose was of Lynn, the freeman 1691, with Mr. before his surname, possibly meant to supply William.

HACK:—William Hack, of Taunton, had William, born at Plymouth 1663, by wife Mary.

REFERENCES:—Ball's Hist. of Lake Co., Ind., 417; Hayden's Virginia Gens., 243; N. E. Hist., and Gen. Reg., XLVII, 453-6.

HACKER:—George Hacker, of Salem, perhaps brother of William, married 1672, Bethia Meacham, perhaps daughter of Jeremiah, had Bethia, born 1673, died soon; Bethia, again, 1675; George 1678; and Sarah 1681; was made prison-keeper, 1698.

WILLIAM HACKER, of Lynn, 1643. Possibly this may be the same as Hackett or Harker. At Southampton, L. I., which was settled chiefly from Lynn, was the name of Hacker; but Farmer suggests that this might be Hagar.

REFERENCES:—Morris' Gen. (1898), 1013; Austin's Allied Fams., 116-9.

HACKERBERRY:—Thomas Hackerberry, one of the soldiers of Moseley's Comp., 1675, marched to Narragansett.

HACKETT:—Jabez Hackett, of Lynn 1644, removed to Taunton, there had John, 1654; Jabesh 1656; Mary 1660; Sarah 1661; Samuel 1664; and Hannah 1667.

JOHN HACKETT, of Boston, by wife Rebecca had Mary, born 1689.

WILLIAM HACKETT, of Dover, 1657, at Exeter had Mary, born 1665, when perhaps his wife died; was of Amesbury, 1666, mariner; married 1667, Sarah, daughter probably of Thomas Barnard of Salisbury, had at S., Sarah, born 1668; Ephraim, 1680; William 1683; Judah 1685; Ebenezer 1687; besides, perhaps Rebecca (earlier than Ephraim), who married Jonathan Whiting of Portsmouth; and these four sons may have been son of another. Perhaps he came from Lynn.

REFERENCES:—Savage's Gen. Dict., II, 326; Sinclair Gen. (1896), 131; Paxton's Marshall Gen.; Hoyt's Salisbury, 190.

HACKFORD:—William Hackford, of Salem 1637. Probably he soon removed.

HACKLINTON, or HACKLETON:—Francis Hacklinton, of Northampton, 1661, a brickmaker, unmarried; perhaps removed next year to Hartford, and married Joanna, daughter of Samuel Wakeman.

HACKWELL:—John Hackwell, came in the Increase, 1635, aged 18; but his residence is not known.

HADAWAY:—John Hadaway, of Barnstable. See Hathaway, the modern name.

HADBORNE:—George Hadborne, from Stepney, near London, a glover, came in the Abigail, 1635, aged 43; with wife Ann, 46; and children Rebecca, 10; Ann, 4; and two servants; where he settled down has not been found.

HADDEN, or HADDON:—Jared, Jerad, Garrett, or Gerard Hadden, of Cambridge, 1632, came probably in the fleet with Winthrop, for he is among the first hundred members of the Boston ch. adm., prior to any second arrival; freeman 1634, a propriet. of Salisbury, 1640; had wife Margaret, and at S., by her, Sarah, born 1640; was living at S., 1663; his wife died 1673.

GEORGE HADDEN, of Cambridge, or at least Harvard Coll., 1647, may have been son of the preceding; unknown afterward. A Catharine Hadden is witness to the will of Thomas Bittlestone at C., and may have been first wife or even daughter of Jared.

HADLEY:—George Hadley, of Ipswich, 1639, living in 1678.

GEORGE HADLEY, of Rowley, 1668, was perhaps the same or son of preceding.

REFERENCES:—Wyman's Charlestown, Mass. Gens., I, 451; Cochrane's Hist. of Francestown, N. H., 739; Hoyt's Salisbury, Mass., Fams., 191; Haywood's Hist. of Hancock, N. H., 625-32; Little's Hist. of Weare, N. H., 890-3; Stearn's Hist. of Ashburnham, Mass., 725.

HADLOCK:—James Hadlock of Roxbury, married 1669, Sarah Draper, had Sarah, born 1670, removed to Salem, there had in 1678, wife Rebecca, daughter probably of Richard Hutchinson; son James, and John, daughters Mary, Hannah, Sarah and Rebecca. But possibly he had some of these by another wife.

JOHN HADLOCK, of Concord, died 1675.

NATHANIEL HADLOCK, of Charlestown, 1643, freeman 1646, after 1658 removed to Lancaster; by wife Mary had Mary, born 1641; and Nathaniel, 1643.

NATHANIEL HADLOCK, perhaps son of the preceding, suffra. 1668 with Quakers, removed to Gloucester, married 1673, Remember Jones, had John, born 1682.

REFERENCES:—Hoyt's Salisbury, Mass. Fams., 192; Herrick Gen. (1885), 167; Babson's Gloucester, 97.

HADWELL:—William Hadwell, a passenger in the Arabella, from London 1671, of whom no more is known.

HAFFELL, or HAFFIELD:—Richard Haffell, of Ipswich, came 1635, in the Planter, aged 54, with wife Martha, 42; and children, Mary, 17; Sarah, 14; Martha, 8; Rachel, 6; and Ruth, 3.

HAFFUT:—William Haffut, given by Mr. Coffin in Geneal. Reg., VI, 341, as aged 48, in 1668, though residence is not shown.

HAGAR, or AGAR:—John Hagar, of Watertown, perhaps son of the first William, a soldier in brave Capt. Davenport's comp. Killed in the great Narragansett battle, 1675.

WILLIAM HAGAR, of Watertown, probably came in the fleet with Winthrop; freeman 1631; nothing more is heard of him.

WILLIAM HAGAR, perhaps son of the preceding, born in England, married, 1645, Mary Bemis, had Mary, born 1645; Ruhamah and Samuel, twins, 1647; Hannah 1649; Sarah 1651; Susanna; William 1659; Rebecca 1661; Abigail and Mehitable; he died 1684; his wife, 1695.

REFERENCES:—Savage's Gen. Dict., II, 328; Ward's Hist. of Shrewsbury, Mass., 327; Child's Gen., 560-76; Barry's Framingham, 268; Craft's Hist. of Whately, Mass., 503-5.

HAGBORNE, or HACKBORNE:—Abraham Hagborne, of Boston, Shoemaker, by wife, Elizabeth, had Eliz.; Sarah, born 1639; Isaac bapt. 1642; and Joseph 1652; freeman 1645, when in Col. Rec. The spelling is Hackburne; he left good estate.

HAGGETT:—Henry Haggett, of Salem, 1642, freeman 1670, probably of Wenham, at his death 1676, in 83rd year, leaving widow, and children, Henry, Moses, Mary, Deliverance and Hannah; had also probably Abigail.

HAILSTONE:—William Hailstone, of Taunton, 1640, an original proprietor, bought in 1646 an estate at Boston; was living 1675. His daughter Margaret married, 1659, Samuel Fletcher of Chelmsford.

HAIMES:—John Haimes, of Boston, by wife Mary had Catharine, bapt. 1682.

HAINES:—See Haynes.

HALBRIDGE, HALBICH, HOLBRIDGE, or HOLBICH:—Arthur, of Boston, 1635, removed to New Haven, said to have come 1638; certainly there, June, 1639; died 1648. His widow received assist. by public contribut.; her children Mercy and John were bapt., 1650.

HALE:—Gershom Hale, of Springfield, had several children before going thither, and one born 1698, when his wife Ann died there; little else is known of him, except that a son and daughter were married 1708.

ROBERT HALE, came probably in fleet with Winthrop, among earliest members of Boston ch.; freeman 1634. artillery comp. 1644, ensign, and selectman 11 years; died 1659. He had, besides John, born 1636, Mary, 1639; Zachary 1641, died soon; Samuel 1644; and Joanna.

SAMUEL HALE, of Hartford, 1640, one of the first propriet. at Norwalk, 1654, had first been at Wethersfield 1642, and with his brother Thomas served in the Pequot War, 1637; was rep. for N., 1657-'8 and '60; went back to Wethersfield and lived in that part which is now Glastonbury; in his will, children named are, Samuel, John, Thomas, Ebenezer, Mary, Rebecca, and Dorothy.

THOMAS HALE, of Roxbury, brother of preceding; a single man, freeman 1634, removed soon after to Hartford, returned for short time, married 1640, Jane Lord, went among first settlers to Norwalk, 1654; not long after removed, and perhaps died at Charlestown.

THOMAS HALE, of Newbury, a glover, came in 1635, with wife Thomasin, and son Thomas, born 1633; freeman 1638; had here John, born 1636, and Samuel; lived some years at Haverhill, where he was selectman; in 1659, perhaps at Salem; but returned to Newbury and died 1682, aged 78; his widow next month.

THOMAS HALE, of Saco, 1653, then made freeman of Mass.

THOMAS HALE, of Charlestown, married 1659, Mary Nash, daughter of William, had John, bapt. 1665; and freeman, 1671; may be same as Thomas of Roxbury.

THOMAS HALE, of Hadley, married Priscilla, daughter of William Markham, had Martha, born 1676; Thomas 1678; John 1680; Samuel 1683, died young; Priscilla 1685; William 1687; and Joseph 1691; removed to Enfield, then had Samuel, again; and died about 1725.

TIMOTHY HALE, of Windsor, married 1663, Sarah, daughter of Thomas Barber, had Sarah, born 1665; Timothy, 1667; John 1670; Thomas 1672; Samuel 1674; Vine, a daughter, 1675, died young, and Josiah 1678; removed to Suffield, had Joanna, 1680, died 1689.

WILLIAM HALE, of Billerica, died 1668, leaving widow Ann.

ARMS:—Gu., three arrows, or, feathered and barbed, arg.

REFERENCES.

MASSACHUSETTS.—Coffin's Hist. of Newbury, 304. Emery's Reminis. of Newbury, 156-60; Longmeadow Centen. app. 64-6; Perley's Hist. of Boxford, 99; Wyman's Charlestown, Mass. Gens., 452-5.

NEW HAMPSHIRE.—Wheeler's Hist. of Newport, 403-6; Randall's Hist. of Chesterfield, 326; Norton's Hist. of Fitzwilliam, 591.

OTHER PUBLICATIONS.—Hale Gen. (1877), 19 pp.; Hale Ancestry in England, (1881)), 8 pp.; Hale Gen., (1889), 415 pp.; Savage's Gen. Dict., II, 329-32; Amer. Ancestry, I, 35; IV, 59; XII, 18, 104; N. E. Hist. and Gen. Reg., VII, 271; XXI, 83-99; XXXV, 358;

HALEY:—John Haley, of Hadley; married, 1681, Ruth, widow of William Gaylord, daughter of John Crow, but no children by her or by second wife, Hannah, daughter of Samuel Bliss; he died, 1688.

THOMAS HALEY, of Wells, or Saco, before 1650; married daughter of John West; had Ann, Lydia, Samuel and Thomas.

WILLIAM HALEY, of Reading, an early settler.

REFERENCES:—Wilson Gen. (1898), 20-6; Ridlon's Saco Valley, Me., Fams., 706-20; Bradbury's Kennebunkport; Haley Gen. (1900), 115 pp.; Updyke's Narragansett Churches, 160; Yarmouth, N. S., Herald, 1896.

HALFORD:—Thomas Halford, a passenger in the Christian from London, 1635, aged 20, of whom we know no more.

HALL:—Andrew Hall, of Boston, mariner; married, 1667, Ann, daughter of Robert Ratchell.

ANDREW HALL, of Newton, 1691.

BENJAMIN HALL, of Dover, 1659; was, perhaps, a Quaker, who removed to Portsmouth, R. I., and married, 1676, Frances, daughter of George Parker; had Mary, born 1678; William, 1680; Benjamin, 1682; George, 1685, and Nathaniel, 1689.

BENJAMIN HALL, of Wrentham; married, 1692, Sarah Fisher; had Sarah, 1697, died soon.

CHRISTOPHER HALL, of Groton; by wife Sarah, had Grace, born 1672, and John, 1681.

DANIEL HALL, of New Haven, merchant; married, 1670, Mary, daughter of Henry Rutherford; but he may have been of another town, and only came to New Haven to be married; died at Barbados, 1675.

EDWARD HALL, of Cambridge, 1636; freeman 1638; had wife Margaret, who outlived him, but no children.

EDWARD HALL, of Duxbury, 1636, or 7; was of Taunton, 1641, but back again next year; a prop. at the Settlement of Bridgewater, '1645, withdrew from the jurisdiction in 1652, but probably was of Rehoboth; in his will, 1670, named wife Esther and son John.

EDWARD HALL, of Braintree, 1640; by wife Esther, had John, born 1651, and Esther, 1654; may have been of Rehoboth, 1658.

FRANCIS HALL, of New Haven, 1639; was at Stratford after 1648, and, 1657, adm. freeman of Conn. jurisdict.; had Isaac and Samuel. At Fairfield he had large estate, but died early in 1690 at S. He brought from England wife Elizabeth and took, 1665, second wife, Dorothy, widow of John Blakeman, daughter of Rev. Henry Smith; he left four daughters, Mary, Elizabeth, Rebecca and Hannah.

GEORGE HALL, of Taunton, 1643-64; had wife Mary, and children John, Samuel, Joseph, Charity and Sarah.

HENRY HALL, of Westerly, 1664; united with Richard Knight, of Newport, in purchase from Indians; seems to have had children Henry, Edward, James and John.

HENRY HALL, of Boston, a soldier in Captain James Oliver's company; killed by Indians in great swamp fight, 1675.

JAMES HALL, of New London, 1662; then was tenant of John Winthrop on Fisher's Island; perhaps in 1669 lived at Westerly, and may have been son of Henry.

JOB HALL, of New Haven, 1646.

JOHN HALL, of Charlestown; came, 1630, it is thought, from Coventry, probably with Winthrop, being No. 19 on list; had wife Bethia, in 1632; freeman 1634; had, besides Samuel, John, 1638; Shebar, 1640, both died young; by wife Elizabeth Larned, had John, 1645; Elizabeth, 1647, died soon; Elizabeth, again, 1648; and he removed to Barnstable and Yarmouth, where more children were born; records at B. tell that there he had Captain Joseph, 1642; Benjamin, 1644, died in a few days; Nathaniel, 1646; Gershom, 1648; William, 1651; Benjamin, again, 1653, and Elisha.

JOHN HALL, of Kittery, 1640.

JOHN HALL, of Dover; brought Ralph, John and Stephen, and perhaps other children from England very early.

JOHN HALL, of Roxbury, who in records has prefix of respect, and was probably freeman of 1635, unless 1640; no further mention is made of him here and perhaps he removed to Conn. and was at Hartford, 1644, and at Middletown, 1654, where he died, 1673. His will mentions sons Richard, John and Samuel, and daughter Sarah.

JOHN HALL, of Lynn, possible as early as 1630; possibly the freeman of 1640, and may have been a short time at Salem, in 1637; became one of the first proprietors in 1640, of Salisbury; married, 1641, Rebecca, widow of Henry Byley; had John, born 1642; and died before 1650.

JOHN HALL, of Boston; was one of the selectmen, 1657, and ens.

JOHN HALL, of Newport, 1638; was freeman there in 1655.

JOHN HALL, of New Haven, 1639; married Jane Wallen or Woolen; had John and Sarah, both baptized 1646;

John, and Sarah, again, in list of next year, the truth of which is disbelieved; Samuel, 1648; Thomas, 1649; Jonathan, 1651, and David, 1653; removed to Wallingford about 1670, and died 1676, leaving widow. Another John, at New Haven, 1648, was servant of John Meigs.

JOHN HALL, of Taunton; married, 1671 (or as Col. Rec. says, 1667), Hannah Penniman; had John, 1672; Joseph, 1674; James, 1675, and Benjamin, 1677.

JOHN HALL, of Roxbury; freeman 1684.

JOHN HALL, of Wethersfield; died, 1692, leaving widow Rebina and child Elizabeth, 9 mos. old.

NATHANIEL HALL, of Dorchester, 1633.

NATHANIEL HALL, perhaps of Duxbury; "a maim. soldier in the Indian war," was allowed £5 per annum.

NATHANIEL HALL, a captain in the Indian war at the E. under Church; fought with great bravery in defense of Falmouth, 1689; married Ann, daughter of Rev. Thomas Thornton; had no children; kept a tavern and practiced as a physician; removed to Hingham, thence to Delaware River.

NICHOLAS HALL, of Boston; by wife Mary, had Thomas, born 1678; we see no more of him. One NICHOLAS was a soldier in Gallop's comp. of the ill-fated expedit., 1690, against Quebec.

RALPH HALL, of Dover, 1639, son of John, of Dover; born in England about 1619; perhaps of Charlestown, 1647; removed to Dover 1650, thence, in 1664, to Exeter again; by wife Mary, had Mary; born 1647, or '8, died soon; perhaps another Mary, who married, 1669, Edward Smith; Huldah, 1649. Ralph, who died 1671; Samuel, who died 1690; Joseph and Kinsley 1652; was lieut., 1656, rep., 1680, and died 1701, leaving Joseph and Kinsley.

RALPH HALL, of Long Island, adm. to be freeman of Conn., 1664.

RICHARD HALL, of Dorchester, 1644, married Elizabeth, daughter of Richard Callicot, had Martha, born 1648; Mehitable, 1650; Samuel, 1652; Elizabeth, 1653; Jonathan, 1659; Experience, 1662; Hopestill, 1663, died soon; Dependence, who died 1667; Sarah, 1669; and Joseph, 1674; was a lieut., died 1691; and his widow died 1693.

RICHARD HALL, of Bradford, freeman, 1676.

RICHARD HALL, of Roxbury, married 1679, Elizabeth Holbrook, had Martha, 1680; and Richard 1683.

SAMUEL HALL, of Ipswich 1636, had been in the country 1633, went late in autumn to explore, and returned from wilderness 1634; perhaps went home that year and came back in the spring of 1635, aged 25, in the Elizabeth and Ann; was of artillery comp. 1638, and after some years went home again, and died, 1680, at Langford, near Maldon, in Essex. [Hutch., I, 43; Winth., I, 123; Felt., Ipswich, 62, and Hubbard, 170.]

SAMUEL HALL, of Salisbury, 1640; may be the person from Canterbury, England, in 1635, or 6, with wife Joan and three servants [3 Mass. Hist. Coll., VIII, 276], but the Eng. volume does not name the ship. He was represent., 1655.

SAMUEL HALL, of Taunton; had Samuel, born 1664, and John, 1666; Nicholas, 1670; Mary, 1672; Sarah, 1674, died young; Ebenezer, 1677; Sarah, again, 1679, and George, 1681.

SAMUEL HALL, of Cambridge, 1648, brother of Edward, of same, whose sole heir he claims to be; freeman 1681; had wife Elizabeth, three daughters, Hannah, Mary and Lydia; probably no sons. Late in his years he married, 1683, Martha, widow of Humphrey Bradshaw, formerly widow of William Russell.

THOMAS HALL, of Woburn; had Elizabeth, born 1674; Abigail, 1681, both died soon.

TRISTRAM HALL, of Barnstable; had Mary, 1645; Sarah; Joseph, 1652; John, 1654, and Hannah, 1656.

WILLIAM HALL, of Portsmouth, R. I., 1638; freeman, there lived in 1655.

WILLIAM HALL, of Guilford, 1639; had wife Esther; son John, born 1648, and Samuel; he died 1669.

ZURIEL HALL, perhaps of Portsmouth, R. I.; had Mary, who married, 1686, Robert Fish, of the same.

REFERENCES.

MASSACHUSETTS:—Atkins Hist. of Hawley, 47; Kingman's No. Bridgewater, 529; Hazen's Hist. of Billerica, 65; Hodgman's Hist. of Westford, 451; Hoyt's Salisbury Fams., 193; Heywood's Hist of Westminster, 682; Draper's Hist. of Spencer, 211; Hammatt Papers of Ipswich, 129-31; Brook's Hist. of Medford, 517-27; Benedict's Hist. of Sutton, 1654-7.

NEW HAMPSHIRE:—Aldrich's Hist. of Walpole, 270-4; Hayward's Hist. of Gilsum, 319; Hayward's Hist. of Hancock, 632-6; Bedford Centennial, 310; Bouton's Hist. of Concord, 707; Chase's Hist. of Chester, 536-9; Cochrane's Hist. of Antrim, 523-6; Cochrane's Hist. of Francestown, 740-4; Morrison's Hist. of Windham, N. H., 555-7; Saunderson's Charlestown, 382-5.

CONNECTICUT:—Whittemore's Hist. of Middlesex Co., 534; Stiles' Hist. of Windsor, II, 363; Orcutt's Hist. of Stratford, 1210; Davis' Hist. of Wallingford, 750-87; Hibbard's Hist. of Goshen, 459-62.

OTHER PUBLICATIONS.

Amer. Ancestry, II, 78; III, 24, 68, 88; V, 68, 158; VI, 69, 106, 203; VII, 109, 167, 175, 238; IX, 96, 188, 204, 233, 237; X, 19, 27, 105, 112, 161; XI, 39; XII, 10, 26; Baldwin Gen., 843; Hall Family of Medford (1855). 12 pp.; Hall Family of Cleveland (1876), 26 pp.; Hall Family of Connecticut (1882), 31 pp.; Halls of N. E. (1883), 790 pp.; Hall Gen. Notes (1886), 192 pp.; Hall Family of Detroit (1892), 105 pp.; Hall Family Ancestry (1896), 507 pp.; Hanson's Old Kent, Md., 87; Savage's Gen. Dict., II, 332-9.

HALLAM:—John Hallam, of Stonington; came, 1677, in run, from Barbados, with a younger brother and his mother Alice, who had married second husband, and died 1683; was a merchant; married, 1683, Prudence, daughter of Amos Richardson; had John, 1684, died young; Prudence, 1686; John, again, 1689, and Amos, 1695; and died 1700, aged 39.

NICHOLAS HALLAM, younger brother of preceding; married, 1686, Sarah, daughter of Alexander Pygan; had Alexander, born 1688; Edward, 1693, and Samuel, 1695. His wife died, 1700; and, in London, where he had gone in prosecution of an appeal to the King in Counc., he married, 1701, widow Elizabeth Meades, whose maiden name was Gulliver; had born there Elizabeth, 1702; came back, and had here, Mary, 1705, and John, 1708; died 1714, aged 49 years. His widow died 1736.

REFERENCES:—Caulkin's N. London, 358; Savage's Gen. Dict., II, 339.

HALLECK:—David Halleck, of Dorchester, 1640; Boston, 1644.

HALLET, sometimes HOLLET:—Andrew Hallet, of Lynn, removed to Sandwich, 1637, soon after to Yarmouth, and about 1645 went home, but soon came again; had Dorcas, baptized 1646, and Jonathan, 1647; John, 1650; Mehitable; Abigail, who married, 1672, Captain Jonathan Alden; and Ruhamah, who married, 1664, Job Bourne; Winsor gives the amount of his estate £1,180. In Lechford's Plain Dealing, p. 41, he is called schoolmaster.

ANDREW HALLET, of Yarmouth, 1643, then called Junior, was son of preceding, and born in England.

GEORGE HALLET, Boston; freeman 1690; then called Senior, so that there was a Junior at the same time there.

JOHN HALLET, of Scituate, brother of Andrew, but perhaps not residing there at same time; had Ann, who married, 1649, Richard Curtis, of S., and he probably removed to Yarmouth after few years, yet seems to have come back to S.

RICHARD HALLET, of Boston; had Alice, who married, 1652, Mordecai Nichols, and next Thomas Clark, of Plymouth. A widow, Lydia H., married, 1661, at Boston, John Drummond.

WILLIAM HALLET, of New London, 1648, carpenter; removed next year. He was an original settler at Greenwich, and in 1652 had land at Newtown, L. I., where, in 1686, he lived with William, Jr., and Samuel, perhaps his son. One Samuel was drowned, 1650, with Thomas Blossom.

REFERENCES:—Freeman's Hist. of Cape Cod; Swift's Barnstable Fams., II, 473-531; Riker's annals of Newtown, N. Y., 402-6; Savage's Gen. Dict., II, 240.

HALES, or HALE: Arms: Gu., three arrows, or feathered and barbed, arg.

ARMS:—Or, a chief engrailed, sa. Over all, on a band; engrailed, gu., three bezants.

CRESTS:—Out of a ducal coronet, or, a demi-lion, arg., holding, in the paws, a bezant.

HALLOWELL, HOLLOWAY, HALLAWAY, or HALLOWAY, the name is also, first, HALWAY:—Andrew Holway, of New Haven, 1654.

SAMUEL, of Taunton; had Samuel, born 1668; Nathaniel, 1670; Esther, 1673; John, 1675.

TIMOTHY, of Taunton, 1643.

WILLIAM, of Marshfield, of Taunton, 1643, where he sold his estate and removed to Boston, 1650; by wife Mary, had Mary, born 1653; William, 1655; Benjamin, 1656.

WILLIAM, of Boston, by his will, 1664, leaves property to children Timothy, Samuel, Nehemiah, Elisha, Malachi and Esther, and made widow Elizabeth extrix.

REFERENCES:—Sullivant Gen.; Hallowell Gen. (1893), 246 pp.; Savage's Gen. Dict., II, 340; Smith's Hist. of Delaware Co., Pa., 466.

HALSALL, HANSELL or HALSEY:—George Halsall, of Dorchester, where he was of their church and recom. to Boston 1642, a blacksmith, born about 1614, by wife Elizabeth had Mehitable, born 1641, died soon; Joseph, bapt., 1644; and Hannah 1647; his wife died not long after, it is presumed, and he married Joan,

daughter of Thomas Ruck, it is thought, and had Sarah, who died soon; Benjamin, 1652; was freeman 1645, and of artillery comp. 1650. He removed to New London, 1661, but remained not long.

JAMES HALSALL, of Boston, 1074, called, in a deed to him, mathematician, freeman 1690.

JOHN HALSALL, came in the Elizabeth and Ann, 1635, aged 24, from London, but where he sat down is unknown.

THOMAS HALSALL, of Lynn, 1637, removed in a few years to Long Island, and was long of Southampton, the richest man in town, engag. in establish. the Conn. jurisd. there and was a represent. 1664; had Thomas, Isaac, Daniel and Elizabeth, named in his will.

WILLIAM HALSALL, of Boston, 1654, by wife Sarah had Asa, born 1655; Joseph 1657; living at Pulling Point, may have removed to New London. A frequent spelling is Halsey.

REFERENCES:—Savage's Gen. Dict., II, 341; Halsey Gen. (1895), 550 pp.; Amer. Ancestry, IV, 154, 182, 226; VII, 36, 132; Stiles Hist. of Windsor, Ct., II, 364.

HALSTEED:—Henry Halsteed, of Concord, 1645.

NATHAN HALSTEED, of Concord, may have been father of preceding. His wife Isabel died, 1642, and he soon after.

NATHANIEL HALSTEED, of Dedham, freeman 1641, died 1644, and may seem same as the preceding.

WILLIAM HALSTEED, of Concord, died 1645, says Farmer; but an error of a year occurs in Geneal. Reg. III, 177, giving date of his will, 13 June, of 1646, while in 3 fall. attest. of witnesses, each proves that it was the farmer, and the inv. was taken in December of the same year. He was unmarried.

REFERENCES:—Amer. Ancestry, XII; Whittemore's Orange, N. J., 406; Amer. Ancestry, II, 49; VI, 13; Baird's Hist. of Rye, N. Y., 474; Halsted Gen. (1896), 34 pp.

HALWORTHY:—Robert Halworthy, passeng in the Arabella from London, 1671. Savage finds no reason to judge him a relative of Sir Matthew, of London, the great benefactor of Harvard College.

HAM:—John Ham, of Dover, 1665, married, 1668, Mary, daughter of John Heard, had Mary, born fall. year; Elizabeth, 1672; Joseph, 1678; John, 1681; and perhaps more; was some years after at Casco; his wife died 1706. Land in which he dwelt is still engaged by his descend.

MATTHEW HAM, Isle of Shoals, 1657.

WILLIAM HAM, of Exeter, 1645, died about 1672.

REFERENCES:—Savage's Gen. Dict., II, 342; Amer. Ancestry, II, 49; IV, 145; Hudson's Hist. of Lexington, Mass., 83; Missouri Pioneer Fams., 265; New Eng. Hist. and Gen. Reg., XXVI, 388-94; Otis Gen., (1851); Wheeler's Hist. of Brunswick, Me., 837; Caverno Gen., 14-6.

HAMANS:—William Hamans, of Scituate, 1636, died soon, or removed, says Deane. No doubt, spelling was otherwise, elsewhere; yet the very same letters are used when he was a planter at Saco, 1643; or adm. freeman of Mass., 1653, at Wells. See Willis, I, 49. It may be the same as Hammond.

HAMBLEN:—James Hamblen, of Barnstable, one of the early settlers, came with wife Ann, probably from London, perhaps brought James, and Hannah; had here Bartholomew, born 1642; John, bapt., 1644; Sarah, 1647; Eleazur, 1650; and Israel, 1652; he died 1690.

REFERENCES:—Andrews Gen. (1890), 195-9; Swift's Barnstable, Mass., Fams., I, 522-36; Hamlin Gen. (1894), 70-130; Hamblin, And. news, New Britain, 273; Kitchell Gen., 54; Pierce's Hist. of Gorham, Me., 171.

HAMBLETON. See Hamilton.

REFERENCES:—Amer. Ancestry, III, 101; Man and Hambleton, Fams., (1876), 124 pp.; Hambleton Gen. (1887), 108 pp.

HAMDEN:—John Hamden, of Plymouth, 1622; "a gentleman of London," says Winslow, "who wintered with us, and desired much to see the country;" went home, 1623.

HAMES:—Mark Hames, of Boston, 1655. Perhaps it is the same as Haines, and he may have been of New Haven, 1641.

HAMILTON or HAMBLETON:—Daniel Hamilton, of Dover, 1666, had Solomon, born that year, and Jonathan, 1672.

DAVID HAMILTON, of Berwick, killed by the Indians, 1691.

JOHN HAMILTON, of Charlestown, 1658.

ROBERT HAMILTON, of Springfield, died 1683.

WILLIAM HAMILTON, of Boston, married 1654, Mary Richardson, had Gustavus, same year, who died soon; Elizabeth, 1655; Sarah, 1657; and Abraham, 1661.

REFERENCES.

MASSACHUSETTS:—Stone's Hist. of Hubbardston, 287; Temple's Hist. of N. Brookfield, 613-5; Temple's Hist. of Palmer, 476-'8, 487; Freeman's Hist. of Cape Cod, II, 603; Heywood's Hist. of Westminster, 684.

NEW HAMPSHIRE:—Leonard's Hist. of Dublin, 348; Little's Hist. of Weare, 894; Randall's Hist. of Chesterfield, 327.

OTHER PUBLICATIONS.—Eaton Gen. (1895); Hamilton Fam. of N. Y. (1893), 32 pp.; Hamilton Fam. of Worcester, (1894), 139 pp.; Humphrey Gen., 103; Savage's Gen. Dict., II, 343; Amer. Ancestry, XI, 85; XII, N. E. Hist. and Gen. Reg., XLIV, 361-5.

HAMLET:—William Hamlet, of Cambridge, or Watertown, born about 1614, married Sarah, widow of James Hubbard; had Jacob, Rebecca, both bapt. at C.; Sarah, and Thomas; was freeman, 1651; removed about 1658 to Billerica. This was one of the first bapt. His wife, Sarah, died at Woburn, 1689.

REFERENCE:—Hazens, Billerica, Mass., 65.

HAMLIN:—Clement Hamlin, of Boston, a soldier in Turner's company, 1676.

EZEKIEL HAMLIN, of Boston, married 1654, Elizabeth Drake, had Ezekiel, born 1655; Joseph, 1657; and Elizabeth, 1661; was a mariner.

GILES HAMLIN, of Middletown, 1650, married 1655. Esther, daughter of John Crow, of Hartford, had John, born 1658; Giles, 1666; William, 1669, and Richard, whose date may be next to John; daughters, Mehitable, or Mable, born 1664, who married Samuel Hooker; Es-

ther, born 1665, married William Southmayd; and Mary, 1663, married 1690, Rev. Noadiah Russell; was represent. 1666, and nearly every year to 1684, assistant 1685 till death, 1689.

REFERENCES:—Talcott's N. Y. and N. E. Fams. 543-51; Amer. Ancestry, IV, 37; V, 160; VIII, 20; Hamlin Gen. (1885), 4 pp.; (1894), 130 pp.; Hinman's Conn. Settlers, 1st ed., 214-9; N. E. Hist. Gen. Reg., III, 133-5; L, 220; Saunderson's Charlestown, N. H., 385-8; Dwight Gen., 504-8; Warren's Hist. of Waterford, Me., 251-3.

HAMMANT:—Francis Hammant, of Dedham before 1650, in that part which became Medford; died 1692. His will names Sam John, Timothy, his wife, and daughter Elizabeth.

HAMMATT, HAMOT, or HAMMETT:—Thomas Hammatt, of Scarborough, own. alleg. and Mass. 1658, made freeman that year, but renewed subjection to the King in 1663, married the widow of John Burrage, but the date is not ascertained.

REFERENCE:—
Bangor Hist. Mag., VII, 174.

HAMMER. See Hammer.

HAMMERSTON:—Edward Hammerston, of Cambridge, buried 1646.

JAMES HAMMERSTON, of Mass., 1642.

HAMMAND, or, as often written, HAMMONS:—Benjamin Hammond, of Yarmouth 1643, by Farmer said to have come from London, and to be son of William and Elizabeth, a sister of William Penn, but this could not be the celebrated William. Farmer adds that he was at Sandwich, married in 1650, and removed to Rochester, where lived John, called his 2d son, born 1663.

GEORGE HAMMOND, Newport, in the list of freemen there, spelt Haman, 1655.

JOHN HAMMOND, of Scituate, 1643.

JOHN HAMMOND, of Gloucester, whose surname is by Felt. written Hamons, Haman, or Heman, married 1660 Mary, daughter of Morris, or Maurice Somes, had Elizabeth; John, 1664; Mary, 1666; Timothy, 1668; and William, 1674.

JOHN HAMMOND, of Watertown, son of William, brought by his mother at the age of 7, in the Francis from Ipswich, 1634, was a lieut.; by first wife, Abigal, had John, born 1654, who died 1658; Elizabeth, 1655; and Abigail, 1658; and another John by second wife Sarah Nichols, married at Charlestown 1664, who died 1688, aged 45, had Sarah, who died 1674, at 8 years; Hannah, 1669; Nathaniel, 1677, died soon; Samuel, 1680, died young; and Hepibah; had 3d wife Prudence, but no children; he died 1709. He was the richest man in town, selectman 1664, and often after.

JOSEPH HAMMOND, of Kittery, 1680, brother of the preceding, a lieutenant, had Joseph, born 1677, and two daughters to outlive him; was probably the major carried prisoner by the French 1695, to Canada, as Hutch. II, 89 and 180, tells; and couns. of Mass.; died 1710. His widow Catharine, daughter of Nicholas Frost, had been widow of William Leighton, and died 1715. His daughter Dorcas married Robert Cutts, Jr.

LAWRENCE HAMMOND, of Charlestown, artillery company 1666, freeman 1666, married 1662, Audrey Eaton, who came, he says, the year before from London, had Francis born 19th August following, and his wife died eight days after. He next married, 1665, Abigail, widow of John Willet, youngest daughter of Deac. Edward Collins, of Medford, had Martha, died soon; Jane, 1670, died young; and Elizabeth, 1672. His wife died 1674, and he married, 1675, Margaret, widow of Deputy-Gov. Willoughby, who bore him no children, and died 1683. Fourth wife, Ann, was widow of William Gerrish, married 1685, and had Lawrence, who died under 5 years, and Francis, again, 1689, who also died soon; his oldest child was killed 1688, by fall on board his ship. He was capt., represent. 1672, and five years more, removed to Boston, and died 1699.

RICHARD HAMMOND, of Kennebeck 1665, killed by the Indians 1676, at same time with Capt. Thomas Lake, when all his family of 16 were killed or carried into captiv. Elizabeth, his widow, married John Rowden, of Salem.

THOMAS HAMMOND, of Hingham 1636, younger brother of 1st William, born at Lavenham, Co. Suffolk, where, it is said, he was bapt. 1587, "perhaps several years before he was born;" freeman 1637, by wife Elizabeth, married probably in England 1623, brought children Elizabeth and Thomas, had Sarah, bapt. 1640, and Nathaniel, 1643; removed to Watertown, thence across the river, 1650, to Cambridge vill., purchased large farm with Vincent Druce, and died 1675, aged 88 years. He had very good estate.

WILLIAM HAMMOND, of Watertown, perhaps as early as 1632, freeman 1636, had good estate, died 1662, aged, it is said, about 87. He married 1605, Elizabeth Payne, sister of William, had William, bapt. 1607; Ann, 1609, died soon; John, 1611; Ann, again, 1616; and Thomas, 1618. The wife had come in the Francis from Ipswich, 1634, with children Elizabeth, 15; Sarah, 10; and John, 7. She died 1670.

WILLIAM HAMMOND, of Lynn, is by Lewis named of 1636, and died next year.

WILLIAM HAMMOND, of Wells, 1656, or earlier, a man of consequence, gr. juror, next year clerk of the writs, and commissr. for small causes until 1679, had Jonathan, and Joseph, perhaps other children, but those outlived him. He died 1702. Gen. Reg. IX, 312.

WILLIAM HAMMOND, who was killed by the Indians 1675, the fourth day of Philip's War, may have been of Rehoboth, for their son William had Elizabeth, born 1661; but this man was of the troop of Capt. Prentiss, which must, we suppose, have chiefly been composed of volunteers of Cambridge and neighboring town of Dedham.

REFERENCES:
—Amer. Ancestry, II, 50; III, 183, 212; V, 42, 49; VI, 17; VII, 109, 113; IX, 210; X, 60, 97, XI, 84; XII, 40; Savage's Gen. Dict., II, 345-8; Wyman's Charlestown, Mass., Gens., I, 461; Hammond Fam. of Vermont (1876), 11 pp.; H. Fam. of N. H. (1890), 17 pp.; H. Fam. of Mass. (1894), 311 pp.; Haywood's Hist. of Gilsum, N. H., 320; Collins' Gen., 148; Dwight's Strong Gen., 50; Amer. Hist. Reg., I, 867-73; Caverly's Hist. of Gloucester, Mass., 97; Chapman's Trowbridge Gen., 242; N. E. Hist. Reg., XXX, 28-33; XII, 167; Paige's Hist. of Hardwick, Mass., 387; Raymond's Tarrytown Monument, 45-59; Washburn's Hist. of Leicester, Mass., 375.

HAMPTON:—Thomas Hampton, of Sandwich, died early, it would seem without wife or children.

REFERENCES:
—Shotwell Gen., 240; Powers' Sangamon, Ills., 396; Richmond, Va., Standard, II, 17.

HAMUCK:—Thomas Hamuck, of Dover, was there taxed 1666 to '72, says Mr. Quint, but he tells no more.

HANBURY:—Daniel Hanbury, came from London 1633, in the Planter, aged 29, but no more is known.

LUKE HANBURY, of Mass., 1637. Felt.

PETER HANBURY, of Sandwich, 1643.

WILLIAM HANBURY, of Duxbury, 1639, married 1641, Hannah Souther, was of Plymouth 1643, but rem. to Boston 1649, here had William, born same year, probably died 1650. He had three children before. Sometimes name is written Henbury.

HANCOCK:—Anthony Hancock, of Wrentham, had been servant of William Sumner, of Dorchester, ment. in will of 1681, by wife Sarah, who died 1700, had probably Henry; Anthony, 1685; and perhaps by wife Ruth, had Mary, 1701; William, 1703; Hannah, 1706; and Silence, 1709.

JOHN HANCOCK, of New Haven, 1679, a propr. 1685, who is not known to have had issue, died 1712. He may have been the man to whom, 1663, grant of 500 acres in Carolina was made by the patentees for discovery there.

NATHANIEL HANCOCK, of Cambridge, by wife Joan had Mary, born 1634; Sarah, 1636; Nathaniel, 1638; John, who died 1643, less than 2 yrs.; Elizabeth, 1645; and Lydia, 1646; and he died, says Farmer, before 1652. The distinguished John Hancock, president of that Cong. which declared Independence, was descendant of Nathaniel.

THOMAS HANCOCK, of Hadley, 1678, removed soon.

ARMS:—Gu, three rams' heads, couped and erect, arg. on a chief, of the last, three cocks, of the first.

REFERENCES.

MASSACHUSETTS:—Ballon's Hist. of Milford, 781; Hudson's Hist. of Lexington, 83-8; Daniels' Hist. of Oxford, 530; Longmeadow Centenn. app., 66-8; Paige's Hist. of Cambridge, 571-4.

NEW HAMPSHIRE:—Runnel's Hist. of Sanbornton, II, 325; Dearborn's Hist. of Salisbury, 625-7.

OTHER PUBLICATIONS:—Amer. Ancestry, VIII, 212; Kelly Gen. (1892); Davis Gen., 61; Lee Gen. (1888), 369-75; Lane Gen. (1891), 235; N. E. Hist. Reg., IX, 352-4; X, 81; XXXVI, 75-7; Prentice Gen., 3,413; Savage's Gen. Dict., II, 348; Thoud's Fenwick Colony, N. J., 85.

HANCOX:—Thomas Hancox, of Farmington, 1670, aged about 25 yrs., married 1685, Rachel, daughter of John Leonard, of Springfield, had Thomas, 1686; John, 1688; William; Abel; Rachel; Daniel; Jonathan; and Mehitable; but the records are uncertain, as he removed to Hartford, was then keeper of the gaol 1691, and the names are found at each town. but without uniformity.

HAND:—John Hand, of Easthampton, L. I., 1648. Wood 40. Perhaps is same who was a proprietor at Guilford, 1685.

JOSEPH HAND, one of the first settlers at Killingworth 1663, and perhaps he married Jane, daughter of Benjamin Wright; another Joseph, of Guilford, married Hannah, daughter of William Seward.

REFERENCES:—Amer. Ancestry I, 35; II, 50; XII; Ely. Gen., 182; Kulp's Wyoming Valley Fams.; Crawford Fam. of Virginia, 84-7; Littell's Passaic Valley Gens., 170-9.

HANDEN:—Benjamin Handen, Providence 1645, or 6. See Herrendean.

HANDFORTH:—Nathaniel Handforth, of Lynn, 1637, came from London, died 1687, aged 78. Lewis 90.

HANDS:—Mark Hands, of Boston, 1645, nailer, came, Savage thinks, in the Jonathan, 1639, aged 20, by wife Abra had Mary born 1646, died soon; by wife Mary had Mehitable, 1652; John, 1654; went on a long voyage 1661, and probably died abroad.

HANFORD, or Handford:—Thomas Hanford, of Scituate, 1643, 1650 freeman of Mass., earlier he had taught school at Roxbury, probably engaged in preaching, in 1652, was of Norwalk; married Hannah, daughter of Thomas Newbury, of Dorchester; by her no children. His second wife, Mary, widow of Jonathan Ince, the New Haven scholar, married 1661, brought him Theophilus, 1662; Mary, 1663; Hannah, 1665; Elizabeth, 1667; Thomas, 1668; Eleazur, 1670; Elnathan, 1672; and Samuel, whose name was probably mistaken for Sarah; he died 1693.

REFERENCE:— Savage's Gen. Dict., II., 349; Amer. Ancestry, IV., 176; X., 136; Chapman Gen., 226; Wentworth Gen., II., 21; Selleck's Norwalk, Ct. (1896), 135-49; Morris' Bontecon Gen., 102.

HANKFORD, or HANSFORD:—Richard Hankford, of Plymouth, died 1633, probably unmarried.

HANMER, or HANMORE:—John Hanmer, of Scituate, 1639, next year at Duxbury, but only short time, and of Marshfield, 1663; had sons John, Joseph and Isaac; daughters Rebecca, Bethia and Hannah. He was living 1673, but for a century the name has failed here.

HANNADOWN:—Roger Hannadown, of Weymouth, ship carpenter, removed to Boston; by wife, Sarah, had Lydia, bapt. 1643.

HANNAH:—Robert Hannah, of Wickford, or some port of the Narragansett country, married before 1690, Mary, daughter of Samuel Wilson; had Robert and Mary; his widow married, 1708, George Webb.

REFERENCE:— R. I. Hist, Sac. Colls., III., 294; Austin's R. I. Gen. Dict., 91.

HANNIFORD, or HANNIFALL:—John Hanniford, of Boston, mariner, by wife Hannah had Samuel, 1645; Joseph, 1652; John, 1653, died soon; besides daughter Hannah, who became, Savage thinks, wife of Mark Hands. He married 1655, Abigail, widow of George Dell, had Sarah, born 1656. He died before 1661; see Geneal. Reg. XIII., 149.

RICHARD, of Marblehead, 1674, printed in Geneal. Reg. VIII., 288, as probably it was sounded, Haniver, and VII., 70, Hannier.

HANNUM:—William Hannum, of Dorchester, an early settler, removed to Windsor, but not with first migrat.; son John born before; at W. had Abigail 1640; Joanna, 1642; Elizabeth 1645; and Mary 1650; probably Joanna died young; removed again about 1655 to Northampton, there died 1677.

REFERENCES:— Futhey's Hist. of Chester Co., Pa., 605; Temple's Hist. of Northfield, Mass., 456; Cope's Dutton Gen., 61; Doolittle's Sketches of Belchertown, Mass., 267; Jackson Gen., 241.

HANSCOM, HUNSCOM, or HANSCOMBE:—James Hanscom, of Essex Co., 1666, may have been son of Thomas of Salem, came with Higginson, 1629.

REFERENCES:— Old Eliot, Me., Monthly, II, (1898), 8, 11.

HAUSE, or HAUNCE:—John Hause, of Dover 1656, still there 1665.

HANSETT, HANDSETT, HANCHET, HANSHUT, or HANSHET:—John Hansett, Boston, 1634, freeman 1637, removed to Braintree, had John, born 1641; his wife died and he soon removed to Roxbury, married 1644, Elizabeth Perry, had Thomas, bapt. 1645; Hannah 1647, died soon; Hannah, again, 1649, died soon; and Peter 1651.

THOMAS HANSETT, perhaps brother of John, had John, born 1649, removed to New London 1651, then 3 years, after intermed. resid. was at Northampton about 1660, deacon 1668, rem. to Westfield, thence to Suffield, where he died 1686. His wife was Deliverance, daughter of George Langton; she married Jonathan Burt; other children were Thomas, Deliverance and Hannah.

REFERENCE:— Savage's Gen. Dict., II., 351-2.

HANSON:—Isaac Hanson, probably of Portsmouth, by wife Mary had Mary, born 1679, who married, 1698, James Libbey.

THOMAS HANSON, Dover, 1657, freeman 1661, prob. died 1666; his widow was killed by the Indians; his children were Tobias, Thomas, born about 1643; Isaac, Timothy and 2 daughters.

REFERENCES:—Wentworth Gen., II., 23; N. E. Hist. and Gen. Reg., VI., 329-32; Hubbard's Stanstead Co., Canada, 315-17; Austin's Allied Fams., 120-3; Am. Ancestry, VI, 64; VII, 148; Coggswell's Hist. of Nottingham, N. H., 693-6; Lee Gen. (1895), 157-9; Hanson's Old Kent, Md., 99 et seq.; Eaton's Hist. of Thomaston, Me., II, 252.

HANWELL:—Ambrose Hanwell, of Pemaquid, took oath of fidelity to Mass. 1674.

HAPGOOD:—Syndrach, or Shadrach Hapgood, of Sudbury, Savage presumes is that passenger from London, in the Speedwell, at Boston, 1656, aged 14, though in Gen. Reg. I, 132, called Hopgood; married 1664, Elizabeth, daughter of Nathaniel Treadway, had Nathaniel and Thomas, last born 1669; besides Mary, and Sarah; in Philip's war was killed, 1675, at Brookfield.

REFERENCES:—Morse's Grant Gen., 65-9, N. E. Hist. and Gen. Reg., XVI; Savage's Gen. Dict., II, 352; Warren's Hist. of Waterford, Me., 253-5; Ward's Hist. of Shrewsbury, Mass., 306; Hapgood Gen., (1859).

HARBERT, or HERBERT:—Henry Harbert, of Charlestown, 1653, married 1668, Elizabeth George, and died 1677.

JOHN HARBERT, of Salem, a shoemaker, came in the Abigail 1635, aged 23, was from Northampton, England, had grant of land at S. 1637, perhaps there had wife Mary; but is better written Herbert.

JOHN HARBERT, of Braintree, freeman 1641, by wife Joel, daughter of first Richard Thayer, probably had several children; John; Mary 1656; and Hannah 1658. A former Hannah had died 1657. In some records his name is Harbour. He was an active merchant, going to W. I. and back 1645 and 6.

SYLVESTER HARBERT, of Boston, married 1652, Lucy Adams, had Samuel, born 1653.

HARBOUR:—Benjamin Harbour, of Hartford, married about 1644, Christian Nethercoat, and many years after a second wife, Jane, but had no children; was freeman 1656, and died after 1685. Wrote his name in advanced years, Harbert.

REFERENCE:— Power's Sangaman, Ills., 354.

HARCHER:—William Harcher, of Lynn, 1636, removed about 1640 to Southampton, L. I., but may have come back and died at L. 1661. Lewis. Perhaps same name as Harker, Hacker, or Hacket.

HARCUTT, HARKER, or HARKETT:—Richard Harcutt, of Warwick, among freemen 1655, married Elizabeth, daughter of Robert Patter of the same, and removed to L. I. His children were Daniel, Isabel, Elizabeth, Mary, Meribah, Mercy, Dorothy, Sarah and Benjamin. He had second wife; name may be Harcourt.

HARD:—John Hard, of Dover, 1648, may have been of Marblehead 1669. This name may be same as Hurd.

HARDEN, or HARDIN:—Edward Harden, of Gloucester, a soldier in Capt. Gardner's company, wounded in great swamp fight 1675.

RICHARD HARDEN, of Boston, 1677.

REFERENCES:—Amer. Ancestry, VII, 112, 256; Eaton's Hist. of Thomaston, Me., 253; Lincoln's Hist. of Hingham, Mass., II, 288; Bellinger Gen. (1895), 9-12.

HARDIER:—Richard Hardier. of Braintree, freeman 1648, died 1657.

HARDING, or HARDEN:—Abraham Harding, of Dedham, early settler, lived first at Braintree; freeman 1645, one of the founders of Medford, died 1655, had by wife Elizabeth, Abraham, probably posthum., besides other children, including John. See Geneal. Reg. IX, 35.

GEORGE HARDING, of Marblehead, 1649. Felt.

JOHN HARDING, the freeman of 1640, may have been of Weymouth, there shared in division of town lands 1682.

JOHN HARDING, of Duxbury 1643, may have been preceding.

JOSEPH HARDING, of Eastman, 1660, married that year Bethia, perhaps daughter of first Josiah Cook; had Martha, born 1662; Mary 1665; Joseph 1667; Josiah 1669; Maziah (?) 1671; John 1673; died 79; Nathaniel 1674; Joshua 1676; Abiah 1680; and Samuel 1685.

PHILIP HARDING, of Boston, married, 1659, widow Susanna Haviland, was at Marblehead 1674.

ROBERT HARDING, of Boston, came with Winthrop in the fleet, no doubt 1630, being No. 11 on list, freeman 1631, married widow Philippa Hammond, who came same time, No. 40 in list; was a captain and selectman but joined in support of Hutchinson faith, was disarmed 1637, yet of Artillery Co. 1638, removed that year to R. I., where he was respect. high, an assistant 1641; yet had his estate at Boston for some years; in 1645 or earlier his widow died and he married that year Esther, daughter of George Willis of Hartford, and next year went home in ship with Thomas Peters, Thomas Fowle, John Leverett and others; in 1651 was merchant of London. Winthrop, I, 248, II, 354.

THOMAS HARDING, of Boston, 1656.

WILLIAM HARDING, of New Haven, 1642.

REFERENCES:—Wight Gen., 24; Rich's Hist. of Truro, Mass., 535; Daniel's Hist. of Oxford, Mass., 531; Amer. Ancestry, VI, 38; Crawford Fam. of Va., 112; Harding Gen. (1864), 84 pp.; Lapham's Hist. of Bethel, Me., 556; Morse's Gen. Reg., IV (1864), 84 pp.

HARDMAN:—John Hardman, of Lynn, 1647. Lewis. He may have removed to Braintree, by wife Sarah, there had Mary born 1652; and John 1654; or perhaps may be that Herdman of Fairfield 1662, who died 1665, leaving children.

HARDY, or HARDIE:—George Hardy, of Newbury, by wife Mary had Mary, born 1693; and he died 1694.

JOHN HARDY, of Salem, freeman 1634, brought from England son Joseph, in whose favor grant of land was made 1644, and perhaps had born here John, for Felt says John, Jr., had grant of land here 1637. John had grant of land 1636, was selectman 1647, and died 1652; his will mentions also daughter Elizabeth, who married Roger Hasell.

RICHARD HARDY, of Concord 1639. Shattuck says: He may be the man, who, at Stamford married Ann Huested, had Mary born 1659, gave son Samuel a house and land in 1683, and not long afterward gives legacies in his will to daughter Elizabeth Persons, Parsons, or Pearson; Susanna Sherman; Sarah Close; Ruth Mead, and Mary Hardy.

SAMUEL HARDY, of Beverley, 1686, one of the witnesses to deed from the Indians that year to Salem, was town clerk 1674, married, 1676, Mary, daughter of Samuel Dudley, had Robert, Mary, Theophilus, and Elizabeth.

THOMAS HARDY, of Ipswich, one of the first 12 who made the settlement 1633, had Thomas, John, Joseph, Jacob, and William, one daughter who married William Hitchins, and Mary, who married, 1670, Samuel Currier of Haverhill; removed to Rowley about 1653, thence in 10 years to Bradford, there died 1678, aged 72. Perhaps he was brother of John.

REFERENCES:—Hayward's Hist. of Hancock, N. H., 637-9; Cochrane's Hist. of Francestown, N. H., 744; Bangor Hist. Mag., V, 178; Temple's Hist, of N. Brookfield, Mass., 615; Worcester's Hist. of Hollis, N. H., 376; Freeman's Hist. of Cape Cod, Mass., II, 157; Poor's Merrimack Valley, 113, 123-6, 160.

HARE:—George Hare, of Boston, by wife Mary had George, Born 1677.

JOHN HARE, of Boston, by wife Joanna had Susanna, born 1670.

REFERENCES:—Amer. Ancestry, I, 36; Stearns' Hist. of Ashburnham, Mass., 729; Kidder's Hist. of New Ipswich, N. H., 383.

HARES:—Gabriel Hares, of New London, 1664, may be either Ayres or Harris.

HARGER, HARDGER, or HARDYEAR:—Jabez Harger, of Stratford, married 1662, Margaret, daughter of Henry Tomlinson; had Samuel, born 1663; Sarah 1666; Ann 1668: Mary 1670; Abigail 1671; Mary, again, 1673; Ebenezer 1674; Abraham 1677, and a posthum. child perhaps named Jabez; removed to Derby, died 1678.

REFERENCES:—Orcott's Hist. of Stratford, Ct., 1211; Orcott's Derby, Ct., 724-6.

HARKER:—Anthony Harker, of Boston, came, no doubt, in the Griffin, 1633, in the employ of Thomas Leverett, freeman 1636, by wife Mary had John, bapt. 1639; Mary 1641; John, again, 1643; Sarah bapt. 1646; Mercy, 1649; and Elizabeth 1652.

EBENEZER HARKER, of Nantucket, married Patience, daughter of Peter Folger, but whether he had issue is not known; his widow married Thomas Gardner.

JOHN HARKER, of York, freeman 1652. See Haz. I, 575; he had married Dorothy, widow of Robert Mill, about 1648.

WILLIAM HARKER, of Lynn, had wife Elizabeth, who died 1661.

REFERENCE:—Savage's Gen. Dict., II, 356.

HARKWOOD. See Hapgood.

HARLAKENDEN:—Roger, of Cambridge, from Earle's Colne, in Essex, born 1611, came in the Defence 1635, with wife Elizabeth, 18, daughter of Godfrey Bosseville, Esq., of Gunthwayte, Co. York, whom, he married that year, and sister Mable, 21, who married Gov. Haynes; freeman next year, same year chosen assist. and so continued until he died, 1638, of smallpox, leaving wife and 2 daughters, Elizabeth, born 1636; and Margaret 1638; the widow married Herbert Pelham, Esq.

REFERENCES:—N. E. Hist. Reg., X, 129; XIV, 319; XV, 327-9; XLVI, 368; Darling Mem.; Harlakenden Chart by Jones (1863), 17x22; Paige's Hist. of Cambridge, Mass., 574; Walworth's Hyde Gen., II, 1162-74.

Arms: Azure, a fess, ermine, between 3 lions' heads, erased, or.

Crest: Between the attires of a stag, or, an eagle, reguardant, wings expanded, arg.

HARLOCK:—Thomas Harlock, of Edgartown, married a daughter of Thomas Mayhew, it is said, had Thomas, born 1659, and John.

HARLOW:—William Harlow, of Lynn, 1637, a youth whose father is unknown, removed that year to Sandwich, and in a few years to Plymouth, married 1649, Rebecca, daughter of Robert Bartlett, had William, born 1650, died soon; Samuel 1653; Rebecca 1655; and William 1657; by second wife, married 1658, Mary, daughter of John Founce, had Mary, born 1659; Repentance 1660; John 1662; and Nathaniel 1664; his wife died that year and he married, 1666, Mary Shelly, had Hannah, 1666; Bathsua 1668; Joanna 1670; Mehitable 1672; and Judith 1676.

REFERENCES:—Ward's Hist. of Shrewsbury, Mass., 329; Amer. Ancestry, III, 193; VII, 88; N. E. Hist and Gen. Reg., XIV, 227-33; Winsor's Hist. of Duxbury, Mass., 264; Pierce's Biog. Coutb.; Lapham's Hist. of Paris, Me., 623-5.

HARLS:—Thomas Harls, of Penaquid, swore fidelity to Mass, 1674.

HARMAN, or HARMON, or HERMAN:—Francis Harman came in the Love 1635, aged 43, from London, with children John, 12; and Sarah, 10; but no more is known of him.

JAMES HARMAN, of Saco, 1655.

JOHN HARMAN, of Springfield, 1644, brought then

John and Samuel; had there Sarah 1644; Joseph 1647; Elizabeth 1649, died young; Mary 1651; Nathaniel 1654; Ebenezer 1657, drowned at 3 years; died 1661. His widow married Anthony Dorchester.

JOHN HARMAN, of Plymouth, 1643, Duxbury 1657, married daughter of Henry Sampson, may have been of Saco 1652, and again 1680, when he was prominent man.

JOSEPH HARMAN, of Kittery, 1674.

NATHANIEL HARMAN, of Braintree, married Mary, daughter of Thomas Bliss of Rehoboth, had Nathaniel, 1641; and Mary 1643; freeman same year; had also Sarah 1653; Jonathan 1654; and Ephriam 1656.

SAMUEL HARMAN, of Boston, 1689, had Samuel, bapt. 1692; and Sarah 1696.

THOMAS HARMAN, York, was drowned 1701.

REFERENCES:—N. E. Hist. and Gen. Reg., XXXI, 165; Amer. Ancestry, IX, 25.

HARMER:—Ephraim Harmer, of Rehoboth, died 1679.

REFERENCE:—Meade's Old Fams. of Va.

HARNDALE, HORNDEL, or HARNDEL:—Benjamin Harndale, of Lynn, 1647, as given by Farmer, was possibly Harnden, which spread at Reading, when Benjamin, John, Richard, and William, perhaps father, and three sons are called early settlers, and Richard was freeman 1691.

JOHN HARNDALE, of Newport, had daughter Mary, wife of John Stanton; and daughter Rebecca, wife of Hugh Moshier. Perhaps he was of New Haven, 1644.

HARNETT:—Edward Harnett, Salem 1640, had grant of land year before, as had also Edward, Jr., probably his son. Perhaps it was the elder who with wife Priscilla, suffered for favoring the Quakers, 1658; but doubt is felt which of them it was that had Jonathan, bapt. 1650; and Eunice, 1652. Probably the younger Edward married a daughter of Jonathan Porter, of Huntington, L. I.

HARNSON:—Edward Harnson, of Wethersfield, 1644.

HARPER:—Joseph Harper, was of Braintree, says Farmer, early, but year is not mentioned. Dorcas, perhaps his daughter, married at Boston, 1657, Isaac Woody.

ROBERT HARPER, of Sandwich, a Quaker, sentenced in 1659, at Boston, to 15 stripes; married, 1666, Prudence Butley, as 2d wife, but by former wife Deborah, had Experience, 1657; Stephen, 1662; and Mary, 1665. By second wife had besides Hannah, Mercy in 1675.

REFERENCES:—Stiles' Hist. of Windsor, Ct., II, 365; Bowie Gen., 189; Freeman's Hist. of Cape Cod, Mass., II, 68; Browne Fam. Notes (1887), 40 pp.; Power's Sangamon, Ill, Settlers, 361; Stearns' Hist. of Ashburnham, Mass., 729; Gould's Hist. of Delaware Co., N. Y., 30-3; Futhey's Hist of Chester Co., Pa., 588.

HARRADEN, HARRADIN, or HARRENDINE:—Edward Harraden, of Gloucester, 1658, may have been of Ipswich in 1651, by wife Sarah had Andrew, born 1659; Ann, 1661; Joseph, 1668; Sarah, 1670, died at 2 yrs.; and Benjamin, 1671. Probably this fam. was perpet. the next generation at Salem.

HARRIMAN:—John Harriman, of New Haven, 1646, innholder, had wife Elizabeth, who died 1681; son John, bapt. 1047; and Elizabeth 1048; and he died 1083.

LEONARD HARRIMAN, of Rowley, 1049, by wife Margaret had John, born 1050, probably that soldier of Lothrop's comp. killed 1075, by the Indians at Deerfield; Matthew, 1052; and Jonathan, 1057; in this last year he was freeman, when name is recorded as Hurryman.

REFERENCES:—Gage's Hist. of Rowley, Mass., 442; Amer. Ancestry, VI, 104; Dow's Hist. of Hampton, N. H., 744; Eaton's Annals of Warren, Me., 548; Herrick Gen. (1885), 279-81; Lamb Gen. (1900), 12-24; Fullonton's Hist. of Raymond, N. H., 234-40; Washington, N. H, Hist., 465; Savage's Gen. Dict., II, 358.

HARRINGTON:—Edward Harrington, of Charlestown, 1643, probably had wife Elizabeth; he died, 1047.

RICHARD HARRINGTON, of Charlestown, by wife Elizabeth, had Elizabeth, born 1643, freeman 1047, and died 1659.

ROBERT HARRINGTON, of Watertown, 1642, married 1648, Susanna, daughter of John George, had Susanna, born 1649; John, 1651; Robert, 1053; George, 1055; killed by Indians at Lancaster, 1676; Daniel, 1057; Joseph, 1059; Benjamin, 1602; Mary, 1004; Thomas, 1605; Samuel, 1666; Edward, 1009; Saran, 1071; and David, 1673, died young; and the father died 1689. His widow married Eleazar Beers the next year, and in 1705, Peter Clayes.

SAMUEL HARRINGTON, of Hatfield, 1679.

REFERENCES:—Amer. Ancestry, V, 120; IX, 99, 110; XI, 32; Savage's Gen. Dict., II, 259; Young's Hist. Chautauqua Co., N. Y., 601; Temple's Hist. No. Brookfield, Mass., 616; Barry's Hist. of Framington, Mass., 270; Chandler's Hist. of Shirley, Mass., 431-3; Norton's Hist. of Fitzwilliam, N. H., 592-4; Ward's Hist. of Shrewsbury, Mass., 317-23; Williams' Hist. of Danby, Vt., 157-60; Wyman's Charlestown, Mass., Gens., I, 466; Leland Gen., 52; Locke Gen., 47, 93, etc.

HARRIS COAT OF ARMS.

Ar—a lion, rampant, sa.—over all a chevron ermine. —Crest, a falcon, with wings expanded. Or"—

HARRIS:—Anthony Harris, of Boston, son of the widow Elizabeth, Artillery Co., 1644, may have lived at Ipswich 1648; but if this were the inhab. of that town he came soon after to B., died at that part called Winnisemet, now Chelsea, 1651; in his will names wife Elizabeth, brothers Daniel and Thomas, but no children.

ARTHUR HARRIS, of Duxbury, 1640, was early settler of Bridgewater, but removed to Boston and died 1674:, leaving wife Martha, and child Isaac, who lived at Bridgewater; Martha, who married Thomas Snell; and Mary, who married John Winchcomb. Mitchell.

BENJAMIN HARRIS, of Boston, bookseller, from London, 1687, proj. a newspaper that·year but was unsuccessful; went home 1694.

BERNARD HARRIS, of Boston, by wife Mary had Hezekiah, born 1666.

DANIEL HARRIS, of Rowley, 1643, perhaps brother of Anthony, married Mary, daughter of Joseph Weld of Roxbury, removed 1652 to Middletown, there in 1660 was appro. to keep an inn, a lieut. 1661 and capt. soon after, had large family; daughters, Mary, Elizabeth, Sarah, died soon; Sarah again, Hannah; sons, Daniel, Joseph, Thomas, William and John; he died 1701; his widow Mary died 1711.

DANIEL HARRIS, of Boston, by wife Sarah, had Sarah 1687.

DAVID HARRIS, of Charlestown, but may have been of Boston, mariner, in 1695, by wife Thomasin had Joseph 1679; Ann, Elizabeth, 1683; Thomasin 1685; Elson 1687.

EXPERIENCE HARRIS, Boston, by wife Abigail had Abigail 1676.

GEORGE HARRIS, Salem, 1636, had in 1638 a family of 6, and died before 1644, when Joseph and another son about 8 years old were bound to apprent.

GEORGE HARRIS, Concord, 1669, married 1671, Lydia Grosse, had Edmund, born 1672; Lydia 1675; John 1677; Hannah 1679; Lydia 1681; he married again, 1688, Sarah Vinting, or Vinton, had George 1691; most of this family went to Lancaster.

GEORGE HARRIS, Boston, died about 1686, leaving widow Joanna.

JAMES HARRIS, Boston, by wife Sarah had Sarah, 1668; James 1673; Margaret 1674; died soon; Mary 1677; Deborah, Elizabeth, Asa, 1680; Hannah 1682; all bapt. 1683; Ephraim 1684; Mary, again, 1686; Ephraim, again, 1688, and perhaps by another wife, James.

JOHN HARRIS, of Rowley, may have been that passenger in the Christian from London 1635, aged 28, freeman 1647, and by wife Bridget had Ezekiel, Nathaniel, both probably died young; John, born 1649; Thomas 1651, probably died young; Timothy 1657; and Mary, who married William Allen, of Salisbury; his wife died 1672.

JOHN HARRIS, of Charlestown, by wife Amy had Samuel, born 1658; John 1661; Thomas 1662, died next year; Thomas, again, 1664; Joseph 1665, and perhaps more.

JOHN HARRIS, of Boston, married 1657, Hannah, daughter of William Briggs, had John 1658.

JOHN HARRIS, Boston, had wife Joanna in 1671, possibly may be same as preceding, but it is not likely, nor that John of B. who married 1675, Susanna Breck of Dorchester, was; or a mariner John of B., who by wife Elizabeth, daughter of William Lane, had seven children and died 1682.

JOHN HARRIS, Ipswich, 1673, had wife Esther, freeman 1685.

JOHN HARRIS, of Marblehead, a fisherman, had in 1673, wife Sarah.

JOHN HARRIS, of Marblehead, 1674, weaver, had wife Hannah in 1692.

JOSEPH HARRIS, of Charlestown, by wife Mary had Mary, born 1672; Richard 1675; Joseph 1676; Sarah 1678; besides two Johns that died infants.

NICHOLAS HARRIS, of Dover, 1665-84.

RICHARD HARRIS, brother of the first wife of Presid. Dunster, whom perhaps he accomp. 1640 from Eng., died 1644.

RICHARD HARRIS, Wethersfield, died 1666, unmarried.

RICHARD HARRIS, of Braintree, by wife Margaret had Sarah 1663; John 1665; another son, prob. Peter, 1667; Samuel 1669; William 1675; and perhaps others.

RICHARD HARRIS, of Charlestown, died 1679.

RICHARD HARRIS, of Salem, mariner, married 1671, Hannah, daughter of Matthew Dow, and he, or another of same name died 1681.

RICHARD HARRIS, of Boston, merchant, by wife Elizabeth had Sarah, 1680; Mercy 1681; Eliz., died soon; Richard, died young; Elizabeth, again, died young; Mary 1689; Richard, again, 1694; and Elizabeth, again, 1695; and he died 1697.

RICHARD HARRIS, of Charlestown, had wife Hannah in 1682.

ROBERT HARRIS, Boston, living in that part called Muddy River, now Brookline, married, 1653, Elizabeth Boughey, or Boffee, had Elizabeth, born 1644; John, Timothy, 1650; Daniel 1652; and Prescilla 1653; up to this date he had perhaps been of Roxbury, was freeman 1650, and probably died 1701. See Geneal. Reg. V, 307.

SAMUEL HARRIS, of Salem, mariner, had been, perhaps, of Manchester, 1667, probably removed to Beverly and died 1682.

THOMAS HARRIS, Roxbury, died in family of John Johnson, 1640, may have been father of first Daniel.

THOMAS HARRIS, Providence 1637, brother of William, an assist. under first charter 1654, and under second 1666-9, had sworn alleg. to Charles II, 1666, died 1686; had Thomas, Richard, Nicholas, William, Henry, Ethelan, who married Nathaniel Brown, Joab, Amity, who married a Morse; Mary, who married Gabriel Bernon; and Job, as Staples declares.

THOMAS HARRIS, of Ipswich, perhaps brother of Anthony, had land in Rowley 1644, married 1647, Martha, daughter of Margaret Lake, had Thomas, born 1648; Martha 1651; John 1653; Elizabeth 1655; Margaret 1657; Mary 1660; William 1661; and Ebenezer, perhaps others.

THOMAS HARRIS, of Providence, not son of Thomas of the same, called Jr., when he took oath of alleg. same day with him, but another Thomas, Jr., of P., swore to his alleg. 1682, was then, if son of the first Thomas of the same, in his 17th year, the right military age; and he married Phebe Brown, but of what family is not known.

THOMAS HARRIS, a Quaker, came from R. I. 1658, to Boston, was fined, imprisoned and cruelly treated.

THOMAS HARRIS, of Charlestown, by wife Hebzibah, had Thomas, bapt. 1687; Hepzibah 1689; William 1692; Silence 1694; and William 1700.

THOMAS HARRIS, Boston, butcher, by first wife had Jane, who married first a Smith, and next Robert Gold, of Hull; he married 2d wife 1679, Rebecca, wid. of John Croakham, daughter of Abraham Josselyn, had Samuel, born 1680; Rebecca 1681; three named Thomas; and Mary; all of whom died young; Mehitable 1691; and Benjamin 1694, and died 1698.

THOMAS HARRIS, Boston, by wife Sarah had Mary, born 1677.

THOMAS HARRIS, of Concord, married 1688, Mary Shepard, had Thomas, born 1689.

WALTER HARRIS, Weymouth, 1632, came in the William and Francis, freeman 1641, in 1649 was of Dorchester, removed to New London 1653, with wife Mary and child Gabriel, and Thomas; and died 1654.

WILLIAM HARRIS, of Salem, 1635, brother of Thomas of Providence, removed with Roger Williams to build Providence 1636, had bitter controv. a few years after with W. and so all the Planta. were divided into two fac-

tions, one for H. another for W. He took oath of alleg. to Charles II, 1666 at P. and eight years later was oblig. to go to Eng. to secure the interpos. of the crown as to the land controv. (for which will be found the King's response to Gov. Winthrop in Conn. Col. Rec. II, 580), returned to P. soon after outbreak of Philip's war; then staid through the war of 1675; in 1678, having made his will, aged 68, he went for home to support cause of Pautuxet proprs., emb. at Boston in the Unity, Capt. Condy, but early in 1679 was taken by an Algerine corsair and sold in Barbary. After more than a year's slavery he was redeemed at a high rate, traveled through Spain and France, and died, 1680, 3 days after reaching London. His widow, Susanna, was not perhaps mother of all his children; Andrew, born 1634 or 5; Mary, who married Thomas Burden; Howlong, who became 2d or 3d wife of Arthur Fenner, 1684; and Toleration 1645.

WILLIAM HARRIS, of Charlestown, 1642, brother of Anthony, and prob. by his mother the widow Elizabeth, in youth removed to Rowley, thence to Charlestown again and in few years to Middletown; by wife Edith had Hannah; Mary 1646; Martha; Elizabeth, and Patience; his wife died 1685 and he married Lydia, widow of Joseph Smith, but he lived to 1717.

WILLIAM HARRIS, of Boston, by wife Hannah had William 1672, died young; John 1673, died soon; Hannah; Hezekiah, both died young; Elizabeth 1680; Mercy 1682; Hezekiah, again, 1684; John 1686; and Samuel 1688.

WILLIAM HARRIS, of Boston, merchant, died before 1684, leaving William, born of first wife, and second wife Susan, who died 1702.

REFERENCES.

MASSACHUSETTS:—Essex, Mass., Inst. Hist. Colls., XXI, 106-10; Gage's Hist. of Rowley, 443; Hammatt Papers of Ipswich, 124-7; Daniel's Hist. of Oxford, 531-4; Wyman's Charlestown, I, 467-75; Ward's Shrewsbury, 325; Mitchell's Hist. of Bridgewater, 522; Hudson's Hist. of Lexington, 99; Barry's Hist. of Framingham, 271.

NEW HAMPSHIRE:—Cochrane's Hist. of Francestown, 745; Coffin's Hist. of Boscawen, 554; Bassett's Hist. of Richmond, 406-9; Stark's Hist. of Dunbarton, 207; Wheeler's Hist. of Newport, 409; Read's Hist. of Swanzey, 362.

OTHER PUBLICATIONS:—Amer. Ancestry, I, 36; II, 52; III, 114; IV, 120; V, 118, 149; VI, 94, 146; X, 103; Harris' Biog. Hist. of Lancaster, Pa.; Harris Family of Roxbury (1861), 56 pp.; H. Fam. of New London, Ct. (1878), 239 pp.; Harris Mem. of T. W. (1882), 14 pp.; Harris Fam. of Ipswich (1883) 135 pp.; H. Fam. of N. J. (1888), 350 pp.; H. Fam. of Va. (1893), Chart Harris Ancestors in N. E. (1887), 32 pp.; Savage's Gen. Dict., II, 360-6; N. E. Hist. Gen. Reg., II, 218; XXV, 185; Ely Gen., 314-6; Anstin's Ancestries 29; Austin's Allied Fams. 125; Austin's R. I. Gen. Dict., 310-5; Preble Gen., 248-50; Robertson's Pocahontas Descend.; Thomas Gen. (1877), 87; Cae and Ward Mem., 68-70.

HARRISON:—Edward Harrison, Boston, perhaps brother of Rev. Thomas, came from Virginia, where, says the rec., he was member of church; by wife Elinor had Joseph, 1646; and John, bapt. 1648.

ISAAC HARRISON, of Hadley, married, 1671, Martha, daughter of Richard Montague, had Abigail and Sarah; was killed after the Falls fight in 1676, by the Indians

JOHN HARRISON, of Salisbury, 1640, a ropemaker, by wife Grace had John, born 1642, prob. died young; rem. 1643 to Boston, freeman 1641; by wife Persis had John, 1652; Elizabeth 1653; and Abraham 1661; had also Ann.

JOHN HARRISON, Wethersford, merchant, freeman of Conn. 1657, died 1666, leaving large estate; had three daughters, Rebecca, Mary and Sarah; his widow Catharine, of unpleasant temper, was indict. as witch and found guilty, but the court had more sense than the jury, set aside the verdict and advis. the prisoner to rem. out of the reach of her timid and malignant neighb.

MARK HARRISON, sign. a memor. to the Gen. Court of Mass. 1654, which may be seen in Hutch. Coll. 255.

NICHOLAS HARRISON, Dover, 1675-1707.

RICHARD and RICHARD HARRISON, JR., were of New Haven 1644, of which the Sr. died 1653, and the Jr. had Samuel; Benjamin, 1655; John; Joseph; George; and Daniel; and rem. to Newark, N. J., where all exc. John, it is said, were heads of families.

THOMAS HARRIS, came from Virginia, where he was a minister whose teachings were not agreeable to Gov. Berkley; here, by Dorothy, daughter of Hon. Samuel Symonds of Ipswich, had Elizabeth, bapt. 1649; and next year went to Eng.; was a celebrated preacher in London, says Calamy, II, 122, and succ. Dr. Thomas Goodwin.

THOMAS HARRIS, New Haven, 1654, married widow of first John Thompson of the same, had Thomas, born 1657, and Nathaniel 1658, perhaps more; was probably of Branford 1667, had married, 1666, as second wife, Elizabeth Stent or Stint of B.

WILLIAM HARRIS, came in the Pied Cow, 1635, aged 55, from London; no more is known.

WILLIAM HARRIS, Boston, before 1686.

(Harrison Ref.)

REFERENCES:— Amer. Ancestry, II, 52; III, 172; IV, 159; VI, 28; IX, 90; XII, 107; Harrison Ancestry (1893), 96 pp.; Savage's Gen. Dict., II, 366; Wyman's Charlestown, Mass., Gens., 475-7; Symmes Gen. 89-92, 118-21; White Gen. (1879), 159-64; Power's Sangamon Co., Ill. Settlers, 358-60; Richmond, Va., Critic (1888); Gold's Hist. of Cornwall, Ct., 298-303; Montague Gen., 62; Munsey's Mag. 1896; Goode Gen., 113, 379, 478, 486; Hayden's Va. Gens., 510-13; Dwight Gen., 675, 723-5; Cabell Gen., 515-31; N. J. Hist. Coll., VI, Supp. 119; Page Gen., 97, 130, 224, 245.

HARROD:—John Harrod, Boston, had John, bapt. 1651, and perhaps by wife Rachel, that Jeremiah bapt. 1656.

JOHN HARROD, Warwick, married 1666, Elizabeth, daughter of John Cooke of same.

JOHN HARROD, Boston, perhaps son of first John, by wife Susanna had Hannah, born 1687.

THOMAS HARROD, Boston, 1680, where Mr. Drake says he was a juror in a sad witchcraft trial. Perhaps Harwood is sometimes the true name.

HART:—Edmund Hart, Dorchester, probably came in the Mary and John 1630, removed to Weymouth, freeman 1634, living 1664, and may be the man of Westfield killed by lightning 1673, whose son Elisha died 1683, and whose daughters were Sarah, wife of John Score; Martha, wife of Edward Neale; and one, wife of John Greet.

EPHRAIM HART, Weymouth, perhaps brother of Edmund.

ISAAC HART, Watertown, came 1637, as servant to Richard Carver, embarked at Yarmouth, was from Scrathby, a parish in that vicinity, aged 22; Lynn 1640, removed to Reading 1647; had Elizabeth, born 1651; Samuel 1657; and his daughter Rebecca died 1670.

JOHN HART, Salem 1637, came in the William and Francis, embarked at London 1632; went home and came again 1635, aged 40, with wife Mary, in the James from London, was a shipwright, of Marblehead 1648, Boston 1651, died 1656; his daughter Judith married Robert Ratchell, or Rachell, and next 1660, Thomas Rease, or 1663 Philip Bullis.

JOHN HART, New Haven, 1656, perhaps that son of Stephen, who, with his father, removed to Farmington, and was freeman of Conn. 1654; had Sarah, born 1653; John 1655; and Stephen 1657; in which all of family except himself and son John were burned with his house; he died 1666.

JOHN HART, Portsmouth, 1665.

JOSEPH HART, Lynn, married 1684, Ruth Chadwell.

LAWRENCE HART, Newbury, married 1679, Dorothy Jones; had Lucy, born 1679; Mary 1681, died in a few days; Ann 1682, died young; Charles 1684; Ann, again, 1685; Lawrence 1687; and John 1689.

NATHANIEL HART, Ipswich, 1636.

NICHOLAS HART, Taunton, 1643, excom. there, came to Boston and next year or follow. was occasion of ex- com. of Sarah, wife of Benjamin Keayne, daughter of Gov. Thomas Dudley.

RICHARD HART, Portsmouth, R. I., had Alice 1687; George Pierce, and perhaps other children.

SAMUEL HART, Lynn 1640; had Mary, who died 1657; Hannah 1657; Joseph 1659; Abigail 1660; John 1666, died at 14 mos.; Rebecca 1668; Ezekiel 1669, died soon; and his wife Mary, who may have been mother of all the preceding, died 1671; he married 1674, Mary Whiting, but Lewis made the name Witteridge; had John, who died 1676; and William, born same year; his widow married, 1684, William Beale.

STEPHEN HART, Cambridge 1632, perhaps brother of first John, or of Edmund, or both, freeman 1634, re- moved to Hartford, thence to Framington, where he was represent. 1647, and most of the time following, to 1660, one of the founders of the church 1652, and its deacon; had John, Stephen, Thomas, besides daughters Sarah, wife of Thomas Porter, and Mary, wife of John Lee; had no children by his second wife Margaret, widow of Arthur Smith; and died 1683; his widow long outlived him.

THOMAS HART, New Haven 1645, perhaps of Ipswich 1648, may be the same man of Newport, who married Freeborn, daughter of Roger Williams; had John, James and Mary, who married Samuel Cranston, and he died before 1674; his widow married, 1683, as third wife Gov. Walter Clark. One Thomas was a soldier in Gal- lap's company for the ill-starred attempt against Que- bec, 1690.

REFERENCES.

MASSACHUSETTS:—Lewis Hist of Lynn, 277; Hammatt Papers of Ipswich, 131.

CONNECTICUT:—Orcott's Hist. of Torrington, 709; Timlom's Southington Sketches, 107-30; Davis' Hist. of Wallingford, 787-9; Andrew's New Britain, 149-51, 170-91.

NEW HAMPSHIRE:-Hayward's Hist. of Hancock, 639-41; Little's Hist. of Weare, 897; Worthen's Hist. of Sutton, 740-4.

OTHER PUBLICATIONS:—Amer. Ancestry, I, 36; II, 52; V, 131, 140, 176; VIII, 112; X, 6, 39; Hart Fam. of Bucks Co., Pa. (1867), 159 pp.; H. Fam. of Conn. (1875), 606 pp.; H. Fam. of Virginia (1882), 82 pp.; Morris Gen. (1853), 38; N. Y. Gen. and Biog. Rec. XV, 108-11; XXI, 36-9; XXVI, 170-7; Poore's Gen., 131-4.

HARTFORD:—William Hanford, a soldier at Northampton 1676, in Turner's company from Boston or Charlestown. Drake's index changes name to Hartley.

REFERENCES:—

HARTLEY:—Richard Hartley, New London, 1656, shopkeeper, from Stanfield, Co. York, where he left wife Mary and only child Martha; freeman 1658, was a serg., died 1662.

REFERENCES:—Amer. Ancestry, III, 165; Life of R. M. Hartley (1882).

HARTSHORN:—Benjamin Hartshorn, Reading, was freeman 1691, perhaps son of Thomas; died 1694.

DAVID and JOSEPH HARTSHORN, perhaps brothers of the preceding, served in Philip's war as soldiers at Hadley, 1676, were freemen 1691.

THOMAS HARTSHORN, Reading, one of the first settlers, freeman 1648; had Thomas 1648; Benjamin 1654; Jonathan 1656; David 1657; Susan 1660; and his wife died same year; he married, 1661, another wife, Sarah, had Timothy next year.

REFERENCES:—Cleveland's Hist. of Yates Co., N. Y., 504; Hill's Dedham, Mass., Rec. I; Secomb's Hist. of Amherst, N. H., 613-9; Whittemore's Hist. of Middlesex Co., Ct., 486; Walworth's Hyde Gen., 157, 725-9; Anderson's Waterbury, I, 61; Hayward's Hist. of Hancock, N. H., 641; Sylvester's Hist. Ulster Co., N. Y., 272.

HARTUB, or HARTOPP:—William, Duxbury 1643.

HARTWAY:—Abraham Hartway, a soldier of Moseley's comp., 1675.

HARTWELL.—William Hartwell, Concord, probably 1636, living in that part now Lincoln, was a valuable citizen, quartermaster in militia; had William, born 1638; John 1641; Mary 1643; Samuel 1645; Martha 1649; and Sarah; freeman 1642: a petur. for grant of Chelmsford, died 1690, aged 90. His first wife was Jessie: had other children, Jonathan and Nathaniel. He came, says tradition, from Kent; had, in 1644, or earlier, second wife Susan, in records made mother of Samuel, he was adm. 1628, and matric. with the rank of pensionwho died 1695.

REFERENCES:—Amer. Ancestry, V. 20; Chandler's Hist. of Shirley, Mass., 135-43; Cochrane's Hist. of Antrim, N. H., 527; Hartwell Fam. Reunion (1885), 15 pp.; (1891), 19 pp.; Hartwell Gen. (1887), 197 pp.; (1895),

176 pp.; Kingsman's No. Bridgewater, Mass., 530; North's Hist. of Augusta, Me., 881; Winchell Gen., 251.

HARVARD:—John Harvard, Charlestown, born near London, probably, for on his entry at the University he is called of Middlesex, educ. at Emanuel, where er, 1631, his A. B. was of 1631-2, and A. M. 1635; came here 1637, and on first Sunday in August united with church, freeman that year, and died next. Half his estate, £779. 17 2, he left to the college which perpet. his ever-honored name. His wife Ann is thought to have been daughter of Mr. Sadler of Patcham in Sussex, probably had by him no children, and in 1639, it is believed, married Thomas Allen.

REFERENCES:—Savage's Gen. Dict., II, 369.

HARVEY:—Edmund Harvey, Milford, 1639, merchant, brought two daughters, one 9 years, the other 4, and perhaps a wife, but probably was a widower, and married about 1640, Martha, had Josiah, bapt. 1640; and Hannah, born 1646; removed to Fairfield, it may be some years before, was represent. 1647, and died 1648, leaving a daughter then in England, aged 22; two more, aged 18 and 14 yrs., all by his former wife, but none of these three daughters are named. His widow married Nathan Gould.

JOACHIM HARVEY, Newcastle or Great Isl., N. H., freeman 1669; died 1678.

JOHN HARVEY, Lynn, or New London, 1682, died 1705, had only children John and Elizabeth; probably he was first of Newbury, and a soldier in the great Narragansett fight of Major Appleton's comp. 1675, in which he was wounded but not disabled, if he be the same who took oath of fidelity at Amesbury 1677.

JOSEPH HARVEY, from Earlscombe in Essex, died on his passage, and spoke of brother John in Wethersfield in old England.

MATTHIAS HARVEY, Hempstead, L. I., had removed there, Savage supposes, after marrying, about 1655, Mary, widow of Robert Cole.

PETER HARVEY, Salem 1692, may have been father of George, aged 46, and Henry, 43, impressed next year by a frigate as they came home from a fishing voyage. Felt, Ann. II, 214.

RICHARD HARVEY, a tailor, came from London in the Planter, 1635, aged 22, with Ann, perhaps his wife, 22, but no more is known of them. He may possibly be the following.

RICHARD HARVEY, Concord, had twin daughters born 1639, soon died, as did the mother, Margaret; he may have removed to Stratford; by another wife had Elizabeth, born 1644; Mary 1647; and Sarah 1650; was living 1659.

THOMAS HARVEY, Taunton 1643.

THOMAS HARVEY, Amesbury, captain, freeman 1690, represent. 1691 and 2, before and after new charter.

WILLIAM HARVEY, Plymouth, married 1639, Joanna, removed to Taunton, was represent. 1664 and 13 years after.

WILLIAM HARVEY, Boston, by wife Joan had Abigail, born 1640; Thomas 1641; Experience bapt. 1644; Joseph bapt. 1645; and probably the same man by wife Martha had William, 1651; Thomas, again, 1652; and John, 1655; he died 1658 and his widow next year married Henry Tewksbury.

REFERENCES:—Amer. Ancestry, II, 52; VI, 24; VI, 76; Green's Kentucky Fams.; Harvey Gen. (1899), 1057 pp.; Hoyt's Salisbury, Mass., Fams., 195; Savage's Gen. Dict., II, 369; Temple's Hist. of Palmer, Mass.; 488; Bemis' Hist. of Marlboro, N. H., 520-3; Carliss' No. Garmault, Me., Mag.; N. E. Hist. and Gen. Reg., XII, 313-5; Sheldon's Hist. Deerfield, Mass., 184; Worthen's Hist. of Sutton, N. H., 745-63; Smith's Hist. of Sunderland, Mass., 394-6.

HARWOOD, or HARWARD:—Edward Harwood, New Haven, 1641.

GEORGE HARWOOD, Boston, carpenter, by wife Jane, had John, born 1639; Joanna, 1642; and Deliverance, who died 1641; perhaps removed to New London about 1651. Of this name, also, was a distinguished merchant of London, who was treasurer of colony, 1629, and never came over the water.

HENRY HARWOOD, Charlestown, came with wife Elizabeth in fleet, no doubt with Winthrop, freeman 1633, had John, baptized 1632. and in October following was one of the founders of the church at Charlestown. His life was shortened by extraordinary suffering in a storm mentioned by Winthrop I 39, and he may have died as early as 1635.

HENRY HARWOOD, Salem, 1638, freeman 1643, died about 1664.

HENRY HARWOOD. Boston, shoemaker, by wife Elizabeth had Elizabeth, born 1665; Henry, 1667; Hannah, 1669; Elizabeth. again, 1671; and Henry, again, 1674; removed to Casco 1675; had command of the forces there before 1683; then went back to Boston.

JAMES HARWOOD, Boston, son of William Harwood, of Biddeford, in Devon, died before 1655.

JOHN HABWOOD, Boston, 1655, freeman, 1649, by wife Elizabeth had Elizabeth, baptized 1650; Hezekiah, 1653; died next year; Hannah, 1655; merchant and perhaps son of first treasurer; sold his estate 1657 to br. Thomas Scottow, went home. and in 1677, was of London, but directing his son John in import operations.

NATHANIEL HARWOOD, Boston, by wife Elizabeth had William, born 1665; perhaps he removed to Concord and was freeman, 1690.

ROBERT HARWOOD, Boston, baker, by wife Joanna had Thomas, born 1674.

ROBERT HARWOOD, Boston, married 1654, widow Rachel Woodward (whose former husband was Robert) daughter of John Smith, the tailor; had Rachel, born 1655, died next year; Jeremiah, 1656; Ann, 1657, died next year; Rachel, again, 1661; and Benjamin, 1663.

HASELTINE:—See Hazeltine.

REFERENCES:—Amer. Ancestry, VIII, 27; X, 173; XII; Chase's Hist. of Chester. N. H., 539-42; Goodwin's Hist. of Buxton, Me., 219; Haseltine Char. (1890), 12x18 inches.

HASEMAN:—Nathaniel Haseman, Braintree, 1662.

HASEY:—William Hasey, Boston, by wife Sarah had William, born 1652; Asa, 1655; Joseph. 1657; and Susanna, 1660: by second wife. Judith had William, again, 1679; and Jacob, 1684; was of artillery co. 1652; living at Rumney Marsh, now Chelsea, and died 1695, leaving widow Judith. Savage presumes he was freeman 1665; spelt Hazzy: others of the name were at Chelsea, and it has been wide spread.

REFERENCES:—Bangor Hist. Mag., IV, 122.

HASKELL, or HASCALL:—Roger Haskell, Salem, 1637, brother of 1st Wm., born about 1613; married Elizabeth, daughter of John Hardy, had John, William, Mark and Elizabeth, was of Beverly, after the incorp. of that town; but some confusion appears in arrang. relationship.

TOBIAS HASKELL, Lynn, 1645. Lewis.

WILLIAM HASKELL, Gloucester, 1642, born about 1617, married 1643, Mary, daughter of Walter Tybbot, had William, born 1644; Joseph, 1646; John, Benjamin, Ruth, Sarah; Mark, 1658, died 1691; Mary, 1660; and Eleanor, 1663; was represent. 1672, and several years mover, lieut. and capt. Descendants are more numerous than any other early settlers of G.

WILLIAM HASKELL, Salem, married 1679, Miriam Hill, had John, born 1680, and William, 1682.

REFERENCES:—Amer. Ancestry, I, 36; VII, 76; Bemis' Hist. of Marlboro, N. H., 525-7; Carliss' No. Yarmouth, Me., Mag.; Daniel's Hist. of Oxford, Mass., 538; Eaton's Hist. of Thomastown, Me., II, 256; Haskell Fam. Tree (1880); H. Gen. (1896), 63 pp. reprint; Haskell Mag. (1898), 100 pp.

HASKETT:—Stephen Haskett, Salem, 1664, soapboiler; by wife Ellen, had Stephen, born 1669; died 2 wks. Elias, 1670; Mary, 1672; Sarah, 1674; Hannah, 1675, and two other daughters; was pressed 1675 for a soldier in comp. of Capt. Corwin. Elias lived some time at Boston in the early part of the 18th century, before which Mr. Felt found evidence of his being Gov. at Providence, Bahama.

REFERENCES:—Austin Allied Fams., 127; Driver Gen. 281.

HASKINS, or HARSKINS:—John Haskins, a soldier of Gallops' company, 1690, in the crusade against Quebec.

ROGER HASKINS, Salem, 1668.

THOMAS HASKINS, Barnstable, 1668.

WILLIAM HASKINS, New Haven, 1643.

WILLIAM HASKINS, Lynn, died 1662, leaving William, who in 1665, had wife Grace. See HOSKINS.

REFERENCES:—Amer. Ancestry, II, 53; Hoskin's Emerson Ancestors, 2-27; Paige's Hist. of Hardwick, Miss., 391; Warren's Hist. of Waterford, Me., 225; Williams' Hist of Danbury, Vt., 159-61.

HASSARD:—Thomas Hassard. See Hazard.

HASSELL:—John Hassell, Ipswich, 1636, freeman 1637; removed probably to Rehoboth with first settlers, 1642. where the record is Hazell, but back again to I. 1648; no wife or children.

RICHARD HASSELL, Cambridge, freeman 1647; by wife Joan had Elizabeth, born 1643; Joseph. 1645; and Esther, 1648. He perhaps removed to Watertown; there had Ann. born 1669; thence to Dunstable. This name may be HASWELL.

HASTINGS:—John Hastings, tanner, of Braintree, freeman 1643; had Walter, born 1631. and Samuel, brought from England, John, born on passage, and Elizabeth, 1643; "both bapt." says Mitchell's Reg. "at Braintree": removed to Cambridge, where in 1652 he had shared in division of the Shawsheen land, married there Ann, widow of John Means, and died 1657.

ROBERT HASTINGS, Haverhill, took oath of fidelity 1677.

THOMAS HASTINGS, Watertown, came in the Elizabeth 1634, aged 29, with wife Susan, 34, from Ipswich, and may be thought a Suffolk man, freeman 1635; his wife died 1651, without children, and he married shortly afterward Margaret Cheney; had Thomas, born 1652; John 1654; William 1655, drowned at 14 years; Joseph 1657; Benjamin, 1659; Nathaniel, 1661; Hepzibah, 1664; and Samuel, 1666; was deacon, represent. 1673; date of his death unknown, but will probated 1685.

REFERENCES:—Amer. Ancestry, XII, 53; Bemis' Hist. of Marlboro, N. H., 523-5; Cochrane's Hist. of Antrim, N. H., 528; Corliss' Gen.; Hastings Gen. (1886), 183 pp.; Kellog's White Gen. 100; N. E. Hist., Reg., XIII, 134; XXI, 350-2; Paul's Hist. of Wells, Vt., 102; Saunderson's Charlestown, N. H., 392-9; Savage's Gen. Dict., II, 372-5; Sheldon's Hist. of Deerfield, Mass., 185-8, 401-8; Stearns' Hist. of Rindge, N. H., 555; Wyman's Charlestown, Mass., Gen. I, 480.

HATCH:—Charles Hatch, York, probably a fisherman, died during or before 1655; his brother Philip was admin. on his estate.

PHILIP HATCH, York, freeman, 1652.

SAMUEL HATCH, was a volunteer in the Pequot war, 1637, says Deane; but he tells no more. Perhaps he was of Duxbury, 1684.

THOMAS HATCH, Dorchester, freeman 1634, removed to Scituate, there died about 1646, but he had probably gone to Barnstable before 1643, and may have returned; left Jonathan, William, Thomas, Alice and Hannah.

THOMAS HATCH, Barnstable, had wife Grace, and probably died 1661; a young man.

WILLIAM HATCH, Scituate, perhaps as early as 1633, but if so he went home, and, 1635, brought in the Hercules from Sandwich, in Kent; wife Jane, 5 child. and 6 servants. He was the first rul. elder of the 2d church founded in 1644, for William Witherell, after long agitations foll. the removal of Lathrop to Barnstable; was brother of 1st Thomas, probably, and died 1651. His widow Jane married, 1653, Elder Thomas King. His children were William, Walter, Ann, Hannah, Jane, Jeremiah, also, perhaps, Lydia.

WILLIAM HATCH, of New London, about 1690.

REFERENCES:—Amer. Ancestry, II, 53; VI, 9, 81, 118; Boyd's Annals of Winchester, Ct., 190; Davis' Landmarks, Plymouth, Mass, 130; Draper's Hist. of Spencer, Mass., 210; Hanover (Mass.) Records (1898); Hatch Fam. of Scituate (1874), 23 pp.; H. Fam. of Hartford (1879), 36 pp.; H. Fam. of Boston (1896), 7 pp.; Hatch Gen. (1879), 36 pp.; Hatch's Hist. of Industry, Me., 638-42; Hayword's Hist. of Hancock, N. H., 1052; Montague Gen., 85; Loomis Gen. (1880), 634; N. E. Hist. Gen. Reg., XIV, 197-9; II, 34-8; Rich's Hist. of Truro, Miss., 535; Savage's Gen. Dict., II, 375; Swift's Barnstable Fams., I, 461-73; Tanner Gen., 66-70; Winslow Gen., II, 740-4.

ARMS:—Gu., two demi-lions, rampant, or.

HATHAWAY, or HADAWAY:—Arthur Hathaway, Marshfield, 1643, married 1652, Sarah Cook, perhaps daughter of Rev. John, had John, born 1653; and Sarah 1656; ten years later was at Dartmouth, and there took oath of fidelity 1684.

JOHN HATHAWAY, Barnstable, perhaps came at 18 years in the Blessing 1635, from London, married 1656, Hannah Hallet, had son born 1657, died soon; John 1658; Hannah 1662; and Edward 1664; removed to Taunton, of which he was represent. 1680-4 inclus., and 1691.

JOSEPH HATHAWAY, Taunton, freeman 1657; was perhaps brother of the first John.

REFERENCES:—Amer. Ancestry, II, 53; X, 128; Cleveland's Hist. of Yates Co., N. Y., 113-7; Hathaway Gen. (1869), 43 pp.; Lapham's Hist. of Norway, Me., 519; N. E. Hist. and Gen. Reg., XXXII, 236; Paige's Hist. of Hardwick, Mass., 394-6; Savage's Gen. Dict., II, 376; Swift's Barnstable Fams., I, 457-61; Slafter Gen., 25-7.

HATCHETT:—William Hatchett, found by Felt; in Mass. 1641, but perhaps only a transient visitor.

HATHERLY:—Arthur Hatherly, Plymouth, 1660. Deane.

GEORGE HATHERLY, Boston, by wife Abigail, had Thos., born 1668, who married, 1693, Lydia Greene; Abigail, 1670; and Samuel, 1678.

TIMOTHY HATHERLY, Scituate, came in the Ann, 1623, to Plymouth; went home next year; was a merchant in London, and came for the residue of his days, arriving in the Charles at Boston, 1632, coming with his wife from Barnstable in Devon, where also is a parish of his name; for 2d wife he married, 1642, Lydia, widow of Nathaniel Tilden, but had no children; was assistant from 1636 to 1657 incl. ex. 1638, and died 1666.

REFERENCE:—Dean's Scituate, 280-2.

HATHORNE, or HAWTHORNE:—Ebenezer Hathorne, Salem, 1669. Felt, I, 286.

JOHN HATHORNE, Salem, 1643, had there baptized, Sarah, 1644; John, 1646; and Priscilla, 1649; removed to Lynn; had there, William, born 1651, died 1676; Mary, 1653, died 1676.

NATHANIEL HATHORNE, Lynn, perhaps brother of first John, as Lewis gave him residence there 1634, but no more is known of him.

WILLIAM HATHORNE, Salem 1636, had before been of Lynn or Dorchester, conflicting claims for each town's assert by Lewis and Harris severally, from 1630, when he came in the Arabella with Winthrop, freeman 1634, represent. 1635, perhaps for D., speaker 1644, and 6 years after, Assistant 1662-79, Milit. Command. as capt. or major in Philip's war and in the following with the Eastern Indians; died 1681 in 74th year; had at Salem Eleazur, born 1637; Nathaniel, 1639; John, 1641; Ann, 1643; William, 1646; Elizabeth, bapt. 1649; and Mary, 1653.

REFERENCE:—Bangor Hist. Mag., VI, 153-5; Essex, Mass. Inst. Hist. Colls. XVII, 153-5; N. E. Hist. and Gen. Reg., XLII, 363; Eaton's Thomaston, 260.

HATLEY:—Philip Hatley, Milford, 1639, went home to London 1649.

RICHARD HATLEY, came in the Hopewell, Capt. Babb, from London 1635, aged 15, of whom no more is known.

HATSELL:—George Hatsell, Boston (by mistake of a letter for Halsall), in record of the town. See Halsall.

HENRY HATSELL, New Haven, came from London, where, after 1656 he had married Susanna, widow of John Evance, had Henry, and died 1667. His widow and child went to London.

HATWELL:—Benjamin Hatwell. See Atwell.

HAUGH:—See Hough. Eaton's Reading Mass., 87.

HAUGHTON:—Henry Haughton, Salem, came 1629, with the fleet of Higginson; was made ruling elder; died same year.

RICHARD HAUGHTON, Boston, removed with Sir Joseph, born about 1639, and Robert 1642, to New London 1651, and may have been first at Milford, had second wife Catharine, widow of Nicholas Charlet, of Boston, who died 1670, and he had third wife, Alice, before 1673. Children by the second were John, Catharine, Sampson, Abigal, James and Mercy. He was a shipwright, and died at Wethersfield 1682 while building a vessel.

REFERENCES:—Caulkins' New London, Ct., 299; Hudson's Hist. of Lexington, Mass., 106; Bakers' Montville, Ct., 486-8.

HAVEN, or HAVENS:—Richard Haven, Lynn, 1645, said to have come from west of England, by wife Susanna had Hannah, born 1646, Mary, 1647; Joseph, 1650; Richard, 1651; Susanna, 1653; Sarah, 1655; John, 1656; Martha, 1659, died at 4 months; Samuel, 1660, died 6 moths; Jonathan, 1663, died next year; Nathaniel, 1664; and Moses, 1667. His wife died 1682; he probably lived many pears.more; was freeman 1691.

THOMAS HAVEN, Dedham, married Mary, daughter of Thomas Hearing, or Herring.

WILLIAM HAVEN, whose name at Portsmouth is spelled Havens, is, in the list of inhabs. recorded 1639, called Heavens; died 1683. His will names wife Dennis, or Dionis, and children, John, Robert, George, Thomas and William, with equal number of unmarried daughters, and Sarah, wife of John Tyler of Bristol; Mary, wife of Thomas Cook; Ruth, wife of ——— Card; Dinah, Elizabeth, Martha, Rebecca and Margaret. Thomas, and perhaps William, went to live at Narrangansett.

REFERENCES:—Ballou's Milford, Mass., 788; Bemis' Hist. of Marlboro, N. H., 527; Haven Gen. (1843), 104 pp.; Haven Family Meeting (1849), 28 pp.; Leland Gen., 49; Wakefield Gen., 158; Wood's Hist. Shrewsbury, Mass., 330-2.

HAVILAND:—Edward Haviland, Boston, by wife Susanna, had Susanna. born 1657. He died early, and his widow married 1659, Philip Harding.

WILLIAM HAVILAND, a freeman there 1653, represent. 1656.

REFERENCES:—Amer. Ancestry, II. 53; Baird's Hist. of Rye, N. Y., 475; Pelletreau's Westchester Wills, 399-410.

HAWES:—Daniel Hawes, Wrentham, by wife Abigail had Abigail, born 1681; Daniel, 1684; Josiah, 1686; Hezekiah, 1688; Ruth, 1691; and Benjamin, 1696.

EDMUND HAWES, Yarmouth. a cutler, of London, came in the James from Southampton, arriving 1635; represent. 1645; and 15 years besides; had John and perhaps other children.

EDMUND HAWES, Dedham, 1655.

JEREMIAH HAWES, Yarmouth, perhaps son of Edmund, or Thomas. represent. 1676. and several more years.

JOHN HAWES. Barnstable. married 1661, Desire, daughter of Capt. John Gorham; perhaps he was brother of the preceding, and may have lived at Yarmouth.

RICHARD HAWES, Dorchester, came in the Truelove, 1635, aged 29, with wife Ann, 26, and children, Ann, 2½, and Obadiah, 6 months; freeman 1638; and here had Bethia, born 1637; Deliverance, 1640; Constance, 1642; and Eleazur.

ROBERT HAWES, Roxbury, joined the church in 1665, and buried 1666, "aged about 84"; names in will children Thomas, John and Mary, and makes son Humphrey Barrett excor.

THOMAS HAWES, Yarmouth, a capt., represent. 1652, and 11 years more, had wife Mary, son Thomas, Joseph and Jeremy, all named in his will 1665.

WILLIAM HAWES, Boston, by wife Susanna had Susanna, born 1652.

REFERENCES:—Amer. Ancestry, I, 36; V, 128; Cochrane's Hist. of Antrim, N. H., 529; Corliss' No. Yarmouth, Me., 841-4; Daniel's Hist. of Oxford, Mass, 539; Hawes Gen. (1895), 28 pp.; Leland Gen., 268; Morse's Sherborn. Mass., Settlers. 99; Wentworth Gen., I, 345-9; Sibley's Hist. of Union, Me., 459-64.

HAWKE, more com. HAWKES:—Adam Hawke, Lynn, 1638, may have came in the fleet with Winthrop and been first a Charlestown. His wife Ann, probably mother of all but one of his children, died 1669; and he married, 1670, Sarah Hopper; had Sarah, born 1671; other children were Adam; John, about 1633; Moses, Benjamin, Thomas, and Susanna. He died 1672, aged 64. See Lewis, 64.

GERSHOM HAWKE, Malden, married Elizabeth, daughter of Richard Pratt, of the same.

JOHN HAWKE, freeman 1634; may have then been of Lynn, as Lewis claims. but more probably of Dorchester, next that inhab. of Windsor, who there had John, born 1643; Nathniel, 1645; Elizabeth, 1647; Ann, 1648; Isaac, 1650; Mary, 1652; Joanna, 1654; Eliezer, 1655; Sarah, 1657; Gershom, 1659; beside two that died young; removed to Hadley about 1600: there was buried 1662. His widow Elizabeth married Robert Hinsdale, and 3rd Thomas Dibble.

MATTHEW HAWKE. Hingham, came in the Diligent, of Ipswich, 1638. embark. at London; arrived 10 Aug. with wife Margaret, and servant John Fearing; was from Cambridge. England: freeman 1642; was town clerk, and died 1684. aged 74 years. leaving only son James, born 1649; but appears to have had others.

THOMAS HAWKE, Salem, 1648.

REFERENCES:—American Ancestry, XII; VI, 119; Barrus. Goshen. Mass., 147; White's Discourse Claremont. Mass., 42; Sheldon's Hist. of Deerfield. Mass., 188-99; Baker Gen. (1867). 50-2; Hawkes' Gen. (1887), 20 pp. reprint.

HAWKESHURST, or HAUXHURST, as he wrote it or HAWXHURST, as sometimes the clerk wrote it:—Christopher Hawkeshurst, Warwick. in the list, freeman. 1655. and represent. the same year: married a daughter of Henry Reddock: removed in few years to L. I.

HAWKESWORTH. often HAUXWORTH:—Thos. Hawkesworth. Salisbury. 1640. an original proprietor. came perhaps. in the Christian 1635: aged 23; unless this be the age of son Thomas (which is not prob.) had wife Mary, and by her had Mary, born 1641: and he died 1642. His wife married Belshazzar Wllix.

HAWKINS:—Abraham Hawkins, Charlestown 1642, freeman 1645; died 1648.

ANTHONY HAWKINS, Windsor, had Mary, born 1644; Ruth, 1649; and John, 1652; by wife who died 1655. Removed 1656, to Farmington; there married Ann, widow of Thomas Thompson, daughter of Gov. Thomas Wells, had by her, who died 1680, Sarah, 1657; Elizabeth, 1660; and Hannah, 1662; was represent. for 17 sessions; is named in the charter of Conn, 1662, and was Assist. 1668-70; died 1674.

GAMALIEL HAWKINS, Salem, 1688, mariner.

GEORGE HAWKINS, Boston 1644, shipwright.

JAMES HAWKINS, Boston 1635, had wife Mary; son James, born 1652, died soon; James again, 1654; Mary; Ruth, Damaris, Elizabeth; Susan, 1646; and Sarah, 1656; beside Peleg, 1648; probably died young.

JOB HAWKINS, came in the Planter from London, 1635, aged 15, at Boston; by wife Francis had Martha, born 1646.

JOHN HAWKINS, Boston, 1630, No. 41 in list of church members; died early.

JOHN HAWKINS, Boston, married 1654, Sarah, daughter of Humphrey Damarill.

RICHARD HAWKINS, Boston, 1637, had wife Jane, suspected of witchcraft, having "much familiarity with the devil in England," as Winthrop asserts, I, 261, and II, 9. Perhaps he removed to Portsmouth, R. I.

RICHARD HAWKINS, a youth of 15, came in the Susan and Ellen from London 1635; perhaps was the freeman Portsmouth, R. I., 1655, or he may have been son of the preceding.

ROBERT HAWKINS, Charlestown, came in the Elizabeth and Ann 1635, aged 25, with Mary, 24, his wife; freeman 1636; had Eleazer, bapt. 1636; Zachary, 1639; Joseph, 1642; and perhaps more.

ROBERT HAWKINS, Boston, freeman 1690.

ARMS:—Arg., three inescutcheons, gu.

THOMAS HAWKINS, of Boston, a man of distinct., was a shipwright in London, had grant of lot 1636 at Charlestown, but living then at Dorchester, and there continued several years, but removed at last to B.; had Hannah, bapt. 1644; artillery co., 1638; freeman 1639; represent. 1639; a capt. and merchant of more enterprise than discretion; died abroad 1648. See Winthrop. His widow, Mary, married 1654, Capt. Robert Fenn, and again, 1662, Henry Shrimpton. Thomas, his only son, was a shipwright of Boston. His daughters, beside Hannah, were Elizabeth, Sarah, Mary and Abigail.

THOMAS HAWKINS, Boston, baker, perhaps brother of Abraham, artillery co. 1649; by wife, Hannah, who died 1644, had Abraham, 1637; Hannah and Job, twins, 1641; Hope, 1643; and by wife Rebecca, had Rebecca, 1645; and Mehitable, 1657, died soon. He kept an inn in his later days. Hannah married 1661, Edward Howard.

TIMOTHY HAWKINS, Watertown, 1635, by wife Hannah, had Hannah, born 1637; Timothy, 1639; and Mehitable; died 1651. Hannah, the widow, married 1653, Ellis Barron.

WILLIAM HAWKINS, New Haven, early had a lot there, but it was sold before 1656; nor was he known as a resident.

WILLIAM HAWKINS, the freeman of Providence 1655, who was called Senr. when he took oath of allegiance 1668; and may have been the man called Hunkings in 3 Mass. Hist. Coll. I, 4,—when with others then praying for protect. of Mass., but who is by Winslow called Hawkins. He lived at P. throughtout war with Philip; perhaps had son William, born about 1647; John, who was eldest; besides Mary, and probably Edward.

WILLIAM HAWKINS, Boston 1666, a butcher, calls himself surgeon in his will of 1685; had wife Dorothy and speaks of children, but names none.

ZECHARIAH HAWKINS, in some part of Long Island, perhaps Brookhaven, adm. freeman of Conn., jurisdict. 1664.

ARMS:—Arg., on a saltire, sa., five *fleurs-de-lis*, or,

CREST:—On a mount, vert., a hind lodged; proper.

MOTTO, *Toujours pret.*

REFERENCES:—American Ancestry, XI, 85; XII; Austin's R. I. Gen. Dict. 94, 316; Green's Kentucky Fams.; Hubbard's Hist. of Springfield, Vt., 327; Lapham's Hist. of Norway, Me., 520; Mead's Old Churches, of Va.; Savage's Gen. Dict., II, 382-4; Wymans Charlestown, Mass., Gen., I, 482; Young's Hist. of Wayne Co., Ind., 341.

HAWLEY:—Joseph Hawley, Stratford 1649, perhaps earlier; by wife Catharine. had Samuel; Joseph, born 1650; Elizabeth, 1651; Ebenezer, 1654; Hannah, 1657; Ephraim, 1659; John, 1661; and Mary, 1663. He was a prominent man, represent. at many sessions, made his will 1689, and died next year, as did Ephraim.

SAMUEL HAWLEY, called Dr. Trumbull, one of the first settlers of Stratford, may have been at Norwalk 1657; but it is altogether uncertain whether it be not an error of the bapt. name.

THOMAS HAWLEY, Roxbury, had Thomas, born 1651, says the town record, and his wife Amy or Emma died same year; he married next year Dorothy Lamb, widow of Thomas; had Joseph, born that year, died soon; Joseph, again, 1654; Elizabeth, bapt. 1656; and Dorothy, 1658. He was killed by the Indians, 1676, at the same time with Capt. Wadsworth and many of his company at Sudbury. His widow died 1699.

REFERENCES:—Am. Ancestry II, 53; VI, 129; XII; Freeman's Hist. Cape Cod, Mass., II, 69, 139; Hawley Fam. of Marblehead (1887). 8 pp.; Hawley Gen. (1890). 608 pp.; Hawley Fam. of Marblehead (1897), 16 pp.; Middlefield Ct. Hist.; Orcutt's Hist. of New Milford, Ct., 709; Power's Sangamon Co., Ills., Settlers, 364; Salem, N. Y., Book of History, 59.

HAWTHORNE:—See Hathorne.

HAXIE, or HAUKSIE:—Lodowick Haxie, Sandwich, married 1662, Mary Presbury, daughter perhaps of John, had Bashua, born 1665; Joseph, 1667; John, 1669; Ann; Gideon, 1673; Hezekiah, 1677; and Solomon, 1679.

HAY:—James Hay, Reading, by Eatoon is named among early settlers.

THOMAS HAY, Boston, by wife Bridget, had Nicholas, born 1687; and Sarah, 1689.

ARMS:—Arg., three in escutcheons, gu.

REFERENCES:—Bond's Watertown, Mass., 295; Wyman's Charlestown, Mass., Gens., 483-7; Richmond, Va.,

Standard, II, 45; Egle's Penn., Gens., 2nd edit., 334-40; Eaton's Hist. of Reading, Mass., 91.

HAYDEN, or HAYDON:—James Hayden, Charlestown, 1635, freeman 1637; by wife Elizabeth, who died 1665, had James, born 1638; John, 1639; Ruhamah, 1641; also Elizabeth; Mercy; Joshua; Sarah, died 1662; and Thomas, who died 1656; and he died 1675.

JOHN HAYDEN, Dorchester, freeman 1634, at Braintree; had John, 1636; Joseph; Samuel; Jonathan, 1640; Hannah, 1642; Ebenezer, 1645; and Nehemiah, 1648.

JOHN HAYDEN, Warwick, R. I., was a freeman 1655.

JOHN HAYDEN, Charlestown; by wife Hannah, perhaps daughter of John Mayne, of Boston, had James, born 1673; he died 1674.

WILLIAM HAYDEN, Dorchester, came probably in the Mary and John, 1630; removed early to Hartford, thence after serving 1637 in the Pequot war, to Windsor; had Daniel, born 1640; Nathaniel, 1644; and Mary, 1648; all at W. His wife died at W. 1655, and he married Margaret, widow of William Wilcockson, removed 1666 to Killingworth; was represent. 1667, and there died 1669. Perhaps he was of Fairchild 1662. Mary married 1670, Judah Evarts, of Guilford. In Conn. name is sometimes Heyton; in Mass., Heiden, or Hoiden.

ARMS:—Quarterly, arg. and azure, a cross, engrailed, counterchanged.

REFERENCES:—Am. Ancestry, IV, 135; VIII, 156; XII, 57; Binney Gen., 30; Hayden Fam. of Conn. (1859), 16 pp.; H. Fam. of Mass. (1877), 46 pp; H. Fam. of Ct. (1885), 20 pp; H. Fam. of Ct. (1888), 329 pp.; Hayden's Virginia Gens., 26; Hay Wells Gen. 145-50; Loomis' Gen. (1880), 591, 736-9; Marshall's Grant Ancestry, 114-8; Savage's Gen. Dict., II, 386; Vinton Gen., 323-30; Wyman's Charlestown, Mass., Gen., I, 488.

HAYES:—George Hayes. Windsor, 1682, had there Daniel, born 1686; George, 1695; and William, 1697; besides four daughters; removed to Simsbury.

JOHN HAYES, Dover, 1680; married 1686. Mary Horne; another wife. or the same, was daughter of John Tuttle; had John 1686; Peter; Robert; Ichabod, 1692; Samuel, 1695; William. 1698; Benjamin, 1700; beside one daughter married Phipps; another married Ambrose, both of Salisbury; and one married Ambrose of Chester; died 1708.

NATHANIEL HAYES. Norwalk, 1652; in 1672 had 7 children; was living 1604. Probably he had for second wife, Mary, daughter of Thomas Kimberley. who names in his will grandchildren, Nathaniel, Elizabeth, and Mary Hayes.

ROBERT HAYES, Ipswich, 1638. Felt.

REFERENCES:—Am. Ancestry, II, 53; III, 25, 161; IX, 148; XII, 33-35; Goode Gen., 83-5; Haye's Gen., (1876), 76 pp.; 2nd edit. (1883). 84 pp.; 3rd edit. (1884), 354 pp; Haye's Wells Gen. 150-8; Maine Hist. and Gen. Rev., III, 118-20; N. E. Hist. and Gen. Reg., VI, 333; XXVII, 76-81; XXXVI, 387-93; Potts' Gen. (1895), 337-40; Runnel's Sanborton. N. H., II. 220-3; Stiles' Hist. of Windsor, Ct., II, 383-5; Selleck's Norwalk. Ct. (1896), 85-91; Hurd's Rockingham Co.. N. H., 632-6.

HAYMAN, or HEYMAN:—John Hayman, Charlestown, rope maker, had liberty in 1662, to spin in Boston; freeman 1688; bore the prefix of respect 1678; was ma-

jor; had wife Grace, who died 1683, aged 70. Frequently names is Heyman or Heman.

NATHAN, or NATHANIEL HAYMAN, Charlestown, probably son of the preceding; married 1674, Elizabeth Allen; had Nathan, born 1675; Elizabeth, 1677; Sarah, 1679; Mary, 1682; and Grace 1685.

SAMUEL HAYMAN, Charlestown, 1656, is thought to be brother of the preceding; by wife, Hannah, who died 1684, aged 39, had Mary, 1673; and Hannah, 1675. By and wife, Mary, daughter of John Anderson, widow of Rev. Thomas Shepard, he had Sarah, 1687, died soon; and Sarah, again, 1678; was represent. 1690, 1 and 2, and named a couns. in the charter of William and Mary, when Hutch II, 15, in error calls him of Maine; was buried 1712.

REFERENCES:—Amer. Ancestry, IV, 75; Wyman's Charlestown, Mass., Gens., I, 489; Savage's Gen. Dict., II, 388.

HAYNES, or HAINES:—Benjamin Haynes, Southampton, L. I., 1639; probably from Lynn; had several children residing there in 1698.

CHARLES HAYNES, New London, 1644, by wife Mary had James, born 1665; Peter, 1666; Charles, 1669; Jonathan, 1674; Mary, 1676, died soon; Mary, again, 1678; and Hercules, 1681; and died 1685.

EDMUND HAYNES, Springfield, 1646, died next year; had Sarah; Hannah and Ruth. His widow Hannah married George Lankton.

JAMES HAYNES, Salem, 1637, freeman 1637; had there bapt. John, 1639; James, 1641, died soon; Benjamin, 1643; Mary, 1646; James, again. 1647; Jonathan and Sarah, twins, 1648; and Thomas, 1651.

JOHN HAYNES, Cambridge, was of Copford Hall, Essex; came with Rev. Thomas Hooker, arriving in the Griffin 1633; freeman 1634; then chosen an Assist. and Gov. of the Col. 1639, and cont. by alternate years to fill that office; died 1654. By first wife he had Robert and Hezekiah, who were left in England; Roger, who went home, died soon; and Mary, who married Joseph Cooke. By second wife Mabel, sister of Roger Harlakenden, who came with her brother in the Defence 1635, aged 21, he had John; Joseph, born 1641; Ruth; and Mabel.

JOHN HAYNES, Sudbury, 1640. son of Walter, born in England; freemtn 1646; represent. 1669; by wife, Dorothy Noyes, had Elizabeth, born 1644; John, 1649; Mary, both died soon; Dorothy, 1651; Peter, 1654; Joseph, 1656, killed in youth by fall of a tree; Thomas, 1658, died young; James, 1660; Daniel. who died a soldier, 1688; Rachel; Ruth; and David, 1671.

RICHARD HAYNES, Beverly, 1671; had wife Mary, and died 1681. John Sampson, of B., married his daughter, whose name is not seen.

ROBERT HAYNES, Isle of Shoals, was in 1681, in 70th year.

SAMUEL HAYNES, Dover, 1640, came in the Angel Gabriel 1635. from Bristol, which was wrecked in great storm at Pemaquid; probably removed to Portsmouth 1646; selectman 1653; was living 1684 His children were Samuel, 1646; Matthias, 1650; and Elizabeth or Mary.

THOMAS HAYNES, Maine, 1658-65. Perhaps he removed to Amesbury, married, 1667, Martha Burnet, of Salisbury, and died 1683, leaving widow, who married

Samuel Buckman, and children as follows: Thomas, 13; Ellen, 9; Aquila, 5; John, 3; and Mary, 1½. He may have been son of Richard.

WALTER HAYNES, of Sudbury, one of the first proprs., a linen weaver of Sutton Mandeville, Co. Wilts. came in the Confidence from Southampton, 1638, aged 55, with wife Elizabeth, sons Thomas, John and Josias, all under 16, and daughters Suffrance and Mary, besides three servants; was freeman 1641; represent. 1641, 4, 8 and 51; selectman 10 years; died 1665.

WILLIAM HAYNES. Salem, 1644; perhaps brother of James or Richard; married Sarah, daughter of Richard Ingersoll; had Thomas, and perhaps other children.

ARMS:—Arg., three crescents, barry, undee, azure and gules.

CREST:—A stork rising: proper.

REFERENCES:—Am. Ancestry,I, 36; VI, 138; ix, 28; Caulkins' Hist. of New London, Ct., 309; Corliss Gens., 241; Darling Mem; Hayne's Gen. (1895), 8 p. reprint; Hayne's Gen. See Haines; Meade's Old Churches of Va.; Moore's American Governors, I, 311; N. E. Hist. and Gen. Reg. ix, 349-51; xxiv, 125, 442; xxxii, 310-2; xlvii, 71-5; xlix, 304-10; Roome Gen. 253; Washington, N. H. Hist., 468; Walworth's Hyde Gen, 1170.

HAYNOR:—William Haynor, Salem, 1660, a tailor from Virginia. Felt.

HAYWARD:—George Hayward, Concord 1635, one of the earliest settlers; freeman 1638; died 1671; by wife Mary, had John, born 1640; Mary; Joseph, 1643; Sarah, 1645; Hannah, 1647; Simeon, 1649; William, 1651; and George, 1654.

JAMES HAYWARD, Charlestown, spelt at London Custon House Haieward; came probably in the Planter, 1625; aged 22, was, perhaps, of Woburn, married Judith Phippen, aged 16; died 1642; had Rebecca, born that year. His widow married, 1644, William Symonds, of Woburn.

JAMES HAYWARD, New Haven 1643, died 1648, probably without family.

JOHN HAYWARD, Watertown 1632, freeman 1634, removed to Dedham, there was constable 1638, represent. 1645, died at Charlestown 1672.

JOHN HAYWARD, Plymouth 1643, had Sarah, born 1647, was after of Dartmouth, with son Daniel, propr. at Little Campton 1675.

JOHN HAYWARD, Boston, 1671, scrivener; by wife Mary had Thomas, 1672; and John, 1674; in 1677 was appointed postmaster for the col.; in 1673 was lieut. of artillery co. and later a notary; had second wife Elizabeth, who had been widow of Samuel Sendayy, and still earlier widow of John Warren; and died 1687.

JOHN HAYWARD, Boston 1676, by wife Silence, had Mary, born 1677.

NICHOLAS HAYWARD, Salem 1643, removed probably to Boston, and by wife Elizabeth had Richard, born 1665; Rebecca, 1666; and John, 1668.

RICHARD HAYWARD, Salem, was of Co. Bedford, came with Higginson 1629.

ROBERT HAYWARD, Windsor, a miller, married Lydia, daughter of first Thomas Kilbourne, had Tabitha, born 1647; Rebecca, 1648; Esther, 1651; Lydia, 1655; besides 3 other daughters, most of whom died young; and Ephraim, 1657; removed to Northampton 1659; but after

some years went back to W, there died 1684. This family is usually called Howard.

ROBERT HAYWARD, Boston, a notary. See Howard.

SAMUEL HAYWARD, Gloucester, married 1641; the first on record, a daughter of Henry Felch, had Samuel 1642; and John, 1643.

SAMUEL HAYWARD, Boston, by wife Isabel, had James, born 1645; Samuel, 1646; and Peter, 1654; and he, or more probably the preceding, was of Mendon, 1672.

SAMUEL HAYWARD, Charlestown, came in the Elizabeth 1635, aged 22, and Savage supposes sat down in that part which became Malden; had Martha, born 1653; Mary, 1654; Sarah, 1656; and Elizabeth, 1658, died young at C. He also had Richard, baptized 1660; Elizabeth, 1661; Deborah, 1662; Nathaniel, 1664.

THOMAS HAYWARD, came in the Hercules 1635, from Sandwich, being tailor of Aylesford, Co. Kent, with wife Susanna and 5 children, but he had perhaps been there as early as 1632, coming with Winslow in the William and Francis, and satisfied with prospects went home to bring them; settled at Duxbury before 1638, probably at Bridgewater 1651, being one of the first proprietors 1645, was freeman 1646; had Thomas, Nathaniel, John, Joseph, Elias, Mary and Martha. He died 1681.

THOMAS HAYWARD, Eufield, had Benjamin, born 1686; but before had Nathan, John and several daughters. It is probable that he was born on this side of the Atlantic.

WILLIAM HAYWARD, Hampton, freeman 1640, had been of Charlestown 1637, was lieutenant and representative 1641-5.

WILLIAM HAYWARD, Braintree 1648, had wife Margery and several children of whom Jonathan is the only one to be traced exactly; was drowned 1659.

WILLIAM HAYWARD, Swanzey, by wife Sarah had Jonathan, born 1672; Margery, 1673.

REFERENCES:—Amer. Ancestry, IV, 35; V, 148; VI, 37; VIII, 86 IX, 136; Austin's Allied Fams., 127-9; Cochrane's Hist .of Autrim, N. H., 530; Hayward Gen. (1853), 1 page; Hayward Fam. Gathering (1879), 35 p.; Hayward's Hist. Gilsum, N. H., 322-5; Hayward's Hist. of Hancock, N. H., 641-51; Leonard's Hist. of Dublin, N. H., 351; Loomis' Gen. (1880), 783; Morse Mem. appendix, 51¼; Potter's Concord, Mass. Fams., 11; Whitman Gen. 116-9; Wood Gen., 109-15; Wyman's Charlestown, Mass. Gens., I, 489; Mitchell's Hist. of Bridgewater, Mass., 176-85; Hyde's Hist. of Brimfield, Mass., 474.

HAYWOOD:—Anthony Haywood, Boston 1671, had wife Margaret, son Powell, born 1674, died young; and Powell again, 1679; was one of the founders of the Episcopal church; died 1689.

JOHN HAYWOOD, postmaster. See Haywa.d.

REFERENCES:—Amer. Ancestry, II, 54; XI, 199; Hubbard's Hist. of Springfield, II, Vt., 328; Bond's Watertown, Mass., Gens. 295; Wheeler's Hist. of No. Carolina, 143.

HAZARD:—George Hazard, Providence, born 1646, was perhaps son of one Thomas, and brother of Thomas, Jr.

THOMAS HAZARD, Boston, 1635, ship carpenter, freeman 1636; removed in few years to R. I., there died 1669. His will names wife Martha; daughter Elizabeth, Hannah and Martha; all married; besides son Robert.

REFERENCES:—Amer. Ancestry, IV, 48; V, 201; Austin's Ancestries, 31; Andrey's Hist. of New Britain, Ct., 311; Austin's R. I. Gen. Dict., 320; Field Gen. (1895), 119; Hazard's Olden Times in R. I. (1897), 291 pp.; Hazard Gen. (1895), 293; pp.; Narragansett Hist. Register, II, 45-51; R. I. Hist. Society Calls, III, 312; Rodman Gen., 73; Savage's Gen. Dict. II, 395.

HAZEL:—John Hazel, Rehobath, was fined and imprisoned 1651, though near 60 years old, for exhibiting sympathy with Obadiah Holmes, when publicly whipped as a Baptist.

HAZELBERRY:—Isaac Hazelberry, Northampton, 1671-4, a single man, removed soon.

HAZELTINE, or HAZELTON:—Charles Hazeltine, Ipswich, 1661-6.

DANIEL HAZELTINE, Bradford, freeman 1676.

JOHN HAZELTINE, Rawley, freeman 1640, had wife Joan Anter, a servant of Mr. Holman, of Bideford, in Co. Devon, a member of Boston Church 1643, and children, Samuel, born 1645; Mary, 1648; Nathaniel, 1656, and probably others.

ROBERT HAZELTINE, Rawley, brother of the preceding and freeman the same day, married 1639 and died 1674. By wife Ann, had Ann, born 1641; Mary, 1642, died soon; Mary, again, 1646; Abraham, -1648; Deliverance, 1651; Elizabeth, 1653; Robert, 1657; Gershom, 1661; and David.

REFERENCES:—Amer. Ancestry, VII, 104; Crane's Rawson Family, 22-7; Page's Hist. of Hardwick, Mass.; Benedict's Hist. of Sutton, Mass., 659; Savage's Gen. Dict., II, 395.

HAZEN:—Edward Hazen, Rawley, 1650-91, perhaps had Elizabeth, who married 1670, Nathaniel Harris; and Edna, who married, 1686, Timothy Perkins, of Topsfield.

REFERENCES:—Amer. Ancestry, IX, 32-4; XI, 213; XII, 128; Cope Gen. 96, 195; Guild's Stiles Gen., 385; Hazen Gen. (1879), 7 pp.; Hollister Gen., 203; Slafter Gen., 66; Tucker's Hist. of Hartford, Vt., 425-46; Warthen's Hist. of Sutton, N. H., 765.

HAZELWOOD:—Francis Hazelwood, Boston, by wife Sarah, had Mary, born 1672. He died early in 1674.

HEAD:—Henry Head, Little Compton, representative to Plymouth, Ct., 1683, being the first of the town, served 4 years, and ,after the charter of William and Mary, was represent. at Boston 1692.

RICHARD HEAD, Marblehead, 1674.

REFERENCES:—Amer. Ancestry, II, 54; Austin's R. I. Gen. Dict., 94; Chase's Hist. Chester, N. H., 542; Eaton's Annals of Warren, Me., 549; Poors' Merrimack Valley Researcher.

HEALD:—John Heald, Concord, came, says tradition, from Berwick-on-Tweed; freeman 1641; had 4 sons and 4 daughters, of whom John may have been born in England, and some two or three others, for we have only these dates, of Dorcas, born 1645, died 1650; Gershom, 1647; and Dorothy, 1649. All were, says Shattuck, by wife Dorothy.

REFERENCES:—Amer. Ancestry, III, 178; VII, 281; IX, 194, 195; Andrew's Gen. (1899), 112-4, 159; Dunster Gen., 245-8; Heald Chart by Drury (1880), 11x17

inches, Lacke Gen., 113; Savage's Gen. Dict., II, 396; Stearns' Hist. of Ashburnham, Mass., 743; Stearns' Our Kindred (1885), 9-11; Whittemore's Orange, N. J., 323.

HEALEY, or HALEY, sometimes on records HALE, or HEALE, and HELE:—Dennis Healey, Watertown, married, 1681, Joanna Bullard, had Ruth, born same year.

GEORGE HEALEY, Boston 1677.

NICHOLAS HEALEY, Pemaquid, took oath of fidelity 1674.

SAMUEL HEALEY, Salisbury, married, 1685, Hannah Smith, had Samuel, born 1685; Nathaniel, 1687; William and Mary, twins, 1690, died in few days; and William again.

WILLIAM HEALEY, Lynn, removed to Roxbury, there by wife Grace had Hannah, bapt. 1644; Samuel, 1646, died soon; Elizabeth, 1647. His wife died 1649, in childbirth; and he married 2nd wife, had Sarah, 1651, died young; William, 1652; removed to Cambridge, there his wife died and he married 1653, 3rd wife, Grace Buttress, had Grace, born 1654; Mary, 1657, died soon; Nathaniel, 1659; and Martha, 1660; and by 4th wife, Phebe, daughter of Bartholomew Greene, had Samuel, 1662; Paul, 1664; and Mary again, 1665; perhaps more. He had fifth wife, married 1677, widow Sarah Brown, and died at Cambridge 1689. He was convicted with 8 others of the ridiculous crime of high treason in 1683, by the tyrant governor of Cranfield, and pardoned by advice of the crown.

REFERENCES:—Barry's Framingham, 281; Dow's Hist. of Hampton, N. H., 745; Fullonton's Hist. of Raymond, N. H., 232-4; Hoyt's Salisbury Fams.. 197; Paige's Hist. of Cambridge, Mass., 579.

HEARD:—Benjamin Heard, Salisbury, by wife Ruth, had Elizabeth, born 1691; Samuel, 1692; and Benjamin, 1702.

JAMES HEARD, Kittery, brother of first John, perhaps, was ensign 1659, of the militia under Charles Frost, lieut. com.

JOHN HEARD, Dover, had perhaps been of Kittery before 1643, and after, married Elizabeth, daughter of Rev. Benjamin Hull, of York, had Benjamin, born 1644; Mary, 1650; Abigail, 1651; Elizabeth, 1653; Hannah, 1655; John, 1659; Joseph, 1661, died soon; Samuel, 1663; Catharine; Tristran, 1667; Nathaniel, 1668; Dorcas; Experience; James; and William; died 1688. His widow was preserved in the assault on the town 1689, by an Indian to whom she showed favor 13 years before; and died 1706. See Niles, Indian wars, in 3 Mass. Hist. Coll. VI, 206. Magn. VII 65.

JOHN HEARD, Eastham, had John, born 1689; Grace, 1693; and Jacob, 1695.

LUKE HEARD, Newbury, went, 1640, to Salisbury, an original propr., freeman 1639; by wife Sarah, had John, 1644, died soon; John again, 1645; removed to Ipswich, there died 1647, leaving widow Sarah, (who was a Wyatt, of Assington, in Co. Suff'k, Eng.,) and sons John and Edmund. His widow married John Bixby.

THOMAS HEARD, Portsmouth, 1630, one of the men sent by Mason, the patentee.

WARWICK HEARD, Kittery, a young man, probably son of James, 1st, killed accident in 1646, by Charles Frost.

WILLIAM HEARD, Plymouth, came in the Ann 1623, of whom no more is known. He was not a partaker in division of cattle, 1627.

REFERENCES:—Amer. Ancestry; Caldwell Gen., 69; Hammatt Papers of Ipswich, Mass., 154-7; Otis Fam. of N. H., (1851); Wentworth Gen. I, 160; 258-62; Heard Gen. (1880), 61 pp.

HEARSEY. See Hersey.

HEATE, or HITTE:—Thomas Heate, Cambridge, a propr. 1635, after which the name is not found.

HEATH:—Bartholomew Heath, Newbury, had John, born 1643; removed to Haverhill; had also Joseph and Josiah.

CHARLES HEATH, Boston, by wife Mary, had Robert, bapt. 1683.

ELIAS HEATH, Boston, married, 1699, Elizabeth Eldridge. No more is know of him than that he had sister, Ann Turner, of Buckland, Co. Surrey; and he died 1706, aged 55.

ISAAC HEATH, Roxbury, came in the Hopewell, Capt, Babb, late in 1635, aged 50, with wife Elizabeth, 40; daughter Elizabeth, 5; and Martha, probably a sister, 30; freeman 1636; was representative 1637 and 8; ruling elder, and died 1661.

JOHN HEATH, brother of Bartholomew, died 1675, in his will names no family of his own.

JOSEPH HEATH, younger brother, perhaps, of Charles, or Elias, or both, had Ebenezer, Mary, Elizabeth and Esther, before he removed to Charlestown, there had bapt. Joseph, Abigail and Lydia; died 1714, aged only 46.

THOMAS HEATH, Boston, perhaps brother of Charles, by wife Mary, had James, bapt. at O. S. Church, 1676; and Charles, 1680. Probably he removed or died before 1695.

WILLIAM HEATH, Roxbury, brother of Elder Isaac, came from London in the Lion, arriving 1632, with wife Mary and 5 children, of whom one may have beeen Mary Spear, daughter of his second wife by former husband. Others were Isaac, Mary, Peleg and Hannah; all probably by first wife; possibly Martha; he was freeman 1633. represent. at first assembly of dep. 1634, 7, 9 to 42 and in 45 for Dover; died 1652, "an able, goodly and faithful br." is Eliot's entry in church records. His widow, Mary, died 1659.

REFERENCES:—Amer. Ancestry, I, 36; II, 54; V, 208; XII, 6, 42; Chambers' Early Germans, N. J., 398-400; Dow's Hist of Hampton, N. H., 744; Hoyt's Salisbury, Mass. Fams., 200-2; Little's Hist. of Weare, N. H., 900; Savage's Gen. Dict., II, 398; Stile's Hist. of Windsor, Ct., II, 386; Thompson Gen. (1890), 177.

HEATHFIELD, or HITHFIELD:—Matthias Heathfield, New Haven, took oath of fidelity 1660.

HEATON:—James Heaton, New Haven 1661-85, married 1662, says Dodd, Sarah, daughter of Rev. Nicholas Streete.

NATHANIEL HEATON, Boston 1634, freeman 1636, by wife Elizabeth had Eleazur, 1636; perhaps Leah; Nathaniel, 1639; and Elizabeth, 1643; he died early, and his widow married, perhaps, William Pell, again was widow and married John Maynard, and outlived him.

NATHANIEL HEATON, New Haven, perhaps son or brother of James, a propr. 1685.

REFERENCES:—Amer. Ancestry, IX, 55; Child's Gen. 539; Goodyear Gen., 85; Read's Hist. of Swanzey, N. H., 365; Tuttle Gen., 657; Wyman's Charlestown, Mass. Gens. I, 491.

HEDGE:—Elisha Hedge, Plymouth, was a sergeant 1671.

JOHN HEDGE, Lynn 1634, then aged about 24.

STEPHEN HEDGE, Fairfield, 1670.

WILLIAM HEDGE, Lynn, freeman 1634, removed to Sandwich, thence to Yarmouth; had Elizabeth, born 1646; Mary 1648; besides Abraham, Sarah Elisha, William, John, Mary, and Lemuel. His 2nd wife was Blanch, and had been widow Hull.

REFERENCES:—Kellog's White Gen., 59; Davis' Landmarks, 132; Morris' Bontecau Gen., 194; Paige's Hist. of Hardwick, Mass., 396; Sear's Gen., 148; Schenk's Hist. of Fairfield, Ct., 376-8; Wood's Hist. of Shrewsbury, Mass., 325.

HEDGER:—Thomas Hedger, Warwick, a resident of many years of whom by record no trace of family is seen.

HEDGES:—Tristram Hedges, Boston, married, 1657, Ann Nickerson, daughter of William, had Grace, born 1659.

WILLIAM HEDGES, Taunton 1648, freeman 1652, married Mary, daughter of Henry Andrews, of the same, had John and Henry, born about 1652; died 1654.

REFERENCES:—Amer. Ancestry, II, 54; Cleveland's Hist. of Yates Co., N. Y., 687; Hedge's E. Hampton, N. Y., 290-301; Littell's Passaic Valley Gens., 172; Chambers' Early Germans of N. J., 400.

HEDLEY:—John Hedley, Newport, by wife Mary had Mary, born 1674; Elizabeth, 1676; John, 1678; and Sarah.

REFERENCES:—Amer. Ancestry, V, 71; Austin's R. I. Gen. Dict., 97.

HEFERMAN:—William Heferman, Wickford 1674, when also Robert, Samuel, and William, Jr., perhaps his sons, were all there.

HEIFOR:—Andrew Heifor, was at Kittery 1640; but in what christian land he got his name is unknown.

HELDRED:—William Heldred, Ipswich 1637. Felt. Perhaps the same as Eldred.

HALE. See Healey.

HELMAN:—John Helman, Nantucket, had Richard, born 1682.

HELME:—Christopher Helme, Exeter 1639, removed to Mass. 1643, thence to Warwick, next year with the Gartonists, there died before 1650, leaving widow Margaret and son William. Belknap, 20, 432; R. I. Hist. Coll. II, 160.

REFERENCES:—Austin's R. I. Gen. Dict., 322; Green's Kentucky Fams.; Jolliffe Gen. (1893), 103; Narragansett Hist., Reg., IV, 132; Power's Sangamon Co., Ills., Settlers 367; Sharpless Gen. 227-352.

HELSON:—John Helson, Saco, married, 1658, Joan, daughter of Henry Warwick, had Ephraim, born 1667; and perhaps others.

HEMAN:—Francis Heman, freeman of Mass. 1646. It may be the same as Hayman.

HEMMENWAY, or HEMINGWAY:—Ralph Hemmenway, Roxbury 1633, freeman 1634; married 1634, Elizabeth Hewes, had Mary, died soon; Samuel, 1636; Ruth, 1638; John, 1641; Joshua, 1643; Elizabeth, 1645; and Mary again, 1647, died young. He died 1677, or 8.

REFERENCES:—Adams' Haven Gen., 25; Amer. Ancestry, III, 182; Bartow Gen., 196; Haven Gen., 25; Haywood's Hist. of Gilsum, N. H., 327; Hemenway Gen. (1880), 92 pp.

HEMPSTEAD:—Robert Hempstead, New London, 1645, one of the four inhab. to assist Winthrop in settlement of the place, had Mary, born 1647; first child born in that town; Joshua, 1649; and Hannah, 1652; it is said that he died 1655, and that his widow married Andrew Lester.

REFERENCES:—Amer. Ancestry, V, 85; Walworth's Hyde Gen., 1014; Iowa Hist. Rec., I, 3-12; Caulkin's Hist. of New London, Ct., 272-4.

HENBURY:—Arthur Henbury, Hartford, was buried 1697, but many years before he was of Windsor and Simsbury, married, 1670, Lydia Hill, had Mary, Hannah, Elizabeth and Susanna.

HENCHMAN, or HINCHMAN:—Daniel Henchman, Boston, schoolmaster 1666, freeman 1672, artillery comp. 1675 perhaps, by wife Sarah, had (besides Richard, Hezekiah and Nathaniel), Susanna, 1667; and William, 1669, who died young; and by wife Mary, daughter of William Poole, married 1672, had William again, 1673; Jane, 1674; Daniel, 1677; and Mary, 1682; the last two probably died young. Having served on the committee of survey on a new planta., now Worcester, about 1665, he became a propr. and in Philip's war, 1675 and 6, was a captain of distinction, and died at Worcester 1685.

EDMUND HENCHMAN, Marshfield 1652, had come with or after Rev. John Fiske, of Wenham; removed, it is supposed to Chelmsford, after 1657, there died 1668; perhaps had daughter, Elizabeth.

JOHN HENCHMAN, Boston, married 1660, Elizabeth, daughter of Thomas Emmons.

JOHN HENCHMAN, Charlestown, perhaps same as Hinckson.

JOSEPH HENCHMAN, Scituate, about 1680, had Elizabeth, 1685; Mary, 1689; Thomas, 1691; Deborah, 1692; Joseph, 1694; William, 1696; Hannah, 1698; Edmund, 1700; and Sarah, 1702.   Deane says he was son of Thomas, of Chelmsford.

THOMAS HENCHMAN, Concord, removed early to settlement at Chelmsford, freeman 1654; had Bridget, and perhaps other children; was represent. 1667, 71 and 6, major of the reg. of Middlesex, and died 1703. Allen says he removed from Wenham.

WILLIAM HENCHMAN, Boston, married 1653, Mary Philbird, if the surname be correct. had William, born 1654; and Mary, 1655.

REFERENCES:—Deane's Scituate, Mass., 282; Secomb's Hist of Amherst, N. H., 624.

HENDER:—Richard Hender, Salem 1668.

REFERENCE:—Wyman's Charlestown, 492.

HENDERSON:—William Henderson, Dover, 1679.

REFERENCES:—Amer. Ancestry, VIII, 149; Caldwell Gen. 172; Driver Gen., 262; Richmond, Va., Standard,

II, 23; Wentworth Gen., I, 387; Wheeler's Hist. of No. Carolina I, 116; II, 102.

HENDRICK:—Daniel Hendrick, Haverhill 1645, had been of Hampton, 1639; born about 1610; married at Boston, 1660, perhaps for 2nd wife, Mary, widow of John Stockbridge, represent. 1681, living 1690, probably had all by first wife Dorothy, daughter of John Pike, Daniel; John, born 1649; Jonathan; Jabez; Israel; Hannah and Dorothy; perhaps Sarah, who married 1682 Samuel Ingalls, at Andover, was his daughter by 2nd wife.

PETER HENDRICK, Windsor 1675, removed perhaps to Wallingford, 1712.

REFERENCES:—Champion Gen., 206; Lyman's E. Hampton, Mass., Hist. Add., 192.

HENDY, HANDY or HENDEE:—Owen Hendy, Marblehead, 1668.

RICHARD HENDY, Norwich 1659, died about 1670. Richard Hendy, son of the preceding, was one of the first proprietors of Killingworth.

REFERENCES:—Caulkin's Norwich, Ct., 178.

HENFIELD:—Edmund Henfield, Salem 1669, master mariner.

JOSEPH HENFIELD, Salem, married Mary, daughter of Lemuel Gardner, but after having Mary and Joseph, she did not live long.

REFERENCE:—Pickering Gen.

HENING, or HENNEN:—Richard Hening, Newbury, had Shubael, born 1671.

REFERENCES:—Goode Gen., 225; Hayden's Virginia Gens., 255.

HENLEY, or HANLEY:—Elias Henley, Boston, married 1657, Sarah Thompson, probably was of Marblehead, 1668-74.

JOSEPH HENLEY, Chelmsford 1680.

REFERENCE:—

HENRICKSON:—Peter Henrickson, Boston, had Mary, born 1640; and John, 1643.

HENRY:—Isaac Henry, Medford 1675.

JOHN HENRY, Topsfield, freeman 1690.

REFERENCES:—Amer. Ancestry, VI, 48; XII; Cabell Gen., 324; Chambers' Early Germans of N. J., 403; Clarke's Old King Wm. Co., Va. Fams; Good's Gen. 375; Marshall Gen. (1884)), 99-102; Lewis Gen. (1893), 84; Randall's Hist. of Chesterfield, N. H., 343-5; Roome Gen., 228; Saunderson's Charlestown, N. H., 400; Slaughter's St. Mark's Parish, 140, 186.

HENRYSON:—John Henryson, Springfield 1661, had there by wife Martha, daughter Elizabeth, born 1663; removed to Haddam, there or at Hartford, died after some years. He had other daughters, Mary, Miriam and Sarah; only son James, who lived at Hartford.

HENSHAW, HINSHAW, or HINSHEW:—Daniel Henshaw, Milton. He was sent to our country with his brother in their youth, says a doubtful tradition, was first of Dorchester; married Mary, widow of Nicholas Allen, who had been widow of Robert Pond, had Daniel, who died unmarried. His widow died 1719, in her 83d year.

JOSHUA HENSHAW, Dorchester, brother of Daniel 1670, by wife Elizabeth, daughter of William Sumner, had William, born 1672; Joshua; Elizabeth, 1675, died in few days; Thankful, 1677; John, 1679; Samuel, 1682; Elizabeth again, 1684; and Catharine, 1687.

ARMS: Argent, a chevron, between 3 heronshaws, sable.

CREST: A falcon, proper belled, or, wings elevated, preying on the mallard's wing, argent, gutee de sang.

REFERENCES:—Bill Gen., 241; Denny Gen., 82; N. E. Hist. Gen. Reg., XXII, 106-15; Ward Gen., 146; Ward's Hist. of Leicester, Mass., 378; Washburn's Hist. of Leicester, Mass., 378; Wyman's Charlestown, Mass., Gens., I, 495; Amer. Ancestry, X, 181.

HENSHER, or HEINSHER:—Thomas Hensher, Woburn, married, 1677, Hannah, daughter of Moses Cleveland, had Elizabeth, born 1678; Thomas, 1680; Hannah, 1683; William, 1685; Samuel, 1688; Ebenezer, 1691; and Josiah, 1695; and died 1700, when the record spells Henshaw.

HEPBURN, HEYPBOURNE, HEBORNE, or HEPBOURNE:—George Hepburn, Charlestown 1635, leather dresser, freeman 1636, had wife Hannah and died 1666. In his will names sons Ludkin and John, who probably had married his daughters, and children Richard. John and Abigail. but perhaps this list was grandchildren, also Sarah, Sally and Rebecca.

REFERENCES:—Egiis' Queries (1897), 24; Tuttle, Gen., 65; Orcutt's Hist. of Stratford, Ct., 1218; Meginness' Hist. Jour., II, 62-64, etc.

HERBERT:—Henry Herbert. Charlestown, died 1677, he had first wife Elinor Miller, probably widow of Richard, and next married, 1668, Elizabeth, widow of John George, and she died 1691, aged about 70.

JOHN HERBERT, Salem 1637, the shoemaker from Northampton, England. who probably came in the Abigail, 1635, age 23, and had wife Mary, who was of the church there, though he was not the freeman of 1641; had Mary, bapt. 1640, and John 1643; probably went to Southold, L. I.. after 1668.

JOHN HERBERT, Reading, captain, married about 1680, Elizabeth, widow of Nathaniel Graves, daughter of Hon. Richard Russell, and died 1712. His widow died 1714. See Harbet.

SYLVESTER HERBERT, Boston, 1652, admitted an inhab. that year.

REFERENCES:—Amer. Ancestry, VI, 73; XII; Bonton's Hist. of Concord, N. H., 665-70; Meade's Old Churches of Virginia; N. Y. Gen. and Biog. Rec., XXI, 41-3, XXVI, 30; Richmond, Va., Standard, III, 30; Thomas Gen. (1877), 87.

HEARNDALE:—Benjamin Hearndale, Providence, 1646, short time, perhaps at Lynn, next year swore alleg. 1666, probably had sons Benjamin, John, Joseph, Thomas and William, or some of them. for the oath of allegiance was taken at P. by Joseph and Benjamin, in 1671; by the other three in 1682.

HERMAN:—Francis Herman, and Nathaniel, Braintree, 1640. See Harman.

REFERENCES:—Mallery's Bohemia Manor; Penn. Mag. of Hist. and Biog., IV, 100-7.

HEROD:—James Herod, Newtown, L. I., 1656. Perhaps this may be the same as Harrod.

HERRICK:—George Herrick, Salem, 1686; came that year in the same ship with John Dunton, who, in his "Life and Errors," speaks kindly of him; by wife Martha, had Martha, San Howett, and George, posthum. born 1696. He was a shopkeeper, yet an officer of justice; had hard work in the witchcraft infatua. and died 1695.

HENRY HERRICK, Salem, 1629, came in the fleet with Higginson, probably, and, 1630, reg. adm. and next year was sworn freeman: married Edith, daughter of Hugh Laskin, of S. Had, besides other sons and daughters not named in will, who probably died young, Thomas; Zechary, bapt. 1639; Ephraim, 1638; Henry, 1640; Joseph, 1645; Elizabeth, 1647; John, 1650; and Benjamin; was one of the founders of the church at Beverly, 1667, and died 1671.

WILLIAM HERRICK, Southampton, L. I., is by Farmer mentioned as one of the grantees in the Ind. deed, 1640.

REFERENCES:—Amer. Ancestry, I, 37; II, 54; III, 26; V, 76; VII, 114; Dodge Ancestry (1896), 17; Driver Gen., 308-19; Guild's Stiles Gen., 221; Hemenway's Vt. Gaz., V, 101-3; Herrick Gen. (1846), 69 pp.; 2d edit. (1885), 516 pp.; Joslin's Hist. of Poultney, Vt., 273; Poor's Merrimack Valley Researches, 145; Williams' Hist. of Danby, Vt., 161-3.

CREST:—A bull's head, couped, argent, horned and eared, sable, garged with a chaplet of roses: proper.

MOTTO:—Virtus omnia nobilitat.

HERRIMAN:—Augustine Herriman, Saybrook, 1651. See Trumbell's Col. Rec., I, 219. See, also, Harriman.

HERRING:—James Herring, Dedham, 1642.

THOMAS HERRING, Dedham, a freeman, 1654, is otherwise unknown, because his wife, Mary, daughter of Robert Pierce, was. by misreading the name, given to Thomas Haven, of Dedham, when there was no such person. A John H. was, in 1687, engaged in London in receiving conveyance from Judith, widow and extrix. of Stephen Winthrop, as he was purposed to come to N. E.

HERRINGBORNE:—George Herringborne, Boston, 1664.

HERSEY:—William Hersey, Hingham, 1635, freeman, 1638; artillery comp., 1652; had wife, Elizabeth, who survived him, and died 1658. His will of that year names sons William, John and James, daughters Frances, Elizabeth and Judith, of whom perhaps some were born in England.

REFERENCES:—Barry's Hanover, Mass., 317; Hersey Chart (1895), 27x32 inches; Swift's Barnstable, Mass., Fams., II, 5-18; Runnell's Hist. of Sanbarnton, N. H., 337-50.

HESSELDEN:—Francis Hesselden, Boston, 1630; came probably with Winthrop, as he was a very early member of the church, and no more is known.

HETHERSAY, or HITHERSEA:—Robert Hethersay, Charlestown, 1640; Dover, 1648, and of York, 1651, acting against Godfrey in favor of Mass., but both became freemen 1652. Haz. I, 575.

THOMAS HETHERSAY, Hampton, 1650.

HETT:—Thomas Hett, of Hingham, 1637; cooper; had been a propr. of Cambridge, 1632; married Ann

Needham, an early member of Boston Church, had Eliphalet, bapt. 1639, and Thomas, was freeman, 1642. Winthrop tells the tale of her insane attempt to drown her children, (I, 236 and II, 65, 129). He lived probably at Rehoboth in 1645 (Baylies, II, 200), certain at Charlestown, 1658 (Frothingham, 153), but probably in that part which became Malden, where birth of son Israel, 1654, is recorded, and he died 1668; his daughter Mary, 1668, married Nathaniel Frothingham, and Mehitable married, 1673, Increase Turner; and his widow died, 1688, aged 75.

REFERENCES:—Savage's Gen. Dict., II, 407; Wyman's Charlestown, Mass., Gens., I, 496.

HEWES:—Christopher Hewes, of Haverhill, 1646.

GEORGE HEWES, of Salisbury; by wife Mary had William, born 1672, and Solomon, 1675.

JAMES HEWES, of Boston; by wife Elizabeth had James, born, 1669; John, 1674; Rachel, 1677; Isaac, 1680; Rebecca, 1682; James, again, 1684; Sarah, 1686, and Joseph, 1689; perhaps more; perhaps he married Bertha, daughter of Thomas Sweetman, of Cambridge, as second wife. Certainly the names of Hughes and Hewes seem interchangeable.

JOHN HEWES, of Scituate, 1632; called the Welshman, had before been at Plymouth, was living 1673, says Deane, who tells, also, that his daughter Mary married, 1657, Jeremiah Hatch, and that his son John died 1661.

JOHN HEWES, of Watertown; married, 1677, Ruth, daughter of Richard Sawtel, had John, bapt. next year; Samuel, 1679, died soon; and Elizabeth, 1681.

JOSHUA HEWES, of Roxbury, came, says the church record, a single man, about 1633, probably in the Griffin, with Cotton and Hooker; freeman next year, married that year, Mary, daughter of Henry Goldstone, of Watertown, who died 1655. at Boston; had Joshua, born, 1639, died soon; Mary, 1641; and Joshua, again, 1644; was represent., 1641; artillery comp., 1643; a merchant of large transactions, a lieut., sent with two others, 1648, to inq. a. complaints against Gorton's comp. at Warwick, over which Mass. always wished to usurp jurisd.; eng. in the Narragansett settlement, of Wickford, whither he removed, 1662, and in May, 1663, was by Conn. jurisd. with others appointed; had married second wife at Boston, 1657, Alice, widow of John Crabtree, and came back to Boston, where he had Hannah, born that year, and died 1676, aged 66.

SOLOMON HEWES, perhaps of Roxbury; married, 1700, Martha, daughter of Robert Calef, but no more is heard.

REFERENCES:—Bangor Hist. Mag., II, 120; Bond's Watertown, Mass., Gens., I, 296; Farrow's Hist. of Islesborough, Me., 224; Hudson's Hist. of Lexington, Mass., 103; Read's Hist. of Swanzey, N. H., 367; Martin's Hist. of Chester, Pa., 405.

HEWETT. See Huet.

HEWINS, HUEN, or HEWENS:—Jacob Hewins. Dorchester; by first wife had Samuel, born 1658. died soon; Mary. 1660; Hannah, 1665; Joseph, 1668; Benjamin, 1670. He married, 1681, Martha, daughter of William Trescott, had Mercy, 1682; Martha, 1687, and Mary.

REFERENCES:—Amer. Ancestry, VI, 205; Morse's Gen. Reg., II (1859), 165-76; North's Hist. of Augusta, Me., 882.

HEWLET:—Lewis Hewlet, Charlestown, 1636.

MATTHEW HEWLET, came to Boston, 1634, in the Hercules, but in what town he first settled is unknown.

REFERENCES:—Queen's Co., N. Y., 432-4; Winslow Gen., 555; Flint's Peters Lineage, 9, 12-4.

HEWSTED:—Angel Hewsted, Stamford, 1666-74; a selectman. The name appears with variations; perhaps in our day Husted. See Huested.

HEYLER, or HILER:—Richard Heyler, came in the Christian, 1635, aged 22, and perhaps settled in Boston, but the spelling of the name at the London Custom House was very uncertain.

HEYWOOD:—John Heywood, Concord; married, 1656, Rebecca, daughter of Thomas Atkinson, who died 1665; had Rebecca, born 1657, died soon; Rebecca, again, 1660; John, 1662; and Benoni, 1665, died in few days. Before the end of that year he married Sarah Symonds, had by her several daughters, and William, 1674; was freeman, 1670, and died 1707.

REFERENCES:—Goode Gen., 171; Lapham's Hist. of Bethel, Me., 560; Marvin's Hist. of Winchendon, Mass., 458; Heywood's Hist. Westminster, Mass., 691-6.

HIBBERT, HIBBARD, or HEBARD:—Robert Hibbert, Salem, with wife Joan was adm. of the church, 1646, and then had children bapt., Mary, born 1641; John, 1643; and Sarah, 1644; Joseph and Robert, 1648; Joanna, 1651; Elizabeth, 1653; Abigail, 1655; and Samuel, 1658; living in that part which became Beverly, then died, 1684, aged 72.

REFERENCES:—Amer. Ancestry, IV, 35; XI, 214; XII; Cleveland Gen., 142; Montague Gen., 124, 439-41; Plumb's Hist. of Hanover, Pa., 423; Sharpless Gen., 142-4, 194-8, 310-7; Temple's Hist. of N. Brookfield, Mass., 624.

HIBBINS. or HIBBENS:—Giles Hibbins, Saco, 1670; married Mary Pennell. Folsom, 188.

WILLIAM HIBBINS, Boston, 1639; merchant, admitted that year, with Ann, his wife, he is then called gentleman; may have came in the Mary and John, 1634; his estates are enumerated among first eight in Town book of possessions; freeman, 1640, representative 1640-1, when he went with Peter and Welde to pray for protection from Parliament for the Colony; came back next year and was chosen assistant, 1643, till his death, 1654. His wife, Ann, an uncomfortable subject for her bad temper in his life, brought no children, but in June, 1656, had prevailed on majority to condemn her as witch, and she was executed on that preposterous charge.

HIBBS:—David Hibbs, Watertown; by wife Elizabeth had David bapt. as was his mother, 1686; and Elizabeth, same month.

JOSEPH HIBBS, Watertown; perhaps brother of preceding; had Abigail and Elizabeth, bapt. 1687. The name is a strange one, and probably is not perpetuated in any part of the country.

HICHBORN:—David Hichborn, Boston, 1650; by wife Catharine had Catharine, born 1654, and Solomon and David, twins, 1661. His wife died a few days after.

REFERENCE:—Lincoln's Hingham, II, 327.

HICKOCKS. HICOCK, or HICKAX:—Joseph, Farmington, 1673; perhaps, after 1680, removed to Waterbury.

SAMUEL HICKOCKS, Farmington, 1673; perhaps brother of 1st Joseph, removed to Waterbury, there died, 1695, when his children are named, Samuel, aged 26; William, 22; Thomas, 20; Joseph, 17; Stephen, 11; Benjamin, 9; Ebenezer, 2; besides Hannah, 24; Mary, 14; Elizabeth, 12, who was bapt. at F., 1682, and Mercy, 6; Joseph and Stephen, probably his sons, were first settlers of Durham. Field, 115.

WILLIAM HICKOCKS, Farmington; an early settler; possibly father of preceding, who sold out his estate before they removed. A Mr. Hickocks, a man of property, was among New Haven people, 1643, but not in the number, 1646, who may have been father of Joseph and Samuel, but, as no more is heard of him, we may presume he went home.

REFERENCES:—Amer. Ancestry, X, 9; Clarke Gen. (1884), 49, 51.

HICKS:—John Hicks, Newport, 1639; Newton, L. I., 1656, and Hempstead, L. I.; was a justice under comm. from Conn., 1664, and representative of H. the same year.

JOHN HICKS, a soldier at Hadley in Philip's War; may have been son of preceding, or perhaps was from Boston.

RICHARD HICKS, Boston, 1649; had wife Mary, and by her, Timothy, born that year; Mary, 1654; Richard, 1657; Elizabeth, 1659; Thomas, 1662, and Rebecca, 1665.

ROBERT HICKS, Plymouth, came in the Fortune, 1621, and his wife, Margaret, came in the Ann, 1623, with her children, who are presumed to have been two sons, Ephraim and Samuel, and two daughters, Lydia and Phebe. He was in 1618 a leatherdresser at London, or rather Bermondsey Street, Southwark.

SAMUEL HICKS, Plymouth, 1643, removed to Eastham. Eldest son of preceding.

THOMAS HICKS, Scituate; brother of Robert; probably from London; had wife Margaret and children Zechariah, Daniel and Samuel.

TIMOTHY HICKS, Boston, shipwright; removed to Salem, had wife, Dorcas, who died 1673.

REFERENCES:—Amer. Ancestry I, 37; II, 54; VII, 76; VIII, 161; XI, 194; Barton Gen. Appendix, 189; Bunker's L. I. Gens., 212-5; Davis Hist. of Bucks Co., Pa., 244; Dwight Gen., 582-6; Hedge's Hist. of E. Hampton, N. Y., 301; Hicks' Lineage (1894), 15 pp.; Lamb's Hist. of N. Y. City, N. Y., 763; Leland Gen., 172; Mott. Gen., 370-81; Swift's Barnstable, Mass., Fams., II, 72; Winsor's Hist. of Duxbury, Mass., 266.

ARMS:—Gu., a fess wavy, between three *fleurs-de-lis*, or.

HICKENS:—Thomas Hickens, Stamford; had Ann, who married after his death, 1683, James Jupp, or Norwalk.

HICKSON:—Robert Hickson, Eastham; married, 1679, Sarah Brewster, or Bruster, perhaps daughter of John, of Portsmouth.

WALTER HICKSON, Hatfield; had been a soldier in Turner's company, there in 1676, from the E., and in 1679 married Sarah, widow of Barnabas Hinsdale, daughter of

John White; had three children, and died 1696. Two of the children died early, and Jacob, born 1683, being taken by the French and Indians at the assault on Deersfield, February, 1704, perished on way to Canada.

HIDDEN:—Andrew Hidden, Rowley, 1655, died at good age, 1701. The name was perpetuated at R.
REFERENCE:—Essex Inst. Call. XXI, 181-4.

HIDE.—See Hyde.

HIGBY:—John Higby, Middletown, died 1688; may have been of Hartford, first; had wife, Rebecca; son, Edward, and probably other children.

REFERENCES:—Phoenix's Whitney Gen., I, 370; Crime Gen. (1895), 46.

HIGDEN:—Peter Higden, came with Anthony Thacher, from Salisbury, in Wilts, and was probably lost soon after in the great storm of August 15, 1635, when his master was wrecked on Cape Ann. Young's Chron. of Mass., 486.

HIGGINBOTTOM:—Richard Higginbottom, New Haven, a tailor, married Elizabeth, daughter of Thomas Munson; had Rebecca, born 1682; a proprietor, 1685; removed before 1692 to Elizabethtown, but came back to Conn., living at Stamford, where his name appears, 1701, and his wife Eunice died, 1710. Spelt in records Hinganbottom.

HIGGINS:—Abraham Higgins, Salem, 1637. Says Farmer.

JOHN HIGGINS, Boston; by wife Susanna had John, born 1656.

JONATHAN HIGGINS, brother of preceding; married, 1661, Elizabeth, daughter of Joseph Rogers; had Beriah, born soon; Jonathan, 1664; Joseph, 1667; and Mr. Hamblen adds, Elizabeth, 1680; Mary, 1683; Rebecca, 1686; James, 1688, and Sarah, 1690; but probably these five last were by second wife.

RICHARD HIGGINS, Plymouth, 1623; married, 1634, Lydia Chandler; removed to Eastham, 1644; was representative, 1647-51; had Jonathan, born 1637; Benjamin, 1640; married, 1651, Mary Yates, had Mary, born 1652; Eliakim, 1654; William, 1654 or 55; Judah, 1657; Zerniah, 1659; Thomas, 1661, and Lydia, 1664.

ROBERT HIGGINS, Boston; married, 1654, Susanna Westoe. He was the public executioner, and died 1665. Of this name were more families at Eastham, in 1801, than of any except Smith.

REFERENCES:—Amer. Ancestry, II, 55; Austin's R. I. Gen. Dect, 98; Field's Hist. of Haddam, Ct., 46; Hatch's Hist. of Industry, Me., 647; Jolliffe Gen. (1893), 95; Leland Gen., 167-9; Orcutt's Hist. of Walcott, Ct., 496-9; Paige's Hist. of Hardwick, Mass., 397; Pierce's Hist. of Garham, Me., 175; Pratt's Hist. of Eastham, Mass., 120; Ridlou's Saco Valley, Me., Families, 727; Walker Gen., 339; Hemenway's Vt. Hist. Gaz., V, 104.

HIGGINSON:—Francis Higginson, Salem, came in the Talbot, 1629, with wife and eight children, of whom

Mary died on the passage at four years of age. He was, it is said, son of Rev. John, born 1588, bred at Jesus Coll, Cambridge, where he took his A: B., 1609, but was of St. John's when his A. M. was given, 1613, though Mather asserts he was of Emanuel1 for several years was minister of one of the parish churches in Leicester, but his growing dislike of conformity prevented him first from advancement, and next from comfort of home, so that he gladly accepted the desire by the Gov. and Comp. of Massachusetts for his emig. hither. He was ordained, 1629, at Salem, and died next year. His widow, Ann, lived some years before and after at Charlestown, but a year or lived at New Haven, there died at the beginning of 1640. His second son, Francis, adm. of the Church of Salem, 1639, went home and studied at Leyden and other places on the continent; was established in church of Kirby Steven, in Westmoreland, where he conformed, and died 1672, aged 55; Timothy, third son, was a mariner, and died unmarried; Samuel, the fifth son, went with his mother to New Haven, there after her death was apprenticed to Gov. Eaton, took oath of fidelity 1644, at same time with elder brother Theophilus; and Charles, born about 1628, was on death of his mother apprenticed to Thomas Fugill, of New Haven. Both these, by the family traditions, became mariners, and adds that Samuel was captain of a vessel of war in Cromwell's day, died aged 44; and Charles, master of a Jamaica ship, died at 49. Neophitus, seventh son, born at Salem, and only child born after leaving England, except second Mary (whose existence is doubted), born about 1630, was by Atherton Hough taken to bring up, and died unmarried under 25 years. Ann, born about 1623, married Thomas Chatfield, of Guildford.

JOHN HIGGINSON, Salem, distinguished in the annals of that place, eldest son of preceding, born 1616 at Claybrook, Co. Leicester (which was dwelling of another family of same name), came with his father, was freeman, 1636; served as chaplain, 1637, at Saybrook, but in 1641 went to Guilford and was same year colleagued with Rev. Henry Whitefield, whose daughter Sarah he married, by whom he had John, Nathaniel, born 1652; H. C., 1670; Thomas, Francis, bapt. 1660, who went to England and was, it is said, sent to the University by his uncle Francis, but died at London, of smallpox, 1684. Henry, 1661, who died 1685 at Barbados, of smallpox; besides two daughters, Sarah and Ann, who both married. On a design of going to England he came in 1659 to Salem, there was prevailed on to remain, ord. 1660, and died among the most honored of our clergymen, 1708. He had second wife, Mary, widow of Joshua Atwater, of Boston, who long survived him.

WILLIAM HIGGINSON, Farmington, whose name is usually Higason, or Higgison, married Sarah, daughter of John Warner, had there bapt., Margaret, Sarah, Elizabeth, 1691, and Mary, 1692; was a proprietor, 1673; left no sons, nor is the date or place of his death known. He is not reckoned of the preceding family.

REFERENCES:—Cleveland Gen. (1899), 487-97; Essex Inst. Call., V, 33-42; W. E. Hist. and Gen. Reg., XLVI, 117; Savage's Gen. Dict., II, 412-4; Symmes' Gen., 35-45; Winslou's Giles Gen., 321-3.

HIGLEY:—John Higley, Windsor, married, 1671, Hannah, daughter of John Drake, had born there John, 1673; Jonathan, bapt. 1676; Hannah, bapt. 1678; Catha-

rine, born 1679; removed to Simsbury, there probably had more children, and died. He was, it is believed, from Frimley in Surrey, a hamlet eight miles from Farnham, about thirty miles from London. Hannah married Joseph Trumbull, and was mother of first Gov. Jonathan.

REFERENCES:—Am. Ancestry, IV, 143; VI, 190-1; Barbour's "My Wife and Mother," app. 59; Higley Gen. (1896), 738 pp.; Humphrey's Gen., 160, 443; Stiles' Hist. of Windsor, Ct., II, 387-91; Brown's West Simsbury, Ct., Settlers, 76-8.

HILAND.—See Hyland.

HILDRETH, sometimes HILDRICK:—Richard Hildreth, Cambridge, freeman, 1643; had wife Sarah, who died 1644; by wife Elizabeth, who died at Malden, 1693, aged 68, had Elizabeth, 1646, and Sarah, 1648. He was serg. of the grantees of Chelmsford, 1653; there had Joseph, 1658; Persis, 1660; Thomas, 1662; Isaac, 1663; besides Abigail, who married Moses Parker of the same. The father died at Chelmsford, 1688, aged 83.

REFERENCES:—Am. Ancestry, X, 61; Cleveland Gen., 90-2; Hatch's Hist. of Industry, Me., 648-50; Hildreth Fam. of Woburn (1857), 8 pp.; second edition (1879), 9 pp.; H. Fam. of Lowell (1892), 71 pp.; Hudson's Hist. of Lex., Mass., 279; N. E. Hist. and Gen. Reg., XI, 7-12; Sheldon's Hist. Deerfield, 200.

HILL, or HILLS:—Abraham Hill, Charlestown, 1636, freeman, 1640; by wife Sarah, daughter of Robert Long, had Ruth, born 1640; Isaac, 1641; Abraham, 1643; Sarah, 1647, died soon; Sarah, again, 1649, died same month; Mary, 1652; Jacob, 1657, and Zechary, perhaps older than the last; died 1670 in Malden.

BENJAMIN HILL, New Haven, 1646, but removed soon after taking oath of fidelity in 1647.

CHARLES HILL, New London, came from Maryland, 1665, but was born in Barlow, near Chesterfield, in Derbysh.; son of George; was a merchant of distinction, partner with the Christophers, going to and from Barbadoes. From that island he brought the first news of the great fire in London, 1666, as set forth in his letter to Gov. Winthrop. (See 3 Mass. Hist. Coll., X, 66.) He married, 1668, Ruth, widow of John Picket; had Jane, born 1669; Charles, 1671; Ruth, bapt. 1673, and Jonathan, 1674; his wife, daughter of Jonathan Brewster, died 1677, and he married, 1678, Rachel, daughter of Deputy Gov. John Mason, who with infant child died next year. He was a useful man, clerk of Co. Court, and recorder of the town; died 1684.

EBENEZER HILL, Dorchester, a soldier of brave Capt. Johnson's comp. in Dec., 1675.

EBENEZER HILL, Newbury, took oath of allegiance 1678.

EDWARD HILL, a soldier from the E. on Conn. river in 1676.

ELIPHALET HILL, Boston, by wife Ann had Mary, born 1670.

FRANCIS HILL, Boston, by wife Hannah had Sarah, born 1664.

HENRY HILL, Woodbury, 1683.

HERCULES HILL, Scituate, 1636, a soldier, next year in Pequot War, went home soon after, and 1666 was of Rochester, Kent.

IGNATIUS HILL, Boston, 1658.

JAMES HILL, Boston, married, 1662, Hannah Henchman; had Hannah, born 1665; James, 1667; Ignatius, 1668, and Elizabeth, 1670; was freeman, 1671.

JOHN HILL, Plymouth, 1630, probably a servant or apprentice, withdrew next year to Massachusetts. See the very curious letter of Plymouth Court to our Gov., in Genealogical Reg., II, 240. He may have been of Salem, and had grant of land, 1650, and of Beverly, 1659, where he was among the principal men, 1681-82; or the man of this name at Lynn, 1655; or of Dover, 1649-72; or of Medfield, 1656, so common was this name, and one was freeman, 1646. This last, by wife, Hannah, had Abigail, born 1658; Samuel, John, 1661; Mary, 1662; Eliezur, 1664; Johnson, 1666, and Ebenezer; and died, 1718, leaving widow, who died 1719.

JOHN HILL, Dorchester, 1641, a blacksmith; by wife Frances had John; Jonathan, born about 1639; Samuel, 1640; Hannah, 1641; Mercy, 1642; Mary, Frances, and two or three or four more, of whom all but Mary died, says tradition, before their father. He died 1664.

JOHN HILL, Rowley, 1641, or earlier.

JOHN HILL, New Haven, 1643, brother of Robert; took oath of fidelity 1644, had no family, and died 1647.

JOHN HILL, Guilford, 1646-8, and later, but after removal had wife Frances, who died 1673, and by her had John, Sarah, James and Elizabeth, and another daughter. He married at Saybrook, 1673, Catharine, probably widow of Alexander Chalker; died 1689. In will names wife Catharine, the two sons and two daughters, Sarah and Elizabeth, who were dead, but left children, and living daughter married to a Tapping.

JOHN HILL, Boston, perhaps brother of Valentine, adm. of our church, 1647; married, 1657, Elizabeth Strong, who may have been daughter—though more probably sister—of Elder John.

JOHN HILL, Dover, 1649-72; by wife Elizabeth had Benjamin, born 1665.

JOHN HILL, Salem, of whom we only know that, in 1666, he was witness to the will of Capt. William Trask.

JOHN HILL, Boston, merchant; by wife Mary had Elizabeth, born 1668, and John, 1673.

JOHN HILL, Portsmouth, 1665; had wife Elizabeth, and perhaps sons Joseph, Nathaniel and Samuel, who were all of P. in 1685.

JOHN HILL, Saybrook, married 1670, Jane Bushnell, had Samuel, born 1671.

JOHN HILL, Saco, perhaps son of Roger, distinguished in wars with E. Ind., 1689-96; was taken 1704 at Wells, carried to Canada and restored next year.

JOSEPH HILL, Charlestown, 1638, was from Malden, in Essex, England, where he was a woolen draper; had brother John, of Barnham, about ten miles from Malden, who may have came over or died several years earlier, with wife Rose, who is thought to have been sister of President Druster, adm. of the ch., 1650, yet not freeman until 1645, though selectman the year preceding; rep. for Malden, 1647, 50 to 6; speaker of the house in the earliest year, but not "the first speaker," as in Geneal. Reg. IX, 34, is said; and leader of the militia of the town. His wife died 1650, and he married, following year, Hannah, widow of Edmond Mellows. Again, in 1656, married Helen Atkinson, called daughter of Hugh, of Kendall, in Co. Westmoreland, and in Newbury, 1665, married for fourth wife, Ann, widow of Henry Lunt. He died at N. 1688, in 86th year. His children were Joseph, born probably in England; Gersham, born 1639; Mehitable, 1641; died young; as did also Nathaniel and John; Samuel, 1652; Hannah, Deborah, 1657, died young; Abigail, 1658, died young, and perhaps Mait.

JOSEPH HILL, Boston, by wife Ellen had Abigail, born 1664.

LUKE HILL, Windsor, 1651, married that year, Mary Hoyt, had Lydia, born 1652; Mary, 1654; Eleazur, at Farmington, and there rec., 1657; Tahan, 1659; Luke, 1662; Abigail, 1664; Elizabeth, 1666, and John, 1668; removed to Simsbury, was living there 1694. Mary married, 1677, John Saxtan.

PETER HILL, Saco, 1648, freeman, 1653, died 1667.

RALPH HILL, married 1638, Margaret Toothaker, probably a widow; removed to Woburn, there had Jonathan, born 1646; was freeman, 1647, and one of the first settlers of Billerica, 1653; died 1663, naming children in his will, Nathaniel, Jonathan, Ralph, Martha and Rebecca; besides widow Margaret, who died 1683, aged 87.

RICHARD HILL, Charlestown, 1638, copper, perhaps brother of Abraham, or Joseph, or both; died unmarried, 1639.

RICHARD HILL, New Haven, 1639.

RICHARD HILL, New Hamp., who died about 1677, may be thought the same, who at Pemaquid, 1674, took oath of fidelity to Mass.

ROBERT HILL, New Haven, 1639, signer of original comp.; had came in the Defence, 1635, to Boston, embarked in July, aged 20 years, on business of Cradock, first Gov. of the Comp. of Mass Bay, at London; died, 1663. He owned land in England. Had Abiah, bapt. 1648, died young; John, bapt. 1651; Hannah, 1653; Ebenezer, 1655, and Nathaniel, 1659, died young. He married second wife, 1662, Adeline, widow of Robert Johnson, and died in August, 1663.

THOMAS HILL, Paxbury, perhaps brother of William, came in 1633, and died next year in the family of Rev. John Eliot, in whose church records it is certified that he was a very faithful and prudent servant, and good Christian.

THOMAS HILL, Plymouth, freeman 1637, soon died or removed to Boston 1638.

THOMAS HILL, Boston, a tanner, had married Eleanor, widow of Thomas Munt, before 1668.

THOMAS HILL, Middletown, by wife Mary had Susanna, born 1678; Elizabeth 1679; Thomas 1682; removed to Hartford; there had John 1692, and died 1701. Had also daughters Mary and Sarah.

VALENTINE HILL, Boston 1636, a mercer from London, Artillery Co. 1638, freeman 1640, and ordained deacon with Jacob Eliot. By wife Frances, who died 1646, had Hannah, bapt. 1639; John 1640, died soon; Elizabeth 1641, died young; Joseph and Benjamin, twins, 1644, both died soon; and by 2d wife, Mary, daughter of Gov. Eaton, had John, bapt. 1647; and Nathaniel, 1660. He was a great public spirit, grantee in 1641, with others, of the town of Bendall's Dock, and the week following was made a selectman, rechosen 1642, 3, 4, 5 and 6, interested in lands at Dover, and probably lived some time there; was representative 1652-3 and 7, and died 1662. His widow married perhaps John Lovering of Dover, and next, Ezekiel Knight of Wells.

WILLIAM HILL, Dorchester, a man of note among the first settlers, probably came in the Maryland, and John freeman 1633; was selectman 1636, and removed to Windsor, of which he was representative 1639-44, thence removing to Fairfield, of which he was representative 1652 and 3, and perhaps had Sarah, who married, 1646, Joseph Loomis at W., and William, and possibly it may have been the latter who was representative 1669.

WILLIAM HILL, Roxbury, came 1632, as a servant, probably in the Lion, freeman 1634, married Phillis, daughter of Andrew Warner of Hadley, and there died 1683; in his will names children William, John, Joseph, bapt. 1650; Benjamin, Jonathan, Hannah, Susanna, Sarah and Mary (always the family employ final s).

WILLIAM HILL, a wheelwright, aged 70, embarked at London in the James, July, 1635, to come to N. E.; but no more is known.

WILLIAM HILL, Dover 1657-71.

ZEBULON HILL, Gloucester 1652, from Bristol, Eng., had grant of land before 1650, removed to Salem, there had bapt. 1662, Joanna, Eliz. and John, Philip, same year; besides Zebulon, Mary, Abigail and Sarah in later days.

REFERENCES:—Massachusetts: Bobsone Hist. of Gloucester, 1046 Ballou's Hist. of Milford, 819; Barry's Hist. of Framingham, 290; Craft's History of Whateley, 501; Daniel's Hist. Oxford, 541; Emerson's Hist. of Douglas, 153-62; Hazen's Hist. of Billerica, 68-72; Hill's Old Dominion, 162; Lincoln's Hist. of Hingham, II, 331; Mitchell's Hist. of Bridgewater, 186-8; Paige's Hist. Cambridge, 581-5; Sewall's Hist. of Woburn, 617; Temple's Histories (N. Brookfield, Palmer, Whately); Wyman's Charlestown, I, 499-502. New Hampshire: Cochrane's Hist. of Francestown, 754; Cogswell's Nottingham; Eaton's Hist. of Candia, 81; Hill Fam. of Dover (1889) 16 p.; Norton's Hist. of Fitzwilliam, 605; Read's Hist. of Swanzey, 368-71; Runnell's Sanbornton, II, 350-4; Washington

Hist. 476. Connecticut: Baker's Hist. of Montville, 422-9; Brown's W. Simsbury Settlers, 70-2; Caulkin's Hist. of N. London, 307; Cothren's Woodbury, 567; II, 1505; Hull Fam. of Fairfield; Hine's Lebanon Hist. Address, 157; Schenck's Hist. of Fairfield; Stile's Hist. of Windsor, II, 392; Todd's Hist. of Redding, 196. Other Publications: Amer. Ancestry, I, 37; VI, 32, 110; VII, 26; VIII, 218; IX, 129; X, 186; Buxton, Me., Centen, 193-8; Chapman Gen., 223; Fogg, Hill and Wood's Gen. 1881; Kilburn Gen., 189; Locke Gen.; U. E. Gen. Reg., XII, 139-45; 261-4; XLI, 52; Pompey, N. Y., Reunion, 322-4; Sharpless Gen., 245; Savage's Gen. Dict., II, 415-21; Young's Hist. of Wayne Co., Ind., 342.

HILLIARD:—Anthony Hilliard, Hingham, 1638, probably had family, and his daughter, Mary, it may have been, who married, 1664, John Farrow, Sec. of the same. Perhaps he too had daughter Ann at H.

BENJAMIN HILLIARD, Salem, 1653, was killed at Hampton by Indians 1677.

EDWARD HILLIARD, Salem, by wife Martha had Elizabeth, born 1658; and (if record be good), Mary, 1659; Edward, 1660; Sarah, 1662; David, 1665; Jonathan, 1668; and Joseph, 1673.

EM^NUEL HILLIARD, Hampton, 1649, lost in a boat going out with 6 others, 1657, had probably Timothy.

H^UH HILLIARD, Salem, freeman, 1634; had wife Margaret, son Job, and Benjamin, and died early. His widow married John Elson, who died 1648, at Wethersfield, and she took third husband, Thomas Wright, of W., and died 1671.

WILLIAM HILLIARD, Boston, came in the Elizabeth and Ann, 1635, a carpenter, aged 21, by wife Esther had Esther, born 1642; Mary, 1644.

REFERENCES:—Austin's R. I. Gen. Dict., 98; Cleveland Gen., 200-4; Dow's Hist. of Hampton, N. H., 746; Swift's Barnstable Fams., II, 69-71.

HILLIER, HEYLER or HILLER:—Hugh Hilliar, Barnstable, had been of Yarmouth, 1639, then by wife Rose had Deborah, born 1643, and Samuel, 1646; died soon after. Widow married Thomas Huckins.

JOHN HILLIER, Windsor, had John, born 1637; Mary, 1639; Timothy, 1642; James, 44; Andrew, 46; Simon, 48; Nathaniel, 51; Sarah, 52; and Abigail, 54; and he died 1655. His name in record is Hilliour, and often name is called Hilliard.

ROGER HILLIER, Charlestown, 1691, married Experience, daughter of Richard Hall of Dorchester, had John, bapt. 1689; and Sarah, 1692; and died 1693, aged 32.

WILLIAM HILLIER, Duxbury, 1639-43, a carpenter; was the first miller in town, says Winsor.

REFERENCES:—Lapham's Norway, Me., 526; Savage's Gen. Dict., II, 422; Stile's History of Windsor, Ct., II, 391.

HILTON:—Edward Hilton, Dover, probably brother of William, fishmonger, which means, it is thought, citizen of London of that company; came and set. down, it is thought, in 1623, at Dover, lived there 20 years, then removed to Exeter, and died early in 1671. Name of first wife not known; by her he had Edward 1630—or 1626; William 1632—or 1628; Samuel, and Charles. After July 1650 he married Catharine, daughter of Alexander Shapleigh, and widow of Thomas Treworthy, who outlived him. Perhaps he had other children, as John, and Jonathan—the latter name being found in tax list at D. 1659; one daughter who married Christopher Palmer, and Mary, who married Henry Moulton of Hampton. Descendants to our day are in good repute.

ROBERT HILTON, Wells, may have been son of Edward, or William, or of neither.

WILLIAM HILTON, Plymouth (it is supposed brother of Edward), came in Fortune 1621, to P., having left his wife and two children to follow in the ship Ann, 1623. The letter he wrote in 1621 is preserved in Young's Chron.; names of children not certain. Removed to Dover, representative 1644. Date of his death is not known, but in 1661 he was constable at Kittery Point. Probably there was a second William, who came to Plymouth in 1623, with his mother in the Ann, and settled at Newbury.

REFERENCES:—Chapman's Weeks Gen., 143; Hilton Gen. (1896), 24 pp.; Hatch's Hist. of Industry, Me., 650; Johnson's Hist. Bristol, Me., 446, 9; Cleveland's Hist. Yates Co., N. Y., 213; Cogswell's Hist. Nottingham, N.H. 404-6; Dudley Gen., 125; N. E. Reg., VII, 50-2, 155; XXI, 179-94; Richmond, Va., Standard, I, 38, 40, 48; Savage's Winthrop's N. E., I, 116; Woodman Gen., app. c 42-8.

HINCKLEY, or HINKLEY:—Samuel Hinckley, Scituate, from Tenterden, in Kent, came in the Hercules of Sandwich 1635, with wife Sarah and 4 children, Thomas, the future Governor, Sussanna, Mary and Sarah. His wife joined church 1635, had Elizabeth bapt. that year. Samuel 1638, died soon; Samuel, again 1639, died soon; removed 1640 to Barnstable, where he had Samuel 1642—by Deane called Sarah, and John 1644; three other children who died. His wife died 1656, and he married 1657, perhaps daughter, but more prob. widow of Robert Bodfish, and died 1662.

THOMAS HINCKLEY, Barnstable, son of above, born in England about 1618, came probably with his father 1035. was represent. 1647, married 1641, Mary Richards, had Mary, born 1644; Sarah bapt. 1646; Meletiah, bapt. 1648; Hannah 1651; Samuel 1653; Thomas, born 1654; Bathsua, 1657; and Mehitable 1659. His wife died 3 mos. after, and he married, 1660, Mary, widow of Nathaniel Glover of Dorchester (daughter of John Smith, born in Lancashire 1630), had Admire, born 1661, died 2 weeks; Ebenezer 1662, died 2 weeks; Mercy 1663; Experience 1665; John 1667; Abigail 1669; Thankful 1671; Ebenezer again, 1673; and Reliance, bapt. 1675, being Sunday of the great Narragansett fight, the hardest battle before Bunker Hill ever fought in New England. He was an Assistant of the Colony, and first Deputy Gov. 1680, and Gov. from 1681 to 1692, when the Massachusetts charter absorbed the old Col.; during period of Andros' power was a counsel; named by the King, and died 1706 in 88th year. His wife had died 1703, in 73d year.

REFERENCES:—Am. Ancestry, III, 184; Deane's Hist. of Scituate, Mass., 284; Dwight Gen., 193; Eldredge Gen. 20-4; Glover Gen., 170, 178; Hinckley Gen. (1859), 7 pp.; Lincoln's Hist. Hingham, Mass., II, 332; Paige's Hist.

Hardwick, Mass., 398; Strong Gen.; Waldo's Hist. Tolland, Ct., 74; Wheeler's Hist. Brunswick, Me., 838.

HINCKES, HINKS, or HINCKS:—John Hinckes, Portsmouth, came in 1672, was a provinc. counsel 1683, and of Sir E. Andros's counc. 1687; Chief Just. of Sup. Ct. 1699 to 1707.

SAMUEL HINCKES, Harvard College 1701, may be his son.

HINCKSON, or HINKSMAN:—John Hinckson, Charlestown, by wife Mary had John, born 1683, bapt. with brother Robert 1687; and Mary, bapt. 1688.

PHILIP HINKSON, Saco, freeman 1653. Sullivan 362.

PETER and SIMON were of Scarborough 1671-6; and Peter, prob. son of one of them, married, 1698, Eliz., daughter of John Parsons.

THOMAS HINKSON, New Hampshire, married daughter of Thomas Walford, but of him we hear no more, except that he died 1664. Hincksman was the common perversion of Henchman.

HINDS:—James Hinds, Salem 1637. See Haynes.

REFERENCES:—Hatfield's Elizabeth, N. J., 78; Heywood's Hist. Westminster, Mass., 697; Hind's Gen. (1899), 394 pp.; N. E. Hist. Reg. XVIII, 267; Randall's Hist. of Chesterfield, N. H., 355; Temple's Hist. North Brookfield, Mass., 629-31.

HINE:—Thomas Hine, Milford, 1646. There the name continues.

REFERENCES:—Anderson's Waterbury, Ct., I, 66; Hine Gen. (1898), 239 pp.; Orcutt's N. Milford, 711-7; Seymour, Ct. Record, Aug. 12, 1897, 1 col.; Whittemore's Orange, N. J., 459.

HINMAN:—Edward Hinman, Stamford, before 1650, removed to Windsor, married Hannah, daughter of Francis Stiles, removed to Stratford, died 1681. His children were Sarah, born 1653; Titus 1656; Samuel; Benjamin 1662; Hannah 1666; Mary 1668; Patience 1670, and Edward 1672.

ARMS:—Vert. on a chevron, or, 3 roses, gu., slipped and leaved, of the first.

CREST:—On a mount, vert., a wyvern; proper—ducally gorged and lived, or.

REFERENCES:—Brown's W. Simsbury, Ct., Settlers, 72; Am. Ancestry, II, 55; IV, 250; X, 125, 191; Dolbeare Gen., 21; Hinman Gen. (1856), 84 pp.; Pompey, N. Y., Reunion, 327; Power's Sangamon Co., Sett., 380.

HINSDALE, HINSDELL, or HINDSELL, sometimes ENSDELL:—Gamaliel Hinsdale, Medfield, is probably error for Samuel.

ROBERT HINSDALE, Dedham,, one of the founders of the church there, 1638, freeman 1639, by wife Ann had Barnabas, born 1639; Gamaliel, perhaps mistake for Samuel, 1642; Mary 1644; Experience 1646; John 1648—but the church record has this child Mary, which may be error; and Ephraim, 1650. He was of artillery co. 1645, removed to Medfield, where he aided in forming church, thence to Hadley, resided several years, married Elizabeth, widow of John Hawks, removed to Deerfield—there was gathering harvest in corn fields and killed with his son Barnabas, John and Samuel, when Capt. Lathrop, with the flower of the Essex, fell at Bloody Brook. His widow married Thomas Dibble.

REFERENCES:—Andrew's Hist. N. Britain, Ct., 185;

Hinsdale Gen. (1883), 31 pp.; Judd's Hist. Hadley, Mass., 511; Sheldon's Hist. Deerfield, Mass., 201-7.

HINTON:—Benjamin Hinton, Springfield 1678; but he was not long there.

HIPDECH, or HIPDITCH:—Joseph Hipdech, Boston, was a blacksmith, married Mary, daughter of Nathaniel Adams, made his will 1678, in which no children were mentioned.

HIRST:—William Hirst, Salem, married 1674, Mary, daughter of Edward Grove of Boston, had Grove, born 1675; Elizabeth 1677; William 1679; died 6 weeks; William, again, 1683; John 1685, died in 2 years; John, again, 1687; Mary 1689, died early; and George 1691, died next year. He was selectman 1686, representative 1693 and 5, a major 1698, and died 1717. Elizabeth married 1716, Walter Price, as his second wife.

HISKETT:—George Hiskett, Boston, mariner; married, 1662, Sarah, daughter of Thomas Clark, was living 1677.

HITCHBORN:—Daniel, Boston, 1668.

HITCHCOCK:—Edward Hitchcock, New Haven 1643, had (15 Dec., 1644, bapt. in right of his wife there), Mary, born 1639; Abigail, and John, born 1643; Samuel, born 1646, and Joseph, 1648; probably was brother of Matthew, and died 1659.

LUKE HITCHCOCK, New Haven, 1644, removed to Wethersfield, died 1659, leaving widow Eliz. and children Hannah, John and Luke, this last born 1655. His widow married 1661, William Warriner of Springfield; and next, Joseph Baldwin, of Hadley.

MATTHEW, or MATTHIAS HITCHCOCK, New Haven, 1639, came to Boston in the Susan and Ellen, 1635, from London, aged 25, had Eliakim, Nathaniel, John and Elizabeth, the last born 1651, died 1669.

RICHARD HITCHCOCK, Saco, assessed there 1636, for support of min. at the lowest rate of any in the list, probably was a young man; constable 1652, freeman 1653, represent. 1660, died 1671. His will of 1670 names wife Lucretia, and six children, Thomas, Jerusha, Lydia, Rebecca, Ann, and Margaret.

SAMUEL HITCHCOCK, Hartford, 1669.

Six of this name had, in 1826, been graduated at Harvard, and ten at the other New England colleges.

REFERENCES:—Anderson's Waterbury, Ct., I, app. 66; Avery Gen. (1893), 86-8; Caverly's Hist. Pittsford, Vt., 1707; Chapman's Trowbridge Gen., 51; Carliss' N. Yarmouth, Me., 1125, 1155; Dickerman Gen., 604; Hitchcock Gen. (1894), 555 pp; Hitchcock Family Excerpts (1897), 4 pp; Kellog White Gen., 121; N. E. Hist. and Gen. Reg., XI, 307-9.

HITCHEN, HITCHINGS, or HICHEN:—Daniel Hitchen, Lynn, called sen. when made freeman 1691; probably removed to Reading.

EDWARD HITCHEN, Boston 1634, freeman 1635.

JOSEPH HITCHEN, Lynn, had Rebecca, born 1662; Joseph 1664; Samuel 1666; Sarah 1671; Martha 1674; Elizabeth 1676; Elnathan 1679, and Ruth 1681.

HOADLY, HOADLEY, or HODLEY:—John Hoadly, Guilford, 1639-58, one of the seven pillars at founding church, 1643; I Mass. Coll. X, 92. He was born 1617, perhaps at Rolvenden. Co. Kent, came with some relations in 1639, married 1642, Sarah Bushnell, who had

been passenger in same ship with him, perhaps daughter of Francis; had Samuel, born 1643; John, 1645, died in few weeks; John, again, 1647, died soon; Athia, 1648, died under 16 years; John, again, 1650; Nathaniel, 1652, died under five years, and Stephen, 1654, died at 3 weeks. Later, in 1653, he, leaving his family here, went home, and was noticed by Cromwell, who made him one of his court chaplains, says tradition, in Conn.; but it was for the garrison in Edinburgh Castle, whither his wife and children followed him in 1655. There he had 3 more children and removed thence in 1662 to Rolvenden, where he had two more, and died 1668. His wife died 1693, and was buried at Halsted, in Kent, where her son John, under diff. ordina, from his father, was the rector.

WILLIAM HOADLEY, Branford, an early settler, probably born in England, one of the covenant planters, 1667; had been of Saybrook, 1663; was a merchant, by wife Mary had William; Samuel; Eliz., 1668, prob. died young; Abraham, John and Mary; was represent. 1678, and several times after. His wife died 1703, and he had second wife Ruth, widow of John Frisbie, daughter of John Bowers, but no issue by her; died 1709, leaving good estate. The name was written by him, Hoadle.

REFERENCES:—Anderson's Waterbury, Ct., I, app. 67; Boyd's Annals of Winchester, Ct., 384; Middlefield, Ct. History.

HOAG:—John Hoag, Newbury, a weaver, born, says Coffin, 1643, married 1669, Ebenezer, daughter of John Emery; had John, born 1670; Jonathan, 1671; Joseph, 1677; Hannah, 1683, and Judith, 1687; perhaps others. Descendants are numerous in New Hampshire.

REFERENCES:—Coggswell's Nottingham, N. H., 407-9; Little's Hist. of Weare, N. H., 900-3; Wight Gen., 136.

HOAR:—David Hoar, Boston, 1650, probably brother of Leonard, the Presid., named in his will; went home and died at London.

HEZEKIAH HOAR, brother of John, was one of the first purchasers of Taunton, there had Mary, born 1654; Nathaniel, 1656; Sarah, 1658; Eliz., 1660; Edward, 1663; Lydia, 1665; Mary, 1669, and Hezekiah, 1678. Deane says he was ensign in the expedition that was proposed against the Dutch of New York in 1654. Baylies, II, 267, 71 and 7.

JOHN HOAR, Scituate, 1643, it is believed, came some years before with his mother, Joanna, brothers Daniel and Leonard, and sisters Margery and Joanna; removed to Concord 1660, had wife Alice, only son Daniel, born 1650.

LEONARD HOAR, Cambridge, brother of John, born in England—though never has it been known who was the father; it is presumed he did not come to the country. His mother, Joanna, who died at Braintree, 1661, brought the three sons and daughters. He was graduated at H. C. 1650, went to England, was min. at Wenstead, Essex, and one of the ejected under the Bartholomew Act; took degree of M. D. at University of Cambridge, 1672, and came again hither to preach by invitation at Third, or Old South Church, but with commend. of strong friends in London that he should be made president of the coll. to succeed Chancery, late dec. He arrived 1672; the same month was chosen to the office; but was sadly unfortunate in his place. A combination against him of three of the corp. created such diffic. that all the students left the inst., and in March, 1675, he resigned, as the Gen. Court in October preced. had not indistinctly desired. On his coming two and a half years before they had voted a salary half as much again as they gave C., on the sole condition that H. be elected.

Same year he died, probably of broken heart for his treatment, aged only 45 years. Cotton Mather was then one of the undergraduates, and may perhaps be believed in what he says of "the unhappy countenance of several very good men" toward the ungovernable youth in their ungovernableness, at least as to the latter portion he was an unwilling, if we may presume he could have been, a good witness. See Magn. IV, 129, among the best, and characteristic pages of that strange work. Contempo. documents should be referred to in the Coll. of Hutch., 435, 45, 52, 64 and 71 ; but the noble Hist. of the Univ. by Quincy, I, 31-5, may seem to be inadequate in its decision. His wife Bridget was daughter of that lady sacrificed by the detestable governm. of James II, and his worthy Ch. Just., Jef fries, 2 Sept., 1685, and of John Lisle, the rigicide (a lawyer of distinct. made by Cromwell one of his commission ers of the Great Seal, sometimes called erroneously, Lord Lisle, because the Protector summoned him to the "other house," who met a death by violence, after the restoration, in Switzerland). Nothing is known of any children by daughter Bridget, born at Cambridge, 1673, who went with her mother, 1687, to England, and before her return, 1697. After death of her second husband, the daughter married Rev. Thomas Cotton, a minister of London, who was a most liberal benefactor of H. C.

NATHANIEL HOAR, Taunton, married, 1682, Sarah Wilbare, perhaps daughter of Shadrach, the honor. town clerk ; had Abigail, born same year.

RICHARD HOAR, Yarmouth, who was represent. 1642 2 and 50, may have hardly been brother of Leonard, as was supposed by Baylies.

SAMUEL HOAR, Concord, freeman 1682.

WILLIAM HOAR, Salem. 1659, may have removed to Boston, where a baker of this name, who married, 1669, Hannah, daughter of Robert Wright, was freeman 1671 ; had William, born 1671. died at 2 mos. ; Samuel, 1673, died at 7 mos. ; Joseph, 1675 ; Benjamin, 1680 ; Paul, 1682 ; William, again. 1685, and Hannah, 1687.

Dorcas. of Beverly, sentenced to die for witchcraft, in the sad Sept. 1692, was not executed, says Hutch. II, 58, and probably saved her life by confession of the idle or ideal crime after conviction.

ARMS :—Arg., an eagle. displayed, with 2 heads, within a bordure, engrailed, az. (sometimes sa.)

REFERENCES :—Andrews' Hist. New Britain, Ct., 352-5 ; Bond's Watertown. Mass., Gens.. 297-9 ; Deane's Hist. Scituate. Mass., 285 : Hoar Fam. Lineage (1898), 56 pp ; H. Fam. Ancestry (1899), 37 pp ; Westminster, Mass., Cent., 19 ; Parson's Gen. (1900), 20-6 ; 69-91.

HOBART :—Edmund Hobart, Hingham, came with wife. children Joshua, Rebecca and Sarah, perhaps also Thomas. and his wife and children, in 1633, with intent. to satisfy inq. of his neighbors in old Hingham, was first at Charlestown, freeman 1634, constable same year, went, as one of the first settlers, 1635, to Hingham, was represent. 1639-42. and died 1646. leaving Edmund, Joshua, Rev. Peter. Thomas. and 2 daughters. There is reason to infer that a widow Lyford, whom he married late in life, was relict of that Rev. John L. who was at Plymouth the first disturber of their church.

PETER HOBART (above meant). born 1604 at Hingham, England. bred at Univ. of Cambridge, where on taking his A. B. 1625-6. and A. M. 1629. he wrote his name Hubberd, was of Magdalen Coll. had preached at divers places, and last at Haverhill, in Suff'k, before coming hither, where he arrived 1635, at Charlestown ; freeman 1635, and in few days was settled at Hingham, with old friends. He brought wife and 4 children, Joshua and Jeremiah, H. C. 1650 ; probably Josiah and Eliz. ; and had here Ichabod in 1633 ; Hannah, 1637 ; both died soon ; Hannah, again, 1638 ; Bathsheba, 1640 ; Israel, 1642 ; Jael, 1643 ; Gersham, 1645, H. C. 1667 ; Japhet, 1647, H. C. 1667 ; Nehemiah, 1648, H. C. 1667 ; David, 1651 ; Rebecca, 1654 ; Abigail, 1656, died unmarried, 1683 ; and Lydia, 1659 ; and the patriarch died 1679. His will named 14 children and wife Rebecca, probably daughter of Richard Ibrook, who was mother of last six children.

SAMUEL HOBART, the freeman of 1635, may have been of the church of Dorchester, or other, before taking the oath, but he was not of Boston, Roxbury, or Charlestown ; nor is anything more known of him.

REFERENCES :—Butler's Groton, Mass., 406 ; Claypoole Gen., 99-101 ; Granite Monthly, Concord, N. H. (1882), 380 ; Hobart Fam., Groton, Mass. (1886), 182 ; H. Fam., Hingham, Mass. (1897), chart. ; Porter Gen., 195-7 ; Hubbard Gen., 145-56 ; Jackson's Hist. of Newton, Mass., 308 ; Thayer Memorial (1835), 100-8 ; Worcester's Hist. of Hollis, N. H., 377.

HOBBS :—Christopher Hobbs, Saco, 1652 ; freeman, 1653 ; appoint. admar. 1654 on est. of brother-in-law William Foster, and died 1673. His will gives to children Christopher, Robert, and Jane, but provides that son John, who had not "came over," should have something if he did.

HENRY HOBBS, Dover, 1657, married daughter of Thos. Cannez.

JOHN HOBBS, a soldier in Lothrop's camp of the flower of the Essex, was killed by the Indians 1675 at Bloody Brook.

JOSIAH HOBBS, came to Boston in the Arabella, 1671, a passenger from London, lived at Woburn, by wife Mary had Josiah, born 1685 ; Mary, 1687 ; Susanna, 1688 ; but the family tradit. in geneal. Reg. IX, 255, makes the eldest son, Josiah, born in Boston, 1684, and the father there to have lived first 18 years after coming. In 1690, says the genealogy, he removed to Lexington, then called Cambridge Farms, and with wife, Tabitha, joined the church there, 1699 ; had Josiah Tabitha, and Mary, bapt. 1699 ; Matthew and Susanna, 1700 ; Ebenezer, 1710 ; and Tabitha, again, 1712 ; and he died 1741, aged 92 years.

MAURICE HOBBS, Newbury, removed to Hampton between 1640 and 5, there married 1678, Sarah, daughter of Benjamin Swett, as second wife, the first being Sarah, daughter of William Eastow, both wives of Newbury ; perhaps had Mary, born 1687, and died 1700, "aged above 80," says Coffin, leaving ten children, whose names are untold, except Bethia.

MAURICE, or MORRIS HOBBS, Hampton, called Jr. when he took oath of fidelity 1678 ; was perhaps son of preceding, as, also, Nehemiah, of the same town, sworn at the same time.

THOMAS HOBBS, Topsfield, freeman 1671, may be same who died at Boston 1690. He was probably father of that soldier killed 1675, of the flower of Essex, in one account called John.

Hist. of Hampton, N. H., 747-55 ; Hatch's Hist. of Indus

REFERENCES :—Bond's Watertown, Mass., 300 ; Daws try, Me., 653 ; Hobb's Gen. (1855), 16 pp. reprint ; Stone's Hist. of Hubbardston, Mass., 293 ; Topsfield, Mass., Hist. Coll. III (1897).

HOBBY:—John Hobby, Greenwich, before 1666; may have been earlier of Newtown, L. I. He died 1707, had four sons and six daughters, all of whom, except John, who died without issue, are mentioned in will. Thomas, Benjamin, Jonathan, Eliz., Prindle, Hannah Burnham, Martha Morehouse, Rebecca Hardy, Mary Holmes and Rachel James. Rebecca was dead but left children.

WILLIAM HOBBY, Boston, merchant, by wife Ann had, besides Charles and John, William, born 1669; Ann, 1670; Mercy, 1672; Judith, 1674; and Eliz., 1676.

REFERENCES:—Savage's Gen. Dict. II, 437; Whitmore's Coppie Hill Epitaphs.

HOBSON:—William Hobson, Rowley, 1652, was from Yorkshire, son of Henry Ilsflate, near Whitgift, in the south part of the W. Riding; by wife Ann, daughter of Humphrey Reyner, had Humphrey, born 1655; John, 1657; and William, 1659. He had a brother killed in the Civil War at a battle near Willoughby.

REFERENCES:—Austin's R. I. Gen. Dict., 99; Buxton, Me., Cent., 243-6; Essex, Mass., Hist. Coll. XXI, 185-8; Page Gen., 104; Richmond, Va., Standard, III, 36.

HOCKADAY:—Nathaniel Hockaday, Isle of Shoals, died 1664.

HOCKING:—John Hocking, killed, 1634, at Kennebec. For full explanation see Geneal. Reg. IX, 80, and the contempo. Govs. Bradford and Winthrop in their several hist.

HODDY:—John Hoddy, New Hampshire, 1675, married 1675, Mary Roddam, had John, born 1679; Arthur, 1681, and Samuel, 1683. His widow married, 1696, Samuel Keais.

HODGDON:—Benoni Hodgdon, Kittery, had his house burned by the Indians, 1675; was represent. at Boston, one of the first under the new charter, 1692.

JEREMIAH HODGDON, Dover, 1666.

JOSEPH HODGDON, Casco, perhaps bro. of Benoni; had grant, after the destruction of the town, of 100 acres, but in 1686 removed to York. Willis I, 167.

REFERENCES:—Little's Hist. Weare, N. H., 903; Sinclair Gen., 390-7; N. E. Hist. and Gen. Reg., VII., 155.

HODGE:—John Hodge, Killingworth, 1664, married 1666, Susanna Denslow, of Windsor; had John, born 1667, at K.; Thomas, 1669; Mary, 1671; Joseph, 1672; Benjamin, 1674; Henry, 1676; William, 1678; all at W. and at Suffield, or possibly at either K. or W.; these, Eliz., 1680; Susanna, 1682; Abigail, 1685, and Samuel, 1686; and perhaps others.

NICHOLAS HODGE, Little Harbor, N. H., 1684.

REFERENCES:—Cochrane's Hist. Francestown, N. H., 755; Judd's Hist. Hadley, Mass., 512; Ransom Gen., 48.

HODGKIN, or HODGKINS:—John Hodgkin, Guilford, 1665, and his heirs were proprs. in 1685. A Thomas Hogkin, possibly of same family, was there 1703.

SAMUEL HODGKIN, New Haven, 1651, perhaps brother of John, had there Joshua, born 1651; Thomas, 1654, and Daniel, 1657; besides Samuel and John, and perhaps daughter also. Died 1663, and his 5 sons were proprs. 1685, under name of Hotchkiss, which is the present spelling; but intermediately it was Hodskis.

WILLIAM HODGKIN, Plymouth, married 1636, Sarah, probably daughter of Robert Cushman, and 1638, Ann Haynes; was one of the first purchasers of Middleborough. Eliz., at Plymouth, who married, 1633, William

Palmer, of Scituate, and later, John Willis, of Bridgewater; was probably his sister.

WILLIAM HODGKIN, Ipswich, 1665, died, says Felt, 1693. Perhaps he is the same mentioned by Eaton among early settlers of Reading.

REFERENCES:—Aldrich Walpole, 274-7; American Ancestry, I, 38; XII, 35; Bemis Hist. of Marlboro, N. H., 535; Eaton's Annals of Warren, Me., 553; Hodgman Golden Wedding (1865), 14 pp.

HODGES:—Andrew Hodges, Ipswich, 1639, freeman 1641; died 1666.

CHARLES HODGES, Lyme, married, 1686, to Ann; but no further report of the family is found.

GEORGE HODGES, Salem, married 1663; had Catharine, born 1664. His wife died 1665, and he married, 1669, Sarah, daughter of Thomas Phippen; had Sarah, born 1670; George, 1672; Mary, 1674; Joseph, 1676; Hannah, 1678; Dorcas, 1680; John, 1682, and Gamaliel, 1685. Tradition makes him son of John, or Richard, both of Salem in 1642; but neither is found in Felt's list.

HENRY HODGES, Taunton, son perhaps of William of the same; married, 1674, Esther, daughter of the brave Captain John Gallop; had Mary, born 1676; Esther, 1678; William, 1680; Charity, 1682; Henry, Benjamin, Joseph, John, Ephraim, Eliz., and Abigail; was elder of church, captain, and died 1717, aged 65.

HUMPHREY HODGES, Boston, 1671, became a Quaker and was whipped 1677.

JOHN HODGES, Salisbury, an original sett., went home to London in 1647.

JOHN HODGES, Charlestown, 1633, with prefix of respect in 1636, yet no more is known of him.

JOHN HODGES, Taunton, 1668, eldest son, perhaps of William; married, 1672, Eliz. Macy; probably daughter of George; had John, born 1673; Nathaniel, 1675; Samuel, 1678; William, 1682; George, 1685; Ebenezer, 1687, and Nathan, 1690, and died 1719.

NICHOLAS HODGES, Plymouth, 1643, in his will of 1665 has an alias—Miller.

THOMAS HODGES, married, 1663, Exercise Razar.

WILLIAM HODGES, Salem, 1638, was called to serve on a jury next year, is thought to have brothers John and Richard, appearing at Salem four or five years later, though nothing more is told of either; and Andrew, George, or Nicholas may, as well, seem to be brethren of this William. But the compiler of records of the Hodges family, without any positive authority, but by conjecture only, presumes him to be the following.

WILLIAM HODGES, Taunton, 1643, had wife Mary and two sons, John, born about 1650, and Henry, about 1652. See also Hedges.

REFERENCES:—Am. Ancestry, V, 8; IX, 120; Bowen's of Woodstock, Ct., 179; Daniel's Hist. of Oxford, Mass., 542; Hodges Gen. (1837), 22 pp; H. Gen., 2d edit. (1853), 71 pp; 3d edit. (1896).

HODGKINSON:—William Hodgkinson, Plymouth, 1623, says Farmer, but it is not known where he derived his informat., for he was not a "first comer," had no share in the division of land. Perhaps name was Hodgkins. A Mary H. married at Boston, 1654, Samuel Bedwell.

HODGMAN:—Josiah Hodgman, Reading, named by Eaton among early settlers, may have been born about

1669. Webber, and early brought up by Thomas H., who gave him land in 1703, called him "Josiah H., alias Webber, who was dutiful to me as a servant while he lived with me." He married, 1691, Elizabeth . . . . who died 1712, and he married, 1724, for second wife, Grace Bautell, widow of the second John of R., by whom he had no children. Nor by the first wife is more than one child heard of—Thomas, born, 1693.

THOMAS HODGMAN, Reading, married, 1663, Mary Morrill, the young widow prob. of Ezekiel of R., is thought to have had no issue, but to have adopted the preceding orphan in early youth. He died 1729; his widow died 1735, in her 96th year.

HODSDON, HODSDEN, or HODSDIN:—Jeremiah Hodsdon, Dover, 1665, perhaps had Esther, who married, 1663, Edward Waymouth.

NICHOLAS HODSDON, Hingham, 1647, removed to Cambridge and Boston, now in Newton and Brighton, and drew several others from H. Name has also been spelled Hudson.

REFERENCES:—Bradbury's Kennebunkport; Lapham's Hist. of Rumford, Me., 345; Old Eliot, Me., Monthly, 11. (1898), 146; Wentworth Gen. I, 420-4.

HODSON, HODGSON, or HODSHAW:—George Hodson, Cambridge, is said to have come very early; by wife, Jane, had Ann, born 1645, and daughter Abiail, 1648.

JOHN HODSON, New Haven, merchant; married, 1651, Abigail Turner; had Abigail 1654; Sarah, 1657, and probably others, besides Nathaniel, H. C. 1693, and John, was a propr. 1685, with prefix of respect, in his will of 1690, provides for his son at college.

ROBERT HODSON, Warwick, married Rachel, daughter of Samson Shatton; had Robert, Alice and Mary. He had come, says Thompson's L. I., in June, 1657, over the ocean, and 2 months later appeared first at New Amsterdam, where he was cruelly beaten and chained as a Quaker, under the government of Stuyvesant. He is called "an ancient friend, and traveller for God's truth;" he died 1696, aged 78 years.

HOGG:—John Hogg, Mass., 1639. Felt. Perhaps he was only trans.

RICHARD HOGG, Boston, a tailor; by wife, Joan, had Joseph, born 1637, not 1636; bapt. 1639; Mary, bapt. 1641, 6 days old and John, 1644; Mary, again, 1647; was freeman, 1640.

THOMAS HOGG, New Haven, 1646, or earlier, was there 1654. Five of the name were landed in Boston 1652, by the John and Sarah, from London, to be sold, having been made prisoners at Worcester fight preceding year, of not one of which is anything heard of after.

REFERENCES:—Cochrane's Hist. Francestown, N. H., 756; Stark's Hist. Dunbarton, N. H., 221; Bedford, N. H., Centennial, 311.

HOGGRIDGE, or HOGGERIDGE:—Abel Hoggridge, Pamaquid, swore fidelity to Mass., 1674.

HOLBEECH, HOLBICH, HOLBIDGE, or HOLBRIDGE:—Arthur Holbeech, Boston, 1635, after 1638 removed to New Haven, where he was 1646; died 1648. See Holbridge. See Halbridge.

HOLBROOK:—John Holbrook, Dorchester, perhaps brother of Thomas the first; freeman 1640; may have removed for a short time to Rehoboth about 1643, thence to

Weymouth; children thought to be Thomas, Richard, Margaret, who became second wife perhaps of Nicholas Rockett, or Rockwood; Daniel, Samuel and Nathaniel; was representative years between 1651 and 92; called lieut. and afterwards capt. Is thought to be same whose wife Sarah died 1644, but what children, if he had any, are unknown, excepting Lois and Eunice, twins, 1658. By wife Elizabeth, daughter of that wid. Stream, who was second wife of John Otis, he also had Experience, 1661; Ichabod, 1662; and earlier or later several more, for his will of 1699 names wife and children John, Samuel and Ichabod, besides Hannah.

RICHARD HOLBROOK, Milford, 1658, was perhaps first at Dorchester; freeman 1648; next, one of the first settlers of Huntington, L. I.; died at M. 1670, leaving, it is probable, many descendants. His daughter Mary married, 1675, Ephraim Wheeler, of M.

THOMAS HOLBROOK, Weymouth 1643, may have come several years earlier at W. (whence removed the first settlement of Rehoboth in that year), and though he was one of the grantees of R., yet for not going to reside there, his share was forfeited 1645. All his children were probably brought from England. Eldest son John, born about 1617; Thomas and William, and 3 daughters by Experience, daughter of the first. Hopeslid Leland, freeman 1643; was of Dorchester 1652, last at Medfield 1668. There he died, it is thought, early in 1677. In will, calls himself of Weymouth.

REFERENCES:—Am. Ancestry I, 38; VII, 6; Austin's Allied Fams, 131-3; Bedford's, N. H., Cent., 311; Deane's Hist. Scituate, Mass., 286; Harris' (W. C.) Ancestors; Hudson's Hist. Lex., Mass., 279; Kingman's N. Bridgewater, Mass., 526; Orcutt's Hist. of Derby, Ct., 729-31; Pompey, N. Y., Reunion, 324-6; Vinton Gen., 185-8, 330-40; Secomb's Hist. Amherst, N. H., 633.

HOLCOMB:—Thomas Holcomb, Dorchester, 1633, freeman 1634; removed with other friends of Rev. John Warham, 1635 or 6, to Windsor; probably with two or three children; had there Abigail, born 1639; Joshua, 1640; Sarah, 1642; Benajah, 1644; Deborah, 1646, died soon; Nathaniel, 1658; Deborah, again, 1651; Jonathan, 1653, died soon, and the father died 1657.

REFERENCES:—Am. Ancestry II, 57; IV, 109; VII, 21; XII; Barbour's My Wife and Mother, app. 60; Loomis Gen. (1880), 471-4, 517-8, 759-6, 766-8; Marshall's Grant Ancestry, 118; Stiles, Windsor, Ct., II, 394-7.

HOLDEN, or HOULDEN:—Justinian Holden, came in the Francis, 1634, from Ipswich, Eng., aged 23, probably younger brother of Richard; owned estate also in Cambridge, near the Fresh Pond; freeman 1657, and was of C. when his wife Eliz. died 1673. He married Mary, daughter of John Rutter, of Sudbury; had Samuel, 1674, John, 1675; Isaac, 1677; Mary, 1679; Grace, 1681; Joseph, 1683, and Elizabeth, 1686. Estate was good. He died about 1691; his widow was living 1714.

RANDALL HOLDEN, Warwick, R. I., came from Salisbury, Co. Wilts. but the time is not known; was of Portsmouth before 1638, in that year was witness with Rogers Williams to the deed of the Island by the Indian sachems; yet, in 1642, was driven from the Island, and soon after sat down at W. before 1643, when the controversy began with Mass. claim of jurisdiction against him and his friends: the force of the heretics was not adequate to maintain the right to their soil, and they were brought prisoners to Boston. He was saved from sentence of death, but shut up in jail till next year at Salem, went home, and from the Parliament obtained vindication of his right in 1645; and again came in 1646; married Francis, daughter of Jeremiah Clarg of Newport; had Francis, born 1649; Eliz., 1652; Mary, 1654; John, 1656, drowned before middle age; Sarah, 1658; Randall, 1660; Margaret, 1663; Charles, 1665; Barbara, 1668; Susan, 1670; and Anthony, 1673; was an Assistant in R. I. and lived in 1676.

RICHARD HOLDEN, probably a Suffolk man, came in the Francis, 1634, aged 25, with Justinian, probably his brother; married Martha, daughter of Stephen Fosdick; had Stephen, born 1642; Justinian, 1644; Martha, 1646; Samuel, Mary, Sarah, Eliz., Thomas and John 1657; all living 1679. He removed to Woburn, there had John, born 1650, who prob. died young; to Cambridge, to Groton, of which he was one of the first proprietors; back to Watertown, and last to Groton again; his wife, Martha, died 1681, and he died 1696.

REFERENCES:—Am. Ancestry I, 38; III, 190; IV, 92; VII, 62; VIII, 67; XI, 33; XII, 114; Austin's Ancestral Dict., 100; Butler's Hist. Groton, Mass., 407, 491; Clapp's Jones Hill, Dorchester, Mass., 65-8; Hartwell Gen. (1895), 74-83; Hazen Hist. Billerica, Mass., 73; Kidder's Hist. New Ipswich, N. H., 390; Hill's Hist. Meson, N. H., 203; Lapham's Hist. Norway, Me., 530; Narragansett Hist. Reg., III, 139-43; Wyman's Charlestown, Mass., I, 307-12.

HOLDER:—Christopher Holder, Providence, a Quaker, of Alverton Co., Gloucester, 9 miles from Bristol, arrived at Boston from London 1656, aged 25, and was imprisoned, whipped next year, and in following had an ear cut off. Went to Providence 1665, there married 1660, Mary, daughter of Richard Scott, had Mary, born 1662; Eliz. 1665; his first wife died soon after; and by second wife, Hope, he had Christopher 1666; Hope 1668; atience 1670; probably died soon; Patience, again, 1671; John 1672; Content 1674; Ann 1676.

NATHANIEL HOLDER, Dorchester, 1634.

REFERENCE:—Austin's R. I. Gen. Dict., 102.

HOLDRIDGE, or HOLDREDS, John, Holdridge, Roxbury, by wife Eliz., had Sarah, 1665; John, 1668; Thomas, 1670; Eliz., 1672, and Mary—all captr. 1674; Samuel, 1676, died young, and Samuel again, 1679; town record adds Mercy.

WILLIAM HOLDRIDGE, Haverhill, 1646, a tanner, of the Parish of St. Alphaze, Cripplegate, London, came in the Elizabeth, 1635, aged 25. Was first at Salisbury, where name is Holdred, by wife Isabella, had Sarah, 1640, died 1641; Mary, 1641, died in a few months; Rebecca, 1643; William, 1647; Sarah, 1650; died within 6 mos.; Mehitable, 1652; Abigail, 1654, died young; Mary, again, 1656, and Samuel, 1659.

REFERENCES:—Am. Ancestry, II, 57; Burleigh's Guild Gen., 91.

HOLDSWORTH:—Joshua Holdsworth, Boston, mariner; married, 1669, Sarah Rawlins; was freeman 1671.

HOLGRAVE, or HALGRAVE:—John Holgrave, Salem, freeman 1633; had probably wife Lydia, and second wife Elizabeth, represent. at the first Assembly, 1634; also 1635; after 1640 had resided at Gloucester; died 1708, aged 94.

JOSHUA HOLGRAVE, Salem, 1640; had bapt. Eliz., 1640, and Love, 1642. Probably he was brother of preceding, and removed with him to Gloucester.

HOLLAND, or HOLLON:—Christopher Holland, Boston, 1652, by wife Ann had John, 1648 Bridget, 1650; Joanna, 1652, died soon; Joanna, again, 1653, died in few months; Eliz., 1655; Hannah, 1658; Deborah, 1661, and Mary, 1663; and died 1704, aged 91.

JEREMIAH HOLLAND, Harvard Coll. 1645, went home, was a minister with a good living in Northamptonshire and died before 1698 by Mather's list; nothing else known of him.

JOHN HOLLAND, Dorchester, 1634, freeman 1636, was a merchant of good est.; had wife Judith, son John; Thomas, Nathaniel, bapt. 1638; and 3 daughters besides Obedience; and died about 1652; his widow married George Kinewright, if this name be not mistaken at Cambridge village, or Newton. Had Relief, another daughter.

JOSIAH HOLLAND, Roxbury, freeman 1690, is not mentioned in town records, as born, married, or dead.

NATHANIEL HOLLAND, Roxbury, freeman 1663, was of Watertown, probably son of first John, may have been born in England, at Charlestown, by wife Mary, had Joseph, born 1659, and at W. by wife Sarah, daughter perhaps of Samuel Hosier, had Sarah 1662; Ruth 1666; Nathaniel, 1668; John, 1674; Eliz., 1676; and Mary 1678, died next month; and he was living 1709.

THOMAS HOLLAND, Yarmouth, had Thomas, bapt. at Barnstable 1641.

REFERENCES:—Aldrich's Walpole, N. H., 277; Bangor Hist. Mag., III., 84-6; Barry's Hist., Farmington, Mass., 291; Holland Chart (1882) by H. W. H.; Pierce Gen. (1894); Ward's Hist., of Shrewsbury, Mass., 323.

HOLLORD:—Angel Hollord, Boston, shoemaker, freeman 1636, then member of Weymouth Church, where, perhaps, were born several of his children, as Thomas, 1635, prob. died young; Hannah, 1638; Elizabeth, 1641, who died in a few months; Hepzibah, 1642; Cubin B. certainly had Thomas, 1644; Sarah, 1646; and by wife Catharine had Joanna, 1653, died soon. His widow Catharine married 1671, John Upham, of Malden.

GEORGE HOLLORD, Boston, 1664, mariner, died 1714, in 90th year. Easaily this surname is perverted to Holland. and has been frequently.

HOLLEY:—Joseph Holley, Dorchester, 1634, Weymouth, 1639, was probably of Sandwich, 1643, and died early 1647; often spelled Holway.

SAMUEL HOLLEY, Cambridge, 1636, in his will, 1643, refers to wife Elizabeth and son John.

HOLLIDAY:—Walter Holliday, Springfield, in 1673 married Catharine, perhaps eldest daughter of William Hunter, had Ebenezer, 1675; and William; removed to Suffield, then had Samuel, 1680; Sarah, 1683; Mary, 1685; Isaac, 1690, and Abigael, 1692.

HOLLIDGE:—Richard Hollidge, Boston, 1638, freeman, 1639; had wife Ann.

HOLLIMAN, or HOLYMAN:—Ezekiel Holliman, Salem, 1637; had been at Dedham before that; brought from England a daughter, whose name is never seen, but it is less certain that he brought her mother, Susanna, daughter of John Oxston, alias Fox, of Stanmore, in Co. Middlesex. He was born at Tring, in the adjoining Shire of Hertford, and married his second wife probably 1638, at Providence, Mary, widow of Isaac Sweet, who seems to have been cast out of the church at Salem, 1639, perhaps for carrying out the opinions of her husband, was perverted in his faith; went to R. I., there at Providence in 1638, was one of the founders of the First Bapt. Church. He lived later at Warwick. Backus, 1, 106, Winth. I., 293. Benedict, Hist. of Bapt.

REFERENCES:—Austins' R. I. Dict., 102; Austin's Allied Fams., 134.

HOLLINGSHEAD:—Richard Hollingshead, Boston, 1634, fisherman.

REFERENCES:—Haine's Ancestry, 13-5.

HOLLINGWORTH—Richard Hollingworth, Salem, came from London in the Blessing in 1635, aged 40, with wife Susan, 30; son William, 7; Richard, 4, and daughters Elizabeth, 3, and Susan, 2. He was a shipwright, and for a casualty (by which one of his workmen was killed), severely fined for benefit of the widow and children in 1641. He died 1654. Perhaps he had children born on this side of the water, Joseph, Abigail, and Caleb.

WILLIAM HOLLINGWORTH, Salem, born in England, was a man of large commercial operations, supposed to be lost at sea about 1677. Felt., II., 240.

REFERENCES:—Hollingsworth Gen. (1884), 144 pp.; Jolliffe Gen. (1893), 145-53; Morris Gen. (1898), 560-3; Radman Gen., 168.

HOLLIS:—John Hollis, Weymouth, by wife Elizabeth had John born 1664; Thomas, 1667; Eliz., 1669; Mercy, 1675, and perhaps others. In December of this last year he was a soldier.

WILLIAM HOLLIS, Salem, 1668.

REFERENCES:—Am. Ancestry, VII., 25; Davis' Landmarks of Plymouth, Mass., 135; Lapham's Hist., Bethel, Me., 567; N. E. Hist. and Gen. Reg., XLV., 51-61.

HOLLISTER:—John Hollister, Weymouth, freeman, 1643, was represent. in 1644 in Mass., and same year in Conn., removed to Wetherfield, where he had been in 1642, when son John was born to him; was an efficient man in Conn., represent. 1655, and often until 1656, but with others engaged in controversy with the church under Rev. John Russell, which caused the pantation of Hadley in 1659; was lieut. and died 1665. By will left good estate to wife Joanna, daughter of first Richard Treat, five sons, John, born in 1642; Thomas, Joseph Lazarus, Stephen; besides daughters Mary,, Eliz., and Sarah.

REFERENCES:— Child Gen., 802; Ely Gen., 261; Glastenbury Ct. Cent., 183; Goodwin's Gen Notes, 97-106; Sedgwick's Hist. of Sharon, Ct., 90; Talcott's N. Y. and N. E. Families, 552-67.

HOLLOWAY, or HOLWAY:—Henry Holloway, Dover, 1662.

JOHN HOLLOWAY, Hartford, came to Boston in the Eliz. of London, 1635, aged 21; was a soldier in the Pegnot war. Married, 1663, but died without children, 1684.

JOSEPH HOLLOWAY, Lynn, 1636, removed to Sandwich, 1637, but probably came back, or left son Joseph, Lynn, who had Joseph, and Edward, twins, born 1673; Mary, 1675, and Samuel, 1677; died 1693.

MALADIS HOLLOWAY, Taunton, 1668.

SAMUEL HOLLOWAY, Taunton.. married 1666, Jane Brayman, had Hannah, 1667; Samuel, Nathaniel and John, born 1667 to 70, was a propr., 1676. His son Sam-

uel was in Gallopis camp in the sad expedit. against Quebec, 1690.

THOMAS HOLLOWAY, Duxbury, 1637, a soldier in the Pegnot war.

TIMOTHY HOLLOWAY, Taunton, 1643-59.

WILLIAM HOLLOWAY, Taunton, 1639-43, removed to Boston about 1650, by wife Mary had Mary, born 1653; and Benjamin, 1656. His daughter Hannah, died 1653, and it is feared that great confusion exists with another William. See Hallowell.

REFERENCES:—Am. Ancestry, IX., 192; Sullivan's Memoirs, 85-95.

HOLLY:—John Holly, Stamford, 1664, represent. 1670, and for Greenwich, 1673. Elizabeth came in the Blessing 1635, aged 30.

REFERENCES:—Huntington Stamford, 41-5; Tuttle Gen., 340-2.

HOLMAN, or HOMAN:—Edward and Gabriel, Marblehead, 1674.

JOHN HOLMAN, Dorchester, 1634 (but in Col. Rec. is mentioned in 1632), Selectman 1636, Ensign 1637, artillery camp. 1638, by wife Ann, who died 1639, had Margaret, or Mary, whose date is not known, and John, born 1638; perhaps a daughter, Ann, who may have been wife of Henry Butler. He married a second wife, but her name is not told, had Thomas, 1641; Abigail, 1642; Samuel, and Patience, bapt. 1648, or 9. He probably died in 1652, for his will of that year is abstracted in General Reg. V., 242. His estate was very good. A John H., perhaps son of the preceding, was of Casco, 1675, or earlier, in that part now Cape Elizabeth; and in the Catal. of H. C., 1700, is a John H., who died 1759; but his descendants are not known.

SOLOMON HOLMAN, 1694, by wife Mary had Mary, born 1695; Solomon, 1697; Edward, 1700, and Eliz., 1701; but we have no clue to his origin from Mr. Coffin.

WILLIAM HOLMAN, Cambridge, came in the Defence, 1635, aged 40, with wife Winifred, 35; and children, Hannah, 8; Jeremy, 6; Mary, 4; Sarah, 2, and Abraham, 3 mos.; at C. had Seeth and Eliz., born 1644. He was from Northampton, Eng., propr. of a lot, of which the Botanic Garden is now a part, and died 1653. His wife, or widow, was slandered as a witch, but permitted to die as a Christian, 1671.

REFERENCES:—Bass' His. Braintree, Vt., 194-51; Bemis' Hist. Marlboro, N. H., 537-9; Collins' Hist. Hilldale, N. Y., app. 64-6; Driver Gen., 305; Paige's Hist., Cambridge, Mass., 587.

HOLMES, or HOMES:—David Holmes, Dorchester, died 1666; by his will provides for wife Jane, son David, two younger sons not named, and daughter Margaret.

GEORGE HOLMES, Roxbury, freeman, 1639, had Nathaniel, 1640; Deborah, 1642, died in a few days; Sarah, bapt. 1644; Deborah, again, 1645, died same year. He died of fever, 1646. Had also Joseph and perhaps other children.

JOHN HOLMES, Plymouth, 1632; nothing else is known save that he was messenger of Gen. Court and continued there 1643. Sarah, perhaps his daughter, died there, 1650.

JOHN HOLMES, Duxbury, was of H. C., 1658, says Farmer; same call him eldest of William, but this is not certain. He married 1661, Mary, daughter of John Wood, or Atwood, of Plymouth, who became third wife of 2nd William Bradford. He had not any children of that union ment. by Minsor; but he says he died 1675.

JOHN HOLMES, Portsmouth, married a daughter of Thomas Walford.

JOHN HOLMES, Northampton, had John, 1678; removed to Deerfield, there died 1692.

JOHN HOLMES, Duxbury, married 1661, Patience, sister of Elder Faunce, had John born 1663; Richard, Patience, Mehitable, Sarah, George, Nathaniel, Ebenezer, Thomas, Joseph, and Desire, and he died 1697.

JOHN HOLMES, New Hampsh., 1689.

JOHN HOLMES, Roxbury, married 1690, Hannah, daughter of Isaac Newell.

JOSEPH HOLMES, Roxbury, 1651, married Elizabeth daughter of Capt. Roger Clap, removed to Boston, had there Joseph, 1661; Eliz., 1662, and Nathaniel, 1664. Perhaps he was son of George, and freeman 1690.

JOSEPH HOLMES, Boston, tailor, 1677.

JOSHUA HOLMES, Westerly, by wife Abigail had Joshua, born 1678; Mary and another son whose name is not seen, and died 1694.

JOSIAH HOLMES, Duxbury, married 1666, Hannah, daughter of Henry Sampson, who was one of the first comers; had Hannah, born. 1667; another daughter (name unknown) 1669; Josiah, 1672; Mary, 1674; John, 1678, and William, 1680.

NATHANIEL HOLMES, Plymouth, marired 1667, Mercy, sister of Elder Fannie, says Winsor.

OBADIAH HOLMES, Salem, 1639, was from Preston in Lancashire, had probably wite Catharine; and bapt. there Martha, 1640; Samuel, 1642; Obadiah, 1644; was perverted in faith and excom. therefor, with John Clark and John Crandall, sentenced to heavy fine or whippng; went to Rehoboth, thence soon to Newport, had 5 more children, was a preacher from 1652, died 1682, aged 76. He had a post in Settling, New Jersey, in 1664. Of his descendants in 1790, the estimate was 5,000.

RICHARD HOLMES, Rawley, 1643, was born 1610, but in 1692 his age was called 88.

RICHARD HOLMES, Norwalk, 1654, had 2 children living in 1672, and was there in 1694.

ROBERT HOLMES, Cambridge, 1636, freeman 1651, by wife Jane, who died 1653, had Dorcas, born in 1638, died 1642; John, 1639; Eliz., 1655; Mehitable, 1645, died same year; Sarah, 1646; Ephraim, 1647, died soon; Samuel, 1653; Sarah, again, 1654; John, Joseph, and Elizabeth.

ROBERT HOLMES, Newburg, married 1669, Esther, daughter of Anthony Morse, had Robert, 1670, and Esther, 1673. He died same year.

ROBERT HOLMES, Stonington, 1670.

SAMUEL HOLMES, Rehoboth, had Samuel, who died 1674; Saumel again, 1675; may have removed to Duxbury, or perhaps the Duxbury man may have been his son, who had there Consider, born 1702, and he of Marshfield, died 1690.

THOMAS HOLMES, Hingham, perhaps at least one of that name came 1637, as servant to William Ludkin, who was of the City of Norwich, and set down here H.

THOMAS HOLMES, New London, born at London, came in 1665; by wife Lucretia, or Lucia, daughter of Thomas

Dudley, of New York, had John, born 1686; he died 1724; his wife, 1688.

WILLIAM HOLMES, Plymouth 1632, was sent next year with armed force to re-establish trading house above Hartford against the Dutch; served in the Pegnot war; was lieut. in Scituate; went home, and got employment in the Civil war, or great rebellion, as the other side called it; came back, and died at Boston 1649, probably without wife of children; was called Major, and his will gives estate in Antigua, and his farm at Scituate, to daughters of his brother Thomas in London, "if they come to N. E." They were too poor to come, as depons. in 1654 show, yet possibly that Thomas Home, who arrived at Boston from London in the Speedwell, 1656, aged 11, may have been a relation. The Major's will mentions "arrears due him for being a soldier and commander in the army and service of the King and Parliament," as if the town of Boston was as good a place to expect such arrears as London. Winthrop, I, 92, 113. Usually Oliver took better care of his soldiers, especially if they had the merit of being hard heads as weil as roundheads.

WILLIAM HOLMES, Scituate, 1646, or earlier, freeman of that colony 1658, had Abraham, 1641; Israel, 1642; Isaac, 1644; Sarah, 1646; Rebecca, 1648; Josiah, 1650; Mary, 1655, and Eliz., 1661, and perhaps John, first born in England; removed that year to Marshfield, and died 1678, probably.

REFERENCES:—MASS., Ballan's Hist. of Milford, 827; Bliss' Hist. of Rehoboth, 207; Bond's Watertown Gens., 302; Daniel's Hist of Oxford, 544; Deane's Hist. of Scituate, 287; Hammatt Paper of Ipswich, 157; Hudson's Lexington, 106; Mitchell's Bridgewater, 188; Temple's N. Brookfield, 633-5.

NEW HAMPSHIRE, Dearborn's Hist. Scituate, 287; Dearbarn's Salisbury, 628; Runnell's Sanbarnton, II., 356; Smith's Peterborough, 110-7.

Other Publications, Andrew Fam. of Kingston; Austin's Ancestries, 71; Holmes' Fam. of Conn., (1865), 76 pp.; H. Fam. of S. Car. (1893), chart; Humphrey Gen. 373; Savage's Gen. Dict., II., 451-4; Taylor Gen. (1886) 69-85; Vinton's Giles Gen., 56-9, 76, 181-234; Whitmore's Copps. Hill Epitaphs.

HOLMSTEAD:—See Olmstead.

HOLSEY:—See Halsall.

HOLT:—Nicholas Holt, Newbury, a tanner from Ramsey in Hunts, came in the James 1635, from Southampton, perhaps arrived at Boston with wife, freeman 1637; had Elizabeth, born 1636; Mary, 1638, and Samuel, 1641; removed to Andover, where he was one of the founders of the church, 1645; then had Henry, Nicholas, James and John, who married 1685; Sarah Geary and died 1607; beside Priscilla, who died young, 1653; he died himself at the age of 104 same year, say records—though Coffin makes her 21 years younger. His first wife died 1654, and he married, 1658, Hannah, widow of Daniel Rolfe, daughter of Humphrey Bradstreet, who died 1665, and married, 1666, widow Preston.

ARMSS:—Az., two bars, or, In chief, a cross, farmée fitchee, of the last.

CREST:—A squirrel sejant, or, holding a hazel-branch, slipped and fructed: all proper.

MOTTOE:—Exaltavit humiles.

SAMUEL HOLT, Andover, freeman 1691, was son of Nicholas.

WILLIAM HOLT, New Haven, 1653, by wife Sarah had John born 1645; Nathaniel, 1647; Mercy, 1649; Eleazur, 1651; Thomas, 1653; Joseph, 1655; the last three bapt. in right of their mother 1656; Benjamin, 1657, and Mary,

REFERENCES:—Abbott's Andover, Mass., 22; Caulkin's New London, Ct., 314; Dawson, Gen., 42; Holt Gen., (1864), 367 pp.; Holt Ass'n (1868), 20 pp.; Holt Assoc. Meeting (1871), 7 pp.; Lapham's eBthel, Me., 563-7; N. E. Hist. and Gen. Reg. xxviii.

HOLTON, or HOLTEN:—John Holton, Dedham, married 1667 Abigail, daughter of 1st Dan'l Fisher, was freeman 1671.

JOSEPH and JOSEPH, JR., of the same were admitted freemen in years 1682 and 1690, respectively. The younger is presumed to be he who was wounded in the great Swampfight, 1675.

NATHANIEL HOLTON, Salem, 1668.

RALPH HOLTON, Lancaster, freeman 1668, is designed for Houghton.

ROBERT HOLTON, Boston, 1633, a slater, freeman 1634, by wife Ann, bapt. 1634; and Jabez, 1637, perhaps posthum. for early in 1638, the widow had become wife of Richard Walker.

WILLIAM HOLTON, Hartford, an original propr., though it is unknown from which of the Mass. towns he removed, came in the Francis, from Ipswich, 1634, aged 23, had John, Samuel, bapt. 1646; William, Mary, Sarah, Ruth, Rachel, and Thomas; probably all born before 1655, when he removed to Northampton, though there are no dates of any; was the first drawn at N., ordained 1663, represent 1664, 7, 9-71, once for neighboring town of Hadley, and died 1691.

REFERENCES:—Benedict's Sutton, Mass., 665; Dwight's Strong Gen., 228; Goodwin's Olcott Gen., 28; Holton Fam. Chart, (1886), 18x24 in.; (1872); Holton's Farewell Gen., 93-101, 155-81; Magenni's Gen., 57-9; William's Danbury, Vt., 167.

HOLYAKE, sometimes HOLLIOCKE:—Edward Holvake, Lynn, 1636, or 7, was from Tamworth Co., Stafford, in the edge of Warwickshire, and with prefix of respect, freeman 1639, living most of his days in that part of Boston known as Rumney Marsh, since Chelsea, but chosen perhaps represent. for several towns between the time he was serving for Lynn, 1639-48. He died 1660, leaving only son Elizur; and daughters Elizabeth, Ann, Mary, Susanna, and Sarah. His wife was Prudence, daughter of Rev. John Stockton of Kinholt, married 1612, bv whom before he came here he had also Edward, who died 1631. in 13th year, and John, who also died in England in 1635.

REFERENCES:—Bangor Hist., Mng. I., 27-9; Lewis' Lvnn, Mass., 121; Pvnchan Gen.; Talcott's N. Y. & N. E. Fams., 568; Tuttle Gen., xxxii.

ARMS:—Azure, a chevron, Argent, Caticed, or, between 3 crescents of the second.

CREST:—A crescent, argent.

HOMAN:—John Homan, Salem, 1668.

HOME:—Thomas Home, (before mentioned), the youth of 11 who came in the Speedwell from London, 1656.

HOMER:—Michael Homer, Boston, in a petition 1676, for releasing a servant from impress. for the war, says he had had one servant killed. Probably by first wife he was father of John; but he took 1693, Mary Burrows, probably as second wife.

REFERENCES:—Bridgeman's Kings Chapel Epit., 199-203; Homer Gen., (1889), 27 pp.; Hyde's Brumfield, Mass., 415-8.

HOMES:—Robert Homes, a soldier in Lathrop's Camp; killed by the Indians at Bloody Brook, 1675.

REFERENCES:—Bowen's Woodstock, Ct., 208-10; Morris' Bontecan Gen., 211; Pierce's My Ancestors, (1864).

HOMWOOD:—William Homwood, Cambridge, by Winifred had Elizabeth, born 1644.

HONET:—Edward Honet, Huntington, L. I., 1664.

HOOD:—John Hood, Lynn, 1650, Kittery 1652, says former; yet of him no more can be learned, but that he was a weaver, had wife Eliz., was in England 1653; except that Mary Truesdale, widow of Richard, in her will of 1672, speaks of "brother John Hood's two children."

RICHARD HOOD, Lynn, 1650, came from Lynn, Regis Co., Norf'k, had Richard born 1655; Sarah, 1657; Rebecca, 1663; John, 1664; Hannah, 1665; Samuel, 1667; Ann, 1673; Joseph, 1674, and Benjamin 1678; freeman 1691, and died 1695.

REFERENCES:—Am. Ancestry, II., 59; Hood Gen. (167), 64 pp.; (1899), 27 pp.; Morris' Bontecon Gen., 64-6; Smith's Hist. of Delaware Co. Pa., 469.

HOOKE:—John Hooke came in the Mayflower, 1620. Servant to Isaac Allerton, and died shortly after arriving.

WILLIAM HOOKE, Taunton, born in Co. Hauts, son of a gentleman, as the register at Oxford University expresses it, on his matric at Trinity Call, 1620. Martha says he was a minister at Exmouth, Devonsh, before he came here, the exact date of which is not marked by any writer, though we are sure he was here in 1639, as in town record his land is there made a boundary, removed about 1644 to New Haven, then had Eliz. bapt. 1645, and Mary, 1647; was in high esteem until he went home in 1656, held in great favor with Oliver, the Protector, (who made him a domestic chaplain), of the character of which a valuable letter to Gov. Winthrop by Hooke gives amusing insight. 3 Mass.. Hist. Call. I., 181. He died 1667, says Trumbell; but Calamy makes it 10 years later.

WILLIAM HOOKE, York, 1633, brother of Francis, removed to Salisbury, freeman, 1640, called by Winthrop III., 125, a jolly gentleman; represent. 1643, and 7; by wife Eleanor had Jacob, born there 1640; died 1654, leaving widow Eleanor, and son Josiah, who died at Salem 1683.

One William was of New Haven, 1647, a shoemaker, called Jr. to distinguish him, it is supposed, from the minister, but perhaps he was not son or any relation.

REFERENCES:—Hoyt's Salisbury Fams., 203-5.

HOOKER:—Nicholas Hooker, Charlestown 1678, had wife Mary, who died that year.

THOMAS HOOKER, Cambridge, born at Markfield, near Leicester, Co. Leicester. about 1586, as Mather tells; he was bred at Emanuel Call., Cambr. where he took his degree 1608 and 11, and was chosen one of the Fellows; first exercised his faculties as a lecturer, when 40 years old, at Chelmsford, in Essex; but after four years his unflinching aversion to same ceremonies, compelled him to withdraw from the pulpit, and he opened a school at

Little Baddaw, about 5 miles from C., where famous John Eliot was his assistant, but being still troubled for his Puritanism, he went within 2 years over to Holland, served in the gospel at Delft, and went thence to assist William Ames at Rotterdam, not without the thought of America in view; his sister had married George Alcock, who was one of the earliest settlers here, hence his desire to come over. Probably he got passage in the Griffin, with Rev. Sam'l Stone, and the great John Eatton, arrived at Boston 1633, next month settled at Cambridge, freeman 1634, and in 1636 went to Hartford with a majority of his parishioners; died 1647, aged 61; though in the verses, which Mather et the end of his life, III., 68, transcribes from Elizah Corlet, the glorious schoolmaster, he is made 75, a preposterous exaggeration that must have delighted the author of the Magn. His children were Joanna, Mary, John, Samuel, and Sarah—the last 3 being under age in 1647, as appears by his will. Both will and inventory of estate are printed in Trumbull, Call. Rec., I., 498-502. A clause of the testament, thought it did not forbid his eldest son from seeking and taking a wife in England, did forbid from "tarrying there." John not only did marry and live in England, but worse than that, in the opinion of his father's friends, being a parish priest aften the Restorator at Marfmouth, Co. Bucks, a short distance from Aylesburg.

REFERENCES:—Cathren's Hist. Woodbury, Ct., 569-77; Dwight Gen. 844, 1043-50; Joslin's Hist. of Poultney, Vt., 274-8; U. E. Hist. and Gen. Reg. XLVII., 189-92; Tuttle Gen. 88.

HOOLE:—Thomas Hoole, of Boston, freeman 1665, is unknown further.

REFERENCE:—Am. Ancestry, XI, 110.

HOOPER:—George Hooper, Boston, 1674, mariner. JOHN HOOPER, Marblehead, 1674, possibly was brother of George.

JOHN HOOPER, Marblehead, married 1691, Mary Litchfield at Boston.

RICHARD HOOPER, Hampton, removed to Watertown before 1684, was a physician and surgeon, by wife Elizabeth, had Hannah, born 1683. died voung, it is said, by mistake; and Henry, 1685; and he died 1690.

ROBERT HOOPER, Marblehead, born about 1607, probably was brother of John; bought dwelling house 1663, and land in 1665; sold in 1681 his house in conjunction with wife Elizabeth. By her had Robert and Henry, and was progenitor of a race of enterprising and most valuable men, of which one—Robert—over a hundred years ago, had usually the title—King Hooper.

SAMUEL HOOPER, Marblehead, married at Boston 1694, Mary White.

WILLIAM HOOPER, Reading, came in the James from London 1635, aged 18, freeman 1648, had Mary. born 1646; Ruth, 1653, Rebecca. 1656; William, 1658: Hannah, 1662; Elizabeth. 1665; Thomas. 1668, and John, 1670; was, perhaps, of Salem in 1668, then bought a tenement of David Thomas. He died 1678.

REFERENCES:—Aldrich's Walpole, 278-82; Bond's Watertown, Mass. Gens., 302; N. E. Hist. and Gen. Reg., XXII, 287; Platt Gen. (1898), 15-9; Wyman's Charlestown, Mass. Gen., I, 513.

HOPEWELL:—Thomas Hopewell, Fairfield, 1670.

HOPKINS:—Edward Hopkins, Hartford, came to Boston 1637, with Rev. John Davenport and Gov. Theop.

Eaton, and went to Hartford perhaps the same year, was chosen Assistant 1639, and Gov. foll. year, and thereafter in alternate years. with John Haynes until he went home in 1652, and even in his absence, through hope of his returning, he was again chosen in 1654. Had been before coming here "a Turkey merchant in London." Says Hutch. I, 82, "of good credit and esteem." Yet, though a thorough Puritan, he was not a member of the Mass. Comp. in London. After reaching home he was made a member of Oliver's Parliament, and a commiss. of the navy; made his will 1657 and died soon, in 58th year, near 10 mos. before Gov. Eaton and within two or three days of his friend, Col. Fenwick. His widow Ann, daughter of David, or Thomas, Yale, after insanity of over 50 years, died 1698.

JOHN HOPKINS, Cambridge 1634, freeman 1635, removed to Hartford, was then an original propr.; died 1654, leaving widow Jane and children; Stephen, born about 1634, and Bethia about 1635, as Goodwin presumes. The widow married Nathaniel Ward of Hadley.

RICHARD HOPKINS, Watertown, was punished 1632 for sale to an Indian of military stores.

RICHARD HOPKINS, a soldier, 1675, in Moseley's comp.

SAMUEL HOPKINS, Milford 1658, at New Haven married, 1667, Hannah, daughter of Capt. Nathaniel Turner, had Wait, Samuel and Hannah, 1670; removed soon after from the colony.

STEPHEN HOPKINS, Portsmouth. came in the Mayflower, 1620, with wife Elizabeth, son Giles and daughter Constance, both by former wife; and by this had Damaris, as also a son born on the voyage, called therefor, Oceanus, but he died within a year. He also brought servants, Edward Datey and Edward Leister, the duellists. Deborah was brought probably in 1622, before the division of land. Other children, also, they had: Caleb, Ruth and another daughter who died, besides Elizabeth. His wife lived at P. over 20 years; and he died 1644; had been an assistant 1633-6.

THOMAS HOPKINS, Providence, 1641; had followed Roger Williams in 1636 from Plymouth, married Eliz., daughter of William Arnold the first, had William and Thomas; swore allegiance to Charles II, 1668, as did Thomas Jr. in 1671; was representative some years. and progenitor of Stephen, the Gov. See Mass. Hist. Coll., I, 4. Possibly he had Joseph, and perhaps other children—certainly William; and died 1699.

WILLIAM HOPKINS, Stratford, 1640; an Assistant 1641-2, but it is unknown whence he came, when he died, or what wife or children he had.

WILLIAM HOPKINS, Roxbury; had William, Thomas and Hannah, all bapt. 1660; and Mary, 1662; but the town records give none of the births but Hannah's—1657.

WILLIAM HOPKINS, Providence; swore allegiance, 1668. married Abigail. daughter of John Whipple, had William (who by wife Ruth, daughter of Samuel and Plain Wilkinson, was father of the venerable Stephen, Gov. of the State, the immortal signer of the Declarat. of Independ., as also of Esek, a distinguished naval officer in the same cause) ; there living through the war, and was rewarded for his constancy.

REFERENCES:—Mass. Davis' Landmarks of Plymouth. 145; Freeman's Cape Cod, II, 384, 508; Hazen's Hist. of Billerica, 74; Judd's Hist. of Hadley, 513; Rich's Hist. of Truro, 536. New Hampshire, Cochrane's Hist. of Antrim, 542-7; Livermore's Wilton, 414; Morrison's Windham, 589-95; Secomb's Amherst, 639. Other publications, Am. Ancestry, II, 59; IV, 83, 218, 227, 237; V, 138, 187;

IX, 82; Hopkin's Gen. (1879), 6 pp.; (1881), 82 pp.; N. E. Hist. and Gen. Reg., V, 43-5; Page Gen., 130; Savage's Gen. Dict., II, 461-3

ARMS:—Sa., on a chevron, between two pistols, in chief, or, and a silver medal, with the French King's bust, inscribed Louis XV., tied, at the top, with a red ribbon, in base; a laurel chaplet, in the center; a scalp, on a staff, on the dexter, and a tomahawk, on a sinister; all proper. A chief, embattled, arg. Also:—

ARMS:—Sa., on a chevron, or, between 3 pistols, of the last, 3 roses, gu.

CREST:—A tower, La., in flames: proper.

MOTTOES:—*Vi et animo*, and *Inter primos.*

HOPKINSON:—Michael Hopkinson, Boston, 1638; was in the employment of Jacob Eliot, say the records of the church when admitted in 1639; same year was dismissed for the gathering of church at Rowley, where he lived; freeman, 1640, died, 1648, having, it is conjectured, married a daughter of Richard Swan, and had Caleb and John named in will of Swan, 1678. Farmer thought that John, who died 1704, and Jonathan, who died 1719, aged 76, at R., were his sons, and perhaps he had a son Michael, for one of the name, at a later day, married Sarah, daughter of Thomas Coleman of Newbury.

REFERENCES:—Guildhall's Vt., 242-4; McKean Gen., 149; Woodbury's Groveland Mass., Epitaphs, 41-8.

HOPPIN:—Stephen Hoppin, Dorchester, 1653; lived on Thompson's Island, married Hannah, eldest daughter of Thomas Makepace, had in 1666, when only 42 years old, Deliverance, John, Stephen, Hannah, Sarah, Thomas, Opportunity, Joseph and Benjamin. Same year he was of Roxbury. Name sometimes perverted to Happie.

REFERENCES:—Am. Ancestry, IV, 45-87; Power's Sagamore Co. Ill. Settlers, 383; Tuttle Gen., 664-6.

HOPSON, see HOBSON:—John Hopson, Guilford, 1664; born, it is said, 1610, which is doubted; embarked 1635 at London in the Globe, was constable 1666, by wife Sarah had John, born 1666; and Francis, who died young. His widow died 1669; and he at Saybrook married 1672, Eliz., daughter of Edward Shipman, had Eliz., born 1674; Abilgail 1677, died young; and Samuel 1684; but probably this last was by Eliz., daughter of John Alling, of New Haven, as 2nd wife is supposed to have died 1683.

REFERENCES:—Hughes' Gen., 108-10; Orcutt's Hist. Torrington, Ct., 720; Paul's Hist. Wells, Vt., 93.

HORN:—Armstrong Horn, Exeter, is given as name of one who took oath of fidelity 1667, but error is suspected.

JOHN HORN, Salem, 1630, came probably in fleet with Winthrop, but may have been earlier, freeman, 1631; was deacon, and, Bentley says, requested assist. by Callea, "as he had been in that office above 50 years;" died 1685, aged 82; had Recompense, Capt, 1636; and Jonathan 1658; both died before the father; had also John; Simon 1649; Joseph; Benjamin; Eliz. Gardner; Jehoadan Harvey; Mary Smith; and Ann Felton 1657. We may presume that his wife was Ann, as that name appears in Felt's list of early church members. An Eliz. Horn died at Newburg, says Coffin, 1672. All descendants in our day spell Orne (as he did in his last will).

WILLIAM HORN, Dover, 1659. at Salisbury, by wife Eliz. had Eliz. 1662; John, 1663; William, 1674; Thomas,

1676; and Margaret 1679; was killed by Indians at assault on Dover, 1689. Perhaps he had also Mary.

REFERENCES:—Barry's Framingham, 292; Felton Gen. (1886), 245.

HORNDEN, or HORNDALL:—John Hornden, Newport, in list of freemen 1655, had Mary, born 1647. See Horndale.

HORNER, or HAWNER:—In Col. Rec., Ephraim, Rehoboth, was buried 1684.

REFERENCES:—Am. Ancestry, IV, 175; XI, 86; Clyde's Irish Sett. in Pa., 63-71; Hayden's Virginia Gens., 188-97.

HORNETT:—Edward Hornett, Huntington, L. I., made freeman of Conn. 1664. Perhaps he is same as Harnett. See that name.

HORRELL:—Humphrey Horrell, Beverly, freeman 1682. Possibly wrong.

HORSLEY:—James Horsley, Newton, married Martha, daughter of first John Parker, had James.

JOSEPH HORSLEY, Rowley, 1672, died 1699.

REFERENCE:—Quade Gen., 70, 132, 261-3.

HORT:—Joseph Hort, and Samuel, Lynn, freemen 1691, perhaps brothers, of which no more is known.

HORTMAN:—Timothy Hortman, a soldier in Philip's war, 1676, for discharge of whom his wife Catherine made petition, because he had served 17 weeks and had 2 children. Once in the papers it is Heardman.

HORTON:—Barnabas Horton, Hampton 1640. went to Southold, L. I., 1662, favored Conn., and was next year made an officer.

BENJAMIN HORTON, perhaps brother of preceding, living at same place, same time, and Caleb, too.

JOHN HORTON, Guilford, was freeman 1669, but not a propr. 1685.

JOSEPH HORTON, Southold, L. I., 1662, made freeman of Conn.; was perhaps brother of Barnabas.

THOMAS HORTON, Windsor, removed to Springfield 1638, died 1641. by wife Mary. who married probably Robert Ashford, had only Jeremiah.

THOMAS HORTON, Charlestown, had Thomas, born 1665; John 1657; and William 1659. died in a few days. The name is spelt without H in early records.

REFERENCES:—Baird's Hist. of Rve, N. Y., 413-5; Bangor. Me., Hist. Mag., V., 197; Ely Gen., 25; Horton Fam. Gathering (1876). 13 pp.; Horton Gen. (1876). 259 pp.; supplement (1870); 80 pp.; Williams Hist. Danbury, Vt., 167.

HORWOOD:—James Horwood, came in the Christian early in 1635, aged 30. But no more is known of him. Possibly same as Harwood.

JOHN HORWOOD, Boston, 1633, perhaps only transient visitor.

HOSFORD:—William Hosford, Dorchester 1633, (Dr. Harris marks him 1630); freeman 1634, when name is spelled Horseford, removed to Windsor with his daughter Sarah; then his wife died 1641; and he married 2nd wife Jane; widow of Henry Fawkes, probably removed to Springfield and there preached from 1652 (when Moxon gave up in disgust), to 1654, and after several years both went home. In England 1656 he gave land to his 2 children and wife, also gave some of her land to the children of W. and others.

REFERENCES:—Joslin's Poultney, Vt., 278; Pearson's Schenectady, N. Y., Settlers, 95; Stiles' Hist. Windsor, Ct., II, 403.

HOSIER:—Samuel Hosier, came probably in fleet with Winthrop 1630, reg. adm. that year and was recorded early in next, married 1657, prob. as 2nd wife, Ursula Streeter, widow of Stephen, died 1665. The widow married William Robinson of Dorchester, and had Griffin Crafts for 4th husband.

HOSKINS, after HASKINS:—Anthony Hoskins, Windsor, freeman 1654, married 1656, Isabel Brown, had Isabel, born 1657; John 1659; Robert 1662; Anthony 1665; Grace 1666; Rebecca 1668, died at 5 years; Jane 1671; Thomas 1673; and Joseph 1675; his wife died 1698; and he died leaving large estate 1707, when all the children but Isabel and Rebecca were living.

JOHN HOSKINS, Dorchester, probably came in the Mary and John, reg. adm. 1630; made freeman next year, represent. 1637; removed to Windsor, there died 1648, leaving wife and only son Thomas to enjoy estate.

JOHN HOSKINS, of what place unknown, freeman of Mass. in 1634.

NICHOLAS HOSKINS, Portsmouth, school-master 1660.

SAMUEL HOSKINS, New Haven, married, perhaps in 1642, Eliz. Cleverly.

WILLIAM HOSKINS, Scituate, of whom no more is told by Deane, was of Plymouth after, freeman 1634, had a son there, born 1647; and Samuel 1654; and died 1695; had perhaps also daughters Mary, Sarah and Eliz.

REFERENCES:—Barber's My Wife, 74; Martin's Hist. of Chester, Pa., 55; Pierce's Biog. Contrib. 139-95; Smith's Hist. of Delaware Co., Pa., 470.

HOSMER:—James Hosmer, Concord, came in the Elizabeth from London 1635, aged 28; with wife Ann, 27; daughters, Mary, 2, and Ann, 3 mos.; and 2 maid servants. He was of Hawkhurst Co., Kent; had here James, born 1637; John 1639; another daughter Mary 1641, died 1642, and the wife called Mary had died 1641. Soon he had another wife in records called Alice, by whom were born Stephen, 1642; Hannah 1644; and Mary 1646; and 3rd wife Mary; though in another place this wife is named Ellen. She died 1665. He was freeman 1637, and died 1685.

THOMAS HOSMER, Cambridge, 1632, then called Newtown, brother of first James, freeman 1635, removed early with Hooker to Hartford, where he had good estate, was constable, selectman and representative several times, had only son Stephen, born 1645; daughters Hannah 1649; Esther; Clemence. He had before removed to Northampton; in old age married at Hartford 1679, Catharine, widow of David Wilton, and died 1687, aged 83, says the oldest monument in graveyard.

REFERENCES:—Brown's Bedford, Mass., Fams., 18; Guild's Stiles Gen., 366; Hosmer Gen. (1861), 16 pp.; Potter's Concord, Mass., Fams., 11; Walworth's Hyde Gen., 911.

HOSSOM, or HOSSUM:—Jeremy Hossum, Dover, 1665, probably left children.

HOTCHKISS:—Daniel Hotchkiss, New Haven, 1688.

JOSHUA HOTCHKISS, New Haven, married 1677, Mary, daughter of George Pardee.

SAMUEL HOTCHKISS, New Haven, married 1678 Sarah Talmage, had Mary, 1680; Sarah 1681; Samuel 1683; James 1684, and.Abigail 1687; was a lieut.; died 1705.

REFERENCES:—Am. Ancestry, XII; Andrews' New Britain, Ct.; A.'s Waterbury, Ct., I, opp., 70-3; Dodd's Hist. E. Haven, Ct., 129; Orcutt's Hist. Derby, Ct., 731; O.'s Hist. New Milford, Ct., 718; O.'s Hist. Torrington. Ct., 721; O.'s Hist. Wolcott, Ct., 502-5.

HOUCHIN, HOUTCHIN, HOWCHEN, or HOWCHENES:—Jeremy Houchin, a tanner, removed early to Boston, freeman 1640, artillery camp 1641, by wife Esther had Mary, born 1640; Jeremy, bapt. 1643, died perhaps on the day given by town records as that of birth; Mehitable 1644; Jeremy, again, 1651, died soon; Jeremy, again, 1652; Sarah, 1654; and John 1655, and the 3 last prob. died young. But he had, also, prob. at Dorchester (to Harris omits the name of so prominent a man), Eliz., who married, 1653, John Endicott, son of the Gov.; and Nathaniel 1658; and Rachel. He was represent. for Hingham 1651-9, exc. 56, and for Salisbury 1663, and died in 1670.

ROBERT HOUCHIN, Newport, by wife Rachel had Mary, born 1666; and Alice, 1668.

HOUGH, or HAUGH:—Atherton Hough, had been mayor of Boston, in Co. Lincoln 1628, and an alderman there 1633, when he resolved to come with his minister, famous John Cotton, and arrived with wife Eliz. in the Griffin that year; freeman 1634, chosen Assistant 1635, left out in 1637 as of Antinomian tendency, and chosen represent. for Boston at the same, and following courts; his wife died 1643, and he took another at Wells, died 1650, leaving widow Susanna and son Rev. Samuel.

WILLIAM HOUGH, Gloucester, housewright, was from Cheshire, son of Edward, and came probably 1640, with Rev. Richard Blinman, married 1645, Sarah, daughter of Hugh Caulkins, had Hannah, 1646; Abiah 1648, and Sarah 1651; removed to New London, there had Samuel, 1653; John 1655; William 1657; Jonathan 1660; Deborah 1662; Abigail 1666; and Ann 1667; was deacon and died 1683.

REFERENCES:—Am. Ancestry, VI, 182; VII, 92, 231, 232; VIII, 6; Aylsworth Gen., 304; Babson's Hist. Gloucester, Mass., 105; Davis' Hist. Wallingford, Ct., 802-6; Pott's Gen. (1895), 229-34.

HOUGHTON:—John Houghton, Lancaster, came in the Abigail from London 1635, with certificate of 2 Justices and the minister of Eaton Bray, near Dunstable Co., Bedford, at the age of 4 years, says the custom house record; was not of Watertown—as has been said—but of Concord, possibly; removed to Lancaster about 1652, had wife Beatrice and child Beatrice, born 1665; Benjamin 1668; Sarah 1672; and was represent. 1690, and several years after new charter.

JOHN HOUGHTON, Woburn, had Henry, born 1676; Joseph and Benjamin, twins, 1678; Mary 1680; Mercy 1682; may have been son of preceding, and probably removed.

RALPH HOUGHTON, Lancaster, cousin of the first John, and alder., no doubt, by wife Jane had Mary, 1654; John 1655; Joseph 1657; Experience 1659; Sarah 1662, and Abigail 1664; freeman 1668; was town clerk, represent. 1673, and 89.

ROBERT HOUGHTON, Woburn, had Isabel, born 1682; but no more is known. Perhaps he was son of John, and may have removed.

WILLIAM HOUGHTON, a butcher, came from London in the Increase 1635, aged 22, went in few years to Conn.

REFERENCES:—Am. Ancestry, III, 175; IV., 229; VII, 154; IX, 113; XII, 8; Douglas Gen., 163-6; Houghton Assoc. Report (1848), 27 pp.; H. A. R (1869), 60 pp.; Lapham's Hist. Norway, Me., 534; Lapham's Paris, Me., 635; Lapham's Woodstock, Me, 225; Waterford, Me., Cent.; Worcester Mag. and Hist. Jour., 281, 342.

HOUNSLOW:—Edward Hounslow, Scarborough, 1676.

HOUSE:—John House, Cambridge, died 1644; may have been child of Samuel.

SAMUEL HOUSE, Scituate 1634, one of the founders of the church, 1635, had Eliz. 1636; Sarah 1641; removed to Cambridge and prob. some other town, where he may have had Samuel before going to S. He probably lived some years at Boston or Cambridge, there had John 1642, who prob. died very young; at Scituate had John, again, bapt. 1645; and died 1661. His wife Eliz. was daughter of William Hammond and sister of William Payne.

WALTER HOUSE, New London, died 1670, leaving wife and child John; but no more is known.

REFERENCES:—Am. Ancestry, II., 59; Deane's Hist. Scituate, Mass., 289; French's Hist. Turner, Me., 54; Hanover, Mass., Records (1898).

HOUSING:—Peter Housing, Casco, 1666-73. Had wife Sarah, children not named in will. Willis, I, 121, 140.

HOUSLEY:—Joseph Housley, Rowley, 1691.

HOVEY:—Daniel Hovey, Ipswich, 1637, by wife Rebecca, daughter of Robert Andrews of same, had Daniel, 1642; John, who may have been the eldest; Thomas, 1648; James killed by Indians 1675, at Brookfield; Joseph; Nathaniel 1657; Abigail, and Priscilla. He removed to Brookfield 1668, thence, before the destruction of the town, in Philip's war, to Hadley; but went back to I. and died aged 73, perhaps 1692. His widow had died 1665.

JOSEPH HOVEY, Cambridge, married 1702, Mary, daughter of John Marrett of the same, had Amos, born 1712, and perhaps others.

THOMAS HOVEY, Hadley, married 1677, Sarah, eldest daughter of Aaron Cook, the sec. of Hadley, had Thomas 1678; Sarah 1680; Abigail 1682; Joanna 1684; Eliz. 1686; Miriam 1689; Hannah 1691, died young; 3 daughter 1693 —born and died same day; Daniel 1694; Dorcas 1697; and Rachel 1699. He was freeman 1681, lieut., represent. 1699 and 1703 and died 1739.

REFERENCES:—Amer. Ancestry, IV, 152; V, 23, 46, 139; Ammidown Gen., 35; Andrew's Gen. (1890), 50-3, 61; Caldwell Gen., 71; Cleveland Gen., 10-20, 99-125, 134-55; 2nd edit., 638-46; Daniel's Hist. Oxford, Mass., 545-8; Hovey Gen. (1893), 31 pp.; Jackson's Hist. Newton, Mass., 311; Paige's Hist. Cambridge, Mass., 589-91.

HOWARD:—Edward Howard, Boston, married 1661, Hannah, daughter of Thomas Hawkins the baker; no more is heard of him.

HENRY HOWARD, Hartford, had been at Wethersfield, there married 1648, Sarah Stone, perhaps a sister of Rev. Samuel, had Sarah, born 1651, died early; Sarah, again, 1653; Eliz. 1656; John and Lydia, twins, 1661; all at W. beside Mary and Samuel, mentioned in his will, but not found in record. He died 1709.

JAMES HOWARD, Boston 1677, of whom no more is learned.

JAMES HOWARD, Weymouth, had Hannah, born 1683.

JOHN HOWARD, Dedham, 1636-60.

JOHN HOWARD, Bridgewater, one of the first settlers, brought up by Capt. Miles Standish, in 1643 was of Duxbury, a carpenter, rep. 1678, and often after, married Martha, daughter of Thomas Hayward, had John, James, Jonathan, Eliz., Sarah, Bethia and Ephraim.

JOSEPH HOWARD, Warwick, married Rebecca, daughter probably of John Lippit.

NATHANIEL HOWARD, probably of Dorchester, freeman of Mass., 1643, of whom no more is known.

NATHANIEL HOWARD, Charlestown, married 1666, Sarah, daughter of Major Simon Willard, had Sarah, born 1667; Nathaniel 1671; and his wife died 1678. He married same year Sarah Parker, probably daughter of Jacob, had Jacob 1679, and lived at Chelmsford. Perhaps he was of Dorchester before Charlestown, artillery co. 1641, and freeman 1643.

ROBERT HOWARD, Windsor, 1643, is named under Hayward, and may be the miller at W. 1683, or his father.

ROBERT HOWARD, Lynn, about 1641, had Edward.

ROBERT HOWARD, Dorchester, freeman 1653, by wife Mary had Jonathan, Robert, Hannah, Jeremiah, Bertha, Mary, Temperance, and perhaps more, of whom Mary and some others were born in England; removed to Boston about 1660, was a notary pub. and died perhaps, early in 1683.

SAMUEL HOWARD, Malden, by first wife whose name is unknown, had Hannah, who married 1666, Isaac Hills, and died before her father; Martha, born 1653; Mary 1654; Sarah 1656; Eliz. 1658, died at 2 years; and by 2nd wife, married in 1662, Eliz., widow of Seth Sweetser, had Mary 1664; and by 3rd wife married 1671, Susanna Wilkinson, had Samuel, 1672; but probably by 2nd wife most of these following: Abigail, Deborah, Ann 1669, died soon; another Eliz., who perhaps died 1686; Nathaniel, and Jonathan; and died 1697.

SAMUEL HOWARD, Boston, by wife Isabel, had Peter, born 1654, died at 2 years, and Hannah, 1657.

THOMAS HOWARD, Lynn, married 1667, Ruth Jones, had Thomas, born 1669.

THOMAS HOWARD, Norwich, 1660, married 1667, Mary, daughter of William Wellman of Killingworth, had Mary, born 1667; Sarah 1669; Martha 1672, died at 1 mo.; Thomas 1673; Benjamin 1675, and died 1676. His widow married 1677 William Moore.

WILLIAM HOWARD, Tapsfield 1650, was living 1666.

WILLIAM HOWARD, Boston 1660, a witness to the will of Wm. Paine, and a legatee also therein.

WILLIAM HOWARD, Malden, had wife Martha, who died 1662. An Eliz. H. died at M. 1686.

WILLIAM HOWARD, Swanzey, 1671, by wife Sarah had Mercy, born 1681.

REFERENCES:—Mass.—Benedict's Hist. of Suttan, 666; Daniel's Hist. of Oxford, 548; Davis' Landmarks Plymouth, 146; Hammott Papers, Ipswich, 166; Kingman's No. Bridgewater, 533-46; Stearn's Hist. Ashburnham, 756; Temple's Hist. N. Brookfield, 636; Wyman's Charlestown Gens., 522. New Hamp.—Bemis Hist. Marlboro, 540; Blood's Hist. of Temple, 227-9; Cochrane's Hist.

Francestown, 770; No. Hayward's Hist. of Gilsum, 332-4; Livermore's Hist. Wilton, 415; Reade's Hist. Swanzey, 381; Secomb's Hist. Amherst, 640.   Other publications— Amer. Ancestry, III, 198; XI, 87; Hanson's Old Kent Maryland, 41-8; Howard Fam. of Conn. (1884), 238 pp.; H. Fam. of Mass. (1897), 71 pp.; Lillie Gen., (1896), 106-14; Locke Gen., 111; Preston Gen. (1870), 58-63; Proctor Gen. (1898), 263-8; Thomas Gen. (1877), 94-6; Thomas Gen. (1896), 362-9; Worcester Mag. and Hist. Journal, II, 13.

ARMS:—Gu., a bend, between 6 cross crosslets, fitchee, arg.

HOWD:—Anthony Howd, Branford, by wife Eliz. had John, born 1673; Anthony, 1674; and Benoni, 1676; died not long before the last was born; his widow married John Nash in 1677.

HOWE:—Abraham Howe, Roxbury, freeman 1638, had Abraham, Eliz., and Sarah, one or more perhaps, born in England; Isaac, born here, 1639; Deborah, 1641; and Israel, 1644. His wife—name unknown—died 1645, "the most sad mortal week that ever Roxbury saw," says Eliot's church record; he removed to Boston, perhaps, however, to Dorchester first, and died 1683. He had probably other children, certainly Esther.

ABRAHAM HOWE, Watertown, married 1658, Hannah Ward, had Mary, born 1659; Joseph, 1661; prob. died soon; and again, Joseph, 1662; removed to Marlborough, had Hannah, 1663; Daniel, 1665; Deborah, 1667; Rebecca, 1668; Abraham, 1670; Sarah, 1672; and Abigail, 1675; and died 1695.   The preceding year he kept the inn at which the Commissioners of Mass. to treat with the Mohawks lodged the first night of their journey.

DANIEL HOWE, Lynn 1630, freeman 1634, artillery comp., 1637, of which he was the first lieut., rep. 1636 and 7, removed to Southampton, L. I., about 1640, where he was one of the earliest settlers.

DANIEL HOWE, Boston, came in the John and Sarah, embarked at London 1651, one of the prisoners, freighted in that ship, to be sold, as they unhappily survived the battle of Worcester.   How long he lived here is unknown.

EDWARD HOWE, Watertown, freeman 1634, ruling elder, after selectman, and represent. 1635, 6 and 9, had a hard law suit with Dudley, of which Winthrop II., 51, speaks fully; he died 1644. His widow, Margaret, married George Bunker.

EDWARD HOWE, Lynn, came in the Truelove 1635, aged 60, with Eliz., his wife, 50, who survived him, and children, Jeremy, 21; Sarah, 12; Ephraim, 9; Isaac, 7, and William, 6; was freeman 1636, represent. at March, May and Sept. courts, 1638, and died very suddenly, 1639, as Winth. I, 295, tells.   A widow H. died at Lynn 1672. Felt.

EPHRAIM HOWE, Tapsfield, 1686.

ISRAEL HOWE, Sudbury, freeman 1680.

JAMES HOWE, Roxbury, freeman 1637, removed to Ipswich before 1648, married Eliz., only daughter of first John Dane of the same, had Sarah, and probably more children, and died 1702, aged 104—possibly an error.   He perhaps came from Hatfield Co., Essex, or the neighborhood.

JOHN HOWE, Tapsfield, born about 1640, freeman 1685.

JOSEPH HOWE, Lynn, 1640, had wife Eliz. and died about 1651.

JOSEPH HOWE, Boston, a cooper, freeman 1657, married 1652, perhaps as 2nd wife, Frances Willey, daughter of Thomas Marshall. He had Joseph, born 1653; and Sarah, 1656.

NATHANIEL HOWE, New Haven, took oath of fidelity 1660.

NICHOLAS HOWE, perhaps of Roxbury, married 1672, Mary, daughter of William Sumner, 2nd.

THOMAS HOWE, Yarmouth, 1640.

WILLIAM HOWE, Dorchester, 1641, says Farmer, who adds that he probably went to Chelmsford about 1656, which is doubted; more probably lived at Concord, there by wife Mary had Daniel, who died in 1657; Sarah, 1658, died young, and Hannah, 1660.

ZACHARIAH HOWE, New Haven, adm. to oath of fidelity 1660, had John, born 1667, says Dodd, but says no more.

REFERENCES:—Mass.—Ballan's Hist. of Milford, 830; Barry's Hist. of Framingham, 292-8; Brook's Hist. of Medford, 528; Draper's Hist. of Spencer, 207-9; Herrick's Hist. of Gardner, 357-9; Hudson's Marlborough, 380-97; Paige's Hist. of Hardwick, 401; Stearn's Hist. Ashburnham, 757-58; Temple's Hist. Northfield, 469; Ward's Hist. of Shrewsbury, 310-7; Wyman's Charlestown Gens., I, 523.   New Hamp.—Bassett's Hist. Richmond, 414-6; Cochrane's Hist, Francestown, 771; Hayward's Hist. of Tilsum, 334; Livermore's Hist. Wilton, 415; Read's Hist. Swanzey, 382; Wheeler's Hist. Newport, 419.   Other Publications—Am. Ancestry, I, 40; IV, 173; V, 86; VI, 148; VII, 135; VIII, 36, 38; X, 28; XI, 204; XII, 58; Dwight Gen., 480; Ellis Gen., 394; Glover, Gen., 356-8; Howe (Rev. J. M.) Biog. (1889), 254 pp.; Howe Family Gathering (1871), 46 pp.; Ireland Gen., 23-7; Little Gen., 162-5; Rice Gen.; Thayer Mem. (1835), 88; Tuttle Gen., 485; Whittemore's Capp Hills Epitaphs; Whittemore's Orange, N. J., 434.

HOWELL:—Abraham Howell may have been son or brother of Rice of Dover, and in 1658 was called 26 years.

EDWARD HOWELL, Lyme, freeman 1639, with prefix of respect, had 500 acres at that place, but removed to Long Island soon, was one of the grantees of Southampton in the Indian deed 1640, and made an assist., or a magistr., 1647, and six years or more after, under jurisdiction of Conn.   He had John, born about 1625; Edmund, Edwind, Richard and Arthur, who may all have been born in England; he died before May, 1656.

MORGAN HOWELL, Saco 1636, but more properly was of Cape Porpoise, some miles east of Saco; freeman 1653, constable 1656, and several years later.   Whether he had family is not known.

RICE HOWELL, Dover, taxed there 1657, and seven years before.

THOMAS HOWELL, Marshfield 1643, died in few years.

REFERENCES:—Am. Hist. Reg., III, 56-78; IV, 59-64; Chamber's Early Germans of N. Y., 421-5; Hughes Gen., 113-5; Kellog's White Gen., 53; Nevins' Gen.; Pott's Gen. (1895), 392; Prime Gen. (1895), 45; Sharpless Gen., 204, 324-7.

ARMS:—Gu., three towers, triple-turreted, arg.

HOWEN, HOWING, or HOWYN:—Robert Howen, Boston 1639, a cutler, by wife Eliz., who died 1653, had John, born 1640, bapt. 1641; and Israel, bapt. 1642: freeman 1642.   Both he and his wife probably died before 1653.

HOWES:—John Howes, Yarmouth, married 1689. Eliz. Paddock, perhaps daughter of Zachariah; may have married second wife 1691, Mary Matthews.

SAMUEL HOWES, Yarmouth 1634, adm. freeman 1635, had Sarah, born 1641; and John, 1645.

THOMAS HOWES, Yarmouth 1638, one of the grantees, constable 1644, represent. 1652, 3, 8, 9, and after, made his will 1665, naming sons Joseph, Thomas and Jeremy and wife Mary; died 1682.

REFERENCES:—Atkin's Hist. of Hawley, Mass., 52; Austin's Allied Fams., 136; Howes Gen. (1892), 208 pp.; Read's Hist. of Swanzey, N. H., 383.

HOWKINS:—Anthony Howkins, as Trumbell, Call. Rec. spells name, is same as Anthony Hawkins.

HOWLAND:—Arthur Howland, Marshfield 1643, or earlier, not thought to be near relation of Mayflower John, by wife, Margaret Read, a widow, had Arthur, Deborah and Mary; beside Martha and Eliz.—as Miss Thomas gives the children; in 1669 was aged and poor, and died 1675. His widow died 1683.

HENRY HOWLAND, Duxbury 1633, may have been brother of 1st Arthur, was a grantee of Bridgewater 1645, but did not remove; died 1670; his widow died 1674. His will of 1670 mentions, beside wife, 8 children, Joseph, Zoeth, John, Samuel, Sarah, Eliz., Mary and Abigail.

JOHN HOWLAND, Plymouth, of the ever-honored passengers who came in Mayflower, 1620. He was a servant or attendant of Gov. Carver, yet is in rank the 13th signer of the covenant, and was reckoned as part of the family of Gov. Carver, which gave occasion, no doubt, to the vain tradit. prevail. for the last two centuries that his wife Eliz. was daughter of the Gov., who, perhaps, never had a child, certainly brought none over. Both the Gov. and his wife died in the first season, and Howland, at time of their arrival, 28 years old, married Eliz., daughter of John Tilley. For correction of the long prevalent error, that he married Gov. Carver's daughter, we are indebted to Bradford's Hist., formerly part of N. E. Library of Prince, in the tower of O. S. church at Boston, discovered 1855, in the library of the Bp. of London at Fulham. He was an assistant 3 years, so early as 1633-5, and after a represent., and died 1673, aged 80; his widow died 1687, aged 80 also. Had children John, Isaac, Jabez, Joseph, Desire, Hope, Eliz., Lydia, Hannah and Ruth.

ZOAR HOWLAND, Newport, by wife Abigail, married 1656, had Nathaniel, 1657; Benjamin, 1659; Daniel, 1661; Lydia, 1663; Mary, 1666; Sarah, 1668; Henry and Abigail, twins, 1672.

REFERENCES:—Aldrich's Walpole, 287-9; Austin's Allied Fams., 137; Bill Gen., 176-8; Davis' Landmarks of Plymouth, 147-56; Eaton's Annals of Warren, Me., 556; Howland Gen. (1885), 463 pp.; Howland Gen. (1887), 12 pp.; Pierce's Contrib., 105-38; Thatcher's Hist. Plymouth, Mass., 129-71.

ARMS:—Arg. two bars sa. In chief 3 lions, rampant of the last.

HOWLET:—John Howlett, Boston, mariner, died before 1676, when his widow, Susanna, sold estate.

THOMAS HOWLETT, Boston 1630, probably came in the fleet with Winthrop, went early in 1633 with young John Winthrop to plant Ipswich. freeman 1634, represent. 1635, married Alice French of Boston, had Sarah, who married John Cummings; died 1667. leaving widow Rebecca, who died 1680, and Samuel, who may have been of Tapsfield, 1661, unless this was the father.

REFERENCES:—Guild's Stiles Gen., III; Hammott Papers, Ipswich, Mass., 153; Tapsfield, Mass., Hist.; Call, (1896), II.

HOWMAN:—John Howman, came probably with Winthrop 1630, requested to be made freeman, but as admission is not found after, perhaps he died soon or went home.

HOYLE:—John Hoyle, Marblehead 1674.

HOYT:—John Hoyt, Salisbury 1640, by wife Frances had Frances, born 1636; John, about 1638; both perhaps born in England; Thomas and Gregory, twins, 1641; Gregory died 1643; Elizabeth, born 1643; his first wife died 1643; by another wife, whose name was Frances, had Sarah, 1645, died soon; Mary, 1646; Joseph, 1648, died soon; 2nd Joseph, 1649, died 1650; Margaret, 1653; Naomi, 1655; Dorothy, 1656; and Mehitable, 1664. From Pike's Journal we learn that he was killed by the Indians probably between Andover and Haverhill, 1696.

JOHN HOYT, Fairfield 1650, freeman 1664.

MOSES HOYT, Fairfield 1658-65 and later, may have been son of Simon.

NICHOLAS HOYT, Windsor, may have been brother of preceding, married 1646, Susanna Joyce, had Samuel, born 1647; Jonathan, 1649; David, 1651; Daniel, 1653, who died 1655, as did both his father and mother.

SIMON, or SIMEON HOYT, Dorchester, had been at Charlestown 1629, freeman 1631, removed about 1639 to Windsor (but had first been at Scituate 1633-6), at W. had Benjamin, born 1644; prob. removed 1650 to Fairfield, soon after removed again to Stamford, and died 1659.

WALTER HOYT, Windsor, son of Simon, born prob. in England, had John and Zerubabel, removed to Norwalk with first sett. about 1653; was represent. 1658 often to 1681. In rec. of Windsor there is on "old quody Hoyt," died 1643, and we may presume she was either mother of Walter or of Simon. His name is usually Haite or Hayte.

WILLIAM HOYT, Amesbury, took oath of fidelity 1677, on being enrolled in the militia, married, 1688, Dorothy, daughter of Samuel Colby, had Eliz., born 1689, Dorothy, 1691; Abner, 1693; Mary, 1694; Susanna, 1696; Philip, 1697; William, 1702; Hope, or Hopestill, a daughter, 1704, and Miriam, 1710; and he died 1728.

REFERENCES:—Am. Ancestry, I, 40; VI, 136, 145; XI, 35, 219; Banton Gen.; Dwight's Strong Gen., 665; Hoyt Gen. (1857), 144 pp.; 2nd edit. (1871), 686 pp.; Hoyt Fam. Meeting (1866), 64 pp.; Hoyt's Salisbury, Mass., Fams., 205-9; Huntington Gen., 77; Morse Mem. (1896), 81-3; Sheldon's Hist. Deerfield, Mass., 213-8; Temple's Hist. No. Brookfield, Mass., 641; Tompkins Gen., 42.

HUATT:—Daniel Huatt, Guilford 1669.

HUBBARD:—Anthony Hubbard, probably of Dedham 1648.

BENJAMIN HUBBARD, Charlestown, 1633, with wife Alice probably came with his momther Eliz., who died at Boston 1644, having named in her will other children, Hannah. Sarah and Rachel; her father or husband not known; freeman 1634, was in 1636 one of only a dozen householders. Enjoying prefix of respect, a cautious friend of Wheelwright, he was made clerk of the writs in 1641, and perhaps removed to Boston; had Benjamin, born 1634; Eliz., 1636; Thomas, 1639; Hannah, 1641, and James, 1644; all at Charlestown. But he certainly went home and wrote Gov. Winthrop a letter from London, 1644, speaking in it of "his invention longitude."

GEORGE HUBBARD, Wethersfield 1636, probably went from Watertown, represent. 1638 in the first. Gen. Assembly, and several times after; removed 1643 to Milford, thence to Guilford, 1650, where he was of importance; prob. represent. to New Haven, certainly after the union of the two colonies, 1665 and 6; died 1683. His will names sons John, Daniel and William, with daughters Mary, Sarah, Abigail, Hannah and Eliz. His wife died in 1676; all above children may not have been by her.

GEORGE HUBBARD, Hartford, perhaps as early as 1639, married Eliz., daughter of Richard Watts of the same; had Mary, born 1642; Joseph, 1643; Daniel, 1645; Samuel, 1648; George, 1650; removed to Middletown, there had Nathaniel, 1652; Richard, 1655, and Eliz., 1660. He was made freeman 1654, and died 1685.

HUGH HUBBARD, New London about 1670, said to be from Derbyshire, Eng., married 1673, Jane, daughter of Carrie Latham; had Mary, born 1674; Lydia, 1676; Margaret, Jane and an infant son, who died; besides Ann, living at his death 1685. His widow married John Williams and died 1739.

JAMES HUBBARD, Watertown, buried 1639, leaving by widow Sarah—who married William Hamlett—Thomas, born 1638; James and Sarah, both perhaps born in England.

JAMES HUBBARD, Lynn 1637, had house and land at Charlestown, went to Long Island 1641, at Gravesend 1664, had a commiss. from Conn. jurisdict.

JOHN HUBBARD, of Boston, whose name is spelt Hubert in town records of Roxbury, there by Rebecca is said to have had Sarah, born 1684, and a daughter without name in 1686; he may have been the soldier in Johnston's comp, 1675.

RICHARD HUBBARD, Boston, freeman, with prefix of respect, 1669.

RICHARD HUBBARD, Dover, 1658, may have been an Ipswich man 1668, but not probably.

RICHARD HUBBARD, Boston, mariner, married Eliz., daughter of Dr. John Clark, had Richard, born 1669, and must have died soon after; his widow married 1703, Rev. Cotton Mather.

ROBERT HUBBARD, Boston, married 1654, Margaret Allen, had Daniel 1655, and John, 1656.

SAMUEL HUBBARD, Newport, had come to Salem, says Backus, in 1663, then a youth; removed to Watertown, thence to Wethersfield, then up the River to Springfield, and was then one of the five founders of the church and had the first children on record—Ruth, born 1640; Naomi, who died 1643; Rachel, 1643, and Bertha, 1646; next year was at Fairfield, and the following year fixed at N.

THOMAS HUBBARD, Middletown, first of Hartford, 1647, perhaps brother of George of the same, though another conj. is that he was son of James the first, but almost certain son of a William; stands at the head of a long list of freemen 1657; by wife Mary—surname unknown—had Mary, Thomas, Ebenezer, John and George. His widow married Deacon John Hall.

THOMAS HUBBARD, Billerica, 1656, died 1662; left widow Eliz.

WILLIAM HUBBARD, Ipswich, came in the Defence 1635, from London, aged 40, with wife Judith, 20; and Martha, 22; Mary, 20; perhaps his sisters; besides John, 15; William, 13; H. C., 1642; Nathaniel, 6, and Richard; 4; H. C., 1653, who may have been his children, emb. in July. Possibly age 25, assigned to his wife, is wrong, unless she was

his 2nd wife. He is called husbandman; freeman 1638; represent. that year and several following; removed to Boston 1662, and died 1670.

WILLIAM HUBBARD, perhaps of Lynn, came, it may be, in the Eliz. and Ann, from London 1635, aged 35, with Thomas, 10.

REFERENCES:—Aldrich's Walpole, 289; Am. Ancestry, III, 106; IV, 156, 232; V, 135, 224; VI, 29, 122; IX, 89, 90, 94, 95, 101, 115, 117, 229, 230, 234; Austin's R. I. Gen. Dict., 106; Bergen Gen., 127, 156; Blake Gen., 71; Ely Gen., 40, 86-9; Hubbard Fam. of Ipswich, Mass., 168-70; H. Fam. of Glastonbury (1872), 34 pp.; H. Gen. (1895), 495 pp.; H. Hist. of Springfield, Vt., 347-51; Hubbard Stanstead Co., Canada, 126-8; Kellog's White Gen., 98; Loom's Gen. (1880), 652-4; Middlefield, Ct., Hist.; Potter's Concord, Mass., Fams., 12; Stiles' Hist. Windsor, Ct., II, 414; Sullivant Gen., 275-8.

ARMS:—Quartered, arg. and sa., on a bend, gu., three lions, passant, or.

CREST:—A boar's head, couped, gu., collared, ringed and lined, arg. In the mouth a spear, sa., headed, of the 2nd.

HUBBELL:—Ebenezer Hubbell, New London, came from Fairfield about 1690.

RICHARD HUBBELL, New Haven, 1647, removed to Fairfield, freeman 1664, was living 1690 there, and also Richard, Jr., and Samuel, perhaps his son. Sometimes with a single l, or Hobbells.

REFERENCES:—Boyd's Annals of Winchester, Ct., 214; Jenning's Hist. Bennington, Vt., 278-82; Ruggles' Gen.; Sears' Gen, 73.

HUBBS, or HUBS:—Robert Hubbs, Newport, in the freemen's list 1655.

REFERENCES:—Cope Gen., 96, 194-5.

HUCKINS:—Robert Huckins, Dover, 1640, had James, only son, and perhaps Sarah, born 1654.

THOMAS HUCKINS, Barnstable, had lived in or near Boston, was of artillery Co. 1637, and bore its standard 1639, married, 1642, Mary Wells; had Lydia, 1644, died soon; Mary, 1646; Eliz., 1648, died soon; his wife died 1648, and he married soon after Rose, widow of Hugh Miller; had John, 1649; Thomas, 1651; Hannah, 1653; Joseph, 1655, and died at sea, perhaps, with his youngest son, 1679. His widow died 1687.

HUCKLEY:—Thomas Huckley, New Haven, took oath of fidelity 1660.

HUDD:—John Hudd, Hempstead, L. I., 1647. Thompson.

HUDDLESTONE:—Valentine Huddlestone, Newport, by wife Catherine had Henry, born 1673, and George, 1677.

HUDDY:—George Huddy, Newbury, took oath of allegiance 1678, then aged 17.

HUDSON:—Daniel Hudson, Watertown about 1640, removed to Lancaster 1664, by wife Joanna had Daniel, 1651; Mary, 1653; Sarah, 1656; Eliz., 1658; Joanna, 1660; John, 1662; William, 1664; Abigail, Ann, 1668; Nathaniel, 1671, and Thomas; was killed, says Willard, by the Indians 1697, with his wife, 2 daughters, and 2 children of his son Nathaniel.

DANIEL HUDSON, Boston, one of the wretched survivors of the crowning mercy of O. Cromwell, 1651, at the bloody field of Worcester, where Daniel was made prisoner, shipped in 1651, and perhaps did not live long after.

FRANCIS HUDSON, Boston 1630, fisherman, came from Chatham, Co. Kent, son of William, probably came with Winthrop, had wife Mary and by her Eliz., 1640; Deborah, bapt.., 1643; Mary, 1643; died soon; Mary, again, 1644; Susanna—also called Hannah, 1645; Samuel, 1650; and Sarah, 1653; freeman 1673; died 1700.

HENRY HUDSON, Hempstead, L. I., 1647. Thompson.

JAMES HUDSON, Boston 1642, by wife Ann had Lydia 1643, died young; Deborah, 1644; James, 1646; Lydia, again, 1648; his wife died 1652, and he soon married Rebecca, daughter of William Brown, who died same year, having borne John, who died soon; by a 3rd wife Mary, had John, again, 1655; Mary, 1656; Lazarus, 1658; Bethia, and Abigail, twins, 1659; Samuel, 1661; Ebenezer, 1662; and Eleazer, 1668.

JOHN HUDSON, Lynn, 1637, an unworthy servant of John Humphreys. Winth. II, 46.

JOHN HUDSON, Boston, obscure.

JOHN HUDSON, New Haven, by wife Abigail, had Abigail, 1654; Sarah, 1657; Mary, 1660, and Samuel, 1664.

JOHN HUDSON, Marblehead, 1674.

JOHN HUDSON, Duxbury, had wife Ann Rogers, daughter of John; had 4 daughters—Hannah, Rhoda, Eliz., and Abigail.

JONATHAN HUDSON, Lyme, married 1686, Sarah, and left descendents.

NICHOLAS HUDSON, Hingham, freeman 1637, is, beyond doubt, the same as Hodsdin, or Hodgen, who was at H., 1635, removed to Boston, that post called Muddy River, sold his Est., 1650.

RALPH HUDSON, Boston, a woolen draper, came in the Susan and Ellen, from London 1635, aged 42, with wife Mary 42, and 3 children—Hannah, 14; John, 12, and Eliz., 5; (but John was his brother, it seems); freeman 1636, died before his widow.

RICHARD HUDSON, Marblehead 1668, may be a soldier under Capt. Turner in 1676, at Northampton.

SAMUEL HUDSON, one of the comp. called "the flower of Essex," under Lothrop, who was killed at Deerfield 1675, and perhaps was of Marblehead 1668.

THOMAS HUDSON, Lynn 1637, had Jonathan, and perhaps other children.

WILLIAM HUDSON, Charlestown 1630, came probably in fleet with Winthrop, freeman 1631, and removed early to Boston, and continued there; brought perhaps son William, and wife Susan, by whom he had Nathaniel, bapt. 1634, as says the town rec., which may be more correct in saying that Richard, their son, died 1641, prob. unbapt. He went home before 1656.

WILLIAM HUDSON, Boston, called the younger, was born about 1619, freeman 1640; may have been son of the preceding, or not; by wife Ann, had Hannah, 1641; died soon; Hannah, again, 1644; before her birth he went to England and served as ensign in comp. of John Leverett, under Israel Stoughton, in the Earl of Manchester's army for the Parliam. The unhappy consequences of his absence, and his wife's exposure to temptations, for which she was whipped, is told by Winthrop II, 249. She had no more children.

REFFRENCES:—Adams' Haven Gen., pt. II, 31; Baird's Hist. of Rye, N. Y., 415; Caverlys' Hist. of Pittsfield, Vt.,

709; Glenn's Gen. Notes, (1898); Hudson Gen., (1892), 28 pp.; Hudson's Hist. of Lexington, Mass., 107-10; Hudson's Marlborough, Mass., 397-401; Hudson's Hist., Sudbury, Mass., 443; Middlefield, Ct. Hist.; Morris' Gen., (1898), 243; Paige's Hist., Cambridge, Mass., 592; Whitmore's Copps Hill Epitaphs.

HUDSHON:—John Hudshon, Hartford 1649. Spelling may be careless in record, and possibly the person is Hodson; but name is unimportant.

HUESTED, or HUSTED:—Jonathan Huested, Greenwich, married Mary, daughter of Robert Lockwood.

ROBERT HUESTED, Boston 1640, had grant for eight heads that year at Mount Wollaston, now Braintree, removed soon after to Stamford, had wife Eliz., and children—Robert, Angel, and Ann. Sometimes spell. Heustis.

REFERENCE:—

HUET:—Ephraim Huet, Windsor, had been a minister of Wraxall, near Kenilworth, in Warwick st., was proceeded against by Archbishop Laud 1638, for neglect of ceremonies, came next year with wife and children—Susanna, Nathaniel, Sarah, Mercy, and Lydia; went from Boston, and reached W., where he became colleag. with Warham; had Mary, 1640; and he died 1644. Sarah and Nathaniel had died 1642.

JOHN HUET, Marshfield, may have been son of Thomas of Hingham has been suggested, though there is no evidence to sustain such opinion; married 1668, Martha, daughter of Christopher Winter, who died 1691, had Solomon, born 1670; Bridget, 1673; Eliz., 1675; Winter, 1678; Christopher, 1681; Mercy, 1686, and Lydia, 1689.

NICHOLAS HUET, Boston, had Zebulan, born 1645.

ROBERT HUET, Hartford 1646, may have been in Mass., 1632, and that year was of the jury.

THOMAS HUET, Hingham, brother of Rev. Ephraim, freeman 1647, had Ephraim, born 1639; James, 1643; Thomas, 1644, and Timothy, 1647. Prob. died 1670.

THOMAS HUET, Stonington 1651, mariner, married 1659, Hannah, eldest daughter of Walter Palmer, by his 2nd wife had Thomas, born about 1660; and Benjamin, 1662, perhaps posthum; went on a voyage 1662, and was never heard of after. His widow married 1670, Roger Sterry of Stonington.

WILLIAM HUET, Marblehead 1668, bought 1681 dwelling-house of Robert Hooper.

REFERENCES:—Lincoln's Hingham, II, 358. See also under Hewitt and Huit.

HUGGINS:—John Huggins, Hampton, by wife Bridget had Susan, 1640; he died 1670, leaving sons—John, Nathaniel and James, who was killed by the Indians at Durham 1689. His widow Bridget married a Clifford.

JOHN HUGGINS, Newbury, took oath of fidelity 1678, then called 26 years old.

ROBERT HUGGINS, Dover 1642.

THOMAS HUGGINS, Barnstable. See Huckins.

REFERENCES:—Davis' Hampton, N. H., 757; Dickerman Gen., 470; Power's Sagamon Co., Ills. Settlers, 390.

HUGHES:—Arthur Hughes, Salem 1676.

JAMES HUGHES, Gloucester, by wife Eliz., had Eliz., born 1670; and Jonathan, 1672.

JOHN HUGHES, a soldier at Hatfield 1676, was from some E. town.

RICHARD HUGHES, Guilford, about 1640-50. His widow, Mary, married 1659, William Stone of G. Sometimes name may be Hewes.

SAMUEL HUGHES, Guilford, perhaps son of preceding, 1665-85.

REFERENCES:—Avery Gen. (1893), 224-9; California Reg. (1900); Freeman's Hist. Cape Cod, Mass., II, 576; Hughes' Gen. (1879), 245 pp.; Perkin's Old Houses of Norwich, Ct., 475.

HUFF:—Jonathan Huff. See Hough.

REFERENCE:—Bradbury's Kennebunkport, 252.

HUGHSON:—John Hughson, Boston, an appraiser on the large estate of William Hanbury, 1650; perhaps was not permanent settler.

REFERENCE:—Am. Ancestry, II, 62.

HULBERT, sometimes HULBURD:—William Hulbert, Dorchester 1630, prob. came in the Mary and John, freeman 1632, removed to Windsor 1636, thence 1655, to Northampton, was but some years before at Hartford, where he had Sarah, 1647, and Ann bapt., 1650. He also had John and William, prob. born at Windsor, and two others, whose names are not mentioned.

REFERENCES:—Hulbert's Gen.; Sedgwick's Hist. Sharon, Ct., 92.

HULL:—Andrew Hull, New Haven 1639, emb. at London for Boston 1635, aged 29, in the Hopewell, Capt. Babb, with Catherine, prob. his wife, 23; had Hannah and Sarah, bapt., 1640. No more is known of him; but his widow married Richard Beech before 1644.

BENJAMIN HULL, Weymouth 1635, was soon after, perhaps, at Bass River, now Beverly; in 1643 at York; certainly at Dover 1659-61. He may have gone home later. Had son here.

BENJAMIN HULL, Portsmouth 1689, a prominent man, was probably son of preceding.

GEORGE HULL, Dorchester 1630, probably of the comp. in the Mary and John; freeman 1633; represent. at the first Gen. Court 1634; removed to Windsor; was represent. for that town most of the time until 1656, and died 1659. The names of his children are not known with certainty.

GEORGE HULL, Beverly 1674, Farmer says: and *Isaac* is found there 1671, who may be the same who was Minister at First Baptist Church in Boston 1675-88.

JOHN HULL, Dorchester, a blacksmith; freeman 1632, Artillery Co. 1638, removed probably to Boston; and probably died 1666.

JOHN HULL, Newbury, died 1670; and his widow Margaret, who had been widow of William Goodridge, says Coffin, died 1683.

JOHN HULL, Boston, merchant, called jr. to distinguish him from the mint-master—son of Robert; married Mary, daughter of Capt. Robert Spencer; died about 1673; she probably married next year William Phips, the shipwright, afterward Sir William, the royal Gov. of Mass. under new charter; in her next widowhood married Peter Sergeant.

JOHN HULL, Stratford 1661-70, had John, born 1662; Samuel 1663; Mary 1666; Joseph 1668; and Benjamin 1672; but he removed to Derby a year or two after and had four more children there: Richard 1675; Ebenezer

1678; Jeremiah 1679; and Andrew 1685; perhaps he was the man who served in Philip's War 1675-6, as Surg. of the Conn. forces; and died 1714.

JOSEPH HULL, Yarmouth 1642; forbidden to be Minister. See Felt. Eccles. His. I., 498.

PHINEAS HULL, York, a sufferer by attack of the Indians, who took his wife 1690, and kept her for their secretary until late the following year. Mather VI., 76.

RICHARD HULL, New Haven 1640, or earlier; had John bapt. 1640; and Hannah 1642; but first living in the Mass Colony, and was freeman 1634, though of what church he was member is not known, yet resided in Boston short time about 1637, died 1662; named in his will of Aug. of that year child Jeremiah, who continued there a propr. 1685; John, Hannah and Mary.

ROBERT HULL, Boston, came in the George Bristol 1635, with wife Eliz., who brought son Richard Storer, and his own—John, and Edward; was a blacksmith; freeman 1637; his wife died 1646, and he married wife Judith Paine of Braintree, who had been widow of Edmund Quincy; he died 1654. She was mother of his son John's wife.

SAMUEL HULL, Fairfield, married Deborah, daughter of Elder James Beers.

THOMAS HULL, Boston, cooper, married 1657, Hannah, daughter of William Townsend; had William 1659, died 1660; Mary 1661, died young; Thomas 1663; Hannah 1664; Mary, again, 1666; and Samuel 1667. He died 1670; later his widow married Lieut. Richard Way.

TRISTRAM HULL, Yarmouth 1643, had Mary, born 1645; Sarah 1647, died soon; Sarah, again, 1650; Joseph 1652; John 1654; Hannah 1657; wife's name Blanch.

WILLIAM HULL, R. I., 1654.

REFERENCES:—Anderson's Waterbury, Ct., I., app. 74; Andrew's Hist. New Britain, Ct., 367; Boutan Gen., Cathren's Woodbury, Ct., 577-9; II., 1509; Greene Gen., Hull Gen. (1863) 36 pp.; Hull Fam. New Haven (1869) 20 pp.; (1895) 78 pp.; Loomis Gen. (1880) 59-107; Orcutt's Hist. Derby, Ct., 732-7; O's Hist. Stratford, Ct., 1225; Stile's Hist. of Windsor, Ct., II., 416; Tuttle Gen., 658-64.

HULLING, or HULLINE:—Obadiah Hulling, Salem, had, says Felt, grant of land 1639; doubtful; a Holme had grant there in 1639.

HULTON:—Richard Hulton, Salisbury, by wife Martha had Dorothy, born 1673; had been earlier of Topsfield.

HUMBER:—Edward Humber, Salem, freeman, 1665.

HUMPHREY HUMBER, Hampton, 1645.

HUME:—David Hume, and 2 or 3 others of same family name came to Boston 1652, as Worcester prisoners, brought in the John and Sarah, with about 270 more, to be sold; no more known of them.

REFERENCES:—Hume Gen. (1891), 2 pp.; Morris' Gen. (1887), 62, 95-7; (1898), 746-8; Martin's Hist. of Chester, Pa., 294.

HUMFREY:—John Humfrey, Lynn, a gentleman of great merit for his services and affection to our country in its first attempts; chosen as its second meeting, 1629, dep.-gov. of the comp. in England; came over in 1634, probably in the Planter; with him, besides his wife Susan, daughter of the illustrious Thomas Clinton, 3d

Earl of Lincoln, and some children—Ann, Dorcas and Sarah, he brought money, goods and cattle for the colony. Here he had at Salem, Theophilus 1637; Thomas 1638; Joseph 1640; and Lydia 1641; Perhaps he had John, and another daughter. Early in 1651 he was of Artillery Co., and in June was made the first Maj.-Gen. of the Col., but having lost most of his property, was tempted by great offers for new plant. in W. Indies. He went home in 1641, in same ship with Rev. John Phillips.

HUMMERSTAN:—Henry Hummerstan, New Haven 1644, married 1651, Joan Walker; had Samuel, born 1653; Nathaniel 1655; Thomas 1656; prob. all died.

HUMPHREY, UMPHRYS, or HUMPHRIES:—Jeremiah Humphrey, Saco, 1653.

JONAS HUMPHREY, Dorchester 1634, tanner, whose pits were employed by six generations; was from Wendover, Co. Bucks, where he was constable; came with children James, Jonas, and prob. Eliz. and Susanna; perhaps with wife Frances, whose daughter Sarah was buried here 1638. For 2d wife he had Jane, widow of George Weeks, who died 1668. He died 1662.

MICHAEL HUMPHREY, Windsor, perhaps had been at Dorchester; was freeman of Conn. 1657; married 1647, Priscilla, daughter of Matthew Grant, had John, born 1650; Mary 1653; Samuel 1656; Sarah 1659; Martha 1663; Abigail 1666; and Hannah 1669; all living 1697, before which he died at Simsbury, whither he removed 1669.

NATHANIEL HUMPHREY, Hartford, married Agnes, daughter of Samuel Spencer. His widow married John Hubbard.

NATHANIEL HUMPHREY, Ipswich, freeman 1680.

THOMAS HUMPHREY, Dover 1660, married 1665, at Hingham, a daughter of George Lane, prob. living at Pemaquid 1674, when he swore fidelity to Mass.

WILLIAM HUMPHREY, Boston, had gone home and died before 1654.

REFERENCES:—Austin's Allied Fams., 141; Ballon's Hist. Milford, Mass., 831; Daniel's Hist. Oxford, Mass., 522-4; Humphrey Gen. (1882); Lincoln's Hist. of Hingham, Mass., II., 360-9; Stile's Hist. Windsor, Ct., 673.

HUNGERFORD:—Thomas Hungerford, Hartford 1639, but not an original propr.; removed to New London 1650, constable 1662, and died 1663, leaving widow and children—Thomas, aged 15; Sarah, 9; and Hannah, 4. His widow Hannah, daughter of Isaac Willey, was his 2d wife, and mother only of last child. She married Peter Blachford, and next, Samuel Spencer of Haddam, whither the family had removed.

REFERENCES:—Anderson's Waterbury, Ct., I., pp 75; Boyd's Annals of Winchester, Ct., 173; Field's Hist. of Haddam, Ct., 47.

HUNKING, sometimes HUNKINS:—John Hunking, Portsmouth 1650; died 1681; by wife Agnes had John, born 1651, died at 15 years in Eng.; Hercules, 1656; John again 1660; Peter 1663; Agnes 1665; William 1668; and Mark 1670.

MARK HUNKING, Portsmouth, perhaps brother of preceding, had wife Ann, and died 1667. Had children Mark, Archelaus and Mary.

MARK HUNKING, Portsmouth, master mariner, in 1679, of a vessel from Barbadoes for Boston; record. of

the Prov. Judge of the Sup. Court., and in 1710 a couns., says Farmer. He may have been son of John; had daughter Sarah; and other children who died young.

REFERENCE.—

HUNKINGS:—William Hunkings, Providence 1651, unit. with Benedict Arnold, William Harris, and others in compl. to their neighbors of Mass. against Sorton and others; prob. name should be Hamkins.

HUNLOCK, or HUNLOKE:—Edward Hunlock, Boston, from Derbysh.; by wife Margaret had Margaret, born 1682; Martha 1684; and Mary 1686; removed to Burlington in Prov. of W. Jersey, whence he wrote to his kinsman, John, at Boston, 1695. In 1699 was appointed by Gov. Hamilton one of the three Prov. Judges, and in the first year of her reign, Queen Anne, by commiss. 1702, to her cousin Lord Cornbury, Gov. of New Jersey, among his 13 counsel, named him the first.

REFERENCE.—

HUNN:—George Hunn, Boston 1635, tanner, freeman 1637, by wife Ann had Nathaniel, and died 1640. His widow married William Philpot.

HUNNIWELL, HUNNUEL, HONGWELL, or HUNNEWELL:—John Hunniwell, Wethersfield, married Eliz., daughter of Daniel Harris of Middletown, was surveyor of the roads 1682.

ROGER HUNNIWELL, Saco, died 1654, Folsom. Had son Richard, who was killed by Indians 1703.

REFERENCES:—Fowle Fam. (1891); Hunnewell Chart (1892); Hunnewell Gen. (1900), 47 pp.; N. E. Hist. of Gen. Reg., LIV., 140-6.

HUNT:—Bartholomew Hunt, Dover, 1640, supposed to be same who was of Newport, 1655, freeman of that Col.; there by wife Ann had Bartholomew, born 1654; Adam 1656; Naomi 1658; and Ezekiel 1663, or 4, beside others.

EDMUND HUNT, Duxbury, 1637. Had, says Winsor, been of Cambridge 1634; was surveyor of roads 1655, and a propr. of Bridgewater, but prob. did not move thither.

EDWARD HUNT, Duxbury, died 1656; is suspected to be same as preceding.

EDWARD HUNT, Amesbury, swore fidelity 1677.

ENOCH HUNT, Weymouth 1650, blacksmith; came from Lee, a parish in Bucks near Wendover, had perhaps been at Newport 1639; but at W. had Sarah 1640; after some years went home, leaving here son Ephraim.

JOHN HUNT, Boston, mariner, was taken by the French.

PETER HUNT, Rehobolt 1644, perhaps had children Mary, Peter, Tabitha, Eliz., and perhaps others; was represent. 13 years, from 1654. Baylies II., 198.

RALPH HUNT, Newtown, L. I., 1656, adm. freeman of Conn. 1664; died 1677. Had children Ralph, Edward, John, Samuel, Ann and Mary. Branches of this family are at Jamaica, L. I., and Newton, L. I., and one went to N. J. Riker 85.

RICHARD HUNT, Boston, by wife Mary had Richard, born 1676, died young; and Richard, again, 1680. He died 1682, aged about 48 years, and was from Plymouth, in Co. Hauts.

ROBERT HUNT, Charlestown, 1638, an original propr. of Sudbury.

SAMUEL HUNT, Duxbury, 1663-90, says Winsor, and no more is learned.

THOMAS HUNT, Boston, by wife Eliz. had Jabez 1655; and John, 1656, who died next year; the father also died soon.

THOMAS HUNT, West Chester, in jurisdict. of N. Y., but claimed by Conn., at whose Gen. Court he was made freeman 1663; represent. 1664.

THOMAS HUNT, Duxbury, killed 1676, in the comp. of Capt. Pierce of Rehobolt, but Winsor does not specify. The battle was one of the hardest of Philip's War. See Newman's dispatch in Deane, 123.

THOMS HUNT, Boston, by wife Joanna had Thomas, born 1677; and by wife Mary had Thomas 1681; Priscilla 1688; Mary 1690; Sarah 1692; Joanna 1695; Martha 1697; Jobez 1698; and Eliz. 1700.

THOMAS HUNT, Northampton, freeman 1684.

WILLIAM HUNT, Concord, freeman 1641, had Samuel, Nehemiah, Isaac, William, who died before his father, and several daughters, of whom perhaps the youngest was Hannah, born 1641. His widow Eliz. died 1661. He removed to Marlborough, married 1664, Mercy, widow of Edmund Rice, who had been widow of Thomas Brigham, whose maiden name was Hurd; died 1667.

WILLIAM HUNT, Boston, by wife Sarah, had Thomas, born 1682; and Ann 1686.

WILLIAM HUNT, Weymouth, by wife Mary had Mary, born 1688; and William, 1693.

ZACCHEUS HUNT, Hull freeman 1680.

REFERENCES:—Mass.—Atkin's Hist. Hawley, 55; Ballon's Hist. of Milford, 832-41; Draper's Hist. of Spencer, 211; Hammatt Papers of Ipswich, 166; Hobart's Hist. of Abington, 404; Hoyt's Salisbury Fams.; 211-3; Paige's Hist. Hardwick, 401-3; Sheldon's Hist. Deerfield, 218.

OTHER PUBLICATIONS.

Dodd's Hist. of Haven, Ct., 131; Hunt Gen. (1862), 414 pp.; Jessup. Gen., 378-87; Read's Hist. of Swanzey, N. H., 384; Sedgwick's Hist. of Sharon, Ct., 91; Stearns Hist. of Rindge, N. H., 262-5; Wetmore Gen., 218; Whitmore's Copps Hill Epitaphs.

ARMS:—Per pale. arg and Sa., a Saltire, counter changed.

CREST:—A lion's head, erased, per pale, arg. and Sa., collared, gu., lived and ringed.

HUNTER:—John Hunter, New Haven, 1654, died 1658, or early 1659, prob. without family.

ROBERT HUNTER, Ipswich, freeman 1650, had wife Mary, but no children. Another Robert, Ipswich, had there several children, of which Thomas was eldest, died early 1687.

THOMAS HUNTER, Springfield 1678.

WILLIAM HUNTER, Boston, married 1657, Cicely, who prob. died young, and by wife Mary, only child of Richard Carter, had Mary, born 1659, died young; Hannah 1661; Sarah 1663; and Mary, again, 1665. He died shortly afterward. His widow married Joseph Cowell.

WILLIAM HUNTER, Springfield, by wife Priscilla had Sarah, born 1664; Priscilla 1665; Mary 1667; James 1669; John 1672; Hannah 1624; and Abilene posthum 1677. He was killed by the Indians 1676. His widow married at Springfield 1678, David Frow.

WILLIAM HUNTER, Barnstable, married 1671, Rebecca, daughter of Austin Bearce.

REFERENCES:—Bartlett Wanton Gen., 129; Bullock Gen.; Hudson's Hist. of Marlborough, Mass., 401; Hunter Fam. of Va. (1895), 50 pp.; H. Fam. of Mass. (1896), 5 pp.; Temple's Hist. of Palmer, Mass., 473; Wheeler's Hist. of Brunswick, Me., 840.

HUNTING:—John Hunting, Dedham, freeman 1639, the first ruling Elder, by wife Esther had John, born prob. in England.; Samuel 1650; Nathaniel 1643, died few days. Margaret, born in England, other daughter Mary, Esther, and another.

REFERENCES:—Ballon's Milford, Mass., 841; Hill's Dedham, Mass., Rec. I.; Hunting Gen. (1888), 83 pp.; Howell's Hist. of Southampton, N. Y., 250.

HUNTINGTON:—Christopher Huntington, Norwich, son of that Simon who died of smallpox on passage from England to Boston, 1633, brought with his brother, says Couteur, ch. rec. of Roxbury, by their mother Margaret, who lived at R. until 1635 or 6, when having married Thomas Stoughton of Dorchester, the family removed to Windsor; before coming of age he was at Saybrook, then living many years, was freeman 1658, but married at Windsor 1652, Ruth, daughter of William Rockwell, had Christopher, again, 1660, the first male of the new town of Norwich; Thomas 1664; John 1666; Susanna 1668; Lydia 1672; and Ann 1675; and he died prob. 1691.

SIMON HUNTINGTON, Norwich, brother of the first Christopher, prob. born in England, was freeman, 1663, married 1653, Sarah Clark, perhaps at Saybrook, had Sarah 1654; Mary 1657; Simon 1659; Joseph 1661; Eliz. 1664, died soon; Samuel 1666; Eliz., again, 1669.

THOMAS HUNTINGTON, Windsor, brother of Christopher and Simon, prob. eldest; was freeman of Conn. 1657, living at Branford; married Hannah, daughter of Jasper Crane, and had Samuel; prob. accomp. many of his neighbors who went with Pierson to found the town and church of Newark.

WILLIAM HUNTINGTON, Salisbury 1640, prob. was of Hampton 1643, but voted in 1650 at S.; had wife Joan, and children—John, born 1643; and May, 1648. Another William was of Amesbury in 1677, to swear fidelity.

REFERENCES.—Aldrich's Walpole, 291; Buckingham Gen., 153-6; Champion Gen., Dolbcare Gen., 20; Huntington Mems. (1857), 119 pp.; N. E. History Reg. V., 163; X, 283; XI. 156; Norwich, ,Ct. Jubilee, 208; Swain Gen., 107-10; Todd Gen. (1867).

HUNTLEY:—John Huntley, Boston 1652; by wife Jane had Moses, born 1654; and Aaron; was of Roxbury 1659; and removed in perhaps one or two years to Lynne; was there when that town was incorp. by Separat, from Saybrook in 1667, having other children, Eliz. and Mary. He married 2nd wife 1669, Mary Barnes; had Sarah and Alice by her and died 1676.

REFERENCES:—Champion Gen., 28; Perkins' Old Houses of Norwich, Ct., 494.

HUNTON:—William Hunton, Hampton 1644, perhaps had Philip, who is seen in New Hampsh. 1689.

HUNTRESS:—George Huntress, Portmouth 1688; was of the Grand Jury that year, and in the next with many others; pray. for jurisdiction of Mass. to be extended to them.

HURD:—Adam Hurd, brother of John the first, living there 1650 to 69, had wife Hannah and son John.

HURD:—John Hurd, Windsor, among first settlers, but not, like most of them, from Dorchester; removed with the early settlers to Stratford, represent. 1659, 56 and 7; still in 1671 a prominent man.

JOHN HURD, Boston, 1639, by wife Mary had John, born 1639; Hannah, 1640; John, again, 1643; Joseph, 1644; Benjamin, 1652; Jacob, Samuel, 1655; and Mehitable, 1657. He was a tailor, freeman 1640, and died 1690.

JOHN HURD, a freeman of Mass., 1652, was perhaps a weaver, of Lynn, with wife Eliz. in 1657.

JOHN HURD, Stratford, the freeman, 1669, married, 1662, Sarah, daughter of John Thompson, of S.; had John, born 1664; Sarah, 1666; Hannah, 1667; Isaac, 1669; Jacob, 1671; prob. died young, Mary, 1673; Esther, 1676; and Abigail, 1679.

REFERENCES:—Bond's Watertown, Mass. Gen., 518; Craft's Gen., 151-3; Hayward's Hist. of Gilsum. N. H., 337-41; Hurlbut, Gen., 410-2; N. E. Hist. & Gen. Reg., XIX, 123-5; Stiles Hist. Windsor, Ct., II, 417.

HURLBUT, or HURLBURT:—Thomas Hurlbut, Wethersfield, served in the Pequot war, 1637, in which he was wounded; by wife Sarah had John, born 1642; Thomas, Samuel and Joseph; all these, except John, lived at Wethersfield some years later.

THOMAS HURLBUT, Woodbury, had Jemima 1680; Jerusha 1683; Thomas 1684; and Gideon 1688.

WILLIAM HURLBUT, Dorchester, 1635, removed to Windsor perhaps as early as 1640, married Ann, widow of Samuel Allen; he died 1694; Ann, 1687.

REFERENCES:—Boyd's Annals, Winchester, Ct., 96-100; Cathren's Hist., Woodbury, Ct., 580-2; Gald's Hist., Cornwall, Ct., 245; Hinman's Conn. Sett., 1st ed., 170; Hurlburt Gen. (1861), 22 pp.; (1888), 545 pp.

HURNDELL:—See Harndale.

HURRY:—William Hurry, Charlestown, by wife Hannah had William, born 1664, also Hannah, Temperance, John, Mathew, Sarah, Rebecca, and Rachel; Rebecca, again, 1673; Abigail 1674; and prob. no more; he died 1690.

REFERENCE.—Wyman's Charlestown, 534.

HURRYMAN:—See Harriman.

HURST:—James Hurst, Plymouth, 1632, a tanner, erected the first works in the town for that object, 1640; one of the purchasers of Dartmouth; was deacon; died 1657.

JOHN HURST, Boston, by wife Alice, had Richard, born 1690.

THOMAS HURST, Hadley 1678, removed to Deerfield, then had Sarah 1685; Eliz. 1687; Thomas 1691; Hannah 1695; Ebenezer 1698; and Benoni 1702. Early in the year he died, and his widow and children were taken, 1704, by the French and Indians to Canada; the youngest was killed en route; the mother with eldest of children got back from captivity, but the other three were kept by the enemy.

WILLIAM HURST, Sandwich, married, 1640, Catharine Thurston; he died 1641.

REFERENCE:—Savage's Gen. Dict., II., 506.

HUSE:—Abel Huse, Newbury, is said to have come from London, 1635; but was not freeman till 1642. His wife, Elinor, died 1663, and he married Mary, prob.

widow of Thomas Sears, had Ruth, born 1664; Abel 1665; Thomas 1666; William 1667; Sarah 1670; John; Amy 1673, died young, and a daughter Ebenezar 1675; he died 1690.

HUSSEY, or HUZZEY:—Christopher Hussey, Newbury, was first of Lynn, to which he perhaps came with Rev. Stephen Batchilor, whose daughter Theodata he had married in England. He was, says Coffin, of Dorking, in Co. Surrey, and was prob. passenger in William and Francis, arriving 1632; removed 1639 to Hampton; was rep. 1658, 9 and 60, and couns. of the Prov.; engaged in settlement of Haverhill; and died 1686 by shipwreck on the Florida coast, says Lewis, aged 87; nearly 90, says Coffin. His widow died 1646, had Stephen, perhaps born in England 1630; John 1636; Joseph; Hulda; Mary 1637; and Theodata 1640; after 1658 he married widow Ann Mingay, who died 1680, and he 1685.

ROBERT HUSSEY, Danbury, 1643-55, in this latter year was witness to will of Rev. Ralph Partridge, and he prob. died twelve years after.

ROBERT HUSSEY, Dover, in the tax list of 1659.

ROBERT HUSSEY, Boston, freeman 1690.

WILLIAM HUSSEY, one of the early settlers at Reading according to the list of Mr. Eaton.

REFERENCES:—Austin's Allied Fams., 142-5; Cushman's Hist. of Sheepscatt, Me., 393; N. E. Hist. Gen. Reg., VII, 157; Daw's Hist. of Hampton, N. H., 758-61.

HUSTING:—John Husting, Manchester 1649.

HUTCHINS, or HUTCHINGS:—Enoch Hutchins, New Hampshire, married 1667, Mary Stevenson, perhaps daughter of Thomas of Dover.

GEORGE HUTCHINS, Cambridge, freeman 1638, by wife Jane had Joseph 1639; Luke 1644; Ann 1645; and Abiah 1658.

JOHN HUTCHINS, Newbury, by wife Frances had William; Joseph 1640; Joseph 1641—perhaps an error of a year or two; Love 1647; Eliz. and Samuel; rem. to Haverhill, and died 1674.

JOHN HUTCHINS, Wethersfield, died 1681, leaving Sarah and Ann.

JONATHAN HUTCHINS, Kittery, a youth of 14 years, taken by the Indians 1698.

JOSEPH HUTCHINS, Boston, married 1657, Mary, daughter of William Edmonds, of Lynn.

JOSEPH HUTCHINS, Haverhill, swore fidelity 1677; was, perhaps, son of John.

NICHOLAS HUTCHINS, Lynn, married 1666, Eliz., daughter of George Farr, had John, born 1668; and Eliz. 1670.

RICHARD HUTCHINS, reg. adm. as freeman 1630, and so may be thought to have come in fleet with Winthrop; but prob. died soon as went home.

SAMUEL HUTCHINS, Kittery, taken by the Indians 1698.

REFERENCES:—Am. Ancestry, I, 42; V, 123; Child's Gen., 383; Carliss' Gen., 237; Forrest's Hist. Norfolk, Va., 55-71; Hutchins (Levi) Autob. (1865); Carliss' No. Yarmouth, Me.

HUTCHINSON:—Edward Hutchinson, Boston, son of Susanna, a widow (who came in 1636 with John Wheelwright, and her daughter Mary, his wife)—but this son came with wife Sarah in 1633, prob. in the Griffin, having fellow passeng. John Cotton, the disting. theol., Elder Truevett, Gov. Brenton, Edmund Quincy, Atherton Hough, and other prom. persons, most of whom were like himself from Lincolnsh. Freeman 1634, had here John, 1634; and Ichabod 1637; went to R. I., thence to England and never returned.

EDMOND HUTCHINSON, eldest son of William, called junr. to disting. him from his uncle, came before his parents, a single man, freeman 1634, Artillery Co. 1638, a capt. 1657, represent. 1658, and served in important rank in Philip's war 1675, in which he was mortally wounded by Indians in treacherous assault, says history, when he was marching to a peaceful meeting with them. He was, with his uncle and father, among the first settlers at Newport, forming their covenant 1638, but in a few years preferred Boston for his residence, and deserves honor for his firmness in opposing cruelty to the Quakers. Geneal. Reg. I. 297, says his first wife Catherine Hamby, daughter of a lawyer at Ipswich; had bapt. Elishua, prob. died young; Eliz. 1639; Elisha 1641; Ann 1643; William 1646, died young; Catharine 1648, died young; Susanna 1649; Edward, perhaps 1652; Catharine, again, 1653; Benjamin 1656, died before his father; and Hannah 1658. A second wife Abigail, widow of Robert Button, survived, and died 1689. She was mother of last four children and daughter of the widow Alice Vermaies, of Salem.

EDWARD HUTCHINSON, Lynn, perhaps son of Samuel of the same, had Thomas, born 1654; Mary 1656; Joseph 1658; and Sarah 1671.

FRANCIS HUTCHINSON, Concord, died 1661.

FRANCIS HUTCHINSON, born in England about 1630, married 1661, Sarah Leighton, who died in a few days. Prob. he removed to Reading, freeman 1685, died 1702, perhaps had Francis, the freeman of 1691.

GEORGE HUTCHINSON, Charlestown, came prob. in fleet with Winthrop, and very early of church of Boston, No. 53, with his wife, Margaret, had Nathaniel, bapt. 1633, freeman 1634, died 1660.

GEORGE HUTCHINSON, New London 1680, had wife Margaret, who, in 1686, obtained divorce for his desertion.

JOHN HUTCHINSON, Salem, by first wife Alice, had Richard, born 1643; had another wife, Sarah, who perhaps was daughter of Thomas Putnam, married 1672, he died 1676.

JOHN HUTCHINSON, New Haven, of whom no more is known than that he took oath of fid. 1644.

RALPH HUTCHINSON, Boston, married 1656, Alice, widow of Francis Bennett, had John, removed to Northampton, there had Mehitable, born 1662, died soon; Judah 1664; Samuel 1666; and Moses 1671.

RICHARD HUTCHINSON, Salem, by wife Alice, had Abigail, bapt. 1636; Hannah 1639; and John 1643, who died 1676; and may have had other children by her; but had two other wives, one, widow Susanna Archer, or Orchar, married 1668, died 1674; the other Sarah, outlived him; and he died 1682, leaving son Joseph and five daughters.

SAMUEL HUTCHINSON, Boston, brother of William, a bachelor, is not known long here, and perhaps did not live here many years before his death, but had grant of land 1638, at R. I., whither he went, no doubt, with his brother William, and had been associated with his brother Wheelwright in purchase from Indians at Exeter and Wells.

SAMUEL HUTCHINSON, who by Lewis is called of Lynn 1637, was prob. of Reading 1670.

SAMUEL HUTCHINSON, Andover, married 1686, Eliz. Parker, who may have been widow of Joseph, had, perhaps, several children, but John, who died 1689, is the only one known.

THOMAS HUTCHINSON, Charlestown 1630, came, no doubt, in fleet with Winthrop, perhaps brother of George, who is next below him in the list of very early members of the church.

THOMAS HUTCHINSON, Lynn 1637, says Lewis, but it is supposed he moved to L. I., where in 1664 he was adm. freeman of Conn.

THOMAS HUTCHINSON, Boston, by wife Mary, had Thomas, born 1672; but name is not found again.

WILLIAM HUTCHINSON, Boston, came in ship with Rev. John Lathrop and Zechary Symmes, 1634, bringing wife and all his children exc. Edward, his eldest son, who came with Cotton (before mentioned), and daughter Mary, wife of Rev. John Wheelwright, who came two years later. He had lived at Alford in Co. Lincoln, and prob. both himself and wife Ann, daughter of Edward Marbury, of Lincolnsh., were drawn hither by their admiration of John Cotton. He was freeman 1635, and two sons, Richard and Francis, were adm. the same day; represent. 1635, and four courts following; had one child, Zuriel, bapt. 1636, but by the violent heats of the relig. controv. in which his friends, Sir Henry Vaue and John Cotton were defeated, and his family, besides others of the party were very severely treated, he was forced with Coddington and other prominent members, to remove to R. I.; there in 1638 formed a new civil compact, not much unlike that of Mass.; was an assistant 1639, and died about 1642. His widow, Ann, who had been the gifted prophetess of the doleful heresies that shook and almost subvert. the colony of Mass., removed next year from R. I. beyond Conn. to the Dutch Prov., and before being fairly estab. in her new planta. was, with several children and servants to the number of sixteen, cut off by the Indians. His daughter, Faith, married at Boston about 1637, Thomas Savage; Susanna married 1651, John Cole; Bridget married a Willis of Bridgewater; and one married Collins, a scholar, of whom Winthrop II, 38 tells. This last, and the son Francis perished with their mother. The widow Susanna, mother of Edward, Richard, Samuel, William, of the wife of Rishwarth, and of Mary, the wife of Wheelwright, went from Boston to Exeter with her daughter's husband in his banishment, and thence to Wells, where she was buried.

REFERENCES.—Am. Ancestry, VI, 122; VII, 50; Bass' Hist. Braintree, Vt., 153-5; Cochrane's Hist. of Antrim, N. H., 551-3; Drake's Hist. Boston, Mass., 227; Haywards Hist. Gilsum, N. H., 341; Hayward's Hist. Hancock, N. H., 677-9; Hist. of Clermont, Ohio, 548; Hutchinson Chart (1888), 14 x 24 in.; H. Gen. (1852) 49 pp.; (1857) 26 pp.; (1865) 9 pp.; (1866) 24 pp.; (1870) 107 pp; Lancaster's Hist. Gelmanton, N. H., 273; Narragansett Hist. Reg., II. 177; Livermore's Hist. Wilton, N. H., 415-21; Temple's Hist. Northfield, Mass., 473; Walworth's Hyde Gen., 1126-8; Whitmore's Copps Hill Epitaph; Wheeler's Hist. Newport, N. H., 424; Updyke's Narragansett, R. I., ch., 106; N. E. Reg., XIX, 13; XX, 355-67; XXII, 236-54; Savage's Gen. Dict., II, 508-13

ARMS:—

HUTHWIT:—John Huthwit, Woodbury, came with his sister Ann, "of gentle blood," orphans early, by the guardian in England defrauded of property and sent over here, by wife Judith, had Eliz. bapt. 1689, died young; Ann 1690; Martha 1693; Mary 1696; and Eliz., again, 1698.

HUTLEY:—Richard Hutley, Ipswich 1639. Perhaps it is same as Utley.

HUTTON:—John Hutton, Wenham, 1675.

RICHARD HUTTON, Wenham, perhaps brother of the preceding, freeman 1672, and born about 1621.

REFERENCES.—Hutton Gen. (1872) ; Jackson Gen., 229, 246-8.

HUXLY:—Thomas Huxly, Hartford, married Sarah, eldest daughter of Thomas Spencer of the same, had Thomas, born 1668; also John, Sarah, Mary, and Eliz.; removed to Suffield, there had Jared, 1680; Hannah, 1682; Nathaniel, 1683, died soon; and William, 1687. His wife died 1712; he died 1721.

HUXSTABLE:—Christopher Huxstable, Marblehead, 1668.

HYATT:—Thomas Hyatt, Dorchester, 1633, called by John Russell, in his will of that year, brother.

THOMAS HYATT, Norwalk, 1672, a soldier in Philip's war, married, 1677, Mary, daughter of Matthias Sension, had Rebecca, born next year, and one or more sons who perpetuated the name, spelling first Hiet, and next Hyett. He was living 1694.

REFERENCES:—Baird's Hist. Rye, N. Y., 411; Hoyt Gen., 633-6; Young's Hist. Wayne Co., Ind., 328.

HYDE, or HIDES:—George Hyde, Boston, ship-carpenter, by wife Ann, had Mary, 1642: and Timothy, 1644; and she became second wife of Daniel Weld, of Braintree, who removed to Roxbury.

HUMPHREY HYDE, Windsor, thence to Fairfield, 1655, and in 1670 divided his lands with John, perhaps his son.

JOHN HYDE, a tailor, of Marlborough, Co. Wilts. came in the James, 1635, arriving at Boston, but it is not known whither he removed.

JOHN HYDE, Stratford, married Eliz. daughter of Richard Harvey, had John, born 1668.

JONATHAN HYDE, Cambridge, living in that part called New C. or C. village, now Newton, freeman 1663, by wife Mary, daughter of William French, of Billerica, had Jonathan, born 1651, died soon; Samuel, and Joshua, twins, 1653; Jonathan, again, 1655; John, 1656; Abraham, 1658; Eliz., 1659; William, bapt. 1662; Eleazer, 1664; Daniel, 1665; and Ichabod, 1668; and she died in her 39th year at B. of her 12th (or as Jackson counts him. 13th) child—Joseph, 1672. He married, 1673, Mary, daughter of John Rediat of Marlborough, had Hannah 1677, died at two years; Sarah, 1679; Ruth, 1682, died soon; Isaac, 1685; Jarat, 1687; Lydia, 1689; and Ann, 1692. He was selectman, 1691; outlived the second wife more than three years, and died 1711, aged 85 years.

RICHARD HYDE, Salem, had there bapt. Isaac, 1642; Rebecca, 1644; Ephraim, 1646; Mary, 1648; Hannah, 1650; Richard, 1652; and Christian, 1654.

SAMUEL HYDE, Cambridge, elder brother of the first Jonathan, came from London to Boston in the Jonathan, 1639, aged 29, had wife Temperance and children—Joshua, 1642, died soon; Job, 1643; Sarah, 1644; Samuel, 1647; and Eliz. He lived at the village which became Newton, was freeman 1649; and died 1689.

WILLIAM HYDE, Hartford, an original propr., removed to Saybrook, thence, about 1659 or 60, to Norwich, there

died 1681. The only children known of are Samuel and Esther, who married John Post.

REFERENCES:—Am. Ancestry, III, 176; VII, 110; VIII, 154; IX, 215; Bliss' Hist. of Rehoboth, Mass., 207; Bond's Hist. Watertown, Mass., 304; Cochrane's Hist. Antrim, N. H., 533; Douglas Gen., 178-80; Dwight Gen., 579; Hyde Gen. (1864), 1446 pp.; Orcutt's Hist. Stratford, Ct., 1218; Richmond, Va., Standard, II, 27; Savage's Gen. Dict., II, 514-4; Ward's Rice Gen., 352; Whitney Fam. of Conn., I, 96.

HYLAND:—George Hyland, Guilford, 1662, died 1692, leaving four daughters of whom two married Hulls, and one had son named Highland—sometimes Hiland, or Hyland.

THOMAS HYLAND, Scituate, 1637, was from Teuterden Co., Kent, had Thomas; Samuel, who died in Philip's war; Deborah; Mary; Sarah, and Ruth.

REFERENCES:—Deane's Scituate, Mass., 290; Johnson's Hist. Cecil Co., Md., 522-4.

IBBROOK:—Richard Ibbrook, Hingham, 1635, Lincoln, 43. He had grant, in 1647, of an island in the harbor; and died 1651. His widow died 1664, as is learned from diary of Rev. Peter Hobart, who married his daughter Rebecca for second wife; a daughter Helen, or Ellen, married, 1638, Joshua Hobart; and another daughter, Margaret, married, 1639 or 40, John Tower.

IDE:—Nicholas Ide, Rehoboth, 1643, probably married a daughter of Thomas Bliss, for in the will of B. he is called son-in-law; and probably he had Mary, Nicholas, Martha, and John. His wife was buried 1676, and son John, probably youngest child, was buried a month later.

REFERENCES:—Dagget's Attleborough, 91; Davis' Hist. Redding, Vt., 157; Ward's Hist. Shrewsbury, Mass., 333.

IGGLEDEN, IGLEDEN, or EGGLEDEN:—Richard Iggleden, Boston, son of Stephen, married, 1660, Ann Prince; his father died in passage to this land in the Castle, 1638; and his widow, Eliz., was a propr. at Roxbury, 1639, married, 1642, Joseph Patcham, and bore him two sons; Eliz., her daughter had married, 1641, Philip Meadow, of R.; another daughter, "about ten years old," died there, 1646; and Sarah Eggleton, who married, 1650, John Nutting, of Woburn, or Ruth Eggleden, who married, 1655, Samuel Blodget, of Woburn, may each be supposed another. Prob. the family came from Co. Kent.

ILES, or HILLS:—Richard Iles, who died at Charlestown, 1639, was a cooper, unmarried; prob. came from Bristol not long before.

ILSLEY:—John Ilsley, barber, Salisbury, probably came in the Confidence from Southampton, 1638, with William, perhaps his brother (though names are printed in Geneal. Reg. Ilsbey), freeman, 1639, in the rec. spelt Ellsley; was an original propr., and by wife Sarah, who died 1673, had John, 1642, or 3; Ruth, 1647, or 8—died young; and Jonathan, 1652; and perhaps Hannah; and he died 1683.

WILLIAM ILSLEY, Newbury, was of Newbury, Wilts, came in the Confidence, 1638, aged 26, a shoemaker, with wife Barbara, 20, and servant, Philip Davis, 12; had John, born 1641; Mary; Elisha; William, 1648; Joseph, 1649; Isaac, 1652; and Sarah, 1655; and he died 1681; aged 73, says Coffin.

INCE:—Jonathan Ince, Hartford, an original propr. removed to Boston before 1640, there died, and his lot at H. was granted to John Cullick. He was prob. the father of that Jonathan, H. C. 1650, employed by the Governor, 1652, as a surveyor for the north boundary of Mass.; he designed to settle at New Haven, and married, 1654, Mary, daughter of Richard Miles, and had Jonathan, born 1656; and he sailed next year in Garrett's ship from Boston for London, with Mayhew, Davis, and Pelham, of which voyage no tidings were ever received. His widow married, 1661, Rev. Thomas Hanford.

INDICUTT, or INDICOTT:—John Indicutt, Boston, by wife Eliz. had Eliz., born 1670; Ann, 1674; Thomas, 1678; Sarah, 1680; John 1686; and Joseph, 1687.

JOHN INDICUTT, Boston, a cooper, by wife Mary, had John, born 1691; and Bayworth, 1693; he, or the preceding, was one of the wardens of King's chapel, 1698. Sometimes this name is written like the Governor's, and sometimes the great man's like this; whether they were relations is unknown.

REFERENCE:—Indicott Gen. (1888), 15 pp.

INES, INNES, IYANS, or IRONS:—Matthias, or Matthew, Boston, in employment of William Colbron, when adm. of the church, 1634, freeman 1636, disarmed 1637, as a supporter of Wheelwright, but was not exiled, as more important persons were; by wife Ann, had John, 1638; Eliz., 1641; Thomas, 1643; Rebecca, 1645; Edward, 1649; and Samuel, 1650; Edward prob. died young; he had also Ann, 1652, died soon; William, who died 1654; Ann, again, 1654, died next mo.; and Catharine, 1655; beside Matthew, who died 1656, perhaps very young. This name, best written Iyans, is sometimes mistaken for Jones.

INGALL, or INGALLS:—Benjamin Ingall, Portsmouth, R. I., married, 1682, widow Mary Tripp, who died 1688, but of whom she had been the widow is not seen.

EDMUND INGALL, Lynn, 1629, if Lewis be correct, was killed by the breaking of bridge three, 1648, leaving widow Ann, and nine children—Robert, Eliz., Faith, John, Sarah, Henry, Samuel, Mary, and Joseph, all perhaps born in England.

FRANCIS INGALL, Lynn, brother of preceding, was there 1629, born about 1601, and had the earliest tannery in Mass.

JOHN INGALLS, Ipswich, 1648.

RICHARD INGALLS, Lynn, had James, born 1684.

SAMUEL INGALLS, Lynn, married, 1682, Hannah Brewer, had Hannah, 1683; and Abigail, 1685; was freeman 1691.

THOMAS INGALLS, Salem, freeman, 1671.

REFERENCES:—Abbott's Andover, Mass., 33; Am. Ancestry, II, 63; III, 28; Bangor Hist. Mag., IV, 149-56; Chase's Hist. Chester, N. H., 549; Lewis' Hist. Lynn, Mass., 111; N. H., Hist. Soc. Coll., VII, 375; Thompson's Hist. Swampscott, Mass.; Washington, N. H., Hist., 488; Wyman's Charlestown, Mass., Gens., I, 540.

INGASON:—John Ingason, New London. See Ingersoll.

INGERSOLL, or INKERSALL:—John Ingersoll, Hartford, 1653, or earlier; married about 1651, Dorothy, daughter of Thomas Lord, had Hannah, born 1652; Dorothy, 1654; and removed to Northampton, where his wife died in giving birth to Margery, 1656. He married 2nd wife, Abigail, daughter of Thomas Bascom, had Abigail, 1659; Sarah, 1660; Abiah, or Abigail, 1663; Esther, 1665; removed to Westfield next year, had Thomas, 1668; and his wife died that year. By 3rd wife Mary, sister of

Jonathan Hunt, the grand-daughter of Gov. Webster, had John, 1669; Abel, 1671; Ebenezer, 1673, died young; Joseph, 1675, who was killed by assault of Indians in Deerfield, 1704; Mary, 1677, died young; Benjamin, 1679, died young; and Jonathan, 1681; he died 1684, and his widow died 1690. Only 13 of the children were living when the estate of their father was divided, and 10 so late as 1707.

RICHARD INGERSOLL, Salem, 1629, came with Higginson, bringing wife and children, was from Co. Bedford; died 1644; his will names wife Ann, and sons, George, John, Nathaniel, son-in-law Richard Pettingell, who married his daughter Joanna, and William Haines, who married his daughter Sarah, that had 2nd husband Joseph Houlton; also daughters Alice, wife of Josiah Walcott, and Bathsheba, the youngest, who married John Knight, Jr., and before 1652, his father John Knight, married her mother, Ann, who died 1677.

REFERENCES:—Am. Ancestry, IV, 218; VI, 6; VIII, 4; Driver Gen., 254; Ingersoll Gen. (1893), 107 pp.; Haye's Wells Fam., 169; Essex. Inst. Call., I, 12, 153; XI, 228-34; Wyman's Charlestown, Mass., Gens., 540.

INGHAM:—John, or Joseph Ingham, Saybrook, married, 1655, Sarah, perhaps daughter of John Bushnell, had Joseph, born 1656; and Sarah, 1658; was freeman 1669; and often the name begins with H.

THOMAS INGHAM, Scituate, 1640, a weaver, had Mary, born 1647; Thomas, 1654; Sarah, 1658; and John, 1663. In 1676 his wife Mary was accused of witchcraft, and he was suspected, but the jury acquitted the wife, and no more nonsense of that kind was brought forward in the old Col. of Plymouth. The great success of the devil in destroying women because they were old, was in the chief Col. of Mass.

REFERENCES:—Davis' Hist. Bucks Co., Pa., 301; Ingham Gen. (1871); Smith's Gen. (1890), 167-72,195.

INGLES, or INGLISH:—Mauditt, or Maudett Ingles, Boston, a fuller of Marlborough, Wilts, came in the James, 1635, had Hannah, born 1639; Mary, 1644; and Samuel, 1647.

REFERENCES:—Penn. Mag. V, 335-9.

ARMS:—A3, a lion rampant, arg. on a chief, of the second three mullets, of the first.

INGLISH:—William Inglish, Boston, 1652, a cordwainer, had wife Mary, and died 1682; had no children that are known of.

INGOLDSBY:—John Ingoldsby, Boston, 1641, spelled without d in record of his adm. of the ch. that year, then a single man, freeman 1642; by wife Ruth, had John, who died 1649; another John, 1653, also died soon; another John, 1655, died in few weeks; Ebenezer, 1656; and Peter, 1659.

INGRAM, or INGRAHAM:—Edward Ingram, Salem, came in the Blessing from London, 1635, aged 18; had grant of land, 1638.

HENRY INGRAM, Boston, by wife Lydia had Deliverance, 1672; and Henry, 1673; prob. rem.

JARED INGRAM, Boston, married, 1662, Rebecca, daughter of Edward Searle, or Seale, had Margaret, 1663; removed to Swanzey, and there had Hannah, 1673; his daughter Mary was buried 1673; and by same wife, had Jeremiah, 1683.

JOHN INGRAM, Hadley, married, 1664, Eliz. Gardner, had, beside four children who died young, or unmarried, at least John, 1666; Samuel, 1670; Nathaniel, 1674; and Jonathan, 1676, who was killed 1704, in the assault in Deerfield by the French and Indians; he was freeman 1683, and died 1722, aged more than 80 years, over 60 of which he had lived at H.

RICHARD INGRAM, Reboboth, 1645, removed to Northampton, there married, 1668, Joan, daughter of William Rockwell, widow of Jeffrey Baker, of Windsor; died 1683; and his wife, by whom he had no children, died soon after.

WILLIAM INGRAM, Boston, 1653, cooper, married, 1656, Mary Barstow, perhaps daughter of William of Dedham; had William, born 1657, died soon; William, again, 1658; Jeremiah, 1664; Mary, 1666; and Eliz. 1669.

WILLIAM INGRAM, Boston, by wife Eliz., had Rebecca, born 1653; Edward, 1657; and Hannah, 1659; he, or the preceding, was freeman 1674.

REFERENCES:—Judd's Hadley, Mass., 519; N. E. Hist. Gen. Reg., XIII, 90.

INGS, or as given in Geneal. Reg. II, 253, INGGS:— Samuel Inggs, Hingham, married, 1673, Mary Beal.

INMAN:—Edward Inman, Providence, 1646, a glover, in list of freemen 1655, took oath of alleg. to the King, 1666; and is ment. 1677; Knowles, 410; Staples.· By wife Barbara he had John, Edward, and perhaps other children, and was dead before 1706.

EDWARD INMAN, Providence, called junr. when he swore alleg. in 1682; prob. was son of the preceding.

REFERENCES:—Austin's R. I. Gen. Dict., 326; Bangor, Me., Hist. Mag., VI, 30; Plumb's Hist. Hanover, Pa., 434-6.

IRELAND:—John Ireland, Charlestown, 1681, had wife Grace, removed probably to Boston, but at C. had Abiel, a daughter, bapt. 1685.

PHILLIP IRELAND, Ipswich, had wife Grace, says Farmer, who died 1692.

SAMUEL IRELAND, Wethersfield, a carpenter, came to Boston in the Increase, from London, 1635, aged 32; with wife Mary, 30; and daughter Martha, 1½; had more children here, and died 1639; his widow married, 1645, Robert Burrows, and died 1672.

WILLIAM IRELAND, the freeman of 1650, was then, perhaps, of Dorchester, but certainly of Boston, living at Rumney Marsh, now Chelsea, 1654, and constable, 1656.

REFERENCES:—Am. Ancestry, III, 91; V, 92; Ireland Gen. (1880) 51 pp.; Wyman's Charlestown, Mass., Gens., 541-4.

IRESON:—Edward Ireson, Lynn, came in the Abigail, 1635; aged 32; with Eliz., prob. his wife, 27; had Hannah, born 1639; Ruth, 1641; Samuel, 1641, perhaps; Eleazer, 1642; Benoni, or possibly Benjamin, 1645; Eliz., 1648; and prob. by 2nd wife, Rebecca, 1657; he died 1675, aged 73.—Lewis.

RICHARD IRESON, Lynn, 1643.

THOMAS IRESON, a passenger in the Hopewell, 1635.

IRISH:—John Irish, Duxbury, by wife Eliz., had John and Elias; removed to Bridgewater, perhaps, at least was a propr. there—though not original—went to Little Campton; died 1677; his wife died 1687. It is possible name may be Frish, for one of the party at Kennebeck under John Howland, 1634, sent to cut the cable of an interloper, Hocking; had son Elias, of Taunton.

REFERENCES:—Am. Ancestry, II, 63; Austin's R. I. Gen. Dict. 110; Davis' Landmarks of Plymouth, Mass., 158; Pierce's Hist. Gorham, Me., 177; Sibley's Hist. Union, Me., 465; William's Hist. Danbury, Vt., 171-6.

IRONS:—See Ines.

ISAAC, or ISAACS:—Joseph Isaac, Cambridge, 1636, freeman 1637; represent. 1638; died 1642, and Eliz., prob. his widow, married, 1643, Nicholas Davis; a passenger in the Eliz. from Ipswich, 1634, aged 36; named Rebecca Isaac, may have been his sister.

THOMAS ISAAC, a merchant of Boston, but perhaps on transient, in 1662.

REFERENCES:—Dwight Gen., 168-70; Hall's Hist. of Norwalk, Ct., 212, 240.

ISBELL:—Eleazer Isbell, New London, son of Robert, freeman of Conn., 1669; married, 1668, Eliz. French; died 1677, leaving only one son and one daughter to care of their grandmother; he went as one of the first settlers to Killingworth (so by perversion made from Kenilworth, the town in Co. Warwick, Eng., whose name was used for this in Conn. because one or more of the earliest inhab. were born there); Field, 106; at K. he had Eliz., 1669; Robert, 1671, died soon; Hannah, 1674; and Robert, again, 1676.

REFERENCES:—Cregar's White Gen.; Isbell and Kingman Gen. (1889), 30 p.

ISLIN:—Thomas Islin, Sudbury, freeman 1640; died 1665.

ISSAM:—John Issam, Barnstable, married, 1677, Jane Parker, had Jane, born 1679; John, 1681; Isaac, 1683; Sarah, 1684; Mary, 1687; Hannah; Patience; Joseph; and Thankful, died 1717; this name may have been changed to Isham.

IVES:—John Ives, New Haven, 1669.

JOSEPH IVES, New Haven, propr., 1686.

MATTHIAS IVES, prob. mistake for Iyans, but may have lived at Watertown.

MILES or MICHAEL IVES, Watertown, 1639; by wife Martha had Sarah, 1639; Mary, 1641; and Hannah, 1643; sold estate and, 1641, removed to Boston, there died, 1684, aged 86.

THOMAS IVES, Salem, 1668.

WILLIAM IVES, New Haven, unit. in the civil compact, 1639, but had prob. come to Boston, 1635, aged 28, in the Truelove from London, had Phebe, bapt., 1642; and John, 1644; died 1648; his will names no children; his widow married, 1648, William Bassett.

REFERENCES:—Am. Ancestry, IV, 36; V. 48; VII, 269; Blake's Hist. of Hamden, Ct., 256-61; Bulkley's Brown Mem., 78-82; Annabell Gen., 101; Driver Gen., 320-67; Hubbard's Stanstead Co. Canada, 271; Tuttle Gen., 463.

IVEY:—James Ivey, Braintree, died 1654; prob. without wife or children.

JOHN IVEY, Newbury, perhaps brother of the preceding, had John, born 1643.

IVORY:—Thomas Ivory, Lynn, 1638, by wife Ann, had Thomas, daughter Lois, Ruth, and Sarah; his widow married William Croft.

WILLIAM IVORY, Lynn, perhaps brother of first Thomas, came in the Truelove, 1635, aged 28, from London, was a carpenter, died at Boston, 1652.

REFERENCES:—Savage's Gen. Dict., II, 526; Wyman's Charlestown, Mass., Gens., I, 545.

IYANS:—Matthias Iyans. See Ines.

JACKLIN, JACKLENE, JACKLYN, or JACK-LING:—Edmund Jacklin, Boston, 1634, glazier, free-man 1635; by wife Susan, had Samuel, born 1640; Susanna, 1643, died few months; Susanna, again, 1644, died very soon; Hannah, 1645; Susanna, again, 1649; Mehit-able, 1654; Mary, 1655, or 6; and Ruth 1658.

JACKMAN:—James Jackman, Newbury, was from Exeter, Co. Devon, had wife Joanna; children—Sarah, 1648; Esther, 1651; James, 1655; Joanna, 1657; Richard, 1660; was freeman 1684, and died 1694.

REFERENCE:—

JACKSON:—Abraham Jackson, Plymouth, apprent. of Secr. Morton, married, 1657, Remember, daughter of the Secr.; had Lydia, 1658; Abraham; Nathaniel Eleazer, 1669; and John; his wife died 1707, and he died 1714.

DAVID JACKSON, Boston, in his will of 1683, gave all his est. to brother Daniel, "*if he return,*" otherwise to Henry Boulton, and Edmund Shore, so we infer he was a bachelor.

EDMUND JACKSON, Boston, 1635, shoemaker, joined church that year; by wife Martha, who died 1652, had Hannah, born 1636; John, 1638; Thomas, 1640; Samuel, 1643; Jeremiah, 1645; Mary, 1647; and Isaac, 1651; he next married, 1653—eight weeks after death of first wife —Mary, daughter of Samuel Cole, wid. of —— Gawdren, if record be right, and had Edmund, 1654, prob. died young; Eliz., 1657; and Elisha, 1659; and this wife died soon after; by third wife, Eliz., he had Sarah, 1660; Martha, 1662; Susanna, 1663, died soon; Susanna, again, 1666; Edmund, 1668, died young; Edmund, again, 1672; and Mary, 1674, and died next year; he was freeman 1636, and prob. came from old Boston.

EDMUND JACKSON, Boston, married, 1660, Eliz. Pilk-ington; if there be no error in record, very possibly he is same as preceding, though there was an Edmund, of Wey-mouth, who by wife Mary had Samuel, born 1691, and may have removed to Abington.

EDWARD JACKSON, Cambridge, a nailer from White-chapel parish, in London, where lived his father Chris-topher, was bapt. 1604, or 5, at Stepney; came about 1643; he was freeman 1645, purchased 1646 the beautiful farm of 500 acres from Gov. Bradstreet, for £140, which had been sold to him for 6 cows by Thomas Mayhew in 1638, before he went to the Vineyard; represent. 1647 and 15 years more. Several times honored with notice as the aid of Apostle Eliot in the evangeliz. of the Indians; died 1681; by first wife, brought prob. from England, named Frances, he had, says the family tradition, four sons, and four daughters, though only six are recorded; others may have been born afterward, however. Israel, 1631, died in infancy; Margaret, 1633; Hannah, 1634; Rebecca, 1636; Caleb, 1638; and Joseph, 1639. In favor of the tradition one may add Jonathan, Sebas, who was born on passage from Eng., and Frances, who died 1648; but that this is the wife is more probable, though the historian of Newton counts her the child; his second wife, married 1659, was Eliz., daughter of John Newgate, widow of John Oliver, the scholar (who died 1709); by her he had Sarah, 1650; Edward, 1652; Lydia, 1656; Eliz., 1658; another Hannah, about 1660; and Ruth, 1664, who died 1692, unmarried.

EDWARD JACKSON, Cambridge, in the village, brother of Abraham, was killed by the Indians at Medfield, 1676, in Philip's war.

GEORGE JACKSON, Marblehead, went as surgeon in the wild Canadian expedition of Phips, 1690, but outlived it; had wife Mary, and bought a farm in Scituate, 1702.

HENRY JACKSON, Watertown, 1637, one of the lessees of the fishing wear at that place, perhaps was freeman of Fairfield 1669, had large estate, may be the man who came from London 1635, aged 29, in the Eliz., and Ann, for no other of the name is found earlier.

JAMES JACKSON, Charlestown, 1640; but Frothingham says no more.

JAMES, PATRICK AND RICHARD JACKSON, unhappy Scotch prisoners from the great battle of Worcester, 1651, sent here in the John and Sarah to Boston, to be sold; all prob. died soon after. But at Dover was one James, taxed 1659 and 61.

JOHN JACKSON, Salem, had grant of land 1637, says Felt; came prob. in Blessing, 1635, from London, aged 40; met wife Margaret, 36; and son John, 2; suffered loss of his house by fire, 1636, as told by Winth. I., 200, and may have been the "godly man" saved from ship-wreck, as he also tells, II., 19; was a fisherman, perhaps the freeman, 1641; died 1656.

JOHN JACKSON, Cambridge, bapt. at Stepney, near Lon-don, 1602; was elder brother of Edward, and prob. came in the Defence, 1635, from London; aged 30; called at the custom house "wholesale man in Burchen lane;" by wife, who perhaps died soon, had, beside perhaps two daughters, Sarah and Theodosia, John (who died 1675, in 36th year, prob. unmarried); was freeman 1641, it may be, though more prob. 1643, and by wife Margaret had Caleb, born 1645, died 2 days; Hannah, 1646, or 7; Abigail, 1648; Margaret, 1649; Edward, 1651; killed by Indians at Medfield, 1676; Mary; Abraham, 1655; De-liverance, 1657; Joshua, 1659; and Grace, whose date is unknown. He bought in 1639 the est. of Miles Ives; was deacon, and died 1675. His wife Margaret died 1684, in 60th year.

JOHN JACKSON, Boston, prob. brother of Henry, came in the Eliz. and Ann, 1635, aged 27, a carpenter; by wife Abigail had Sarah, born 1639; bapt. 1640; Abigail, 1641; John, 1643; Hannah, 1645; Peter, 1647, died young; Mary, 1649; Benjamin, 1651, died young; and Mary, again, 1652; died after 1673.

JOHN JACKSON, Ipswich, prob. freeman 1641; left widow, Catherine, who married 1648; one son and 5 daughters.

JOHN JACKSON, Boston, married, 1657, Jane, daughter of Evan Thomas; had John, born 1659; one John took oath of fidelity at Exeter, though of what import, is less clear. See General Reg., VIII, 77.

JOHN JACKSON, Scarborough, 1663.

JOHN JACKSON, Portsmouth, died about 1654, leaving widow Joanna, and son Richard; perhaps born in Eng-land.

JOHN JACKSON, New Haven, by wife Mary, who died 1665, had one child, born 1654, another 1655, neither of whose names is mentioned in the record; Mary, 1657; Grace, 1659; Mehitable, 1660; and Hannah, 1663. But among proprs. in 1685 this name does not appear.

JOHN JACKSON, Cambridge, lieut., had wife Sarah, who died 1700; by 2nd wife, Deborah, daughter, perhaps, of

GILES FIFIELD, of Charlestown, had Fifield, born 1702; John, 1704; James, 1706; Xene, 1708; and he died 1709. See Harris.

MANUS JACKSON, Charlestown, by wife Rebecca had Rebecca, born 1643.

NICHOLAS JACKSON, Rawley, 1643, had Samuel, born 1649; Jonathan, 1650, and Caleb, 1652; was of Salem, in 1668.

RICHARD JACKSON, Cambridge, a gent. of distinct., represent. 1637, 8, 9, 41, 8, 53, and 61; died 1672, aged almost 90; had taken 2nd wife in 1662, Eliz., the widow of Richard Brown; she died 1677. He left no children.

ROBERT JACKSON, Hempstead, L. I., 1665; Wood's Hist.

SAMUEL JACKSON, Scituate, came in from Plymouth, says Deane; joined the church, 1638, and had daughter Ann bapt. soon after, though born 2 or 3 years before; his wife died year following baptism. He married, 1639, Esther, daughter of Richard Sealis; had Bettria, bapt. 1641; Esther, 1643, and Samuel, 1647; was freeman of that colony 1644; removed to Barnstable about 1645, and died 1682, aged 72.

SEABIS, SEBIS, SEBAS, SEBES, or SEBAT JACKSON, Cambridge, son of the first Edward, born perhaps on the passage, whence may have sprung the un-Christian name, which was, says tradition, Seaborn; living at the village now Newton, freeman 1690; married, 1671, Sarah, daughter of Thomas Baker, of Roxbury; had Edward, born 1672; Sebas, 1674; John, 1676, died soon; Sarah, 1680; Eliz., 1683; John, again, 1685; Jonathan, 1686; Mary, 1687; and Joseph, 1690. He died 1690, and his widow died 1726, aged 84, says the historian of Newton, not remembering that she was born 1650.

THOMAS JACKSON, Plymouth, a servant who ran away from his master, with 3 others, on their way to Providence, robbed and murdered a solitary Indian (fully told in Bradford's Hist., 362-5), for which he and Arthur Peach and Richard Stinnings, in 1638, were hanged.

THOMAS JACKSON, Portsmouth, married Hannah, daughter of James Johnson, had Mary.

THOMAS JACKSON, Reading, in Mr. Eaton's list of early settlers, may have removed to Boston to be the freeman of 1690; and he, or another of the same name, married Elizabeth and Priscilla, daughters of Nathaniel Grafton. See note in General Reg., VIII, 270.

WALTER JACKSON, Dover, 1658, was of Portsmouth in 1667, but chiefly residing at D.; there was taxed 1661-75; had grant of land, 1666; was dead 1698. Perhaps he was brother of James of the same.

WILLIAM JACKSON, Rawley, 1639, had wife Deborah; only son John, who died before his father. Perhaps had 3 daughters.

WILLIAM JACKSON, Saybrook, 1648.

REFERENCES:—Am. Ancestry, I, 42; III, 88; V, 78, 230; VIII, 169; IX, 212; Austin's Ancestries, 35; Baird's Hist. Rye, N. Y., 415; Barry's Hist. Framingham, Mass., 300; Brown's Bedford, Mass. Fams., 19; Bunker's L. I. Gens., 220-6; Cole. Gen., 21; Davis' Landmarks of Plymouth, 159-62; Elderkin Gen.; Goode Gen., 149; Jackson Chart (1829), 25 x 27 in.; Jackson Gen. (1878), 371 pp.; Jackson's Hist. Newton, Mass., 326-53; Kingman's N. Bridgewater, Mass., 546-8; Lapham's Hist. Paris, Me., 642-7; Orcutt's Hist. New Milford, Ct., 720; Paige's Hist. Cambridge, Mass., 592; Roome Gen., 330-5; Temple's Hist. N. Brookfield, Mass., 643; Wyman's Charlestown, Mass., I, 546.

ARMS:—

JACOB or JACOBS:—Bartholomew Jacob, New Haven, 1668; a propr. in 1685.

GEORGE JACOB, Salem, living in village now Danvers, charged with witchcraft, sent to Boston because the gaol in Essex Co. couldn't hold half of the accused prisoners; condemned and executed 1692. See full account in Essex Hist., Call., I, 52. Had wife Ann, daughter Ann, and son George. See also Hutch. II, 38-40; Felt, II, 477-82.

NICHOLAS JACOB, Hingham, came in 1633, with wife and 2 children, John and Eliz.; residing first at Watertown, but removed 1635 to the new settlement; freeman 1636; had also Josiah, born 1642, died in a few days; was represent. 1648 and 9; died 1657, leaving widow Mary; sons John and Joseph; daughters Eliz., Mary, Sarah, Hannah and Deborah.

PETER JACOB, Hartford, 1647.

RICHARD JACOB, Ipswich, came in Mary and John 1634; freeman 1635; married Martha, daughter of the first Samuel Appleton; had Richard, Thomas, John, Samuel, Nathaniel, Joseph, Martha and Judith; but no dates are found; died 1672 or 4. His second wife, Joan, had been widow of Deacon Robert Hale of Charlestown, and died 1681, in 78th year, at C.

SAMUEL JACOB, Newbury, with prefix of respect, says Coffin, died 1672. He was prob. son of Richard of Ipswich, and died before his father, leaving widow and one child, Lydia.

REFERENCES:—Austin's Allied Fams., 149; Barry's Hist. Hanover, Mass., 319-35; Deane's Hist. Scituate, Mass., 291; Hobart's Hist. Abington, Mass., 405.

JAFFREY:—George Jaffrey, Newbury, married, 1665, Eliz. Walker; had Sarah, 1667; removed to Boston, and again, about 1677, removed to Great Island, or Newcastle, N. H.; in 1683 was petnr. against Gov. Cranfield; after was represent. and speaker, Couns. 1702; died at house of Col. Appleton, in Ipswich, 1707, leaving good estate. His widow, Hannah, married Penn. Townsend, of Boston.

REFERENCES:—Jaffray's Hist. Jaffray, N. H.; N. E. Hist. Gen. Reg. XV, 14; Wentworth Gen., I, 303-5.

ARMS:—

JAGGER:—Jeremy Jagger, Wethersfield, one of the first sett.; may therefore have been of Watertown; served in the Pequot war, 1637; removed, 1641, to Stamford; then was master of a trading vessel, and went to the W. I. four years before his death, 1658, abroad. His widow, Eliz., married, 1659, Robert Usher; and in 1671 grants for his conduct in the old war were made to his 3 sons, John, Jeremiah and Jonathan.

JOHN JAGGER, Southampton, L. I., 1641, perhaps brother of the first Jeremy, was living 1664.

JONATHAN JAGGER, Stamford, brother of first John, was living there 1673, and not in 1687, but whether he had family then, or after, is unknown.

REFERENCES:—Howell's Southampton, 327; Huntington's Stamford, Ct. Fams., 56.

JAMES:—Charles James, Gloucester, married, 1673, Ann Collins; had Charles, born 1674; and Francis, 1677.

EDMUND JAMES, Newbury, may or may not be the same who, having come in the fleet with Winthrop, required adm. as freeman, 1630, but we see no evidence of his becoming one. Perhaps he went home before the time of adm. next year, and came again. The early settler was prob. of Watertown, and his wife, Reana. However, the man at N., who had Edmund, born 1670; and Benjamin, 1673, and in that year died, as says Coffin, could not be the Watertown settler, because his widow, Reana, by contract of marriage, 1640, says Bond, 800, became wife of William Andrew.

ERASMUS JAMES, Salem, 1637, then had grant of land, was of Marblehead, 1648; died about 1660, leaving widow, Jane Felt. He had prob. son of the same name.

FRANCIS JAMES, Hingham, came in the Diligent, 1638, with wife and 2 servants, Thomas Tuckling and Richard Baxter, from old Hingham; freeman 1643. He lost house by fire in May, and died 1647.

GOWDY JAMES, Charlestown, 1639, freeman 1642; had leave to inhabit at Boston, 1657; by wife Ann had, perhaps, no children. Sometimes Gardy.

JOHN JAMES, Derby, 1694-1706, had preached in Haddum as early as 1683; by Mather, in Hecatompolis, erron. marked as bred at Harvard; he is not in the Catal. of Alumni, yet may be the gentleman to whom, in 1710, was given A. M., being the 3rd honor degree ever confer. by the Inst.; and by Farmer he was thought son of Rev. Thomas, of Charlestown, but Dr. Field says that he was "supposed to be a native of Wales;" he died at Wethersfield, however, 1729, having there lived in privacy some years.

HUGH, JAMES, Portsmouth, sent over by Mason 1630, or 1.

JOSEPH JAMES, Fairfield, 1674, died before 1688, leaving widow Mary, and daughter Mary, who married Nathan Adams.

PHILIP JAMES, Hingham, prob. brother of Francis; came, 1638, in the Diligent, with wife, four children, and 2 servants, William Pitts and Edward Mitchell (children's names not mentioned), from Hingham, in old Norfolk. He died soon after, and his widow married, 1640, George Russell.

RALPH JAMES, Weymouth, 1650, may be thought the man who married that year, at Plymouth, Mary Fuller, daughter, perhaps, of Samuel, of the Mayflower.

SAMUEL JAMES, Scituate, thought by Deane to be father of William.

THOMAS JAMES, Charlestown, bred at Emanuel College, Cambridge, where he had his degree, 1614 and 1618; had preached in Co. Lincoln, where prob. he was born; came in the William and Francis, 1632, with wife Eliz., and prob. son Thomas; freeman 1632; had John, bapt. 1633. After few years he went to New Haven, where, in 1639, a lot was granted him; made a freeman of that colony 1640; he had Nathaniel, bapt. 1641; thence, 1642, sailed to Virginia, in company with Knowles and Tomson, but came back next year, and before 1648 went home; never returned.

THOMAS JAMES, Providence, 1637, one of the founders of the first Bapt. ch.; a physician; strong friend of Williams, a good servant in the cause of humanity, as is seen in Hist. of Bradford, 364, and Winthrop, I, 268.

THOMAS JAMES, Dedham, may be the man who had grant of land at Salem, 1638, and the same who married at Plymouth, 1650, Mary Fuller, perhaps daughter of the beloved physician of the Mayflower. He came from Marlborough, Co. Wilts, 1635, by the James, from South-

ampton; his name may be misprinted. By wife Margaret he had John, 1641; and perhaps soon removed.

THOMAS JAMES, Lancaster, died shortly after 1660.

WILLIAM JAMES, who reg. adm. as freeman 1630, but never took the oath, prob. came in fleet with Winthrop, and perhaps went home soon. Felt thinks him the same who had grant of land at Salem, 1637. But this man, it seems more likely, came in the Lion, arriving 1632. Either of these Williams may have been the planter at Kittery, 1651.

WILLIAM JAMES, Scituate, 1673, had wife Mehitable, but no children.

REFERENCES:—Am. Ancestry, VII, 243-281; IX, 95, 143; Austin's R. I. Gen. Dict., 111: Babson's Hist. Gloucester, Mass., 107; Deane's Hist. Scituate, Mass., 292-4; Savage's Gen. Dict., II, 535-7; Richmond, Va. Standard, II, 6; Wyman's Charlestown, Mass., Gens., I, 547.

JAMESON:—Andrew Jameson, Boston, 1657, one of the first members of the Scots' Charit. Soc. that year.

ROBERT JAMESON, Watertown, 1642.

WILLIAM JAMESON, Charlestown, supposed to have been a soldier in Turner's Comp., 1676, and whose name is thought to be called Jennison in Frothingham's list of householders, 1678, page 183, because in Budington is found as church member, 1681, Goodman William Jimmison, and such name is not seen in F.; had wife Sarah, whose gravestone says she died 1691, aged 38, by whom he had John, bapt. 1686; William, 1689, and Mary, 1691; and 2nd wife Sarah died 1710, aged 61; and 3rd wife Mary, died 1718, aged 67; he having died 1714, aged 61. At Dover, in 1658, an inhabitant was recorded called Patriarch Jameson, says Mr. Quint, but perhaps the clerk should have written Patrick.

WILLIAM JAMESON, Casco, about 1685.

REFERENCES:—Am. Ancestry, III, 29; IV, 44; Cochrane's Hist. Antrim, N. H., 544-62; Cogswell's Hist. Henniker, N. H., 631; Eaton's Hist. Thomaston, Me., II, 281-4; Kulp's Wyoming Valley Fams.; Morrison's Hist. Windham, N. H., 605; Stark's Hist. Dunbarton, N. H., 240; Savage's Gen. Dict., II, 537.

JANES, or JEANES:—William Janes, New Haven, 1643, then had family of 5, perhaps one or more born in England; had Ruth, born 1650; removed, 1657, to Northampton, where his wife Mary died, 1662. By her he had, also, Abel, Ebenezer and Jonathan; the last two were killed by the Indians, 1675, at Northfield; and also Nathaniel and Elisha; both died at Springfield, 1663. He married in a few months Hannah, widow of John Broughton, daughter of Thomas Bascom; had Samuel, born 1664; Hepzibah, 1666; Hannah, 1669; Benjamin, 1672; and, perhaps, William, of Hartford, about 1700, may also have been his son. He was among the first settlers at Northfield, and preached to the people there under an oak tree; but twice that planta. was broken up, and he was driven down to Northampton; there died, 1690. His descend. spell the name Janes, though he always had e before the a.

REFERENCES:—Am. Ancestry, I, 42; IX, 214; Hyde's Hist. Brimfield, Mass., 421-5; Janes Gen. (1868), 419 pp.; Loomis Gen. Female Branches, 394-417; Morris and Flynt Gen., 58.

JANSEN, or JANSON:—Hendrick Jansen, Newtown, L. I., 1656, a Dutchman, willing to endure the jurisdict. of Conn.

REFERENCES:—Am. Ancestry, II, 64; IV, 133; V, 57; VI, 158; Bergen's Kings Co., N. Y., Settlers, 153-66; Munsell's Albany, N. Y., Call., IV, 137; Pearson's Schenectady, N. Y., Settlers, 97; Prime's Hist. L. I., N. Y., 360; Schoonmaker's Hist. Kingston, N. Y., 482; Sylvester's Hist. Ulster Co., N. Y., 338.

JACQUES:—Henry Jacques, Newburg, a carpenter, came 1640; married, 1648, Ann, perhaps daughter of Richard Knight; had Henry, born 1649; Mary, 1651, died young; Mary, again, 1653; Hannah; Richard, 1858; Stephen, 1661; Sarah, 1664; Daniel, 1667; Eliz., 1669; Ruth, 1672, and Abigail, 1674. He was freeman, 1669; died 1687, and his widow died 1705.

REFERENCES:—Whitehead's Perth Amboy, 365; Wyman's Charlestown, Mass., Gens., I, 548.

JAQUITH:—Abraham Jaquith, Charlestown, married Ann, daughter of James Jordan of Dedham, whither it is thought he soon removed; had Abraham, 1644; Mary, 1646; and 3 other children. He was freeman 1656. Written Jackewish when the spelling was by sound.

REFERENCES:—Cutter's Jaffrey, N. H., 377-80; Davis' Gen., 79; Hayward's Hist. Gilsum, N. H., 344; Hayward's Hist. Hancock, N. H., 679; Hazen's Hist. Billerica, Mass., 77; Sewall's Hist. Woburn, Mass., 618; Stearn's Hist. Ashburnham, Mass., 763; Washington, N. H., Hist., 489-92.

JARRATT:—John Jarratt, Rawley, freeman 1640; died 1648. Names in his will wife Susanna, and daughter Elizabeth.

REFERENCE:—Powers' Sangamon Co., Ill Sett., 408.

JARVIS:—John Jarvis, Boston, merchant, died 1656; but probably he was only a visitor.

JOHN JARVIS, Boston, shipwright, married, 1661, Rebecca, daughter of Elias Parkman; had Nicholas, bapt., 1666; and Samuel, 1674; but prob. the elder died young. In his will, 1689, he names wife Rebecca, and 3 children, all minors—Samuel, Mary and Abigail.

STEPHEN JARVIS, perhaps of Huntington, L. I., married a daughter of Jonathan, of the same, before 1670.

REFERENCES:—Am. Ancestry, III, 166; VIII, 3; IX, 228; Eaton's Annals of Warren, Me., 559; Jarvis Gen. (1879), 369 pp.; Whitmore's Copps Hill Epitaphs.

JAY:—Jonathan Jay, a soldier, 1676, under Capt. William Turner.

WILLIAM JAY, Boston, married, about 1653, Mary, daughter of John Hunting of Dedham.

REFERENCES:—Alden's Am. Epitaphs, V, 246-50; Am. Ancestry, VI, 151; Baird's Hist. of Rye, N. Y., 479-85; Bolton's Westchester Co., N. Y., II, 196; Flanders' Chief Justices of N. Y., I, 11-8; Holgate's Am. Gen., 234; Lamb's Hist. of N. Y. City, I, 602, 697; N. Y. Gen. Biog. Rec., VII, 110-6; X, 114.

ARMS:—

JECOCKES, or JECOXE:—Francis Jecockes, Stratford, 1646.

JEFFORD:—John Jefford, Lynn, 1675.

JEFFREY, JEFFRIES, or JEFFERY:—David Jeffrey, Boston, merchant, married, 1686, Eliz., daughter of John Usher; had Jane, born 1687; John, 1689; David, 1690; Eliz., 1692; Rebecca, 1693; Sarah, 1695; Francis, 1696, and Peter, 1697; all of these living when his wife died, 1698, as Sewall tells, in Geneal Reg., VI, 77.

DIGORY JEFFREY, Kittery, was a constable in 1664.

EDWARD JEFFREY, came in the Truelove, 1635, aged 24, from London, but it is not known where he sat down.

FRANCIS JEFFREY, Falmouth, about 1685. Willis, 1, 218.

GEORGE JEFFREY, Windsor, had then Mary, born 1669; Hannah, 1671; Eliz., 1675; removed to Suffield; there had James, 1681, who was of Westerly, R. I., 1709; also he had Sarah, and perhaps other children, and died 1683.

GEORGE JEFFREY, Boston, 1676, a merchant from Scotland, may have been, 1684, of Portsmouth.

GREGORY JEFFREY, Wells, was freeman 1653, constable 1658; had wife Mary, and son John, an infant. He died 1662; his widow married John Lux.

ROBERT JEFFREY, Charlestown, came in the Eliz. and Ann, 1635, aged 30, bringing wife Mary, 27, and children—Thomas, 7; Eliz., 6; and Mary, 3; two maid servants, Susan Brown, 21, and Hannah Day, 20; he removed to R. I., 1638, where he was in high repute as physician, and treasurer of Newport, 1640, and there was living 1646.

THOMAS JEFFREY, Dorchester, freeman 1634, removed before 1634 to New Haven, prob. with Eaton in 1638, had served with reput. in the Pequot war; was called a serg. when he died, 1661, in good esteem; had a sister Sarah, wife of George Betty, in Co. Somerset.

WILLIAM JEFFREY, Weymouth, one of the earliest settlers in Mass. Bay, before Gov. Winth. or even Capt. Endicott; prob. first at Cape Ann, and may have drifted along shore to Manchester, early called Jeffry's Creek. or as far as Salem; and Felt claims him for Ipswich, but, of course, this would be some years later; he was sworn freeman 1631; may have had Mary, born 1642, and tradition gives him son John. He may be the brother of Robert, who was in R. I., 1638, and certainly is seen in list of freemen at Newport, 1655, where he died 1675, aged 84. His will names wife Mary, eldest daughter Mary, son Thomas, other daughters Sarah, Priscilla and Susanna.

REFERENCES:—Salter's Monmouth, N. J.; Savage's Gen. Dict., II, 539.

ARMS:—

JEFTS, or JEFFS:—Henry Jefts, Woburn, 1640, married, 1647, Ann Stowers, and next, 1649, Hannah Borth, or Births, perhaps Booth; had John, born 1651; Hannah, who died 1653; Hannah, again, 1655; Joanna, 1656; Henry, 1659, and possibly others before or after, but all these, since the first, at Billerica, of which he was one of the first settlers, and died 1700, aged 94. Strangely is the name spelt Sciffs, in 2 Mass. Hist. Call., II, 162.

JOHN JEFTS, Boston, 1656, mariner, had Mary, born 1656, by wife Sarah, who took admin. upon his estate 1670, because "nigh twelve years since depart. and no news of him."

WILLIAM JEFTS, Rhode Island, 1652.

REFERENCES:—Hazen's Hist. Billerica, Mass., 78; Hill's Hist. Mason, N. H., 203; Sewall's Hist. Woburn, Mass., 618; Stearn's Hist. Ashburnham, Mass., 763; Washington, N. H., Hist., 492-4.

JEGGLES:—Daniel Jeggles, Salem, 1639.

DANIEL JEGGLES, Salem, perhaps son of Thomas, or possibly of the preceding, was master of a vessel taken by the French, 1689. See Rev. in N. E., Justif., 43.

THOMAS JEGGLES, Salem, perhaps brother of the first Daniel, married, 1647, Abigail, daughter of Elder Samuel Sharp; had Abigail, born 1648; Thomas, 1650; William, 1653, died in few days; Samuel, 1654; Eliz., 1656; William, again, 1659; Daniel, 1661; Mary, 1665; Nathaniel, 1666; all exc. the third, bapt. 1668; John, born 1669; Ebenezer, 1672, and Benjamin, 1674.

WILLIAM JEGGLES, Salem, 1637, shipwright, prob. brother of first Daniel, and perhaps of first Thomas, died 1659. He had wife Mary, and son John; but perhaps a 2nd wife, Eliz., was admx. Another William, of Salem, who came from Virginia, died 1674. Giggles, Gyggles, and other forms are used.

REFERENCE:—Savage's Gen. Dict., II, 541.

JELLETT:—John Jellett, Boston, died 1656, yet it might seem that he was only trans., since we see no other mention of him; but the record of marriage contains that of William Wardell with widow Eliz. J., and under Gillet may be read more of her.

JELLICOE:—Thomas Jellicoe, Middletown, had wife Mary, but prob. no children; died 1684.

JEMPSON, GIMSON, or JEMSON:—James Jempson, Boston, had wife Sarah, 1647, and son James, born 1651, who prob. died soon; and James, again, 1655; and died 1662. Perhaps he may have written the name Jameson.

JOHN JEMPSON, Amesbury, possibly son of the preceding, married, 1670, Esther, daughter of George Martin, of Salisbury; took oath of fidel. 1677.

PATRICK JEMPSON, at Dover, adm. an inhab. in 1659, and there was taxed several years. See Jameson.

JENKINS, or JENKIN:—Edward Jenkins, Scituate, 1643, prob. came with Nathaniel Tilden, for in his will, 1641, he is called his servant; was represent. 1657, died 1699, leaving Thomas.—Deane.

HENRY JENKINS, New Hampshire, died about 1670.

JOEL JENKINS, Braintree, had Lydia, born 1640, and Theophilus, 1642; was freeman 1646; removed to Malden; has Theophilus, his son; died there 1660.

JOHN JENKINS, Plymouth, 1643, prob. removed to Barnstable, there married, 1653, Mary Ewer; had Sarah, born 1653; Mehitable, 1655; Samuel, 1657; John, 1659. Mary, 1662; Thomas, 1666, and Joseph, 1669. He may or may not be the passenger in the Defence, from London, 1635, called 26 years of age. A few weeks later, Eliz. J., aged 27, embarked in the Truelove at London, for N. E. She may be the person who died at Sandwich, 1649.

LEMUEL JENKINS, Malden, 1671, married, 1670, Eliz., daughter of Thomas Oakes; had Lemuel, born 1672, and Eliz., who died 1698, unless she was a grandchild.

OBADIAH JENKINS, Malden, married, 1677, Mary Lewis; had Sarah, born 1685; Ann, 1687, and Obadiah, 1690; was freeman 1690.

REGINALD JENKINS, Dorchester, 1630, is prob. the man who removed, says Winth. I, 89, to Cape Porpus, and there was killed by the Indians, 1632.

REGINALD JENKINS, Kittery, who submitted 1652, to the jurisdict. of Mass., removed to Dover; there, by wife Ann, had Philadelphia. He may have been son of the preced.

ROBERT, of Dover, 1657, called Junkins, prob. the same named Jenkins, at York, 1674, where he took the oath of alleg., 1681, to the King.

SAMUEL JENKINS, Greenwich, 1672, may have been he who married, 1670, Mary, widow of Eleazer Famer, of Dorchester.

REFERENCES:—Am. Ancestry, I, 42; IV, 174; VI, 171; Deane's Hist. Scituate, Mass., 294-6; Freeman's Hist. Cape Cod, Mass., II, 87; Hayward's Hist. Hancock, N. H., 680; Hobart's Hist. Abington, Mass., 406-9; Mitchell's Hist. Bridgewater, Mass., 203; Norton's Hist. Fitzwilliam, 617; Spooner Gen., I, 471-83; Wyman's Charlestown, Mass., Gens., I, 550.

JENKS:—Joseph Jenks, Lynn, 1645, blacksmith, employed at the iron works, came, a widower, is the tradition of the family, from Hammersmith, or Hounslow, Co. Middlesex, or Colebrook, in the edge of Bucks, near London; had child Joseph, born in England, and perhaps another son that may have gone south, and be progenitor of the name in N. C.; and by 2nd wife Eliz. who died 1679, had prob. Sarah; certainly Samuel, born at Lynn 1654; Deborah, 1658; John, 1660; and Daniel, 1663; and died 1683. He was an ingenious workman; in 1652 was engaged to cut the dies for our coinage, says report; and Boston, 1654, gave power (we find by the record) to its selectmen to contract with him for engines to carry water in case of fire.

REFERENCES:—Am. Ancestry, III, 141; Ammedown Gen., 45; Corliss' No. Garmault Gen.; Draper's Hist. Spencer, Mass., 213; Driver Gen., 147; Essex Inst. Hist. Call.; Savage's Gen. Dict., II, 542-4; Wyman's Hunt Gen., 114.

JENNER, GINNER, or JENNERS:—David Jenner, Boston, 1685, freeman 1691; prob. was of Charlestown before and afterward; and by wife Mabel Russell, married 1688, had Mabel, 1690, and Rebecca, 1692. In B. had Thomas, 1693; Eliz., 1696, and David, 1699; and died 1709, aged 46.

JOHN JENNER, Dorchester, perhaps soon went to Stratford, where he might be 1650, or of Brookhaven in L. I., 1655; had prob. married Alice, only child of Robert Pigg, of New Haven.

THOMAS JENNER, Roxbury, about 1634 or 5, removed soon after to Weymouth; was minister there but a few months or years; freeman 1636; represent. 1640, and went to Saco; there preached not long, but went home, and in 1651 was in Norf'k, so poor as to sell his library. Another Genner was of Weymouth, at the same time with this minister, and if his name of bapt. were Thomas, might be that freeman of 1639.

THOMAS JENNER, Charlestown, 1658, prob. the same to whom Frothingham, 86, says liberty of residence was given 1636; was not a freeman of the colony, but perhaps Esther, who joined the church 1648, was his wife.

THOMAS JENNER, Charlestown, perhaps son of the preceding, born in England; married, 1655, Rebecca, daughter of Nicholas Trerice, who died 1722, aged 86; had Rebecca, born 1656, and prob. other children; we know Thomas and another child were bapt. 1660; David, 1663; Sarah, 1667; Samuel, 1669; Eleanor, and Eliz., twins, 1671; and Eleanor, 1674; united with the church 1681, yet was not made freeman, though it is less remarkable, since in 1682, only two men of that town are found sworn, and only three others in 1690, among several hundreds from other towns who took that privilege, 1692. He was of the artillery comp, 1673, a capt., and prob. that master of the ship from London to Boston, 1685, with whom came Honest John Dunton, who calls him a man with "some smatterings of divinity in his head;" and died about 1699.

REFERENCES:—Caverly's Pittsford, Vt., 710; Cathren's Hist. Woodbury, Ct., 602; Jenner Gen. (1865), 3 pp. reprint; N. E. Hist. Gen. Reg. XIX, 246-9; Wyman's Charlestown, Mass., Fams., 551-3.

JENNESS:—Francis Jenness, Hampton, baker, married a daughter of Moses Coxe; had Thomas, born 1671, died at 25 years; Hannah, 1673; Hezekiah, 1675; John, 1678; Eliz., 1681; Mehitable; and Richard, 1686. Descendants are numerous. Sometimes name appears Jennings.

REFERENCES:—Bedford, N. H., Cent., 312; Coggswell's Hist. Nottingham, N. H., 411-9; Dow's Hist. Hampton, N. H., 765-9.

JENNINGS:—John Jennings, Hartford, 1639, removed about 1641 to Southampton, where he was 1644. Another John, of mean character at Hartford, was whipped 1649.

JONATHAN JENNINGS, Norwich, 1684, left descendants.

JOSHUA JENNINGS, Fairfield, 1656, had, in 1648, lived in same town on the river, prob. Hartford, where he married, 1647, Mary Williams, but whose daughter she was is unknown. He gave offense; died at F. 1676, leaving family and good estate.

NICHOLAS JENNINGS, Hartford, came in the Francis from Ipswich 1634, aged 22; prob. a Suff'k man, and perhaps brother of John; forfeited his grant of a lot by non-residence, attracted, possibly, to Saybrook.

RICHARD JENNINGS, Ipswich, came in 1636 with Rev. Nathaniel Rogers, being a Suff'k man, born at Ipswich; went home in 1638 or 9; obtained the living at Combs, whence, by the Act of Uniform., he was ejected 1662. Calamy, 649.

RICHARD JENNINGS, Bridgewater, 1666, had probably been apprenticed to Robert Bartlett, 1635; may have been father of that Susanna who died at Plymouth 1654, and lived afterward at Sandwich, whence he removed to B., and had there a family of children.

RICHARD JENNINGS, New London, 1675, came from Barbados, 1678; married Eliz. Reynolds, who came from the same island; had Samuel, born 1679; Richard, 1680, and Elinor.

SAMUEL JENNINGS, Portsmouth, R. I., in the list of freemen 1655.

STEPHEN JENNINGS, Hatfield, married, 1677, Hannah, daughter of John Dickinson, the widow of Samuel Gillet, killed at the Falls fight the preceding year. At the assault on Hatfield the Indians carried her to Canada, where, several months later, was born the daughter called after getting home the same year, Captivity. Other children were Stephen, born 1680; Joseph, 1682; Sarah, 1684; Benjamin; and Jonathan, 1691. He was freeman 1690; removed to Brookfield.

THOMAS JENNINGS, Portsmouth, R. I., in the list of freemen 1655; perhaps brother of Samuel.

WILLIAM JENNINGS, Charlestown, 1630.

REFERENCES:—Aldrich's Walpole, 293; Austin's R. I. Gen. Dict., 114; Barry's Framingham, Mass., 300-3; Bartow Gen. Appendix; Butler's Hist. Farmingham, Me.,

505-9; Hall's Record Norwalk, Ct., 266, 294, 301; Hatch's Hist. Industry, Me., 662; Jennings' Assoc. Report (1863), 34 p, (1866) 10 p.; Jennings Fam., by Albert Welles (1881); Morse's Hist. Sherborn, Mass.; 155; Savage's Gen. Dict., II, 544-6; Shourd's Fenwick Colony, N. J., 119-21; Temple's N. Brookfield, Mass., 649-50; Schenck's Hist. Fairfield, Ct., 383-6; Montague Gen., 653-8.

JENNISON:—John Jennison, Amesbury, 1680; possibly son of William.

ROBERT JENNISON, Watertown, 1636, by wife Eliz. (in the record called Grace, probably by mistake), had Eliz., 1637; first wife died 1638; and by second wife, Grace, who died 1686, had a daughter, Michal, 1640; Samuel, 1642, died soon; and Samuel, again, 1645; was freeman 1645; died 1690.

WILLIAM JENNISON, Watertown, brother of Robert, came prob. in the fleet, 1630, with Sir Richard Saltonstall and Winth.; freeman 1631; was ensign 1633, served in the Pequot war 1636, as Underhill tells; lieut. and capt. afterward; represent. 1635, and very often later; artillery comp. 1638; went home 1651.

REFERENCES:—Aldrich's Walpole, 293-6; Benedict's Hist. Sutton, Mass., 668; Bond's Watertown, Mass., 306-10, 800-14; Fiskes of Amherst, N. H., 147; Hemenway Gen. Rec., 12; N. E. Hist. Gen. Reg., VII, 71; Ward's Hist. Shrewsbury, Mass., 337.

JENNY:—John Jenny, Plymouth, who was a brewer of Norwich, went to Holland in his youth, lived at Rotterdam, came in the James, a little vessel of 44 tons, built for the Pilgrims at Leyden; arrived 1623, with wife Sarah (whom he married at Leyden 1614, by the name of Carey), and children—Samuel, Abigail and Sarah—at same time with the ship Ann, therefore with her passengers reckoned "old comers;" had born here John and Susanna; was an assistant 1637-39, and represent. 1641; he died 1644.

REFERENCE:—Temple's Whately, Mass., 243.

JEPSON, or JEPHSON:—Christopher Jepson, Dorchester, 1646.

JOHN JEPSON, Boston, 1647, married, 1656, Emma, daughter of John Coddington; had John, born 1657, who died soon.

ROGER JEPSON, Saybrook, removed to Middletown, died 1680, leaving Samuel, aged 8; Jonathan, 6; one daughter, Martha, 5, and Roger, 18 mos.; his widow Martha married Thomas Allyn of M.

THOMAS JEPSON, Boston, by wife Hannah had Richard, born 1692; Hannah, 1693, and Emma, 1696.

REFERENCE:—Sigourney Gen., 25.

JERMON:—Edward Jermon, Providence. See Inman; for so Judge Staples reads the name.

JEWELL:—Thomas Jewell, a miller, aged 27, unless custom house records mistake the name, came from London 1635, in the Planter.

JESS, JESSE, JOSE, or JOYCE:—David Jess, Boston, goldsmith, married before 1698 Mary, daughter of Phineas Wilson of Hartford; had David, born 1700;

Mary, 1701; Phineas, 1702; Eliz., 1704; and Susanna, 1706. He had good estate with his wife, and died 1708. His widow Mary married, 1717, Joseph King.

WILLIAM JESS, Windsor, where the name was Joyce, removed to Springfield; there had Abigail, 1645; and was drowned at Enfield Falls, in the river, same year.

JESSAN:—Jacat Jessan, Boston, merchant, agent of his brother Abraham, ironmonger of London, was of artillery comp., 1673.

JESSOP:—Edward Jessop, Stamford, about 1650; Newton, L. I., 1656; was of Westchester, 1664, and in 1653, or earlier, sold land in Fairfield, but took estate there again in 1689.

JOHN JESSOP, an early sett. at Wethersfield, might seem to have died at or near Hartford, 1637, as by order of the Gen. Court, Feb., 1637, all creditors were to produce claims 3 mos. later, but that means credit. of John Oldham, and Jessop may have been one prosecuting a suit before death of O., who might well cause this mention of him; so prob. this is the construction. He united with others in 1640 to go to settle Stamford; removed to Greenwich; was represent. 1664 for that town, prob. with Westchester or Rye, and made commissioner with authority at Westchester; but in 1673 lived at Southampton, on L. I.

PHILIP JESSOP, a soldier, 1676, in Phillip's war.

REFERENCES:—Howell's Southampton, 332-5; Huntington's Stamford, Ct., Sett., 57; Jessup Gen. (1887), 463 pp.; Prime's Sands Gen., 87-90; Savage's Gen. Dict., II, 547.

JEWELL:—George Jewell, Saco, mariner, may be that unhappy man whose loss in 1637 is related by Winth., I, 244. See Folsom, 33, 125.

JOSEPH JEWELL, Watertown, by wife Martha had Joseph, born 1673, and Martha, 1675. Perhaps he was there only as transient resident, driven away by fear of Indian hostility.

SAMUEL JEWELL, Boston, 1655.

THOMAS JEWELL, Braintree, 1639, had grant at the meeting on Monday, Feb. 24, 1640, of 12 acres, which was the common allowance for 3 heads—himself, wife and prob. child Thomas; by wife Grizell had Joseph, 1642; Nathaniel, 1648; Grizell, 1652, and Mercy, 1653. His widow married Humphrey Griggs, 1656.

REFERENCES:—Am. Ancestry, I, 42; VII, 202; Dunster Gen., 255; Hudson's Hist. Marlborough, Mass., 403; Jewell Gen. (1860), 104 pp.; N. E. Hist. Gen. Reg., XXII, 436; Runnel's Hist. Sanbornton, N. H., II, 399; Savage's Gen. Dict., II, 547; Loomis Gen. Female Branches, 626-33; Waterford, Me. Centen. (1879), 261.

JEWETT:—John Jewett, Ipswich, freeman 1676; of descent unknown to Savage. By wife Eliz., daughter of the first Isaac Cummings, who died 1679, he had Sarah, born 1668; Abigail, who died 1672; Abigail, again, 1675, died at 2 mos.; David, 1677, and Mary, 1679. He married Eliz., widow of Benjamin Chadwell, of Lynn; had Daniel, 1681; Jonathan, 1685; Dorcas; and Rebecca, 1690.

JOSEPH JEWETT, Dorchester, thence soon to Rawley;

freeman 1639; represent. 1651-4, and 60; died 1661. Beside 4 daughters by wife Mary, perhaps one of whom was Patience, who married at Lynn, 1666, Shubael Walker, he had Jonathan; Nehemiah, 1643; Joseph, 1656; last-named child was by Ann, widow of Bozoan Allen, of Boston, married 1653.

MAXIMILIAN JEWETT, Rawley, brother of the first Joseph, came from Bradford in the W. Riding, of Yorksh., at the gathering of the church, 1639, chosen deacon; freeman 1640; represent. 1641, and for 16 years later; had 2nd wife, married 1671, widow Elinor Boynton; and died about 1684, leaving, besides widow Sarah, the child Ezekiel; Joseph; Ann; Eliz., wife of Robert Hazeltine; Mary Hazeltine; Faith Dowse, and Sarah, prob. wife of Philip Nelson.

NATHANIEL JEWETT, Concord, freeman 1681.

THOMAS JEWETT, Hingham, married, 1672, Susanna, prob. daughter of John Gilford; had Mary, bapt. 1674; Thomas, 1676; Hannah, 1681, died at 2 years; and John, 1683.

REFERENCES:—Am. Ancestry, III, 154; IV, 139; V, 130; VI, 149; Andrew's Hist. New Britain, Ct., 316; Blood's Hist. Temple, N. H., 229; Bond's Hist. Watertown, Mass., 903-5; Butler's Hist. Groton, Mass., 409, 473; Cregar's White Gen.; Cutter's Hist. Jaffrey, N. H., 382-4; Davis' Gen., 471, 484-6; Gage's Hist. Rawley, Mass., 445; Guild's Stiles Gen., 101-4; Hall's Genealogical Notes, 74, 79-81; Hanson's Hist. Gardiner, Me., 137, 158; Hatch's Hist. Industry, Me., 663; Hayward's Hist. Hancock, N. H., 681; Haye's Wells Fam., 157; Little Gen., 69; North's Hist. Augusta, Me.; Savage's Gen. Dict., II, 548; Stearns' Hist. Ashburnham, Mass., 763-5; Temple's Hist. Whately, Mass., 240; Wood Gen., 154-66; Worcester's Hist. Hollis, N. H., 378.

AFTER HUTCHINSON ref—p 102

ARMS:—Per pale, gu, and az., semée of cross crosslets, or, a lion, rampant, arg.

AFTER JACKSON ref—p 123

ARMS:—Gu, a fess, between three shovelers, tufted on the head and breast, arg., each charged with a trefoil, slipped, vert.

CREST:—A shoveler, as in the arms.

MOTTO:—Innocentiæ Securus.

AFTER JAFFREY reference—p 124

ARMS:—Paly of six, arg. and sa., surmounted by a fess, of the first, charged with 3 stars of the second.

CREST:—The sun shining through a cloud; proper.

MOTTO:—Post nubila Phœbus.

AFTER JAY ref—p 132

ARMS:—Az., a chevron, or. In chief, a demi-sun, in its splendor, between 2 mullets. of the last; in base, on a rock, two birds (or one single bird), all proper.

AFTER JEFFREY ref—p 135

ARMS:—Sa., a lion rampant, or, between 3 scaling ladders, of the last.

MOTTO:—Fac recte et nil time.

CORRECTIONS UNDER LETTER H.

HARTSHORNE:—Richard Hartshorne of Middletown, N.J., a prom. Quaker lawyer, came from Lancester, England, with his three servants and purchased land from the Indians at the Highlands of Navesink, Monmouth County, N. J. in 1669. Estate still owned by his decendants. One of the proprietors of East Jersey, commissioner of boundaries in 1683. Deputy in Gov. Lowerie's Council, 1684; member of assembly from Middletown, N. J. 1683 and 1685; Speaker 1686-98. Member of Provincial Council 1684, 1695, 1698, 1702; High Sheriff 1683; Judge of Sessions 1695, 1698; Member of Gov. Barre's Council 1698, to surrender of the government to the Crown. Married Sept. 27th., 1670,Margaret Carr, dau. of Robert Carr of Newport, R. I. from London in the ship Elizabeth and Ann, 1635. A freeman of Newport March 16, 1641; member of assembly Oct. 26, 1670. His son Caleb Carr was Governor of R. I. in 1695. Richard Hartshorne had dau. Sarah, who married John Taylor of Middletown, N. J.

REFERENCES:—N. J. Archives, Vol. I, p. 220; Journal of Representatives, Vol. XIII, p. 78. Smith's History if N. J., p. 1175; Rhode Island Col. Records.

HUBBARD, James, Gravesend, L. I., came to Salem, Mass. in 1637 with Lady Deborah Moody, from Langham, Rutlandshire, England where he said his family could trace their lineage back 124 (One hundred and twenty-four) generations. On account of his Baptist faith took refuge with the Dutch at Gravesend, L. I., in 1643. Commissioner of Indian Affairs, Schout Fiscael, Surveyor, Commissioner in Land Office, Magistrate of Gravesend in 1650, '51, '53 and '63. Represented Gravesend in the convention held at New Amsterdam in 1653. Laid out the town of Gravesend in 1645. He was Sergeant at Law in the English Court, before emigrating to America. Married Elizabeth Baylies Dec. 31, 1664; had James, Samuel and Elias.

REFERENCES:—Town records of Gravesend; Bergen Family (Genealogy) foot notes 314 and 315; Bergen's Kings Co. Settlers; O'Callaghan's Trans. Dutch Man.

HOLMES:—Rev. Obadiah Holmes of Newport, R. I., was a Congregationalist minister who with his wife Katherine Preston came to Salem and Lynn, Mass. from Manchester, England before 1639. Became a Baptist, and was publicly whipped in Lynn, from the tail of a cart, for saying his prayers with his hat on, and baptising on Sunday. Later he took refuge in Providence, and at Newport, R. I., where he was made freeman in 1655. Representative to the General Court of R. I. in 1656, '57, '58; member of special Governor's Council in King Philip's war; a patentee of Monmouth Co., N. J., and instrumental in forming that patent in 1665. Mostly resided at Newport, R. I. where he was pastor of the Baptist Church for twenty-five years and died in 1682. He brought the first pendulum ("Grandfather's Clock") clock to this country, now at the Long Island Historical So. at Brooklyn, N. Y. Had Jonathan, born in 1637. John in 1639. Martha, 1640. Samuel, 1642. Obadiah, 1644. Mary. Hope and Lydia. JONATHAN born in England, prominent both in N. J. and R. I.; member of Gen'l Assembly in N. J., 1668 to '72 and '80 and Com. Captain, 1783. Deputy in R. I., 1689 to 1701; Speaker; Member of Govnor's Council, Gen'l Treasurer, 1704.

REFERENCES:—Gen. Dictionary of R. I., pp. 103-104;

Salter's Hist. of Monmouth Co.N.J.; Elli's Hist. of New Jersey, p. 26; Old Times in Old Monmouth, Beekman and Salter.

ADD TO HUNT.

EDMUND (alias EDWARD) came on the ship "Fortune" landed at Plymouth 9th of Nov. 1621, was one of Capt. Miles Standish' Company; located at Duxbury in 1637; lived at Houndsditch near Blue River in 1664; his will and inventory probated at Duxbury 20th July 1656; died (says Winser) Christmas day 1655. (?) had a son named SAMUEL. b. 1647.

REFERENCES:—Pierce's Col. Lists; Hist. Soc. Col. Mass.; Memoirs Plymouth Colony; Winser's Hist. Duxbury.

ENOCH, came with his two young sons Ephraim and Peter from England to Weymouth in 1635. M. Sarah Paine in 1668, (second wife). In 1640 was Church Collector; in 1660 m. Dorothy Baker (third wife) they had

SARAH, b. 4 July, 1660 (a deaf mute who m. Matthew Pratt also a deaf mute) ; wife Dorothy died in 1662 and ENOCH returned to England.

REFERENCES:—Memoirs Plym. Col. vol. IV, pp. 84-89

EPHRAIM, son of Enoch came with his father and brother Peter from Eng., 1635 to Weymouth; m. Ioana made freeman 1671, was Sergeant Weymouth Militia and Ensign, 16th Mass, 1680. Captain, 1690. Representative, 1689-91; served in the expedition to St. Lawrence (Canada) under Sir William Phipps also against the Indians at Groton, 1706-7; was assistant, 1703-1713. He owned the whole town of Ashfield, given him for service in the Canadian expedition, and actually deeded to his descendants forty years after; wife Joanna died leaving a son Peter; and a son, Ebenezer, b. 6 Apr., 1694; 2d lieut. in Continental army; after a few years Ephraim m. Amanda (dau. of Thos. and Welthian Richards) was promoted to a colonelcy and died 1713-14, a very distinguished man.

REFERENCES:—Mass. Rec., vol. LXIII, p. 285; Farmer's First Families N. E. p. 9; Barber's Hist. Colonial Wars p. 225.

JONATHAN, b. Northampton Co., Eng., 1637; was son of John and Mary (Webster) Hunt of Sudburrowe, Thrapstone Co., Northampton, Eng., came to Connecticut 1658; m. 3 Sept., 1662, Clemence (dau. of Thos. Hosmer of Hartford), and removed to Northampton, Mass., took oath of allegiance 16 Feb., 1678; made freeman 19 May 1680; was Deacon, 1681; Representative 1690-91 and died, 29-30 Sept., 1691 (his widow Clemence m. John Smith of Milford Conn. she d. 8 July, 1699) had Thomas, b. 23 Jan., 1663, was one of the 9 who organized the church at Hartford. Jonathan, b. 20 Jan. 1664 died same year JONATHAN, (2) b. 20 Jan., 1665 d. 1 July, 1738.

JOHN, b. 22 Dec., 1667; d. (unm.) 4 Apr., 1712.

HANNAH, b. 7 Jan., 1669-70; m. 19 Dec., 1690 to Ebenezer Wright.

CLEMENCE, b. 8 Jan., 1671; d. 8 July, 1689.

EBENEZER, b. May, 1673; d., 1675.

EBENEZER (2), b. 5 Feb., 1675; m. 27 May, 1698 to Hannah Clark.

MARY, b. 24 Mar., 1679; m. 16 Dec., 1701 to Ebenezer Sheldon; she died, 1767.

SARAH, b. 20 July, 1682 and Samuel, b. 15 Sept., 1684.

REFERENCE:—Savage-Farmer

PETER, made freeman at Plymouth, 5 June 1651; deputy, 1653; Lieut. in Miles Standish's Company, 1654; m., 24 Dec., 1673 to Rebecca Paine; 1668 was selectman; large tract of land granted to him at "Attleburrough;" he died, 1675, sine prole.

REFERENCES:—Court Orders, Plymouth, p. 84; Hist. Plymouth; Hist. of "Attleburrough."

PETER, of Rehoboth, son of Enoch of Weymouth; came as a youth with his father in 1635; m., 10 Dec., 1645 to Elizabeth (dau. of Henry Smith of Rehoboth; selectman in 1646. Town clerk, 1649; surveyor of highway, 1650; deputy, 1652; representative, 1660-5 and again, 1672-83; 1674 was townsman; 1664, collector of excise; was commissioned a lieutenant and promoted to a captaincy, 1682, d., 1692; had a son Ephraim, b., 9 May, 1661.

REFERENCES:—Pierce's Col. Lists, p. 70 and 27; Hist. Rehoboth; Essex Collections.

RALPH, son of Francis and Dorothy (Durand) Hunt of London, Eng.; came with his bro. Thomas to Newtown, Long Island and became patentees there, 1663-4; in 1663 Ralph was a "Schepen." In 1664 magistrate and surveyor of Indian lands; same year was made lieutenant of militia, 21 Apr., 1665; his sons were Ralph, Edward, John and Samuel.

REFERENCES:—Riker Hist. Harlem; N. E. Gen. Reg., vol. 30, p. 404; Bodge N. Y. in Rev., 499; Doc. Hist. N. Y., p. 592.

ROBERT, the first of the name in America, was born in County Kent, England; he was vicar of Reculver in 1594, resigned that office in 1602 and sailed from Blackwall, Eng., 19 Dec., 1606, as chaplain to Newport's fleet· and landed at Jamestown, Virginia, 28th April, 1607. Rev. Robert Hunt preached the first gospel sermon in America, officiated at the first marriage (Anne Burras to John Layden in 1608), the first baptism and the first Holy Communion; the Sacrament was administered the third Sunday after Trinity, June 27th, 1607, in a barn-like structure which was burned the next year and the year in which Reverend Robt. Hunt died.

REFERENCES:—Smith's Hist. Generale; Lossing's Cyclopedia U. S. History, p. 659, and many Colonial histories.

WILLIAM, b. Halifax, Eng., 1605, came to America in 1635; settled at Concord. Aug. 12, m. Elizabeth Best, who bore him Nehemiah, 1631; Samuel, b. 1633; Elizabeth, b. 1636; Hannah, b. 12 Dec., 1641; Isaac, b. 1647; Nehemiah (2), b. 1631; d. 6 Apr., 1717; wife Elizabeth, b. 1636; Hannah, b. 12 Dec., 1640; Isaac, b. 1647; in 1664, and he died at Malborough, 1667, Oct. 10th.

REFERENCES:—Bancroft's U. S. Hist.; Hunt Family, by Alfred Wyman Hoar.

JOCELYN. See JOSSELYN.

JOHNS:—WILLIAM JOHNS. Hingham, died about 1663; having no relatives in this country.

REFERENCES:—Dodds' East Haven, Ct., 131.

JOHNSON:—ANDREW JOHNSON is the name of a soldier borne on the list of Moseley's camp 10 days before the decisive battle of Philip's War, Dec., 1675.

CALEB JOHNSON is the name of a servant of John Osgood of Andover, ment. in the will of 1650· who was drowned in Merrimack river, 1656.

CHARLES JOHNSON, New London, before 1690.

DAVY JOHNSON, Dorchester,came pub. in the Mary and John, 1630, reg. adm. that year and was made freeman next year, though no further mention of him is found; but in 1636 mention is made of the widow of David.

EBENEZER JOHNSON, Stratford, perhaps son of Peter of Fairfield, married 1667, Eliz. daughter of Edward Worster, Worcester, or Wooster, had Eliz. born, 1672; removed to Derby 1676, there had Eunice 1678, Hannah, 1680; Peter 1684; and Ebenezer 1687; and perhaps more. He was freeman 1678, and being one of the chief of the town, its represent. 1685, and after Lieut. Major and Colonel, continuing propr. 1717.

EDMUND JOHNSON,Hampton, came in the James from London 1635, aged 23, died 1654, leaving child Peter, who was bapt., 1639, and drowned 1674, John, 1641, James and Dorcas, beside widow Mary, who married 1651, Thomas Coleman, and died 1663.

EDWARD JOHNSON the famous capt. and author of the curious hist. called "Wonder Working Providences of Zion's Saviour in N.E." came, no doubt, in fleet with Winthrop 1630, took oath of fidelity following year; he was of Hernehill· a parish near Canterbury; after being some time at Charlestown or Salem, and other Planta., to satisfy himself he went home to bring his wife Susan, 7 children and three servants in 1636 or 7, and was settled at C. 1637, became one of the founders of the church at W. represent, 1643-71 except the year 1848, and was speaker, 1655, was town clerk almost 30 years, and did other valuable service, died 1672. See 3 Mass. Hist. Coll. VIII., 276. In will mentions children, Edward, George, William, Matthew and John; also James Prentice, whose wife was his daughter Susanna.

EDWARD JOHNSON, York. admitted freeman of Mass., 1652, with prefix of respect., and in later days it is thought lived at Wells; was in high esteem by all parties in their time of confusion, from 1656 to 80, and after that swore allegiance to Charles II. Perhaps may be father, of that Edward, though he may be the same, unfavorably mentioned in Winth. II., 210.

EDWARD JOHNSON, Branford, married Esther, daughter of Thomas Wheaden, had Eliz., born 1690; Amos, 1693; Experience, 1695; Edward, 1697; Esther, 1700; and Ebenezer, 1703.

FRANCIS JOHNSON, Salem, 1630; freeman, 1631; perhaps brother of Capt. Edward, and may have came with him; was nephew of Christopher Caulson (an asst. chosen at the first election after the charter, 1629). By wife Joan he had bapt. there, Naomi, 1638; Ruth, 1640; Eliz., 1642; Francis, 1644; Samuel, 1649; Joan, 1651; and Sarah, 1654. Prob. his wife married in a few years more and he married at Boston, 1656, Hannah, probably widow of William Hanbury; may be the F. Johnson in Frothingham's Hist. of 1677, at Charlestown (certainly not entitled in 1648 to the double name of Walsingham, given him by Dana); was 82 years old in 1686, and died 1691, prob. at Boston.

ISAAC JOHNSON, Salem, son of Abraham, grandson of Robert of Clipsham, Co., Rutland (who was arch. deac.

of Leicester, 1684, and parson of N. Luffanham in said Co., whose lineal descendant, Ezekiel, in 1727, was lord of the manor of Clipsham), and his mother, wife of Abraham, was a daughter of William Chadderton, D.D., the Puritan Bp. of Lincoln. He had larger estate than any of the patentees that came to our country; was an assistant named in the royal charter; next is Sir Richard Saltonstall, and in the list of members of the Boston church formed at Charlestown, stands after Winthrop and Dudley, and before Wilson, their minister. He came with Winthrop in the admiral ship of the fleet, formerly named the "Eagle," but after purchased by the Gov. and Comp. for this expedition called "Arabella," in complim. to the illustr. passengr., his wife. She was one of the daughters of Thomas Clinton, 3d Earl of Lincoln, and sister of Theophilus, the 4th Earl, ancest. of the Duke of Newcastle; she left, says Mather, I, 21, "an earthly paradise in the family of an Earldom to encounter the sorrows of a wilderness, for the entertainment of a pure worship in the house of God, and then immediately left that wilderness for the heavenly paradise." She died in a few weeks after landing at Salem, and was buried there; in a month Isaac followed her.

ISAAC JOHNSON, Roxbury, eldest son of John of the same; born in England, freeman, 1635; married, 1637, Eliz. Porter; had Eliz., born, 1639, died 1661; Mary, 1642; Isaac, 1644; Joseph, 1645, died soon; Nathaniel, born, says town record, 1647, bapt., says ch. rec., same day, by name of Nehemiah, which may be error. He was of Artillery comp., 1665, its capt., 1667; represent., 1671; was killed by the Indians at the head of his comp. in the great Narragansett fight, 1675. Hutch., I. 299, or Mather, VII, 50. The widow died, 1683.

ISAAC JOHNSON, Charlestown, by wife Mary had Eleazer, and Mary, bapt., 1676; Isaac, 1677; William, 1680; Eliz. and Hannah, twins, 1681; Nicholas, 1684; Abigail, 1686; Hannah, 1689; Nathaniel, 1692; and Abigail, again, 1694. He died, 1711, aged 62.

JAMES JOHNSON, Portsmouth; sent over by Mason in 1630 or 1; is said to have died about 1678, aged 79.

JAMES JOHNSON, Boston, 1635, a glover, freeman, 1636; artillery, comp.; a capt. in 1656, and he married 1667; his wife, Margaret died, 1643, and he married Abigail, daughter of Elder Thomas Oliver; had Joseph, born 1644, died very soon, Abigail, 1645; Abigail, again 1647; James and John, twins, 1653; Eliza., 1655; perhaps died in few months; Mary, 1657, and two named Hannah, of whom the youngest was born, 1661.

JEREMIAH JOHNSON, New Haven, 1662.

..JOHN JOHNSON, prob. came in the fleet with Winthrop, bringing wife. Margery, who died in 1655, and his children, Isaac and Humphrey, prob. others, as his will speaks of 5; possibly the other 3 were daughters, and all born in Eng. Freeman, 1631; a man of estate and distinction; represent. at the first general court, 1634, and many years following: artillery comp., 1638; surveyor-gen. of arms and ammunit. He married Grace, wid. of Barnabas Fawer, and died, 1659.

JOHN JOHNSON, Newport, 1638; may have been of Wickford, 1674.

JOHN JOHNSON, Sandwich, 1634.

JOHN JOHNSON, New Haven, 1653, counts 5 in family; prob. the propr. with others of the name, 1685; may be

he who came from London in the James, 1635, aged 26, with wife, Susan, 24; Eliz., 2, and Thomas, 18 mos.; which may be thought a blunder by the custom house clerk for 8 mos. At New Haven had Daniel, 1648; Samuel, bapt., 1654; Hannah, 1657: Sarah, 1664, and Abigail. Perhaps he was brother of Edmund, a fellow passenger, but uncertain; another John came from London, 1635, in the Eliz., aged 23, of whom nothing is sure, unless he was John who, for service in Pequot war, 1637, had grant in Conn. of 50 acres in 1671. He may be the freeman of Guilford, 1669, or of New Haven. The Guilford John married Eliz. Disbrow, 1651, who had been divorced that year for offense of her husband, Thomas Relph, Rolfe, or Ralfe. who ran off to R. I. He had 4 children by her: John; Ruth, 1654; Isaac, 1656; and Abigail, 1659. His widow died 1669, and he died 1681; in his will naming these children.

JOHN JOHNSON, Rawley, 1650; married 1655, Hannah, daughter of Anthony Crosby, had John, born 1668, and Samuel, 1671; beside 2 daughters. He prob. had served in Philip's war, for in 1667 he was made capt. of the town by the Gen. Court.

JOHN JOHNSON, Lancaster, 1654; may be he of Sudbury, who married 1657, Deborah, daughter of William Ward, who died 1697, aged 60 and lived at Marlborough, where he had John, born 1672, died soon; Daniel, 1675; Eliz., 1677, and Deborah, 1678; was freeman, 1690, and died, 1713.

JOHN JOHNSON, Charlestown, married, 1656, Eliz., daughter of Elias Maverick; had John, born 1657; and prob. others—certainly Ruth, who in 1681 is named in the will of grandfather Maverick; removed before 1662 to Haverhill; was the first blacksmith there; freeman, 1666; represent., 1690.

JOHN JOHNSON, Boston, a turner, m. Sarah daughter of, James Neighbors.

JOHN JOHNSON, Watertown, married, 1659, Mary, daughter of Thomas King; had Hannah, who married, 1697, Francis Pierce, her father having giving her in month preceding houses and lands at Cambridge Farms, now Lexington, whither he had removed.

JOHN JOHNSON, New Hampshire, married, 1661, Eleanor Brockett; had John,, born 1662; Rosamond, 1665; Hannah, 1670; James, 1673, and Ebenezer, 1676.

JOHN JOHNSON, Rehoboth; had Eliz., born 1673; Joseph, 1677; Rebecca, 1679; Rachel, 1681, died in 4 mos.; Jonathan, 1683.

JOHN JOHNSON, Norwich, 1677; has large posterity.

JOHN JOHNSON, Oxford, one of the Huguenots who prob. came, 1686 from Rochelle in France, after the persecution began the year before, and wrote his name Jean Jeanson; had wife, Susan; was, with 3 of his children, killed by the Indians, 1696. His widow married,1701, her cousin, Daniel Johonnot, who rescued her from that fate, as the family tradition credibly reports.

JOHN JOHNSON, Salem, 1691; a lighterman. Felt.

JOSEPH JOHNSON, Lancaster, died 1668, leaving widow, Susanna.

MARMADUKE JOHNSON. Cambridge. 1661; printer, sent over by the Society for Prop. the Gospel to put Eliot's Indian Bible to press; ought to have more told of him than that he was sick of his residence here and went home in 1664, a little before finishing the work.

NATHANIEL JOHNSON, Medfield, married 1671, Mary Plimpton; died in Marlborough, prob., 1718.

PETER JOHNSON, an early adventurer with Byran Binks in the settlement of Sagadahock; see Col. Rec., I, 98. He and his associates prob. went to Virginia—at least, Winth., I, 58, gives them no prominence.

PETER JOHNSON, Boston, called a Dutchman when, in 1638, Richard Rawlings was allowed to purchase his house; he removed and was of Fairfield about 1649. His wife, Eliz., had a child born in prison, where, perhaps, she died. We find not the occasion of her imprisonment, which was very long, but conjecture is that she was insane, and that the child was posthumous, named Moses, and had elder brothers, John and Ebenezer.

RETURN JOHNSON, Hampton, swore alleg., 1678, but had at Andover, 1673, married Mary Johnson.

RICHARD JOHNSON, Charlestown, or Watertown; came in the employment of Sir Richard Saltonstall, 1630, and removed to Salem; had grant of land, 1637; but prob. lived at Lynn that year; freeman; had children, Daniel, Samuel, Eliz., and Abigail, and died, 1666.

RICHARD JOHNSON, Swanzey; by wife, Eliz., had Richard, born, 1684.

RICHARD JOHNSON, New Haven, had no family, but is called old Richard Johnson in record of his death, 1679.

ROBERT JOHNSON, New Haven, 1646: died, 1661 and in his will names children, Thomas, John and William.

ROBERT JOHNSON, the graduate of H. C., 1645. Is altogether unknown to Savage.

ROBERT JOHNSON, Marblehead, 1674.

SAMUEL JOHNSON, Boston, a mariner; by wife, Mary, had Peter, born 1653, and he died soon after.

SAMUEL JOHNSON, one of the soldiers in Gallup's comp., 1690, in the sad expedit. of Sir William Phips, of whom no more is known.

SOLOMON JOHNSON, Sudbury, 1638; freeman, 1651; by wife, Hannah, had Joseph, or Joshua, and Nathaniel, twins, born, 1640; Mary, 1644, and by wife, Elinor, had Caleb, 1646, casually killed at 8 years; Samuel, 1654; Hannah, 1656, and Caleb again, 1658; and died, 1690.

STEPHEN JOHNSON, Andover, married, 1661, Eliz., daughter, perhaps, or sister of Rev. Francis Dane; had Eliz., who died, 1668; Stephen; Francis, born, 1666; Ann., who died, 1669; Joseph; Mary, who died, 1673; and Benjamin. He died, 1690.

THOMAS JOHNSON, Hartford, a cobbler, as the record of his admin., 1640, calls him.

THOMAS JOHNSON, Hingham, 1635, came, perhaps, in the Hopewell, Capt. Babb, in the autumn of that year from London, aged 25 (though the name in the custom house record may be taken for Ireson, and inspect. leaves it uncertain); is prob. the man who was in peril on a raft, 1646, as told by Winth., II, 305. and was drowned, says Boston record, in the harbor, 1656. Had no children by his wife, Margaret.

THOMAS JOHNSON, Dover, 1648-57, had only child, a daughter, that died prob. soon after her father, who died, 1661.

THOMAS JOHNSON, of H. C., 1661; is, like Robert, wholly unknown to Savage. In Mather's catalogue, 1698, both are starred.

THOMAS JOHNSON, New London, 1682.

THOMAS JOHNSON, Andover, married, 1657, Mary, daughter of Nicholas Holt, who died, 1700, had Thomas, John, James, Peter and Josiah living at his death, in 1719. He was freeman, 1691, and, perhaps, had other children, for Penelope J. was killed by the Indians at Andover, 1698.

TIMOTHY JOHNSON, Andover, married, 1674, Rebecca, daughter of John Aslett, and died, 1688.

WALTER JOHNSON, middletown, 1684; of whom nothing is known.

WILLIAM JOHNSON, Charlestown, 1634, perhaps bro. of Capt. Edward, had wife, Eliz., and Ruhamah, a daughter, bapt., 1635; Joseph, 1637; Eliz., 1639, and Jonathan, 1641; and by second wife, Judith, James, born 1643; prob. others, and, certainly, Eliz., who was in 1668 wife of Edward Myer. William died, 1677.

WILLIAM JOHNSON, Guilford, married, 1651, Eliz. Bushnell, perhaps daughter of Francis, an important man, represent., 1665, and after, far above twenty years after, was a deacon; had Eliz., born 1652; Hannah, 1654, who may be guessed to be called Ann in the will or other records; Mary, 1657; Sarah, 1658, died soon; Martha, 1660, died in a few weeks; Abigail, 1661, died young; Mercy, 1665; Sarah, again, 1667, died at 2 years; Samuel, 1670, and Nathaniel Apr. 17, 1672. The mother died 10 days after, the last child in a few weeks, and the father died, 1702.

WILLIAM JOHNSON, Stonington, 1670, died, 1696, leaving children.

WILLIAM JOHNSON, Andover, married, 1678, Sarah Lovejoy; had Susanna, who died, 1683. and prob. other children; was freeman, 1691.

WINGLE, or WINDLE JOHNSON, New Haven, married, 1664, Sarah, daughter of John Hall; had William, born 1665, and John, 1667; was freeman, 1669.

ZECHARIAH JOHNSON, Charlestown, 1672, by wife, Eliz., had Eliz., bapt., 1673; Jephtha, 1675; Sarah, 1677, and Zechariah, 1680; William, 1683; Sarah, again, 1684, and Mary, 1688; and he was freeman, 1676.

Of this name the occurrence is so frequent in all parts of N. E. that out of inquiry confined exclusively to it, a large volume would grow.

REFERENCES:—Abbott's Andover, 35; Aldrich's Hist. Wolpole, N. H., 296-8; Am. Ancestry, I, 42; II, 64; III. 154; IV, 122, 166; VI, 87; VII, 30, 35, 49, 91, 162, 240; VIII, 50, 88; Austin's Allied Trans., 154; Austin's R. I. Gen. Dict., 114; Baldwin's Hist. Milford, Mass., 844-8; Barry's Hist. Framingham, Mass., 303; Brown's West Simsbury, Ct., Settlers, 88; Bond's Hist. Watertown, Mass., 539-42; Butler's Hist. Farmington, Me., 509-14; Champion Gen.; Chase's Hist. Haverhill, Mass., 276, 634-7; Child Gen., 422; Clute's Hist. Staten Island, N. Y., 392-4; Coffin's Hist. Boscamen, N. H., 560-2; Cogswell's Hist. Henniker, N. H., 632; Cogswell's Nottingham, N. H., 726-30; Collins' Hillsdale, N. Y., 14 App., 68-74; Cope. Fam. of Pa., 52-115; Corliss No. Yarmouth, Me.; Cathren's Woodbury, Ct., 600-2; II, 1510; Cutter's Hist. Arlington,

Mass., 265; Davis' Landmarks Plymouth, Mass., 162; Davis' Hist. Wallingford, Ct., 830-6; Deane's Hist. Scituate, Mass., 296; Densmore's Hartwell Gen.; Davis' Hist. Hampton, N. H., 770-5; Driver Gen., 510-2; Eaton's Hist. Thomaston, Me., II, 284; Ellis' Hist. Roxbury, Mass., 122; Emery's Rem. Newbury, Mass., 201-14; Essex Inst. Hist. Coll., XXII, 121-5; Felton's Johnson Gen. (1879); Tax's Hist. Dunstable, Mass.· 246; Gage's Hist. Rawley, Mass., 446; Gilmer's Georgians, 90, 102, 105; Gold's Hist. Cornwall, Ct., 253; Goode Gen., 174, 321; Guild's Stiles Gen., 394; Hatch's Hist. Industry, Me., 663-73; Hayward's Hist. Hancock, N. H., 682-6; Heraldic Journel, III, 43-5, 182; Holgate's Am. Gen., 22; Hubbard's Stanstead Co., Canada, 273; Hudson's Hist. Lexington, Mass., III; Hudson's Hist. Marlborough, Mass., 403-6; Johnson's Wonder Working Providence; Poole's Ed., Introduction, 140; Johnson's Gen. (1876), 85 p.; (1878) 12 p.; (1879) 16 p.; (1885) by Paxton; (1891) 27 p.; (1892) 200 p.; Kellog's White Gen., 37; Kulp's Wyoming Valley Trans.; Lapham's Hist. Norway, Me., 537; Leland Gen., 249; Littell's Passaic Valley Gen., 193-5; McKeen's Hist. Bradford, Vt., 297-305; Martin's Hist. Chester, Pa., 156; Meade's Old Families of Va.; Miller's Hist. Colchester Co., N. S., 266-81; Mitchell's Hist. Bridgewater, Mass., 204-6; Marris and Flynt Gen., 16; Morse's Gen. of Sherburn, Mass., 155; N. E. Hist. Gen. Reg., VIII, 232, 358-62; XXXIII, 60-6; 81-91; 333-9; XXVIII, 407-10; N. J. Hist. Coll., VI, Supp., 121; N. Y. Gen. Rec., XVIII, 150-2; XIX, 67-9; North's Hist. Augusta, Me., 894-6; Norton's Hist. Fitzwilliam, N. H., 618; Old Kent, Md., 50-9; Orcutt's Hist. Derby, Ct., 737-41; Orcutt's Hist. Stratford, Ct., 1226; Orcutt's Hist. Torrington, Ct., 726; Orcutt's Hist. Wolcott, Ct., 588; Paige's Hist. Cambridge, Mass., 593-5; Paige's Hist. Hardwick, Mass., 404-6; Pearson's Schnectady, N. Y. Settlers, 97; 'hœnix's Whitney Gen., I, 345; Pierce's Gorham, Me., 180; Poor's Hist. of Researches, 107; Power's Sangamon Co., Ills., 21, 410-4; Queens Co. N. Y. Hist., 248; Richmond· Va., Standard, III, 14-29; Ridlon's Harrison, Me. Settlers, 83-6; Runnell's Hist. Sanbornton Mt., II, 402-8; Salisbury Mems. (1888); Sanderson's Charlestown, N. H., 457; Savage's Gen. Dict., II, 549-59; Sewall's Woburn, Mass., 73-6; 165-8; 617; Sharp's Seymour, Ct., 200-3, 222; Shourd's Fenwick Colony, N. J., 103-10; Slaughter's St. Mark's Parish. 124; Stearn's Hist. Ashburnham, Mass., 765; Stearn's Hist. Rindge, N. H., 579; Stiles' Hist. Windsor, Ct., II, 420; Stone's Johnson Orderly Book (1882); Temple's Hist. N. Brookfield, Mass.. 650-4; Temple's Hist. Northfield, Mass., 477; Temple's Gen., 98-101; Timlow's Hist. Southington, Ct., 137; Tuttle Gen., 666-8; Vinton's Richardson Gen.. 208: Walworth's Hyde Gen., 561-4; Ward's Hist. Shrewsbury, Mass., 334-6; Washburn's Hist. Leicester. Mass.. 379; Waren's Hist. Waterford, Me.· 264; Watson's Johnson Gen. (1872); Whitmore's Copp's Hill Epitaphs; Williams' Hist. Danbury, Vt., 178; Wyman's Charlestown. Mass., I, 554-63; Young's Hist. Wayne Co., Ind., 229.

ARMS:—Gu, on a chevron, between 3 *fluer-de-lis*, arg., three escallops of the field.

CREST:—An arm, couped at the elbow, erect, holding an arrow: proper.

MOTTO.—*Deo regique debeo.*

JOHONNOT:—DANIEL JOHONNOT, Boston, a Huguenot youth, born about 1668; came from Rochelle in France, attending his uncle, Andrew Sigourney, prob. in 1686, and lived at Oxford with those other noble exiles until driven away by the Indians in 1696, when he saved, says tradition, his cousin, Susan Johnston (before men.) whose husband and three children were then killed. He married her, 1701; had Zechray, born, 1702; Susan, 1703; Daniel, 1704, died at 17 years; Andrew, 1705; Marian, 1706, and Francis, 1709. His wife died after 1731, and he died 1748.

REFERENCES:—Bridgeman's Granary, 181; Hemingway's Vt. Gaz., IV, 917-9; U. S. Hist. Reg., VI, 357-66; VII, 141-4; Porter's Eddy, Gen. Appendix; Savage's Gen. Dict.· II, 559.

JONES:—ABEL JONES, Northampton; freeman, 1690.

ABRAHAM JONES, Hull, 1657; freeman, 1673; was represcnt., 1689. In his will of 1717 he mentions wife, Sarah, and his seven sons, Benjamin, Thomas, Abraham, Josiah, Joseph, John and Ephraim; another Abraham, perhaps, was freeman, 1690.

ALEXANDER JONES, Portsmouth, 1631, who married a daughter of Thomas Walford the same, and had Alexander; was one of those sent by Mason, the patentee.

BENJAMIN JONES, Malden, 1681; perhaps is the man who married at Hingham, 1686, Susanna Beal.

BENJAMIN JONES, New Haven; married, 1687, Hannah Brown; is by same supposed to be son of dept.-gov. William, but this is doubtful.

CHARLES JONES, who came 1635; aged 21, in the Abigail from London, may be thought brother of Thomas, who came at the same time in that ship; if so, was probably of Dorchester.

CORNELIUS JONES, Stamford, 1670; called senior, so that perhaps he had son of the same name.

DAVID JONES, Dorchester; freeman, 1665; married, 1669, Sarah, daughter of Clement Topliff; had Jonathan, born 1660, died under 22 years; Eliz., bapt., 1662, died under 20 years; David, 20, bapt. 1664; John, bapt. 1667; Praise-ever, 1671; and Jonathan, again, 1683; his wife died the same year, aged 44, and he died 1694, aged 66. Perhaps he was the leader of Turner's comp. who, with a few others did not march all the way to the place of their hard service on Conn. River, but was left at Suaboag· 1676.

EDWARD JONES, Charlestown; freeman, 1631, with prefix of pespect.; was prob., therefore, in the fleet with Winthrop yet no more is known of him but that he was there in 1636, prob., and by wife, Ann, daughter of George Griggs of Boston, had Mary, bapt. 1637; Eliz., born 1643. His widow married Robert Latimore.

GRIFFIN, or GRIFFITH JONES, Springfield, 1646; freeman, 1649; had Mercy, born 1647; Hepzehah, 1649; Samuel, 1651; Ebenezer, 1653; Thomas, 1655; Griffith, 1658, died soon; Griffith, again, perhaps, 1660; Experience, 1662: Peletiah, 1664: beside Benoni, whose date is not found. and died in 1677.

HENRY JONES, Lynn, 1642.

ISAAC JONES, Casco; had lands on Presumscut River,

1681. Willis thinks he came from Charlestown that year and was at Falmouth.

ISAAC JONES, Boston; by wife, Mary, had Mary, born 1687; and John, 1691.

JACOB JONES, New Haven; died, 1675.

JAMES JONES, freeman of Mass., 1644; may have belonged to Roxbury, or Charlestown, or Boston, or other town after that date, where the surname was common.

JEFFREY JONES, Southold, L. I., 1664; was of Salem, 1668.

JENKIN JONES, Dover, 1666; married Abigail, daughter of John Heard.

JOHN JONES, Concord; came in the Defence from London, 1635 to Boston, with wife, Sarah, aged 34, and children, Sarah, 15; John, 11; Ruth, 7; Theophilus, 3; Rebecca, 2; and Eliz., 1-2. He was ordained 1637, pastor to the church gathering of year preceding; had Eliphalet, morn 1641; in 1644 went with many of his parish to Fairfield. Perhaps the wife and Theophilus died at C. He died early in 1665.

JOHN JONES, Providence, 1646; was in the list of freemen, 1655, and swore alleg. to the King, 1666. His daughter, Mary, married James Greene.

JOHN JONES, Portsmouth; prob. came in the Susan and Ellen, 1635, aged 20, from London; had Francis, Mary, Nathaniel, James and John, and died about 1667. Belkn., I, 28.

JOHN JONES, New Haven, died, 1657. Whether he had wife or children is unknown.

JOHN JONES, Cambridge, 1648; perhpas was the youth of 15, passenger in the Abigail, 1635; by wife, Dorcas, had Samuel, born 1648; removed to Concord, then had Ephraim, 1650; Eliz., 1652; Joseph, 1654; John, 1656; Dorcas, 1659; and Rebecca, 1663; and, perhaps, William, who died unmarried, 1691, at C. He was freeman, 1650, and died, 1673.

JOHN JONES, Boston; by wife, Eliz., had John, born 1665; William, 1668, and Jotham, 1672.

JOHN JONES, Swanzey; buried, 1675; killed, no doubt, by the Indians on the first day of Philip's War.

JOHN JONES, Charlestown, whose name is by Frothingham, 183, misprinted John James; by wife Rebecca, daughter, it is thought, of Manns Sally, had Rebecca, bapt. 1672; John, 1673, died young; Thomas, 1674; John, again, 1677; and Catharine, 1680. In 1681, says Willis, was at Falmouth, yet came back to C. and had bapt. Rebecca, 1688, and Sarah, 1690. May have been brother of Isaac of Casco.

JOSEPH JONES, Hingham, had his house burnt by the Indians, 1676. He had married at Weymouth, 1657, Patience, daughter of Thomas Little. One, Joseph, was a soldier in Gallup's comp. in the sad expedit. of Phip's, 1690 to conquer Canada.

LEWIS JONES, Roxbury, with wife, Ann, who died 1680 aged 72, or 78, is found among members of the church about 1640; had Phoebe, born 1646, died few months later by a scald, says church record; he had elder child, Lydia, perhaps born in England; also Josiah, born 1643; and Shubael, 1651. This last was probably infirm in mind. He was long at Watertown, and there died, 1684.

LEWIS JONES, Saybrook; had Margaret, born 1667; Catharine, 1671; Jonathan, 1673; Samuel, 1676; and Ephraim, 1685.

MATTHEW JONES, Boston; by wife, Ann, had Rebecca, born 1645; Matthew; and Sarah, about 1660; removed to New London where Sarah married John Prenitce.

MORGAN JONES, Newton, L. I., 1680; son of John of Bassaleg, near Newport, Co. Monmouth; bred at Jesus College, Oxford; left a place in Glamorganshire for the Uniformity act of 1662, and might, therefore, from other non-conformists expect better treatment than to be called a tanner from Wales,, of whose deception in evangelis. at Killingworth and Branford, indignant story is given in Magn., VII, 34. Riker's Hist. of Newtown, 99-115, overthrows all the credit of Mather's relation with great modesty.

PHILIP JONES, buried at Boston, 1684; as Sewall tells, was prob. only transient.

RALPH JONES, Barnstable; married, 1650, Mary, daughter of Capt. Matthew Fuller; had Shubael, born 1654; Jedediah, 1656; John, 1659; besides 5 others whose names are not found.

RICE JONES, Boston; by wife, Ann, had Matthew, born 1651; Sarah, 1654, died 1661.

RICHARD JONES, Dorchester, 1635; died, 1641, leaving widow, Alice, and children, Timothy, Samuel, Eliz. and Mary. The widow married John Kingsley.

RICHARD JONES, Hingham, 1636; has still descend. there, unless Lincoln, 44, has given this name by mistake for Robert.

RICHARD JONES, Farmington; after one of the first settlers at Haddam, died, 1670; had David, born 1663, who died early after his father; Eliz., 1666; Mary, 1668, and Patience, posthum., 1671.

ROBERT JONES, Hingham, 1637; removed to Rehoboth, 1644, back in a few years to H.; had Robert, born, possibly, in Eng.; Ephraim, 1649, at H.; John, 1652; Joseph, 1658; and Thomas, 1659. Deane, 298. He is prob. man called son-in-law in will of John Biddle, 1653, whose daughter, Ann, was his wife. One, Robert, taxed at Dover, 1657 and 62, may not be easily found elsewhere.

ROBERT JONES, Salisbury; married Joan, daughter of William Osgood; had William, born 1659; Robert, 1660; Joseph, 1664; Eliz., 1666; and Mary, 1668.

ROGER JONES, a soldier of Turner's comp., 1676; therefore belonging to Boston or Charlestown, prob.

STEPHEN JONES, Dover; freeman, 1672; married, 1664, Eliz. Field. In the Indian war his house was a garrison defended with success in 1694.

TEAGUE JONES, Yarmouth, 1653; had Teague, Jeremiah, Joseph, and Samuel, perhaps, but dates are not seen.

THOMAS JONES, Dorchester, 1635; came that year, aged 40, with wife, Ellen, 36; Isaac, 8; Esther, 6; Thomas, 3; and Sarah, 3 mos.; besides Mary, 30 years, who may have been a sister, all embarked in the Abigail from London, says the custom house record; prob. son, Thomas, died on passage. Here he had Hannah, 1636; and Rebecca, 1642; was freeman, 1639; selectman, 1644, and many years more, represent., 1638, 9 and 49; died, 1667.

THOMAS JONES, Newberry, 1637; removed to Hampton 1639; by wife Abagail had Susanna born that year. He may be the freeman of 1652 at Kittery.

THOMAS JONES, Hingham, 1638; freeman, 1646; had Joseph, prob. born in Eng., and, possibly, Benjamin, also, as he was born 1637; Thomas, 1640; and prob. others. Deane, 298. Perhaps this is the man who came in the Confidence, 1638, from Southampton, called himself a tailor, aged 36, with wife, Ann, and 4 children under 10 years, whose names are not given, and 2 servants. He was of Caversham, in south part of Oxfordshire; in the same ship was a William Jones under 11 years. This Thomas may, in his later years, have lived at Hull, and married at Boston, 1657, widow Abigail Elithrop.

THOMAS JONES, Charlestown; butcher; came in the Mary Ann from Yarmouth, 1637, aged 25, being from Elsing in Co. Norfolk; had wife, Abigail, and died 1666. His will names daughter, Susanna, widow of William Goose; he left 2 dwellings and a slaughter house. The widow married a Chadwell.

THOMAS JONES, Gloucester; by wife, Mary, daughter of Richard North, had Thomas ,born 1640; Nathaniel and Ruth, twins, 1645; Samuel, 1647; Ephraim, 1649; Benjamin, 1651; Remember, 1653; removed, 1651, to New London, back same year and died, 1671, unless this date belonged to the Thomas, Jr., and 1672 be the father's. The widow died, 1682.

THOMAS JONES, Taunton; had Lydia, born 1659; Thomas, 1662; Joseph, 1664; and Hannah, perhaps, 1657, or else 1675.

THOMAS JONES, Concord, removed to Fairfield; there freeman, 1669; represent., 1685; may have been brother of Rev. John.

THOMAS JONES, Huntington, L. I., 1664; may possibly be same as preceding, but prob. not. See Trumbull Col. Rec., I, 428, with II, 83.

THOMAS JONES, Guilford, 1639; by wife, Mary, who died 1650, had Sarah; Samuel; Nathaniel; and Thomas-born 1650, died one month after the mother. He soon after married widow Carter, went home and died in England, 1654, of small-pox.

THOMAS JONES, Boston; married, 1654, Lydia, daughter of Robert Saunderson.

THOMAS JONES, Springfield, 1678.

THOMAS JONES, Charlestown, not son of Thomas of the same; was, perhaps, a householder in 1678; died, 1686, in 35th year. His will shows that he was a mariner; had mother, Catharine, sister, Catharine and brother, William; prob, no wife or children.

TIMOTHY JONES, Gloucester; by wife, Eliz., had Thomas, born 1680.

WILLIAM JONES, Cambridge, 1635; may be the inhabitant of Charlestown in 1658, a mason.

WILLIAM JONES, Portsmouth, 1640; in 1644 lived at that part named Bloody Point. Belkn., I, 28.

WILLIAM JONES, Scituate; died, 1672, as not mentioned by Deane, may have only been transient.

WILLIAM JONES, New Haven; idly said to be son of that Col. John, the regicide, executed 1660, who had, late

in life, many years after the birth of this William, married second or fifth sister of famous Oliver Cromwell, widow of Roger Whetstone, by the Protector called to be one of the lords or "other house," as he termed in contempt of the work of his own hands, chiefly was it so surmised, prob. because he came from England shortly before the suffering of his supposed father. True it is that he arrived in Boston from London (where he was born, 1624, and had been a lawyer), 1660, in the same ship with the celebrated regicides, Wholley and Goffe and brought sons William and Nathaniel, born to him by first wife. But he had motive sufficient to come wtihout the vain fear of being pointed at for a son of that tool of Oliver, because in virtue of a marriage contract of 1659, he, by the style of W. J. of the parish of St. Martin's in the Field, Co. Middlesex, had married Hannah Eaton of the parish of St. Andrew, Holborn, London, spinster, youngest daughter of Gov. Theophilus Eaton, and was well inclined to take care of her estate at New Haven; brought a child, Hannah, the offspring of that union, born same season of the embarkation; had there Theophilus, 1661, died in 3 days; Sarah, 1662; Eliz., 1664, but bapt. by the name of Mary; Samuel, 1666, died at 6 mos.; John, 1667, H. C., 1690; Deodat, March, 1670, died next month; Isaac, 1671; Abigail and Rebecca, twins, 1673, died both in 5 days; and Susanna, 1675; of Caleb, by Increase Mather, called a son, we may well doubt, as he tells of his death at sea, 1676. He was of good talents, a very active public servant, assist. and dep. gov. of the col. of New Haven, and after assist., 1678 of the United Col. of Conn.; died, 1706.

REFERENCES:—Am. Ancestry, I, 43; II, 64; III, 96, 124, 165, 171; IV, 33; V, 55, 140, 209; VI, 76, 133, 205; VII, 23, 73, 190, 268; VIII, 190; Andrews' Hist. New Britain, Ct., 311; Austin's Ancestral Dict., 33; Babson's Hist. Gloucester, Mass., 107; Ballon's Hist. Milford. Mass., 846-60; Bangor Hist. Mag., III, 57; IV, 55-7; Barry's Hist. Farmington, Mass., 304-7; Blake's Hist. Franklin, Mass. 255; Bond's Hist. Watertown, Mass., 310-22; Bullock Gen.; Bunker's L. Cent., 106; Densmore's Hartwell Gen.; Draper's Hist. I. Gen., 227; Butler's Hist. Farmington, Me., 515; Champion Gen.; Chapman Gen., 52, 220; Chapman's Trowbridge Gen., 52; Clapp's Jones Hill, Dorchester, Mass., 1-8; Cleveland's Hist. Gates Co., N. Y., 671; Clute's Hist. Staten Island, N. Y., 395; Cooley's Trenton, N. J. Gen., 150-2; Carlin's North Yarmouth, Me.; Cushman's Hist. Sheepscott, Me., 394; Davis' Hist. Reading, Vt., 139; Davis' Hist. Wallingford, Ct., 886-8; Deane's Hist. Scituate, Mass., 297; Dennyside, Me. Cent., 106; Densmore's Hartwell Gen.; Draper's Hist. Spencer, Mass., 214; Dyer's Hist. Plainfield, Mass.; Eaton's Annals Warren, Me., 559-69; Eaton's Hist. Thomaston, Me., II, 285; Freeman's Cape Cod, Mass., II, 208, 476; French's Hist. Turner, Me., 55; Goode Gen., 36, 205, 232, 236; Goodwin's Gen. Notes, 129-36; Green's Kentucky Farms; Hayward's Hist. Hancock, N. H., 686; Hazen's Hist. Billerica, Mass., 79; Hill's Old Barnstable, Mass. (1878); Hinman's Conn. Settlers, 1st ed., 179; Hollister's Hist. Pawlet, Vt., 208; Howell's Southampton, N. Y., 335-8; Hudson's Hist. Lexington, Mass., 280; Hughes Gen., 233; Huntington's Stamford Ct., Settlers, 38; Jameson's Hist. Medway, Mass., 496-8; Jenkins' Hist. Gwynedd, Pa., 367, 378; Jones (Ipswich) by Caldwell (1888), 7 p.; Jones (of Queens Co., N. Y.) (1849), 99 p.; Jones (of Virginia) Gen. (1891), 295 p.; Jones (of Roxbury) by Trask (1878), 75 p.; Jones'

New York in Rev. War, I, 58-67; Jones' Stockbridge, Mass., 148-50; Joslin's Hist. Poultney, Vt., 285-7; Kidder's Hist. of Ipswich, N. H., 393; Kingsman's N. Bridgewater, Mass., 549; Lancester's Hist. Gilmanton, N. H., 273; Lapham's Hist. Paris, Me., 647; Leonard's Hist. Dublin, N. H., 355; Little's Passaic Valley Gen., 186; Livermore's Hist. Wilton, N. H., 422; Locke Gen., 34, 64, 117-22; Meade's Old Fams. of Virginia.; Morse's Gen. of Sherborn, Mass., 156; Morse Mem. Appendix, 66; N. E. Hist. Gen. Reg., VI, 260, 279-82; XIII, 34; XLIV, 158-67; XLVII, 470-2; N. Y. Hist. Soc. Coll., New Series, II, 490; Orcutt's Hist. Stratford, Ct., 1227; Paige's Gen., 100; Paige's Hist. Cambridge, Mass., 595; Palmer and Trimble Gen., III, 22; Paxton's Marshall Gens., 145; Penn Mag. of Hist., IV, XIII, 180; Phœnix's Whitney Gen., I, 193; Pierce's Hist. Gorham, Me., 179; Potter's Old Fams. Concord, Mass.; Power's Hist. Sangamon Co., Ills., 414-20; Queen's Co., N. Y, Hist,, 552-4; Richmond, Va. Standard, II, 44, 52; III, 4, 6, 44; Runnell's Hist. Sanbarnton, N. H., II, 410; Savages' Gen. Dict., II, 560-8; Schenck's Hist. Fairfield, Ct., 387-91; Lecomb's Hist. Amherst, N. H., 376; Sedwick's Hist. Sharon, Ct., 94; Shuttuck's Hist. Concord, Mass., 376; Slaughter's Bristol Parish, Va., 138; Slaughter's St. Mark's Parish, 191; Stearn's Hist. Ashburnham, Mass., 767-72; Stearn's Hist. Rindge, N. H., 580; Stiles' Hist. Windsor, Ct., II, 421; Strong Gen., 159-62; Swift's Barnstable Fams., II, 106-12; Thayer Mem. (1835), 89; Temple's Hist. N. Brookfield, Mass., 654; Thomas Fam. of Maryland, 101; Timlow's Hist. Southington, Ct., 138-43; Vinton's Giles Gen., 278; Walker Gen., 40; Washington, N. H., Hist., 494-507; Wheeler's Eminent N. Carolinians, 202; Wheeler's Hist. N. Carolina, 188; Whitman Gen., 11-3, 202-8; Whitmore's Copps' Hill Epitaphs; Wilkesbarre Hist. Rec., V, 6; Wyman's Charlestown, Mass., Gens., 563-6; Young's Hist. Chautauqua Co., N. Y., 565; Young's Hist. Wayne Co., Ind., 180.

JORDAN, JOURDAINE, or JOURDAN:—FRANCIS JORDAN, Ipswich, 1634; married, 1635, Jane Wilson; had Sarah, born, 1636; Hannah, 1638; Mary, 1639, died in 4 mos.; Mary, again, 1641; Lydia, 1643; and Deborah, 1645; made his will, 1678, in which he names his wife, Jane, and a grandchild, Mary Simson.

JAMES JORDAN, Dedham; died, 1655; had son, Thomas; daughter, Mary, and Ann.

JOHN JORDAN, Guilford, 1639; signed the covenant of that year by his name, Jurden; was there in 1668; perhaps died next year.

JOHN JORDAN, Plymouth, 1643; who hay have been father of that Jehosabeth that married, 1665, John Robbins of Bridgewater; at least there had Baruch born 1651, may have removed to Portsmouth.

ROBERT JORDAN, Casco; came as a preacher before 1641; prob. having deacon's or priest's orders from Episc.; author; married Sarah, only daughter of John Winter, the great leader of all that coast, and slid easily into civil life, ,but was not cautious enough to conciliate the Mass. chief men who imprisoned him, 1654, but in 1658 he was sworn freeman of this jurisdiction. His est. was on the Spurwink, now Scarborough. In the Indian hostilities, 1675, he withdrew to Portsmouth and there died, 1679, aged 68. His wife and children, John, Robert, Dominicus, Jedediah, Samuel and Jeremiah, are will carefully provided for. Willis, 154, 238.

STEPHEN JORDAN, Ipswich, 1634; came that year in the Mary and John; removed to Newburg; died, 1670, leaving wife, Susanna, who died, 1673, and 2 daughters who had married Robert Cross and John Andrews, both at Ipswich.

THOMAS JORDAN, Guilford, 1650; came from same part of Kent, Eng.; went home in 1651, and was of distinct. there. A daughter married Andrew Leete.

THOMAS JORDAN, Rehoboth; married, 1674, Esther Hall, daughter of Edward of the same.

REFERENCES:—Am. Ancestry, II, 65; V, 122; VI, 36; VIII, 48; Bangor, Me., Hist. Maj., IV, 71; Collins Hist. Hillsdale, N. Y., 76; Corliss' No. Yarmouth, Me.; Eaton's Annals Warren, Me., 562; Eaton's Hist. Thomaston, Me.; II, 286-8; Gilmer's Georgian's, 144; Jordan Gen. (1882), 488 p.; Lapham's Hist. Bethel, Me., 569; Lapham's Hist. Norway, Me., 538-41; Me. Hist. Soc. Coll., I, 153-6; Mellick Story of an Old Farm, 675; Neill's Virginia Carolorum, 282; Paige's Hist. Hardwick, Mass., 406; Savage's Gen. Dict., II, 568; Walker Gen., 153; Wheeler's Hist. Brunswick, Me., 841.

JOSE:—CHRISTOPHER JOSE, Portsmouth; had lived at Isle of Shoals, where he was constable, 1656; by wife, Jane, had Richard, born, 1660; Thomas, 1662; Joanna, 1664; Margaret, or Mary, 1666; John, 1668; Jane, 1670; Samuel, 1672; and Mary, 1674; and he died, 1678.

REFERENCES:—Wentworth Gen., 298

JOSSELYN, JOCELYN, JOSELIN, or JOSLIN:—ABRAHAM JOSSELYN, Scarborough; of the grand jury, 1658; was, perhaps, brother of Henry, Esquire, and John, the traveller; but whether he went home or died here, is unknown.

HENRY JOSSELYN, Scarborough, son of Sir Thomas of Co. Kent; came, perhaps, as early as 1631; certainly was here in 1634, but this was in employment of Mason, patentee of N. H., after whose death he engaged under Sir F. Gorges, and most faithful was his servant from 1636; freeman, 1658; he married Margaret, widow of Capt. Thomas Cammock; was for a long time the second person in authority in Maine; in 1665 of course he enjoyed the favor of the royal commissioners, but again became loyal to the usurp. governm. of Mass. In 1676 he was subdued by the Indians, and prob. went to the westward; but no more is known. See Williamson, Sullivan, 369, supposed that he went to Plymouth, and Willis, 128 followed that mistake. The indefatigable historian of Portland discovered that he was at Pemaquid in 1682, and died early next year.

JOHN JOSSELYN, Scarborough, the well-known author; brother of the first Henry, came in the Nicholas, chartered by Edward Tyng; arrived from London at Boston, 1638; made a short excursion to S. to see his brother; went home in the Fellowship from Boston and reached Bideford, 1639. His next visit brought him to Boston 1663, whence, after spending a few weeks, he went to his brother at S. and remained 8 years. He went home and published in 1672, his book, "New Eng. Rarities," more curious than trustworthy.

RICHARD JOSSELYN, Saybrook, a freeman of Conn., 1669; spelt Joseland.

THOMAS JOSSELYN, Hingham; a husbandman, aged 43; with wife, Rebecca, 43, and children, Rebecca, 18; Dorothy, 11; Nathaniel, 8; Eliz., 6; and Mary, 1; beside Eliz. Ward, a servant, 38; came from London, 1635, in the Increase; was among grantees of Sudbury, 1640; not resident; but after some years removed to Lancaster, where he signed the civil compact, 1654; having, perhaps, for a short time lived at Boston; at Lancaster he died, 1661.

REFERENCES:—Barry's Hanover, 335-47; Deane's Hist. Scituate, Mass., 299; N. E. Reg., II, 306-10; XIV, 15; XL, 290-4; Savage's Gen. Dict., II, 570-2; Spooner Gen., I, 430-4; Stiles' Josselyn Gen. (1868), 126 pp.

ARMS:—Chequy, gu, and az., on a fess of the first, an armulet, or.

JOY:—ISAAC JOY, Guilford; died 1674; was prob. only transient.

JACOB JOY, Fairfield; removed to Killingworth: married, 1672, Eliz. Wellman, who was daughter of William Spencer of Hartford, and widow of William W. of New London and Killingworth; had Deborah, born 1673; Jacob, 1675; Walter, 1677; Mary, 1680.

THOMAS JOY, .Boston, 1638; a house carpenter; by 1640, bapt., 1641; John, 1641; Thomas, 1643; both prob. died young; Joseph, 1645; Ephraim, 1647; in the year 1646 was arrested, and kept 4 or 5 days in irons, as a too ardent lover of liberty; soon removed to Hingham; had there more children—Sarah, Eliz., and Ruth; freeman, 1665; artillery comp. the same year, and died, 1678.

WALTER JOY, Milford, 1650.

REFERENCES:—Austin's R. I. Gen. Dict., 115; Bangor Me. Hist. Mag., IV, 74; Dyer's Hist. Plainfield, Mass.; Joy Gen. (1876), 37 pp.; Schenck's Hist. Fairfield, Ct., 391.

JOYCE, or JOICE:—JOHN JOYCE, Lynn; removed, 1637, to Sandwich, thence to Yarmouth in 1643, being in list of those able to bear arms that year in both towns; had Abigail, 1646 at Y., where she died, 1666. His widow Dorothy died, 1680. In his will names only Hosea, Mary and Dorcas.

WALTER JOYCE, Marshfield, 1667. Winsor.

WILLIAM JOYCE, Boston, who died, 1648; was only transient; had wife in London.

REFERENCE:—Savage's Gen. Dict., II, 573.

JOYLIFFE:—JOHN JOYLIFFE, Boston, 1656; married, 1657, Ann, widow and extrix. of Robert Knight, who had also been widow and extrix. of Thomas Cromwell, the wealthy privateersman; had only child Hannah, born, 1660. He was freeman, 1673; many years a selectman; one of the patriots in 1689 who put Andros in prison; town recorder in 1691, and was made by Increase Mather one of the council in the charter of William and Mary; died, 1702. Hutch., I, 374 and II, 14.

JAYNES:—JOHN JAYNES, aged 18; emb. at London, 1635 for N. E. in the Hopewell, Capt. Bundock; but no more is known.

REFERENCES:—Meade's Old Fams. of Va.; Richmond, Va., Standard, II, 34.

JUDD:—ROGER JUDD, Boston; freeman, 1690; by wife, Eliz., who died, 1720, aged 69, had Jonathan; Eliz., born ,1678; David, 1680, died young; and David, again, 1682, bapt. at O. S. church with Jonathan and Eliz., 1684; Ebenezer, 1686; and Experience, 1690.

THOMAS JUDD, Cambridge, 1634; freeman, 1636; had 2 or 3 children born at C.; removed to Hartford before 1639, and was of orig. propr.; had there John, 1640; Benjamin, 1642; removed, 1645 to Farmington, prob. after birth of Mary, about 1644; had there, Ruth, bapt., 1647; Philip, 1649; and Samuel, 1651; or, perhaps, 1653. Was represent., 1647, and often after until 1679; one of the founders of the church, 1652, and soon one of its deacons. Of the three eldest children, we judge Thomas, born about 1638, the youngest; may have been born at H., while we are ignorant of the 2 elder, which was the first born, Thomas or Eliz., or whether he had married when he left England; yet it is prob. that he brought wife, though her name is not seen; and it may be that one child was born before the father came; later in life his wife died and he removed to Northampton; there married, 1679, Clemence, widow of Thomas Mason, and died 1688; perhaps near 80, or quite. The widow died, 1696.

REFERENCES:—Andrew's New Britain, Ct., 140-8; Bronsan's Hist. Waterbury, Ct., 508-13; Goode Gen.; 290; Jones' Gen., 80; Judd Gen. (1856), 112 pp.; Judd's Hist. Hadley, Mass., 520-2; Kellog's White Gen., 44-71; N. E. Hist. and Gen. Reg., XIV, 288; Strong Gen., 275-81; Timlow's Hist. Southington, Ct., 115-8.

JUDKIN, or JUDKINS:—JOB JUDKIN, Boston, 1658; had, by wife, Sarah, who died 1657, Job, born 1637, died soon; Samuel, 1638, bapt. 1641; as was also on same day son Job, born 2 mos. before; Joel, 1643; and Sarah, 1645.

SAMUEL JUDKIN, Hingham; married, 1667, Eliz., daughter of John Leavitt; had Samuel, born same year; the father fell in Turner's comp., 1676; the son perished with many of his townsmen by small-pox, 1690, in Philip's expedition against Quebec.

THOMAS JUDKIN, Gloucester, 1651; married, 1665, widow, Ann Howard; died, 1695, aged 66.

REFERENCES:—Babson's Gloucester, 109; Lapham's Norway, Me., 541; Savage's Gen. Dict., II, 575.

JUDSON:—SAMUEL JUDSON, Dedham, 1646, or earlire. Savage remarks that his widow, Bridget, died that year, according to church records; but we presume that it is error for wife, as he states that Samuel married Mary, widow of Henry Aldrich. Mary had 2 sons by A. and 3 daughters—Mary, Sarah and Esther by Samuel. She afterward married John Hayward of the same.

WILLIAM JUDSON. Concord, 1635; came the year preceding with wife and three sons; removed, 1639, to Hartford, yet seems not to have been an original propr. nor long there, for in 1644 he was at Stratford, and engaged in 1644 there to obtain aid for the infant colony at Cambridge. A few years later he removed to New Haven, where his wife, Grace, died, 1659, and he married, next year, Eliz., widow of Benjamin Wilmot· and died 1661; or, as Goodwin says, 1662. His will only names son, Joseph, born 1619; and Jeremiah· 1621; but he had another son Joshua, of whom we know nothing as to place of birth or date.

REFERENCES:— Am. Ancestry, I, 43; II, 65; V, 209; IX, 24; Deacon's Stoddard Gen.; Goodwin's Gen. Notes· 137-44; Goodwin's Foote Gen., 275; Goodwin's Olcott Gen., 32; Judson Chart. (1860) 15x20 in.; Sprague's Hist. Gloversville, N. Y., 121; Timlow's Hist. Southington, Ct., 143-6;

JUELL. See JEWELL.

JUNKINS. See JENKINS.

JUPE:—GRACE JUPE, .Boston; sister of Robert Keayne, had Anthony, Mary, and Benjamin.

JUPP:—JAMES JUPP, Norwalk, 1672; was in Philip's war· for serving in which the town voted him grant of land; married, 1683, Ann, daughter of Thomas Hickens of Stamford.

K.

KATES. See CATES.

KATHERICK. See CATHRICK.

KEAIS:—SAMUEL KEAIS, New Hampshire; married, 1696, Mary, widow of John Haddy; had Samuel, born 1697, and William, 1699.

KEATS:—RICHARD KEATS, Boston, 1677; bricklayer.

KEAYNE:—BENJAMIN KEAYNE, Boston, 1638; only son of Robert· born in London, came with his father, freeman 1639, artillery co. 1638, married before 1639, Sarah daughter of Gov. Thomas Dudley had only child Ann, lived some short time at Lynn, was a Major, went home in disgust with his wife about 1645; and repud. her, died 1668. She had been disciplined 1646 for irregular prophesy and was excom. in 1647, and sadly degraded, but was made the wife of one Pacey.

JOHN KEAYNE, Hingham, died, 1650, of whom no more is known· but that his name appears sometimes Cane.

ROBERT KEAYNE, Boston, merchant of the Merch. Taylor's comp. of London, came in the Defence, 1635, aged 40, with wife, Ann, 36, and a son Benjamin, 16 (ment. before). In 1624 he had been one of the undertakers, who encouraged the Plymouth Pilgrims; he was freeman, 1636; represent., 1638 and 9; one of the founders of Ar-

tilery comp.; died, 1656· and his widow married Samuel Cole, 1660. William, Boston, had wife, Agnes, who joined the church, 1646.

KEBY, or KEBBY. See KIBBY.

KEDALL, KEDELL, or KEEDEL:—A strange name of 2 maids that married very reput. at Watertown, viz., Mary, 1655, Thomas Whitney; and Bethia· 1666, Theophilus Phillips; and long and large inquiries have been followed as to their origin.

KEDEN:—BENJAMIN KEDEN, Boston, 1661; servant of Rice Jones.

KEELER:—RALPH KEELER, Hartford; had a lot in 1640, though not orig. propr.; had there Rebecca, born 1651; and Eliz., who may have been born at Norwalk; besides an elder daughter who married Thomas Moorhouse. He was freeman, 1668; had John, Ralph, Samuel, and Jonah, who died 1676; and died 1672. He had married Sarah· widow of Henry Whelpley.

WALTER KEELER, Norwalk, 1651; perhaps a nonentity.

KEELEY:—EDWARD KEELEY, New Haven; a propr. in 1685; may be he who came from London, 1635, in the Hopewell, Capt. Bundocke, aged 14.

KEEN, or KEAN:—ARTHUR KEEN, Boston; died, 1687. His will mentions wife, Jane; son, John; and daughter· Sarah Pierce, who was wife of William.

JAMES KEEN, Braintree, 1645; was Capt.

JOHN KEEN, Boston, 1662; mariner, and in a few years innholder; may be that passengr. in the Confidence from Southampton, 1638, aged 17, with Martha, 60, who may have been his mother; Eliz., Martha· Josias, and Sarah, prob., his brother and sisters.

JOSIAH KEEN, Duxbury, married Hannah, daughter of John Dingley; had John, bapt. 1661; Josiah; Matthew; and Hannah.

WILLIAM KEEN, Salem, 1638; of which Felt says, he had in that year a grant of land, and nobody else tells anything.

REFERENCES:—Am. Ancestry, V, 22; VII, 168; Eaton's Hist Thomaston· Me., 290-2; Mitchell's Hist. Bridgewater, Mass., 206; Penn. Mag. of Hist., I, 3; II, 325-35; III, 334-41; IV., 242-5; 343-60; 444-500; V, 85, 101, 217-9.

KEENY, KENY, or KEENEY:—ALEXANDER KEENY, Wethersfield; freeman· 1667; died, 1680, leaving Alexander, 18; Thomas, and Sarah, twins, 16; Joseph, 14; Lydia, 11; Ebenezer, 8; and Richard, 6. His wife, Alice, died, 1683.

WILLIAM KEENY, Gloucester; by wife· Agnes, had Susanna; Mary; and John, born about 1640; removed to New London about 1651; in 1662 was about 61; and his wife, 63; he died 1675.

REFERENCES:—Cunnabell Gen., 90; Orcutt's Hist. Derby, Ct., 742-4; Young's Hist. Warsaw, N. Y., 285.

KEEP:—JOHN KEEP, Springfield, 1660; freeman, 1669; married, 1663, Sarah Leonard; had Sarah, born 1666; Eliz., 1668, died young; Samuel, 1670; Hannah, 1673; and Jabez, who was, with his mother, taken by the Indians, 1676, when the father was killed as were the mother and son soon after.

REFERENCES:—Hodgman's. Westford,. Mass.· 456; Longmeadow, Mass., Cent., 70-3; Temple's Hist. N. Brookfield, Mass., 657-8.

KEESE:—JOHN KEESE, Portsmouth, R. I.; married, 1682, Ann, daughter of Shadrach Manton; had Alice, born 1683; William, 1685; Patience, 1690; John, 1693; Shadrach, 1695; Ann, 1698; and he died, 1700.

REFERENCES:—Austin's R. I. Gen. Dict., 115; Hurlbut Gen., 441.

KEET:—FRANCIS KEET, Northampton; had come from east part of the colony on service in Philip's war; was at the Falls fight· 1676; married Hannah, daughter of John French, had Francis, John, and, perhaps, Thomas.

KEETCH:—JOHN KEETCH, Boston; by wife, Hannah, had Mary, who died 1656· says the record.

KEISAR:—See KEYSAR.

KEITH:—JAMES KEITH; first minister of Bridgewater; bred at one of the coll. in Aberdeen; came about 1662; was ordained early in 1664, undr 21 years of age; died, 1719, aged 76; his first wife was Susanna, prob. daughter of deacon Samuel Edson; and his second, 1707, was Mary Williams of Taunton, widow of Thomas; and all his children were by the first; one daughter· Susanna, probably married Jonathan Howard, 1689, at T. Progeny of his sons James, Joseph, Samuel, Timothy, John, and Josiah, is scattered through the U. S. Had also daughters, Margaret and Mary.

REFERENCES:—Am. Ancestry, VI, 32; IX, 113; Child Gen., 475-8; Crane's Rawson Gen., 176; Eaton's Hist. Thomaston, Me., II, 292; Green's Kentucky Fams.; Hudson's Hist. Lexington, Mass., 280; Keith Gen. (1873), 24 pp.; (1889)· 115 pp.; Leland Gen., 63-5; Paxten's Marshall Gen., 27; Pierce's Grafton, Mass., 509-12; Spooner Gen., I, 208-11; Whitman Gen., 126, 333-5.

KELLEN, KILLIN, or KELLING:—JAMES KELLEN, Charlestown; married, 1679, Hannah Trarice· perhaps daughter of John; had James; Samuel, 1682; and Margaret, 1684.

KELLOG:—DANIEL KELLOG, Norwalk, 1655; by 1st wife (name unknown), had Mary, 1663; Rachel, 1664. as second wife he had Bridget, 1665; daughter of John Bouton; by her had Sarah, 1666; Eliz. 1668· who died young; Daniel 1671; Samuel 1674; Lidia 1676; Benjamin and Joseph twins, 1678;of whom Joseph died before 1703; was rep. 1670, and 6 or 7 times after; and died 1688.

JOSEPH KELLOG Farmington, weaver, freeman 1654, had John, bapt. 1656, and Martin; removed 1659 to Boston had Edward 1660; next year sold his prop. in B. and went to Hadley; where his first wife Susanna died 1666; and he married next year, Abigail daughter of Stephen Terry, besides these children he had Samuel 1662; Joanna 1664; and Sarah 1666; all by 1st; and 2nd wife had Stephen 1668; Nathaniel 1669; Abigail 1671; Eliz. 1673; Prudence 1675; Ebenezer 1677; Jonathan 1679; Daniel 1682; died 2 years; Joseph 1684; and Ephraim 1687; died young. All the daugthers were married. In the Falls fight he was lieut. and command. the men of H· He died, 1707, then having 14 adult children.

NATHANIEL KELLOG, Farmington, 1653; had been one of the sett. at Hartford, 1640, though not original propr.; had, perhaps, Eliz., born 1652; Joseph, 1653; and Nathaniel, bapt. 1654, who all died early, and he died after short residence at F.

SAMUEL KELLOG, Hatfield; perhaps brother of the 1st Joseph; married, 1664, Sarah, widow of Nathaniel Gunn, daughter of Robert Day; had Samuel, born 1669; Nathaniel, 1671; Ebenezer, 1674; and Joseph, 1676; who was killed with his mother, 1677, by the Indians, who carried young Samuel off to Canada, whence he came back. He maried, 1679, Sarah Root of Westfield; had John, born 1680; and Thomas, 1681; who both died at H. unmarried, over 70 years of age, and Sarah, 1684.

REFERENCES:—Am. Ancestry, IV, 169; VI, 66, 85; IX, 192; Barry's Hist. Framingham, Mass., 307; Chapin Gen.; Oweight Gen., 309; Eaton's Warren, Me., 403; Eaton's Thomaston, Me., 298; Kellog Meeting (1858), 8 p; (1860) 8 p.; Nash. Gen., 85; Savage's Gen. Dict., III, 4-6; Sedgwick's Hist. Sharon, Ct., 95; Temple's Hist. No. Brookfield, Mass., 659; Thayer Mem., 61.

KELLOND:—THOMAS KELLOND, Boston: merchant; recent. from England; had warrant. 1661, from Gov. Endicott, for pursuit that was fruitless of the regicides, Whalley and Goffe; married Abigail, daughter of Capt. Thomas Hawkins, widow of Samuel Moore; had Susanna, born 1665; John, 1667, died young; John, again, 1669, died young; Thomas, 1670. died young; Samuel, 1671; Eliz., 1673; Thomas, again, 1674; John, again, 1678; and Richard, 1681; died, 1686; and his widow married 3rd husband, Hon. John Foster, whom she outlived.

THOMAS KELLOND, Boston; by wife, Eliz., had Eliz., born 1687, died soon; Eliz., again, 1689; Mary, 1697; and Thomas, 1699.

KELLY:—ABEL KELL, Salem; freeman, 1641; where he removed to is not known.

BENJAMIN KELLY, a freeman of Mass., 1669; can be assigned to no town with confidence.

DAVID KELLY, Boston; by wife, Eliz., had David, born 1647; and Samuel, 1653; and another Samuel, 1657; he died, 1662; his widow married, 1663, Robert Smith.

HENRY KELLY, Lancaster; freeman, 1668, if the printer have not mistaken the name; that, perhaps, was intended for Kerley.

JOHN KELLY, Newburg; among the first settlers; came, says Coffin, from Newbury in Berks. 1635; had Sarah. born 1641; and John, 1642; died, 1644 A John Kelly was admitted freeman of Conn., 1658, but his residence is not known.

RENALD, or REGINALD KELLY, Pemaquid; took oath of fidelity, 1674.

ROGER KELLY, Isle of Shoals, 1668; married at Exter, 1681, Mary, daughter of William Holdbridge of Salisbury; was rep. at the first gen. Ct. in Boston, says Farmer, under the new charter, 1692.

REFERENCES:—Am. Ancestry, V, 169; Austin's Allied Fams., 156-9; Chase's Hist. Chester, N. H., 530; Guild's Stile's Gen., 544-6; Kelly Gen (1887), 154 pp.; Savage's Gen. Dict., III, 6.

KELSEY:—WILLIAM KELSEY, Cambridge, 1632; freeman, 1635; removed to Hartford, thence, about 1663, to Killingworth; at H. the only children born were Abigail, 1645; Stephen, 1647; and Daniel, 1650; but, no doubt, others were omitted in the record or were earlier born at C.; was rep. in 1671, when the record is Callsey, but after it is Kelse, Kelso, Kelsea, Kelsa, or Kelsy.

REFERENCES:—Adams' Fairhaven, Vt., 406; Buckingham Gen., 237-9; Chandler's Hist. Shirley, Mass., 1487-90; N. E. Hist. Gen. Reg., XIX, 242; Stiles' Hist. Windsor, Ct., II, 421; Stone Gen., 43; Wentworth Gen.,I, 645-8.

KELSON:—THOMAS KELSON, Reading.

KEMBLE, or KEMBALL:—See KIMBALL.

REFERENCE:—Wyman's Charlestown, 568.

KEMPE:—EDWARD KEMPE, Dedham; freeman, 1639; prob. was of Wenham, 1651; and afterward a blacksmith, and died 1668, at Chelmsford, to which he removed, 1655. His will names only daughter, Esther, wife of Samuel Foster, and her son, Samuel, and his own kinsman, Samuel of Groton.

ROBERT KEMPE, Dedham, 1639; adm. with wife of the church that year, as was Esther, 1646.

SAMUEL KEMPE, Billerica, 1659; afterward prob. at Andover, and at Groton, where the family widely extended; by wife, Sarah, had Jonathan, born 1668; Mehitable, 1673; and Bethea, 1683.

WILLIAM KEMPE, Duxbury, is called in custom house

certificate from Southampton, 1635; a servant, passenger in the James, arriving in Boston that year; but may be a mistake. Had William, and died, 1641; leaving widow, Eliz.

WILLIAM KEMPE, Dover, 1664; of whom no more is known.

REFERENCES:—Butler's Hist. Groton, Mass., 409; Page Gen., 75; Hazen's Hist. Billerica, Mass., 80; Worcester's Hist. Hollis, N. H., 379.

KEMPSTER:—DANIEL KEMPSTER, Cambridge; freeman, 1647; Abigail, his daughter, more prob. his wife, died 1657; his will names no wife nor children, however.

KEMPTHORNE:—DANIEL KEMPTHORNE, Cambridge; is in list of creditors of James Atwood "for keeping. his," sons 1653.

SIMON KEMTHORNE, Charlestown; perhaps son of Daniel; married Mary, daughter of Robert Long; had Sarah, born 1656, who died 1671. In 1656 he brought from Barbadoes, as master of the ship Swallow, two women, the first Quakers in the colony, for which he was blamed by the court of assist.; he died about 1657. His widow died 1675.

KEMPTON:—EPHRAIM KEMPTON, Scituate; perhaps brother of Manassch; is included in the list of those able to bear arms, 1643, with Ephraim, Jr.; but his name is erased, because, no doubt, he was too old or infirm, and he died 1645. He came some time after 1627.

MANASSEH KEMPTON, Plymouth; one of the old comers, prob. in the Ann, 1623, though name in the division of lands is printed Faunce; had wife, Julian, sister of Gov. Bradford, widow of George Martin; was rep., 1639, at the first assembly in the colony, and for 9 years more; was one of the first purchasers with Gov. B. of Dartmouth, and died 1663; and the record adds: "He did much good in his place, the time God lent him." His widow died 1665, in 81st year. See Russell's Guide to Plmouth, Appx., XI.

REFERENCES:—Davis' Landmarks, 163-5; Rickertson's N. Bedford, Mass., 203, 205, 209; Wheeler's Hist. Newport, N. H., 450.

KEN:—ROBERT KEN, Reading; among early settlers.

KENDALL:—FRANCIS KENDALL, Woburn, 1640; married, 1644, Mary Tidd; had John, born 1646; Thomas, 1649; Mary, 1651; Eliz., 1653; Hannah, 1655, Rebecca, 1657; Samuel, 1659; Jacob, 1661; and Abigail, 1666; was freeman, 1647; in 1700 swore he was fourscore years old. His wife died 1705.

JOHN KENDALL, Cambridge 1647; died 1661. His daughter, Eliz., married, 1647, Morris Somes of Glouster.

ROBERT KENDALL, Mass., 1640. Felt.

THOMAS KENDALL, Lynn, brother of Francis, freeman, 1648; had one son who died young, and another daughter beside the eight following; Ely, 1643; Rebecca, 1645; Mary, 1647; Hannah, 1650, removed to Reading, had Sarah, 1653; Abigail, 1655; Susanna, 1658; and Tabitha, 1660; was deacon and died 1681. His widow Rebecca died 1703, aged 85.

REFERENCES:—Am. Ancestry, III, 189; Ballou's Hist. Milford, Mass., 863; Barry's Hist. Framingham, Mass., 307-10; Densmore's Hartwell Gen.; Douglas Gen., 265; Ely Gen., 299-301; Kendall Gen.; Locke Gen., 20; Morse's Hist. Sherborn, Mass., 157; N. E. Hist. Gen. Reg., XXXIX, 17-23; Savage's Gen. Dict., III, 9; Secomb's Hist. Amherst, N. W., 652-5; Sewall's Hist. Woburn, Mass., 619-23; Stearn's Hist. Ashburnham, Mass., 776; Temple's Hist. Northfield, Mass., 478; Vinton's Richardson, Mems., 255; Well's Am. Fam., Antiq.; Wyman's Charlestown, Mass., Gen., II, 569.

KENNARD:—John Kennard, Haddam, about 1674, married Rebbeca, daughter of Jared Spencer, of the same, and died 1689, leaving John, 6 years old; and Eliz., 2. His widow married John Tanner.

KENNEDY:—Alexander Kennedy, Plymouth, by wife Eliz., had Hannah, born 1678; Eliz., 1682; Lydia, 1685; William, 1689; Sarah, 1693; Annable, 1698; and John, 1703. Descendent's are at Middleborough.

REFERENCES:—Cushman's Sheepscott, 396; Eaton's Annals Warren, Me., 2nd Ed., 566; Kennedy, Gen. (1888), by E. D. Kennedy; Wentworth Gen., I, 640-4.

KENNET:—Richard Kennet, Boston, died 1693. Probably he was an apothecary.

KENNICUT:—Roger Kennicut, Malden, married 1661 Joanna Sheperson, had Joanna, born 1664; Lydia, 1667; and John, 1669; was freeman, 1670, but sold his estate 1679, he and his wife then called of Swanzey.

KENNISTON or KINISTON:—Allen Kenniston, Salem, 1638, or earlier, for Dorothy K., his wife, is by Felt, recent, 1636, but in 1638 a grant of land was made to him; was freeman, 1642; and died 1648.

CHRISTOPHER KENNISTON, Portsmouth, married at Exeter, 1677, Mary Mushamore; perhaps he was son of Welham.

JOHN KENNISTON, Dover, 1663, Greenland, 1625; was killed by the Indians and his house burned 1677. Belkn. I. 81.

WILLIAM KENNISTON, Dover, 1646-71.

REFERENCES:—Dow's Hampton, N. H., 776; Eaton's Thomaston, 229.

KENNY, or KENNEY:—Andrew Kenny, Malden, by wife, Eliz., had Samuel, born 1690.

HENRY KENNY, Salem, 1653; had John, bapt. 1654; Mary, 1659; Sarah, 1662; and perhaps others.

HENRY, KENNY, perhaps son of the preceding, married 1691, Priscilla Lewis, had Jermima, born 1693; Priscilla, 1696; Dinah, 1698; and Mary, 1701.

JOHN KENNY, Salem, had Hannah, bapt. 1657, who prob. died young, as his will names only Sarah; and he died 1670, says Felt.

RICHARD KENNY, New Hamp., 1680.

THOMAS KENNY, Gloucester, 1664. Gibbs.

REFERENCES:—Jameson's, Medway, Mass., 498.

KENRICK, KENERICK, after Kendrick:—Caleb Kendrick, Boston, 1652.

GEORGE KENRICK, Scituate, 1634, freeman, 1635, joined the church with wife 1637; Joseph, born 1620; rep. 1642 and 1644; removed to Rehoboth, 1645, says Deans, but more prob. to Boston, where is recorded the birth by wife Jane of Joseph; and Deborah, 1646. His son Isaac died 1676.

JOHN KENRICK, Boston, 1639, prob. had come the former year, if not earlier, and there is no slight reason to think he came with mother in the James from Bristol, 1635; by wife Ann, sister prob. of Robert Smith, from London, had Hannah, bapt. 1640, who died soon; John, 1651; Elijah, 1644, then 6 days old, died soon; Eujah, again, or Elisha, as the false record has it, 1645; and Hannah, again, 1652. He lived after 1652, when he sold his estate in Boston proper, in that part of B. called Muddy river, now Brookline, where wife died 1656; 1658 removed to Cambridge, village of Newton, there died 1686. His widow Judith died, says Roxbury rec., 1687.

JOHN KENRICK, Ipswich, or Rowley, married 1657, Lydia Cheny.

JOHN KENRICK, Rehoboth, married 1681, Mary Perry, had Jehiel, born 1682; and Mary, 1684.

REFERENCES:—Jackson's, Newton, 354-9.

KENT:—James Kent, Newburg, brother of Richard, Jr., freeman 1669, had only son John, born 1641, possibly in England; died 1681.

JOHN KENT, Dedham, 1652, freeman, 1654; but of whom no more is learned.

JOHN KENT, Charlestown, by wife Hannah Grissell, who died 1696, had Hannah, born 1667; Mary, 1670; Joshua, 1672, died soon; Joshua, again, 1673; Joseph, 1675; Samuel, 1678, died at 25 years; Ebenezer, 1680; and Lydia, 1683.

JOSEPH KENT, Dedham, brother of John.

JOSHUA KENT, Dedham, 1643, prob. brother of 1st Adm. of the church, 1644, went home, and came again, 1645, bringing two brothers, it is said, but perhaps only one; freeman, 1646; by wife Mary, had Lydia, born 1647; went with wife again to England that year, but came again 1648; that year had Sarah, bapt. in 1650; and Mary, 1651.

JOSEPH KENT, New Hamp., 1689.

OLIVER KENT, Dover, 1648, died about 1670, leaving widow, Dorothy

RICHARD KENT, Ipswich, 1634, came that year, with another of the same christian and surname, perhaps a cousin, in the Mary and John; freeman 1635; removed with first settlers to Newbury; left in England Sarah, and other daughters, of which one, Rebecca, had married in Eng., Samuel Scallard, and after his death she came, and perhaps brought daughter Mary, who married 1656, John Rolfe, and the mother married 1647, John Bishop; but here, says Coffin, he had John, born 1645; and he died 1654.

RICHARD KENT, Newbury, 1635, came the year before in the Mary and John, brother of James, had wife Jane, who died 1674, and he married 1675, Joanna, widow of Nicholas Davison, of Charlestown, and died 1689, without children, and gave estate to his nephew, John.

STEPHEN KENT, Newbury, brother of 1st Richard, came, says Coffin, 1635, but if so he went home, and came again 1638, in the Confidence from Southampton, with wife Margery, and 4 or 5 servants. Sworn freeman 1639; had Eliz. 1642, died at 11 years; Hannah 1644; Stephen 1648; Rebecca 1650; David 1657, and Mary. Had 3 wives. Ann, the 2nd, died 1660; he married 1662, Eleanor, widow of William Leadlock, of Saco, and removed to Haverhill, thence to Woodbridge, N. J.

THOMAS KENT, Gloucester, 1643, died in 1658; and his widow died 1671.

THOMAS KENT, Gloucester, perhaps son of the preceding, married 1659, Joan, daughter of Thomas Penny, had Thomas, born 1660; Mary, 1662; Mercy and Joan, twins, 1665, both died in 6 days; Joan again, 1666; and John, 1667; was of Brookfield, 1671; freeman 1690.

WILLIAM KENT, Boston, 1662, married, Mary, widow of John Mears; of artillery comp. 1667, its ensign 1673, died 1691. Seven of this name, had, in 1634, been graduated at Harvard, and 9 at other New England colleges.

REFERENCES :—Am., Ancestry, IX, 133; Babson's Hist. Gloucester, Mass., 110; Bangor, Me., Hist. Mag., V. 238; Chase's Hist. Chester, N, H., 551; Deane's Hist. Scituate, Mass., 300; Dwight, Gen., 405, 421-8. Futhey's Hist. Chester Co., Pa., 620; N, E. Hist. Gen., Reg., XV, 273; Power's Hist. Sangamon Co., Ills., 425; Savage's Gen. Dict., III, 11; Secomb's Hist. Amherst, N, H., 658; Tuthill and Kent, Chart (1880) 2x2 ft., Waldo's Hist. Tolland, Ct., 126; Wyman's Charlestown, Mass., Gens., 570-3.

KERLEY, CARSLEY, or CARSLY :—Edward Kerley, of Ashmore Co., Dorset, near Shaftsburg, husbandman. Embarked in the Confidence, 1638, aged 22, at Southampton; but no more is known of him.

WILLIAM KERLEY, Hingham, 1637, of Sudbrug, about 1641, removed to Lancaster, freeman 1647; in his old age married 2nd wife, 1664, Rebecca, widow of Thomas Josslyn, and died 1670, leaving William and Henry.

REFERENCES :—Savage's, Gen., Dict., III, 13; Worcester Mag. and Hist. Journal, II, 281.

KESKEYS :—Henry Keskeys, Boston, by wife Ruth had Henry, born 1656.

KETCHAM :—Edward Ketcham, Ipswich, 1635, freeman, 1637, may reasonably be thought progenitor of all the name, in our country. Perhaps Edward of Stratford, who died before 1678, was his son whose daughter Rebecca married, 1678, Thomas Taylor of Norwalk, and Edward K. married Mary, daughter of Richard Harcutt, but probably he was of L. I.,—yet may have been the Stratford man, who in his will 1655 names 3 daughters—Mary, Hannah and Esther.

HENRY KETCHAM, Ipswich, 1638, probably son of preceding.

JOHN KETCHAM, Ipswich, 1648, prob. son of Edward, removed to that part of L. I., called Setauket, now Brookhaven, constable, stood up for the jurisdict. of Conn., was honored, 1662, with a commis. to make his neighb. swear and represent. 1664. In 1668 he removed to Newton, there was a man of influence to his death, 1689. Riker, 89.

JOSEPH KETCHAM, Norwalk, 1672, possibly son of the preceding, or grandson of Edward, married, 1697, Mercy, daughter of Deacon Henry Lindall, of New Haven, had Nathaniel, born 1680; and Sarah, 1672; was in town service, 1701.

SAMUEL KETCHAM, Newtown, L. I., 1655, prob. brother of John, was of Setauket, freeman of Conn., 1664, and with Edward, who may also have been bred at Huntington, 1672.

REFERENCES :—Bunker's, L. I., Gens., 230; Savage's, Gen. Dict., III., 14; Sedgwick's, Hist. Sharon, Ct., 94; Sylvester's, Hist. Ulster Co., N. Y., 101.

KETTLE :—John Kettle, Gloucester, by wife Eliz., daughter of the 1st William Allen of Salem, had Eliz., born 1658; Mary, 1660; Samuel, 1662; and James, 1665. Prob. from him is derived the name of Kettle Cove at the adjoining town of Manchester.

PETER KETTLE, came in the Abigail, 1635, aged 10, from London; nothing else known about him.

RICHARD KETTLE, Charlestown, 1633, butcher, freeman, 1635, by wife, Esther, daughter of Samuel Ward, had Hannah, bapt. 1637; John, 1639; Joseph, 1641; Samuel, 1642; Nathaniel, 1644; Jonathan, 1646.

REFERENCES :—Babson's Gloucester, III.; Munsell's Albany Call, IV, 137; Pearsons's, Schenectady, N. Y., Settler's, 99. Savage's Gen. Dict., III, 14-6.

KEY :—John Key, Dover, had James, taken about 1690 by the Indians, and soon killed. But he and another John called Jr., perhaps his son, were prisoners from Piscataqua, at Quebec, 1695.

REFERENCES :—Hanson's Kent, Md., 38; Hayden's Va., Gens., 167; Paxton's, Marshall, Gen., 28; Richmond, Va., Standard, III, 20; Smith's Hist. Delaware Co., Pa., 476

KEYES :—Robert Keys, Watertown, 1633, by wife Sarah, had Sarah, born that year; Rebecca, 1638; Mary, 1639; died soon. Mary, again, 1642; died soon; Elias, 1643; removed to Newbury, then had Mary, again, 1645; may have returned to Watertown, perhaps had Peter, and others, and he died, 1647. His widow married 1658, John Gage.

SOLOMAN KEYS, Newburg, married 1653, Frances Grant, had Hannah, born 1654; Sarah, 1656; Mary, 1658; Jane, 1660; and Judith, 1662; removed to Chelmsford, there he had Soloman, bapt. 1665; and was tythingman, 1679.

REFERENCES :—Am. Ancestry, I., 43; Blakes's, Lucy Keyes, Biog. (1893) 23 pp.; Cochrane's Hist. Antrim, N. H., 567; Davis' Hist. Reading, Vt., 140; Keyes Gen. (1857) 15 p.; (1880) 192 p.; (1880) 319 p.; Keyes' W. Boylston, Mass., Reg., 26; Merrill's Hist. Ackworth, N. H., 233; Savage's Gen. Dict., III., 16; Stearn's Hist. Ashburnham, Mass., 777; Ward's Hist. Shrewsbury, Mass., 339-47; Whitcomb Gen., 9; Young's Hist. Chautauqua Co., N. Y., 366.

KEYSAN, or KEZAN :—John Keysan, Haverhill, married Hannah, daughter of John Davis, of Dover.

KEYSER, of KEASUR :—George Keyser, Lynn, a tanner, freeman, 1639, removed to Salem, married Eliz., daughter of Edward, Holyoke, had Elizur; George, born 1657; and Edward, 1659. His wife died 1659, and the last child followed soon after; and he died 1676, or by another account, 1690, aged 73.

THOMAS KEYSER, Lynn, 1638, perhaps brother of George, by wife Mary, had Rebecca, born, 1640; and Thomas; Timothy, 1646.

REFERENCES:—Am. Ancestry, V., 29; Keysur, Reunion (1889), 161 p.; Plumb's Hist. Hanover, Pa., 438-40; Welles' Washington Gen., 261.

KIBBY, KIBBE, or KIBBEE:—Arthur Kibby, Salem, fisherman, or mariner, by wife, Abigail, daughter of William Ayer of the same, had Abigail, born 1659; Arthur, 1660; William, 1661; and probably Mary; Joseph; Hannah; Sarah; and Jerusha. He prob. died early in 1685.

EDWARD KIBBY, Boston, 1645, a sawyer, living at Muddy River, had Reuben, bapt. 1653; and Eliz., 1655, both at Roxbury, also prob. James; Elisha; Joshua; Rebecca; Edward; and perhaps, Hannah.

ELISHA KIBBY, Salem, married Rachel Coak, had John, born 1668; Edward, 1670; Elisha, 1673; died young; and James, 1675; removed to Enfield, 1682, then part of Springfield, had Isaac, the 1st male child born in E., 1683; and Rachel, 1688; and perhaps others. Probably he was son of the preceding, or of the following.

HENRY KIBBY, Dorchester, tailor, freeman 1642; Artillery Co. 1644; died 1661.

JOSEPH KIBBY, Salem, married Abigail, daughter of William Anger.

JOSHUA KIBBY, Sherborn, by Morse, the autocrat of S., regarded as son of Edward, married 1668, at Woburn, Mary Comey, daughter of David, had Edward; Sarah, 1708; and Joshua 1712.

WILLIAM KIBBY, Hull, 1642.

REFERENCES:—Coggswell's Henniker, 634; Savage's Gen. Dict., III., 17; Wheeler's Hist., Newport, N. H., 452.

KIDBY:—John Kidby, Duxbury, 1640.

LEWIS KIDBY, Boston, 1640, fisherman.

KIDD:—James Kidd, Dover, 1657, took oath of fidelity 1677; was of Exeter 1688.

KIDDER:—Edward Kidder, by Eaton called one of the first settlers at Reading; it is probable that he was the man of Wrexam, in Co. Denbigh, 1675, who bound himself to serve 4 years in Boston, Theophilus Gale, of Chester, in England, as a shoemaker.

JAMES KIDDER, Cambridge, 1649, son of James, born in England, at East Grinstead, Co. Sussex, 1626, by wife Ann, daughter of Elder Francis Moore, married 1649; had Hannah born 1650; Dorothy 1651; James 1654; John 1656; Thomas 1657; Nathaniel, bapt. 1659; Ephraim 1661; at Billerica had Stephen 1662; Enoch 1664; Samuel 1666; Sarah 1667; and Joseph 1670; and died about 1683.

STEPHEN KIDDER, Berwick, 1633, in the employment of Mason the patentee. See in Belkn. I., 425, letter of Ambrose Gibbons.

THADDEUS KIDDER, Marblehead, 1674.

REFERENCES:—Adams, Fairhaven, Vt., 406; Am. Ancestry, VI., 161, 181; Bass Hist. Braintree, Vt., 157; Guilds' Stiles Gen., 84; Kidder Gen. (1876) 32 pp. (1886) 175 pp.; Kidder's New Ipswich, N. H., 394-414; Paige's

Hist. Cambridge, Mass., 596; Ransom Gen.; Savage's Gen. Dict., III., 18; Secomb's Hist. Amherst, N. H., 659; Upham Gen., 38-40; Wyman's Charlestown, Mass., Gens., 585-8.

KILBOURN, or KILBORNE:—George Kilbourn, 1636, freeman 1640, in church record is called servant, removed to Rowley, by wife Eliz. had Mary, born 1649; Joseph 1652; Jacob 1655; one of the flower of Essex in Lothrop's camp. Killed by the Indians 1675 at Bloody Brook; Samuel 1656; Isaac 1659; and Eliz. 1653. He was son of Thomas, Capt. at Wood, Ditton Co., Cambridge, 1612.

JOHN KILBOURN, Wethersfield, 1647, son of Thomas, born in England, came in the Increase with his father 1635, by wife Naomi, who died 1659, had John, born 1651; Thomas 1653; and Naomi; and by wife Susan, perhaps daughter of John Brownson, of Hartford, had Ebenezer, born 1665; Sarah; George, 1668; Mary; Joseph about 1672; and Abraham 1675. He was represent. 1660, 1 and 2; made his will 1688, but lived many years afterward at Glastonbury, and died 1703; and his wife died 1711.

THOMAS KILBOURN, Wethersfield, from Wood Ditton, in Co. Cambridge, came to Boston in the Increase 1635, aged 55, with wife Francis 50; and children Margaret, Lydia, Mary, Frances, and John, before mentioned. He died 1640; his widow 1650.

THOMAS KILBOURN, who came in the Elizabeth from Ipswich 1634, aged 24, with wife Eliz. 20, was eldest son of preceding, bapt. 1609. Sent by his father in advance to make preparations for the family migrat., but no more is known of him.

REFERENCES:—Coffin's Boscawen, 562-6; Freeman's Hist. Cape Cod, Mass., II., 648; Kilbourn Gen. (1845) 151 pp. (1856) 488 pp.; N. E. Hist. Gen. Reg., XIII., 372; XVIII., 226; Ridlon's Harrison, Me., Settlers, 90; Savage's Gen. Dict., III., 18-20.

KILBY:—Christopher Kilby, Boston, by wife Sarah had Nathaniel, born 1694; Miriam 1696; John 1699; Rebecca 1701; Samuel 1706; Sarah 1708; and Mary 1712.

EDWARD KILBY, Boston, married 1662, Eliz., widow of Edward Yeomans, daughter of Thomas Josselyn.

JOHN KILBY, Boston, perhaps brother of Christopher, by wife Rebecca had Eliz. 1686; John 1688; Sarah 1692; Christopher 1693; prob. died soon; Richard 1695; William 1698; Catharine 1700; Rebecca 1702; Christopher, again, 1705; Nicholas 1708; and Ebenezer 1711.

REFERENCES:—Dennysville, Me., Centen., 107; Heraldic Journal, II., 48; Savage's Gen. Dict., III., 20; Titcomb's Early N. E. People, 94-101; Wilder Gen., 354.

KILCUP:—Roger Kilcup, Boston, perhaps son of William, freeman 1690, married 1695, Abigail, daughter of Joseph Dudson, had Dudson, was of artillery comp. and died 1702, aged 52. It is presumed his widow married, 1704, Ezekiel Lewis.

WILLIAM KILCUP, Boston, 1659, in few years was of Charlestown with wife Grace, and called a sieve-maker; may have had daughter Sarah married to Richard Wilson before 1654, though in Geneal. Reg., VIII., 277, a different conjecture is given.

KILHAM, KILLAM, KELHAM, or KEELUM:—Austin, or Augustine Kelham, Salem, 1637, had then, says Felt, a grant of land, but was of Dedham soon after, and may have short time lived at Ipswich; by wife Alice had Lot, born 1640; and Sarah 1642; was freeman 1641. He was of the church at Wenham before 1655, when he removed to Chelmsford.

DANIEL KILHAM, Wenham, artillery comp. 1645.

DANIEL KILHAM, son of the preceding, freeman 1680.

JOHN KILHAM, Dedham, 1645; perhaps was of Brookfield 1690, and his family in poverty.

REFERENCE:—Fiske Fam. of Amherst, 135.

KILTON:—Robert Kilton, is on the list of Gallop's comp. in Phip's crusade against Quebec 1690, but further is not known.

REFERENCE:—Austin's R. I. Gen. Dict., 116.

KIMBALL, sometimes Kemball:—Ebenezer Kimball, Rowley, 1691.

EPHRAIM KIMBALL, Wenham, freeman 1690.

GILES KIMBALL, Charlestown, 1656, brother of Thomas, died at Boston 1659.

'HENRY KIMBALL, Watertown, prob. brother of Richard the 1st, came in the Eliz. 1634, from Ipswich, aged 44, with wife Susanna 35; children Eliz. 4; and Susan 1½; and servant Richard Cutting 11; freeman 1638; had John, born 1638, died soon; Mary 1641; Richard 1643; and John, again, 1645; and he died 1648. His widow married again, and died 1684.

HENRY KIMBALL, Charlestown, married 1656, Sarah, perhaps daughter of John Fawnell, who died next year. He married 2nd wife Mary, daughter of Thomas Brigden, had Zechary, Mary, Sarah, and Henry.

JOHN KIMBALL, Newburg, married 1665, Mary Hobbs, had Mary, born 1667; and John 1668, and the father died same month.

JOHN KIMBALL, Amesbury, took oath of fidelity 1677, and was made freeman 1690.

JOHN KIMBALL, Boxford, freeman 1690.

RICHARD KIMBALL, Watertown, prob. brother of Henry of the same, came from Ipswich. Old England, 1634, aged 39, in the Elizabeth, with wife Ursula; children Henry 15; Richard 11; Mary 9; Martha 5; John 3; and Thomas 1; and servant John Laverick 15; was freeman 1635; removed 1638 to Ipswich, there had more children and died 1675, leaving Henry, Richard, Mary, Thomas, Benjamin, Eliz., Caleb, Sarah, and another daughter, wife of John Severns.

SAMUEL KIMBALL, Wenham, freeman 1682.

SAMUEL KIMBALL, Boston, mariner, perhaps eldest son of Thomas of the same, may have been a soldier in Mosely's comp. 1675, and died 1684.

THOMAS KIMBALL, Charlestown, 1653, merchant, by wife Eliz. Trarice. perhaps eldest daughter of Nicholas. had John, born 1656, removed to Boston and had Sarah 1666: Rebecca 1668; Henry 1670; and Eliz. 1671. He was buried on Copp's Hill; died 1689 and was born 1622.

THOMAS KIMBALL, Dover, 1660. Spelling is often Kemble.

REFERENCES:—Am. Ancestry, III., 30, 90; IV., 88; VII., 97; VIII., 76; Andrew's Gen. (1890), 190-5; Bond's Hist. Watertown, Mass., 323-5; Buxton, Me., Centen. 142-7; Cochrane's Hist. Antrim, N. H., 569-71; Collins' Hist. Hillsdale, N. Y., App., 88-90; Driver Gen.,

368-86; Dudley Gen., 126; Dunster Gen., 288-99; Hammatt Papers Ipswich, Mass., 79; Kimball Gen. (1885), 103 pp.; N. E. Hist. Gen. Reg., XXVIII., 271; Perley's Hist. Boxford, Mass., 51-3; Pierce's Hist. Grafton, Mass., 512-4; Saunderson's Hist. Charlestown, N. H., 460; Savage's Gen. Dict., III., 21-3; Secomb's Hist. Amherst, N. H., 660; Wentworth Gen., I., 162-5.

KIMBER:—Richard Kimber, born probably at Wantage, England, grandson of Richard, of Grove, Berkshire, England, born 1610, an officer of Horse in the Parliamentary Army under Cromwell 1643-1644; married Mary Preddy, emigrated to America, sailing from Bristol, England, and settled in Pennsylvania. He was a farmer. By a warrant dated April 5, 1749, he obtained a patent for sixty-seven acres of land and allowance, the patent being dated August 15, 1753. He died in 1753. By his will dated February 15, 1753, and proved February 26, 1753, he gave half of his property to his wife, and the other half to his son, Richard Preddy (called Preddy in the will, but always known as Richard Preddy after his father's death), and his daughter Sarah. Children: Isaac, died young; Sarah married Daniel Hart; Mary married Joseph Underwood, removed to Virginia; Richard Preddy, born 1737, died 1822, married Gertrude Griffith.

REFERENCE:—"The Descendants of Richard Kimber," Boston, 1894.

KIMBERLY:—Thomas Kimberly, Dorchester, 1635, had wife Alice, with whom he removed to New Haven 1639; his estate was then small. His wife, by whom he had Eleazer, bapt. 1639; and Abiah 1641; besides 5 or 6 others, before or after, died 1659, at New Haven; he married again and removed to Stratford, there died 1673; in his will of that year he names sons Thomas, Abraham, Nathaniel, and Eleazer, wife Mary, and several daughters.

THOMAS KIMBERLY was freeman in 1669, had wife Hannah, and with Nathaniel, propr. at New Haven 1685; but T. had no children, and it is said Nathaniel left son of same name.

REFERENCES:—Am. Ancestry, IX., 222; Orcutt's Hist. Stratford, Conn., 1232; Orcutt's Hist. Tarrington, Conn., 728; Savage's Gen. Dict., III., 23.

KIME:—William Kime, Dover, 1668-71.

KIMWRIGHT:—George Kimwright, Dorchester, married about 1653, the wealthy widow of John Holland; removed to Cambridge about 1664.

KINCAID:—Daniel Kincaid, New Hampsh., came 1689, probably from Scotland.

KIND:—Arthur, Kind, Boston, by wife Jane had Sarah, born 1646; James, who died 1654; Mary, who died 1655; James, again, 1655; Nathaniel, 1658; Thomas 1659; Mary 1662; and William 1665.

KING:—Alexander King, Wickford, R. I., 1674.

CLEMENT KING, Marshfield, by Miss Thomas, in Geneal. Reg., VIII., 192, is favored with wife Susanna, who died or was buried 1669; but whose son, or whose daughter, or when born or married, is not easily known.

DANIEL KING, Lynn, 1647, a merchant, born 1601, died 1672. His will names wife and children, Daniel, Hannah, Eliz., and Sarah. His widow Eliz. who had been widow Corwin, says Lewis, died 1677 or 8. His estate was very good.

EDWARD KING, Windsor, an Irish servant, had grant of land 1663, living on Long Island when he died 1702; had 2 daughters named Mary Hilliard and Saray Cady.

GEORGE KING, freeman of Mass. 1637, came in the Hercules 1634, and by Farmer is set down at Newbury, but he must soon have removed, for Coffin names him not.

HENRY KING came in the James from Southampton 1635, is called a laborer, but no more is known.

HEZEKIAH KING, Weymouth, by wife Mary had Mary, born 1679; and Samuel 1686; and prob. others.

ISAAC KING, Weymouth, a soldier in Capt. Johnson's comp. in the great Narragansett fight, 1675, when he was wounded. Prob. he is called Hezekiah in the list of Geneal. Reg., VIII., 242.

JAMES KING, Suffield, died 1722, leaving James; William 1679; Annis 1681; Benoni 1685; Joseph 1687; and Mary 1692.

JOHN KING, Northampton, is by Hinman said to have come at the age of 16 in 1645, living at Hartford, and 5 years after married Sarah Holton, daughter of John; but part of this is erron., for he married 1656, Sarah, daughter of William Holton, who, of course, was sister, not daughter of John; had John born 1657; William 1660; Thomas 1662; Samuel 1665; Eleazur 1667, who died at 32 years unmarried; Joseph 1669, died next year; Sarah 1671; Joseph, again, 1673; Benjamin 1675; Thankful 1679; David 1677, or 1681; and Jonathan, 1683; and his wife died soon after; was represent. 1679 and 89; married 2nd wife Sarah, widow of Jacob Mygatt, daughter of William Whiting, was a capt., and died 1703.

JOHN KING, Weymouth, by wife Esther had Fearnot, born 1655; John 1659, died soon; John, again, 1661; Esther 1664; and Patience 1668. Perhaps he was son born in England of an elder John of the same, who had Mary, born 1639; and Abigail 1641.

MARK KING, Charlestown, 1658, by wife Mary had Mark, besides Mary, both bapt. 1659; 2 children bapt. 1660, whose names are not found; Hannah 1664, died soon; Hannah, again, 1666; and Samuel 1671.

PETER KING, Sudbury, 1654, deacon and represent. 1689 and 90, died 1704. Prob. he had children of whom one may have been Peter, freeman 1690.

PHILIP KING, Weymouth, 1672. His daughter Mary married John Leonard.

RALPH KING, Lynn, 1648, married 1644, Eliz. Walker, had Ralph, born 1667; Daniel 1669; Sarah 1671; Richard 1677; and Mary 1679; freeman 1680; was capt., and died 1689.

RICHARD KING, prob. of Salem. had died, and his widow married Richard Bishop, of Salem, to whom, in her right, was granted admin. of est. of K. as early as 1635. Felt.

ROBERT KING, came in the Confidence from Southampton 1638; aged 24; a servant, but no more is known.

SAMUEL KING, Plymouth, 1643, had Samuel, born 1649, and Isaac 1651.

SAMUEL KING, Weymouth, by wife Experience had Susanna, born 1659; Eliz. 1662; Experience 1664; Sarah 1666; and Samuel 1671; was freeman 1681. Another Samuel at Weymouth, or the same, had Abigail, born 1681.

THOMAS KING, Sudbury and Lancaster, by wife Ann, who died 1642, had Thomas, born same year, who died 1645. The father also soon died. Possibly he was that youth of 15 who came from Ipswich at the same time, in 1634, with the other Thomas, a few years older.

THOMAS KING, Watertown, 1640, prob. in the Frances from Ipswich, 1634, aged 19, came with so many, who sat down at that place, but first was prob. at Hampton; by wife Mary had Thomas, born 1641; Mary 1643; and died 1644. His widow married, 1645, James Cutler.

THOMAS KING, Scituate, came in the Blessing from London 1635, aged 21, in comp. with William Vassall, united with the church 1638, but did not remove next year with the pastor and his many friends; by wife Sarah had Rhoda, born 1639; George 1642, who, it is thought, died young; Thomas 1645; Daniel 1648; Sarah 1650; and John 1652, who died in a few weeks, and the wife died soon after. He next married 1653, Jane, widow of Elder William Hatch, who died soon after. Had 3d wife, Ann; but children of the first wife only are heard of; was Ruling Elder and died 1691.

THOMAS KING, Sudbury, married 1655, Bridget Davis.

THOMAS KING, Taunton, died 1713, aged 70, says gravestone. He may be that Weymouth inhab. who by wife Mary had John, born 1670; Mary 1673; and, perhaps, had child after removing to Taunton.

WILLIAM KING, Salem, came from London in the Abigail, 1635, aged 28; freeman 1636, though Felt says he had grant of land 1637, and was freeman after it; had then bapt. Mehitable 1636; John 1638; and Deliverance 1641.

WILLIAM KING, Isle of Shoals, died 1664, leaving William.

WILLIAM KING, Boston, who by wife Sarah, daughter of George Griggs, had William, born 1655, is, perhaps, father of that man, honored by Dunton in 1686, who died 1690. The widow of William married before 1662, Roger Burgiss, and died 1664.

REFERENCES:—Massachusetts, Atkins' Hist. Hawley, 44-97; Ballau's Hist. Milford, 869; Benedict's Hist. Sutton, 670-81; Bond's Hist. Watertown, 326; Davis' Landmarks Plymouth, 167; Deane's Hist. Scituate, 301; Hobart's Hist. Abington, 410; Jackson's Hist. Newton, 359; Taylor's Great Barrington, 117-20; Temple's Hist. N. Brookfield, 663; Temple's Northeld, 479; Temple's Palmer, 469-501; Wilson's Address at Palmer (1852); Wyman's Charlestown Gens., 589.

OTHER PUBLICATIONS:—Am. Ancestry, I., 44; II., 66; III., 30; IV., 160; VI., 10, 107, 166; VII., 186; VIII., 76, 160; IX., 188; Austin's R. I. Gen. Dict., 117; Bulloch Gen.; Corliss' No. Yarmouth, Me.; Cutts Gen., 64; Driver Gen., 236; Dwight Gen., 119, 550-2, 952-72; Elderkin Gen., 152-66; Essex Inst. Hist. Coll. (1880); Goode Gen., 25 ʃp.; Goodwin's Olcott Gen., 30; King Chart (1887) 22 x 27; (1892) 22 x 26; (1892) 23 x 28; King Gen. (1866) 28 pp.; Lapham's Hist. Paris, Me., 650-3; Livermore's Hist. Wilton, N. H., 430-2; Longmeadow Mass. Centen., 73; Loomis Gen. Female Branches, 651; Me. Hist. Records, I., 1-8, 33-40, 182-6, 209-11; Maine Hist. Soc. Call., III., 214; Meade's Old Fams. of Va.; N. E. Hist. and Gen. Reg., XI., 357-9; XVI., 144-50; XLVI., 370-4; Phoenix Fam. of Vt. II., 1275; Powers Hist. Sangamon Co., Ills., 428-31; Richmond, Va., Standard, II., 9; III., 13; Savage's Gen. Dict., III., 23-7; Strong Hist., 256, 578, 1256; Thomas Fam. of Maryland, 104; Walter's King Fam. Rec.

(1880); Walworth's Hyde Gen., 285; Wentworth Gen., I., 299-304; Whitman Gen., 28; Whitmore's Copps Hill Epitaphs; Young's Hist. Wayne Co., Ind., 187.

KINGMAN:—Edward Kingman, Wentworth, a soldier in Capt. Johnson's comp. 1675, in the Narraganset campaign.

HENRY KINGMAN, Weymouth, freeman 1636, represent. 1638 and 52; his wife Joan died 1659; son Henry, perhaps eldest, died 1660. In his will of 1666, he calls his age 74, or thereabouts, ment. sons Edward, Thomas, John, and daughter Holbrook; Davis, wife of Tobias, married 1649; and Barnard; of whom the last was dead, leaving 5 children.

REFERENCES:—Am. Ancestry, II., 66; VI., 75, 85, 116; Isabell and Kingman Gen. (1889) 30 pp.; Kingman's No. Bridgewater, Mass., 216-20; Savage's Gen. Dict., III., 27; Whitman Gen., 145.

KINGSBURY:—Henry Kingsbury, Ipswich, 1638, came with wife Margaret and 2 or more children in the Talbot, one of the fleet of Winthrop 1630; of him we learn no more, but possibly he was of I. (I.) 1648. Winth. Appx. A. 41 and 45.

HENRY KINGSBURY, Ipswich, calls himself 54 years old in a depon. of 1669; with wife Susanna, by whom he had Susanna, who married Joseph Pike; John; James, perhaps; Joseph, born about 1656, and other children, prob. Samuel, and Thomas; may be the son of Margaret the preceding, living at I. 1660, at Rowley 1662, and who died at Haverhill 1679; and he died there 1687. Perhaps he had Ephraim.

JAMES KINGSBURY, Haverhill, perhaps son of Henry, or of Thomas; took oath of fidelity 1677; had married 1674, Sarah, daughter of Matthias Button. Removed later to Conn. and in 1730 was of Plainfield.

JOHN KINGSBURY, Watertown, freeman 1636, removed that year to Dedham, of which he was represent. 1647. From his will it is learned that his wife was Margaret, and only child John.

JOSEPH KINGSBURY, Dedham, brother of the first John of the same, freeman 1641; by Millicent had Mary, born 1637; Eliz. 1638; Joseph; John 1643; Eleazur 1645; and prob. others, of whom one may have been Sarah, who died 1646.

REFERENCES:—Am. Ancestry, IV., 49; Blake's Hist. Franklin, Mass., 256; Blood's Hist. Temple, N. H., 230; Caulkin's Hist. Norwich, Conn., 234; Corliss' Gen., 240; Hayward's Hist. Gilsum, N. H., 348; Hughes Gen., 207-11; Locke Gen., 106; N. E. Hist. Gen. Reg., XIII., 157-6; XVI., 327, 332-41; Pierce's Hist. Grafton, Mass., 514; Savage's Gen. Dict., III., 28; Stile's Hist. Windsor, Conn., II., 426-8; Temple's Hist. No. Brookfield, Mass., 664.

KINGSLEY, or KINSLEY:—John Kingsley, Dorchester, 1635, came prob. with some friend of Mather and was here before him; at least was one of the 7 pillars on formation of the new Church for him 1636, and was the last surviv.; had Freedom Eldad, born 1638; Enos; Edward; and Renewal, 1644: removed to Rehoboth after 1648, when he was in office, and 1658; there lived and suffered Indian hostilities, of which in a letter of supplication for relief, in 1676, most sad picture is given. It is printed in Trumbull, Col. Rec., II., 445.

JOHN KINGSLEY, Milton, married Abigail, daughter of James Leonard; had Abigail; Mary 1676; John;

Stephen; Samuel; and Eliz., and died 1698, leaving widow and children here named.

SAMUEL KINGSLEY, Billerica, freeman 1651; married Hannah, daughter of Capt. Richard Brackett; died 1662.

STEPHEN KINGSLEY, Dorchester, perhaps brother of John, freeman 1640, rep. 1650, removed to Braintree, there had Mary, born 1640; he removed finally to Milton, was rep. 1666; in his will provides for son John, three sons-in-law, besides children of his son Samuel, prob. deceased.

REFERENCES:—Am. Ancestry, V., 173; VI., 207; VIII., 49; Caverly's Hist. Pittsford, Vt., 712; Coit Gen., 174; Mitchell's Hist. Bridgewater, Mass., 220; Ruggles Gen.; Savage's Gen. Dict., III., 29; Montague Gen., 416-8, 621-7, 634-6; Stanton Gen., 279; Strong Gen., 885-90, 1405-13; Warren-Clark Gen., 104.

KINGSNOTH, or KINGSWORTH:—Henry Kingsnoth, Guilford, 1639; signed the cov. for settlement of June 1; married Mary, daughter of John Stevens, of the same; died 1668, and his widow married 1669, John Collins, as his 2nd wife.

KINGSMILL:—William Kingsmill, a Quaker, punished at Boston with 15 stripes.

KINNICUT:—See Kennicut.

KINSMAN, or KINGSMAN:—Robert Kinsman, Ipswich, 1635; came the year preceding in the Mary and John; had soon after a grant of land; married a daughter of Thomas Boreman, and died 1665.

ROBERT KINSMAN, Ipswich, son of the preceding; freeman 1674; married Rebecca, eldest daughter of Andrew Burley of the same; was a warm oppon. of Andros, rep. 1692.

KIRBY:—Henry Kirby, a soldier 1676, served in Turner's comp. on Conn. river, who may be the Salem freeman 1677, spelled in list Kirrey, unless, as seems more prob. that he intend. for Skerry.

JOHN KIRBY, Middletown, whither Dr. Field thought he removed from Boston, and Hinman made him of Hartford 1645; but before the sett. of M. he had been at H. and Wethersfield, and at Plymouth 1643; had Eliz. born at Hartford 1646; and at W. Hannah, 1649; John and Eunice, twins, 1651. He owned an estate at Rowington, near Kenilworth, in Warwicksh. His son John was killed by the Indians 1676; and he died 1677. leaving widow Eliz., and children Mary, the wife of Emanuel Buck, aged 32; Hannah, wife of Thomas Andrews, 27; Esther, wife of Benajah Stone. 25; Sarah, wife of Samuel Hubbard, 23; Joseph 21; Bethia 18; Susanna 13; and Abigail 11; beside Eliz. wife of David Sage.

RICHARD KIRBY, Lynn, removed 1637 to Sandwich; by wife Jane had Increase, and prob. Abigail, twins, born 1650, of whom Abigail died soon and Increase same year; also the mother and her son Richard. The father was imprisoned as a Quaker 1658; may have taken oath of fidel. at Dartmouth 1684, where he married 1678, Abigail Rowland of D. perhaps as 2nd or 3rd wife. By former wife Patience he had at D. Sarah, born 1667; John 1673; and Robert 1675. Perhaps he was of Oyster Bay, L. I., 1685.

ROBERT KIRBY, Dartmouth, 1684, or near that time.

WILLIAM KIRBY, Boston, by wife Eliz., had Eliz., born 1640, who died 1642. He was the executioner of 1657 and 8, living in 1667, may be that freeman of 1647, printed Kerley.

REFERENCES:—Am. Ancestry, II., 67; Savage's Gen. Dict., III., 30.

KIRGE:—Joseph Kirge, is the un-Eng., name given to one of "the flower of Essex," who fell at Bloody Brook under Capt. Lothrop, 1675. Name prob. should be spelled King.

KIRK:—Henry Kirk, Dover, 1665.

THOMAS KIRK, Boston, merchant from London, or, as Sir Thomas Temple wrote, then here, capt. of a ship, was sent with Thomas Kellond, bearing warrant from Gov. Endicott, 1662, to arrest in Conn. the regicides Whalley and Goffe. Hutch. I., 215; 3 Mass. Hist. Call., VIII., 325. Full report of their search, a curious paper is in Hutch. Call. 334.

ZECHARIAH KIRK, Boston, 1686, married Abigail, daughter of Joshua Rawlins.

REFERENCES:—Am. Ancestry, III., 170; Cogswell's Hist. Henniker, N. H., 638; Cregar's Haines Ancestry, 148-50; Futhey's Hist. Chester Co., Pa., 624; Kirk Gen. (1872) 252 pp.

KIRKEETE, KARKEET, or CARKEET:—William Kirkeete, Saco, died 1662. The name seems strange, yet one William K., of Lynn, who may have come from Saco, by wife Lydia had Robert, born at Salem, 1697.

KIRKHAM:—Thomas Kirkham, Wethersfield, 1648, had Samuel, and, perhaps other children, but not on record.

KIRMAN:—John Kirman, Lynn, 1632, freeman 1633, represent. 1635.

KIRTLAND, or KERTLAND, now commonly KIRKLAND:—John Kirtland, Saybrook, by tradition called one of the first settlers, but very likely was not; was son of Nathaniel, of Lynn; married 1679, Lydia, daughter of Lieut. William Pratt, had John, born 1681; Priscilla 1683; Lydia 1685; Eliz. 1688; Nathaniel 1690; Philip 1693; Martha 1695; Samuel 1699; Daniel 1701; and Parnell 1704; was a lieut., and died 1716.

NATHANIEL KIRTLAND, Lynn, came in the Hopewell, Capt. Bundock, from London, 1635, aged 19, called of Sherington, in Co. Bucks, near Olney, went to Long Island with first settlers there, but after few years came back to L. There, by wife Parnell, had Ann, born 1658; John 1659; Hannah 1662; Eliz. 1664; Martha and Mary, twins, 1667; and he died 1686.

PHILIP KIRTLAND, Lynn, came in the Hopewell, Capt. Bundock, from London, 1635, aged 21, prob. brother of above, and from same place in England; went with him to settle on L. I., but came back sooner than he; was a shoemaker, Lewis says; by wife Alice had Mary, born 1640; Sarah 1646; Susanna 1652; Hannah, and Ebenezer, twins, 1654. He had elder brother John whose residence is unknown, and died in or before 1659, and his wife Alice married Evan Thomas, of Boston, who in favor of children made conveyance of estate in trust 1661.

REFERENCES:—Brown's Simsbury, Ct., 89; Burk and Alvord Gen., 187-94; Kirtland Gen. (1894) 5 pp.; Muzzey's Reminiscences; N. E. Hist. Gen. Reg., XLVIII., 66-70; Wetmore Gen., 584-7; Young's Life of J. T. Kirkland, 78-80.

KIRTSHAW:—John Kirtshaw, Newton, L. I., 1655.

KISKEYES, or KESKEYS:—Henry Kiskeyes, Boston, married, 1656, Ruth, daughter of Richard Graves, had Henry, born 1657; misprinted in Geneal. Reg., X., 68.

KITCHELL:—Robert Kitchell, Guilford, 1639, had wife Margaret; son Samuel; Hannah; and Sarah, who died 1657; was given power in 1665, to hold court at G., but next year removed to N. J., where he was distinguished, and is called in hist. the benefactor of Newark. His widow removed to Greenwich, there died 1679.

REFERENCES:—Kitchel Gen. (1879) 80 pp.; Savage's Gen. Dict., III., 32; Tuttle Gen., 667.

KITCHEN:—John Kitchen, Salem, 1640, freeman 1643, shoemaker, by wife Eliz. had there bapt. Eliz. and Hannah, 1643; Joseph 1645; John 1646, died soon; Mary 1648; John, again, 1652; and Robert 1655; was chosen sealer of leather 1655, and died 1676.

KITCHERELL, KETCHERWELL, KETCHERING, or KECHERELL, sometimes with the first letter C.:—Joseph Kitcherell, Charlestown, 1636.

SAMUEL KITCHERELL, Hartford, by wife Martha had Martha; Samuel, and Hannah, born 1646; and he died 1650. His widow married 1651, Anthony Dorchester, of Springfield, where Samuel died 1651, and Hannah 1658, and Martha married 1659, Abel Wright.

KITTREDGE:—John Kittredge, Billerica, 1661, or earlier; the ancestor of the many thousands of the name in our land, came, it is said, in youth with his mother, was a farmer; had John, born 1666; James 1668; Daniel 1670; Jonathan 1674, who died 1696; and Benoni 1677, posthum., for the father died 1676.

REFERENCES:—Aldrich's Walpole, 303-5; Am. Ancestry, VI., 32; Chase's Hist. Chester, N. H., 552; Draper's Hist. Spencer, Mass., 217; Hazen's Billerica, Mass., 85-8; Secomb's Hist. Amherst, N. H., 661; Temple's N. Brookfield, Mass., 1664-7.

KNAPP:—Aaron Knapp, Taunton, 1643, may have been father of Eliz., who married 1674, Nicholas Stoughton; and besides had Mary, bapt. at Roxbury, 1659; and he died before 1676. Baylies, II., 267, 278.

JOHN KNAPP, Taunton, married 1685, Sarah Austin.

NICHOLAS KNAPP, Watertown, may have come in the fleet with Winthrop and Saltonstall 1630; by wife Eleanor had Jonathan, who was buried 1631; Timothy 1632; Joshua 1635; Caleb 1637; Sarah 1639; Ruth 1641; and Hannah 1643; removed to Stamford; there, it is supposed, had Moses and Lydia. His wife Eleanor died 1658, and he married next year Unity, widow of Peter Brown, who had been widow of Clement Buxton; died 1670.

ROGER KNAPP, New Haven, 1643-7, Fairfield 1656-70, and prob. later; had made his will 1673, named wife Eliz. and children Jonathan, Josiah, Lydia, Roger, John, Nathaniel, Eliz., and Mary.

THOMAS KNAPP, Sudbury, married at Watertown 1688, Mary, daughter of John Grout, and died beyond sea, leaving widow and children, Sarah aged 9 and Mary 6.

WILLIAM KNAPP, Watertown, 1636, died 1658, "aged about 80 years." Perhaps he came as early as Nicholas, and had in his will of 1655 not named any wife, but referred to children, of whom several were brought by him from England. They were William; Mary; Eliz.; John, born 1624; James 1627; Ann; and Judith.

REFERENCES:—Am. Ancestry, II., 68; IV., 162; VII., 166, 207; Baird's Hist. Rye, N. Y., 416; Benedict's Hist. Sutton, Mass., 682; Bond's Hist. Watertown, Mass., 327; Cleveland's Yates Co., N. Y., 149, 711; Cleveland Gen., 228-31; Draper's Hist. Spencer, Mass., 215; Hemenway's Vt. Gaz., V., 149; Huntington's Stamford, Ct., Settlers, 61-4; Jackson's Hist. Newton, Mass., 360; Joslin's Hist. Poultney, Vt., 294-6; Knapp Gen. (1878); Lapham's Hist. Rumford, Me., 365; Paige's Hist. Hardwick, Mass., 408.

KNEELAND:—John Kneeland, Boston, one of the founders of the Scots Charitable Soc. 1657; by wife Mary had Mary, born 1659, died next year; Hannah 1663; Mary, again, 1666; John 1668; Solomon 1671; and Ruth 1673. He died at Roxbury, aged 59.

PHILIP KNEELAND, Lynn, 1637.

REFERENCES:—Am. Ancestry, V., 45; Champion Gen.; Herrick's Hist. Gardner, Mass., 364; Hodgman's Hist. Westford, Mass., 459; Ridlon's Harrison, Me., Settlers, 86-9.

KNELL, KNEALE, or KNILL:—John Knell, Charlestown, perhaps son of Nicholas, removed to Boston, had wife Eliz., who became 3rd wife of Nathaniel Bachiler, of Hampton, 1689. Children of K. were John, born 1679; bapt. 1680; Hannah bapt. 1681; and Rachel 1683.

NICHOLAS KNELL, Stratford, 1650; married Eliz., widow of Thomas Knowles, of New Haven, had John, born 1651, died soon; Eliz. 1653; Isaac 1655; John, again, 1657; by the government was granted in 1668 50 acres, and as much more next year; and died 1675.

PHILIP KNELL, Charlestown, perhaps brother of John, by wife Ruth, married 1666, as wid. Allen, had Ruth, 1670; Eliz. 1674; and Philip 1675.

REFERENCES:—Orcutt's Stratford, Ct., 1233.

KNIGHT, or KNIGHTS:—Alexander Knight, Ipswich, 1635, had kept an Inn at Chelmsford, Eng., says Vincent in his Hist. of the Bequot war. Perhaps he came in the Defence—at least in the same ship that year came from London, Sarah K., aged 50, and Dorothy, 30, of whom one might be widow and the other sister or daughter.

APSIA KNIGHT, Charlestown, 1637, of the force of Frothingham, 57 and 88, can render such a name credible; perhaps it might have been Apphia.

CHARLES KNIGHT, Salem, a soldier of Gardner's comp. wounded in great Narragansett fight 1675.

DANIEL KNIGHT, York, 1640, perhaps in Indian war, removed to Lynn, died 1672. He may have been son of Jacob.

EZEKIEL KNIGHT, Salem, of the grant of land 1637, which Felt mentions drew him thither, but most of his days were at Braintree; by wife Eliz., who was buried 1642, had Ezekiel, born 1641, died at 7 mos.

EZEKIEL KNIGHT, Wells, 1645, prob. had wife and children in early life, and may be the same as the preceding; was commiss., i. e., represent. 1661, at York, much betrust. in public service, and afterward, 1662,

married Mary, daughter of Gov. Theophilus Eaton, widow of Valentine Hill, of Dover, formerly of Boston; and next, the widow of John Lovering, and she died before June, 1675. His will mentioned son Ezekiel, and daughter Eliz. Wentworth, of Dover, who is believed to have been wife of Ezekiel W.

FRANCIS KNIGHT, Pemaquid, 1648.

GEORGE KNIGHT, Hingham, came 1638, in the Diligent, with wife and children from Barrow, a parish of Co. Suffolk, near Bury, St. Edmunds.

GEORGE KNIGHT, Scarborough, died 1671, in his will of that year mentions wife Elinor, son Nathan, and daughter Eliz. His widow married Henry Brooking.

GEORGE KNIGHT, Hartford, 1671, died 1699, leaving widow Sarah, several daughters, but no sons.

JOHN KNIGHT, Dorchester, 1634, with prefix of respect. prob. removed, but may be that John who died in a town not mentioned 1634.

JOHN KNIGHT, Newbury, came from Southampton 1635 in the James; was a tailor of Romsey in Hauts. adm. freeman with his brother Richard 1635, had wife Eliz., who died 1645, and by her, or a former wife, had John, born 1622. His next wife was Ann, widow of Richard Ingersoll, of Salem, and he died 1670.

JOHN KNIGHT, Watertown, 1636, a maulster, prob. not the freeman of 1636, as Bond thought; was among original proprs. of Sudbury 1642; prob. the freeman of 1643, was of Woburn 1653, first signer of a petition for church liberty.

JOHN KNIGHT, Lynn, had Martha, born 1657.

JOHN KNIGHT, Northampton, freeman 1676.

JOHN KNIGHT, Charlestown, not son of John of the same; by wife Persis had Persis, bapt. 1669, died young; . Mary 1670; Persis, again, 1672; John 1673; Samuel 1675; perhaps several more, and some of them may belong to the other John of C., for Mr. Wyman says, no John of C. had wife Persis.

JOHN KNIGHT, not son of 1st John of Charlestown, married 1681, Abigail, eldest child of John Craggin; had Abigail 1681; John 1684, died next year; John, again, 1686; Benjamin 1688, died under 10 years; Samuel 1690; Ebenezer 1695; Rebecca 1698; Benjamin 1700; and Amaziah 1703.

JOHN KNIGHT, perhaps son of Richard of the same, married Leah, widow of Benedictus Tarr, it is said, but no more is known of him except that his inv. was brought in 1700.

JONATHAN KNIGHT, Salem, 1670, married prob. at Woburn 1663, Ruth Wright, and had Jonathan; Ebenezer; Enos; Ruth; and Deborah; and he died 1683. He was probably son of 1st Philip. A John, with wife Mary, and Joseph, with wife Hannah, early at Watertown, are ment. by Bond, but no issue is found in his volume.

JOSEPH KNIGHT, Woburn, freeman 1652, had Sarah, born 1651; Samuel 1652, died next year; Hannah 1654; John 1656; Eliz. 1658; Mary 1660, died at 10 mos.; Dinah 1661; Samuel, again, 1663; Mary, again, 1672, died in a few months; Joseph 1673; Edward 1677; Isaac 1680, died next mo.; James 1681, died soon; Ruth 1882: Ebenezer 1684; and Amos 1687; but most prob. by more than one wife, and quite prob. by 2 Josephs. The senior died 1687, and wife Hannah died 1695.

JOSEPH KNIGHT, named by Thomas Spaule, of Boston, in his will 1671, as the husband of testator's daughter Mary, and having children, and to her and them mankind resid. devise aft. that to his own wife dur. wid., was prob. of B.

MAUTLYN, or MACKLIN KNIGHT, Boston, 1643, had wife Dorothy.

MICHAEL KNIGHT, Woburn, married 1657, Mary Bullard, had Mary, born 1658; Jonathan 1662; Joshua 1665; Lydia 1674; and he had been adm. freeman 1654.

PHILIP KNIGHT, Charlestown, had wife Margery, children Jonathan, Philip, Rebecca, Eliz., and Mary, who, at his death were of the ages respect. about 26, 23, 17, 13, and 11; but he had removed long before to Topsfield, or near it, and died 1668.

RICHARD KNIGHT, Newbury, prob. younger brother of the first John, came with him from Southampton in the James, 1635, called in the custom house record tailor of Romsey, in Hauts; married, says Coffin, Agnes Coffley, who died 1679; had Rebecca, born 1643; Sarah 1648; Ann; and Eliz. He was sworn freeman 1636, was deacon, and died 1683, aged 81.

RICHARD KNIGHT, Weymouth, 1637, mentioned by Winthrop, II., 348; may be he who was recorded an inhab. of Boston early in 1642, a slater, being adm. of the church, and perhaps son of a widow Susan; freeman 1642; by wife Dinah had Samuel 1643, died soon; Joseph, 1645; and by wife Joanna had Joanna 1653; James 1655; but it may be very difficult to distinguish him from others of the name.

RICHARD KNIGHT, Hampton, perhaps Portsmouth, 1643, was perhaps of Dover, 1659, or before 1668, of Boston, a merchant.

RICHARD KNIGHT, Boston, by wife Joanna had James, who died 1652; Sarah 1656; and Mary 1659.

RICHARD KNIGHT, Newport, 1648, next year chosen Gen. Sergent, whatever that may mean, and many years bought land of Indians on the Contin. 1665 in conjunct. with Henry Hall, of Westerly. He had eldest son John, of Norwich, as from law papers Savage learns; and this may imply that he had other children.

RICHARD KNIGHT, Boston, 1673, bricklayer, was called to serve in Philips' war on Conn. river in Capt. Turner's comp. Perhaps he married Sarah Kimball, and had daughter Eliz., to whom her uncle, John Kimball, gave estate. This Richard was bred a carver, but married a wife of superior mind, Sarah, daughter of Thomas Kemble, or Kimball, of Charlestown.

ROBERT KNIGHT, Hampton, 1640, removed to Boston, had, by first wife, Samuel, born 1642, who prob. died young. He married Ann, the young widow of Thomas Cromwell, the rich privateersman, early in 1650, and may therefore have spent a year or more in Maine, but had Edward, born 1652; and Martha 1653; besides James, in 1654, who prob. died soon; and he died 1655.

ROBERT KNIGHT, Marblehead, 1648, may be he who died at Cambridge 1652; but nothing more is known.

ROBERT KNIGHT, Kittery, 1647, removed to York, died 1676; his will ment. son Richard, living in Boston.

ROGER KNIGHT, Portsmouth, 1631, among the people sent by Mason, the patentee. Belkn., I., 425.

SAMUEL KNIGHT, Roxbury, married 1685, Sarah, perhaps daughter of Abraham Howe of the same, had Mehitable, born 1686, died under 17 years; Samuel, who died 1689; and Ebenezer 1694.

THOMAS KNIGHT, Salem, 1661, a mason, perhaps son of Walter.

TOBY KNIGHT, Newport, 1638.

WALTER KNIGHT, Salem, 1626, had been here in 1622, and is now sent over by the Dorchester people to strengthen Conant; perhaps was of Duxbury 1638, and in 1653 giving evidence about something that occurred in 1622, perhaps only hearsay; he called his age 66.

WILLIAM KNIGHT, Salem, a mason, had grant of land 1637, yet seems rather to belong of Lynn; freeman 1638; had John, Ann, Francis, Hannah, all by 2nd wife, Eliz. Jacob, Daniel, Eliz. and Mary, and died 1650. From Lewis was this account derived from Farmer; yet there is evidence that he had John and Francis, Joanna, and Mary only, all brought from England, and that the sons both went home, and there Francis died without issue; but John, after serving the parliam. cause in the civil war, obtained possession of estate in England that was his father's, and died in that country.

WILLIAM KNIGHT, Topsfield, came, perhaps, in 1638, or else not before 1639, in which year he had grant of 200 acres at Ipswich.

REFERENCES.—Massachusetts—Ballou's Hist. Milford, 870; Coffin's Hist. Newbury, 307; Draper's Hist. of Spencer, 216; Hudson's Hist. Lexington, 280; Lyman's Hist. Eastonhampton, 181-3; Sewall's Hist. Woburn, 624; Stearn's Hist. Ashburnham, 782; Temple's Hist. N. Brookfield, 667-9; Temple's Northfield, 580; Wyman's Charlestown Gens., 590-2.

New Hampshire.—Cochrane's Hist. Antrim, 571; Hayward's Hist. Gilsum, 350; Hayward's Hancock, 699-721; Kidder's Hist. Ipswich, 415; Livermore's Hist. Wilton, 432; Norton's Hist. Fitzwilliam, 623-5; Secomb's Hist. Amherst, 662.

OTHER PUBLICATIONS.—Am. Ancestry, II., 68; V., 121; Austin's Ancestries, 37; Cregar's Haine's Ancestry, 50-2; Essex Inst. Hist. Coll., I., 186; Hinman's Ct. Settlers, I., 321; Knight (Frederick) Biog. (1855); Lapham's Hist. Norway, Me., 542; Lapham's Paris, Me., 654-6; Lapham's Rumford, Me., 366-8; N. E. Hist. Gen. Reg., XV., 269; Richmond, Va., Standard, III., 8; Thomas Family of Md., 104-6; Wentworth Gen., I., 137-9, 467; Wilder Gen., 160, 172.

KNOCKER:—George, and Thomas Knocker, misprinted in Geneal. Reg., III., 80, for Knower, of Charlestown.

KNOLLYS:—Hanserd Knollys, Dover, was born, it is said, 1598, at Cawkwell, in Co. Lincoln, bred at the University of Camb., ordained 1629, as a priest by the Bp. of Peterborough, renounc. the Church of England in 1636, and in 1638 came to N. E., though some Eng. books say a year earlier. On arriving at Boston he was refused permission of resid. thro. suspic. of antinomtaint, so that he went to New Hampshire jurisdict. and in 1641 home, reaching London last of that year. See Winth., I., 326; II., 27.

KNOTT:—George Knott, Sandwich, 1637, perhaps removed thither from Lynn, died 1648, leaving widow Martha, son Samuel, and daughter Martha.

JAMES KNOTT, a soldier on Conn. river 1676, under Capt. Turner.

RICHARD KNOTT, Marblehead, 1678, a surgeon with prefix of respect.

KNOWER:—George Knower, Charlestown, 1631, may have came in the fleet with Winthrop, lived on the Malden side, died 1675, leaving prop. to wife Eliz., son Jonathan, born 1645, and daughter Mary Mirable; mentions in his will another daughter, wife of Joses Bucknam.

JOSEPH KNOWER, of Massachusetts, 1639. Felt.

SAMUEL KNOWER, Malden, by wife Eliz. had Samuel, born 1690; is in Geneal. Reg., VI., 336, an error, for the father's name is Kenny.

THOMAS KNOWER, Charlestown, perhaps brother of George, was punished 1632, and it is supposed went home, but came again in 1635, then called 33 years, with Nell (perhaps Moll), 29; and Sarah, 7; thought to be wife and daughter in the Abigail. He died 1641.

REFERENCE:—Savage's Gen. Dict., III., 40.

KNOWLES:—Alexander Knowles, a freeman of Mass. 1636, whose residence is unknown; but in few years he removed to Fairfield, there was in good esteem, and was chosen an Asst. of the Col. of Conn. 1656. He died 1663, and in his will mentions sons John and Joshua, daughter Eliz. Ford, and perhaps another daughter.

HENRY KNOWLES, Warwick, on list of freemen 1655, in 1644 was of Portsmouth, R. I., and had, it is supposed, married a daughter of Robert Potter, of Warwick; and 1671 was in his 62nd year; in will he names sons John, William, and Henry, daughters Mary Lippit, and Martha Eldredge.

JOHN KNOWLES, Watertown, the 2nd minister of that town, was born in Lincolnshire, bred at Magdalen Coll., Cambridge; came over in 1638, and joined with church at Boston next year, having married prob. in Eng. the widow of Ephraim Davis; next year was dism. to go to aid Phillips at W. and there was ordained 1640 as pastor; went on a mission 1642, to Virginia, back next year, freeman 1650, and next year went home, and for some time preached at Bristol, was silenced by the act of 1662, and during the plague of London, 1665, was then with wife Eliz.; on the death of Presid. Chauncy, 1672, he was proposed to succeed him at Harvard College. He had a W., by wife Eliz., Mary, born 1641; Eliz. 1643; and Hannah. He died 1685.

JOHN KNOWLES, Hampton, took oath of allegiance 1678.

RICHARD KNOWLES, Cambridge, 1638, by wife Ruth had James, born 1648; may be he that died at Hampton 1682.

RICHARD KNOWLES, Plymouth, had Samuel, born 1651; removed to Eastham, had Mehitable 1653; Barbara 1656; and, perhaps, Mercy and others, before or after.

THOMAS KNOWLES, New Haven, 1655, was dead, leaving Eleazer and Thomas, before 1648. His widow married Richard Krill, of Stratford.

REFERENCES:—Austin's R. I. Dict., 332; Austin's Allied Fams., 160; Bangor, Me., Hist. Mag., V., 199; Chase's Hist. Chester, N. H., 552; Dow's Hist. Hampton, N. H., 778-81; Freeman's Hist. Cape Cod, II., 393, 736; Rich's Hist. Truro, Mass., 538; Savage's Gen. Dict., III., 41; Schevek's Hist. Fairfield, Ct., 392;

Thomas Fam. of Md., 106; Walker Gen., 46; Wyman's Charlestown, Mass., Gens., 592.

KNOWLTON:—Benjamin Knowlton, Springfield, married 1676, Hannah Mirick; had Mary, born 1677; Benjamin 1679; Sarah 1682; Mercy 1685, died young; Joseph 1687; and Mercy, again, posthum. He died 1690.

JOHN KNOWLTON, Ipswich, freeman 1641, died about 1654, leaving wife Margaret, children John, Abraham, and Eliz.

JONATHAN KNOWLTON, Malden, by wife Sarah, had Eliz., born 1688.

NATHANIEL KNOWLTON, Ipswich, freeman 1683, was a man of consequence.

SAMUEL KNOWLTON, Wenham, freeman 1680.

THOMAS KNOWLTON, Ipswich, 1648, brother of the first John, married 1668, Hannah Green, was deacon and prison keep.; died 1692.

WILLIAM KNOWLTON, Hingham, 1635, was, says Felt, the bricklayer, who died at Ipswich 1644.

REFERENCES:—Am. Ancestry, IV., 45; III., 208; IX., 244; Barry's Hist. Framingham, Mass., 311; Butler's Hist. Farmington, Me., 516-24; Cogswell's Hist. Nottingham, N. H., 734-6; Eaton's Hist. Thomaston, Me., II., 302; Hayward's Hist. Hancock, N. H., 721; Hill's Hist. Mason, N. H., 204; Morse's Hist. Sherborn, Mass., 160; N. E. Hist. Reg., XV., 344-6; XXXIV., 386; Savage's Gen. Dict., III., 42; Temple's Hist. No. Brookfield, Mass., 348-55.

KNOX:—John Knox, Watertown, by wife Hannah had Sarah, bapt. 1686; John 1689; and James 1690.

REFERENCES:—Bangor Hist. Mag., V., 129; Bent's Hist. Whiteside Co., Ills., 279; Eaton's Hist. Thomaston, Me., II., 303; Goode Gen., 122; Hanson's Old Kent, Md., 134-6; Knox Anniv. (1873), 107 pp.; Knox Gen. (1890), 34 pp.; Richmond, Va., Standard, II., 47; Temple's Hist. Palmer, Mass., 496 Wentworth Gen., I., 252-4.

KOLDOM, the other spelling of Coldham, which see.

KOSTLO:—John Kostlo, ———, by wife Sarah had Sarah, born 1663, and John 1666.

KOWDALE:—Edward Kowdale. See Cowdall.

L

LACOCK:—Lawrence Lacock, Boston, 1644; ship carpenter; had wife Alice.

LACY:—Lawrence Lacy, Andover, had Lawrence, born 1683; Abbot, 39. He was "the first person she afflict.," as poor Eliz. Johnson was driven to confess in the sad delusion of 1692.

MORGAN LACY, Saco, about 1660.

REFERENCES:—Am. Ancestry, II., 68; VIII., 115, 143; Cutter's Hist. Jaffrey, N. H., 390-3; Littell's Passaic Valley Gens., 204-7; Orcutt's Hist. Stratford, Ct., 1353.

LADD:—Daniel Ladd, Ipswich, came in the Mary and John 1634, by tradition called son of Nathaniel, was one of the first townsmen of Salisbury, about 1639, but, perhaps, not so long there, and became permanent inhab. of Haverhill after birth of one or two children. By wife Ann he had Eliz., born 1640; Daniel 1642; Lydia 1655; the three being on record at S.; Mary 1647; Nathaniel 1652; Ezekiel 1654; and Sarah 1657. Both he and his wife were living 1678.

JOHN LADD, married at Woburn, 1678, Eliz. Fifield.

JOSEPH LADD, Portsmouth, R. I., whose will of 1669 names children Joseph, William, Daniel, Mary, and Sarah.

REFERENCES:—Am. Ancestry, V., 50, 151, 224; Austin's R. I. Gen. Dict., 118; Corliss' Gen., 238; Cutts Gen., 364; Farrow's Hist. Islesborough, Me., 228; Hubbard's Hist. Stanstead Co., Canada, 176; Kitchell Gen., 58; Ladd Gen. (1890), 413 pp.; Savage's Gen. Dict., III., 43; Stiles' Hist. Windsor, Ct., II., 429; Walworth's Hyde Gen., 652-65.

LAHORNE:—Rowland Lahorne, Plymouth, 1636, Charlestown, 1649, had wife Flora.

LAIGHTON, or LEIGHTON:—George Laighton, Portsmouth, R. I., 1638, freeman there 1655; married Eliz. daughter of Thomas Hazard of the same.

JOHN LAIGHTON, Ipswich, 1648, may have been 10 years before at Newport.

RICHARD LAIGHTON, Rowley, 1643. His will of 1682 names children John, Ezekiel, Mary, and Sarah, daughter, perhaps, of the 1st Samuel Graves, had Eliz., born 1681; Samuel 1683, died at 2 days; and perhaps others.

THOMAS LAIGHTON, Lynn, freeman 1639, represent. 12 years betw. 1646 and 61, had Thomas, Margaret, Samuel, Rebecca, and Eliz.

THOMAS LAIGHTON, Saco, 1645, had John, who married 1665, Martha, daughter of Robert Booth.

THOMAS LAIGHTON, Dover, 1648, died 1672, leaving only son Thomas, Mary, Eliz., and Sarah. His widow Joanna married 1673, Job Clements, outlived him and died 1704.

THOMAS LAIGHTON, Portsmouth, R. I., 1638, freeman there 1655, perhaps was brother of George.

WILLIAM LAIGHTON, Kittery, married before 1650, Catharine, daughter of Nicholas Frost, had John, born 1661, and Eliz. about 1663, who died young; and he died 1666.

LAKE:—Henry Lake, Salem, 1649, a currier, perhaps the same who was of Dorchester, 1658, brother of Thomas of the same.

JAMES LAKE, Masachusetts, 1647. Felt. Perhaps only transient.

JOHN LAKE, Boston, 1643, a tailor, freeman 1644; by wife Mary, sister of Matthew and Richard Coy, had Caleb 1646, but prob. died young; and the father died 1677, leaving widow Lucy.

LANCELOT LAKE, Boston, 1695, physician, of whom nothing is known but that he married 1708 widow Catharine Child.

THOMAS LAKE, Dorchester, freeman 1641, died 1678, 7 days after his wife, leaving no children.

THOMAS LAKE, Boston, where he owned lands before his residence, an eminent merchant, came from London to New Haven, there married Mary, daughter of Stephen Goodyear, the deputy-gov. of that colony; had Stephen 1650; Mary 1653. died in few weeks; Thomas 1657; Mary, again, 1659, died soon; Edward 1661, died soon; Edward, again, 1662, died soon; Ann 1663; John 1666; Nathaniel 1668; Rebecca 1670; and Sarah 1671. He purchased 1654, from John Richards, half of Arousick isl. in the Kennebec, and many years had a trading house there; was freeman 1671, selectman, had large

transactions with the Indians, by whom he was killed 1676, being on a visit. It is learned from his will that he was brother of John, that his wife had sister Lydia, and not much more.

REFERENCES:—Austin's R. I. Gen. Dict., 118; Bergen's Kings Co., N. Y., Settlers, 179; Clute's Hist. Staten Island, 398; Crawford Fam. of Va., 110-2; Savage's Gen. Dict., III., 44; Stearn's Hist. Rindge, N. H., 590-3; Williams' Hist. Danbury, Vt., 183.

LAKEMAN:—William Lakeman, represent. of the Isle of Shoals 1692, says Farmer.

REFERENCES:—Pierce's Gorham, Me., 181; Runnel's Hist. Sanbornton, N. H., II., 431.

LAKIN:—John Lakin, Reading, prob. younger brother of William, was driven from Groton, Savage supposes, during the Indian war, but had by wife Mary, Sarah 1662; William 1664; Abigail 1667; Joseph 1670; Benjamin 1672; and Josiah 1675; and prob. went back to G., where he was ensign and had been of the first settlement, 1697. His father was son of William, and died in England, says Butler, and his widow married William Martin; he had daughters Mary and Sarah.

WILLIAM LAKIN, Groton, freeman 1670, died 1672, in 90th or 91st year.

WILLIAM LAKIN, Reading, brother of John, by wife Lydia, daughter of 1st Abraham Brown, had William, born 1655; John 1658; and Jonathan 1661; removed to Groton and had Abraham 1664, died soon; William 1665; Abraham, again, 1667; and Elias 1669; was prob. freeman 1672, died 1700.

REFERENCES:—Butler's Groton, 410-2; 473; Densmore's Hartwell Gen.; Green's Groton, Mass., Epitaphs, 242; Green's Early Groton. Mass., Settlers, 8; Hayward's Hist. Hancock, N. H., 722-35; N. E. Hist. and Gen. Reg., XLVIII., 444-6; Runnel's Hist. Sanbornton, N. H., II., 432; Savage's Gen. Dict., III., 45.

LAMB:—Edward Lamb, Watertown, 1633, had wife Margaret; children Hannah 1633; Mary 1635, died soon; Samuel 1637; Mary, again, 1639; John and Increase, twins, 1640, died both in a week; removed to Boston, there had Eliz. 1648. His widow married Samuel Allen. Coll. Rec., III., 216, and IV., pt. I., page 31.

JOHN LAMB, New London, 1664-9, was offered in the latter year to be made freeman; in 1677 lost a son by being struck by a mill-wheel, as told in Bradstreet's Journ. He perhaps was in 1712 in that part made Groton.

SAMUEL LAMB, Springfield. freeman 1690.

THOMAS ROXBURY, came 1630, in the fleet with Winthrop, brought wife Eliz. and 2 children, Thomas and John; req. adm. and was made freeman next year; had Samuel; Abel 1633; Decline. the 1st daughter, 1637; and Benjamin 1639, died soon, as did the mother. He married 1660, Dorothy Harbottle, "a godly sis. of the church"; had Caleb 1641; Joshua 1642; Mary 1644; and Abiel 1646. He died following year.

WILLIAM LAMB, Boston, 1668, died 1685.

REFERENCES:—Am. Ancestry, V., 125; VIII.. 124; Barry's Hist. Framingham. Mass., 311-3; Bass' Hist. Braintree, 158; Davis' Gen., 29-31, 98; Draper's Hist. Spencer. Mass.. 217-20; Eaton's Hist. Thomaston, Me.. 303; Ellis' Hist. Roxbury. Mass.; Littell's Passaic Valley Gens., 207; Miller's Hist. Colchester Co.. N. S., 341; Paul's Hist. Wells, Vt., 109-14; Powers' Hist. Sangamon Co., Ills., 435-7; Savage's Gen. Dict., III., 46-8; Stearns' Hist. Rindge, N. H., 594; Temple's No. Brookfield, Mass., 670; Temple's Hist. Palmer, Mass., 506.

LAMBERT :—Ezra Lambert, Salem, fisherman, taken by the French 1689.

FRANCIS LAMBERT, Rowley, freeman 1640, by wife Jane had John; Ann, brought from England prob. with other children, and here had Jonathan, born 1639; Gershom 1643; and Thomas 1645; and died 1648.

JESSE LAMBERT, Milford, 1680, married 1688, Deborah, daughter of William Fowler the 2nd, had Rachel; Martha, who died at 20 years unmarried; Richard, died young; Sarah; Jesse, born 1693; Deborah, died unmarried; Eliz. and David 1700. He had 2nd wife Joanna, and died 1718.

JOHN LAMBERT, Lynn, a fisherman about 1644, Salem 1663, at Lynn again till death, 1676.

JOHN LAMBERT, Saybrook, married 1668, Mary Lews.

JOHN LAMBERT, Hingham, removed, says Deane, to Scituate, there had John born 1693.

MICHAEL LAMBERT, Lynn, 1647, had wife Eliz., who died 1657, and he married 1659, Elinor, widow of Strong Furnell, had Michael, and Mary born 1662; and, perhaps by 3rd wife, Moses 1673, and died 1676.

RICHARD LAMBERT, Salem, 1637, had then grant of land, and perhaps daughter Esther, who married 1659, Jeremiah Bootman.

RICHARD LAMBERT, Salem, perhaps son of preceding, not possibly the same, was killed by the Indians 1675, at Bloody Brook, with the flower of Essex, under Capt. Lothrop.

ROBERT LAMBERT, Boston, came from Dartmouth, in Devon, it is said, was among the founders of the first church of Bapt. in Boston, 1665.

THOMAS LAMBERT, Dorchester, 1637, may be the illspelling of Lombard.

WILLIAM LAMBERT, came in the Susan and Ellen, from London 1635, aged 26; but where he sat down is unknown.

REFERENCES :—Am. Ancestry, II., 69; Blake Gen., 42; Cathren's Woodbury, Ct., 667-12, 1512; Essex Inst. Hist. Coll., XXII., 133-5; Lambert's Hist. New Haven, Ct., 207-16; Lambert Gen. (1892), 56 p.; Littell's Passaic Valley Gens., 208-11; Savage's Gen. Dict., III., 48; Winsor's Duxbury, Mass., 274.

LAMBERTON :—George Lamberton, New Haven, 1641, prob. merchant from London, was one of the chief inhabs. employed 1643 in project. a settlement at Delaware, but resisted by the Swedes, who vindicated their right; by wife Margaret had Mercy, bapt. 1641; Desire 1642; and Obedience 1655; went in January, 1646, for England in the ship of 80 tons, "cut out of the ice 3 miles," with Mr. Gregson, the wife of Dep.-Gov. Goodyear, and others, which was never heard of. He left widow, who married Dep.-Gov. Stephen Goodyear, and, perhaps, daughter Eliz., who married 1654 Daniel Sillevant; Desire. married 1659, Thomas Cooper, Jr., of Springfield; Hannah, married Samuel Wells, and, next, Col. John Allyn; and Obedience, who married 1676 Samuel Smith. Yet it is not sure that these were his daughters, and possibly another family may have come, for at Jamaica, L. I., was a Thomas, 1686.

REFERENCES :—Am. Ancestry, IX., 135; Hyde's Ware, Mass., 52; Kulp's Wyoming Fams.; Savage's Gen. Dict., III., 48; Stile's Hist. Windsor, Ct., II., 429; Temple's Hist. Palmer, Mass., 505.

LAMBSHEAD :—Thomas Lambshead, Marblehead, 1666. Felt. Sister L. was of the church in Boston, 1673.

LAMPHEAR :—See Lampfear.

REFERENCE :—

LAMPREY, LAMPHREY, LAMPER, or LAMPRELL :—Henry Lamprey, Boston, 1652, a cooper, by wife Julian had Mary, born 1653, and Mary, again, 1657, but elder children he perhaps had before coming, Henry, Daniel, and Elizabeth. He prob. removed to Hampton, or Exeter, perhaps both in different times, was of grand jury 1684, when was, also, a David L. there. In 1678 he, and Benjamin, and Daniel took oath of alleg. Henry, the son, not the father, it is supposed, married 1686, Eliz. Mitchell.

REFERENCE :—Dow's Hampton, 782-97.

LAMSON :—Barnabas Lamson, Cambridge 1635, had brought Joseph, prob. other children, perhaps all those named in his will, Geneal. Reg., II., 104, which distributed them to near friends in the church; Mary, Sarah, Barnaby, Martha, and Joseph. He died before 1642.

JOHN LAMSON, Ipswich, freeman 1674; if it may be assumed that the name printed in Col. Rec., V., 536, as likewise Mr. Paige's list, Lumpson, is wrong.

SAMUEL LAMSON, Reading, among early settlers, freeman 1677, died 1692, whose Samuel, Jr., might be his son.

THOMAS LAMSON, New Haven, died 1664, in his will names only 2 children, Jonathan, who was bapt. 1645, and Zubah, who married 1670, Joshua Wills, of Windsor.

WILLIAM LAMSON, Ipswich, freeman 1637, died 1659, leaving widow Sarah, and 8 children, whose names are not seen. His widow married 1661, Thomas Hartshorn, of Reading.

REFERENCES :—Am. Ancestry, IV., 131; V., 206; Bell's Hist. Exeter, N. H., 27; Bond's Hist. Watertown, N. H., 329; Burnet's Dod Gen., 112; Goode Gen., 291; Leland Gen., 163; Orcutt's Hist. Stratford, Conn., 1235; Savage's Gen. Dict., III., 49; Secomb's Hist. Amherst, N. H., 644-6; Temple's Hist. N. Brookfield, Mass., 670; Wyman's Charlestown, Mass., Gens., 594-7.

LANCASTER, or LANKASTER :—Henry Lancaster, Dover, 1634, testif. in 1882, that he knew Walford, of Portsmouth, 50 years before. It may be the same as Langstaff.

JOSEPH LANCASTER, Salisbury, by wife Mary had Joseph, born 1666; Mary 1667; and Thomas 1669; removed to Amesbury; freeman 1690.

WILLIAM LANCASTER, Fairfield, 1654, had lands perhaps never occupied, but removed soon.

WILLIAM LANCASTER, Providence, did not remove in 1676.

REFERENCES :—Cogswell's Nottingham; Lancaster's Hist. Gilmanton, N. H., 274; Merrill's Hist. Ackworth, N. H., 236-8; Runnel's Sanbornton, N. H., II., 433-6.

LANCLON, easily mistaken for Langdon, which may be referred to.

LAND:—Edward Land, Duxbury, 1666.

LANDDIER:—Charles Landdier, Dover, 1672. It seems an unusual name, but may not be impossible.

LANDER:—John Lander, Portsmouth, or Kittery, 1639, a fisherman, died before 1646. Belkn., I., 28.

THOMAS LANDER, came in the Abigail from London 1635, aged 22, removed 1637 to Sandwich, there had John, born 1651.

WILLIAM LANDER, Marshfield, 1643, died 1648.

LANDFEAR, or LAMPHEAR:—George Lamp-iear, Westerly, R. I., 1669, had Richard, Shadrack, John, Theodosius, Seth, and daughters of whom one was wife of Eber Crandall; Mary, Sarah, and Eliz.

LANDON:—James Landon, Boston, or Charles-town, member of the first Bapt. church 1670. Mr. Wy-man thinks this name was Lowden.

REFERENCES:—Am. Ancestry, II., 69; Va. Mag. of Hist. and Biog., II. (1895); Wyman's Hunt Gen., 116.

LANE:—Ambrose Lane, Portsmouth, 1648-50, then called (as from its original settle. it had been), Straw-berry bank, shipmaster, was, perhaps, brother of Sam-son, who mortgaged to him that year all his prop. for £1,000.

DANIEL LANE, New London, 1652, married Catha-rine, widow of Thomas Doxy, removed 1661 to L. I., was one of the grantees of Brookhaven 1666.

EDWARD LANE, Boston, a merchant, came in the Speedwell, from London, 1656, aged 36, having bought, 1651, estate of Robert Harding; married 1657, Ann, daughter of Benjamin Keayne; had Ann, born 1660, died soon; and Edward 1662. He next year sold est. at Malden to Richard Dexter, and lived not long after. His widow married Nicholas Paige.

GEORGE LANE, Portsmouth, freeman 1672.

ISAAC LANE, Middletown, 1669, that year married Hannah, only daughter of Nathaniel Brown; had Han-nah, born 1671; Eliz. 1673; Eleanor 1674; Isaac, and John, twins, 1675, both died soon; John, and Sarah, twins, 1677, both died soon; John, again, 1681; Na-thanial, 1682, died soon; Isaac 1683; Benoni 1685, died at 4 years; Mary 1687, died soon; Mary, again, 1688, died soon; Abigail, 1690, died very soon; and Nathaniel, again, 1694, died at 8 years; and the father, who in 1704, called his age 65, died 1711.

JAMES LANE, Boston, carpenter, had come from Ply-mouth in Old England with son Francis. Had wife Dousabel, and son James, who prob. remained at home.

JOB LANE, Rehoboth, 1644, was in England 1647, when his kinsman, Thomas Howell, of Marshfield, made his will, naming him to be excor., but he declined that trust, yet after some years came back, and settled at Malden, freeman 1656, had by wife Sarah, who died 1659, Rebecca, born 1658, died young. He married 1660, Hannah, or Ann, daughter of Rev. John Reyner; had John, born 1661; Ann 1662, died in few weeks; Je-mina 1666; Dorothy 1669; and Rebecca, again, 1674; removed to Billerica, was represent. 1676-9, and for Malden 1685, and under the new chart. in 1692. He died 1697, and his widow 1704. From his will we learn that he had other daughters, Mary Avery; another Ann, wife of James Foster, of Dorchester; and Sarah, wife of Samuel Fitch.

JOHN LANE, Milford, 1640, perhaps, or soon after had good estate, freeman 1665.

JOHN LANE, Boston, 1674, cordwainer.

JOHN LANE, of Falmouth, before 1690.

JOSHUA LANE, a soldier under Capt. Turner, 1676, on Conn. river, from E. part of Col.; was after at Falmouth.

ROBERT LANE, Stratford, 1665-85. He may be the man, by Field 107, said to be from Derbysh. and an early settler, but with no more precise date, at Killing-worth.

SAMSON LANE, Portsmouth, 1631, one of Mason's men, said to have come from Teignmouth in Devon; purch. 1646 the est. that had been Thomas Wannerton's, and was then called master of the Neptune, of Dart-mouth; in 1650 mortgaged the estate and his other prop., includ. a ship on the stocks, to Ambrose L., be-fore ment., and prob. went home.

SAMUEL LANE, Hadley, had been a soldier 1676, from the E. under Capt. Turner; married 1677, Sarah, daugh-ter of 1st John Dickinson, of H. Had Samuel and Sarah; removed to Suffield, then had Mary, born 1684; John 1686; and Eliz.; and he died about 1690, leaving these 5 children; and his widow married 1691, Martin Kellog.

WILLIAM LANE, Dorchester, 1641, from whose will, made 1651, we learn that he had sons Andrew, and George, both of Hingham; daughters, Mary Long and Eliz. Rider, besides others whose bapt. names are not seen, wives of Nathaniel Baker, and of Thomas Lin-coln, of Hingham.

WILLIAM LANE, Boston, 1651, freeman 1657, by wife Mary had Samuel, born 1652; John 1654; and Mary 1656, says record in Geneal. Reg., IX., 312. His wife died 1656, by G. R., X., 220; and he married soon after Mary, daughter of Thomas Brewer, of Roxbury; had Sarah 1657; William 1659; and Eliz. 1662.

REFERENCES:—Massachusetts.—Bason's Hist. Glou-cester, 111, 257; Brown's Bedford Fams., 19-23; Clark's Hist. Norton, 84; Hazen's Hist. Billerica, 88; Hobart's Hist. Abington, 411-4; Stearn's Hist. Ashburnham, 783-91; Temple's Hist. No. Brookfield, 571; Temple's Hist. of Northfield, 480; Wyman's Charlestown Gens., II., 597.

New Hampshire.—Aldrich's Walpole, 309; Chase's Hist. of Chester, 553-5; Dow's Hist. Hampton, 798-808; Eaton's Hist. Candia, 86; Fullonton's Hist. Raymond, 240-7; Livermore's Hist. Wilton, 433; Runnel's San-bornton, II., 436-51; Sanderson's Charlestown, 469; Wheeler's Hist. Newport, 457-9.

OTHER PUBLICATIONS:—Am. Ancestry, II., 69; III., 31; Buxton, Me., Centen., 198-205; Goodwin's Buxton, Me., 260-2, 286, 296; Gregory's Hist. Northfield, Vt., 153-6; Lane Gen. (1856), 6 p.; (1857), 24 p.; (1885), 35 p.; (1886), 58 p.; (1888), 12 p.; (1891), 296 p.; N. E. Hist. Gen. Reg., II., 360; X., 356; XIII., 141-52; XXVII., 176-81; Savage's Gen. Dict., III., 50-4; Whit-more's Copp's Hill Epitaphs; Williams' Hist. Danbury, Vt., 184.

LANESON:—Jacob Laneson, Weymouth; by wife Susanna had Abigail, born 1680, and Susanna 1683.

LANFEAR:—See Landfear.

LANG:—John Lang, Portsmouth, married a daugh-ter of William Brooking.

REFERENCES :—Coffin's Boscawen, N. H., 571; Driver Gen., 287; Essex Inst. Hist. Coll., VI., 257; Lapham's Hist. Rumford, Me., 368; Montague Gen., 302-4; Runnel's Hist. Sanbornton, N. H., II., 452-5.

LANGBURY :—Gregory Langbury, Pemaquid, took oath of fidelity 1674.

JOHN LANGBURY, a soldier, killed 1676 at the Falls Fight. As he was of Turner's comp. he was from the E.

LANGDEN :—Thomas Langden, New Haven, 1650, a taverner, who had wife and one son at least. He prob. went home to England.

LANGDON :—David Langdon, Boston, by wife Martha had David, born 1685; Samuel 1686; Jonathan 1688; Mary 1698; Martha 1701; and Sarah 1704; and he died 1725, aged 75.

JOHN LANGDON, Boston, 1648, sailmaker, had Sarah; Benjamin; Abigail 1660; and perhaps others.

JOHN LANGDON, Farmington, joined the church there 1653, was a deacon, married the widow of Thomas Gridley.

JOHN LANGDON, Boston, by wife Eliz. had Eliz., born 1686; Josiah 1687; Ephraim 1690; Mary 1691; Joanna 1693; Nathaniel 1695; Margaret 1697; John 1698; and Margaret, again, 1703. He died 1732, aged 82.

PHILIP LANGDON, Boston, brother of the 2nd John of the same, a mariner, by wife Mary had Philip; Susanna, born 1677; John 1682; James 1685; Samuel 1687; Mary 1690; and Paul 1693. He died 1697, and his widow died 1717.

TOBIAS LANGDON, Portsmouth, 1662, had wife Eliz. and prob. several children; died 1664.

TOBIAS LANGDON, Portsmouth, perhaps son of the preceding, married 1686, Mary Hubbard, had Eliz. 1687; Tobias 1689; Martha 1692; Richard 1694; Joseph 1696; Mark 1698; Samuel 1700; William 1702; and John 1707.

REFERENCES :—Am. Ancestry, II., 69; IX., 208; Brewster's Portsmouth, II., 53-61, 362-6; Champion Gen.; Currier's Castleton, Vt., Epitaphs; Cutts Gen.; Green's Todd Gen.; Jordan's Leighton Gen. (1885); Langdon Gen. (1876), by Alger; N. E. Hist. Gen. Reg., XXX., 33-7; Savage's Gen. Dict., III., 54; Wentworth Gen., I., 329-36.

LANGER :—Henry Langer, Boston, 1655, by wife Ann had Susanna, born 1646.

RICHARD LANGER, Hingham, 1636, very aged, when he made his will 1660, in which he refers to daughters Dinah and Elizabeth, and Margaret, wife of Thomas Lincoln.

LANGFORD :—John Langford, Salem, moved in from another town, but which is unknown—possibly Sudbury; freeman 1645; was living at Salem 1689, says Farmer.

RICHARD, written LANKFORD, Plymouth, 1632.

REFERENCES :—Am. Ancestry, V., 132; Austin's R. I. Gen. Dict., 336; Narragansett Hist. Reg., II., 302-5.

LANGHORNE or LONGHORNE: — Richard Langhorne, Rowley 1649, died 1669.

THOMAS LANGHORNE, Cambridge 1644, by wife Sarah, daughter of Bartholomew Green, had, beside Thomas, who was born 1647, buried 1648, Sarah 1649, Eliz. and

Mary, Samuel 1660; Mercy 1662, and Patience 1664. He was the town drummer, and died 1685, aged 68 years.

REFERENCES :—Paige's Cambridge, 599; Lynchburg, Va., Sketches, 164-7; Paxton's Marshall Gen., 296; Savage's Gen. Dict., III, 55.

LANGLEY :—Abel Langley, Rowley 1651.

DANIEL LANGLEY, Boston 1689, mariner, went with others that year to take a piratical ship in Vineyard Sound, of which in Geneal. Reg. II, 393, is account.

JOHN LANGLEY, Hingham, married 1666, Sarah, daughter of Thomas Gill, was a soldier in the company of brave Capt. Johnson, of Roxbury, Dec. 1675; an innholder 1695. Of his children is known only Sarah, born 1668, who married 1686, Jonathan May of H.

WILLIAM LANGLEY, Lynn, freeman 1639, in 1677 was, it is thought, of Charlestown. But it may be well to see Longley.

REFERENCES :—Cogswell's Nottingham, 215; Essex Inst. Hist. Coll., XXII, 209; R. I. Hist. Mag., VI, 304-10.

LANGMEAD :—Richard Langmead, Boston perhaps, mariner, died 1660, leaving wife Ellen, who had administered 1661.

LANGMADE :—Hubbard's Stanstead, 178.

LANGSTAFF: — Henry Langstaff, Portsmouth 1631, or soon after, sent over by Mason, the patentee, was of the grand jury 1643, and at Dover 1648. Had Sarah, who married Anthony Nutter, also Henry; and died by a fall, says Pike's Journal, 1705, nearly 100 years old.

LANGTON, LANCKTON or LANKTON :—George Langton, Springfield 1646, married a second wife 1648, Hannah, widow of Edmund Haynes, had Esther (strangely called son in Geaneal. Reg. IX, 171), born 1649, and no more children; but had formerly been at Wethersfield, and by first wife had there, or in England, several children; removed about 1658, to Northampton, there died 1676. He will mentions son John, daughters Pritchet, Corbee, Hanshet (who was Deliverance, wife of Thomas), Hannum (who was Esther, wife of John), and grandson Samuel.

JOSEPH LANGTON, Ipswich 1648, may have been son of Roger.

ROGER LANGTON, Ipswich, freeman 1635. He may have died that year.

LANGWORTH :—Andrew Langworth, Newport, 1656, married about 1661, Rachel, daughter of Samuel Hubbard.

LAPHAM :—John Lapham, Malden, married 1671, a Hollis, no more is known of him.

JOHN LAPHAM, Providence, married Mary Mann, daughter William and Frances (Hopkins) Mann; had Mary (or Mercy), born 1673, John 1677 and William 1679. Was called 45 years old in 1680.

THOMAS LAPHAM, Scituate 1635, joined Lothrop's church 1636, married 1637, Mary, daughter of Nathaniel Tilden; had Eliz., bapt. 1638, Mary; Thomas, born 1643; Lydia, Rebecca 1645, Joseph 1648; in which year the father died.

REFERENCES :—Am. Ancestry, II, 70; III, 63; Austin's Ancestral Dict., 34; Austin's R. I. Gen. Dict., 120;

Ballou's Gen., 672-80; Cutt's Gen., 203; Deane's Hist. of Scituate, Mass., 302; Hanson's Hist. Gardiner, Me., 138; Lapham Gen. (1873) 31 pp.; Lapham's Hist. Bethel, Me., 578-81; Lapham's Hist. Paris, Me., 657-9; Lapham's Tabular Pedigree, 1864; Lapham's Hist. Woodstock, Me., 234; Savage's Gen. Dict., III, 56; Stearn's Hist. of Rindge, N. H., 594; Williams' Hist. Danbury, Vt., 184-7.

LAPTHORNE:—Stephen Lapthorne, Scarborough 1640.

LARAN:—John Laran, Jamaica, L. I., 1656.

LARGE:—Jervice Large, Scituate, a servant of Samuel Hinckley, brought probably from Co. Kent, was buried 1636.

JOHN LARGE, Branford 1672, perhaps came over from L. I., may be the man who married at Saybrook, 1659, Phebe, daughter of Thomas Lee, and possibly was son of William.

WILLIAM LARGE, Hingham 1635, removed with wife to Cape Cod, perhaps further.

REFERENCE:—Thomas Family of Md., 106; Savage's Gen. Dict., III, 56.

LARGIN:—Henry Largin, Boston, by wife Ann had Susanna, born 1646; by wife Alice had Joseph, born 1653, who died in few weeks.

JOHN LARGIN, a soldier from the East under Capt. Turner, at Hatfield 1676.

LARKHAM:—Mordecai Larkham, Beverly 1681, has numerous descendants, it is believed write name Larcom.

LARKIN:—Edward Larkin, Charlestown 1638, by wife Joan had John, born 1640, Sarah 1641, another record says Eliz. about same date, Thomas 1644, and probably Edward: certainly Sarah, again, 1648; was freeman 1640, artillery co. 1644. He died before middle life prob. and his widow married John Pentecost, and she died 1686, aged 70.

EDWARD LARKIN, Newport, in the list of freeman 1655, was represent. 1663. He was of Westerly, in the same colony 1669, and by wife Eliz., daughter of the first Henry Hall, had Edward and John, probably also Roger, and daughter Hannah to dwell there ten years later.

EDWARD LARKIN, Charlestown, perhaps son of the first Edward, married 1688, Mary Walker, had Edward, who died 1689; John, bapt. 1690, Mary 1693, John, again, 1695; Edward, again, 1696, Joanna 1699, and Samuel 1701.

JOHN LARKIN, Charlestown, perhaps brother of first Edward, by wife Joan had Hannah, born 1643, who married 1665, John Newell, outlived him, and died 1704.

REFERENCES:—American Ancestry, I. 48; Austin's R. I. Gen. Dict., 121; Clermont Co. Ohio Hist., 357; Morris and Flynt Gen., 57; Palmer and Trimble Gen., 200-3; Savage's Gen. Dict., III. 57; Winslow Gen., II, 565-70; Wyman's Charlestown Gen., 599-605.

LARRABEE:—Greenfield Larrabee, Saybrook, had, by his wife (supposed to have been a Brown of Providence), Greenfield, born 1648, John 1650, Eliz. 1653, Joseph 1655, died young, and Sarah 1658.

ISAAC LARRABEE, Falmouth, about 1680, being driven off by the Indians, went to Lynn, says Willis; had Benjamin, born 1666, at Casco; Samuel and Thomas. In Maine the name spread much.

WILLIAM LARRABEE, married at Malden 1655, Eliz., perhaps daughter of George Felt; was freeman 1690. Sometimes this name is perverted to Leatherby, as very often it was sounded.

REFERENCES:—Chandler's Shirley, 496; Corliss' No. Yarmouth, Me.; Eaton's Hist. of Thomaston, Me., II, 304; Libby Gen., 41; Machias, Me., Centen., 168; Savage's Gen. Dict., III, 57; Stearn's Hist. of Rindge, N. H., 595; Wheeler's Hist. of Brunswick, Me., 841.

LARY:—Cornelius Lary, Exeter, took oath of fidelity 1677.

LASKIN:—Hugh Laskin, Salem 1636, freeman 1639, died 1659.

LATCOME:—William Latcome, a passenger in the Hercules 1634, as printed in Geneal. Reg. IX, 267, which may be error for Larcom, or Larkham; but nothing can be known.

LATHAM:—Cary Latham, Cambridge, married Eliz., daughter of John Masters, and probably widow of Edward Lockwood; had Thomas, born 1639, Joseph (?), removed early to New London, where he was of active service; represent. 1664, and after to 70. He had there Elizabeth, who married 1678 John Leeds; Jane married Hugh Hubbard, Lydia married John Packer, and Hannah, who married probably John Lockwood. He died 1685.

LEWIS LATHAM, Newport, of whom no more is known, but that his daughter Frances married Jeremiah Clark, and was mother of Gov. Walter and others; but it may be that he never came to our shores.

ROBERT LATHAM, Cambridge, perhaps brother of Cary, lived two years or more with Rev. Thomas Shepard; removed to Marshfield, where he was constable 1643; thence to Plymouth, where he married Susanna, daughter of John Winslow, in 1649, and had Mercy, born 1650; before 1667 removed to Bridgewater; had sons James, Chilton, Joseph; daughters Eliz., Hannah and Sarah. Mitchell thinks him son of William. Hannah married Joseph Washburn.

WILLIAM LATHAM, Plymouth, came in the Mayflower 1620; servant to Gov. Carver, only a youth, and, in 1627, had shared in the division of cattle, being in the lot with Gov. Bradford, yet was never named as one of Mayflower company in 1620 when a boy under Carver's charge. By the discovery of Bradford's Hist. his right to passage in the first ship is proved. He was of Duxbury 1637-9, and Marshfield 1643, and 8, and in Bradford we see, that after so long resid. here, he went home to England, thence to the Bahamas, and died of starvation. Of one Latham in our country, there is idle tradition that he was brought up with Charles I, but no benefit or evil of the companionship is boasted.

REFERENCES:—Amer. Ancestry, II, 71; IV, 108; Austin's Ancestries, 127; Austin's Allied Fams., 161; Caulkin's Hist. New London, Ct., 312; Lapham's Hist. Norway, Me., 543; Mitchell's Hist. Bridgewater, Mass., 222-4; Powers' Hist. Sangamon Co., Ills., 445; Savage's Gen. Dict., III, 58.

LATHROP:—See Lothrop.

ARMS:—Gyronny of eight, az. and gu., an eagle displayed, arg. Also.

ARMS:—Quarterly, gu. and sa., an eagle displayed, arg.

CREST:—A Cornish chough: proper.

LATIMORE or LATIMER:—Christopher Lattimore, Marblehead 1648, in 1663 sold dwelling house to Robert Hooper, but was there living in 1674.

HUGH LATTIMORE, Marblehead, perhaps son of preceding, married 1669, Mary, daughter of William Pitt.

JOHN LATTIMORE, Wethersfield, had Rebecca, born 1646, Naomi 1648, Abigail 1649, John 1650, Elisheba 1652, Jonathan 1655 and Bezaleel 1657; he died 1662.

ROBERT LATTIMORE, New London, mariner, about 1660, married prob. at Boston, Ann, widow of Matthew Jones, and daughter of George Griggs, had Robert born 1664 and Eliz. 1667, and he died 1671.

REFERENCES:—Am. Ancestry, I, 48; II, 71; Bartow Gen., Part 2, 132-5; Brown's W. Simsbury, Ct., Settlers, 90; Caulkin's Hist. New London, Ct., 288; Clyde's Irish Settlement, Pa., 87-90; Coit Gen., 280; Freeman's Hist. Cape Cod, Mass., II, 590; N. E. Hist. Gen. Reg., XIX, 243, 317; Savage's Gen. Dict., III, 59; Stile's Hist. Windsor, Ct., II, 430; Thomas Family of Md., 107-17; Walworth's Hyde Gen., 192-953.

LATTING, LETTEN or LETTIN.—Richard Latting, Concord, had Josiah, born 1641, and another son 1643, but record gives not the name; removed to Fairfield, and thence in few years to L. I., about Huntington. In 1663 he was ordered to depart for not submit. to jurisdict. of Conn., and in 1672 was by New York denounced for disloyal speech against the duke.

REFERENCES:—N. Y. Gen. Rec., II, 8, 22, 54, 68; Savage's Gen. Dict., III, 59.

LAUGHTON:—Thomas Laughton, Boston 1660.

REFERENCES:—Savage's Gen. Dict., III, 59; Hudson's Lexington, 114; Vermont Hist. Gaz., V, 57-61.

LAURENSON:—James and John Laurenson, Newtown, L. I., 1686, were probably of Dutch descent.

LAURIE:—Francis Laurie, Salem, of whom Hist. Coll. of Essex Inst., II, 15, gives all that can be learned that will of 1665 mentions son-in-law John Neal and wife Mary, and grand children Jeremiah, John, Jonathan, Joseph and Lydia. But conjecture is bold enough to suggest that the same man is intended where Felt. II. 447, places the graveyard "on the hill above Francis Lawe's house," and there is no doubt of the soundness of conjecture after turning to the article Lawes in this volume.

GILBERT LAURIE, Boston 1686, went to preach that year in absence of Moody, at Portsmouth, was probably a Scotchman, and may be presumed to have gone home in 1689.

LAVENUKE:—Stephen Lavenuke, a Frenchman. married 1672, Mary Dival, perhaps French also, had Isabella, born 1673, Judith 1677, who died 1758, and Stephen 1678, who died 1764.

LAVERICK:—John Laverick, perhaps at Watertown, as servant of Richard Kimball. came at the age of 15, in the Elizabeth from Ipswich 1634.

LAVERS:—George and Jacob Lavers, Portsmouth

1683, petitioners to the King against Gov. Cranfield that year. Belkn. I, 473.

LAW:—Andrew Law, Hingham 1654, had Joshua, Josiah and Caleb, is by Farmer erroneously given, says Savage, for Lane, whom see.

JOHN LAW, Concord, married 1660, Lydia, daughter of Roger Draper, had John, born 1661, Thomas 1663, Stephen 1665 and Samuel.

JONATHAN LAW, Milford 1667, freeman 1669, perhaps only son of Richard, married Sarah, daughter of George Clark, Sr.; by her had Jonathan, born 1674, Harvard Coll. 1695, who was chief justice 16 years, and a distinguished Gov. of Conn.

LYMAN LAW, Gravesend, L. I., 1650.

RICHARD LAW, Wethersfield 1638, may, therefore, have first been at Watertown, married Margaret, eldest daughter of Thomas Kilbourne, had Abigail, Jonathan and Sarah, and probably more children; removed early to Stamford, may have been represent. in New Haven, Ct.; certainly was, after the union, in Conn. 1665, 6, 9 and 72. His daughter Abigail married Jonathan Sellick and Sarah married John Sellick.

WILLIAM LAW, Rowley 1643. Records show that he was dead 1669, leaving wife Faith and 4 children. Fifteen of this name, often in old records having es. final, had, in 1829, been graduated at the N. E. colleges, mostly Yale.

REFERENCES:—Cinc., Ohio, Criterion (1888), II, 476; Am. Ancestry, IX, 196; Essex Inst. Hist. Coll., XXII, 210; Hall's Gen. Notes, 104-12; Hall Gen. by T. P. Hall (1892), 11; Kilbourne Gen., 39-41; Power's Hist. Sangamon Co., Ills., 447; Savage's Gen. Dict., III, 60.

LAWES:—Francis Lawes, Salem, a weaver, born at Norwich, England, embarked at Ipswich, arrived at Boston 1637, with wife Lydia, aged 49, one child, Mary, and 2 servants, Samuel Lincoln 18 and Ann Smith 19. He was freeman 1641, and died about 1666. Mary married John Neal, and, next, Andrew Mansfield. See Laurie.

LAWRENCE:—David Lawrence, New Hampshire 1683, died 1710, leaving widow Mary, children Joseph, David and Phebe, and grand. ch. David and Jonathan.

GEORGE LAWRENCE, Watertown, married 1657, Eliz., daughter prob. of Benjamin Crispe, had Eliz., born 1659. Judith 1660, Hannah 1662, John 1664; killed by accident at 10 years; Benjamin and Daniel, twins, 1666; George 1668. Sarah 1671, Martha, and Grace 1680. His wife died 1681. and he married 1691, Eliz., perhaps widow of Joseph Holland. had Joseph, and Rachel and Patience, twins, 1694. He died 1709. Eliz. married 1679, Thomas Whitney; Judith married John Stearns; Hannah married prob. Obadiah Sawtell; Sarah married Thomas Rider; Mary married 1689. John Earle, and, next, Michael Flagg; Martha married 1697, John Dix, and Grace married an Edes.

HENRY LAWRENCE, Charlestown 1635. See Frothingham, 84. A widow Christian, whom Bond thought to be his, died 1648.

JOHN LAWRENCE, Watertown. freeman 1637, by wife Eliz. had John, born 1636. Nathaniel 1639. Joseph 1642, died at 2 months; Joseph, again, 1643, Jonathan, perhaps his twin brother, died soon; Mary 1645, Peleg 1647, Enoch 1649. Samuel. Isaac, Eliz. 1655. Jonathan, again, and Zechariah 1659, all at W. except Eliz., born at Boston, who may, however, have been another John's. He removed about 1662 to Groton, and his wife died there 1663, and he married 1664, Susanna, daughter of William Batchelor, of Charlestown, had Abigail, born 1666, prob. died young, and Susanna 1667. He died 1667, and his widow removed to Charlestown, there died 1668.

JOHN LAWRENCE, Newtown, L. I., one of the patentees of Hempstead, 1644, was there in 1655, but was first of Ipswich; came at the age of 17 with his mother, Joan Tuttle, and 16 other Tuttles, in the Planter, from London 1635; after conquest of New York, removed thither and was an alderman, mayor of the city, judge of the Sup. Ct. of the Prov., died 1699. He had Joseph, John, Thomas, Martha, Susanna, and Mary, who were all married, though none left issue to reach maturity except this last, whose husband was William Whittingham.

JOHN LAWRENCE, Boston, married 1654, Eliz. Atkinson, had Eliz., born 1655.

JOHN LAWRENCE, Boston, of that part called Muddy River, now Brookline, married 1657, Sarah, daughter of Thomas Buckminster, or by record, Buckmaster.

JOHN LAWRENCE, Wrentham, by wife Sarah, who died 1684, had Mary, born 1682.

NICHOLAS LAWRENCE, Charlestown 1648, may have been that brother of first John designed by his will.

RICHARD LAWRENCE, Branford 1646, had Bethia and Esther, both bapt. at New Haven, 1651, who are not found on record of birth at B., but others are; Eleazer 1652, Eldad 1655, died soon, and Sarah 1657. He signed the agreement for removal to New Jersey 1665, and was established at Passaic 1668.

ROBERT LAWRENCE, Falmouth 1680, married Mary, widow of Thomas Munjoy, daughter of John Phillips of Dorchester, was a man of distinction, lieutenant of the town, killed at the taking 1690, by the French and Indians, and his widow had 3rd husband, Stephen Cross, 1690, at Boston. Willis, I, 212.

THOMAS LAWRENCE, Hingham 1638, married Eliz., daughter of James Bates, of Dorchester, had Nicholas, born at H.; Mary and Eliz. at D., died 1655, and his widow removed to Dorchester with her children, Nicholas; Mary, who married Thomas Maudesley; and Eliz., who married 1658, William Smead.

THOMAS LAWRENCE, Milford 1639, an original settler, died 1648.

THOMAS LAWRENCE, Newtown, L. I., 1656, may have been of Stamford 1670, was brother of John and William, of Newtown, and much engaged in the politics of New York 1689; died 1703. Account of him and his brothers with large genealog. details is in Riker's Ann. of Newtown, 281-290.

WILLIAM LAWRENCE, Duxbury 1643. At D. he married a daughter of Francis Sprague.

WILLIAM LAWRENCE, Newtown, L. I., 1645, may be the youth who was emb. in the Planter at London 1635, aged 12, with elder brothers John and Thomas; living first at Ipswich with his mother, was a man of great energy, died 1680, had children by 2 wives, and his widow married Sir Philip Cartaret, Gov. of N. J. Seven of this name had been graduated at Harvard, and six at other N. E. coll. in 1834.

REFERENCES.

MASSACHUSETTS:—Ballou's Hist. Milford, 872;

Blake's Hist. of Franklin, 257; Bond's Watertown 330-3, 817-50; Brook's Hist. Medford, 529; Butler's Hist. Groton, 413-6, 474; Green's Early Groton Settlers, 9; Green's Groton Epitaphs, 243; Hodgman's Hist. of Westford, 459; Hudson's Hist. Lexington, 114-8; Paige's Hist. Hardwick, 410; Stearn's Hist. Ashburnham, 791-98; Temple's Hist. No. Brookfield 673; Wyman's Charlestown, II, 606-10.

NEW HAMPSHIRE:—Bassett's Hist. Richmond, 427; Cochrane's Hist. Antrim, 572; Hayward's Hist. Hancock, 735-7; Hill's Hist. Mason, N. H., 196-8, 204; Livermore's Hist. Wilton, 434; Secomb's Hist. Amherst, 667-9; Washington Hist., 506-8; Worcester's Hist. of Hollis, 380.

NEW YORK:—Bolton's Westchester Co., I, 247; Cleveland's Hist. Yates Co., 639-42; Kip's Olden Times in New York; Lamb's Hist. of N. Y. City; Thompson's L. I., II, 362-7.

OTHER PUBLICATIONS:—Bergen Gen., 140; Corliss' No. Yarmouth, Me.; Eaton's Annals of Warren, Me., 568; Eaton's Thomaston, Me., II, 305; Hanson's Hist. Gardiner, Me., 106, 161; Hinman's Conn. Settlers, 169; Kip's Historical Notes, 39-45; Lawrence Gen. (1847) 64 p.; (1848) 20 p.; (1853) 70 p.; (1856) 20 p.; (1857) 191 p.; (1858) 240 p.; (1860) 48 p.; (1869) 332 p.; (1876) pamphlet; (1881) 96 p.; (1883) 107 p.; (1888) 94 p.; (1888) 215 p.; (1888) 223 p.; N. E. Hist. Reg., X, 295; XI, 208; XLVI, 149, 51; N. Y. Gen. Rec., III, 10-20, 26-9, 121-31, 178, 83; Ruggle's Gen.; Salter's Monmouth Co., N. J., XXXV; Savage's Gen. Dict., III, 60-3; Winchell Gen., 251.

ARMS:—Arg. a cross, raguly, gu. Also, Add to blazoning above: On a chief, of the second, a lion passant guardant, or.

LAWSON:—Christopher Lawson, Exeter 1639, removed to Boston, by wife Eliz. had Thomas, born 1643, and Mary 1645; was a cooper; removed to Maine before 1665, there purchased Swan Island in Kennebec River from the Indians, and was an important man. Sullivan, 290; Holmes, I, 349; Folsom, 128; Williamson, II, 172. Yet so ill did he agree with his wife that their mutual complaints came to the Gen. Ct. 1669.

DEODATE LAWSON, son of Rev. Thomas, of Denton, Co. Norfolk, Eng., is first heard of at Martha's Vineyard 1676, had been bred to divinity, it is presumed, for nothing is known, or even Catton Mather, though he gives him a place among his contempo. fellow serv. in Hecatompolis, felt unable to introduce him into either of his three classes; living after few years at Boston, joined with the third, or Old South, church. He took oath of freeman 1680, was called to preach 1683 at Salem village, now Danvers, where no church was yet formed; but George Burrows had taught the people above two years and they would have ordered Lawson in the latter part of 1686; but having lost his first wife and her daughter Ann, he luckily for him went to settle at Scituate, second church, of which he was 3 minister, and dismissed in 1698 for having been absent more than 2 years, gone home. At Boston, by wife Jane he had Deodate, born 1682, and he had 2nd wife, Deborah Allen, married 1690, by whom he had at Scituate Deborah, born 1694, and Richard 1696. Deane, 195; Calamy, II, 629.

HENRY LAWSON, Massachusetts, probably came 1630, and died early in 1631.

JAMES LAWSON, Dartmouth, swore fidelity 1684.

JOHN LAWSON, Boston 1690, had Ann, bapt. 1700, Sarah 1702, and John and Savil 1704, the record at Mather's church being "twin of John, lately died."

ROGER LAWSON, Boston, mariner 1690.

REFERENCES:—Cogswell's New Boston, 419; Forrest's Hist. Norfolk, Va., 71; Hanson's Old Kent, Md., 173-5; Mallery's Bohemia Manor; Powers' Hist. Saugamon Co., Ills., 449; Savage's Gen. Dict., III, 63; Shourd's Hist. Fenwick Colony, N. J., 139-41.

LAWTON:—George Lawton, Portsmouth, R. I., had Isaac, born 1650, George, perhaps, and certain Robert; but no more can be learned of him, except that his daughter Ruth married 1681, William Wodell, and Mercy married 1682, James Tripp; prob. he died 1693; at least, one George then died and the record adds, "his son Job died 1697."

JAMES LAWTON, Suffield, son of John, had Jacob, who was several years represent. and, from caprice, adapted in his business as a lawyer, the name of Christopher Jacob L.

JOHN LAWTON, Newton, L. I., 1656, may be the one who married at Boston 1659, widow Joanna Mullins; and had 2nd wife, perhaps that Mary, daughter of Matthew Boomer, or some such name, who next married 1678, Gideon Freeborn, as his 2nd wife, at Portsmouth, R. I.

JOHN LAWTON, Suffield, had James, Benedicta, Mary and perhaps others, died 1690, and his widow Benedicta died 1692. Both of the daughters were married 1683.

THOMAS LAWTON, prob. of Portsmouth, R. I., may have been an early settler, for his daughters Eliz. married 1657, Peleg Shearman of that place; Sarah married 1667, George Sisson, and Ann married 1669, Giles Slocum.

REFERENCES:—Austin's R. I. Dict., 121-3; Austin's Allied Fams., 164; Chandler's Hist. Shirley, Mass., 497-501; Paige's Hist. Hardwick, Mass., 411-3; R. I. Hist. Mag., IV, 195; V, 236-8; Savage's Gen. Dict., III, 64.

LAY:—Edward Lay, Hartford 1640, removed to Saybrook 1648, on E. side, or Lyme, died before 1657, or perhaps removed to Portsmouth, R. I., where in 1679 he was living, 71 years old.

JOHN LAY, Saybrook 1648, perhaps brother of preceding, was on the side of the river incorp. 1667, as Lyme; in his will of 1675 he calls himself aged, names sons John and James, by former wife, and Peter and John of his present wife Abigail, daughters Abigail, Susanna and Eliz. John, and, perhaps, others of these children, were born in England. James one of the sons, died about 1683, and the widow Abigail died 1686.

JOHN LAY, Lyme, son of preceding, born in England. prob. was badly wounded in the great swamp fight 1675, had wife Sarah, and children, Sarah born 1665, Rebecca 1666, Edward 1668, Catharine 1672, Abigail 1673, Marah 1678, Eliz. 1681, John 1683 and Phebe 1685, and died 1696, aged 63; and his widow died 1702. Possibly this Lyme may be the same as Laigh or Lee.

ROBERT LAY, Lynn 1638, removed to Saybrook, prob. 1647, same year was married; had Phebe born 1652 and Robert 1654; was freeman 1657, represent. 1666; his wife Sarah died 1676, aged about 59, and he died 1689, aged 72. Phebe married 1667, John Denison of Stonington.

WILLIAM LAY, Boston, by wife Mary had Susanna born 1690. It is spelled Ley sometimes, and also Lee.

REFERENCES:—Am. Ancestry, II, 72; Champion Gen.; Chapman Gen., 106; Salisbury Gen.; Savage's Gen. Dict., III, 64; Walworth's Hyde Gen., II, 880-4; Whittemore's Middlesex Co. Ct., 574.

LAYLAND:—See Leland.

LAYTON:—See Laighton.

LAZELL:—Henry Lazell, Barnstable, of whom no more is heard.

JOHN LAZELL, Hingham 1647, married 1649 Eliz. daughter of Stephen Gates, had John bapt. 1650, died under 15 years; Thomas born 1652, Joshua 1654, Stephen bapt. 1656, Eliz. 1658, who died at 18 years; Isaac born 1660, Hannah 1662, Mary 1664, Sarah 1666, John, again, 1669, and Israel 1671; was freeman 1678. His will, 1695, mentions four sons living beside grandchild Joshua, son of his son Joshua, and the 2 children Isaac and Abiah, son and daughter of his son Isaac. The daughters were named Hannah Turner, Mary Burr and Sarah, who married 1693, Peter Ripley.

THOMAS LAZELL, Duxbury, married 1685, Mary Allen, removed to Plympton, Falmouth, C. C., and Windham, says Windsor. Early this name seems Lassell, or Lasell.

REFERENCES:—Mitchell's Bridgewater, 227-9; Savage's Gen. Dict., III, 65; Winsor's Hist. Duxbury, Mass., 275.

LEA:—John Lea, a youth, aged 13, came 1634 in the Francis from Ipswich, prob. as servant to William Westwood.

WILLIAM LEA, a youth of 16, came in the Planter 1635 from London. Possibly this may be same as Lee.

REFERENCES:—American Ancestry, III, 116; Savage's Gen. Dict., III, 66.

LEACH:—Ambrose Leach, Boston 1648, is spoken of in Hutch. Coll. 298, and, in 1663, was concerned in Narraganset, or the King's Province.

EDMUND LEACH, New Haven 1647-9 and may be longer.

GILES LEACH, Weymouth 1656, but removed to Bridgewater before 165, says Mitchell, who mentions that he married Ann Nakes 1656; had Sarah born 1656 or 7. Eliz., Samuel 1662. David, John, Eebenezer, Benjamin, and perhaps others. Sarah marreid John Aldrich and Eliz. married John Emerson.

JOHN LEACH, Salem 1637, then had, says Felt, grant of land, was brother of Lawrence, died 1658.

LAWRENCE LEACH, Salem 1629, came in one of the fleet with Higginson, req. adm. 1630, and was sworn freeman 1631, died 1662. aged 82, or 85, leaving all his estate to widow Eliz., who died 1674. Of his sons, beside John and Robert. Clement lived in England and Richard died here 1647. leaving sons John and Robert.

RICHARD LEACH. Salem 1639, married Ann Fuller, freeman 1665, lieut. 1675, and capt. 2 years after; died 1687, leaving 7 children, of whom it is only known that Hannah was bapt. 1662, and Sarah married 1667. Joseph Herrick.

ROBERT LEACH, Charleston 1637, where Mary united with the church 1630, might be thought his wife, but Felt gives him grant of land at Salem 1637, and the freeman of 1644 was member of neither of the churches in those towns, yet he is said to be son of Lawrence, and to have died before his father. However, we may presume that there was one at each, and he of Charlestown was householder in 1658 and 78, chosen tythingman 1679, and died 1688, aged about 80, says the record.

ROBERT and SAMUEL LEACH, were inhabitants of Manchester, and in favor of that small town petit. for relief in 1686, from expense of support. worship. See Geneal. Reg., X, 322.

SETH LEACH, Bridgewater, married Mary, daughter of Thomas Whitman. The name was frequent. A Margaret, aged 15, was passenger in the Planter, another Margaret, 22, in the Susan and Ellen, both from London 1635.

THOMAS LEACH, New London 1680, married Abigail, daughter of Richard Haughton, who died soon after; her child Sarah was born 1684. By two other wives he had 10 children more before 1719.

REFERENCES:—Am. Ancestry, I, 48; IV, 17, 113; Caverly's Hist. Pittsford, Vt., 712; Davis' Landmarks of Plymouth, Mass., 169; Dow's Hist. Hampton, N. H., 809; Eaton's Annals Warren, Me., 569; Hollister's Hist. Pawlet, Vt., 209; Kingman's N. Bridgewater, Mass., 573-5; Mitchell's Bridgewater, Mass., 229-34; Plumb's Hist. Hanover, Pa., 452; Savage's Gen. Dict., II, 66; Stone's Hist. Beverly, Mass., 29; Temple's Hist. N. Brookfield, Mass., 674; Walworth's Hyde Gen., 788; Wyman's Charlestown, Mass., II, 610.

LEADBETTER:—Henry Leadbetter, Dorchester, married 1660, Sarah, daughter of Thomas Tolman, had Sarah, born 1660, Catharine 1662, Henry 1664, Deliverance 1667, Increase 1672, Ebenezer 1676 and Israel 1678; was freeman 1671, and constable 1673; and died 1722. His widow Relief died 1743, aged 92. She had been widow of Timothy Foster, and first of John Dowse, being daughter of John Holland. Sarah married 1684, Henry Withington, and Catharine married 1684, Ephraim Payson, of the sons Henry and Israel, were married as well as the following:

INCREASE LEADBETTER, Dorchester, son of preceding, had wife Sarah, who died 1634, aged 53 years, and he died 1737.

REFERENCES:—Barry's Framingham; Savage's Gen. Dict., III, 67.

LEADER:—George Leader, submitted to Mass. 1652.

RICHARD LEADER, Lynn 1645, supt. of iron works, tried copper wire in Endicott's farm at Salem, meeting ill success, went, 1650, to Berwick, had grant of exclus. use of the Little River to erect mills, and was a magistrate. Winth., II, 356; Belkn., I, 56; Lewis, 6; Sullivan, 326. In 1654 he was called of Strawberry Bank.

THOMAS LEADER, Dedham 1640. His wife Susanna was recorded of the church 1641; he removed to Boston 1647, his second wife Rebecca died 1653, and he died 1663. His will proves that he had 3d wife Alice, son Thomas, deceased, and that he well provided for his widow and 3 children of Thomas, and his other son Samuel.

REFERENCE:—Savage's Gen. Dict., III, 68.

LEAGER, LEGARE, or LEGER:—Jacob Leager, Boston, tailor, freeman 1641, had Hannah born 1655, and died 1664, leaving widow Ann. daughter of William Blake, of Dorchester, a 2d wife, who married a Hallowell, and daughter Bethia, who married Fearnot Shaw. His will of 1662 provided for wife and daughters Bethia and Hannah.

LEAMAN:—Samuel Leaman, Charlestown, by wife Mary had Joanna, born 1676, died soon; Nathaniel, died young; Rebecca, died young, and Eliz. 1684. Eaton calls him one of the first settlers of Reading.

LEAR or LEARE:—John Lear, Salem 1658.

TOBIAS LEAR, Portsmouth 1665, married Eliz. daughter prob. eldest of Henry Sherburne, and died about 1681, leaving Tobias, who may have been of Newcastle 1727. A Mrs. L. died at Portsmouth 1775, in 105th year.

TOBIAS LEAR, Harvard Coll. 1783, private secretary of Washington, died 1816.

LEARNED, LARNED or LARNET, sometimes LARNIT and LERNET:—Isaac Learned, Woburn, only son of William, born in England, freeman 1647, married 1646, Mary, eldest child of Isaac Stearns, had Mary, born 1647, Hannah 1649, William 1650; removed to Chelmsford, there had Sarah 1653, Isaac 1655 and Benoni 1656; was a selectman, and died 1657. His widow married 1662, John Burge, and died next year; Mary married Moses Barron; Hannah married 1666, Joseph Farwell, and Sarah married Jonathan Barrett.

WILLIAM LEARNED, Charlestown 1632, may have come 2 years before, but is first heard of in joining the church with his wife Goodith in Dec., being the first adm. since the separation from Boston church; was freeman 1634, selectman 1636, and in the same office first at the settlement off town of Woburn, to which he removed 1641. In the great trouble of 1637 he was on the side of moderat. so far as to disappr. the banishment of Wheelwright; died 1646. A widow Sarah, says record, died 1661, at Malden, but Savage finds admin. same year on estate of widow Jane (but no doubt the same person), of M.; perhaps she was 2d wife of William.

REFERENCES:—Am. Ancestry, I, 48; III, 32; IV, 175; VII, 81; Ammidown's Hist. Coll., 254-6; Austin's Allied Families, 166; Barry's Hist. Framingham, Mass., 314-6; Bond's Watertown, Mass., 333-7, 850; Cait Gen., 183-6; Davis. Gen., 15, 33-5, 110-7; Harris' Watertown, Mass. Epitaphs, 35; Learned Gen. (1882), 346 pp.; Leonard's Hist. Dublin, N. H., 359-61; Merrill's Hist. Acworth, N. H., 272; Morse's Gen. of Sherborn, Mass., 170; Savage's Gen. Dict., III, 68; Sewall's Woburn, Mass., 624; Washburne's Livermore, Me., 24.

LEATHERS:—Edward Leathers, Dover 1665. Perhaps he was commonly regarded as of Gipsey blood.

REFERENCE:—Stearn's Ashburnham, 798.

LEAVENWORTH:—David, and Thomas Leavenworth, Woodbury, as Cothren in his Hist. p. 612, tells by aid of tradition, came about 1690 from Germany; and that David was drowned in youth; and of Thomas, nothing.

REFERENCES:—Am. Ancestry, VIII, 44; Bronson's Hist. Waterbury, Ct., 515-8; Cothren's Hist. Woodbury, Ct., II, 1513; Leavenworth Gen. (1873), 376 pp.; Orcutt's Hist. Stratford, Ct., 1236.

LEAVER:—Thomas Leaver, Rowley 1643, town clerk, married Damaris, daughter of James Bayley, of same; and we hear no more, but that he died 1683, leaving prob. Thomas, and perhaps others; certain. Prudence, born 1645, who married 1671, Benjamin Gage, as his 2d wife, and, next, 1674, Samuel Stickney.

REFERENCE:—Essex Inst. Coll., XXII, 210.

LEAVITT:—John Leavitt, Dorchester 1634, removed to Hingham, freeman 1636, was represent. 1656, 64, a deacon, died 1691, aged 83. By wife Sarah, who died 1700, he prob. had John. Hannah, bapt. 1639; Samuel 1641, Eliz. 1644, Jeremiah 1646, Israel 1648, Moses 1650, Josiah 1653, Nehemiah 1656, Sarah 1659, Mary 1661, Hannah, the second, 1664, and Abigail, bapt. 1667.

JOHN LEAVITT, Exeter, or Dover, 1645.

THOMAS LEAVITT, Exeter 1639, may have been brother of first John, before 1644 removed to Hampton, and died 1696, leaving, says Farmer, sons Hezron, Aratus, born 1646; John, Thomas, James, 1652, died young; also Isabel, Jemima and Heriah, but the order is unknown. His wife Isabel died 1700. His name is used as a grantee with John Wheelwright and two others in that enormous forgery of the deed of the whole S. and E. part of the Province of N. H. with the Isle of Shoals from Indian sachems 1629, certain. more than 7 years before the principal W. came to this country, and near 9 years before that honest purchase by W. of all lands for 30 miles between the great rivers Merrimack and Piscataqua. Nor can any evidence be discovered that L. was here a single year earlier than W.

REFERENCES:—Bell's Hist. Exeter, N. H., 28; Cothren's Woodbury, Ct., 614; Dearborn's Hist. Parsonfield, Me., 384; Dow's Hist. Hampton, N. H., 809-20; Dwight Gen., 406-13; French's Hist. Turner, Me., 581; Leavitt Gen. (1853), 16 pp.; Loomis Gen. Female Branches, 810; Prescott's Mems. W. Prescott, 514-9; Runnel's Hist Sanbornton, N. H., 455-61; Sanborn Gen. (1894), Savage's Gen. Dict., III, 69-71; Secomb's Hist. Amherst, N. H., 669-71.

LE BLONDE:—James Le Blonde, Boston 1689, prob. a Huguenot, whose wife Ann united 1690 with Mather's church, had there bapt. James 1690, died soon; James, again, 1691; Ann 1693, died soon; Peter 1695, Gabriel 1698, Ann, again, 1700; Phillippa 1704, Marion 1706, and Alexander 1709.

LECHFORD:—Thomas Lechford, Boston, a lawyer from one of the Inns of Court at London, came 1637, left here, after vain attempt to earn bread, and being artillery Co. 1640, in same ship with Hugh Peter, Thomas Welde and John Winthrop, the younger. He got his book through the press almost 2 years before Welde's, and Cotton says he died shortly after its pub.

LECK, LECKE or LEEKE:—Ambrose Leck, Wickford 1674.

LEDDRA:—William Leddra, Boston, convict. Sept. 1660 of being a Quaker and hanged next year. An excellent letter to the wife of his bosom is preserved. Sewel Hist., I, 336, 459, 65, 8. Hutch, I, 202, calls him Ledea.

LEE:—Abraham Lee, Dover 1680, a man of some skill in natural science, married 1688, Esther, widow of Henry Elkins, and daughter of Major Richard Waldron, was killed with the father of his wife by Indians 1689 His widow married Richard Jose, sheriff of the Prov. outlived him, and died in the Isle of Jersey, says pedigree of W. in Geneal. Reg., V, 182.

EDWARD LEE, Hartford 1648, is by Savage thought to be same as Lay.

HENRY LEE, Manchester 1650, was brother of Thomas of Ipswich, and prob. removed to Boston 1656.

JOHN LEE, Ipswich 1640, had, it is said, come about 1635 from London, had John, born about 1639, and Joseph, 1643; died 1671. Family tradition makes him marry on our side of the water, yet tells not the name of the wife, but gives him 4 daughters, 3 without names, of which one married a Patch, one a Hunkins, another a Tuttle, and exact account of the other is that she was called Ann, died unmarried 1691. On same evidence it is shown that original name was Leigh, and the son of this man agreed to change it.

JOHN LEE, Saco 1645, was of the grand jury that year, but in Dec. 1647 was dead, or removed.

JOHN LEE, Farmington 1653, died 1690, had wife Mary, daughter of Stephen Hart, and children John, born 1659, Mary 1664, Stephen 1667, Thomas 1671, David 1674 and Tabitha 1677. His widow married 1691 Jerediah Strong, as his 3d wife; Mary married Stephen Upson 1682; Tabitha married Preserved Strong, of Northampton, and they removed to Coventry, whither also removed her brother David after some years at N.

ROBERT LEE, Plymouth 1636, was prob. from London, adm. freeman 1637, may have been short time in 1638 at Lynn; had wife Mary and children Ann and Mary, was living 1654. Either he or his wife, who left them part of their est. See Geneal. Reg., IV, 173, and V, 260. Mary married 1651, John Howland, Jr.

SAMUEL LEE, Boston, may seem only a transient visitor, as he is called of Virginia in the record of his marriage 1655 to Eliz. Rowland of B. Yet perhaps he was the Malden man who had Eliz. born 1670, and she may have married 1690, Jonathan Howard.

SAMUEL LEE, Boston, born in London 1623, bred at Magdalen Coll., Oxford, there created M. A. 1648, and, in violat. of their rights, made 1651, one of the Proctors of the Univ. See Wood's Fasti Oxon., II, 164. He came over hither 1686, and became set. min. of B. 1687; preached at public fast in B. 1691, and embarked for home; on voyage was taken by a French privateer, carried into St. Maloes, there died in prison same year. Mather, III, 223, makes some amends for the brevity of his narrative, by the praise of its subject. But Baylies follows Eliot in more sober estimate of him. See 4 Mass. Hist. Coll., II, 122.

SAMUEL LEE, Malden, freeman 1671, died 1676, aged 36, married 1662, Mercy Call, daughter of Thomas. He may have had Mercy to marry 1686, Richard Wicks; and his widow married 1677, John Allen.

THOMAS LEE, Ipswich 1648, brother of Henry, and John, died 1662, aged about 82.

THOMAS LEE, Lyme, came about 1641 with his mother and two sisters, Phebe, and Jane, the father, whose name was Thomas, having died, as tradition was, on the voyage of smallpox. The surv. came from Boston to Saybrook, though the father of the mother by the same authority, is called Brown of Providence. This son must have been very young, for Lyme rec. gives him children up to 1692, and his first, John, by wife Sarah Kirkland, was born 1670; Thomas 1672, Sarah 1675; and after this wife died, 1676, he married for second wife Mary, perhaps daughter of Balthazar De Wolf, and had Phebe, born 1677; Mary 1679, Eliz., William 1684, Stephen, Hannah, and four more children, one of whom died young. He was ensign, represent. 1676, and died 1705, and his widow Mary became second wife of Sec. Matthew Griswold. His sister Jane married 1659, Samuel Hyde, of Norwich, and Phebe married 1659, perhaps, John Large, of Saybrook.

WALTER LEE, Windsor, freeman of Conn. 1654, removed to Northampton 1656, thence about 1665 to Westfield, there died 1718, at great age. His children were John, born 1657; Timothy 1659, died soon; Stephen 1662 and Nathaniel 1663, all at N.; this last recorded at Westfield, by, perhaps, some years after birth: Mary 1665, Eliz. 1667, died young, Hannah 1668 and Abigail 1670. His wife died 1696 and he married 1705, second wife Hepzibah, widow of Caleb Pomeroy, who died 1711. Often spelling is Laigh, but it may sometimes be Lay, which see.

REFERENCES.

MASSACHUSETTS:— Shattuck's Hist. Concord, 377; Temple's Hist. Palmer, 505; Wyman's Charlestown Gens., 612.

NEW HAMPSHIRE:—Hayward's Hancock, 737; Kidder's Hist. New Ipswich, 416.

NEW YORK:—Bolton's Westchester Co., II, 734; Cleveland's Hist. Yates Co., 644-50; Roe's Sketches of Rose, 309.

CONNECTICUT:—Andrew's Hist. New Britain, 141-5; Stile's Hist. Windsor, II, 432; Timlow's Southington, 154-6; Todd's Hist. Redding, 205.

Lee (of Virginia).

OTHER PUBLICATIONS:—Amer. Ancestry, IV, 4, 30, 82, 83, 91, 112, 162, 214, 218, 219, 227, 229; VII, 22, 197; VIII, 120, 148, 231; Austin's Ancestral Dict., 35; Campbell's Spotswood Gen., 22; Campbell's Hist. Va., 659, 745; Carter Tree of Va.; Hayden's Va. Gens., 96; Hemenway's Vt. Gaz., 315-8; Hine's Lebanon, Ct., Address, 159; Hubbard's Stanstead Canada, 155-9; Lee Gen. (1851), 31 pp.; (1868), 114 pp.; (1872), 11 pp.; (1874), 8 pp.; (1878), 180 pp.; (1884) (1885), 116 pp.; (1888), 500 pp.; (1890), 11 pp.; (1893), 14 pp.; Meade's Old Fams. of Va., II, 135-45; New Eng. Hist. Gen. Reg., XI, 329; XXVI, 61, 69; XXVIII, 394-401; XXXVIII, 6-7; XLIV, 103-11; XLVI, 64-78, 161-6; XLVII, 21-3; Pickering Gen.; Plumb's Hist. Hanover, Pa., 444; Richmond, Va., Critic (1888); Richmond, Va., Standard, I, 44, 48; III, 38, 40; IV, 2, 8, 18, 21; Salisbury Gen.; Savage's Gen. Dict., III, 71-4; Scranton Gen., 31; Slaughter's British Parish, 156; Southern Bivouac (1886), 51; Strong Gen., 956-64; Tilley's Mag. of N. E. Hist., III, 48-61; Walworth's Hyde Gen., 34.

ARMS:—Gu., a fess, chequy, az. and or, between ten billets, arg.—four in chief, three, two, and one in base.

LEEDS:—John Leeds, New London 1674, mariner, from Staplehoe, Co. Kent, called himself 39 years old in 1680, married 1678, Eliz., daughter of Cary Latham, had John, bapt. 1681, Eliz. 1681, William 1683, Gideon and Thomas. He lived on Groton side, where William lived 1712.

JOHN LEEDS, Waterbury, had, says, Bond, Eliz., John, Edward, Joseph, Abigail and Deborah, bapt. 1688 but he could not name the wife.

RICHARD LEEDS, Dorchester, embarked 1637, at Great Yarmouth, Co. Norf'k, aged 32, with wife Joan, 23, and a child whose name is not found in English records; had a grant of land that year at Salem, says Felt, but did not continue there; had Benjamin and Joseph, twins, born 1637, bapt. 1639, freeman 1645, a selectman 1653, constable 1664, died 1693, aged about 98, a s inscription above grave, whereas his declaration in 1637 would prove him to be 88. Will names only sons

Joseph and Benjamin; daughter, Hannah Clap, wife of Samuel, who was bapt. 1640; daughter-in-law Miriam, wife of Joseph, and grandson Joseph.

REFERENCES:—Amer. Ancestry, III, 33; Caulkin's Hist. New London, Ct., 335; Cregar's White Gen.; Eaton's Annals of Warren, Me., 570; Faxton Gen., 80; Glover Gen., 350, 383; Huntington's Stamford Co. Fams., 65; Leed's Fam. Chart (1886), 2x2 ft.; Powers' Hist. Sangamon Co., Ill., 449; Savage's Gen. Dict., III, 74.

LEES:—Edward Lees, Guilford, perhaps son of Hugh, married at Saybrook 1676, Eliz. Wright, was a propr. 1685.

HUGH LEES, Saybrook 1648, living there 1664; prob. had son William of Norfolk, besides preceding.

LEETE:—William Leete, Guilford, signed plant covenant 1639, was an Assist. of New Hamp. Col. 1643 to 57, dep.-gov. 1658, gov. 1661 to 65; on the union to Conn. became Assist. to 1669, then dept.-gov. to 1676, when, on death of Gov. Winthrop, he was chosen to that office, and so by ann. elect. till his death at Hartford 1683. He was often commissr. of the Unit. Col. of N. E. from 1655 to 79. Of 3 wives first is presumed to be Ann, who died 1668, and was prob. mother of all the children; John, born 1639, Andrew, William, Abigail, Caleb, died at 21 years; Graciana 1653, Peregrine 1658, died young; Joshua died 1660, prob. very young; and Ann 1662.

REFERENCES:—Barbour's Wife and Mother, 57; Brown's W. Simsbury, Ct., Settlers, 89; Dwight's Strong Gen., 359; Leete Gen. (1884), 168 pp.; Savage's Gen. Dict., III, 75; Stone Gen., 8, 13, 28.

LEETH:—John Leeth, Boston, by wife Hannah had Martha, born 1654. May be same as Leathe.

LEFFINGWELL, sometimes in old records read LEPPINGWELL, or LAPPINGWELL:—Michael Leffingwell, Woburn, had Hannah, born 1643, died in few weeks; Hannah, again, 1646; Sarah 1647, Thomas 1649, Ruth 1650, Michael 1651, died in week; Rachel 1653, Abigail 1655, Esther 1657 and Tabitha 1660, and he died 1687; Geneal. Reg., VII, 284.

THOMAS LEFFINGWELL, Saybrook 1637, prob. on E. side of river, had Rachel, born 1648, Thomas 1649, Jonathan 1650, Joseph 1652, Mary 1654 and Nathaniel 1656. Was one of the purchasers of the tract from the Indians 1659, now includ. Norwich and several other towns, and with the first sett. of N., its represent. 1662, and many following years, was an active partisan when he was a lieut. in Philips' war.

REFERENCES:—Am. Ancestry, IX, 126; Caulkins' Hist. Norwich, Ct., 189-92; Coit Gen., 104; Elderkin Gen., 86-8; Huntington Gen., 81; Joslin's Hist. of Poultney, Vt., 302; N. E. Hist. Gen. Reg., XXV, 295; Savage's Gen. Dict., III, 76; Sewall's Hist. Woburn, Mass., 625; Tuttle Gen., 204; Walworth's Hyde Gen., 30, 383, 1083-7.

LEGAT or LEGGETT:—John Legat, Hampton 1640, Exeter 1642, clerk of the write, kept school in each; at H. in 1849; married 1644, Ann, Thomas Wilson's widow.

REFERENCES:—Amer. Ancestry, II, 72; V, 214; Bolton's Westchester Co., N. Y., II, 446; Savage's Gen. Dict., III, 76.

ARMS:—Az., on a bend, arg., three hearts, gu. On a chief, of the second, three martlets, sa.

LEGAREE:—Francis Legaree, Boston 1690, a Huguenot goldsmith, with 2 sons.

LEGGE:—John Legge, Salem 1631, servant of John Humfrey, came in the fleet with Winthrop, living at Marblehead, was freeman 1635, died 1674.

JOHN LEGGE, Marblehead, son perhaps of the preceding, freeman 1680, had Samuel, who was a mariner of Boston 1671, and John of M. 1691.

LEGROVE:—Nicholas Legrove, Salem 1668.

LEIGH:—John Leigh, a soldier in Moseley's comp. 1675, of whom is known no more.

JOSEPH LEIGH, Ipswich 1651. Perhaps it is the same as name of like sound—Lee.

THOMAS LEIGH, nephew of Capt. Thomas Brattle, died 1694, aged 30.

REFERENCES:—Richmond, Va., Standard, II, 4; III, 14; IV, 2; Watkin's Gen., 40.

LEIGHTON:—See Laighton.

REFERENCES:—Am. Ancestry, III, 106; Cushman's Hist. of Sheepscatt, Me., 398; Dennysville, Me., Centen., 108; Essex Inst. Hist. Coll., XXII, 211; Hodgman's Hist. Westford, Mass., 460; Leighton Family (1885) 127 pp.; Milliken's Narraguagus Valley, Me., 6-8; Runnel's Hist. Sanbornton, N. H., II, 461; Savage's Gen. Dict., III, 44; Wentworth Gen., I, 217-9, 498.

LEISTER or LISTER:—Edward Leister, a youth from London, in the employ. of Stephen Hopkins, came in the Mayflower 1620. But we know no more of him, except his punishment for fighting a duel with another youth from London, and Bradford, who calls him Lister, 4 Mass. Hist. Coll., III, 455, says, he went to Virginia, and there died.

REFERENCES:—Bolton's Westchester, 380; Leister Gen. (1877) 6 pp.; New York Gen. Biog. Rec., VII, 145-51; Valentine's N. Y. City Man. (1860) 594.

LELAND:—Hopestill Leland, Weymouth, in very recent time ascertained to be the ancestor of all the numerous tribe, derived through only son Henry, who was before thought the progenitor of our side of the water. Perhaps he had several daughters beside Experience, who married the first John Holbrook, in England. He died at Medford 1655, aged 75. Morse exults in his honor, as "one of the most ancient, if not the most ancient," that ever came to our country, yet presumes the time of his coming was 1624, when he, of course, could not be over 43 years old.

REFERENCES:—Adam's Haven Gen., 27, 48; Ballou's Hist. of Milford, Mass., 875-8; Benedict's Hist. of Sutton, Mass., 684-6; Crane's Rawson Gen., 50; Haven Gen., 48; Hodgman's Hist. of Westford, Mass., 461; Leland Gen. (1850), 278 pp.; Morse's Sherborn, Mass., Settlers, 160-70; Pierce's Hist. Grafton, Mass., 515-30; Savage's Gen. Dict., III, 76; Stone's Hist. of Hubbardston, Mass., 304; Young's Hist. of Chautauqua Co., N. Y., 421.

LELLOCK:—Joseph Lellock, Boston, found in the second copy of record to have, by wife Joanna, born to him son Martin 1658. Savage considers this almost an impossible name, occurring in no other place of county, town, or church record.

LEMON, LEAMOND or LEMOND, sometimes LEMAN:—Joseph Lemon, Charlestown, came in youth from England, where he was born about 1662, married 1690, Mary Bradley, had Joseph, bapt. 1692, who was father of Joseph, Harvard Coll. 1735.

ROBERT LEMON, Salem 1637, by wife Mary had there bapt. Grace, and Mary, 1639; Martha 1640, John 1642, Eliz. 1643, John 1645 and Hannah 1650, who married 1668 Samuel Beadle; was freeman 1642, when the name is recorded Leoman, or Looman. His widow married 1674 Philip Cromwell.

SAMUEL LEMON, Groton, married Mary, daughter of William Longley, had Samuel, born 1667. It is supposed he was driven to live at Charlestown, and there was impressed into Mosely's comp. 1675.

REFERENCES:—Wyman's Charlestown, 614; Pickering Gen.; Powers Hist. of Sangamon Co., Ills., 450: Temple's Hist. Palmer, Mass., 502; Wyman's Charlestown Gens., II, 615.

Same arms as the Baronets Lenman, or Lemon, of Northaw, Co. Herts. (Ext. 1762), descended from Sir John Lemon, Mayor of London (1616).

LENOX:—Ralph Lenox, New Haven, had John, born 1655; but some doubt is felt about this name.

LENTHALL:—Robert Lenthall, Weymouth, 1637, not pleasing the government of our colony, was forbidden to be ord. Went to Newport next year, where his name is spell. Lintell, when adm. a freeman in 1640, kept a school, but was glad to go home in 1642. See Lechford; Callender, 62; Winth. I., 287.

LENTON:—Lawrence Lenton, Ipswich, 1673. Felt.

LEONARD:—Henry Leonard, Lynn, had wife Mary in 1650, it is said, and children, perhaps one or more born in England, Samuel, Nathaniel and Thomas, but certain at L. Henry, born 1656, died next year; Sarah 1663; Mary 1666, died next year; was aged 37 in 1655, freeman 1668 of Rowley, perhaps, 1674, when certainly his 3 sons engaged there in iron works; removed, it is thought, to New Jersey, where the iron works (in which he had been engaged at Lynn, Braintree, and Taunton at several times, though chief. at L.), now under the government of Cartaret, promis. better.

JAMES LEONARD, Providence, 1645, Taunton 1652, from Pontypool. Monmouthsh., son of Thomas, who come not, with his brother Henry, inspect. iron works, at Lynn and Braintree; had Thomas, born about 1641; James, about 1643; Abigail; Rebecca; Joseph, about 1655; Benjamin; Hannah, who died 1675; and Uriah, 1662; besides John, who died, says family tradition, about 20 years old, the first two, perhaps, in England. He had second wife, Margaret, who bore him no children. Died before 1691, and his widow died about 1701. Baylies Hist. of Plymouth II, 268; III, 120. His daughter Hannah married, 1678, Isaac Deane.

JOHN LEONARD, Springfield, 1639, married 1640, Sarah Heald, had John, 1641, died young; Joseph 1643, died soon; Joseph again, 1644; Sarah 1645; Mary 1647; Martha 1649; Lydia 1651; John, again, 1652, died young; Benjamin 1654; Abel 1656; Josiah 1658; Hannah 1659; Rebecca 1661; Deborah 1663; and Rachel 1665; and he was killed by the Indians early in 1676, and his widow married, 1677, Benjamin Parsons, and again, in 1690, the worshipful Peter Tilton; and she died at S. 1711, 71 years after first marriage; but it is not known (remarks Savage) that she had any more children than those 15 she bore to L. Eight sons and four daughters were married.

PHILIP LEONARD, Marshfield, brother of the first Henry and James, was son of Thomas of Pontypool, in Wales, had wife Lydia, who died 1707, and only daughter Phebe, who married, 1694, Samuel Hill of Duxbury, whither he removed, and died 1708.

RICE LEONARD, Rehoboth, 1654, had Rachel, born 1674; Sarah 1676; and his wife Sarah was buried next year.

SOLOMON LEONARD, Duxbury, 1637, removed Bridgewater 1645, had Solomon, Samuel, John, Jacob, Mary and Isaac. He died 1686, leaving widow Mary.

REFERENCES:—Adam's Fairhaven, 426-9; Amer. Ancest., I, 49; II, 72; IV, 78; VI, 104; Ammidown Mems. 46; Austin's Ancestral Dict., 36; Baldwin Gen. 1138; Blake Gen., 55; Caverly's Hist., Pittsford, Vt., 713; Clark's Hist. of Norton, Mass., 86; Werman's Hist. Cape Cod, I, 611; Haugh's Hist. Lewis Co., N. Y., 150; Leonard Gen. (1851), 28 pp.; Mass. Hist. Soc. Coll. 1st series, II, 173; Mitchell's Hist. Bridgewater, Mass., 235-8; Morris and Flint Gen., 54; N. E. Hist. Reg., V, 40, 13; XXXII, 269-71; Paige's Hist. Hardwick, Mass., 413; Parsons and Leonard Gen. (1867), 36 pp.; Lead's Hist. Swanzey, N. H., 395; Savage's Gen. Dict., III, 78-80; Sprague's Hist. of Gloversville, N. Y., 122; Temple's Hist. of Whately, Mass., 245; Thayer Mem. (1835), 160, 279-310; Walker Gen., 31; Walworth's Hyde Gen., 346; Winsor's Hist. Duxbury, Mass, 346.

ARMS:—Or, on a fess, gu., three fleurs-de-lis, of the field crest; out of a ducal coronet on heraldic tiger, arg., maned and tufted, or.

MOTTO:—*Pour bien desirer.*

LEONARDS:—Thomas Leonards, freeman of Conn. 1658; but his residence is unknown.

LEONARDSON:—Jacob Leonardson, Newtown, L. I., 1655. Thompson.

LESTER:—Andrew Lester, Gloucester, an early settler, freeman 1643, then called Lister, by wife Barbara had Daniel, born 1642, Andrew 1644, Mary 1647 and Ann 1651; removed that year to New London, where his wife died 1654. By second wife, Ann, he had Timothy, born 1662, Joseph 1664, besides Benjamin, whose date is not given. He died after 1699, when two elder sons were proposed for freemen. Ann married 1670 Nathaniel Millet, of Gloucester.

REFERENCES:—Am. Ancestry, II, 73; Caulkin's Hist. of New London, Ct., 411; Walworth's Hyde Gen., 1138.

LETHERLAND or LITHERLAND:—William Letherland, might rather be inserted here than Lytherland, where Farmer first placed the name.

LETHERMORE:—John Lethermore, freeman of Massachusetts 1635, whose residence is certain, perhaps at Watertown; but Bond names him not.

LETTIS or LETTICE:—Thomas Lettis, Plymouth 1638, may be that passenger in the Elizabeth 1635, from London, aged 23, in the custom-ho. records called Lettyne. His will names wife Ann, who died 1687 in 80th year. He had Thomas, who died 1650, and prob. no other son.

WALTER LETTIS, at Newport, 1659, was stabbed by Capt. George Wright, as in a letter of Roger Williams is told, 3 Mass. Hist. Call. IX, 280.

LEVENS or LEAVENS:—John Levens, Roxbury, freeman 1634, came 1632, with wife Eliz. in the William and Francis. His wife died 1638, and he married 1639, Rachel Wright, "a godly maid," had John, born 1640, James 1642, Peter and Andrew 1644, "twin child of John L. in the 63d year of his age, a double blessing," but Peter died in Jan. following; had also Rachel, bapt. 1646, and next year he died.

LEVER or LEVAR:—Richard Lever, a soldier from the E. under Capt. Turner, at Hadley 1676.

LEVERETT:—Thomas Leverett, Boston, came in the Griffin, arrived from London 1633, having in July preceding resigned his place as one of the aldermen of the borough of Boston, Co. Lincoln, with wife Ann, daughters Jane and Ann, and prob. son John (afterward Governor); was soon made ruling elder, and selectman, in each place; continued till his death, which occurred 1650. He had 13 children, as by the registry of the borough, certified copy of which was sent to Governor L. by a friend, as follows: John, bapt. 1612, Jane 1613, Jane again 1614, John again 1616, Thomas 1618, Ann 1619, James 1621, Sarah 1622, Mary 1623, Jabez 1627, Israel 1628, Elisha 1630 and Nathaniel 1632, and we may believe that all but the 3d, 4th and 6th died young. A perfect mem. of his family is cont. in Geneal. Reg., IV, 121, and a pedigree in same work, XII, 289, that is quite deficient in accurate dates.

REFERENCES:—Goodwin's Gen. Notes, 188; Leverett Gen. (1850), 19 pp.; (1856), 203 pp.; Moore's Mem. American Governors, I, 374-6; N. E. Hist. Gen. Reg., IV, 121; XII, 288; Paige's Hist. of Cambridge, Mass., 598; Savage's Gen. Dict., III, 82-4.

ARMS:—Arg., a chevron, between three leverets, courant, sa.

LEVERICH, LEVERAGE, LOVERIDGE or LEVERIDGE:—Caleb Leverich, Newtown, L. I., 1664, that year made freeman of Conn., by wife Martha, widow of Francis Swaine, had John, Mary and Eleanor, and so by son John, the head of large and reput. progeny, died 1717, aged 79; was eldest son of Rev. William.

ELEAZER LEVERICH, Newtown, L. I., 1662, brother of preceding, married Rebecca, daughter of Nicholas Wright, but had no children.

HENRY LEVERICH, a tailor, came from Southampton 1635 in the James, called of Salisbury, Co. Wilts, arrived at Boston that year, but no more is known.

WILLIAM LEVERICH, Sandwich, came with Wiggin 1633 in James from London, but went into Salem, where they landed, but to Dover, being engaged for that plant., but in 1635 came to Boston, and joined church; was at Duxbury and a lot was laid out for him 1637, but in 1639 or 40 was established at Sandwich, and years after employed by the commissioners of the United Colony to instruct the Indians on Cape Cod, thence removed 1653 to Oyster Bay, and with early settlers to Huntington, L. I., there was in 1664 made freeman of Conn., and continued until 1670, and at Newtown 1674; died in 1677; Riker 98.

LEVETT:—Christopher Levett, an explorer of the coast of Maine 1623 and 4, whose valuable work printed in London 1628 is repub. in 3 Mass. Hist. Coll. VIII·

159. See Hubbard 186. He may be the man called Captain at Salem 1630, when Winthrop arrived, and, perhaps, was here again 1632, and carrying letters from here, they were exposed by his daughter on the voyage, to unfriendly eyes at home.

LEWISTON :—Daniel Lewiston, York. Killed by Indians 1694.

JOHN LEWISTON, Billerica, about 1679, a Scot, whose 5 young children and the mother of his wife were killed by the Indians 1695, and one daughter carried away by them. Memoir of Billerica, 13, as cited by Farmer.

LEWIS :—Daniel Lewis, Westerly, R. I., 1679, perhaps was son of John of the same, married Mary Button, daughter prob. of Peter, and in his will of 1718, names eldest son John, Jonathan, Mary, Dorcas, Daniel and Hannah.

DAVID LEWIS, Westerly, brother of preceding, married Eliz., daughter of the 2d James Babcock.

DAVID LEWIS, Salem, died prob. June 1662, for Samuel Archard of Salem was ordered to admin. in behalf of the country, so that perhaps he was only transient.

EDMUND LEWIS, Lynn, was first at Watertown, removed about 1643, not, as Lewis has it, 1640, came in the Eliz., from Ipswich 1634, aged 33, with wife Mary 32, and 2 children, John 3 years and Thomas 9 mos.; had James born 1636 and Nathaniel 1639, born at W., beside a child buried 1642, 10 days old, and had 2 more children born at L., where he died 1651. His will, probated 1651, names wife extrix. and sons John and Thomas. His widow Mary died 1658.

FRANCIS LEWIS, Boston 1663, a boatman.

GEORGE LEWIS, Plymouth and Scituate, where he joined church 1635, a clothier, was from E. Greenwich, in Kent before 1633, and removed to Barnstable before 1641, had in England married Sarah Jenkins, by her had several children born there, as Mary, who married 1643 John Bryant; prob. George, and Thomas; perhaps Edward; Jabez, who died unmarried, and James; but at S. had John 1638 and at B. had Ephraim 1641, and Sarah 1644; his death was prob. after 1663, for his will was brought forward 1664. It names wife Mary, sons Ephraim, George, Thomas, James, Edward, John, and daughter Sarah. John was killed by the Indians 1676, under Capt. Pierce.

GEORGE LEWIS, Cesco, before 1640 had grant of land. Mr. Willis, in Vol. I, 37 and 174, conject. that he was son of first mentioned George, but he may have been son of Thomas, and he died without male issue, according to Willis. He lived and died at Falmouth, had son John, to whom were granted 100 acres as early as 1657, and Philip, besides 4 daughters, Ann, Susanna, Mary and Hannah.

JAMES LEWIS, a soldier, killed at Hatfield by the Indians 1675.

JAMES LEWIS, Boston, freeman 1684, with prefix of respect.

JOHN LEWIS, Charlestown 1634, freeman 1646, by wife Margaret had John, born 1638; Joseph and Mary, twins, bapt. 1640; Samuel 1641, Eliz. 1642, Sarah 1647; lived on Malden side, there wife died 1649, and he married 1650, Mary Brown, perhaps daughter of Abraham the first of Watertown, had Abraham, born 1650; Jonathan

1652, died 1 month; Mary 1653, Hannah, Isaac and Trial, posthum. 1658. He died year preceding. His widow married a cutler.

JOHN LEWIS, Scituate, by Deane called brother of first George, was of Tenterden in Co. Kent, and came in the Hercules 1635 with wife Sarah and one child, as the Vicar of T. and the Mayor certify for him. He removed in a few years to Boston, where his wife died 1657.

JOHN LEWIS, New London 1648, commonly noted as senr. because, beside other children, of whose birth nothing is seen on record, he had son John, was freeman before 1669 and died 1676.

JOHN LEWIS, brother of George of Barnstable, was very early, perhaps 1638, at Yarmouth, but not long continued; may be same as preceding.

JOHN LEWIS, Lancaster, freeman 1665.

JOHN LEWIS, Boston, a butcher, married 1659, Alice, widow of Nathaniel Bishop, daughter of James Mattock, who, in his will, refers to her; had Samuel, born 1662, Joseph 1663 and Benoni 1665. Another John of Boston is called mariner in 1669.

JOHN LEWIS, Saybrook, died prob. 1670, for in June of that year inventory was rendered, says the record by Lord, his admor.

JOHN LEWIS, Westerly 1669, had John, Daniel, James, David, Israel and Samuel.

JOHN LEWIS, Windsor, had Samuel, born 1677, Mary 1679, Eliz. 1682, Sarah 1684 and John 1694.

JOHN LEWIS, Hingham, married 1682, Hannah, daughter of Daniel Lincoln.

JOSEPH LEWIS, Swanzey, by wife Mary had Joseph, born 1672, Sibill 1674, and he was buried 1675, prob. killed by the Indians.

JOSEPH LEWIS, New London 1666, may have been son of John of the same, perhaps of Windsor 1675, and died at Simsbury 1680, married Eliz. eldest daughter of John Case of S. about 1674, had Eliz., born 1675, Joseph 1677, and John, posthum. 1681. His widow married 1684 John Tuller.

NATHANIEL LEWIS, New London 1666, perhaps brother of preceding.

PHILIP LEWIS, Portsmouth 1665, prob. of Dover 1672, rep. 1680, at the first assembly under Provinc. Gov.

ROBERT LEWIS, Newbury, came from Bristol to Salem, says Coffin, and died after removing to N. 1644. It is supposed he embarked in the Blessing at London 1635, aged 28, with, perhaps, wife Eliz., aged 22.

ROBERT LEWIS, Charlestown, spelt Luist in the record, by wife Rebecca had Robert, bapt. 1683, Thomas 1685 and David 1687; perhaps removed to Boston.

THOMAS LEWIS, Saco, before 1630 had prob. ranged the coast to ascertain the most agreeable spot for his patent, was assess. £3 quarterly for support of ministry before 1640. Willis I, 16; Belkn. I, 9.

THOMAS LEWIS, Northampton, had Mary born 1663, Esther 1665, and Thomas 1666. In 1667 Thomas died. but which of the two is not known. No more is heard of the family.

WILLIAM LEWIS, Roxbury, in absurd family tradition, by which Farmer was mislead, often made the same as the foregoing; adm. freeman 1642, brought, it is said, John, born 1635, and Christopher, 1636, both in England, and the town record has Lydia, born 1640, and Josiah, 1641; so careless was that keeping that we willingly miss the latter children. Perhaps he removed to Boston 1644, and continued to worship with Apostle Eliot; at least we find at R. bapt. Isaac 1644, Mary 1646, and Hannah 1649, and may be that propr. of Lancaster 1654, who died 1671. His will names wife Amy, who with Isaac, are made excors. Other children were John, Lydia, Mary and Hannah.

REFERENCES:—Connecticut—Andrew's Hist. of New Britain, 160-7; Bronson's Waterbury 518; Caulkin's Hist. of New London, Ct., 295; Davis' Hist. of Wallingford, 841-5; Field's Hist. of Haddam, 46; Meade's Hist. Greenwich, Ct., 216; Orcutt's Hist. Stratford, 1237-41; Orcutt's Wolcott, 513-8; Stile's Hist. Windsor, II, 432; Sedgwick's Hist. Sharon. 96; Timlow's Southington, 156-66. Massachusetts—Davis' Landmarks of Plymouth, 172; Deane's Hist. Scituate, 303; Freeman's Cape Cod, I, 614; II, 285; Hazen's Hist. Billerica, 91; Hill's Dedham Records; Hudson's Lexington, 281; Judd's Hist. Hadley, 330; Lewis' Hist. Lynn. 180-2; Rich's Hist. Truro, 543; Wyman's Charlestown Gens. 617-9. Maine—Bradbury's Hist. Kennebunkport, 257; Corliss' No. Yarmouth; Pierces' Hist. Gorham, 181-3 Ridlon's Harrison Settlers, 97-5. Other Publications—Alden's American Epitaphs, V. 68; Am. Ancestry, III, 153, 170; V, 35, 97, 104, 106, 175. 190. 194; VI. 37, 71. 156; VIII. 64, 117; Austin's R. I. Gen. Dict., 124; Bartow's Gen., Part 2. 170-2; Borton Gen.; Burr Gen.; Bullock Gen.; Carter Tree of Va.; Dwight Gen., 552; Gilmer's Georgians, 42. 105; Green's Kentucky Fams.; Guild's Siles' Gen., 307; Hayden's Va. Gens., 379-94; Howe's Hist. Coll. of Va.. 181-3; Kulp's Wyoming Valley Fams.; Lewis's Letter, Monthly (1887-94); Lewis Gen. of Va. (1893). 454 pp.; Livermore's Block Island, R. I., 336; Marshall Gen. (1884). 104-6; Meade's Old Fams. of Va., II. 231-3, 325; Mellick's Story of An Old Farm. 650; N. E. Hist. Gen. Reg., XVII, 162-6; Paul's Hist. of Wells. Vt.. 114-20; Pearson's Schenectady. N. Y., Settlers, 104; Richmond, Va., Standard. II. 32; III, 23, 24, 38. 40; IV, 1. 10. 14; Robertson's Pocahontas Descendants; Savage's Gen. Dict., III, 84-90; Slaughter's Fry Memoir. 74; Slaughter's St. Mark's Parish, 184; Smith's Hist. Delaware Co., Pa., 478-80; Spooner Gen. (1871)), 163-89; Sullivan Gen.. 337-40; Virginia Hist. Reb.. V, 24; Winslow and Lewis Chart. (1877); Young's Hist. Wayne Co., Ind., 229.

LEY:—Henry Ley, Boston, by wife Mary, had Richard, born 1657.

JOSHUA LEY, Boston, by wife Mary had Benjamin born 1691.

LIBBEY:—Anthony Libbey, Scarborough, 1676, removed about 1685 to Portsmouth.

JAMES, HENRY, DAVID, MATTHEW, DANIEL and SAMUEL LIBBEY were brothers of preceding, and sons of John, who, as well as John, Jr., probably first born of the family, was there 1663, and thus the name has continued. The father died 1683. He came, it is said, from Broadstairs, in the Isle of Thanet, County Kent. Of the children, James married Mary. daughter of Isaac Hanson, who probably lived at Portsmouth.

REFERENCES:—Dow's Hampton, N. H., 821; Eaton's Warren, Me., 574-7; Eaton's Hist., Thomaston, Me., II.

308; Hubbard's Hist. Stanstead Co., Canada, 167; Lapham's Hist., Paris, Me., 651-3.

LIDGETT:—Peter Lidgett, Boston, a rich merchant, partner in many voyages with John Hull, was freeman of 1673, when it is spelled Lydgett, had wife, Eliz. Scammon and children Eliz., Charles, born 1650, and Jane, 1676. His widow married, 1680, Hon. John Saffyn, as his second wife, and Eliz. married John Usher, stationer of Boston, afterwards Lieut.-Gov. of New Hampshire.

LIGHT:—Henry Light, New Hampshire; died about 1677.

JOHN LIGHT, Salisbury; by wife, Dorothy, had Joseph, born 1676; removed to New Hampshire 1676; had Mary 1678; Robert, 1680; John, 1682, and Dorothy, 1685.

REFERENCES:—Eagles' Lebanon Co., Pa., 245; Ransom Gen., 64.

LIGHTFOOT:—Francis Lightfoot, Lynn; freeman, 1636; said to have come from London; died 1646.

JOHN LIGHTFOOT, Boston, 1653; Haz. II., 210.

WILLIAM LIGHTFOOT, Marblehead, 1674.

REFERENCES:—Meade's Old Fams. of Va.; Powers' Hist. Sangamon Co., Ills., 455; Slaughter's Fry Gen. Slaughter's St. Mark's Parish, Va., 142-4.

VILFORD, or LILFORTH:—Francis Lilford, Rawley, 1643; drowned 1672.

THOMAS LILFORD, Rawley, 1643, perhaps brother of the preceding; removed to Haverhill 1654; had wife Eliz. and was freeman 1666. It may reward investigation, whether that passenger in the Susan and Ellen from London, 1635, aged 13, whose name appears Ann Liefard, was not a sister.

EDWARD LILLY, Boston, 1670, a cooper.

GEORGE LILLY, Reading; married 1659, Hannah, but record does not insert surnames; had Hannah, born 1660; John, 1662; besides others probably, and died 1691.

JOHN LILLY, Concord, by wife Dorothy, had Israel, born 1660.

JOHN LILLY, Woburn; by wife Hannah had John, born 1691; Hannah, 1694; Sarah, 1696; Rebecca, 1699; Susanna, 1702; Phebe, 1705.

LUKE LILLY:—Marshfield, 1643.

SAMUEL LILLY, Boston, 1686; merchant, at whose grave, it is supposed, in 1689, occurred the indecent dispute about the burial service, of which Increase Mather had fine account from his gossip corresp. Joshua Moody. See Hutch. I., 356.

SAMUEL LILLY, Boston, 1682, perhaps son of the preceding; had Theophilus, bapt. 1690; Samuel, 1692; Mehitable, 1694; Eliz., 1696; Edward, 1698, and Abigali,, 1699.

SAMUEL LILLY, Reading, freeman 1691. Often the name is Lilley.

REFERENCES:—Benedict's Sutton, Mass., 686; Eaton's Hist. Reading Mass., 95; Savage's Gen. Dict. III., 90; William's Hist. Danbury, Vt., 188; Lilly Gen. (1881) 4 pp.

LINCOLN:—Daniel Lincoln, Hingham, 1644, a young man of whom we are not sure that he was a relative of any earlier person bearing this surname, by wife Susanna, who died 1701, had Susanna, born 1654; Daniel, 1657; died young; Hannah, 1659; Daniel, again 1662; Sarah, 1664; Ephraim, 1667, and Rachel, 1671; and he died 1699.

SAMUEL LINCOLN, Hingham; came from the city of Norwich, with Frances Lawes, a weaver, probably his apprent., 1637, but the old Cushing MSS. says he was of Old Hingham, aged 18; went, perhaps, on reaching his majority, to H., where lived his brother Thomas, a weaver, also by wife Martha; had Samuel, bapt. 1650; Daniel, 1653; Mordecai, born 1655, died soon; Mordecai again, 1657; Mary, born 1662; Thomas, 1664; Martha, 1667; a daughter, 1669, prob. died without a name; Sarah, 1671, and Rebecca, 1674, and he died 1690. His widow died 1693.

STEPHEN LINCOLN, Hingham, 1638; came that year from Wymondham, a town about 9 miles from Norwich, bringing mother, wife and son Stephen, but prob. not in the Diligent, arriving that year; and his wife, whose name is unknown, died soon after; the daughter died 1649, and he died 1658.

THOMAS LINCOLN, Hingham, 1636, the weaver, elder brother of the first Samuel; was two years or more at Watertownw and Charlestown, having, says the Cushing MSS., come with Nicholas Jacob, a relative, in 1633; had grant of land in 1635; may have been the freeman of 1638, or of 1642. His first wife, Susanna, died 1641, and he had another wife, Mary, who by one report, prob. erron., outlived him, and died 1675, leaving no children.

THOMAS LINCOLN, Hingham, the miller, prob. came 1635; certainly had house lot 1636; brought several children, perhaps two or three; removed about 1652 to Taunton, where 1665 he took second wife, Eliz. Streete, prob. widow of Francis. He, in his will of 1683, calls himself "eighty years or thereabouts," and mentions with these children of former wife Thomas, John, Samuel, Sarah, Mary and son-in-law Joseph Willis, perhaps husband of Sarah, and Sarah's son Thomas. In Gen. Reg. VI., 188, it is printed Linton.

THOMAS LINCOLN, Hingham, 1638, the husbandman, brother of first Stephen, prob. younger; had grant of land 1638; came, says the Cushing MSS., in 1638 from Wymondham Co., Norf'k, with Jeremiah Moore; perhaps is the freeman of 1642; had wife Margaret, daughter of Richard Langer, and children Caleb, bapt. 1643, died soon; Joshua and Caleb, twins, 1645, of whom the latter prob. lived not long; Susanna, Mary, 1648; Sarah, 1650; Thomas, 1652; Eliz. and Ruth, born 1664. He died 1692.

WILLIAM LINCOLN, Roxburg, a soldier in the comp. of his townsman, the brave Capt. Johnson; was wounded 1675, in the great Narragansett Battle and died soon after.

REFERENCES: Massachusetts—Deane's Hist. Scituate, 304; Hyde's Hist. Brimfield, 429; Kingman's Hist. N. Bridgewater, 571-3; Mitchell's Bridgewater, 238; Temple's No. Brookfield, 675; Wall's Rem. Worcester, 345; Wyman's Charlestown Gens. II., 620..

Maine—Cushman's Sheepscott, 400; Eaton's Annals Warren, 577; Eaton Thomaston, Me., II., 308..

OTHER PUBLICATIONS.—Amer. Ancestry, VI., 56, 141, 163, IX., 157, 176, 191; Ellis Gen., 107-10; Heminway's Vermont Gaz., V. 103; Holland's Life of Abraham Lincoln, 18-21; Huntington Gen, 82; Lincoln Gen. (1865) 10 p., (1885) by J. L., (1887) 7 p., (1895) 1009 p; Muzzy's Reminiscences, N. E. Hist. Reg. XIX., 357-61; XLI., 153-7; XLVIII., 327; New York Gen. and Biog. Rec. III., 69-71; Phoenix Whitney Gen., I. 753; Robbins' Sermon on Noah Lincoln, 35-49; Savage's Gen. Dict., III., 91-5; Shackford's Lincoln Lineage (1887) 7 p.; Whitmore's Copp's Hill Epitaphs.

LINDALL, LYNDALL or LINDALE:—Henry Lindall, New Haven, 1646, sometimes spelled Lindon, was a deacon, died late in 1660 or early 1661; had Mary, bapt.

1646, who married John Hoyt, of Norwalk; Sarah, 1648; Hannah, 1651; Rebecca, 1653, who married 1674 John Fitch, of Norwalk; Grace, 1656, and Mercy, 1658, who married 1679 Joseph Ketchum, of Norwalk.

JAMES LINDALL, Duxbury, 1640, a propr. of Bridgewater, 1645; had Abigail, who married Capt. Samuel Wadsworth; died 1652, as did his wife Mary soon after. His will names two minor children (committed by the Ct. to care of Constant Southworth), Abigail and Timothy, who was born 1642, says the family Bible tradition, which carries other less definite matters, as that he was from the North of England, and had James, Caleb and Joshua, who died of the plague before he came over.

JAMES LINDALL, Boston; was a soldier in Oliver's comp. and wounded in the terrible day of Narragansett. By wife Susanna he had Eliz., born 1680, and James, 1684.

REFERENCES:—N. E. Hist. Reg. VII., 15-24; Savage's Gen. Dict., III., 95; Vinton's Giles Gen., 311-38; Winsor's hist. Duxbury, 276.

LINDON, or LYNDON:—Augustine Lindon, Boston; mariner 1652, by wife Jane had Samuel, prob. born 1653, and both mother and child died same month; his wife Eliz. died at Charlestown 1657, and he married third wife, 1658, Phebe, widow of William Franklin; was freeman 1660, and an iron-monger 1672, at B.

JOHN LINDON, New Haven, prob. a workman at the iron works; died 1667.

LINDSAY, or LINDSEY:—Christopher Lindsay, Lynn, 1630 perhaps, died 1669, and his widow Margaret died same year, leaving sons John and Eleazer.

DANIEL LINDSAY, came 1637 in the employment of Samuel Dix, from the city of Norwich, but no more is known of his master or him.

REFERENCES:—Amer. Ancestry I. 49; Lindsay Gen. (1889) 300 pp.; Page Gen. 202; Power's Hist. Sangamon Co., Ills., 21, 460; Savage's Gen. Dict., III., 96.

ARMS: Quartered—1st and 4th; gu., a fess, chequy; arg. and az.; 2nd and 4th. Or, a lion, rampant, gu., the shield, debruised of a ribbon, in hand, sa., over all.

LINES, LAINES, or LINE:—Gabriel Lines, freeman of Conn. 1656, most prob. died or removed soon.

HENRY LINES, New Haven, son of John of Badby, 2 miles from Daventry, 13 from Northampton Co., Northampton; had John, born 1656, died young, it is thought; Joanna, 1658; Samuel, 1660, and Hopestill, 1661, and he died 1663, leaving widow.

JOHN LINES, Isle of Shoals, who died about 1675. Savage thinks was a fisherman.

RALPH LINES, New Haven, perhaps brother of Henry; may have had Samuel, freeman, 1670; Ralph, born 1652, and certainly John, 1655; Joseph, 1657, and Benjamin, 1659; perhaps others; was freeman before 1669.

ROGER LINES, Jamaica, L. I., 1656.

SAMUEL LINES, New Haven, 1687; perhaps son of Ralph, of the same; had wife Mary, daughter of John Thompson, the 2nd, of the same.

REFERENCES:—Amer. Ancestry, V. 82, VII. 206; Runker's L. I. Gens., 234-8; Mansfield Gen., 57-61; Orcutt's Hist. New Milford Ct., 723; Tuttle Gen. 207-9.

LING:—Benjamin Ling, Charlestown, 1636; went to New Haven prob. with Gov. Eaton; had his estate laid out 1640; was a freeman with prefix of respect, living in what is now East Haven, died 1673, leaving no children, but giving good property to some friends, and large to wife Joanna, who married soon after Col. John Dixwell, the regicide, and died in few weeks.

LINN:—See Lynn.

LINNELL, or LYNNELL, often printed LINNETT or LYNNETT:—

DAVID LINNELL, perhaps son of Robert, born in England; married 1653 Hannah Shelley, or Shilley; had Samuel, born 1655; Elisha, 1658, and Hannah, 1660, who married 1681, the second Dolor Davis, beside Jonathan.

JOHN LINNELL, Barnstable, who was son possibly of the preceding, or of Jonathan, of whom we know from Hamblen only that he was a settler of B. before 1700, and may have been a brother of David, or of John; married Ruth Davis; had Thankful, born 1696; Samuel, 1699; John, 1702; Bethia, 1704; Joseph, 1707; Hannah, 1709; and Jabez, 1711.

ROBERT LINNELL, with wife, Scituate, 1638; removed to Barnstable next year; had Bethia, bapt. 1641; left widow and several children and prob. grandchildren.

THOMAS LINNELL, Hampton, 1643. Deane made the last letter of the name t.

REFERENCES:—Savage's Gen. Dict., III., 97; Swift's Barnstable Fams., II., 148-61.

LINSLEY:—John Linsley, Guilford, 1650, or earlier, removed long before 1667 to Branford, when John, Jr., was there.

LINTON:—Richard Linton, prob. at Gov. Chadwick's planta.. Medford, 1630, and Watertown, 1638, one of the first settlers of Lancaster, 1643; died 1665. His estate was small, and very little is known of him but that his daughter Ann married Lawrence Waters, of Lancaster.

REFERENCES:—Am. Ancestry, IV. 150; Linton Gen. (1881) 15 pp.; Savage's Gen. Dict., III., 97.

LIPPET, or LIPPIT:—John Lippet, early a townsman of Providence, and afterward freeman at Warwick, 1655; had, perhaps, Nathaniel, certain John, Moses and Joseph, prob. Rebecca, who married, 1665, Joseph Howard, and next, 1669, Francis Budlong; yet Joseph and Nathaniel died perhaps early.

REFERENCES:—Austin's Ancestries, 39; Austin's R. I. Gen. Dict., 339; Fuller's Hist. Warwick, R. I., 112-4; New Eng. Gen. Reg., XXVII. 70-3; Richmond, Va., Standard, II., 147; III., 37; Updyke's Narragansett R. I. Ch., 371-4.

LIPPENCOT:—Bartholomew Lippencot, Dover, 1658. RICHARD LIPPENCOT, Dorchester, freeman, 1640, removed to Boston 1644; by wife Abigail had Remembrance, bapt. 1641 at D. and at B. had John, born 1644; Abigail, 1647, died in few weeks. In a few years he disagreed with his brethren of the church, who cast him out from their communion, 1651, though only for his conscientious scruples, and soon after he went home, where more liberty was encouraged by Cromwell than our people liked. There he had Restore, born at Plymouth, prob. 1653, and at some other town in Devonshire, Treedam, 1655; Increase, 1657, and Jasah, 1660; in 1663 came again over the ocean, and at R. I. had Preserved, 1663, who died at 3 years. In a few years more he removed to N. J. and at Shrewsbury in that colony he was a patentee of the charter, 1669, and his descend. have continued.

REFERENCES:—Savage's Gen. Dict., III., 98.

LISCAME, or LISCOM:—Nicholas Liscame. Marblehead, 1663—Felt. Perhaps he had grant of land, 1637, and is the man whose name is by Felt, 1., 169, printed Listen, seems a very uncommon surname, and mistakes

might easily arise by reading c as t, which in the old engross. hand it so much resembles as to have a thousand times been so taken. Possibly the modern family of Luscome, at Salem, may be thus derived.

LISLE:—See Lyall.

LISTER:—Andrew Lister, see Lester.

REFERENCES—Babson's Gloucester, 112.

LITCHFIELD:—Lawrence Litchfield, in Plymouth Colony, before 1639, probably Kent, England, was a townsman of Barnstable, in 1643, and on the roll of Lieut. Thomas Dimmock; joined Ancient and Honorable Artillery Company of Boston, 1640; was in Scituate about 1646, and died there about 1650. His wife was Judith, daughter of William Demnis, who married, secondly, William Peakes. Children: Experience (a son), born prob. Barnstable, about 1642, died in Scituate, 1673, unm.; Remember (a daughter), born about 1844, prob. Barnstable, married Henry Luce, of Martha's Vineyard, and had at least nine children; Dependence (a daughter), born Scituate, Feb. 15, 1646, prob. died unm.; Josiah, born in Scituate, prob. April 3 or 4, 1648, married Sarah Baker, dau. Rev. Nicholas Baker, and became the father of seven children, from whom descends the Litchfields of New England.

"DEBORAH LITCHFIELD married John Cowen" 1687 (Deane's Scituate, page 244). Is not this an error? Who was this Deborah? If an error, who was the wife of John Cowen (Cowing)?. See Litchfield Genealogy, page 36.

DEPENDENCE "LEICHFEELD," and ELIZA "FAIRFEELD," married in Boston, Dec. 5, 1718, by Rev. Benjamin Wadsworth. Presbyterian minister.

THOMAS "LEICHFEILD," freeman in Dorchester, 1679. Had wife, Mary, from whom he was divorced (?), before 1690, in which year she married, 3d, John Hooper, in Boston. Her first husband (who died in Aug., 1676) was Joseph Long, son of Joseph and Mary (Lane) Long (see Lane Gen.). She had one daughter, Mary Long, who married Henry Straight, of East Greenwich, R. I., before 1693. (See Boston and Suffolk County records.) Dorchester records give birth of a daughter of Thomas L., born Aug. 18, 1678. Her name was Anne.

THOMAS LITCHFIELD, witness in 1690, to inventory of Philip Foxwell's estate (York County, Maine, deeds).

THOMAS LITCHFIELD married Sarah Davis, born Aug. 5, 1658, daughter of James Davis, Jr., and his wife, Elizabeth Eaton.

REFERENCES (on Litchfield): Dean's Scituate, page 305; N. E. Hist. Gen. Reg., xix., pp. 181, 209; Farmer, p. 280; Savage's Gen. Dict.; Barry's Hanover, p. 319; Otis's Barnstable County Families, part 2, p. 217; Freeman's Cape Cod, vol. ii., p. 255; Hurd's Hist. Plymouth County, p. 110; Pope's Pioneers; Pierce's Colonial Lists, p. 73; Roberts's A. & H. A. Co., vol. i., p. 107; Scituate town records: Plymouth County registry records: Litchfield Family in America, part I., No. 1. (1901), pp. 1-101.

LITTLE:—George Little. Newburg, 1640, a tailor from London, married Alice Poor, had Sarah, born 1652, died at 6 mos.; Joseph, 1653; John, 1655, died at 17 years; Moses, 1657; Sarah again, 1651; his wife died 1680, and he married 1681, Elinor, widow of Thomas Barnard, of Amesbury (who outlived him a short time), and died 1694.

JONAS LITTLE. Scituate. 1663, of whom no more is known.

RICHARD LITTLE, New Haven, freeman 1670, a propr. 1685.

THOMAS LITTLE, Plymouth, 1630, married 1633, Ann, daughter of Richard Warren, removed to Marshfield 1650, where son, Ephraim, was born that year. Beside him and Isaac, he had Thomas, killed at Rehoboit fight 1676, and Samuel, and perhaps, daughters—certainly Hannah, Mercy, Ruth and Patience; and he died 1671.

THOMAS LITTLE, Cambridge, had daughter, Patience, said on record at Boston to have married at Weymouth, 1657, Joseph Jones, of Hingham, and anything else is not known.

REFERENCES:—Amer. Ancestry, I, 49; IV, 184; VII, 147; VIII, 31, 78; Ball's Lake Co., Ind., 448-52; Bangor Hist. Mag., V, 34; Chandler's Hist. Shirley, Mass., 501-13; Cochrane's Hist. Antrim, N. H., 573-6; Coffin's Hist. Boscawen, N. H., 572-87; Cushman's Hist. Sheepscott, Me., 401; Davis' Landmarks, Plymouth, Mass., 173; Deane's Hist. Scituate, Mass., 306; Emery's Newbury. Mass., Rem., 125-34; Hayward's Hist. Hancock, N. H. 739; Hubbard's Stanstead Co., Canada, 252-4; Little Gen. (877) 16 p., (1877) 82 p., (1882) 620 p.; Loomis Gen. Female Branches, 719; Poore Gen., 109-11; Power's Hist. Sangamon Co., Ills., 461; Savage's Gen. Dict., III, 99; Smith's Hist. Peterborough, N. H., 133-5; Temple's Hist. Palmer, Mass., 507; Upham Gen., 41-4; Wheeler's Hist. Newport, N. H., 462.

LITTLEFIELD:—Daniel Littlefield, Wells, married Mary, daughter of Capt. Roger Hill, and numerous descend. prosper there.

EDMUND LITTLEFIELD, Exeter, 1639, removed to Wells in or before 1655, was there a man of distinction as commiss. with Ezekiel Knight and Thomas Wheelwright; is called "old Edmund L," died 1661, by his will of that date gave guad. pradis. to wife Ann, to eldest son Francis, and other sons, Anthony, Thomas, John, and youngest, Francis; to daughters, Eliz. Wakefield, Mary Barrett and Hannah L.

FRANCIS LITTLEFIELD, Woburn, had Mary, born 1646, and his wife Jane died soon after.

JOHN LITTLEFIELD, Dedham, 1650, by wife Mary had Rebecca, born 1651; Experience 1659; John 1664; and Ebenezer 1669; was freeman 1671; living in that part which was incorporated as Wrentham. His wife died 1675 and he removed.

JAMES LITTLEFIELD, Wells, killed by the Indians, 1690.

JOHN LITTLEFIELD, Wells, constable 1661, made a lieut. in 1668 by the Commissurs., who created Francis, Jr., ensign; so that we may reckon him older, if a brother, or superior in influence, if not. His daughter, Mary, married Matthew Austin.

THOMAS LITTLEFIELD, Dover, 1648, afterward at Wells, swore to Mass. in 1653, was there still in 1680 to swear alleg. to the K. In the Bevis, from Southampton, 1638, came Alice L., with six children; she was 38.

REFERENCES:—Amer. Ancestry, I, 50; III. 211; Ballan's Hist. Milford, Mass., 880; Bangor's Hist. Mag. VI, 30; Barry's Hist. Framingham, Mass., 317; Bradbury's Hist. Kennebunkport, Me., 257; Littlefield Gen. (1881); Livermore's Block Island, R. I., 333-6; Mitchell's Hist. Bridgewater, Mass., 238; Morse's Gen. Sherman, Mass., 171-3; Savage's Gen. Dict., III, 99; Thayer Mem. 37.

LITTLEHALE:—Richard Littlehale, came in the Mary and John, 1634, and prob. was first sett. atIpswich. thence at Newbury, married 1647, Mary Lancton, had

twelve children, says Coffin, but he names only John, born 1650, who was a soldier in Lothrop's Comp. "the flower of Essex," killed 1675; and adds that he died at Haverhill, 1694. Mirick says he was clerk of the writs. His widow married 1665, as his 3d wife, Edmund Bridges. No doubt some of the children spread the name.

REFERENCES:—Lapham's Bethel, Me., 581; Littlehale Gen. (1880) 10 p.; (1889) 128 p.; Savage's Gen. Dict., III, 100.

LIVEEN:—John Liveen, New London, where it was commonly written, came from Barbados, 1677, with wife Alice, who had by former husband, John and Nicholas Hallam; died 1689; his widow died 1698.

LIVERMORE:—John Livermore, Watertown, was prob. son of Peter, of Little Thurlow, in the W. of Co. Suff'k, came in the Francis from Ipswich, 1634, aged 28, but with no wife or children, yet it is thought that wife followed from England, with daughter, Hannah, born 1633; went to Wethersfield, there he owned lands in 1640, but was, in 1639, of New Haven, then signed the coven. with family count. four, there had bapt. Samuel, 1641; Daniel, 1643; a daughter, 1645; and Mary, 1647; beside Eliz. and Sarah, but sold 1650, to Theophilus Higginson, his house and land and removed back to Watertown. By wife Grace at W., he had Edmund, who died soon ofter birth, in 1659. Hannah married 1655 John Coolidge; Sarah married James Townsend, of Charlestown; and Martha married, 1682, Abraham Jarker, Jr., of Chelmsford. His will of 1683, was prob. 1684.

THOMAS LIVERMORE, Charlestown, by wife Mary, had John, 1687; and Thomas 1688. Seven of this name had, in 1834, been graduated at Harvard, and nine at other N. E. and Princeton coll., of whom three were members of the U. S. Congress. In early records it may easily be mistaken for Lethermore.

REFERENCES:—Barry's Framingham, 318; Bond's Watertown, Mass., 338-52; 852-4; Brewster's Portsmouth, N. H., II, 145-7; Chandler's Hist. Shirley, Mass., 513-9; Clarke Fam. of Watertown, Mass., 44, 79; Draper's Hist. of Spencer, Mass., 214; Dwight Gen., 642; Harris' Watertown, Mass., Epitaphs, 36-9; Hudson's Hist. Lexington, Mass., 118; Isbell and Kingman Gens., 27; Livermore Gen. Notes (1874); Livermore's Hist. Wilton, N. H., 435-9; Savage's Gen. Dict., III, 101; Temple's Hist. No. Brookfield, Mass., 677; Washburn's Hist. Leicester, Mass., 381; Washburn's Notes on Livermore, Me., 15-7.

LIVINGSTON:—John Livingston, Boston, 1659, then adm. of the Scot's Charit. Soc.

REFERENCES:—Alden's Epitaphs, V, 265-8; Aldrich's Hist. of Walpole, N. H., 312-5; Amer. Ancestry. I, 50; II, 73; IV, 181; Ball's Lake Co., Ind., 433; Caulkins' Hist. New London, Conn., 364; Cochrane's Hist. Antrim, N. H., 576; Cogswell's Hist. Henniker, N. H., 640-2; Cogswell's Hist. New Boston, N. H., 439; Gunn's Life of J. H. Livingston (1829); Heraldic Journal, Ill, 76-8; Holgate's Am. Gen., 155; Hunt's Life of E. Livingston (1864); Jones' Hist. New York in Rev. War I, 413; Kip's Olden Times in N. Y. (1872); Lamb's Hist. N. Y. City, I. 276; Livingston Gen. (1887-8); Mag. of Am. Hist., VI. 276-8; Morris' Bontecon Gen. 158; Munsell's Albany, N. Y.. Coll., IV, 143; N. Y. Gen. Biog. Rec., VI, 276-8; O'Callaghan's N. Y. Doc. Hist., III, 609; Phenix's Whitney Gen.. I, 913; Schuyler's Colonial New York; Sedgwick's Life of Wm. Livingston, 17-24; Smith's Hist. Dutchess Co., N. Y., 396; Smith's Hist. Peterborough, N. H., 135-8; Smith's Hist. Rhinebeck, N.

Y.; Strong Gen., 607-9; Washburn's Hist. Leicester, Mass., 380.

ARMS: *Quarterly*—1st and 4th: Three gilly-flowers, gu., within a double tressure, flory counter-flory, vert. for Linlithgow. 2nd quarterly-quartered—1st and 4th: Gu., on a chevron, arg., a rose (or fleur-de-lis), two lions, passant combattant, of the first, for Hepburn; 2nd and 3rd: Az. three martlets or. 3d—Grand quarter; Sa. a bend, between six billets, or, for *Callendar*.

ADD. and CORR.;—The father of the emigrant quartered simply the arms of *Linlithgow* and *Callendar*, and used *cinque-foils*, not *gilly-flowers*, in the 1st and 2nd quarters. Above the shield he used four Hebrew characters, signifying *Ebenezer*.

LLOYD:—Edward Lloyd, Charlestown, spelled sometimes with a single *l*, by wife Hannah, had Hannah, bapt. 1682; Edward, born 1684; Elizabeth bapt. 1689; and Martha 1693.

JAMES LLOYD, Boston, probably merchant from Bristol, as family tradition said, had came about 1670 to Newport, but 1673, as fixed at B. Married Griselda, daughter of Nathaniel Sylvester, of Shelter Island, and died 1693. He married second wife, 1691, Rebecca, daughter of Governor John Leverett. His son, Henry, of Queens Co., L. I., was father of James, a distinguished physician of Boston, born 1728, died 1810; whose son James, Harvard College, 1787, a U. S. Senator, died 1831, without issue.

WALTER LLOYD, came in the Hopewell, Capt. Babb, in the autumn of 1635, aged 27; but where he sat down is unknown.

REFERENCES:—Amer. Ancestry, VIII, 211; IX, 200; Gregg's Old Cheraws, 77; Hanson's Old Kent, Md., 29-40; Heraldic Journal, III, 73; Hill Gen. (1584), 27-34; Lloyd Gen. (1870), 88 p.; (1884) 7 p.; Meginness' Biog. Annals, 18, 7; N. E. Hist. and Gen. Reg., XXXVIII, 425; Smith's Lloyd Family of Penn.; Strong Gen., 635.

ARMS: Gu., a lion rampant, or, within a bardure, of the last.

ARMS: *Quartered*—1st and 4th: sa., a he-goat, passant, arg. 2nd and 3rd; az, three cocks, arg., armed and

CREST:—A he-goat, salient. combed, gu..

Motto: Esto vigilans. (Be watchful).

LOBDELL or LOBDEN:—Isaac Lobdell, Hull, 1658, may have several years before been at Plymouth, freeman 1673. It is stated that his wife was Martha, daughter of Samuel Ward.

JOHN LOBDELL, perhaps brother of the preceding, married, 1659, Hannah, daughter of John Leavitt, who died 1682, and he died 1673, same year in which he was freeman.

NICHOLAS LOBDELL, Charlestown, by wife Eliz. had Nicholas, bapt. 1688; Eliz., 1689.

SIMON LOBDELL, Milford, Hartford, 1655, freeman 1657; removed to Springfield, there from 1666 to '74, was prison-keeper; had Eliz., born 1669; and Joshua 1671; removed to Me. and there had Rebecca, bapt. 1677, and perhaps other children. Lambert is, perhaps, wrong by 30 years in making him of Milford, 1645. Eliz., possibly his sister, married at Boston, 1651, Jonathan Burt, of Springfield; and Ann, another sister perhaps, married 1660, Samuel Terry, of S.

REFERENCES:—Amer. Ancestry, VIII, 99; Pope Gen.; Savage's Gen. Dict., III, 102; Williams' Hist. Danbury, Vt., 190-4.

LOCKE:—John Locke, Dover, 1645, removed to Hampton, married about 1652, Eliz., daughter of William Berry, had John, Eliz., Nathaniel, born 1661; Alice, Edward, Tryphena, Rebecca, Mary, William, 1677; James and Joseph was killed by the Indians 1696.

WILLIAM LOCKE, Woburn, is probably the child of 6 years brought over by Nicholas Davis, in the Planter, 1635, from London, where probably he was born, 1628, no doubt living first at Charlestown, married 1655, Mary, daughter of William Clark, of Watertown, who died 1715; had William, 1657, died in two weeks; William again 1659, John 1661, Joseph 1664, Mary 1666, Samuel 1669, Ebenezer 1674, James 1677, and Eliz. 1681; was deacon and died 1720.

REFERENCES:—Adam's Haven Gen., 36; Amer. Ancestry, VI, 70, 150; VIII, 123; Barry's Hist. Framingham. Mass., 318; Chase's Hist. Chester, N. H., 556; Cutter's Hist. Arlington, Mass., 268-74; Dow's Hist. Hampton, N. H., 821-6; Haven Gen., 36; Hayward's Hist. Gilsum N. H., 353; Hagin's Billerica, Mass., 92; Hubbard's Stanstead Co., Canada, 179, 312; Hudson's Hist. Lexington, Mass., 119-26; Lapham's Hist. Bethel, Me., 582; Lapham's Paris, Me., 663; Locke Gen. (1853), 406 pp.; Norton's Hist. Fitzwilliam, N. H., 626-31; Paige's Hist. Hardwick, Mass., 414; Pope Gen., Salisbury Gen., Saunderson's Charlestown, N. H., 470-2; Savage's Gen. Dict., III, 102-4; Sewall's Hist. Woburn, Mass., 177, 625-7; Stearn's Hist. Ashburnham, Mass., 800; Stearn's Hist. Rindge, N. H., 596-8; Williams' Hist. Danbury, Vt., 194-7; Wyman's Charlestown, Mass., Gens., 622-4.

LOCKHART:—George Lockhart, Falmouth, 1688, by Sir Edmund Andros, made commander of the fort, seized by the patriots on the Revo. as partaker of his tyranny Willis, I, 196.

REFERENCE:—Amer. Ancestry, V, 190-2.

LOCKWOOD:—Edmund Lockwood, Cambridge, came prob. in the fleet with Winthrop as he requested, 1630, to be made free when he hears the prefix of respect; was admitted following year; was a man of good repute, constable and on the finance comtee., 1632, for the col.; died 1635, leaving widow, Ruth, as strangely reads Mass. Rec., I, 134, when her name was Eliz., had children (perhaps more than one), John, born 1632, though record calls parents Edward and Eliz. "Elder children" by order of Ct., 1635, to be disposed of, leaves no doubt of a former wife. Perhaps the widow was daughter of John Masters, who in his will 1639, leaves handsome sum to his grandchild, John L. She married Cary Latham.

EDMUND LOCKWOOD, Stamford, 1651, perhaps son of the preceding, on death of his brother John without issue in 1683, had his estate, and died 1683, leaving children, John, Daniel, Edmund, and Abigail, of whom John was old enough to be taxed in 1687.

RICHARD LOCKWOOD, Maine, was 40 years old when he gave evidence in 1672.

ROBERT LOCKWOOD, Watertown, perhaps brother of Edmund, ot whom. in 1635, he was excar.. freeman 1637, by wife Susanne had Jonathan, born 1634, Deborah 1636, Joseph 1638, Daniel 1640, Ephraim 1641, Gershom 1643; removed to Fairfield after 1645 but before 1652; died 1658. His widow, Susanne, married Jeffry Ferris, and was dead 1661. All children before named, except Deborah, partook of his estate, and four others, John, Abigail, Sarah and Mary, perhaps all born at Fairfield.

REFERENCES:—Amer. Ancestry, III, 34; VI, 61; Austin's Ancestral Dict., 37; Anstin's R. I. Gen. Dict., 125; Austin's Allied Fams., 167; Barlow Gen.; Bolton's Westchester Co., N. Y., II, 745-8; Hall's Hist. Norwalk, Conn. 184, 265; Huntington's Stamford, Conn., Settlers, 67-9; Lockwood Gen. (1889), 910 pp.; Mead's Hist. Greenwich, Conn. 313; Paige's Hist. Cambridge, Mass., 599; Savage's Gen. Dict., III, 104; Schenck's Hist. Fairfield, Conn., 392; Sedgwick's Hist. Sharon, Conn., 97; Slaughter's St. Mark's Parish, 160.

LOFT:—Richard Loft, a malster, from Kent, England, died here 1690, by his will he gave all property to widow Eliz.

LOGYN or LOGAN:—Alexander Logyn, Charlestown, one of the Scot's Charit. Soc., 1684, by wife Susanna had Alexander, bapt. 1685; John same time, James 1687; Jonathan 1690, Ebenezer 1692, Isaac 1695.

JACOB LOGYN, a proprietor at Watertown, 1642, says Bon, who tells no more.

REFERENCES:—Amer. Ancestry, VIII, 127; IX, 42; Green's Kentucky Families; Loganian Lib. Phil. Cat. (1867); Miller's Hist. Colchester Co., N. S., 118-26; Power's Hist. Sangamon Co., Ills., 465; Richmond, Va., Standard, III, 39; Ruttenber's Hist. Orange Co., N. Y., 407; Wyman's Charlestown, Mass., Tens., II, 624.

LOHUN:—William Lohun, Swansey, had Nathaniel, born 1675, and was killed by the Indians soon after.

LOKER:—John Loker, Sudbury, had, before 1652, married Mary Draper.

LOLLENDINE:—John Lollendine, Dunstable, an original settler about 1673, continued a householder, 1699.

LOMBARD, LUMBORT or LUMBART:—John Lombard, Springfield, 1646, married at New Haven 1647, Joanna Pritchard, had John, born 1648, David 1650, and Nathaniel 1654; died young; and he died 1672. This name at S. was written Lumbard, as sounded.

JOSHUA LOMBARD, Barnstable, son perhaps of Bernard, prob. born in England, but may be more prob. of Thomas, married 1651, Abigail, daughter of Robert Linwell, had Abigail 1652, Mercy 1655, Jonathan 1657, and Joshua 1661.

RICHARD LOMBARD, Scituate, 1640, was of Tenterden Co., Kent, and went home that year, says Deane.

THOMAS LOMBARD, Dorchester, came, prob. bringing Bernard and two other children, in the Mary and John, 1630, requested to be made freeman and was admitted next year; removed in few years, perhaps to Scituate first, but to Barnstable by 1640, had Jedediah there, bapt. 1641, and Benjamin 1643. That he had other children, of whom one or two must have been born in England, is plain enough from his will 1663, in which, while he names these, he mentions that he formerly gave property to sons Barnard, Joshua, Joseph, born about 1638, and son-in-law Edward Colman, who married 1648, his daughter Margaret, provides for wife Joyce, and son Caleb. Perhaps he had also Jemima, who may have been a runaway match with Joseph Benjamin, at Boston, 1661, and lived many years after her father at New London.

REFERENCES:—Amer. Ancestry, VI, 146; VIII, 87; Bendict's Hist. Sutton, Mass., 686; Dinney Gen., 30; Cutter Gen., 124, 327; Deane's Hist. Scituate, Mass., 307; Freeman's Hist. Cape Cod, II, 330, 567; Lombard Gen. (1883), 71 pp.; N. E. Hist. Gen. Reg., XII, 249-53; XVIII, 186-8; Pierce's Hist. Gorham, Me., 184; Reade's Hist. Swanzey, N. H., 396; Rich's Hist. Truro, Mass., 539-43; Savage's Gen. Dict., III, 105-7; Swift's Barnstable Families, II, 217; Vickery and Lombard Gen. (1864), 5 p.

LOMMAKS:—Nathaniel Lommak, Dover, 1672 to 88, was son of Edward. See Loomis.

LONDON:—John London, Windsor, was soldier in Philip's war. Trumbull, Coll. Rec., II, 396, 9. The Conn. council of war (for his coming from the army without license in 1676, calumn. the officers, and report. many notorious lies), sent him to prison, but he was soon relased, on acknowledg. of his offence, and promise to do good service. He was engaged in the work of befooling Sir Edmund Andros in 1680, about the regicide Goffe, and swore, 1680, in N. Y., where A. was then Governor, that G. was in April, 1678, living at Hartford, and that James Richards, who was the oldest member of the council, and richest man in the colony, was agent of G., and that if he, L., discovered the matter it would tend to his ruin; and much other preposterous stuff he testif. See the curious matter in Conn. Hist. Coll., III, 284, et seq. showing how the letter of Gov. Andros from New York, of May 18, was received on June 10, twenty-three days from date, and travel almost 6 miles a day. Perhaps Gov. Leete was innocent of the deception, but he must have been blind, or deaf, or both, not to have suspect. the contrivance, and distrust. the agent.

LONG:—Joseph Long, Dorchester, 1660, son of Mary, the widow of Joseph Farnsworth, by wife Mary, whose surname is not known, married 1662, he had Mary, and died 1676. His widow married Thomas Litchfield, from whom she was divorced, and died about 1703. The daughter, Mary, married Henry Straight, of Greenwich, R. I.

PHILIP LONG, Ipswich, 1648, removed to Boston, married prob. as second wife, Ann, widow of Thomas Constable, had Joseph, born 1652; his daughter, Sarah, married 1656, Benjamin Briscoe, and he had another daughter. In 1656 he was of Edgartown, on the Vineyard, in 1658, made his will, bound to sea, and no doubt died next year.

RICHARD LONG, Weymouth, 1635.

RICHARD LONG, Salisbury, by wife, Ann, daughter of Joseph French, of the same, had Eliz., born 1680, William 1682, Richard 1684, Susanna 1685, Joseph 1688, Sarah 1689, Eleanor 1691, and Sarah 1693.

ROBERT LONG, Plymouth, was passenger in the Ann. 1623, had shared in the division of land, but was removed before 1627, when the division of cattle was made, unless he died in the interval. Morton's Memor. Davis's Ed., 379.

ROBERT LONG, Charlestown, came in the Defence from London, 1635, aged 45, with whom no doubt his wife. Eliz., 30, says the custom house record, but prob. 33, and 10 children. Michael, 20; Sarah, 18; Robert, 16; Eliz., 12; Ann, 10; Mary, 9; Rebecca, 8; John, 6; Zachary, 4, and Joshua, 9 mos.; had here Hannah, born 1637; Ruth, 1639, Deborah 1642, and was freeman 1636. He had been an innholder at Dunstable, Co. Bedford, 30 miles from London, therefore well known to Rev. Zechariah Symmes. rector in that church (in whose honor, perhaps, he called one of his sons), Artillery Co., 1639, was a selectman. kept the inn, and died 1664, leaving good estate. His will names his widow, who lived to 1687, aged 84, and eleven children, being all those he brought except Robert, who had died nearly 7 years before, beside Ruth and Deborah. The register of Dunstable, Eng., which mentions the bapt. of his son Zechary, 1630, relates also that a Sarah was buried 1631, so she was not his daughter.

ROBERT LONG, Newburg, married 1647, Alice Stevens, had Mary, born 1649, Abiel 1650, Susanna 1656, Shubach

1661, Martha, John and Rebecca; was freeman 1655, deacon, and died of smallpox 1690, and his widow died in three weeks.

SAMUEL LONG, Ipswich, 1648, may have been brother of Philip.

THOMAS LONG, Roxbury, had Thomas, born 1688. Perhaps he was brother of Joseph, of Dorchester.

REFERENCES:—Amer. Ancestry, VI, 75; IX, 21, 58; Austin's R. I. Gen. Dict., 126; Brewster's Portsmouth, N. H., II, 275-9; Davis' Hist. Bucks Co., Pa., 431; Davis' Landmarks Plymouth, Mass., 173; Eaton's Hist Thomaston, Me., II; 310; Gilmer's Georgians, 227; Goode Gen. 242; Lancaster's Hist. Silmanton, N. H., 275; Littell's Passaic Valley Gens., 262; Power's Hist. Sangamon Co., Ill., 465; Read's Hist. Swanzey, N. H., 397; Savage's Gen. Dict., III, 107-9; Slaughter's St. Mark's Parish, 164, 179; Stiles' Hist. of Windsor, Conn., II, 452; Temple's Hist. of Northfield, Mass., 583; Wyman's Charlestown, Mass., Gens., 625-8.

LONGBOTTOM:—James Longbottom, Newport, 1660, was one of the purchasers of Misquamicut, or Ascomicut, now Westerly, R. I., Hist. Coll., III, 251, and R. I. Coll. Rec., I, 450.

LONGDON:—Andrew Longdon, New London, had been before 1643 on the river Conn., died about 1680, without children.

ANTHONY LONGDON, perhaps of Hartford, 1647. This is diverse from Landon,

LONGFELLOW:—William Longfellow, Newbury, born about 1651, in Co. Hants, came in youth to N., married 1678, Ann, daughter of Henry Sewall, then 16 years old; had William, born 1679; Stephen 1681, died under 3 years; Ann, 1683; Stephen again, 1685; Eliz., 1688, and Nathan, 1690. He went, in 1687, Judge Sewall says, to England, to obtain his patrimony in Yorksh., after his return was ensign of the comp., embarked in wild project of Sir William Phips against Quebec, and with 9 others perished by shipwreck in that. At Anticosti, as Coffin, 155, takes from Sewall's diary, whose first report was Cape Breton. His widow married, 1692, Henry Short.

REFERENCES:—Dummer Acad. (1863); Machias, Me., Centen.. 169; Pierce's Hist. Gorham, Me., 185; Savage's Gen. Dict., III, 110; Titcomb's Early New England People, 230-7.

LONGHORN:—See Langhorn.

REFERENCE:—Essex Inst. Coll., XXII, 213.

LONGLEY:—John Longley, Groton, son of William, by wife, Hannah, had William, born 1669; Margaret, 1671, and Mary, 1673; fled in Indian War, thinks Savage, to his native town, there had Nathaniel, 1676.

RICHARD LONGLEY, Lynn, 1636, had William and Jonathan. See Lewis, Ed. 2nd., p. 91.

WILLIAM LONGLEY, Lynn, son of preceding, from England perhaps. yet in 1661 he was able to prove there was no Richard, but he was the person to whom, in the partition of lands, in 1638, was granted by name of Richard. See the blind story in Geneal. Reg. VII, 188. He may be that freeman of 1639 called Langley, was clerk of the writs 1655, by wife Joanna (who soon after his death married Benjamin Crispe. outlived him, and by her will, of 1698, gave to two Shattucks. her granddaughters) had Sarah, born 1660, but he had elder children. John. Ann. Mary. Eliz.. who married James Blood. and died before her father, and William. beside Lydia, who may have been younger. He removed to Groton, there died, 1680;

in his will names four daughters, Mary, wife of Samuel Lemont or Leman; Hannah, wife of Thomas Tarbell, Jr.; Lydia, wife of James Nutting, and Sarah, besides two sons, John and William. Sarah married, 1679, Thomas Rand, of Charlestown, whither in Indian war he prob. removed.

REFERENCES:—Amer. Ancestry, II, 155; Atkins' Hist. Hawley, Mass., 42-4, 95-7; Butler's Hist. Groton, Mass., 416, 493; Chandler's Hist. Shirley, Mass., 519-50; Chase's Hist. Haverhill, Mass., 637-9; Green's Groton, Mass., Settlers, 10-2; Green's Groton, Mass., Epitaphs, 244; Savage's Gen. Dict., III, 110; Smith's Hist. Peterborough, N. H., 138; Warren's Hist. Waterford, Me., 270-2.

LOAK:—Thomas Loak, Lynn., had Thomas, born 1646; Sarah, 1648; Jonathan, 1651; Mary, 1654, and Eliz., 1656. Jonathan was of Topsfield, 1684.

REFERENCES:—Hatch's Industry, Me., 674; Walworth's Hyde Gen., 764.

LOAKER, or LUKER:—Henry Loaker, Sudbury Artillery comp. 1640, was freeman 1643, by wife Mary had Mary, 1653; he died two months before.

MARK LOAKER, Newport, 1644, a freeman there 1655 was an old member of the Baptist Church and ruling elder; died 1676.

LOOMAN, or LOOMER:—Stephen Looman, New London, 1687, died 1701, and his widow married Caleb Abell of Norwich. He left children, as Miss Caulkins, in her elaborate history of that town, mentions.

LOOMIS, LOOMAS, LOOMYS, LOMES, LOAMAX, LUMAX, LUMMAX, or LUMMIS:—Edward Loomis, Ipswich, 1658, came in the Elizabeth from London 1635, aged 27, but in the same month at London we find Edward Lummus embarked in the Susan and Ellen, aged 24, which was, thinks Savage, the same person, and playing a delusion upon the custom house officers. He had four sons, Jonathan and Samuel, who lived in Ipswich; Edward, who went to N. J., and Nathaniel, of Dover; and a daughter who married John Sherring. See Lommaks. Probably the descend. adhered to the spelling Lummus.

JOSEPH LOOMIS, Windsor, was not first at Dorchester perhaps, and the family tradition, that he came in the Mary and John is wrong, and more likely it is, though no evidence is found, that he accompanied Rev. Ephraim Huet, in 1638, and brought sons Joseph, John, Thomas, Samuel and Nathaniel, beside daughters Mary, wife of John Skinner, who when wid. married, 1651, Owen Tudor; Eliz., who married, 1641, Josiah Hull, and one who married Nicholas Olmstead. His wife died 1652; he died 1658.

NATHANIEL LOOMIS, Windsor, brother of 2nd Joseph, born in England, freeman 1654, married, 1654, Eliz., daughter of John Moore, had Eliz., born 1655; Nathaniel, 1657; Abigail, 1659; Josiah, 1661; Jonathan, 1664; David, 1668; Hezekiah, 1669; Moses, 1671; Mindwell, 1673; Ebenezer, 1675; Mary, 1680, and Rebecca, 1682. He died 1688, when, it is thought, all the children were living. His widow married John Case, long outlived him, and died 1728, aged 90.

SAMUEL LOOMIS. Farmington, perhaps son of Joseph the first, born in England. freeman 1654, married 1653 Elizabeth, daughter of Thomas Judd; had Ruth. 1660; Sarah, 1663; Joanna, 1665; Benjamin, 1668; Nehemiah, 1670; William, 1672; removed to Westfield, there had Philip, 1675, and Mary, 1678; he was a lieut. and died 1689.

THOMAS LOOMIS, Salem, 1668, signed petit. against impost that year.

REFERENCES:—Amer. Ancestry, I, 50; II, 74; III, 215; VIII, 97, 151; IX, 109; Ballan's Hist. Milford, Mass., 882; Barbour's My Wife and Mother, App., 71; Bass' Hist. Braintree, Vt., 159; Boyd's Annals Winchester, Conn., 59, 117-9; Ely Gen., 154; Guild's Stiles Gen., 220; Hines' Lebanon, Ct., Address, 160-3; Hollister's Hist. of Pawlet, Vt., 211; Hurd's Hist. New London Co., Ct., 513; Kellog's White Gen., 30; Loomis Gen. (1870), 292 p., (1875) 611 p., (1880) 1132 p.; Marshall's Grant Ancestry, 119-24; Morris and Flint Gen., 63; Orcutt's Hist. Torrington Ct., 730-7; Savage's Gen., Dict., III., 111-5; Stiles' Hist. Winsor, Ct., II, 432-52; Strong Gen., 804-7; Temple's Hist. Palmer, Mass., 502-5; Temple's Hist. Whately, Mass., 245; Waldo's Hist. Tolland, Ct., 134; Wentworth Gen., II, 290; Wright's Williams Gen., 26-8, 36-46.

LOPER:—James Loper, Nantucket, 1672, was the first person, says Macy's Hist., 28, that undertook the catching of whales there. See large extract in General Reg., XIII, 311. But Felt, II, 223, says that his petit. in 1688, for a patent for making the oil asserts that he had been engaged 22 years.

REFERENCE:—Goode Gen., 197.

LORD:—John Lord, Hingham, 1637; may be the man who died at Watertown 1669, as Bond says.

JOHN LORD, Kittery, was of the grand jury 1651.

JOHN LORD, son of Thomas, born in England, had first wife, Rebecca, daughter of Francis Bushnell, of Guilford, who died before 1647, and he married, 1658, Adrian Raye, the surname prob. being, with profuse expense, Baysey; but he soon abandoned her, and in Sept., 1651 an order from the court for securing her apparel and a bed is found in Trumbull, Col. Rec. I, 224. He had fled in debt to Virginia, and there wrote a letter to his creditor's nephew, Richard, Feb., 1664, which is printed by Porter, p. 11, that serves to show him little changed; and he was named in his mother's will 1670.

JOHN LORD, Watertown, died 1669.

NATHAN, or NATHANIEL, LORD, Kittery, freeman 1652. In same records the name is Lawd. Farmer thought him father of the Capt. Samuel, the ancestor of several families of this name in the parts adjacent, of whom one descendant is Rev. Nathan, presid. of Dart. Coll.

RICHARD LORD, Cambridge, 1632, son of Thomas, who perhaps had sent him to look out for the most desirable place for his friends, Gov. Haynes and Rev. Thomas Hooker; was freeman 1635, but next year removed with Hooker and his father to Hartford, and Gov. Haynes soon followed. He was an original propr. and one of the earliest settlers, capt. of the first troop in the Union chart of 1662, but before it was brought over died at New London, 1662, prob. in 51st year. See Caulkin's Hist. of New London. Porter says he died 1664, but he says also he was rep. to his death and the latest year of his service was 1661; and Goodwin makes his death 1662, only a week difference from Caulkins. His widow was Sarah; the children, Richard, born 1636; Sarah, 1638, and Dorothy. He was the capt. relied on in conjunct. with John Pyncheon for securing the person of the regicides, Goffe and Whalley, that they might be brought to justice in England, as Sir Thomas Temple wrote to Sec. Morrice. His loyalty in this went beyond his judgment. See 3 Mass. Hist. Coll. VIII, 326. Sarah married Joseph Haynes.

ROBERT LORD, Ipswich, freeman 1636, rep. 1638, was clerk of the courts, marshal, town clerk and reg. of deeds,

Coffin thought; married Mary Waite; had Thomas, born 1633; Robert, about 1634; Samuel, 1640; Joseph, died young; Nathaniel, died 1658; and daughters Abigail, who married, 1666, Jacob Foster; Hannah, and another, who married a chandler; and he died, perhaps, 1650. A widow, Catharine L., who had grant of land at I. 1641, may have been his mother, and it was probably his sister who died 1696.

ROBERT LORD, Boston, by wife Rebecca (daughter thinks Savage, of Christopher Stanley, by Susanna, his wife, who afterward marred William Phillips, and in her will calls Rebecca her daughter, in 1650) had Robert, born 1651; Thomas, 1653; died young; and died, as Farmer thought, in Charlestown, 1678. Perhaps, as he came in same ship with Stanley and his wife, he may be son of the first Thomas; by Porter, called sea capt., but we know nothing more of him, except that his mother in her will, 1670, names him, unless he were that Robert, of London, sued in 1675 by his nephew, Richard.

SAMUEL LORD, Charlestown, perhaps son of Robert, of Ipswich, by wife Eliz., had Joshua, Robert and Eliz., all bapt. 1676; Nathaniel, 1680; and his wife died and he married, 1684, Rebecca Eddington, died 1696, aged 56, says gravestone.

THOMAS LORD, Hartford, came in the Eliz. and Ann, 1635, from London, aged 50, with wife Dorothy, 46, and children, Thomas, 16; Ann, 14; William, 12; John, 10; Robert, 9; Annie, 6, and Dorothy, 4; called at the London custom-house a smith, but that may have been a godly deception. His eldest son, Richard, had been sent over three years before, and Thomas stopped at Boston, or Cambridge, a year or more, but was an original propr. and among the first settlers at H. Date of his death is not ascertained. His widow, Dorothy, who died 1676, made her will 1670, in which she names children of her deceased son, Thomas, daughter Ann, wife of Thomas Stanton; William, John, Robert, Annie, wife of John Gilbert; grandson Richard and grandchildren Hannah, Dorothy and Margaret, child of daughter Dorothy, wife of John Ingersoll.

THOMAS LORD, Boston, married 1652, Hannah Thurston, but of him no more is known, and it may be that he did not inhab. at Boston, but came here only to be married by Bellingham. At least no issue is known.

WILLIAM LORD, Salem,, 1636, a cutler, said to have been born about 1590, freeman 1639, was constable next year; perhaps had wife Mary, died 1673, wild tradition says, in his 96th year.

WILLIAM LORD, Salem, 1670, perhaps son of the preceding; had William. His widow, Abigail, extrix. of his will, married, 1674, Resolved White.

REFERENCES:—Amer. Ancestry, II, 75; Bradbury's Kennebunkport, Me., 258-60; Child Gen., 351-5; Cleveland Gen., 108-13; Dearborn's Hist. Parsonsfield, Me., 385; Freeman's Hist. Cape Cod, II, 596; Goodwin's Gen Notes 347-55; Hubbard's Stanstead Co., Canada, 279; Kellog's White Gen., 22; Lapham's Hist. Norway, Me., 544; Locke Gen., 109; Lord Gen. by F. B. L. (1865), 6 pp.; New Eng. Hist. Gen. Reg., XXXI, 211; Porter's Hartford, Ct., Settlers, 8-12; Runnel's Hist. Sanbarnton, N. H., II, 462-6; Salisbury Gen. (1892), 13; Savage's Gen. Dict., III, 115-7; Schenck's Hist. Fairfield, Ct., 393; Secomb's Hist. Amherst, N. H., 671; Sedgwick's Hist. Sharon, Ct., 97; Stanton Gen., 13; Stiles' Hist. Windsor. Ct., II, 452-6; Temple's Hist. Whately, Mass., 246; Walworth's Hyde Gen., II, 733-43; Wentworth Gen., I, 242; II, 408-15; Wyman's Charlestown, Mass., II, 628-31.

LORING:—Thomas Loring, Hingham, freeman, 1636; came from Axminster Co., Devon, says the family tradit. with wife, who was Jane Newton, and children, Thomas and John, the latter born 1630, and they left their home 1634, stopped first at Dorchester, but it could not be long, for his house lot was drawn at H. Sept. after embark.; had bapt. there Isaac, 1640, died soon, and Benjamin, 1644; was early a deacon, removed to Hull, died 1661, and his widow died 1672.

REFERENCES:—Bridgeman's Copp's Hills, 221; Bridgeman's Granary Epitaphs, 350-7; Corliss' No. Yarmouth, Me., 875; Davis' Landmarks Plymouth, Mass., 174; Draper's Hist. Spencer, Mass., 221; Hudson's Hist. Lexington, Mass., 126-8; Hudgan's Hist. Marlborough, Mass., 410-2; Loring Gen. (1891), 22 pp.; Mitchell's Bridgewater, Mass., 239, 380-2; N. E. Hist. Gen. Reg., VII, 163, 326; Orcutt's Hist. Stratford, Ct., 1241; Pickering Gen.; Savage's Gen. Dict., III, 117-9; Smith's Hist. Peterborough, N. H., 139; Whitmore's Copp's Hills Epitaphs; Winsor's Hist. Duxbury, Mass., 276-80; Wyman's Charlestown, Mass., Gens., 631.

ARMS—*Quarterly,* arg. and gu., a bend, engrailed, sa.

LORPHELIN:—Peter Lorphelin, Boston, a Frenchman, put in the pillory 1679, for clip. money, prob. went away as soon as he could.

LOTHROP, LATHROP, LOTHARP, or LOWTHROP:—John Lothrop, Scituate, the first minister, was bred at Oxford, if the tradition may be trusted, but prob. he was there only for a short time, preached, perhaps, at Egerton, in Kent, but certainly in London, where Bp. Laud caused him to be imprisoned for it for two years, in which time his wife died, by whom he had all his children, except those by second wife: Barnabas, bapt. at Salem 1636; Abigail, who was bapt. at Barnstable 1639, the first in that church; Bathsheba, bapt. 1642; John, 1645, and two, who died soon after birth, 1638 and 1650. On liberation from prison he embarked for Boston, 1634, having fellow passengers Rev. Zachary Symmes, celebr. Ann Hutchinson and many others; went to Salem, there married second wife, Ann, who long outlived him, dying 1688. He removed to Barnstable with a large part of his flock, 1639, and was held in honor to his death, 1653. His will provides for wife and eldest son, Thomas, and Benjamin, beside John, who was in England, and daughters Jane and Barbara. See 2 Hist. Coll. I, 163. Children beside those already named were his second and third son, Samuel and Joseph, both brought from England.

MARK LOTHROP, Salem, 1643, removed to Duxbury, and thence to Bridgewater, 1656, died about 1686. He had Eliz., Mark, Samuel and Edward.

THOMAS LOTHROP, Salem, freeman 1634, artillery co. 1645, lieut. and capt. rep. 1647, 53 and 64, and for Beverly 1672 and more years, where he was one of the founders of the church 1667; though no account is known of his wife or children; Savage conjectures he was same who was capt. in fight at Bloody Brook, 1675, near Deerfield, killed by the Indians, with almost every man of his company, called "the flower of Essex." He left, perhaps, no children, but his widow, Bethia, daughter of Darriel Rea, married Joseph Grafton, as his second wife, and next married Deacon William Goodhue.

REFERENCES:—Amer. Ancestry, VII, 51; IX, 31; Bass' Hist. Braintree, Vt., 160; Bond's Hist. Watertown, Mass., 453; Davis' Landmarks Plymouth, Mass., 175-7; Deane's Hist. Scituate, Mass., 167; Eaton's Hist. Thomaston, Me., II, 311; Freeman's Hist. Cape Cod, I, 139; II, 243; Holmes' Amer. Annals, I, 228-55; Mass. Hist. Soc. Coll., 2d series, I, 163; N. E. Hist. Reg. II, 64, 195; III, 273; Sprague's Annals of Am. Pulpit, I, 49; Stone's Hist. Beverly, Mass., 24-8; Swift's Barnstable Fams., II, 162-211, 215.

LOUD:—Soloman Loud, a soldier from the East, was at Northampton in Turner's comp. 1676.

REFERENCE:—Davis' Landmarks, 177.

LOVE:—John Love, Boston, 1635; prob. only transient resid.

JOHN LOVE, New Hampshire, made a couns., 1692. Belkn. I, 124.

THOMAS LOVE, Boston, married 1652 Harnah Thurston.

LOVEJOY:—John Lovejoy, Andover, married, 1651, Mary, daughter of Christopher Osgood, who died 1675; was freeman 1673; had 2nd wife, married 1678, Naomi Hoyt, daughter of John the first of Salisbury, and died 1690. Beside Benjamin, who died in service as a soldier early in 1689, at Pemaquid, he had John, William, Christopher, who married, 1685, Sarah Russ, and died 1737, in 78th year; Joseph, Nathaniel, who married 1694 Dorothy Hoyt, and died 1758, aged 84, and Ebenezer, who married, 1693, Mary Foster, and died 1759, in 86th year. Mary, who married, 1670, Joseph Wilson; Sarah, who married, 1678, William Johnson; Ann, who married, 1685, Jonathan Blanchard, and Abigail, who married, 1691, Nehemiah Abbot, were, it is presumed, his daughters.

REFERENCES:—Abbott's Andover, Mass., 27; Am. Ancestry, II, 75; Eaton's Hist. Thomaston, Me., II, 312; Hazen's Hist. Billerica, Mass., 92; Lapham's Hist. Bethel, Me., 584; Lapham's Hist. Norway, Me., 545; Livermore's Hist. Wilton, N. H., 439-43; Orcutt's Hist. Stratford, Ct., 1241; Roe's Sketches of Rose, N. Y., 237; Runnel's Hist. Sanbornton, N. H., II, 470-4; Savage's Gen. Dict., III, 122; Secomb's Hist. Amherst, N. H., 672-7; Stearn's Hist. Rindge, N. H., 599-601; Worchester's Hist. Hollis, N. H., 380.

LOVELAND, LOVEMAN, or LOVENAM:—John Loveland, Hartford, died 1670; had wife and possibly children, but no more is known. Perhaps the family was perpet. at Glastonbury.

ROBERT LOVELAND, Boston, 1645, a witness then to deed from Bendall to Yale, may have removed to Conn., was taxed at New London 1666; had four years before a lawsuit with Bigot Eggleston, of Windsor, about hides to be tanned, and a widow Lovenam pursued a remedial action for trespass 1649.

THOMAS LOVELAND, Wethersfield, 1670, proposed for freeman that year; had grant of land 1673; perhaps ten years later was of Hartford.

REFERENCES:—Amer. Ancestry, III, 139; Caverly's Hist. Pittsford, Vt., 714; Hayward's Hist. Gilsum, N. H., 355-7.

LOVELL:—Alexander Lovell, Medfield, 1649; married, 1658, Lydia Albee, daughter of Benjamin, of the same.

DANIEL LOVELL, Boston, 1640; lived with his mother in the part which became Braintree.

JAMES LOVELL, Weymouth, by wife, Jane, had Deborah, born, 1665; James, 1667; Hannah, 1668; a son, 1670; Mary, 1674; John, 1675; Eliz., 1679, and Joseph, 1684. Perhaps he removed to Barnstable,

JOHN LOVELL, Weymouth; perhaps elder brother of James of the same, by wife, Jane, daughter of William Hatch, of Scituate, who, in his will of 1651, names her and grandson, John L., who died young; had, also, Eliz., who died 1657; Phebe, 1656; John, again, 1658; Eliz., 1660; James, 1662; William, 1665; Andrew, 1668; Jane, 1670, and probably removed to Barnstable, where Phebe married, 1679, Thomas Bumpas, and Eliz. married, 1684, Thomas Ewer.

JOHN LOVELL, Lynn; had Zacheus, who died 1681, unless the record means that date for the father.

ROBERT LOVELL, the freeman of Mass. 1635, was, thinks Savage, then of Weymouth, and may have brought John, and here had James.

THOMAS LOVELL, Ipswich, 1647, currier; had been at Salem, perhaps in 1640, and was one of the selectmen at I. 1681. He came from Dublin 1639; had Alexander, born 1657, died at two years, and Nathaniel, 1658; was in 87th year of his age in 1707. Another Thomas, of Ipswich, called junr., may not have been son of preceding, died 1710, leaving widow Ann and children, John, Thomas, Eliz., Perkins, Hannah, Dutch and Mary Downton.

WILLIAM LOVELL, Dorchester 1630; was capt. of a small vessel coasting in the neighbor. seas, from whom, perhaps, Lovell's Island, in Boston harbor, got its name. Harris, 62; Winthrop I, 174.

REFERENCES:—Aldrich's Walpole, N. H., 315; Amer. Ancestry, IX, 59; Benedict's Hist. Sutton, Mass., 686; Birney Gen., Jameson's Hist. Medway, Mass., 499; Keyes' W. Boylston, Mass., Reg., 27; Saunderson's Hist. Charlestown, N. H., 471; Savage's Gen., Dict. III, 123; Sedgwick's Hist. Sharon, Ct., 97; Slaughter's St. Mark's Parish, 179; Temple's Hist. N. Brookfield, Mass., 676; Wall's Remin. of Worcester, Mass., 340; Welles's Washington Gen., 202, 226.

LOVERING:—John Lovering, Watertown, freeman 1636, was born Dedham Co., Essex, a selectman 1636-7; died early, made a nuncup. will, in which he gave all to his wife, except £100, which was to be given his brother that had children, and £20 to the children. Who that brother was, or whether he was on this side of sea is unknown. Barry says, and Bond confirms, that his widow Ann, in 1644, married Rev. Edmund Brown, of Sudbury.

JOHN LOVERING, Dover, 1657, had prob. lived before at Ipswich, was drowned 1668 or '9, leaving several young children. His widow, who had, perhaps, been widow of Valentine Hill, married Ezekiel Knight, and died before 1675.

MARK LOVERING, Salem 1668.

THOMAS LOVERING, Watertown, son of William in Oldham Co., Suffolk, came about 1663; had wife Ann, but no children.

REFERENCES:—Dow's Hampton, 828-30; Fullonton's Raymond, N. H., 247; N. E. Hist. Gen. Reg., XVIII, 336; Norton's Hist. Fitzwilliam, N. H., 631.

LOVETT:—Alexander, Medfield, Mass., 1678.

LOVETT, DANIEL, Braintree, 1662, married Joanna, daughter of Robert Blott; removed to Mendon, was freeman 1673; probably all his children were born at Braintree: James, born 8th July, 1648; Mary, born 7th March, 1652; Matilda, born 7th June, 1654; Hannah, born 30th March, 1656; perhaps others, but his wife was dead before the will of her father in 1662.

LOVETT, JOHN, Salem, 1639, had that year grant of land. Had wife, Mary, children baptized at Salem: Simon, Joseph and Mary on 8th September, 1650; his wife united with church that year with the children; Bethia, 13th June, 1652; and Abigail, March, 1655; porbably, also, John, perhaps others, for the name has much prevailed there; dwelt on Beverly side; died 5th November, 1687, in 76th year.

LOVETT, JOHN, Mendon, perhaps son of Daniel; died 26th July, 1668.

LOVETT, THOMAS, Boston, 1645, owned a lot bounding on Christopher Lawson's, looking probably toward the common.

REFERENCES:—American Ancestry, IV, 207; Ballou's Milford, Mass., 883; Calnek's Annapolis, N. S., 541; Daniels, Oxford, Mass., 596; Eaton's, Thomaston, Me., II., 313; Lincoln's, Hingham, Mass., III., 43; Livermore's Wilton, N. H., 439; Milliken's Narraguagus Valley, Me., 17; Stone's Beverly, Mass., 31.

LOVEWELL:—John, Boston, 1660; nothing known of him, excepting that he was a witness that year to will of Thomas Rawlins.

LOVEWELL, JOHN, Dunstable in 1690, had John, born 14th October, 1691; celebrated for his services and sagacity in Indian warfare; killed at Pequawket 8th May, 1725; Hannah; Zaccheus, 22d July, 1701, who was colonel of a N. H. regiment in the French war, 1759; and Jonathan, 14th May, 1713, a preacher, representative and judge, he is said to have been 120 years old, and probably was near 100 at his death about 1754.

REFERENCES: Bond's Watertown, 353; Fox's Hist. Dunstable, Mass., 246; Heywood's Hist. Westminster, Mass., 753; Stone's Hist. Hubbardston, Mass., 305.

LOW, or LOWE:—Ambrose, Hingham, Mass., married February, 1688, Ruth Andrews.

LOW, ANDREW, New Haven, Conn., 1639; married Joan, widow of Henry Peck; died 1670; in his will, probably gave some property to four children of his wife by her former husband, and mentions only, son Andrew, who was then in England. Anthony, Boston, son of John, a wheelwright, removed after 1654 to Warwick; had wife, Frances, and son, John; perhaps other children. He was afterwards at Swansey, his house at Warwick having been burned in March, 1676. In July, that year, performed good service for the famous Captain Church.

LOW, or LOWE, Arthur, Marshfield, son of John, of same place; married in 1714 to Elizabeth, perhaps daughter of Daniel Crooker, had Hannah, 1717; Elizabeth, 1720, and Jeremiah, 1735.

LOW, FRANCIS, residence not known, while on the road from Swansey to Boston, was killed by lightning 15th July, 1685.

LOW, JOHN, Boston, 1637, a wheelwright, had wife, Elizabeth, and died 1st December, 1653.

LOW, JOHN, Sudbury, 1641.

LOW, JOHN, Hingham, married February, 1650, Elizabeth, daughter of John Stodder, Sr., and in September, 1659, Hannah Lincoln, who perhaps died in a few years, as we find on 25th September, 1679, he married Ruth, daughter of Thomas Joy. By first wife he had John, 3d April, 1655, and Elizabeth, to each of whom in the will of their grandfather, John Stodder, dated 20th November, 1661, a legacy is given; also Tabitha, 7th January, 1653, who died in 1654.

LOW, or LOWE, JOHN, Concord, by wife Lydia had John, born 7th March, 1661.

LOW, or LOWE, JOHN, Ipswich, son probably of

Thomas, married 10th December, 1661, Sarah, daughter of John Thorndike.

Low, or Lowe, John, Marshfield, whose father is not named, married Elizabeth, daughter of Arthur Howland, had Arthur, born 1665, and Hannah, born 1670; he was killed by the Indians 1676 at Rehoboth.

Low, or Lowe, John, Warwick, son of Anthony, married 3d March, 1675, Mary, daughter of Zachery Rhoades.

Low, or Lowe, Joseph, Charlestown, a soldier of Moseley's company in the battle of Narragansett, 19th December, 1675.

Low, or Lowe, Richard, Rye, 1663, one of the first settlers, perhaps a merchant of Salem, 1672.

Low, or Lowe, Robert, 1649, a vintner.

Low, or Lowe, Thomas, Ipswich, 1644, died 8th September, 1677, leaving Thomas, John and several daughters, descendants very numerous.

Low, or Lowe, William, Kettery, one of the grand-jury in 1662.

REFERENCES:—American Ancestry, VII, 119; Austin's R. I., Gen. Dic., 338; Babson's Hist. Gloucester, Mass., 113-5; Cleveland's Hist. Gates Co., N. Y., 379; Hammatt Papers of Ipswich, Mass., 215-7; Hayward's Hist. Hancock, N. H., 740-2; Lincoln's Hingham, Mass., III, 41-6; Low Family of Boston (1890) Chart; McKeen's Hist. Bradford, Vt., 349-52; Penney Genealogy, 61-9; Riker's Hist. Harlem, N. Y., 519; Schoonmaker's Hist. Kingston, N. Y., 482; Secomb's Hist. Amherst, N. H., 677-9; Eaton's Thomaston, Me., II, 313; Hale Genealogy, 319-21; Morton's Hist. Fitzwilliam, N. H., 631; Savage's Gen. Dic., III, 125; Stearn's Hist. Ashburnham, Mass., 801-4; Temple's Hist. N. Brookfield, Mass., 677.

LOWDEN:—John, Charlestown, son of Richard, married 27th May, 1662, Sarah, daughter of And'w Stephenson; had John and Richard, both baptized 29th March, 1668; Andrew, 2d August, 1668; Mary, 22d January, 1671; Sarah, 16th November, 1673; Joseph, 27th February, 1676; and by wife, Elizabeth, had Elizabeth, baptized 13th March, 1687; was freeman 1668.

LOWDEN, Richard, Charlestown, 1638, freeman 18th May, 1642, by wife, Mary, had John, born 10th May, 1641; Jeremy, born 8th March, 1643; buried 11 months after; Mary, born 24th February, 1645; Samuel, who died September, 1682, in his 33d year; Elizabeth, baptized 23d September, 1656, and Martha, baptized 6th April, 1659. His wife, Mary, died 6th October, 1683, aged 65. He died 12th July, 1700, in the 88th year. Martha married John Call.

LOWELL:—formerly written LOWLE

LOWELL, Benjamin, Newbury, son of the first John, married 17th October, 1666, Ruth, daughter of Edward Woodman; had Ruth, born 4th September, 1667; Elizabeth, 16th October, 1669; Benjamin, 5th February, 1674; Sarah, 15th March, 1676; Mary, Joseph, 12th September, 1680, and John, 25th February, 1683; was made a freeman 1669.

LOWELL, John, Newbury, came in 1639, it is said, with his father, Percival, and brought children by his wife, Mary, born in England: John, Peter, Mary and James, beside an apprentice, Richard Dole; had here Joseph, born 28th November, 1639; was a freeman 2d June, 1641; had second wife, Elizabeth Goodale, by whom he had Benjamin, born 12th September, 1642; Thomas, 4th June, 1644, probably died young, he not being mentioned in will of his father; and Elizabeth, 16th February, 1646;

he died 10th July, 1647, being town clerk that year. His will dated 29th June, 1647. His widow, Elizabeth, died April, 1651; and daughter, Elizabeth, married, as his second wife, Philip Nelson, of Rowley, 1st January, 1667.

LOWELL, John, Boston, a cooper, born in England, son of above John, married 3d March, 1653, Hannah, daughter of George Proctor, of Dorchester; had John, born 26th August, 1655, died young; Mary, 7th January, 1658; after death of his wife moved to Scituate; there he married on 24th January, 1659, Elizabeth, daughter of Richard Sylvester; had John, born 7th April, 1660; Joseph, died soon; Patience, 7th October, 1662; and Elizabeth, who died soon; also Ruth, 11th July, 1665. He married for his third wife, Naomi, sister of his second, in 1666; removed to Rehoboth, there had Phebe, who died soon; Margaret, 20th October, 1667; Samuel, 1st August, 1669, died soon; Samuel, 30th January, 1671; died soon; Mehitable, 7th January, 1678; Benjamin, 5th November, 1679; and Nathaniel, 25th February, 1681. He came back to Boston, and had Ebenezer, in 1675, though the birth is not entered on the record, and died there 7th June, 1694. His widow, Naomi, administered the estate. His son, Ebenezer, was a shoemaker, was father of Rev. John, who graduated from Harvard College 1721, and was ordained at Newbury, 19th January, 1726, who was father of John, a graduate of Harvard College in 1760, and afterwards became a distinguished judge.

LOWELL, Joseph, a cooper, brother of the preceding, married 8th March, 1660, Abigail, daughter of George Proctor, of Dorchester; had Joseph, born 1st August, 1661, died soon; Hannah, 31st January, 1663; Joseph, 9th November, 1665; Abigail, 4th February, 1667, died soon; James, 27th March, 1668; Abigail, 9th March, 1671; and Samuel, 13th July, 1678.

LOWELL, Percival, Newbury, a merchant, came from Bristol, 1639, bringing sons, John and Richard, his wife, Rebecca, died 28th December, 1645, and he died 8th January, 1665. Family tradition says he was eldest son of Richard, who married a Percival, and drew his descent through eight generations by the eldest son of each, from Walter of Yardley, in Co. Worcester.

LOWELL, Percival, Newbury, son of Richard, married 7th September, 1664, Mary Chandler; had Richard, born 25th December, 1668, who lived till 29th May, 1749; Gideon, 3d September, 1672; Samuel, 13th January, 1676; and Edmund, 24th September, 1684.

LOWELL, Richard, Newbury, brother of John, of same place, came with his wife, 1639, but no children that is known; had Percival, before mentioned, born 1639, and Rebecca, 27th January, 1642; his wife died in 1642, and by second wife, Margaret, had Samuel, 1644, and Thomas, 28th September, 1649, and died 5th August, 1682, aged 80. A number of the descendants of first Percival have been graduated from Harvard College, and four have been of the corporation of the University.

REFERENCES:—American Ancestry, I, 50; x 134; Bridgeman's Granary Epitaphs, 304; Butler's Farmington, Me., 524-30; Currier's Ould Newbury, Mass., 577-9; Cutt's Genealogy, 359; Eaton's Hist. Thomaston, Me., II., 313; Hoyt's Salisbury, Mass., Families, 233-5; Lapham's Hist. Bethel, Me., 584; Lowell Genealogy (1899); New England Hist. and Gen. Reg., LIV., 315-9; Ridlon's Harrison, Me., Settlers, 95-7; Savage's Gen. Dic., III, 126; Stearn's Hist. Rindge, N. H., 601; Washington, N. H., History, 519-23; Whitmore's Heraldic Journal, I, 25-7.

LOWGIE, or LOUGEE:—John, came at the age of 16, in the Confidence of London, from Southampton, 1638, with Grace, perhaps his sister, as servant of John Stephens, of Caversham, Oxfordshire. This name is still found in New Hampshire, but the tradition of the family derives it from John, who came from the Isle of Jersey, about 1700.

REFERENCES:—Lancaster's Gilmarton, 275; Runnel's Sanbornton, N. H., II, 466-70.

LUCAS:—Thomas, Plymouth, had John, born 15th July, 1656; Mary, 15th March, 1658; Benoi, 30th October, 1659; Samuel, 15th September, 1661; and William, 13th January, 1663; was killed by the Indians in King Philip's war.

LUCAS, WILLIAM, Middletown, married 12th July, 1666, Esther, perhaps daughter of John Clark, of New Haven, who died 15th April, and he died 20th April, 1690, leaving William, born 26th April, 1667; John, 14th October, 1669, Mary, 5th December, 1672; Thomas, 1676; and Samuel, 15th April, 1682.

LUCAS—A Mr. Lucas was of New Haven, 1643, with a family of six, of whom no more is heard. He probably was one of the London associates who soon went home. A Lucas family of good estate, in New England, is of French descent, but came not early across the ocean. The first emigrant, Augustus, writes of himself, "I married 6th January, 1696, at St. Malo, in Bretagne."

REFERENCES:—Chamber's N. J. Germans; Davis' Landmarks, 177-9; Emery Genealogy, 210; Hibbard's Hist. Goshen, Conn., 480-6; Middletown, Conn., History; N. E. Hist. and Gen. Reg., XXV., 151-3; Savage's Gen. Dic., III, 126.

LUCE, or LUCY:—Henry, Rehoboth, 1668.

LUCE, or LUCY, Thomas, Charlestown, had Samuel, born 1644, says Farmer, to which nothing can be added, probably removed soon. The name is common at Martha's Vineyard. A "Lucy," at Portsmouth, married Mary, daughter of William Brooking, and had Benjamin.

REFERENCES:—American Ancestry, I, 51; Bass' Hist. Braintree, Vt., 160; Child Genealogy, 244, 779-82; Cleveland Genealogy (1899), 429-31; Davis' Landmarks, 179; Densmore's Hartwell Genealogy; Hatch's Hist. of Industry, Me., 675-719; Mallman's Shelter Island, N. Y., 214.

LUCKIS, or LUCKIN:—William, Marblehead, 1648.

REFERENCES:—Penn. Mag., XXIII, 270.

LUDDEN:—Benjamin, Weymouth, perhaps son of James, by wife, Eunice, daughter probably of John Holbrook, had daughter, Abia, born 22d December, 1679; a son whose name is not known, 13th March, 1681; and James, 9th November, 1689.

LUDDEN, JAMES, Weymouth, had Mary, born 17th December, 1636; Sarah, 15th November, 1639, died soon; Sarah, 5th June, 1642; and John, 13th January, 1657; by wife, Alice, who may have been mother of the others. Perhaps this man was the guide, in October, 1632, in honor of whom, when traveling on foot from Plymouth to Weymouth, named a fording place in the North river. In Vol. IX, p. 171, of N. E. Hist., and Gen. Register, he is called Laddon.

LUDDEN, JOHN, Weymouth, may have been son of the preceding (James), was a soldier on Connecticut river under Captain Turner in March, 1676. This name is often found in the western part of Massachusetts.

REFERENCES:—Draper's Spencer, Mass., 224; Lyman's

Hist. East Hampton, Mass., 191; Thayer Memorial (1835), 47-9; Savage's Gen. Dic., III, 126.

LUDDINGTON:—William, Charlestown, 1642, lived in the part now called Malden; by wife Ellen, had Mary, born 6th February, 1643; Matthew, 16th December, 1657, died next month; removed to New Haven, but the date not known, and there had William; Henry, who died 1676; Hannah, John and Thomas, and died at the East Haven iron works, 1662. His widow married George Rose.

LUDDINGTON, WILLIAM, New Haven, probably the eldest surviving son of above, married Martha, probably daughter of George Rose; had Henry; Elinor, and William, born 25th September, 1686. By second wife, Mercy Whitehead, whom he married in 1690, had Mercy, born 31st May, 1691; Hannah, 13th March, 1693; John, 31st January, 1695; Eliphalet, 28th April, 1697; Elizabeth, 1699, died young; Dorothy, 16th July, 1702; and Dorcas, 16th July, 1704. The name is very rare of any other stock. In the spring of 1635 a Christian Luddington, aged 18, embarked at London, on board the Hopewell, nothing further known of him.

REFERENCES:—Andrews' New Britain, Anderson's Waterbury, Conn., I App. 86, Dodd's Hist. East Haven, Conn., 132-4, Ludington Gen. (1886), Savage's Gen. Dic. III, 128.

LUDECAS, or LEUDECOES.—Daniel, at Dover, 1659. His wife died 1st Nov., 1662; he died in 1664.

REFERENCES:—Savage's Gen. Dic. III, 128.

LUDKIN:—Aaron, Charlestown, probably son of George or William, but may have been a younger brother of them, or otherwise related; came, probably, from Norwich, England; owned several pieces of land in Hingham, Mass., which were sold by him in 1671. His wife, Hannah, perhaps daughter of George Hepbourne, was received into the church April, 1650. He was chosen deacon February, 1672. In relation to his children we hear only of Hannah, wife of Samuel Dowse, joined the church 15 June, 1673. He died 26th March, 1694, in his 76th year, and his widow, Hannah, daughter of Richard Miller, who had been widow of Nathaniel Dade, and of John Edmunds, whom he had married 22d May, 1684, died 13th December, 1717.

LUDKIN, GEORGE, Hingham, one of the first drawers for house lots, in 1635, came from Norwich, County of Norfolk, with wife and son, a freeman 3d March, 1636; removed to Braintree; died there 22d February, 1648.

LUDKIN, WILLIAM, Hingham, perhaps brother of the above, a locksmith, born at Norwich, arrived at Boston 20th June, 1637, from Ipswich, Eng., with wife, Elizabeth, aged 34, and one child, also a servant, Thomas Hawes; freeman March, 1638; his daughter Esther was buried October, 1645. Belonged to the artillery company 1651; chosen constable 8th March, 1652, and was drowned 27th of same month, leaving widow, Elizabeth, and two children.

REFERENCES:—Savage's Gen. Dic. III, 128; Wyman's Charlestown, Mass., Gens., 635.

LUDLOW:—George, a gentleman with prefix of respect, requested admission as freeman 19th October, 1630. Was, perhaps, kinsman of Roger L., then one of the assistants and may have accompanied him in the Mary and John to Dorchester, but probably went home in spring of the following year.

LUDLOW, HENRY, Huntington, N. Y., admitted freeman of Connecticut 1664; may have been son of Roger.

LUDLOW, ROGER, Dorchester, came in the Mary and John from Plymouth, May, 1630, an assistant chosen at the last General Court in London, 10 February, 1630, and first attended court in Charlestown August following. In 1634 was made Deputy-Governor, but left out the next year, having infirmity of temper. He removed, 1635, to Windsor, and in the civil line was chief of a commission of eight from Massachusetts, with unlimited power, 1636, for some time; was engaged in the Pequot War, and the first Deputy-Governor of the Colony of Connecticut; removed to Fairfield 1639, and early in 1641 bought from the Indians the territory on east side of Norwalk river; was employed in 1646 for reducing their laws to a system, and was commissioner 1651-'2 and '3 in the Congress of the United Colonies of New England, but went off next year to Virginia in some disgrace, and there passed the remainder of his days under a charge of carrying away the town record, which was long afterward refuted by finding the volume in the town. He had a child, born at Windsor, but the record does not tell the name; and his daughter Sarah married Rev. Samuel Brewster, of Brookhaven. That the habitual heedlessness of Mather made his name William is less matter of surprise than that Farmer was blinded by the blunder. Its origin was probably reading Mr. as an abbreviation for William.

REFERENCES:—American Ancestry II, 75, v. 43; Fowler's "Our Predecessors," 41-52; Howell's Southampton, N. Y., 339-11; Littell's Passaic Valley Gens., 264-72; Ludlow Hall Memorial App. (1866), N.Y. Gen. and Biog. Rec., XXVI, 5; Ruttenber's Orange Co., N. Y., 399-401; Savage's Gen. Dic., III, 129; Thomas' Genealogy (1877), 120.

LUDWELL:—John, a passenger, aged 50, in the Confidence from Southampton, 1638; nothing more known of him.

REFERENCES:—Keith's Harrison Ancestry, 49; Lee Genealogy (1895), 127-30; Ludwell Gen. (1879); Meade's Old Churches of Virginia, I, 195; N. E. Hist. & Gen. Reg., XXXIII, 220-2; XXXIX, 162; Richmond, Va., Standard I, 44; Southern Bivouac (1886) 649.

LUFKIN:—Hugh, Salem, 1654.

THOMAS, Gloucester, perhaps son of Hugh; by wife, Mary, had Joseph, born 16th Nov., 1674; Ebenezer, 18th May, 1676; Abraham and Isaac, twins, 14th and 16th February—no year given; both died same month; and Thomas, 9th April, 1682. The name is also spelled Lovekin, or Loufken. Lufkin is a name at Dedham, Eng.

REFERENCES:—American Ancestry IX., 206; Babson's Hist. Gloucester, Mass., 112; Chase's Hist. Chester, N.H., 557; Corliss' Nor. Yarmouth, Me., 1077-85; Lapham's Hist. Rumford, Me., 369-71; Little's Hist. Weare, N. H., 934; Poor's Merrimac Valley Researches, 113.

LUGG, or LUGGE:—John, Boston, 1637, by wife Jane had Elizabeth, born 7th March, 1638; baptized 24th March, 1639, the month after his wife joined the church; Mary, born August, 1642, but the record of her baptism (25th September) adds, "about four days old;" and John August, 1644, about two days old; he died 1647. He is probably the man whom Felt enumerates among Salem people as John Luff, having a grant of land 1637, because that name never occurs elsewhere except in the list of passengers to pass for New England in the Mary and John, who took the oath of supremacy and allegiance 24th March, 1634. Final letters are easily mistaken: and very many of such grants were ineffectual. In the will of Samuel Hagborne, of Roxbury, 24th July, 1643, are given "unto my brother, Lugg, four bushels of corn and my suit of apparel." His daughter, Mary, married 11th

February, 1659, Nathaniel Barnard. Possibly these were both Luff and Lugg with the common name of John, but it appears very unlikely.

REFERENCE:—Savage's Gen. Dic., III, 130.

LINN:—Henry, Boston, by wife Sarah had Sarah, born 20th August, 1636; Elizabeth, 27th March, 1638, and Ephraim, 16th January, 1640.

REFERENCE:—Savage's Gen. Dic., III, 130.

LUKE:—George, Charlestown, by wife Hannah, had George, baptized 6th March, 1687.

REFERENCES:—American Ancestry I, 51; Green's Kentucky Families; Munsell's Albany Coll., IV, 144.

LULL:—Thomas, Ipswich, freeman 1672.

REFERENCES:—Caldwell Gen. (1873); Hammatt Papers of Ipswich, Mass., 223; Little's Hist. Weare, N. H., 934; Stanton Genealogy, 92; Washington, N. H., 523; Winslow Genealogy, II, 570-2.

LUM:—John, Southampton, L. I., in 1641; perhaps was living in 1673, when John Knowles, of Fairfield, Conn., writes the name in his will "Loom."

REFERENCE:—Little's Passaic Valley Gens., 273.

LUMBARD, or LUMBART:—See Lombard.

LUMAS:—See Loomis.

LUMPKIN:—Richard, Ipswich, from Boxted, in Essex; was freeman 2d May, 1638, and Representative same year, died 1642, probably without children. His widow married Deacon Simon Stone, of Watertown, and died 1663; in her will dated 25th March, 1663, mentions no children by either husband, but gives her property to her husband, Stone, to kinsmen John and Daniel Warner and Thomas Wells.

LUMPKIN, WILLIAM, Yarmouth, 1643, by wife, Thomasine, had Thomasine, born 1626, who married Samuel Mayo, of Barnstable, and John Sunderland for second husband; perhaps Hannah, who probably married John Gray; another daughter married an Eldridge, but no son, and died 1671. His will of 23d July, 1668, names his wife, Thomasine.

REFERENCE:—Savage's Gen. Dic., III, 130

LUND:—Thomas, Boston, merchant, brought from London in 1646, power from certain citizens of London to collect debts.

LUND, THOMAS, Dunstable, an early settler and Selectman, had Thomas, born 9th September, 1682; Elizabeth, 29th September, 1684, and William, 19th January, 1686. His son Thomas left descendants, but was killed by the Indians 5th September, 1724.

REFERENCES:—Belknap's Hist. N. H., I, 207; Fox's Hist. Dunstable, Mass., 247; Wheeler's Hist. Newport, N. H., 464.

LUNDALL:—Thomas, Dover, 1658.

LUNERUS:——— A German or Polish doctor in Boston, who married 1st July, 1652, Widow Margaret Clemens. In 1654, by the records of the General Court, it appears that he was to determine when an offender should be whipped, the offender being then too ill.

REFERENCE:—Savage's Gen. Dic., III, 131.

LUNT:—Daniel, Newbury, eldest son of Henry, married 16th May, 1664, Hannah, daughter of Robert Coker; had Hannah, born 17th May, 1665; Daniel, 1st May, 1667; Henry, 23d June, 1669; John, 10th February, 1672; Sarah, 18th June, 1674; Mary, 24th July, 1677. His wife died 29th January, 1679, and he married Mary, widow of Samuel Moody, by whom he had Joseph, 4th March,

1681; Ann, 28th January, 1683, and Benjamin, 15th March, 1686. Was freeman 1683, and killed by the Indians 27th June, 1689, at the house of Major Waldron, in Dover.

LUNT, HENRY, Newbury in 1635, one of the passengers in the Mary and John, who took the oath of supremacy and allegiance 26th March, 1634; was perhaps first at Ipswich; made freeman 2d May, 1638; by wife, Ann, had Sarah, born 8th November, 1639; Daniel, 17th May, 1641, before mentioned; John, 20th November, 1643; Priscilla, 16th February, 1646; Mary, 13th July, 1648; Elizabeth, 29th December, 1650, and Henry, 20th February, 1653. He died 10th July, 1662. In his will, made two days before his death, and probated 30th September, 1662, the widow and seven children are well provided for. His widow married 8th March, 1665, Joseph Hills.

LUNT, HENRY, Newbury, son of the preceding, by wife Jane had Skipper (if Coffin is right), born 29th November, 1679; Mary, 16th January, 1682; Abraham, 10th December, 1683; John, 1st February, 1686; William, 4th July, 1688; Daniel, 1st January, 1691; Jane, 9th November, 1693; and Samuel, 26th March, 1696.

LUNT, JOHN, Newbury, brother of the preceding, married 19th November, 1668, Mary Skerry; had John, born 22d October, 1669; Elizabeth, 12th October, 1671, and Henry, 22d February, 1674, and died 17th September, 1678, unless Coffin is mistaken, for one John Lunt married 26th October, 1696, Ruth, widow of the third Joseph Jewett, daughter of Thomas Wood, who long outlived him.

LUNT, THOMAS, Newbury, married 17th January, 1679, Opportunity, daughter of Stephen Hoppin, of Dorchester.

REFERENCES:—Coffin's Newbury, Mass., 308; N. E. Hist. and Gen. Reg., XXII, 232-4; Savage's Gen. Dic., III, 131; Wheeler's Hist. Brunswick, Me., 842.

LUPTON:—Christopher, Southampton, L. I., in 1673; may have been son of Thomas.

LUPTON, THOMAS, Norwalk, 1654, one of the first settlers and admitted to be a freeman 1664, but was not actually accounted so in 1669; had two children, but we did not learn their names, and perhaps they died young. On page 61 of Hall's Norwalk (1847) his Peter Lupton should be Clapton, or Clapham. He was living in 1687, but a widow Lupton is mentioned next year. She was probably his, and was Hannah, daughter of Thomas Morris, of New Haven, married in 1652.

REFERENCES:—Howell's Southampton, 341; Jolliffe Genealogy (1893), 126; Savage's Gen. Dic., III, 131.

LUSCOMB:—Humphrey, Boston, 1686; was a major; died 10th June, 1688, and probably his widow or daughter had died 1st February, 1687, as given by Sewall.

LUSCOMB, WILLIAM, Salem, 1686, a cooper, perhaps had wife and children, for the name is continued there.

REFERENCES:—Driver's Genealogy, 387-93; Savage's Gen. Dic., III, 132.

LUSHER:—Eleazer, Dedham, 1637, one of the founders of the church, 1638; freeman 13th March, 1639, a member of the artillery company 1638 as one of the founders, Representative 1640, and for many years after, assistant from 1662 until his death, captain in 1644, and head of the regiment later; had for second wife Mary, widow of John Given, of Charlestown, but not any children, unless Mary, who, the record says, died 28th December, 1638, was one. He was of high character, and, as Johnson states in his "Wonder-Working Providence," page 110, "one of the right stamp, and pure mettle, a

gracious, humble and heavenly-minded man." His will was made 25th September, 1672, and his widow on the 26th January following made her will; both were probated together 6th February after.

REFERENCES:—Johnson's Wonder-Working Providence, 110; Savage's Gen. Dic., III, 132.

LUSON, or LENSON:—John, Dedham, 1637, one of the founders of the church, freeman 13th March, 1639, died May, 1661; his will of 15th February, 1639, in which he disposes of his estate, names no children nor near relatives; Thomas, Robert and Susan, children of Robert Luson, in England, late deceased, to whom a legacy is given to be equally divided within two years after the death of his wife, Martha. He also names his kinswoman, Ann, wife of William Bristow, of Scituate, but he gave the larger part of his estate to his neighbor, Thomas Battelle, specially remembering his children, John and Mary.

REFERENCE:—Savage's Gen. Dic., III, 132.

LUTHER:—Hezekiah, Swansey, had Edward, born 27th April, 1674.

LUTHER, JOHN, Taunton, 1639, given by Bayliss, I, p. 286, as one of the purchasers, yet may have been of Gloucester 1647.

LUTHER, SAMUEL, Rehoboth, 1662, was second Baptist minister at Swansey, ordained 22d July, 1685; died 1717. He had child, Experience, born 3d March, 1675. The town of Rehoboth sent many in the mad expedition of Gov. Phips against Quebec in 1690, of whom one was Samuel, perhaps son of the preacher. Progeny in that quarter is very much diffused.

LUTHER, SAMUEL, Norwich, 1675. A captain of a vessel trading to Delaware from Boston, of this name, in 1644, was killed by the Indians in that river.

REFERENCES:—American Ancestry V, 5; XI, 103; Benedict's Hist. Baptist Denomination I, 426; Cleveland's Hist. Yates Co., N. Y., 135; Draper's Hist. Spencer, Mass., 221; Savage's Gen. Dic., III, 132.

LUX:—John, Saco, in 1664 had three daughter Mary and son Joseph, supposed by his first wife, for he had only lately married Mary, widow of Gregory Jeffries, who in her will of 8th September, 1664, provided for her son, John, by former husband, with the proviso that if he died before 17 years of age Mary and John Lux should have that portion; thought to have lived many years after, as it is found there was a John in Boston 1676, called junior, as if there was an elder of that name.

LUX, WILLIAM, Exeter, takes oath of allegiance to Massachusetts 14th July, 1657.

REFERENCES—Savage's Gen. Dic., III, 132.

LUXFORD:—James, Cambridge, by wife, Elizabeth, had Elizabeth, born September, 1637, and Reuben, February, 1641.

LUXFORD, REUBEN, Cambridge, son of the preceding married 22d June, 1669, at Lancaster, Margaret———, and had a daughter Margaret 27th July, 1673; was made freeman in 1674. His wife died 31st August, 1691.

LUXFORD, STEPHEN, Haddam, died 1676, leaving wife, but no children.

REFERENCES:—Paige's Hist. Cambridge 600: Savage's Gen. Dic., III, 132.

LYALL, LYSLE, LISLE, LIOLL, OR LOYAL:—Francis, Boston, 1637, a barber-surgeon of some importance, admitted to the church 29th September, 1639; may be that freeman of 13th May, 1640, whose name is printed

Seyle by Paige in N. E. Hist., and Gen. Reg., Vol. III, p. 187; and by Shurtleff in Colonial Record, as it had been in Winthrop's History, Vol. II, Appendix of Edition of 1826; by wife Alice had Joseph, born 10th October, 1638, baptized 6th October, 1639, died 10th February, 1640; Benjamin, baptized 5th January, 1640; buried 1st March following; Mary, baptized 14th February, 1641, four days old, when the record of the town says she was born that day; Joseph, baptized 26th March, 1642. He went to England with Leverett, Bourne, Stoughton, and others to serve in the cause of the Parliament, and became surgeon in the life guard of the Earl of Manchester, whence he had the wisdom, like most of his townsmen, to come back in 1645. See Snow's History, 118. Farmer said that his son, Joseph, was a lawyer, which may be less probable than that he was of the artillery company in 1668, which Savage doubts. His daughter, Mary, married Freegrace Bendall, and to him was given, in conjunction with Joseph, administration on estate of Alice, 1st November, 1666, who probably outlived her husband.

REFERENCES:—American Ancestry, VI, 132; VII., 205; Egle's Notes and Queries (1898) 300; Goode Genealogy, 118; Green's Kentucky Families, Lyle Genealogy, Richmond, Va., Standard, III, 2; Savage's Gen. Dic., III, 133.

LYDE:—Allen, Portsmouth, married 3d December, 1661, Sarah Fernald; had Allen, born 29th July, 1666; perhaps other children, and died about 1671.

LYDE, ALLEN, Portsmouth, son of the preceding; had Allen, born 15th November, 1691, and Francis, 28th September, 1695.

LYDE, EDWARD, Boston, married 4th December, 1660, Mary, daughter of Rev. John Wheelwright; had Edward and died before June, 1663. The name in the record of the marriage is Loyd. The widow married October, 1667, Theodore Atkinson. Wheelwright in his will provides for the grandson.

LYDE, EDWARD, Boston, son of the preceding, married 29th November, 1694, Susanna, daughter of Captain Geo. Curwen, and for his second wife married 22d October, 1696, Deborah, daughter of Hon. Nathaniel Byfield; had Byfield, a graduate of Harvard College, 1722; but strangely the name is given as James in Judge Sewall's Diary in N. E. Hist. and Gen. Reg., Vol. VI, p. 76.

REFERENCES—Savage's Gen. Dic., III, 133.

LYFORD:—Francis, Boston, a mariner, married about 1670 a daughter of Thomas Smith and removed to New Hampshire and there married, 21st November, 1681, Rebecca, daughter of Rev. Samuel Dudley.

LYFORD, JOHN, Plymouth, in 1624; came that year probably in the Charity with Edward Winslow, bringing wife and children, probably four; soon bred disturbances and was obliged to leave; went to preach to the fishermen at Nantucket, and next at Cape Ann, and thence (Felt thinks) accompanied Conant, in 1626, to Naumkeag; but about 1627 removed with some adherents to Virginia and there died, soon, it is thought. It is a reasonable conjecture that he had wife, Ann, and children, Ruth and Mordecai, left at Nantasket, and that his widow Ann, who died July, 1639, had married Edmund Hobart, of Hingham. Ruth, in 1641, and Mordecai, next year, give to him discharge, as their stepfather, of certain tobacco and other chattels, in the will of their father, John, given to them. Ruth married 19th April, 1643, James Bates.

LYFORD, MORDECAI, Hingham, 1642, son of John.

REFERENCES:—Cogswell's Genealogy, 107; Hubbard's Stanstead Co., Canada, 182.

LYMAN, BENJAMIN:—Northampton, son of John

of same place, had Medad; Joseph, born 22d August, 1699; Benjamin, 6th December, 1701, died young; Hannah, 1709; Caleb, 1711; William, 12th December, 1715; Daniel, 1717; Elihu and Susanna.

LYMAN, CALEB, Northampton, youngest son of John, distinguished for his bold and short campaign against the Indians in 1704; removed to Boston, died without issue.

LYMAN, JOHN, Hartford, son of Richard the first, born in England and brought by his father in the Lion, November, 1631, by wife Dorcas, who in a tradition of little value is called daughter of Rev. Ephraim Huit (who in his will names no such child, and she was the daughter of John Plum, of Wethersfield), married 12th January, 1655; had Elizabeth, born at Branford 6th November, 1655, and removed soon to Northampton; there had Sarah, born 1658; John 1660; Moses, 1663; Dorothy, 1665; Mary, 1668; Ephraim, 1670, died young; Joseph, 1671; died aged 21 years; Benjamin, 1674, and Caleb, 1678, before mentioned, was in the Falls fight 1676, a freeman in 1690, perhaps, and died 20th August, 1690, 66 years old, says the gravestone truly, for he lacked only a month of 67.

LYMAN, JOHN, Northampton, eldest son of the preceding, married 19th April, 1687, Mindwell, widow of John Pomeroy, daughter of the first Isaac Sheldon.

LYMAN, MOSES, Northampton, son of the first John, married Ann in 1686; had Ann, born, 1688; Moses, 1690; Martha, 1695; Bethia, 1698, beside four who died young; was freeman 1690, and died 1702.

LYMAN, RICHARD, Roxbury, 1631, born at High Ongar, where he was baptized 30th October, 1580; came with Eliot, in the Lion, bringing, so says the church records, "Phillis, baptized 12th September, 1611, at High Ongar; Richard baptized 24th February, 1618; Sarah, baptized 8th February, 1621; John, born September, 1623, and another," known now to be Robert, born September, 1629; and it goes on to tell how he went to Connecticut, "when the great removal was made," and suffered greatly in loss of his cattle; was freeman 11th June, 1633, and among the original proprietors of Hartford, where he died 1640. His will, of 22d April, 1640, is the first in the valuable work of Trumbull, Colonial Records of Connecticut, Vol. I, pp. 442-3, followed by the Inventory. His widow, Sarah, died not long after. All the children are named in the will, and Phillis is called wife of William Hills.

LYMAN, RICHARD, Windsor, eldest son of the preceding, born in England, married Hepzibah, daughter of Thomas Ford, and had Hepzibah, Sarah, Richard, Thomas, Elizabeth and John, all born at Windsor before 1655, when he removed to Northampton; there had Joanna, 1658, died soon, and Hannah, 1660. He died 3d June, 1662, and his widow married John Marsh, of Hadley, who thereupon removed to Northampton. Hepzibah married 6th November, 1662, Josiah Dewey; Sarah married, 1669, John Marsh, Jr.; Elizabeth married 20th August, 1672, Joshua Pomeroy, and Hannah married 20th June, 1677, Joseph Pomeroy.

LYMAN, RICHARD, Northampton, eldest son of the preceding, married, 1675, Elizabeth Cowles, daughter of John, of Hatfield; had Samuel, born 1676; Richard, 1678; John, 1680; Isaac, 1682; Jonathan, 1684; Elizabeth, 1686; David, 1688, and Josiah, and removed to Lebanon, 1696, where he had Ann, 1698.

LYMAN, ROBERT, Northampton, youngest son of the first Richard, born in England; married 5th November,

1662, Hepzibah, daughter of Thomas Bascom; had Sarah, born 1664; John, 1664; Thomas, 1666, all of whom died young; Samuel died before manhood; Thankful, 1671; Hepzibah, 1674; Preserved, 1676; Wait, 1678, died at the age of 19 years, and Experience, 1680. Two of his daughters were married. He was freeman 1684, living his last ten years in a "distracted condition," giving his time solely to fishing or hunting and perished, as the tradition goes, on a hill in Northampton, still named Robert's Hill, but the date of his death is not found in the records.

LYMAN, THOMAS, Northampton, 1678, brother of the third Richard; married in 1678, Ruth, widow of Joseph Baker, daughter of William Holten; had Thomas, Mindwell, Ebenezer, Elizabeth, Noah and Enoch; was freeman 1690, and removed to Durham. Noah was father of Gen. Phineas. Forty-seven of this name, says Farmer, had been, in 1834, graduated at New England colleges, of which thirteen were clergymen and three members of Congress, and of those twenty-eight were of Yale, only six of Harvard.

REFERENCES:—Adams' Fairhaven, Vt., 484; American Ancestry, I, 51; VI, 45, 116; VII., 24, 185; IX, 106; XI, 104, 231; Austin's Ancestries, 41; Barbour's "My Wife and Mother," App. 23; Barnes' Hist. Goshen, Mass., 150-2; Bartlett's Wareton Genealogy, 131; Doolittle's Belchertown, Mass., 253; Dwight's Genealogy, 124-6, 541, 556-76, 906-8; Hibbard's Hist. Goshen, Conn., 486-93; Hine's Lebanon, Conn., Hist. Add., 163; Huntington Genealogy, 131; Hind's Hist. New London Co., Conn., 513; Hyde's Hist. Brimfield, Mass., 532; Judd's Hist. Hadley, Mass., 531; Kellogg's White Genealogy, 101; Litchfield Co. Hist. Conn. (1881), 355; Loomis Genealogy (1880), 333-63, 686-8, 739; Lyman Genealogy (1865); Lyman Genealogy (1872); Lyman Family Reunion (1871); Lyman's Hist. East Hampton, Mass., 161-8; Middlefield, Conn., Hist.; Montague Genealogy, 200-2; Orcutt's Hist. Derby, Conn., 744; Orcutt's Hist. Torrington, Conn., 744-8; Pickering Genealogy; Powers' Sangamon Co., Ills., Settlers, 467; Savage's Gen. Dic., III., 134; Smith's Hist. Sunderland, Mass., 438; Strong Genealogy, 1203-7; Temple's Hist. Whately, Mass., 844-9. 844-9.

LYNDE:—Benjamin, Boston, son of Simon, studied at the Middle Temple, and became a barrister before he came home; was married to Mary, daughter of Hon. William Brown, on 22d April, 1699, and had Benjamin, born 5th October, 1700, who graduated from Harvard College, 1718: was made Chief Justice of the Supreme Court of Massachusetts, and died 3d October, 1781: and William, born 27th October, 1714, graduated at Harvard College, 1733, a merchant at Salem: was sworn as one of the judges of the Supreme Court 25th July, 1712, afterward was Chief Justice of Massachusetts, and died 28th January, 1745, and his widow died 12th July, 1753.

LYNDE, JOHN, Malden, by wife, Mary, had Thomas, born 24th October, 1685; Ann, 13th August, 1687; Abigail, 4th December, 1689; Samuel, 29th November, 1690, and perhaps his wife died 22d December, 1690. By second wife, Elizabeth, had Dorothy, born 20th December, 1692; Joanna, 22d February, 1697; Mehitable, 11th March, 1698, and his wife died 19th January, 1699. He was a captain and died 17th September, 1723, about 75 years of age.

LYNDE, JOSEPH, Charlestown, son of the first Thomas of the same place, a freeman in 1671, Representative 1674-'9, and '80, member of artillery company 1681, a patriot in the Committee of Safety 1689, made by Mather

and King William in the charter of 1691 a counselor, but was left out at the first election by the people; married 24th March, 1665, Sarah, daughter of Nicholas Davison; had Nicholas, born 1665, died soon; Sarah, 5th December, 1666, baptized 13th January following; Margaret, 24th January, 1669, baptized on the 30th; Joseph, 15th, baptized 21st May, 1671, who was lost at sea 16th October, 1694; Nicholas, 2, baptized 14th July, 1674; Joanna, 4, baptized July, 1676, and Thomas, 1678, who was lost at sea with his brother, Joseph. His wife died 13th December, 1678, aged 31, and his second wife was Emma, widow of John Brakenbury, and daughter of John Anderson, who died 1st September, 1703, and his third wife was Mary, widow of Hon. Adam Winthrop, whom he married 13th March, 1706; she died 30th October, 1715; was Lieutenant-Colonel, and died 29th January, 1727, aged, so says Sewall, about 90.

LYNDE, JOSEPH, Malden, son of the second Thomas, freeman 1678, died 2d January, 1736, aged 83, says the gravestone; by wife, Elizabeth, daughter of Peter Tufts, had Mary, born 30th April, 1686, died in few days; Joseph, 1687, died 13th February, 1688; Ann, 29th May, 1688; Joseph, 2d September, 1690; perhaps others; certain Mary, 25th August, 1692; Sarah, 12th November, 1694; Rebecca, 14th July, 1696, and Thomas, 21st April, in 1683 Susanna, daughter of Deputy-Governor Francis 1702.

LYNDE, NATHANIEL, Saybrook, son of Simon, married in 1683 Susanna, daughter of Deputy Governor Francis Willoughby; had Susanna born 6th August, 1685, died at four months old; Samuel, 29th October, 1689; Nathaniel, 22d October, 1692; Elizabeth, 2d December, 1694; and four others, and died 5th October, 1729.

LYNDE, SAMUEL, Charlestown, son of Thomas by wife Rebecca, had Thomas, born and died 1678, and Rebecca, baptized 10th February, 1682, when the mother joined the church as a widow, but when the father died is not known.

LYNDE, SAMUEL, Boston, brother of Nathaniel, was a merchant and freeman 1690, died December, 1697.

LYNDE, SIMON, Boston, 1650, born in London June, 1624, son of Enoch, who died there 25th April 1636, and of Elizabeth, who long survived her husband; married 22d February, 1653, Hannah, daughter of John Newgate; had Samuel, born 1st December, 1653, before mentioned; Simon 26th September, 1655, died soon; John, 8th November, 1657; Nathaniel, 22d November, 1659, before mentioned; Elizabeth, 25th March, 1662; Benjamin, 22d September 1666, graduate of Harvard College, 1686, before mentioned; Hannah, 19th May, 1670, and Sarah, 25th May, 1672, besides John, Joseph, Enoch, who was baptized 1st February, 1674, and James, who all died young: member of the artillery company 1658, and died 22d November, 1687, and his widow died 20th December, 1689. He was bred to trade in Holland, and after coming to Boston and residing several years went to London, and for some time was engaged there, and partook, in 1672, of a design for planting near Stonington, as land speculator. The daughter Elizabeth married George Pordage; Hannah had three husbands, but no children, and died 9th August, 1723, and Sarah married her cousin, Nathaniel Newgate, or Newdigate, as it was written in England.

LYNDE, THOMAS, Charlestown, 1634, made freeman 4th March, 1636, representative 1636-'7-'45 and several years more, selectman 14 years, and a deacon; died 30th December, 1671, in his 77th year. By first wife he had Thomas, born in England, where probably she died; and Mary, who was brought over in 1635, by John Winthrop, Jr., in the Abigail, then aged 6 years; beside six others, who died before him, one being Henry, who died 9th

April, 1646; and by second wife, Margaret, widow of Thomas Jordan, and daughter of John Martin, had Joseph, born 3d. baptised 5th June, 1636; Sarah, baptised 14th April. 1639; Hannah, born 2d, baptised 8th May. 1642; William; and Samuel, born 14th October, 1644. This wife died 3d August, 1662, and he married, 6th December, 1665, Rebecca, widow of Captain Nicholas Trerice, who long outlived him, and died 8th December, 1688. His will, made only ten days before he died, with a codicil of a single day before, mentioned wife Rebecca, sons Joseph, Samuel and Thomas, son-in-law Robert Pierpont. daughters Hannah Trerice and Mary Wicks of Succonesset. The inventory was of a good amount. Mary married a Wicks; Hannah married. 1663, John Trerice; and Sarah married 18 Feb'y, 1657, Robert Pierpont of Roxbury.

LYNDE, THOMAS, Malden, son of the preceding, born in England, freeman 1645; had Thomas, born 25th March, 1647 or 1648; Elizabeth. 20th April, 1650; Joseph, 13th December, 1652; and perhaps others, died 15th October, 1693, aged 78 years; his wife Elizabeth, aged 81, having died six weeks before. Elizabeth married, 26th August, 1670, Peter Tufts.

LYNDE, THOMAS, Charlestown, probably son of the preceding, by wife Mary, had Mary baptised 18th May, 1684. Between the families of Boston and of Charlestown with this name no relationship is discovered. The spelling in various records is Lind, Linds. and even Lines. Six had been graduated at Harvard College, to 1834, and five at Yale.

REFERENCES:—Davis Genealogy, 85; Dorr Genealogy; Draper's Hist. Spencer, Mass., 225; Goss' Hist. Melrose, Mass., 10-2; Heywood's Hist. Westminster, Mass., 754; Malden, Mass., Bi-Centennial, 232-4; N. E. Hist. and Gen. Reg., IX, 323; Oliver's Lynde Diaries, 1880. App. 251; Prime's Bowdoin Genealogy, 28; Salisbury's Family Histories (1892), 350-425; Savage's Gen. Dic. III, 135; Sheldon's Hist. Deerfield, Mass., 233-5; Sherburne. N. Y., News for Aug. 31, 1889; Washburn's Hist. Leicester, Mass., 382; Wyman's Charlestown, Mass., II, 637-41.

LYNN OR LYME:—Henry, Boston, 1630, probably came in the fleet with Winthrop, who speaks of his dissatisfaction with our government, I, 61; by wife Sarah had Sarah, born 20th August, 1636; Elizabeth, 27th March, 1638; Ephraim, 16th January, 1640; and Rebecca, 15th February, 1646, all of whom he (as Widow Lynn, having married Hugh Gunnison) brought to baptism 23d May, 1647. The church record indicates the age of each of the children, and these dates, excepting for the youngest concur, but this is said to be 5 years and about 3 months, and we may therefore believe the record of birth to be incorrect. He was of York, 1640, probably, and in 1645 went to Virginia, carrying most of his property there; died soon, for his widow and four children only £4.18.10 remained after his debts were paid. Joanna, perhaps his daughter, married, 19th July, 1660, William Williams.

REFERENCES:—Clark's King William, Va., Families; Richmond Standard, III, 13, 51; Sullivan's Memorial, 281-94; Penna. Mag. of Hist., XVII, 376; Powers' Sangamon Co., Illinois Settlers, 470; Savage's Gen. Dic., III, 137.

LYON:—George, Dorchester, 1666, freeman in 1669. Nothing is known of him beyond that, in 1678, he joined the new church gathered at Milton.

LYON, HENRY, Milford, 1646, was of Fairfield. 1652, where he married the only daughter of William Bateman.

LYON, JAMES, Roxbury, had Ann; born 4th March, 1683.

LYON, JOHN, Salem, 1638, when, Felt says, he had a grant of land. Lived probably on Marblehead side in 1648.

LYON, JOHN, Roxbury, eldest son of first William, married, 10th May, 1670, Abigail, daughter of John Polley, had John, born 14th May, 1673; William, 15th September, 1675; Joseph, 10th February, 1678; Benjamin, 1680, died soon; Abigail, 12th July, 1682; Benjamin, 18th December, 1684; Berthia, 20th October, 1690; Ebenezer, 10th March, 1693; Nehemiah, 23d July, 1695; and Hannah, 22d April, 1698, died December following. He and his wife were buried in one grave, 15th January, 1702, so says the record. He had lived at Dorchester, and was freeman 1690.

LYON, JOSEPH, Roxbury, son of the first William, was a soldier of Turner's Company, March, 1676; married, 23d March, 1681, Mary, daughter of John Bridge. and had Mary, born 9th January following, died soon; Joseph, 4th July, 1684; and perhaps removed, for no more is said of them in the records, unless he be that one who died 19th June. 1724, but is said to be in his 47th year by the inscription, which may be an error. See N. E. Hist. and Gen. Reg., VII, 331.

LYON, PETER, Dorchester, freeman 1649, had Mary, born 4th November, 1650; Elkanah or Elhanan, 23d September, 1652; Nathaniel, 28th December, 1654; Susanna, 25th March, 1658; Ebenezer, 20th February, 1661; and perhaps others. His second wife, Hannah or Ann, was daughter of Thomas Tolman, and died November, 1689.

LYON, PETER, Dorchester, freeman 1690, may have been son of preceding.

LYON, RICHARD, Cambridge, sent by Sir Henry Millmay as tutor for his son William at Harvard College, 1644-5, and perhaps went home with him after graduating in 1647; but probably assisted President Dunster in his revision of the N. E. version of the Psalms, of which the first edition was printed at Cambridge 1640.

LYON, RICHARD, Fairfield, 1649, recommended to be freeman 1664, but not qualifying before 1669.

LYON, SAMUEL, Roxbury, son of the first Willliam, had, says the church record, Ebenezer, baptised 29th September, 1678, and is supposed to have removed to Rowley, but came back, and the records of the town says, by wife Deliverance had Margaret, born 24th August, 1685; and by wife Maria, who died 25th April, 1704. had John, born 7 days before, unless this refers to his nephew Samuel, as seems likely; and he died 7th April, 1713.

LYON, THOMAS, Fairfield, 1654-70, may be the soldier under Captain Turner, in the Falls fight, killed by the Indians after his victory, 19th May, 1676.

LYON, THOMAS, Roxbury, second son of first William, married, 10th March. 1669, Abigail Gould, had Thomas, born 4th September following if the record be correct; Sarah, 26th August, 1672; both baptised 20th April, 1673; Jonathan, 24th June, baptised 23d August, 1674, died in October of next year; Jonathan, 25 August, 1676, record of baptism not found; Esther, 13th October, 1678, baptised June 8. 1679; Mehetable, 17th March, baptised 24th April, 1681; Ann, who died soon, in 1683; Jonathan, died soon;Eliphalet, 20th September, 1687; and Ann, 28th April, 1689, died at the age of 4 years.

LYON, WILLIAM, Roxbury, came in 1635, aged 14

years, in the Hopewell, Captain Babb, probably under charge of Isaac Heath, a passenger, with his family, in the same ship; married, 17th June, 1646, Rachel, daughter of Thomas Ruggles, had John, born 10th April, 1647; Thomas, 8th August, 1648; Samuel, 10th June, 1650, all before mentioned; William, 12, baptised 18th July, 1652; Joseph, 30th November, baptised 3d December, 1654, when the church record calls him John; Sarah, baptised 8th March, 1657, whose birth is not in town records; Jonathan, 5th September, 1666, who died before another Jonathan, born late in 1668 or early in 1669; was of the artillery company, 1645, freeman 1666, and died 21st May, 1692; and his widow died 4th August, 1694.

LYON, WILLIAM, Roxbury, son of the preceding, married, September, 1675, Sarah Dunkin, perhaps daughter of Samuel, had William, born 9th December, 1677; Samuel, 20th September, 1679; Hannah, 11th August, 1681; Benjamin, 29th March, 1683, died in a few days; Mehitable, 24th March, 1684; his wife died 9th February, 1689, and by wife Deborah he had David, 31st October, 1692; Martha, who died soon; and Jacob, 4th June, 1696; he died 10th August, 1714. His widow Deborah died 12th March, 1717.

REFERENCES:—American Ancestry, I, 51; V, 117; X, 104; XII, 33; Baird's Hist. Rye, N. Y., 422-5; Baker's Hist. Montville, Conn., 450-4; Bangor, Me., Hist. Mag., III, 209; Barrus' Hist. Goshen, Mass., 150; Bass' Hist. Braintree, Vt., 161; Bolton's Westchester County, N. Y., II, 748; Chandler's Hist. Shirley, Mass., 559-61; Egle's Penn. Gens., 2d ed., 383-407; Ellis Genealogy, 238, 376; Goode Genealogy, 158; Hyde's Hist. Brimfield, Mass., 433; Littell's Passaic Valley Gens., 274-6; Mansfield Genealogy, 51; Mead's Hist. Greenwich, Conn., 313; Morris Genealogy (1887), 31; N. J. Hist. Colls., VI, Supp. 125; N. Y. Gen. and Biog. Rec., XXVIII, 75-9, 235-7, XXIX, 98-100; Norton's Hist. Fitzwilliam. N. H., 631; Powers' Sangamon Co., Ills., Settlers, 469; Redfield Genealogy, 49; Savage's Gen. Dic., III, 137; Schenck's Hist. Fairfield, Conn., 393-5; Stone's History Hubbardston, Mass., 305; Todd's Hist. Redding, Conn., 205; Ward's Hist. Shrewsbury, Mass., 357; Well's Amer. Fam. Antiquity, II, 93-111; Whitman Genealogy, 74-6; Wight Genealogy, 99; Williams' Hist. Danby, Vt., 189; Woodward's Life of Nath. Lyon, 349-56.

LYSCOM OR LISCOM:—Humphrey, Boston, a member of the artillery company in 1678. He was a merchant, of whose estate administration was given 23d June, 1688, by Sir Edmund Andros, calling him Major, to Abigail Kelloud, his mother-in-law, and on her resignation the next month, it was given to his brother Thomas.

LYSCOM, JOHN, Lynn, by wifef Abigail had Samuel, born 16th September, 1693.

REFERENCE:—Savage's Gen. Dic., III, 138.

LYTHERLAND, LETHERLAND, or LITHERLAND:—William, Boston, 1630, came, no doubt in the fleet with Winthrop, in the employment of Owen Roe of London, who was one of the company of adventurers to Massachusetts, who never came here, but was made a member of the High Court of Justice, so called for condemnation of the King. and affixed his seal, as one of the regicides, to the warrant for execution. He joined church 24th November, 1633, and became, it is supposed, a freeman 4th March following, when the name in the list is Netherland; was a supporter of Mrs. Hutchinson's opinions, for which he was disarmed and went to Rhode Island, was many years town clerk of Newport, had wife Margaret, but whether any children is unknown. In 1684 he was called to give testimony as to the purchase from the Indians, in his first coming to settle here, and then gave his age as 74.

LYTHERLAND, ZIBION, or more probably Zebulon (both names being used in the records, though the former more frequent and latest), Boston, by wife Rachel had Margaret, born 4th July, 1670; William, 5th March, 1673; and Deborah 2d October, 1678.

REFERENCE:—Savage's Gen. Dic., III, 139.

MACCALLOM or MAKCALLOM:—Malcolm, Boston, 1657, one of the first members of the Scot's Charity Society. By an error in Drake's History of Boston, page 455. the name is given Maktallome.

REFERENCE:—Savage's Gen. Dic., III, 139.

MACCANE:—William, Wrentham, by wife Ruth had William, who was accidentally killed in youth; Mary, born 1st February, 1670; Sarah, 10th August. 1671; and Deborah, 23d May, 1674; probably others.

REFERENCE:—Savage's Gen. Dic., III, 139.

MACCARTY:—Florence, Boston, 1686, a butcher, was one of the founders of the first society for Episcopal worship in New England. By wife Elizabeth had Elizabeth, born 25th December, 1687; Thomas, 5th February, 1689; William, 3d February, 1691; and by wife Sarah had Esther, 1st July, 1701; and Margaret, 29th March, 1702, if the record be correct. He died 13th June, 1712, at Roxbury, and a third wife, Christian, with his son William administered the estate.

MACCARTY, THADDEUS, Boston, by wife Elizabeth had Charles, who died 25th October, 1683, aged 18; Francis, born 21st March, 1667; Thaddeus, 12th September, 1670; Margaret, 25th September, 1676; and Samuel, baptised at Roxbury, 3d November, 1678. He was a member of the artillery company 1681, died at Boston, 18th June, 1705, aged 65; and his widow Elizabeth died 7th June, 1723, aged 82. A Thomas graduated from Harvard College in 1691, who was dead in 1698. See Hutchinson's Hist. Colony of Mass. Bay, 2d ed., Vol. I, p. 392; and a Charles, badly wounded in the expedition 1690, against Quebec, are of unknown descent.

REFERENCES:—Allen's Worcester, Mass., 82; Lincoln's Worcester, Mass., 150; Savage's Gen. Dic., III, 139.

MACARTER, MAKARTA, MAGARTA or MECARTA:—John, Salem, married, 27th January, 1675, to Rebecca Meacham, daughter perhaps of Jeremiah, had John, born 13th January, 1676; Rebecca, 4th February, 1678; Jeremiah, 9th September, 1679; Peter, 1st November, 1681; Andrew, 6th June, 1684; James, 17th November, 1686; all baptised 16th November, 1687; Isaac, 3d June, baptised 28th September, 1689; and Rebecca, born 6th February, 1691.

REFERENCE:—Savage's Gen. Dic., III, 139.

MACCLARY, or McCLARY:—John, Haverhill, 1655, was a Scotchman, possibly one of the prisoners at Dunbar or Worcester, shipped over here for sale; but not the ancestor of a distinguishd family in N. H., who had been of the Protestant defenders of Londonderry, and emigrated from Ireland, so late as 1725.

REFERENCE:—Savage's Gen. Dic., III, 140.

MACCOOME, or MACOMB:—Alexander, Boston, 1659, one of the "Scot's Charitable Society," of that year. Drake gives this name as Mackcowmes

REFERENCES:—Anthon's Narrative, 22; Drake's Hist. Boston, 455; Hall Genealogy (1892), 84-6; Navarre Genealogy, 239-56; Savage's Gen. Dic., III, 140.

MACCULLOCK, or Mc CULLOCK:—Alexander and Thomas, Boston, 1684, were of the "Scot's Charitable Society."

REFERENCES:—Drake's Hist. Boston, 455; Savage's Gen. Dic., III, 140.

MACDANIEL, or MAGDANIEL:—Dennis, Boston, by wife Alice had Dennis, born 25th November, 1671; and Elizabeth, 7th May, 1674.

MACDANIEL, JOHN, Boston, married, 17th May, 1658, Elizabeth Smith, had John, born 13th September, 1659; Elizabeth, 3d September, 1661; Martha and Mary, twins, 14th September, 1663; Michael, 26th July, 1666; William, 21st September, 1671; and Mary, 11th October, 1674.

MACDANIEL, NEAL, Newton, 1678.

REFERENCE:—Savage's Gen. Dic., III, 140.

MACDOWALL:—Sturgis. Boston, a member of the "Scot's Charitable Society," 1684.

REFERENCES:—Savage's Gen. Dic., III, 140; Drake's History of Boston, 454.

MACE:—William, probably of Warwick, as one of this name married Sarah, daughter of Samuel Gorton.

REFERENCES:—Dow's Hampton, N. H., 830-4; Savage's Gen. Dic., III, 140.

MACGINNIS:—Daniel, Woburn, married 10th February, 1677, Rose Neal, had Rose. born 19th November, 1677; removed to Billerica. 1679, but in Woburn had Edmund. 23d March. 1685.

REFERENCE:—Savage's Gen. Dic., III, 140.

MACK:—John, Salisbury, married, 5th April, 1681. Sarah Bagley, had John, born 29th April, 1682.

REFERENCES:—American Ancestry, I, 51; II, 76; Bedford, N. H., Centennial, 313; Hayward's Hist. Gilsum, N. H. . 357; Lancaster's Hist. Gilmanton, N. H., 278; Livermore's Hist. Wilton, N. H., 443; Mack's Genealogy; Olin Genealogy, 45; Parker's Hist. Londonderry, N. H., 278-80; Savage's Gen. Dic., III, 140; Secomb's Hist. Amherst. N. H., 680-3; Sheldon's Hist. Deerfield, Mass., 235.

MACKANEER:—Alexander, perhaps of Boston, but not certain. Inventory of his estate on the 5th December 1670. shows £123 9s.

REFERENCE:—Savage's Gen. Dic., III, 140.

MACKAY:—Archibald. Newton, probably son of Daniel, by wife Margaret had Hannah, born 24th February, 1694; William, 25th December, 1695; John, 22d September, 1698; Nathaniel, 5th January, 1702; Abigail, 6th January, 1705; Edward, 21st July, 1706; Elizabeth. 20th February, 1712, died at 4 years; Nehemiah, 14th February. 1715; and Mary, 14th January, 1721.

MACKAY, DANIEL, Newton, by wife Sarah had Mary, born 25th September, 1673; Jacob, 14th March, 1675; Hannah, 29th March, 1677; and Ebenezer, 20th October, 1680; besides Archibald, before mentioned, and perhaps others. He was a Scotchman, and is supposed to have come from Roxbury, but in that town the name is not found at so early a date.

REFERENCES:—Savage's Gen. Dic., III, 140.

MACKINTOSH:—John, Dedham, married, 5th April, 1659, Rebecca, daughter of the first Michael Metcalf, who died before him, and by another wife had William, baptised 25th November, 1665, probably other children; died 1691, and in his will, made 13th August, 1691, and probated 28th October following, mentioned wife Jane, and children William and Rachel.

REFERENCES:—Savage's Gen. Dic., III, 140.

MACKLATHLIN. MACLOTHLIN. MACKLATHIN or MEGLATHLIN:—Robert, Brookfield,

perhaps a Scotch prisoner of Cromwell's field of triumph, either at Dunbar or Worcester, sent to this country to be sold for years. May have married, at Brookfield. a daughter of the first John Warner, as Mr. Judd infers, from the fact that one of two orphan daughters of Macklathlin's appears at Hadley in 1685, named Joanna, and married, that year, Samuel Smith of Hadley, and another daughter married at the same place, in 1699, a man whose name is not plain in the record.

REFERENCES:—Savage's Gen. Dic., III, 140.

MACLOUD:—Mordecai, Lancaster, 1658, was with wife and two children, killed by the Indians, 22d August, 1675.

REFERENCES:—Savage's Gen. Dic., III., 141; Nourse's Early Records of Lancaster, Mass., 323.

MACKMALLEN, or MACKMILLAN:—Alister, Salem, aged 30 years in November, 1661, perhaps had wife Elizabeth and daughter Elizabeth. His daughter supposed to have married. 17th December, 1677, Henry Bragg, and his widow perhaps married. 4th November, 1679. John Baxter, both at Salem.

REFERENCE:—Savage's Gen. Dic., III, 141.

MACKMAN:—James, Windsor, married, 1690, Elizabeth. daughter of Thomas Stoughton, had no children, died 18th December, 1698. He was a merchant, and left a good estate, and his widow married John Eliot of Windsor. Sometimes this is spelled Mackmin, never Markham. as Hinman gives it on page 153 "First Puritan Settlers of Connecticut."

MACOMBER, or MACUMBER:—John, Taunton, 1643. had Thomas, born 30th July, 1679; William, 31st January, 1684; beside probably John, as the record shows that John, Sr., married. 7th January, 1686, Mary Badcock.

MACOMBER, THOMAS:—Marshfield, married. 20th January, 1677, Sarah Crooker, daughter of Francis.

MACOMBER, WILLIAM, Duxbury, 1643. was there in 1638. possibly a brother of Thomas, may have removed to Marshfield, where Sarah, perhaps his daughter, married. 6th November, 1666. William Briggs; removed afterwards to Dartmouth, was living there 1686.

REFERENCES:—American Ancestry, XII; Davis' Ancient Landmarks of Plymouth, Mass.. 180; Stackpole's Hist. Durham. Me., 215-7; Savage's Gen. Dic., III, 141.

MACCOONE, MACKOON or MACCOUNE:—John. at Cambridge, married, 8th November, 1654, Deborah Bush. who died 20th February, 1665; had Hannah, born 31st October, 1659; Deborah. 31st December, 1661; Elizabeth, 31st January, 1663, died 1664; and Sarah, 15th February, 1664; he married, 14th June, 1665, Sarah Wood, had John, 14th June. 1666; Daniel, 18th February, 1669; Elizabeth, 17th January, 1670; Margaret, 20 February. 1672; and Peter, 21st February, 1674.

MACOONE, JOHN, of Westerly, 1669. in his will of 15th December, 1732, names wife Ann, eldest son John, other children Daniel; Rachel, who married, 17th April, 1721, James Hall; Mary, who married a Larkin; Abigail, who married a Brown; William and Joseph.

MACOONE, JOHN, of Westerly, son of the preceding, in his will of 2d April, 1754, mentions wife Patience, children William, Samuel, Lois and Sarah.

MACOONE, JOSEPH, of Westerly, brother of the preceding, had wife Jemima, and died before 1750.

REFERENCES:—Austin's R. I: Dic., 126; Savage's Gen. Dic., 141.

MACRANNEY:—William, Springfield, Mass., married. 1685, Margaret, daughter of John Riley.

REFERENCE:—Savage's Gen. Dic., 141.

MACKRENEL:—James, a soldier under Captain Turner, and so known to be from Boston or Cambridge, killed at Northampton, 14th March, 1676, by the Indians.
REFERENCE:—Savage's Gen. Dic.. III, 141.
MACREST:—See Makrest.
MACURNMORE:—John. Newport, 1639.
MACWORTH:—Arthur. Casco, 1636, one of the most respected settlers of the early times, married Jane, widow of Samuel Andrews; but probably he had wife and children before that union, when he lived at Saco, whither Willis thinks he came with Vines in 1630, and where he served on the grand jury in 1640. He died 1657, leaving Arthur, John and several daughters, all of whom would not be children of the widow Jane, who died at Boston 1676, though it may be difficult to discriminate those she bore to Andrews and to him. His daughter Rebecca married Nathaniel Wharff.
REFERENCES:—Savage's Gen. Dic., III, 142; Willis' Hist. of Portland, Me., 75.
MACY:—Francis. married Sarah, daughter of Jeremiah Norcross of Watertown, but it is said, not known whether he was ever in this country, and Bond was uncertain whether his name was Merry or Massey.
MACY, GEORGE, Taunton in 1643, was a lieutenant in Philip's war, representative 1672 for six years, died 17th August, 1693, leaving several daughters (of whom one was probably Elizabeth, who married, 15th May, 1672, John Hodges: another might be Rebecca, who married Benjamin Williams, 18th March. 1690), but no son.
MACY, JOHN, Nantucket, son of Thomas; married Deborah, daughter of the first Richard Gardner, and she next married Stephen Pease.
MACY, THOMAS, Newbury, came, it is said, from Chilmark, Co. Wilts, freeman 6th September, 1639, married Sarah Hopcot, who died 1706, aged 94; removed to Salisbury; had Sarah, born 9th July, 1644. died young; Sarah, again, 1st August, 1646; Mary, 4th December, 1648; and Thomas, 2d September, 1653; was representative 1654, removed to Nantucket about 1659, being one of the first settlers there. Had six children, and died 19th June, 1672. in his 74th year. His daughter Sarah married, 11th April, 1665, William Worth; Mary married, 11th April, 1669, William Bunker; and Bethia married, 30th March, 1670, Joseph Gardner.
REFERENCES:—Amer. Ancestry, II, 76; VI, 49; Hoyt's Salisbury, Mass., Families, 236; Huntington Genealogy, 92; Macy Genealogy (1868); Savage's Gen. Dic., III, 142.
MADDOCKS, MADDOCK. MATTOCKS or MADDOX:—Edmund, of Boston, married, 14th January, 1652, Rebecca Munnings, had Mary, born 4th January, 1656; and John, 12th March, 1657.
MADDOCKS, HENRY, Saco, 1653, swore fealty that year to Massachusetts. removed to Boston, had wife Rachel and daughter Rachel, born 24th July, 1673, who died soon; Rachel again, born 2d September, 1677.
MADDOCKS, HENRY, Watertown. married, 21 May, 1662, Mary, only daughter of Roger Wellington, had only child John, born 16th May, 1663; and his widow married, 16th September, 1679, John Coolidge.
MADDOCKS, JAMES, Lynn, came, it is said, from Bristol, 1642, and died at Newbury.
MADDOCKS. JOHN, Boston. perhaps elder brother of the preceding, came in the Planter, from London, early in 1635, called a sawyer, aged 43, was at Lynn and last at Newbury. where he died, 24th April, 1643.

MADDOCKS, JOHN, Watertown, son of Henry of the same. married, 23d June, 1689, Ruth, daughter of Caleb Church, had Ruth, born 13th or 19th February, 1691; John, born 22d January, 1693; Mary, born 4th December, 1694; Sarah, born 22d December, 1696; Henry, born 18th October, 1698; Caleb, born 29th August, 1700; and Joanna, born 4th October, 1702. He died 1st February after. and his widow married, 25th July, 1705, Joseph Child.
REFERENCES:—Bond's Watertown, 354, 855; Eaton's Thomaston, 321; Bangor Hist. Magazine, III, 220; Savage's Gen. Dic., III, 142; Shourd's Fenwick Colony, 142.
MADER:—Robert, Boston, freeman 1643, nothing more is known of him excepting he joined the church 16th April, 1643.
REFERENCE:—Savage's Gen. Dic., III, 142.
MADIVER:—Joel, Casco, son of Michael, driven by the Indian war in 1676 to Boston, there by wife Rebecca had Mercy. born 12th August, 1677; returned after the peace; and in the third war was killed by the French, August, 1703. His son Joel lived at Falmouth.
MADIVER, MICHAEL. Casco, was in the part called Perpoodick, now Cape Elizabeth, after 1658. Owned land on west side of the Spurwink river. which makes the east boundary of Scarborough, and there first lived. His inventory, August, 1670, was small. He married a widow Carter. Often this name is found Madeford, also Madinde and Maddine.
REFERENCE:—Savage's Gen. Dic., III, 143.
MAGOON, MAGOUN, McGOWN or MAKOON:—Elias, Duxbury, son of the first, by wife Hannah had David, born.1st November, 1703; Mary, born 24th March, 1705; and Elias, born October, 1707; Recompense, and Ruth; but perhaps his second wife Ruth was mother of the last. He lived in that part which was made Pembroke, 1712, and died 1727. His will of 13th August, probated 25th September of same year, names wife Ruth and the sons and daughters, and son-in-law John Clark perhaps husband of Mary. Of this stock was the late well-known shipbuilded of Medford.
MAGOON, HENRY, Dover, 1657-83, at Exeter took oath of allegiance in 1677, had sons Alexander and John.
MAGOON, JAMES, Duxbury, eldest son of John of Scituate, by wife Sarah had James, born 25th March, 1697; Thomas; Isaac, who probably died young; and Sarah. He died 1705, and his widow Sarah administrated his estate before close of which. about 1720, James was dead. His widow Sarah married, 23d November, 1710, Stephen Bryant.
MAGOON, JOHN, Scituate, before 1662, was among freeholders 1666, had married at Hingham, and had a daughter before 1663, whose name is not mentioned, but was perhaps Hannah; James, 25th June, 1666; and at Scituate had John, born 1668; Elias, 1673; and Isaac. 1675. His will of 20th May, 1697, probated 27th June. 1712, names wife Rebecca, eldest son James, the other three sons and daughter Hannah Lovett.
MAGOON, JOHN, Marshfield, son of the preceding, probably had John, and perhaps others.
MAGOON, JONATHAN, Hingham in 1657.
REFERENCES:—American Ancestry, VIII, 96; Barry's Hist. Hanover, Mass., 349; Hubbard's Stanstead, 240; Hyde's Hist. Address at Ware, Mass., 47; Magoun Gen., 1891; Magoun Gen. Sup., 1893; Savage's Gen. Dic., III, 143; Temple's Hist. Palmer, Mass. 511; Winsor's History Duxbury. Mass., 281.

MAGSON:—Richard, Boston 1634, in the employ-ment of James Everill, as the church records of his admission 2d October mentions, but no more is known.
REFERENCE:—Savage's Gen. Dic., III, 143.

MAGVARLO, MACVARLO, or MACFARLO:—Purdy of Hingham, married, July, 1667, Patience Rus-sell, had several children, of whom probably was Mar-garet, who married, 26th May, 1690, David Stodder.
REFERENCE:—Savage's Gen. Dic., III, 143.

MAHOONE:—Dermin or Dorman, of Boston, 1646. by wife Deiner or Dinah, had Daniel, born 4th December, 1646; and Honor, 29th Ooctober, 1648; and his wife Dinah died 8th January, 1657.
REFERENCE:—Savage's Gen. Dic., III, 143.

MAINE, or MAYEN:—Ezekiel, of Stonington, in 1670, offered to be freeman 1673.

MAINE, EZEKIEL, of Stonington, son of the preced-ing, married, 14th January, 1689, Mary Wells.

MAINE, JOHN of Boston, in a petition to Andros and the Council in 1687, says that thirty years since he had purchased house and lands at what is now North Yarmouth, and when the Indians burned his house and killed two of his sons-in-law, he and his wife and rest of his family hardly escaped. But he was of York in 1681, when his name is written with a "y" as he took the oath of allegiance, and he died at Boston, 27th March, 1699.
REFERENCES:—Tanner Genealogy, 26-28; Savage's Gen. Dic., III, 144.

MAJOR:—George, of Newbury, was from Isle of Jersey, says Coffin, took wife Susanna, 21st August, 1672, had Hannah, born 18th May, 1673; and George, 20th November, 1676.
REFERENCE:—Savage's Gen. Dic., III, 144.

MAKEPEACE:—Thomas, of Dorchester 1636, came with a large family. Belonged to the artillery company 1638, married in 1641, for his second wife, Elizabeth, widow of Oliver Mellows, and had Joseph, baptised 20th September, 1646, who died, probably, be-fore his father removed some years later to Boston, and there died. In his will of 30th June, 1666, he names eldest son Thomas, to whom he had before given house and land in England, where he then lived, and William; eldest daughter Hannah, wife of Stephen Hoppin; Mary, wife of Lawrence Willis; Esther, wife of John Brown of Marlborough; and Waitawhile, wife of Josiah, not Thomas Cooper (as Gen. Reg., V, 402, has it), nine children of Hoppin, whose mother was Opportunity, four of Brown, and two of Cooper.

MAKEPEACE, WILLIAM, of Boston, son (probably) of the preceding, married, 23d May, 1661, Ann Johnson, removed to Taunton, where the name was long kept up.
REFERENCES:—Makepeace Gen., 1858; Savag'e Gen. Dic., Vol. III, 144.

MAKREST:—Benoni, of Salisbury, by wife Lydia Fifield, married, 12th September, 1681, had Samuel, born 3d September, 1682, died aged 2 months; Joseph, born 28th August, 1683; Benjamin, born 16th November, 1685; Lydia, born 27th March, 1688; and Mary, born 15th April, 1690; and he died 7th August, 1690, leaving widow.
REFERENCE:—Savage's Gen. Dic., Vol. III. 144.

MALBON:—John, of Salem, 1629, supposed to have been skilled in iron works, came in fleet with Higginson, and probably went home the next year.

MALBON, RICHARD, of New Haven, an early assist-ant (but not as Mather II, Captain 12, writes in 1637). Had daughter named Martha. He removed or perhaps

went home in 1648 or 9, and it would have been better if he had gone before. He was dead before May, 1661.
REFERENCE:—Savage's Gen. Dic., Vol. III, 144.

MALINE, or MELLIN:—See Melyen.

MALINS:—Robert. of Newport, married, 1st Janu-ary, 1675, Patience, daughter of Peter Easton, had Mary, born 21st October, 1675; and Robert, 22d January, 1677; and died 26th August, 1679, and it is said his wife died same day, "each aged 30 years," though she was only 24.
REFERENCES:—Austin's R. I. Gen. Dic., 127; Sav-age's Gen. Dic., Vol. III, 144.

MALLARD:—Thomas, of Boston, member of the Artillery Company 1685. perhaps removed to New Hamp-shire, where the name occurs.
REFERENCE:—Savage's Gen. Dic., Vol. III, 144.

MALLORY:—John, of New Haven, son of the first Peter, had John, born 6th September, 1687; Eliza-beth, born 1st May, 1691; Rebecca, born 15th September, 1693; Mabel, born 19th December, 1695; Silence, born 13th October, 1698; John, born 1st March, 1701; and Obedience, born 11th April, 1704.

MALLORY, JOSEPH, of New Haven, brother of the preceding, married Mercy, daughter of Thomas Pinion, had Mercy and Thankful, twins, borns August, 1694; Abigail, born August, 1696; Joseph, born 5th November, 1698; Benjamin, born 5th November, 1701; and Hannah, born 1st September, 1709.

MALLORY, PETER, of New. Haven, signer of the Plan-tation Covenant in 1644, had Rebecca, born 18th May, 1649; Peter, born 27th July, 1653; Mary, born October, 1655, died soon; Mary, born 28th November, 1656; Thomas, born 15th April, 1659; Daniel. born 25th November, 1661; the last three were baptised 12th July, 1663, not 11th, as church records state; John. born 10th May, 1664; Joseph, born 1666; Benjamin, born 4th January, 1669; Samuel, born 10th March, 1673; and William, born 3d September, 1675.

MALLORY, PETER, of New Haven, son of the pre-ceding, married, 27th May, 1678, Elizabeth, daughter of James Trowbridge, had Peter, born April, 1679, died young; Caleb, born 3d November, 1681; Peter, born August, 1684, died young; Elizabeth, born 27th April, 1687; Judith, born 2d September, 1689; Benjamin, 3d April, 1692; Stephen, born 12th October, 1694; Ebenezer, born 29th November, 1696; Zechariah, born 2d May, 1699; Abigail, born 5th August, 1701; Zipporah, born 15th December, 1705; and Peter, born 1 March, 1708.

MALLORY, THOMAS, of New Haven, brother of the preceding, married, 26th March, 1684, Mary Umberfield, had Thomas. born 1st January, 1685, who died 21st July, 1783. aged 98 years 6 months and 9 days old, not "one hundred and one years," as in Cothern; and Daniel, born 2d January, 1687, was a proprietor as were also his father and brothers Peter, Daniel and John, in 1685; he died 15th February, 1691. Often the second syllable of the name has "e" and sometimes "a."
REFERENCES:—Amer. Ancestry, VIII, 161; Boyd's Annals of Winchester, Conn . 286; Cothren's Woodbury. Conn., 615-8, II, 1514; Cutter's Hist. of Arlington, Mass., 275; Dodd's Hist. of East Haven, Conn., 134; N. E. Hist. and Gen. Reg., LIV, 320-5; Orcutt's Hist. of Strat-ford, Conn., 1242; Orcutt's Hist. of New Milford, Conn., 725; Paul's Hist. of Wells, Vt., 121; Power's Sangamon Co. Ill. Settlers, 471; Savage's Gen. Dic., III, 144; Todd's Hist. of Redding, Conn., 206.

MALONE, or MALOON:—Hendrick of Dover in 1660.

MALONE, LUKE, in Dover, 1670, married, 20th November, 1677, Hannah Clifford, perhaps daughter of John, first of same, had Sarah, born 1679; Joseph; Samuel, Luke, Elizabeth and Nathaniel; but dates and order of births are not known.

REFERENCES:—Power's Sangamon. Ill., 472; Nottingham, N. H., 419-25; Savage's Gen. Dic., III, 145.

MALTBY:—John, of New Haven, married Mary, daughter of Richard Bryan of Milford, had John and Mary, was lost at sea, as in 1676 was concluded. and 10th of June that year his inventory of only £58 was brought in, yet he has the prefix of respect, and was a valuable man. Mary married Rev. John Fordham.

MALTBY, WILLIAM, of Branford, 1667, in 1673 was cornet of the New Haven troop and left descendants.

REFERENCES:—Amer. Ancestry, IX, 201; Davenport Genealogy, 207, 218; Davis Genealogy, 1888; Maltby Genealogy, 1895; Savage's Gen. Dic., III, 145.

MANCHESTER:—Stephen, Portsmouth, R. I., married 13th September, 1684, Elizabeth, daughter of Gershom Wodell.

REFERENCE:—Austin's R. I. Dic., 127; Savage's Gen. Dic., III, 145.

MANLY:—Ralph, Charlestown, probably come in the fleet with Winthrop, and died September. 1630.

MANLY, WILLIAM, Weymouth, by wife Rebecca had Sarah, born 5th October, 1675; in March following was a soldier in Turner's company, outlived the campaign, and had Thomas, born 11th July, 1680; and by wife Sarah had Rebecca, born 6th March, 1687; perhaps he removed to Boston, and was a freeman of 1690.

REFERENCE:—Savage's Gen. Dic., III, 145.

MANN:—Abraham, of Providence, 1676, was one of the few that did not remove in King Philip's war. He took the oath of allegiance May, 1671.

MANN, FRANCIS, of Providence, of whom there is only known that his daughter Mary married, 6th April, 1673, John Lapham.

MANN, JAMES, of Newport, freeman in 1653.

MANN, JOHN, of Boston, 1670, a baker, by wife Mary had Joseph, born 30th June, 1672.

MANN, JOSIAH, a soldier, probably from Boston or Charlestown, under Captain Turner, 1676, at Hadley.

MANN, NATHANIEL, of Boston, 1670,- perhaps brother of Josiah, by wife Deborah had William, born 19th February, 1672.

MANN, RICHARD, of Scituate, 1646, was reckoned a youth in Elder Brewster's family, who could claim to have come in the Mayflower, 1620; but that is rejected for the person who had share with Brewster in the division of cattle in 1627 was More, not Mann; he had Nathaniel, born 1646, and died about 1656; Thomas, born 15th August, 1650; Richard, born 1652; and Josiah, born 1654. The last is probably the soldier of whom no more is known. Deane says Nathaniel lived in Scituate, had no family, and gave his estate to his brothers Thomas and Richard. He must have been of Boston for a short time.

Thomas saw hard fighting and was badly wounded in the Rehoboth day, when Pierce was ambushed, but lived to have four sons and three daughters. Richard had three sons and four daughters. No doubt this "Mann" should be "More" or "Moore." See that name.

MANN, SAMUEL, of Dedham, 1642.

MANN, SAMUEL, of Wrentham, only son of William, had the engagement to keep the school in Dedham for one year for £20, "to be paid in coin at the current price," and continued seven years in that honorable employment; married, 19th May, 1673, Esther, daughter of Robert Ware, of Dedham, who died 3d September, 1734, and was freeman in 1678; ordained 13th April, 1692, in the place formerly part of Dedham, where he had preached many years, and died 22d May, 1719. His children, by the Wrentham records, were Mary, born 7th April, 1674; Samuel, born 8th August, 1675; Theodore, born 8th February, 1681; Thomas, born 24th October. 1682; Hannah, born 12th June, 1685; Beriah, born 30th March, 1687; Pelatiah, born, 2d April, 1689; Margaret, born 21st December, 1691; and Esther, born 26th June, 1696; besides whom were Nathaniel and William, born after the settlement was broken up by Philip's war, and before his return, March, 1676, and August, 1680, all these six sons and five daughters were married. Of this family most have written but a single "n" in the name.

MANN, THOMAS, of Rehoboth, had wife Rachel, who died June, 1676, and a child at the same time. He married, 9th April, 1678, Mary Wheaton; had Rachel, born 15th April, 1679; Mary, born 11th January, 1681; Bethia, born 12th March, probably 1683.

MANN, WILLIAM, of Cambridge, 1634, came, it is said, from Kent, born 1607, the youngest of eleven children; married, 1643, Mary Jarrad, or perhaps Garrad, had share in the Shawshin division, 1652, but may have been of Providence in 1641, as Farmer had it; yet he could not long have continued there. He had by first wife Samuel. before mentioned, born 6th July, 1647, of Harvard College in 1665; and married, 11th June, 1657, second or third wife, Alice Teel, and died 7th March, 1662. In his will, dated 10th December, 1661, names no children but Samuel. Six of this name had, to 1819, been graduated at Harvard, and nine at other New England colleges.

REFERENCES:—Amer. Ancestry, IV, 90, VII, 89, 102; Austin's Ances. Dic., 38; Austin's R. I. Gen. Dic., 129; Ballou's Hist. of Milford, Mass., 890; Bangor, Me., Hist. Mag., VI, 88; Barry's Hist. of Hanover, Mass., 350-2; Bass' Hist. of Braintree, Vt., 162-4; Bemis' Hist. of Marlboro, N. H., 562; Blake's Hist. of Franklin, Mass., 258; Corliss' North Yarmouth, Me.. Magazine; Davis' Hist. of Bucks Co., Pa., 670; Deane's Hist. of Scituate, Mass., 309; Dearborn's Hist. of Salisbury. N. H., 659; Dedham, Mass., Hist. Reg., VI, 124-9; VII, 28-33, 60-5, 140-5; Heywood's Hist. Westminster. Mass., 755-7; Hills' Hist. of Mason, N. H., 204; Hinman's Conn. Settlers, 1846; Hudson's Hist. of Lexington, Mass., 128; Jameson's Hist. of Medway, Mass., 500; Mann Genealogy, 1873 and 1884; New England Hist. & Gen. Reg., XIII, 325-8, 364; Oneida Hist. Society, Trans. II, 120-3; Orcutt's Hist. of Stratford, Conn., 1243; Page Genealogy, 51; Pierce's Hist. of Gorham. Me., 193; Power's Sangamon Co., Ill. Settlers, 473; Savage's Gen. Dic., III, 145; Slafter Genealogy, 20; Stone's Hist. of Hubbardston, Mass., 306-8; Temple's Hist. of Palmer, Mass., 516; Washington, N. H.. History, 524-6.

MANNERING:—Edward, Scarborough in 1663.

MANNERING, JOSEPH, a passenger in the William and Francis from London, 1632, embarked in March and reached Boston 5th June, with Edward Winslow; but no connection with him is known nor is this name heard of for many years except by judgment of court, 4th March, 1634; it was found that he had paid £5 on account of which Joseph Twitchell had been charged. Several who we know to have been on board that ship could not have obtained leave from the government.

REFERENCE:—Savage's Gen. Dic., III, 147.

MANNING:—George. Boston in 1653, a shoe-maker, perhaps an original proprietor in 1640, of Sudbury; married, 15th July, 1653, Mary Harraden; and another record says that he married. 13th March, 1655, Hannah, widow of William Blanchard, daughter of James Everill, had George. born 24th November, 1655; Elizabeth, born 19th March. 1657, died young; Mary, born 15th December. 1659. died young; Elizabeth, born 13th October, 1661; James. born 6th March, 1663; Hannah, born 20th April, 1665; Mary, born 3d November, 1666; Sarah, born 19th March, 1668; John, born 11th October, 1671; and Joseph, born 6th November, 1674.

MANNING, JOHN, Boston, a merchant, member of the artillery company in 1640, by wife Abigail, who died 25th June, 1644. had John, born 25th May, 1643; and Mary. born 3d June. 1644; and by wife Ann, daughter of Richard Parker, who joined our church 15th May, 1647, had Ann. born 12th March, 1652; and Ephraim. born 10th August, 1655. Ann married John Sandys in 1669.

MANNING, JOHN, Ipswich in 1634. of whom nothing more is known.

MANNING, JOHN, in Maine, whose inventory of £115 was returned 5th October. 1674.

MANNING, NICHOLAS, Ipswich, was probably a son of Richard, had the command of a vessel at Salem in 1677, in 1681 had wife Elizabeth. was in 1688 appointed by Andros a judge in the remotest eastern part of his jurisdiction near Kennebec, and as one of his adherents was the next year imprisoned.

MANNING, RETURN, Boston, married at Hingham, December. 1664. Sarah Hobart. probably daughter of Edmund the second of the name, had daughter Mary, mentioned in the will of her grandfather Hobart. From whence he came is not known. At Boston he had Sarah, born 7th April, 1669; and Rebecca, born 21st September, 1670, and perhaps shortly afterward moved away.

MANNING, RICHARD. Ipswich, by wife Anstis had Nicholas, born 23d June, 1644; Richard. born 22d June, 1646; Anstis, born 8th January, 1655; Margaret, born 9th October, 1656; Jacob, born 25th December, 1660, who was of Salem. and died 24th May, 1756; Thomas. born 11th February, 1665; and Sarah, born 28th August, 1667, who married. 8th December, 1686. John Williams of the same. His descendants are numerous.

MANNING, SAMUEL, Billerica. son of the second William, made freeman in 1670. selectman in 1680, representative in 1695. and town clerk for 6 years; died 22d February, 1711, aged 66 years.

MANNING, THOMAS, Ipswich. in 1636, was perhaps an elder brother of Richard. died about 1668, aged 74 years.

MANNING, THOMAS, Swansey. married, 28th October, 1674, Rachel Bliss, perhaps daughter of Jonathan.

MANNING, THOMAS, a soldier of Ipswich, perhaps son of Thomas the first, or more probably his grandson. Killed with the "flower of Essex." under Lathrop, 18th September, 1675, at Bloody Brook. Deerfield.

MANNING, WILLIAM, Cambridge in 1634, a freeman 13th May, 1640, brought from England William and probably other children, perhaps Timothy, who died 8th November, 1653, was one. His wife Susanna was buried 16th October, 1650, but when he died is not known.

MANNING, WILLIAM, Cambridge, son of the preceding, born in England. made freeman 10th May, 1643, by wife Dorothy had Hannah, born 21st June, 1642;

Samuel, born 21st July, 1644, before mentioned; Sarah, born 28th January, 1646; Abigail, born 15th January, 1648, died aged 4 months; John, born 31st March, 1650; who died of smallpox, 25th November, 1678; and Mary. He was selectman 1667, and many years after. sent in 1670 to England to induce Urian Oakes to come over to be president of the college, though that vacancy did not occur, by the death of Chauncy, until 1672. The grave-stone that tells his death, 14th March, 1691, aged 70 years, may be true, but one may expect some exaggeration in that, for his wife Dorothy, when it makes her 80 years at the death, 26th July, 1692. Sarah married, 11th April, 1671, Joseph Bull of Hartford; and Mary married, 21st October, 1674, Rev. William Adams of Dedham. "From Ormsby. in County Norfolk, came, in 1637, aged 17, Ann Manning as servant of Henry Dow," says th: record of his declaration before embarking, as found at Westminster Hall.

REFERENCES:—Amer. Ancestry, I, 52; III, 199; Bedford, N. H., Centennial, 313; Bond's Watertown, Mass. 527-9, 945; Daniel's Hist. Oxford, Mass., 598; Eaton's Hist. Thomaston, Me., 322; Emmerston's Gleanings, 72; Essex Inst. Hist. Coll., XVII, 73-6; Hammatt Papers, 225; Hayward's Hist. Hancock, N. H., 742; Hazen's Hist. Billerica, Mass., 93-5; Lapham's Hist. Norway, Me., 546; Manning Family Chart, 1887; Manning Family Notes, 1897; New England Hist. & Gen. Reg., L. 221; LI, 389-406; Paige's Hist. Cambridge, Mass., 601-3; Perkins' Old Houses of Norwich, Conn., 527-9; Savage's Gen. Dic., III, 147; Secomb's Hist. Amherst, N. H., 687; Washington, N. H., History, 526; Wyman's Charlestown, Mass., Gens., 650-2.

MANSFIELD:—Andrew, Lynn in 1639, had been at Boston in 1636, came from Exeter in Devon. it is said, bringing son Andrew, born 1630, and, it is supposed, wife Elizabeth, daughter of Rev. William Walton. who died 8th September, 1673, aged above 80 years. by whom probably he had other children, as perhaps each of the following: Joseph. John; who died 16th October. 1671; Robert, who died 16th December. 1666; Samuel; and Elizabeth. This last married, 10th June. 1675. Joshua Wit; and he died 1692 in his 94th year.

MANSFIELD, ANDREW. Lynn, son of the preceding, born in England, was representative from 1680 to 1683; by wife Bethia had Bethia, born 7th April, 1658. died aged 14 years; Mary. born 7th March. 1660, died 1661; Lydia, born 15th August, 1662; Deborah, born 1st January, 1667; and Daniel, born 9th June, 1669. He had second wife. 4th June, 1673, Mary, widow of John Neaic, daughter of Francis Lawes, who died 27th June. 1681; and he married, 10th January. 1682, Elizabeth Conant.

MANSFIELD, ANDREW, Lynn, a freeman in 1691, may have been son of the preceding or of Robert.

MANSFIELD, DANIEL, Lynn, son of the second Andrew, was freeman 1691.

MANSFIELD. JOHN, Boston, son of Sir John, came in the Regard, 1634, sent out by charity, with his family, so Winthrop I, 150, states. His widow mother died that year in London, at the house of Robert Keayne, whose wife was a daughter, and Elizabeth the wife of Rev. John Wilson was another, but he seems to have done little here but worry his brothers, Wilson and Keayne, in the will of the latter most curious details are related. Yet Keayne gave something to the two children and their father seems to have held on a long time, dying at Charlestown in 1674.

MANSFIELD, JOHN, Lancaster. son of the preceding.

became a proprietor in 1654, had 500 acres given him by his aunt, Ann Keayne, as Rev. John Wilson of Medfield testifies, 11th February, 1675.

MANSFIELD, JOHN, Lynn, perhaps a younger brother of the first Andrew, came in the Susan and Ellen, from London, 1635, aged 34, a freeman 1643, may be the one who died in 1671, above designated as perhaps son of Andrew.

MANSFIELD, JOHN, Charlestown in 1658.

MANSFIELD, JOHN, Hingham, freeman in 1684, in his will, dated 19th February, 1689, and probated 20th August, same year, names only wife Elizabeth, who was perhaps daughter of Joseph Farnsworth of Dorchester. and two children, Mary and John, born 15th November, 1656, who had married Sarah Neal.

MANSFIELD, JOHN, Windsor, married, 13th December, 1683, Sarah, daughter of Samuel Phelps, had John, born 1684, died at 6 years of age; Sarah, born 1686; Samuel, born 1687; Mary, born 1689, and perhaps more.

MANSFIELD, JOSEPH, Lynn, son of the first Andrew, was probably born in England, by wife Elizabeth had Joseph, born 20th March, 1661, and may have had other children earlier. She died 25th February, 1662; and he was called senior, as Felt notes from the record when his daughter Deborah died, 14th February, 1678.

MANSFIELD, JOSEPH, New Haven, son of Richard, probably born in England, had Mary, born 1658; Martha, born 1660; and perhaps others; is in list of freemen 1669, and proprietor in 1685.

MANSFIELD, JOSEPH, Lynn, son of the first Joseph, married, 1st April, 1678, Elizabeth, daughter of Isaac Williams of Salem, had Elizabeth, born 6th February, 1679; twins born 25th October, 1680, died soon; Joseph, born 18th August, 1681; and Sarah, born 22 January, 1684; freeman in 1691.

MANSFIELD, MOSES, New Haven, son of Richard, born in England, was a very valuable man in town business 1673, lieutenant and captain in the Indian war, representative in 1676-7, a proprietor in 1685, had Samuel, at Harvard College in 1690, who kept the grammar school at New Haven same year, became a merchant and died in 1701, perhaps before his father.

MANSFIELD, PAUL, Salem, signed the petition against imposts in 1668.

MANSFIELD, RICHARD, New Haven, 1643, perhaps earlier, died 10th January, 1655, leaving widow Gilian, who married Alexander Field, and children Moses and Joseph, before mentioned.

MANSFIELD, ROBERT, Lynn, in 1642, may have been son of the first Andrew, or more probably his brother, born in England, who died in 1666.

MANSFIELD, SAMUEL, Lynn, perhaps son of the first Andrew, married, 3d March, 1674, Sarah Barsham, had Andrew, born 4th January, 1675; Sarah, born 6th November, 1676; and Bethia, born 13th March, 1679; and he died 10th April following.

MANSFIELD, SAMUEL, Springfield, representative in 1680-3 and 4.

MANSFIELD, THOMAS, Lynn in 1642. One of this family name came in the Regard, 1634, who was from Exeter, England, and was not found to be a desirable inhabitant, as mentioned by Winthrop I. 150.

REFERENCES:—Amer. Ancestry, II, 78; VII, 204; X, 202; XI, 103; Bond's Watertown, Mass., Gens., 355; Daniel's Hist. Oxford, Mass., 599; Davis' Hist. Wallingford, Conn., 847; Hayward's Hist. Gilsum, N. H., 359; Hemenway's Vermont Gaz., Vol. V, 198, 211-3; Kidder's

Hist. New Ipswich, N. H., 416; Lincoln's Hist. Hingham, Mass., III, 50-2; Mansfield Gen., 1885; Orcutt's Hist. Derby, Conn., 745; Savage's Gen. Dic., III, 148; Stiles' Hist. Windsor, Conn., 691; Tuttle Gen., 667-9; Walworth's Hyde Gen., 122.

MANSIR, MANSER, or MANSUR:—Robert, Charlestown in 1678, a householder, of whom nothing more is known.

REFERENCES:—Blood's Temple, N. H., 231; Heywood's Hist. Westminster, Mass., 757; Hubbard's Stanstead Co., Can., 171; Lapham's Hist. Rumford, Me., 372; Livermore's Hist. Wilton, N. H., 444-6; Savage's Gen. Dic., III, 149; Wyman's Charlestown, Mass., Gens., 652; Young's Hist. Wayne Co., Ind., 188.

MANSON:—May or may not be found in New England before 1692, but as yet he has been sought in vain. Yet in the Blessing from London, 1635, there was brought a Thomasia Manson, aged 14 years, who may have followed her father.

MANTON:—Edward, Providence, son of Shadrach, of Providence, married, 9th December, 1680, Elizabeth, daughter of John Thornton, made freeman in 1655, swore allegiance May, 1682. He was the only son of three, that had a son to perpetuate the name, and of his three sons, two died in infancy, while his son Daniel at the age of 16 years, it is said, was the only male on this side of the sea with this surname. He left eight sons and three daughters, all of whom married and had children.

MANTON, SHADRACH, Newport in 1668, swore allegiance 1st June, 1668, had besides two other sons, Edward; and Ann, who married, 18th September, 1682, John Keess.

REFERENCES:—Austin's Ancestral Dic., 39; Austin's R. I. Gen. Dic., 342; Narragansett Hist. Reg., IV., 296-9; Savage's Gen. Dic., III, 149.

MANWARING:—Nathaniel, residence unknown, member of the artillery company 1644.

MANWARING, OLIVER, New London 1664, in the tax list of 1666 his name being spelled "Mannering", married Elizabeth, daughter of Richard Raymond, but Miss Caulkins calls her Hannah had Hannah, Elizabeth, Prudence, and Love, all baptised in 1671; Richard, 13th July, 1673; Judith, April, 1676; Oliver, 2d February, 1679; Bathsheba, 9th May, 1680; Ann, 18th June, 1682, and Mercy, whose baptism is not found nor the birth of any one, but of the five preceding the last we may be content with dates of baptism. He died 3d November, 1723, aged 90, when all those children were living and the eight daughters married, though we have not the names of the husbands of any excepting Love, who married John Richard; and it is said Elizabeth married, 7th July, 1686, Peter Harris.

MANWARING, PHILIP, New Hampshire in 1683.

REFERENCES:—Baker's Montville, Conn., 244-50; Caulkins' New London; Savage's Gen. Dic., III, 150; Walworth's Hyde Gen., II, 1009-15, 1111-8.

MAPES:—John, aged 21, came from Ipswich in the Francis, 1634; but this name is so very rare in this country that unless he died in a few years we can hardly mistake in supposing he was of Long Island, where in 1662 "goodman Mapes" of Southold, was allowed to be made freeman of Connecticut. Perhaps he had first been of Salem, at least Dickinson, who was at the same time with him at Southold, had lived at Salem some years.

MAPES, JOSEPH, Setauket, L.I. in 1655, says Thompson. He may be the same, or Thomas, who is placed by Wood in his history, at Southold, 1640.

REFERENCES:—Amer. Ancestry, XI, 103; Savage's Gen. Dic., III, 150; Weygant's Family Record, 1897.

MARBLE:—John, Boston, by wife Judith had John, born 10th November, 1646.

MARBLE, JOSEPH, Andover, married, 30th May, 1671. Mary Faulkner, probably daughter of Edmund; had Deborah, who died 30th June, 1673; and probably other children.

MARBLE, JOSEPH, Andover, perhaps son of the preceding, married, 23d April, 1695, Hannah Barnard.

MARBLE, NICHOLAS, Gloucester, in 1658.

MARBLE, SAMUEL, Andover, 1660. married, 26th November, 1675. Rebecca Andrews, probably his second wife.

MARBLE, WILLIAM, Charlestown, or Malden, by wife Elizabeth, had Mary, born 10th April, 1642: perhaps he moved, for Frothingham, in his list of 1658, does not include the name nor do we see it among church members, though he was freeman in 1654.

REFERENCES:—Austin's Allied Families, 171; Benedict's Hist. Sutton, Mass, 687-9; Daniel's Hist. Oxford, Mass., 599; Lapham's Hist. Paris, Me., 667; Lincoln's Hist. Hingham, Mass., III. 53-6; Read's Hist. Swanzey, N. H., 400; Stearn's Hist. Ashburnham, Mass., 804-9; Stiles' Hist. Windsor. Conn., 465; Savage's Gen. Dic., III. 150. Wyman's Charlestown, 653.

MARCH:—George, Newbury, brought by Stephen Kent. in the Confidence as a servant from Southampton, 1638, aged 16, and he may be that freeman at Boston, 1666, whose name is printed "Marg" in the Genealogical Record.

MARCH. GEORGE, Newbury. son of Hugh, freeman in 1683, married. 12th June. 1672. Mary, daughter of John Folsom of Exeter, had George, born 6th October, 1674; John, 18th August. 1676: Mary. 28th August, 1678, died before three months old: Stephen. 19th September. 1679, died before 5 years old; James, 19th June. 1681; Israel, 4th April, 1683; Sarah. 6th July, 1685; Stephen. 16th November, 1687; Henry. 31st July. 1694. perhaps; George, 24th April. 1698; and Jane. 8th May, 1699; besides Hugh, probably the eldest, a sergeant, and killed by the Indians at Pemaquid, 9th September, 1695. His widow married. 28th June, 1707. Joseph Herrick as his third wife.

MARCH, HUGH, Newbury, brother probably of the first George, came in the Confidence, 1638, from Southampton, aged 20 years, as servant of Stephen Kent, a carpenter: by wife Judith, who died 14th December. 1675, had George, born 1646: Judith, born 3d January, 1653: Hugh, born 3d November, 1656; John, born 10th June. 1658; and James, born 11th January. 1664. He married, 29th May, 1676. Dorcas Blackleach, who died 22d November. 1683; and he married third wife 3d December, 1685, Sarah Healy, and died 12th December. 1693, aged 73; and his widow died 25th October, 1699.

MARCH, HUGH, Newbury, son of the preceding, married. 28th March, 1683, Sarah, daughter of Caleb Moody; had Sarah, born 27th April, 1684; Henry, born 22d September. 1686; Samuel, born 2d March, 1689; Elizabeth, born 27th October, 1691; Hannah, born 4th September, 1694, died next month: Daniel, born 30th October, 1695; Mehitable, born 3d January, 1703; and Trueman, born 14th November, 1705. He was a captain.

MARCH, JAMES, Newbury, brother of the preceding, was a lieutenant; by wife Mary had Benjamin, born 23d November, 1690; Nathaniel, born 2d September, 1693; and Tabitha, born 20th June. 1696; removed probably to Salisbury, there had Judith, born 13th May, 1698.

MARCH, JOHN, Charlestown 1638, probably had wife Rebecca, and his son. Edward died 4th October, 1638; as did John, another child, 2d May, 1641; on 15th May of next year he joined the church and on 18th was admitted freeman; perhaps had more children; was there a householder in 1658.

MARCH, JOHN, Newbury, son of the first Hugh, married 1st March. 1679, Jemima True; had Judith, born 21st March, 1682; Mary, born 2d April, 1684; Joseph. born 8th May, 1687; John, born 26th September, 1690; Abigail, born 4th September, 1693; Hugh, born 8th January, 1696; and Elizabeth, born 6th September, 1698; was a soldier, captain in Phip's disastrous expedition against Quebec in 1690. and a major in defence of Falmouth in 1703. Two of this name had, in 1834, been graduates from Harvard College and four from other New England colleges.

REFERENCES:—Amer. Ancentry I, 52; IV, 63; Benedict's Hist. Sutton, Mass., 689; Bradbury's Hist. Kennebunkport, Me.,261; Brewster's Portsmouth,N.H., II, 129; Chapman's Weeks Gen., 146; Coffin's Hist. Newburyport, Mass., 309; Hoyt's Salisbury, Mass., Families, 237-9; Lapham's Hist. Norway, Me., 547; March Genealogy, 1899; N. E. Hist. & Gen. Reg., LIII, 121; Runnel's Sanbornton, N. H., II, 474-7; Savage's Gen. Dic., III, 150; Sedgwick's Hist. Sharon. Conn., 99.

MARCHANT:—See Merchant.

MARDEN:—Richard, New Haven in 1646, took oath of fidelity next year, soon removed.

REFERENCES:—Chase's Chester, N. H., 558; Cochrane's Hist. Francestown, N. H., 821; Cogswell's Hist. New Boston, N. H., 377-9; Livermore's Hist. Wilton, N. H., 341; Morrison's Hist. Windham, N. H., 621-4; Savage's Gen. Dic. III, 150.

MARGERUM or MARGORUM:—Richard of Salem. in 1655; was not perhaps a permanent resident.

REFERENCES:—Essex Coll., I., 67; Savage's Gen. Dic., III, 151.

MARGERSON:—Edmund, a single man, came in the Mayflower, as one of the passengers to Plymouth, December, 1620; died early in 1621.

REFERENCES:—Savage's Gen. Dic., III, 151; Calnek's Annapolis N. S., 542.

MARGIN:—Richard, Dover, 1659; married at Andover, 21st May, 1660. Rebecca, probably daughter of William Holdredge of Haverhill.

MARINER:—James. Falmouth. 1686; was supposed to have come from Dover, probably had children at Falmouth, when in his age he left there, and was of Boston in 1731, aged 80.

REFERENCES:—Savage's Gen. Dic., III, 151; Wheeler's Brunswick, 842.

MARION:—Benjamin, one of Gallup's company in the expedition against Quebec, 1690.

MARION, ISAAC, Boston, son of first John of Boston; by wife Phebe had Mary, born 4th December. 1682.

MARION, JOHN, Watertown, cordwainer, married Sarah, daughter of John Eddy, freeman in 1652; had Mary, buried 24th January, 1642, aged 2 months; John, born 12th May. 1643; Isaac, born 20th January, 1653; Samuel, born 1655; removed to Boston, was selectman 1693, and died 7th January, 1705, aged 86.

MARION, JOHN, Cambridge, probably son of the preceding, removed to Boston; married Ann, daughter of John Harrison, had John, born 30th May, 1683, died soon; John, born 17th August, 1684. died young; Joseph, born 10th August, 1686; John, born 29th August. 1687. died soon: and John. born 28th June. 1689: freeman in 1679;

was deacon. selectman in 1698, and member of the artillery company in 1691.

MARION, SAMUEL, Boston, son of the first John. from Sewall in his Diary we learn of the sad manner of the death of his wife Hannah, 4th April, 1688; and from the records that he had John, born 25th December, 1681; Hannah, born 23d June, 1685; and Mary, born 18th June, 1687. He married a second wife, Mary, and had Samuel, born 8th June, 1689; Catherine, born 15th September, 1690; Edward, born 2d December, 1692; Isaac, born 8th March, 1694; Elizabeth, born 21st November, 1695; Joseph, born 18th December, 1698, probably died young; Joanna, born 10th May, 1701; John, born 5th April, 1703; and Joseph, 22d July. 1705. The name is sometimes spelled Merion.
REFERENCES:—Bridgeman's Kings Chapel Burial Ground, 263-9; N. E. Hist. & Gen. Reg., XIV, 86-8; Savage's Gen. Dic., III, 152.

MARK or MARKS:—John, or other name beginning with J., of Middleborough; died July, 1675. of a wound by the Indians.

MARK, PATRICK, Charlestown 1677, by wife Sarah had Mary, baptised 20th January, 1689, aged 18 years. the mother having been admitted to that rite 10th April, 1687, aged 50.

MARK, ROGER, Andover, a soldier of Maj. Appleton's company; wounded by the Indians at the fight 19th December, 1675; lost his wife Sarah 22d December, 1690. by smallpox.
REFERENCES:—Amer. Ancestry, IX, 54; Hayward's Gilsum, N. H., 360; Orcutt's Stratford, Conn., 1243; Parthermore Gen., 135; Richmond, Va., Standard, II, 24; Savage's Gen. Dic., III, 152; Temple's Hist. North Brookfield, Mass, 680; Tuttle Gen., 269.

MARKHAM:—Daniel, Cambridge, married, 3d November, 1669, Elizabeth, daughter of Francis Whitmore, had James, born 16th March, 1675, perhaps freeman in 1674, removed to Middletown and married Patience, daughter of William Harris.

MARKHAM, JAMES, Cambridge, son of Daniel., married, 14th October, 1700. Elizabeth, youngest child of the first William Locke; removed to Middletown; had James. born 22d November, 1701; Elizabeth, born 18th January, 1704; William, born 28th January, 1706; John, born 28th December, 1708; Mary, born 14th May, 1710; Abigail. 22d July, 1712; Martha, born 18th June, 1714; Hannah, born 6th September, 1716; and Nathaniel, born 27th February. 1719; and died 8th June, 1731. His widow died 25th September, 1753, but gravestone says 17th.

MARKHAM, JEREMIAH, Dover, 1659.

MARKHAM, NATHANIEL. Watertown, freeman in 1682; was perhaps father of the Nathaniel of Charlestown. whose death, 26th September, 1673, is noted by Farmer.

MARKHAM, WILLIAM, Hadley, of the first settlement, but before that had William, who was killed by the Indians with Captain Beers at Northfield, 4th September. 1675 ,and daughters Priscilla and Lydia; at Hadley had John, born 1661, died at less than 3 years of age; and Mercy, born 1663, died young; was freeman in 1661, on the 15th October. 1681, swore he was in his 60th year, and died about 1689. Priscilla married Thomas Hale, about the year 1675; Lydia married Timothy Eastman in 1682. and her descendants named Smith lived at the ancient homestead of Markham. who had much estate from Nathaniel Ward of Hadley, whom he called uncle. The name is sometimes written Marcum and Marcom.

REFERENCES:—Amer. Ancestry, VI, 114; Hinman's Conn. Settlers. 1st ed., 171; Locke's Genealogy. 23; Merrill's Hist. Acworth. N. H., 240; Paxton's Marshall Gen., 16; Savage's Gen. Dic., III. 152; Virginia Magazine of History, V. 205-6, 334-6, 439-40; VI, 80-2.

MARLO. MORLEY. or MARLOW:—Edward, Hartford in 1667.

MARLOW, THOMAS. Westfield. married. 8th December. 1681. Martha, daughter of the first Abel Wright, had Martha. born 7th September. 1682; Thomas, 14th September. 1684; Mary, 30th October. 1686; Abel, 18th January. 1689; Elizabeth, 23d June. 1691; Thankful, 28th February. 1693; Mary. 14th November, 1695; John, 1st May. 1699; and Ebenezer. 22d March. 1701. The family may be still at Westfield, but the name long since became Morley.

MARLO. WILLIAM. a soldier under Captain Turner in March, 1676.
REFERENCES:—Amer. Ancestry, IX, 22; Savage's Gen. Dic., III, 153.

MARRETT:—Amos. son of John, of Cambridge. married, 12th November. 1681. Bethia Longhorn. who died 20th November. 1730. in the 70th year of her age; had Amos. and perhaps others; and he married, 2d November. 1732. Ruth Dunster. probably a widow. died 17th November, 1739. He was a lieutenant. and his son Amos married. 21st September. 1732. Mary Dunster, perhaps a daughter of her who a few weeks after married the father.

MARRETT, JOHN, Cambridge. son of Thomas of Cambridge; was brought by his father from England when 5 years old; married, 20th June. 1654. Abigail Richardson; had Thomas. born 15th December, 1655; John, born, 13th December. 1656, who died 7th March. 1658; Amos, born 25th February, 1658; Susanna, born 19th January. 1660; John. born 29th January, 1662. died next year; John. baptised 6th June. 1664; and Abigail. born 19th August. 1666; beside Hannah, born 17th August, 1668. died soon; Edward, born 2d August, 1670; Mary, born 7th March, 1672; and Lydia. born 22d February, 1674; was freeman in 1665; owned estate at Watertown as early as 1642. Mary married, 10th December, 1702. Joseph Hovey. who died at Cambridge, giving her by will dated 28th June. 1735, all his property. and became second wife of Nathaniel Parker of Newton, 27th January, 1737; and Abigail married Timothy Rice. 27th April, 1687.

MARRETT NICHOLS or NICHOLAS, Salem. 1636: was of Marblehead 1648, born 1613.

MARRETT, THOMAS. Cambridge, 1635, freeman 3d March, 1636; brought with him from England son John before mentioned; Susanna. Thomas. and Abigail, besides wife Susanna, and had also Hannah. who may have been born at Cambridge, and died unmarried 9th December, 1668; and he died 3d June, 1664, aged 75. His will of 15th October. 1663. mentions his aged wife, four living children (being all. except Susanna. who had married George Barstow, and died not long after him), beside children of George Barstow. deceased. other grandchildren. Lydia. Amos. John, and Jeremiah Fisher; also Thomas. Amos, Susanna and John Marrett. who all appear to be children of John. Abigail had married, 17th November. 1641. Daniel Fisher of Dedham. The widow died 23d February. 1665. His name in the Colony Records is Marryott. but in the town records is slightly changed.

MARRETT. THOMAS. New London. 1666: may have been son of the preceding.

REFERENCES:—Dunster Gen., 66-9; Hodson's Hist. Lexington. Mass., 128-30; Paige's Hist. Cambridge, Mass., 603-5; Savage's Gen. Dic., III. 153.

MARRIOTT:—John. Marblehead in 1674.

MARSH:—Alexander, Braintree, was freeman in 1654; married, 19th December, 1655. Mary, daughter of Gregory Belcher; was representative under the new charter. 1692; died 7th March, 1698, aged 70 years, so says gravestone. His will of 19th March, 1697, probated 31st March, 1698, mentions wife Bathsheba, son John, daughters Rachel, Phebe, Ann, wife of Samuel French, besides granddaughter Mary French, son-in-law Dependence French, and Samuel Bass. His son John was then a minor, and possibly was father of the John who was a graduate from Harvard College in 1726. His widow died 8th January, 1723, aged about 82, says the gravestone at Dorchester.

MARSH, DANIEL, Hadley, son of John of Hadley; married in 1676 to Hannah, widow of Samuel Crow, daughter of William Lewis of Farmington; was made a freeman in 1690, representative under the new charter in 1692, and many times after, died in 1725, aged 72 years. He had children, but their names and dates of birth are not given other than of Joseph, who was a graduate of Harvard College in 1705, who was minister of Braintree, and died 8th March, 1726, and had Joseph; yet I find that Elisha, first minister of Westminster and Perez, a physician of Dalton, were also his grandchildren.

MARSH, EPHRAIM, Salem. son of John of Salem: signed a petition against imposts in 1668.

MARSH, GEORGE, Hingham, 1635, a freeman 3d March, 1636, died 2d July, 1647, wife Elizabeth surviving. His will made the same day provides for her, sons Thomas and Onesiphorus. daughters Elizabeth Turner and Mary Paige. Rev. John of Wethersfield was a descendant.

MARSH, JOHN, Charlestown, 1638, died 1st January, 1666; in his will made that day, names wife Ann and her grandchild. Sarah Bicknor, son Theophilus and his son John, daughter Frances Buck and her children.

MARSH, JOHN, Salem: had grant of land in 1637. probably came in the Mary and John, 1634; and at Salem his children baptized were Zechary, on the 30th April, 1637: John. 9th May, 1639; Ruth, 5th May, 1641; Elizabeth. 13th September, 1646; Ezekiel, 29th October, 1648; Bethia. 1st September, 1650; Samuel, 2d October, 1652; Susanna. 7th May, 1654; Mary, 14th September, 1656; Jacob, 10th April, 1659; and a daughter 12th June, 1664, whose name is not known. His will of 20th March, 1674, probated 26th November, 1674, names wife Susanna, sons Zechary. Samuel, Jacob, Ezekiel, Benjamin and daughter Bethia.

MARSH, JOHN, Hartford, 1636; married, Ann, daughter of Gov. John Webster; with him removed to Hadley in 1659-60; before he removed had Joseph, baptized 24th January, 1647, died soon: Joseph, born 15th July, 1649; John, Samuel, Jonathan, Daniel, Hannah, and Grace. His wife died 9th June, 1662, and he married in 1664, Hepzibah, widow of Richard Lyman of Northampton, daughter of Thomas Ford, and removed to that place, and had Lydia. He died in 1688. Grace married, 16th January, 1672, Timothy Baker. By will, dated 1676, of his brother Joseph at Braintree, County of Essex, estate was given to these children, and obtained by suit at law, so it is presumed he came from that part of England.

MARSH, JOHN, Hartford, eldest son of preceding; married, in 1666. Sarah, daughter of Richard Lyman, and of the wife of his father, freeman in 1670, died 1727.

MARSH, JOHN, Boston, in 1672.

MARSH, JONATHAN, Milford in 1649; removed to Norwalk, one of the first settlers in 1655; not mentioned after 1659. Do not know as he had wife or children.

MARSH, JONATHAN, Hadley, brother of Daniel; married, in 1676, Dorcas, widow of Azariah Dickinson, had Jonathan, a graduate of Harvard College in 1705, who became minister of Windsor; was freeman in 1690, representative in 1701; died in 1730, aged 80.

MARSH, ONESIPHORUS, Hingham, son of George; married 6th January, 1655, Hannah Cutter; had Onesiphorus, born 5th November, 1655; Hannah, born 28th June, 1657; was freeman 1672, and of Haverhill in 1690, at least one of the same name lived there so called his son.

MARSH, SAMUEL, New Haven; had Mary, born 1648; Samuel, born 12th February, 1650; Comfort, born 2d August, 1652; all baptized 20th March, 1653; Hannah, born 22d July, 1655, baptized next month, but not on the day mentioned in the church record; Elizabeth, born 27th December, 1657, baptized in February following; John, born 2d May. 1661; a child without name born 1st April, 1663.

MARSH, SAMUEL, Hatfield, brother of Daniel: married in 1667 to Mary Allison; was freeman in 1690, representative in 1705-6, died in 1728, leaving several children.

MARSH, THOMAS, Hingham, son of George, born in England; married, 22d March, 1649, Sarah, daughter of John Beal, and died 2d August, 1658, leaving four children named in his will. Thomas, Sarah, Ephraim, born 11th July, 1655, and Mary, born 22d February, 1658. His son John, born 20th February, 1654, probably died young. His widow married, 1st September, 1662, Edmund Sheffield of Braintree.

MARSH, ZECHARY, Salem. son of John of Salem; was freeman in 1680.

REFERENCES:—Aldrich's Walpole, N.H., 319; Amer. Ancestry I, 52; III. 125, 138, 148; X, 64; XI, 117; Atkin's Hist. Hawley, Mass., 49; Austin's R. I. Gen. Dic., 130; Baird's Hist. Rye. N. Y., 486; Bangor Hist. Mag., IV. 35-7; Barbour's My Wife and Mother, app. 22; Bass' Hist. Braintree, Vt., 164; Benedict's Hist. Sutton. Mass., 689-91; Cogswell's Hist. Henniker, N. H., 643; Cogswell's Hist. Nottingham, N. H., 230; Craft's Hist. Whately. Mass., 514-6; Dana's Hist. Woodstock. Vt., 614-8; Daniel's Hist. Oxford, Mass., 600; Draper's Hist. Spencer. Mass., 233; Dwight's Genealogy, 841-4; Eaton's Hist. Thomaston, Me., II, 323; Gold's Hist. Cornwall, Conn., 282; Hatfield's Hist. Elizabeth, N. J., 81; Heywood's Hist. Westminster. Mass., 758; Hine's Lebanon, Conn., Hist. Ad., 164; Hurd's Hist. New London Co., Conn., 514; Hyde's Hist. Address at Ware, Mass., 50; Judd's Hist. Hadley, Mass., 533-5; Lincoln's Hist. Hingham, Mass., III. 36-64; Marsh Genealogy (1886); Marsh Family of Hingham (1887); Marsh Family of Salem (1888); Marsh Family of Hartford (1895); Morse's Sherborn, Mass. Settlers; Orcutt's Hist. New Milford, Conn., 726-30; Paige's Hist. of Hardwick, Mass., 418; Perkins' Old Houses of Norwich, Conn., 531; Pompey, N. Y., Reunion. 332-4; Power's Sangamon Co., Ills. Settlers, 474; Randall's Hist. Chesterfield, N. H., 379-82; Savage's Gen. Dic., III, 154; Sinclair Genealogy (1896); Smith's Hist. Sunderland, Mass., 443-7; Stiles' Hist. Windsor, Conn., II. 465; Temple's Hist. Whately, Mass., 247; Tucker's Hist. Hartford, Vt., 448-52; Wyman's Charlestown, Mass., Gens. 654.

MARSHALL:—Benjamin, Ipswich, son of the first Edmund; married, 1677. Prudence Woodward, had Edmund, Ezekiel, John and four daughters; died in 1716.

MARSHALL, CHRISTOPHER, Boston, 1634, a single man on joining the church late in August, 1634, freeman 6th May, 1635; was of Cotton's party in the great schism of 1637, but not disarmed as a dangerous heretic, so that he was perhaps a student of divinity, and certainly married here, for his daughter Ann was baptized 13th May, 1638, at our church, adhered to Wheelwright at Exeter, and with him had dismissal January, 1639, from our church and probably went home in 1640 or 1641, and may be that man who Colamy says was partly educated by our Rev. John Cotton, minister of Woodkirk, in Yorkshire, and died February, 1673, aged 59.

MARSHALL, DAVID, Windsor, son of Captain Samuel; married, 9th December, 1686, Abigail Phelps, daughter, probably, of Samuel; had Abigail, born 9th January, 1687; Hannah, born 8th December, 1689; and David, born 14th April, 1692, who died at 33 years of age.

MARSHALL, EDMUND, Salem, 1636; had there, perhaps by wife Milicent, Naomi, baptized 24th January, 1637; Ann, 15th April, 1638; Ruth, 3d May, 1640; Sarah, 29th May, 1642; Edmund, 16th June, 1644; and Benjamin 27th September, 1646; was a freeman 17th May, 1637, and removed either to Ipswich or Newbury.

MARSHALL, EDMUND, Newbury, a shipwright, perhaps son of the preceding; had Edmund, born 5th October, 1677, and John, born 7th July, 1682; but may have had older children before living at Newbury, and possibly removed to Suffield; there had Martha, 1685, and Elizabeth, 1689; it is certain one of that name lived there, and died, for by his will, made in 1721, though not probated until a long time after, mentions these children with others, John, Benjamin, Mary and Abigail.

MARSHALL, EDWARD, Warwick; by wife Mary had Edward, born 10th April, 1658; John, born 12th May, 1660; Thomas, born 1st March, 1663; Mary, born 1st July, 1666; Charles, born 28th June, 1668; and Martha, born 16th March, 1670.

MARSHALL, EDWARD, Reading, among the early settlers; may be the same who was made freeman at Malden, 1690.

MARSHALL, ELIAKIM, Boston, son of Thomas, the shoemaker; removed to Stratford, and in 1665 sold his estate in Boston, but came back in a few years; was of Lothrop's company in Philip's War, and killed at Bloody Brook 18th September, 1675.

MARSHALL, ELIAKIM, Windsor, son of Captain Samuel; married, 23d August, 1704, Sarah Liet of Guilford, if that be the correct name; had Dorothy, born 1st October, 1705; Sarah, born 27th June, 1709, probably died soon; Sarah, born 29th January, 1711; Mary, born 14th March, 1715; and Eliakim, born 15th July, 1720, died in a few days.

MARSHALL, FRANCIS, Boston, a master mariner; came in the "Christian" from London, 1635, aged 30; was living in 1659.

MARSHALL, JOHN, Duxbury, had been of Leahorn in ter. in Devonshire; did not long continue here, and perhaps was the man expected in vain to settle at New Haven, 1643, when his estate was valued at £1,000; his family of five and his lot, transferred to Richard Mansfield. He sold his Windsor estate, and may be that "rich merchant" referred to in Winthrop, Vol I, p. 150.

MARSHALL, JOEL, Hartford, 1682, perhaps son of Thomas of same place.

MARSHALL, JOHN, Duxbury, had been of Leahorn in County Kent, son and heir of Sybil Marshall, by which description in November, 1631, he enters into contract of marriage with Mary, eldest daughter of Rev. Ralph

Partridge of Sutton, near Dover, to whom and his brother, Jervase P., citizen and cordwainer of London, as trustee, he made conveyance of estate in County Kent as jointure of his wife if she outlived him. This instrument, with a bond in the penal sum of £200, to secure, etc., are recorded in Vol. III of our Suffolk Register of Deeds; but it is curious that these documents were not recorded here before January, 1661, some years after death of the Rev. Ralph, who in his will notices Robert and John, sons of his daughter Mary M.

MARSHALL, JOHN, Providence, 1639.

MARSHALL, JOHN, Boston, came, perhaps, in the Hopewell, Captain Babb, from London, 1635, aged 14 years. By wife Sarah had John, born 10th December, 1645; Thomas, born 11th May, 1656; Benjamin, born 15th February, 1661; and Christopher, born 18th August, 1664.

MARSHALL, JOHN, Billerica, 1659, freeman in 1683; had John, who was probably the freeman at Billerica in 1690.

MARSHALL, JOHN, Boston, a mariner from Barnstaple, County Devon, died 1662; and his brother Thomas of Alwington, in Devon, took administration of his estate in England and in 1670 claimed and obtained the assets from John Sweete, who was administrator in 1662.

MARSHALL, JOHN, Boston; by wife Ruth had Mary, born 2d January, 1661; John, born 2d October, 1664 (who was a mason of Braintree, kept that valuable diary, formerly quoted often by Dr. T. M. Harris, who procured it for the Historical Society as Fairfield's); Thomas, born 6th February, 1666; Samuel, born 14th July, 1669; and Joseph, born 14th April, 1672; was probably the freeman of 1671, and died November, 1672. His widow Ruth married Daniel Fairfield.

MARSHALL, JOHN, Braintree, son of the preceding; married, 12th May, 1690, Mary, widow of Jonathan Mills, daughter of Edmund Sheffield; had a daughter Deborah. In the Diary 25th December, 1700, John writes: "Brother Thomas came to Boston to visit, after being absent 17 years and a half, tarried three weeks and returned." Whence he came for this visit to his native town is not known.

MARSHALL, JOHN, Greenwich, 1672.

MARSHALL, JOHN, Boston, 1681-4; had an office under the Colonial government, with a salary of £13 per year; may have been freeman in 1690, and died in 1694.

MARSHALL, JOHN, Windsor, youngest son of Captain Samuel; by wife Abigail, who died 29th February, 1698, had Abigail, born 10th December, 1693, who died in a few weeks; and Hannah, born 16th April, 1695.

MARSHALL, NOAH, Northampton, died 15th December, 1691.

MARSHALL, PETER, Newbury, with prefix of respect; by wife Abigail had Thomas, born 1st July, 1689; and Ruth, born 31st December, 1690; perhaps removed to Boston.

MARSHALL, RICHARD, Taunton; married, 11th February, 1676, Esther Bell.

MARSHALL, ROBERT, Salem, 1637, perhaps soon removed to New Hampshire, as one of the name died there in 1663.

MARSHALL, ROBERT, Plymouth, son of John, grandson of Rev. Ralph Partridge; married, 1659, Mary, daughter of John Barnes; had John; Robert, born 15th August, 1663; and perhaps more.

MARSHALL, ROBERT, Boston, in 1668, merchant; may be the same as preceding.

MARSHALL, SAMUEL. Windsor, son of Thomas, the shoemaker of Boston; born in England, was a tanner; by Stiles, in his history, page 692, is made to own lot a dozen years too early, and representative in 1637, and magistrate in 1638, when he never gained either of these honors. Thomas was mistaken for this Samuel, who married, 6th May, 1652, Mary, only child of David Wilton, not Wilson, as the Genealogical Register, Vol. V, page 229, prints the name; had Samuel, born 27th May, 1653; Lydia, born 13th February, 1656; Thomas, born 23d April, 1659, died soon; David, born 24th July, 1661; Thomas, born 18th February, 1664; Mary, born 8th May, 1667, died at nine years of age; Eliakim, born 10th July, 1669; John, born 10th April, 1672; and Elizabeth, born 27th September, 1674. He was freeman in 1654, and in the war against Philip had short but most honorable service. On 30th November he was made a captain in place of Benjamin Newbury, who was disabled, for the projected winter campaign, and on 19th December, 1675, in the great swamp fight, the hardest ever known in New England, he was killed, with many of the men under him. His widow died 25th August, 1683. Lydia married, 24th September, 1676, Joseph Hawley of Northampton, where the oldest son lived, while the others continued at Windsor.

MARSHALL, SAMUEL. Barnstable; by wife Sarah had Sarah, who died 2d August, 1690, and father and mother had died the month previous.

MARSHALL, SAMUEL. Charlestown, freeman in 1690, says the record, but Budington has not given his name among the church members.

MARSHALL, SAMUEL. Northampton, eldest son of the brave Captain Samuel; married, 1675, Rebecca, daughter of Captain Benjamin Newbury of Windsor; had Mary, born 1676, died soon; Samuel, born, 1679; Abigail, born 1682; Sarah, born 1685; Preserved, born 1691; Lydia, and Mercy; was made freeman 1690.

MARSHALL, SAMUEL. Boston, in 1681; had wife Ruth, freeman in 1691.

MARSHALL, THOMAS. Dorchester, in 1634; freeman 6th May, 1635; removed, it is thought, to Windsor; was representative in March and April, 1638; but no more is known of him. In Stiles, History, page 698, he is said to have married, 2d March, 1637, Mary Drake, who may have been daughter of the first John; and we might suppose, from the same line, the same man married, 10th May, 1660, Bethia Parsons, though upon the same page he says that Thomas Markell married the same day that same woman; and great distrust springs up, when we see him on page 735, give the same woman, the same day, to Thomas Haskell.

MARSHALL, THOMAS. Boston, shoemaker or ferryman, or both, called widower on admission to church, 31st August, 1634; freeman 4th March, 1635; had brought from England probably sons Thomas and Samuel, and daughters Sarah and Frances; and here by second wife Alice had Eliakim, born 1st March, 1637, yet not baptized until April, 1638, no doubt on account of the quarrel in the church for acting with the major part of which in support of Wheelwright he was required in November, 1637, to surrender his arms; but like most of the rest, thus abused, regained high esteem; was selectman 1647 to 1658, deacon and representative 1650, and died, perhaps, in 1665. Frances married, 16th July, 1652, Joseph Howe, and Sarah married James Penniman.

MARSHALL, THOMAS. Boston, 1643, a tailor, admitted to the curch 17th February, 1644, and had Thomas, baptized 7th January, 1644, 5 days old; freeman in May,

1644, and in June following was excommunicated. Probably went to New Haven, after recovering, in 1646, the favor of his former fellow-worshippers.

MARSHALL, THOMAS. Reading, came probably in the James from London in 1635, aged 22 years; had Hannah, born 7th June, 1640; Samuel, born 1st September, 1643, died in one week; Abigail; Sarah, died young; Thomas and Rebecca, twins, born 20th February, 1648; Elizabeth; Sarah, born 14th February, 1655; was made freeman in 1653, a lieutenant; very probably is that man of Lynn, always called captain, who there had Joanna, 15th September, 1657; John, born 14th February, 1660; Ruth, born 14th August, 1662; and Mary, born 25th May, 1665; a member of the artillery company in 1640, and perhaps a freeman 4th June, 1641; he was a representative 1659-60-3-4-7 and 8; died 23d December, 1689; and his widow Rebecca died August, 1693. Hannah married at Lynn, 17th June, 1659, John Lewis; Sarah married, 15th July, 1674, Ebenezer Stocker; and Mary married, 7th April, 1685, Edward Baker. Lewis seems to have confused father and son and to have misled Farmer.

MARSHALL, THOMAS. Salem, 1657.

MARSHALL, THOMAS. Middletown, 1669, then offered as freeman; may have had Thomas, Joel and Mary, who married, 24th July, 1665, John Catlin, but it is not certain.

MARSHALL, THOMAS, died at Northampton, 3d June, 1663, but he may have been but a visitor.

MARSHALL, THOMAS. Andover, ought to have more told of him than is found in Farmer, that he died January, 1708, almost 100 years old, and that Joanna died there in May following, aged about 100. Perhaps it was his daughter Mary who married, 6th July, 1659, Robert Russell.

MARSHALL, THOMAS. Charlestown, 1684.

MARSHALL, THOMAS. Hartford, had sister Mary, who married John Catlin, but who their father was is not ascertained. He had Mary, born 10th May, 1670; John, born 24th February, 1672; William, born 21st April, 1674; Thomas, born 3d October, 1676; Elizabeth, born 23d October, 1678; Sarah, born 27th March, 1681; and Benjamin, born 22d February, 1684, and died in 1692. His son Thomas, a mariner, married after the date of his will, 15th February, 1697, Mary Chantrel of Boston, a spinster, and she had it probated 19th September, 1700, as his widow, in which he gave memento to his sister Elizabeth, a spinster, and brother Benjamin, and uncle John Catlin, all of Hartford, as he also styles himself, but all the residue to his beloved friend Mary Chantrel.

MARSHALL, THOMAS. Windsor, son of Captain Samuel; married, 3d March, 1686, Mary Drake, probably daughter of John; had Thomas, born 14th January, 1687, died young; Mary, born 21st February, 1689; Samuel, born 23d July, 1691; Thomas, born 6th February, 1694; Rachel, born 12th April, 1696; Catherine, born 11th April, 1699; John, born 3d April, 1701; Noah, born 24th April, 1703, died young; Daniel, born 1705; Benjamin, born 8th August, 1707, died in a few months; and Eunice, born 3d May, 1709.

MARSHALL, WILLIAM. Salem, 1638; had then a grant of land. He probably came in the Abigail, 1635, from London, aged 40 years.

MARSHALL, WILLIAM. Charlestown; married, 8th April, 1666, Mary, daughter of William Hilton, who died 15th July, 1678, aged about 33; had William and Mary, baptized 4th February, 1672, she having joined the church a few days before; John, born 20th April, 1673; Edward, born 16th April, 1676; and by second wife Lydia had

Samuel, baptized 31st August, 1684; Hannah, born 25th September, 1687.

REFERENCES:—Amer. Ancestry, II, 79; IV, 224, 237; VI, 102, 172; Austin's R. I. Gen. Dic., 130; Ballou's Hist. Milford, Mass., 891; Barry's Hist. Framingham, Mass., 320; Bond's Watertown, Mass,. Gens., 574-8; Calnek's Hist. Annapolis, N. S., 542-5; Carter Family. Tree of Virginia; Chute Genealogy. app. 114-24; Cothren's Woodbury, Conn., 631-3; II, 1575; Davis' Landmarks of Plymouth, Mass., 184; Eaton's Hist. Thomaston, Me., II, 323; Egle's Notes and Queries (1897), 178; Farrow's Hist. Islesborough, Me., 230-2; Freeman's Hist. Cape Cod, Mass., II, 444; Futhey's Hist. Chester Co., Pa., 649-52; Goode Genealogy. 469; Green's Kentucky Families; Guild's Stiles Genealogy. 406; Hatch's Hist. of Industry, Me.. 732; Haven Genealogy, 28; Hayward's Hist. of Hancock, N. H., 743; Hazen's Hist. Billerica, Mass., 95-7; Heyward's Hist. Westminster. Mass:, 759; Holton's Winslow Mem., I, 103, 118-29; Howell's Hist. Southampton, N. Y., 342; Huntington's Stamford, Ct., Settlers, 73; Joslin's Hist. of Poultney. Vt., 306-8; Kingman's North Bridgewater, Mass., 579; Lamborn Genealogy, 272; Lapham's Hist. Paris, Me., 669; Lee Genealogy (1895), 512-4; Leonard's Hist. Dublin, N. H., 361; Littell's Passaic Valley Gens., 277; Little's Hist. Weare, N.H., 1026-31; Marshall Family of Pennsylvania (1884); Marshall Family of Virginia (1885); Marshall's Grant Ancestry. 125; Meade's Old Churches of Virginia, I, 216, 244; Morris Genealogy (1898): Morse Memorial, app. 21; Morse's Sherbourn. Mass., Settlers, 175; New York Gen. & Biog. Rec., XXVI, 84; Norton's Hist. of Fitzwilliam, N. H., 632; Orcutt's Hist. Torrington, Conn., 737-9; Richmond Standard, II, 7, 32; III, 14, 16, 39; IV, 1; Savage's Gen. Dic., III, 155-9; Smith's Hist. Delaware Co., Pa., 482; Stark's Hist. Dunbarton. N. H., 253; Stiles' Hist. Windsor, Conn., II, 465-72; Sullivant Gen., 324-34; Symmes Gen., 131; Thomas Gen. (1896); Vinton's Giles Gen., 221-3, 345-62; Walworth's Hyde Gen., 224; Washington, N. H., History, 527; Wheeler's Hist. Newport. N. H., 446; Wyman's Charlestown, Mass.. Gens., II. 657.

MARSHCROFT. MASHCROFT or MASCROFT:—Daniel of Roxbury; married, 23d May, 1665, Mary, daughter of John Gorton, probably lived at some other place; there had Elizabeth, until the death of his wife's father, after which we find in the records of Roxbury, Hannah, born 6th May, 1677; but perhaps he removed again to some neighboring town and had Samuel, brought to baptism with Mehitable. 3d February, 1684, where we see the record of birth of the latter only, under date of 28th February. 1683. He had also Mary, whose birth is not given, but she died 8th June. 1688; and he died, perhaps, before middle age, and his widow died 30th June, 1703. Elizabeth married, at Roxbury, 18th March, 1700, Samuel Spencer; and Hannah married, 15th July, 1701, Samuel Frost.

REFERENCE:—Savage's Gen. Dic . Vol. III. 159.

MARSHFIELD:—Josiah, Springfield. son of Samuel; married. 22d September. 1686; Rachel, daughter of Jonathan Gilbert; had six children born at Springfield; was freeman in 1690. and after 1700 removed to Hartford; there had a son born 17th March. 1704.

MARSHFIELD, SAMUEL, Springfield. son of Thomas. born in England; married. 18th February. 1652. Esther. daughter of deacon Samuel Wright; had Mercy. born 10th June. 1653; Thomas. born 6th September. 1654. both died young; Sarah. born 2d February, 1656; Samuel. born 1659. died young; Hannah. born 1661; and Abilene.

born 2d April, 1664. His wife died next day, and he married, 28th December, 1664, Catherine, widow of Thomas Gilbert. daughter of Samuel Chapin. and had been widow first of Nathaniel Bliss; had Josiah. born 29th September, 1665; Esther, born 6th September. 1667; and Margaret, born 3d December, 1670; was a proprietor of Westfield in 1666, but never lived there; representative in 1680-3 and 4. sheriff of the county, and died 8th May, 1692. Sarah married, in 1676. William Holton, Jr.; Hannah married Joseph Bedutha; Abilene married Thomas Gilbert; Esther married Ephraim Colton; and Margaret married Ebenezer Parsons.

MARSHFIELD, THOMAS, Windsor; may have removed with Warham. from Dorchester, but no certainty is reached. The first that can postitively be learned is by a letter from him. as Marshfield, to Samuel Wakeman, 6th May. 1641. on page 12 of Vol. I of Register of Deeds, strange as the place is. where an extract is inserted by Gov. Winthrop. and next year he withdrew from the country, as by Conn. Record, 14th October, 1642, when the court appointed trustees to manage his estate for the use of the creditors. Perhaps he was lost at sea, but at least no more was ever heard of him. His widow and family removed to Springfield, the chidren being Samuel, before mentioned; Sarah, who married Thomas Miller, and another daughter.

REFERENCES:—Morris and Flynt Ancestors (1882), 36; Morton Ancestry, 144-6; Savage's Gen. Dic., III, 159.

MARSTON:—Benjamin, Salem, son of John; married Sarah, daughter probably of Hilliard Verin; representative in 1696: was, it is presumed, father of Benjamin, of Harvard College in 1689, a man of distinction.

MARSTON, EPHRAIM, Hampton, son of Thomas; married. 19th February, 1678, Abigail, daughter of John Sanborn; took oath of allegiance in 1678, as also did, in the same town, the same year, Isaac, James and William, who perhaps were his brothers or cousins. of which Isaac, married 23d December, 1669. Elizabeth. daughter of John Brown; had Caleb, born 19th July, 1672; Abigail, born 25th December, 1673, died in six months; Elizabeth, born 30th April, 1675; Mary, born 18th April. 1677; Sarah. born 6th November, 1680; Abigail, born 7th May. 1682; and Bethia. born 6th July, 1687.

MARSTON, JACOB, Andover; married 7th April. 1686. Elizabeth Poor; had Jacob, who died 31st March. 1688; and John. who died 20th November, 1700. Probably Mary. who married, 1st December, 1680, Stephen Parker. was his sister, and possibly Hannah. who married, 2d January. 1689. Benjamin Barker. and Sarah. who married, 24th May. 1692. James Bridges, all at Andover. may have been.

MARSTON, JAMES, Hampton. son probably of Thomas: by wife Dinah Sanborn had Abigail, born 17th March. 1679, who married, 5th August. 1701. John Prescott of same place and died 14th November, 1762; and Ann, born 16 February. 1681, who married, 30th December, 1702, Nathaniel Prescott, and died 30th December. 1761.

MARSTON, JOHN. Salem: came in 1637. aged 30 years. as servant of widow Mary Moulton. from Ormsby. County Norfolk. England: was a carpenter: made freeman 2d June. 1641: had baptized John. on the 12th September, 1641; Ephraim, 10th December. 1643; Manasseh. 7th September. 1645; Sarah. 19th March. 1648; Benjamin, 9th March. 1651. before mentioned; Hannah. April. 1653; Thomas, 11th October. 1655; Elizabeth, 30th August. 1657; and Abigail. 10th April. 1659. He died 19th December. 1681. aged 66 years. so says the gravestone.

MARSTON, JOHN, Barnstable; married, 1st July, 1657, Martha, daughter of Bernard Lombard; had John, born 15th June, 1658; and George, 4th October, 1660; removed to Swansey; there by wife Joan had Melatiah, born 31st August, 1673.

MARSTON, JOHN, Andover, 1667, perhaps was father of Jacob and Mary, Hannah and Sarah, above mentioned, and of John; but means of certainty are beyond reach, and all we know is that he had wife Martha, was a freeman in 1691, and that his daughter Sarah married, 24th May, 1692, James Bridges of Andover.

MARSTON, JOHN, Salem, probably son of the first John; had wife Mary, who died 25th May, 1686, aged 43 years, by the inscription on her gravestone; nothing more is known of him, than he was a freeman in 1671.

MARSTON, JOHN, Andover, probably son of John of the same place; married, 2d May, 1689, Mary, daughter of Christopher Osgood; had son John, who died 25th January, 1694; John, born 13th May, 1699; and perhaps others. His wife died 5th April, 1700, having suffered in the delusion of 1692, being imprisoned as a witch.

MARSTON, MANASSEH, Salem, brother of Benjamin; was a blacksmith; freeman in 1677; captain, and representative in 1691; died in 1705.

MARSTON, ROBERT, Hampton, 1636.

MARSTON, THOMAS, Salem, 1636; freeman 2d June, 1641; removed to Hampton, as one of the first settlers; was the husband of Mary, daughter of William Estow of Hampton, and probably father of Ephraim; perhaps of Isaac, James and William, as well as of Mary, who married, 1st January, 1681, the second William Sanborn, unless one or more were the children of William; representative in 1677.

MARSTON, WILLIAM, Salem, 1637, perhaps brother of Thomas; had grant of land in 1637, but was of Hampton in 1640, and back to Salem in a few years; had there baptized Hannah, Sarah and Elizabeth, all on the 10th April, 1659; Deliverance in August, 1663; removed to Newbury, but for only a short time, then again to Hampton, where he was a freeman in 1666; there died, 30th June, 1672, according to Coffin, who says his wife was Sabina, daughter of Robert Page, and that he left five children, Thomas, William, John, Tryphena and Prudence Cox.

MARSTON, WILLIAM, Hampton, son of the preceding; married Rebecca Page; had Mary, who married, 6th March, 1695, James Prescott.

REFERENCES:—Amer. Ancestry, I, 52; III. 158, 159, 200; Cogswell's Nottingham, N. H., 425-32; Cutts Genealogy, 77; Dearborn's Hist. Parsonsfield, Me., 386; Dow's Hist. Hampton, N. H., 834-53; Eaton's Annals of Warren, Me., 583; Freeman's Cape Cod, Mass., I, 373; II, 324; Howland Genealogy, 304; Lapham's Hist. of Norway, Me., 547; Marston Genealogy (1873); Marston Genealogy (1888); N. E. Hist. & Gen. Reg., XXVII, 291-307, 390-403; XXXIX, 165; Oxford, N. H., Centennial, 118-21; Savage's Gen. Dic., III., 160; Swift's Barnstable, Mass., Families, II., 219; Watson's Marston Genealogy (1873).

MARTEN:—Abraham, Hingham, 1635, a weaver, at Rehoboth in 1643. His will was probated 9th September, 1669.

MARTEN, AMBROSE, Weymouth, 1638; in Concord, 1639; had Joseph, born 8th November, 1640; and Sarah, born 27th October, 1642.

MARTEN, ANTHONY, Middletown; married 10th or 11th March, 1661, Mary, daughter of Richard Hall; had Mary, born 1st January following, died soon; John, born 17th March, 1663; Mary, born March, 1667; and Elizabeth, born 3d August, 1671; he died 16th November, 1673, leaving a widow.

MARTEN, CHARLES, York, 1680; swore allegiance next year.

MARTEN, CHRISTOPHER, Plymouth; came in the Mayflower; was of Billericay, in County Essex; came with wife and two servants, Solomon Prower and John Langemore. All died shortly, the servant Solomon before landing, 24th December, 1620, and the husband on the 8th January following.

MARTEN, EDWARD, Boston, 1679.

MARTEN, EMANUEL, Salem; signed the petition against imposts in 1668.

MARTEN, GEORGE, Salisbury, blacksmith; by wife Hannah, who died soon; had Hannah, born 1st February, 1644; married, 11th August, 1646, second wife Susanna, daughter of Richard North; had Richard, born 29th June, 1647; George, born 21st October, 1648; John, born 26th January, 1651; Esther, born 7th April, 1653; John, born 2d November, 1656; Abigail, born 10th September, 1659; William, born 11th December, 1662, died very soon; and Samuel, born 29th September, 1667. Hannah married, 4th December, 1661; Ezekiel Worthen; and Esther married, 15th March, 1670, John Jameson.

MARTIN:—Isaac, Rehoboth, 1643.

MARTIN, JOHN, Charlestown, 1638; freeman 13th May, 1640; by wife Rebecca had Sarah, baptized 9th September, 1639; Mary, born 14th March, 1641; John, born 1st May, 1642; and by wife Sarah had Mehitable, born 1st October, 1643.

MARTIN, JOHN, Dover, 1648; of the grand jury in 1654; married Esther, daughter of Thomas Roberts; was freeman in 1666, but in 1673 was in Jersey.

MARTIN, JOHN, of Barnstable; married, 1st July, 1657, Martha, daughter of Bernard Lombard; had John, born June. 1658; George, born October, 1660; and Desire, born 1st January, 1663. He removed to Martha's Vineyard.

MARTIN, JOHN, Chelmsford; freeman in 1665.

MARTIN, JOHN, Marblehead in 1674.

MARTIN, JOHN, Swansey; had John, born 15th March, 1675, and the Colonial Records transcription, of Swansey, gives him by wife Joan, Joanna, born 15th February, 1683.

MARTIN, JOHN, Rehoboth; married, 27th June, 1681, Mercy Billington, daughter of Francis; thought to have had John, born 10th June, 1682; Robert, born 9th September, 1683.

MARTIN, JOHN, Middleton, son probably of Anthony; had wife Elizabeth, who died 26th July, 1718. His children were John, who died young, 14th March, 1687; Nathaniel, born 17th March, 1688; Elizabeth, born 24th September, 1689; John, born 4th April, 1692; Ebenezer, born July, 1694; Daniel, born October, 1697; Hannah, born 23d May, 1699; and Mary, born 31st May, 1701.

MARTIN, JONATHAN, Farmer says was of New Hampshire, and freeman in 1668.

MARTIN, MICHAEL, Boston, a mariner; married, 12th September, 1656, Susanna, daughter of Edward Holyoke.

MARTIN, RICHARD, Caseo, 1646; married a widow Atwell, perhaps was of Scarsborough; a freeman in 1658; died early in 1673, his will of 11th January, 1673, being probated in April of that year. In it he shows that he had wife Dorothy, son-in-law Robert Corbin and his wife Lydia, and gives to Benjamin Atwell, who had probably married another daughter, perhaps dead, for he also gives to grandchild Joseph Atwell, and this Joseph in 1679 was only eight years old, is called only heir. He brought from England two daughters, of whom Lydia married Robert Corbin, and possibly the other was Mary, executed at the age of 22 years in Boston for the murder of her illegitimate child, as given in Winthrop II, 302. See also Willis I, 134.

MARTIN, RICHARD, Boston, a merchant; married, 1st February, 1654, Sarah, daughter of John Tuttle; had Mary, born 7th June, 1655; Sarah, born 2d July, 1657; and married, in 1660, a second wife, Elizabeth, daughter of John Gay of Dedham; had John. born 2d August, 1661; Richard, born 24th March, 1663; Elizabeth and Mary, twins, born 15th April, 1665, perhaps both died; Elizabeth, born 25th July, 1667; Abigail, born 14th November, 1669; and a posthumous child, Lydia, born 8th February, 1672. He died between 19th of July, the date of a deed to serve for his will, and 6th November, 1671, when administration papers were given to his widow. Perhaps he came in the Elizabeth and Ann from London in 1635. aged 12 years, and may have been brother of John of Boston.

MARTIN, RICHARD, of Charlestown, a captain, died 2d November, 1694, aged 62 years, and his widow Elizabeth died 7th January, 1726, aged 84 years, says the gravestones, but he had not lived there most of his days, for the list of householders in 1678 does not give the baptized name, but simply "Mr. Martin," and it is not thought to mean either John or Thomas, and Coffin authorizes the conjecture that he was of Newbury; had son Richard, born 8th January, 1674. A former wife, Elizabeth, died 6th October, 1689; and his second wife married, 28th November same year, was widow of Joshua Edmonds.

MARTIN, ROBERT, a freeman of Massachusetts 13th May, 1640; was perhaps, of Weymouth, then, soon removed to Rehoboth, 1643, and Swansey.

MARTIN, ROBERT, New Haven; had Mary baptized, perhaps 24th May, 1646; John. 28th May, 1648; and Stephen, perhaps 13th May, 1652, but for the first and last wrong dates are given in the church record.

MARTIN, SAMUEL, Wethersfield, in 1646; went to New Haven, and married the widow Bracey, but this may have been before his permanent settlement at Wethersfield; her name was Phebe, daughter of Mr. Bisley of London, who provided for her and her children by buying estate at Wethersfield. He had son Samuel, and, perhaps, Richard; went to London in 1652, soon returned, served in Philip's War as a lieutenant, and in October, 1677. had a grant of 50 acres "to him and his heirs forever, prohibiting him the sale of the same, or any alieniation thereof from his heirs," showing that his courage was valued higher than his thrift. He died 15th September, 1683.

MARTIN, SAMUEL, Andover; married. 30th March, 1676, Abigail Norton; had Samuel, who died 1st February, 1683; was an ensign and died 16th November, 1696.

MARTIN, SOLOMON, Gloucester, ship carpenter; came in the James, it is thought, in 1635. from London, aged 16 years; married, 21st March, 1643, Mary, daughter of Henry Pindar; had Samuel, born 16th April, 1645; and Mary, born 9th January, 1648. His wife died 9th February following, and he married, 18th June next, widow Alice Varnum of Ipswich; perhaps removed to Andover. at least he sold his Gloucester estate in March, 1651, and next year was freeman of Andover.

MARTIN, THOMAS, Charlestown. 1638. a freeman 22d May, 1639, perhaps removed to Cambridge; there by

wife Alice Ellet, married, 1st June, 1650, had Abigail, born 22d August, 1653; may have been of New London in 1666, having prefix of respect, at least was not a householder at Charlestown in 1658.

MARTIN, THOMAS, Boston, mariner; married, 1670, Rachel, daughter of John Farnham.

MARTIN, THOMAS, Marlborough, 1675; made freeman 1690.

MARTIN, WILLIAM, Reading, 1641; one of the earliest selectmen; freeman in 1653, perhaps removed to Groton, there died 23d March, 1673; his wife Mary, who had been widow Lakin, having died 14th August, 1669, made provision of his will, dated 6th March, 1673, probated 1st April same year, more liberal. To his wife's children, William and John Lakin, to the children of William Lakin and to sister Allen and her children. excepting Hannah, are bequests to three neighbors, release of debts, and £10 is given to the town for the purchase of a bell for the meeting-house. Uniform use of "y" in the name belongs only to the New Hampshire family.

REFERENCES:—Aldrich's Walpole, N. H., 321; Amer. Ancestry, I, 52; II, 78; IV, 195; VI, 167; XI, 235; Avon, N. Y., Gen. Rec., 26-9; Babson's Hist. Gloucester, Mass., 115; Bass' Hist. Braintree, Vt., 164; Bassett's Hist. Richmond, N. H., 432; Bedford, N. H., Centennial, 316; Buckingham Genealogy, 107-12; Champion Genealogy, 90-4; Chase's Hist. Chester, N. H., 557; Cleveland's Hist. Yates Co., N. Y., 482; Cochran's Hist. Francestown, N. H.; Cothern's Woodbury, Conn., 630-3; II, 1515; Daniel's Hist. Oxford, Mass., 602; Davis' Hist. Wallingford, Conn., 845-7; Eaton Grange, 79-82; Eaton's Hist. Thomaston, Me., II, 324; Egle's Notes and Queries (1896), 130, 234-9; Futhey's Hist. Chester Co., Pa., 652; Guild's (Calvin) Ancestry, 25; Hayward's Hist. Hancock, N. H., 744; Heywood's Hist. Westminster, Mass., 760; Hough's Hist. Lewis Co., N. Y., 172-4; Hoyt's Salisbury, Mass., Families, 239-42; Hubbard's Hist. Stanstead Co., Can., 143; Joslin's Hist. Poultney, Vt.. 309; Kitchell Genealogy, 59; Lapham's Hist. Rumford, Me., 372-5; Lewis Genealogy (1893), 359-76; Littell's Passaic Valley Gens., 278; Little's Hist. Warren, N. H., 935-7; Livermore's Hist. Wilton, N. H., 447; Martin Genealogy (1880); Martin's Hist. Chester, Pa., 102-5, 328-37; McKeen's Hist. Bradford, Vt., 158-62; Meade's Old Churches of Virginia; Minor's Meriwether Gen., 11-3; Montgomery Genealogy (1897), 62-4; Neill Family of Delaware, 94-8; Neill's Virginia Carolonum, 20; New Eng. Hist. & Gen. Reg., LIV, 27-31; Palmer Genealogy (1886). 65-7; Palmer and Trimble Gen., 139-42; Powers Sangamon Co. Ills., Settlers, 475; Richmond, Va., Standard, III, 44; Ridlow's Saco Valley. Me., Families, 908-12; Salem. N. Y., Book of History, 61; Savage's Gen. Dic., III, 161-4; Sedgwick's Hist. Sharon, Conn., 99; Sharpless Genealogy, 342; Smith's Hist. Duchess Co., N. Y., 248; Stearn's Hist. Ashburnham, Mass.; Temple's Hist. North Brookfield, Mass.. 680; Washington, N. H., History, 527; Wells' Amer. Fam. Antiquity, III, 61-107; Wheeler's Hist. North Carolina. II, 182, 405; Wetmore's Copps Hill Epitaphs; Wyman's Charlestown, Mass., Gens., II. 658; Young's Hist. Chautauqua Co., N. Y., 451; Young's Hist. Warsaw, N. Y. 294; Young's Hist. Wayne Co., Ind., 350.

MARTYN:—Edward, New Hampshire, 1674; may have been son of John of Dover.

MARTYN, RICHARD, Portsmouth, was one of the founders of the first church there, 1671; representative in 1672 and 1679, speaker of the house and a counsellor of the Province, 1680; died 2d April„ 1694. He had Richard, born 10th January, 1660; Elizabeth, born 1662; Hannah, born 1665; Michael, born 3d February, 1667; John, born 9th June, 1668; and Elias, born 18th April, 1670. He married second wife Mary, widow of John Denison, daughter of Hon. Samuel Symonds of Ipswich; and third wife was Mary, widow of Samuel Wentworth.

MARTYN, RICHARD, Portsmouth, son of the preceding; was a schoolmaster and preached, but probably did not wish for a settlement; died 6th December, 1690.

REFERENCES:—Allen's Worcester, Mass, 63; Wentworth Genealogy, 116; Savage's Gen. Dic., III, 164.

MARTUGAL:—Saunders; sworn as freeman of Connecticut 9th of May, 1667, if Trumbull has given correctly, the odd name in Colonial Records, II, 58. What town he lived at is unknown, but in 1669, as this name is not among the freemen of any town, it may be thought he was dead or had removed.

REFERENCE:—Savage's Gen. Dic., III, 164.

MARVIN:—John, Lyme, eldest son of the second Reynold; married, 7th May, 1691, Sarah, daughter of Henry Graham or Grimes; had Sarah, Mary, John, born 9th August, 1698; Elizabeth, Joseph, born, 1703; Benjamin, Mehitable, and Jemima; and died 11th December, 1711. His widow married Richard Sears, and died 14th December, 1760, aged 90 years.

MARVIN, JOHN, Norwalk, son of the second Matthew; married, 22d March, 1704, Mary Beers; had John, born 22d July, 1705; Nathan, born 4th March, 1708; Seth, born 13th July, 1709; David, born 24th August, 1711; Elizabeth, born 23d October, 1713; Mary, born 20th December, 1716; and Elihu, born 10th October, 1719. His wife died 17th April, 1720, and on 27th April, 1721, he married Rachel, daughter of Matthias St. John, and had Hannah, born 4th December, 1722; Joseph, born 20th May, 1724; Rachel, born 24th December, 1725, died in two days; Benjamin, born 14th March, 1728, died in three days; Rachel, born 27th March, 1729; Sarah, born 18th May, 1733, died in three days; and Ann, born 7th September, 1741.

MARVIN, MATTHEW, Hartford, 1638, an original proprietor, came in the Increase, 1635. from London, aged 35, a husbandman, with wife Elizabeth, aged 31, and children, Elizabeth, in the custom-house record called 31, probably by error for 11; Matthew, aged 8; Mary, aged 6; Sarah, aged 3; and Hannah, aged 6 months. He was one of the original grantees of Norwalk, and settled there in 1653; was a representative in 1654. At Hartford he had Abigail, born before 1641; Samuel, baptized 16th February, 1648; and Rachel, born 30th December, 1649; and died 1687. Elizabeth married John Olmstead, survived him, and made her will 15th October, 1689. Mary married, 11th October, 1648. Richard Bushnell of Saybrook, and. in 1680, deacon Thomas Adgate as her second husband; had children by each, and died 29th March, 1713. aged 84 years; Sarah married, 4th October, 1648. William Goodrich of Wethersfield; Hannah married Thomas Seymour, January, 1654; Abigail married. 1st January, 1657, John Bouton; and Rachel married Samuel Smith.

MARVIN, MATTHEW, Norwalk. son of the preceding. born in England: a freeman in 1664; by wife Mary had Matthew, Sarah, Samuel, Hannah, John, born 2d September, 1678; and Elizabeth; besides others. for in 1672 he counted six children; was representative in 1694 and 1697. Of the children the account is imperfect, as is so

frequently found in the third generation. Matthew married Rhoda, daughter of Mark St. John, and had one daughter, Mary, born 7th October, 1689, and he died in 1691; Sarah married, January, 1681, Thomas Betts; Samuel was representative in 1718, and left descendants by sons Samuel and Matthew, and also had Josiah; Hannah married Epenetus Platt; John is before mentioned; and Elizabeth married, 6th November, 1700, Joseph Platt. Mary, who married Daniel Benedict of Norwalk, may be a daughter.

MARVIN, RENOLD, REYNOLD or REGINALD, of Hartford, 1639, not an original proprietor; was probably a younger brother of the first Matthew; removed to Farmington, soon after to Saybrook; a freeman in 1658; died between 13th of May, the date of his will, and 28th of October. 1662, date of inventory of his estate, leaving only Reynold and Mary, perhaps both were born in England. Mary married William Waller of Saybrook.

MARVIN, REYNOLD, Lyme, son of the preceding; probably born in England; freeman in 1658; was a deacon, a representative in 1670-2-3-4 and 6; died in 1676. By wife Sarah, daughter of George Clark, had John, born 1665; Reynold, born 1669; and Samuel, born 1671; besides Mary and Sarah, whose birth dates are unknown, as also all else, excepting that Mary married Richard Ely of Saybrook. The gravestone tells of his military rank. His widow married Joseph Sill or Scill, the distinguished soldier, survived him, and was living 28th May, 1702. His descendants are very numerous.

MARVIN, REYNOLD, Lyme, son of the preceding; by wife Phebe had Phebe, born 3d December, 1696; Reynold born January, 1702; Lydia, born 12th January, 1704; Esther, born 3d April. 1707; and his wife died 21st October, 1707. In 1708 he married Martha, daughter of Thomas Waterman of Norwich; had Martha, born 3d April, 1710; Elisha, born 26th September, 1711, died young; James, born 26th May, 1713; Sarah, born 8th March. 1716; Elisha, born 8th March. 1718; and William, born March, 1720. He was a deacon and captain, and died 18th October, 1737. From him through his ninth chold descends Hon. Theophiles R. Marvin of Boston.

MARVIN, SAMUEL, Lyme, brother of the preceding; married, 5th May, 1699, Susanna, daughter of Henry Graham or Grimes; had Samuel, born 10th February, 1700; Zachariah, born 27th December, 1701; Thomas, born 4th March, 1704; Matthew. born 7th November, 1706; Abigail, born 13th September, 1709; Elizabeth, born 1st June, 1712; Nathan, born 21st November, 1714; Nehemiah, born 20th February, 1717; Mary and a twin sister, who both died soon; was a representative in 1711 and 1722; died 15th March, 1743.

MARVIN, THOMAS, Newbury; died 28th November, 1651.

REFERENCES:—Amer. Ancestry, I, 52; III, 311; IV, 25; Barlow Genealogy, 223-7; Daniel's Hist. Oxford, Mass., 602; Hall's Norwalk, Conn., Records, 181, 285; Hinman's Conn. Settlers; Marvin Genealogy (1848); N. E. Hist. & Gen. Reg., XVI. 235-54; XXXI, 212; XXXII, 82; LI, 330; Porter's Hartford, Conn., Settlers, 12; Salisbury's Family Hist., III. 77, 213; Savage's Gen. Dic., III, 164; Sedgwick's Norwalk, Conn., 150-3; 371; Talcott's Gen. Notes, 592-609; Walworth's Hyde Genealogy, 567, 795; Young's Hist. Chautauqua Co., N. Y., 367.

MASCALL or MASKELL:—John, Salem; there had baptized 23d February, 1651, John; Stephen, born 13th March. 1653; Mehitable, born 3d June. 1655; Thomas, born August, 1657; James. born 26th May. 1662; and Nicholas, born 5th June, 1664; was freeman in 1678 or possibly in 1671, where the name is Masker in the list.

MASCALL, ROBERT, Boston, 1640, in the family of William Pierce; went home and had letters of dismissal from our church, 5th July, 1646, to church at Dover, England.

MASCALL, THOMAS, Windsor, where it is written Maskell; married, 10th May, 1660, Bethia Parsons; had Bethia, born 6th March, 1661; Thomas, born 19th March, 1662, died soon; Abigail, born 17th November, 1663; Thomas, born 2d January, 1666; John, born 19th November, 1667; Elizabeth, born 19th October, 1669; and he died in 1671. His widow married, 8th August, 1672, John Williams. Hinman, 52, 53 and 153, means one only.

REFERENCES:—Ewing Genealogy (1858) ;, Savage's Gen. Dic., Vol. III, 165.

MASON:—Arthur, Boston; married, 5th July, 1655, Joanna, daughter of Nicholas Parker; had Ann, born 10th August, 1656, died at 1 year; Mary, Abigail, David, born 24th October, 1661; Joanna, born 26th March, 1664; Arthur, born 16th April, 1666, died soon; Alice, born 26th June, 1668; Arthur, born 18th, baptized 31st January, 1674; Jonathan, baptized 23d April, 1676, died at Dorchester, 9th March, 1723; and Lucy or Lois, born 11th August, 1678. It is said he came to America in 1639, but he was only 77 years old at his death, 4th of March, 1708. His wife had died 2d January, 1708. He was a constable and well disposed to magnify his office, for an amusing proof of which see Hutchinson, Vol. I, 254; he wrote his name with "ss." Mary married, in November, 1678, Rev. John Norton of Hingham; Joanna married a Perry; Alice married Samuel Shepard; his son Arthur, who was a mariner, married, 26th January, 1701, Mary, daughter of Sampson Stoddard, who died 19th September, 1746.

MASON, DANIEL, Watertown, youngest son of Hugh of same place; studied for a profession, and went as surgeon of a vessel from Charlestown, of which James Ellson was master, in 1678-9; was captured, as family tradition says, by an Algerian corsair, and probably died in Barbary.

MASON, DANIEL, Stonington, in 1673, son of Major John; removed that year to New London or Norwich; married a wife for whom he had obtained liberty to come to Roxbury to her relations in the early spring of 1676, and for this year to dwell there; his son Daniel was baptized at Roxbury 9th April, 1676, and after her return probably she died, and he at Hingham married, in October, 1679, Rebecca Hobart. He was that year schoolmaster at Norwich; removed from there to Lebanon, and finally to Stonington, where he died in 1736.

MASON, EDMUND, Watertown, a proprietor in 1642.

MASON, EDWARD, one of the early settlers at Wethersfield, of whom no more is known, excepting that in 1640, after his death, the inventory of his estate is found in the records, but no family is heard of.

MASON, ELIAS, Salem; had three baptized Sarah, and Mary on the 23d May, 1647; Hannah, born 14th January, 1649; Martha, born 18th May, 1651; and Elias, born 29th May, 1653. His will, dated 1st May, 1684, probated 13th June, 1688, mentions wife Elizabeth and no children, but Sarah, wife of John Robinson, with grandchild John; and Mary, wife of George Cox, with grandchild George. Emma, a widow of Eastwell, County Kent, who came in the Hercules, 1635, and had a grant of land in 1637 at Salem, may have been his mother though no child in the ship's list of passengers is given.

MASON, HENRY, Scituate, 1643, perhaps removed to

Dorchester, and may be the freeman of 1650, after 1656 a brewer in Boston, who died in 1676, and in his will, dated 6th October, 1676, probated the next month, mentions wife Esther, daughter of the first Abraham Howe, no children, and cousin, that is, neice, Mary, daughter of Joseph Eliot.

MASON, HENRY, Boston, servant to James Everell; died 10th November, 1653.

MASON, HUGH, Watertown, a tanner; came in the Francis from Ipswich, County Suffolk, in 1634, aged 28 years, with wife Esther, aged 22; made freeman 4th March, 1635; had Hannah, born 23d September, 1636; Elizabeth, born 3d September, 1638, died young; Ruth, buried 17th December, 1640; Mary, born 18th December, 1640; John, born 1st January, 1645; Joseph, born 10th August, 1646; Daniel, born 19th February, 1649, probably at Harvard College in 1666; and Sarah, born 25th September, 1651; was a representative in 1644-5, 60 and often later to 1676-7; a captain in 1652, and died October, 1678.

MASON, JOHN, Dorchester, though thought by some to have come, 1630, with Winthrop, probably came early in 1632; was in that year sent as a lieutenant with 20 men against a pirate, for which he was paid £10, and became captain next year; was first in the list of freemen, 1635, representative 1635 and 6, and removed with Warham to Windsor; of great service in military and civil life; finished the Pequot war in 1637, being in chief command; representative 1637 to 41, then Assist. to 59. then Deputy Governor for eight years; major-general and commissioner for the Congr. of N. E., 1647, 54, 5, 6, 9 and 61. From Windsor he removed, 1647, to Saybrook, thence to first settlement of Norwich, 1659. By first wife, who died at Windsor, no children are known, but he took second wife, 1639, named Peck, and had, perhaps, Isabel; certain, Priscilla, born 1641; Samuel, 1644; John, 1646; Rachel, 1648; Ann, 1650; Daniel, 1652; and Elizabeth, 1654, and died 1672, aged 72. All that the diligence of Prince, the annalist, could gather to prefix to his history of the Pequot War may be read in Mass. Hist. Coll., VIII, 122; and later inquiries add little; yet in Sparks's Amer. Biog., Vol. III, of second series, is a copious biography of the great captain, written with much felicity, by the Rev. George E. Ellis.

MASON, JOHN, Portsmouth, R. I., 1655; was perhaps of Westerly, 1669.

MASON, JOHN, Watertown; an early settler, perhaps older brother of Hugh; was a captain, died 1678, aged 73, by the gravestone.

MASON, JOHN, Salem; bricklayer, 1661; may be he who married at Charlestown, 1659, Ann Colliham.

MASON, JOHN, Concord, who died 1667; had married, 1662, Hannah Ramsden, and children were John, born 1664, and Hannah.

MASON, JOHN, Hartford, died 1698, leaving good estate for these children, Mary, then aged 20; Hannah, 17; John, 13; Joseph, 10; Abigail, 7; Jonathan, 4; and Lydia, 1.

MASON, JOHN, Boston; merchant, came about 1678. from London; married Sarah, daughter of Robert Pepper, had Sarah, born 1681; Susanna, 1687; Samuel, 1689; Jonathan, 1692; Abigail, 1693; Benjamin, 1695; and John, 1697. He died, 1698.

——— Another John of Boston had wife Prudence, and children a few years later.

MASON, JOSEPH, Portsmouth, in 1667; conveyed his estate to brother Robert of Southam Co. Berks, in trust for his three daughters.

MASON, JOSEPH, Watertown, son of Hugh; married, 1684, Mary, daughter of John Fiske; had Mary, born 1685; Esther, 1686; Joseph, 1688; and Sarah, 1691; was freeman 1690, and died 1702. His widow died 1725.

MASON, NICHOLAS, Saybrook, 1648; may be thought father of that Nicholas who married, 1686, Mary, Peat, daughter of William Dudley. One Nicholas, perhaps from the east, was at Northampton, a soldier, 1676, in Capt. Turner's company.

MASON, NOAH, Rehoboth, 1675; was perhaps son of Sampson. His wife Martha died 1676, and he married at Taunton, 1677, Sarah Fitch; had Noah, born 1678; John, 1680; Mary, 1682.

MASON, RALPH, Boston; came in the Abigail from London, 1635; was a joiner of Southwark, aged 35; with wife Ann, 35, the age perhaps carelessly inserted, and children Richard, 5; Samuel, 3; and Susan, 1; had here Zuriel, born, 1637; John, 1640; Jacob, 1644; and Hannah, 1647. But his will of 1679 names only aged wife and the children Richard, Samuel, Susanna, John and Jacob. Susaana married, 1659, William Norton.

MASON, ROBERT, Roxbury, where his wife died, 1637; removed to Dedham, there died 1667. His sons John, Robert, and Thomas, who may all have been born in England, had administration of his estate.

MASON, ROBERT, Boston; by wife Sarah, daughter of Robert Reynolds, had Robert; Sarah, 1657; Nathaniel, 1659; Philip, 1662; and Elizabeth, 1669. He was freeman 1673.

MASON, ROBERT, Roxbury; married, 1680 or 2, Eliz. Chandler, who died 1688; had Robert, born 1684; Elizabeth, 1686; and John, 1687, died in a few days.

MASON, ROGER, Hartford 1670; then propounded for freeman.

MASON, SAMPSON, Dorchester 1651; shoemaker; had probably Sampson, who served in Philip's war; and John, born about 1656; was of Rehoboth 1657, Swanzey 10 years lter. He lived to 1676. See Bliss, 48.

MASON, SAMUEL, Hingham; married, 1670, Judith Smith.

MASON, THOMAS, Watertown 1637; perhaps removed to Hartford before 1651, and thence, in 1656, to Northampton; had wife Clemence, and only child Samuel, who was killed by the Indians 1675, and he died 1678. His widow married Deacon Thomas Judd, and died 1696.

MASON, THOMAS, Dedham 1642; probably son of the first Robert, born in England; married, 1653, Margery Partridge; had John, born 1655; and Mary, 1658; lived in that part which became Medfield, and was killed by the Indians 1676. His house was probably burned at the same time.

REFERENCES:—Massachusetts—Ballou's Hist. of Milford, 892; Bond's Watertown, 356-64; 855-7; Draper's Hist. of Spencer, 230; Hill's Dedham Records; Hudson's Hist. of Lexington, 131; Jackson's Hist. of Newton, 364; Jameson's Hist. Medway, 500-2; Morse's Gen. of Sherborn, 175; Paige's Hist. Cambridge, 605-8; Temple's Hist. Northfield, 491; Temple's Hist. Palmer, 516-8; Ward's Hist. Shrewsbury, 376; Wyman's Charlestown Gen.s, II, 659. New Hampshire, Aldrich's Hist. Wapole, 322-5; Dow's Hist. Hampton, 854-7; Hayward's Hist. Hancock, 745; Livermore's Hist. Wilton, 447; Merrill's Hist. Acworth, 240; Norton's Hist. Fitzwilliam, 633; Reade's Hist. Swanzey, 401-3; Runnels' Sanbornton, 477-81. Other publications—Adams' Ancestry, IV, 31, 143, 188; V, 115; VI, 164; IX, 70; Ammidown Gen., 47; Ayer (James) Biog. (1892); Bangor,

Me., Hist. Mag., II, 238; Bridgeman's Granary Burial Ground, 148; Bulkeley's Brown Mem., 84; Campbell's Hist. of Virginia, 648-50; Chandler Gen., 41, 140; Carter Tree of Virginia; Caulkin's Hist. Norwalk, Ct., 146-8; Corliss' North Yarmouth, Me.; Dunster Gen., 300-4; Ely Gen., 271-3; Goode Gen., 236; Harrison's Old Kent, Md., 269; Harris' Ancestors of W. C. Harris; Hatch's Hist. of Industry, Me., 732-4; Hayden's Va. Gens., 109; Hines Lebanon, Ct., Address, 165; Hurd's Hist. New London County, Ct., 527-9; Lapham's Hist. Bethel, Me., 585-90; Lapham's Hist. Paris, Me., 671; Leonard's Hist. Dublin, N. Y., 363-70; Mason (Capt. John) Memoirs, 33-43; Mason Gen. (1892), 15 pp.; Meade's Old Farms Va., II, 229; Morse Mem. Appendix, 43; Me. Hist. Gen. Reg., XVI, 117-22, 217-24, 318; XVII, 39-42, 214-9; XVIII, 246-54; Page Gen., 242; Paxton's Marshall Gen., 327; Powers' Hist. Sangamon Co., Ill., 476-8; Savage's Gen. Dict., III, 166-70; Schroeder's Boardman Mem., 561-71; Shourd's Fenwick Colony, N. J., 150-2; Southern Bivouac (1886), 727; Spark's Amer. Biog., 2d series, III, 435-8; Stiles Hist. Windsor, Ct., II, 472-5; Young's Hist. Wayne Co., Ind., 286.

MASSEY:—Jeffrey, Salem, one of the first members of the church there; freeman 1634; was clerk of the market 1642, died 1677, aged about 84; had John, born 1631, who by Dr. Bentley was called the first born male of the town; but Felt differs from that argument, though the cradle in which he was rocked was long admired, and perhaps acknowledged as proof.

REFERENCES:—Dwight's Strong Gen., 637; Penn. Mag., VII, 473; Smith's Hist. Delaware Co., Pa,. 483.

MASSON:—See Mason.

MASTERS:—Abraham, Cambridge 1639; probably son of John, but may have been grandson.

MASTERS, GILES, Boston, died 1688. He probably had lived here only a short time, and with no sympathy towards our people, as in Sewall's diary he is described merely as the "King's attorney."

MASTERS, JOHN, Cambridge, perhaps came in the fleet with Winthrop; freeman 1631, with prefix of respect; a man of skill and enterprise; died 1639, and Jane, his wife, died a few days after. His will names daughter Sarah Dobyson, or Dobson, but we know nothing of her or her husband; daughter Lydia Tabor, perhaps wife of Philip, grand child John Lockwood, probably by his daughter Elizabeth, son of Edmund; Abraham and gives residence Nathaniel Masters, probably son and grandson, and gives residue of estate to Elizabeth, wife of Cary Latham.

REFERENCES:—Paige's Cambridge, Mass., 609; Savage's Gen. Dict., III, 170.

MASTERSON:—Richard, Plymouth 1630; came probably the year preceding; a deacon of the "goodly company of the Pilgrims at Leyden," before the death of Rev. John Robinson, 1625; chosen probably 1620, when Gov. Carver, Elder Brewster, and Samuel Fuller, who had probably all been predecessors in that office, embarked for New England in the Mayflower. He brought wife Mary, named Goodall, of Leicester, in the documents at Leyden; was married 1619; child Nathaniel, before mentioned, and Sarah, who married John Wood, or Atwood. The widow married Rev. Ralph Smith. It has been doubted whether the deacon ever came to this country, but the doubt relies, says Savage, mainly on the negative fact of mention of him being hardly found, and yet it is known from Bradford that he died at Plymouth in the great sickness, 1633.

REFERENCE:—Savage's Gen. Dict., III, 171.

MATHER:—Cotton. Boston, eldest son of Increase, freeman 1680, when he was only 17 years old, so that he came forward with strange rapidity (having joined the church of his father in 1679), which is the more striking, as his father was never admitted freeman that we find; and if his course at college were a full one he must have entered at 11½ years. Yet more than two or three have been ministers in Boston younger than he; but with less sagacity than his father he was ordained at Second Church, colleagues with him, 1685; distinguished as a scholar above most of his contemporaries, but known in modern days chiefly as author of the Magn. in seven books. London, 1702, a work of no little value, yet more curious than valuable. Died 1728. He married, 1686, Abigail, daughter of John Phillips of Charlestown, who died 1702, having born to him 9 children, of whom 5 died young, three before baptism; and he married, 1703, Elizabeth, daughter of Dr. John Clark, widow of Richard Hubbard, mariner, with a good estate, had 6 more children, of whom Rev. Samuel 1706, Harvard College, 1723, attained no humble share of celebrity, and she died 1713. He next married, 1715. Lydia, daughter of Rev. William Lee, widow of John George, who long survived. 12 of his children with dates of baptism and names, are in the appendix to Rev. Chandler Robbins's Hist. of the Second Church, but 6 of them are by the second wife. In the pious labor of his son, Rev. Samuel, on the biography of his father, he is more copious than exact. The most agreeable of all the copious writings of Mather will, perhaps, be found in some apologies designed to magnify the merits of his father in obtaining the new charter, for which, however, little favor was found in the mind of Calef. They may be seen in 3 Mass. Hist., Call. I, 126, 133. But his epistolary exercises are more frequently referred to, and they are very numerous. As the sample of his style, and also highly illustrating the politics of the day, that his father was too much engaged in for the larger part of his life. See letters in I Mass. Hist. Coll., III, admonish. Gov. Dudley by father and son, each, as if in rivalry, more venemous than the other.

MATHER, ELEAZER, Northampton, son of Richard; was the first minister at M. ordained, 1661; married, 1659, Esther, youngest daughter of John Warham; had Eunice, born 1664; Warham, 1666; H. C. 1685; and Eliakim, 1668; and died 1669, only three months after his father. His widow married Rev. Solomon Stoddard, outlived him, and died 1736, in her 92d year.

MATHER, INCREASE. Boston, younger brother of Eleazer, having taken at Harvard College his A. B., went at 18 years of age to his brother Samuel at Dublin, and studied there for his A. M. in 1658; preached in several places, as Co. Devon and Isle of Guernsey, leaving the latter after the restoration, but returned at the end of August, 1661, to New England. He was chosen president of the college, 1685, and filled the office until 1701, when the increase of dissatisfaction long prevailed, at his refusal to give up the pulpit in Boston and reside at Cambridge, compelled his resignation. Next year he feared the glory of New England was departing and that the college under the direction of Willard of the Old South Church should "become a nursery, not of plants of renown, but of degenerate plants, who will forsake thou holy principles of truth." etc., etc. But his talents had new scope in the intermediate time, for in the last dangerous year of Sir Edmund Andros, he was sent in disguise on board a ship, to intercede with King James, and sailed 1688, being absent from his college

duties, on political engagement, until 1692, when Sir William Phips, the Governor of his own nomination, landed with him, bringing the new charter of William and Mary. Unhappily the desire to manage state affairs ever afterward possessed him, and lessened his usefulness, beside embittering his life. He died 1723, and was buried with the greatest marks of esteem and affection. He married, 1662, Mary, sometimes spelled Maria, daughter of famous John Cotton, who died 1714: had Cotton, Harvard College, 1678, before mentioned, born 1663; Maria, 1665; Elizabeth, 1667; Nathaniel. Harvard College, 1685, baptised, 1669, whose great promise of distinguished talents was cut off 1688 at Salem; Sarah, 1671; Samuel, Harvard College 1690; Abigail, 1667; Hannah, 1680; Catharine, 1682, died soon; and Jerusha, 1684. He married second wife, 1715, Ann, daughter of Thomas Lake, widow of Rev. John Cotton of Hampton, who outlived him and died at Brookline, 1637.

MATHER, NATHANIEL, Dorchester, son of Richard, born at Toxteth, near Liverpool, Eng.; went some years after his graudation at Harvard College to England; had the living at Barnstable, 1656, by presentation of Oliver Cromwell, it is widely said, meaning, perhaps, by his recommendation for ecclesiastical patronage had ceased, ejected 1662; preached at Rotterdam; after some years was at Dublin, successor to his brother Samuel, whence he sent contributions for relief to the sufferers in Philip's war, 1676, and last in London, 1697; had served at the altar 47 years, in England, Holland, Ireland, and England again.

MATHER, RICHARD, Dorchester, son of Thomas, born 1696, of an ancient family, as his grandson Cotton in Magn., III, c. 20, assures us, at Lowton, in the parish of Winwick, Lancaster: was employed in teaching a school some years before going to the university, but at length, 1618, was entered of Brazen Nose College, Oxford, yet soon called to Toxteth, where he had taught the school, preaching his first sermon 30th November of thatyear. There most faithful he served 15 years, and was then suspended for non-conformation, and feeling the true sense of his office, resolved in expatriation. In disguise he embarked at Bristol in the James, arriving 1635, after peril in the remarkable storm Aug. 15, and two months later with wife Catharine joined church of Boston. He had married, 1634, that daughter of Edmund Holt. Esq., of Bury, in Lancaster; had Samuel, born 1626, Harvard College 1643; Timothy, Nathaniel, 1630, Harvard College 1647, before mentioned; and Joseph, who died in childhood; after coming to N. E. had Eleazer, 1637, Harvard College, 1656, and Increase, 1639, Harvard College, 1656, before mentioned. He was a man of excellent discretion, of less learning, it is probable, than his ambitious son, Increase, and less brilliancy, it is clear, than his eccentric grandson, the never-dying author of Magnalia, but in true service as minister happier than either and better than both. He was settled at D. 1636; his wife died 1655, and he married, 1656, Sarah, widow of his great friend, John Coton, and died 1669.

MATHER, SAMUEL, Dorchester, eldest son of of the first Richard, born in England, freeman 1648; after large preparation for his profession went home, preached in England, Scotland, and Ireland; settled in Dublin, was made a fellow of Trinity College; then, says family tradition, married a sister of Sir John Stevens, and died 1671.

MATHER, TIMOTHY, Dorchester, son of Richard, born in England; married Catharine, daughter of Humphrey Atherton; had Samuel, born 1651, Harvard College, 1671, before mentioned; Nathaniel, born, 1653. probably died soon, which may explain the failure of entry of birth; Richard, 1653, before mentioned; Catharine, 1656; Nathaniel, again, 1658; Joseph, 1661; and Atherton, 1663; and he died 1685, by an accident. His widow Elizabeth, whom he had married 1680, died 1710, aged 70.

REFERENCES:—Alden's Epitaphs, I, 120-8; Amer. Ancestry, I, 53; III, 79; VIII, 45; IX, 103; Andrews' New Britain, Ct., 148, 176, 203; Goodwin's Gen. Notes, 150-6; Hall's Gen. Notes, 101-3, 106; Hayward's Hist. Hancock, N. H., 745; History of Hamden, Ct., 263; Huntington's Stamford, Co. Settlers, 74; Lamb's Hist. New York City, I, 339; Marshall's Grant Ancestry, 125-8; Martin's Hist. Chester, Pa., 171; Marvin Gen. (1848), 34-6; Mather Gen. (1848), 76 p. (1851), (1890). 540 p.; Mather's Magnolia, I, 12; N. E. Hist. and Gen. Reg., V, 460; VI, 20; XLVII, 171-85; XLIX, 29-34 Phoenix's Whitney Gen., I. 759; Powers' Sangamon Co., Ill., 510-2; Savage's Gen. Dict., III, 171-5; Stiles Hist. Windsor, Ct., II, 482-92; Temple's Hist. Whately, Mass, 247; Walworth's Hyde Gen., 73, 585-7; Washington, N. H., Hist., 528.

ARMS:—Ermine, a fess embattled, gules.

CREST:—A hand erect, issuing from a cloud, holding an arrow, point downwards; all proper.

MATSON:—Thomas, Boston, 1630; gunsmith, probably came in the fleet with Withrop; feeman 1634; by wife Ann, who was sister of Abigail, the first wife of Theodore Atkinson; had Thomas, baptized 1633; John, 1636; removed to Braintree, having been disarmed as one of the recusant friends of Wheelwright, in 1637; had there Joshua, 1640; and Abigail, perhaps eldest of all; was a military officer after the religious heats had assuaged; died after 1666.

REFERENCES:—Am. Ancestry, V, 30; Brown's W. Simsbury, Ct., Settlers, 90; Buck's Hist. Montgomery Co., Pa., 26; Collin's Hillsdale, N. Y., 94; Savage's Gen. Dict., III, 175; Walworth's Hyde Gen., 164

MATTHEWS:—Francis, Portsmouth 1631. of the men sent over by Mason, was of Exeter 1639 to 46, removed to Dover. probably died 1647. when perhaps, his widow Thomasine (with children Benjamin, Walter, and Martha, who married first a Snell, and next a Browne), was on the estate he purchased, 1640. of William Beard. Descendants who write the name Mathes are numerous.

MATTHEWS, HUGH. Newbury, married, 1683. Mary Emerson; had John, born 1688; Judith, 1689; Joanna, 1690; Hugh, 1691, died soon; and Hugh, again, 1696.

MATTHEWS, JAMES, Charlestown 1634, probably removed before 1634 to Yarmouth, where he had Samuel, born 1647; Sarah, 1649; Esther, 1651; probably others; and was representative 1664.

MATTHEWS, JOHN. Roxbury; had Gershon, born 1641; and Elizabeth, 1643. He was freeman, 1642, when the Col. record spells it Mathis.

MATTHEWS, JOHN, probably removed to Springfield; married, 1644, Pentecost Bond; had two children. who died. one Sarah, buried 1650, and the wife was killed by the Indians 1675. He married second wife, and had son who died young, and he died 1684.

MATTHEWS, JOHN, Boston 1645, a tailor.

MATTHEWS, JOHN. Charlestown, married, 1659, Margaret Hunt, and he died son after.

MATTHEWS, JOHN, Marlborough, Barry thinks, in 1681; married Mary, daughter of Jonathan Johnson;

had Lydia, born 1691, died at 15 years; Ruth, 1693; John, 1695; and Daniel, 1697. His wife died 1710, and he married, 1713, Sarah Garfield.

MATTHEWS, MARMADUKE, Malden, was son of Matthew of Swansea. in Glamorgaush. and in his 18th year Matric., 1624, at All Souls. Oxford; came from Boston in a ship from Barnstable, 1638, and his wife Catharine joined church early next year. He preached at Yarmouth, 1639 to 43, for in August of this latter year his wife was dismissed from Boston Church to that of Yarmouth; was admitted freeman of Plymouth Colony 1641; had Manasseh, baptised 1641, by Lathrop, at Barnstable, but came to Hull about 1644; some years later taught at Malden, where his troubles were copious, detailed by Frothingham, in Hist. of Charlestown; he had there been ordained, but against the good will of the heavens; he was forced to depart; was then employed at Lynn and other places; finally went home, and Calamy says he died at his native place about 1683.

MATTHEWS, MORDECAI. Harvard College 1655, presumed to have been son of preceding, and, as no more is heard of him, probably he went to England.

MATTHEWS, ROGER, Dorchester; had grant of land 1635, but soon removed.

MATTHEWS, SAMUEL, Jamaica, L. I., 1656; Thompson.

REFERENCES:—Amer. Ancestry, VI. 126, 138; VII, 23; Barry's Hist. Warrington, Mass., 321; Clement's Neton, N. J., Settlers; Cogswell's Hist. Henniken, N.H., 644; Eaton's Hist. Warren. Me., 584; Eaton's Hist. Thomaston, Me., II, 326; Freeman's Cape Cod, II, 180-2, 214-6, 225; Gilmer's Georgions, 73; Hayward's Hist. Hancock, N. H., 746-56; Herrick's Hist. Gardner, Mass., 367; Hudson's Hist. Marlborough, Mass., 412; Lapham's Hist. Paris, Me., 672; Meade's Old Farms of Va.; N. E. Hist. Gen. Reg., VII, 257; XXXIX, 73; Peyton's Hist. Augusta Co., Va., 317; Powers' Hist. Sangamon Co., Ill., 481-3; Reade's Hist. of Swanzey. N. H., 403; Savage's 'Gen. Reg., III, 176; Stanton Gen., 266; Stearn's Hist. Ashburnham. Mass, 809; Temple's Hist. N. Brookfield, Mass., 681; Timlow's Hist. Southington, Ct., 167-9.

MATTHEWSON:—James, is by Farmer put into the list of earliest settlers of Rhode Island, but Savage finds nothing to add. except that at Providence he took the engagement if alleged to Charles II. in May, 1666, and probably had Ruth. who married, 1686, Benjamin Whipple.

MATTHEWSON, JOSEPH. who married, 1715, Sarah, daughter of the second Valentine Whitman, is called son of Daniel, of whom naught seems to be known.

MATTOCKS:—David. Braintree. freeman 1650; had wife Sarah, and daughter Elizabeth, who was decrepid. one son and daughter at Roxbury before 1654; he died 1655. The widow married, 1656. Thomas Rawlins of Boston.

MATTOCKS, JAMES, Boston, a cooper; came from Bristol, perhaps before 1635 (at least his daughter Alice was then wife of Nathaniel Bishop) ; joined the church 1639, and was made freeman same year. Perhaps all his children were born in England. In his will, made 1667, he names son Samuel, and daughters Alice, wife of John Lewis, who had been widow of Nathaniel Bishop, and Mary, wife of Samuel Brown, married, 1661.

MATTOCKS, RICHARD, New Haven, married, 1669, Grace Todd, but it is not certain that he was resident long. He had deserted his wife before 1686, when her father died.

REFERENCES:—Savage's Gen. Dict.. III. 177; Wheeler's N. Car. II. 158.

MATTOON:—Hubertus, or Herbert. Kittery 1652; when he submitted to jurisdiction of Massachusetss; probably removed to Saco before 1683. Folsom, 174.

MATTOON, PHILIP, a soldier from the east part of the Colony, in the spring of 1676; was in Turner's company and took part in the Falls fight, then settled at Springfield; married Sarah, daughter of John Hawkes of Hadley; had Margaret, born 1678; Philip, 1680; John, 1682; Isaac, 1684; Sarah, 1687; removed to Deerfield; there had Eleazer, 1689; Gershom, 1690; Nathaniel, 1693; Ebenezer. 1695; and Mary, posthum. 1697. He died 1696, and his widow married Daniel Belden. as third wife, and died 1751, in 95th year. Of his son Philip, with wife Rebecca. daughter of Godfrey Nims. and only child were killed at the second destruction of Deerfield by the Indians and French, 1704; John settled at Wallingford: Isaac and Nathaniel at Northfield; Eleazer at Amherst, but was first at Northfield; and Gershom at Lebanon; Ebenezer died at 21 years.

MATTOON, RICHARD or ROBERT, Exeter, probably son of Herbertus; swore fidelity 1657; married Jane, daughter of Edward Hilton, Jr.; was killed by the Indians 1706, with his son Hubertus. Belknap, I, 172.

REFERENCES:—Amer. Ancestry, II, 79; Davis' Hist. Wallingford, Ct., 847; Judd's Hist. Hadley, Mass., 535; Savage's Gen. Dict.. III, 177; Temple's Hist. Northfield, Mass., 491-5.

MAUDE:—Daniel, came in the James with Richard Mather; was bred at Emanuel, Cambridge, where he had his A.B. 1606, and his A.M. 1610; kept the school for some years, joined the church 1635. freeman next year, yet without prefix of respect; for second wife married Mary Bonner, a widow with four children; went to Dover; there was first minister in settlement found, 1642, to his death in 1655. He left no children by either of his wives.

MAUDSLEY:—Henry. Braintree; came in the Hopewell, Capt. Babb, in the autumn of 1635, aged 24; had Mary, born 1638 Samuel, 1641; and, perhaps. others; artillery company. 1643; freeman 1646; name of wife unknown, also any other items. Dr. Harris claims him of Dorchester. 1630. but without sufficient warrant. yet he had grant of a house lot 1637.

MAUDSLEY, JOHN. Dorchester, freeman 1639; by wife Elizabeth had Joseph, born 1638. as printed in Gen. Reg., V, 244, though it is thought son called Joseph may have been John; but whether any more, and when that wife died, is unknown; died 1661: by wife Cicely's will are named sons John and Thomas, and daughter Elizabeth. This Cicely, who may seem to be same as wife Elizabeth, died 1661. The name was spelled with many variations as Mawdesly, Modesly. Madesly, but long has been fixed as Moseley, yet liable to be much mistaken. as in Geneal. Reg., VI, 268. printed Moreley.

MAULE, or MAULD:—Thomas, Salem 1669, a shopkeeper, from England; came, he says in his book. via Barbadoes; was whipped for ill words, being a Quaker, in May of that year; married. 1670. Naomi Lindsay; perhaps as second wife: had Mary. daughter of John Keyser of the same, and in 1695 punished again. for "Truth held forth," etc Still he showed great fondness for Salem, and in his will, about 1723, he left a bequest to its use. of which part was to be applied to

support the writing-school. He had son John. and third wife Mary, who survived.

MAURY:—See MOREY.

MAVERICK:—Antipas, Isle of Shoals 1647; attended before commissioners of Massachusetts and submitted to her jurisdiction 1652; was of the grand jury of the Colony 1654; was dead before 1682, when administration of his estate was granted to Edward Gilman and Stephen Paul, in behalf of their wives. His daughter Abigail married Edward Gilman.

MAVERICK, ELIAS. Charlestown 1632; was of the church in February of next year, and freeman; lived at Winnesemet, then part of Boston, now Chelsea: married Ann, daughter of a widow Elizabeth Harris, who became the wife of Deacon William Stetson: had John, born 1636; Abigail, 1637; Elizabeth, 1639, died young probably: Sarah, 1641. died young perhaps; Elias, 1644; Peter; Mary; Ruth; Paul, 1657; and Rebecca, 1660; was of artillery company, 1654; died about 1684. He had perhaps other children.

MAVERICK, JOHN. Dorchester; came in the Mary and John. 1630. from Plymouth. with colleague Warham, desired to be admitted freeman, and is first in list of those who took the oath, 1631; died 1636, while preparing to accompany his friends, who removed to Windsor—though perhaps, say Blake's Ann., he would have continued with Mather. He was in 60th year. and accounts of his education or earlier days is not found.

MAVERICK, JOHN, Boston, possibly son of preceding, as Farmer thought, but Savage thinks same very improbable; by wife Jane had John. baptised with his sister Jane. as his mother. 1653; and Dorothy, 1655. Perhaps his wife died soon after, as well as son John, and by second wife Rebecca he had John. again, 1662.

MAVERICK, MOSES. Salem. perhaps brother of the first Elias; freeman 1634. though Felt inscribes his name with wife in the list of church members under 1637. and so we must believe he had been accepted in another town; had Rebecca, baptised 1639; Mary. 1641, died at 15 years; Abigail. 1655; Elizabeth, 1646. died soon. Samuel. 1647; Elizabeth. again. 1659. who married. 1665. Nathaniel Grafton; Remember, 1652; Mary, again. 1657; and a son whose name is not in the record, 1663; besides Sarah, who is not found in record. He lived on Marblehead side; was one of the founders of the church, 1684. and died 1686. aged 76. which date, Farmer says. Dana mistook. His wife Remember, daughter of famous Isaac Allerton (but in Gen. Reg., VIII. 270. she is called Sarah, and possibly he had both, though it seems not probable). died after 1652, and he married. 1656. Eunice, widow of Thomas Roberts. His daughter Rebecca married. 1658. John Hawkes of Lynn, and died soon after birth of son Moses next year. His will. probably 1686, names wife and Moses, the only surviving child of his deceased daughter Rebecca; four children of his deceased daughter Abigail. viz.: Samuel Ward, Abigail Hinds. Mary Dollabar, and Martha Ward; and four living daughters, viz.: Elizabeth Skinner, Remember Woodman, Mary, wife of Archibald Ferguson; and Sarah, wife of John Norman.

MAVERICK, SAMUEL, Boston: found here in Noddles Isl. by the Mass. Company in 1630, having built a little fort with four small pieces of artillery, so that we may be sure that he was here in 1629, perhaps same in 1628, too late for liability to expense of the expedition of Endicott against Morton. He desired administration 1630, into the company, but did not take the freeman's oath until 1632. Against all improbability he is called son of Rev. John by a writer of more animation than exactness, in Hist. of E. Boston; and even the careful Hist. of Dorchester, 404, confidently says the same. For his habit of hospitality, he was required in the spring of 1635, to change his residence and move to the peninsula, but that tyranny was not enforced, and in the autumn of same year he went to Virginia to buy corn; was absent almost a year. He as one of the King's commissioners, 1665, and in a deponent 1665 swore he was 63 years old. Of his family only wife Amias, daughter Mary. and sons Nathaniel and Samuel are known. Nathaniel, who was a merchant in a convey· nce by his father and mother, 1650, of the island to some creditors is styled heir of Noddles Island, and he joined in the security. But we never hear more of him. Mary married, 1656, John Palsgrave, and next, 1660, Francis Hooke. She, in a petition to Andros, a few weeks before his overthrow, tells a strange story about her elder brother defrauding his father of the title to Noddle's Island, which had above 17 years been owned by Col. Samuel Shrimpton, under sale from Sir Thomas Temple. It may be, that as Shrimpton was opposed to Sir Edmund A., though one of his council, that this was a contrivance to get rid of him. See Geneal. Reg., VIII, 334.

REFERENCES:—Maverick Gen. (1894), 8p.: N. E. Hist. and Gen. Reg., XLVIII, 207-9; Savage's Gen. Dict., III, 179-82; Sumner's Hist. of E. Boston, 161-77; Titcomb's N. E. People, 244-55; Wyman's Charlestown, Mass., Gens., 661.

MAWER:—Moses, a Huguenot, who escaped from France soon after 1685, and as Potter in his history tells sat down in that part now E. Greenwich, probably bringing wife and children, of whom two are named. Peter and Mary. Mary married in New York.

MAWER, PETER, Providence, son of the preceding; married Mary, daughter of the second Pardon Tillinghast; had, as we learn from the will of their grandfather without any indication of order. Sarah, Amey, Lydia, Mary, John. born. 1718, and Peter. By a second wife, whose name Potter has not given, he says there were three, perhaps named Elizabeth. Mercy and Pardon, but the want of precision is unavoidable. The name is one of the perversions suffered in change of their alleg. since in France it was spelled "Le Moine."

REFERENCES:—Savage's Gen. Dic., III, 182; R. I. Hist. Coll., III, 3, 4.

MAXCY:—Alexander, a soldier in Gallup's company for the sad expedition 1690, of Phips against Quebec.

REFERENCES:—Daggett's Attleborough, 92; Eaton's Annals, Warren, Me., 585; Powers' Hist. Sangamon Co., Ill. 484; Sibley's Hist. Union, Me., 469.

MAXFIELD:—Clement, Dorchester 1658; came with his wife from Taunton. but they had years before been members of Dorchester church: had married Mary Denman, probably daughter of John, constable, 1664; had Samuel, and perhaps John: died 1692. and his widow died 1707, aged 86.

MAXFIELD. JOHN. Salisbury 1652; was of Gloucester 1679; but this may be the Mayfield of Lynn in Felt's list Geneal. Reg., V, 339, who married Rebecca Armitage. See that.

MAXFIELD, JOHN, Salisbury; by wife Elizabeth had John, born 1680; Timothy, 1682; Mary, 1685; Margery, 1686; Nathaniel, 1689; Joseph, 1692; Elizabeth, 1695; and William, 1699; and died suddenly 1703.

MAXFIELD, SAMUEL, Dorchester; married Mary.

daughter of Thomas Davenport; had John; Ebenezer, born 1675; Mary, and Mehitable. His widow Mary died 1707.

MAXSON, or MAGGSON:—John, Westerly, perhaps son of Richard; was representative 1685; may have been father of a minister who served the the Seventh Day Baptist congregation (as mentioned by Collender), at Westerly, 1738, and died 1720, aged 82. Descendants have been numerous. He married Mary Mosher; had John, born 1666; Joseph. 1672; Dorothy; Jonathan; Hannah; and Mary. His wife died 1718, aged 77.

MAXSON, RICHARD, Newport 1638, of whom no is known but that he was a blacksmith.

REFERENCES:—Austin's R. I. Dict., 342; Cope Family of Pa., 80, 179; Greene Gen.

MAXWELL:—James, Boston 1684. a member of the Scott's Chart. Society; was doorkeeper for the Gen. Court 1693. The name may be same as Maxfield.

MAXWELL, JOHN, the freeman of 1669; may have then been of Andover.

REFERENCES:—Cunnabell Gen., 51; Littell's Passaic Valley Gens., 279-81; Maine Hist. and Gen. Rec., IV, 263-6; Phoenix Gen., 17; Powers' Hist. Sangamon Co., Ills., 481-3; Temple's Hist. Palmer, Mass., 515.

MAY:—George, Boston; married 1656, Elizabeth, daughter of William Franklin; as an iron-manger, artillery company. 1661; freeman 1665.

MAY, JOHN, Roxbury, written Mayes and Mays in the early record of town and church, but Maies in Col. record; came as early as 1640 or before, with wife and probably children John and Samuel; freeman 1641; died 1670. aged 80. His nuncup. will made four days before, names sons John and Samuel; his widow Sarah died next year. This was not that wife he brought from England for in record of church, Eliot had written under 18th June, 1651: "Sis. Mayes died a very gracious and savory Christian." Nor was she that Sarah recorded by dismissal from Dorchester church as the same hand notes "an aged woman joined here 29th April, 1660." Farmer was informed that he was of Mayfield Co., Sussex.

MAY, JONATHAN, Hingham; married, 1686, Sarah, daughter of John Langley of the same; had Mary, born 1687, and no more. He died of smallpox. 1690; a soldier in the lamentable expedition of Phips against Quebec.

MAY, THOMAS, Malden. one of Moseley's company in 1675 for Narragansett campaign.

REFERENCES:—Amer. Ancestry, III, 88; Barrus' Hist. Goshen, Mass., 153-5; Child Gen., 418-21; May's Journey to Ohio in 1718, 7-11; Davis' Landmarks of Plymouth. 184; Draper's Hist. of Spencer. Mass., 232; Futhey's Hist. of Chester Co., Pa., 654; Hayward's Hist. Gilsum, N. H., 361; Hayward's Hist. Hancock, N. H., 756-8; May Gen. (1878), 210 pp.; Morris and Flint Gen., 22; Norton's Hist. Fitzwilliam, N. H., 633; Pierce Gen. (1894); Savage's Gen. Dict., III, 183; Slaughter's Hist. Ashburnham, Mass, 800; Stiles' Hist. of Windsor, Ct., II, 492; Temple's Hist. N. Brookfield, Mass., 682; Walker Gen., 25; Washington, N. H., Hist., 529.

MAYBEE:—Henry, Newtown, L. I., 1656. Thompson.

MAYBEE, NICHOLAS, Windsor; was buried 1667, with very small estate, and neither wife nor children.

MAYER:—Henry, Boston, butcher; by wife Alice had Joseph, born, 1686; and by wife Hannah had Patience, 1698.

MAYER, ROBERT, Boston; by wife Hannah had Hannah, born 1683.

MAYER, THOMAS, Hingham 1638; came from Co. Norfolk that year in the Diligent.

REFERENCE:—Mayer Family (1878), 179 p.

MAYFIELD:—John, Lynn; married Rebecca, daughter of Godfrey Armitage of the same; had Benoni, born 1666.

MAYHEW:—John, Chilmark, son of the second Thomas; labored all his short life in teaching the Indians chiefly in the vineyard; died 1689, in 37th year, leaving son Experience to carry on work on a large scale, born 1674, died 1758, who married. 1695, at Barnstable, Thankful, daughter of Gov. Hinckley, and father if an illustrious line, Joseph, Harvard College 1730; Nathan, Harvard College, 1731; Zachariah, a missionary to the Indians, who died 1806, in 89th year; and Jonathan, Harvard College 1744, one of the most distinguished divines of our country, prematurely taken from his service, in 44th year, by dying at Boston, 1766.

MAYHEW, JOHN, New London, mariner; was from Devonshire; married, 1676, Joanna, daughter of Jeffrey Christophers; had John, born 1677; Wait, 1680; Elizabeth, 1683; Joanna; Mary; and Patience; and died 1696. His son John served as one of the pilots for the fleet of Sir Hovenden Walker, in the abortive expedition, 1711, against Quebec, and was sent to England to give evidence of the cause of its failure, should any inquiry ever be instituted. See Hutch., II, 197.

MAYHEW, THOMAS, Watertown, born early in 1591; came in the Griffin 1633, if we might so infer from the fact of his taking the oath as freeman 1634, when Gov. Haynes and Gov. Brenton, besides Cotton, Hooker, and Stone, passengers in that ship, were admitted. But that inference would be wrong, for in Col. Rec., I, 95, is a report signed by him and two other gentlemen for setting out the bounds between Watertown and the new town, 1632, and in July, 1633, he was appointed admor. of Ralph Glover, while Cotton and fellow passengers did not arrive before September next, so that he must have been here in 1631, and he served as a merchant at Southampton, Eng., as Bond relates, and here as representative 1636-44 etc. 42; was active in trade, first at Medford, afterward at Watertown, but was induced to remove to the Vineyard about 1647, where he was propr.'s gov. and preacher to the Indians above 33 years; died 1681, almost 90 years old. It is indistinct pronounced by tradition that first wife, who died in England, had been Martha Parkhurst, and second was probably brought with him. Grace, widow of Thomas Paine of London, and by her he had Hannah, born 1635; Bethia, 1636; and Mary, 1640. It is not known that he had any son but Thomas.

REFERENCES:—Ballou's Milford, Mass. 894-7; Barry's Hist. Framingham, Mass., 322; Caulkins' Hist. New London, Ct., 336; Dennysville, Me., Centen. 110; Kellog's White Gen., 67; Savage's Gen. Dict., III, 184.

MAYNARD:—John, Duxbury, 1643.

MAYNARD, JOHN, Sudbury 1640, an original propr. freeman 1644; was one of the petitioners for grant of Marlborough in 1656, and died 1672. He had two wives, if not more; by first was born John, date unknown; and perhaps others; he married, says Barry, 1646, Mary Axdell, or Axtel; had Zechary, born 1647; Elizabeth. 1649; Lydia; Hannah 1653; and Mary, 1656. Hannah died probably young, as she is not mentioned in his will of 1672, in which he calls John eldest son, but makes wife, with Zechary, executors; calls Elizabeth

wife of Joseph Moore; and the youngest daughter unmarried, but she married, 1674. Daniel Hudson of Lancaster, and died 1677. Perhaps the first wife was daughter of Comfort Starr, and second may have been married a dozen years later than Barry tells.

MAYNARD, JOHN, Dorchester or Boston 1648, a carpenter; freeman 1649, married widow Eliz. Pell (that had before been widow of Nath. Heaton), and died 1658, leaving her once more a widow.

MAYNARD, WILLIAM, New London; came from Hampsh., Eng.; married, 1678, Lydia, daughter of John Richards; had William, born 1680; and three more children, of which three were under age in 1751, when he died. This name is spelled with many variations.

REFERENCES:—Aldrich's Walpole, 325; Amer. Ancestry. IX, 101, 224; Ballou's Hist. of Milford, Mass., 897; Barry's Hist. of Framingham, Mass., 322-5; Caulkins' Hist. New London, Ct., 354; Goode Gen., 209; Hayward's Hist. Gilsum, N. H., 362-4; Hayward's Hist. Hancock, N. H., 758; Hudson's Hist. Marlborough, Mass., 413-6; Humphrey's Gen., 425; Norton's Hist. Fitzwilliam, N. H., 633; Rice Gen.; Savage's Dict., III, 185; Stearn's Hist. Ashburnham, Mass., 810-4; Ward's Hist. Shrewsbury, Mass., 358-65.

MAYNE, or MAYEN:—See Maine.

MAYO:—John, Barnstable, min. colleag. with Lothrop; came in 1638, probably as he was sworn freeman 1640, and ordained soon after; brought from England children Hannah, Samuel, John, Nathaniel, and, perhaps, Eliz., who may, however, have been born here; removed to East ham 1646, thence, discouraged at Eastham, drawn to Boston, where he was inst. 1655, min. of the sec. or N. church, and Michael Powell ordained ruling Elder, the same day; dismissed 1673, in advanced age, after having more than 20 years had joint service with Increase Mather, he went to Barnstable, there, and at Eastham and Yarmouth lived the short resid. of his days with one or another church, and died at Yarmouth 1676, leaving widow Thomasine, who died 1682, but we know not whether she had been his first wife in England. The agreement, 1676, for settlement of the small estate between widow, children and grandchildren is on record.

MAYO, JOHN, Roxbury, came in 1633; a young child brought by Robert Gamblin, Jr., as son of his wife by former husband; married, -654, Hannah, daughter of John Graves; had Hannah, born 1657, died soon; John, 1659; Hannah, again, 1661; Rebecca, 1614, died at 21 years; Joseph, 1667; Mehitable, 1669; Thomas, 1670; Benj., 1672, died soon after, as died also Thomas, the predecessor; Thomas, again, 1673; yet the town record makes this last 1676. He died 1688.

REFERENCES:—Amer. Ancestry, V. 28; VI, 47; Davis Gen., 14, 58; Davis' Landmark, Plymouth, Mass., 185; Freeman's Cape Cod, II, 358-89, 757; Meade's Old Farms of Va.; Merrill's Hist. of Acworth, N. H., 242; Paige's Hist. Hardwick, Mass., 420; Pratt's Hist. Eastham, Mass., 23; Preble Gen., 259; Rich's Hist. of Truro, Mass., 543; Savage's Gen. Dict., III, 186-9; Swift's Barntable Families, II, 220-2.

MAYSANT:—William, Branford 1646 and 8; then owned lands; probably removed, for no more is known.

McDONALD:—John, Boston 1657.

REFERENCES:—Eaton's Thomaston, 317; Pearson's Schenectady, N. Y., Settlers, 108; Pierce's Hist. Gorham, Me., 189; Powers' Hist. Sangamon Co. Ills., 498; Richmond, Va., Standard, IV. 3; Roome Gen., 290.

McDOUGALL:—Alister, Boston 1658.
REFERENCE:—Lindsay Gen.

McEWEN, or McKUNE, McCUNE, or ME-
CUNE:—Robert, Stratford 1686, a Scotchman, came
in the Henry and Francis, a ship of 350 tons, chartered
by the laird of Pitlochie, os Whitehead, in Hist. of Perth
Amboy tells, or in the Caledonia (by another rep.);
a man-of-war of 50 guns, to transport covenanters
releas. from the tallbooths of Edinburgh, Glasgow and
Sterling, on condition of transportation to the
colonies. No little of historic interest attaches to this
colony that landed their precious freight at Perth
Amboy. McEwen himself, which by tradition is derived
from Dumfries, explains: "In June 18, 1679, I was in
an engagement in Scotland, at Bothwell brigg, then of
the age of 18 years. The 5th of September, 1685, we set
sail to come to America, and landed at Amboy, 18th
December, and 18th February following I came to Stratford.". Here he was a tailor, made leather breeches for
the record says: John as born 1697; and Eliz., whom
he calls Betty, 1699. Other children were Robert, 1702;
Sarah, 1704; Timothy, 1707; and Gershom, 1711; and
the father died 1740.
REFERENCES:—Boyd's Winchester, 56-8; Orcutt's
Hist. Stratford, Ct., 1244-6; Savage's Gen. ict., III, 189.

MEACHAM:—Isaac, son probably of Jeremiah
the first, lived many years at Salem; married, 1669,
widow Deborah Perkins: had Deborah 1670, died next
year; Isaac, 1672; Jeremiah, 1674; Israel, 1676, who
both died without children; Ebenezer, 1678; Ichabad,
men, stays and mantys for women; and he says he married, 1695, Sarah Wilcoxson, daughter of Timothy, as
1679; Deborah, again, 1681; and John, 1682. He removed next year from Salem, and at E. had Mary,
1684; Joseph, 1686. Harvard College 1710, the first
minister of Coventry, 1713; and Benjamin, 1687; and
died 1692.

MEACHAM, JEREMIAH, Salem 1660, a fuller: married Deborah, daughter of John Brown of Watertown;
had probably Isaac, and Jeremiah, besides daughters
Rhoda, who married a West and died before her father,
leaving Samuel; Sarah, who married, 1668, William
Gill; Bethia, who married, 1672, George Haeker; and
perhaps Rebecca, who married, 1675, John Macarty. He
died 1695, aged 81.

MEACHAM, JOHN, Salem: married, 1697, Mary,
daughter of William Cash.
REFERENCES:—Adams's Fairhaven, Vt.; Austin's
Allied Families, 173; Benton's Hist. Guildhall, Vt., 257;
Hinman's Conn. Settlers, 1st ed., 171; Humphrey's Gen.,
345; Odiorne Gen.; Powers' Hist. Sangamon Co., Ills.,
512-4; Savage's Gen. Dict., III, 190; Stiles' Hist. Windsor, Ct., 492.

MEADE, MEADES, or MEDE:—David, Cambridge Village, perhaps son of Gabriel; married at
Watertown, 1675, Hannah Warren, perhaps daughter of
David; had Hannah, born 1676; and David, 1678; removed to Billerica: freeman 1683; removed to Woburn;
there had John, 1685; Sarah, 1688; Susanna, 1690; and,
perhaps, removed again. Hannah married, 1701, Ebenezer Locke.

MEADE, GABRIEL, Dorchester: freeman 1638; died
1666 in 79th year; his will, probated 1667, names wife
Johanna, who probably was a second wife; son David,
and four daughters—Lydia, Experience, Sarah, and Patience.

MEADE, ISRAEL, Woburn, probably son of the preceding: married, 1669, Mary, daughter of widow Mary
Hall; had Margaret, born 1676; Mary, 1682; Ruth,
1684; Ebenezer, 1686; and, perhaps, some earlier. Margaret married Joseph Locke as second wife.

MEADE, JAMES, Wrentham: by wife Judith had
Grace, born 1692, and James, 1694; and his wife died
on same day.

MEADE, JOHN, Greenwich, probably son of Joseph;
propound. for freeman 1670.

MEADE, JOSEPH, Stamford 1657; removed to Greenwich; was freeman 1662, rep. 1669.

MEADE, NICHOLAS, Charlestown 1680; had by wife
Eliz., who joined church 1681; Susanna, baptised 1681;
Eliz., 1681; and, perhaps, removed.

MEADE, RICHARD, Roxbury 1663; freeman 1665;
had Richard, a mariner, who died before 1679, when the
father took admin. on the estate. The father married,
1678, Mary, a second wife, and died 1689.

MEADE, WILLIAM, Gloucester 1641; one of the
selectmen 1647; removed to New London before 1653,
when he was represent., but never after, though lived
1669.

MEADE, WILLIAM, Roxbury, brother of Richard;
had wife Rebecca, and died 1683, and his widow 8 days
afterward.
REFERENCES:—Amer. Ancestry, IX, 105; Campbell's Hist. Virginia, 690; Goode Gen., 477; Meade's
Old Families of Va., I, 291-8; N. E. Hist. and Gen.
Reg., XXXVIII, 107; Page Gen., 77; Robertson's Pocahontas' Descendants; Savage's Gen. Dict., III, 190.

MEADER:—John, Dover, 1653; by wife Abigail
had Eliz., born 1665; John; Sarah, 1669; and Nathaniel,
1617, who was killed by the Indians 1704, and, perhaps,
Nicholas. Sarah married, 1692, Edward Wakeham.
Belknap I, 168; and Niles, in 3 Mass. Hist. Coll, VI, 254.
REFERENCES:—Amer. Ancestry, VI, 20; Austin's
Allied Families, 174; Hatch's Hist. Industry, Me., 734-
8; Wentworth Gen., I, 162.

MEADOWS:—Philip, Roxbury; married, 1641,
Eliz., daughter of Stephen Iggulden or Iggleden; had
Hannah, 1643. Perhaps he removed, for no more is
found of him in the record.

MEAKINS, or MEEKINS:—John, Hartford; is
in the list of freemen 1669; died 1706, leaving widow
Mary, daughters Mary Belden, Sarah Spencer, besides
Rebecca, and Hannah, unmarried, when his will of 1702
was made, and three sons—John, Joseph, and Samuel.
Of these John was a lieutenant, died 1739, aged 76;
Samuel was a lieutenant, died 1733, in 60th year. The
widow, who may have been second wife, was daughter
of John Biddle, and she died 1725, in 78th year.

MEAKINS, THOMAS, Boston 1633; came probably
in the Griffin; adm. with wife Catharine of Boston
church, then called "servant to our brother Edmund
Quincy;" freeman 1637; probably died in few years,
and his widow went to live at Roxbury with son
Thomas; there died "an aged woman," as Elliott writes,
"mother of brother Meakins," Feb. 3, 1651.

MEANE, or MEANS:—John Meane, Cambridge;
by wife Ann; had John, born 1638, who died next year;
Sarah, 1640; Mary, 1644; John, again, posthumous; the
father died 1646; the widow married John Hastings outlived him, and died 1667.
REFERENCES:—Paige's Cambridge, Mass., 609; Am.
Ancestry, VII, 279; Carliss' No. Yarmouth, Me.; Hayward's Hist. Hancock, N. H., 761; Livermore's Hist.
Wilton, N. H., 449; North's Hist. Augusta, Me., 902.

MEARS:—John, Boston; by wife Lydia had John,
born 1678

MEARS, ROBERT, Boston, tailor; came in the Abigail
1635, from London, aged 43, with wife Eliz., 30;
Samuel, who probably died soon; and John, 3 months,
and his wife Eliz. joined church 1636; had Stephen,
1636 or 7; Samuel, 1641; and James, 1654.
REFERENCES:—Joslin's Hist. Poultney, Vt., 311;
Mears Gen. (1873), 31 pp.; Savage's Gen. Dict., III,
192; Secomb's Hist. Amherst, N. H., 689; Smith's Hist.
Petersborough, N. H., 143; Stiles' Hist. Windsor, Ct.,
II, 492.

MEASURE, or MASEUR:—William, New Lon-
don 1664; married that year, Alice, widow of John
Tinker; removed to Lynn before 1671; was represent.
1676; died 1688, and admin. of his estate was given
same year to Alice. his widow, by Sir E. Andros.

MECOCK, MEACOCK, MAYCOCK, or ME-
COKE:—Peter, Newton, L. I., 1656. His widow Mary
married Thomas Case of Fairfield before 1661.

MECOCK, THOMAS, Milford 1656 removed to Guilford 1667; was a propr. 1685.

MEDBURY:—John, Swansey; by wife Sarah had
Benjamin, born 1681 or 3.

MEECH:—John, Charlestown, record says; was
there 1629, but no more is ever heard. Young's Chron.,
375.
REFERENCE:—Hemenway's Clarke Papers.

MEEK:—Richard. Marblehead, 1668.

MEEKER, MECAR, or MEAKER:—Robert, New
Haven; married, 1651, Susan Tuberfield; removed to
Fairfield before 1670.

MEEKER, WILLIAM, New Haven 1657; sued Thomas
Mulliner that year for slander in bewitching his pigs.
REFERENCES:—Hatfield's Elizabeth, N. J., 81; Lit-
tell's Passaic Valley Gen., 282-4; Todd's Hist, Redding,
Ct., 207.

MEGAPOLENSIS:—John, son of a minister of
the same name; came in the summer of 1642, aged 39,
with wife, 42, to New York. from Holland, and was
first employed by the patroon. Van Rensselaer, up the
river, but soon afterward is found at the city, and lastly
on Long Island. While at Albany, he wrote, 1655, his
account of the Marquas or Mohawks. He had Helle-
gord, Dirck, Jan, and Samuel, of the ages, respectively,
14, 12, 10 and 8, it is supposed at time of arrival.
Samuel was sent to Harvard College, 1657; studied
three years; thence to Leyden Univ., where he was
admitted M. D.; was licensed as minister. came back to
New Amsterdam, and was the dominie, yet of such good
capacity for worldly affairs, that Gov. Stuyvesant made
him one of the Commissioners for adjusting the terms
of surrender of that Province, 1665, to the English.

MEIGS:—John, Weymouth. son of Vincent. born
in England; had John, born 1642, removed probably to
Rehoboth 1643, next to New Haven. about 1647; not
long afterward, about 1654, to Guilford, thence, last,
about 1662. to Killingworth, where both he and son
John are in the list of freemen 1669. Died 1672. He
had only one son, four daughters—Mary, wife of
William Stevens: Concurrence, wife of Henry Crane;
Trial, wife of Richard Hibbell, who had died before her
father. He was a tanner; had large estate and some
books, of which one was a Latin and Greek Dict.

MEIGS, VINCENT, New Haven 1646, probably carried thither by son John above mentioned, he being an
old man, having only two children known to us; removed to Guilford, and again removed; died at what
is now Killingworth, Dec., 1658.

REFERENCES:—Amer .Ancestry, IV, 50; VII, 83;
IX, 102; Andrew's Hist. New Britain. Ct., 381; Coth-
ren's Hist. Woodbury, Ct., II, 1516; Holton's Winslow
Mem., I, 402; Hubbard's Hist. Stamstead Co., Canada,
146; N. E. Hist. Gen. Reg., IV, 91; Savage's Gen. Dict.,
III, 193; Scranton Gen., 28; Wilcoxson. Gen.

MELBY:—Nathaniel, Hull; freeman 1680; seems
to Savage a wrong name, he never having heard of it
in N. E.

MELCHER:—Edward, Portsmouth 1684; died
1695.
REFERENCES:—Dow's Hampton, N. H., 857;
Wheeler's Brunswick, Me., 843.

MELLEN, MELIN, MELLING, or other variations:—Isaac, New Haven 1657; removed soon after
1665, probably to Virginia.

MELLEN, JACOB, New Haven, brother of Isaac. See
Melyen.

MELLEN, RICHARD, Weymouth; freeman 1639; removed to Charlestown; had James, 1642. He had, also
at Weymouth, if the date be right, Sarah, 1643; probably Mary, and perhaps others. Of no family in the land
is the investigation more difficult. the spelling more
various, the dates more perperse, the deficiecies more
numerous.

MELLEN, SAMUEL, Fairfield; died before 1659, and
John Ufford, of Medford; had admin. It may be that
this gentleman was Dutch, from Monhadoes, now New
York.

MELLEN, SIMON, Boston, on Winnisemet side, perhaps
son of Richard; by wife Mary had Simon, born 1665;
removed to Malden; had Thomas, 1668; Richard, 1672;
Mary; James. about 1682; and John. at Watertown,
1686; removed to Sherborn, and died 1694. From him,
through Thomas, descended Prentiss. Harvard College,
1784, distinguished as first chief justice of Maine.
REFERENCES:—Allen's Worcester, 78; Amer. Ancestry, II, 79; Ballou's Hist. Milford. Mass., 898-903;
Barry's Framingham, Mass., 325-30; Bassett's Hist.
Richmond, N. H., 444; Lapham's Hist. Paris, Me., 676;
Leland Gen., 182; Morse's Gen. Sherborn. Mass., 176;
Norton's Hist. Fitzwilliam, N. H., 634-7; Prentice Gen.,
177-9; Rockwood Gen., 95-101; Savage's Gen. Dict., III,
194; Temple's Hist. N .Brookfield. Mass., 684; Wash-
ington, N. H.. Hist., 536; Wyman's Charlestown Gens.,
II, 644.

MELLOWS, or MELLHOUSE:—Abraham,
Charlestown, adm. of the church, wife Martha and son
Edward 1633; freeman 1634; died as early as 1639.
leaving 6 children, says Felt, and Frothingham asserts
that he adventur. £50 in the comp., which
it is presumed was before coming from England. His
will was brought into court in .June, 1639.

MELLOWS, OLIVER, Boston 1634, with wife Eliz.
admitted of our church that year; freeman soon after;
disarmed in 1637, as one of the supporters of Wheelwright; had Samuel. baptised 1634; Martha, 1636; and
Mary, 1638; soon after died at Braintree. and there
probably had lived. His widow married, 1640, or 1,
Thomas Makepeace of Dorchester.

MELLVILLE:—David Mellville, Barnstable 1691.
merchant; removed to Eastham; there by wife Mary,
daughter of Rev. Samuel Willard. had Thomas, born
1697; Mary, 1699; Abigail and Eliz., twins, 1702; and
David, 1704.

MELVIN:—John Melvin, Charlestown; by wife Hannah, who died 1696, aged 41, had John, born 1679, baptised 1681; Hannah, 1681; Robert, 1684; James, 1686; Jonathan, 1688; David, 1690; and Benjamin, baptised 1695.

REFERENCES:—Chase's Chester, N. H., 564; Densmore's Hartwell Gen.; Leland Gen., 75; Stearn's Hist. Ashburnham. 816; Wyman's Charlestown, Mass., II, 665.

MELYEN, MELYNE. or MALINE:—Isaac, New Haven, brother of Jacob, whose father (always called Mr. without name of baptism as on list of those sworn to fidelity, 1657), had probably brought them both from Holland or New York: but of their son the last mentioned is 1663, and whether he had wife and family or not is unknown. It must be very easy to distinguish this family from the numerous Mellens.

MELYEN, JACOB, New Haven; took oath of fidelity with his father (who had been then seated in the church as early as 1655, probably a Dutchman from New York) ; married, 1662, perhaps, Hannah, daughter of George Hubbard, but after 1663 had removed to Boston; was a leather dealer, constable seven years. before and after 1695; he had been chosen guardian 1693, by his nephew; called himself son of Isaac, late of Virginia, planter. His will names wife Hannah, and only two children, Samuel, Harvard College, 1696, and Abigail Tilley, wife of William. after of Hon. Samuel Sewall. chief justice

MELYN, SAMUEL, Fairfield, perhaps brother of Jacob, and uncle of preceding; had died before 1660.

REFERENCE:—Hatfield's Elizabeth, N. J., 82.

MENDAM. MENDALL, or MENDON:—Richard, Kittery 1663; may have been son of, if not the same as, the following.

MENDAM, ROBERT, Duxbury 1638, or earlier; sold, in 1639, house and land: removed to Kittery before 1647. and 1652, submitted to Massachusetts; was constable that year and in 1666 was of the grand jury.

MENDAM, WILLIAM, Braintree 1667.

MENDLOVE:—Mark Mendlove, Plymouth 1637, Duxbury 1640.

MENDLOVE, WILLIAM, Plymouth 1633. Yet in 1643 the name is not seen.

MENTOR:—Thomas, a soldier. killed 1675, by the Indians at Bloody Brook, with "the flower of Essex," under Lothrop.

MEPHAM:, MAPHAM, or MIPHAM:—John, Guilford 1639, one of the seven pillars at founding of the church in 1643, and died 1647, leaving only child John, who was remembered in the will of Timothy Baldwin.

MEPHAM, JOHN, Southampton, L. I., 1673, printed Mepdam in a valuable paper, 3 Mass. Hist. Coll., X. 88; was probably son of preceding.

MERCER:—Thomas, Boston; died 1699. In his will he names wife Eliz. and their children—William, the eldest, Thomas and Sarah. Perhaps he had, in 1665, been of Sheepscot. Sullivan, 287.

MERCER, TIMOTHY, Windsor 1649, of whom all we know is he was fined that year. A Lucy M. came in the Defence, 1635, aged 19, from London.

REFERENCES:—Am. Ancestry, II, 80; VIII, ·168; Carter Tree of Va.; Meade's Old Families of Ba., 205; Richmond Standard, I, 14, 28; II, 33, 35.

MERCHANT, or MARCHANT:—John, Braintree, whose wife Sarah died 1638; removed, it is thought, to Rhode Island, and 1639 was allowed inhabit. of

Newport. Perhaps he was after of Yarmouth; there had Mary, born 1648; Abijah, 1651.

MERCHANT, WILLIAM, Watertown 1639; by wife Mary had Mary, born 1642, and removed to Ipswich; there died 1668.

REFERENCES:—Am. Ancestry, I, 55 VI, 175; Todd's Hist. Reading, Ct., 208.

MEREDITH:—See Ameredith:—Jonah M., was one of the soldiers in Gallup's company in the doleful serv., 1690.

MERIAM:—George. Concord: freeman 1641; by wife Susanna had Eliz., born 1641; Samuel, 1642; Hannah, 1645; Abigail, 1647; Sarah, 1649; and Susanna. His wife died 1675, and he soon after.

MERIAM, JOHN. Boston, freeman 1647: by wife Sarah had Samuel. baptised 1655; Sarah, 1658; Thomasine, 1660; and Mary. 1663: was selectman 1681.

MERRIAM, JOHN, Concord, freeman 1690: may have been son of William the first, and possibly of Hampton; there took oath of allegiance 1678.

MERRIAM, JOSEPH, Concord, brother of George: freeman 1639; had Joseph. probably born in England, and John, 1641. He had died in January of this year. His wife was Sarah and he had other children.

MERIAM, ROBERT, Concord. freeman 1639, town clerk 1654-76, representative 1655-8, deacon; died 1682, aged 72, leaving no children.

MERIAM, SAMUEL, Lynn. perhaps son of William; married, 1669, Eliz. Townsend; may have removed to Concord: there became the freeman of 1690.

MERIAM, SAMUEL. Charlestown; by wife Mary had Samuel, baptised 1691: Catharine, 1691; Edward, 1693; and Isaac 1694.

MERIAM, WILLIAM, Concord 1635: freeman 1649: then perhaps of Boston .but in short time of Lynn: had wife Sarah, and children Joseph, Williams. and John; died 1689.

REFERENCES:—Am. Ancestry, IV, 142: IX, 194; Jackson's Hist. Newton, Mass., 367: Locke Gen., 26, 42, 82-5: Meriam Gen. (1888), 52 pp.

MERING:—Joseph, a soldier at Hatfield 1676, in Turner's company, from the East.

MERLAN:—John. Hampton 1649.

MERRELLS:—Thomas. Hartford: had Thomas, baptised 1646. Perhaps the name was Merrill.

MERRICK:—James. Marblehead 1668.

MERRICK, JOHN, Hingham; died 1647, leaving John, and probable widow Eliz., who sold estate there in 1649, to Thomas Thaxter.

MERRICK, THOMAS, Springfield. by tradition said to have come from Wales through Roxbury, and reached Springfield in 1636, but there is evidence that he was of Hartford early in 1638. He was very young. if he left. as is said, his native land in 1630; and no trace is seen at Roxbury of him, or of his father or mother, brother or sister, nor can the name be found there before 1649. At Springfield he married. 1639. Sarah, daughter of Rowland Stebbins, who was the third man in that town. of any English; had Thomas, born 1641, third birth on the town record, died young: Sarah, 1643; Mary, 1645, died soon; Mary, 1647; and Hannah, 1650. In 1653 he married Eliz. Tilley; had Eliz.. born 1654, died young; Miriam, 1656, died at 28 years; John, 1658; Eliz., again, 1661; Thomas, 1664; Tilley. 1667: James. 1670: and Abigai, 1673: as freeman, 1665, and died 1704.

MERRICK, WILLIAM, Duxbury 1640; was one of the original proprs. of Bridgewater; early removed to Eastham; by wife Rebecca had William, 1643; Stephen. 1646;

Rebecca, 1648; Mary, 1650; Ruth, 1652; Sarah, 1654; John, 1657; Isaac, 1661; Joseph, 1662; and Benjamin, 1665; was an ensign, and died about 1688.

REFERENCES:—Corliss' Gen . Appendix; Eaton's Hist. Thomaston, Me., II, 228; Freeman's Cape Cod, II, 365, 391, 507, 736; Hyde's Hist. Brimfield, Mass., 433; Merrick Gen. (1860), 9 pp.; Savage's Gen. Dict., III, 198; Underwood's Pollard Gen.; Wilbraham, Mass.-Centen., 301-4; Winsor's Hist. Duxbury, Mass., 282.

MERRILL, or MERRILLS:—Jeremiah, Boston; bv wife Sarah had Jeremiah, born 1652; and Sarah, 1655.

MERRILL, JOHN, Newbury, one of the first settlers; freeman 1640; died 1673; by wife Eliz., who died 1682, had Hannah, born in England, who married, 1647, Stephen Swett; and died 1662.

MERRILL, NATHANIEL, Newbury, brother of John; had wife Susanna, and had Nathaniel, born 1638; John, Abraham, Susanna, Daniel. 1642; Abel, 1644; and died 1655.

REFERENCES:—Amer. Ancestry, III, 89; Andrews' Hist. New Britain, Ct., 226; Bangor, Me., Hist. Mag., V, 199; Barbour's Wife and Mother App., 15-21; Bouton's Hist. Concord, N. H., 679; Bradbury's Kennebunk-port, Me., 262; Brown's W. Simsbury, Ct., Settlers, 109-11; Buxton. Me., Centen., 163-7; Chases's Hist. Chester, N. H., 565; Chase's Hist. Haverhill, Mass., 276; Clute's Hist. Staten Island, N. Y., 405-7; Coffin's Hist. Newbury, Mass., 309; Corliss' No. Yarmouth. Me.; Dearborn's Hist. Parsonfield, Me., 387; Douglas Gen., 125; Eaton's Hist. Thomaston. Me., II, 327; Hatch's Hist. Industry, Me., 738; Hubbard's Hist. Stamstead Co., Canada, 193; Lapham's Hist. Bethel, Me., 590; Lapham's Norway, Me.; 549-53; Lapham's Paris, Me., 677-9; Little's Hist. Warren, N. H., 555; Me. Hist. and Gen. Record, I, 192; III, 178-81; Montague Gen., 435-7; Morrison's Gen., 99, 118; Morrison's Hist. Windham, N. H., 641-8; Nash Gen., 48; N. E. Hist. and Gen. Reg., XLV, 304; Orford, N. H. Centen., 122; Paul's Hist. of Wells, Vt., 12; Phoenix's Whitney Gen., I, 152; Poore's Gen., 86; Poore's Hist. Researches, 115, 132, 169; Redfield Gen., 32; Runnel's Hist. Sanbornton, N.H., II, 48; Savage's Gen. Hist., III, 99; Secomb's Hist. Amherst, N. H., 698; Slaughter's St. Mark's Parish, 160; Stearn's Hist. Ashburnham, Mass., 825; Washington, N. H., Hist. 538; Wheeler's Hist. Brunswick. Me., 843; Winslow Gen., II, 830-9; Worcester's Hist. Hollis, N. H., 38; Young's Hist. Warsaw, N. Y., 300.

ARMS:—Arg., a bar, az.: between three peacock's heads. erased; proper.

MERRIFIELD:—See Merryfield.

MERRIMAN:—Nathaniel, New Haven; had Nathaniel, Hannah, born 1651; Grace 1653; Sarah, 1655; Eliz., 1657; Abigail, perhaps 1659; John, 1660; Mary; he was one of the first settlers at Wallingford. its representent. 1674, lieut., and late in 1675, capt. of the dragoons of the Co., and continued propr. at New Haven; died 1694, aged 80.

REFERENCES:—Am. Ancestry. IX, 194, 241 Bontecon Gen., 67; Davis' Hist. Wallingford. Ct., 848-51; Hubbard's Hist. Stanstead Co., Can., 269; Powers' Sangamon Co., Ills., 517-9; Temple's Hist. Northfield, Mass., 595-7; Timlow's Hist. Southington. Ct., 169-75; Wheeler's Hist. Brunswick. Me., 344.

MERRITT:—Ezekiel. Newport 1639.

MERRITT, HENRY. Scituate: his wife joined the church 1637. died 1653: he had Henry and John.

MERRITT, JAMES, Boston 1655.

MERRITT, JOHN, a soldier. killed by the Indians at

Bloody Brook, with the "flower of Essex," under Capt. Lothrop, 1675.

MERRITT, JOHN, Marblehead, perhaps son of Nicholas; was freeman 1664.

MERRITT, JOHN, Scituate; had wife Eliz., and died 1740, aged 80. and his widow died 1746, aged 82.

MERRITT, NICHOLAS, Marblehead 1648 or earlier; in his will of 1685, probated 1686, names his children Martha Owens, Rebecca Chin, helpless daughter Mary, John, James, Samuel and Nicholas.

MERRITT, WILLIAM, Duxbury, constable 1647.

REFERENCES:—Adams' Fairhaven, Vt., 432; Amer. Ancestry, III, 194; Baird's Hist. Rye. N. Y., 426-8; Bunker's L. I. Gens., 239-48; Cleveland's Hist. Yates Co., N. Y., 503; Deane's Hist. Scituate. Mass., 311; Paige's Hist. Hardwicke, Mass., 421; Ruttenber's Hist. Newburgh, N. Y., 363; Savage's Gen. Dict., III, 200; Stearn's Hist. Ashburnham, Mass., 825; Temple's Hist. Palmer, Mass., 516; Wetmare Gen., 249.

MERROW, or MERO:—Henry Merrow, Woburn; married, 1660, Jane Wallis; had child, born 1662; probably was most of his days at Redding, freeman 1677, died 1685; probably had John and Samuel, as Eaton gives thier names among early seetlers at Redding.

REFERENCES:—Eaton's Reading, Mass., 96; Wentworth Gen., I, 260.

MERRY:—Cornelius, Northampton, an Irishman; had grant of land 1663; married Rachel Ballard; had John, who died soon; John, again, 1665; Sarah, 1668; Rachel, 1670; Cornelius, Leah, and perhaps others; was in the Falls fight, and after the war removed. John, the son, went to L. I.; Cornelius at Hartford. had nine children born 1702-18.

MERRY, JOHN, Boston: by wife Constance had Jonahtan, born 1663.

MERRY, JOSEPH, Haverhill 1650, perhaps removed to Hampton, thence to Edgarton, about 1678.; had wife Eliz. there, and died 1710, in 103d year, says tradition. A daughter if his was wife of Timothy Hilliard of Hampton, 1669.

MERRY, WALTER. Boston. shipwright; had wharf and dwelling and warehouse convenient for his trade. at the point bearing his name. later called N. Battery: by wife Rebecca, admitted to church 1633. and he soon after; had Jeremiah, baptised 1634. died soon: Rebecca. 1636; and Jeremiah. 1638. died soon. and wife died perhaps not long after. He married second wife. Mary Dolens, or Dowling. 1653; had Sylvanus. 1655. died soon: and Walter, 1656: was freeman 1634: and was drowned 1657. His widow married. 1657. Robert Thornton of Taunton. There Walter continued to reside with his mother. This Walter is often written as Waters, and was, by Farmer, brought in again as an inhabit. by name Merry Waters.

REFERENCES:—Eaton's Warren. Me., 586: Hatch's Hist. Industry, Me., 741-5; Hubbard's Hist. Stanstead Co., Can., 263; Savage's Gen. Dict., III. 200.

MERRYFIELD:—Henry, Dorchester 1641: by wife Margaret had John, Eliz., and Ruth, all baptised 1649; Hannah, 1650: Mary, 1652; Abigail, 1656: Benjamin. 1658: Martha, 1661; and Henry. 1664.

MERWIN:—Miles. Milford. where Lambert reports him in 1645; had Eliz.. John. Abigail, Thomas, Samuel, born 1656: and Miles. 1658: Daniel. 1661. died young; Martha and Mary. twins. 1666: Hannah. 1667; and Deborah, 1670; all the first six named in the will of his aunt Abigail. widow of Rev. John Warham, who had before been widow of John Branker, made in 1684, when he calls him 60 years old, but in 1692 says aged 70. He died 1697, aged 74; in his will, 1695, names third wife Sarah, and all sons living, four in number, and seven grandchildren. The inventory, 1697, names six daughters, by the surnames of their husbands. His first wife, name untold, died 1664; his second wife was Sarah, widow of Thomas Beach, who died 1670. Eliz. married a Canfield; Abigail married a Scofield; Martha married James Prince; Mary married a Hull; Hannah married Abel Holbrook; and Deborah married a Burwell.

REFERENCES:—American Ancestry, II, 80; Collin's Hillsdale, N. Y., App. 76-88; Orcutt's Hist. of New Milford, Ct., 797; Savage's Gen. Dict., III., 201.

MESSER:—Edward Messer, New Hampshire, 1689. Kelly.

REFERENCES:—Aldrich's Walpole, N. H., 333; Amer. Ancestry, IV, 239; Bangor, Me., Hist. Mag., IV, 162; Corliss Gen., Sibley's Hist. of Union, Me., 472.

MESSINGER:—Andrew Messinger, Norwalk 1672, may have been as early as 1639 at New Haven; in 1687 had good estate; no mention of him after is found.

MESSINGER, EDWARD, Windsor; had Dorcas, born 1650; Nathaniel, 1653; but no more is heard of him. Dorcas married Peter Mills.

MESSINGER, HENRY, Boston; by wife Sarah had John, born 1641; Sarah, 1643; Simeon, 1645; Henry, Ann, baptised 1650; Rebecca, 1652; Lydia and Priscilla, twins, 1656; Thomas, 1661; and Ebenezer, 1665. He was a joiner, Artillery Co., 1658; freeman, 1665, perhaps a short time, 1656; at Jamaica, L. I., one of that name is mentioned in Thompson's Hist. His will, 1678, gives little light on family; his estate was not appraised before 1681.

MESSINGER, NATHAN, Windsor, probably son of Edward, though record calls him Nathaniel; married, 1678, Rebecca, eldest child of Mark Kelsey; had Hannah, 1682; Nathan, 1684; Rebecca, 1686; Joseph, 1687; John, 1689; Return, 1691 and Nathan, again, 1693.

REFERENCES:—Brown's W. Simsbury, Ct., 112-4; Chipman's Hist. Harrington, Mass., 106; Hayward's Hist. Hancock, N. H., 762; Mesinger Gen. (1863.. 14 p. (1882), reprint; Morse's Gen. Sherborn, Mass., 177; N. E. Hist. Gen. Reg., IX, 59; XVI, 308-14; Savage's Gen. Dict., III, 201. Stiles' Hist. of Windsor, Ct., II, 493.

METCALF:—Frequently Medcalf in early records.

METCALF, JOHN, son of the first Michael, born in England; married, in 1647, Mary, daughter of Francis Chickering; had John, 1648; Michael, 1650; Mary, 1652; Joseph, 1658; and Hannah, 1664. He was freeman 1647; died 1675, unless this date belongs to his eldest son John, New Haven, 1645, a brickmaker, as below.

METCALF, JOHN, New Haven 1645, a brickmaker; may have been son or brother of Stephen, as about the year 1647 he removed.

METCALF, JOSEPH, Ipswich, freeman 1635; reported in that year, and often after; died 1665, aged 60. By his will we learn that his wife was Eliz., his son, Thomas, born in England, probably; and grandchildren Joseph, Mary, and Eliz. His widow married, 1670. Edward Beacham.

METCALF, MICHAEL, Dedham, born 1586, at Tatterford, in Co. Norfolk; was a dornock weaver at Norwich, and free of the city, where all his children were born; married Sarah,. 1616; had Michael, 1617, died soon; Mary, 1618 or 1619; Michael, again, 1620; John, 1622;

Sarah, 1624; Eliza, 1626; Martha, 1628; Thomas, 1629 or '30; Ann, 1631 or 4, died soon; Jane, 1632; and Rebecca, 1635; his wife was born at a village near Norwich, he says, 1593, but possibly the figures have been mistaken, as in examination one week before sailing of ship, called, it is thought Rose of Yarmouth, from Yarmouth, 1637, he calls him 45 years, and wife 39. Arrived at Boston "three days before mid-summer with wife and nine children, and a servant, Thomas Comberback, aged 16. He was freeman in 1640, or 1642. His wife died 1645, and he married Martha, widow of Thomas Piggs or Pidge; he died 1664.

METCALF, STEPHEN, New Haven 1639, a brickmaker; after 1647 probably remained; was in good repute.

REFERENCES:—Adams' Haven Gen., 26, 47; Amer. Ancestry, III, 181; VI, 77, 103; VII, 136; Ballou's Hist. of Milford, Mass., 905-7; Barry's Hist. of Framingham, Mass., 331; Bemis' Hist. of Marlboro, N. H., 579; Blake's Hist. of Franklin, Mass., 259-62; Clarke's Kindred Gen. (1896), 131-6; Chute's Hist. of Staten Island, N. Y., 412; Daniel's Hist. of Oxford, Mass., 614; Dedham Hist. Reg., IV, 166-70; V, 22-31; Driver Gen., 394-432; Eaton's Hist. of Thomaston, Me., II, 329; Freeman's Hist. of Cape Cod, Mas., II, 442; Goodwin's Gen. Notes, 157-62; Green's Kentucky Farm; Hammott Papers of Ipswich, Mass., 775; Hill's Dedham, Mass., Records, I; Hyde Gen., I, 348-54; II, 1055-63; Jameson's Hist. of Medway, Mass., 502; Metcalf Fam. of Deadham (1867), 12 pages; Metcalf Fam. of Franklin (1894), 16 pages; N. E. Hist. Gen. Reg., VI, 171-8; XVI, 180; Read's Hist. of Swanzey, N. H., 405; Saunderson's Charlestown, N. H., 476-81; Savage's Gen. Dict., III, 202-4; Stearn's Hist. of Ashburnham, Mass., 826-4; Stearn's Hist. of Rindge, N. H., 602-4; Tuttle Gen., 433; Washington, N. H., Hist., 540-2; Wheeler's Hist. of Newport, N. H., 471-3; Whipple-Hill Families (1897), 87-9; Wright's Williams Gen., 34.

METHUP (with five variations):—Daniel, Watertown; married, 1664, Bethia, perhaps daughter of Anthony Beers; had Bethia, 1665; Mary, 1666; Daniel, 1668; Robert, 1671; Isaac, 1672; Sarah, 1675; Abigail, 1678; and Hannah, 1681. He died 1717, and his widow, 1711.

REFERENCES:—See Mettup's Bond's Watertown, 366.

MEW:—Ellis, New Haven; took oath of fidelity 1654; is one of the freeman 1669; by wife Ann, daughter of William Gibbons; had Ann; and Dodd, 135, tells no more. In his list of deaths is Ann, only child, 1681, and Ann, widow, 1704.

REFERENCES:—Austen's R. I. Gen. Dict., 133.

MICO:—John, Boston 1689, merchant; married Mary, daughter of Thomas Brattle; died 1718. His widow 1733.

REFERENCES:—Savage's Gen. Dict., I, 239.

MIDDLEBROOK:—Joseph, Concord; went with Rev. John Jones to Fairfield, 1644; in 1670 was propr. there; died probably 1686. ' He married Mary, widow of Benj. Turney, the first; had son same name, and daughter Phoebe, wife of Samuel Wilson, the only heirs.

REFERENCES:—Am. Ancestry, II, 81; VII, 283; Orcutt's Hist. of Stratford, Ct., 1246-8; Schwenke's Hist. of Fairfield, Ct.

MIDDLECOTT:—Richard, Boston; came from Warminster, Co. Wilts, bringing son Edward; married here second wife Sarah, widow of Tobias Payne, who had been widow of second Miles Standish, and daughter of John Winslow; had Mary, 1674; Sarah, 1678; Jane, 1682; was freeman 1690; named one of the councillors in the new chart. by Mather, and left out at first popular election; died 1704. His widow died 1728. Mary married Henry Gibbs; and next Othniel Haggell of Barbadoes; Sarah married, 1702. Louis Boucher; and Jane married, 1703, Elisha Cooke, Jr.

REFERENCE:—Payne and Gove Gen., 12.

MIDDLETON:—James, Dover 1658; removed to Maine, 1665.

MIDDLETON, WILLIAM, Boston; by wife Eliza. had Eliza., born 1673; Abigail, 1680; Alice, 1684; and Joanna, 1687. He died 1699, aged 74, as, says the gravestone found, 1850, in the wall of the tower of the Old South Church.

REFERENCES:—Am. Ancestry, VIII, 192; New York Gen. and Biog. Rec., XXVIII, 167, 239-41.

ARMS:—Arg., fretty, sa., on a canton, per chevron, or and sa., a unicorn's head, erased per chevron, gu and or, the horn, sa.

MIGHILL:—Ezekiel, Rowley 1691, son of Thomas of the same.

MIGHILL, SAMUEL, Rowley, son of Thomas, born before coming to our country; married, 1657, Elizabeth, daughter of Abraham Toppan, of Newbury; was taxed in 1691.

REFERENCES:—Essex Inst. Coll., XXII, 214-9; Gage's Hist. of Rowley, Mass., 447.

MILBURNE:—William, Saco; was the minister 1685; accompanied Folsom, 137; probably died at Boston 1699.

REFERENCE:—Am. Ancestry, VII, 34.

MILBURY, or MILLBURY:—Henry, of York, 1680; had a family, for the will of William Dixon gave something to his children.

REFERENC:—Calnek's Anapolis, N. S., 549.

MILDMAY:—William, son of Sir Henry of Graces, in Essex, H. C., 1647. though sent by his father, with a tutor from England, Richard Lyon, is ranked lowest in his class. yet had his A. M. in regular course. Sir Walter, of the same family, was founder, in the time of Queen Elizabeth, of Emanuel College, at the University of Cambridge, which supplied N. E. in its early days with some of the chief lights that illumined its churches and well be added the venerable Gov. Bradstreet.

MILES:—Benjamin, Dedham. son of Samuel; freeman, 1678

MILES, JOHN. Concord 1637; freeman 1639; by wife had Mary, 1640. His wife died 1678, and he married Susanna, widow of John Rediat; had John, 1680; Samuel, 1682; Sarah. 1686: died 1693.

MILES, JOHN, Boston. minister of the first Baptist church; removed. 1683. to Swanzey.

MILES, JOSEPH, Kittery; submitted, 1652, to jurisdiction of Massachusetts.

MILES. JOSEPH: arraigned as a Quaker 1659; may have been the passenger who took the oath of supremacy and allegiance, 1634. to pass for N. E. in the Mary and John. though it may be it was his son. for we hear not where the passenger sat down.

REFERENCES:—Allen's Worcester. Mass., 165; Am. Ancestry, VI, 15; Anderson's Waterbury, Ct., I, App., 90; Chapman's Trowbridge's Gen. 49, 51; Davis' Hist. of Wallingford. Ct., 852; Heywood's Westminster, Mass., 776-82; Hibard's Hist. of Goshen, Ct., 495-502; Hill's

Hist. of Mason's, N. H., 205; McKean Gen., 126; Miles Family of Mass. (1840). 12 pages; Miles Family of Philadelphia (1895). 182 pages; Morris' Bontecon Gen., 109-13; Morton's Hist. of Fitzwilliam, N. H., 638; Orcutt's Hist. of New Milford, Ct., 731; Pierce's Hist. of Grafton, Mass., 537-9; Potts' Carter Gen., 180; Runnel's Hist. of Sanbornton, N. H., II, 482; Savage's Gen. Dict., III. 206, 8; Smith's Hist. of Del. Co., Pa., 485; Tuttle Gen., 163; Ward'st Hist. of Shrewsbury, Mass., 368-70; Westminster, Mass., Centennial. 30.

MILK, or MILKE:—John, Salem; authorized chimney 1663.

REFERENCE:—Journal of Smith and Deane. 223.

MILLARD:—John, Rehoboth, tanner; had son of same name, perhaps before 1658. Baylis, II, 208.

MILLARD, THOMAS, Boston; had a lot for five heads, granted him at Mount Wolaston, 1639.

REFERENCES:—Am. Ancestry, I, 55; Loomis Gen. (1880), 803; Sedgwick's Hist. of Sharon, Ct., 100.

MILLER:—Abraham, Charlestown; had Susanna, baptized 1698. He was perhaps son of James the Scotchman.

MILLER, ALEXANDER, Dorchester, 1637; freeman 1638.

MILLER, ANDREW, Enfield, an early settler, died 1708, aged 60; had David, who married, 1713.

MILLER, ANTHONY, Dover; was rep. 1674-6.

MILLER, HUMPHREY, Reading; among early settlers; married at Cambridge, 1677. Elizabeth Smith.

MILLER, JOHN, Dover, 1647; was perhaps of Kennebec, 1665, as in Sullivan, 287, and swore allegiance to the King, 1681.

MILLER, EPHRAIM, Kittery, before 1690; had, besides Samuel, Martha, who married John Wentworth of Dover, and Mary, who married Ephraim Wentworth.

MILLER, GEORGE, Easthampton, L. I., 1660. Thompson.

MILLER, JAMES, Charlestown, perhaps son of Richard; married, 1673, Hannah, daughter of John George, who joined church 1677, and was then baptized; had James. born 1674; Hannah, 1677; Elinor, 1680; James, again, 1682; Richard, 1684; Eliz., 1686; John, 1688; Mary, 1690; and Ruth. 1693; and he died 1705, aged about 64. His widow died 1733, aged 78. This now may be confused with other James.

MILLER, JAMES, Norwalk, 1671, of whom we hear no more except that he lived at Rye 9 years after.

MILLER, JOHN, Dorchester. 1636; by some thought (not by Savage) perhaps son of Richard the first; had share in 1637. says Harris, of the lands in the neck, now South Boston: but he was more probably of Roxbury, for there is record of his daughter Mehitable. born 1638. and with wife Lydia he belonged to Eliot's church, of which he was an elder: was bred at Gonville and Cainus Coll., Cambridge. where he took his A.B., 1627; freeman 1639, without the prefix of respect: brought from England John. born 1632. perhaps had there another child, or after coming here. may have had at Roxbury, or Rowley, some not mentioned; went to be minister, 1639, at Rowley, and was also the first town clerk there. where he had Lydia, born 1640: soon after accepted the call at Yarmouth. Cape Cod, yet he can hardly have been long resident there. At Roxbury again he was living; had Susanna. born 1647. who died at Charlestown, unmarried, 1669; Eliz., 1649: his wife died at Boston, 1658, and he died at Groton, 1663.

MILLER, JOHN. Rehoboth 1643; may have gone from Dorchester, but not so probable as that he was father of John, Ichabad and Robert, who all appear there in division of lands, 1668. His wife Eliz. was buried 1680.

MILLER, JOHN. Wethersfield, one of the first settlers about 1636; removed, 1642, to Stamford; there died very soon, leaving widow and sons John, Jonathan and Joseph, all living 1666.

MILLER, JOHN, Easthampton, L. I., 1650. Thompson.

MILLER, JOHN. Springfield; freeman 1690.

MILLER, JONATHAN, Springfield, 1678.

MILLER, JOSEPH, came in the Hopewell, Capt. Babb, 1635, from London, aged 15; perhaps son of some one that had come before; may have been of Dover, 1647. and may be same as the next.

MILLER, JOSEPH, Newbury; had wife Mary, who, Coffin says, had been widow of Capt. John Cutting, and died 1663; but in another place, 1664; and he died 1681.

MILLER, JOSEPH, Marlborough; freeman 1685; may be the man of Cambridge, who married Mary, only daughter of Walter Pope; had Thomas, born 1675; Samuel, 1678; and probably Joseph of Newton, who died 1711; and Jane, who died 1719. He died 1697; and his widow died 1711. Perhaps he was son of Richard.

MILLER, LAZARUS, Springfield, son of Obediah; took oath of allegiance 1678, as did at the same time Obadiah, and Obadiah, Jr.

MILLER, NICHOLAS, Plymouth, whose will of 1665 bears the name Hodges, also, may therefore be of the same person borne in the list of those able to bear arms, 1643.

MILLER, PAUL, Boston; by wife Eliz. had Sarah, born 1692; and he lived not long after.

MILLER, RICHARD. Charlestown: came perhaps in 1637; and had grant of a lot, it is said, in 1638; but as neither Frothingham, in the history of thet own, nor Budington, in that of the church, mentioned him, we may suppose he died early. Elinor, who joined the church 1643, may have been his wife or widow. She married Henry Herbert, and died 1667; and her daughter Hannah M. married, 1663, Nathaniel Dade, and after his death married, 1667, John Edmands, and next, 1664, married Deacon Aaron Ludkin, long outlived him, and died 1717.

MILLER, RICHARD, Kittery; had Samuel, Martha and Mary; was dead before June, 1694, and his widow Grace married Christopher Benfield. Mary married Ephraim Wentworth. But she may, as also the brother and sister, belong to Ephraim M., as claimed by the Wentworths.

MILLER, ROBERT, a soldier under Capt. Turner, probably present in the Falls fight; may have come from Rehoboth, certainly from some eastern part; at Rehoboth had Solomon, born 1674; Mary, 1680.

MILLER, ROBERT, Boston; by wife Lydia had Lydia, born 1666; is possibly same as the preceding.

MILLER, SAMUEL, Springfield; freeman 1690.

MILLER, SAMUEL, Rehoboth; married, 1682, Esther Brown; had Esther; and, perhaps, he had second wife Rebecca, daughter of Joseph Belcher.

MILLER, SAMUEL, Kittery, son of Richard, or Ephraim.

MILLER, SYDRACH, Salem, 1629, a cooper; probably came with Higginson.

MILLER, THOMAS, Rowley, 1646; had license to sell wines next year.

MILLER, THOMAS, Boston, planter; had estate of

about three acres adjoining the town common; sold in 1668, to Thomas Deane.

MILLER, THOMAS, Springfield; married, 1649, Sarah, daughter of Thomas Marshfield; had Sarah, born 1650; Thomas, 1653; Samuel, 1655; John, 1657; Joseph, 1659, died soon; Josiah, 1660; Deborah, 1662; Martha, 1664, soon; Martha, again, 1665; Ebeneazer, 1667; Mehitable, 1669; Joseph, again, 1671; and Experience, a daughter, in 1673; and he was killed by the Indians 1675, as may have been his son John next year, in the great Falls fight. Five daughters and four sons were married at Springfield.

MILLER, THOMAS, Middletown, an early settler; by wife Isabel, who died 1666, had Ann, who married about 1653, Nathaniel Bacon; and when above 56 years old took, 1666, second wife, Sarah, daughter of Samuel Nettleton of Branfield, a girl, probably not older than his daughter Ann; had Thomas, born 1666; Samuel, 1668; Joseph, 1670; Benj., 1672; John, 1674; Margaret, 1676; Sarah, 1679; and Mehitable, posthumous, 1681. He He died, 1680. Children named in division of estate are: Thomas, 14; Samuel, 12; Joseph, 10; Benjamin, 8; Margaret, 4; and Sarah, 1. His widow married a Harris, perhaps Thomas.

MILLER, WILLIAM, Ipswich 1640; probably removed with earliest settlers to Northampton; by wife Patience had Mary, Rebecca, died young; Patience, born 1657; William, 1659; Mercy, 1662; Ebenezer, 1664; Mehitable, 1666; Thankful, 1669; and Abraham, 1672; was freeman 1690, and died 1690.

REFERENCES:—Adams' Fairhaven, Vt., 440-2; Am. Ancestry, II, 81-6; III, 225; IV, 63; Baird's Hist. of Rye, N. Y., 428; Blake's Hist. of Franklin, Mass., 262; Bouton's Genealogy; Brown's West Simsbury, Ct., Settlers, 108; Caulkin's Hist. of New London, 327; Chambers' Early Germans of N. J., 155-7, 448, 590; Douglas Gen., 96-9; Eaton's Hist. of Thomaston, Me., 329; Hedge's Hist. East Hampton, N. Y., 305-11; Jackson's Hist. of Newton, Mass., 365; Maine Hist. and Gen. Recorder, VIII, 238-42; Miller and Morris Gen. (1876), 300 p.; Munsell's Albany Collections. IV, 148; Pott's Gen. (1895), 245-59; Richmond, Va., Standard, III, 2; Stiles' Hist. of Windsor, Ct., II, 494; Whitmore's Heraldic Journal, 39, 42.

MILLERD, MILLARD, or MILWARD:—Benjamin, Joseph, Robert, and Samuel, Rehoboth, 1690.

MILLERD, THOMAS, Gloucester, a fisherman or mariner; was selectman 1642; removed to Newbury; had Ann, Rebecca and Elizabeth, after; did not sell his estate before 1652; died 1653:

REFERENCES:—Am. Ancestry, I, 55; Loomis Gen. (1880), 803; Sedgewick's Hist. of Sharon, Ct., 100.

ARMS:—Ermine, a fess, gules, between three wolves' heads, erased, azure.

CREST:—A wolf's head, erased, azure.

MILLET:—Thomas. Dorchester: came in the Elizabeth, from London, 1635, aged 30, with wife Mary, 29, and children Thomas, John, born 1635; Jonathan, 1638, died next month; Mary, 1639; Mehitable, 1642; perhaps also Bethia, who married, 1666, Moses Eyres or Ayres (as Mr. Eben. in General. Reg. V, 402, says), and died 1669. He was freeman 1637, had his wife, married in London, was daughter of John Greenway.

MILLETT, THOMAS, Gloucester, 1642; had John, Nathaniel, and Thomas, who were of adult age in 1664.

REFERENCES:—Am. Ancestry, III, 225; Driver Gen., 142-50; Washington, N. H., Hist. 547; Am. Ancestry,

IV, 9, 125; VI, 34; Wentworth Gen., I, 385-8.

MILLING:—Simon, Watertown, an old man; had five children—Simon, Richard, James and John, all baptised 1686. No mother mentioned; may have been dead, and he had lately removed thither. Rare will be the mention of the name.

MILLINGTON:—John, Windsor; married, 1668, Sarah Smith; removed to Suffield, where had John, 1675; Henry, 1679; and probably others.
REFERENCE:—Stiles' Windsor, II, 493.

MILLS:—Simon, Windsor, 1639; married, that year, probably second wife Joan; wife died childless. Date of his death unknown.

MILLS, JOHN, Boston; came probably in the fleet with Winthrop, for among the members of the first church his name is No. 33, and his wife Susanna next; admitted as freeman 1630, and was sworn 1632. His daughters Joy and Recompense, were baptised in 1630, being the first on our church record. He removed to Braintree, and with wife was recommended in 1641, to church there; was town clerk, 1653. Susanna, his wife, died 1657, in her 80th year. He made his will, 1678, in which he names daughters Mary Hawkins and Susanna Davis, and his son John is charged to bring up one of his sons, until earning, that he may be fit for the ministry, which was, he says, the employment of my predecessors. to third, if not fourth, generation.

MILLS JOHN, Scarborough; had John, James, Sarah, and Mary, who were all charged with neglect of public worship; and Sarah's defense subjected her to stripes.

MILLS, PETER, Windsor; in a tradition of very light esteem, probably a modern exercise of wit. said to have come from Holland; a tailor. with the name of Van Molyn (turned into English Mills). when relations between the two nations had long been hostile, strangely said to have been so late as 1666; married before 1672, Dorcas. daughter of Edward Sessinger, who died 1688; had Peter. and probably other children. perhaps Samuel, certainly Ebenezer, who died 1687; Return died 1689; and Eleazer 1698. all probably young. date of birth not seen. Married, 1691, a second wife, Jane Warren, or Fannin, of Hartford; he died 1702.
REFERENCES:—Am. Ancestry. III, 208; IV, 185; X, 186; XI, 196, 207; XII, 41. Brown's W. Simsbury. Ct., Settlers, 91-104; Eaton's Hist. of Thomaston, Me., II, 330; Hayward's Hist. of Hancock, N. H., 766; Mills Genealogy (1896), 36 pages; Savage's Gen. Dict., III, 213-5; Vinton Gen., 341-.

MILNER:—Michael, Lynn; came in the James, from London, 1635, aged 23; removed to Long Island, 1640, says Lewis.
REFERENCES:—Calnek's Annapolis, N. S., 551; Cope Gen., 58, 135-7.
ARMS:—Sa., three snaffle bits, or.
CRESTS:—(a) A snaffle-bit, of the shield. (b) A horse's head, couped, arg., bridled and maned, or, charged on the neck with a bit.
MOTTO:—Addit frena feris. (He reins in the untamed beasts.)

MILOM, or MYLOM:—Humphrey, Boston 1648; by wife Mary, Savage thinks, daughter of John Gove, of Roxbury, had Mary, 1652; Constance, 1653; Abigail, 1660; Hannah, 1663; Ruth, 1666; beside Mary and Sarah; was a cooper; in his will, 1667, names Mary and five daughters, of whom Constance married John Alcock.

MILTON:—George, New London, 1663.

MINARD:—Thomas, Hingham, 1636. Lincoln.

MINGAY:—Jeffrey, Hampton; freeman, 1640; represent., 1650; died 1658. Ann, probably his widow, married Christopher Hussey, and died 1680.

MINGO:—Robert, Newbury; by wife Elizabeth had Thomas, born 1689; and Robert, 1697. Savage thinks the name identical with MINGAY.

MINOR, or MINER:—Thomas, Charlestown 1632, son of William of Chew Magna, in Co. Somerset; one of the founders of the church, in Frothingham, 70, as well as Budington, 184, said to be dismissed for that purpose from Boston church that year; removed to New London soon after 1645; had married, 1634, Grace, eldest daughter of Walter Palmer; had John, 1635; Thomas, Clement, born 1642; Manasseh, Ephraim, Joseph, Judah, Samuel, Ann, Elizabeth, Eunice, and Mary. He was a very valuable man; representative for Stonington. A diary kept by him, for several years, furnishes some good information. Sometimes in Connecticut this name is Myner; and in 1834, nine of the family had been graduated at Yale.
REFERENCES:—Am. Ancestry. V, 162; Caulkins' Hist. of New London, Ct., 326; Hayden's Virginia Gen., 371; Minor's Meriwether Gen., 46-51; Orcutt's Hist. of Stratford, Ct., 1248.
ARMS:—Gu., a fess, arg., between three plates.

MINORD:—James, Boston; by wife Mary had Amander, a son, 1645.

MINOT:—George, Dorchester. son of Thomas, born 1594. at Saffron. Walden. Co. Essex; was an early settler; freeman 1634; representative. 1635; ruling elder 30 years; died 1671. By wife Martha had John, 1626; James, 1628; Stephen, 1631; all born in England, and Samuel, 1635. His wife died 1657, aged 60.
REFERENCES:—Potter's Concord. Mass., Families, 12; Whittemore's Orange, N. J., 372; Savage's Gen. Dict., III. 216-8.

MINTER:—Tobias, New London, son of Ezer; came from Newfoundland, 1672; died next year.

MINTER, TRISTRAM, New London; died before 1674, when his widow married Joshua Baker.

MIRABLE. ———, Charlestown, 1651; had wife Elizabeth, who was one of the friends of Matthews. Perhaps the true name was Marble, whom See. Yet in the will of George Knower, Mary Mirable is called his daughter.

MIRIAM:—John, Boston: was a selectman. 1691.

MIRICK:—James. Newbury, 1656: had Hannah, 1657; Abigail, 1658; Joseph, 1661; Isaac, 1665; Timothy, 1666; and Susanna, 1670. Coffin says he was born 1612; but it is not known when he died.
REFERENCES:—Cogswell's Henniker, 646; Jackson's Hist of Newton. Mass., 366; Temple's Hist. N. Brookfield, Mass, 685.

MITCHELL:—Edward. Hingham: came in the Diligent, 1638, but we know no more of him, except that he was from Old Hingham.

MITCHELL. EXPERIENCE, Plymouth, a youth: came in the Ann. 1623; had been one of the goodly company at Leyden. where he left a brother Thomas, who died there. Perhaps he was under the care of Francis Cook. at least he is of his company. in partaking share of cattle. 1627, and soon after married his daughter Jane.; was of Duxbury, after 1631. and long after removed to Bridgewater; died there 1689, aged above 80 years. His children were Elizabeth, who married, 1645, John Washburn; Thomas; Mary, married, 1652, James Shaw, and died 1679; Edward, Sarah, Jacob, John and Hannah, but the order of birth is uncertain, and so may be the mother, for he had second wife Mary.

MITCHELL, JONATHAN, Cambridge; came with his father, Matthew, in the James, from Bristol, 1635, being then 9 or 10 years; was bred at Harvard College, where, 1647, he had his A. B.; ordained 1650; married 1650, Margaret, widow of Rev. Thomas Shepard, his predecessor, but was before betrothed to Sarah, daughter of Rev. John Cotton, who died; had children Margaret, 1653, died next year; Samuel, 1660, Harvard, 1681. It is certain he had Jonathan, Harvard, 1687, who died 1695; and Margaret, again, who married, 1682, Stephen Sewall of Salem, and only through her is the blood of the distinguished ancestor come down now.

MITCHELL, MATTHEW, Charlestown; came in 1635, with Rev. Richard Mather, in the James, of Bristol, bringing wife and children David and Jonathan; perhaps more; removed to Concord, and soon Springfield; there signed compact with Pynchon and others in 1636; soon after to Saybrook, for a short time, where in the Pequot war he was protected by Lyon Gardiner, but he says the Indians took one of the "old man's sons, and roasted him alive." He was represent. in 1637, one of the asstist. of the Col. that year.

MITCHELL, THOMAS, Block Island 1684; was troubled by a French invasion. 1689, as Niles, a fellowsufferer, tells in his Indian wars, 3 Mass. Hist. Coll., VI. 272. He lived there many years.

MITCHELL, WILLIAM, Newbury; married, 1648, Mary Sawyer; had Mary, 1649; John, 1651; William, 1653; and Elizabeth, posthumous, 1655. He died 1654; and his widow married Robert Savoy in 1656.

REFERENCES:—Am. Ancestry, II, 86; III. 161; XI, 116, 176; XII. 34; Corliss' North Yarmouth. Me., 247-56; Hanson's Old Kent, Md., 119; Hinchman's Nantucket Settlers. 83-7; Livermore's Hist. of Block Island. R. I., 337; Mitchell's Hist. Bridgewater, Mass., 241-7; Savage's Gen. Dict., III. 219-21; Wooden Genealogy, 53-8. 69-72.

MITCHELSON. oftener MICHELSON. or MITCH-ENSON (as the vulgar made it):—Edward, Cambridge 1636; artillery company 1639; Marshall-Gen. of the Colony 1654. at salary of £50. for many years: had the sad office of executing the Quakers; though he was by Mitchell's reg. in full communion with the church, yet not found; in the list of freemen: died 1682, aged 77. By wife Ruth Bushell. who came 1635. aged 23, in the Abigail, had Thomas. 1637, died soon; Ruth. 1638. who married John Green: Bethia. 1642. who married Daniel Weld; Edward. 1644. H. C., 1665, lost on voyage to England, next year; and Elizabeth. 1646, who married Theodore Atkinson. Jr.. and. in 1676. Henry Deering.

MITCHENSON. WILLIAM. Cambridge; married, 1654. Mary Bradshaw: had Mary, 1655; Thomas, 1657; and Alice, all baptised 1663; Ruth. 1663; and Abigail. 1666; and he died 1668.

REFERENCES:—Mitcheson. Paige's Cambridge, 610-2.

MITTEN:—Michael. Falmouth. 1637; associated with George Cleves. whose only child, Elizabeth. he married; had Ann. who married Anthony Brackett; Elizabeth, born 1644. married Thaddeus Clarke; Mary married Thomas Brackett; Sarah married James Andrews: and Martha. married John Graves. who removed from Kittery to Little Compton; beside only son Nathan-

iel, who was killed by the Indians, 1676, unmarried. He was constable in 1640, freeman 1648. See Winthrop II, 302. He died 1660. His widow married a Harvey.

REFERENCE:—Austin's Allied Families, 176.

MIX, or MEEKS:—Thomas, New Haven 1643; married, 1649, Rebecca, daughter of Capt. Nathaniel Turner; had John, the eldest, born 1649; Nathaniel, 1651; Daniel, 1653; Thomas, 1655; Rebecca, 1658; Abigail, 1659; Caleb, 1661; Samuel, 1664; Hannah, 1666; Esther, 1668; died within two years; and Stephen, 1672, H. C., 1690. He died early in 1691.

MIX, WILLIAM, New Haven, perhaps brother of the first Thomas: married Sarah, daughter of William Preston; had Benjamin, 1650; Nathaniel, 1651; Sarah, 1654; Mary, 1656; Thomas, 1659; and probably others; and died before 1685. The name was first written Meekes.

REFERENCES:—Blake's Jonathan Mix, 78-98; Davis' Hist. Wallingford, Ct., 853-7; Savage's Gen. Dict., III. 222.

MIXER:—Isaac, Watertown; came in the Elizabeth, from Ipswich, 1634, aged 31, with wife Sarah, aged 33, and son Isaac, 4; was freeman, 1638; had born here Sarah, who married John Stearns. He was selectman 1651; died about 1655, and his widow died 1681.

REFERENCES:—Bond's Watertown, Mass., 367-70, 858; Savage's Gen. Dict., III, 223; Ward's Hist. of Shrewsbury, Mass., 366.

MOGER:—John, Brookhaven, L. I., 1655. Thompson.

REFERENCE:—Orcutt's Stratford, Ct., 1250.

MOHONAS:—Teague, Boston; perhaps a fisherman: appointed administrator, 1651. on estate of Matthew Collane, who died at Isle of Shoals.

MOISES:—Henry, Salem, 1676, a householder.

MOKUM:—Robert, Boston; by wife Hannah had William, 1668; may be the same as Mokey, which Mr. Felt found at Ipswich, 1639.

MOLT:—James, a soldier in Philip's war, under Capt. Turner, at Hatfield, 1676.

MONK:Christopher, Boston; by wife Mary had Christopher. 1686, perhaps died soon: Thomas. 1690; Ebenezer, 1692; Susanna. 1696: and Mary, 1700. He had been a mariner, was neighbor of Mather, who, in his Magn. VI. 7. has wisely given the relation of capture by Algerine in August. 1681. and recapture next month.

MONK, GEORGE. Boston, vintner. at the Sign of the Blue Anchor; by wife Lucy. who was daughter of Thomas Gardner. and widow of John Turner. had George. born 1683; and William. 1686. By second wife Elizabeth. widow of John Woodmansey. who survived, he had probably no children. He died 1698.

REFERENCE:—Wentworth Genealogy I. 528.

MONTAGUE. or MOUNTAGUE:—Griffin. Brookline. 1635. then a part of Boston. called Muddy River; was of Cape Porpoise in 1653. when he swore fidelity to Mass. By his will, probated 1671. gave all to wife Margaret.

MONTAGUE, RICHARD. Boston; said to be son of Peter. of the parish of Burnham. Co. Bucks; by wife Abigail had Sarah. died four days after; Martha, 1647; removed to Wethersfield; there had Peter. 1651; thence to Hadley; 57 years old in 1671; freeman 1681. and died that year.

REFERENCES:—Am. Ancestry, XII; Ballou's Hist. of Milford. Mass.. 908: Montague Family of Virginia (1894). 494 p.; New Eng. Hist. and Gen. Reg.. XIX,

318; Savage's Gen. Dict., III, 224; Titcomb's Early New Eng. People, 268.

ARMS:—Arg., three fusils, conjoined in fess, gu., between three pellets.

MOODIE:—Thomas, Boston, 1684, one of the Scot's Charit. Soc.

MOODY, or MOODEY:—William, Newbury; came in 1634; a saddler, from Ipswich, Co. Suffolk; freeman 1635; had wife Sarah and children Joshua, probably born in England; Caleb and Samuel; was probably a proprietor, of Salisbury, 1650; died 1673.

MOODY, JOSHUA, Portsmouth, son of William, born in England, Harvard College 1653; was first minister, of the first church; ordained, 1671; was called to preach the Gen. Election sermon of Mass., 1675; and by strange driven to Boston, and settled, 1684, at first church, the same year. Of his humane boldness, in the delusion of 1692, extraordinary instance is preserved, in Eliot's Biog. Dict. Allen in Biog. Dict. says, that "his zeal against witchcraft delusion occasioned his removal from the church where he was preaching." His wife was daughter of Edward Collins of Cambridge, prob. Martha; his daughter Martha married, in 1680, Jonathan Russell; and Sarah married, 1681, Rev. John Pike, and died 1686. He died while on a visit to Boston, 1697.

MOODY, DEBORAH, the lady who purchased, in 1640, the plantation of John Humfrey, at Lynn; was a member of Salem church, which admonished her, for error, as to baptism of infants, making her life so uncomfortable that she removed, after 1643, to the Dutch Col. and settled on Long Island, where Sir Henry Moody lived, who may have been her son, but more certain in Wood's Hist. is called one of the original patentees. There she resided long; had from Gov. Stuyvesant allowance to nominate magistrate, in 1654, for Gravesend, as Increase Mather had from King William to dictate for Mass. in her new charter.

REFERENCES:—Alden's Am. Epitaphs II, 120; Am. Ancestry, VII, 206; IX, 197; Eliot, Me., Early Settlers, 17-23; Fogg's Eliot, Me., Settlers, 13, 19; Kimball Gen., 85-8; Savage's Gen. Dict., III, 225-7; Wentworth Genealogy, 170; Hayward's Hist. of Hancock, N. H., 767.

MOONE:—Robert, Boston, tailor; by wife Dorothy had Ebenezer, 1645.

REFERENCES:—Austin's R. I. Gen. Dict., 133; Walker Genealogy, 170.

MOORCOCK, or MORECOCK:—Nicholas, Wethersfield; probably came, 1635, in the Elizabeth and Ann, from London, to Boston, aged 14, with Bennett, 16, and Mary, 10, who may have been brother and sister, certified by the minister of Beninden, in Co. Kent; one of this name married a daughter of Thomas Burnham of Windsor.

MOORE, or MOOR:—Francis, Cambridge; freeman, 1639; brought wife Catherine, who died 1648; had children Francis, Samuel, John, and perhaps Ann. also Thomas, named with John in the will of brother Francis; married second wife 1653, Elizabeth, widow, perhaps. of Thomas Periman. He died 1671, aged 85, and his widow died 1683, aged 84. Ann married James Kidder.

MOORE, GEORGE, Scituate; had been a servant of Edward Dotey; at Plymouth, 1630, kept the ferry on Jones River in Kingston 1633-8; had much land 1642; fell distracted in 1664. when guardians had power to sell some of his estate, and died 1677 suddenly.

MOORE, GOLDIN, Cambridge, 1636; freeman, 1641; married Joan, widow of John Champney; had Hannah,

1643; Lydia, and Ruth; was a settler on the farms, 1642, now Lexington; removed to Billerica; died there, 1698, in 89th year.

MOORE, MILES, Milford, 1646; removed as early as 1657, to New London; freeman 1663; left descendants through daughter Miriam, wife of John Willey; besides Abel.

MOORE, RICHARD, Plymouth; brought by Elder Brewster,.with a brother, both as servants, in the Mayflower, 1620; the brother died in a few weeks; at the division of cattle, 1627, when the name of every man, woman and child is given, he was still associated with Elder Brewster; but by Gov. Bradford's Hist., 451, he married in 1651; had four or five children living. Gov. Bradford did not mention names of children or mother. Perhaps he removed to one of the newer settlements. Winsor's Duxbury tells that he sold his land, 1637; and after long search, Savage is convinced that he is the Richard of Deane, in history of Scituate. called Mann, as the other four passengers with this baptismal name of Richard were all then adult. See Mann.

MOORE, RICHARD, Cape Porpoise, now Kennebunk; had grant of acres in 1647, and less than 20 years after was of Scarsborough; had wife Bridget; became pauper 1679, and died 1681.

MOORE, THOMAS, Portsmouth, one of the first settlers sent by John Mason, the patentee, 1631.

MOORE, JONATHAN, Boston, youngest son of Ann, widow of William Hibbins. the assistant in the will of his mother, 1656, shortly before her execution. for the preposterous crime of witchcraft, speaks of him and his brothers John and Joseph, as if all were in England, and in the codicil acknowledges "the more than ordinary affection 'of this one,' in the time of my distress," as he had arrived to attend the result of the execrable fanaticism. She was probably the richest person ever hanged in this part, and the prejudice against witches long slumbered.

MOORE, JASPER, Plymouth. servant boy of Gov. Carver, who died soon after arriving in the Mayflower, by careless reading often supposed to be son of the Governor, who had no children, though many thousands have prided themselves on being his descendants.

MOORE, JEREMY, Hingham; came in 1638, by the Diligent; was from Wymondham, a large town in Co. Norfolk; removed to Boston, 1643; was freeman, 1645; died before 1669, leaving Jeremiah, Samuel, and Mary. who married John Cotton.

MOORE, JOHN, Newtown, Long Island. 1656; was then first minister, says Riker's Hist.

MOORE, JOHN, Dorchester, 1630; came in the Mary and John, probably, for he was freeman, 1631; a deacon; went with Warham, 1635, to Windsor; was there a chief man; mentioned often in 1643, 1665; died Sept., 1677. He had Abigail, 1639; Mindwell, 1643; and John. 1645; had. probably. older daughters: Hannah. who married, 1648. John Drake; and Elizabeth, who married Nathaniel Loomis; Abigail married, 1655, Thomas Bissell; Mindwell married. 1662, Nathaniel Bissell.

MOORE, ISAAC, Norwalk; one of the first settlers; had first been of Farmington; married at Hartford, 1645, Ruth, daughter of John Stanley, a sergeant in 1649, may be that youth of 13, who came in the Increase, 1635, from London, to Boston; was representative for Norwalk. 1657; had Ruth, 1657; Sarah. 1662; Mary, 1664 Phebe. 1669; no sons; went back to Farmington, 1660; was a deacon; married daughter of Rev. Henry Smith, who had been widow of three husbands.

MOORE, WILLIAM, Exeter, 1645; was a representative in the Assembly of New Hampshire.

MOORE, WILLIAM, York, 1652, when he submitted to the Massachusetts government to 1680, when he took the oath of allegiance to his Majesty.

MOORE, WILLIAM, Westerly, 1669; may be the same who, at Norwich, married, 1677, Mary, widow of Thomas Howard, who was killed at the great battle of Philip's war, 1675; married daughter of Thomas Wellman; had Elizabeth, 1678; Experience, 1680; Martha, 1682; Joshua, 1683; William, 1685; and Abigail, 1687. His wife died 1700, and he married, in 1700. Mary, widow of Joshua Allen of Windham, who died 1727; and he married, 1728, Tamison Simmons, and died 1729.

REFERENCES:—Adams' Fairhaven, Vt., 443; American Ancestry I, 56; II, 86; IV, 126; V, 102, 225; XII, 60; Barry's Hist. of Framingham, Mass., 334; Campbell's Spotswood Family of Va., 20-3: Cleveland's Hist. of Yates Co., N. Y., 517; Davis Genealogy, 36, 122-4; Eaton's Hist. of Thomaston, Me., II. 333; Foote's Hist. of Va., first series, 506; Green's Kentucky Families; Harris Hist. of Lancaster Co., Pa., 399; Littell's Passaic Valley Gencalogies, 294; Mitchell's Hist. of Bridgewater, Mass., 248; New York Gen. and Biog. Rec., XV, 57-68; Old Northwest Gen. Quarterly II, 104-6; Power's Sangamon Co., Ill., Settlers, 528-30; Roberts' Old Richland, Pa., Families, 171-3; Stearns' Hist. of Ashburnham, Mass., 831; Temple's Hist. of Palmer, Mass., 508-10; Wyman's Charlestown, Mass., Gens., II, 683.

MOORES:—Edmund, Newbury; Coffin says, came 1640, aged 26; by wife Ann, who died 1676, had Martha, 1643; Jonathan, 1646; Mary, 1648; Edmund, who died 1656; Richard, 1653; Sarah, 1661.

MOORES, MATTHEW, Newbury; married, 1662, Sarah Savory; had Sarah, 1663; William, 1666.

MOORES, SAMUEL, Newbury; married, 1653, Hannah Plummer, who died 1654, and he married, 1656, Mary Ilsley, daughter of William of the same.

REFERENCE:—Hayward's Hancock, 772.

MOREHOUSE, or MOOREHOUSE :— John, Fairfield; ensign in 1676.

MOORHOUSE, JONATHAN, Fairfield; married Mary, daughter of Edward Wilson, before 1684.

MOOREHOUSE, THOMAS, Wethersfield, 1640; perhaps was at Stamford next year, but in 1653 at Fairfield.

REFERENCES:—Am. Ancestry, VII. 7; Collamer's Genealogist, 17; Morehouse Genealogy (1895), 40 p.; Todd's Hist. of Redding, Ct., 208.

MORFIELD, or MOORFIELD:—John, Hingham; came in the Diligent, 1638, from old Hingham.

MORELL:—William; came, 1623, with Robert Gorges, to Weymouth; soon went to Plymouth, after Gorges left him and home within a year. His verses, Latin, and translated into English, show he was a fair scholar; and his prudence was proved by not producing the ecclesiastical commission he had to rule on this side of the water.

REFERENCES:—Am. Ancestry, IX, 160; Hudson's Hist. of Lexington, Mass., 141.

MOREY:—Roger, Providence, 1649; had early been one of Salem church; by wife Mary had Bethia, Mehitable, Roger, 1649; Thomas, 1652; Hannah, 1656; he died 1668.

MOREY, GEORGE, Duxbury, 1640; died that year; may be the passenger, 1635, from London, aged 23, by the Truelove.

MOREY, JONATHAN, Plymouth; married, 1659,

Mary, widow of Richard Foster, daughter of Robert Bartlett.

MOREY, BENJAMIN, Wickford, 1674; was some relation, probably, of Isaac Heath, of Roxbury, who names Mary and Benjamin in his will, 1661.

REFERENCES:—Am. Ancestry, II, 87; Bolton's Westchester Co., N. Y., I, 238; Lincoln's Hist. of Hingham, Mass., III, 73; Morey Genealogy (1890), 30 pages.

MORGAN:—Miles, Springfield; by family tradition, said to have arrived at Boston, 1636, with two brothers, from Bistol; by wife Prudence had Mary, 1645; Jonathan, 1646; David, 1648; Pelatiah. 1650; Isaac, 1652; Lydia, 1654; Hannah, 1656; Mercy, 1658; his wife died 1661. He marired, 1670, Elizabeth Bliss, daughter of Thomas; had Nathaniel, 1671; died 1699.

MORGAN, ROBERT, Salem. 1637; adm. of the church, 1650; June that year had baptised Samuel. Luke, Joseph, and Benjamin, and December following Robert; Bethia, 1653; Aaron, 1663; was one of the founders of the church at Beverly, 1667. His will, 1672, names wife Margaret, son Samuel w. s. f. Norman, sons Benjamin, Robert, Bethia, Joseph, and Moses.

MORGAN, JAMES, Roxbury, 1640; married Margery Hill; had Hannah, 1642; James, 1644; John, 1645; Joseph, 1646; Abraham, 1648; was freeman 1643; removed to New London; was representative 1657, when he swore he was fifty years old; representative for the last time in 1670.

REFERENCES:—Am. Ancestry, III, 36; IV, 180; Clement's Newtown, N. J., Settlers; Daniels' History of Oxford, Mass; Meade's Old Churches of Virginia, II, 302; Paxton's Marshall Genealogy, 290; Temple's History of Northfield, Mass.

ARMS:—Vert, a lion, rampant, or.

MORLEY:—John, Braintree; freeman, 1645; removed, 1658, to Charlestown, he and his wife being recorded into the church that year. He names in his will his sister, Ann Farmer. In his wife's will is more instruction for genealogy, as she mentions her brother Joye (perhaps meaning Joseph) Starr, her sister Ann Farmer, her sister Suretrust Rous, nephew John Starr, cousins Mercy Swett and Simon Eyre, Elizabeth, wife of John Fernside, and Elizabeth and William Edmunds. No doubt she was sister of the first Comfort Starr.

REFERENCES:—Am. Ancestry, IX, 22; Savage's Genealogical Dictionary, III, 333.

MORRILL:—Abraham, Cambridge, 1632; perhaps came in the Lion, with brother Isaac, 1638; removed with original proprietors to Salisbury, where, in 1650, only four men were taxed higher; died 1662. He married Sarah, daughter of Robert Clement of Haverhill; had Isaac, 1646; Jacob, 1648; Sarah, 1650; Abraham, 1652; Moses, 1655; Aaron, 1658; Richard, 1660; Lydia, 1661; Hepzibah, 1663, posthumous. His will names wife Sarah, children Isaac, the eldest, Abraham, Jacob, Moses, Lydia, and Sarah, besides his brother, Job Clement. His estate was £507. Lydia married Ephraim Severance.

MORRILL, ISAAC, Roxbury, brother of Abraham, said to have been born 1588; came in the Lion, 1632, bringing wife and probably Sarah and Catharine; freeman, 1633, by wife Sarah had here Isaac, 1632; died next year; Isaac, again, 1634, died young; Hannah, 1636; Elizabeth, 1638; Abraham, 1640. Sarah married Tobias Davis, 1646; Catharine married, 1647, John Smith; and Hannah married, 1652, Daniel Brewer. His will names grandchildren John, Isaac, Francis, Mary and Abraham Smith, and Sarah Davis.

REFERENCES:—Bourne's Hist. of Wells, Me., 759; Chase's Hist. of Chester, N. H., 571; Hoyt's Salisbury, Mass., Families, 251-6; Little's Hist. of Weare, N. H., 94; Morrill Family, Cambridge, Mass. (1886) Chart.; Runnel's Sanbornton, N. H., II, 489-93.

MORRIS:—Edward, Roxbury: married, 1655, Grace Burr; had Isaac, 1656; Edward, 1659; Grace, 1661; Ebenezer, 1664; Eliz., 1666; Margaret, 1668; Samuel, 1671; Martha, 1675; was representative 1678-1686; removed to New Roxbury, since called Woodstock; died 1692; when administered his estate was great. Grace, his daughter, married Benjamin Child, 1683; and Elizabeth married, 1685, Joshua Child; and Margaret, in 1689, John Johnson.

MORRIS, RICHARD, Boston, 1630; came probably in the fleet with Winthrop; he and his wife were very early of the church Nos. 64 and 5; freeman 1631, with title of sergeant, and so perhaps a hired officer at Roxbury soon after, and was representative 1635-1637; but, favoring the cause of Rev. John Wheelwright, was disarmed, and with that heresiarch went to Exeter, 1638; dismissal was granted, 1639, to Wheelwright and eight others, including him, "unto the church of Christ at the Falls of Paschataqua, if they be rightly gathered and ordered." The spelling is Morrys.

MORRIS, THOMAS, New Haven, 1639; by wife Elizabeth had John, Hannah, 1642; Eliz., John, Eleazer, 1648; Thomas and Ephraim, twins, 1651; and Joseph, 1656; wife died 1668, and he died 1673. Hannah married, 1652, Thomas Lupton.

REFERENCES:—Am. Ancestry, III, 66; IV, 243; V, 108, 172; VI, 16; Bolton's Westchester Co., N. Y., II, 455; Morris Family of Woodstock (1887), 423 p.; Shourd's Fenwick's Colony, N. J., 161-3; Stanton Genealogy, 265; Thomas Genealogy (1877), 121; Whitmore's Heraldic Journal, III, 72; Wyman's Charlestown, Mass., Gens., II, 685.

ARMS:—Quartered, 1st and 4th: Gu., a lion, reguardant. or. 2d and 3d: Arg., three torteaux.

MORRISON:—Andrew, New Haven, 1690.

MORRISON, DANIEL, Newbury, 1690; by wife Hannah had Daniel, 1691; John, 1693; Hannah, 1696; Ebenezer, 1697; and Mary.

REFERENCES:—Adams' Genealogy (1894), 76-9: Am. Ancestry, III, 37, 177; Butler's Hist. of Farmington. Me., 534-6; Harris' Hist. of Lancaster Co., Pa., 401; Leonard's Gen. of W. Smith, appendix; Strobridge Genealogy, 159-226.

MORSE:—Anthony, Newbury. a shoemaker of Marlborough. Wiltshire: arrived at Boston, 1635, in the James from Southampton; said to have been born 1606: freeman. 1636; by wife Mary had Anthony, Benjamin, 1640; Sarah. 1641: Hannah, 1642; Lydia, 1645, died; Lydia. again, 1647. died in a few months; Mary, 1649; Esther, 1651; Joshua. 1653; had second wife Ann, who died 1680: he died 1686. Sarah married Amos Stickney. Esther married Robert Holmes, 1669.

MORSE, DANIEL, Watertown. son of Samuel, born in England, 1635; removed to Dedham; there by wife Lydia Fisher had Obadiah, 1639; Daniel, 1641; Jonathan. 1643; Lydia. 1645; Bethia, 1647; Mary, 1650; at Medfield had Bathshua. 1653; Nathaniel, 1658; Samuel, 1661. His original parchment deed conveyed. with consent of wife Lydia, to John Hull, part of his estate in Medfield. 1666. His last residence was in Sherborn. where he died, in 1688, aged 70.

MORSE, JOHN, Boston, tailor; married, 1652, Mary

Jupe. niece of Robert Keayne; had Mary, 1654; was probably the freeman of 1654, and went home, but came back in the Speedwell, 1656, aged 40, and may be the person whose death is mentioned in 1657. In that ship at that time, came the first Quakers.

MORSE, SAMUEL, Dedham, perhaps brother of Daniel; came in the Increase, from London, 1635, aged 50, with wife Elizabeth, aged 48, and son Joseph, who died 1654; he gives wife Elizabeth all his estate, but after her life to be divided among children John, Daniel, and Mary, wife of Samuel Bullen.

MORSE, WILLIAM, brother of Anthony; came with him in 1635, in the James from Southampton; had been a shoemaker at Marlborough; by wife Elizabeth had Elizabeth, 1655; Ann, perhaps before her, yet may be the daughter named by Coffin, 1641; perhaps John or Jonathan, Joseph, Timothy, 1647; Abigail, 1652. Ann married Francis Thorla. Mather Magn., VI, 68, exults on the wondrous diabolical operations within and without her dwelling, of which all were traceable to a roguish person. It was Increase Mather that first published the full relation of those follies as wonders, much of the evidence. how the devil was played in 1679, for which poor tormented Elizabeth was sentenced to be hanged for a scapegrace, but happily pardoned before the grim adversary's full triumph was gathered.

REFERENCES:—Aldrich's Walpole, N. Hampshire, 337-9; Am. Ancestry, III, 225; Ammidon Genealogy, 49-53; Ballou's History of Milford, Mass., 910; Barry's History of Framingham, Mass., 335-7; Bond's Watertown, Mass., 317-4; 859, 895; Chase's History Chester, New Hampshire, 566-9; Daniel's History of Oxford, Mass., 624; Hale Genealogy, 87-90; 172-80; Lapham's History of Paris, Me., 680-2; Leonard's History of Dublin, N. H., 370-6; Morse Family Meeting (1895), 44 pages; Preble Genealogy, 258; Wakefield Genealogy. 158.

MORTIMER, MORTIMORE, or MALTIMORE: —Edward, Boston, merchant: by wife Jane had Dorcas, 1674; Edward, 1676; Elizabeth, 1678; Richard, 1680; Jane, 1686; and Robert, 1688. He is highly commended by John Dunton, who says he came from Ireland.

MORTIMER, RICHARD, Boston. perhaps brother of the preceding; by wife Ann had Mary. 1664.

MORTIMER, THOMAS, New London: was constable 1680; had wife Eliza. and two daughters—Mary. who married Robert Stoddard, and Elizabeth married Abraham Willey. He died 1710.

REFERENCES:—Thomas Gen. (1896). 452; Welles' American Family Antiquity. II. 241-60.

MORTON:—Charles. Charlestown. eldest son of Rev. Nicholas, who died at Southwark, near London, having a parish: descended from an ancient family at Morton, in Co. Notts, where was the seat of Thomas Morton, secretary of Edward III: was born 1626, in Cornwall. bred at Wadham. Coll. Oxford; settled at Bisland. in his native county. as minister: ejected in 1662: he lived several years at Newington Green. near London, engaged teaching in private seminary. until 1686. when he embarked for Boston. and was ordained: a nephew. Nicholas. Harvard College 1686. died at Charlestown 1689, had come a year earlier than his uncle. He was chosen vice-president of the college

MORTON. GEORGE, Plymouth, born at Austerfield, in Yorkshire: baptised 1599: no doubt related to that numerous family; came in the Ann. 1623: married at Leyden. 1612. Juliana. daughter of Alexander Carpenter: four or five children, counted with Experience Mitchell, for eight in the division of lands, 1624; died same year; widow married Manasseh Kempton, and thought to have been sister of Gov. Bradford; died 1655, aged 81, beside children Nathaniel and Patience, who married in 1633, a fellow passenger. John Faunce, friend of the celebrated Elder: John, 1616; Sarah, 1618, married, 1644. George Bonham; and Ephraim, before mentioned.

MORTON, JOHN, Boston; by wife Martha had John, 1649.

MORTON, JOHN, Salem, petitioner against imposts, 1668.

MORTON, NATHANIEL, Plymouth, eldest son of George, born in England, 1613; came with his father; freeman 1635, and that year married Lydia Cooper; had Remember, 1637; Mercy, Lydia. Elizabeth, 1652; Johanna, 1654; and Hannah, besides Eliezer and Nathaniel, who both died in early youth. He was secretary of the colony from 1645-1685; first wife died 1673; he married, 1674, Ann, widow of Richard Templar, of Charlestown, who survived him; died 1690, aged 66.

MORTON, RICHARD. Hartford, blacksmith; was freeman there, 1669; had Richard and Thomas; removed, 1670. to Hatfield; had John. 1670, died soon; Joseph, 1672; John. again, 1674, died young; Abraham, 1676; Elizabeth, 1680; Ebenezer, 1682; and Jonathan, 1684; was freeman 1690; died 1710. His widow Ruth died 1714; all his executors lived at Hatfield.

MORTON, THOMAS, Plymouth; came in the Ann, 1623, in company with George, who may have been his brother; is called junior in the division of cattle, 1627; the other Thomas is not named; was residing there 1641.

MORTON, THOMAS, Braintree, the pettifoger of Clifford's Inn, London; came June, 1622: seems much to have displeased all the settlers in other plantations; perhaps in no small degree for calling his plantation Merry Mount; was seized and sent home. 1628, for causes well set down by Gov. Bradford in Hist. Coll., III, 62; soon returned and followed similar courses, and by Gov. Winthrop was sent off; he was infatuated with New England, punished and died in poverty at York, 1646. He published New England Canaan, one of the most amusing, and not least valuable books descriptive of our country.

MORTON, WILLIAM, New London, one of the first settlers in 1646; constable 1658, and after; died 1668 without children.

MORTON, WILLIAM, Windsor; freeman in 1669; died 1670; had William, who died before his father; John, Thomas, who died before his father; left children.

REFERENCES:—Am. Ancestry, IV, 234; VIII, 263; IX, 74, 101; Collin's Gen., III, 3; Davis' Landmarks of Plymouth, Mass., 187-92; Hayden's Virginia Genealogies, 35; Lincoln's History of Hingham, Mass., III, 75; Martin's History of Chester, Pa., 142-6, 157; Morton Family Ancestry (1894), 191 pages; Savage's Gen. Dict., III, 243, 5; Watkin's Gen., 18, 30-4.

MOSES:—Aaron, New Hampshire, 1690, perhaps son of John; crav. jurisdic. of Mass. that year.

MOSES, HENRY, Salem; married Remember, daughter of Edward Gyles; had Hannah, 1660, died next year; Henry, 1662; Elizabeth, 1664; John, 1666; Remember, 1668; Edward. 1670; Eleazer. 1673; and Samuel, 1677.

MOSES, JOHN, New Hampshire. 1658.

MOSES, JOHN, Windsor, 1647; married, 1653, Mary Brown; had John, 1654; William, 1655; Thomas, 1659; both the last died before the father; Mary, 1661; Sarah,

1663; Margaret, 1666; Timothy, 1670; Martha, 1672; Mindwell, 1676. He died 1683, and his widow 1689; his daughter Mary married, as his second wife, Samuel Farnsworth, in 1685.

REFERENCES:—Am. Ancestry, IV, 52; VII, 104, 142. 174; IX, 82; Ballou Gen., 296-303; Moses Gen. (1890), 138 pages.

MOSIER. or MOSHIER:—Arthur, Boston; by wife Rebecca had Lydia, 1678; Thomas, 1679; Samuel, 1683.

MOSIER, HUGH, Falmouth, 1640; came perhaps in the Jane from London, eight weeks' voyage; was inhabitant of Newport, 1660; engaged in the purchase of Misquamsitt; died before 1666, leaving James and John. He married Rebecca, daughter of John Harnden, of Newport; as second wife, unless another Hugh be intended, in her will filed 1685.

REFERENCES:—Am. Ancestry, I, 56; Paul's History of Wells, Vt., 124; Corliss' N. Yarmouth, Me.; Pierce's History of Gorham, Me., 194.

MOSMAN:—James, Wrentham; by wife Ann had Elizabeth, 1675; died soon. He probably removed to Roxbury; ther had Timothy, 1679; and Elizabeth, 1696; it is not certain if by the same wife, or whether other children had not been born.

REFERENCES:—Eaton's Thomaston, Me., 336; Heywood's History of Westminster, Mass., 798-803.

MOSS:—John, New Haven, 1639; signed the original comp. 1643; had John, probably 1640, died young; Samuel, 1641; Abigail, 1642; Joseph, 1643; Ephraim, 1645; Mary, 1647; Mercy (male), 1649; John, again, 1650; Elizabeth, 1652; Esther, 1654; Isaac, 1655. He was represent. 1667-70, and then removed to Wallingford, 1670, of which he was represent, 1671-3, yet continued prop. at New Haven; died 1707, aged 103.

MOSS, JOSEPH, Portsmouth, Mass., 1665.

MOSS, JOSEPH, Boston; by wife Mary had Joseph, 1687; and Joseph, again, 1689.

REFERENCES:—Anderson's Waterbury, Ct., I, 92; Leavenworth Genealogy, 68-73; Sharpless Genealogy, 183; Shourd's Fenwick Colony, N. J., 173-5.

MOTT:—Adam. Hingham, a tailor from Cambridge. England; came in the Defence, 1635, aged 39, with wife Sarah, 31, and children John, 14; Adam, 12; Jonathan, 9; Elizabeth, 6; and Mary, 4; was first of Roxbury; freeman 1636; went, 1638, to Rhode Island with family; there had, perhaps, more children, and was with Adam, Jr., John, and Jonathan; perhaps his son lived at Portsmouth as freeman, 1655.

MOTT, JOHN. Newport; perhaps brother of the first Adam; signed the compact at the same time with him, 1638; was of Block Island, or one of the same name, 1684.

MOTT, NATHANIEL, Scituate; able to bear arms 1643; removed to Braintree; married, 1656, Hannah Shooter; had Nathaniel, 1657.

A Margaret More came in Speedwell, 1656, aged 12.

REFERENCES:—Am. Ancestry, I, 56; VIII, 72; IX, 220; Austin's Rhode Island Dictionary, 135, 344; Bunker's Long Island Genealogies, 252-60; Deane's History of Scituate, Mass., 313; Mott Genealogy (1890), 418 pages; Rhode Island Historical Magazine; V, 34-6; VII, 289-93; Talcott's New York and New England Families, 610-5.

MOULD:—Hugh, New London, 1660; shipbuilder; married, 1662. Martha, daughter of John Coit; had been perhaps first at Barnstable; died 1692, leaving widow Martha, and six daughters. Susanna married, 1683, Daniel White; and Mary, in 1693, Joseph White, and the mother of the girls married the father of their husbands, as his second wife.

MOULD, SAMUEL, Charlestown; by wife Mary had Mary, baptised 1689. the mother having been, in 1687, aged 20.

REFERENCE:—Coit Genealogy, 28.

MOULDER:—Nicholas, Boston, merchant; by wife Christian had Nicholas, born 1672. He was abused as a Quaker, by Gov. Bellingham, and removed to whence he came. They abused him, changing his Christian name. for the Friends' record proves that it was Edward, born 1669, and at Boston Nicholas, 1671, who probably died soon; and Nicholas, again, by Boston record, June, 1672.

REFERENCE:—Coit's Genealogy.

MOULTHROP, or MOULTROP:—Matthew, New Haven, 1639; by wife Jane had Matthew, Elizabeth, and Mary, perhaps the first two born in England; Elizabeth born 1638, and Mary in 1641; were baptised in 1642. He died 1668. and his widow died in 1672. Elizabeth married, 1663, John Gregory.

REFERENCES:—Am. Ancestry, VIII, 10; Dodd's History of East Haven, Ct., 137-9; Sharp's Hist. of Seymour, Ct., 224-6.

MOULTON:—Benjamin, Hampton, son of William; took oath of fidelity, 1678; was living in 1690.

MOULTON, HENRY, Hampton, 1640, probably son of John, born in England. His will, 1654, names wife Mary, Savage thinks daughter of Edward Hilton; children Jonathan and David.

MOULTON, JACOB, Charlestown, 1663, says Barry.

MOULTON, JAMES, Salem; joined the church 1637, as did wife Mary next year; had baptised James, 1638; Samuel, 1642; was freeman 1638; lived at Wenham, 1667. His will, 1679, names two sons and daughter Mary Friend.

MOULTON, JEREMIAH, York, perhaps son of Thomas; took oath of allegiance 1681; representative 1692, and after of the Council, 1727, in 77th year.

MOULTON, JOHN, Newbury; came from Ormsby, in Co. Norfolk, near Great Yarmouth; embarked 1637; called husbandman, aged 38, wife same age, Ann; five children, Henry, Mary, Ann, Jane and Bridget; two servants, Adam Goodwin, 20, and Alice Eden, 19; had John, baptised 1638; removed to Hampton, 1639; there had Ruth, baptised 1640, died 1651; had other children, William and Thomas, Jane and Bridget: were twins, who died on same day; aged 64. Cotton Mather wrote to Woodward of the Royal Soc. a memoir of these maidens. His will, 1650, names wife Ann; sons Henry, John, and Thomas, daughters Mary Sanborn, Ann, Jane, Bridget, and son Sanborn.

MOULTON, ROBERT, Salem, a shipbuilder; came 1629, in fleet with Higginson, but went to Charlestown; freeman 1631; was one of the first selectmen, and representative at the first court, 1634, and for Salem in 1637; was that year disarmed as a friend of Wheelwright; died 1655, leaving Robert and Dorothy, wife of one Edwards, as also grandson Robert, named in his will.

MOULTON, THOMAS, Charlestown, 1631, perhaps brother of Robert; lived on Malden side; had wife Jane, and child John; baptised 1633; Martha, 1637; Hannah, 1641; Elizabeth, 1642; beside Jacob, who died 1657. A

daughter Mary, Savage thinks, married, 1655, Thomas Mitchell.

MOULTON, THOMAS, Newbury, 1637; removed with Rev. Mr. Bachilor, in 1639, to Hampton; by wife Martha had Thomas, baptised 1639, and Daniel, 1641; was freeman 1639; died 1665.

MOULTON, THOMAS, York; constable 1661.

MOULTON, WILLIAM, Hampton; came 1637, aged 20, as servant of Robert Page of Ormsby, Co. Norfolk, and his daughter Margaret; had Joseph, Benjamin, Hannah, Mary, Robert, and Sarah, who was born 1656; all mentioned in his will, 1664, besides provision for unborn child, perhaps called Ruth. Mary married, 1674, Jonathan Haynes of Hampton, who died soon, and he next married, same year, Sarah, daughter of W. Moulton.

REFERENCES:—Am. Ancestry, III, 209; VI, 74; XI, 43; Daniels' History of Oxford, Mass., 625; Dow's History of Hampton, N. H., 860-78; Emery Genealogy (1890), 76-91; King Genealogy (1897), 43-70; Moulton Genealogy (1873), 44 pages; Moulton Genealogy (1893), 99 pages; Temple's History of N. Brookfield, Mass., 688.

MOUNTAIN:—Richard, Boston; had wife Abigail, who joined the church April 4, 1646.

MOUNTFORD, MUNFORD, or MUMFORD:—Benjamin, Boston, merchant; came, it is said, 1675, in the Dove, from London, aged 30; artillery company, 1679; was one of the wardens of King's Chapel, 1690; died 1714.

MOUNTFORT, EBENEZER, Boston, 1676, when the sec. church was burned; his house was also burned.

MOUNTFORT, EDMUND, Boston, tailor; by wife Elizabeth had Edmund, 1664; Henry, 1666; Benjamin, 1668; John, 1670; Sarah, 1672; Hannah, 1673; Joshua, 1675, and Jonathan, 1678.

MOUNTFORT, HENRY, brother of Edmund; by wife Ruth, perhaps daughter of Elder John Wiswall, had Henry, 1688, died young; in his will, 1691, names Ebenezer, then minor, as only child; yet remembering two sisters in England, Hannah and Sarah.

MOUNTFORT, JOHN; took oath of allegiance 1671.

MOUNTFORT, WILLIAM, Boston. mason; by wife Ruth had Ruth, 1671; Lydia, 1672; William, 1677; Elizabeth, 1679; Naomi, 1681; perhaps one not rec. in Philip's war.

REFERENCES:— Bridgeman's Granary Burying Ground, Boston. Epitaphs, 112; Vinton's Giles Genealogy, 148; Whitmore's Copps. Hills Epitaphs; Whitmore's Heraldic Journal.

MOUNTJOY:—Benjamin, Salem; died 1659.

MOUNTJOY, WALTER, Salem; married, 1672, widow Elizabeth Owen.

REFERENCE:—Garrard Genealogy, 103-7.

MOUSALL:—John, Charlestown, 1634; with wife joined church; also freeman, 1635; artillery company, 1641; deacon and selectman, 1642; removed to Woburn; died 1665. Possibly he was tempted to Salem; a John Mousall had grant of land there 1639, and a church member 1646. Ruth Mousall, names closely resembling. His daughter Eunice married, 1649, John Brooks. His will, 1660, probated 1665, names wife Joanna, son John and John Brooks, executors, with mention of grandchildren Sarah, Eunice, and Joanna Brooks.

MOUSALL, JOHN, Charlestown, son probably of Ralph, born in England; by wife Elizabeth had Elizabeth, 1659; was perhaps soldier in Moseley's Comp., 1675; died 1704, aged 74.

MOUSALL, RALPH, Charlestown, brother of the first John; came, perhaps, in the fleet with Winthrop, he being No. 72, and wife Alice No. 73 in the list of Boston church members, desiring adm. as freeman, 1630; was sworn the May following, when the name appears Mashell, and in Geneal. Reg., VII, 30, Moushole. He was one of the founders of the church at Charlestown, representative in 1636, but, being a favorer of Wheelwright, was ejected, yet later recovered his reputation; was deacon 1657. leaving John, who was probably in England: Thomas, baptised 1633; Mary Goble, Ruth Wood, and Elizabeth. His will, 1633, names cousins, Nathaniel Ball and Mary Wayne, in a codicil, mentions son Thomas, having a son born. His widow died 1667.
REFERENCES:—New England Historical and Gen. Register, XLVII. 462-7; Savage's Gen. Dict., III, 250; Wyman's Charlestown, Mass, II, 688-92.

MOUSSETT:—Thomas, Boston; by wife Catherine had Peter, born 1687; was probably a Huguenot, and one of the four ruling elders of that communion. The name is not found in Boston any more, though he owned land in Roxbury, 1698, and lived at Braintree.

MOWER:—Richard, Salem, 1638, probably passenger in the Blessing from London, 1635, aged 20; a mariner; joined the church 1642; had Samuel and Thomas baptised that year; Caleb, 1644; Joshua, 1646; Richard, 1648; Susanna, 1650; Christian, 1652; was freeman 1643; employed by government 1654; had Mary, born 1662; was living 1696.
REFERENCES:—Cleveland's Yates Co., 377; Mower Genealogy (1897), 12 pages; Wall's Reminiscences of Worcester, Mass., 351; Washburn's Hist. of Leicester, Mass., 384.

MOXON:—George, Springfield, 1637, the first minister; came from Yorkshire; had been bred at Sidney College, in the Univ. of Cambridge; took his A. B. 1623; with wife Ann sat down first at Dorchester, after being freeman, 1637; was attracted to Springfield by his former neighbor, Pynchon, who was intimate; had three sons, Union, 1642; Samuel, 1645, and another, 1647, whose name is not mentioned in the record, but elder children Martha and Rebecca were, in 1651, said to be bewitched by Mary, wife of Hugh Parsons, who was, on trial, found not guilty.

MOWRY:—John, may be written Morey; at the London customs house Mory; a passenger, aged 19, in the Blessing from London, 1635; spelled with a "w."
REFERENCES:—Am. Ancestry, V, 119; VI. 121; VII, 19; Austin's R. Island Gen. Dict., 346-9; Ballou's Hist. of Milford, Mass., 911; Mowry Family of R. I. (1878), 343 pages.

MOYSE:—Joseph, Salisbury. His wife Hannah died 1655.

MUDDLE, or MUDDLES:—Henry, Gloucester; died before June, 1663, when inventory was taken. Philip, Gloucester, perhaps son or brother of preceding, petitioned against imposts, 1668.

MUDGE:—James, one of the "Flower of Essex," under Capt. Lothrop, killed by the Indians 18th Sept, 1675. at Bloody Brook.

MUDGE, JERVIS. Wethersfield, 1643; married, 1649, the widow of Abraham Elsen; removed to New London; died there, 1652, leaving that widow and two sons, probably born of a former wife

MUDGE, THOMAS. Malden, 1658; had Samuel, born 1658; and perhaps Martha, wife of Rev. Michael Wig-

glesworth. A George Mudge died, 1685, at Malden or Charlestown.
REFERENCES:—Bangor Hist. Mag., IV, 19; Mudge Genealogy (1865), 8 pages; Mudge Geneal. (1868), 443 pages; Phoenix's Whitney Geneal., II, 1013; Temple's Hist. of Northfield, Mass., 503.

MUDGET:—Thomas, Salisbury; married, perhaps, for second wife. 1665, Sarah Morrell, eldest daughter of Abraham the first; had Mary, 1667; and Temperance, 1670; was freeman, 1690. Another Thomas, Salisbury, perhaps a son, or the same, by wife Ann, had William, 1696; Thomas, 1699, probably died soon; Thomas, again, 1700.
REFERENCES:—Dearborn's Parsonsfield, 389; Hoyt's Salisbury, Mass., Families, 262; Little's History of Weare, N. H., 943.

MULFORD:—John, Easthampton, L. I., 1650; one of the first settlers, says Wood, 44; perhaps went home for some time, and came again in the Speedwell, 1656, from London, when the name appears Mulfoot; was chosen Assist. 1658; had commission from Conn. as a magistrate, and 1674 as a judge.

MULFORD, THOMAS, Easthampton; by wife Hannah, had John, born 1670; Patience, 1674; Ann, 1677; his widow died 1718.

MULFORD, WILLIAM, Easthampton, L. I., 1650.
REFERENCES:—Freeman's Cape Cod, 375; Mulford Genealogy (1880), 12 pages; reprint; Southold, N. Y., Record, 172; Sulfolk County, N. Y., History, 30-2.

MULLIGAN, MULLEGIN, or MULLEKIN:—Hugh, Boston; by wife Elinor had Robert, 1681; in 1684 was admitted member of the Scot's Charit. Soc.

MULLIGAN, ROBERT, Rowley, perhaps brother of the preceding; by wife Rebecca had Robert, 1688; John, 1690; Mary, 1692; and others.

MULLERY:—John, Boston; by wife Abigail had Elizabeth, 1672; John, 1674; Ann, 1677; Abigail, 1681; Susanna, 1684; Robert, 1686; Joseph, 1688; besides Sarah, baptised 1690, and Benjamin, 1691.

MULLINER:Thomas, New Haven, 1640; was a gr. purchaser of Branford, by its Indian name of Totoket in that year; had division of lands there in 1646 and 8.

MULLINER, THOMAS, New Haven, probably son of the preceding; sold out his lands at Branford, 1651; by wife Martha had Martha, 1656; and Elizabeth, 1658; removed, 1658, to West Chester, and was living there in 1691 with wife Martha.

MULLINS, or MOLINES:—William, Plymouth; came in the Mayflower, 1620, with wife, two children, Joseph and Priscilla, and a servant, Robert Carter; but the wife died a few days before or after him, who died 1621; and the sons and servant died the same season, but his daughter Priscilla married John Alden, and had eleven children.

MULLINS, WILLIAM, Duxbury, 1642; had lands in Middleborough, 1664. Good estate as well as character is told of the pilgrim.

MULLINS, WILLIAM, Boston; married, 1656. Ann, widow of Thomas Bell.
REFERENCES:—Littell's Passaic Valley, 297; Winsor's History of Duxbury, Mass., 283.

MUMFORD:—Edmund, Boston; married Elizabeth, widow of Joshua Carwithy, 1663.

MUMFORD, STEPHEN, Newport; came from London, 1664, and was the same preacher of the sect of the seventh day Baptists which prevails in a part of the State.

MUMFORD, THOMAS, Newport; had Thomas, 1656; Peleg, 1659; George, and Abigail, who married, 1682, Daniel Fish. Yet he does not appear a constant resident at Newport, though he joined with Brenton, John Hull and others in purchase of Pettaquamscuck. Possibly the name is the same as Mountfort. The name of his wife is not known, nor the time of his death, but it was before 1692.

MUMFORD, WILLIAM, a Quaker, whipped at Boston, 1677.

REFERENCES:—Am. Ancestry, V, 195; Cleveland's History of Yates Co., N. Y., 406-8; Narragansett Hist. Reg., IV, 135; Savage's Gen. Dict., III, 253, 264.

MUN, or MUNN:—Benjamin, Hartford; served in the war with the Pequots, 1637; removed to Springfield; married, 1649, Abigail, widow of Francis Ball, daughter of Henry Burt; had Abigail, 1650; John, 1652; Benjamin, 1655; James, 1657; Nathaniel, 1661; died 1675. His widow married Lieut. Thomas Stebbins, and his daughter Abigail married Thomas Stebbins, Jr.

MUN, DANIEL, Milford; died 1666, leaving will. Inventory of his estate £42.

MUN, SAMUEL, Wodbury, 1680, wheelwright; may well be of different family, from any preceding; he came from Milford; had Jane and Amy, baptised 1680; Mary, 1681; Daniel, 1684; Samuel, 1687. In modern times the name has double "n."

REFERENCES:—Baldwin Gen. Supp., 1122-4; Longmeadow, Mass., Centennial, 75; Shaw's Hist. of Essex Co., N. J., II, 725-8.

MUNDAY, or MONDAY:—Henry, Salisbury; freeman, 1640; was rated, 1652, higher than any other inhabitant but one. He has prefix of respect in town record.

MUNDAY, WILLIAM, passenger in the Mary and John, 1634; may have been father of the preceding; at least we know that several of the early settlers at Salisbury came in that voyage.

MUNDEN:—Abraham, Springfield; married, 1644, Ann Munson; had Mary, 1645; he was drowned at Enfield Falls, the same year. This daughter was complained of, 1676, at Northampton, for "wearing silk, and that in a flaunting manner."

MUNGER:—Nicholas, Guilford; married, 1659, Sarah Hull; had John, 1660; Samuel. 1668.

REFERENCES:—Adams' Fairhaven, Vt., 435; Temple's History of Palmer, Mass., 517.

MUNJOY, or MUNGY:—Benjamin, at Boston, master mariner, or ship carpenter. 1655; his estate, administered in Essex Co., 1659, by his wife's brother, £19, 2, 5.

MUNJOY, GEORGE, Boston, master mariner. or ship carpenter, 1647; son of John of Abbotsham, near Biddeford, Devonshire; adm. of the church 15th May, and same month freeman; married Mary. only daughter of John Philips, Boston; had John, baptised 1653; George, 1656; when church record calls him John; and Josiah, 1658; next year bought the Noah's Ark Tavern in Boston, but removed soon to Casco, to have charge of the great purch. from Cleves, by his father-in-law; had at Falmouth, Mary, brought up to Boston for baptism, 1665; and Hepsibah, besides sons Phillips, Benjamin. Peletiah and Gershom; all living in 1675, when the Indian war began. He died 1681, leaving widow Mary. Mary married John Palmer of Falmouth; Hepsibah married a Mortimore; and the widow married Robert Lawrence. and, in 1690. Stephen Cross.

MUNJOY, WALTER, Marblehead, 1668; petitioner against imposts.

REFERENCES:—Heywood's Westminster, 804-6; Maine's History Soc. Collections. I, 170.

MUNNINGS, or MULLINGS:—Edmund, Dorchester; came in the Abigail, 1635, aged 40, with wife Mary, 30. and children Mary, 9; Ann, 6; and Mahalaleel, 3; at Dorchester had Hopestill. 1637; Returned, 1640; and Takeheed, 1642. He was a proprietor late as 1658, but Savage thinks he had gone to Malden, Co. Essex; was connected there with Joseph Hills.

MUNNINGS, GEORGE, Watertown; came from Ipswich, Co. Suffolk, in the Elizabeth. 1634, aged 37, with wife Eliza. 41; and children Elizabeth, 12; Abigail, 7; freeman 1635; perhaps had Rebecca, who married, 1652, Edmund Maddocks, at Boston; was active in church and town; lost an eye in service, Pequot war. 1637; was an original propr. of Sudbury, but resided at Boston, 1645; several years kept the goal; died 1658; will, made day before death, gives estate to his wife Johanna.

REFERENCES:—Bond's Watertown, 374; Savage's Gen. Dict.. III, 255.

MUNROE, or MONROE:—Alexander, whose place of residence not sure; had before 1651, lawsuit in Mass. with Elias Parkman.

MUNROE, WILLIAM, Cambridge, in the part now Lexington; freeman, 1690; by wife Martha had John, 1666; Martha, 1667; William, 1669; and George; by second wife Mary, he had Daniel, 1673; Hannah, Elizabeth, Mary, 1678; David, 1680; Eleanor, 1683; Sarah, 1685; Joseph, 1687; and Benjamin, 1690. He died 1717, aged 92. It has been conjectured (see Savage) that he was a prisoner, taken by Cromwell at the decisive battle of Worcester. 1651, shipped in November, to be sold here, where the 272 unhappy men arrived the May after; Hugh, John, Robert, and another without baptismal name, all Monrows, formed part of the sad freight. Of his daughters, Martha married, 1688, John Come of Concord; Hannah, 1692, Joseph Pierce, as his second wife; Elizabeth married a Rugg; Mary married. perhaps, a Farwell; Eleanor married, 1707, William Burgess of Charlestown; and Sarah married a Blanchard.

REFERENCES:—Barry Hanover, Mass. 353; Cutter's History of Arlington, Mass., 277; Hudson's History of Lexington, Mass., 144-61; Munroe Genealogy (1858), 15 pages. reprint; Spooner's Mem. of W. Spooner. 93; Ward's History of Shrewsbury, Mass.

MUNSON, or MONSON:—Richard, New Hampshire: was one of the petitioners in the winter 1689-90 for Mass. jurisdiction.

MUNSON, THOMAS, Hartford. 1641; removed next year to New Haven; had Samuel. baptised 1643; and Hannah. 1648; was respresentative 1666. 9. 70-5. and served in the Indian war. He died 1685; in division of estate. another child named Elizabeth, wife of Richard Higginbotham; Hannah married. 1667, Joseph Tuttle. Susan. who came in the Elizabeth to Boston. 1634. aged 25, was probably his wife.

REFERENCES:—Anderson's Waterbury. Ct.. 92; Munson Family Reunion (1887). 88 pages: Munson Family Reunion (1896). 43 pages: New Eng. Hist. Gen. Reg.. XXIX, 139-41; Trowbridge Genealogy: Tuttle Genealogy, 672.

MUNT, or MOUNT:—Thomas, Boston, 1635; mason. His wife Dorothy died in 1640. and by wife Elinor he had Faith, who died soon; and Faith, again.

1645; besides two more daughters, names not seen. He died 1664. His widow married, 1668, Thomas Hill. Faith married, 1660, Clement Short.

MURDOCK:—Robert, Roxbury; married. 1692, Hannah Stedman; had Hannah. 1693; Robert. 1695: John, 1696; Samuel, 1698; Benjamin, 1701; removed, 1703, to Newton; there had Hannah, 1705. He is by Jackson supposed to have come from Plymouth Col. His wife died 1727; had second wife, Abigail; died 1754, aged 89.

REFERENCES:—Am. Ancestry, VIII. 215: IX, 38, 162; Buckingham Genealogy, 177-9; Egle's Notes and Queries, 2d ser., II, 42-5; Hedges' History of East Hampton, N. Y., 316; Keyes' West Boyleston. Mass.. Reg., 30.

MURPHY:—Bryan, Boston, an Irishman; married, 1661, widow Margaret Mahone.

REFERENCES:—Am. Ancestry, I, 56; IV, 216; VII, 28; Lincoln's History of Hingham, Mass., III, 76.

MURRY:—James, Dover, 1658.

MUSGROVE:—Jabez, a soldier under Capt. Turner, 1676; at Hatfield, shot by an Indian, with a ball "in the ear, and out at his eyes." He may have come from Concord, for one Mary Murry died there, 1649, but in 1680 he was of Newbury.

REFERENCES:—Harris' Lancaster, Pa., 404.

MUSHAMORE:———. Portsmouth, 1677. Mary, perhaps his daughter. married that year Christopher Kenniston.

REFERENCE:—Savage's Gen. Dict., III, 258.

MUSSELWHITE:—John. Newbury; came in the James, 1635, from Southampton; called in the custom house record of Longford. which is near Salisbury, Wilts, laborer; was first of Ipswich; freeman 1639; died 1671, leaving estate in Lavenstock, close to Salisbury, to brothers, Thomas. John, and sister Eda.

REFERENCES:—Savage's Gen. Dict., III, 258.

MUSSEY, or MUZZEY:—Abraham, a passenger who took the oath of supremacy and allegiance to pass for N. E., 1634, in the John and Mary of that year.

MUSSEY, BENJAMIN, Malden, perhaps living some time in that part of Boston called Rumney Marsh; married Alice, daughter of Richard Dexter; had Benjamin. 1657; Joseph, 1659.

MUSSEY, ROBERT, Ipswich, one of the first settlers; freeman 1634. died 1644.

MUSSEY, THOMAS, Cape Porpus. 1631-8-, in which last year he swore allegiance to the King.

Among Cambridge proprietors, 1632. appears Esther Mussey, a widow. who married. 1635 or 6, William Rusco, Rosco. or Rescue. probably his second wife. He sold part of her estate, as her husband. 1636. Often this is spelled Muzzy or Muzzey.

REFERENCES:—Barry's Framingham. 338; Morse's Mem. Appendix, 52; Ward's History of Shrewsbury. Mass., 373.

MUSSILLOWAY:—Daniel. Newbury, an Irishman; had been, 1665, servant to Joseph Plummer; married, 1672. Ann. widow of Aquila Chase. who died 1687; and by second wife, Mary. had Daniel. 1688, lived three days; Daniel. again. 1690; and John, 1693; and died 1711. Coffin thinks this name has become Siloway. and was easily mistaken for Musselwhite.

MUSTE:—Edward. Mass., of whom no more is found than that he was admitted freeman. 1634.

MYCALF:—James. Braintree; married, 1657 or 8.

Mary Farr; had James, born 1659; and twin sister Rebecca, who married, 1679, Richard Thayer.

MYATE. MYGATT, sometimes MAYGOTT, or MEGOTT:—Joseph, Cambridge; came in the Griffin, with famous Cotton and Hooker, 1633; freeman, 1635; removed to Hartford; representative, 1658, and often after; deacon; calls his age 70, in 1666; had only two children, Jacob thought. born 1633; and Mary, 1637. ..is widow Ann, born 1602. survived him; he died 1680, aged 84. Mary married, 1657, John Deming, the sec.

REFERENCES:—Baldwin's Gen. Supp., 1264-5; Mygatt Gen. (1853), 116 pages; Orcutt's Hist. of New Milford, Ct., 738-40.

MYLAM, or MILOM:—Humphrey, Boston, 1648; by wife Mary, daughter, perhaps of John Gore, of Roxbury, had Mary, born 1652; Constance, 1653; Abigail, 1660; and Sarah: was a cooper; in his will of 1667. names Mary and five daughters, of whom Constance married John Alcock; one of his wives, if he had two, was daughter of John Gore.

MYLAM, JOHN, Boston, probably elder brother of the preceding; a cooper; freeman 1636; by wife Christian had Benjamin, baptised 1636, died at 4 years; Constance, 1638; John, 1640; Eliasaph, 1642; baptised Eleazer, Samuel. 1644; Ebenezer, 1646; Samson, 1649; and Joseuh and Mary, twins. 1652; by another wife, Mary, had Sarah. 1656.

MYLES:—John, Swaney; came from Swansea, in Wales, 1662; first formed his ch. at Rehoboth, 1663; died 1683, leaving widow Ann, daughter of John Humphrey. and children John, Susanna. and Samuel, then, says his will. at Harvard College, 1684.

NALY:—Richard. Kittery: disfranchis. 1669, as a Quaker.

REFERENCES:—Hayden's Virginia Gens., 730.

NANEY, or NANNY:—Robert, Boston; sent by Robert Cordele, a goldsmith of Lombard St., London, in the Increase, 1635, aged 22; was first at Dover, perhaps. or Saco: had good character before coming, in 1652, to Boston. By wife Catharine, daughter of Rev. John Wheelwright, had John, 1654, died soon; John, again, 1656; Joseph, 1658; James, 1659; Mary, 1661; Elizabeth. 1663: and he died same year; his will, made five days before, names wife and children only Samuel, who was born before his father came from the E.. and Mary, and one anticip.; so probably the others died early. He was a merchant. owned estate in Barbadoes, perhaps in company with Richard Hutchinson of London. whom he calls uncle: by inventory, show £1,089, 14. 1½. His widow married Edward Naylor.

REFERENCE:—Savage's Gen. Dict., III. 260.

NARRAMORE:—Richard, Mass.; master of the Ketch Sparrow, 1687; brought persons from the Bahamas; suspected of piracy by Sir E. Andros, our Gov.

NARRAMORE, THOMAS, Dorchester, 1664. a fisherman; perhaps brother of preceding; removed to Boston. where wife Hannah joined the sec. church, 1681; by her had Hannah, 1671: Sarah. 1672; James, 1674; John, 1676; Sarah. 1686. Probably he removed to New Hampshire and early in 1690 prayed for jurisdic. of Mass.

REFERENCES:—Barrus' Goshen. Mass., 156; Bassett's Hist. of Richmond, N. H., 446.

NASH:—Edward. Norwalk, 1654; in 1672 had two children .in his family. probably others. He is not in the list of freemen 1669. though accepted conditionally. 1664. yet had good estate.

NASH, FRANCIS, Braintree, a soldier of Capt. Johnson's company, 1675.

NASH, GREGORY, Charlestown, 1630; came probably in fleet with Winthrop; he and his wife died following February.

NASH, ISAAC, Dover, 1657, perhaps removed to York; there died, 1662. His widow, Phebe, married John Pierce.

NASH, JACOB, Weymouth, son of James; by wife Abigail had Joseph, born 1669; Alice and Benjamin, twins, 1685; Sarah, 1688; beside Alice, and perhaps more; was freeman, 1666; representative, 1689 and 90. Jacob, Weymouth, son of James, probably, was freeman, 1686.

NASH, JAMES, Weymouth; fondly thought to have been a seetler there, in 1628, but may have been 1638; freeman, 1645; had James, Jacob, and perhaps other children; was representative, 1655, 62 and 7.

NASH, JOHN, New Haven, 1642, son of Thomas, born in England; had by wife Elizabeth, daughter probably of Edmund Tapp, of Milford, who died 1676, Elizabeth, baptised 1647; Sarah, 1649; Mary, 1652; Hannah, 1655; was lieutenant, 1652; representative, 1665; at the first Ct. after the union, and in 1672, chosen an assist., in which place he was cont. acc. the custom of ann. elect. to his death, 1687. Elizabeth married, 1676, Aaron Cook; Sarah married, 1689, Thomas Yale; Mary, 1679, Philip Paine; and Hannah married, 1673, Eliphalet Ball. and next, 1689, Thomas Trowbridge.

NASH, JOHN, Salisbury, 1660; had probably been 8 years before at Newbury.

NASH, JOHN, Boston, cooper; married Rebecca, daughter of Laurence Smith, of Dorchester; had Mary, 1667; John, 1672.

NASH, JOSEPH, Weymouth; by wife Elizabeth, daughter, probably, of John Holbrook; had Joseph, born 1674, probably died young, if, as Deane says, he removed to Boston; there had Joseph, born 1678, and had estate at Scituate in 1670, but Deane probably was in error (see Savage), for Joseph, Scituate, son of the preceding, married, 1700, Hannah, daughter, probably, of John Curtis; had Joseph, born 1701; John, 1703; Hannah, 1705; James, 1708; Elizabeth, 1709; David, 1712; Mary, 1713, died soon; Ephraim, 1715; Mercy, 1718; Simeon, 1720; Elisha, 1722; and Mary, 1724. He died 1732, aged 58, says the gravestone.

NASH, JOSHUA, Boston; married, 1659, Elizabeth, daughter of Edward Porter; had Thomas, born 1660; Elizabeth, 1662; Sarah, 1664; Robert, 1666; and Joseph, 1672.

NASH, ROBERT, Boston, butcher, in 1643; had been of Charlestown; died 1661. His wife was Sarah, and daughter Elizabeth married, 1654, John Conney.

NASH, SAMUEL, Plymouth, 1630, perhaps, but certain in beginning of next year; he was taxed half as high as Capt. Standish; in 1643 was of Duxbury; was sheriff of the Col. 1652; representative, 1653, and was living in 1682, in his 89th year. His daughter married William Clark: another daughter married Abraham Sampson.

NASH, THOMAS, New Haven, 1643, or earlier; had in 1639 been at Guilford; died 1658. His wife Margery, daughter of Nichalos Baker, of Herts, died 1656, and by his will, 1657, names eldest son John; Joseph, Mary, wife of Roger Allen; Sarah, wife of Robert Talmage; and Timothy, all brought from England.

REFERENCES :—Amer. Ancestry, II, 88; IV, 28;

Bliss Gen., 650; Judd's Hist. of Hadley, Mass., III, 78; Nash Gen, (1853), 304 pages; Steele Gen. (1896); Wheeler's Hist. of North Carolina, II, 1; Wyman's Charlestown, Mass., Gens., II, 695.

NASON :—Richard, Kittery, 1649; submit. 1652 to Mass.; was ensign 1653, and in 1656 chosen representive, but disallowed by the General Court, and three years later was fined for receiving Quakers, and disfranch. He had John, Joseph, Benjamin, and Baker; named in will, 1694, prob. 1696, in which he names wife, who had been widow of Nicholas Follett, and not mother of these children.

REFERENCES :—Nason Gen. (1859), 8 pages; Old Elliott Monthly Me., III (1899), 4; Pierce's Hist. of Gorham, Me., 195; Trask's Elias Nason Memoir, 36 pages.

NAYLOR :—Edward, Boston, merchant; came perhaps not before 1665; married Catharine, widow of Robert Nanney, daughter of Rev. John Wheelwright; had Tabitha, born 1667; and Lydia, 1668. His estate was taken in 1673, in execution for debt to John Freake.

REFERENCE :—Pott's Gen. (1895), 404.

NAZITER :—Michael, Saco, 1666; had Michael, born 1664; John, 1666; and Jane; his daughter, probably, married, 1669, Richard Peard.

NEAL :—Andrew, Boston, 1664, a taverner; by wife Milicent had Sarah, 1665; Mary, 1666; Andrew, 1668; Elizabeth, 1670, died soon; Elizabeth, 1671; and Mary, again, 1674.

NEAL, EDWARD, Weymouth, 1662; may have removed to Westfield; there by wife Martha, daughter of Edmund Hort, had Deborah, 1670; Abigail, 1672; Mary, 1675; Martha, 1677; Edward, 1679; Esther, 1680; Elizabeth, 1683; and he died 1698. His daughter Abigail married, 1694, Ephraim Stiles, the sec.

NEAL, FRANCIS, Falmouth; married a daughter of Arthur Macworth; had Francis, 1693; and Samuel, who survived; was great propr. at Scarsborough, 1657; representative, 1670; removed from the Indian devastation, to Salem, and died 1696, leaving widow.

NEAL, HENRY, Braintree, 1640; by wife Martha had Martha, born 1643; Samuel, 1647; Henry, 1650; and by a second wife, Hannah Pray, perhaps sister of John of the same, married, 1656, had Abigail, 1657; Hannah, Joseph, 1660; Sarah, 1661; Mary, 1664; Rachel, 1666; Deborah, 1667; Benjamin, 1669; Ruth, 1670; Lydia, Elizabeth, 1675; Joanna, 1680; Rebecca, no date, and five more of unknown names. Ruth married, 1680, Ebenezer Thayer. In the will, probated 1691, is provision for four sons, for wife Hannah, and for eleven daughters, Abigail Scott, Hannah, wife of Nehemiah Hayden; Sarah Mansfield, Mary Thayer, Ruth Thayer, Deborah, Lydia, Rebecca, Rachel, Elizabeth, and Jóanna; but to the last six, perhaps children of the surviving wife, only £50 cash was given. The boast on his gravestone is, that he was father of 21 children, but far better is it thought to provide for 15.

NEAL, JOHN, Salem, freeman, 1642, but Felt does not include his name with church members; perhaps had united with some other church, before going thither; he had baptised there John, 1642; John, again, 1644; Jeremiah, 1646; Lydia, 1650; Jonathan, 1652; Mary, 1655; and John, again, 1658; and Joseph, 1663, died 1672. As Mary is among church members, 1647, she was perhaps his wife, only child of Francis Lawes, and she married next Andrew Mansfield.

NEAL, WALTER, Portsmouth; came early in 1630, by the Warwick, as Gov. of the plantation of Georges and Mason; went home, 1633, sailed from Boston. Both his coming and going is proof of the falsity of the gr. Ind. deed to wheelwright, 1629, seven years before the grantee came, and one year before this witness arrived. Much stronger is the evidence of forgery of a letter, pretending to be of Neal and Wiggin, to the patentee, John Mason, 1633, who was by the managers of the fraud, intended for a buttress of the splendid grant. That letter purports to be written at Northam, which was the name some years later for Dover, on the Piscataqua, by Hist. of Gov. Winthrop, on that same day Neal was in Boston, with comp. of eight friends, to embark in the Elizabeth Bonadventure, sailing for England that month; and from same Vol. that Wiggin was in London on the date of that forgery letter, embarking at Gravesend for Salem, the day Neal left Boston for England. Farmer thinks Walter of New Hampshire, 1660, who by wife Mary had Samuel, born 1661, was in 1673 lieutenant in company of Capt. James Pendleton, might have been his son. He joined most of his neighbors in desir. jurisdiction of Mass., 1690.

REFERENCES:—Andrews' New Britain. Ct., 255; Dow's Hist. of Hampton. N. H., 880; Lincoln's Hist. of Hingham, Mass., III. 79; Ridlon's Harrison. Me.. Settlers, 97; Ruggles Gen.; Savage's Gen. Dict., III, 263, 5.

NEAVE:—Margaret. Salem; came from Yarmouth, in Co. Norfolk, 1637, a widow, aged 58, with gr. ch. Rachel Dickson, in the Mary Ann, and ten years after joined the ch.

NEEDHAM:—Anthony, Salem; with wife Ann, only child of Humphrey Potter, charged as Quakers, 1658, then 30 years old, and the wife after being often fined for absence from public worship in vain, was in June, 1660, sentenced to be whipped twelve stripes. Yet they had long lives, both acting in 1696, and he in 1705, beside good success in rear. ch.; by deed of 1703, we see that Anthony, Isaac, Thomas, Rebecca, Hannah, Elizabeth, Mary, Abigail, and Rachel should enjoy the estate of their mother.

NEEDHAM, EDMUND, Lynn, 1639, one of the grantees of Southampton; next year probably not there; died at Lynn, 1677; perhaps his wife Joan died 1674, aged 65.

NEEDHAM, JOHN, Boston; by wife Elizabeth, daughter of Zechariah Hicks; married, 1679; died, 1691; buried at Cambridge; had Elizabeth, 1680; Margaret, 1683; Zechariah, 1685; Mehitable, 1687; and by second wife Kesiah, had John, 1692; and perhaps others.

NEEDHAM, BOSTON, who died 1690; left sons William and John, to be remembered by a Rinsman to whom he was indebted.

NEEDHAM, NICHOLAS, Exeter, 1638, one of the 35 who formed the original compact there; was a witness to the true deed from Ind. sachems, made to Wheelwright and others, not the spurious one, bearing date 7 or 8 years before W. came from England; was living 1652.

NEEDHAM, WILLIAM, Braintree; may have been of Newport, 1638, and came after to Mass.; freeman 1648; removed perhaps to Boston; in will, 1690, wiven one-third of his estate to Old South Church, opp. to which was his residence, and two-thirds to William and John, sons of his kinsman, John N., late of Boston, deceased, and he minutely disposes of his furniture; died 1690.

REFERENCES:—Am. Anc., III. 147; IV, 213; Caverly's Hist. of Pittsfield. Vt., 716; Lapham's Hist. of Norway, Me., 559-61; Wales. Mass., Centennial, 8.

NEFF:—William, Newbury; removed to Haverhill; married, 1665, Mary, daughter of George Corliss; died at Pemaquid in soldier's service, 1689, aged 47. His widow was taken by the Indians, in the assault on Haverhill, 1697, and carried towards Canada, in company with the celebrated Mrs. Duston, in whose remarkable rescue she participated, and died 1722.

REFERENCES:—Bass' Hist. of Braintree, Vt., 166; Corliss Gen., 237; Neff Gen. (1886), 352 pages.

NEGUS, NEGOS, or NEGOOS:—Benjamin, Boston, shopkeeper; by wife Elizabeth had Elizabeth, 1640; Benjamin, 1641; Mary, baptised, 1643; Samuel, 1645; Hannah, born 1653; was freeman 1648. Elizabeth married Richard Barnard.

NEGU, ISAAC, Taunton, cooper, 1675; styles himself sole heir of Jonathan N., late of Boston; married, 1679. Hannah Andrews.

NEGUS, JABEZ, Boston, 1673, carpenter; was freeman, 1691.

NEGUS, JONATHAN, Boston, 1634; is said to have been at Lynn, 1630; freeman, 1634; by wife Jane had Mary, 1653, who probably died young. He was clerk of the writs, 1651, and several years after. Negus had estate at Muddy River, and his sister, Grace, married Barnabas Fawer.

REFERENCE:—Vermont Hist. Gaz., V. 69.

NEIGHBORS, or NABORS::—James, Boston, cooper; by wife Lettice had Rebecca,-1657; she probably died young, for in his will, prob. 1672, he gave estate to five daughters, Mary, wife of Daniel Matthews; Sarah, Johnson, Elizabeth, wife of William Wills, in Carolina; Rachel, wife of Peter Codner; and Martha, called youngest, wife of John Hunt; and to a granddaughter Mercy. He lived several years at Huntington, L. I.; died there. Robt. Gibbs, in court, recovered large damages from him, in 1661.

REFERENCE:—Chambers' N. J., Germand, 450.

NELSON:—John, Boston, a relation of Sir Thomas Temple; artillery company, 1680, captain; one of the chief actors in the revolt against Andros, 1689; taken by French and Indians; long imprisoned at Quebec and in France. He died probably 1721. In right of his wife Elizabeth was heir and excor. with others, of Lieut.-Gov. Stoughton. He was son of William, to whom Sir Thomas, who he calls his uncle, had made lease of his patent rights in Nova Scotia.

NELSON, MATTHEW, Portsmouth, 1684; had wife Jane; in 1690 solicit. for jurisdict. of Mass.

NELSON, THOMAS, Rowley, 1638; freeman, 1639; representative, 1641; brought from England Philip and Thomas, and by wife Joanna had Mercy and Samuel; went home in 1647 or 8; his will, made in contemplation of the voyage, in 1645, with codicil, made in England, designing to return hither, in 1648, wherein his uncle, Rich. Dummer, and Gov. Bellingham have trusts as excors. and care of the children.

NELSON, WILLIAM, Plymouth, 1640; marrried Martha Ford, daughter of the widow passenger in the Fortune, 1627; one of the purchasers, 1662, of Middleborough; had perhaps John, born 1647; Jane or Joan, 1651. In 1668 the wife of a William of Plymouth was Martha. His daughter Jane married, 1672, Thomas Faunce.

REFERENCES:—American Ances., I, 57; V. 31; Bolton Gen., 72; Carter Family Tree of Va.; Nelson Family of Mass. (1867), 25 pages; Strong Gen., 636; Whitmore's

Heraldic Jour., I, 94; Worthen's Hist. of Sutton, N. H., 829-42.

NEST:—Joseph, New London. 1678; had wife Sarah, who died before him, and daughter Susannna. who married George Way. He died 1711.

NETHERLAND:—William: in list of freemen 1635, and on jury, on Peter Fitchew's body, found drowned, 1639; Savage thinks he must be that Lytherland, a well-known member of Boston church.

NETTLETON:—John, Killingworth, 1663; propounded to be made freeman 1670; mal have been son of Samuel, and lived at Milford in 1713.

NETTLETON, SAMUEL, Milford, 1639, or soon after: had Hannah. who married, 1656, Thomas Smith; Martha. 1656, who married John Ufford, perhaps other children; was propr. there 1713, unless another Samuel were the man.

REFERENCES:—Anderson's Waterbury, 94; Loomis Gen. (1880), 69-71, 78-81; Wheeler's Hist. of Newport. N. H., 477-80.

NEVENS:—Richard, Woburn, by wife Martha had Samuel, born 1689; Mary, 1694; and Martha, 1698.

REFERENCE:—Sewall's Woburn. Mass., 627.

MEVINSON:—John, Watertown, 1670; came two years before from East Horsley, Co. Surry; son of Rev. Roger; by wife Elizabeth, married probably in England. had John. Sarah, 1672; Elizabeth, 1675; Ann, 1678; William. 1681;a nd Mary, the oldest, born in England. He died 1695. Soon after the widow married William Bond. Both sons died unmarried, the elder 1692, the younger in 1711. Sarah married, 1713, Nathaniel Stearns. and next Samuel Livermore; Elizabeth married. 1694. Samuel Hastings; Ann married. 1716, Joshua Grant; and Mary married Samuel Hastings, after death of her sister, his first wife.

REFERENCE:—Bond's Watertown. 375-860.

NEWBERRY:—Benjamin. Windsor, son of Thomas of Dorchester. born in England; married. 1646, Mary. only daughter of Matthew Allyn; had Mary. 1648; Sarah. 1650; Hannah. 1652, died at 11 years; Rebecca, 1655; Thomas, 1657; Abigail. 1659; Margaret, 1662; Benjamin. 1669; Hannah. again. 1673; and he died. 1689; his wife died 1703. A tradition reports that he married Abigail. widow of Rev. John Warham. and had two daughters. He was representative at 22 sessions, and an assistant 1685. a captain in war with King Philip, and member of the Council of War. His daughter married John Maudslev. Newberry calls him Marshall; Sarah married, 1668. Reserved Clapp; Abigail married, 1684. Ephraim Howard; Margaret married, 1689. Return Strong; and Hannah. 1703, John Wolcott.

NEWBERRY, JOHN, Windsor, early settler; probably removed or died before middle age; was born of the preceding.

NEWBERRY, JOSEPH, Windsor. born of the preceding: died early or removed, perhaps; but one of the sons of his father was called probably to go home to look after property of the testator.

NEWBERRY, RICHARD, Weymouth; freeman 1645; by wife Sarah had Tryal. Joseph, and Dorcas, beside Benjamin, 1660. In this year he purchased land at Malden, and removed thither: made imperfect will 1685. inventory the month following. Benjamin was probably dead long before his father: of the three named in will Joseph was dead before 1702. when the widow Sarah was living. and Tryal and Dorcas, who married, perhaps. Joseph Burrill,

and she had been administratrix, having by will of the father most of his property, but charged to take care of her mother.

NEWBERRY. THOMAS, Dorchester: may have come in the Mary and John, 1630; freeman 1634: representative 1635: was engaged to go with Warham and most of his congregation to plant Windsor. but died before the migration: by his will, 1635, leaves large property. of which £200 to wife Jane. beside what she brought at marriage, and residue equally to childr. exc. that the three youngest daughters should each have £50 less than the others. Instead of £50. as Savage reads some years before, Mr. Trask. usually a careful copier of old writings. gives 50 s. in that abstr. which might. in case of some petty estate. seem large enough. The inventory. taken 28th January following (including land in England at £300). was £1,520, 4. 7. Sarah married. 1640. Henry Wolcott: Mary. 1644. married Daniel Clarke: Rebecca was second wife of Rev. John Russell of Hadley; and Hannah married Rev. Thomas Hanford: died early.

NEWBERRY, WALTER, Newport: married. 1675. Ann Collins of London: had Sankey. 1676, probably died young; Samuel. 1677: Sarah. 1680: Walter. 1682: Sankey. again. 1684; Elizabeth and Martha. twins. 1686. of which the latter probably died soon: Martha. again. 1689: and Mary. 1691: one of the Council, 1687, to Sir G. Andors.

REFERENCES:—Austin's Gen. Dict.. 137: Dwight's Strong Gen.. 99-100: Ely Gen.. 76. 100-2: Stiles' Hist. of Windsor. Ct.. II. 516-33.

NEWBY:—George. Boston: by wife Mary had John... 1680: he may have had second wife Elizabeth.

NEWBY, WILLIAM, a passenger in the Mary and John. from London. 1634. who took the oath of supremacy and allegiance 1634. bound for N. E. but where he pitched his tent is unknown.

NEWCOMB. or NEWCOME:—Andrew. Boston. mariner: married Grace. widow of William Rix: had Grace. 1664. By his will. 1683. probated 1686. his wife and daughter. Grace Butler. and grand child. Newcomb Blake. were cared for.

NEWCOMB, FRANCIS, Boston. 1635: came in the Planter. aged 30. that year. with wife Rachel. 20. and two children. Rachel. 2 years. and John. 9 months: lived after at Braintree: died 1692. upwards of 100 years: had Hannah. baptised 1637; Mary. 1640: Sarah. 1643; Judith. 1654; Elizabeth. 1658: when the folly of tradition would make her mother over 66 years old. Mary married. 1657. Samuel Dearing.

REFERENCES:—Am. Ancestry. XII: Daniel's Hist. of Oxford. Mass.. 627: Lincoln's Hist. Hingham. Mass.. III. 81-3: Orcutt's Hist. of Derby, Ct.. 747.

NEWCOMEN:—Elias. Isle of Shoals: constable in 1650.

NEWCOMEN, JOHN, Plymouth. a youth waylaid and killed by John Billington, for which he was executed. 1630.

NEWELL:—Abraham, Roxbury: came in the Francis. 1634. aged 50. from Ipswich. with wife Francis. 40, and child Faith. who in the church record is named Ruth. 14: Grace. 13: Abraham. 8; John. 5; Isaac. 2; and Jacob. born on the passage: freeman 1635; died 1672. aged 91: and his widow, 1683, aged 100. says the record of the town. Ruth married a Bennett. for whose children John. the grandfatehr. provided liberally. Grace married. 1644. William Tay of Boston. and died 1712, aged 91. town record.

NEWELL, ANDREW, Charlestown, merchant from Bristol, whose widow died 1684, in her 78th year, says the gravestone.

NEWELL, ANDREW, Charlestown; married, 1665, Hannah, daughter of John Larkin, and died 1704, in 71st year. His widow died same year, aged 62.

NEWELL, THOMAS, Farmington, 1652; married Rebecca Olmstead, sister of John and Richard O.; had nine children to partake division of his estate, 1689, Rebecca Woodford, then aged 46; Mary, wife of Thomas Bascom of Northampton, 44; John, 42; Thomas, 39; Esther Stanley, 37; Sarah Smith, 34, who was baptised 1655; Hannah North, 31, baptised 1658; Samuel, 1660; and Joseph, 1664, who died.

REFERENCES:—Adams' Haven Gen., II, 23; Ballou Gen., 161-3, 221, 390-5; Bullock Gen.; Freeman's Hist. Cape Cod, Mass., II, 763; Stackpole's Hist. of Durham, Me., 225-8; Stiles' Hist. of Windsor, Ct., II, 533.

NEWGROVE:—John, Dover, 1648.

NEWHALL:—Anthony, often confused with Newell, Lynn, 1636; some time at Salem; died 1657; mentions grandchildren Richard and Elizabeth Hood.

NEWHALL, THOMAS, Lynn, 1630, Mr. Lewis thinks, brother John; had Thomas, the first English child born in that town. His wife died 1665, and he died 1674. His will, prob. 1674, names two sons, John and Thomas, and daughter Susanna, wife of Richard Haven, and her five children, Joseph, Richard, Sarah, Nathaniel, and Moses; and Mary, wife of Thomas Brown and her children, not named them.

REFERENCES:—Daniell's Hist. of Oxford, Mass., 627; Newhall Gen. (1882), 109 pages.

NEWLAND:—Jeremiah, Taunton; had Anthony, born 1657.

NEWLAND, WILLIAM, Sandwich; had removed thither Lynn, 1637; was freeman of the Col. 1641; representative 1642, 3 and 4, but disfranchised 1659 for abetting Quakers; married, 1648, Rose Holloway; had Mary, 1649; John, and Mercy, who married an Edwards, and administered her father's estate, 1694.

REFERENCES:—Clarke's Morton, Mass., 87; Freeman's Hist. of Cape Cod, Mass., II, 69; Paige's Hist. of Hardwick, Mass., 426.

NEWMAN:—Daniel, Stamford, 1670.

NEWMAN, FRANCIS, New Haven, 1638, an assist. 1653 and after, until made Gov., 1658, to his death, 1660. He also served in the important place of Commr. of the Unit. Col., 1654 and 8, and in the troublesome relations with the Dutch of New Netherlands. In his barn was formed the compact, 1639, or civil const, by which the Col. many years was rued. His widow married, says Emery, Rev. Nicholas Street, of ch. Elizabeth, who married Thomas Knowles, and next Nicholas Knell.

NEWMAN, JOHN, a sergeant in Capt. Turner's company, 1676, stationed at Hadley; must have come from the East. A John N., was at Ipswich, 1679, owning Commons.

NEWMAN, NOAH, Rehoboth, son of Rev. Samuel, who he succeded, 1669; Joanna, daughter of Rev. Henry Flint; had Sybel, 1675, and died in few months; besides Samuel, who was buried in 1677, and Henry, Harvard College, 1687; librarian at the college, and agent in England for Rev. Prov. of New Hampshire, and died 1678. The widow, by her will, prob. 1680, gave her estate to Henry. But in case of his death to children of her brother, Rev. George Shove, who had married Hopestill Newman.

NEWMAN, SAMUEL, Rehoboth, born at Banbury, Oxfordshire; baptised 1602, son of Richard; was matricul. of Trinity College, Oxford, 1620, in his 17th year, but on proceed. A. B. of that year is titled in Wood's Fasti, I, 392, of St. Edmund Hall; had a small benefice, 1625, at Midhope, part of parish of Ecclesfield, in the W. Riding of Yorkshire. He came to New England, perhaps, 1636, though Elizabeth, aged 24, who may have been his wife or sister, came in the James from London, 1635. Mather makes him come in 1638; Spend a year and a half at Dorchester, five years at Weymouth, and 19 years at Rehoboth. He was admitted freeman 1639, no doubt of Weymouth, where his daughter Hope was born, 1641. He deserves esteem for service in framing the Concordance. said to have been written by light of pine knots; he died 1663, aged 61; in his will names wife Sybil. sons Samuel, Antipas, Noah, to whom he gave his library; and daughter Hopestill or Hope, who married, 1664, Rev. John Shove, and died 167. Patience, an elder daughter, married, 1649, Nathaniel Sparhawk of Cambridge.

NEWMAN, THOMAS, Ipswich, 1639; had come 1634 in the Mary and John; took oath of supremacy and allegiance 1676, leaving wife, who died 1679, and sons Thomas, John, and Benjamin.

NEWMAN, WILLIAM, Stanford, 1665; may have removed to Narragansett after 1669. Five of this name had in 1834 been graduated at Harvard, and two at other N. E. colleges.

REFERENCES:—Amer. Ancestry, I, 57; VIII, 85; Clarke's Old King Wm. Co., Va., Families; Delamater Gen., 96-9; Locke Gen., 42; Newman's Rehoboth, Mass. (1860), 62-8.

NEWMARCH:—John, Ipswich, 1638, at Rowley, perhaps, 1643, and back to Ipswich 1648; married Martha, daughter of Zaccheus Gould; had, as learned from will, prob. 1697, John, Thomas, Zaccheus, Martha, who married, 1675, Samuel Balch; Phebe, Pennywell, and Sarah Berry. It made wife Martha executrix, and named grandchildren Thomas Gould and Martha Balch. Sometimes it is Newmarsh.

REFERENCES:—Hammott Papers, 233.

NEWPORT:—Richard, Boston; by wife Ruth had Ruth, 1668.

NEWTON:—Anthony, Dorchester; of Braintree, 1640; engaged 1652 in settling of Lancaster; was freeman 1671.

NEWTON, BRYAN, Jamaica, L. 1., 1656.

NEWTON, EDWARD, New Haven; took oath of fidelity 1645.

NEWTON, JOHN, Dorchester, 1632; freeman 1633; removed to Dedham; was kinsman of Edward Alleyn of Dedham, who, dying suddenly at Boston, where he was a representative, 1642, by nuncup. will give his estate to him and another relative; had Henry, baptised 1643.

NEWTON, RICHARD, Sudbury, 1640; by wife Ann or Hannah had John, born 1641; Mary, 1644; Moses, 1646; Joseph, 1655; Elizabeth, Sarah, Isaac, and Hannah, who died 1654. He took the freeman's oath 1645; after 1656 removed to southern part of Marlborough, now Southborough; was living 1675; Mary married Jonathan Johnson; Elizabeth married a Dingley; and Sarah married a Taylor.

NEWTON, ROGER, Farmington, the first minister: married at Hartford, Mary, eldest daughter of Rev. Thomas Hooker, who died 1676; had at Hartford Samuel. baptised 1646; was ordained the day the church was formed, 1652; there had John, baptised 1656; probably other children before and after; went to England 1657; returned to Milford; was inst. 1660; died 1683. His will names Samuel, Roger, Susanna, John, Ezekiel, baptised 1660; Sarah, 1662; Alice, 1664; and Mary. His daughter Susanna married John Stone of M., and Sarah, 1683, John Wilson of New Haven.

NEWTON, THOMAS, Fairfield, one of the first five settlers; a man of consequence; chosen representative 1645; had frequent suits at law with his neighbors, and in 1652 charged with a capital crime, probably witchcraft, or imagin. offense; he escaped from prison, took refuge with the Dutch, who believed him innocent. He lived at Newton, L. I., 1656; a purchaser that year of Middlebury and was a captain under Stuyvesant.

NEWTON, THOMAS, 1688; came from New Hampshire; supposed to have been born 1661, and was Sect. of that Prov. until 1690; was controller of the customs at B., judge of the admr. and Attorney-General in the witchcraft prosecut.; died 1721. His opinion must have led to the cure of that internal delusion, for, in 1693, he wrote to Sir William Phips, the Gov. of the 52 charg. at Salem that court, the three convicts should have been acquainted like the rest.

REFERENCES:—Am. Anc., 1, 57; IV, 78; VI, 16, 24, 70; Bemis' Hist. of Marlboro, New Hampshire, 585-90; Loomis Gen. (1880), 725; Meade's Old Churches of Virginia, II, 151; Newton Gen. (1897), 39 pages; Temple's Hist. of N. Brookfield, Mass., 692.

NICHOLET:—Charles, Salem; came 1672, from Virginia; preacher to 1673; by vote of the town, with dissatisfaction of both the church and its pastor, went to England.

NICHOLS:—Adam, New Haven, 1645, or earlier; married Ann, daughter of John Wakeman; had John, baptised 1645; Barachiah, 1647; Esther, 1650; Lydia, 1652; in 1655 was of Hartford; removed, 1661, to Hadley, where his son John was drowned next year. His father-in-law, in his will, probated 1661, mentioned these children of his daughter Ann N., viz.: John, Hanah, Sarah, and Ebenezer, born probably at Hartford, and some time later he had Esther. Next he was of Boston; freeman 1670; in his Col. Rec. returned to Hartford, and died, 1682, when his only child was Esther Ellis.

NICHOLS, ALLEN or ALLYN, Barnstable; married, 1670, Abigail, daughter of Austin Bearse; had Nathaniel, born 1671; Mary, 1673; Josiah, 1676, died at 2 years; Joseph, 1678; Abigail, 1681; Priscilla, 1682, died next March; Experience, 1684; was baptised with Nathaniel, Mary and Joseph, 1688; and James, born 1689, baptised with Abigail May following.

NICHOLS, CYPRIAN, called Siborn in the records of Hartford, 1668; made freeman next year; was from Witham Co., Essex, and had vot. before com. estate of William Whiting, merchant of London, 1664; Gent. that was prop. of the f. of WI. in our country; perhaps came with son Cyprian in 1667; was nominated, 1668, freeman, with prefix of respect; was selectman, 1670, 5 and 6, and in other town offices.

NICHOLS FRANCIS, Stratford; died 1650; was father of Isaac, Caleb, and John, who were all born in England. His estate was small; of which is no record.

NICHOLS, HUGH, Salem, married, 1694, Priscilla Shattuck, daughter of Samuel of the same, and died before 1701.

NICHOLS, ISAAC, Stratford, 1639, son of Francis, born in England; one of the first settlers. Savage thinks was that sergeant appointed to train the men in militia

discipline this year; was representative, 1664; at the October session; had Mary, born 1648, who married, 1667, Isreal Chauncey, the minister of the town; Sarah, 1649; Josiah, 1652; Isaac, 1654; Jonathan, 1655; Ephraim, 1657; Patience, 1660; Temperance, 1662; Margery, 1663; Benjamin, 1666; and Elizabeth, 1668. He was a soap boiler; had good estate; made his will 1694. He names wife Margaret and all the children but Josiah, who had died. Yet three other sons, Isaac, Jonathan and Ephraim, were also dead, but to their children each a small legacy was directed by that instrument, because each family had been portioned. Sarah married, 1674, Stephen Burritt, and Elizabeth, 1691, Rev. Joseph Webb.

NICHOLS, JAMES, Malden; married, 1660, Mary, daughter of George Felt; had Mary, 1661; James, 1662; Elizabeth; Nathaniel, 166; Ann, Samuel and Caleb; was freeman 1668; died 1694.

NICHOLS, JOHN, Watertown, a proprietor 1636 or 7. He may well seem to be the man of Fairfield, buying land before 1653, perhaps residing there after a temporary one at Wethersfield, and the brother of Isaac and Caleb. By wife Grace, he had Isaac, Sarah, and John, named on return of his inventory, 1665, with hopes of another world, who was the Samuel, probably, named by the widow, 1659, when, giving deed to her son Isaac, she requires him to pay her children Sarah, John and Samuel certain sums. The widow married Richard Perry of the same, who was deceased in 1658. His son John served in Philip's war, and died in the first year of it, unmarried.

NICHOLAS, JONATHAN, a soldier of Moseley's company, 1675, and next year under Capt. Turner on Conn. river in Philip's war.

NICHOLS, MORDECAI, Boston; mariner; married, 1652, Alice, daughter of Richard Hallet; had John, 1653; and Samuel, 1658, who died young. He died not long after, for 1664, his widow gave inventory and prov. for the only child John in court, for the reason, says the record of the widow, "being ready to dispose of herself." She soon married Thomas Clark of Plymouth.

NICHOLS, NATHANIEL, Charlestown; died before 1687, when his widow Joanna brought, says the church record, to baptise her children Elizabeth and Hannah. One of the name from Hingham was in Johnson's company, 1675; may have outlived the hard service. His widow, who was, perhaps, daughter of Richard Shute, married Joseph Buckley of Boston. Hannah married, 1702, Jonathan Mountford.

NICHOLS, RANDOLPH or RANDAL, Charlestown; had wife Elizabeth, daughter perhaps of Thomas Pierce, senr., and children Sarah, born 1643; Elizabeth, Hannah, 1647; John, 1654; Nathaniel, 1655; William, 1657; and Daniel, 1658; was living in 1678; a householder at Charlestown. His daughter Sarah, in the will of Nicholas Shapleigh of Charlestown, 1662, and his son Joseph, was advised to marry, or at least a bequest was made on condition that he should do so. Elizabeth married Thomas Tuck.

NICHOLS, ROBERT, Watertown; married, 1644 or 5, Sarah, widow of John Goss; may be the man to whom with many others our Col. Governor, in 1680, made grant of land at the bot. of Casco Bay, 5 miles square and two of the islands adjoining.

NICHOLS, ROBERT, Saybrook, 1664-73.

NICHOLS, ROBERT, Falmouth, 1679, perhaps son of the first Robert; was killed by the Indians, 1675, at Scarborough.

REFERENCES:—Aldrich's Walpole, 341-3; Am. Anc.,
II, 89; III, 38; V, 77, 159; VI, 90; VII, 25; VIII, 42,
117; Bass' Hist. of Braintree, Vt., 167-9; Bouton Gen.,
22; Corliss' North Yarmouth, Me., Magazine; Hurlbut
Gen., 439, 453-6; Nichols Gen. (1882), 17 pages;
Williams' Hist. of Danby, Vt., 206-10.

NICHOLSON:—Edmund, Marblehead, 1648;
died 1660, it is presumed, for his inventory taken that
year, was brought six days after by Elizabeth, his widow,
who was prosecuted as a Quaker the same year. His
children then were aged, as the rcord shows, Christopher,
22; Joseph, 20; Samuel, 16; John, 14; Elizabeth, 11; and
Thomas, 7. Joseph, Thomas and Elizabeth, then widow
of Nicholas Andrews, all united in a deed, 1672, to their
brother Samuel.

NICHOLSON, ROBERT, Scarsborough; had Robert
and John; his inventory is 1676.

NICHOLSON, WILLIAM, Yarmouth, 1641, fined for
disrespect to religion; next year had William, baptised
at Barnstable, 1646.

REFERENCES:—Austin's R. I. Dict., 139; Clement's
Newtown, N. J., Settlers; Savage's Gen. Dict., III, 283;
Shroud's Fenwick Col. N. J., 164-6.

NICK, or NECK:—Christopher, Marblehead, 1668.

NICK, JOHN, Lynn; married, 1676, Mary Richards;
had William, born 1676, died next year Bathsheba, 1678,
died soon; Bathsheba, again, 1682. If this be the same
name with Nicks, he may have been son of that Matthew
Nicks who had, Felt says, grant of land at Salem, 1639;
but the same year he mentions Matthew Nixon, as
grantee of land from the town, and probably he was the
same.

NICK, WILLIAM, Marblehead, 1674; May have been
brother of John; possibly it is an abbreviation for
Nicholson.

NICKERSON, WILLIAM, Boston, weaver, from Norwich, England, aged 33, with widow Ann, eldest daughter of Nicholas Busby (who came in same ship), aged
28, and four children, Nicholas, Robert, Elizabeth and
Ann, embarked at Ipswich, or Yarmouth, 1637, arrived
June at Boston, thence to Watertown; after he is found
at Yarmouth, where he had Joseph, 1647; Elizabeth,
married, 1649, Robert Eldred.

NICKERSON, WILLIAM, Eastham; married, 1691,
Mary Snow; had Mercy, 1692; and Nicholas, 1694.

REFERENCES:—Am. Anc., II, 89; XI, 108. 9; Davis
Landmarks of Plymouth, Mass., 194; Lincoln's Hist. of
Hingham, Mass., III, 91.

NICKISON:—John, Salisbury, 1650; probably
misprint for Neckerson.

NIGHTINGALE:—Benjamin, Braintree, 1689.

NIGHTINGALE, WILLIAM, Braintree, 1689, or earlier;
died 1747, aged 77.

REFERENCES:—Austin's Anc., Dict., 41.

NILES:—John Dorchester, 1634. Braintree, 1636;
freeman, 1647; had wife Jane, and children Hannah,
born 1637; John, 1639; Joseph, 1640; Nathaniel, 1642;
Samuel, 1644; Increase, 1646; Benjamin, 1651; his wife
died 1654. He went to Block Island perhaps, but before
removing by wife Hannah, perhaps had Isaac, 1658.

REFERENCES:—Stiles' Hist. of Windsor, Ct., II;
534, 6; Vinton Gen., 344-51; Whitman Gen., 181.

NIMS:—Ebenezer, Deerfield, son of Godfrey; in
the assault Feb. 29, 1704, by the French and Indians,
when most of the family were destroyed, was taken;
carried to Canada, adopted by an Indian squaw; had

there a wife and one child; was liberated, 1714, and
came home.

NIMS, GODFREY, Northampton, 1668; was a soldier
in Philip's war; married Margaret, widow of Zebediah
Williams; had Rebecca, born 1678, died soon; John and
Rebecca, twins, 1679; Henry, 1882; went to Deerfield;
there had Thankful, 1684; and Ebenezer, 1687; his wife
died next year, and he married Mehitable, widow of
Jeremiah Hull, daughter of William Smead; had
Thomas, 1693, who died at 4 years; Mehitable, 1696;
Mary, and Mercy, twins, 1699; and Abigail, 1701. Henry
was killed, 1704, at the surprise of the town by French
and Indians. Mehitable, Mary and Mercy were at the
same time burned to death in the cellar of his house, and
his wife carried off, but killed on the way to Canada,
whither John, Ebenezer and Abigail were carried. John
failed to escape in his first attempt, but got free in the
second from Montreal, 1705. His daughter Rebecca had
married Philip Mattoon, and was killed with him and
their only child.

REFERENCES:—Am. Anc., III, 39; Savage's Gen.
Dict., III, 285; Sheldon's Hist. of Deerfield, Mass, 250-7.

NIXON, or NICKSON:—John, R. I., 1663.

NIXON, MATTHEW, Salem, 1639; was petitioner,
1668, against imposts, signed for self and company.

REFERENCES:—Am. Anc., VIII, 207; Hudson's Hist.
of Sudbury, Mass., 410-2.

NOAKES, or NOAKE:—Robert, Boston, by wife
Mary, perhaps daughter of Robert Wright, who in his
will Noakes calls his son; had Arthur, 1665; Mary,
1667; Robert, 1670; Joseph, 1671; and Robert, again,
1676.

REFERENCES:—Cope's will of Wm. Nookes (1869),
6 pages.

NOBLE:—Thomas, Boston, 1652; removed to
Springfield; married Hannah, only daughter of William
Warriner; removed to Westfield, 1669; freeman, 1681;
representative 1682. He had John, 1662; Hannah, 1664,
who married John Goodman of Hadley, and next, 1728,
Nathaniel Edwards of Northampton; and Thomas, 1667;
Mary, 1680; Rebecca, 1683. He died 1704, and widow
married deacon Medad Pomeroy.

NOBLE, WILLIAM, Flushing, L. I.; was in 1664, employed by the Conn. Coll.

REFERENCES:—Collin's Hillsdale 6, 740-7; Davis'
Hist. of Buck's Co., Pa., 217.

NOCK:—Thomas, Dover, 1655; by wife Rebecca,
probably daughter of Henry Tibbets, had Elizabeth,
1663, died at 3 years; Henry, posthumus, 1667; besides
others earlier, as Sylvanus and Rebecca. He died 1666,
and his widow married, 1669, Philip Benmore, outlived
him, and died 1680. It is said this name has become
Knox, in some branches.

REFERENCES:—Lapham's Knox Genealogy.

NODDLE:—William, Salem; came probably in
fleet with Winthrop; freeman 1631; was drowned 1632.
Prince, II, 29, thinks Noddle's Island was named for him.

NORCROSS:—Jeremiah, Watertown, 1642, perhaps the freeman, 1653, whose baptismal name is not
given on the records; died in England, 1657; in his will,
1654. besides sons Nathaniel and Richard, he names
daughter Sarah, widow of Francis Macy, though Bond,
376, reads the name Merry or Massey, son Richard,
daughter Mary, and John Smith, son of his wife Adrean,
and speaks of grandchildren in England.

NORCROSS, NATHANIEL, Salem, 1639; joined the
church there, 1641; freeman 1643; was, Bond says, that

son of the first Jeremiah, born in England, bred at Catherine Hall, in the University of Cambridge, where he had his A. B. 1636-7; lived 1647, at Watertown, and probably preached a little, having declined the request of the first settlers of Lancaster, two or three years before, and probably went back to England; may have had a church at Walsingham, in Norfolk, whence, Calamy says, he was ejected, at the great day of triumph after the restoration.

REFERENCES:—Bond's Watertown, 376-81; Hudson's Hist. of Lexington, Mass., 168; Ward's Hist. of Shrewsbury, Mass., 388.

NORCUT, or NORCOTT:—Daniel, Boston, sailed in the Pied Con, 1635, for England, and because she was not heard of next year administration of his estate was given to John Coggan, who probably was a creditor, 1637.

NORCUT, WILLIAM, Marshfield; married Sarah Chapman; had William, 1663; John, 1664; Thomas, 1670; Ralph, 1673; Isaac, 1675; Ephraim, 1683; and Ebenezer, 1691; besides four or five daughters; died 1693.

NORDEN:—Nathaniel, Marblehead, a captain and freeman, 1690; also representative same year and the former.

NORDEN, SAMUEL, Boston, shoemaker, perhaps brother of the preceding; by wife Joanna had Samuel, 1651; Nathaniel, 1653; Benjamin; his wife died; second wife he married, 1656, Elizabeth, daughter of Philemon Pormont; had Elizabeth, 1657; Susanna, 1659; Joseph, 1664; Joshua, 1666; Mary, 1669; Isaac, 1672; and was freeman, 1666.

NORMAN:—Hugh, Plymouth; married, 1639, Mary White; removed to Yarmouth before 1643; had Elizabeth, who was drowned, 1648, aged 6 years; removed to Barnstable.

NORMAN, JOHN, Salem, 1631; by wife Arabella. had John, 1637; Lydia, baptised, 1640; Ann or Hannah, baptised, 1642; Arabella, 1644; Martha, 1647; Richard, 1651; Joseph, 1653, died soon; Joseph, again, 1656; he was in 1640, at Jeffrey's Creek, now Manchester; of Marblehead, 1648, and back again to Salem; died 1673 in his 6oth year; and his widow in 1679. His daughter Arabella, married, 1664, John Baldwin.

NORMAN, RICHARD, Salem, perhaps brother of first John; came in 1626, as Felt thinks, probably from Dorchester, in England, with son Richard, to each of whom he assigns that year, but John, who was the elder, may have been left in England. Farmer thinks he had also William, living at Marblehead, 1648, and says the elder Richard died 1683, though it may seem as probable that he was the son of that name, who, he says, was born 1623, and lived, 1672, at Marblehead. It seems to Savage that the elder died probably before this last date, and that second Richard was the freeman of 1680.

REFERENCES:—Essex Inst. Hist. Coll., I, 191; Perkin's Old Houses of Norwich, Ct., 542.

NORRIS:—Edward, Salem, fourth minister at that church, ordained 1640; had joined the Boston church, 1639, as did next month his wife Elinor; his daughter Mary united with the church at Roxbury soon after; freeman 1640. died 1659; his will, probated 1660. Mather includes him in his first classes, yet omits his name of baptism. He was ordained by a bishop, in the last days of Eliz.

NORRIS, NICHOLAS, Exeter, 1666; took oath of allegiance, and in 1690 desired jurisdiction of Mass.

REFERENCES:—Am. Anc., III, 193; VII, 195, 256-63; Dow's Hist. of Hampton, N. H., 881; Norris Gen. (1892), 107 pages Martin's Hist. of Chester, Pa., 36; Power's Sangamon Co., Ill. Settlers, 545; Sinclair's Gen., 405-18.

NORTH:—John, Farmington, an early settler, probably he who came, 1635, aged 20, in the Susan and Ellen, to Boston; was freeman of Conn. 1657; had Thomas; John, 1641; Samuel and Mary, twins, 1643; James, 1647; Sarah, 1653; Nathaniel, 1656; Lydia, 1658; and Joseph, 1660; died late in 1691, his inventory being early in 1692. Mary married John Searle; and Sarah married the second Matthew Woodruff of Farmington.

NORTH, RICHARD, Salisbury, 1640, one of the first proprietors; freeman 1641; removed to Salem; made his will, 1649, in which wife Ursula, children Mary, Saran, who married an Oldham, and Susanna, are mentioned. Mary was wife of Thomas Jones of Gloucester, died 1682, as his widow; and Susanna of George Martin of Salisbury.

NORTH, THOMAS, New Haven, 1644; had by wife Mary, daughter of Walter Price, of Newington Butts, near London, who had been widow of Philip Petersfield of Holborn, three children—Thomas, John, and Bathshua. She outlived him and married Thomas Dunck of Saybrook, and died in England, whither she went, 1670, to recover estate descended to her, leaving Dunck to get another wife before 1677.

REFERENCES:—Andrews' New Britain, Ct., 180-2; North Gen. (1860), 30 pages; Savage's Gen. Dict., III, 289.

NORTHAM:—James, Hartford, 1655; may have been 10 years before at Wethersfield; freeman 1658; engaged next year with the seceders, who would remove to Hadley, but he was unable to fulfill his design, and died before 1662. He married widow Isabel Catlin; had only Samuel, yet it may be he was by a former wife. His widow removed to New Jersey, but afterwards to Hadley, where she married Joseph Baldwin.

NORTHCUT:—William, Yarmouth, 1643, then able to bear arms.

NORTHEND:—Ezekiel, Rowley, 1645; was born 1622; married Edna, widow of Richard Bailey; had besides four daughters, John, 1658; and Ezekiel, 1666; was selectman 1691. His daughter married Humphrey Hobson, and next Thomas Gage; Edna married Thomas Lambert.

NORTHEND, EZEKIEL, Rowley, perhaps son of preceding, a corporal 1691, when he was the richest man in town; married, 1691, Dorothy, daughter of Henry Sewall of Newbury; had John, 1692; Ezekiel, 1697; Samuel, 1701; besides six daughters. Possibly some were by second wife. John was representative 1715-17.

NORTHEND, JOHN, Wethersfield, one of the first settlers; removed probably to Stamford, where final settlement was added.

REFERENCES:—Essex, Me., Inst. Hist. Colls., XII, 71-84; XXII, 226; Northend Gen. (1874), 16 pages reprint.

NORTHEY:—John, Marblehead, 1648, born 1607, and probably fathr of that John of Scituate, who served in Philip's war, became a Quaker, and married, 1675, Sarah, daughter of Henry Ewell; had James, born 1687, of whom is still a line of descendants at Scituate.

NORTHOP, NORTHRUP, NORTROP, or NORTHUP:—Joseph, Milford, an early settler; will probated 1669. Twelve proprietors of this name were connected in 1713, at that place, including two or three widows.

NORTHROP, STEPHEN, Providence, 1645; admitted freeman 1658, and perhaps of Wickford 1674.

REFERENCES:—Am. Anc., IX, 130; Austin's R. I. Gen. Dict., 140.

NORTON:—Francis, Portsmouth, 1631, a steward, sent by Mason and other patentees; removed to Charlestown, says Frothingham, as early as 1637; was freeman 1642, ar. co. 1643, a captain and representative between 1647 and 61; died 1667. His widow Mary married, 1670, Deacon William Stilson; probably he had no sons, but of daughters. Abigail married John Long; Mary married, 1656, Joseph Noyes; Elizabeth married, 1671, Timothy Symmes; Deborah married Zechary Hill, and next Matthew Griffen; and Sarah was unmarried.

NORTON, FRANCIS, Wethersfield, one of the first settlers; was of Milford 1660, thence removed, 1662, to New Haven, where he was drowned, 1667, leaving no children, but in his will. 1666, names cons., i. e. nephew John N.

NORTON, GEORGE, Salem; was probably that carpenter who came in the fleet with Higginson, 1629, from London; freeman 1634: by wife Mary had Freegrace, born probably 1635; John, baptised 1637; Nathaniel. 1639; George, 1641; removed to Gloucester; was there selectman, 1642-3. and representative 1642-4; and there Mary was born. 1643; unless it were a mistake for Henry; Mehitable, Sarah, Hannah; and Abigail, 1651; removed again, perhaps for a short time, to Ipswich, but soon to Wenham, where was baptised; his daughter Sarah, 1647. and Elizabeth, 1653; h died 1659, leaving wife and ten children. His widow married Philip Fowler.

NORTON, HENRY, York, 1656; was marshal of the Colony; had, four years earlier, sworn allegiance to Massachusetts, but probably went home next year.

NORTON, HUMPHREY, Plymouth, 1657, a Quaker, who probably had come but few months before; he was expelled from the Colony in October, being "found guilty of divers horrid errors." and driven to Rhode Island. There the quiet of toleration sent him back in the spring to court persecution. and at the June court attracted attention enough to be whipped, imprisoned and made to pay fees therefore; but the severity of that minor jurisdiction, even after the death of Gov. Bradford, rose not to the sublime of folly exhibited by Mass., and Humphrey went home in 1658, to avoid what he first sought.

NORTON, JAMES, New Haven, 1640.

NORTON, JOHN, Charlestown; may have come in 1629, but certain was here next year; had gone to York, where Stone. on a trading voyage along shore, took him up in 1633 for a companion to Virginia, near the mouth of the Connecticut; the Pequots, in a quarrel, cut off the whole party. He was called captain in Charlestown.

NORTON, JOSEPH, Salisbury; married, 1662. Susanna, daughter of Samuel Getchell: had son born 1662, died soon: Samuel, 1663; Joseph, 1665; Priscilla, 1667; Solomon, 1670: Benjamin, 1672: Caleb. 1675: Flower, 1677; and Joshua. 1680.

NORTON, NICHOLAS, Weymouth: had Isaac. born 1641: and Jacob, 1644.

NORTON, RICHARD, Boston. a cooper; by wife Dorothy had Richard. born and died 1650: and the father died 1657. when his estate was appraised.

NORTON, THOMAS, Guilford, one of the signers of the first compact, 1639; died 1648, leaving widow Grace, sons Thomas and John. daughters Ann, Grace, Mary and Abigail, who married. 1667, Ananias Trians; Ann married, John Warner at Hartford; Grace married. 1651. William Seward; and Mary married, 1660, Samuel Rockwell of Windsor.

NORTON, WILLIAM, Boston, 1658; married, 1659, Susanna, daughter of Ralph Mason: had John, 1660; William. 1662; David, 1664; Mary, 1668; William, 1670; Mary, again, 1671; and Susanna, 1676. Twelve of this name had. in 1834, been graduated at Yale, seven at Harvard; and 4 at other N. E. Colleges.

REFERENCES:—Adams' Fairhaven, Vt., 444-6; Butler's Hist. of Farmington, Me.. 536-47; Chase's Hist. of Chester. N. H., 572; Goode Gen., 383; Ireland Gen.. 36-41; Norton Fam. (1856), 26 pages; Norton Gen. (1859), 10 pages reprint.

NORWICH:—John, freeman, 1640, of whom we know no more; the freeman's list has his name between a Brown of Newbury and a Pitts of Hingham.

NORWOOD:—Francis, Gloucester; married, 1663. Elizabeth Coldum, probably daughter of Clement the second: had Thomas. born 1664; Francis, 1666; Elizabeth, 1669; Mary, 1672; Stephen, 1674; Deborah, 1677; Hannah. 1679; Joshua, 1683; Caleb, 1685; and Abigail. 1689; he died 1709.

NORWOOD, RICHARD, Cambridge; died 1644.

REFERENCES:—Babson's Gloucester. 118-20; Bassett's Hist. of Richmond, N. H.. 452; Hallowell Gen., 193-201.

NOSEWORTHY:—Robert, Boston, 1675. mariner.

NOTT:—John. Wethersfield, 1640 or earlier; had Hannah, born 1649; John, 1651; and Elizabeth, who was eldest; was aften a representative, from 1665-1682. leaving as in his will two years preceding mentioned widow Ann and those children. of whom Hannah married John Hale; and Elizabeth married Robert Reeves.

REFERENCES:—Am. Anc., I, 1-58; VII, 243; Hubbard's Hist. of Springfield, Vt., 400.

NOWELL:—George, Boston, blacksmith; art. co. 1662.

NOWELL, INCREASE, Charlestown, 1630; came in fleet with Winthrop, probably in the Arbella; was one of the founders of first church in Boston, his being the fifth name on the list of men, and wife Parnell fourteenth: had here Increase, baptised, 1630, died young; Abigail, baptised, 1632; Samuel, 1634, H. C. 1653; Eleazer, 1636. died soon; Mehitable, 1638; Increase, again, 1640; Mary, 1643; Alexander, 1645, H. C. 1664. His wife was Parnell Gray, daughter of widow Catherine Coytemore, who came over with the family of N. and elder sister of Capt. Thomas Coytemore, but the wife of N. was by her first husband, Gray; and the prop. of Coytemore, before the law made half blood to be heirs, was adjudged to descend of Coytemore alone. He was always in public service. having early given up the place of church elder: was Secretary of the Colony many years, and assistant from the election in England before the royal charter to his death, 1655. His widow died 1687, aged 84. Mehitable married William Hilton, and next Deacon John Cutler, died 1711; Mary married. 1666. Isaac Winslow. and next, 1674, John Long.

NOWELL, PHILIP, Salem, mariner; drowned 1675.

NOWELL, ROBERT, Salem; married, 1668. Mary Tatchell; had William and Robert. twins, both died in few days; Mary, 1670; Robert. 1672.

NOWELL, THOMAS, Windsor, an early settler, though it is not thought that he had been at Dorchester; had wife Elizabeth, but no children; in his will, 1648, after small gifts to his kindred, Robert Wilson, and Isabel Phelps, devises a compet. estate to wife for life, fee to Christopher Nowell, son of Edward of Wakefield. Yorkshire. Yet he calls neither his brother. A remarkable conjecture may arise, from the moderate distance between Wakefield and Clitheroe, less than 40 miles, that the stock of this Windsor wayfarer and our Secretary of Mass. was in the sixteenth century the same, though Savage finds no evidence of their ever meeting in our country.

REFERENCES:—Whitmore's Copp's Hill Epitaphs: Winchester, Mass., Records I, 27; Wyman's Charlestown, Mass., Gen., 710-2.

NOYES, NOYCE, or NOISE:—James, Newbury, one of the two first ministers, born 1608, at Charlestown, in Wilts. near the edge of Hants, between Amesbury in W. and Andover in H. S. of Rev. William, who was instituted, 1602, as rector of that diocese; in 1621 resigened in favor of Nathan Noyes. His mother was sister of Robert Parker, a very learned Puritan, driven to Holland for his heterodoxy and forms; he was bred at Brazen Nose, Oxford, as his nephew, Rev. Nicholas, in his acco. for Magn. III, cap. 25, Append., writes, and was called away by his cousin Thomas Parker, to assist him at the school of Newbury, in Berkshire. He married, 1634. Sarah, eldest daughter of Joseph Brown of Southampton, and embarked for New England in company with his brother Nicholas and cousin Parker. in the Mary and John of London, preaching a short time at Medford: was freeman. 1634. and invited to Watertown church. but in 1635 went to Newbury. and though younger than his collea. cons.. died first. 1656. His will. made five davs before, mentioned wife Sarah and children, brother, Rev. Nicholas Noyes, and cousin, Rev. Thomas Parker: the inventory shows good estate and children were Joseph. born 1637; James. 1640. H. C. 1659: Sarah. 1641; Moses. 1643. H. C. 1659: John, 1645; Thomas. 1648; Rebecca. 1651; William, 1653; Sarah. again. 1656; and his wife died 1691. Sarah married Rev. John Hale of Beverly.

NOYES, JOHN. Boston: freeman 1676; was that year constable : married Sarah, daughter of Peter Oliver: had Sarah, John and Oliver, born 1675, baptised 1676, H. C. 1695.

NOYES, JOSEPH, Salisbury. 1640; had perhaps Mary, who married, 1657, John French of Ipswich; but this name in Geneal. Reg., III, 55 and 6 is Moys.

NOYES, JOSEPH, Charlestown; married. 1656, Mary. daughter of Francis Norton; she died 1657. being bound on a voyage when he made his will, 1659. probably 1661. in which he calls Peter and Thomas of Sudbury his brothers and "father Norton's four daughters" his sisters ; gives land in England. All which may indicate him as son of the first Peter.

NOYES, NICHOLAS, Newbury, younger brother of the first James, born 1616; came with him: freeman 1637. married Mary, daughter of Capt. John Cutting; had Mary. 1641; Hannah, 1643: John. 1646: Nicholas. 1647. H. C. 1667: Cutting, 1649: Sarah. 1651, died soon: Sarah, again, 1653; Timothy, 1655; James, 1657: Abigail. 1659: Rachel. 1661: Thomas, 1663: Rebecca. 1665, who died at 18 years. He was representative 1660. 79 and 80, and died 1701. Hannah married, 1663, Peter Cheney: and Sarah married. 1674, Matthew Pettingill.

NOYES, PETER, Sudbury, 1639; came in the Confidence, 1638, from Southampton, aged 47, with son Thomas, 15; daughter Elizabeth, and three servants; is called yeoman in custom house record, but after arrival gentleman. He was of Penton, in Co. Hants. which is near Andover; went home after short visit here, well pleased with what he saw at Watertown, and next year came again in the Jonathan, with several friends, and Nicholas, Dorothy, Abigail and Peter, all probably his children, besides John Waterman. Richard Barnes. William Street, Agnes.Bent, Elizabeth Plimpton, and Agnes Blanchard, who Savage judges might be his servants, as he paid for their passages; but such was not Agnes Bent. for she paid for herself, for daughter Agnes, Thomas Blanchard's wife, and Richard Barnes, son of said Blanchard's wife, and probably Elizabeth Plimpton. Blanchard's wife with infant daughter died on passage. 15 days out. and Barnes' grandmother died this side of the Banks. He had share in first division of lands in the town, and again in the second and third, made 1640; was freeman 1640, selectman 18 years, representative 1640, 1 and 50; deacon of the church; died 1657. Three years before he gave his estate in old England to his eldest son Thomas, and in his will, of which Thomas was made executor. made the day before his death. names his other children, Peter, Joseph, Elizabeth, wife of Josiah Haynes: Dorothy, wife of John Haynes; Abigail. wife of Thomas Plympton: daughter-in-law. Mary, wife of his son Thomas: and kinsman, Shadrach Hapgood.

REFERENCES:—Adams Gen. (1895), 34, 43; Carter's Hist. Pembroke. N. H., II, 245-52; Darling Memorial: Noyes Gen. (1861). 13 pages; Noyes Gen. (1889), 32 pages; Noyes Inscription (1894), 4 pages; Noyes Pedigree (1899), 11 pages.

NUDD:—Thomas, Hampton, son, it is said of Roger; was a minor with his widowed mother, at Watertown. who, before 1645, married Henry Dow, and removed from Watertown to Hampton: Thomas married. 1659, Sarah, daughter of Godfrey Dearborn. and had seven children, of whom one was Samuel. and perhaps another Joseph.

REFERENCES:—Dow's Hampton, N. H., 883-8.

NUNN:—Richard, a passenger in the Increase, from London to Boston, 1635, aged 19, but no more is heard.

REFERENCES:—Chambers' N. J. Germans.

NURSE:—Francis, Salem, in that part now Danvers; by wife Rebecca, daughter of William Towne, had John, Samuel, Rebecca, Mary, Francis, born 1661; Benjamin, 1666; Michael, and a daughter, who married William Russell; Rebecca married, 1669, Thomas Preston; and Mary, 1678, John Tarbell. The unhappy mother of these children suffered death in 1692; twice the jury failed to find a verdict, to which they last assented from her not giving satisfactory answers to their questions in open court, that from her deafness she failed to understand. Sir William Phipps, hearing this, prepared a reprieve, but by solicitation of others. weakened, withheld it, and the dreadful sentence was executed on 19th July; and she survived till November, 22, 1695, aged 77. Her sister. Sarah Cloyce, not less guilty, escaped with her life. Twenty years after the sufferer was hanged, the opprobrious deed was cancelled.

NURSE, JOHN, Salem, brother of the first Francis; married. 1672, Elizabeth Smith; had John, 1673; and he married second wife. 1677, Elizabeth Very; had Elizabeth, 1678; Samuel, 1679; Sarah, 1680; Jonathan, 1682; Joseph, 1683; Benjamin, 1686; Hannah, 1687; and Deborah; he died 1719.

REFERENCES:—Norton's Fitzwilliam, 647-9; Putnam's Hist. Mag., III, 96-102; Red's Hist. of Rutland, Mass., 142; Ward's Hist. of Shrewsbury, Mass., 379-81.

NUTBROWNE:—Francis, a youth of 16, passenger, 1635, in the Defense, from London to Boston, who is not again heard of.

NUTE:—James, Dover, 1631, one of the men sent by Mason and other patentees; was still there in 1659; had James, born 1643; and Abraham, 1644.

REFERENCES:—Dearborn's Parsonfield, Me., 390; Lapham's Hist. of Woodstock, Me., 241.

NUTT:—Miles, Watertown; freeman 1637; brought from England daughter Sarah, who married, 1644, at Woburn, John Wyman, and next, 1684, Thomas Fuller; but he died at Malden, 1671. There he had lived several years; was one of the petitioners of the church; made contract of marriage, 1659, with widow Sibell Bibble, which was for the benefit of herself, and daughter, widow of Robert Jones of Hull, afterwards of Lancaster, probably 1674, by James Cary and Thomas Carter, who had with Solomon Phipps been witness of his will. In that will John Wyman sen. excor. provides for the second wife, names daughter Sarah, her son John. Inventory of the estate was with the volume of records burned. The widow married, 1674, John Doolittle of that part of Boston called Rumney Marsh, who died 1681, and she died 1690, aged 82.

REFERENCES:—Cope Gen., 73, 159; Eaton's Hist. of N. H., 710; Thomaston, Me., II, 340; and Secombs' Hist. of Amherst.

NUTTER:—Hatevil, Dover, 1641; was in 1649 of the grand jury in Maine, but soon back on the W. side of the river; much betrusted; a ruling elder, active against the Quakers. says Sewall. I. 564. who perverts his good name to Nutwell; had besides Anthony and perhaps other children, a daughter. who married Thomas Leighton; Mary, who married John Wingate; he died 1675, aged 71.

REFERENCES:—Dearborn's Parsonfield, 391; Robinson's Items of Ancestry (1894), 26-30.

NUTTING:—John, Groton; married at Woburn, 1650, Sarah Eggleston or Eggleden, or Iggleden, perhaps daughter of Stephen; there had a son, born 1651, who may have been John, and other children certain at Chelmsford, Mary, 1656; and John, James, and Mary were baptised 1656; Sarah, born 1660, died soon; but at Groton record gives these names: Sarah, 1663; Ebenezer, 1666; and Jonathan, 1668; was freeman 1660.

REFERENCES:—Am. Anc., XII; Bassett's Richmond, 453; Cutter's Hist. of Jaffrey, N. H., 408-11; Paige's Hist. of Cambridge, Mass., 615; Savage's Gen. Dict., III, 301.

NYE:—Benjamin, Lynn; removed to Sandwich, 1637, where he was progenitor of a very numerous line, yet of a single son only, Jonathan, born 1649, is the birth known, and of Mary, 1652.

REFERENCES:—Am. Anc., VI, 113; IX, 114, 204; Davis' Landmarks of Plymouth, Mass., 195; Gibb's Blandford, Mass., Hist. Address, 60; Lincoln's Hist. of Hingham, III, 95-7; Olin Gen , by Nye (192, 405·25.

OAKES:—Edward, Cambridge; freeman, 1642; brought from England with Jane and children Urian, H. C., 1649; and Edward; had here Mary, and Thomas, H. C. 1662, this last born 1644; both baptised at Cambridge; was lieutenant of Prentice's company in Philip's war; selectman 26 years, between 1643-78; representative 15 years, between 1659 and 82, and of Concord 1684, where he died, 1689.

OAKES, GEORGE, Lynn, 1654; had George, John, born 1664; Mary, 1666; Richard, 1668; Sarah, 1671; and Elizabeth, 1674; died 1688. Lewis gives the name of wife Jennet.

OAKES, RICHARD, Boston; had grant of a lot 1635, which he did not improve; perhaps went home.

OAKES, SAMUEL, Boston; freeman 1690.

OAKES, THOMAS, Cambridge, brother of the first Edward; freeman 1642; by wife Elizabeth had Elizabeth, 1646, died young; Thomas, 1648, died at 2 months; Elizabeth, again, 1650; Hannah, 1657; probably Mary, who died 1659; and Thomas, posthumus; baptised 1659, to whom the father in his will of 1658 left double portion; and made his widow executrix; town record says he died August, 1665; widow married again. Seth Sweetzer of Charlestown, and next, married Samuel Hayward of Malden, whom she outlived, and in her will of 1686 takes notice of the portion of personal estate that came to her from her first husband, which she gives to daughter Abigail that she bore to Hayward, with condition that if it be more than £20, Samuel, son of her late husband by former wife should have 20s. Elizabeth married, 1670, Lemuel Jenkins; and Hannah married, 1672, Joseph Waite, both of Malden.

REFERENCES:—Atkin's Hist. of Hawley, Mass., 49; Paige's Hist. of Cambridge, Mass., 616; Wyman's Charlestown, Mass., Gens., 11, 713.

OAKLEY:—— Was the name of a widow, probably Sarah, at Charlestown, who united with the church, 1634. Nottingham shows her residence, and February, 1654, an Elizabeth Oakley, perhaps her daughter, married at Boston, Edmund Brown.

REFERENCES:—Am. Anc., 11, 89; Bockee Gen., 71-4; Little's Passaic Valley Gens., 304-6.

OAKMAN:—Samuel. Scarsborough, 1658; acknowledged allegiance to Mass., under his hand (by affixing his mark); had Samuel and perhaps Elias; was selectman, 1679, and died next year.

REFERENCES:—Corliss' North Yarmouth, Me.; Maine Hist. and Gen. Recorder, III, 157-8, 229-37; IV, 127-33.

OATES:—John: is the name of a soldier in Moseley's company, 1675, killed by the Indians.

REFERENCES:—N. E. Hist. Gen. Reg., VI, 150-2.

OBBINSON:—William, Boston, 1675, a tanner; may have been driven in that year by the Indian war, from some outlying settlement; had wife Mary, but no children, and he with his wife gave their estate to Paul, then called the oldest surviving son of the Gov. Joseph Dudley.

OBER:—Richard, Salem 1668; Beverly 1679; married Abigail, daughter of Richard Woodbury of Beverly; had Hezekiah, born 1681; Ann. Richard, 1684; and Nicholas, 1686. Farmer says this name, sometimes written Obear, prevails near Beverly, and is found in New Hampshire. In the Watertown record Dr. Bond finds a name Obear, Thomas, with variations, Obear and Ober, for which he suggests Hobart, but by wife Mary had Samuel, 1640; and Judith, 1643.

REFERENCES:—Am. Anc., I, 158; Hayward's Hist. of Hancock, N. H., 788; Washington, N. H., Hist., 560-2.

OCKINGTON, or OKINGTON:—Samuel, Watertown: may have been father of hat Mary O., who married. 1692, Edward Harrington.

OCKINGTON, WILLIAM, Boston; by wife Mary had Matthias, born 1667; and Mary, 1669.

ODELL, or ODLE:—John, Fairfield, perhaps son of William; freeman 1665.

ODELL, WILLIAM, Concord, 1639, probably brought wife and children from England; here had James, born 1640. died next year; and Rebecca, 1642; removed to Southampton, L. I., and soon after to Fairfield, and was called sen. in 1670.

REFERENCES:—Am. Anc., 1-58; Greene's Todd Genealogy; Odell Memoranda (1892), 3 pages; Odell Chart. (1894), 25x36 in.

OLDERIC:—John, Newcastle, 1660, of grand jury 1686; died 1707.

ODLIN, ODLYN. original AUDLEY or AUDLIN:—John, Boston, one of the early settlers, No. 39 on the church list; was a cutler or armorer; disfranchised 1637; by wife Margaret had John, 1635, died soon after, says the town record, but in the church baptism March following; Elisha, baptised, 1640; John, again, 1642; Hannah, 1643; and Peter, 1646. His will of 1685, of which Elisha was executor, names the three children and grand-children, Hannah Bumsted, but whose daughter she was is not known.

REFERENCES:—Bell's Hist. of Exeter, N. H., 34; Oldlin Families (1887), 9 pages reprint.

OFFITT:—Thomas, Roxbury, 1632; came in the Lion; arrived at Boston with wife Isabel and children Thomas, John and a daughter, who married Roger Terrill. This uncommon name is spelled Uffitt, as the church record of Roxbury shows, or Uskitt, in the record of his qualification, at London; adm. freeman 1633; removed, 1635, with Pynchon to Springfield, where the name is Ufford. as the descendants now write it, but passing into Connecticut, at Milford, 1639, where he and wife joined church, 1645, it became Uffoote. A year or two before his death he married, at Stamford, Elizabeth, widow of Nicholas Thele, who outlived him very little time, and died 1660.

REFERENCES:—Savage's Gen. Dict., III, 305.

OFFLEY:—David, Boston; Artillery company, 1638, removed to Plymouth, 1643, but by letter of Gov. Bradford to Gov. Winthrop on complaints of Indians against O. Dec. 11, 1645, Savage infers that he may have come back to Boston.

OFFLEY, THOMAS, Salem, Collector of the Port, 1686-9.

OFIELD:—Thomas, Boston, mariner; had wife Maudline, and several children, yet in his will 1677, though he mentions wife and children; gives name of wife only.

OGDEN:—John, Stamford, 1641; agreed next year with Gov. Kieft of New York, to build a stone church for 2,500 guilders, in 1644; was a patentee of Hempstead. L. I.; lived, 1651, at Southampton, L. I.; in 1656 was chosen an assistant; re-elected to 1660; is named in the royal charter of 1662, and chosen again that year as assistant, but went to New Jersey, and Gov. Carteret made large purchase; was representative for Elizabethtown, in first assembly of that province, 1668.

OGDEN, RICHARD, Fairfield, 1667, brother of first John; had been partner with him in the contract with Krift when he was of Stamford : freeman, 1668, and large proprietor of Fairfield, 1670. Had descendants.

REFERENCES:—Am. Anc., II, 90; XII, 118; Norris Gen. (1898), 878; Ogdens of South Jersey (1894), 35 pages; Shroud's Fenwick Col. N. J., 167-72.

ARMS:—Gyronny of eight, arg. and gu. dexter gyron, arg.; in chief, an oak branch feructed; proper crest; an oak tree; proper—a lion rampant, against it.

MOTTO :—Et st ostendo non jacto (Showing is not boasting).

OGLEBY:—James, Scarsborough, 1676.

OKEY:—John, Boston; by wife Mary had Mary, born 1686; and Tacey, 1688.

OLCOTT:—Thomas, Hartford, an original proprietor, whose lot is exhibited on the ground plan, with his name written Alcock, and often it appears Alcot; was a merchant, who died in 1654 or 5; his inventory of large estate for that day had Thomas, Samuel, Elizabeth, baptised, 1645; John, 1650; and Hannah. His widow Abigail made her will and died 1693, aged 78. Eliza married Timothy Hyde of Wethersfield.

REFERENCES:—Chandler .Gen., 285; Olcott Gen. (1845), 64 pages; Olcott Gen., 2d ed. (1874), 124 pages.

OLD:—Robert, Windsor; married Susanna Hanford (Stiles, 728, calls her Hosford); had Robert, born 1670; Jonathan, 1672 or 3, at Windsor; removed to Suffield; there had Mindwell, 1675; Hanford, 1678; William, 1680; Susanna, 1683; and Ebenezer, 1688; in which year this wife died and he married Dorothy Granger; had John, 1691; of the children, Robert was of Springfield; Hanford of Westfield.

REFERENCES:—Stiles' Hist. Windsor. Conn., II, 537; Temple's Hist. of North Brookfield, Mass., 697.

OLDAGE, OLDIGE, OLDRIDGE, or OLDERIDGE:—Richard, Windsor; before 1640, possibly went from Dorchester, but was not known there to Dr. Harris; died 1661, and the name is extinct. His only child, Ann, married, 1645, John Osbon.

OLDEN:—John, Boston; by wife Eliz. had Nathaniel, 1668. Perhaps it may be Holden.

REFERENCES:—Rodman Genealogy, 157.

OLDFIELDS:—John, Southampton, L. I., 1641, and Jamaica, L. I., 1686.—Thompson.

OLDHAM:—John. Plymouth; came in the Ann, 1623, with a comp. so that in division of lands next year he was reckoned for ten heads; in less than two years gave offense by siding with Rev. Mr. Lyford, and was punished with more contempt than severity; driven to Nantasket, thence, with Conant, to Cape Ann; home in 1628, with their prisoner, mischief-making Morton, back to N. E. late in 1629, or 30; freeman 1631, with prefix of respect; lived at Watertown, engaged in trade with the Indians, representative in the first Gen. Court, 1634; was killed by the Indians in his shallop, 1636, at the mouth of Narragansett Bay. Administration of his estate was in Massachusetts. Not certain if he had wife and children.

REFERENCES:—Deane's Hist. of Scituate, Mass., 317; Mallery's Bohemia Manor; Smith Gen. (1895), 91-6.

OLIN:—John, West Greenwich, R. I., said to have come, 1678, in his youth, from Wales; hd by wife unknown John and Henry, and perhaps Justin and Joseph.

REFERENCES:—Olin (Ezra) Gen. (1892), 441 pages; Olin (John) Gen. (1893), 324 pages.

OLIVER:—John, Boston, 1632; younger brother or perhaps nephew of elder Thomas; came with him in the William and Francis; disarmed 1637; was chosen representative 1638, rejected by the house, as a supporter of the cause of Wheelwright; removed to Newbury; was freeman 1640; married Joanna Goodale, probably daughter of Elizabeth, and sister of Richard the first; had only Mary, born 1640, and he died 1642.

OLIVER, PETER, Boston, son of the elder Thomas, born in England, 1618, admitted freeman 1640; an eminent trader; one of the founders of the old South or 3d Church, which honor in the value of Boston History, by Mr. Drake, is inadvertently given to his fourth son, Hon. Daniel, then only 5 years old. He married Sarah, daughter of John Newgate; had Sarah, 1644; Mary, 1646, H. C., 1675; James, 1659, H. C. 1680; and Daniel, 1664; was of Artillery company, 1643, its captain 1669, and died 1670. His widow Sarah died 1692. His daughter Sarah married John Noyes, and died 1707; Mary married, 1666, Jonathan Shrimpton, who died 1673, and she next year married Nathaniel Williams.

OLIVER, SAMUEL, Boston, son of the elder Thomas; born in England; admitted to the church 1643; Artillery company 1648; had wife Lydia, adm. of the church 1647, and son Vigilant, baptised 1647; Patience, who died 1653; and Deborah, baptised 1652; was drowned 1652, leaving widow Lydia, who married, 1654, Joshua Fisher, sec. of Dedham.

OLIVER, THOMAS, Boston 1632, son of John and grandson of Thomas of Bristol, Eng.; came in the William and Francis, from London 1632, bringing wife Ann, who died 1635, daughter Abigail, and certain six sons, and Nathaniel, killled at 15 years by fall of a tree on Bocton neck, 1633; and Daniel, who died 1637. He was from Bristol; freeman 1632, selectman afterward; had in old age second wife Ann, who was of Dorchester; died June, 1658, "9 years old," says diary of John Hull. His daughter Abigail married James Johnson; another daughter married Richard Wolfall.

OLIVER, THOMAS, Salem, a calendar from Norwich; came at age of 36, in the Mary Ann, of Yarmouth, 1637, with wife Mary, 34, two children, Thomas and John, and two servants, Thomas Doged, 30, and Mary Sape, 12. The wife had too free speech, had suffered in England for neglect of some custom of trifling import in the solemnities of the church, and was punished here for siding with Roger Williams, in 1638, and for berating our elders as late as 1646. He was in office 1670 as a measurer of wood. A Bridget Oliver of Salem, charged with witchcraft, 1680, perhaps was daughter of the free-speaking woman.

REFERENCES:—Jackson's Hist. of Newtown, Mass., 373; Oliver Anc. in England (1867), 36 pages; Oliver Family of Boston (1868), 7 pages; Oliver Family of New York (1888), 27 pages; Richmond, Va., Standard, IV, 23.

OLMSTEAD:—James, Cambridge; came to Boston 1632, in the Lion, from London, with two children and others; was recorded as freeman: constable some years at Cambridge, but removed with earliest settlers to Hartford, 1636, of which he was an original proprietor, with large lots of land; died 1640. His will names two children, Nicholas and Nehemiah; but niece, Rebecca Olmstead, whom he brought over, has also a small provision, and his kinsman Richard, and John O., brothers perhaps of Rebecca, received a small portion of the estate.

Probably was their own property held by him in trust. It also provides for his servant, William Corbee or Corby.

REFERENCES:—Am. Anc., X, 157; Goodwin's Olcott Gen., 18; Olmstead Gen. (1868), 30 pages; Selleck's Norwalk, Ct. (1896), 266, 282-5.

OLNEY:—Thomas, Salem, shoemaker, of Hertford, Eng.; came in the Planter to Boston, 1635, from London, aged 35, with wife Mary, aged 30; son Thomas, 3, and Epenetus, 1; was freeman 1637; had Nehemiah, who died young; soon afterwards went to Providence, joined Roger Williams in purchase of Providence, and in founding the first Baptist church on our continent. There he probably had Stephen, . . . 's' the Lydia; took the oath of allegiance 1666, and died 1682. Of his daughters, Mary married, 1663, John Whipple; and Lydia married, 1669, Joseph Williams.

REFERENCES:—Am. Anc., IV., 149; VIII, 15, 91; Austin's Ancestries, 43, 83, 105; Olney Gen. (1889), 293 pages.

OLT, sometimes written AULT:—John, Portsmouth 1631; sent out by Mason, the royal proprietor; lived at Dover, 1648 to 1657, in which year he was 73 years old, and was living 1679. By wife Remembrance had John: Remembrance, who married John, Rand; and another daughter, who married Thomas Edgerly.

OLVERTON:—William, probably a soldier, killed 1675, by the Indians at Hatfield.

ONGE:—Francis, Watertown; came with wife and children in the Lion; arrived at Boston, 1631; died in a few years; and Francis Onge, in the Watertown record of burial, 1638, is named widow; was perhaps mother of his children to whom, in 1643, a mortgage is found. Simon, in 1646, and Isaac, in 1649, who married, 1670, Mary, daughter of Joseph Underwood, were of Watertown, but Simon got across the river to Newton, 1676; and Jacob, in 1678, was of Groton. Mary, aged 27, a passenger, 1634, from Ipswich, in the Francis, may have been sister or daughter.

ONION:—John, Braintree, 1640.

ONION, ROBERT, Roxbury; came in the Blessing, from London 1635, aged 26; married at Roxbury, but his wife mary died with her first child, 1643; removed to Dedham, 1645; freeman 1646; had second wife Grace, who died 1647; and he married Sarah, daughter of Michael Metcalf; had Susanna, born 1649; Mary, 1651; Hannah, 1656; Joseph, baptised 1663; Grace, 1666; and possibly others.

REFERENCES:—Ballou's Milford. Mass., 934; Hill's Dedham, Mass., Records, I.

ONTHANK:—Christopher, one of the Warwick freemen, 1655. Often is written Unthank.

REFERENCES:—Austin's R. I. Dict., 211.

ORCHARD:—Robert, Boston, merchant; by wife Sarah had Mary, 1668; was involved in controversy at the admiralty, 1666, and complained to the King, 1682. Bradford, to Gov. Winthrop, as to complaints of Indians against the Col.

ORCUTT:—William, Scituate; had perhaps born at Weymouth, William, in 1664; and Andrew; but at Scituate had John, born 1669; Martha, 1671; Joseph, 1672; Mary and Hannah, twins, 1674; Thomas, 1675; Benjamin, 1679; Elizabeth, 1682; and Deborah, 1683. Mitchell adds Susanna, born probably after his removal to Bridgewater, and says that all the children except Elizabeth and Deborah, perhaps then not living, were named in his will of 1694. Mary married, 1697. Daniel Hudson.

REFERENCES:—Lincoln's Hist. Hingham, Mass., III, 98-101; Paige's Hist. of Hardwick, Mass., 432.

ORDWAY:—Abner, Watertown, 1643; married, perhaps as second wife, 1656, Sarah, widow of Edward Dennis, of Boston.

ORDWAY, JAMES, born, it is said, in Wales, 1620; removed to Newbury; married, 1648, Ann Emery, perhaps daughter of Anthony; was taxed, 1649, at Dover, where Emery had lived; had Ephraim, 1650; James, 1651; Edward, 1653; Sarah, 1656; John, 1658; Isaac, 1660, died at 8 years; Jane, 1663; Hananiah, 1665; Ann, 1670; Mary, 1673; his widow died 1687; was freeman 1668, and died after 1702.

REFERENCES:—Coffin's Newbury, Mass., 255; Emery Gen. (1890), 7; Runnel's Hist. Sanbornton, N. H., II, 535-7.

ORMES:—John, Salem; by wife Mary had Mary, born 1656; John, 1658; Elizabeth, 1660; Joseph, 1663; Benjamin and Jonathan, twins, 1665, of the latter next year; Edonia, 1668 and James, 1670; the last was dead when mother took administration of his estate, 1693.

ORMES, RICHARD, Boston; by wife Rebecca had John, born 1682; and Richard, 1685.

REFERENCES:—Bond's Watertown, 382; Temple's Hist. of N. Brookfield, Mass., 698.

ORMSBY, or ORMSBEE:—Edward, Boston, perhaps son of that widow Ann who was admitted of our church, 1634; had grant of land 1637, and in Sept., 1639, was recommended to church of Dedham, wither she had no doubt removed.

ORMSBY, RICHARD, Saco 1641; removed to Salisbury; there by wife Sarah had Thomas, born 1645; Jacob, 1647; and probably John, before either, may have been born at Saco; was at Haverhill, 1653; and probably died at Rehoboth, 1664, where his inventory was taken that year.

REFERENCES:—Daniel's Oxford, Mass., 636; Am. Anc., VII, 117; McKeen's Hist. of Bradford, Vt., 352-8.

ORNE, or HORN:—John, Salem, 1630; came probably in the fleet with Winthrop, but may have been earlier; freeman 1631; was deacon, and Bentley says, in 1680, required assist. by collea. "as he had been in that office above 50 years;" died 1685, aged 82; had Recompense, baptised 1636; and Jonathan, 1658; both died before the father, besides these who outlived him, John, Simon, 1649; Joseph, Benjamin, Elizabeth, Gardner, Jehoadan Harvey, Mary Smith, and Ann Felton, 1657. We may presume his wife was Ann, as that name appears in Felt's list of the earliest children mentioned. All descendants in our day spell Orne (as did he in his last will).

REFERENCES:—Am. Anc., VII, 89; Clarke's Kindred Geneal. (1896), 102-36.

ORRIS, ORIS, or ORRICE:—George, Boston; blacksmith, came 1635, aged 21, in the Elizabeth and Ann; by wife Elizabeth, who joined our church 1645, had Mary, baptised same year, a year and seven months old; John, born 1647; Sarah, 1653; Jonathan, 1656; Samuel, 1659; Nathaniel, 1664; and Experience; and his wife died 1673.

REFERENCES:—Savage's Gen. Dict., III, 317.

ORTON:—Joseph, Rye, 1669, propounded next year for freeman, with the spelling Horton; was representative 1671, a lieutenant, and seems to have served much as la surveyor.

ORTON, THOMAS, Windsor; married, 1641, Margaret Pale, or Paul, not, as the copy in Geneal. Reg., V, 230, has it (with additional mistake of the man's name,

Josias for Thomas); had John, 1648; Mary, 1650; Sarah, 1652; and Elizabeth, 1654; removed, 1655, to Farmington; there had Hannah, baptised 1656. In 1688, to avoid the extortionate rule of Andros, requir. wills to be recorded at Boston, for all parts of N. E., he divided his estate among the four children John, Mary Root, Sarah Dewey, and Elizabeth Lewis.

ORTON, THOMAS, Charlestown, 1642; by wife Mary, who joined the church 1650, had Mary, 1648; and he was a householder 1658 and 77; died 1687. His children baptised there were William, 1660; Samuel, 1661; Ebenezer, 1664; Thomas, 1665; Annie, 166; and Abigail, 1669; possibly others.

REFERENCES:—Orton Chart (1886), 16x21 in., Orton Geneal. (1896), 220 pages; Stiles' Hist. of Windsor, Ct., II, 539.

ORVIS:—George, Farmington; married, 1652, Elizabeth, widow of David Carpenter; had Samuel, 1653; Hannah, 1655; Roger, 1657; Ebenezer, 1660; Margaret, 1661; and Mary, 1663; was freeman, 1658, and died 1664. His widow married Richard Bronson.

REFERENCES:—Hemenway's Vt. Gaz., V, 89; Savage's Gen. Dict., III, 317; Temple's Hist. of Northfield, Mass., 508-10.

OSBILL:—John, New Haven; freeman 1669.

OSBORN, or OSBURN:—Christopher.

OSBORN, JAMES, Springfield; married, 1646, Joyce Smith; had Elizabeth, born 1647; Mary, 1650; James, 1654; Sarah, 1658; and Samuel, 1664; removed to Hartford; there died 1676.

OSBORN, JEREMIAH, New Haven; perhaps brother of Richard; tanner; by wife Mary had Rebecca, 1642; Increase, 1643; Benjamin, 1647; Jeremiah, 1652, died soon; Mary, 1653; Elizabeth, 1655; both baptised 1655; Jeremiah again; Joanna, 1658; Thimos, born and probably died 1660; and Elizabeth again, 1665. He was representative 1672-4; died 1676. His widow, son Jeremiah, and other heirs were proprietors 1685.

OSBORN, JOHN, Braintree; had Matthew, who died 1641.

OSBORN, JOHN, Windsor; married, 1645, Ann, only child of Richard Oldage; had John, 1646; Ann, 1648; Nathaniel, 1650; Samuel, 1652; died soon; Mary, 1655; Hannah, 1657; Samuel again, 1660; Esther, 1682; Isaac, 1664, died at 9 years; and Sarah, 1667. He died 1686, when were living beside John, Nathaniel and Samuel, all the daughters except Ann, who married, 1663, Humphrey Prior, and had left two sons; Mary married, 1674, Josiah Owen; Hannah married Elias Shadduck, and next married, 1678, Benjamin Eggleston.

OSBORN, RECOMPENSE, New Haven; was by the late lamented Prof. Kingsley thought to be son of Thomas, H. C., 1661, though it is less probable from Geneal. Reg., XI, 345, than that he was son of William, and afterwards leaving coll. taught the school at New Haven, until he removed to East Hampton, on Long Island. His death was before the Magnolia of 1698.

OSBORN, RICHARD, Hingham, one of the first settlers 1635; removed soon to Conn.; served in the Pequot war, 1637; next to New Haven before 1640, where he had one child as early as 1643. Thence he removed to Fairfield, 1653, a grant of 80 acres for his services in the old war. Yet he had in 1666, interest in lands at Newtown, L. I., and some years before his daughter lived at West Chester, then thought to belong to Conn.; it is thought he had five children, John, Daniel, Elizabeth, Priscilla, and another child he calls his oldest daughter.

OSBORN, THOMAS. Charlestown, 1644; freeman 1648; by wife Hannah had Sarah, 1647; Thomas, 1649, Mary, 1652; another child, 1654; and Martha, 1656; beside John, baptised 1660. He liven on Malden side; there had wife Sarah, who in October, 1651, stood up manfully, with her sisterhood, in defence of Rev. Mr. Matthews against the Gen. Court. In February, 1662, he and his wife were recorded in the church of Charlestown, by dismissal from Malden; but probably he haa a hankering for heresy, as he next year united with Gould, as a Baptist, having embraced the opinions ot that sect as early as 1658, though their church was not formed until 1665. The name is sometimes Ozbon in records of Middlesex.

OSBORN, THOMAS, New Haven, perhaps brother ot Richard, with far better estate; counted a family of six, in a few years; removed to East Hampton, L. I., 1650; there perhaps had Thomas, Jeremiah, and John, yet may have been born before he left England.

OSBORN, WILLIAM, Salem, 1630; freeman 1639; by wife called in Felt's list of church members 1641, Frezwith or Freesweed; had there no children; removed to Dorchester, and there town records mention by Frodis werd, his wife, had Recompense, born 1644, H. C., 1661, at Braintree had Hannah, 1646; Bezaleel, 1650; and some years after at Boston, by probably the same wife called Frediswerth, and in Prov. rec. Freeswerd, had Joseph, 1652; and Jonathan, 1656. He was a merchant; died in middle life; his inventory, 1662, shows over £1,000; well for that time. His widow married John Mulford of South Hampton, Yorkshire E. Riding, and in 1670 sold to Rev. Antipas Newman of Wenham, that 110 acres granted to Osborn.

REFERENCES:—Am. Anc., I, 58; II, 90; IV. 26; X, 103; Cope Gen., 74, 164-6; Diamond Geneal., 102; Little's Passaic Valley Gens., 306--11; Osborn Geneal. (1891), 11 pages; Wyman's Charlestown, Mass., 716-8.

OSGOOD:—Christopher, Ipswich; came in the Mary and John, 1634; freeman 1635; died 1650, leaving wife Margery, who was daughter of Philip Fowler, and children Mary, Abigail, Elizabeth, Deborah, Christopher, born 1643; and Thomas, probably posthumu;. Mary married, 1651, John Lovejoy; and Abigail married, 1657, as seems probable Shoreborn Wilson of Ipswich.

OSGOOD, JOHN, perhaps brother of first Christopher; came from Andover, in Hampsire, England, where he was one of the founders of the church, 1645, and the first representative of the town, 1651; died that yeai. A widow, Sarah Osborn, died at Andover. 1667. His children were Sarah, John, born in England, 1631; Stephen, 1638; Mary. Elizabeth; all before he went to Andover. and there had Hannah, 1644; and probably Leborah. Sarah married, 1648, John Clement; Mary married, 1653, Henry Ingalls; Elizabeth married, 1659, John Brown of Reading; Hannah married, 1660, Samuel Archer; and Deborah married, 1663, John Russ.

OSGOOD, WILLAM, Salisbury, 1640. a proprietor of that date; born about 1605; had, by record at Salisbury, John and William, twins. born 1648; Mary, 1650; Joseph, 1651; Sarah, 1653; and Joseph, again, 1656.

REFERENCES:—Abbott's Andover, Mass., 19; Binney Geneal. 37-9; Field Geneal. (1895), 123; Hammatt Papers of Ipswich, Mass, 237; Osgood Geneal. (1894), 478 pages.

OSIER. or OSYER:—Abel, a soldier of Capt. Lothrop's Company, called "The Flower of Essex;"

killed at the Bloody Brook. 1675. His inventory of 28th June following, shows £3. 1, 10, that was given to his brother by order of the court.

OSLAND:—Humphrey, Cambridgeville or Newton; shoemaker; married, 1667, Elizabeth, daughter of Samuel Hyde; had Elizabeth, 1668; John, 1669; Hannah and Sarah, 1683; and died 1720. His widow died 1723. Elizabeth married Nathaniel Wilson, as his second wife. Hannah married, 1696. John Prentice, and Sarah married Edward Prentice.

REFERENCES:—Jackson's Newton, Mass., 375; Paige's Hist. of Cambridge, Mass., 620.

OTIS, or OTTIS:—John, Hingham; came some weeks before Rev. Peter Hobart, and company with which he associated in settlement of that town, 1635, born about 1581, at Glastonbury, Co. Somerset; perhaps son of Richard; had before leaving England three children, there bur. beside Richard. baptised 1617, and John, 1622; and daughters older as well as younger, brought over probably all by wife Margaret, who died 1653; was admitted freeman 1636, selectman often. After death of his wife removed to Weymouth; there took second wife, whose name was probably Elizabeth Streame, a widowed mother of Thomas and Bejamin Streame (in her will, 1672, probated 1676, names a son John S. giving him £80; speaks of son-in-law John Holbrook, who should pay that sum; and daughter Elizabeth H., and her child Ichabod); and died 1657; had his will made one day before signed it by mark. in which he provides for wife*and son John: he gives to daughter Margaret, wife of Thomas Burton, and her three children, to daughter Hannah, wife of Thomas Gill, and two only of hei many children. Mary and Thomas, and to his daughters Ann and*Alice, who were probably unmarried.

Mr. Otis, the assiduous antiquary of Yarmouth, from which Savage has gained much knowledge of Scituate. Barnstable, and Yarmouth early settlers, is derived from another stock, emigrating at least 80 years later than the Hingham pioneer, and coming from a part England widely remote from the first.

REFERENCES:—Am. Anc., V, 43; VIII, 149, 199; IX, 205; XI, 44; Ely Gen., 170; Otis Family of Hingham (1850), 39 pages; Otis Family of Dover. N. H., 1851, 48 pages; Swift's Barnstable Family, II, 222-4. 238-40; Williams' Hist. of Danby. Vt., 211-5.

ARMS:—Argent. a soltire, engrailed between four cross crosslets, fitchie. azure.

CREST:—An arm embowered, vested, gules; the hand, proper, holding a bunch of laurel.

OTLEY:—Abraham, Lynn, 1641.

OTLEY, ADAM. Lynn, 1641. perhaps brother of the preceding; Artillery Company, 1641; married a daughter of John Humphrey. Esquire, says Lewis. Perhaps it is the same as Utley.

REFERENCES:—Morris' Bontecon Gen., 162; Paige's Hist. of Hardwick. Mass., 519.

OTWAY:—John. Boston. 1657; owned land in Lynn; may be of same family as the last William Otway, Taunton, 1654.

OVELL:—Nathaniel, a cordwainer, from Dover, Co. Kent; came with a servant 1636; where he settled unknown.

OVERMAN:—Thomas, Boston; married Hannah, widow of Mahaleel Munnings, daughter of John Wiswall; was freeman 1671; dief before 1675; of his widow Hannah, admin. was given 5th June, 1694, to Matthew Johnson of Woburn.

OVERTON:—Robert, Boston; had wife and son John, and died at sea 1673, having made his will aboard ship, in latitude about 24 degrees, and probably was foll. by those who saw him die.

REFERENCES:—Am. Anc., III, 40; IV, 17; Chambers' Early Germans of N. J., 458; Lincoln's Hist. of Hingham, Mass., III, 104.

OVIAT, or OVIETT:—Thomas, Milford, 1665, proposed for freeman 1673.

REFERENCES:—Humphrey's Geneal., 294; Orcutt's Hist. of New Milford, Ct.

OWDRIE:—John, a youth of 17, came in the Increase, 1635, to Boston, from London.

OWEN:—John, Windsor, said to be born 1624; married, 1650, Rebecca Wade, perhaps daughter of Robert of Hartford; had Josias, 1651; John, 1652, died soon; John again. 1654, died at 16 years; Nathaniel, 1656; Daniel, 1658; Joseph. 1660; Mary, 1662; Benja-. min, 1664. died soon; Rebecca, 1666; Obadiah, 1667, and Isaac, 1670; was freeman, 1667, and removed to Simsbury, and died 1690. Mary married, 1681, Nathaniel Williams of Windsor.

OWEN, RICHARD, Newtown, L. I., 1656-86. Thompson and Riker.

OWEN, SAMUEL, Springfield; married, 1681, Ann, widow of John Pettee; had Sarah, born 1682; Abigail, 1685; Samuel, 1688; removed to Brookfield; there kept an inn.

OWEN, THOMAS, Boston; Artillery Co., 1639; imprisoned 1641. perhaps unjustly, for Samuel Maverick befriended him.

OWEN, WILLIAM, Braintree; freeman 1657; called by Chas. Grice. in his will, son-in-law; m 1661 had Daniel, born 1651; Deliverance, 1655, who married, May 1st, 1672, John Eddy, as his second wife, and Ebenezer, before mentioned.

REFERENCES:—Am. Anc., II, 90; Brown's West Simsbury, Ct., Settlers, 115; Humphrey Geneal., 258-60.

OXENBRIDGE:—John, Boston, son of Daniel, who was a daughter of Physic, born 1606, at Daventry, Co. Northampton; matriculated at Lincoln Coll., Oxford, 1623, in his 18th year. After wads of Magdalen Hall; continued there a tutor until disquieted with increasing church ceremonies. he went. 1634, to Bermuda and preached; went home again, but being ejected on the act of uniform. 1662, took departure for Surinam, thence to Barbadoes, and in 1669 to Boston; was installed as colleague with Allen in the first church a few days after the loss of the Davenport; admitted freeman 1670; died 1674. He had three wives. first, Jane Butler, who died 1655; next married, 1656, Francis, only daughter of Rev. Hezekiah Woodward, vicar of Bray. in Co. Berks.; died next year; the third is known by her will to have been named Susanna. His daughter, Bathshua, wife of Richard Scott, Esq., of Jamaica, was sole executrix. and had good estate. A younger daughter, Theodora. married, 1677, Rev. Peter Thatcher, of Milton.

OXMAN:—William. Salem, 1668; then 35 years or

PACEY. or PACYE:—Nicholas, Salem, 1639, when, Felt says. he had grant of land; joined the church, 1650.. Perhaps Catherine, of the same church was his wife. who was the unfortunate man procured to be united with Sarah. daughter of Gov. Thomas Dudley. after her husband Benjamin Keayne, had cast her off. neither Dudley nor Capt. K. informs us, though both

in their wills mention her, as does also. in his will, young Thomas Dudley speaks of his aunt P. Possibly it was Thomas P., named in inventory of John Mills, as one of his debtors, 1651.

REFERENCES:—Chambers' N. J. Germans, 459.

PACKARD:—Samuel, Hingham, 1638; came in the Diligent, with wife probably Eliza and one child; had been of Wymondham, in Co. Norfolk; removed to Weymouth, first, perhaps, where he had John, born 1655; thence to Bridgewater by 1664; had elder children Samuel, Zaccheus, Elizabeth, Mary, beside Hannah, Thomas, Joel. Isreal, Deborah, Deliverance, and Nathaniel. Elizabeth married, 1665, Thomas Alger of Taunton; Mary married Richard Phillips of Weymouth; Hannah married Thomas Randall; Joel married, 1672, John Smith; Deborah married Samuel Washburn; and Deliverance married Thomas Washburn. This name was first written as pronounced.

REFERENCES:—Allen's Worcester. 146-8; Bass' Hist. of Braintree, Vt., 169; Dyer's Hist. of Plainfield, Mass.; Lee Geneal. (1871), 85 pages.

PACKER:—George, Portsmouth, R I.., 1655.

PACKER, JOHN, New London, 1655; by first wife Eliza, who died 1674. had probably John, Samuel and Richard; by second wife Rebecca, widow of Thomas Latham, daughter of Hugh Wells, married. 1676: had James. baptised 1681: beside Joseph, Benjamin and Rebecca, as Miss Caulkins in her Hist. judges. He died 1689; his widow married a Watson of Kingston, R. I.

PACKER, THOMAS, Salem, whose wife Hepzibah, died, 1685, aged 25 years.

PACKER. THOMAS, Portsmouth, 1686. a physician from London: was Col. Judge of province, and a counsel. in 1719; died 1728. His wife Eliz. married, 1687; died 1717, in her 62d year.

REFERENCES:—Caulkins' New London. 324; Savage's Gen. Dict., III. 327; Wentworth Geneal., I. 182.

PADDLEFORD. PADELFORD, sometimes PADDLEFOOT:—Jonathan, Cambridge; in records spelt, Padlfoote; married, 1652, Mary Blandford, probably daughter of John of Sudbury; had Jonathan, born 1653, died soon: Mary, 1654; Jonathan again. 1656; Zechariah, 1657; these three baptised 1659, and Edward, 1669. His widow married, 1662, Thomas Eames of Sherburne. She was killed by the Indians in 1676, and at the same time nine of his children, whereof most were hers also, were either killed or taken. The name is frequent at Providence and the vicinity; four had, in 1834. says Farmer, been graduated at Yale and Brown Colleges.

REFERENCES:—Dean (John G.), Biog.. 32.

PADDOCK:—Ichabod, the subject of a trifling tradition, that he was invited, 1690, from Cape Cod to Nantucket. to teach the art of killing whales, when 18 years before James Loper had there been so engaged. Neither name was of permanent residence before the last was certain at Nantucket.

PADDOCK. ROBERT, Plymouth, 1643, and probably some years before perhaps was never a freeman of the Colony: had Robert. born 1634; Zechariah. 1636; Mary, 1638; Alice; 1640; John, 1643; and Susanna, 1649; his wife is not known. He died 1650. Mary married, 1651; Thomas Roberts; Alice married 1663, Zechariah Eddy; and Susanna married. 1665, John Eddy, and died 1670.

REFERENCES:—Am. Anc., I. 59; Craft's Geneal., 239; New Eng. Hist and Gen., Reg., XII. 220-2.

PADDY:—William, Plymouth; came in the James, 1635, from Southampton, embarked 6th April, arrived at Boston 3d June: called in the customs house Clarence, skinner, late of London: he was perhaps of that company of skinners, and a liveryman of the metropolis, who could not at London have obtained the liberty to leave home, as he probably was a subsidy man, that would not be spared: married, 1639, Alice, daughter of Edmund Freeman; had Elizabeth, born 1641; John, 1645; Samuel, 1645; Thomas, 1647: Joseph, 1649, died in a few months; and Mercy; was one of 4 representatives from his town in the first general court of deputies for that Colony, June, 1639. His wife died 1651, and he married at Boston, same year, Mary widow of Bezaleel Payton, sister of William Greenough the first; had William, 16th September, 1652, died under 20 years; removed to Boston; was in Artillery Company, 1652; here had Nathaniel, born 1653, died under 19 years; Hannah, 1656; Benjamin, 1658; and Rebecca, posthumus, baptised 1659, whose birth in the town records is strange, put 3d August of that year when her father died 24th August preceding, aged 58. His will of 20th August, probated 9th September following, names all his nine children, besides the two Paytons, and provides for the expected one. His widow died 1675, aged 60. Elizabeth married John Mensley; and Mercy married Leonard Dowden. Nathaniel who was probably unmarried, died soon after making his will, 1680, in which he gave estate to his sister Mary Shove, aunts Sarah Phillips, and Eliz. Greenough, cousin Eliz. Greenough, and others.
REFERENCES:—Savage's Gen. Dict., III, 328-30.

PADNER:—Ezekiel, Boston: by wife Ruth, born September, 1668.

PAGE:—Abraham, Boston, 1645. a tailor. from Gt. Baddon, in Essex; by wife Mary, of Braintree Church, had Abraham, 1646, at Boston, died same month, and perhaps he removed.

PAGE, ANTHONY, Dover. 1662-6.

PAGE, BENJAMIN, Haverhill; married 1666, Mary, probably daughter of Thomas Whittier; had nine children, says Barry.

PAGE, CONELIUS, Haverhill. 1677; may have been brother of preceding.

PAGE, EDWARD, Boston, cooper; by wife, daughter of William Beamsley, had Elizabeth, who died 1653; Sarah, born 1656; Edward, 1658; Jonathan, 1660; Penerel, 1663; Eliz., 1666; Humility, 1673; was of Artillery Co., 1661.

PAGE, FRANCIS, Hampton. 1678, oldest son of Deacon Robert; may be that deacon who died 1706, aged 76.

PAGE, GEORGE, Saco, 1653; married daughter of Nicholas Edgecomb, and she married next, John Ashton of Scarborough.

PAGE, GEORGE, Branford. 1667; may be the same one who was an ensign and died at Boston, where in August, 1675, his inventory was taken.

PAGE, HENRY, Hampton. freeman 1666.

PAGE, ISAAC, Boston; married, 1653, Damaris Shattuck; was probably the bricklayer at Salem, 1658.

PAGE, JOHN, Watertown: came in the fleet with Winthrop: made constable, 1630, when he requested to be freeman: was admitted 18th May following; was from Dedham, Co. Essex, with wife and two children, whose sufferings in the first winter were duly thought of by his former minister, blessed John Rogers. His wife

was Phebe, sister of William Paine, and of the wife of William Hammond of Wtertown, nam. Eliz., who died 1677, in 87th year; he died December preceding, aged 90; and their children were John, probably one of the two brothers from England; Samuel, born 1633. Daniel, 1634, died very soon; and Eliz., Mary and Phebe, of whom one may have been born in England. Phebe was third wife of James Cutler.

PAGE, JOHN, Dedham; freeman 8th October, 1640.

PAGE, JOHN, Haverhill, 1646, died 1687, and his widow died November, 1697.

PAGE, ONESIPHORUS, Salisbury; married, 1664, Mary, daughter of Thomas Hawskworth; had Mary, born 1666; Joseph, 1670; Abigail, 1672; Mary, 1674; Sarah, 1677; Onesiphorus, 1679; Cornelius, who died 1683; and Mary again, September, 1686. His widow died May, 1695; and he married, July following, Sarah Rowell; had John, born 1697, and died 1706.

PAGE, ROBERT, Salem, from Ormsby, near Yarmouth, Co. Norfolk; came in 1637, aged 33, with wife Lucy, 30; three children, Francis, Margaret and Susanna; and two servants, William Moulton, aged 20, and Ann Wadd, 15; freeman May, 1642; removed to Hampton, representative in 1667, 1668 and died September, 1679. His will, of 9th September, in that year, names oldest son, Francis, daughter Margaret, who mentions William Moulton, no doubt the fellow passenger; Mary, wife of Samuel Fogg; Thomas; Rebecca, wife of John Smith; Hannah, wife of Henry Dow; Robert, son of his son Thomas; and a grandson John; beside son-in-law William Marston.

PAGE, THOMAS, Saco. 1636; came probably in the Increase to Boston from the parish of All Saints Staynings, Marklane, London; a tailor, aged 29, with wife Elizabeth, 28, and children Thomas, 2, and Catharine, 1. He was of grand jury 1640, and, perhaps, removed to Casco.

REFERENCES:—Am. Anc., IV, 183; V, 89; VI, 5; VII, 211; XI, 152; Bangor, Maine. Hist. Mag., IX, 215-8; Bond's Watertown, Mass., Gens., 383, 865; Carter Family Tree of Virginia; Page Genealogy (1883), 250 pages; Page Genealogy (1893), 275 pages; Richmond, Virginia, Standard, III, 4, 29, 37.

CREST:—Out of a ducal coronet, a demi-griffen, both per pale, or and gules, counterchanged.

MOTTO:—Spe labor levis (Hope lightens work).

PAIGE:—John, Saybrook, 1684.

PAIGE, NATHANIEL, Roxbury. 1686; had seven children, probably born in England, and here had James, baptised 1686, died at 6 months; removed, 1688, to Billerica; was freeman 1690; had Christopher, born 1691. By Joseph Dudley, as Presid. was made, in 1686, marshall of the Co. Suffolk. He died April, 1692. His will names wife Joanna, his daughter Elizabeth married, 1698. John Simpkins of Boston; Sarah married, 1699, Samuel Hill, Jr., of Billerica. His son, Nathaniel died at Bedford, 1755, aged 75. and Christopher was the first deacon at Hardwick, where he died, 1774.

PAIGE, NICHOLAS, Boston, 1665, perhaps brother of the preceding; came from Plymouth, Co. Devon; carried Ann, widow of Edward Lane. daughter of Benjamin Keayne; was on service in Philip's war, 1675; was captain and later a coloney Artillery Company, 1693, and its commander. His wife died June, 1704, and he died probably 1717; his will probated January following. His wife was daughter of the sister of Joseph Dudley. In the weakness of that parent, she was suspected of inheriting a melancholy share, and was indicted and found "guilty of much wickedness," but great leniency was exhibited towards her, and on acknowledgement of offences she was discharged.

REFERENCES:—Am. Anc., III, 188; Davis Geneal., 191; Paige's Hist. of Hardwick, Mass, 433-50; Welles ..ashington Gen., 263; Winslow Gen., I, 148-56; II, 533-8.

PAINE:—Anthony, Portsmouth, R. I., rec. to be an inhabitant, 1638; had wife Rose, who married a Weeden, and may seem to have had family, from his release, of 1650, to share of property of Portsmouth, who died about 1640.

PAINE, ARTHUR, Portsmouth, R. I., 1655, in the list of freemen.

PAINE, JAMES, Newport; by wife Amy had Amy, born 18th January, 1660.

PAINE, PHILIP, New Haven; married, 1679, Mary, daughter of Capt. John Nash; removed to Northampton: freeman 1690; lived some years there, and Seth. who died, 1689, may have been his child; and had Mary, born 1690. but removed again to Connecticut, and part of his days was of Windham.

PAINE, ROBERT, Ipswich, born 1601; was probably from Co. Suffolk, as his wife Ann was daughter of John Whiting of Hadleigh in that shire; freeman 1641; representative 1647-9; had good estate and liberal; was ruling elder, teacher of Essex Co. 18 years; had second wife Dorcas, who died 1681, and he died 1684, leaving son John, and Robert, Harvard College.

PAINE, STEPHEN, Hingham, 1638, from Great Ellingham, near Attleburgh, Co. Norfolk; miller, came that year in the Diligent, with wife Rose, three children, and four servants; freeman 1639; representative 1641: removed to Rehoboth, 1645: representative 1647, and 18 years more. His wife died 1661, and next year he married Alice, widow of William Parker. I presume of Taunton, who outlived him, and he died 1678. His will of that year and inventory of very large estate was taken, 11th September following.

PAINE, STEPHEN, Dedham, married, 1652. Ann, daughter of Francis Chickering, of whom can find no more, unless he be the Rehoboth man and his widow, married, 1679, Thomas Metcalf of Dedham.

PAINE, STEPHEN, Charlestown or Malden; freeman 1665; by wife Elizabeth had Mary, born 1658, and was tything man 1679 at Charlestown near Malden.

PAINE, THOMAS, Salem, a weaver from Wrentham, in Co. Suffolk: came 1637, aged 50, in the Mary Ann of Yarmouth, with wife Eliz., 53, and six children, Mary, born 1611; Thomas, 1613; Eliz,. 1615; Dorothy, 1618; John, 1620, and Sarah. 1622; in a very trustworthy document he is called son of Thomas and Catharine, of Cooklie, near Halesworth, in Co. Suffolk; is said to be born 1686; married this wife November, 1610, and beside the six children brought over, had Peter, 1617, who probably died young; and Nathaniel, 1626, who died under 10 years. He had grant of land 1637; was freeman 1641. unless it was sister then admitted, which seems more probable; made his will 1638, and by the before mentioned document is supposed to have died 1640. Mary married Philemon Dickinson.

PAINE, THOMAS, Yarmouth; was representative 1639; removed to Eastham ,of which he was representative 1671. and six years more; had, beside Eleazer. born 1659. who died young; Thomas, Joseph, Nicholas. Samuel, Elisha, John, James, Mary ,and Dorcas. Mary married, 1670. James Rogers, Jr., and next, 1679. Isaiah Cole; and Dorcas married Benjamin Vickery. The will of the father was probated October 2, 1706, unless there be confusion between father and son of the same baptismal name.

PAINE, THOMAS, Boston; married, 1659. Hannah, daughter of Thomas Bray of New Haven; had Thomas, born 1665. He was. Savage thinks, that son of Thomas of London. born 1632, who, 1647. chose for his guardian, Thomas Mayhew, who had married in London, his mother Jane.

PAINE, THOMAS, Newtown. L. I., 1656.

PAINE, THOMAS, York; swore allegiance 1680.

PAINE, THOMAS, Dover, 1659; constable 1687; made his will 1694. probated 1700; mentions wife Eliz., who was named executrix, and children Thomas, Jane. Eliz.. Catharine. and Ann, said to be all minors.

PAINE, THOMAS, Newport, 1683; very active as captain of a privateer many years and one of the founders of the Episcopal church in that place, of which much may be seen in the valuable Hist. of Arnold. I, 471. and afterward.

PAINE, TOBIAS, Boston; came from Jamaica; married. 1665. Sarah, widow of Miles Standish, Jr., daughter of John Winslow: had William, born 1669, H. C. 1689. He died 1669, with so short notice, will incomplete. In it he provides only for this son, and the widow. who obtained third husband Richard Middlecot.

PAINE, WILLIAM, Ipswich; came in the Increase from London, 1635, aged 37, with Ann, probably his wife, 40; beside Susan, aged 11: William, 10: Ann, 5; John, 3, and Daniel, 8, weeks; freeman 1640; may have been first at Watertown; some few years had large estate used in a public spirit; removed to Boston. and died 1660. leaving only son John before mentioned. His will made 8 days before. provides £200 to his wife Hannah, and the dwelling house for life; £1,500 to the children of his daughter Hannah, wife of Samuel Appleton, viz.: Hannah. £600; Samuel, £500; Judith, £400; a liberal allowance for son John, to six children of Simon Eyre, deceased, viz.: Benjamin, Mary. Rebecca, Christian, Ann and Dorothy, £5 each; and to Simon, who was older than most of them £5 (from this Savage conjectures, also, from being felllow-passenger, that the wife of Ayres was the testator of this) ; to my sister Page £3 per annum. and to her children John. Samuel, Eliz., Mary and Phebe, £5 each; to children of my sister Hannah, John, Eliza, and Hannah, £5; to my kinswoman, Eliz., daughter of Samuel Howse, £10; to two daughters of my cousin John Tall, 40s. each; Samuel Appleton, £10; William Howard, £15; Jeremiah Belcher. 40s; Anthony Stoddard, £10; Christopher Clark, £10; Joseph Taintor, £10; Oliver Purchase, £10: to an Indian servant, 40s. yearly: to the free church at Ipswich his land at Jeffreys Neck; to the Coll. at Cambridge, £20 as a stock forever, and to friends in the ministry, Norton. Wilson. Sherman. Brown. Cobbett, Fiske. Phillips, and Mayo, 40s. each.

PAINE, WILLIAM, Salem, shoemaker; may be that passenger in the Abigail, 1635, aged 15, and at Salem to Eliz. Perhaps his wife or mother, Felt says, grant of land was made 1640, and he was probably the freeman of 1650; died about 1660.

REFERENCES:—Am. Anc., I, 59; III, 92, 97, 100, 109; IV, 34, 117; V, 78; VI, 179; VII, 126; Austin's Allied Families, 190; Chandler Gen., 236-45; Griffin's Journal of Southold, N. Y.; Paine Family Reg. (1857-9), 64 pages; Paine Family of Ipswich (1881), 184 pages; Whitmore's Heraldic Journal, III, 189.

PAINTER:—Thomas, Hingham, 1637; removed perhaps to Providence, at least Roger Williams gives him deed of a lot there, among home lots, but he was after at Boston; by wife Catharine, who died 1641, had Eliz., William and Thomas, all died between 30th Sept., 1639, and 24th April following, says the town record, which may so far be true, but another Thomas by the church record baptised 1640, the father being admitted 5 preceding, and freeman 12th October, 1640; removed to Charlestown, New Haven, Rowley, and back to Hingham, before 1644; there had another wife and child, and suffered severely for unwilling, to bring children to baptism, as told in Winthrop, II, 174. Savage thinks he removed next to Providence, thence again to Newport before 1655, when his name is enrolled among freemen, and probably his last removal was to Westerly with its first settlers in 1661.

PAINTER, WILLIAM, Charlestown, a sea captain and merchant; died Aug., 1666. His will, made 4 days preceding, names wife Eliz., speaks of estate in Barbadoes and Carolina.

REFERENCES:—Anderson's Waterbury, 98; Cape Gen., 38, 129; Painter Genealogy (1869), 20 pages.

PALFREY, PALFERY, PALFRY, or PALFRAY:—John, Cambridge, brought from England, perhaps by his mother, who married George Willis, sometimes written Willowes; by wife Rebecca, daughter of William Boardman, married, 1664, had Rebecca, born 15, baptised 17th September, 1665; John, 12th, baptised 14th April, died in few weeks; Eliz., baptised 1668; Martha, 1670; Thomas, 1672, who died 1677; Ruth, 1677, who died unmarried at Medford, aged 60; John, 1689, who died 1759, says epitaph, in 71st year and unmarried. There were two or three daughters, one was Mary, who married, 1700. Ebenezer Williams. He died 1689; in his will he provides for the new baby John, and six daughters, but does not name them. Rebecca became second wife, Nov. 1716, of Joseph Hicks; and Martha married, 1689, Benjamin Goddard.

PALFREY, PETER, Salem, 1626; came, perhaps with Conant, or soon after req. admission as freeman, October, 1630, and took oath May following; representative 1635; by wife Edith, had Jonathan, baptised, 1036; Jehoiadan, died early; Remember, baptised 1638; Mary, 1639; and at least two daughters more: removed to Reading, there died 1663. He married second wife Eliz., widow of John Fairfield, and had three daughters; wife Alice named in his will, 1662. He names no son; probably had given most of his estate during the inventory of residue being small. The widow lived to 1677. Remember married, 1662, Peter Aspenwall, besides whom he names other sons-in-law Matthew Johnson, who had married Hannah, 1656, who died 1662; Samuel Pickman; and Benjamin Smith, who alone of the four lived at Reading, there daughter Mary probably unmarried. We fail to gain knowledge of the mother of son Descent, however, from

this patriarch is claimed by many, of whom one is the learned Professor Palfrey, the diligent historian of New England.

REFERENCES:—Pickering Gen. Essex Inst. Hist. Coll., I, 185; Savage's Gen. Dict., III, 339.

PALGRAVE, or PALSGRAVE:—Richard, Charlestown, a physician; came in the fleet with Winth., from Stepney, Co. Middlesex, adjoining London, with wife Ann, and daughters Mary and Sarah, and, perhaps, other children; had here Rebecca, born 1631; John, baptised March, 1634; Lydia, baptised January, 1636; and Bethia, baptised 1638; all these baptised were in Boston church, of which the father and mother were both members. Nos. 105 and 6, and did not transfer then relation to the Charlestown church. He required admission as freeman October, 1630, and took the oath May following; died about 1656, and his widow removed to Roxbury: died 1669, aged 75; in her will made six days before, names eldest daughter Mary, wife of Roger Wellington, the child of her deceased son and daughter John and Sarah Alcock, with whom she had lived since the death of her husband and John Heylet, or Aylet, son of her daughter Lydia, who was wife of Edmund of Stephney, near London.

REFERENCES:—Prime's Sands Gen. (1886); Savage's Gen. Dict., III, 339.

PALMER:—Abraham, Charlestown, merchant from London, who there had joined the company of faithful patentees of Mass.; gave £50 to promote its object, 1629; was with Higginson, most active and intelligent town officer; required admission October, 1630, and was made freeman 18th May following; Boston church with wife Grace, No. 68 and 9, and of the founders of church at Charlestown; was in first assembly of representatives, 1634, serj. in the Pequot war; went to the Barbadoes, 1652, in the Mayflower of Boston. in which his share or adventure was 3-5, and that of Edward Burt 2-5, to be accounted for in London; there died 1653. His widow Grace died 1660, and Lieut. Thomas Lothrop had administration.

PALMER, GEORGE, Boston, wine cooper 1640; Artillery Co., 1641; removed to the E. before 1660, and he or another of the name was at Warwick, R.I., before 1655, though the place of residence is not told. He died 1669. In 1670 a Boston creditor, James Neighbors, had grant of admission.

PALMER, HENRY, Newbury 1637; freeman 1642; removed to Haverhill. from where he was representative, 1667, 74. 6-9, and died 1680. Perhaps he was of Hampton in his latter days. His daughter Eliz. married, 1659, Robert Ayer of Haverhill, and Mehitable married, 1676, Samuel Dalton.

PALMER, HENRY, Wethersfield; by wife Catherine had Deborah, born 1642; Hannah, 1645; a son whose name is not distinguishable in the records, 1648; Dorcas, 1650; freeman, 1657, and living 1663.

PALMER, HENRY, Pemaquid: swore fidelity to Mass. 1674.

PALMER, JOHN, Hingham; came in 1635; freeman 1639; removed perhaps to Scituate: Deane makes him, in Hist., 319, to be freeman of Plymouth Col., 1657, to have children then John and Elnathan, afterwards Josiah and Bezaleel.

PALMER, JOHN, Charlestown: perhaps came in the Elizabeth, 1634. from Ipswich, aged 24; was freeman June, 1641, and died 1677, aged 62.

PALMER, JOHN, Portsmouth; by Mr. Wentworth. copied from list of members of the church May, 1640. He served in Philip's war, then being inhabitant of Hampton.

PALMER, JOHN, Falmouth, 1689; consulted by the council of war for the defence of that town, 1689; was wounded 21st September; had married Mary, daughter of George Munjoy.

PALMER, MICHAEL, Branford, 1667, an original signer of the plantation covenant, 1668; freeman 1669.

PALMER, NICHOLAS, Windsor; freeman 1669; was an early settler; had Mary, born 1637; Hannah, baptised 1640; Timothy, 1642; and Eliz., 1644. His second wife, Joan, widow of John Purchase, married, 1646, died 1683, and hed ied 1689.

PALMER, RICHARD, Saco, or Wells, 1676; may be the passenger of 1635, aged 29, in the James from London to Boston.

PALMER, WALTER, Charlestown, 1629, probably younger brother of Abraham; charged in September, 1630, with killing Austin Bratcher, freeman 1631; was constable 1633; in June of that year he with new wife Rebecca, and daughter Grace, united with the church. Had Hannah, baptised 1634; Elihu, 1636; Nehemiah, 1637; Moses, 1640; Benjamin, 1642; all by Rebecca Short, a member of Roxbury church, who came in 1632, as a servant, says the record of Roxbury church, removed to Rehoboth; was representative 1646 and 7, being the first from that town; had more children and removed again to Stonington, 1653. His will, of May, 1658, made at Stonington, probated 1662, cont. in Suffolk reg. (for Stonington, then called Southerton, was claimed as part of our Co., strange as such geography now seems), names wife Rebecca and eleven children, John, Grace, Jonas, William, Grshom, Elihu, Nehemiah, Moses, Benjamin, Hannah, wife of Thomas Huet; and Eliz., and omits to name Rebecca, who married, 1665, Elisha Cheesborough; and was perhaps unable to count the grandchildren.

PALMER, WILLIAM, Plymouth; came in the Fortune, 1621, with son William, and his wife Francis came in the next year, the Ann, 1623; had share in the division of cattle, 1627; removed to Duxbury; married a young wife; had Henry and Bridget, but perhaps by former wife; both named in the will, and grandchild Rebecca, and died probably early in 1638; his will of 1637 was probated March, 1638.

PALMER, WILLIAM, Watertown, 1636; Newbury, 1637; owned land at Great Ormsby, Co. Norfolk; free man 1639; removed to Hampton; had by first wife son Edward, Christopher and Stephen, beside daughter Martha, who married. Savage thinks, John Sherman of Watertown. For second wife he had Grace, widow of Thomas Rogers, who survived him, and married Roger Porter. Ten of this name had in 1834 been graduated at Harvard, six at Yale, and six at the other N. E. colleges.

REFERENCES:—Am. Ancestry, II, 90; III, 101; V, 137, 211; IX, 68. 217; XI, 152; Barlow Genealogy, 395; Dow's Hist. of Hampton, N. H., 899-906; Huntington's Stamford, Conn., Settlers, 79; Palmer Family of Conn. (1881), 295 pages; Palmer Family of Conn., Sup. (1882), 119 pages.

PALMERLY:—John, a passenger in the Elizabeth and Ann, from London. 1635, aged 20; may be the same as Parmely or Parmarly of Guilford; sworn as freeman of Conn. 1665.

PALMES:—Edward, New Haven, 1659, a merchant; removed next year to New London; married Lucy, daughter of Gov. John Winthrop; freeman 1667, representative 1671-4 and 7; was a major in the Great Indian war. By first wife, who died 1676, six months after her father, he had no child, and next year he married Sarah Davis. widow of Captain William of Boston. as Miss Caulkins thinks; had Guy, baptised 1678; Andrew, 1682, Harvard College 1703; and Lucy. He died 1715, in 78th year, leaving good estate; in his will to only Lucy and Andrew. Lucy married Samuel Lynde, or Saybrook. He was named in the royal commiss., 1683, to adjust claims in the King's Province or Narragansett country.

PALMES, WILLIAM, Salem; married Ann, eldest daughter of John Humfrey, Esq., who after his death married Rev. John Wyles.

REFERENCES:—Caulkin's New London. Conn., 360; Ogden Gen. (1898), 84, 131; Arms of the Palmes of Naburn, Co. York.

ARMS:—Gu. three fleur-de-lis, arg.; a chief, vair.

CREST:—A hand holding a palm branch; proper.

MOTTO:—U't palma justus (As straight as a palm).

PALMETER:—Nathaniel, Killingworth 1667, then called Kenilworth; freeman 1668, whose name is spelled Palmerley in the return of the officers of the town; possibly same as Palmerly.

REFERENCE:—Am. Ancestry, II, 90.

PANNLY:—Alexander; is in Paige's list of freemen of Mass., 1660; name may be perverted by some clerk.

PANTON:—Richard, Westchester 1656; a man of influence, who died after 1700; took side of Conn., 1662, against the Dutch at Newtown, L. I.

PANTRY, or PANTREE:—John. Hartford, born in England; freeman 1650; married Hannah Tuttle of Boston, who was probably daughter of Richard; had beside Mary and Hannah, John, baptised 1652; and died probably 1653. His widow married .1654, Thomas Wlles. Hannah died 1672. unmarried.

PANTRY, Cambridge, 1634; came in May by same ship with Simon Willard, excused from military duty, by reason of age; freeman 1635; removed next year with Hooker's friends to Hartford, where he was among the chief proprietors.

REFERENCES:—Porter's Hartford Settlers, 15; Tuttle Genealogy, 83, 100.

PAPILLANS, or PAPILLON:—Peter, Boston. 1679; by wife Joan had Mary. born 1680; and Peter, born 1681; he was one of that company who broke off from the new North church when Rev. Peter Thacher was brought in 1718 to be collea. with their first minister, and in 1722 had command of a ship employed against pirates on the coast. He came into Boston 28th June from his cruise. having seen nothing of the great object of his outfit. the famous pirate Low, who long harassed the trade of New England. but brought in a brigantine that had been in possession of the foe. Supposed to be a Huguenot name.

PARD:—Samuel. Boston: by wife Mary had Samuel. born September, 1671.

PARDEE:—George. New Haven, a youth, apprenticed 1644 to Francis Brown, of whose origin or coming nothing is known: married, 1650, Martha. daughter of Richard Miles: had John, born 1657, died young: John. again. 1653. died before his father: George, 1656: Mary. 1658: Eli., 1660: the last three baptised 1662. He married second wife, 1662. Dodd says, Rebecca (but Catherine, reads another) Lane; had Joseph, 1664: Rebecca, 1666, baptised; Sarah, born 1608; and Hannah, 1672; and he died 1700, aged 71. His will, of 14th April, names all the daughters and sons George and Joseph. Married, 1677, Joshua Hotchkiss; Eliz. married, 1679, Thomas Gregory, and in the will of her father is called an Olmstead; Rebecca married, 1699, Samuel Alling; and Hannah married Edward Vickers. The name is widespread.

REFERENCE:—Am. Ancestry, VI, 104.

REFERENCES:—Am. Ancestry, VI, 104; Orcutt's Hist. of Wolcott, Ct., 536; Sedgwick's Hist. of Sharon, Ct., 103.

PARODY:—William, Mass. freeman, 1645.

PARENTS:—John, Haddam; sett. about 1662, died 1686, leaving two daughters.

PARIS, or PARRIS:—Christopher, Boston, 1649.

PARIS, JOHN, Braintree; married, 1664, says Farmer, Mary Jewell, probably daughter of Thomas.

PARIS, THOMAS, Newbury 1685. son of John, a dissenting clergyman of Ugborough, in Co. Devon; had come two years before to Long Island; removed to southern part of Mass., perhaps Plymouth; grandfather of Rev. Martin of Marshfield, and ancestor of Gov. Albion K. of Maine.

PARISH:—Thomas, Cambridge; came in the Increase, 1635, aged 22; was a physician, though in custom house record called, perhaps for misleading, a clothier, freeman 1637; by wife Mary had Mary, born 1638; Thomas, 1641, Harvard College 1659; and Mary, again, 1642. Probably he went home, lived at Nayland, Co. Suffolk, as his atty., Thomas Danforth, calls him.

REFERENCES:—Am. Ancestry, XII; Parish Genealogy (1897), 31 pages; Strong Geneal., 153, 372-4; Thurston Geneal. (1892), 29.

PARKE, or PARKS:—Edward, Guilford, 1685; died 1690; and there the name continues 20 years.

PARKE, JACOB, Mass. freeman 1657; may have been of Concord, or possibly of Rowley; his name stands in Paige's list between the inhabitants of these towns.

PARKE, RICHARD, Cambridge, 1636; a proprietor at the Farms, now Lexington, 1642; died at Cambridge village (where he had lived 18 years), 1665, leaving will of that year providing for wife Sarah, who had been a widow of Love Brewster, and was living at Duxbury 1678; two daughters and only one son, Thomas. The inventory showed good estate. Isabel, one of his daughters, married Francis Whittemore; and Sarah, the other daughter, 1699.

PARKE, ROBERT, Wethersfield, 1639; freeman 1640; may have sent another, beside his eldest son William some years before he came to our shore, as permanent resident. Savage thinks he came back same year, carrying an order by our Gov. to his son John in England to pay money, which is in my possession, and may be the earliest bite of exchange draft on our side of the water, but was not guided by the decision of the s. as to his plantation. Representative 1641; removed 1649 to New London, where his barn was the first place of worship; selectman 1651; representative 1652; called an aged man 1662, and died 1665. His will, May, 1660, probated March, 1665, names only three children, William, Samuel and Thomas, but a daughter, Ann, had accompanied her brother William to Roxbury; there married, 1640, Edward Payson, and died following September. In his favor was the curious order of 30th May, 1644, by our general court, that he might "proceed in marriage with Alice Thompson, without further publishment."

PARKE, WILLIAM, Roxbury, eldest son of Robert; came in the Lion; arrived at Boston, February, 1631, with Roger Williams; was perhaps sent by his father to look out good spot for plantation; one of the earliest church members; freeman May, 1631; married Martha, daughter of John Holgrave of Salem; had Theoda, 1637; Hannah, 1639, died 1655; Martha, baptised 1642; Sarah, baptised 1643, who died September following; John, baptised 1645, died next June; Deborah, baptised 1647, whose birth the town record omits, but inserts her death, 1649; John, again, 1649, died at 14 years; Deborah, again, baptised 1651; son and daughter, twins, buried June, 1653; William, baptised 1654, died young; and Hannah, again, September, 1658; Artillery Company 1638; was representative 1635 and 32, various years after, the longest term of service in that rank under the old charter. He was many years deacon; died 1685. His will provided for the wife of his youth, mentions two surviving daughters, and Mary, grandchild, besides brothers, Thomas, deceased, and Samuel. Gravestone, Gen .Reg., makes the death 1683. The widow Martha died 1708, aged 94. Theoda married, 1654, Samuel Williams, and so was mother of Rev. John, Harvard College 1683, of Deerfield, the famous "Redeemed Captive;" another daughter, Martha, married Isaac Williams, whose son William, Harvard College 1683, minister of Hatfield, the grandfather, says he had taken care of from the age of 3 years, besides part of Stonington land to other sons; and another daughter married John Smith, and to them he gives part of his Stonington land. Five of this name, in its several spellings, had been graduated at Harvard in 1834, and thirteen at other N. E. colleges.

REFERENCES:—Biddle Geneal. (1892), 39-46; Meade's Old Churches of Virginia; Potter's Am. Monthly, VI, 85.

PARKER:—Abraham, Woburn; married, 18th November, 1644, Rose Whitlock; had Ann, born 1645; John, 1647; Abraham, 1650, died next year; Abraham, again, 1652; removed to Chelmsford; there had Mary, 1655. baptised April following; Moses, Isaac, born 1660; Eliz., 1663; Lydia, and Jacob, 1669. He was freeman 1645, and died 1685; and his widow died 1691.

PARKER, AZRIKAM, Boston, 1662; mariner.

PARKER, BASIL, York, 1649; recorder of the province, and made by Gorges one of the counc.; died before 1651, when administration was given to John Alcock.

PARKER, EDMUND, Roxbury; married, 1647, Eliz., probably daughter of the first Abraham Howe; had there baptised Eliz., 1648, died soon; Eliz., again, 1649; 1649; Abraham, 1652; Mary, Esther. Deborah, June, 1656, perhaps not all born in one day; for he may have removed to Lancaster, where he was proprietor 1654, and there brought these children to baptism and probably had others later.

PARKER, EDWARD, New Haven 1644; married Eliz., widow of John Potter; had Mary and John, baptised 1648; Hope, born and baptised 1650; and Lydia, 1652; and he died 1662. In 1666 Mary married John Hall: in 1667 Hope married Samuel Cooke: and Lydia married, 1671, John Thomas.

PARKER, ELISHA, Barnstable; married, 1657, Eliz. Hinckley, sister of Gov. Thomas; had Thomas, born 1658: Elisha, 1660; and Sarah, 1662.

PARKER, GEORGE, Portsmouth, R. I., 1638; may be that carpenter from London, who came, 1635, in the Elizabeth and Ann, aged 23, was serj. gen.: died 1656.

leaving widow and daughter Francis, who married, 1676, Benjamin Hall, beside Mary, who married Ichabod Sheffield.

PARKER, GEORGE, York; freeman 1652; constable there 1659.

PARKER, JACOB, Chelmsford; by wife Sarah had Sarah, born 1654; Thomas, 1656; both with elder brother Jacob, baptised 1656; Tabitha, 1658; Rebecca, 1661; Rachel, 1665, and Mary, 1667, and perhaps others. He died in few months; widow Sarah presented inventory in 1669.

PARKER, JACOB, Roxbury; married 1687, Thankful, daughter of John Hemmenway; had Thankful, died 1688, a few days old; Sarah, 1689; Jacob, 1691; soon after Thankful again, 1692; Jacob, again, 1697; Mary, 1699; Eliz., 1700; and Experience, 1705.

PARKER, JAMES, Dorchester, early, perhaps. as 1630; freeman, 1634; removed to Weymouth, and was representative 1639-42; thence to Portsmouth, where he invited to be their minister, but preferred to continue in trade, though he preached a few years; went to Barbadoes, whence a good letter to Gov. Winthrop from him is given by Hutch. Coll., 155; died on a visit to Boston, 1666.

PARKER, JAMES, Woburn, 1640; married, 1643, Eliz., daughter of Robert Long of Charlestown; had Eliz., born 1645; Ann, 1647; John, 1649 (who was killed by the Indians 27th July, 1694); was freeman 1644; and a grantee of Billerica; removed to Chelmsford and had Josiah, 1655; Samuel, 1656; Joshua, 1658; Zechariah, 1659; and Eleazer, 1660; was captain; removed to Groton and perhaps by second wife had very late in life Sarah, again, 1697; and he died 1701 in 84th year.

PARKER, JOHN, Boston, 1635, a carpenter of Marlborough, Co. Wilts; came that year in the James; arrived from Southampton, with wife Jane; had Thomas, 1635, baptised 1637, his wife having united with the church; Noah, baptised 1638; beside John, and Margaret ,who may have been brought from England. He lived at Muddy River, now Brookline, and died in a few years, for in 1656 his widow Jane had married Richard Tare, and then sold her house and garden, and to Stephen Greenleaf, who came from Newbury.

PARKER, JOHN, Saco 1636; the purchaser of Parker's Island, now Georgetown, on eastern side of Kennebec River, near the mouth; is by Williamson thought to have first settled in 1629, on the west side of the river, but his purchase was in 1650; tradition says he was from Biddeford, Co. Devon, and before June, 1661. died. By wife Mary he had Thomas, John, and Mary, but all may have been in England, though tradition makes John born at Saco, 1634. Mary married Thomas Webber, it is said, who died at Charlestown before 1695. She was widow on joining the church that year.

PARKER, JOHN, Hingham, 1636; removed to Taunton, of which with William, elder brother, was a purchaser, 1637; was representative 1642, and died 1668.

PARKER, JOHN, Boston, 1644; shoemaker; had wife Sarah, who joined church in August of that year, and probably daughter Sarah, who married, 1653. Isaac Bull, perhaps he was the freeman of 1650.

PARKER, JOHN, Woburn 1653; removed probably to Billerica; was there first town clerk; died at Charlestown 1669.

PARKER, JOHN, Cambridge. in the part which became Newton; had come from Hingham, with Druce. Hammond and Winchester; induced to remain by Nicholas Hogdon; was perhaps the freeman of 154; by wife Joanna had Mary, born 1648; Martha, 1649; John, 1652; Joanna. 1654; Jeremiah, 1656, died early; Thomas, 1658, died at 21 years; Sarah, 1660; Isaac, 1663; Jonathan, 1665; and Lydia, 1667; but the first two were brought from Hingham; he died 1686, aged 71; his widow died 1688. Mary married Peter Hanchett of Roxbury; Martha married James Horsley; Sarah married, 1686, Samuel Snow of Woburn; and Joanna married a Stone.

PARKER, JOSEPH, Newbury; came in the Confidence, from Southampton, 1638, aged 24; was a tanner of Newbury, Co. Berks.; had Joseph, born 1642; removed to Andover, where he was one of the founders of the church. October, 1645, and had more children, of whom were Stephen, born 1651, and Samuel, Thomas, non compos. and daughter Sarah, Mary and Ruth, who all outlived him; also John, killed by the Indians, 1678; and he died 1678. All his estate in Rumsey, Co. Hauts, about 8 miles from Southampton, devised to his wife by last will; her name was Mary, and a widow of that name died 1695.

PARKER, JOSEPH, Chelmsford; married, 1655, Rebecca Read; had Ann, born 1656; Mary, 1657; John, 1659; and John, 1660; but the record gives not mother of first two. and for the third names Mary; and Margaret for the fourth. It may be probable that one wife, either Mary or Margaret, brought all. and perhaps there were more.

PARKER, JOSEPH, Dunstable, though a proprietor, only a temporary resident; had by wife Margaret, as seen on Chelmsford record. Joseph, born 1653; Ann, 1653, died young; Mary. 1657; John, 1660. died soon; Ann, 1663; perhaps confusion between husband of Margaret and Rebecca; in the record of their church must have occurred, as each had Mary born on the same day.

PARKER, NATHAN, Newbury, an early settler; removed to Andover; was brother of Joseph of the same. married, 1648, Sarah. or Susan Short. who died 1651, by another wife. Mary. he had John. 1653; James. Robert, and Peter; and died June, 1685. Perhaps this man may be he who was entered as Nathaniel, of London, a baker, aged 20. in 1638, when Stephen Dummer brought him in the Bevis from Southampton.

PARKER, NICHOLAS. Roxbury; came in 1633, either with Cotton in the Griffen, or in the Bird (both which arrived 4th September), with wife Ann, children Mary, and Nicholas; freeman 1634; had Johanna, born 1635, says the Roxbury church record; removed soon after to Boston; had a child born 1637. died soon; Jonathan. 1640; Abiel, 1642; Joseph, 1643; no mention of his death. His daughter Mary married William Davis; Johanna married, 1655. Arthur Mason, the stout patriot. constable; and Jonathan lived in London.

PARKER, RALPH. Gloucester 1647; removed to New London 1651; had Mary by afor mer wife and by Susan. na. daughter of William Keeny, had Susanna. Jonathan. Ralph. born 1670; Thomas, Hannah, Mehitable. and Rebecca; was a master mariner and merchant, and died 1683. Mary married a William Condy; Susanna married. 1666. Thomas Forster; Hannah married Richard Wyatt, it is said; Mehitable married William Pendall; and Rebecca married. 1685, John Prentiss. as his second wife.

PARKER, RICHARD, Boston, merchant; by wife Ann had Joseph, born 1638, died in few months; Sarah, baptised 1641; was freeman 1641, and probably died soon after, but may have had second wife, for in the book of possessions Jane, widow of Richard, had an estate. His daughter Ann, born probably in England, married, 1651, John Manning, as second wife, and their daughter Ann married, 1669, John Sands: and Sarah married, 1659, John Paine.

PARKER, ROBERT, Boston; called on admission to the church, 1634, "servant to our brother William Aspenwall;" was a butcher; possibly came from Woolpit, near Bury St. Edmunds, Co. Suffolk; freeman; removed early to Cambridge; married Judith, widow of Richard Bugby of Roxbury; had Benjamin, 1636; Sarah, 1640; John, baptised at Roxbury, in right of his wife, 1642, and Savage judges him to be the H. C. graduate 1661; Nathaniel, 1643, died young; and Rachel, who died before her father. His wife died 1682, aged 80, and in his will, 1684, probated 1685, calls his age 82 years. The sons Benjamin and John, had full share, and are dead, so he names daughter Sarah, wife of Thomas Foster, sole heir, and to her children after, with double portion to her son Thomas.

PARKER, ROBERT, Barnstable; married, 1657, Sarah James; had Mary, 1658; Samuel, 1660; Alice, 1662; and Jane, 1664. He married a second wife, 1667, Patience, daughter of Henry Cobb; had Thomas, 1669; Daniel, 1670; Joseph, 1672; Benjamin, 1674; Hannah, 1676; Sarah, 1678; Elisha, 1680; and Alice, again, 1681, both baptised 1684; an erroneous date of his death is given, 1680.

PARKER, SAMUEL, Hingham, 1638; may have been of Haverhill 1677, but owned land in 1682 at Weymouth.

PARKER, SAMUEL, Dedham; married, 1657, Sarah, daughter of William Holman, of Cambridge; had Sarah, 1658, died next year; Samuel, 1659; Ann, 1661; Sarah, again, 1662; Nathaniel, 1664, died at 3 months; Susanna, 1667; Margaret, 1668; Nathaniel, again, 1670; and Mary, 1675; and his wife died November following and he died December, 1678. Administration was given on his estate 1680, to Capt. Thomas Prentice and Mr. Timothy Dwight.

PARKER, THOMAS, Lynn; came in the Susan and Ellen, 1635, with his wife, being fellow passenger; freeman, 1637; removed to Reading; had Hannah, born 1638; Thomas, Joseph, 1642, died soon; Joseph, again, 1645, died at 4 months; Mary, 1647; Martha, 1649; Nathaniel, 1651; Sarah, 1653, probably died young; Jonathan, 1656; and Sarah, again, 1658; beside John; was there one of the founders of the church and many years deacon till his death, 1683. His will of that year provides for wife Amy, sons John, Thomas, Nathaniel, daughters Mary and Martha, beside grandchildren Samuel and Sarah, and makes Hannah sole executor. His widow died 1690.

PARKER, WILLIAM, Hartford, an original proprietor, 1636; removed to Saybrook, after having several children. Sarah, born 1637; Joseph, died in a few weeks; John, 1642; Ruth, 1643; William, 1645; Joseph, again, 1647; Margaret; Jonathan, 1653; David, 1656; and Deborah. 1658; was representative 1672; his wife Margery died 1660, and he died 1686.

PARKER, WILLIAM, Taunton 1643, perhaps elder brother of John of the same; a purchaser in 1637; in his will of 1660, being 60 years old, names wife Alice, but no children and gave small legacy to his nephew, James Phillips. His widow married, 1662, the first Stephen Paine of Rehoboth.

PARKER, WILLIAM, Watertown; by wife Eliz. had Ephraim, of whom the record says he died in 1640, six months old; and Ruhannah, 1641; was freeman 1641. He was one of the original proprietors of Sudbury.

PARKER, WILLIAM, Scituate; married, 1639, Mary, daughter of Thomas Rawllyns; had Mary, born 1640; William, 1643; and Patience, 1649; and his wife died August, 1651. He married, November, 1651, Mary, daughter, of Humphrey Turner; had Lydia, 1653; Miles, 1655; Joseph, 1658; and Nathaniel, 1661, who perished in Phip's expedition against Quebec, 1690; and died 1684. Mary married Theophilus Wetherell; Patience married a Randall; one daughter married Thomas Totman; and in his will are also named daughters Lydia and Judith; this Lydia was probably second wife of Theophilus Wetherell, and died 1719, aged 67. Forty-one of this name had in 1834 been graduated at Harvard, and thirty-eight at all other New England colleges.

REFERENCES:—Abbot's Andover, Mass., 20; Am. Anc., I, 59; II, 91; III, 167; V, 202; VI, 22, 179; X, 201; XI 45; Avery Gen. (1893), 211-4; Bedford, N. H., Centennial, 323; Butler's Hist. Groton, Mass., 421, 476, 494; Chambers' Early Germans of N. J., 460; Cutts Geneal., 242-4; Dickey Geneal., 32-7; Egle's Penn. Geneal., 2d ed., 579-604; Freeman's Cape Cod, II, 438, 466, 642; Green's Kentucky Farm; Hill's Hist. of Mason, N. H., 205; Jackson Geneal., 299; Lamb's Hist. of New York City, I, 706; Parker Family of Roxbury (1890), 10 pages; Parker of New York (1877), 18 pages; Shattuck Geneal., 375-7; Whitehead's Perth Amboy, N. J., 128-38; Wyman's Charlestown, Mass., Gens., 726-9.

PARKHURST:—George, Watertown; freeman 10th May, 1643; brought from England son George, daughter Phebe, and perhaps other children. Barry says his wife was Susanna. In 1643 he married second wife Susanna, widow of John Simpson; sold his estate in 1645, and removed to Boston; was living there in 1655. Phebe married Thomas Arnold. In the early records the name is Parkis or Perkis.

REFERENCES:—Am. Anc., I, 60; XII; Bemis' Hist. of Marlboro, N. H., 595; Parkhurst Geneal. (1883), 19 pages; Stone's Hist. of Hubbardston, Mass., 328; Temple's Hist. of Palmer, Mass., 527.

PARKINSON:—William Dover, 1684.

REFERENCES:—Cochrane's Hist. Francestown, N. H., 866-9; Mills Geneal. (1893), 13-5; Power's Sangamon Co., Ill., Settlers, 556.

PARKMAN:—Elias, Dorchester, 1633; freeman 1635; removed to Windsor early; there had Elias, Rebecca, Samuel, born 1644; and George, who died 1645; he probably had an establishment for trade at New Haven, 1640, but finally removed to Boston; there had Mary, baptised 1648; Deliverance, baptised 1651; and Nathaniel, baptised 1655. His wife was Bridget. He was a mariner: traded from Boston to Conn. River, and perhaps on longer voyages, in one of which he was probably lost, for his wife presented inventory 2d July, 1662, made two days before recit. that he was "supposed to be dead;" and as it amounted to only £37, 15s., we may think that most of his property was lost at the same time. Rebecca married, September, 1661, John Jarvis, and perhaps his widow married, September, 1672, Sylvester Eveleth, of Gloucester.

REFERENCES:—Allen's Worcester, 56; Ballou's Hist. of Milford, Mass., 941-51; Breck Geneal., 20-32; Whitmore's Copps Hill Epitaphs.

PARMELEE:—John, Guilford, 1639; was of New Haven 1659, when he made his will, 8th November, and died soon afterward; to his only son large part of his property was given, residue to grandchildren, Nathaniel and Hannah, wife of John Johnson, after providing for his own wife Eliza, who married John Evarts. Sometimes this name is spelt Parmelin.

REFERENCES:—Am. Anc., III, 195; X, 195; Davis Hist. of Wallingford, Conn., 884; Salisbury's Fam. Hist. (1892), I, 219-33; Whitemore's Hist. Middlesex Co., Ct., 211.

PARMENTER (Often in old records Parminter): —Benjamin, Salem 1637, when, Felt says, he had grant of land, but perhaps he did not live there, exc. on Marblehead side. Yet called of Salem when freeman, 1678, many years before; had wife Mary and daughter Mary, and was of Gloucester, 1684; said to have been born about 1610.

PARMENTER, JOHN, Watertown, 1638; one of the first settlers of Sudbury, 1639; freeman 13th May, 1640; selectman and deacon; had brought from England son John, and perhaps other children, with wife Bridget, who died April, 1660, and he removed to Roxbury; there married, August, 1660, Ann, or Annis, widow of John Dane, who had before been widow of William Chandler; and he died May, 1671, aged 83. In his will he names this wife and son-in-law John Woods, husband of his daughter Mary, and grandson John, his son of that name being some years; died and this grandson made one of the executors. The will of his widow, November, 1672, probated eleven years after, names her first husband's children John, Thomas and William Chandler; Hannah, wife of George Abbott, and Sarah, wife of William Cleaves.

PARMENTER, JOHN, houseright; by wife Judith had Judith, born 1667, died soon; Eliz., February, 1668; John, 1670; died soon; Judith, again, July, 1672; John, again, November, 1674; and Lydia, 1677; and by second wife Hannah, daughter probably of Richard Williams of Taunton, had Eliz., again, September, 1688.

PARMENTER, ROBERT, Braintree; freeman, 1650; by wife Leah had John, born Oct., 1653, died next month; Joseph, 1655; Eliz., 1657; and Hannah, 1659; and was deacon and died 1696, in his 74th year. The name is pronounced Parmiter.

REFERENCES:—Barry's Framingham, 353; Draper's Hist. of Spencer, Mass., 236; Savage's Geneal. Dict., III, 359; Temple's Hist. of Northfield, Mass., 511.

PARNELL:—John, Dover, 1668-8, perhaps had wife Mary, daughter of Henry Stacy.

PARNELL, THOMAS, Pemaquid; swore fidelity to Mass., 1674.

PARNELL, FRANCIS, captain; died at Boston, October, 1724.

PARR:—Abel, Boston; freeman June, 1641.

PARR, JAMES, one of the soldiers sent to seize Groton, and his comp. was of unknown residence.

PARR, SAMUEL, Salem, 1665.

PARROTT, PAROTE, or PARRETT:—Frances, Rowley; freeman, May, 1640; was town clerk, 14 years representative, 1640 and 2, being the earliest from that town; went home, and died about 1656. His will mentions wife Elizabeth and six children; one was probably that Faith who married Ezekiel Jewett.

REFERENCES:—Austin's Rhode Island Gen. Dict., 144; Homer Geneal., 18-20; Orcutt's Hist. of Stratford, Ct., 1354.

PARRY:—Edward, came from London in the Truelove, 1634, aged 24, but where he settled, unknown.

REFERENCES:—Am. Anc. VI, 67; VII, 20; Fell Geneal. 88; Parry Geneal. (1877), 38 pages; Youngs' Hist. of Wayne Co., Ind., 353.

PARSONS:—Benjamin, Springfield; said to have come, perhaps was brought, in childhood, from Torrington, about 30 miles from Exeter, in the northwest part of Devonshire; married Sarah, daughter of Richard Vore, of Windsor; had Sarah, born 1656; Benjamin, 1658; Mary, 1660, died young; Abigail, 1663; Samuel, 1666; Ebenezer, 1668; Mary, 1670; Hezekiah, 1673, and Joseph, 1675. His wife died 1676 or 7, and he married widow of John Leonard, who took after his death third husband, Hon. Peter Tilton; was deacon, and died 1689. Sarah, married Dorchester; Abigail, married 1680 John Mun, and 1686 John Richards; and Mary married 1691 Thomas Richards.

PARSONS, GEORGE, Boston; by wife Elizabeth daughter; Savage thinks of Rev. John Wheelwright; had Joseph, 1667; and Wheelwright, 1674.

PARSONS, HUGH, Springfield; married 1645, Mary Lewis from Wales; had Hannah, born 1646; Samuel, 1648, died next year; and Joshua, October, 1650, killed by his mother 4 Mar. following, and she pleaded guilty in May after having been just before acquitted of the absurd charge of witchcraft on a charge of the Rev. Mr. Moxon. The unhappy woman had, in her native land, suffered abuse by a former husband, who several years before she came hither, abandoned her, and her character was so fair we must believe her insane. But the husband was less lucky, the jury convicted him of a similar crime, when, in 1652, the sentence of death was refused by the court, and the Gen. Court had sense enough to discharge the prisoner. Soon after both harmless felons removed to Watertown. There he died 1675, and his widow, Ruth, died 1676. The first wife Savage thinks suffered death for the murder of her child.

PARSONS, JEFFERY, Gloucester; married November, 1657, Sarah, daughter of William Vinson; had James, born 1658; Jeffery, 1661; Sarah, 1663; John, 1666; Elizabeth, 1669; Jeremiah, 1672; Nathaniel, 1675; Abigail, 1678; Ebenezer, 1681, died soon; and Ebenezer, again 1682. He was, it is said, born about 1631 at Alphington, near Exeter, adjoining Topham, Co. Denn, and died 1689; and his widow died 1708. His grandson, Moses, minister of Byfield parish in Newbury, who died 1783, was father of Theophilus, Harvard College, 1769; Chief Justice of Massachusetts, one of the principal framers of the constitution of this Commonwealth. He was the most learned lawyer in the general opinion of his contemporaries that ever appeared on our side of the Atlantic.

PARSONS, JOSEPH, Springfield; brother of the first Benjamin, witness to the deed from the Ind. to Pynchon, July, 1636; married, 1646, Mary, daughter of Thomas Bliss of Hartford; had Joseph, born 1647; Benjamin, died 1649; John, 1649, died soon; John again, 1650; and Samuel, 1653; removed to Northampton, there had Ebenezer, 1655, who is said to be the first white born there, and was killed by the Indians at Northfield, 1675; Jonathan, 1657; David, 1659, died young; Mary, 1661; Hannah, 1663; Abigail, 1666; and Esther, 1672. His wife, charged with witchcraft 1674, was sent to Boston, tried, May 1675, and acquitted by the jury; lived to January, 1712. He was freeman, 1669; cornet of the horse; one of the richest men of the town; removed 1679 back to Springfield, and died 1683. Mary, married 1685, Joseph Ashley and next, 1699, Joseph Williston; Hannah, married 1688, Peletiah Glover, Jr.; Abigail, married 1690, John Colton; and Esther, married 1698, Rev. Joseph Smith, after of Middletown.

PARSONS, RICHARD, Windsor, 1640; there made freeman in April; was soon after at Hartford, probably went home.

PARSONS, ROBERT, Lynn; freeman, 1639, of whom no more is known, unless he were the man who died at North Haven, 1648.

PARSONS, SAMUEL, East Hampton, L. I.; 1650.

PARSONS, THOMAS, Boston; seems to have by the old book of possessions, an estate bound E. by Elder Thomas Leverett, and this before 1639.

PARSONS, THOMAS, Windsor; was soldier in the Pequet war, 1637, for which some of his children had grant of land many years after; married, 1641, Lydia Brown; had Bethia, 1642; Abigail, 1644; Thomas, 1645; John, 1647; Mary, 1652; Ebenezer, 1655; Samuel, 1657; and Joseph, 1661; beside William in some earlier year not specified, and died 1661. His widow married Eltweed Pomeroy. Of these children, Ebenezer, Samuel, William, and Joseph lived at Simsbury, and some, if not all, had families. Bethia married, 1660, Thomas Mascall, and next, 1672, John Williams of Windsor.

PARSONS, WILLIAM, Boston; came probably in the James from Southampton, 1635, then by the custom house clearance described as a tailor of Salisbury, though called a joiner on his admission to the church 1644; by wife Ruth, had Ruth, baptized 1645; was freeman, 1645; Ar. Co. 1646, and died January, 1702, in 87th year. REFERENCES:—Am. Anc. I, 60; II, 92; III, 206; IV, 199; V, 166; VII, 37, 104, 265, 273; VIII, 68; X, 165. Barnes' Hist. of Goshen, Mass., 162-5. Coe and Ward Memorials, 56-60. Daniell's Hist. of Oxford, Mass., Eaton's Annals of Warren, Me., 597; Hall Geneal. (1892), 14; Jordan's Leighton Geneal.; Montgomery Co. N. Y. Hist., 211; Parson's Fam. of Hartford (1877) chart; Parson's Fam. of Parsonsfield, Me. (1879) chart; Parson's Fam. of Springfield (1900), 109 p.; Winslow Gen. I. 318-23, 345, 354; II, 710-5.

PARTRIDGE:—Alexander, came in 1645, with wife and family to Boston, and was found to be dangerous by his opinions, which he had imbibed in the Parliament, or, rather, Cromwell's army, so that he could not be permitted to reside here, but was forced away before the first winter to Rhode Island. He was made Captain of the force of that col. 1648, and was living at Newport 1655.

PARTRIDGE, GEORGE, Duxbury; perhaps brother of Rev. Ralph, being mentioned in the record 1636, the same year that Ralph came; married, 1638, Sarah, daughter of Stephen Tracy, of Plymouth; had Sarah, born 1639; Mercy, Tryphosa, Ruth, Lydia, John, born 1657; and James, who lived to 1745, but had probably no children; was proprietor, 1645, of Bridgewater, and one of the original purchasers of Middleborough in 1662. His daughter Sarah married, 1658, Samuel Allen, of Bridgewater; Tryphosa married, 1668, Samuel West; Ruth married, 1670, Rodolphus Thatcher; and Lydia married, 1672, William Brewster.

PARTRIDGE, NATHANIEL, Boston; tailor; had wife Ellen, who joined our church, 1643, and he four weeks after was freeman, 1644.

PARTRIDGE, OLIVER, Dorchester, 1636; was member of the church with wife Sarah, before 1639.

PARTRIDGE, RALPH, first minister of Duxbury; arrived at Boston in a half year passage from London, 1636, in company with blessed Nathaniel Rogers. He had been well instructed and was many years a preacher at Sutton, Co. Kent, near Dover, as is learned from bond of conveyance of land by John Marshall of Lenham, November, 1631, made in consideration of marriage with Mary,

daughter of P., who, with Jervase P. (probably his brother), citizen and cordwainer of London, were made trustees. His own will, September, 1655, probably May, 1658, names daughter Elizabeth, wife of Rev. Thomas Thacher, married May, 1643, her sons, Thomas, Ralph, and Peter, beside her eldest daughter Patience Kemp; also his eldest daughter Mary M., and her sons Robert and John. His wife, Patience, was dead and the inventory of his library is counted 400 volumes, which, for that time on this side of the sea, was very respectable.

PARTRIDGE, WILLIAM, Salisbury, 1638; freeman, 1639; is said to be son of John of Olney in Co. Bucks; died 1654; left widow, Ann; perhaps mother of the children John, Hannah, Elizabeth, born 1643; Nehemiah, May, 1645; Sarah, 1647; Rachel, 1650; and, possibly, William, posthum. His widow married, 1656, Anthony Stanion, and died 1689. Elizabeth married, 1661, Joseph Shaw of Hampton; Sarah married, 1666, John Heath of Haverhill, and Rachel married, 1671, Joseph Chase of Hampton and died 1718.

PARTRIDGE, WILLIAM, Hartford; came, it is tradition, from Berweck on Tweed, married, 1644, Mary Smith, only sister of four brothers who are Christopher, of Northampton, Joseph, of Hartford, Simon, of Hartford, and nameless one, died 1680; had Samuel born, 1645; was one of the two constables, 1655; removed to Hadley, 1660; there died 1668. His name uniformly ends pigy. His daughter Mary married, 1663, John Smith.

PARTRIDGE, WILLIAM, Medfield, 1649; freeman, 1649; freeman, 1653; married, 1654, Sarah Pierce, who had Eleazer three days before she died May, 1656; and November following he married Sarah Colburn; had Nathaniel, baptized at Dedham, 1660; John, 1662; Elisha, 1665; Joseph, 1668; William, 1669; Priscilla, 1672; Sarah, 1674; and Mary, 1682.

REFERENCES:—Ballon's Hist. of Milford, Mass., 951-3; Dedham Hist. Reg. VII, 51-6, 100-6, 148-51; VIII, 14-9; Eaton's Hist. of Thomaston, Me., II, 348; Tapham's Hist. of Norway, Me., 573; Morse's Sherborn, Mass., Settlers, 186-90; Strong Geneal., 1129-31. See also Partridge.

PARUM:—William, Boston; by wife Frances; had John, born 1657, says the substitute record used in place of the original that may have been lost near 200 years.

PARY, or PARRY:—William, adm. freeman of Mass., 1646; he was known to be of Watertown, 1642, and Bond thinks he came from Scituate.

PASCO:—Hugh, Salem, 1668.

PASCO, JOHN, Boston; by wife Rachel, had Dorothy C., 1685; and Thomas, 1688; in 1696, or later, removed to Enfield, there died 1706.

REFERENCE:—Stiles' Windsor, Ct., II, 555-7.

PASMORE, PASMER, or PASMERE:—Bartholomew, Boston; an early proprietor whose estate is described in book of possessions; had Abigail, 1641.

PASMORE, JAMES, Concord; by wife Alice, had Stephen, born 1642; and Hannah, 1644.

PASMORE, RICHARD, Ipswich, 1674.

PASMORE, WILLIAM, Boston; by wife Rebecca, had Robert, born 1674; and Rebecca, October, 1679.

REFERENCES:—Am. Anc. V, 15; Sharpless Geneal., 185, 298.

PASSAM, PASSANT, or PASSON:—Hugh, Watertown, 1649; died 1675, aged about 63; had wife Ruth, who died 1676. They were very poor and had relief as paupers. But the real name was Parsons, says Savage. "See Parsons."

PATCH:—Edmund, Salem, 1639; had Abraham, baptised, 1649; died, 1680.

PATCH, JAMES, Salem, 1646; lived on Beverly side; by wife Hannah, had Mary, born 1647, died at 2 years; Mary, again, 1650; prob. James, who died 1653; Eliz., 1654; James, again, 1655; and Nicholas, 1657; who died January following; died 1658; in his will of that year names wife Hannah, son James, daughters Mary and Eliz., bros. Nicholas Woodbury and John P. His daughter Mary married, 1688, Paul Thorndike; and Eliz. married Richard Thistle. The wife died at Ipswich.

PATCH, NICHOLAS, Salem; had grant of land 1639, says Felt; was one of the founders of the church at Beverly, 1667, with Eliz., probably his wife, who was, says a wild tradition, the first girl of English parents born in the Col. of Mass. and died 1715, aged 86. He died 1673, leaving sons John and Thomas.

REFERENCES:—Am. Anc. III, 137; Brook's Hist. of Medford, Mass., 532; Norton's Hist. of Fitzwilliam, N. H., 655; Savage's Gen. Dict., 368.

PATCHIN, or PATCHING:—Joseph, Roxbury; married, 1642, Eliz., widow of Stephen Iggleden; had Joseph, born 1643; John, 1644; another child died 1649; and after the parents joined to the church, Joseph and John were baptised 1650. He removed to Fairfield, and in 1666 called his age 56 years.

REFERENCE:—Cleveland's Yates Co., 248.

PATEFIELD, or PLATFIELD:—John, Charlestown; by wife Amy had Mary, born 1654; and Rebecca, 1657; was then living 1678.

PATESHALL, PATTESHALL, or PADDESHALL:—Edmund, Pemaquid, 1665; swore fidelity to Massachusetts 1674; may be he whose depon. is referred to by Chalmers, 504.

PATESHALL, RICHARD, Boston, 1665; freeman, 1678; by wife Abigail, had Edward, born 1670; and by wife Martha, had Martha, born 1674; Ann, 1678; Edmund, 1683; and Robert, 1685.

PATESHALL, ROBERT, Boston, 1652, merchant; was captain and magistrate in the temporary Co. of Devonshire, Me.; perhaps was the man killed by the Indians, 1689, at Pemaquid.

PATIE:—Peter, Haverhill; took oath of allegiance November, 1677.

PATRICK:—Daniel, Watertown, one of the two captains in regular pay; brought in the fleet by Winthrop, 1630; freeman, 1631; was short time of Cambridge, but at W. selectman, 1638; removed to Connecticut; had a Dutch wife and was killed by a Dutchman, 1643, at Stamford.

PATRICK, WILLIAM, Hartford; had Samuel, born 1654.

REFERENCES:—Am. Anc. II, 92; See Gen. (1888), 370-7; Paige's Hist. of Cambridge, Mass., 623; Welles' Wash. Gen., 251.

PATTEN:—Nathaniel, Dorchester, 1640; died 1661, leaves widow Justine, and large estate on which the widow admin. and died 1675. Suppose he left no children, for his brother and heir, John, from Crewkerne, in Co. Somerset, sent his son Thomas to dispose of estate in Boston.

PATTEN, THOMAS, Salem, 1643.

PATTEN, THOMAS, Boston, 1671; came from Bristol; was son of John, sent by his father to look after the estate of Nathaniel the first.

PATTEN, WILLIAM, Cambridge; brought from England, wife Mary, by whom he had Mary, baptised in England; Thomas, born 1636; Sarah, 1638; Nathaniel, 1643; William, bur. 1646, quite young, besides probably a former Nathaniel, who died 1640; freeman, 1645; one of the original proprietors of Billerica, 1658, and died 1668.

REFERENCES:—Am. Anc., I, 60; Blood's Hist. of Temple, N. H., 238; Daniels' Hist. of Oxford, Mass., 639; Hurlbut Geneal., 418; Reed's Hist. of Bath, Me.; Savage's Gen. Dict. III, 369-376.

PATTERSON, or PATTISON:—Andrew, Stratford; came from Scotland, it is said, 1685, by the Henry and Francis, to Perth Amboy. He was accompanied by Robert McEwen and ten other passengers who fled from the severities of the administration against the covenanters, as McEwen writes in his journal of his share in the fight of Bothwell Bridge, a few years before and he is careful to note the day of sailing, 5th September, the day of landing, 18th December, and the day of reaching Stratford, to which they came on foot, 18th February following, as feeling more confident of security in Connecticut than could be expected under the proprietary government of East Jersey. No battle of ancient or modern times is more exactly described than this, from which the friends of the sufferers escaped to New England, as the pen of Sir Walter Scott depicts it. Patterson married, 1691, Eliz. Peat, had Sarah, born 1694; Charles, 1696; William, 1698; Eliz., 1701; Hannah, 1703; Mary, 1706; and John, 1711, Yale College, 1728, who lived to 1806, and his name is mentioned in the town records of Salem, late as March, 1735.

PATTERSON, DAVID, is the name of one of those wretched Scotch prisoners from Worcester fight, sent out by the John and Sarah, from London, November, 1651, to be sold in Boston, where they arrived May following.

PATTERSON, EDWARD, New Haven, 1639; probably the man named by Mason in his Hist. as one of the soldiers in the Pequot war, 1637, in which he did much service, and perhaps the passenger from London in the Christian, 1635, aged 33; had wife in 1647, but only ch. ment. were Eliz., baptised 1644, who married Thomas Smith of the same, and John in January following obtained a grant of land 1670, sixty acres, "where he can find it;" he probably died without sight of it.

PATTERSON, EDWARD, Rehoboth, 1643; Hingham, 1652; where he had Faith, born 1656.

PATTERSON, JAMES, Billerica; perhaps brother of David; came probably in the sad freight list of the John and Sarah, from London, 1651, and, if so, he is one of only four or five that prospered here among the great crowd of romantic followers in Scotland of Charles II., who in the bloody days of the successful years, 1650 and 1651; was captain on the fields of Cromwell's glory at Dunbar and Worcester, and transported to the colonies, to be sold in the shambles like other cattle, of which the cargoes to Boston would amount to as many hundreds. He was of B. perhaps carr. by his owner, 1659; freeman, 1690; married, 1662, Rebecca, daughter of Andrew Stevenson of Cambridge; had Mary, born 1666; James, 1669, died young; Andrew, 1672; John, 1675; Joseph, 1678; Rebecca, 1680, died young; James, again, 1683; and Jonathan, 1686. He served in the great war with the Indians, 1675, and with other soldiers; was sixty years after rewarded with grant of land in Narragansett, November 6, and his grandsons drew the proper share. His will, probably 1701, names brother-in-law, Andrew Stevenson. Mary, the eldest, married, 1689, Peter Proctor of Chelmsford.

PATTERSON, PETER, Saybrook; married June, 1678, Eliz. Rithway.

REFERENCES:—Andrews' New Britain, Conn., 128, 133. 152: Boyd's Hist. of Conesus, N. Y., 225; Lewis Gen. (1893). 275-9; Patterson Geneal. (1847), 103 pages; Patterson Geneal. (1867), 8 pages; Roome Geneal., 199; Young's Hist. of Warsaw, N. Y., 313-6.

PAUL:—Benjamin, New Haven: may be the man mentioned by Felt at Salem, 1647, with a final y added to his name.

PAUL, DANIEL, New Haven, 1643; perhaps brother of Benjamin; may be the man who lived at Kittery, 1652, when he acknowledged the government of Massachusetts and was of the grand jury.

PAUL, RICHARD, Boston; a soldier, hired in 1636, for the castle, was two years after one of the proprietors of Taunton. Perhaps Hannah, born at Taunton, 1657, was his child.

PAUL, SAMUEL, Dorchester, married 1667 Mary, daughter of Edward Breck; had Samuel, 1670; Hannah, 1672; Mary, 1675; Eliz., 1677; Ebenezer, 1680; Priscilla, 1682; and Susanna, 1685; was constable, 1627; chosen clerk, 1689, and he died November 3, 1690. His widow married, 1692, John Tolmon, died 1720.

PAUL, WILLIAM, Taunton; had James, born 1657; John, 1660; Edward, 1665; Mary, 1667; Sarah, 1668; and Abigail, 1673; and he died 1704.

REFERENCES:—Beckwith's Creoles, 28-37; Paul fam. Chart, by Geo. H. Paul (179); Paul Gen. (1896), 7 pages; Paul's Hist. of Wells, Vt., 122-8; Wakefield Geneal., 176.

PAYSON:—Edward, Roxbury; freeman 1640; married, 1640, Ann Parke, perhaps sister of William; she died following year, having born Mary, 8 days before, who probably died young; he married, 1642, Mary Eliot, daughter of Philip, perhaps; had John, baptised 1643: Jonathan, 1644; Ann, 1647, died at 3 years; Joanna, 1649; Ann, again, 1651; Susanna, 1653. died next year; Susanna, again, 1655; Edward, 1657; H. C., 1677; Ephraim, 1659; Samuel, 1662: and Mary, 1665; the last three are not in town record as he had moved to Dorchester. His wife or widow died 1697. Susanna married, 1673, Samuel Capen; and Mary, 1682, Preserved Capen, and she died 1708.

PAYSON, GILES, Roxbury; came in the Hopewell, Capt. Bundock, from London, 1635, aged 26; probably an Essex man, and perhaps born of the first Edward; was freeman 1637; married Eliz. Dowell; had Eliz., 1640, died in few days; Samuel, 1641; Eliz. again, 1645; Sarah, 1648; and possibly others. He removed to Dorchester, where the town records were destroyed by fire. He was deacon at Roxbury and died 1689, aged 78. Sarah married, 1678, Elisha Foster, and next, 1685, Ebenezer Wiswall and died 1714. Eliz. married, 1667, Hopestill Foster, and next Edmund Brown.

REFERENCES:—Am. Anc. VI, 125; XII, 64; Gage's Hist. of Rowley, Mass., 449; Savage's Gen. Dict. III, 372, 4; Sinclair Gen., 230-2; Wentworth Gen. I, 357-60, 683-94.

PAYTON:—Bezaleel, Boston, 1642; mariner; married that year Mary Greenough, of Sandwich, sister of William of Boston; had Sarah, baptised 1643; Mary, 1646; perhaps also Bezaleel, who died probably on distant land; his invt. was rend. 1651, and his wife married third of next month William Paddy. Sarah married, 1661, Hudson Leverett; and Mary married Sampson Shore.

PAYTON, ROBERT, Lynn, 1639.

PEABODY, PABODIE, or PAYBODIE:—Francis; came in the Planter, 1635, aged 21; was freeman, 1642; married Mary, daughter of Renold Foster; had John, born 1643; Joseph, 1644; William, 1646; Isaac, 1648; Sarah, 1650; Hepzibah, 1652; Lydia, 1654; Mary, 1656; Ruth, 1658, died before her father; Damaris, 1660, died same year; Samuel, 1662; died at 15 years; Jacob, 1664; Hannah, 1668, died soon; and Nathaniel, 1669; and died 1698. His widow died 1705. Sarah married a How, probably Ephraim, or John of Topsfield, whither the family removed before 1657. Hepzibah married a Rea of Salem; Lydia married Jacob Perley; and Mary married John Death of Sudbury or Framingham.

PEABODY, JOHN, Duxbury; one of the proprietors of Bridgewater, 1645; made his will 1649; names his wife Isabel; eldest son Thomas; second, Francis; youngest, William; daughter Annis Rouse; John, son of John Rouse; and John, son of William.

PEABODY, WILLIAM, Duxbury; perhaps brother of Francis; married, 1644, Eliz., eldest daughter of John Alden, who died at Little Compton, 1717, aged 93, and he died 1707 in his 88th year. Bradford says there were five children in 1650. His son John, named in the will of his uncle John, was killed by casualty 1669, but he must have had other son. Eliz., his daughter, married, 1666, John Rogers of Duxbury; of his daughters Hannah married Samuel Bartlett; Martha married Samuel Seabury; and Priscilla married the Rev. Ichabod Wiswall, who was indignant at Increase Mather's Abolition of the independ. of Plymouth Col. He had been representative 1659, most of the years to 1678.

REFERENCES:—Alden Mem., 5; Chandler's Hist. of Shirley, Mass., 599; Peabody Gen. (1848), 21 pages; Peabody Gen., 2d edition (1867), 61 pages; Smith's Hist. of Peterborough, N. H., 223; Winsor's Hist. of Duxbury, Mass., 285.

PEACH:—Arthur, Plymouth; a young Irishman, who came from Virginia 1636, whither he had gone the year preceding, aged 20, in the Plain Joan, from London; served in the Pequot war; though of good parentage and fair conditioned, was, as Winth. tells us, "with exempla. justice, hanged for a very cowardly murder, with two associates, in detection of which Roger Williams gained much credit. But in the proper study of the case, study the contempo. hist. of Gov. Bradford.

PEACH, JOHN, Salem or Marblehead, 1648-79; said to be born 1612, of whom Felt finds mention in 1630; may have been father of John, Jr., M. freeman, 1683.

REFERENCES:—N. E. Gen. Reg. LIV, 276-9.

PEACHE or PEACHY:—John, Marblehead, 1648; may be the same as Peach.

PEACHE, THOMAS, Charlestown, 1678; Mary, perhaps his widow, died 1691, in 59th year.

REFERENCES:—Bitsche Gen., 7-30, etc.; Meade's old Families of Virginia; Wm. and Mary College Hist. Reg. III, 111-5.

PEACOCK:—John, New Haven, 1638; at Milford early, perhaps even in 1639, certainly before 1650, removed to Stratford, there died 1670; in his will names wife Joyce, and daughters Phebe, wife of Richard Burgess; Mary, who married, 1673, Benjamin Beach; and Deborah, wife of James Clark.

PEACOCK, WILLIAM, Roxbury, 1652; came probably in the Hopewell from London, Capt. Bundock, 1635, aged 12 years, with such a comp. of Eliots and Ruggleses; he may well be thought to have sprung from Nazing or some neighboring parish to Stanstead, in the border of Hertfordshire; married, 1653, Mary Willis; had William, born 1655, died soon; William again, 1657; and Samuel, 1659.

REFERENCES:—Evans' Fox Gen., 225-32; Randall's Hist. of Chesterfield, N. H., 398; Secomb's Hist. of Amherst, N. H., 724.

PEAKE:—Christopher, Roxbury; freeman 1635; married, 1637, Dorcas French; had Jonathan, born 1637; Dorcas, 1640; Hannah, baptised 1643, died at 17 years; Joseph, baptised 1645; Ephraim, born 1652; and Sarah, 1656; and he died 1666.

PEAKE, WILLIAM, Scituate, 1643; married, 1650, Judith, widow of Lawrence Litchfield; had Israel, born 1655; Eleazer, 1657; and William, 1662. The sons William and Israel had families.

PEAKE, WILLIAM, New London, 1660; had Sarah, who married, 1671, Abraham Deane or Dayne; had William; and John. He died about 1685. In the Hopewell, Capt. Bundock, from London, embarked Mary Peak, aged 15; but whether she was related to any of the foregoing or to John Peak, who was a fellow passenger, aged 38, is not known.

REFERENCES:—Morris' Gen. (1894), 27-30; Morris and Flynt Ancestors (1882), 19-21; Savage's Gen. Dict. III, 377.

PEAKEN:—John, New Haven; died 1658. His inv. was taken February that year.

PEALE:—Daniel, Marblehead, 1651.

REFERENCES:—Am. Anc. VIII, 133; Hanson's Old Kent, Md., 333.

PEARD:—Richard, Saco; married, 1669, Jane Naziter, perhaps daughter of Michael.

PEARSALL:—John, Newtown, L. I., 1656.

REFERENCES:—Bunker's L. I. Gens., 268-71; N. Y. Gen. and Record XVI, 1-3.

PEARSON:—John, Lynn, 1637; had Mary, born 1643; Bethia, 1645; Sarah, 1648; removed to Reading; had John, 1650; and James, 1652. He died 1679, aged 64. His will mentioned wife Maudlin, son John daughters Mary Burnap, Bethia Carter and Sarah Townsend. Mary married, 1663, Thomas Burnap.

PEARSON, JOHN, Rowley, 1643; then set up the earliest fulling mill in America; by wife Dorcas had Mary, born 1643, died young; John, 1644; Eliz., 1646; Samuel, 1648; Dorcas, 1650; Mary again, 1652; Jeremiah, 1653; Sarah, 1655, died in few months; Joseph, 1656, who was of Lothrop's company and fell in battle 1725 near Hatfield; Benjamin, 1658; Phebe, 1660; Stephen, 1663; and Sarah, 1666, died in few months; was freeman of 1647; representative 1678 and several years later, especially after overthrow of Anders, and the anxious ones before his command; deacon, 1686; died 1693. His widow died 1703. In the Col. Rec. the name of the rep. is more commonly spelled it with A; Mary married, 1671, Samuel Palmer; Eliz. married, June, 1676, John Hopkinson; and Phebe married, 1682, Timothy Harris.

REFERENCES:—Am. Anc. II, 92, XII; Bangor, Me., Hist. Mag. VI, 294; Pott's Geneal. (1895), 287-9; Stiles' Hist. of Windsor, Ct. II, 558; Wheeler's Hist. of North Carolina II, 385.

PEASE:—Henry, Boston, 1630; came that year no doubt with wife Susan, and daughter Susan, who was old enough to join with the church August, 1635, father and mother being earlier; freeman 1634. His wife was buried 1645, and he had second wife, Bridget, adm. of our church 1647. and he died 1648.

PEASE JOHN, Salem; came in the Francis from Ipswich, Co. Suffolk, 1634, aged 27, with child Robert, 3, and two servants in company with his brother Robert. They were probably from Great Baddon, near Chelmsford, in Co. Essex. He perhaps had grant of land 1637; was not, we may safely judge, one of the first four settlers of Martha's Vineyard; reported dead 1639. His widow Margaret, who united with the church 1639, had come with his son John, probably in a later ship. She died 1644, and in her will of that year mentions brother Robert, and son Robert.

PEASE, JOHN, Norwich; was complained of, 1672, for living alone and not going to church.

PEASE, ROBERT, Salem; brother of John the first; came in the same ship, 1634, aged 27, by cus. house list, which gives same age to the brother. He joined the church 1643; had baptised his children Nathaniel, Sarah and May; was living in 1655, being keeper of the cattle, 100 cows in one part of the town.

PEASE, SAMUEL, Boston; had command of a vessel, fitted out to pursue a pirate, and in the vineyard sound made her his prize, though mortally wounded.

REFERENCES:—Am. Anc. VIII, 268; Chandler Gen., 84; Dwight Gen. 314-6, 417-20; Pease Gen. (1847), 42 pages; Pease Fam. Hist. (1869), 96 pages.

PEASLEE:—Joseph, Newbury, 1641; freeman 1642; beside ch. brot. prob. from England of wife Jane, who married, 1646, John Davis, was one; had Sarah, born 1642; Joseph, 1646; and Eliz. removed to Haverhill and Salisbury; at one time was the gifted bro. in lieu of a minister to the church at Amesbury; died 1661; in his will names wife Mary, and child Mary, beside those three, and grandchild Sarah. Mary married Joseph Whittier of Haverhill; Joseph, his son, married Ruth Barnard about 1680.

REFERENCES:—Am. Anc. VII, 268; Chandler Geneal., 84; Emery Geneal. (1890), 31; Montague Geneal., 69; New Eng. Hist. and Gen. Reg. III, 27-30.

PEAT:—John, a husbandman from Duffill parish in Co. Derby; came in the Hopewell, Capt. Bundock, from London, 1635, aged 38; but where settled not known, unless he was of Stratford, and there died early in 1678, leaving wife Sarah, and children Samuel, John, Joseph, Sarah, Eliz. and Jane. At Stratford, 1691, Eliz. Peat married Andrew Patterson, a refugee from Tyranny in Scotland five years before.

REFERENCES:—Orcutt's New Milford, Ct., 804; Orcutt's Hist. of Stratford, Ct., 1263-6.

PECK:—Henry, New Haven; by wife Joan, had Eleazer, born 1644, died soon; Joseph and Benjamin, twins, 1647; Eleazer, again; and Eliz., born 1650. He died soon, for his will was made October, 1651, and his invt. next month. The property was given to wife and four children, of whom only Joseph is named.

PECK, ICHABOD, Rehoboth; was of Gallup's company, 1690, in the expedition of Sir William Phips against Quebec.

PECK, JEREMIAH, Saybrook; son of William, born in London probably 1623; was brought about 1637; in Mather's Hecatompolis is marked H. C.; kept a school at Guilford, 1656-60. He married, 1656, Joanna, daughter of Robert Kitchell; taught the grammar school at New Haven, 1660, and next year was min. at Saybrook, but in 1667 removed to Newark, N. J.; there resided to 1674, and at Elizabethtown to 1678, after which he removed to Greenwich, where he was minister to 1689; then went to Waterbury as first minister; there died June, 1699, aged 76. His children were Samuel, born 1659; Ruth, at New Haven, 1661; Caleb, at Saybrook, 1663; Ann, at Saybrook, 1665; Jeremiah, at Newark, 1667; and Joshua, at Newark, 1673. His widow died 1711. Ruth married, 1681, Jonathan Atwater; and Ann married, 1696, Thomas Stanley of Farmington; and Joshua died 1736.

PECK, JOHN, Hadley, 1669; may be that soldier killed by the Indians 1675 at Northfield.

PECK, JOSEPH, Hingham; came in the Diligent; arrived at Boston, 1638, from Ipswich in Suffolk, with wife, three children, two men and three maid servants; freeman 1639; representative 1639-42; removed to Rehoboth, there died 1663. Probably he had lived at Hingham in Norfolk, for his supposed brother Robert was minister there many years.

PECK, NATHANIEL, perhaps son of Joseph; may have been sent by his father from England in 1635; removed to Rehoboth, there had division in share of land 1668; by wife Deliverana had Elisha, born 1675; and she died same month. He died 1676.

PECK, NATHANIEL, Boston; required to give security 1687 to Sect. Randolph for license to be made during the odious government of Sir E. Andros.

PECK, PAUL, Hartford, 1639; was not an original proprietor nor is it known from what town in Massachusetts he went; the name of his wife was Martha, and of children, Paul, born 1639; Martha, 1641; Eliz., 1643; John, 1645; Samuel, 1647; Joseph, 1650; Sarah, 1653; Hannah, 1655; and Mary, 1662, who married John Andrew and lived to 1752. His will of June, 1695, was pro. January following, he having died 23 December, aged 87 years. Martha married John Cornwell; Eliz. married, it is said, a House of Wallingford; Sarah married Thomas Clark of Hartford; and Hannah married, 1680, John Shepherd of Hartford. Two more daughters are by some given to this first Paul, one, without name of baptism, is said to have married Joseph Benton of Tolland; and the other, called Ruth, is made to marry, 1680, Thomas Beach of Wallingford.

PECK, RICHARD, came in the Defence from London, 1635, aged 33, with Margery, perhaps his wife, aged 40, and Israel, 7, with Eliz., 4, both likely enough to be his children.

PECK, ROBERT, Hingham; probably brother of Joseph; was bred at Magdalen Coll., Cambridge, where he had his degree of A. B. and A. M.; the latter 1603; was minister over 30 years at Hingham, Co. Norfolk, yet was harass. for non-conform. to some of the ceremonies by Bishop Harsnet, his diocesan, whose impudence in honor of the church was so great as to excite complaint from the people of Norwich in 1623, to the House of Commons in Parliament. Two successors were milder, but when Wren came to the Cathedral, no Puritan could long serve at the altar. Peck embarked October, 1641, with wife and son Joseph for home, and went back to his old parsonage; there died 1656.

PECK, THOMAS, 1652, shipwright; constable, 1673; by wife Eliz. had Eliz., born 1653; Rachel, 1655; and Joseph, 1656; besides Thomas, elder than either, who was a shipwright after his father. Possibly John, who was a skilful shipbuilder, father of the eminent naturalist, William D. Peck, H. C., 1782, may have been of this family.

PECK, WILLIAM, New Haven; a merchant from London, born 1601; with wife Eliz. and son Jeremiah, came probably in the Hector, as companion with Govs. Eaton and Hopkins, Rev. John Davenport, and the son of the

Earl of Marlborough; arrived at Boston 26 June, 1637; was one of the first compact for New Hampshire in June, 1639; an original proprietor; freeman 1640; deacon from 1659 to his death; had John; Joseph, baptised 1641; and Eliz., 1643. His wife died on a visit to her son at Lynne, and he married Sarah, widow of William Holt, and died 1694. His grave stone can still be seen in the cemetery. He died aged 90. The only daughter, his youngest child, married, 1661, Samuel Andrews. In his will, 1689, made at New Hampshire, the second wife and his four children are mentioned, but no more.

REFERENCES:—Am. Anc. I, 61; II, 93; IV, 225; V, 123, 196; VII, 151; XI, 112; Ballou Geneal., 492-4; Peck Geneal. (1868), 442 pages; Peck fam. of New Haven (1877), 253 pages; Tuttle Geneal., 137-9.

PECKER:—James, Charlestown, 1658; said to have been born 1622; perhaps had wife Eliz., daughter of John Friend, of Salem, aft. at Haverhill, and last a. 1682, Boston.

REFERENCES:—Morrison's Windham, 734.

PECKHAM, or PECKUM:—John, Newport, 1639; probably the same person called by Farmer, Joseph, who was one of the founders of the Baptist church. He is in the list of freeman, 1655.

REFERENCES:—Am. Anc. IX, 94; Austin's Allied Families, 191-5; Hazard Gen., 94-6.

PECKIT:—John, Stratford, 1670; perhaps the name was obscure in the M. S.

PEDRICK, JOHN, Marblehead, 1674; had been there many years. His will was August, 1686, and mentioned wife Meriam, eldest son John, and eight more children, Benjamin, Agnes, Mary, Ann, Sarah, Meriam, Eliz. and Joanna. One of these daughters was probably wife of John Stacy; one of John Parrot; and another of Henry Prentall, as he calls some of these his sons-in-law.

PEEK:—George, Marblehead, 1674.

REFERENCES:—Munsell's Albany Colls. IV, 153; Pearson's Schenectady Settlers, 135-40.

PELHAM:—Herbert, Cambridge; brought in 1638, died Penelope, when he came over after befriending our cause ten years as a member of the comp. in London, where he may have been a lawyer; married second wife Eliz., widow of Roger Harlakenden, d. of Godfrey Basseville, Esq., of Co. York, here had Mary, born probably 1640; Francis, 1643; Herbert, 1645, who died 1646. He was a gentleman from County Lincoln, matriculated at Magdalen Hall, Oxford, 1619, in his eighteenth year, and Gov. Hutchinson says he was of that family who attained the highest rank in the peerage one hundred years ago as Duke of Newcastle. He was much engaged in public service, promoting plantations of Sudbury, where he had grant of land, 1644, ar. co. 1639, was chosen an assistant 1645, being made a freeman at that time; first treasurer of Harvard College, 1643; went home in 1649; lived at Buer's hamlet, Co. Essex, but was buried in Suffolk, 1673. His will of that year names children Waldegrave, Edward, Henry and Penelope, perhaps all, certainly first and last by his first wife, who was a Waldegrave. His widow died 1706 in her 84th year and was buried at Marshfield. Penelope married, 1657, Gov. Josiah Winslow.

PELHAM, JOHN, perhaps brother of Herbert; came in the Susan and Ellen, from London, 1635, aged 20, with Penelope 16, "she being to pass to her brothers plantation," as the custom house record says. The young lady united with the children in Boston, 1639, and in 1641 married the Gov. Bellingham, who prevailed on her to give up another engagement.

PELHAM, WILLIAM, Sudbury; perhaps brother of John; came in the fleet with Winth., losing his passage with the Governor's son Henry, by going on shore at Cowes, from the Arbella, and trusting fortune for another ship; regularly admitted as freeman, 1630; was captain of militia, 1644; selectman, 1645 and 6, and representative 1647; was in England, 1652, when Johnson wrote his book.

REFERENCES:—Austin's R. I. Dict., 149; Davis' Landmarks of Plymouth, Mass., 199; Paige's Hist. of Cambridge, Mass., 625.

PELL:—Thomas, New Haven; came from London in the Hopewell, Capt. Bundock, 1635, aged 22; called in custom house paper a tailor; he of course, sat down somewhere in Massachusetts. Perhaps he went early to Saybrook; in the Pequot war, 1637, served under Mason; and probably in three or four years he followed the attractions of Gov. Eaton; after 1646 married the widow of Francis Brewster; removed to Fairfield; was made freeman 1662; representative 1665; died soon after; date of his will, 1669. It gave most of his estate to his nephew John, son of his only brother, Rev. John of London, D.D.

PELL, WILLIAM, Boston, 1634; tallow chandler; freeman 1635; disarmed for his dangerous opinions, 1637; had Mary, baptised 1634, who married, 1655, Richard George of Boston; Nathaniel, baptised 1638, died in few months; Hannah, 7 days old, 1640; Deborah, 1644; and perhaps more. He may have taken as second wife, Eliz., widow of Nathaniel Heaton. If so she had third husband John Maynard and outlived him.

REFERENCES:—Am. Anc. IX, 202; Bolton's Hist. Westchester Co., N. Y., II. 40; Pell's Howlands Journal (1890), 17-20; Thomas Geneal. (1896), 458-62; Whitmore's Heraldic Journ. III, 75.

PELLET, or PELLATE:—Thomas, Concord; married 5 March, 1660, Mary Dane or Deane; perhaps daughter of Thomas; was freeman, 1690.

REFERENCES:—Temple's N. Brookfield, 701-3.

PELTON:—John, Boston; very early had estate descrip. in the book of possessions; removed to Dorchester; his elder son, John, was baptised 1645. In his will, 1681, pro. March following, he names wife Susanna, sons John, Samuel and Robert, the youngest, beside daughter Mary. To Samuel was given admin. of Robert, lost at sea, 1683.

REFERENCES:—Guild's Stiles Geneal., 188-90; Pelton Geneal. (1892), 722 pages; Stiles Hist. of Windsor, Ct., II, 558-61.

PEMBER:—Thomas, New London, 1686; had there baptised, 1692, Mercy, Thomas, and Eliz.; 1694, Ann; and in 1696, John; only four of these with wife Agnes were living at his death by drowning, 27 Sept. 1711.

REFERENCES:—Paul's Hist. of Wells, Vermont, 138; Walworth's Hyde Geneal., 40-145.

PEMBERTON:—James, Charlestown; came probably in the fleet with Winth, req. adm. as freeman, 1630, but that he ever took the oath does not appear; by wife Alice, who joined church in 1633, had James, baptised September of that year, died young; Mary, 1636; Sarah, 1638; and John, 1642; perhaps removed to Hull for a short time, about 1647; but died at Malden 1662. His will 1661, made at Malden, mentions son John, and his wife Margaret, daughters Sarah, and Mary, with her husband Edward Barlow, and their children. Sarah married, 1668, Samuel Gibson.

PEMBERTON, JAMES, Newbury, 1646; freeman 1648; had John, born 1648; removed to Boston, became one of the founders of O. S. church; by wife Sarah, had Thomas, born 1653; Joseph, 1655; Benjamin, 1660; Mary, 1662; Benjamin, again, 1666; Jonathan, 1668; Elinor, 1672, probably the same as that Ebenezer, baptised 1672; H. C. 1691, before mentioned; died 1696.

PEMBERTON, JOHN, 1632; freeman, 1634; removed to Newbury; and Coffin says his wife died 1646. Perhaps he returned to Boston; married Sarah, daughter of Thomas Marshall, the shoemaker, and in 1662 lived at that part called Winnesemet.

REFERENCES:—Am. Anc. I, 61; Pemberton Geneal. (1890), 26 pages; Pemberton Geneal. (1892), 9 pages; Titcomb's early New England people, 38-56.

PEMBROKE:—Elkanah, Boston; one of the founders of Brattle st. church; may have sprung from Dedham, where, in 1643, was one with his surname.

PENDALL:—William, New London, 1676; shipwright; married Mehitable, daughter of Ralph Parker.

PENDLETON:—Bryan, Watertown; an early settler; freeman 1634; helped to settle Sudbury, of which he was selectman some years but rep. before and after for Watertown between 1636 and 48, six years; removed to Ipswich, perhaps, certain to Portsmouth, of which he was a rep. some years, then removed to Saco, Winter harbor; after a dozen years driven by the Indian war; 1676 went again to Portsmouth, there made his will, 1677, which was prob. 1681. He was Captain and Major many years; left wife Eleanor, son James and daughter Mary, who married Seth Fletcher.

PENDLETON, CALEB, Westerly, 1679.

PENDLETON, JOSEPH, Boston, 1651; witness that year to the will of Robert Truner; may have been son of Bryan.

REFERENCES:—Alden's Epitaphs V, 19; Am. Anc. II, 93; Dwight Geneal., 554; Meade's old churches of Va. II, 298; Savage's Gen. Dict. III, 388.

PENFIELD:—Samuel, Lynn, 1650; married, 1675, Mary Lewis; had Samuel, born 1676; and Mary, 1678; and at Rehoboth, John, 1681, or after; in 1688 living at Bristol with wife and four children.

PENFIELD, THOMAS, Rehoboth; had Sarah, born 1681.

PENFIELD, WILLIAM, Middletown, 1663; Hinman, 62.

REFERENCES:—Andrews' New Britain, Ct.; Caverly's Hist. of Pittsford, Vt., 718; Tuttle Gen., 707.

PENNY:—Henry Penny, secr. of the Prov., 1683, and a captain; died, 1709, leaving son Henry in England. Adams 106.

PENNY, ROBERT; had grant of land, 1638.

PENNY, THOMAS, Gloucester, 1652; of whom knowledge is incomplete, as that his wife Ann died 1667 and he married, 1668. Agnes Clark, who died 1682; and he married soon after that Joan Bradbrook perhaps widow of Richard. But when he took the first wife, what her surname was, or how many children they had, is untold; and though the name was continued in the town to a third and fourth generation, we see in his will about 1692, only one mentioned, that Joan, who had married 1658, Thomas Kent.

REFERENCES:—Amer. Ancestry, VIII, 230; Babson's Hist. Gloucester, Mass., 98; Hudson's Hist. Lex., Mass., 177; Penny Gen.—see Penney; Power's Sangamon Co., Ill., Settlers; 504; Ruttenber's Hist. Newburgh, N. Y., 281; Ruttenber's Hist. Orange Co., N. Y., 374; Wyman's Charlestown, Mass., Gens. II, 736.

(To be continued.)

PEMBER:—Thomas, New London, 1686; had there baptised, 1692, Mercy, Thomas, and Eliz.; 1694, Ann; and in 1696, John; only four of these with wife Agnes were living at his death by drowning, 27 Sept. 1711. REFERENCES:—Paul's Hist. of Wells, Vermont, 138; Walworth's Hyde Geneal., 40-145.

PEMBERTON:—James, Charlestown; came probably in the fleet with Winth. reg. adm. as freeman, 1630, but that he ever took the oath does not appear; by wife Alice, who joined church in 1633, had James, baptised September of that year, died young, Mary, 1636; Sarah, 1638; and John, 1642; perhaps removed to Hull for a short time, about 1647; but died at Malden, 1662. His 1661, made at Malden, mentions son John, and his wife Margaret, daughters Sarah and Mary, with her husband Edward Barlow, and their children Sarah married. 1668, Samuel Gibson.

PEMBERTON, JAMES, Newbury, 1646; freeman 1648; had John, born 1648; removed to Boston, became one of the founders of O. S. church; by wife Sarah, had Thomas, born 1653; Joseph, 1655; Benjamin, 1660; Mary, 1662; Benjamin, again, 1666; Jonathan, 1668; Elinor, 1672; probably the same as that Ebenezer, baptised 1672; H. C. 1691, before mentioned; died 1696.

PEMBERTON, JOHN, 1632; freeman, 1634; removed to Newbury; and Coffin says his wife died 1646. Perhaps he returned to Boston; married Sarah, daughter of Thomas Marshall, the shoemaker, and in 1662 lived at that part called Winnesemet. REFERENCES:—Am. Anc. I, 61; Pemberton Geneal. (1890); 26 pages; Pemberton Geneal. (1892), 9 pages; Titcomb's early New England people, 38-56.

PEMBROOKE:—Elkanah, Boston; one of the founders of Brattle st. church; may have sprung from Dedham, where, in 1643, was one with his surname.

PENDALL:——William, New London, 1676; shipwright; married Mehitable, daughter of Ralph Parker.

PENDLETON:—Bryan, Watertown; an early settler; freeman, 1634; helped to settle Sudbury, of which he was selectman some years but rep. before and after for Watertown between 1636 and '48, six years; removed to Ipswich, perhaps, certain to Portsmouth, of which he was a rep. some years, then removed to Saco, Winter harbor; after a dozen years driven by the Indian war; 1676 went again to Portsmouth, there made his will, 1677, which was prob. 1681. He was Captain and Major many years; left wife Eleanor, son James and daughter Mary, who married Seth Fletcher.

PENDLETON, CALEB, Westerly, 1679.

PENDLETON, JOSEPH, Boston, 1651; witness that year to the will of Robert Truner; may have been son of Bryan. REFERENCES:—Alden's Epitaphs, V, 19; Am. Anc. II, 93; Dwight Geneal., 554; Meade's old churches of Va. II, 298; Savage's Gen. Dict. III, 388.

PENFIELD:—Samuel, Lynn, 1650; married 1675, Mary Lewis; had Samuel, born 1676; and Mary, 1678; and at Rehoboth, John, 1681, or after; in 1688 living at Bristol with wife and four children.

PENFIELD, THOMAS, Rehoboth; had Sarah, born 1681.

PENFIELD, WILLIAM, Middletown, 1663; Hinman, 62. REFERENCES:—Andrews' New Britain, Ct.; Caverly's Hist. of Pittsford, Vt., 718; Tuttle Gen., 707.

PENNY:—Henry Penny, secr. of the Prov., 1683, and a captain; died, 1709, leaving son Henry in England. Adams 106.

PENNY, ROBERT; had grant of land, 1638.

PENNY, THOMAS, Gloucester, 1652; of whom knowledge is incomplete, as that his wife Ann died 1667 and he married, 1668, Agnes Clark, who died 1682; and he married soon after Joan Bradbrook perhaps widow of Richard. But when he took the first wife, what her surname was, or how many children they had, is untold; and though the name was continued in the town to a third and fourth generation, we see in his will about 1692, only one mentioned, that Joan, who had married 1658, Thomas Kent. REFERENCES:—Amer, Ancestry, VIII, 230; Babson's Hist. Gloucester, Mass., '98; Hudson's Hist., Sex., Mass., 177; Penny Gen.—see Penney; Power's Sangamon Co., Ill., Settlers; 504; Ruttenber's Hist., Newburgh, N. Y., 281; Ruttenber's Hist. Orange Co., N. Y., 374; Wyman's Charlestown, Mass., Gens. II, 736.

PENOYER, or PENNYER:—Robert, embarked in the Hopewell, capt. Babb, 1635, aged 21, with Thomas 10, perhaps brother or cousin, at London, where Mr. Somerby, from the Custom Ho. records, found the name Pennaire, but Savage knows that he wrote it Penoire. Where he first sat down after landing at Boston, is uncertain. Yet in Col. Rec. it is found he was sentenced to be whipped in 1639, for some failure, and that, perhaps, made him remove; but to what part of Mass. it was, he had left in 10 years, being then near Gravesend on L. I., and not long after it Stamford, where he married, probably not first wife, the widow of Richard Scofield, and 1671, giving Capt. Jonathan Sellick power to act for him in England, he calls himself of Rye. He was brother of William, a merchant of London, who was liberal in his benefact. to H. C. by whose will, 1670, a bequest to him was made. He, or Thomas, or both, left issue, and the benefit of his relative's generosity was, in our day, more than a century and a half since the donor's death, partaken by an undergraduate of the univ. on claim of blood relationship. REFERENCES:—Huntington's Stamford, 80; Smith Gen. (1870).

PENTICUS:—John, Charlestown, 1638 or earlier, freeman 1640, by wife Joanna, who was widow of Edward Larkin, had John, born 1659, and died 1687, aged near 90. Perhaps he had former wife. He and wife Joanna joined church 1639. See Buddington's Hist. Often in record of town and church the name is Penticost.

PENTLAND:—Nathaniel Pentland, Lynn.

PENWELL, or PENEWELL:—Joseph Penwell, Saco, died early.

PENWELL, WALTER, Saco, died 1683, leaving widow Mary, prob. daughter of Robert Booth, and son Walter, brother of Joseph, of whom he had been admor.

PEPPER:—Francis, Springfield, 1645, died 1685; had prob. no wife nor children.

PEPPER, RICHARD, Roxbury, came in the Francis from Ipswich, 1634, aged 27, with wife Mary, 30, and daughter Mary, 3½; besides Stephen Beckett, of 11 years, united with church early as did his wife; freeman, 1635; but of father, mother or child nothing is known, beyond that, according to a meagre note, he was living in 1648. He may have removed to long distance in Conn. Mr. Drake gave this man the name of Pepy in his transcript for Geneal. Reg. XIV, 331 and 2, but in latter page has it both ways.

PEPPER, ROBERT, Roxbury, perhaps brother of the preced., married 1643, Eliz. Johnson; had Eliz. bapt. 1644, died in few days; Eliz. again; 1645; John, 1647; Joseph, 1649; Mary, 1651; Benjamin, 1653, died young; Robert, 1655; Sarah, born 1657; Isaac, 1659; and Jacob, 1661. He was freeman, 1643; his wife died 1684; he died soon after.

REFERENCES:—Barry's Framingham, 357; Ellis' Hist. Roxbury, Mass., 126; Freeman's Hist., Cape Cod, Mass.; II, 153; Green's Kentucky Fams.; Hollister's Hist. of Pawley, Vt., 221; Savage's Gen. Hist., III, 391.

PEPPERELL:—William, Kittery, came from Cornwall, or Devonshire, a fisherman, about 1676, to Isle of Shoals, thence in 3 or 4 years removed to K.; married Margery, daughter of John Bray, of K.; had Andrew, born 1681; Mary, 1685; Margery, 1689; Joanna, 1692; Meriam, 1694; Dorothy, 1698; and Jane, 1701; besides the famous Sir William, 1696. He was a wealthy merchant, and died 1734, at the age of 85, says Farmer. His widow died 1741.

REFERENCES:—Essex Inst., XXXI, 54; Leighton Gen., 117-20; Maine Gen. and Biog. Recorder (1875) 20; N. E. Hist. Gen. Reg., XIII, 138; XX, 1-6; Parson's Life of Sir William P., 335-41; Pepperell Gen. (1866), 6 pp. reprint.; Savage's Gen. Dict., III, 392; Titcomb's Early New Eng. People, 265; Wentworth Gen., I, 307-9.

PEPYS:—Richard, Boston, 1642, or earlier; took estate that was of William Blaxton, by purch. and desired to buy more, as in records is found that the selectmen, 1643, appointed Colbron and Eliot, a committee "to view a parcel of land toward Mr. Blaxton's Beach, which Richard Peapes desires to purchase of the town, whether it may be conveniently sold unto him." Prob. he was from Cottenham in Cambridgesh. for the pronounc. we see, in one syllable as also his own spelling of the name, both quite rare, are the same as that of the late Lord Cottenham, the Chancellor of Great Britain, and of Saml. Pepys, F. R. S., the diary-maker.

PERCIVAL, PASSEVIL, PASSAVIL, or PARCYFULL and, in Col. Rec. PURSUALL:—James, Sandwich, had Eliz. born 1675.

PERCIVAL, JAMES, possibly son of preceding; had John, born 1706; and Timothy (by wife Abigail), 1712.

PERCIVAL, JOHN, Barnstable; had Eliz., born 1704; and James, 1711. Perhaps he was brother of preceding.

REFERENCES:—Am. Ancestry, XII; Barry's Hanover, Mass., 354; Freeman's Cape Cod, Mass., II, 155, 339.

PERCY, PEERCE, PIERCY, or PERCIE:—John; Gloucester; married 1673, Jane, widow of Philip Stanwood.

PERCY, MARMADUKE, Salem, 1637; came the year before from Sandwich, Co. Kent; a tailor, with wife, Mary, and one servant.

PERCY, ROBERT, New London; bought a house 1678, says Caulkins, and sold it next year.

REFERENCES:—Am. Ancestry, V, 144; Cothren's Woodbury, Ct. Settlers, 674; Rhode Island Hist. Mag., V, 40-8.

PERHAM, PERRUM, or PERAM:—Abraham, Rehoboth, had Sarah and Rebecca, twins, born 1679; and latter died in 3 days.

PERHAM, JOHN, Rehoboth, 1643; supposed by Farmer to be an early settler at Chelmsford, but the contin-

ued residence of him and descend. at R. as shown by Baylies, II, 199, 203, 8, 16, and IV, 85, satisfy as to the contrary. He had Noah, born 1679.

PERHAM, JOHN, Chelmsford, 1666; freeman, 1690. In the same year John of Roxbury appears in the list of freemen, but Savage suspects an error of the records as that name is not found in R. at that time. Possibly John Perry may have been mentioned.

REFERENCES:—Am. Ancestry, IV, 156; Ballou's Hist. of Milford, Mass., 959-61; Butler's Hist. of Farmington, Me., 548-552; Lapham's Hist. of Paris, Me., 691; Lapham's Hist. Woodstock, Me.; 247; Livermore's Hist. Wilton, N. H., 463; Maine Gen., I, 33-9; Norton's Hist. Fitzwilliam, N. H., 659.

PERIGO:—Ezekiel, Saybrook; prob. son of Robert, said to be born 1658; went as a soldier to Northampton, 1707, and that year married Mary Webb.

PERIGO, ROBERT, Saybrook, had suit 1665, in Ct. of Assist. in Mass..

PERIT:—Benjamin, Stratford; 1669.

PERKINS:—Abraham, Hampton; by wife, Mary, who died 1706, aged 88, had Mary and Abraham, bapt. 1639; freeman, 1640. Other children were Humphrey, born 1642, died young; James, 1644; Timothy, 1646; both died young; James, again, 1647; Jonathan, 1650; David, 1653; Abigail, 1655; Timothy, 1657, died in few months; Sarah, 1659; and Humphrey, 1661; besides Caleb and Luke of doubtful date.

PERKINS, BENJAMIN, Newbury; had Daniel, 1684.

PERKINS, EDMUND, Boston, 1675, married Susanna, widow of John Howlett, daughter of Francis Hudson; had Edmund, born 1678, died young; John, 1680; Edmund, again, 1683; and Jane, 1687.

PERKINS, EDWARD, New Haven; married, 1650, Eliz. Butcher; had John, 1651; Mehitable, 1652; Jonathan, 1653; David, 1656; and perhaps others. He and three sons were proprs. in 1685.

PERKINS, ELEAZER, Hampton; 1678.

PERKINS, ISAAC, Hampton, prob. brother of first Abraham; freeman, 1642; by wife, Susanna, had perhaps Lydia; Isaac, bapt. 1639; Jacob, 1640; Lydia and Rebecca, both of whom may have been elder; Daniel, who died young; Caleb; Benjamin, 1650; Susanna, 1652; Hannah, 1656; Mary, 1658; Ebenezer, 1659; and Joseph, 1661; and the time of his death is uncertain.

PERKINS, JACOB, Ipswich, youngest son of first John of the same, born in England; by wife, Eliz., had Eliz., born 1650; John, 1654; Judith, 1655; Mary, 1658; Jacob, 1662; Mathew, 1665; Joseph and Jabez; is usually called serg. and has very long line of descend. His wife died 1686, and he, 1701, aged 76.

PERKINS, JACOB, Edgartown, 1674-85.

PERKINS, JOHN, Ipswich; born about 1590, it is said, at Newent in Co. Gloucester; came prob. in the Lion to Boston, 1631, with Roger Williams, bringing also wife Judith, son John, born about 1614; and prob. other children, certainly Mary, and Eliz. He, with his wife, soon joined church; had Lydia; bapt. 1632; was freeman, 1631, and in 1633 went to I. with John Winthrop, the younger; represent. in 1636; died 1654, leaving John, Thomas, born about 1616, and Jacob about 1624, born in England; Lydia married a Bennet.

PERKINS, JONATHAN, Norwalk, 1671-7.

PERKINS, THOMAS, Dover, 1665; born, it is said, in 1628, took oath of fidelity 1669, and gave land, 1693, to son Nathaniel.

PERKINS, WILLIAM, Roxbury, a minister, but where educated is unheard; son of William, of London, a merchant tailor (who was son of George, of Warwick); was born 1607, and his son having given to the company for our plantation £50, was a member, and to this son grant of 400 acres was made. He came in the William and Francis, leaving London 1632; was freeman, 1634; artillery co. 1638; married 1636, Eliz. Wootton; had William, born 1639; died few weeks; William, again, 1642; removed 1643 to Weymouth; there had Eliz. 1643; Tobijah, 1646; and Catharine, 1648; was represent., 1644, a capt. 1645; removed again, it is supposed, to Gloucester; there had Mary, 1652; preached 1651-5, and became Minister of Topsfield; there had John 1655; Sarah, 1657; Timothy, 1658; and Rebecca, 1662. He died 1682, leaving these nine children who all were married.

PERKINS, WILLIAM, Dover, 1662; took oath of fidelity, 1669; was born, says tradition, in 1616 and died at Newmarket, 1732.

REFERENCES.

MASSACHUSETTS:—Adams Fam. of Kingston, 22-25; Cleveland's Bi-Cen. Topsfield, 60-2; Crowell's Hist. Essex, 255; Davis' Landmark's Plymouth, 199-202; Kingman's Hist. N. Bridgewater, 619-23; Mitchell's Hist. Bridgewater, 265-8; Temple's Hist. Palmer, 527; Wyman's Charlestown Gens., II, 738.

NEW HAMPSHIRE:—Cochrane's Hist. Antrim, 642; Cutter's Hist. Jaffrey, 418-20; Dow's Hist. Hampton, 907-16; Livermore's Hist. Wilton, 464; Morrison's Hist. Windham, 734-8; Runnel's Sanbornton, II, 548-53; Stearn's Hist. Rindge, 630; Washington History, 564.

OTHER PUBLICATIONS:—Adam's Hist. Fairhaven, Vt., 450; American Ancestry, IV, 137; V, 8; IX, 41-146; Bradbury's Hist. Kennebunkport, Me., 267-71; Butler's Hist. Farmington, Me., 552; Champion Gen.; Crawford Fam. of Va., 100-3; Douglas Gen., 113-32; Dudley's Archæolog. and Gen. Coll., plate 5; Eaton's Annals Warren, Me., 2nd Edit., 602; Eaton's Thomaston, Me., II, 352; Essex Inst. Hist. Coll., XI, 222-7; XIX; XXI; XXII; 103-20; 193-208; XXIIII, 46-58, 97-112, 185-200, 281-96; Hanson's Old Kent, Md., 189-97; N. E. Hist. Gen. Reg., X, 211-6; XI, 315; XII, 79-83; XIV, 113-20; XVII, 63; XLVII, 483; Perkin's Chart (1873) 17 x 22 in.; Perkin's Gen. (1860), 8 pp.; (1872); (1882-9); (1885) 29 pp.; Savage's Gen. Dict., III, 394-8; Upham Gen., 611-20; Young's Hist. Warsaw N. Y., 316-8.

PERLEY:—Allen, Ipswich; came in the Planter from London, 1635, aged 27; freeman, 1642; and Coffin says he was from Wales. He had, beside Nathaniel, who died 1668, aged 24, John, Thomas, Samuel, Sarah, Martha and Timothy. He died 1675, leaving widow Susanna, who died 1692; but whether she was mother of all the children is unknown.

PERLEY, JOHN, Boxford; perhaps son of the preceding; born in England; was freeman, 1690; and Farmer says representative 1689-91. One John at Ipswich, by wife Jane; had Hannah, born 1699; but he was not prob. the represent. and may be grandson of Allen.

PERLEY, WILLIAM, Marlborough. Other than that his house was a garrison in Oct. 1675, Savage knows no more.

REFERENCES:—Am. Ancest., II, 94; III, 96; VI, 177; Gage's Hist. Rowley, Mass., 451; Hammatt Papers of Ipswich, Mass., 259; Herrick's Hist. Gardner, Mass., 373; Perley Gen. (1877) 13 pp.; Perley's Hist. Boxford, Mass., 74-8; Ridlon's Harrison, Me., Settlers, 104-6; Runnel's Hist. Sanbornton, N. H., 553; Stark's Hist. Dunbarton, N. H., 254.

PERMET:—See Partmount.

PERRIMAN:—Thomas, Weymouth, 1652; an indent. apprent. of Dorothy Hunt. At Cambridge, Frances P. married Isaac Amsden, 1654, and Rebecca P. married 1660, Daniel Farrabas, but it is not known who they were. Perhaps these maidens were sisters of the apprentice, and they may have been brought from England after death of father.

PERRIN, PERRAN, or PERING:—Abraham, Rehoboth, perhaps son of the first John, married 1677, Sarah, eldest daughter of Philip Walker, who died 1693, and he died soon after. He had Eliz., born 1681; Daniel, 1683; and Nathaniel, 1685.

PERRIN, HENRY, Newport, 1656; Brookhaven, L. I., 1657, says Thompson, and may have been admitted freeman of Conn. 1664, but his name does not appear in the list of 1669.

PERRIN, JOHN, Braintree, had Mary, born 1641, removed perhaps to Rehoboth. It would seem that a John, sr., should be looked for in the same town, whether father of Abraham or not, for in Col. Records is seen that John, sr., was buried 1674. Ann. (Savage supposes his daughter), married, 1675, Thomas Read of Rehoboth.

PERRIN, JOHN, Rehoboth, called jun., had Mary, born 1673; Nathaniel, 1675, died young; Mehitable, 1677.

PERRIN, THOMAS, Ipswich, married before 1669, Susanna, widow of Robert Roberts, was living 1679.

REFERENCES:—Daniel's Oxford, Mass., 641; Dearborn's Hist. Salisbury, N. H., 686; Hemenway's Vermont Gaz., IV, 62; Morris Gen. (1887), 183; N. E. Hist. and Gen. Reg., XXXII, 178-81; Page Gen., 125; Perrin Gen. (1885), 224 pp.; Savage's Gen. Dict., III, 299; Welles' Washington Gen., 262.

PERRY or PURY:—Anthony, Rehoboth, 1658-78; was represent. 1674, says Baylies, IV, 85. Perhaps he had Jariel and Mehitable, both died by Col. Rec. Sept. 1676, and he died 1683.

PERRY, ARTHUR, Boston, 1638; a tailor; by wife Eliz. had Elishua, a daughter, born 1637, died in few months; Seth, 1639; John, 1642; and Eliz. 1647; artillery co., 1638; Sarah, 1647; Deborah, 1649; was the town drummer; freeman, 1640; and died 1652. Both of the sons followed the trade of their father.

PERRY, EDWARD, Sandwich; from being named as son in the will of Edmund Freeman, it may be thought he had married a daughter of that gentleman, but more prob. his mother had become second wife of Freeman; by wife Mary, who may have been daughter of that Edmund Freeman, or of Edward Freeman, he had Samuel, born about 1664; and prob. others.

PERRY, EZRA, Sandwich; married 1652, Eliz., only daughter of Thomas Burge of the same, had Ezra, born next year. Deborah, 1654; John, 1657; Samuel, 1667; Benjamin, 1670; and Remembrance, 1676 or 7.

PERRY, FRANCIS, Salem, 1631; a wheelwright, born about 1608; had wife Jane who joined the church 1641, and had bapt. Sarah, and Benjamin same year; David, 1641; Samuel, 1642; and Elisha, 1644; he removed, but where is not known.

PERRY, HENRY, Salem, 1652, as the diligence of Coffin picked out of records of County, but the equal diligence of Felt discerned not in rec. of town or church.

PERRY, ISAAC, Boston, 1631; prob. arrived with the apostle Eliot in the Lion, and entered in church list; freeman, 1632; but no more is known.

PERRY, JOHN, Roxbury, brother of Isaac, came prob. in the Lion 1632, very early of the church there, being No. 17 on the list of freemen, 1633; had Eliz., born 1638,

John, 1639; and Samuel, 1641. He died 1642, of consumption.

PERRY, JOHN, Newbury, 1651; had wife Demaris. He may be the man named in Felt's list, 1637.

PERRY, JOHN, Medfield, 1678; perhaps son of Roxbury, John; married, 1665, Bethia, daughter of Daniel Morse the first; had John, born 1667; Samuel and Joseph, twins, 1674; Nathaniel, 1671, died under ten years; Nathaniel again; Bethia, 1685, perhaps Eleazer, 1680.

PERRY, JOHN, New Haven; a proprietor, 1685.

PERRY, JOHN, Taunton, 1643.

PERRY, JOHN, Watertown, 1674, then aged 61; may have been father of that John, Watertown, who married 167, Sarah, daughter of John Clary; had John, born 1668, died in few weeks; John, again, 1670; Joanna, 1672; Sarah, 1675; Josiah, 1677, died young; Eliz. 1681; Josiah, again, 1684; Joseph, 1691; and Sarah, 1694.

PERRY, JOSEPH, Seacunk, i. e., Rehoboth, 1651; perhaps was brother of Anthony of the same, or of Thomas of Scituate.

PERRY, NATHANIEL, Rehoboth; married 1683, Sarah Carpenter, daughter of Samuel of the same, as presumed Savage.

PERRY, RICHARD, New Haven, 1640; had Mary bapt. same year; Micajah, 1641; Samuel, 1645; John, 1647; and Grace, 1649; perhaps removed 1651, and was at Fairfield 1650. Share in division of land there is given to Nathaniel but not to Richard, who may have died before and this may have been his heir. Perhaps he was admitted as an inhabitant, 1637, of Charlestown, who is not found long residing there; and at Fairfield married Grace, widow of John Nichols after 1653, and was dead in 1658; but the identity is uncertain, for in 1655 one of the name was at Providence, it is said. This, too, was the name of a merchant in London, one of the Assistants named in the Royal Charter, 1629, who aided our cause by money, but never came over.

PERRY, THOMAS, Ipswich, 1648.

PERRY, THOMAS, Scituate, 1643; married Sarah, daughter of Isaac Stedman; had Thomas, William, Henry, Joseph, John, and perhaps more.

PERRY, WILLIAM, Scituate, 1638; perhaps brother of first Thomas; may have removed to Watertown, 1640; by wife Ann had Eliz., born 1641; and several other children of whom he names five in his will, 1681, when 75 years old—Obadiah, Samuel, Sarah, Ann, and Abia. He died 1683.

REFERENCES.

MASSACHUSETTS:—Ballou's Milford, 961-5; Barry's Hanover, 354-8; Bond's Watertown, 402; Cutter's Arlington, 282; Daniel's Oxford, 641; Davis' Landmarks Plymouth, 202; Deane's Scituate, 322; Fox's Dunstable, 248; Freeman's Cape Cod, II, 153; Hanover Records, (1898); Heywood's Westminster, 824; Hudson's Lexington, 177; Hudson's Sudbury, 446; Hyde's Brimfield, 445; Morse's Sherborn Settlers, 190-5; Paige's Hardwick, 452; Stearn's Ashburnham, 846; Temple's N. Brookfield, 703; Temple's Northfield, 514; Wall's Reminisc. of Worcester, 109-11; Wyman's Charlestown Gens., II, 739.

NEW HAMPSHIRE:—Bassett's Richmond, 459-61; Bemis Marlboro, 248-51; Cochrane's Antrim, 643; Coggswell's Dublin, 680; Hayward's Hancock, 806; Leonard's Dublin, 378-80; Livermore's Wilton, 464; Norton's Fitzwilliam, 662-6; Read's Swanzey, 418; Stearn's Rindge, 631-4; Wheeler's Newport, 503-5.

OTHER PUBLICATIONS:—Adams' Haven Gen., 40; Am. Ancestry I, 61; II, 94; III, 99, 104, 189; IV, 10;

VII, 138; X, 3, 32, 162; XI, 148, 150; Austin's Ancestral Dict., 46; Austin's Ancestries, 45; Austin's R. I. Gen. Dist., 150; Bangor, Me., Hist. Mag., V, 8; Brigg's Hist. Shipbuilding, 84; Cleveland's Yates Co., N. Y., 483, 679; Cole Gen., 43; Conn. Quarterly, III (1897), 109, 137, 352, 480; Cothren's Woodbury, Ct., 660-8; II, 1543; Dearborn's Parsonsfield, Me., 393; Eaton's Thomaston, Me., II, 352-5; Fisk Gen., 149; Goode Gen., 353; Hazard Gen., 103-6; Kimball Family News (1898) 201-8; Lapham's Norway, Me., 575; Lapham's Paris, Me., 694-6; Lapham's Rumford, Me., 381; Leavenworth Gens., 53-64, 73-7; Leland Gen., 207-10, 212-4, 217, 247; Narragansett Hist. Reg., V, 275-8; Orcutt's Derby, Ct., 750; Orcutt's Stratford, Ct., 1267; Perry Memo. (1878), 28 pp.; Perry of Prov, Ancestors (1889), 9 pp.; Perry Family of Topsham (1890), 13 pp.; R. I. Hist. Mag., V, 29-36, 317-27; Savage's Gen. Dict., II, 389-410; Sharpe's Hist. Seymour, Ct., 213-5; Stile's Windsor, Ct., II, 561; Todd's Redding, Ct., 209; Walker Gen., 141; Wight Gen., 156.

PERSON:—George, Reading; died 1679, as Eaton cites the grave stone, aged 64. See PARSONS.

PERWIDGE, or PERWYDGE:—William, an odd name, found 1644, at Hartford or the neighborhood.

PESTER or PESTOR:—William, Salem, 1637; when with a grant of land he had the prefix of respect, yet abandoned the country in 1642, and 10 years later, not being heard of, his wife Dorothy had leave to marry again.

PETCOCK:—See PIDCOCK.

PETERS:—Andrew, Boston, 1659; a distiller, married Mercy, widow of Michael Wilborne, daughter of William Beamsley; removed to Ipswich, 1665; thence to Andover, where, 1689, his sons Andrew and John were killed by the Indians; and other children were Mercy, who married 1686, John Allen, Mary, who married on same day, Thomas Chandler, and Elizabeth, who married 1692, James Johnson; William and Samuel; and he died at the age of 77. Curious it must appear to this later generation that his name in one deed is Peters, and in another relating to the same estate it is Peterson.

PETERS:—Hugh, Salem; the fourth minister there, was born 1599, at the Parish of St. Ewe, or, as commonly said, in the town of Fowry, Cornwall, bred at Trinity Coll., Cambridge, where he had his degrees 1617, and, 22, preached in London with great success, until driven to Holland, there taught, with the famous William Ames, the English church at Rotterdam, and for some two years after death of Ames. Probably came in the Abigail, 1635, though his name does not appear at the London custom ho. and perhaps he got on board in the Downs, arriving in company of 2nd John Winthrop, the mother of whose 1st wife he had married, as it seems; was freeman, 1636; settled in the church at Salem; in 1641, with Hibbins and Welde, as agents for the colony he went home, by way of Newfoundland, in the ship with John Winthrop, the younger, and Lechford, the lawyer, engaged with great zeal in the civil war, and partook largely in the triumphs of this cause, and for the detestation felt at his violence was executed soon after the restoration, 1660, being (thinks Savage) the only clergyman of several thousand who thus suffered. He had not, probably, brought over his first wife by whom he had no children, but married here Deliverance Sheffield, one of the church of Boston, by whom he had Elizabeth, bapt. 1640, the only child to whom his dying legacy was addressed.

PETERS, JOHN, Gravesend, L. I., 1650. THOMPSON.

PETERS, SAMUEL, probably youngest son of Andrew, married 1696, Phebe Frye, daughter, probably, of Samuel of the same, but no more is known.

PETERS, THOMAS, New London, younger brother of Hugh, of far milder temper, said to have been bred at Oxford, but on uncertain authority, was a minister in his native shire of Cornwall, whence driven in 1643 by the royalist forces, he came next year to this country, assisted the younger Winthrop in his plantation, 1646, having served before at Saybrook in the church, yet continued but short time, having been invited home by former parish, in 1646, and went next year.

REFERENCES:—Abbot's Andover, Mass., 37; Amer-Ancestry, II, 94; VII, 249; Bangor Magazine, I, 199-205; III, 240; V, 207; Bartow Gen., 131; Bassett's Hist. Richmond, N. H., 461-3; Bliss Gen., 683-90; Buckminister's Hastings Gen., 167; Coggswell's Hist. Henniker, N. H., 681-3; Eaton's Annals Warren, Me., 602-4; Heraldic Journal, I, 190-2; McDonald's Peters Gen. (1881); McKeen's Hist. of Bradford, Vt., 126-40; N. E. Hist. Gen. Reg., II, 58-64; Palmer and Trimble Gen., 391-3; Peters' Hist. of Rev. Hugh Peters, 155; Powers' Hist. of Sangamon Co., Ills., 564; Savage's Gen. Dict., III, 401-3.

PENHOLLOW:—Samuel, Portsmouth; born 1665 at St. Mabyn, near Bodmin, in Cornwall, as he tells us, and verifying the jingle of Camden's Remains:

By Tre, Ros, Pol, Lan, Caer, and Pen
You may know the most Cornish men.

He came with Rev. Charles Morton, under whom he had prob. studied at Newington Green, arrived at Charlestown, 1686, joined the church there late in 1687, went soon to Portsmouth, married 1687, Mary, daughter of Pres. John Cutt, was counsellor, secretary, and many years treasurer of the Prov., Judge of the Supreme Ct. 1714, and Ch. J., 1717, to his death, 1726; yet in our day most thought of as the historian of the later Indian wars. His children were John, who married Ann, daughter of Hon. Jacob Wendell, was captain, and died before 1736. Eliz., Joseph, Richard, Susanna, and Benjamin, H. C., 1723; died young; and descendants are still found at P.

REFERENCES:—Am. Ancestry, IX, 153; Cutt's Gen., 18-20, 57-60, 116-20; N. E. Hist. Reg., XXXII, 28-35. Penhollow Genealogy (1878) 22 pp.; P. Gen., 2d edit. (1885) 47 p., Wentworth Gen., I, 293-5, 326-8.

PENNINGTON:—Ephraim, New Haven; swore alleg. 1664; had Ephraim, born 1645; and Mary 1646, both bapt. 1648; and he died 1660, leaving widow and these two children.

REFERENCES:—Amer. Ancest. V, 56; Morris Geneal. (1898) 919; N. E. Gen. Ren., XXV, 286-91; 335-8; Pennington Gen. (1871), 18 pp.

PENLEY:—Samson, Falmouth, 1658; was living after the first destruction of the town, 1676, left widow Rachel, and three daughters, Jane, Dorcas, and Mary.

REFERENCES:—Lapham's Norway, Me., 573; Lapham's Hist., Paris, Me., 689-91.

PENN:—James, Boston; came in fleet with Winthrop, reg. 1630 to be made freeman, though it does not appear that he took the oath, as represent. 1648-9, beadle first and marshal aft., ruling elder; died 1671. In his will mentions wife Catharine; no children named, but perhaps had Mary.

PENN, WILLIAM, Charlestown, 1630, came, no doubt, in fleet with Winthrop; settled at Braintree; late in his days removed to Boston; yet in his will, 1688, directs his burial to be at Braintree; gives legacy to church and school there; to several Thompsons, Stephen Paine and their children, but chiefly to cousin Hannah Hill, and Edward Hill, Jr., and Hannah Hill and Edward Hill, Sr., and Sarah Hill, having, he says, sent for his kinswoman, Deborah, wife of said Edward, Sr., out of England, promising to make her his heir, so we may be sure his wife and children, if he had any, were dead; who was the Christian Penn, a passenger in the Ann, to Plymouth, 1623, who soon after married Francis Eaton, is perhaps beyond the reach of all but conjecture.

REFERENCES:—Am. Hist. Reg., I, 559-66; Clermont Co., Ohio, Hist. 379; Egle's Notes and Queries (1896) 233; Meade's Old Churches of Va.; N. E. Hist. and Gen. Reg., XLIV, 186-93; Penn Family, by Smith, (1867) 25 pp.; Penn Family, by Coleman (1871) 24 pp.; Penn Family, by Lea (1890) 51 pp.; Penn Family, by Jenkins (1898) 270 pp.; Penn Family, by Lea (1900) 46 pp.; Penn Mag. of Hist., Vols. 14 to 22; Savage's Gen. Dict., III, 389; Wheeler's Hist. of N. Carolina, II, 163; Whitmore's Heraldic Journal, III, 135-9.

PENNELL:—Walter Pennell, Saco; freeman 1653, married, 1647, Mary, daughter of Robert Booth; had Walter and perhaps others; in the Indian War, 1675, removed to Salem.

REFERENCES:—Maris Gen., 147; Ridlon's Saco Valley, Me., Fams. 1103-6; Sharpless Gen., 87, 231, 360; Smith's Hist. Delaware Co., Pa., 492; Wheeler's Hist. of Brunswick, Me., 847.

PENNIMAN:—James, Boston; came prob. in the Lion, 1631, with John Winthrop, Jr., for he, with Lydia, who survived him, were adm. of the church before the son, but after the wife of the gov. freeman, 1632, the same day with John and Jacob Eliot, whom Savage reckons as fellow passengers. Had James, bapt. 1633; Lydia, 1635; John, 1637; removed to Braintree, there had Joseph, born 1639; and Sarah, 1641; Samuel, 1645; Hannah, 1648; Abigail, 1651; and Mary, 1653; all by wife Lydia; and he died 1664. Abigail married, 1678, Samuel Neal; and Mary married, 1678, Samuel Paine, of the same.

REFERENCES:—Ballou's Milford, 957-9; Eaton's Hist. Thomaston, Me., I, 351; Heywood's Hist. Westminster, Mass., 823; Jameson's Hist. Medway, Mass., 511; Morton's Hist. Fitzwilliam, N. H., 657-9; Savage's Gen. Dict., III, 389; Vinton Gen., 76-8, 351-4; Washington, N. H., Hist., 563.

PENNINGTON:—Ephraim, New Haven; see Thomas Penington, took oath of allegiance and fidelity, 1678.

PETERSON:—Cornelius, Boston, 1685.

PETERSON, HENRY and JOHN PETERSON, of Lyme, were of the train band 1678, and no more is known of either, except that John was afterward of Duxbury, and married Mary, daughter of George Soule; and that Henry, by wife, Marah, married 1683, had Sarah, born 1686.

REFERENCES:—Amer. Ancestry, II, 94; III, 182; Bergen's Kings Co., N. Y., Settlers, 223-5; Davis' Landmarks Plymouth, Mass., 203; Richmond, Va., Standard, II, 31; Slaughter's Hist. Bristol Parish, Va., 205; Wheeler's Hist., Brunswick, Me., 847; Winsor's Hist. Duxbury, Mass., 289.

PETTIFORD, PETFORD, or PITTFORD:—Peter, Salem, 1641; Mr. Felt found mention of, but nothing is told of him, except that he resided at Marblehead, 1648. Among Charlestown bapt. is Samuel, son of Mary Pettiford, brother Baker's daughter, in 1669.

PETTELL:—Anthony, Marblehead, 1653; a fisherman, perhaps from Guernsey.

PETTIBONE:—John, Windsor; freeman, 1658; married 1665, Sarah, daughter of Bigot Egglestone; had John, born 1665; Sarah, 1667, died young; Stephen, 1669, besides Samuel, and several daughters of whom another was Sarah of uncertain date. He had estate in that part named Simsbury, was one of the first settlers and there with John, Stephen, and Samuel, was living in 1712. REFERENCES:—Brown's Simsbury, 115; Humphrey Gen.; Marshall's Grant Ancestry, 129; Stiles' Hist. Windsor, Ct., II, 562; Tuttle Gen., 710-2.

PETTENGELL, or PATTINGGELL:—Richard, Newbury, came from Staffordsh. tradition says, was first at Salem; there married Joanna, daughter of Richard Ingersoll; had Samuel, bapt. 1645; freeman, 1641; was some years at Wenham; and at N. had Mary, born, 1652; and Nathaniel, 1654; besides Matthew and Nathaniel, before or after. Mary married 1670, Abraham Adams.

PETTES, or PETTIT:—Gilbert, Salem, 1668.

PETTES, JOHN, Roxbury, 1639; of whom Mr. Ellis in his history says nothing, but the name occurs, yet with family of several heads, probably removed to Stamford, or Long Island, where Savage finds at Newtown, Thomas in 1660; Nathaniel in 1667; and John, 1686; yet it may well be that his son, John, who married Sarah, daughter of Daniel Scofield, was of Stamford, 1669.

PETTES, THOMAS, Exeter, 1639; a signer of the original combination; in 1647 was the chief military man. REFERENCES:—Amer. Ancestry, II, 94; Huntington's Stamford, Ct., Settlers, 82; Sedgwick's Hist. of Sharon, Ct., 105.

PETTS:—John; a soldier, killed by the Indians, 1675, at Hatfield.
REFERENCE:—Hayward's Hist., Gilsum, N. H., 375.

PETTY, or PETTEE:—John, Springfield; had lived at Windsor, but married at Boston, 1662, Ann Canning; had at W. James, born same year; and at S. Hannah, 1666, died soon; John, 1667; Mary, 1670; Joseph, 1672; Ann, 1675; and Ebenezer, 1678; and he died 1680. His widow married Samuel Owen. James and John each had families at S.

PETTY, PETER, sailed from Salem on fishing voyage, killed by Indians in Autumn of 1677; Felt, II, 213.

PETTY, PETER, Haverhill, 1680. Mirick, 85. It may be same as Pattee, which is seen in New Hampshire. REFERENCE:—Temple's Hist. Northfield, Mass., 514-5.

PETYGOOD, or PETGOOD:—Peter, Marblehead, 1641.

PETYGOOD, RICHARD, Ipswich, 1641.

PEVERLY:—John, Portsmouth; one of the men sent over, 1631, by Mason, the Patentee.

PEVERLY, THOMAS, Portsmouth; perhaps son of the preceding, died after 1670, leaving by wife, who may have been daughter of Thomas Walford, sons John, Thomas, Lazarus, Samuel, and Jeremiah.

PHENIX:—Alexander, Wickford, 1674.
REFERENCES:—Austin's R. I. Geneal. Dict.

PHELPS:—Christopher, Salem; married, 1658, Eliz. Sharp, and no more is known save that he signed petition against imposts, 1668.

PHELPS, EDWARD, Newbury; removed to Andover; by wife Elizabeth, daughter of Robert Adams, had, besides others, John, born at N. 1657, who was killed by Indians in service at Scarborough, 1677; and he died, 1689.

PHELPS, EDWARD, Andover; prob. son of preceding; married 1682, Ruth Andrews, had prob. others besides Edward and Bathsheba, who died 1694; and Elizabeth, born 1690; removed to Lancaster and died 30th Nov. of uncertain years, and there Elizabeth married Samuel Willard of L.

PHELPS, EPHRAIM, Simsbury; son of Edward, married 1691, Mary Jaggers, and died 1697.

PHELPS, GEORGE, Dorchester; freeman 1635; removed with Warham to Windsor; by first wife said to be named Philbury, daughter of Philip Randall, who died 1648, had Isaac, born 1638; Abraham, 1643; and Joseph, 1647, who died soon, as did Abraham in same year. He married 1648 Frances, who had been widow Clark, and then was widow of Thomas Dewey, and had Jacob, 1650; John, 1652; and Nathaniel, 1653; removed to Westfield, there had more children, and died 1687, but Stiles in History, 743, says 1678.

PHELPS, HENRY, Salem; from London, came in the Hercules 1634; married 1652, Hannah Bassett, but Savage thinks as second wife, for there is some prob. that he had married a daughter of Thomas Tresler, by whom he had son John, remembered in the will of his grandmother. Perhaps he was a Quaker, at least Felt II., 582, for Hannah P. in Oct., 1659, was admonished; but she may have been wife of Nicholas P.

PHELPS, JAMES, Boston, 1657.

PHELPS, JOHN, Charlestown; by wife Catharine had Catharine, born 1659, says the Middlesex rec., and the same authority adds that Catharine Phelps died foll. month. But Savage finds no Phelps in Charlestown, for a long time before or after, and John Phillips at that time had wife Catharine, who may have had that child. In some records the name is plain Philps, and this shows how easily one may be converted to the other.

PHELPS, JOHN, Salem; perhaps son of Henry, by wife Abigail had Abigail, born 1669; John, 1671; Henry, 1673; Joseph, 1675; Abigail, 1678; Samuel, 1680; and Hannah, 1683.

PHELPS, JOHN, son probably of John, of Salem; married 1701 Eliz. Putnam, prob. daughter of John.

PHELPS, NICHOLAS, Salem, 1658; a Quaker, whose wife was censured that year, and in 1661 fined for misuse of her tongue. Felt II., 581, 3.

PHELPS, RICHARD, Dorchester, 1633, of whom no more is known, and conjecture is useless.

PHELPS, SAMUEL, Boston; by wife Eliz. had Eliz., born 1681; and Grace, 1687.

PHELPS, SAMUEL, Andover; perhaps son of Edward the first; married 1682, Sarah Chandler, had Sarah, born soon after; Samuel, 1684; John, 1686; Joseph, 1689; Hannah, 1691, died young; Henry, 1693; Thomas, 1695; Elizabeth, 1698; Annis, 1701; and Deborah, 1703.

PHELPS, WILLIAM, Dorchester; came prob. in the Mary and John, 1630, from Plymouth, and may well be thought a Devonshire man, and perhaps brother of George, though more prob. his father; requested to be admitted freeman Oct. of that year, and was sworn following May; brought wife, whose name is not found, and children William, Samuel, Nathaniel, Joseph, and Sarah, yet one or two of these may have been born at D. Was represent. at the first Gen. Ct. of Mass., 1634, and Selectman, 1634-35; went next year with Warham to Windsor, there had Timothy, born 1639; and Mary, 1644. He was of the earliest Assistants, 1636-42, a represent. 1645-57, Assist. again 1658 to 1662, but not under the new charter; and died 1672. Sarah married William

Wade, 1658, and Mary married, 1665, Thomas Barber.

PHELPS, WILLIAM, Boston; mariner, whose first wife is unknown, but for second wife he married Jane, widow of Henry Butterfield, who having power of dispos. gave her estate by will of Feb., 1692, to him for life, remainder to John and William P., sons of her present husband, so that it may be inferred that she had no children by either of her husbands.

REFERENCES:—Abbot's Hist., Andover, Mass., 38; Brown's W. Simsbury, Ct., Settlers, 166-8; Chandler's Hist. Shirley, Mass., 600-3; Doolittle's Hist. Belchertown, Mass., 263-4; Hall's Hist. Eastern Vt., 689-94; Hines' Lebanon, Ct., Address (1880), 166; Hinman's Ct. Settlers, 1st edit., 175-6; Hudson's Hist. Lex., Mass., 178-9; Hudson's Hist. Marlborough, Mass., 428-9; Huntington's Mems., with general notes, 101-2; Judd's Hist. Hadley, Mass., 550-1; Leland Gen., 269; Loomis Gen., Female Branches, 451-54; Lyman's Hist. Easthampton, Mass., 190-1; Nash Gen., 88-9; N. E. Hist., Gen. Reg., XXV, 190; Orcutt's Hist. New Milford, Ct., 750-1; Orcutt's Hist. Torrington, Ct., 754-5; Orford, N. H., Centen., 134; Phelps'. Gen. of Othniel Phelps (1862) (1868); Phelps' Hist. Simsbury, Ct., 172; Phelps' Letters on Phelps' Families (1878); Phœnix's Whitney Gen., I., 712; Power's Hist. Sangamon Co., Ills., 565-6; Savage's Gen. Dict., III., 404-8; Secomb's Hist. Amherst, N. H., 728-9; Stiles' Hist. Windsor, Ct., 738-45; Stone's Hist. Hubbardston, Mass., 331-2; Strong Gen., 1155-7; Temple's Hist. Northfield, Mass., 515-6; Turner's Hist. Phelps' and Gorham's Purchase, 150-1; Worcester's Hist. Hollis, N. H., 383-4.

ARMS:—Arg., a lion, rampant, sa., between six cross crosslets, fitchée, gu.

PHESE or PHESEY:—Samuel, a soldier from the east part of the colony, 1676, sent up to Conn. River in the Indian War, was prob. from Braintree, and son of William.

PHESE, WILLIAM, Braintree, or possibly Watertown, freeman 1643, may be indebted to a careless clerk for this spelling of a name that should prob. be spelled Veazie with confidence.

PHILBRICK, or PHILBROCK, sometimes FILBRICK:—James, Hampton, 1644; prob. son of Thomas, was first perhaps at Watertown; had wife Ann, daughter of Thomas Roberts, of Dover, and by her had Bethia, who married, 1677, Caleb Perkins; James, and perhaps others; was perhaps a mariner, and drowned 1674.

PHILBRICK, JOHN, Hampton, 1639; who may have been brother of the first James; had Hannah, Sarah, John, but dates are not seen; was lost, 1657, with seven others, of whom were his wife Ann, and daughter Sarah, in a boat going out of harbor.

PHILBRICK, JONATHAN, prob. son of Welsh or Cornish, but the printed Col. Rec. V., 539, makes the surname Bengilley. Savage prefers the reading of Page, yet admits the usual correction of the State chirographer, Pulsifer.

PHILBRICK:—Joseph, Hampton; perhaps brother of James the second; had Joseph, born 1686, died soon; prob. Joseph again; and perhaps more.

PHILBRICK, ROBERT, Ipswich, 1639, or earlier, was a soldier in the Pequot War, 1636, but after 1648 may have removed. The town record has FILBRICK.

PHILBRICK, SAMUEL, Hampton, 1678; was prob. son of Thomas the first, and another Samuel, the same year took oath of allegiance there.

PHILBRICK, THOMAS, Watertown, 1636, where the record gives the spelling Filbrick, removed early to Hampton; sold his estate at W. 1646; had many children that he brought from England by wife Ann, daughter of William Knapp, but none prob. born here; died 1667. His will of 1664 calls himself very aged; mentions son James, grandson John, son Thomas, daughters Eliz. Garland, Hannah, Mary, and Martha, grandchildren, James Chase, and Martha, widow of John Cass. His daughter Eliz., probably the eldest, had before 1643 married Thomas Chase, after whose death, leaving five children by her, she married, 1654, John Garland; and again, 1674, married Henry Roby. Mary married, about 1647, Edward Tucke; and Martha married John Cass, the ancestor of the distinguished diplomatist, Lewis Cass.

PHILBRICK, THOMAS, Hampton; prob. son of the preceding, born in England about 1624, freeman 1668, had perhaps Thomas (as a junior is named for taking oath of allegiance 1678, some months before Thomas, Sr.), and prob. several others, as Savage thinks he had second wife Hannah, daughter of John White, young widow of John White, and by her had Hannah, who married Joseph Walker, of Portsmouth, and next, 1686, John Seavey.

PHILBRICK, THOMAS, Hampton; perhaps son of preceding, by wife Mehitable, had Eliz., born 1686.

PHILBRICK, WILLIAM, Hampton; may have been son of Thomas the second, by wife Mary had Walter, born 1690; and Mary 1692.

REFERENCES:—Chapman's Philbrick Gen. (1884); Cochrane's Hist. Antrim, N. H., 644-5; Hammatt Papers, Ipswich, Mass., 109; New England Hist. Gen. Reg., XXXVIII, 279-86; Runnel's Hist. Sanbornton, N. H., II, 554-7; Savage's Gen. Dict., III, 408-9; Stearn's Hist. Rindge, N. H., 634-5.

PHILLIPS:—Andrew, Charlestown; by wife Eliz. had Andrew; Eliz., born 1657; and Ephraim, 1659; perhaps others.

PHILLIPS, ANDREW, son prob. of preceding; married, 1683, Sarah, daughter of Michael Smith, of Malden; had Andrew, born 1687; Ebenezer, 1695; Joanna, 1697; and perhaps more.

PHILLIPS, BENJAMIN, Marshfield; married, 1682, Sarah Thomas, prob. daughter of Nathaniel.

PHILLIPS, CALEB, Roxbury; by wife Eliz. had Caleb, bapt. 1682; John, 1684, died in few weeks; Eliz., 1685; Mary, 1688; and Ebenezer, 1690.

PHILLIPS, CHARLES, Lynn; had David, born 1656, died at 5 months; Abigail, perhaps, 1657; but the record is doubtful; John, 1658, died young; George, 1663; and John again, 1667.

PHILLIPS, DANIEL, Newtown, L. I., 1686; by Riker called brother of Theophilus, was town clerk, superseded on the revolution 1689, and may have been of Gallup's company, 1690, against Quebec.

PHILLIPS, DAVID, Milford, 1655-60.

PHILLIPS, GEORGE, Watertown; the first minister, came in the Arabella, the admiral ship of the fleet, with Winthrop, 1630, bringing son Samuel, and wife, beside Eliz., and perhaps Abigail, an only child, sister by another father of John Hayward, of Watertown and Charlestown, who died soon after landing at Salem. He was son of Christopher, born 1593, at Rainham, St. Martins, near Rougham, in the hundr. of Gallow, Co. Norfolk, not Raymond, as says Mather, III, cap. 4; but Brook, in Lives of Puritans, II, 493, says Rondham, in the same Co.; yet Dr. Fuller, writing to Gov. Bradford, particularly calls him a Suffolk man; however, more important it is that he was bred at Gonille and Caius Coll., Cambridge, matricula. 1610; took degrees 1613 and 1617; was settled in Boxted, Co. Essex. By a second wife, married prob. in 1631, Elizabeth; by Bond, with happy conjecture, thought to be widow of Capt. Robert Welden, he had Zarobabel, born 1632; Jonathan, 1633. Theophilus, 1636; Amabel, late same year, died soon after; Ephraim, buried 1640, very young; Obadiah, born 1641; and a daughter Abiel, perhaps that Abigail who married, 1666, James Barnard. He died 1644, his widow in 1681.

PHILLIPS, GEORGE, Dorchester; freeman 1631; may be presumed to have come in the Mary and John; removed early to Windsor; for his slender health in 1648 and 1655 was excused from milit. watch. His wife died 1662, leaving him no children, and he was so unfortunate, 1676, as to be involved in a wordy controv. with the authority of the colony, who disfranch. him next year, of which some account is in Trumbull's Rec., II, 307; he died in 1678. His estate was disputed for by remote heirs.

PHILLIPS, HENRY, Dedham; freeman 1639; artillery co. 1640; had wife Eliz. Brock, who died 1640; and married, 1641, Ann Hunting, prob. sister of Elder John; had Eleazer, 1642, died in few days; Hannah, 1643; Abigail, 1645; and by third wife, Mary, daughter of John Dwight, had Nathaniel, 1653; and Eleazur, 1654; was ensign of the military comp. 1648; removed to Boston to follow his trade of butcher; had there Henry, 1656, died before his father; Timothy, 1658; Mary, 1660; Samuel, 1662; Elisha, 1665; Jonathan, 1666; Mehitable, 1667; John, 1669, died soon; John, again, 1670; and Elizabeth, 1672. In this year he was made represent. of first church and represent. for Hadley. Judge Sewall, in his diary, chronicles his burial 1686.

PHILLIPS, HENRY, New London; on the tax list of 1667, but never again on any record there, says Miss Caulkins.

PHILLIPS, HENRY, Charlestown; may have been son of Henry of Dedham, though it is not very prob., for by wife Mary, he had Joseph, born 19th Feb., 1675; of course less than 18½ years younger than his father.

PHILLIPS, JOHN, Dover, or Portsmouth; died 1642.

PHILLIPS, JOHN, Dedham; 1638; a famous minister of Wrentham (which is about 30 m. n.e. from Ipswich, Eng.), where he obtained his living as a rector, 1609, and married, 1612, Eliz., a sister of famous Dr. Ames, which gave him favor in the eyes of Puritans; was desired to accept office here in several places, espec. Cambridge, perhaps in connection with the newly begun college, but preferred to go home in the autumn of 1641; Felt, I, 212, thinks he was made townsman of Salem, but the prob. is at least equal that another man was thus honored. He was accompanied to England by John Humphrey, Esq., and then honored in the triumph of the cause, made one of the assembly of divines at Westminster; was founder of the Congreg. Church, 1650, after the N. E. pattern, and died 1660, aged 78. Calamy, Cont., II, 797; Winthrop, II, 86; Lamson.

PHILLIPS, JOHN, Dorchester; a baker, came prob. in the Mary and John, 1630; desired that same year to be made freeman, but was not sworn until 1632; by wife Joanna had Mary, born 1633, died at seven years; John, 1635; Martha, 1636; died soon; Mary, again; Israel, 1642, died next year; by the Gen. Ct. appointed constable 1636; removed to Boston, became one of the founders and a deacon of Second Church, 1650. His wife died 1675, and three months later he married widow Sarah Minor; and he died 1682, aged 77. His only child that reached maturity, Mary, married George Munjoy, of Falmouth, and after him Robert Lawrence, of the same.

PHILLIPS, JOHN, Plymouth, 1640; afterward of Marshfield, had John and other children, born in England; married for second wife, 1667, Faith, widow of Edward Dotey, who died the same year, and he died 1677, says Winsor. But Shurtleff, who gives a full memoir of him, says he was of Duxbury, 1643; by first wife, whose name is unknown, he had John, Samuel, Jeremiah, and Mary; the eldest, prob. John, was killed by lightning 1658, as by the coroner's inquest is shown; that his second wife was Grace, married 1654, widow of William Holloway, and she, with his son Jeremiah, was killed by lightning, 1666, when William Shurtleff, ancestor of the distinguished antiquarian, was killed by the same bolt; and that the third wife, Faith, died 1667; by whom he had no children, but by the second had Hannah; Grace, Joseph, born 1655, who was, says Miss Thomas, killed at Rehoboth fight, 1676; and Benjamin; and that he prob. died 1691, almost 90 years old, leaving Samuel, Benjamin, and Mary. Both of these sons had families. See also Thomas' Memo. of Marshfield.

PHILLIPS, JOHN, Duxbury, 1643; may be that apprentice who went from Boston 1631, but there is no certainty as to that apparent.

PHILLIPS, JOHN, Wenham, 1647; named in the will of Christopher Young as trustee, with charge to take his son.

PHILLIPS, JOHN, called a Welshman, Casco, 1642; perhaps freeman of 1658; removed to Kittery, was living 1684, aged 77. Willis, I, 19.

PHILLIPS, JOHN, Boston; by wife Mary had Mary, born 1652, Sarah, 1654, died same day; and Mary again, 1658; and the same, or another of same name, by wife Sarah had John, 1662.

PHILLIPS, JOHN, Charlestown; perhaps brother of Henry; was a master mariner; married, 1655, Catharine, daughter of John Anderson; had Catharine, 1662; Samuel, 1664; both died early; Mehitable, 1668; Abigail, 1670; Catharine again, 1672; John, 1673, died at 2 years; Mary, 1675; Anderson, 1680; and Henry, 1681. He was freeman, 1677; artillery co. 1680, its captain 1685; represent. 1683-6, of the Committee of Safety on the revolut. against Andros, named in the new charter of the Council, but by popular vote chosen before and so continued to 1716; col. of the milit.; treas. of the Prov.; judge of the County Ct.; and such services were successiv. enjoyed by him. His wife died 1699, aged 59; and soon after he became husband of Sarah, daughter of John Stedman, of Cambridge, who had successiv. been wid. of John Brackett, Samuel Alcock, and Thomas Graves; and she outlived him, though he did not die until 1726, aged 93 years, 9 months.

PHILLIPS, JOHN, Marshfield; married, 1677, Ann Torry.

PHILLIPS, JOHN, Lynn; may have been son of Charles of the same; by wife Hannah had John, born 1689, and Hannah, 1694; and he died soon after. Lewis says others of this family, perhaps earlier, had settled at Lynn.

PHILLIPS, JOHN, Charlestown; son of Col. John, Savage thinks bapt. Anderson; was a mariner; married 1694, Mary, daughter of Samuel Hayman; had Samuel, born 1695, died.soon; John, 1697; Samuel again, 1699. His wife died 1702, and he married soon after Ann, daughter of Col. Joseph Lynde, widow of Isaac Greenwood; had Abigail, born 1712, died young; Anderson, 1715; and Abigail, again, 1716.

PHILLIPS, JOSEPH, Newtown, L. I., 1686; then named by Gov. Dongan, in his grant of chart., but he had been a freeholder there for 20 days (Riker.) He may have been brother of Theophilus, but who shall discover their father will be fortunate.

PHILLIPS, JOSEPH, Providence; took oath of alleg. 1682.

PHILLIPS, JOSEPH, Boston; by wife Bridget had Joseph, born 1684; Benjamin, 1685; and Nathaniel, 1689; perhaps others.

PHILLIPS, MARTIN, Medfield, 1664.

PHILLIPS, NICHOLAS, Dedham, 1638; brother of Henry; removed to Weymouth perhaps late in life; freeman 1640; had Experience, born 1641; Caleb, 1644; was deacon, and died 1672. His will of 1671, probated 1672, makes Richard, his eldest son, excr., but wishes brother Henry to act as overseer; divides estate to his children Richard, Joshua, and Benjamin, Alice or Eliz. Shaw, Experience King, Hannah White and Abigail P.

PHILLIPS, NICHOLAS, Boston; married, 1651, Hannah Salter; had Elizabeth, born 1653; Hannah, 1654; Nicholas, 1657, died soon after; Nicholas, again, 1660; Abigail, 1662; Sarah, 1665; and Thomas, 1667. He died, thinks Savage, in 1670, for Hannah, his widow, renders inv. about that time. He seems to have been a storekeeper.

PHILLIPS, NICHOLAS, Boston; butcher; by wife Phillipa had Nicholas, born 1665; John, 1667, died soon; John, again, 1669; Joseph and Benjamin, twins, 1671; and Mary, 1674.

PHILLIPS, PHILIP, Boston; may be that youth of 15 from Olney, Co. Bucks, arriving in the Hopewell, Capt. Bundock, 1635, servant to John Cooper, who set down prob. at Lynn, and went to L. I. Had by wife Rachel at B. Susanna, who died 1651; Susanna, who died 1656; and David, born 1660, died 1669, and admin. was given the month following to William Dennison, of Milton, in behalf of the eldest son John and two other sons, born before he came to Boston.

PHILLIPS, SAMUEL, Taunton; married, 1676, a widow Cobb; had Mehitable, born next year.

PHILLIPS, SAMUEL, Rowley; son of first George, born in England, 1625, at Boxted, in Essex, if Prince, II, 45, seems better authority, as usual, than Mather, who calls it Boxford; Harvard Col. 1651, ordained 1652; colleague with Ezekiel Rogers; married same year, Sarah, daughter Samuel Appleton, of Ipswich; had Samuel, born 1654, died young; Sarah, 1656, who married Stephen Mighill; Samuel, again, 1658; George, 1659; Eliz., 1661; Ezekiel 1663; all three died soon. George, again, 1664; H. C., 1686; Eliz., 1665, who married, 1683, Rev. Edward Payson, and died 1724; Dorcas, 1667; Mary, 1668; and John, 1670. The last three also died young. He died 1696, and his widow died 1713, aged 85.

PHILLIPS, SAMUEL, Boston, 1681; distinguish as a bookseller in Thomas' Hist. of Print., II, 411, and John Dunton, in the curious book of his Life and Errors; married Hannah, daughter of Capt. Benjamin Gillam; had Hannah, born 1682; Gillam, 1686; Faith; Samuel, 1693; Ann, 1701; and Henry, 1706, prob. H. C., 1724; and he died 1720, aged 58. Hannah, the eldest child, married, 1700, David Anderson, of Charlestown, and next, 1703, Habijah Savage, of Boston; Gillam married Mary Faneuil; Faith married, 1710, Arthur Savage; Samuel was drowned near home, on return from London; Ann married Peter Butler; and Henry died 1729, at Rochelle, in France; confident. thought to be that unhappy man who killed his intimate companion, Benjamin Woodbridge, on Boston Common, in a private duel.

PHILLIPS, SAMUEL, Boston; by wife Sarah had Sarah, born 1682; Ann, 1685; William, 1688; and Bridget, 1692.

PHILLIPS, THEOPHILUS, Newtown, L. I., 1672; had prob. been several years on the island, perhaps as early as 1663; grandson of Rev. George, as Riker thought, but who could be his father. Married Ann, daughter of Ralph Hunt; had Theophilus, born 1673; William, 1676; and Philip, 1678. Riker says he had two more wives, but he names no issue. He was a very useful man; in 1676 chosen to one town office, and next year town clerk, to his death 1689. To Savage it seems highly prob. that he was son of Rev. George, the first, but Riker, 105, supposes him grandson.

PHILLIPS, THOMAS, Pemaquid, 1674; and perhaps his son of the same name, there took oath of fidelity; or one may have been brother, another son, of William.

PHILLIPS, THOMAS, Boston; perhaps son of Nicholas of the same; by wife Hannah had Hannah, born 1690.

PHILLIPS, WALTER, Wiscasset, 1661; born, it is said, about 1619; was at Salem 1689; perhaps driven from the east by the Indian hostilities. Is called senior when made freeman 1690; residing at the village now Danvers, and was living 1700.

PHILLIPS, WILLIAM, Taunton, 1643; and prob. some years earlier, as he was among purch. 1637; in his will, 1654, calls himself "threescore years and ten at the least;" out of his small estate gives wife Eliz. and son James, who was excr., but if he died without issue, then to children of his daughter Eliz., wife of James Walker. Baylies, II, 267, 282; and General Reg., V, 260, comp. with VI, 93 and 95.

PHILLIPS, WILLIAM, Hartford, 1639; perhaps earlier, but not an original paper.; died after 1653, leaving widow Ann, but no children, as is thought. Without doubt she or husband was relat. of famous Hooker.

PHILLIPS, WILLIAM, Charlestown; with wife Mary adm. of the church, 1639; freeman 1640; had Phebe, born 1640; Nathaniel, 1642; Mary, 1644. His wife died 1646; and he removed to Boston; married Susanna, widow of Christopher Stanley, and by her, who died 1655, had there prob. William, Eliz., and Sarah.

PHILLIPS, WILLIAM, Boston; a mariner, called jr. to distinguish him from the preceding, though prob. not son; married, 1650, Martha Franklin; had William, born 1652, who may have died young, and Martha, 1654. Prob. his wife died before long, and by another wife, Joan, he may have had William, again, 1671, who was a butcher; and by the same or another, William, of Boston, possibly son of the next but last preceding; by wife Deborah had William, born 1690; and Sarah, 1692.

PHILLIPS, ZECHARIAH, Boston; artillery co., 1660; by wife Eliz. had (if we accept the truth of the record) Zechariah, who died Sept. 2, 1652; Zechariah, who died Sept. 4, 1652; Zechariah, again, who died 1654; Zechariah, again, born 1657, died young; Eliz., 1661; Sarah, 1662; Zechariah, again, 1664; Joseph, 1669; and Hannah, 1671. He was killed by the Indians, 1675, when the party under Capt. Edward Hutchinson, going by appointment to treat about peace, was treacherously cut off.

PHILLIPS, ZAROBABEL, Southampton, L. I., 1663-73; Savage judges to be the eldest son by sond wife of George the first, though family geneal. does not indicate his residence, nor give anything but the birth. He married at S. Ann, widow of John White, who had been of Lynn before the settlers came there. Savage states that he once presumed that the two uncles, Zarobabel and Theophilus, being of L. I., drew thither Rev. George, their nephew, but some facts appear irreconcil. with this presumption.

REFERENCES:—Ballou's Hist. of Milford, 965; Barry's Framingham, 358; Berkshire Co. Hist. Soc. Coll., I; Bond's Hist. of Watertown, 904; Butler's Hist. of Groton, 426; Jameson's Hist. Medway, 511; Mitchell's Hist. Bridgewater, 270; Paige's Hist. Cambridge, 627; Pierce's Hist. Grafton, 543-6; Stearn's Hist. Ashburnham, 848-51; Stowe's Hist. Hubbardston, 332; Winsor's Hist. Duxbury, 291; Wyman's Charlestown Gens., 740-8; Davis' Landmarks of Plymouth, 204-7; Boston *Daily Advertiser*, Ap. 15 (1878).

Other Publications:—American Ancestry, II, 94, 95; III, 40, 213; IV, 205; V, 30; VI, 66, 137; VII, 118; VIII, 43, 228; IX, 72, 165; Austin's R. I. Gen. Dict., 152; Austin's Allied Fams., 198; Banger, Me., Hist. Mag., V, 170-1; Binney Gen., 25; Bauton Gen., 240-2; Bridgeman's Granary Burial, 275-7; Buckingham Gen., 27; Cooley's Trenton, N. J., Gens., 181-92; Corliss' No. Yarmouth, Me.; Dwight Gen., 101; Ellis Gen., 99-104, 377-83; Essex Inst. Hist. Coll., XXIII, 134; French's Hist. Turner, Me., 55; Hayward's Hist. Gilsum, N. H., 375; Jackson Gen., 132, 144-7; Jameson's Hist. Medway, Mass., 511; Leonard's Hist. Dublin, N. H., 380; Meade's Old Fams. of Va., II, 482; Morton's N. E. Memoir, 457; N. E. Hist. Gen. Reg., VI, 273; XV, 279; Norton's Hist. Fitzwilliam, N. H., 667-70; Ormsby Gen., 28-32, 37-40; Pearson's Schenectady, N. Y., Sett., 141; Phillips' Chart, by Hoyt (1887) 18x24 in.; P. Gen. (1885) 233 pp.; Phoenix and Phillips Chart (1875) 1x2½ ft.; Roe's Sketches of Rose, N. Y., 163; Salisbury Gen., II, 563-610; Savage's Gen. Dict., III, 409-17; Taylor's Mem. Hon. Samuel Phillips, 345-7; Thompson's L. I., N. Y., II, 459-61; Updyke's Narragansett Churches, 120; Wentworth Gen., I, 203; Whitman Gen., 143; Williams' Hist. of Danbury, Vt., 224-8.

PHILPOT:—Thomas, Watertown, 1642; fell insane 1647, but lived at Salem 1668; well enough to petitn. against taxes, and was, says Bond, a pauper in 1674.

PHILPOT, WILLIAM, Boston, 1645; called saltmaker, married, 1651, Ann, widow of George Hunn.

REFERENCE:—Wentworth Gen., I, 453.

PHINNEY, FINNEY, or FENNYE:—Isaac Phinney, Medfield, 1657.

PHINNEY, JOHN, Plymouth; by wife Christian, who died 1649, had John, born 1638, and perhaps others; removed to Barnstable; married, 1650, Abigail, widow of Henry Coggin, who died 1653; and for third wife, 1654, Eliz. Bayley, had Jonathan, 1655; Robert, 1656; Hannah, 1657; Eliz., 1659; Josiah, 1661; Jeremiah, 1662; and Joshua, 1665. Hannah married the second Ephraim Morton.

PHINNEY, ROBERT, Plymouth; prob. brother of John the first, and perhaps elder, came with his mother, supposes Savage; married, 1641, Phebe Ripley; was deacon 1667, and died 1688, near 80; and his widow died 1710, "suppos. 92 years old."

REFERENCES:—Freeman's Cape Cod, 333; Hudson's Hist. Lexington, Mass., 179-81; Machias, Me., Centen., 172; Mitchell's Hist. Bridgewater, Mass., 271; Nash Gen., 120; New Eng. Hist. Gen. Reg., III, 274; Paige's Hist. Hardwick, Mass., 453; Pierce's Hist. Gorham, Me., 198-200; Ridlon's Harrison, Me., Settlers, 100-2; Savage's Gen. Dict., III, 417; Swift's Barnstable Families, II, 225-7.

PHIPPEN, FITZPEN, FIPPENNY, or PHIP-PENNEY:—David, Hingham, 1635; was from Weymouth or Melcombe Regis in Co. Dorset, and son of Robert, perhaps brother of George, the rector of St.

Mary's, Truro, who in that church set up a tablet in honor of his oldest brother Owen, for rescuing himself with great boldness from slavery, after seven years' service in an Algerine corsair, and died 1637, as may be read in the volume of Cornwall in Lyson's Magna Britannia. He brought wife Sarah, children Joseph, Rebecca, Benjamin, Gamaliel, Sarah, and George; and here had John, born 1637, died soon; John, again, 1640, died soon; was freemaan 1636; removed to Boston, 1641, and died before 1650, when his will was probated. His widow married George Hull, of Fairfield. Rebecca married George Vickary; the other daughter married Thomas. Yeo. Geneal. Reg., VII, 233, has abstract of his will. Whether Judith, a maid of 16, who came in the Planter 1635, from Stepney Parish, London, were a relative is not to be suggest. with any ground of conjecture.

PHIPPEN, JOSEPH, Hingham, 1637; son of David; prob. the eldest born in England, married Dorcas Wood, had a child buried 1642; Joseph, bapt. 1642; Mary, 1644; removed to Boston and was made freeman that year; had Sarah, born 1645; David, 1647; Samuel, 1649; and Eliz., 1652, died next year. He had been a year or two before at Falmouth very active, constable 1661, yet in 1658 had a quarrel at Scarborough with Foxwell; and was represent., but settled 1665 at Salem, where he was in good repute; made his will 1687, in which his wife and five children are named, and died soon after. Willis, I, 140. His daughter Sarah married, 1669, George Hodges, of Salem; and had Sarah, as in Essex Inst., II, 151.

PHIPPEN, THOMAS, Salem; son of Benjamin prob., or perhaps of the second David, though less likely; married Mary, eldest daughter of Timothy Tindall. One Judith P., aged 16, came in the Planter from London, 1635, with James Hayward, who married her. Both were servants of Nicholas Davis, of Charlestown.

REFERENCES:—Driver Gen., 89; Phippen Gen. (1868); Pickering Gen.; Savage's Gen. Dict., III, 418.

PHIPS, or, in modern days, PHIPPS:—James, from Bristol, Eng., a gunsmith, set down near the mouth of the Kennebeck River before 1649, having had very many children by the same wife—21 sons and 5 daughters in all, if credulity be sufficiently dilated to embrace the story; one of the youngest, the celebrated Sir William (equival. to all the sons in the opinion of his biographer), being born 1651.

PHIPS, JOHN, Reading; by Eaton classed among the earliest settlers.

PHIPS, SOLOMON, Charlestown, 1641; carpenter; was admitted of the church and made freeman in 1642; by wife Eliz. had Eliz., born 1643; Solomon; Samuel, Harvard Col., 1671; Mehitable, who died 1657; Mehitable, again, 1659; Joseph, bapt. 1661; and perhaps others; died 1671, aged 52. His will of 1670 makes Eliz. extrix. provides for the son Samuel at college, Solomon, and Joseph, besides daughters Eliz., Ray and her child, daughter Mary, meaning perhaps Solomon's wife and her children, yet unbapt. The widow died 1688.

REFERENCES:—Ballou's Milford, Mass., 966-8; Bangor, Me., Hist. Mag., V, 9; Chandler's Hist. Shirley, Mass., 603; Hamden, Ct., Hist., 277; Paige's Hist. Cambridge, Mass., 627; Tuttle Gen., 190-2, 197; Wyman's Charlestown, Mass., II, 749-55; Heraldic Journal, I, 152-4; Morse's Gen. Sherborn, Mass., 195-202; Savage's Gen. Dict. III, 419-22.

PICKARD:—John Pickard, Rowley, 1645; married Jane Crosby; had John, born 1653; Samuel, 1663, and three, or by another story, six daughters; was represent. 1661 and 1695, unless this last year belongs to his son, and died 1697, aged 75. His widow died 1716, aged 89. Mary, one of his daughters, married, 1671, John Pearson, the second.

REFERENCES:—Essex Inst. Hist. Coll., XXIII, 135-9; Gage's Hist. Rowley, Mass., 451; Little Gen., 442-4; Temple's Hist. N. Brookfield, Mass., 705.

PICKE:—John, Cambridge; by wife Mary had Abigail, born 1642. Perhaps it is spelt otherwise in some places.

PICKERMAN, or PICKRAM:—George, Watertown; prob. son of John; brought by his father from England 1630; united with his widow mother Esther, 1646, in sale of estate.

PICKERAM, JOHN, Watertown; died 1630. He prob. came in the fleet with Winthrop; had by wife Esther, son, George, besides John, who was buried 1639, and daughter Joan, who died 3 days after her father. None of this name is found in div. of Shawshin lands 1652, among people of Cambridge and W. May be same as Pickering.

PICKERING:—John, Ipswich, 1634; a carpenter; removed to Salem 1637, had there grant of land; by wife Eliz. had John, prob. born that year; Jonathan, 1639; Eliz., 1644, died soon; and Eliz., again, 1645, prob. died young; and he died 1655 or 1657.

PICKERING, JOHN, Portsmouth, 1635; perhaps had been as early as 1630; may have removed to Cambridge; by wife Mary had Lydia, born 1638; removed to Portsmouth, prob. there died, 1669; but one of this name is claimed by Lewis for his town of Lynn, 1639, who, if transient resident may be either of first two.

REFERENCES:—Amer. Ancest., I, 62; IV, 94; VI, 63; Ballou's Hist. of Milford, Mass., 968; Bassett's Hist. Richmond, N. H., 463-7; Brewster's Portsmouth, II, 49-52, 103-6; Chapman's Weeks Gen., 151; Driver Gen., 295; Hayward's Hist. Gilsum, N. H., 376; Pickering Gen. (1884), 36 p.; (1884), 28 p.; (1887), 2 vols.; Savage's Gen. Dict., III, 422.

PICKES:—John, Piscataqua, i.e., prob. Dover or Kittery, 1640; but Mr. Judd, on examin. of the original, presum. the name to intend Pike.

PICKET:—Christopher, Boston; in that part called Muddy riv., now Brookline; married, 1647, Eliz. Stow, daughter of John; had John, born 1657; was living at B. 1661; and 1675 at Scarborough; prob. a soldier; witness to nuncup. will of Arthur Alger.

PICKET, JOHN, Salem, 1648; had John, James, Thomas, and Sarah, in Nov. of that year, bapt. together; Rebecca, 1650; and Daniel, 1652. He removed, 1660, to Stratford; there was constable, 1667, one of the selectmen 1669, and represent. 1673 and 1675. His wife Margaret died 1683, and he died soon after. Sarah married, 1665, Robert Lane, of S.; and Rebecca married, 1673, James Sention, of Norwalk.

PICKET, JOHN, of Boston, whose son John, by wife Eliz., died 1657, may be the same as the preceding.

PICKET, JOHN, New London; married Ruth, daughter of Jonathan Brewster; had Mary, Ruth, William; John, born 1656; Adam, 1658; and Mercy, 1661. He was an active merchant, had good estate, and died 1667. His widow married Charles Hill, who, in 1670, obtained from the Col. confirmat. of a grant of 600 acres, made by Uncas to P.; Mary married, 1672, Benjamin Shapley; Ruth married Rev. Moses Noyes, of Lyme; and Mercy married, 1682, Samuel Fosdick, and next, John Arnold. Boyd's Conesus, N. Y., 168; Orcutt's Hist. New Mil-

ford, Ct., 751; Orcutt's Hist. Stratford, Ct., 1268; Savage's Gen. Dict., III, 423; Stiles' Hist. Windsor, Ct., II, 607.

PICKLES:—Jonas, Scituate, 1650; married, 1657, Alice, daughter of William Hatch; had Jonas, 1659; Mary, 1660; Nathan, 1661; Lydia, 1662; and Jonas, 1663; next year he died suddenly.

PICKMAN, often written PITMAN:—Nathaniel, Salem, 1654; came from Bristol with wife Tabitha, and Mary, beside Bethia, who all married; the last, 1673, with John Silsbee; Mary, 1665, with Robert Hodges, and Tabitha, 1664, with Edmund Feveryear; had sons Benjamin, Nathaniel, Samuel, and William.

REFERENCES:—Heraldic Journal, II, 26; Vinton's Giles Gen., 330.

PICKTON:—Thomas, Salem; had, says Felt, grant of land 1639, was on Beverly side; by will gave all his estate to wife Ann, who died 1683, aged 83.

PICKWORTH:—Amariah, Salem; had, says very good authority, daughter Rachel, who married the second John Sibley; but Savage feels "no little degre of hesitation because the first John S. married Rachel Pickworth, as is said."

PICKWORTH, JOHN, Salem, 1637; had gone from some part of the bay to Plymouth, 1631; got a wife and went back, says Gov. Bradford, in letter, 1632. His wife Ann joined the church 1638, and had bapt. Ruth, Hannah, and John that year; Samuel; Joseph, 1643; Rachel, 1646; Benjamin, 1648; Sarah, 1650; Abigail, 1652; and Jacob, 1654. He had grant of land at New London, 1651, but forfeit. for non-residence. Ruth married Nathaniel Masters; Rachel married John Sibley; and Sarah married Joseph Mazury.

PICKWORTH, ELIAS, of Beverly, 1687; may have been another son, or perhaps a grandson.

REFERENCE:—Savage's Gen. Dict., III, 425.

PID:—Richard; freeman of Mass., 1642; is wholly unknown to Savage.

PIDDELL:—Corbitt, of Conn.; as strange a name as the preceding, had a suit in court 1649.

PIDCOCK, or PIDCOKE:—George, Scituate; married, 1640, Sarah Richards, who lived 1670; and Deane, 324, says no family is heard of.

PIDGE:—See Pigg.

PIERCE, PEARSE, PEARS, PEIRSE, or PEARCE:—Abraham, Plymouth, 1629; had shared in division of cattle that year, of Duxbury, 1643; was a propr. of Bridgewater, 1645; by wife Rebecca had Abraham, born 1638; Isaac; and three daughters, of whom Alice was bapt. at Barnstable, 1650, and died at D. 1673. Haz., I, 326; Baylies, II., 254.

PIERCE, AZERIKAM, or AZRAKIM, Warwick; is supposed to have come in fgrom Rehoboth, or Swanzey; had children Samuel and Tabitha, perhaps others.

PIERCE, BENJAMIN, Woburn; son perhaps of Robert, more prob. of Thomas of the same; by wife Mary had Benjamin, born 1689; Mary, 1692; Esther, 1696; Rebecca, 1698; Deborah, 1700; Thomas, 1702; and Zurishaddai, 1705.

PIERCE, DANIEL, Watertown; blacksmith; came in the Elizabeth from Ipswich, Co. Suffolk (but called of London by Coffin), 1634, aged 23; freeman 1638; removed to Newbury; by wife Sarah had Daniel, born 1642; Joshua, 1643; and Martha, 1648. He swore fidelity 1652, and married, 1654, Ann, perhaps widow of Thomas Millerd, and died 1677, leaving good estate.

His widow died 1690; and his daughter married perhaps a Thorpe.

PIERCE, DAVID, Dorchester; freeman 1636; but Mr. Paige, in his very careful list, General. Reg. III, 94, reads it Price.

PIERCE, EDWARD, Watertown, 1639; says Bond, who thinks he went to Wethersfield, but nothing certain is known of the man.

PIERCE, EPHRAIM, Weymouth; perhaps son of Michael; by wife Hannah, daughter of John Holbrook of the same, had Azrikam, born 1672; probably Ephraim; and perhaps others.

PIERCE, GEORGE, Boston; a smith; married Mary, daughter of Richard Woodhouse; had Mary, born 1660, and he died 1661.

PIERCE, GEORGE, Portsmouth, R. I.; married, 1687, Alice, daughter of Richard Hart; had Susanna, born 1688; and perhaps more.

PIERCE, GILES, Greenwich, R. I., 1687.

PIERCE, ISAAC, Boston; tailor; married Grace, daughter of Lewis Tucker, of Casco.

PIERCE, JAMES, Boston; killed in youth by lightning, at Plymouth, 1660.

PIERCE, JOHN, the patentee under the Pres. and Counc. of N. E., 1620-3, though connected with the pilgr. of Plymouth, never came, thinks Savage, to this shore, yet Willis seems contra., I, 13.

PIERCE, JOHN, Dorchester; came perhaps, in the Mary and John, 1630, or in the Lion, 1631; is called mariner, from Stepney, one of the modern London parishes; freeman 1631; by wife Parnell had Joseph, born 1631; Abia, 1633; John, 1635, died soon; Nehemiah, 1637, died 39; and his wife died same month. He was Selectman 1636 and 1641, rep. 1639; removed, 1642, to Boston; married sec. wife 1654, Rebecca, widow of Thomas Wheeler, and died 1661.

PIERCE, JOHN, Watertown; freeman 1638; a man of very good estate, projected settlement at Sudbury and Lancaster, died 1661; in his will provides for wife Eliz., eldest son Anthony, and other children without naming; but his widow, in her will of 1667, when she died, aged 79, supplies the deficiency, naming children Anthony, John, Robert, Esther Morse, wife of Joseph, Mary Coldam, whose husband Savage knows not, besides grandch. Mary Ball, and another Ball, Esther Morse, and the children of Anthony and Robert. He had also daughter Eliz., who married, 1655, Francis Wyman, but she died before her father.

PIERCE, JOHN, Boston; by wife Eliz. had John and Eliz., twins, born 1643; and of him nothing more is known, unless he may be that man called John Peirse, to whose four children John Mills, of Boston, in his will of 1651, made gift.

PIERCE, JOHN, Woburn; probably son of John of Watertown, and born in England; had John, born 1644; Joseph, 1646; and Thomas, 1649; perhaps others before or after; was freeman in April and rep. May, 1690.

PIERCE, JOHN, Gloucester; husbandman; freeman 1651; married, 1643, wife Eliz.; had Mary, born 1650; and John, 1653; his wife died 1673, and he married, two months after, Jane Stanwood, and died 1695. His widow died 1706.

PIERCE, JOHN, Hartford, 1640; a youth who prob. removed soon. John, Charlestown, 1652, may have removed to Kittery, and died 1673, leaving widow Elinor.

PIERCE, JOHN; Boston; a mariner, in 1654, was perhaps he who married, 1656, Ruth, daughter of Nathaniel Bishop; had Hannah, born 1660; may have been admitted an inhabitant 1657. Another John, of Boston,

perhaps by wife Isabel, had Samuel, born 1660; and died 1661.

PIERCE, JOHN, Sudbury; perhaps brother of Anthony; had wife Eliz., who died 1655. One John, a weaver, came from Norwich, Co. Norfolk, 1637, aged 49, with wife Eliz., 36, and four children, John, Barbara, Eliz., and Judith, and one servant, John Gedney, 19; may have been this Sudbury man or not as the commonness of thename prevents distinct.

PIERCE, JOHN, Woburn; son, perhaps eldest, of John of the same; married, 1663, Deborah, daughter of James Converse; had Deborah, born 1666; John, 1671; Thomas, 1672; James, 1674, died at 11 years; Daniel, 1676; James, again, 1686; and Joseph, 1688.

PIERCE, JOHN, Salem, 1675; was then chosen lieut. of Capt. Gardner's comp., of whom, therefore, more ought to be known. Felt, II, 497.

PIERCE, JOHN, Boston, 1670; a bricklayer; a daughter of his had married William Talmage.

PIERCE, JOHN, Springfield; married, 1677, Lydia, daughter of Miles Morgan; had Nathaniel, born 1679; John, 1683; Jonathan; removed to Enfield; there had Lydia, 1693, and he died 1696, leaving the widow and these children.

PIERCE, JOHN, York, 1680; took oath of allegiance next year; had several years before married Phebe Nash, widow of Isaac.

PIERCE, JOHN, Woodbury; by Cothren suppos. to be son of John, of Wethersfield, yet who it was is not mentioned; married the defraud. orphan Ann, sister of John Hathwit; had John, bapt. 1683; and Eliz., 1685; and he died 1731.

PIERCE, LAUNCELOT, Pegypscot; married a daughter of Thomas Stephens; had William. Willis, I, 163.

PIERCE, MARK, Cambridge, 1642; removed next year to New Haven.

PIERCE, MARMADUKE, Salem, 1639; charged with killing his apprentice. See Winthrop, I, 318-9, where the surname seems Percy or Perry. He came 1637 from Sandwich, in Kent, with wife Mary and a servant. In Boys' Hist. of Sandwich, p. 752, it is spelled Peerce, and in Felt, I, 169, Percie, but in Ib., II, 458, Pierce.

PIERCE, MICHAEL, Hingham, 1646; had there bapt. that year Persis; other children were Benjamin, John, Ephraim, Eliz., Deborah, Ann, Abia, and Ruth, all named in his will, besides prob. Abigail, born 1662, when his wife died. Soon after he removed to Scituate, took second wife, Ann, was a captain of great bravery in command of 50 English and 20 friendly Indians from Cape Cod, in Philip's War, and was, with most of them, killed 1676, at Pawtucket fight in Rehoboth. Deane, 122, 325.

PIERCE, NEHEMIAH, Boston, 1661; a cooper; artillery co. 1671; married, perhaps second wife, 1684, Ann, widow of Capt. Samuel Mosely, eldest daughter of Isaac Addington, and died 1691.

PIERCE, RICHARD, Portsmouth, R. I., had perhaps other children beside that Susanna, who married, 1673, George Brownell.

PIERCE, RICHARD, Pemaquid; a carpenter; Savage thinks he is that man to whom, in 1642, an Indian Sagamore made large grant of lands and islands, as may be seen in Geneal. Reg., XIII, 365; took oath of fidelity 1674.

PIERCE, RICHARD, Boston; printer; married, 1680, Sarah, daughter of Rev. Seaborn Cotton. Thomas Hist., I, 282. For Benj. Harris, bookseller, he pub., 1690, the *first* number of a newspaper, of which the *second* never appeared. See Felt, II, 14.

PIERCE, ROBERT, Dorchester, perhaps 1630, but not very likely; may have been brother of John, the mariner; by wife Ann, daughter of John Greenway, had Deborah, born 1640, died in few weeks; was freeman 1642, and died 1665, leaving only son Thomas, and Mary, who married Thomas Herring, not (as often said) Haven, of Dedham; and his widow died 1695, "the oldest person that ever lived in D.," says the Hist., 261, aged "about 104 years."

PIERCE, ROBERT, Ipswich; married Abigail, daughter of Mark Symonds, of the same.

PIERCE, ROBERT, Charlestown; married, 1657, Sarah Eyre.

SAMUEL PIERCE, Malden, whose wife's name is not found, had Mary, born 1656; Thomas, 1658; John, and perhaps Joseph, 1659; of whom John died very soon; and Eliz. 1666; probably more, for Savage supposes him to have removed to Charlestown, and may be person whose wife Mary joined the C. Church 1670, and brought to bapt. Samuel, Thomas, Joseph, Jonathan, John, Mary, Eliz. and Persis, all 1670; Abigail, 1670; Hannah, 1671; and Benjamin, 1675.

PIERCE, THOMAS, Charlestown, 1634, freeman, 1635; by wife, Eliz., had Abigail, bapt. 1639, unless she were child of another Thomas, as seems not unlikely, for no other is ascribed to this one, who died 1666; in his will mentions his age as 82 years, his wife Eliz. 71, son John, Randall, Nichols, besides grandch. Mary Bridge and Eliz. Tufts; and gave legacy to the college. His widow, Eliz., mother of Mary, wife of Peter Tuffts, was perhaps his second wife.

PIERCE, THOMAS, Woburn; 1643, may not improb. seem to be son of preceding, born in Eng., living first at Charlestown, and may have been father of that Abigail; but at W. had John, born 1644, died prob. soon; Thomas, 1645; Eliz. 1646; Joseph, 1648, died soon; Joseph, again; 1649; Stephen, 1651; Samuel, 1654, died at two years; Samuel, again, 1656; William, 1658; James, 1659; and Abigail, 1660. He was freeman in 1677 and that year sold land in Charlestown. Thomas, father of Stephen, could not be, as the biogr. supposes, the same Thomas that died 1666, aged 83 years.

PIERCE, THOMAS, Setauket, L. I., 1661, had that year a commiss. as a magistrate of Conn.

PIERCE, THOMAS, Gloucester; had wife Ann, who died 1668; perhaps daughter Eliz. died 1673.

PIERCE, WILLIAM, Boston; a distinguished shipmaster, made more voyages than any other person in the same years to and from Boston, was killed by the Spaniards at Providence in the Bahamas, 1641. Winthrop, II, 33. Prince says in Ann., II, 69, he was ancestor of Rev. James, a distinguished theologian of Exeter, Eng., who died 1730.

PIERCE, WILLIAM, Boston; came in the Griffin, arrived 1633, with Cotton, Hooker, Gov. Haynes, and other churchmen; was freeman, often a selectman, died 1661. He had early married Sarah, daughter of William Colbron; had daughter Sarah, named Sarah Colpit in the will of her grandf. But name may be wrong; at least such a name is not known in Boston. See the note in Winthrop, I, 109.

PIERCE, WILLIAM, Barnstable; 1643.

PIERCE, WILLIAM, Bost.; 1653, a mariner, died 1669, leaving small prop. to his widow. By wife Esther, supposes Savage, he had Mary, born 1656; Martha and Mary, twins, 1659.

PIERCE, WILLIAM, Falmouth; 1680, in the second destruction of the town, 1690, removed to Milton. Willis, I, 163.

PIERCE, WILLIAM, Suffield; married, 1688, Esther Spencer; had Thomas, born 1688.

PIERCE, WILLIAM, Woburn; perhaps son of Thos. of the same; married, 1690, Abigail Somers, alias Warren.

REFERENCES.

MASSACHUSETTS.—Ballou's Hist., Milford, 969-71; Bond's Watertown, 393-9, 869-71; Davis's Landmark of Plymouth, 206-8; Deane's Hist. Scituate, 325; Draper's Hist. Spencer, 246; Hudson's Hist. Lexington, 181-5; Hyde's Hist. Brimfield, 446; Judd's Hist. Hadley, 552; Mitchell's Hist. Bridgewater, 272; Pierce's Hist. Grafton, 540-3; Sewall's Hist. Woburn, 628; Stowe's Hist. Hubbardston, 333; Whitmore's Copps Hill Epitaphs; Wyman's Charlestown Gens., II, 756-62.

NEW HAMPSHIRE.— Blood's Hist. Temple, 239; Brewster's Portsmouth , II, 359-62; Cochrane's Hist. Antrim, 645; Cutter's Hist. Jaffray, 420-8; Dow's His-t. Hampton, 927; Hayward's Hist. Hancock, 807-9; Livermore's Hist. Wilton, 469; Norton's Hist. Fitzwilliam, 670; Read's Hist. Swanzey, 420; Smith's Hist. Peterborough, 226; Worcester's Hist. Hollis, N. H., 384.

OTHER PUBLICATIONS.

Am. Ancestry, I, 62; II, 95; III, 93; IX, 95; Austin's R. I. Gen. Dict., 153; Blake Gen., 46, 62-9; Cleveland's Hist. Yates Co., N. Y., 591; Cothren's Hist. of Woodbury, Ct., 669-72; Eaton's Hist. Thomaston, Me., II, 358; Gold's Hist. Cornwall, Ct., 244; Memenway's Vermont Gaz., V, 101; Hubbard's Stanstead Co., Canada, 128-31; Lapham's Hist. Norway, Me., 576; Locke gen., 32, 56, 86-9, 317-20; Loomis Gen. Female Branches, 535; Meade's Old Families of Va.; New Eng. Hist. Gen. Reg., VI, 276-9; XXI, 61-5; 157-62, 257-64, 340-50; XXII, 73-9, 17485; XXIX, 273-81; Pierce Gen. (1864) 5 p. (1870), 490 p. (1882), 376 p. (1889) 441 p.; Pope Gen., 316-8; Power's Hist. Sangamon Co., Ills., 571; Rhode Island Hist. Mag., V, 70-8; Savage's Gen. Dict., III, 426-32; Smith's Hist. Dutchess Co., N. Y., 498; Spooner's Mem. W. Spooner, 109; Stiles' Hist. Windsor, Ct., II, 607; Walker Gen., 206; Whitcomb and Pierce Gen. (1888) 23 p.; Whitehead's Hist. Perth Amboy, N. J., 359.

PIERPONT:—James, Ipswich; had wife Margaret, left sons John and Robert whom he brought from England.

PIERPONT, ROBERT, Ipswich, 1648; brother prob. of James, may, supposes Savage, be regarded as father of that Robert of I. who was admitted freeman 1676.

REFERENCES:—Am. Ancestry, V, 89; VII, 249; Darling Mem., 40-4; Ellis' Hist. Roxbury, Mass., 126; Hamden, Ct. Hist., 266; Pierpont Gen. (1868) 23 p.; Savage's Gen. Dict., III, 432; Tuttle Gen., 695-8; Walworth's Hyde Gen., 298-304, 307-9.

PIERSON, PEARSON, PORSUNE, or PERSON:—Abraham, Branford, was of Yorkshire, came to Boston 1640, joined the church that year, when he is called "a studient," of which we may doubt the meaning, as we know he was bred at Trinity Coll., Cambridge, where he took his A.B. 1632, and he is in Mather's first Classis as a minister before coming over, though this may well seem incorrect; became minister of the church gathering in Lynn, 1640, to go to sett. at Southampton, L. I.; thence about 1647 went to Branford, and thence in the autumn of 1667, with a part of his congregation, to Newark, N. J. See his letter to John Winthrop, 3 Mass. Hist. Coll., X, 69 and 84. He had Abraham, born at Lynn 1641, H. C. 1668; Thomas, John, and Abigail, before his remov. from S., and at B. were born Grace, 1650; Susanna, 1652; Rebecca, 1654; and Theophilus, 1659; beside Isaac, and Mary. He died 1678.

PIERSON, BARTHOLOMEW, Watertown, 1639; by wife Ursula, written Azlee, Uzlah, Uzlee in the records, had Bartholomew, born 1670, died soon; Bartholomew again, 1642, died in few months; Martha, 1653; perhaps Mary; Jonathan, 1648; Joseph, 1650; Sarah, 1653; and Bartholomew, again, who died in few years. In 1648 he was made freeman, spelling Porsune in the records, and in 1653 he removed to Woburn; was selectman 1665 and 1666, and died 1687. His widow died 1694.

PIERSON, HENRY, Hempstead, L. I., 1686.

PIERSON, HUGH, Watertown, 1649, had, in 1654, wife Alice and daughter Ruth, then 9 years old; and he died 1675, very poor, as he had lived.

PIERSON, JOHN, Middletown, died 1677, leaving wife and son 3 years old.

PIERSON, PETER, a Quaker, to be whipped at the cart's tail 1660, thro. Boston, Roxbury, and Dedham. Hutch., I, 203.

PIERSON, STEPHEN, Derby, 1679; had prob. other children beside Stephen and Sarah; for the name of Abraham is found in the list of estate 1717, and this may lead to the presumption that Stephen was son of the first Abraham.

PIERSON, THOMAS, Branford, 1668, not (as often he is called) son of Rev. Abraham the first; married, 1662, Mary, daughter of Richard Harrison; had Samuel, born about 1663, removed to Newark and there died. He swore alleg. to the Dutch in 1673. He was prob. brother, possibly nephew, of the first Rev. Abraham, and his will of 1698, with codicil of 1701, was probated in May following. It names sons Samuel and Thomas, daughters Hannah and Eliz.

REFERENCES:—Amer. Ancest., I, 62; II, 95; VIII, 104; Avon, N. Y., Gen. Rec., 4-16; Condit Gen.; Howell's Hist. Southampton, N. Y., 348-53; Kitchell Gen., 44; N. J., Hist. Coll., VI, Supp. 2; Orcutt's Hist. Derby, Ct., 751; Pierson Gen. (1878) 104 pp.; Power's Hist. Sangamon Co., Ills., 568; Sewall's Hist. Woburn, Mass., 629; Stiles' Hist. Windsor, Ct., II, 607.

PIGG, PIDGE, or PIGGE:—John, Dedham, prob. son of Thomas, freeman 1690; printed in the list Pidg, as the name of his mother in the Metcalf genealogy is spelt Pidge, which may show the truth.

PIGG, ROBERT, New Haven, 1644; died 1660, or very early next year. In his will mentions wife Margaret, who married, 1662, William Tharpe or Thorpe, daughter Alice, meaning wife of John Jenner, perhaps, her son Thomas, "and her other children." Possibly he was brother of Thomas of Roxbury, freeman 1634, who brought from England wife Mary, and sev. children; had here Martha, bapt. 1643; and he died that year.

PIDGEN:—Thomas, Lynn, 1647. Lewis.

PIGGOTT:—Christopher, Boston, 1655, in 27 Apr. of which year an order was passed, that his wife shall be forthwith sent to him at Muddy River by the constable.

PIGHOGG:—Mr., Boston, admitt. a townsman 1652, with prefix of respect, and entitled a "churrergeon." See Rec., I, 103, which gives no name of bapt.

PIGROM:—William, Dorchester, 1653, perhaps only transient.

PIKE:—William, Marblehead, 1668.

PIKE, HUGH, Newbury, a soldier under Turner; at Hatfield, in 1676; married, 1685, Sarah, daughter of Francis Brown; had Hugh, born 1686, and Joseph.

PIKE, JAMES, Charlestown, 1647; then adm. of the church and made freeman; removed to Reading, had two wives, Naomi, and Sarah; two sons, John, born 1654; and Zachariah, 1658; but of which wife either was son, or whether there were more children, or their names, if there were more, as is prob., etc., Jeremiah, or when either of the wives or the children died, Savage does not know. He died 1699.

PIKE, JEREMIAH, Reading, prob. son of the preced., had Jeremiah, born 1674; James, 1676, died soon; as did Elieser or Ebenezer, born next year; Michael, born next year; Michael, 1678; James, again, 1679, died young; Rachel, 1681; James, again, 1682; Nathaniel, 1685; William, 1687; Naomi, 1689; was of Framingham, a selectman 1700, and died 1711.

PIKE, JOHN, Newbury, came in the James, 1635, from Southampton, called in the clearance from the customhouse laborer of Langford, which church was at Ipswich first; in 1640 of Piscataqua, and removed early to Salisbury, but more probably only established there on his estate; second son died 1654, leaving will, made two days before, in which he provides for grands., John, son of John, and grands., John, son of Robert, three daughters, Dorothy, wife of Daniel Hendrick, by whom we discover the error of Genealog. Reg., VI, 342, where she is called daughter, instead of sister of Robert; Israel, wife of Henry True; and Ann.

PIKE, JOHN, Roxbury; had Jessie, born 1685.

PIKE, JOSEPH, Charlestown, 1683; had wife Susanna, killed by the Indians 1694, near Dover.

PIKE, RICHARD, Newbury, 1655; was settled at Falmouth 1675. Willis, I, 140, 3.

PIKE, ROBERT, Salisbury, son of John the first, brought from England, was first at Newbury, freeman 1637; married, 1641, Sarah Sanders, perhaps daughter of John or his sister; had Sarah, born 1642; Mary, 1644, died young; Dorothy, 1645; Mary again, 1647; Elizabeth, 1650; John, 1653; Robert, 1655; and Moses, 1659; was one of the early church members at S., represent. 1648, and some years following; lieut., capt., major in comm. of one of the Essex regim., an Assist. 1682, to the subvers. of the chart; one of the counc. of Safety on the overthrow of Andros, 1689; and in William and Mary's Charter, 1691, again made one of the council. His wife died 1679, and he died 1706 in his 91st year. Sarah married 1661, Wymond Bradbury; and next, 1671, John Stockman; Dorothy married Joshua Pierce; and Eliz. married William Carr.

PIKE, ROBERT, Providence, 1645; may have been only trans. inhab.

REFERENCES:—Amer. Ancestry, V, 223; Austin's R. I. Gen. Dict., 153; Barry's Hist. Framingham, Mass., 350-63; Bell's Hist. Exeter, N. H., 37; Hatch's Hist. Industry, Me.; 791; Lapham's Hist. Norway, Me., 576-9; Morse's Hist. Sherborn, Mass., 202; Rich's Hist. of Truro, Mass., 551; Runnel's Sanbornton, N. H., II, 570-2; Savage's Gen. Dict., 435-7; Wentworth Gen., I, 82-4; II, 406-8; Wheeler's Hist. Newport, N. H., 506-9; Whitehead's Perth Amboy, N. J., 360-3; Weyman's Charlestown, Mass., Gens., II, 762.

PILE:—William, Salisbury, 1659, removed to Nantucket, thence to Dover, bef. July, 1663.

PILLING, or PILLEN:—John, Kittery, 1639; a fisherman; was prob. of Dover, 1653.

PILLSBURY:—William, Dorchester, 1641; married that year, prob. Dorothy Crosby; had Deborah, born 1642; Job, 1643; Moses; Abel; removed to Newbury; there had Caleb, 1654; William, 1656; Experience, 1658; Increase, 1660; Thankful, 1662; and Joshua, 1671; freeman 1668; died 1686, aged 71.

REFERENCES:—Amer. Ancestry, V, 80, 146; Bangor, Me., Hist. Mag., V, 208; Caverno Gen. Rec., 35; Coffin's Hist. of Newbury, Mass., 314; Cogswell's Hist. Henniker, N. H., 683-90; Cogswell's Hist. Nottingham, N. H., 763; Eaton's Hist., Thomaston, Me., II, 358; Poor's Hist. Gen. Researches, 136, 150; Savage's Gen. Dict., III, 437.

PIMORE:—Thomas, New Haven, a propr., 1685.

PINCKNEY:—Philip, Fairfield, 1650; perhaps he was not there much after 1653; certainly was at East Chester, 1665. His son John lived there 1690, and perhaps he had other children, beside Abigail, who married David Osborn.
REFERENCES:—Bolton's Westchester, 249; Savage's Gen. Dict., III, 439.

PINDAR, PINDER, or PINTER:—Henry, Ipswich, 1642; perhaps was father of Mary, who married, 1643, Solomon Martin; and of Joanna, who married, 1643, Valentine Rowell. He had come prob. as early as 1635 at least, for in that year embarked at London, in the Susan and Ellen, to come hither, were Mary, aged 53, with six children; Francis, 20; Mary, 17; Joanna, 14; Ann, 12; Catherine, 10; and John, 8.
PINDAR, JOHN, Ipswich, 1648; may have been son of the preceding; married a daughter of Theophilus Wilson, and had son Thomas; and perhaps removed to Watertown; there died 1662.
PINDAR, SAMUEL, Ipswich, 1683.
REFERENCES:—Austin's R. I. Gen. Dict., 153; Ipswich, Mass., Chronicle (1882).

PINGRY, PINGREW, PINGREE, or PENGRY:—Aaron, Ipswich, 1648.
PINGRY, MOSES, Ipswich, 1642; perhaps brother of the preceding, a saltmaker; married Abigail, daughter of first Robert Clement; was represent. 1665, and deacon; died 1695, aged prob. 85 years.
PINGRY, JOHN, prob. son of Aaron, or Moses, took lease of the school farm in 1680; married Faith, perhaps daughter of the first Joseph Jewett.
REFERENCES:—Little Gen., 288-90; Pingry Gen. (1881), 186 pp.

PINION:—Nicholas, Lynn, 1647; perhaps worked at the iron mine; removed to New Haven; there wrought at the iron works. By wife Eliz., who died 1667, had Ruth, Hannah, Mary, Thomas, and Robert, and died 1676.
PINION, ROBERT, Lynn, 1647, may have been son of the preceding.
PINION, THOMAS, Sudbury, 1661; may have been son of Nicholas. Sett. at New Haven; by wife Mary had Christiana, Mercy, and Abigail, and died 1710. Doubts as to this name have been expressed in Conn., for it might easily be read Pineon, or Pineo, and the sound of either is not much unlike the others, it is said, and was seldom uttered in public.

PINKHAM:—Richard, Dover, 1648; hired to call the people to church by beating the drum. Had sons Robert and John, and perhaps Thomas.
REFERENCES:—Cushman's Sheepscott, 413; Milliken's Narraguagus Valley, Me., 18; N. E. Hist. Gen. Reg., VII, 353-5; Otis Family of New Hampshire, (1851).

PINNEY, or PYNNY:—Humphrey, Dorchester, born in Somersetshire; came, as once was thought, in the Mary and John, 1630, but Stiles, in Hist. of Windsor, 745, shows that in 1831 he was engaged in England;

freeman 1634; married at Dorchester, Mary, daughter of George Hull; had Samuel; removed to Windsor; there had Nathaniel, born 1641, bapt. 1642; Mary, 1644; Sarah, 1648; John, 1651; Abigail, 1654; and Isaac, 1664. He died 1683, and his widow died 1684.
PINNEY, JOHN, Charlestown; married, 1682, Eliz., daughter of Thomas Rand; had John, Edmund, and Eliz., all bapt. 1687.
PHINNEY, THOMAS, Gloucester, 1671; freeman 1672; and was there ten years after.
REFERENCES:—Loomis, Gen., Fem. Branch, 666; Savage's Gen. Dict., III, 438; Stiles' Hist., Windsor, Ct., II, 608-19; 842-4.

PINSON, PINCHIN, or PINCIN:—Andrew, Wethersfield; died 1697, after more than 30 years inhab., aged 74, and prob. without even wife or children.
PINSON, EDMUND, Cambridge, 1665; married Ann, daughter of John Cooper; had Ann, who died 1666, infant. He had second wife, Sarah, daughter of Richard Dexter.
PINSON, THOMAS, Scituate, 1636; married, 1636, Jane, daughter of Richard Stanlake; had Thomas, born 1640; Hannah, 1642; Waitstill, 1650; John, 1655, and Joshua, 1658.
REFERENCE:—Mitchell's, Bridgewater, 272.

PIPER:—Nathaniel, Ipswich, 1665, is thought to have come from Dartmouth in Devonsh. His will of 1676 names wife Sarah, and children, Sarah, Nathaniel, Josiah, John, Thomas, Mary, Margaret, Samuel, and Jonathan.
PIPER, RICHARD, Haddam, 1669; was then constable, in 1674 rep., died 1678. No children are named in will.

PIPON:—John, master of a ship at Salem, 1673, was prob. that capt. in the forces to whom Andros gave command at the castle. Felt, I, 359. Perhaps Andros officer, in 1678, command at Pemaquid, was Joshua. See Mass. Hist. Call., VII, 180.

PITCHER:—Andrew, Dorchester, 1634; freeman 1641; by wife Margaret, had, beside eldest son Samuel, John, Jonathan, and Nathaniel named in his will, Experience, 1642; Mary, 1644; Ruth, 1647; and another son 1652, who died young, as prob, did Mary; died 1661.
PITCHER, JOHN, Bridgewater, 1666, servant of Francis Godfrey, who names him in his will.
REFERENCES:—Amer. Ancestry, II, 96; Pompey's N. Y. Reunion, 337-41.

PITHOUSE:—See Pittice.

PITKIN:—William, Hartford, 1660, freeman 1662, was son of Roger who was of London 1666, though family tradition brings him from city of Norwich; had prob. been bred a lawyer in England, here first taught a school, was soon made attorney for the colony; rep. 1675, treasurer, 1676; married Hannah, only daughter of Ozias Goodwin; had Roger, born 1662; William, 1664; John; Nathaniel; George, 1675; Ozias, 1679; Hannah; and Eliz., 1677; all named in his will, as also is brother Roger; was an Assist. several years and died 1694, aged 58; and his widow died 1724, aged 86. He brought from England or she followed him, as tradition says, Sister Martha, who married, 1661, Simon Wolcott; was mother of the first Gov. W. who, in the funeral sermon upon him, is said to have never gone to any school, but to have been solely educated by her at home, and after. married Daniel Clark.
REFERENCES:—Amer. Ancest. IV, 116; V, 199, 200, 205; Huntington's Memoirs, 103; Kellog's White Gen.,

62; Pitkin, Gen. (1887) 418 pp.; Salisbury's Memorials, (1888) (1892); Savage's Gen. Dict., III, 440; Stiles' Hist. Windsor, Ct., II, 619.

PITMAN, oft. PITNAM:—Ezekiel, New Hamp., 1683.

PITMAN, JOHN, Salem; a capt., freeman; 1690 lived in what became Danvers.

PITMAN, JONATHAN, Stratford, married, 1681; Temperance, elder daughter of John Welles of the same; had Jonathan, born 1682, died soon; Jonathan again, 1687; Robert, 1689; and Samuel, 1692, and died 1727.

PITMAN, JOSEPH, died 1658, says Farmer, but a doubt is raised whether he was not casual resid., for neither as townsman nor churchman does name appear.

PITMAN, JOSEPH, Dover; in service of William Taskett, discharged by the court in 1686, for cruelty by the master; killed by the Indians, 1704.

PITMAN, MARK, Marblehead, 1674, called 50 years old, may have been soldier; killed next year at Hatfield.

PITMAN, NATHANIEL, Salem, 1639; had there, says Felt, grant of land. He is usual. named Pickman.

PITMAN, SAMUEL, Salem, 1670.

PITMAN, THOMAS, Marblehead, 1648, perhaps had son Thomas.

PITMAN, THOMAS, Marblehead; called junior, aged 17 in 1669; may be the man titled senior, in 1683, then made freeman.

PITMAN, WILLIAM, Dover; married at Boston, 1653, Barbara Evans; had prob. that Mary, who married, 1674, Stephen Otis; and he may have lived 1677 at Boston.

REFERENCES:—Guild's Stiles Gen., 342; Pitman Gen. (1868) 48 pp.; Savage's Gen. Dict., III, 424, 441; Thurston and Pitman Gen. (1865) 80 pp.

PITNEY:—James, Boston, 1652; had been of Ipswich, 1639. His wife, Sarah, had come in the *Planter*, 1635, from London, aged 22, with Margaret, 22, who perhaps was his sister and 2 children, Sarah, 7, and Samuel 1 and ½. He was of Marshfield, 1643, and after death of his wife, 1658, removed to M. again, for there his daughter, Sarah, married, 1648, John Thomas, and there he died, 1663, by nuncupative will giving his little property to his children James, Abigail, and John, and Sarah Thomas, and her children. He was 80.

PITT:—William, Plymouth; came in 1621, in the *Fortune*; had share in division of lands, 1624, but was not present at the division of cattle, 1627; and may have removed to N. shore of the Bay. He was possibly at Marblehead, 1674; at least, one Hugh Latimer, of M. seems to have married, 1669, Mary, daughter of a man of this name, who lived there, 1665. See Morton's Memo. by Davis, 378; and Baylies I. 85.

PITTEE, PITTY, or PITTEY:—Joseph, Ipswich, freeman, 1680.

PITTEE, WILLIAM, an early settler, by wife Mary, had, Savage conjectures, (though record makes Samuel the father) Samuel, born 1657; and William, 1661; others, also, much earlier; John, born 1639, who was drowned; and Mary, 1643, who married, 1660, Henry Adams.

REFERENCE:—Porter Gen. (1878) 15.

PITTICE:—John, Ipswich, 1648, may be the passenger in the *James* from Southampton, 1635, who was of Marlborough in Wilts', says the custom-ho. rec., spelling it Pithouse; and possibly the Pettis or Pittis populat. may be thus derived.

PITTS:—Edmund, Hingham, from Hingham in England; came with wife and children; was a weaver;

freeman 1640, and had brother Leonard in comp.; had John, born 1653; and Jeremy, 1657; Deborah, who married, 1672, Daniel Howard; May, who, 1672, married John Bull or Bullen; and Eliz., who 1673, married Thomas Jones, were his daughters, or they or some may have come of another family.

PITTS, PETER, Taunton, 1643-60; had, perhaps, married Mary, daughter of Henry Andrews, widow of William Hodges or Hedges, who, in her will after 1654, provided that Peter P. should perform its conditions "in case I make him my husband."

PITTS, SAMUEL, Taunton; married 1680, Sarah Bobbett, daughter of Edward of the same.

PITTS, WILLIAM, Hingham; came in the *Diligent*, 1638, from Old Hingham, may be the man of whom Winthrop II, 305, tells, and may have been of Marblehead, 1654; next year married Susanna, widow of Philip Alley, was a trader, and prob. lived at Boston, but his wife, Susanna, died at M. on a visit, 1668. See Essex Inst. Call, II, 69.

REFERENCES:—Pitts Gen. (1882) 63 pp.; Richard Mowry Gen., 223; Riddon's Harrison, Me. Settlers, 99; Savage's Gen. Dict., III, 442.

PITTUMS, or PITTOMS:—John, Boston; by wife Mary had Nathaniel, born 1678; Mary, 1680, bapt. 1681; and Eliz., whose birth is not seen; but bapt. 1685.

PIXLEY:—William, Hadley; married, 1663, Sarah Lawrence, had Sarah, born 1665; Thomas, 1667; removed ot Northampton, there had William, 1669; Joseph. 1671; died young; Joseph, again, 1676; Ebenezer, 1678; removed to Westfield, there had Anthony, 1681, who died 1697; beside Mary, who died 1735, at Westfield, unmarried, date of birth unknown; he died 1689; and his widow died, 1713. Sarah married, 1680, John Lee. Thomas and Ebenezer, as well as Joseph, had children in W., but their names have not been learned. The name is still found.

REFERENCES:—Amer. Ancestry, V, 13; Savage's Gen. Dict., III, 443.

PLACE, sometimes PLAISE:—Enoch, Kingston, R. I., from whose will, 1695, Savage learns that he was 64 years old, and had wife, Sarah; married, 1657, at Dorchester, as in Geneal. Rec., XI, 332, is seen without her surname, and children, Enoch, Peter, Thomas, and Joseph, the youngest, beside Sarah, wife of * * * Cook. The same Dorchester records ment. that Dinah P. died that year.

PLACE, PETER, Boston; came in the *Trulove*, 1635, from London, aged 20, freeman, 1646; by wife Alice had Hannah, 1643; Eliz., 1644; Joseph, 1646; Peter, 1649; Eliz. again, 1652, who died young; Sarah, 1657.

PLACE, PETER, Providence; perhaps son of the preceding, swore alleg. to Charles II, 1682.

PLACE, THOMAS, Braintree or Dorchester; freeman, 1640.

PLACE, WILLIAM, Salem; blacksmith, had grant of land, 1637, when Felt notes he was called "old Mr. William P." He had wife but no children, and died 1646.

REFERENCE:—Austin's R. I. Gen. Dict., 155.

PLANE, or PLAIN:—William, Guilford, 1639, execut. 1646, at New Haven, for monstrous crimes. Winthrop, II, 265.

PLASTOW:—Josiah, Boston, 1631; banished. Winthrop, I, 52, 61, 2. It is said he died before June, 1632.

PLATT:—Abel, Rowley, 1678.

PLATT, ISAAC, Huntington, L. I.; admitted freeman of Conn., 1664.

PLATT, JAMES, Rowley, 1691.

PLATT, JOHN, Norwalk, 1663; freeman, 1668; by wife Hannah, daughter of George Clark, the first of Milford, had John, born 1664; Josiah, 1667; Samuel, 1671; Joseph, 1673; Hannah, 1674; and Sarah, 1678.

PLATT, JONATHAN, Rowley; married, 1655, Eliz. Johnson, made his will 1680, naming wife Sarah, and son.

PLATT, RICHARD, Milford, 1639; then member of the church where he had lands, 1646, in the list of freeman, 1669; was deacon and died, 1684 or 5; had prob. brought from England Mary, John, Isaac, and Sarah, and at M. had bapt. Epenetus, prob., 1640; Hannah, 1643; Josiah, 1645; Joseph, 1649; and his wife, Mary, died or was buried 1676.

PLATT, SAMUEL, Rowley; represent., 1681; perhaps the freeman of 1684; prob. had family.

PLATT, SAMUEL, Rowley; perhaps son of the preceding; was town clerk 19 years and died 1726.

PLATT, THOMAS, Boston, 1669; a butcher. Often the name is found with final "s."

REFERENCE:—Amer. Ancestry, VII, 125; VIII, 109, 112; Boyd's Annals Winchester, Ct., 180; Green's Todd Gen.; Hall's Norwalk, Ct., 86-8, 92-7, 200, 249; Oneida Hist. Soc. Trans., II, 83-90. Platt Gen. (1891) 398 pp.; Platt's Old Times, Huntington, L. I. (1876); Savage's Gen. Dict., III, 444; Stearns' Hist. Rindge, N. H., 637-44; Strong Gen., 702; Thompson's L. I., N. Y., II, 4, 72-5; Timlow's Hist., Southington, Ct., 205-7; Todd's Hist. Redding, Ct., 210; Walworth's Hyde Gen., 544-6.

PLATTS:—James. See Platt.

REFERENCES:—Essex Inst. Hist. Coll., V, 15; XXIII, 141-5; Norton's Hist. Fitzwilliam, N. H., 671-4; Poor's Hist. Gen. Researches, 116-30; Stearne's Hist. Ashburnham, Mass., 851.

PLAYES:—Enoch, Wickford, 1674.

PLIMPTON:—See Plympton.

REFERENCES:—Amer. Ancestry, V. 34; Ammidown's Hist. Coll., II. 365-7, 560; Ammidown Fam., 31; Keyes' W. Boylston Mass. Gen. Reg., 33; Norton's Hist. Fitzwilliam, N. H., 674; Plimpton, Gen., (1885) 240 pp.; Wight Gen., 56-8.

PLOTT:—Josiah, Milford, 1671; as printed in Trumbull. Cal. Rec. II. Savage thinks may be son of Richard Platt.

PLUMB. or PLUM:—John, Dorchester; removed to Wethersfield before September, 1636, and before deputs. to Gen. Ct. were introduced in Conn. Was a sort of ruler in 1637, rep. 1641, 2 and 3, had Samuel, and Dorcas, who married, 1655, John Lyman, was nomin., 1643. for election as Assist.. but did not succeed in the choice, made custom-ho. officer, 1644; sold his estate and removed to Branford before 1646, and there died. His will was probated 1648. Yet is not known where he first landed in our country. or whence he came. Perhaps he was father of John, New London, born about 1621, where after 1665, he seems much connected though prob. living at Hartford, a mariner who traded up and down the river, freeman, 1669; yet before 1677 establ. at N. L., where he had Mercy, bapt. 1677; George, 1679; and Sarah, 1682. Miss Caulkins is confid. that he had elder children: John, Samuel, of which one thinks he was born 1659; Joseph and Greene. His wife was fined, 1671, for sale of liquor to Indians, but at N. L.

he was constable, 1680; and an innholder, and died 1696. John, Samuel, and Joseph were at Milford, but John came back to N. L. and was deacon many years, says Caulkins, who sends George to Stonington. One John was a soldier in Lothrop's comp.; killed by the Indians at Deerfield, 1675; but another John, Dorchester, is only mentioned as partaking of bounty to the poor in 1680. See Hist. of D., 239. But prob. he had long lived there, and had daughter, Waiting, born 1657.

PLUMBE, ROBERT, Milford, 1639; married Mary, daughter of Sylvester Baldwin; had Mary bapt., 1645, who married, 1668, the second Matthew Woodruff; John, 1646; Robert, 1648; Samuel, 1650, died young; Samuel, again, 1653; and Joseph, posthum. 1655; and died 1655.

REFERENCES:—Maltby Gen., 104; Caulkins' New London, Ct., 336; Kellog's White Gen., 56; Savage's Gen. Dict., III, 445.

PLUMLY:—Alexander, Braintree; by wife Esther, had son, Submit, born 1654. He was one of the promoters of settlement at Menden, 1663.

PLUMMER:—Francis, Newbury, 1635; linen weaver; came in 1633, says one tradit. from Woolwich, near London, but another says from Wales; we know not in which town he was first inhab., but he was freeman, 1634, brought wife, Ruth, who died 1647, and several children, certainly Samuel and Joseph. He married, 1648, widow Ann Palmer, who died 1665, and he married next month, Beatrice, widow of William Cantlebury, and died 1673.

PLUMMER, JOHN, at Hatfield; killed by the Indians, 1675; may have been a soldier, not inhab. of H., but came from Dorchester in Johnson's company.

PLUMMER, SAMUEL, Newbury; eldest child of John; born in Eng. about 1619; freeman 1641; by wife Mary, had Samuel, born 1647; Mary, 1650; John, 1652; Ephraim, 1655; Hannah, 1657; Sylvanus, 1658; Ruth, 1660; Eliz., 1662; Deborah, 1665; Joshua, Lydia, 1668; and Bathsheba, 1670. He kept the ferry over the Merrimac, was rep. 1676, and died 1702.

REFERENCES:—Chandler Gen., 217; Coffin's Hist. of Boscowen, N. H., 601-4; Cogswell's Hist., Henniker, N. H., 601-3; Goode Gen., 233; Lapham's Hist., Bethel, Me., 598; Lee Gen. of Ipswich, 295-7, 312; N. E. Hist. and Gen. Reg., XXXVIII, 67; Plummer Hall Proc., Salem, Mass. (1858); Savage's Gen. Dict., III, 446; Shourd's Fenwick Colony, N. J., 176; Warren's Hist. of Waterford, Me. 279; Wentworth Gen., I, 170.

PLYMPTON, or PLIMPTON:—Henry of Boston, died prob. early in 1653, for his inv. was brought in that year.

PLYMPTON, JOHN, Dedham, 1642; perhaps brother of preceding, came prob. some years before for Dr. George Alcock of Roxbury, in his will 1640, calls him his servant, meaning apprentice, may be the freeman of 1643, printed Plimton; by wife Jane (prob. daughter of Richard Dummer, brought from England, married 1644), had Hannah, born 1645; John, 1646, died soon; Mary, 1648; John, again, 1650; Peter, 1652, and the following at Medfield, of whom only dates of birth appear: Joseph, 1653; Mehitable, 1655; Jonathan, 1657; Eleazer, 1660, died soon; Eleazer, again, 1661; Rhoda, 1663, died soon; Jane, 1664, died soon; and Henry, 1666, who died 1668. He removed after the war began, supposes Savage, to Deerfield, where he was serg.; his son, Jonathan, was killed by the Indians, 1675. at Bloody Brook, and the father was taken two years and one day after death of Jonathan, by the Indians, carried towards Canada, and killed, one report says, by burning at the stake. The Hampsh. Prob. rec. takes notice, 1678, of his wife, Jane, and that the children were to have the lands; all removed in few years to the old settlement near Boston. His widow married, 1679, Nicholas Hide.

PLYMPTON, ROBERT, New London; was chosen to office, 1681, and died before 1686.

PLYMPTON, THOMAS, Sudbury, 1643; by wife Abigail, daughter of Peter Noyes, had Abigail, born 1653; Jane, 1655; Mary, 1656; Eliz., 1658; Thomas, 1661; Dorothy, 1664; and Peter, 1667; and was killed at Sudbury fight, 1676.

REFERENCES:—Chase's Plympton Gen. (1885); Cleveland's Hist. Yates Co., N. Y., 695-7; Savage's Gen. Dict., III, 447; Ward's Hist., Shrewsbury, Mass., 410.

POCHER:—George, Braintree, died 1639.

POCOCK:—John, a soldier in the list of killed by the Indians at Hadley, 1675; may be misspell. of Peacock.

POD:—Daniel, Ipswich, 1642.

POD, SAMUEL, came in the *Susan and Ellen*, aged 25, from London.

POLE:—George, Plymouth, or perhaps, Yarmouth, 1646, with Anthony Thatcher, was, as Drake, Book of the Ind., p. 20, tells, on a committee against tobacco. Possibly the name had double "o."

POLLARD:—George, Salem; before 1646, says Felt., in his will pro., 1646, he is called of Marblehead.

POLLARD, WILLIAM, Boston; innholder, by wife, Ann, had John, born 1644; Samuel, 1646; Hannah, 1649; William, 1653; Eliz., 1655; Joseph, 1657; Sarah, 1659; Benjamin, 1663; Ann, 1664; Jonathan, 1666, and David, 1668. The last, with eight others, were bapt. in Old South Church at one time, 1670. One Ann P., at Boston, prob. his widow, died 1725, in 105th year, it is said, in Franklin's N. E. Courant, though somewhat exaggerated, as we know from her own testimony 12 years before, that she was 89.

REFERENCES:—Amer. Ances., IX, 86; Fox's Hist. Dunstable, Mass., 248; Hazen's Hist., Billerica, Mass., 112-4; Kidder's Hist., New Ipswich, N. H., 428; Meade's Old Laws of Va.; Pollard Gen. (1891), 20 pp.; Richmond, Va., Standard, II, 45; Savage's Gen. Dict., III, 448-50; Stearn's Hist. Ashburnham, Mass., 852; Stowe's Hist., Hubbardston, Mass., 334; Walworth Hyde Gen. 469.

POLLY, or POLLEY:—George, Woburn; married 1649, Eliz. Winn, perhaps daughter of Edward; had John, 1650; Joseph, 1652; George, 1656; Eliz. 1657; Samuel, 1661, died in 2 weeks; Hannah, 1662, died same day; Hannah, again, 1663; and he died 1683.

POLLY, JOHN, Roxbury, perhaps son of preceding; had Mary and Sarah twins, bapt. 1650; Hannah, 1652; Abigail, 1654; Bethia, 1659; and Susanna, 1661. His wife, Susan, died 1664; and he by second wife, Hannah, had Rebecca, born 1668, and Joanna, 1670. This wife died 1684, and he married third wife Jane Walter, who died 1701. He died 1689 aged 71.

REFERENCES:—Stearn's Ashburnham, 853; Savage's Gen. Dict., III, 450; Sewall's Hist., Woburn, Mass., 629.

POMEROY, POMROY, PUMMERY, or PUMRY:—Eltweed, Dorchester, by Dr. Harris marked as of 1630 and if so, came prob. in the *Mary and John*, freeman, 1633, removed about 1636 or 7 to Windsor, carrying Mary, who died 1640; John, who died 1647; and Eldad, all prob. born at D.; the two former died at W.; had at W. Medad, bapt. 1638; Caleb, 1642; Mary, again, 1644, died under 15 years; Joshua, 1646; and Joseph, 1652. His wife died 1655, and he married Lydia, widow of Thomas Parsons, removed 1672 to live with his sister Medad at Northampton, there died 1673. His son, Eldad, died unmarried, 1662, having been admitted freeman of Conn., 1658, and betroth. to Susanna Cunliffe.

POMEROY, JOHN, Boston; shipwright, made his will 1690, bound to sea, and gave his property to Mary Brookings, prob. daughter of John; he was, no doubt, a young unmarried man, prob. engaged to marry the devisee.

POMEROY, THOMAS, whose name is written Pummery, was of Portsmouth; married before 1679, Rebecca, daughter of William Brooking of the same.

REFERENCES:—Amer. Ancestry, IV, 168; VII, 67, 72, 153; Collin's Hist. Hillsdale, N. Y., App., 101-3; Hubbard's Stanstead Co., Canada, 122-5; Judd's Hist., Hadley, Mass., 535; Kellogg's White Gen., 66; Lawrence Gen. (1881) 70-81; Lyman's Hist., Easthampton, Mass., 188-90; Mack Gen., 70; N. E. Hist. and Gen. Reg., CLXIX, 39-43. Pomeroy Gen., by Rodman, (1889) 14 pp.; Rodman's Pomeroys in America (1889) 14 pp.; Savage's Gen. Dict., III, 450-2; Stiles' Hist., Windsor, Ct., II, 620; Temple's Hist., Northfield, Mass., 517-20; Corliss' No. Yarmouth, Me.; Read's Hist., Swanzey N. H., 421.

POMFRET:—William, Dover, 1640; was early town clerk and lieut.; died 1680. His daughter, Martha, married William Dame, and another daughter married Thomas Whitehouse.

POND:—Daniel, perhaps son of first Robert; may have been born in England, freeman, 1690; died 1698. His first wife was Abigail, daughter of Edward Shepard of Cambridge, prob. had sev. children, but by another wife Ann, who survived, some of the foll, may have come: John; Ephraim; William; Daniel; Robert; Caleb; and Jabez; seven sons beside Abigail, who married Ralph Day; Hannah Devotion, prob. wife of John; Rachel Stow, dec.; and Sarah, unmarried at death of her father.

POND, ISAAC, Windsor; prob. son of Samuel of the same; married 1667, Hannah, daughter of John Griffin, had Hannah, born 1668; and he died next year.

POND, JOHN, son of one of Winthrop's old neighbors; came 1630, with the Gov., as also did a brother whose name is not ment.; when the Gov. in his first letter after arriving to his eldest son at Groton, directs him to tell "old Pond" both his sons are well, and remember their duty.

POND, ROBERT, Dorchester; though not found in the list of Dr. Harris, was there to partake, 1638, in Division of Cow commons. His widow married Edward Shepard of Cambridge.

POND, SAMUEL, Windsor; by wife Sarah, married, 1642, had Isaac, born 1646; Samuel, 1648; Nathaniel, 1650; and Sarah, 1653; and he died 1655. His son, Nathaniel, was killed with his Capt. Marshall in the great Narragansett fight, 1675.

POND, SAMUEL, Branford, 1668; signed the planta. and church covenant, and may therefore be thought of another family or possibly was son of the preceding. He married, 1670, Miriam, daughter of Thomas Blatchley, of B.

POND, THOMAS, (though surname is doubtful in record of the custom-ho. and by Mr. Hunter thought as near Pount as Pond), a passenger in the *Elizabeth and*

Ann, from London, 1635, aged 21. See the later reading of Geneal. Reg. XIV, 313.

POND, WILLIAM, Dorchester, 1648; perhaps son of first Robert of the same; born in England; married Mary, daughter of George Dyer; had Samuel, who died 1657; Eliz. and Martha, twins, born 1658, both died in a few days; Judith, 1659; Thankful, 1662; George, 1666; and Mindwell, 1667; and perhaps William; was constable 1659, and died 1690, called serg. and Judge Sewall says he died suddenly. His widow, it is said, died 1711.

REFERENCES:—Adams, Haven Gen., 2d part, 10; Amer. Anc., VI, III, IX, 215; Ballou's Hist. Milford, Mass., 972-8; Blake's Hist. Franklin, Mass., 265-73; Caverly's Hist. Pittsford, Vt., 721; Hill's Dedham, Mass Records; Huntington's Stamford, Ct., Settlers, 82; Jameson's Hist. of Medway, Mass., 513; Joslin's Hist. Poultney, Vt., 319-28; Morse's Gen. Sherborn, Mass., 203; Orcutt's Hist. Torrington, Ct., 755; Parker-Bond-Peck Gen. (1892), 51 pp.; Pond Gen. (1873), 210 pp.; (1875), 126 pp.; Power's Hist. Sangamon Co., Ill., 576; Savage's Gen. Dict., III, 452; Stiles' Hist. Windsor, Ct., II, 620; Stowe's Hist. Hubbardston, Mass., 335-8; Wight Gen., 164.

PONDER:—John, Westfield; married, 1668, Temperance, daughter of Thomas Buckland, had Susanna, born 1669; John, 1670, died young; Mary, 1672; Eliz. 1675; Nathaniel, 1677; John, again, 1680; Thomas, 1682; Martha, 1684; and Sarah, 1686, died at four years. He died 1712; and his wife died 1732.

PONTON, or PONTING:—Richard, Boston, a husbandman, adm. of the church, 1649, had been bound 1641, for eight years with his own assent to John Read, of Braintree, removed to Hartford, 1662; freeman 1663; died or removed before 1669.

PONTUS:—William, Plymouth, 1633; in 1643 not in the list of those able to bear arms, i. e., under the age of 60; died 1653; having made his will 1650, leaving two children only, with very small estate.

REFERENCES:—Savage's Gen. Dict., III, 454; Pope Gen.

POOLE, POAL, or POLE:—Edward, Newport, 1638; prob. was of Weymouth most of his days; had Samuel, Isaac, Joseph, Benjamin, John, Sarah, and Jacob, named in this order in his will, 1664; of which his wife was Extrix.; her name is not seen.

POOLE, ELIZABETH, Taunton, 1637; the chief cause of building at T.; was maiden sister of William, and elder than him, of a good family in heraldry, as well as religion; may be regarded as one of the most decided proofs of the deep roots that puritanism had attained in England. She died 1654, aged 65, having made her will four days before in which John, eldest son of her brother, was named Excar. Abstract in Geneal. Reg., V, 262. See Winthrop, I, 252.

POOLE, HENRY, Boston, died 1643; may have been infant.

POOLE, JOHN, Cambridge, 1632; went to Lynn before 1638, when he had there 200 acres, and last of Reading, where his wife Margaret died 1662; and he died 1667

POOLE, JOHN, Beverly; a carpenter; married Sarah, widow of Richard Woodbury, who died 1716; had Jonathan, born 1694; Miriam, 1695; Robert, 1697; Ebenezer, 1699; and Joshua, 1700; removed to Gloucester and had Caleb, 1701; and John, 1703. For second wife he had

Deborah Dodge, daughter prob. of Samuel, but she died 1718; and his third wife, Elizabeth Holmes, perhaps daughter of John of Salem, died 1720; and he took fourth wife 1721, Abigail Ballard of Lynn, says Babson, and had Return in 1722; and Abigail, 1725; and he died 1727.

POOLE, RICHARD, New London, died about 1662, without wife or children, gave estate to wife and children of George Tongue.

POOLE, SAMUEL, Boston; adm. of the church, 1642; called Merchant with prefix of respect; had Ann that year; yet Savage knows nothing more of him, unless he were that captain who married Silence, daughter of Rev. Peter Saxton, of Scituate, who died before 1651; or perhaps of Reading, where Eaton calls one early settler of his name.

POOLE, SAMUEL, Weymouth, son—prob. eldest—of Edward, by wife Mercy had Mary, born 1668.

POOLE, WILLIAM, Dorchester; perhaps as early as 1630; yet most remarkable is it, that he was at Taunton sev. years after 1637, there called capt.; represent. 1641, being brother of the patron saint of that newer town, but in records of Dorchester described as town clerk ten years and after school master, while we do not know whether these functions were fulfilled before he went or after his return, or partly both, certainly at D. he had Theophilus 1660, and this may render prob. that his elder sons and daughters John, Nathaniel, Timothy, Mary and Bethesda, were born at T. He died at D., 1675, aged 81; and his widow who had been married as early, it is judged, as 1638, perhaps Mary, daughter of John Richmond, died near the end of 1690. Timothy was drowned at T., 1667; of Nathaniel nothing is heard except in the will of his Aunt Eliz., and it may be that he died young; nor is more told of Theophilus than his birth and bapt.; Mary was second wife of Daniel Henchman, and Bethesda Poole (whose father showed his religion, we may regret, more than his judgment, in taking for the daughter's name that of the intermit. fountain, of which the power is so beautiful, told in the narrative of the Evangelist), married, 1686, John Filer, as his second wife. He had son William, who was bapt. 1658, at Roxbury. Baylies derives the family from Taunton in Co. Somerset.

POOLE, WILLIAM, Brookhaven, L. I., 1680; perhaps was son of the preceding Thompson.

REFERENCES:—(POOL) Amer. Ancestry, V, 25; Babson's Hist. Gloucester, Mass., 126-9; Barry's Hist. Hanover, Mass., 359; Hobart's Hist. Abington, Mass., 427-30; Hubbard's Stanstead Co., Canada, 292; Lapham's Hist. Norway, Me., 581; Temple's Hist. Palmer, Mass., 527.

(POOLE) Amer. Ancestry, IV, 62, 160; Bridgeman's Granary Burial Ground, 157; Eaton's Hist. Reading, Mass., 106-9; Mitchell's Hist. Bridgewater, Mass., 273; Morrison's Hist. Windham, N. H., 739; Poole Gen. (1893), 164 pp.; Savage's Gen. Dict., III, 454-6; Vinton's Giles Gen., 324, 538-40.

POOR, or POORE:—Daniel, Andover; is that youth, thinks Savage, aged 14, whose name on the list of passengers in the *Bevis* from Southampton, 1638, is Dayell, coming with Alice or Alice P., aged 20, prob. has sister, and Samuel P., 18, prob. their brother and others, under the designation of servants of Richard Drummer; married, 1650, Mary Farnum, perhaps daughter of Ralph; and died 1713, it is said, aged 85, which, is one of the very few instances of under estimate. Only sons—Daniel and John, are named; and of John the death is so early as 1690, that perhaps he was never married. But seven female Poors are as early found to marry, and all may have been his daughters, viz. Martha, with John Granger, 1680; Hannah, with Francis Dane, Jr., 1681; Eliz., with Jacob Marston, 1686; Priscilla, with Abraham Moore, 1687; Deborah, with Timothy Osgood, 1689; Ruth, with John Stevens, 1689; and Lucy, with Samuel Austin, 1691.

Poor, John, Newbury; an early settler, said to have emigrated from Co. Wilts, was, thinks Savage, elder brother of Daniel and Samuel; had Jonathan; John, 1642; Hannah, 1655, died young; Eliz., 1647; Hannah, again, 1649; Henry, 1650; Mary, 1652, died at 6 mos.; Joseph, 1653; Mary, again, 1654, who married, 1670, Samuel Pearson; Lydia, 1656; Edward, 1658; Abigail, 1660, died soon; and Abigail, again, 1661; and he died, 1684, aged 69. His widow died, says Coffin, 1702.

Poor, John, Hampton; married, 1661, Sarah, daughter of John Brown of the same; had Sarah, born 1661; John, 1664; Richard, 1666; John, again, 1668; Sarah, again, 1671; Mary, 1673; and Deborah, 1675. He was a mariner of Charlestown, where all but two of these children were born, and his widow died, 1678, of small pox, and there he married, 1680, Eliz., daughter of John Burrage, widow of Thomas Dean; had Thomas, born 1682; Bethia, 1684; and Silence, posthlm., 1686; but the last two died soon; and he died 1686.

Poor, Nicholas, Lynn, 1637, Lewis.

Poor, Samuel, Newbury; prob. that passenger in the *Bevis* from Southampton, 1638, aged 18, who may be brother of Daniel, Alice and John, fellow-passengers, had Rebecca, born 1649; Mary, 1651; Samuel, 1653; Edward, 1656; Eliz., 1659; Joseph, 1661; Sarah, 1664; Benjamin, 1667; and Mary, 1671; and he was freeman, 1673, died 1683, by Coffin called 60, but prob. was older.

Poor, Thomas, Andover, 1645; may be he whose death is on record, 1695.

REFERENCES:—(POOR) Abbot's Andover, Mass., 26; Amer. Ancestry, IX, 193; Chase's Hist., Chester, N. H., 574; Cochrane's Hist. Antrim, N. H., 646-8; Fullonton's Hist. Raymond, N. H., 271-6; Gage's Hist. Rowley, Mass., 452; Hayward's Hist., Hancock, N. H., 809; Poor Fam. Gathering (1890), 107 pp.; (1893), 52 pp.;

(POORE) Poore Gen. (1881) 332 pp.; Savage's Gen. Dict., III, 456; Titcomb Early N. E. People, 201-13.

POPE:—Ephraim, Boston; died 1677; in his will of 1676, names only Ephraim, and Eliz. as his children. The son died of smallpox, 1678.

Pope, John, Dorchester; came prob. 1633, with wife Jane, was a shoemaker, freeman, 1634; perhaps brought two or three children and here had John, born 1635; Nathan, who was born, as is said, but certainly died 1641; and by wife Alice had Thomas, 1643, and perhaps that Margaret, wife of John P., whose gravestone says, she died 1702, or 1672, as sometimes read, aged 74, was his third wife. He was one of the founders of the new church for Richard Mather, 1636; died 1646.

Pope, John, Springfield, 1678; prob. removed to Windsor, 1683; there died that year unmarried, it is thought.

Pope, Joseph, Salem; came in the *Mary and John* of London, 1634; freeman, 1637; there by wife Gertrude, had Damaris, bapt. 1643; Hannah, 1645, died young; Hannah, again, 1648; George, 1649, who prob. died young; Joseph, 1650; Benjamin, 1653; and Samuel, 1656;

besides Enos, not bapt.; in 1658 was punished for going to Quaker meeting, and died about 1667.

Pope, Richard, Dorchester, 1635; but Mr. Clapp thinks was not long there, and he is called brother by Joseph in his will.

Pope, Samuel, Salem; brother of the preceding; married, 1686, Exercise Smith; had Damaris, born 1687, died in few months; Samuel, 1689; Margaret, 1691; Enos, 1695; Hannah, 1697; Eliz., 1698; Eunice, 1700; and Ruth, 1705, died soon.

Pope, Seth, Darmouth, 1686.

Pope, Thomas, Plymouth, 1631; married 1637, Ann, daughter of Gabriel Fallowell, had Hannah, who married Joseph Bartlett, and died 1710, aged 71. When this wife died is not told, but he married second wife, 1646, Sarah, daughter of John Jenny; had Seth, born 1648; Thomas, 1651; John, 1653; and Susanna, who married 1666, Jacob Mitchell, and being called in 1663 *eldest* daughter of said P. by wife Sarah requires us to believe that another daughter followed. In 1675, he was 67 years old.

Pope, Thomas, Dorchester: perhaps brother of John of the same; had Thomas, born 1670; and Alice, 1676; as says Gen. Reg. V, 465, where it adds that he married 1681, Margaret Long.

Pope, Thomas, Suffield; by wife Margaret had Mindwell, born 1687; and his wife died next year at Springfield. One of these two Thomases, though which of them may be hard to guess, was of Hempstead in L. I.

Pope, Walter, Charlestown, 1634; died before 1640, leaving one child to whom the town made a grant. Frothingham, 80.

Pope, Walter, Charlestown; had Mary, who married Joseph Miller.

REFERENCES:—Amer. Ancestry, III, 150, 187, 223; V, 147; VII, 81; Cogswell's Hist., Henniker, N. H., 693; Davis' Landmarks, Plymouth, Mass., 208; Draper's Hist. Spencer, Mass., 245; Eaton's Hist., Thomaston, Me., II. 360; Essex Inst. Hist. Coll., VIII, 104-18; Freeman's Hist. Cape Cod, Mass., II, 152; Glover Gen., 306-8; Hatfield's Elizabeth, N. J., 89; Meade's Old Fams. of Va.: Mitchell's Hist., Bridgewater, Mass., 273; N. E. Hist. and Gen. Reg., XLII, 45-62; Norton's Hist., Fitzwilliam, N. H., 675; Paige's Hist., Hardwick, Mass., 454; Pope Gen. (1862), 68 p.; (1879), (1882), 7 p.; (1880), 22 p.; (1888), 340 p.; Richmond, Va., Standard, II, 34, 111, 35, 36; Ricketson's Hist., New Bedford, Mass., 205-7; Savage's Gen. Dict., III, 457-9; Spooner's Mem., W. Spooner, 77-82; Winslow Gen., II, 890-917.

PORTAGE: George, Boston; merchant, by wife Eliz., daughter of Simon Lynde, had Judith, born 1685, died young; Hannah, 1687; Samuel, 1689; Judith, again, 1691; Eliz., 1696, died next year, and George, who died without children. Savage thinks he removed from Boston, prob. from the Prov.

REFERENCE:—Prime's Bowdoin Gen., 17.

PORTER:—Abel, Boston; was unmarried when adm. of the church, 1641; by wife Ann, who had been widow of William Simmons, had John, 1643; prob. also Abel, and perhaps others. He may have been adm. freeman 1641, and the name written Parr, died 1685, aged 73, says the gravestone.

Porter, Abel, Boston; perhaps son of preceding, freeman 1672; then called junr.; was one of a new milit. comp., 1677.

Porter, Daniel, Farmington; a surgeon, for sev. years had pay from the Col.; by wife Mary had Daniel, born 1653; Mary, 1655; Nehemiah, 1656; Richard, 1658; Ann, 1661; John, 1662; and Samuel, 1665; all except Mary, in 1688, provided for by deed in Aug. of that year to avoid making a will under Andros admin.; he died 1690; of the descend. some went to Waterbury.

PORTER, EDWARD, Roxbury; came 1636, with two children, John, about 3 years old; and William, about 1 year; and by wife Eliz. here had Eliz., bapt. 1637; Hannah, born 1639; Mary, bapt. 1642; Joseph, 1644; Deborah, 1646; was freeman 1637; removed to Boston; there Eliz. married 1659, Joshua Nash; Hannah married 1663, Fathergone Dinly; and Mary married Peter Bennett.

PORTER, GEORGE, Salem, 1647; Felt.

PORTER, ISRAEL, Salem; died 1678, aged 32.

PORTER, ISRAEL, Hadley, freeman, 1684.

PORTER, JOHN, Windsor; among the earliest settlers, 1638; and so it is by some presumed that he went from Dorchester, but more prob. is it that he had been a short time only in Mass., and accomp. Rev. Ephraim Hewlett, bringing beside the six children ment. in his will, Sarah and Joseph, named by Goodwin, was constable, 1640; rep., 1646 and 7; and add. to church by wife Rose, born prob. in England at W.; had Nathaniel, born 1640; and Ann, sometimes called Hannah, 1642; and Parsons, in Geneal. Reg. V, 359, says he died 1648. His will gives eldest son John, £100; second James, £60; Samuel, Nathaniel, Rebecca, Rose, Mary, and Ann, each £30. His widow was buried 20 days after him.

PORTER, JOHN, Roxbury; freeman, 1633; had wife Margaret; removed to Boston; there a supporter of Wheelwright and disarmed 1637; soon removed to R. I.; signed there compact, 1638; was an Assistant, 1641, and after for some years, lived at Portsmouth, R. I., 1655, and Wickford, 1674; Haz. II, 612. He had a daughter perhaps named Hannah, who married the second Samuel Wilbor.

PORTER, JOHN, Hingham, 1635; was represent., 1644, and that year removed to Salem; had Sarah, bapt. 1649; had many elder children as is shown by his will, 1673, probated, 1676; died aged 80. To his eldest son, John, who had been a prisoner at Boston, 1665, for abuse of his paents (whose case taken up against the Col. by the royal conunrs. that year made such a stir among the people), who died 1684, he gave only £150, he having wasted much (and this is not a fifteenth part of the father's estate) to Joseph; Benjamin, who died without children; Samuel, who died long before; and Israel; beside daughters Mary, wife of Thomas Gardner, with her three children, and Sarah, prob. unmarried, adequate provision, almost naming Samuel's son John. He was represent. 1668. His wife, Mary, survived to 1684, but whether she be that Mary who joined the church, 1639, or in 1644, is not known.

PORTER, JOHN, Weymouth; by wife Deliverance, had Mary, born 1663; Susanna, 1665; John, 1667; one whose name is not given, 1672; and Ruth, 1675.

PORTER, JOHN, Hudley, freeman, 1690.

PORTER, JONATHAN, Salem, 1637; then had grant of land; freeman, 1641; had Mary bapt., 1645; and Jonathan, 1648; was of Beverly side. Mary married, 1669, Thomas Gardner.

PORTER, JONATHAN, Salem, 1636; a sergeant in 1647, and that year had grant of 200 acres; was selectman, 1653 and 4 but late in that year conveyed his estate at S. to James Chichester on condition that he should provide for his widow Eunice if she outlived him, and removed to Huntington, L. I.; had died before 1660, when Eunice sued for her right that year, and in 1670 estate

was divided to the heirs, who were all females. His three daughters married respectively James Chichester, Edward Harnett, and Stephen Jarvis; and widow Eunice married Giles Smith of Fairfield.

PORTER, NATHANIEL, Salem, 1638; had lived elsewhere, for he was freeman, 1637, and is not in Felt's fine list of church members.

PORTER, RICHARD, Weymouth; had Ruth, born 1639; was freeman 1653.

PORTER, ROBERT, Farmington, one of the first settlers, married 1655, Mary, daughter of Thomas Scott of Hartford, had Mary, born 1646; John, 1658; Thomas, 1650; Robert, 1652, died young; Eliz., 1654; Joanna, 1656; Sarah, 1657; Benjamin, 1660; Ann, 1664; and Hepzibah, 1666. He took second wife Hannah Freeman, a widow, and died 1689.

PORTER, ROBERT, Northampton; married, 1688, Sarah Burt; had John, born 1689, who, with his mother, died sóon. In 1691, he married Eliz. Rising; had John, again, 1692; Eliz., 1695; James, 1698; William, 1702; and Thomas, 1705. Both William and his father died 1712.

PORTER, ROGER, Watertown; went home prob. in 1637, and again came in the Confidence, from Southampton, 1638, aged 55, a husbandman of Long Sutton, Hants, with Joan, Susan, Mary and Rose, his daughters, was freeman, 1639; selectman, 1648, and died 1654, aged 71. His widow Grace, who had been widow of William and first of Thomas Rogers, died 1662, in her will naming gr.-child Daniel Smith, and John, Martha, Mary, Sarah, and Joseph Sherman. These last were part of the children of Capt. John Sherman, who had married her daughter Martha; and another daughter Elizabeth had married Daniel Smith. Hereby we discover that P. had been with part of his family at W. for this daughter Eliz. is not named among passengers in the Confidence, nor is the wife, Grace, who was left, no doubt, as W. in her husband's absence to gov. the family, but this is made more certain from our knowing that Sherman's wife had her first child born here, less than 5 months after the arrival of that ship.

PORTER, SAMUEL, Salem; died about 1659; had not long before married Hannah, daughter of William Dodge. His will early that year, made in anticip. of a voyage to Barbadoes, names son John. Perhaps Hannah was second wife. His widow married Thomas Woodbury.

PORTER, STEPHEN, Andover; freeman, 1691.

PORTER, THOMAS, Hartford; married, 1644, Sarah, daughter of Stephen Hart; removed to Farmington; had Sarah, born 1646; Thomas, 1648; Joanna, 1652; who were all bapt. 1653, prob. Dorothy bapt. 1654; Thomas, again, 1656; Samuel; and Ruth, who married, 1687, Samuel Smith, and next Joseph Root. He died 1697, and his will of 1691 names only Thomas, Dorothy and Samuel. Perhaps his daughter, Sarah, married, 1664, Nathaniel Winchell, and Joanna married, 1676, Stephen Taylor.

PORTER, THOMAS, Weymouth; had Thomas, posthum.. born 1673.

REFERENCES:—Aldrich's Walpole, N. H., 344; Amer. Ancestry, II, 97; IV, 74, 84, 103; VII, 210, 254; VIII, 75; Andrew's Porter Gen. (1881); Austin's R. I. Gen. Dict., 155; Bangor, Me., Hist. Mag., 59-61; Bronson's Hist. Waterbury, Ct., 519 24; Brook's Hist. Medford, Mass., 534; Butler's Hist. Farmington, Me., 553-7; Cleveland's Topsfield, Mass., Bi-Cent., 23; Cothren's Hist. Woodbury, Ct., 668; Cuyahoga Co., Ohio, Illust. Hist., 440; Eaton's Hist., Thomaston, Me., II. 360; Goodwin's Gen. Notes, 170-4; Hayward's Hist. Gilsum,

N. H., 378; Herrick Gen., 134-51; Hines' Lebanon, Ct., Address, 166; Hollister's Hist., Pawlet, Vt., 224; Huntington Gen., 200; Judd's Hist. Hadley, Mass., 553-7; Lapham's Hist. Norway, Me., 582; Lapham's Hist. Paris, Me., 697-9; Loomis Gen. Female Branches, 789; Maine Genealogist, I, 45-9; Martin's Hist., Chester, N. H., 85-7; Mitchell's Hist., Bridgewater, Ct., 274; Nash Gen., 72; N. E. Hist. Gen. Reg., IX, 54; XXX, 460; Osgood's Hist. Sketch, N. Danvers, 17; Orcutt's Hist., Stratford, Ct., 1272; Penn. Mag., IV, 292-7; Porter Gen. (1878), 350 p.; (1882), 125 p.; (1893), 888 p.; Richmond, Va., Standard, III, 28; Saunderson's Charlestown, N. H., 523-5; Savage's Gen. Dict., III, 459-64; Stiles' Hist. Windsor, Ct., II, 620-4; Temple's Hist. N. Brookfield, Mass., 707-8; Thayer Mem., 6-8; Timlow's Hist., Southington, Ct., 206-10; Whitman Gen., 502-14; Wyman's Charlestown, Mass., Gens., II, 766.

ARMS:—Arg., on a fess, sa., between two barrulets, or, three church bells, of the first.

CREST:—A portcullis; proper-chained, or.

MOTTO:—*Vigilantia et virtute.*

PORTIS, or PORTOUS: Robert, Boston, 1645; married 1659, Alice Greenwood.

PORTMART, PORMONT, PURMONT, or PERMONT:—Philemon, Boston, adm. of the church with wife, Susan, 1634; prob. brought one child, if not more; was freeman, 1635, and the first grammar school-master; had Lazarus, 1636; Ann, 1638; favored the cause of Wheelwright and followed him to Exeter, and afterward to Wells, having letters of dism. from church, 1639; but prob. came back after prob. not a few years; had Pedaiah, born 1640; his wife died 1642, and by second wife Eliz., had Martha, 1653. His daughter, Eliz., born prob. in England; married 1652, Nathaniel Adams; but another pretend. rec. says Samuel Norden, in Geneal. Reg., XI, 202.

POST:—Abraham, Saybrook, 1664; son prob. of Stephen; freeman, 1665; ensign, 1667; had Stephen, born 1664; Ann, 1667; Abraham, 1669; James, 1671; Esther, 1672; died in few days; Daniel, 1673; Gurdon, 1676; Joseph, 1678; Mary, 1680; and Elinor, 1682; and his wife died 1684. In the will of Uncas, four thousand acres were devis. to him, yet in Geneal. Reg., XIII, 234, his name is Past.

POST, ISAAC, Huntington, L. I., 1666.

POST, JOHN, Woburn; married, 1650, Susanna Sutton; but whether she had children or how long she lived is not told; yet Savage finds that he married second wife, 1662, Mary Tyler, and had Mary, born 1664; Joanna, 1666; and John, 1669.

POST, RICHARD, Southampton, L. I., 1640; named by Thompson, may easily be thought the same as that one of the first settlers of New London, 1646 or 7, a blacksmith, who sold his estate, 1651 or 2, to Amos Richardson, and removed, but whither is not known, nor whether he had children or not.

POST, STEPHEN, Cambridge, 1634; removed, 1636, to Hartford, an original propr.; had John, Thomas, and Abraham, prob. Catherine, who married Alexander Chalker, in 1649, was of Saybrook, where he died 1659.

REFERENCES:—Amer. Ancestry, II, 97; IX, 40; Bolton's Westchester Co., N. Y., II, 754; Buckingham Gen., 272-5; Bunker's L. I. Genealogies, 263-5; Caulkins' Hist. Norwich, Ct., 194-6; Chapman Gen., 81; Clute's Hist. Staten Island, N. Y., 417; Eaton's Hist. Thomaston, Me., II, 361; Howell's Hist., Southampton, N. Y., 353-6; Huron and Erie Co., Ohio, Hist., 123;

Hyde's Hist. Address, Ware, Mass., 628; Pearson's Schenectady, N. Y., Settlers, 145; Roome Gen., 322-9; Savage's Gen. Dict., III, 465; Sewall's Hist., Woburn, Mass., 630; Walworth's Hyde Gen., II, 4, 11-14, 1033-8.

POSTER:—Abel, is the name given to a freeman of Mass., 1674, but where he lived is unknown, and error is suspected.

POTTER:—Abel, Dartmouth; married, 1669, Rachel, youngest daughter of John Warner; removed to Warwick; in his will of 1692, names eldest son George, youngest Stephen, and other child. Abel, Benjamin and Mary.

POTTER, ANTHONY, Ipswich, 1648; married Eliz., prob. daughter of deacon John Whipple of the same; had several children who with wife outlived him, as John, Edmund, Elizabeth, Kimball, Lydia Putnam, prob. wife of Jonathan, beside Thomas and Anthony.

POTTER, GEORGE, Newport, 1638.

POTTER, HUMFREY, Salem; had only child Ann, who married 1656, Anthony Needham.

POTTER, ICHABOD, Portsmouth, R. I.; perhaps son of Robert, the friend of Garton, married Martha, daughter of Thomas Hazard.

POTTER, INDIGO, or perhaps INIGO, Charlestown: married, 1663, Mary Lawrence, daughter of John of Groton; may have lived in some other town; by wife Mary had children, Mary, John, Richard, Inigo, Margaret, all bapt. at C., 1681, and Margaret, again, 1682. John was a grantee of Sudbury in 1640, but where he resided or anything else concerning him is unknown.

POTTER, JOHN, New Haven, perhaps 1639; had John and Samuel, bapt. 1641; perhaps died before 1643, as a widow P., with two children, is that year mentioned. She may also have married again, for Eliz. Rose, in 1677, by her will ment. her son John and Samuel; P., beside several daughters. Coffin made the surname Polter.

POTTER, NICHOLAS, Lynn, 1651; much engaged in the iron works; removed to Salem, 1660, there called a bricklayer; had Hannah, bapt. 1661; and Mary, 1663; Samuel, born 1665, died at one year; Hannah, again, 1666; Lydia, 1667, died next year; Bethia, 1668; Samuel, 1669; Lydia, again, 1670, died next year; Benjamin, 1671; and Joseph, 1673. His wife, Mary, died soon after and he died 1677. That he had children by both wives is inferred, and that second wife, Mary, was daughter of John Gedney appears in Essex Inst., II, 275; but for the bapt. name of the mother of the children Robert, Eliz., Sarah, who were prob. born at Lynn by first wife, certainly is unattainable, though from the transcript of the will it may seem that each wife brought both Samuel and Benjamin. A flickering of light comes from p. 301, indicative that first wife was Alice, who died 1659.

POTTER, ROBERT, Lynn, 1630; freeman, 1634; removed to Newport, where, 1638, he was adm. an inhabitant and in 1641 united with Gorton in settlement of Shaomet, which they called Warwick, and two years later was seized with the whole comp. and brought prisoner to Boston, where the government sentenced them to be confined in various places, enjoining them not to preach their monstrous absurd doctrine on pain of death. Soon, however, as sympathy for such suffering was unavoidably exciting, they all were banished, and he went to England and obt. justice by restorat. to their estate. He kept an inn at W., in 1649, and died in the autumn of 1655, or soon after, leaving son John, born about 1639, and daughters, Deliverance, wife of James Greene; Eliz., who married Richard Harcutt of the same; beside widow Sarah, not mother of either of the children, who became wife, 1657, of John Sandford, the schoolmaster of Boston. Of his first wife the name is not known, but Gorton in his narrative of the invasion and assault by the Mass. forces upon the new settlement of W., tells that she died at that time, perhaps of trepidation.

POTTER, ROBERT, Roxbury, 1634; in joining the church had wife Isabel, of neither of which does Savage find any ment. in records of town or church, but there he was buried, 1654; yet in Boston ch. he had his daughter, Deliverance, bapt., 1637, and in the record of death is error, no doubt, of Robert for William. Prob. he removed.

POTTER, THOMAS, Portsmouth, R. I.; perhaps grandson of Nicholas of Lynn; married, 1687, Susanna, daughter of John Tripp; had Susanna, born 1688; Sarah, 1690; and Ichabod, 1692.

POTTER, VINCENT, Boston; came in the *Eliz. and Ann* from London, 1635, aged 21; was next year a soldier at the castle. [Winthrop, II, 346;] went home in 1639, in the same ship with John Josselyn, who ment. p. 30, that he was afterwards questioned for a Regicide. He was prob. one of the madcap millenarians with Venner, of Salem, but not of sufficient importance to be put to death.

POTTER, WILLIAM, Braintree; came perhaps in the *Increase* from London, 1635, aged 25; one of the early members of that church, 1639; freeman, 1640; removed to Roxbury; married, 1646, Judith Graves, widow of John. She survived him and married Samuel Finch.

POTTER, WILLIAM, New Haven; had Mary, and Sarah, prob. not twins, bapt. 1641; Hope, 1641; Rebecca, 1643; and Nathaniel, 1644.

REFERENCES:—Amer. Ancestry, II, 97; III. 220; IV, 179; V, 178; Austin's Allied Fams., 200; Austin's Ancestries, 47; Austin's R. I. Dict., 155, 354; Bouton's Hist., Concord, N. H., 683; Champion Gen.; Cochrane's Hist., Antrim, N. H., 648; Dodd's Hist., E. Haven, Ct., 142-4; Driver Gen., 51-7; Greene Gen.; Dwight Gen., 543; Ipswich, Mass., Antiq. Papers, June (1883); Montague Gen., 453-7; N. E. Hist. Gen. Reg., XVIII, 150-3; North's Hist., Augusta, Me., 924-6; Norton's Hist., Fitzwilliam, N. H., 645-9; Potter Gen. (1888), 270 p.; Potter's Old Fams., Concord, Mass. (1887); Rhode Island Hist. Mag., VI, 203, R. I. Hist. Soc. Coll., III, 294; Savage's Gen. Dict., III, 466-8; Stearn's Hist. Ashburnham, Mass., 853; Temple's Hist. N. Brookfield, Mass., 708-13; Washburn's Hist. Leicester, Mass., 388; Wheeler's Hist. Brunswick, Me., 848; Wyman's Charlestown, Mass., Gens., II, 768.

POTTS:—Richard, Kennebeck; whose wife was killed by the Indians at Arowsie Isl., 1676; Willis, I, 148.

POTTS, THOMAS, Dover; by wife, Joanna, had Mary, born 1690, and another daughter, 1693.

REFERENCES:—Amer. Ancestry, I, 62; II, 97; VII, 120; IX, 171; Cooley's, Trenton, N. J., Settlers, 192-5; Holstein Gen.; Neill Fam. of Delaware, 99-111; Potts' Carter Gen., 192; Potts Gen. (1874), 416 pp.; Richmond, Va., Standard, IV, 10.

POTUM (if this be a possible name):—Charles, of Cape Porpus, being dead, administ. was given 1678 to John Barrett.

POULTNER:—John, Billerica, 1658; from Rayleigh in Co. Essex, married, 1662, Rachel Eliot of Braintree, daughter of Francis; died at Cambridge, 1676, aged 41, as inscription on gravestone is given by Harris, Epit. 6. His widow married, 1677, John Whitmore, and his sister, Hannah, perhaps, married John Dudley, as did, 1655, Eliz., with Jonathan Danforth, the first; and Mary, 1687, with Samuel Winship. All were, no doubt, children of John P., early settlers at B., but dec. before last date. Prob. he was driven in by Indian hostilities. But a John of Cambridge, perhaps his son, was living there, 1698, and Savage thinks married Hannah, daughter of Lieut. John Hammond, the richest man of Watertown. He may have removed to Boston, and in 1713 been chosen to a town office.

REFERENCES:—Hazen's Billerica, 114; Hudson's Hist., Lexington, Mass., 187.

POUND:—Thomas, a pirate in the Vineyard Sound, 1689; taken and brought in.

POUT, or POAT:—William, Marblehead, 1668-74.

POW:—William, Marblehead, 1674; Dana, 8. It is strange that we never find his name, espec. as it bears the prefix of respect in Dana.

POWELL:—Abel, Newbury, and Caleb, his brother, actors in the direful nonsense of witchcraft, 1679, against or upon William Morse and his wife, Eliz., of which in Hist. of Newbury, 122 134, and in Essex Inst., II, 30; 31 and 212, more than enough may be read. See also a few words in Savage's Dict., III, 242, under Morse.

POWELL, JOHN, Charlestown; by wife, Sarah, had John, bapt., 1669; but the father had died year preceding and the young widow joined to the church and soon married John Blaney.

POWELL, MICHAEL, Dedham, 1639; by wife Abigail had perhaps that Sarah who married 1653, Timothy Dwight, and may have been born in England; Eliz. 164; Dorothy, 1643; and Michael, 1645; beside Margaret, bapt. 1648, about 8 days old; was freeman 1641, removed to Boston, 1647; and without ordination taught in the new church bef. sett. of a minister there, or, indeed, before the gathering of a church, which occurred year following, when he was ord. a ruling elder, the government forbid. his being min. for want of education; had Margaret, bapt. 1649; and died, 1673.

POWELL, RALPH, Marshfield; married 1676, Martha Clement.

POWELL, ROBERT, Exeter; toow oath of fidelity, 1677.

POWELL, ROWLAND, Gloucester, 1657; by wife Isabel, had Rowland, and a daughter, twins, born, 1658, of whom the daughter died next day; Mary, 1660; and Stephen, 1662.

POWELL, THOMAS, New Haven; had Hannah, born 1641, bapt. 1643; Priscilla, 1642; Mary, 1645; Martha, 1649; prob. died soon; Martha, again, 1651; and Esther, prob. bapt. 1653, all in right of wife Priscilla; may be same who, 1664, was of Long Island, adm. to be sworn freeman of Conn. by commsnrs. of Huntington. He was dissatisfied prob. with the recusancy of that Col. to the union with Conn. as by the royal charter provided and may have been of Springfield, 1665; at least bought land there, but did not continue long, and went back to New H. but not to be in the list of 1669, and died 1681.

POWELL, THOMAS, Saco, 1670.

POWELL, THOMAS, Windsor; married 1676, Alice Traharen, had Ann, born 1678; Thomas, 1680; and Hannah, 1682, died at 2 years; and he died 1685.

POWELL, WILLIAM, Charlestown, 1636; by wife Eliz. had Mary, born 1637; Martha, 1639; Joshua, 1641; died soon; Eliz., 1642; and Joshua, again, 1644; the wife died that year. He may be that man, said by Farmer to have died at Salem, 1670.

POWELL, WILLIAM, Taunton, 1643.
REFERENCES:—Amer. Ancestry, II, 97; IV, 210; VII, 56; Babson's Hist. Gloucester, Mass., 129; Bunkers' L. I. Gens., 29-71; Chase's Hist. Chester, N. H., 575; Corliss' No. Yarmouth, Me.; Fowler's Our Predecessors; Hayden's Virginia Gens., 508; Kulp's Wyoming Valley Fams.; Maine Hist. Soc. Coll., VII, 230-8; Meade's Old Fams. of Va., II, 277; Ruttenber's Hist. Newburgh, N. Y., 304-6; Ruttenber's Orange Co., N. Y., 401-3; Savage's Gen. Dict., III, 469; Slaughter's St. Mark's Parish, 193; Smith's Hist. Delaware Co., Pa., 493; Van Kleeck's Thos. Powell Biog. (1857).

POWER:—John, Charlestown; by wife Sarah, had Peter, born, 1643.

POWER, NICHOLAS, Providence; an early settler soon after Roger Williams, died 1657, leaving widow, Jane, and son, Nicholas, and daughter, Hope, both under age. He never dwelt at Shaomet, Staples says, though of the number of purch. of that territory and so suffered very slightly in the monstrous proceed. against Gorton and his comp. at Warwick, 1643. Yet he is one of the signers of the declarations of their rights, 1652. Tradition has been very rich, and as usual, very false about this man and his son of the same name. The father was here to sign the claim of rights, 1642, and was one of the purchasers with Gorton and the other misbelievers of Warwick, and was next year brought a prisoner to Boston, yet the mythical honor makes him to have left Drogheda, "during the siege in 1642, for Surinam, where the family had large estates." Authentic hist. makes the siege of Drogheda a dozen years later. In favor of the second Nichoas, that authority makes his wife "daughter of Sir Zachary R. a Cheshire baronet," but it wisely omits to tell how his title was acquired. Most curious is the document called his will, made 1667 (near ten years after his death by the municip. officers pub. in authentic form. R. I. Hist. Coll., II, Apx. 14.

POWER, NICHOLAS, Providence; son of preceding; freeman, 1655; took engagement of allegiance, 1670; married, 1672, Rebecca, daughter of Zachary Rhodes, had Hope, who died young; and Col. Nicholas, born 1673; and tradition tells that he was killed accidentally by his own friends at the Swamp Fight, 1675, in Phillip's War. His widow married, 1676, Daniel Williams.

POWER, WALTER, Malden, 1660; married 1661, Trial, daughter of Ralph Shepard; had William; Mary; Isaac; Thomas; Daniel, born in 1669; Increase, 1671; Walter, 1674; Jacob, 1679; and Sarah, 1683; and died at Littleton about 1718.

REFERENCES:—Amer. Ancestry, II, 98; Austin's R. I. Gen. Dict., 356; A's Ancestral Dict., 47; Narragansett Hist. Reg., VII, 17-24; Power's Hist. Sangamon Co., Ills., 578; Savage's Gen. Dict., III, 470.

POWES:—Thomas, Boston, of whom Savage sees nothing but that Sewall says he was drowned, 1684.

POWNING, or POUNDING:—Henry, Boston; freeman 1644, but he was of another church of what town Savage is ignorant; had Henry, born 1654, who, perhaps, was of artillery co., 1677; Hannah, 1656, died next year; and Sarah, 1659. In 1695, a widow P. was a householder in B., and Daniel P., artillery co., 1691, a deacon, died 1735.

POWSLAND, POWSLEY, POWLAND, POWLLEN, PAUSLAND, POUSLIN, or PAUSLY:—James, Salem; married 1670, Mary Barnes, wid. prob. of Thom-

as, 1675, was employed as a gunner. Felt, II, 486. He lived, 1674, in Marblehead Side.

POUSLAND, RICHARD, Falmouth, 1674-90. Willis, I, 71, 133.

PRANCE:—Philip, Salem, 1689, master mariner. Felt.

PRATT:—Abraham, Charlestown, a surgeon having in Col. rec. 1630, when he required to be made free, the prefix of respect came, we may well infer, in the fleet with Winthrop, and was living, 1631, at C. He, with his wife Joanna, early joined the church of Roxbury, but removed again to C. and his wife died 1645, and he died, as the gravestone says, on same day.

PRATT, BENEJAH, Plymouth; son perhaps of Joshua or of Phineas, married 1655, Persis Dunham, prob. daughter of first John, had Abigail, born, 1657.

PRATT, DANIEL, Hartford; son prob. of John, freeman, 1657, had Daniel, seven daughters, and died 1691. The daughters were Hannah, married 1678, sec. Daniel Clark; Eliz., wife of Nathaniel Goodwin; Sarah Phelps; Mary Sandford; Rachel Skinner; Esther; and another whose name is not known. Esther, in 1702, died, unmarried; in her will refer. to brother Daniel, and five sisters, so that we infer one was dead since the father.

PRATT, EPHRAIM, Weymouth, by wife, Phebe, had Ephraim, born 1698.

PRATT, JOHN, Cambridge, an expert surgeon, possibly brother of Abraham, was of Hooker's church and freeman, 1634; but he had been so early as 1629 engaged for Boston company, and came in the Lion's Whelp, but returned in same ship, and when next he came, sat down first at Braintree, in 1635, was animadvert. on for ill report of the country, removed to Hartford, prob. 1637, was represent. 1639-42, but not after, excus. from watch, according to previous promise, in 1644, but went for home few months after with his wife, having no children, and above 60 years od, and was drowned in shipwreck on the coast of Spain. Winthrop, I, 173, and II, 239, with Trumbull Col. Rec. II, 27, 108, and 150.

PRATT, JOHN, Hingham, lost his house by fire, 1646, and perhaps removed to Weymouth, and may have been father of John, Joseph, Matthew, Samuel, and Thomas of that town, or of some of them.

PRATT, JOHN, Hartford; an orig. propr. was prob. a carpenter, and was father of John, and Daniel, died 1655. His will names wife, Eliz., and the two sons. He has been sometimes confused with the surgeon who owned no land, whereas this man owned several lots. See Trumbull, Col. Rec. I, 230.

PRATT, JOHN, Dorchester, freeman, 1643, had John, born about 1630, and Timothy, and died, 1647, leaving widow Mary, who married William Turner; Timothy settled in Boston; John, at Medfield.

PRATT, JOHN, Kingston; by wife, Ann, had Deliverance, born 1664; Mary, 1666; John, 1667; Ebenezer, 1669; Phineas, 1671; Joshua, 1673; Jeremy, 1674; and Mercy, 1676.

PRATT, JOHN, Medfield, 1666; was son of John of Dorchester, but prob. born in England, and Savage knows nothing more, except that he had John, Mary, Priscilla, Hannah, and Sarah, and wife, Rebecca, all named in his will, 1707.

PRATT, JOHN, Malden; son of Richard of the same, by first wife, Mary, had Richard; John, born 1686; and by wife, Martha, married 1686, had John born 1687; and Martha, 1690; and he may have removed to Reading, where Mr. Eaton settles one of the name before 1700;

but more prob. he was the deacon who died at M., 1742, aged over 81 years. His widow died 1744, aged 83; unless she died as his wife 1742, aged 79. However, it may be that the long-lived John was son of Phineas, and that his wife, Martha, was daughter of Richard Pratt. The decision is not easy upon Geneal. Reg. IX, 325. Another JOHN, or the same, of Malden, by wife, Mary, had Mary, born 1696, perhaps John, Thomas, Hannah, Ebenezer, Joseph, William, Caleb, Abigail, and Joshua, or some of them, for the children of this surname as the flowers of the field are spread about; but the gravestones in Malden prove that one John's wife, Mary, died 1710, in 56th year, and her husband, John, had died 1708.

PRATT, JOHN, Weymouth, by wife, Mary, who may have been daughter of John Whitman of the same, had Samuel, born 1686, and by wife Mercy, prob. the same Mary, had John, 1692; and John, again, 1696. One JOHN, of Boston, married 1691, Margaret Maverick, but of him or wife Savage knows no more.

PRATT, JONATHAN, Plymouth, brother perhaps of Benejah, married 1664, Abigail Wood, had Abigail, born 1665; Bathsheba, 1667; Jonathan, 1669; Hannah, 1671; Jabez, 1673; Meletiah, 1676; and Bethia, 1679.

PRATT, JOSEPH, Weymouth; by wife, Sarah, had Sarah, born 1664; Joseph, 1666; and John, 1668; was freeman, 1672, and perhaps sworn again 1674, when he lived perhaps at Nantucket, and had there Mary, 1675.

PRATT, JOSEPH, Charlestown; perhaps son of Phineas, married, 1675, Dorcas Folger, had Joseph, born 1677; Bethia, 1680; Benjamin, 1682, died soon; Dorcas, 1683, died soon; Phineas, 1684; Joshua, 1686; Lydia, 1688.

PRATT, JOSHUA, Medfield, 1649.

PRATT, MATTHEW, Weymouth; freeman 1640, had Joseph, born 1637, prob. died soon; and perhaps others, and may have, before 1643, removed to Rehoboth.

PRATT, MATTHEW, Weymouth, perhaps son of preceding, by wife, Sarah, had Matthew, born 1665; Mary, 1667; Hannah, 1670; William, 1673; may have removed to Boston in Philip's war; had son Samuel, bapt. 1676, and gone again to W., there had Ann, 1682; and Susanna, 1684. Prob. he was son but may have been nephew of preceding. He became deaf at 12 years, and almost lost speech, and his wife was deaf and dumb after 3 years.

PRATT, MICAH, Weymouth; had John, born 1691.

PRATT, PETER, Lyme; married 1679, Eliz., that daughter of Matthew Griswold who had been three years before divorced from John Rogers for his heresy; had Peter, and died 1688, and 1691, his widow married Matthew Beckwith. It is not known whose son he was, though sometimes it has been guessed that he was William's of which the probability is remote.

PRATT, PHINEAS, Plymouth; came in 1622, as one of Capt. Weston's men, planted at Weymouth, but soon after, as Gov. Winslow tells in Young's Chron. of the Pilgr. he went to P., had share in the division of land, as if he had come in the *Ann* with Joshua, who may have been a brother, and so may we excuse the error of Mitchell, 279, who says he came in the *Ann*, when it is plain he was here one year earlier; married, 1630, a daughter of Cuthbert Cuthbertson, it is said, removed after many years to Charlestown.

PRATT, RICHARD, Charlestown; born, it is said, youngest of nine children, to John, of Malden, in Co. Essex, and there bapt. 1615; by wife, Mary, had Mary, born 1643; Thomas, 1646; Mercy, 1650, died young; John, 1655; Eliz.; Martha, 1663; and Hannah. He lived in Malden Side, and died 1691.

PRATT, SAMUEL, Weymouth; a carpenter, freeman 1666; by wife, Hannah, perhaps daughter of John Rogers of the same, had Judah, born 1661; another child whose name is out, 1663; Hannah, 1665; Mary, 1668; Samuel, 1670; Experience, 1673; and perhaps Martha, 1675. He was engaged in settlem. of Mendon, 1663.

PRATT, SAMUEL, Wickford, 1674.

PRATT, THOMAS, Watertown, freeman 1647, unless Barry overlooked one generation and it was not that freenan, but his son, who had, partly before and partly after, removed Framingham, after being of Sudbury; these eleven children, Thomas, 1656; John; Ebenezer; Joseph; Philip; David; Jabez; Nathaniel; Abial, fem. Ephraim; and Jonathan; in 1682 had land set to him at Sherborn, and died about 1692; at least, admin. that year was given to widow Susanna and son John. All these ten sons married and had families. It seems prob. that the father of these many children was he who swore fidelity in 1652, rather than the freeman of 1647, who may have been his father.

PRATT, THOMAS, Weymouth; had William, born 1659. A Serg. Pratt, of Weymouth, perhaps not this man, but Joseph, Matthew, or Samuel, was killed by the Indians in Phip's war, 1676.

PRATT, THOMAS, Malden, by wife, Sarah, had Sarah, bapt. 1661, died young; Eliz., 1662; John, 1665; Sarah, again, 1666; Robert, 1668, died young; Edmund, 1670; Hannah, 1672; William, 1674; Deborah, 1676; and Robert, again, 1684.

PRATT, WILLIAM, Hartford; an original propr. prob. brother of John, the second of the same, by wife, Eliz., daughter of John Clark of Milford, ad Eliz., born 1642; John, 1645; removed that year to Saybrook; there had Joseph, 1648; Sarah, 1651; William, 1653; Samuel, 1655; Lydia, 1660; and Nathaniel, perhaps before the last, but not named in second, but by his father in a deed to him; was lieut. in 1661, rep. 1666, and eleven years more. His eldest daughter married William Backus of Norwich; Sarah, married, 1670, Isaac Waterhouse; and Lydia, married, 1679, John Kirtland of Saybrook.

PRATT, WILLIAM, Weymouth; freeman, 1651.

PRATT, WILLIAM, Weymouth; may have been son of first William of the same, or nephew, freeman 1680, by wife, Eliz., daughter of Richard Baker of Dorchester, had Thankful, 1683; and by wife, Experience, had Joanna, 1692; and William, 1695. He removed to Dorchester.

REFERENCES.

MASSACHUSETTS:—Barry's Hist. Framingham, 363-9; Barry's Hist. Hanover, 359; Bond's Hist. Watertown, 551; Chandler's Hist. Shirley, 605; Clark's Hist. Norton, 88; Davis's Landmarks Plymouth, 809; Deane's Hist. Scituate, 326; Eaton's Hist. Reading, 109; Kingman's Hist. N. Bridgewater, 623-5; Mitchell's Hist. Bridgewater, 275-9; Morse's Gen. Sherburn, 203; Paige's Hist. Cambridge, 628; Paige's Hist. Hardwick, 456; Pierce's Hist. Grafton, 546; Stearn's Hist. Ashburnham, 853; Ward's Hist. Shrewsbury, 392-9; Wyman's Charlestown, Mass., Gens., 770-3.

NEW HAMPSHIRE:—Blood's Hist. of Temple, 242-5; Hayward's Hist. Hancock, 811; Kidder's Hist. New Ipswich, 419; Norton's Hist. Fitzwilliam, 679-84; Worcester's Hist. Hollis, 385.

CONNECTICUT:—Andrew's Hist. New Britain, 242-287; Gold's Hist. Cornwall, 267-72; Porter's Hartford Settlers, 17-9; Sedgwick's Hist. Sharon, 106; Timlow's Hist. Southington, 211-3.

OTHER PUBLICATIONS:—Amer. Ancestry, I, 62; II, 98; IV, 229; V, 3, 229; IX, 125; Austin's R. I. Gen.

Dict., 157; Barbour's My Wife and Mother App., 25; Bass' Hist. Braintree, Vt., 172-5; Buckingham Gen., 211-3; Chapman Gen., 256-62; Chapman's Pratt Gen. (1864); Corliss' No. Yarmouth, Me.; Davis Gen., 159; Futhey's Hist. Chester Co., Pa., 689; Hollister's Hist. Pawlet, Vt., 226; Ketchum's Hist. Buffalo, N. Y., II., 174; Lapham's Hist. Paris, Me., 700-2; Loomis Gen. Female Branches, 668; Orford, N. H., Centen., 130-3; Paul's Hist. Wells, Vt., 142; Pompey, N. Y., Reunion, 341-7; Porter's Pratt Gen. (1860) 8 p.; (1864), 420 p.; (1890) 226 p.; Savage's Gen. Dict., III, 471-6; Spooner Gen., I, 762; Walker Gen., 54; Walworth's Hyde Gen., 407-9.

PRAY:—Elisha, Providence; swore alleg. 1682.

PRAY, EPHRAIM, Braintree; son, prob. eldest, of John of the same; married Eliz., daughter of John Hayden; had Ephraim, born 1681; John, 1683; Eliz., 1685; Hannah, 1607; Ruth, 1689; Samuel, 1692; Joseph, 1695; Mary, 1697, and Sarah, 1700.

PRAY, EPHRAIM, Providence, 1676; "who staid and went not away," says the record through the war. He married the widow of Benjamin Herenden.

PRAY, JOHN, Braintree; married 1657, Joanna Dowman; had John, 1658, who probably died before his father, beside Ephraim, Samuel, Joseph, and two daughters, Hannah Bell and Dorothy Furbush, to divide his estate 1699; but Savage knows not the husband.

PRAY, JOHN, Providence; swore alleg. 1671; another of those not frightened away in 1676.

PRAY, QUINTIN and RICHARD, says Lewis, were of Lynn 1645; the former is among debtors, 1655, to estate of Joshua Foote, and the latter by Farmer is put among first settlers of R. I., and in Philip's war refusing to quit Providence. He had sworn alleg. to the king 1668.

PRAY, WILLIAM, Providence; swore alleg. 1682.

REFERENCES:—Austin's R. I. Gen. Dict., 358; Dearborn's Hist. Parsonsfield, Me., 398; Paul's Hist. Wells, Vt., 143; Pope Gen.; Wentworth Gen., I, 468-70.

PREBLE:—Abraham, Scituate, 1637; married Judith, daughter of Nathaniel Tilden; had Abraham, born about 1642; Nathaniel, bapt. there 1648; though some years before he had removed to York, where he perhaps had Benjamin and others; was magistrate 1650; submitted soon to Massachusetts, and freeman 1652; treasurer of the Co., 1659; and died 1663, leaving wife Judith, and several children, of whom one daughter was married. Willis, I, 102.

PREBLE, JOHN, NATHANIEL and STEPHEN; who took oath of alleg. to his majesty at York 1680, were prob. sons of above.

REFERENCES:—Amer. Ancestry, V, 143; VII, 100; Corliss' No. Yarmouth, Me.; Journals of Smith and Dean, 251; N. E. Hist. Reg., XXII, 311; XXIV, 253; Preble Gens. (1850), 28 p., (1868),-336 p.; Ruggle's Gen.; Savage's Gen. Dict., III, 477.

PRENCE:—Thomas, Plymouth; came in the Fortune, 1621; was son of Thomas of Lechlade; in Co. Gloucester, near Cricklade, in Wilts; mar. 1624, Patience, daughter of Elder William Brewster; had Thomas, Rebecca, Hannah, Mercy, and Sarah. His wife died 1634, and he removed to Duxbury; married 1635 Mary, daughter of William Collier, and was chosen Gov. that year, and for two or three years after an Assistant, and Gov. again in 1638, after an Assist. for many years. By this wife he had Jane, born 1637; and prob. Mary, Eliz. and Judith; in 1645 removed to Eastham, there again chosen Gov. 1658, and there his wife died. A third wife, Mary, in 1662, was widow of Samuel Freeman, Sen.; and he

removed again, 1663, to Plymouth; there died, 1673; leaving widow Mary. The son Thomas went to England; married and died young; leaving widow and daughter Susanna.

REFERENCES:—Savage's Gen. Dict., III, 477; Winsor's Hist. Duxbury, Mass., 293.

PRENTICE:—Henry, Cambridge, 1640; was an original propr. of Sudbury; freeman 1650; died 1654. His first wife Eliz. died 1643; and by second wife Joanna, he had Mary, born 1644; Solomon, 1646; Abiah, 1648; Samuel, 1650; Sarah, and Henry. His widow married, 1662, John Gibson; and Mary married, 1664, Nathaniel Hancock.

PRENTICE, JAMES, Cambridge, on that side which became Newton, may have been son of Robert of Roxbury; born in England by wife Susanna, daughter of famous Capt. Edward Johnson; had James, born 1656; Susanna, 1657; Hannah, 1659; Eliz., 1660; Sarah, 1662, and Rose; was freeman, 1690; selectman, 1694; and died 1710; aged 81.

PRENTICE, ROBERT, Roxbury; died 1666; and his inv. was given in by his brother, Capt. Thomas; but nothing is known of his coming, or whether he had wife or children.

PRENTICE, THOMAS, Cambridge, on S. side of the river, now Newton, brought from Eng. wife Grace, and daughter Grace; bapt. there; had here Thomas and Eliz., twins, born 1650; Mary; John, 1654, died next year; John, again, 1655; and Hannah, 1661; was freeman 1652; rep. 1672-4; in 1675, on the first day after Philip began hostil. went to the war in command of a troop of horse, and with great reputation served through it. His influence was great in obt. separation of Newton, in which his estate was. The wife died 1692; and he died 1710, in 89th year.

PRENTICE, THOMAS, Cambridge, in that part now Newton; prob. brother of James, possibly nephew of preceding; born in England; it is thought married Rebecca, daughter of Edward Jackson, Sen.; had Frances, Thomas, John, Edward, James, Ebenezer, Enos, Rebecca, and Sarah; was freeman 1680; selectman 1686, and sev. years afterward; and died 1724, at great age, perhaps above 90.

PRENTICE, VALENTINE, Roxbury; came in 1631; prob. with Eliot in the Lion, bringing wife, Alice, and son, John; having buried one child at sea; freeman 1632; perhaps had one child born here, and died prob. before end of next year; for town record has it that widow married, 1634, John Watson. One Alice P., who possibly was daughter of his, died at Concorn, 1644.

REFERENCES:—Allen's Worcester, 55; Amer. Ancestry, I, 63; II, 155; Bond's Hist. Watertown, Mass., 407; Caulkin's Hist. New London, Ct., 328-30; Cogswell's Hist. Nottingham, N. H., 765; Cothren's Hist. Woodbury, Ct., 672; Cutter's Hist. Arlington, Mass., 284-6; Fox's Hist. Dunstable, Mass., 248; Hayward's Hist. Hancock, N. H., 812-4; Jackson's Hist. Newton, Mass., 389-95; Kidder's Hist. New Ipswich, N. H., 420; Leland Gen., 98-100; Morse's Gen. Sherborn, Mass., 204; N. E. Hist. Gen. Reg., VII, 74; VIII, 333; Paige's Hist. Cambridge, Mass., 628-36; Pierce's Hist. Grafton, Mass., 547-52; Power's Hist. Sangamon Co., Ill., 579; Prentice Gen. (1852), 280 p., (1883), 446 p.; Savage's Gen. Dict., III, 478-80; Stanton Gen., 74-7; Temple's Hist. Northfield, Mass., 520-2; Wyman's Charlestown, Mass., II, 773-6.

PRESBURY:—John, Sandwich, 1643; was buried 1648.

PRESBURY, JOHN, Saco; in 1670 was constable there; died 1679, leaving only child, Nathaniel.

PRESCOTT:—James; by wife Mary, daughter of Nathaniel Boulter, had Joshua, born 1669; James, 1671; Rebecca, 1673; Jonathan, 1675; Mary, 1677; Abigail and Temperance, twins, 1679; John, 1681; and Nathaniel, 1683.

PRESCOTT, JOHN, Lancaster; blacksmith; came about 1640; as is said, with wife Mary Platts (a Yorkshire girl, while he was born in Lancashire, but lived in Sowerby in the parish of Halifax in the W. riding of Yorkshire), and several children, sat down first at Watertown, removed 1645 or 1646 to the foundation of a new sett. at L. Children were Mary, Sarah, Martha, and John, all supposed to have been born abroad; Lydia, born 1641; Jonathan and Jonas, 1648; the last prob. the only one at L. He took oath of alleg. 1652, but was not admitted freeman before 1669; was with his family removed shortly after the doleful day of Feb. 10, 1676, and the town was wholly abandoned for several years so that no white man lived between the towns on Conn. river and those on the Concord. In 1682 the number of families was not more than one-third as large as seven years before. But of these, Prescott's was one, and the year assigned for his death is 1683.

PRESCOTT, PETER, Salem; freeman, 1682; lived in the village that became Danvers, and had part in the trouble of Rev. Mr. Paris. He had married, 1679, Eliz. Redington.

REFERENCES:—Alden's American Epitaphs, II, 59; Amer. Ancestry, III, 219; IV, 111; Butler's Hist. Groton, Mass., 428; Chase's Hist. Chester, N. H., 575; Coggswell's Nottingham, N. H., 437 44; Cutter's Hist. Jaffrey, N. H., 441-6; Eaton's Hist. Thomaston, Me., II, 363; Greene's Early Groton, Mass., Settlers, 15-7; Greene's Groton, Mass., Epitaphs, 249-51; Hayward's Hist. Hancock, N. H., 814; Hodgeman's Hist. Westford, Mass., 466-9; Keyes' W. Boylston, Mass., Gen. Reg., 34; Lancaster's Hist. Gilmanton, N. H., 283; Morrison's Windham, N. H., 740; N. E. Hist. Gen. Reg., VI, 274; X, 297; XXII, 225; Norton's Hist. Fitzwilliam, N. H., 684-6; Palmer Gen. (1886), 41; Prescott Gen. (1870), 1653 pp.; Runnel's Hist. Sanbornton, N. H., II, 586-96; Savage's Gen. Dict., 480-2; Shattuck's Hist. Concord, Mass, 381; Thurston's Hist. Winthrop, Me., 191; Titcomb's Early New Eng. People, 133-43; Tuttle Gen., XXVII.

PRETIOUS, or PRETIOSE:—Charles; Boston; blacksmith or nailer; married, 1653, Rebecca Martin; had Mary, born 1654.

PRICE:—David, Dorchester; freeman 1636.

PRICE, JOSEPH, Salem; killed by the Indians, 1675, in the Narragansett fight, says Felt, II, 505; but whose son he was is not told; yet possibly of Walter.

PRICE, MATTHEW, Charlestown, 1654; of whom is only known that by wife, Elizabeth, he had Joseph, born 1656; and he was a householder in 1658. Perhaps he was of Salem, 1668, to sign memorial against impost with Walter and sons.

PRICE, RICHARD, Boston; artillery co., 1658; married 1659, Eliz. Cromwell, daughter of Thomas, the prosperous privateersman, had Thomas, born 1660; Jayliffe, 1662; Eliz., 1664; and Richard, 1667; was freeman with prefix of respect 1664.

PRICE, RICHARD, Boston; married 1662, Grace, daughter of Gamaliel Waite, had Ebenezer, born 1663; and Richard, 1664.

PRICE, ROBERT, Northampton; had Sarah, born 1678; Mary, 1681; Eliz., 1683; and John, 1689; removed to Deerfield, and thence, again, 1715.

PRICE, WALTER, Salem, 1641; merchant from Bristol,

Eng., brought wife, Eliz., and they joined church next year; freeman, 1642; had Eliz., bapt., 1642; Theodore, 1643; John, 1646; Hannah, 1648; William, 1650; Samuel, 1665; and died 1674, aged 61. Probably had other children.

PRICE, WILLIAM, Watertown; married, 1657, Mary Marplehead; had William, born 1658; Matthew, 1660; Mary, 1662; John, 1665; Sarah, 1667; Benjamin, 1670; Grace, 1672; James, 1675; Joseph, 1677; Eliz., 1680; and Hannah; and he died 1685. Sometimes his name appears Priest.

REFERENCES:—Ballou's Milford, Mass., 979; Bond and Price Gen. (1872), by D. P.; Cope Fam. of Pa., 82, 181; Embree and Price Biog. (1881), 67 p.; Greene's Kentucky Fams.; Hatfield's Elizabeth, N. J., 90; Lancaster's Hist. Gilmanton, N. H., 284; Meade's Old Fams. of Va.; Mitchell's Hist. Bridgewater, Mass., 279; Penn. Mag. of Hist., XV, 125; Price Gen. (1864), 86 p.; Richmond, Va., Standard, III, 12; Rodman Gen., 163-6; Savage's Gen. Dict., III, 484; Sullivan's Gen., 221.

PRICHARD, or PRITCHARD:—Benjamin; Milford, 1713; may have been son of Roger.

PRICHARD, HUGH, Gloucester, 1641-45; removed to Roxbury; freeman, 1642; had, by wife Elinor, Abigail, a daughter, according to town records, but church record says son Abiel, bapt. 1641; Zebediah, 1643, prob. died soon; Phebe, bapt. 1644; in church record very naturally called a daughter, but town records state a son, without a name; and a child without a name, buried 1649; was of artillery co. 1643; represent., 1643, 4 and 9; capt., 1647; went home, prob. in 1650. In giving deed of his estate some years later, his attys. describe him as of Broughton, Denbighsh, which perhaps was the place of his nativity.

PRICHARD, RICHARD, Yarmouth, 1643; was with wife Ann, and daughter, Templar, adm. 1660 of the church at Charlestown; died 1669, at great age. His will names wife Margery, daughter Hannah, wife of Richard Templar, who was made extrix., and her children James, Samuel, and Deborah, grandchild Hannah, wife of Alexander Stewart; and her children James and John; besides Richard, son of Richard Taylor; perhaps another grandson, and possibly it was meant Templer.

PRICHARD, ROGER, Springfield, 1643; freeman, 1648. His wife Frances died 1651, and he removed, 1653, to Milford; married that year Eliz., widow of William Slough, daughter of James Prudden; removed thence to New Haven; there died 1671. Alice, perhaps his daughter at Salem, married, 1655, William Bradlee, of New Haven; and Joan, perhaps another daughter, married at N. H., 1647, John Lumbard of S.

PRICHARD, WILLIAM, Lynn, 1645; Ipswich in 1648; became one of the first settlers at Brookfield; was clerk of the writs; had William, John, Joseph, and Samuel; was serg. of the military; and with son Samuel, at the same time that Edward Hutchinson fell, was killed by the Indians 1675. Often the serg.'s name is called Joseph; it is not mentioned in Wheeler's narrative, and by Coffin, 389, in a list almost officially he is called John.

REFERENCES:—Bedford, N. H., Cent., 326; Bronson's Hist. Waterbury, Ct., 524-6; Kidder's Hist. New Ipswich, N. H., 424-8; McKeen's Hist. Bradford, Vt., 339-49; Bontecau Gen., 152-5; Orcutt's Hist. Derby, Ct., 753; Savage's Gen. Dict., III. 485; Wyman's Charlestown Mass., Gens., II, 777.

PRIDE:—John, Salem, 1637; there had a grant of land; was a brickmaker in 1641; died about 1647.

PRIDE, JOHN, Permaquid; who took oath of fidelity to Mass., 1674; may have been son of preceding.

PRIEST:—Degary, Plymouth, 1620; died in few days after landing from the *Mayflower*, Jan. 1, 1621; and his wife, who was, says Gov. Bradford, sister of Mr. Allerton, and their children came after. He was formerly thought the first married of any of the Leyden exiles, but the record there shows that his intent was pub. 1611, and the marriage with Sarah Vincent, widow of John of London, one month later, and we know that both Isaac Allerton and his sister had a few weeks earlier been married. Dutch record states that after hearing of the death of Priest so early at P. his widow married that same year one, who was, thinks Savage, the Cuthbert Cuthbertson, who brought her and the child in the *Ann*. He had been admitted a citizen of, Leyden late in 1615, then called a hatter, no other of his friends except Bradford and Allerton having enjoyed that distinction.

PRIEST, EMANUEL, Marblehead, 1668; known only as Signer with John, perhaps his brother, against impost.

PRIEST, JAMES, Weymouth; freeman, 1643; and though twice inserted in the list, we may be confident as the same carelessness attaches to two other names, that only one man is intended; had James, born 1640; and by wife, Eliz., had Lydia, born 1658, died young; and Lydia, again, 1662; and he died at Salem 1664.

PRIEST, JOHN, Weymouth, 1657.

PRIEST, JOHN, Salem; married 1673, Eliz. Gray; had Eliz., born 1680.

PRIEST, JOHN, Woburn; had Eliz., born 1679; John, 1681; Daniel (Bond, 911, has Hannah), 1686; and perhaps others.

PRIEST, WILLIAM, Watertown, 1672; perhaps by wife Leah had William, who died 1688; and William, again, born 1689. But Bond leaves it in no doubt that the name was Price, whom see

REFERENCES:—Adams' Fairhaven, Vt., 449; Bond's Hist. Watertown, Mass., 408; Brown's W. Simsbury, Ct., Settlers, 118; Guild's Stiles Gen., 306; Hayward's Hist. Hancock, N. H., 815-21; Savage's Gen. Dict., III, 486; Stearns' Hist. Rindge, N. H., 645; Wood Gen., 137-43; Wyman's Charlestown Mass., II, 777.

PRIME:—James, Milford, about 1654; propound. for freeman, 1669; and died 1685, leaving widow, son James, daughter Sarah, wife of Thomas Prior, and Rebecca, who married 1677, Walter Smith. Among proprs. in 1713 was JAMES, son of preceding, who had son James and other children, and perhaps Ebenezer, Yale C., 1718, minister of Huntington, L. I., who died 1779, aged 79, was another.

PRIME, MARK, Rowley, 1643; by wife Ann had Samuel, born 1649.

REFERENCES:—Cothren's Woodbury, Ct., 674; Dowd Gen.; Essex Inst. Hist. Coll., XXIII, 145-7; N. Y. Gen. and Biog. Rec., XVII, 197-208; Orcutt's Hist. New Milford, Ct., 753; Prime Gen. (1887?) pamphlet, (1888), 118 p.; Prime's Autobiog., (1873); Queens Co., N. Y., Hist. (1882); Read's Hist. of Swanzey, N. H., 423; Resseguie Gen., 71-3; Wetmore Gen., 62.

PRIMIDAYS:—See Pringrydays.

PRINCE:—John, was perhaps of Cambridge, or more prob. of Watertown when freeman, 1635; son of Rev. John, who had been bred at Oxford, and was minister of East Shefford, often called Little Shefford, a few miles from Newbury, in Co. Berks; prob. removed to H. before birth of any children, of which he had prob.

by wife Margaret, John, born 1638, died 1690; Eliz., 1640; Joseph, 1642; Martha, 1645; Job, 1647; Mary, 1649, says rec.; Samuel, at Boston, 1649, says tradit.; Sarah, 1651, died soon; Benjamin, 1652, who prob. died young; Isaac, 1655; Deborah, 1657; and Thomas; he took second wife, Ann, widow of William Barstow; was ruling elder; and died 1676, aged 66. His will of three months before, names only 8 children.

PRINCE, NATHANIEL, Salem; in 1664 was one of the selectmen.

PRINCE, RICHARD, Salem, 1639; a tailor; freeman, 1642; had there bapt. John, 1642; Joseph, 1643; Mary, 1648; Samuel, 1651; Richard, 1655; and Jonathan, 1657; perhaps by wife Mary, a member of the church, 1648; all except first two; was a deacon and died 1675, aged 61.

PRINCE, ROBERT, Salem; may have been brother of first Richard; and Felt says had grant of land 1649. He married, 1662, Sarah Warren; had James, born 1665, died soon; James, again, 1668; Eliz., 1670; and Joseph; and he died 1674. His estate was good.

PRINCE, THOMAS, Gloucester, 1649; by wife Margaret had Thomas, born 1650; John, 1653; Mary, 1658; and Isaac, 1663; Babson, 129, says his widow died 1706.

PRINCE, WILLIAM, Dover, 1671.

One MARY PRINCE, a Quaker, came in the *Speedwell*, 1656; but of her no more is known than Hutchinson, I, 197, tells of her denounc. judgm. of God from her window in the prison against Gov. Endicott as he went by on Sunday from the church.

REFERENCES:—Amer. Ancestry, V, 141, 229; Babson's Hist. Gloucester, Mass., 129; Benedict's Hist. Sutton, Mass., 702; Corliss' No. Yarmouth, Me., 51-78; Davis' Landmarks Plymouth, Mass., 209; Deane's Hist. Scituate, Mass., 327; Denny Gen., 215-7; Drake's Rev. Thos. Prince (1851), 12 p.; Dudley's Arch. and Gen. Coll. Plate 4; Eaton's Annals Warren, Me., 604; Eaton's Hist. Thomaston, Me., II, 364; Ely Gen., 194; Essex Inst. Coll., XIV, 249-57; XXVII, 171-82; Freeman's Hist. Cape Cod, Mass., I, 357; II, 363; Gage's Hist. Rawley, Mass., 453; Guild's Stiles Gen., 44-6; Hemenway, Vt., Gaz., V; Maine Genealogist, III, 103; Mitchell's Hist. Bridgewater, Mass., 384-6; Nealley and True Chart; N. E. Hist. and Gen. Reg., V, 375, 383; Orcutt's Hist. Stratford, Ct., 1273; Pickering Gen.; Poore Gen., 57-61; Pratt's Hist. Eastham, Mass., 12-4; Prince Gen. (1888), 32 pp.; Queens Co., N. Y., Hist., 124; Savage's Gen. Dict., III, 487; Secomb's Hist. Amherst, N. H., 731-7; Sullivant Gen., 2238; Walworth's Hyde Gen., 936; Winsor's Hist. Duxbury, Mass., 293.

PRINDLE:—John, Milford, 1645; possibly name is same as following:

PRINGLE:—William, New Haven; married, 1655, Mary Desbraugh; had Phebe, born 1657; John, 1658; Mary, 1660; and perhaps others; was a propr. 1685; and so was Joseph, who may have been a son. This is now changed to Prindle, it is said.

PRINGRYDAY'S, or PRIMIDAYES, as given in Geneal. Reg., IX, 87; or PRIMRIDES, as by Rev. Mr. Russell in Coffin's Newbury, 390; Edmund, Springfield, married 1666, Mary, daughter of Miles Morgan; in the assault by the Indians when they burned the town, 1675, he was mortally wounded. The widow married Nicholas Rust.

PRIOR, or PRYOR:—Humpherey, Windsor; married, 1663, Ann, daughter of John Osborn; had John, born 1665; and Daniel, 1667; and his wife died before her father.

Genealogical Guide to the Early Settlers of America.—Continued.

PRIOR, EDWARD, Kennebec, 1665.

PRIOR, MATTHEW, Salem, 1638; when he had grant of land; removed to Long Island, and was of Brookhaven in 1665. His daughter Sarah married John Gould, of Newport, and next, 1711, became fourth wife of Gov. Walter Clark.

PRIOR, THOMAS, Scituate; came 1634 from London, with Lothrop; died 1639; in his will that year names sons Thomas and Samuel; daughters Elizabeth and Mary; probably also had sons Daniel and John, perhaps Joseph.
REFERENCES:—Bunker's L. I. Gens., 272; Little's Passaic Valley, 338; Savage's Gen. Dict., III, 488; Stiles' Hist. Windsor, Ct., II, 630-2; Temple's Hist. Northfield, Mass., 524; Winsor's Hist. Duxbury, Mass., 294.

PROCTOR:—Benjamin, Ipswich, 1678; prob. son married, 1662, Eliz., daughter of John Thorndyke; had of first John.

PROCTOR, GEORGE, Dorchester; freeman, 1637; by wife Edith had Hannah, born perhaps in England; Abigail, born 1637; Thomas, 1638; if we may dare to contradict the record, which is 1637, or it has been thought that the 1637 day was that of his burial, and he removed in few years to Salem; perhaps freeman 1690; may have been brought from England. Samuel, 1640; and he died 1662.

PROCTOR, JOHN, Ipswich; came 1635, aged 40, from London, in the Susan and Ellen, with wife Martha, 28; and children, John, 3; and Mary, 1; and in few years was settled at Salem. His wife died 1659; but he took second wife of same bapt. name who outlived him. His will of 1672 names wife and children John, Joseph, Benjamin, and Hannah Weeden, or some such name.
daughters Martha White, Abigail Varney, Sarah Dodge,

PROCTOR, JOHN, son of preceding; born in England; prob. by second wife, Eliz. Bassett. married 1674, William, born next year; Sarah, 1677; Samuel, 1686; Elisha, 1687; died next year; and Abigail, 1692; of which the eldest two were imprisoned in the execrable fanaticism of 1692. These children were prob. discharged without trial; but the mother was one of the first accused of witchcraft, and her husband (to whom the first wife had brought children Martha, born 1666; Mary, 1667, died soon; John, 1668; Mary, again, 1670; and Thorndike, 1672; and that wife died one month after last birth), for showing proper regard for her, as Hutchinson, II, 26 and 55, tells, fell under equal suspicion. Both were tried and condemned on Aug. 5, 1692, and on Aug. 19 he was executed, while she escaped by reason of her pregnancy.

PROCTOR, JOSEPH, Ipswich; married Martha, daughter of Francis Wainwright; had Daniel, born 1680.

PROCTOR, RICHARD, Yarmouth, 1643.

PROCTOR, RICHARD, Boston; freeman, 1690.

PROCTOR, ROBERT, Concord; freeman, 1643; married, 1645, Jane Hildreth, perhaps daughter of Richard; had Sarah, born 1656; Gershom, 1648; Mary, 1650; removed to Chelmsford; had Peter; Eliz., 1657; and Lydia, 1660; died at 6 months.
REFERENCES:—Amer. Ancestry, III, 208; Bridgeman's King's Chapel Bur. Ground, 270; Cogswell's Hist. Henniker, N. H., 696, 700; Felton Gen., 246; Hodgeman's Hist. Westford, Mass., 469; Journals of Smith and Dean, 204; Livermore's Hist. Wilton, N. H., 471; Lock Gen., 106; Marrison's Hist. Windham, N. H., 741-4; Power's Hist. Sangamon Co., Ill., 584; Preble Gen., 250-2; Proctor Gen. (1868), 46 p.; (1873), 19 p.; Savage's Gen. Dict., III, 489; Stearn's Hist. Ashburnham, Mass., 855;

Warren's Hist. Waterford, Me., 281-3; Washington, N. H., Hist., 570-8; Whitemore's Copps Hill Epitaph; Worcester's Hist. Hollis, N. H., 385.

PROSSER:—Roger, Boston, 1672; bought 500 acres at Quinebang.

PROSSER, THOMAS, Roxbury, 1649; perhaps next year was of Weymouth.
REFERENCES:—Meade's Old Fams. of Va.; Poore Gen., 269-71.

PROUSE:—John, Salisbury; by wife, Hannah, perhaps daughter of William Barnes, had Abigail, born 1666; was there living 1680.

PROUSE, ROGER, Boston; by wife, Hannah. had Peter, born 1686.

PROUT:—Timothy, Boston; shipwright; an early inhabitant; adm. of the church and freeman, 1644; by wife, Margaret, had Timothy, born 1645; Susanna, 1647; John, 1649; Joseph, about 1651; William, 1653; Benjamin, 1655, died 1669; Ebenezer, 1657; was represent. for several years, 1685, 9-92; and died 1702. His second wife, Eliz., died 1694; and his will mentions son Timothy as long absent. prob. dead; John. Joseph made excor.; William and Ebenezer; beside grandchildren and great grandchildren without names. He became propr. at Concord before 1680; and perhaps sometimes residing there.
REFERENCES:—Savage's Gen. Dict., III, 490; Wyman's Charlestown, Mass., Gens., II, 779.

· PROUTY:—Richard, Scituate, 1670; beside Edward and Isaac had son William. who left descendents, and daughter, Margaret, who died unmarried at great age. Descendents are numerous.
REFERENCES:—Amer. Ancestry, VIII, 135; Deane's Hist. Scituate, Mass., 328; Draper's Hist. Spencer, Mass., 237-45; Hemenway's Vermont Gaz., V, 451; Hyde's Hist. Brimfield, Mass., 447; Temple's Hist. N. Brookfield, Mass., 714.

PROVENDER:—John, Charlestown; took oath of fidelity 1674.
REFERENCES:—Corliss' N. Yarmouth, Me.

PRUDDEN:—James, Wilford, 1639; perhaps brother of Peter; died 1647. His daughter Ann married Samuel Coley about 1640; and Eliz. married William Slough.

PRUDDEN, PETER, Milford; arrived with famous Davenport at Boston; and at New Haven spent some time next year and the following, where was gathered the church of M. over which he was settled 1640; and died 1656, in 56th year. Was he ever of Wethersfield as the diligent writer in Geneal. Reg., XI. 102. says? Mather says he had been a successful preacher about Herefordshire and near Wales; but caution is useful in receiving the word of M. We know nothing of his parentage or education. He left good estate here besides his lands in Edgeton in Co. York, where perhaps he was born, and certainly there married Joanna Boyse. He had six daughters and two sons, John. bapt. 1646. Howard Coll., 1668; and Samuel, the eldest son, who prob. was the propr. at M., 1713; besides Peter, bapt. 1652, died soon. His widow, Joanna, who had married 1671, Capt. Thomas Willet, and next Rev. John Bishop, in her will, 1681, names the sons and five daughters, Joanna, bapt. 1640; Eliz., 1643; Abigail, 1647; Sarah, 1650; and Mildred. 1653; beside Mary Walker, her daughter deceased. whose portion was to go to two children, Abigail, married 1667; Joseph Walker; Mildred married, 1671, Sylvanus Bald-

PUDEATER:—Jacob, Salem; married, 1666, Isabel Mosier, who died 1677; and took second wife. Nothing is mentioned of him except that his widow, Ann, was one of those innocents charged with the preposterous ofwin; but what was the bapt. name of the husband of Mary remains unseen.

fense of witchcraft, 1692; shut up in Boston jail, at the same time with Philip English and his wife, tried in Sept. and with seven other executed on 22d day. See Felt, II, 477-80; Essex Inst., II, 187, 8; and Hutch., II, 58.

PUDINGTON, or PUDDINGTON:—George, York, 1640; Maine Hist. Coll., I, 273, and I Mass. Hist. Coll., I, 101. A widow, P. Savage finds in the record of that jurisdiction, 1649, licensed to sell wine.

PUDINGTON, JOHN, Portsmouth, 1654; Adams, 40. He may have been of York, 1680, when he swore alleg. and lieut. in comm. of fort, 1640, at Kennebec. 3 Mass. Hist. Coll., I, 86.

PUDINGTON, ROBERT, Portsmouth, 1640. Belkn., I, 28. Prob. it was the same man at Newton, L. I., 1656. See Riker, 43. But he owned estate at P., 1660.

PUDNEY:—John, Salem; married, 1662, Judith, daughter of Henry Cooke, of the same; had John, born next year; Judith, 1665; Joanna, 1668; Samuel, 1670; Joseph, 1673; and Jonathan, 1678.

PUFFER, or PAFFER:—James, Braintree, 1665; by wife, Mary, had Richard, born 1658; Martha, same year.

PUFFER, MATTHEW or MATTHIAS, Braintree; perhaps brother of James; had James, born 1668, at Mendon, of which he was one of the first settlers; and for second wife married Abigail, daughter of Richard Everett, when, Savage thinks, he lived at Wrentham. Other children he had, and another wife Mary. The children were John, James, Jonathan, and Esther, who married, 1697, William Sumner, of Milton.

PUFFER, WILLIAM, Wrentham; by wife, Ruth, daughter of Joseph Farnsworth, of Dorchester, had William, born 1686.

REFERENCES:—Barry's Framingham, 369; Hudson's Hist. Lexington, Mass., 188; Hyde's Hist. Brimfield, field, Mass., 447; Lapham's Hist. Rumford, Me., 383; Morse Gen. app. No. 41; N. E. Hist. Gen. Reg., XXII, 288-90; Puffer Gen. (1868) (1882), 9 p.; Savage's Gen. Dict., III, 492; Smith's Hist. Peterborough, N. H., 229; Stearn's Hist. Ashburnham, Mass., 855.

PULLMAN:—Jasper, York; took oath of allegiance to his majesty, 1681.

PULSIFER:—Benedict, Ipswich, 1664; was in some part of the land after 1662; had daughter Eliz., born 1669; but of the mother we know only that she died 1673. Soon after he married Susanna, daughter of Richard Waters of Ipswich; had Richard, born 1675; William, 1676; Susanna, 1678; Joseph, 1680; Benjamin, 1683; David, 1685; Jonathan, 1687; Joanna, 1691; and Margaret, 1694. In 1688 N. Yarmouth he was one of the first to begin hostilities with the Indians, as in his Decennium Luctuosum Mather shows. Magn. VII, 63.

PULSIFER, JOHN, Gloucester, 1680; perhaps son of Benedict; married, 1684, Joanna, daughter prob. of Thomas Kent of the same; had John, born 1685, died at 22 years; Joanna, 1688; Mary, 1691; a son 1693; Ebenezer, 1695; Mary, again, 1697; David, 1701; and Jonathan, 1704.

REFERENCES:—Amer. Ancestry, IX, 69; Leland Gen., 97; Montague Gen., 497-9; Savage Gen. Dict., III, 493.

PUNCHARD:—William, Salem; by tradition said to have come from Isle of Jersey; married, 1669; Abigail, daughter of Richard Waters, of the same; had Abigail, born 1670; Mary, 1674, died young; William, 1677; John, 1682; and Sarah, 1685. His name is Punshin in Geneal. Reg., IX, 86.

REFERENCE:—Punchard Gen. (1857), 68 p.

PUNDERSON, or PONDERSON:—John, Boston or the neighborhood; for short time only; came from Yorkshire, 1637; went to New Haven, 1639; one of the pillars of the first gathering of that church; by wife, Margaret, had Ruth, born 1643; and Hannah, 1642, who married, 1670, John Gibbs, and died 1681.

REFERENCES:—Amer. Ancestry, II, 100; VIII, 123; Chapman's Trowbridge Gen., 46-8; Savage's Gen. Dict., III, 493.

PURCHASE, or PURKAS:—Abraham, Salem, 1680; by wife, Ruth, daughter of John William of the same, had Ruth, born 1702; and Benjamin, 1706.

PURCHASE, JOHN, Hartford, about 1639; died prob. before middle age. His widow, Joan, married Nicholas Palmer; and his daughter Mary married Jared Speck, and daughter Eliz. married Richard Case.

PURCHASE, JOHN, Boston; by wife Eliz. had Sarah, who died 1652; Sarah, again, 1655; John, 1656; and Mary, 1660.

PURCHASE, OLIVER, Dorchester, 1635; freeman, 1636; removed early to Taunton, where enrolled 1643 in the militia; was ensign 1651; and in good esteem; but few years after removed to Lynn; there his wife Sarah died, 1671; and he married, 1672, Mary, daughter of Rev. William Perkins; was represent., 1660; and often after, last in 1689 at four courts; removed to Concord about 1691; there died 1701, in 84th year. He was chosen one of the Assistants 1685, but refused to take the office prob. because the old charter had been annulled. Savage supposes that Priscilla, who married, 1663, William Wilson, was his daughter.

PURCHASE, THOMAS, Kennebec; an adventurer of good discretion and perseverance; perhaps elder brother of preceding; came first in 1628; and was principal of the Pegypscott sett. on both sides of Androscoggin, near its mouth; appears in first leaf of Vol. I of Maine Record as one of the commrs. at Saco, on New Year's day, 1636, with the friends of Sir Ferd. Gorges, at his planta., which is now Brunswick. His wife Mary died at Boston, 1656. The Indians began hostilities, 1675, by plunder of his house, and he removed to Lynn. He left widow Eliz., who married, 1678, when Thomas died, John Blancy, of Lynn. He left son Thomas; made excor. of his will, 1677; daughters Jane and Eliz., beside three more children as the widow says. Folsom, 31, 153; Willis, I, 14, 156; Sullivan, 372; Haz., I, 58; and Hubbard, Indian Wars, 14.

PURDY:—Frances and Mary, Fairfield, 1644; are witnesses to the will of William Frost. Possibly first was a man.

REFERENCES:—Baird's Rye, N. Y., 434-40; Bolton's Westchester Co., N. Y., II, 754-6; Cleveland's Hist. Yates Co., N. Y., 499; Davis' Hist. Buck's Co., Pa., 202; Huron and Erie Co.'s, Ohio, Hist., 288; Hunting Stamford, Ct., Sett., 83; Ruttenber's Hist. Newburgh, N. Y.,

277; Ruttenber's Hist. Orange Co., N. Y., 367; Walworth's Hyde Gen., 1024.

PURPLE:—Edward, Haddem, 1674; married Hannah Ackley, prob. daughter of Nicholas. In this vicinity the name is found in our day.
REFERENCES:—Purple Gen. (1879); Temple's Hist. Northfield, Mass., 525.

PURRINGTON:—Benjamin; is only use of a wrong surname, which in his case is Parmenter, in the abstract of will of Thomas Cawly, Essex Inst. Hist. Coll., II, 71.
PURRINGTON, JOHN, Kennebunk; was clerk of the writs 1668.
PURRINGTON, ROBERT, Portsmouth, 1665; freeman, 1672; had John, born about 1635; and Robert, about 1638; perhaps both born in England; may have removed to Sudbury; and had other children; may easily be mistaken for Pudington. The name is much diffused, and often found written without g but with single r.

PURRYER:—William, Ipswich; from Olney in Bucks, emb. at London early in 1635; aged, by the customho. records, 36: in the *Hopewell* with wife Alice, 37, and children Mary, 7; Sarah, 5; and Catharine, 1½. Often Felt says, the y is changed to i Savage thinks he removed to Southold, L. I., and was admitted freeman of Conn. 1662; but whether the name is perpetuated is unknown.

PURY:—See Perry.

PUTNAM:—John, Salem, 1640; is said to have come with wife Priscilla, children, Thomas, born about 1618; Nathaniel, 1621; John, 1630; and Elizabeth; from Aston Abbots, near Aylesbury, in Co. Bucks, though family tradition has the name of a place in Co. Warwick, where it is unknown; freeman, 1647, says Farmer by mistake, though true it is he was admitted into the church that year, as had been his wife in 1641; died, 1662. Thirteen of this name had in 1832 been deacons of the first church of Danvers; and of the name, perverted to Putmun in 1828, had been twenty-five graduated at Harvard, two at Yale, and seven at other N. E. Coll.
REFERENCES:—Adams' Fairhaven, Vt., 453; Brown's Bedford, Mass., Families, 28; Cutter's History of Arlington, Mass., 287; McKeen's Hist. of Bradford, Vt., 265-7; Putnam family address (1855) 37 pages; Savage's Gen. Dict., 111, 495-7; Vinton Geneal., 477-80; Young's Chautauqua Co., N. Y., 566-8.

PYGAN, PYGON, PIGGIN, or PIGGON:—Alexander, New London, 1665, perhaps earlier; from Norwich Co. Norf; married, 1667, Judith, daughter of William Redfield; had Sarah, born 1670; and Jane, 1671. His wife died 1678; and in short time he removed to Saybrook; there was an Inn holder; married, 1684, Lydia, widow of Samuel Boyes; had only Lydia, born 1685; and went back to New London before her birth; there he died 1701; and the widow died 1734. Sarah married, 1686, Nicholas Hallam; Jane married, 1694, Jonas Greene; and Lydia married, 1709, Rev. Eliphalet Adams. In the modest model memoir of that clergyman by Miss Caulkins the first article of 4 Mass. Hist. Coll., I, unacish particulars of his father in-law, the only male of this name may be read.
REFERENCES:—Caulkins' New London, Ct., 341; Redfield Geneal., 11.

PYNCHON, or PINCHEON:—John, Springfield; only son of William, born in England, 1625; brought

with three sisters and their mother, by his father in the fleet with Winthrop, 1630; married, 1645, Amy, daughter of George Wyllys, of Hartford, who died 1699; had Joseph, born 1646, H. C., 1664; John, 1647; May, 1650; William, 1653, died in few months; and Mehitable, 1661, died young. He was freeman, 1648; rep., 1659, 62, 3 and 4; in 1665 an Assist., and ever after to the abolition of the old form of governm., 1686; next of the council to Andros, major of the Hampsh. reg. from its formation and during the usurpation of Andros called Col., and was the chief man in all the W. yet Mathew unwisely dictated to the king who took somebody else for the honor of the council, in his new chart. 1692, but the people next year corrected that blunder, and he was chosen until 1702, every year except 1699; and Phips made him Judge of Pro. in 1692. He died 1703. Mary married, 1670, Joseph Whiting, of Westfield, as the record has it, but Goodwin says 1669.
PYNCHON, WILLIAM, Roxbury; an Assist.; came in the fleet with Winthrop, 1630; had been associated with the patentees, 1628, who purchased from the Plymouth Co. that year, and named to office by the royal chart. of 1629; brought four children, Ann, Mary, John and Margaret with their mother, says the record of Roxbury church, of which his name is first. His widow died in the first season before return of the ship in which they came; and after some years he married Frances Sanford, a grave matron of the church of Dorchester; and about 1636 removed to found the town of Springfield, so named, perhaps, from the place of his residence near Chelmsford, in Old England. He was a man of great enterprise, and highly honored as treasurer before his leaving the sea coast, and as couns. after, until his publication of the dangerous judgment as to religion, which he had formed thirty years before. For this he suffered indignity in 1651, when his book was by our governm. ordered to be burned, and lest the same form of purification might reach the author, he went home, as more freedom was enjoyed in his native land. See the letter, in full, to Sir H. Vane, from our Gov. Endicott and his council of Assist. in 3 Mass. Hist. Coll., I, 35. At Wraisbury, on the Thames, near famous Runnymede, in Co. Bucks, he died 1662, in 72d or 74th year, his wife having died there 1657. Ann married Henry Smith, son by her first husband of the second wife of her father; Margaret married, 1644, Capt. William Davis, of Boston; and Mary married, 1640, Capt. Elizur Holyoke; and died 1657. Four of this name had been graduated at Harvard, and three at Yale, 1825.
REFERENCES: — Clarke's Kindred Genealogies (1896), 137-41; Ellis' Hist. of Roxbury, Mass., 128; New Eng. Hist. and Geneal. Reg., XX, 243; XXXVII, 361; XXXVIII, 46-8; XLVIII, 249-63; Whitmore's Heraldic Journal, 11, 49-53.

PYNE:—Hartford, 1647; may have been only transient inhabitant there or at Fairfield. See Trumbull, Col. Rec., I, 130, 158.
PYNE, THOMAS, the freeman of Mass., 1635; was, by Farmer thought to be the same as Pinney.
REFERENCE:—Lincoln's Hingham, III, 122.

QUARLES:—William, Ipswich, 1678; probably came in from Salisbury or some other town, where in 1665 he was 18 years old, but no more is known of him except that his Inv. is found of 1690.
REFERENCE:—Clarke's King William Families.

QUELCH:—Benjamin, Boston; by wife Elizabeth, had Nathaniel, born 1692; and Benjamin, 1694; probably removed soon, as he is not in the list of inhabitants, 1695.

QUELVES:—Robert, is the name written by the Secretary in our Col. Rec., 1645; among the petitioners for a new plantation, that our rulers would have gained from R. I. or Providence jurisdiction, no doubt it was Twelves, of Braintree, the freeman of 1663, and in later vols. of the rec. restitution was made.

QUICK:—Nathaniel, New Hampshire; died 1677. Quick, William, Charlestown, 1636; a mariner, as seems from Trumbull. Col. Rec., I, 6, removed to Newport, where he was admitted an inhabitant 1638. Probably his religious opinions or those of his friends led to that, and he sold house and land 1644. Ann Quick, perhaps his mother, sold her house and land 1640.
    REFERENCE:—Plumb's History of Hanover Pennsylvania, 466.

QUIDDINGTON:—Abraham; one of the soldiers killed by the Indians 1675, at Hatfield, but of what town is not known.

QUILTER:—Mark, Ipswich, 1637; came probably with Rev. Nathaniel Rogers the year before, bringing some children, and died perhaps 1654; his will being of that year. His children were Joseph, Mark, Mary, Rebecca, and Sarah; the two first may have been born in England. His daughter Mary is named in the will of Rev. N. Rogers, 1655, as his maid servant.

QUIMBY, or QUINBY:—John, Stratford, 1654; had one child born there; but after some years removed and was one of the patentees of East Chester in 1664, where the family has continued.
    Quimby, Robert, Salisbury, 1663; had Lydia, born 1658; William, 1660; John, 1665; and Thomas, 1668; and prob. died 1677. Lydia married, 1674, William Holdridge.
    Quimby, William, Amesbury; perhaps brother, perhaps son, of preceding; took oath of fidelity, 1677.
    REFERENCES:—Bolton's Westchester, 706; Chase's Hist. Chester, N. H., 577; Coffin's Hist. Boscawen, N. H., 607; Colliss' No. Yarmouth, Me.; Hubbard's Hist. Stanstead Co., Ill., 168; Runnel's Hist. Sanbornton, N. H., II, 596-8.

QUINCY:—Edmund, Boston; arrived 1633 with John Cotton; making it probable that he came from the same Co., Lincoln, though really he was of Wigsthorpe Co., Northampton; son of Edmund; and bapt. 1602; and was, with wife Judith, married 1623, adm. of the church 1633; and within four months five of his servants joined it; freeman, 1634; and represent. at the first Gen. Ct. of Mass. that year; received grant of land in Braintree, 1635; still enjoyed by his descendents; and died soon after in his 33d year. His widow married Moses Paine, who died 1643; and in a few years she married Robert Hull, and died 1654; as in his Diary is told by John Hull, the mintmaster, who married 1647 his daughter Judith, born in England 1626.
    Quincy, Edmund, Braintree; only son of preceding, born in England about 1628; married, 1648, Joanna, daughter of widow Joanna Hoar, and sister of Presdt. Hoar; had Mary, born 1650; Daniel, 1651; but through misreading of numerals in Advertisem. to Hull's Amer. Diary, p. 117, by the scrupulous editor of Archæol. Amer repeat., p. 275, is made five months too early; John, 1652, died young; Joanna, 1654; Judith, 1655; Elizabeth 1656; Edmund, 1657, died at 4 months; Ruth, 1658, Ann, who died 1670, after 3 days' illness, aged 13, as her

gravestone tells; and Experience. His wife died 1680; and he married next year Eliz., daughter of Hon. Daniel Gookin, widow of John Elliot, Jr., who died 1700; by her had Edmund, again, born 1681, H. C., 1699; and Mary, again, 1684. He was freeman, 1665; major and lieut.-col. of the Suffolk regim.; represent. 1670, 3, 5, 9, and last in the trying time, May, 1692, and died 1698 in 70th year.
    REFERENCES:—Amer. Ancestry, IV, 159; Bond's Hist. Watertown, Mass., 909; Corlin's Hist. Hillsdale, N. Y., App., 103; Cutt's Gen.; Heraldic Journal, III, 178-82; Jackson's Tab. Ped. Quincy Fam.; Muzzey's Reminiscences; N. E. Hist. and Gen. Reg., XI, 71-3. 157; Quincy Gen. (1841), 9 p., (1857), 8 p.; Salisbury Mem., I, 295-370; Savage's Gen. Dict., III, 500; Vinton's Giles Gen., 147.

QUING, or QUIN:—Arthur, Boston, 1677.
    REFERENCE:—Hayward's Hancock, N. H., 830.

QUOITMORE:—Thomas; a perverse spelling in some records of Coytmore.

RABEY, or RABBE:—Catharine, Salem; a waterman's widow from Yarmouth, in Co. Norfolk; embarked 1637, aged 68, to come hither, "to remain with her son," as the official document in Westminster Hall, or her Majesty's Remembrancer's office, says; who he was is unknown, but she united with the church of S. 1641.

RABUN, or RABONE:—George, Exeter, 1639; by Belknap, I, 432, spelled Rawbone.

RADDEN:—Thaddeus, Marblehead, 1674; as printed in Geneal. Reg., VIII, 288, which Savage presumes to be same person as T. Reddam, Redden, and Raddin, in Essex Inst., II, 279 and 280; with less probable name in Geneal. Reg., VII, 70; Thaddeus Kidder or Kiddar.
    REFERENCE:—Littell's Passaic Valley, 339.

RAGLAND:—John, Boston; died 1690; in his will gave all estate to wife Mary.

RAINES, or RAYNES:—Francis, York; swore freeman of Mass., 1652, with prefix of dignity; lieut. 1654; had a daughter married John Woodman, of Dover; as a capt. swore allegiance to the king 1680; made his will 1693.
    Raines, Nathaniel, York; son perhaps of Francis; swore alleg. to the king 1681.
    Raines, Richard, Edgartown, 1659.

RAINSBOROW:—William, Charlestown, 1639; was of artillery co. that year, and had next year estate at Watertown; was prob. desirous of living on this side of the ocean; purchased in the first year of his residence the old meeting house at Budington, 195, has shown, but went home before the civil war, in which he acquired distinction. He is called brother of Stephen Winthrop (perhaps by marriage of W. with sister of R.), whose excors. conveyed to Edward R. prob. son of William, large estate in Lynn, half of 1,500 acres, and also half of Prudence isle in Narragansett Bay. Edward in 1672 was of London. Clarendon in Hist. of Rebellion gives account of William's death, 1648.

RAM:—George; came in the Abigail from London, 1635; aged 25; but nothing more is known of him. In Geneal. Reg., XIV, 318, Mr. Drake is positive that this name in the custom-house record is RUM.